Rick Steves®

ITALY

D1286208

CONTENTS

Welcome to Rick Steves' Europe

Travel is intensified living—maximum thrills per minute and one of the last great sources of legal adventure. Travel is freedom. It's recess, and we need it.

I discovered a passion for European travel as a teen and have been sharing it ever since—through my bus tours, public television and radio shows, and travel guidebooks. Over the years I've taught millions of travelers how to best enjoy Europe's blockbuster sights—and experience "Back Door" discoveries that most tourists miss.

This book offers a balanced mix of Italy's lively cities and cozy towns, from brutal but *bella* Rome to *tranquillo*, traffic free Riviera villages. It's selective: Rather than listing dozens of hill towns, I recommend only the best ones. And it's in depth: My self-guided museum tours and city walks give insight into the country's vibrant history and today's living, breathing culture.

I advocate traveling simply and smartly. Take advantage of my money- and time-saving tips on sightseeing, transportation, and more. Try local, characteristic alternatives to expensive hotels and restaurants. In many ways, spending more money only builds a thicker wall between you and what you traveled so far to see.

We visit Italy to experience it—to become temporary locals. Thoughtful travel engages us with the world, as we learn to appreciate other cultures and new ways to measure quality of life.

Judging by the positive feedback I receive from readers, this book will help you enjoy a fun, affordable, and rewarding vacation—whether it's your first trip or your tenth.

Buon viaggio! Happy travels!

Rick Steves

ITALY

Bell'Italia! Italy has Europe's richest, craziest culture—bubbling with emotion, traffic jams, strikes, rallies, religious holidays, crowds, and irate ranters shaking their fists at each other one minute and walking arm-in-arm the next. Promise yourself to relax and accept it all as a package deal—the exquisite and the exasperating. If you take Italy on its own terms, you'll experience a cultural keelhauling that actually feels good.

After all, Italy is the cradle of European civilization—established by the Roman Empire and carried on by the Roman Catholic Church. As you explore Italy, you'll stand face-to-face with some of the world's most iconic images from this 2,000-year history: Rome's ancient Colosseum and playful Trevi Fountain, Pisa's Leaning Tower, Florence's Renaissance masterpieces (Michelangelo's *David* and Botticelli's *Venus*), and the island city of elegant decay—Venice.

Beyond these famous cities, there's even more: German-flavored Alps, timeless hill towns, peaceful lakes lined with 19th-century villas, the business center of Milan, and Mediterranean beaches. Italy is reasonably small and laced with train lines and freeways, so you're never more than a half-day's journey from any of these places.

Wherever you go, Italy's top sights are its people. They're outgoing and social. They have an endearing habit of speaking Italian to foreigners, even if they know you don't speak their language—and it somehow works. If a local starts chattering

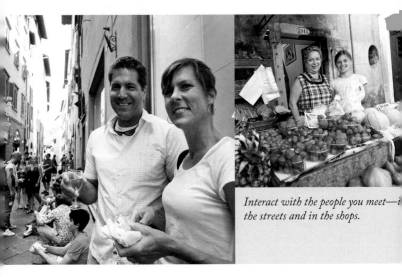

Interact with the people you meet—i the streets and in the shops.

at you in Italian, don't resist. Go with it. You might understand more than you'd expect.

Italian food is a cut above. If America's specialty is fast food, Italy's is slow food—bought daily, prepared with love, and enjoyed convivially. Three-hour restaurant meals are common; dinner is the evening's entertainment. To "eat and run" is seen as a lost opportunity. Wine complements the meal; Italy is the world's number-one wine producer (just ahead of France). For just a quick sandwich or a coffee, Italians stop by a bar. The bars aren't taverns, but cafés…good for a light meal anytime, with all ages welcome.

Early evening is the time for the ritual promenade— called the *passeggiata*—up and down main street. Shoppers, people watchers, families, and young flirts on the prowl stroll and spread their wings like peacocks. You might hear sweet whispers of *bella* (pretty) and *bello* (handsome). You can be a spectator, sipping a drink at a sidewalk table, or better yet, join the promenade, with a gelato in hand.

As you stroll, it's fun to window-shop. While no longer a cheap country, Italy remains a hit with shoppers for glassware and Carnevale masks in Venice; gold, silver, leather, and prints in Florence; and high fashion in Rome and Milan.

Italy's biggest business is tourism—the country is considered the world's fifth-most-visited tourist destination.

Buon Appetito!

Italian cuisine is sightseeing for your palate. The recipe: Start with fresh ingredients and talented cooks, mix in the owner's personality, and add a happy restaurant crowd. Eating in Italy is a joy you can't get anywhere else. Be adventurous, and try the regional specialties and culinary customs. You can eat well, even on a budget.

In Florence and the hill towns of Tuscany, enjoy hearty farmer's food: grilled meats, beans, fresh herbs, and high-quality seasonal vegetables. Popular dishes are *ribollita,* a savory bean-and-bread soup, and *bistecca alla fiorentina,* a grilled T-bone steak. Forage through Florence's gourmet food hall. For light fare, try an *enoteca* (wine bar), where appetizers and salads are paired with fine wine. For dessert, decide for yourself if Florence really does have Italy's most flavorful gelato.

Venetian cuisine features catch-of-the-day fish and shellfish, risotto, polenta, and some exotic choices. *Nero di seppia* is squid in its own black ink, served over pasta. Tourists are drawn to the pricey, romantic, canalside eateries. (Hint: Pizza is the least expensive item on the menu.) But I prefer to dine on the cheap, dropping into atmospheric *cicchetti* bars to munch bite-size appetizers that add up to a fun, tasty meal. Try both!

Trendsetting Milan claims to have created the *aperitivo* happy hour—a drink with free appetizers—that's catching on elsewhere in Italy. In stylish Milan, even the deli food is photogenic. The most famous dish is *risotto alla milanese* paired with *ossobuco* (saffron risotto with veal shank). The Lake District features whitefish on the menu with sublime views included in the cost. In the mountainous Dolomites, the hearty cuisine is Germanic, with pork, game, ▶▶▶

Take your taste buds for a spin, from Florence's bistecca alla fiorentina *(grilled steak) and Venice's* nero di seppia *(inky squid over pasta) to this popular pairing in Milan:* risotto alla milanese *and* ossobuco *(saffron risotto with veal).*

▶▶▶ potatoes, dumplings, and strudel. Passersby will wish you a *"Guten Appetit!"*

In coastal regions such as the Cinque Terre, Riviera, and Amalfi Coast, seafood is the specialty (add pesto and focaccia for the Cinque Terre). For that quintessential beach experience, settle in at a waterfront café on a sunny day. Sample *antipasti frutti di mare*—a plate of mixed "fruits of the sea"—with a glass of wine as the Mediterranean shimmers before you.

Roman cuisine, strongly flavored and unpretentious, features meats, fish, some fried foods, and fresh vegetables. Numerous food-and-wine-tasting tours, offering an insider's look, can fill you in and fill you up. Roman specialties are *spaghetti alla carbonara* (with an egg-and-bacon sauce created here) and *saltimbocca alla romana* ("jump in the mouth" veal). Dine at a sidewalk café with the rust-colored facades of Rome as your backdrop.

Italians say the best pizza is in Naples, its birthplace. The soft, chewy crust is topped with mozzarella and tomato sauce, and baked in a wood-burning oven. At a Neapolitan pizzeria, pizza is often the only thing on the menu.

For an affordable splurge anywhere in Italy, have a glass of wine or cup of coffee in an elegant café or on a classic square. If you sip your pricey drink slowly in a prime people-watching zone, it's an excellent value. Raise a toast: *La vita è bella!* Life is good. ■

In coastal towns, seafood is always on the menu. When in Rome, eat what the Romans eat: saltimbocca alla romana *(veal with prosciutto). Pizza is best in its hometown, Naples.*

Culturally, there are two Italys: The North tends to be industrial, aggressive, and "time is money" in its outlook (though Venice is a world apart). The South is hotter and more crowded, poor, relaxed, farm-oriented, and traditional; families usually live in the same house for many generations. Loyalties are to family, city, region, soccer team, and country—in that order.

Italians are obsessed with soccer (called *il calcio*). Star players are treated like movie stars, and fans are passionate. On big game nights, bars are packed with fans watching TV screens. After a loss, they drown their sorrows. After a victory, they celebrate by driving through the streets honking horns and waving team flags.

Home of the Vatican, Italy is still mostly Catholic. Although Italians will crowd into St. Peter's Square with rock-concert energy to catch a glimpse of *"il Papa,"* they're not particularly devout. They baptize their kids at the local church (there's one every few blocks), but generally don't attend church regularly and hold modern opinions on social issues, often in conflict with strict Catholic dogma. Italy is now the land of legalized abortion, a low birth rate, nudity on TV, socialist politics, and a society whose common language is decidedly secular. The true dominant religion is life: motor scooters, fashion, girl-watching, boy-watching, good coffee, good wine, and *il dolce far niente* (the sweetness of doing nothing).

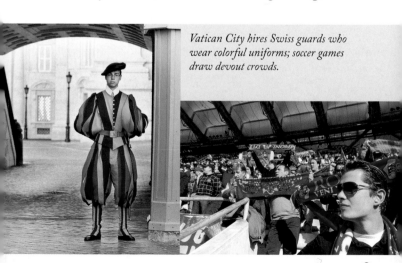

Vatican City hires Swiss guards who wear colorful uniforms; soccer games draw devout crowds.

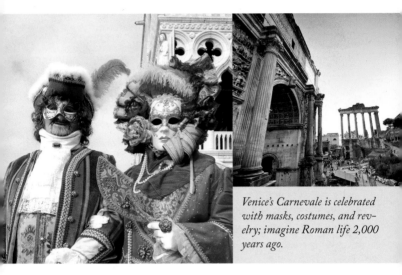

Venice's Carnevale is celebrated with masks, costumes, and revelry; imagine Roman life 2,000 years ago.

Italians are stylish. They strive to project a positive image in manner and dress—a concept they call *la bella figura*. They'd rather miss their bus than get sweaty and mussed-up rushing to catch it. And no matter how hot it gets, Italian men wear long pants—not shorts (except at the beach).

Traditions remain important. On festival days, locals still dress up in medieval or fanciful garb to celebrate Carnevale (Venice), play soccer (Florence), or race horses (Siena). Traditional ways are carried on by choice. Italians are wary of the dangers of a fast-paced global lifestyle. Their history is long, and they're secure in their place in the world.

Zero in on Italy's fine points, and don't dwell on the problems (just call them "cultural experiences"). Savor your cappuccino, dangle your feet over a canal (if it smells, breathe through your mouth), and imagine what it was like centuries ago. Ramble through the rabble and rubble of Rome and mentally resurrect those ancient stones. Sit silently on a hill-town belvedere and get chummy with the winds of the past. Write a poem over a glass of local wine in a sun-splashed, wave-dashed Riviera village. Italy is for romantics.

Italy's Top Destinations

Mamma mia! There's so much to see in Italy and so little time. This overview categorizes the country's top destinations into must-see places (to help first-time travelers plan their trip) and worth-it places (for those with extra time or special interests). I've also suggested a minimum number of days to allow per destination.

SWITZ.

AUSTRIA

SLOVAKIA

SLOVENIA

CROATIA

DOLOMITES

THE LAKES

NEAR VENICE

MILAN

VENICE

FRANCE

BOSNIA-HERZ.

RIVIERA TOWNS

CINQUE TERRE

FLORENCE

PISA & LUCCA

SIENA

HEART OF TUSCANY

VOLTERRA & SAN GIMIGNANO

ASSISI

ORVIETO & CIVITA

ROME

NAPLES

POMPEII & NEARBY

AMALFI COAST & PAESTUM

Sardinia

SORRENTO & CAPRI

Sicily

PLACES COVERED IN THIS BOOK

▲▲▲ Must See

▲▲ Try Hard to See

▲ Worthwhile

100 Kilometers

100 Miles

MUST-SEE DESTINATIONS

Italy's major cities are Rome, Florence, and Venice. Each has a distinctly different flavor, from ancient Roman to Renaissance art to a romantic island. If you have just two weeks for your first Italian trip, include these cities, add the coastal Cinque Terre and the town of Siena, and you'll get an unforgettable introduction to the best (if most touristy stops) that Italy has to offer. Here they are, listed north to south, as they appear in this book:

▲▲▲Venice (allow 1-2 days)
Venice is Italy's dreamy island city, powerful in medieval times and famous today for St. Mark's Basilica, the Grand Canal, and singing gondoliers. Idling on St. Mark's Square—best at night while the orchestras play—is one of Italy's grand experiences.

▲▲▲Cinque Terre (2-3 days)
The lovely Cinque Terre is a string of five idyllic Riviera hamlets tucked along a rugged coastline, connected by scenic hiking trails and boats, and dotted with beaches. The region is revered by hardy hikers, sun worshippers, and photographers.

▲▲▲Florence (1-2 days)
If you love art, you'll enjoy Florence. This surprisingly compact city, which Michelangelo called home, was the cradle of the Renaissance. You'll marvel at the Uffizi Gallery's priceless paintings (starring Botticelli's ethereal *Birth of Venus*, shown above), Brunelleschi's dome-topped cathedral, and Michelangelo's *David*. And anyone can appreciate Italy's best gelato.

Gliding through Venice; Florence's shop-lined Ponte Vecchio; enjoying views on a Cinque Terre hike; a parade in Siena

▲▲▲Siena (1 day)

Nearby Siena is Florence's smaller and (some say) more appealing Tuscan rival, with its magnificent Il Campo square, striking striped cathedral, and medieval pageantry, spurred by its Palio horse race. On any night, if you hear the low throb of drumming signaling a parade in a proud neighborhood—seek it out!

▲▲▲Rome (2-3 days)

Rome is Italy's capital, the sprawling Eternal City, studded with impressive Roman ruins: the Forum, Colosseum, and Pantheon. It's home to Vatican City and the astonishing Sistine Chapel. Wandering through Rome's floodlit-fountain squares at night, happening upon the Trevi Fountain...you won't be the only romantic tossing in a coin with a wish to return.

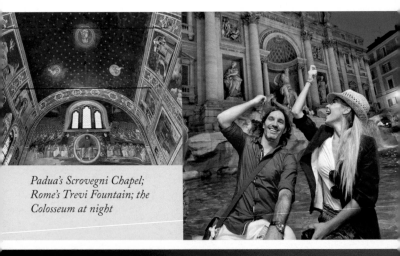

Padua's Scrovegni Chapel; Rome's Trevi Fountain; the Colosseum at night

WORTH-IT DESTINATIONS

You can weave any of these destinations—rated ▲ or ▲▲—into your itinerary. It's easy to add some destinations based on proximity (if you're going to Florence, Pisa is next door), but some out-of-the-way places can merit the journey, depending on your time and interests.

▲▲Milan (1 day)

Many travelers arrive in Milan in northern Italy. With three airports, it's a major transit hub. This powerhouse city of commerce and fashion boasts the prestigious La Scala opera house, pink-marble Duomo, and Leonardo's *Last Supper*.

▲The Lakes (1 day)

For a lakeside stop just an hour from Milan (as a day trip or overnight), consider the Lakes—ideally the quaint village of Varenna on Lake Como, where you can cruise the lake, wander, sunbathe, and dine al fresco. If relaxation is on your agenda, so is Lake Como. Another popular stop is Lake Maggiore and the town of Stresa, where tourists come to see manicured islands and elegant villas.

▲Near Venice (1 day)

Near Venice are several intriguing towns: Padua, known for Giotto's gloriously frescoed Scrovegni Chapel; little Vicenza for its Palladian architecture; and Verona for its ancient Roman amphitheater and Romeo and Juliet sights. Each town is an easy, quick stop on the main train line between Venice and Milan.

▲The Dolomites (1-2 days)

The Dolomites are Italy's mighty Alps, featuring Bolzano, home of Ötzi the Iceman; the charming village of Castelrotto; and Alpe di Siusi, a vast alpine meadow laced with lifts and

The Dolomites; fashionable Milan; view from Lucca's wall; lovely Lake Como hiking trails. Near Austria, the region is sausage-and-sauer-kraut Germanic and can be time-consuming to reach, but if the weather's good, hikers will be in paradise.

▲Riviera Towns (1 day)
You're near Riviera Towns when you're in the Cinque Terre. The coastal towns are little Levanto, double-beached Sestri Levante, the larger Santa Margherita Ligure, gem-like Portofino, and resorty Porto Venere. Choose one—or more!

▲Pisa and Lucca (1.5 days)
These towns make two good stops or day trips from Florence. Pisa has the iconic Leaning Tower, set in the stunning Field of Miracles. The pleasant town of Lucca, a delight for window-shoppers, has an inviting old center, encircled by a wide medieval wall you can stroll or bike.

▲Volterra and San Gimignano (1.5 days)
In Tuscany, these villages are tempting: Volterra is vibrant and rustically real, while multitowered San Gimignano is more photogenic and touristy.

▲▲Heart of Tuscany (1-3 days)
Italy's many hill towns, as sleepy as if they've been caught napping, are popular for good reason. From Florence or Siena, several hill towns are within striking range by public transportation. Those with a car can discover far more. Wine lovers savor a cluster of picturesque, wine-soaked villages amid rolling hills in the Heart of Tuscany: mellow Montepulciano, Renaissance Pienza, and Brunello-fueled Montalcino.

▲▲Assisi (1 day)
Perched on a hilltop, Assisi is the hometown of St. Francis, with a divinely Giotto-decorated basilica dedicated to the humble saint who extolled the virtues of love and simplicity. Assisi is located between Florence and Rome, but will always feel off the beaten track.

▲▲Orvieto and Civita (1 day)
Near Rome, Orvieto offers more hill-town adventures, featuring classic views, Classico wine, and an ornate cathedral, plus nearby Civita di Bagnoregio, a pint-sized hill town reachable only by a narrow, steep bridge.

▲▲Naples (half-day)

A swing south from Rome, from Naples to Paestum, gives you the best of southern Italy. Naples, a good stop en route to the genteel home base of Sorrento, is a gritty port city with nonstop street life and a top archaeological museum starring the treasures from ancient Pompeii.

▲▲Pompeii and Nearby (half-day)

South of Naples are the ruins of famous Pompeii (worth ▲▲▲) and smaller Herculaneum, with their nemesis, Mount Vesuvius, looming on the horizon. The ancient sites are an easy stop between Naples and Sorrento; of the two, Pompeii is better.

▲Sorrento and Capri (1.5 days)

Sorrento is a seaside resort port—a well-located home base for the many sights in the region, including the jet-set island getaway of Capri (worth ▲▲) with its eerie Blue Grotto, just a short cruise away. Also nearby is the...

▲▲Amalfi Coast and Paestum (1-2 days)

From Sorrento, you can travel the cliff-hanging road along the Amalfi Coast, overlooking the sparkling Mediterranean, to visit villages spilling down to beaches.

South of the Amalfi Coast is a site so ancient it predates most Roman sites—Paestum, crowned with well-preserved Greek temples from a time this storied land was Magna Graecia, or Great Greece.

Naples' vibrant street life; the hilltop perch of Civita di Bagnoregio; Cinque Terre's Manarola at night (opposite)

Planning Your Trip

To plan your trip, you'll need to design your itinerary—choosing where and when to go, how you'll travel, and how many days to spend at each destination. For my best general advice on sightseeing, accommodations, restaurants, and more, see the Practicalities chapter.

DESIGNING AN ITINERARY

As you read this book and learn your options...

Choose your top destinations.

My recommended itinerary (see the sidebar on the next page) gives you an idea of how much you can reasonably see in 21 days, but you can adapt it to fit your own interests and time frame. If you like Renaissance art, linger longer in Florence. Exploring Italy's hill towns could soak up a week. For mountains, make tracks to the Dolomites. And if you've always wanted to ascend Pisa's Leaning Tower, now's the time for the climb.

Decide when to go.

Italy's best travel months are May, June, September, and October. They're also the busiest and most expensive times to visit (with the north remaining busy straight through the summer). Crowds aside, these months combine the convenience of peak season with pleasant weather.

The heat in July and August can be grueling, particularly in the south, where temperatures hit the 90s. Fortunately most midrange hotels come with air-conditioning. August is

Italy's Best Three-Week Trip by Public Transportation

Day	Plan	Sleep
1	Arrive in Milan	Milan
2	Milan to Lake Como	Varenna
3	Lake Como	Varenna
4	To Dolomites via Verona	Bolzano/Castelrotto
5	Dolomites	Bolzano/Castelrotto
6	To Venice	Venice
7	Venice	Venice
8	To the Cinque Terre	Vernazza
9	Cinque Terre	Vernazza
10	To Florence via Pisa	Florence
11	Florence	Florence
12	Florence, late to Siena	Siena
13	Siena	Siena
14	To Assisi	Assisi
15	To Orvieto and Civita	Orvieto
16	To Sorrento via Naples	Sorrento
17	Capri	Sorrento
18	Amalfi Coast	Sorrento
19	Morning to Rome via Pompeii	Rome
20	Rome	Rome
21	Rome	Rome
22	Fly home	

Notes: If you have less time, drop the out-of-the-way Dolomites or save the Amalfi Coast for another trip. With extra time, add a day to sight-filled

also when many Italians take their summer vacations; big cities tend to be quiet (with discounted hotel prices), but beach and mountain resorts are jammed (with higher hotel prices).

Winter offers cooler temperatures and fewer tourists, except on major holidays. Expect shorter hours for sights and fewer activities. Beach towns are nearly shut down and battered by waves; skip the Cinque Terre and Amalfi Coast.

For weather specifics, see the climate chart in the appendix.

Connect the dots.

Link your destinations into a logical route. Determine which

Florence or Rome, or slow down in the countryside with more hill towns (check public transportation options first—not all towns are well-served).

Adding a Car: Tour most of Italy by train, then use a car to explore a region or two (even if it means backtracking a few hours by train or car). These stops are easier by train than by car: Venice, the Cinque Terre, Florence, Rome, and the cluster south of Rome (Naples, Pompeii, Sorrento, Capri, and the Amalfi Coast). Drivers will find a car most helpful for exploring the hill-town region. Major car-rental agencies have offices in many towns.

cities you'll fly into and out of. Begin your search for transatlantic flights at Kayak.com.

Decide if you'll travel by car or public transportation, or a combination. A car is particularly helpful for exploring the hill-town region (where public transportation can be sparse), but is useless in big cities (park it). Trains are faster and more expensive than buses (which don't run as often on Sundays).

To determine approximate travel times between destinations, study the driving map in the Practicalities chapter or check Google Maps; visit Trenitalia.it for train schedules. Compare the cost of any long train ride in Europe with a budget flight; check Skyscanner.com for intra-European flights.

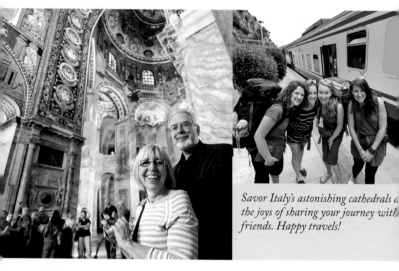

*Savor Italy's astonishing cathedrals ɑ
the joys of sharing your journey wit/
friends. Happy travels!*

Write out a day-by-day itinerary.

Figure out how many destinations you can comfortably fit in
your time frame. Don't overdo it—few travelers wish they'd
hurried more. Allow enough days per stop (see estimates in
"Italy's Top Destinations," earlier). Minimize one-night stands.
It can be worth taking a late-afternoon drive or train ride to
settle into a town for two consecutive nights—and gain a full
uninterrupted day for sightseeing. Include sufficient time for
transportation; whether you travel by train or car, it'll take you
a half-day to get between most destinations.

Staying in a home base (like Florence or Sorrento) and
making day trips can be more time-efficient than changing
locations and hotels.

Take sight closures into account. Avoid visiting a town on
the one day a week its must-see sights are closed. Check if any
holidays or festivals fall during your trip—these attract crowds
and can close sights (for the latest, visit Italy's tourist website,
www.italia.it). Note major sights where advance reservations
are smart or a free Rick Steves audio tour is available.

Give yourself some slack. Every trip, and every traveler,
needs downtime for doing laundry, picnic shopping, people-
watching, and so on. Pace yourself. Assume you will return.

Trip Costs Per Person

Run a reality check on your dream trip. You'll have major transportation costs in addition to daily expenses.

Flight: A round-trip flight from the US to Milan or Rome costs about $900-1,500, depending on where you fly from and when.

Public Transportation: For a three-week trip, allow $550 for buses and second-class trains ($750 for first class). You'll usually save money buying train tickets in Italy, rather than buying a rail pass before you leave home. In some cases, a short flight can be cheaper than taking the train.

Car Rental: Allow roughly $300-500 per week, not including tolls, gas, parking, and insurance (theft insurance is mandatory in Italy).

AVERAGE DAILY EXPENSES PER PERSON

$175
Applies to cities, figure on less for towns

Lodging
Based on two people splitting the cost of a $160 double room with breakfast
$80

Meals
$15 for lunch, $30 for dinner, and $5 for gelato
$50

City Transit
Buses, Metro, or *vaporetti* (in Venice)
$10

Sights and Entertainment
This daily average works for most people.
$35

Budget Tips

To cut your daily expenses, take advantage of the deals you'll find throughout Italy and mentioned in this book.

City transit passes (for multiple rides or all-day usage) decrease your cost per ride.

Avid sightseers buy combo-tickets or passes that cover multiple museums. If a town doesn't offer deals, visit only the sights you most want to see, and seek out free sights and experiences (people-watching counts).

Some businesses—especially hotels and walking-tour companies—offer discounts to my readers (look for the RS% ▶▶▶

Rick Steves Italy

▶▶▶ symbol in the listings in this book).

Reserve your rooms directly with the hotel. Some hotels offer discounts if you pay in cash and/or stay three or more nights (check online or ask). Rooms can cost less in spring and fall (May, June, Sept, and Oct). And even seniors can sleep cheaply in hostels (most have private rooms) for about $30 per person. Or check Airbnb-type sites for deals.

It's no hardship to eat inexpensively in Italy. You can get tasty, affordable meals at delis, bars, takeout pizza shops, street food joints, and Italian restaurants, too. Cultivate the art of picnicking (but avoid it at major sights).

When you splurge, choose an experience you'll always remember, such as a food tour or a gondola ride. Minimize souvenir shopping; focus instead on collecting wonderful memories. ▮

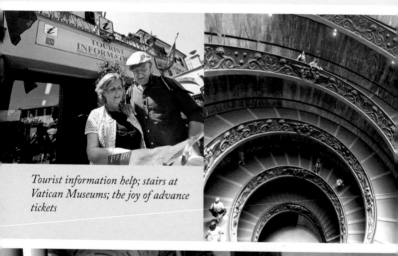

Tourist information help; stairs at Vatican Museums; the joy of advance tickets

BEFORE YOU GO

You'll have a smoother trip if you tackle a few things ahead of time. For more details on these topics, see the Practicalities chapter and RickSteves.com, which has helpful travel-tip articles and videos.

Make sure your travel documents are valid. If your passport is due to expire within six months of your ticketed date of return, you need to renew it. Allow six weeks or more to renew or get a passport (www.travel.state.gov). Check for current Covid entry requirements, such as proof of vaccination or a negative Covid-19 test result.

Arrange your transportation. Book your international flights. Overall, Kayak.com is the best place to start searching for flights. Figure out your transportation options. It's worth thinking about buying essential train tickets online in advance, getting a rail pass, renting a car, or booking cheap European flights. (You can wing it once you're there, but it may cost more.) Drivers: Consider bringing an International Driving Permit (sold at AAA offices in the US, www.aaa.com) along with your license.

Book rooms well in advance, especially if your trip falls during peak season or any major holidays or festivals.

Reserve ahead for key sights. Make reservations or buy tickets in advance for major sights. In Venice, it's smart to book ahead for St. Mark's Basilica, the Doge's Palace, and the Campanile bell tower. For Padua, book well in advance for Giotto's Scrovegni Chapel. For Milan, reserve weeks ahead for Leonardo's *Last Supper*. In Florence, reserve ahead for the Uffizi Gallery (Renaissance paintings), Accademia (Michelangelo's David), and to climb the cathedral dome (mandatory). For Pisa, you can book a time to climb the Leaning Tower.

In Rome, reservations are essential for the Borghese Gallery (Bernini sculptures), Vatican Museums (Sistine Chapel), the Colosseum, and the Roman Forum.

Consider travel insurance. Compare the cost of insurance to the cost of your potential loss. Check whether your existing insurance (health, homeowners, or renters) covers you and your possessions overseas.

Call your bank. Alert your bank that you'll be using your debit and credit cards in Europe. Ask about transaction fees, and, if you don't already have one, get a "contactless" credit card (request your card PIN too). You don't need to bring euros for your trip; you can withdraw euros from cash machines in Europe.

Use your smartphone smartly. Sign up for an international service plan to reduce your costs, or rely on Wi-Fi in Europe instead. Download any useful apps you'll want on the road, such as maps, translators, transit schedules, and Rick Steves Audio Europe (see sidebar).

Pack light. You'll walk with your luggage more than you think. I travel for weeks with a single carry-on bag and a day pack. Use the packing checklist in the appendix as a guide.

Rick's Free Video Clips and Audio Tours

Travel smarter with these free, fun resources:

Rick Steves Classroom Europe, a powerful tool for teachers, is also useful for travelers. This video library contains about 500 short clips excerpted from my public television series. Enjoy these videos as you sort through options for your trip and to better understand what you'll see in Europe. Check it out at Classroom.RickSteves.com (just enter a topic to find everything I've filmed on a subject).

Rick Steves Audio Europe, a free app, makes it easy to download my audio tours and listen to them offline as you travel. For this book (look for the 🎧), these audio tours cover sights and neighborhoods in Venice, Milan, Florence, Siena, Assisi, Rome, Naples, and Pompeii. The app also offers interviews (organized by country) from my public radio show with experts from Europe and around the globe. Find it in your app store or at RickSteves.com/AudioEurope.

Travel Smart

Many people think Italy is a chaotic mess and any attempt at efficient travel is futile. This is dead wrong—and costly, in terms of time and money. Italy, which seems as orderly as spilled spaghetti, actually functions quite well. If you have a positive attitude, equip yourself with good information (this book), and expect to travel smart, you will.

Read—and reread—this book. To have an "A" trip, be an "A" student. Note opening hours of sights, closed days, crowd-beating tips, and whether reservations are required or advisable. Check the latest at RickSteves.com/update.

Be your own tour guide. As you travel, get up-to-date info on sights, reserve tickets and tours, reconfirm hotels and travel arrangements, and check transit connections. Visit local tourist information offices (TIs). Upon arrival in a new town, lay the groundwork for a smooth departure; confirm the train, bus, or road you'll take when you leave.

Outsmart thieves. Pickpockets abound in crowded places where tourists congregate. Treat commotions as smokescreens for theft. Keep your cash, credit cards, and passport secure in a money belt tucked under your clothes; carry only a day's spending money in your front pocket or wallet. Don't set valuable items down on counters or café tabletops, where they can be quickly stolen or easily forgotten.

Minimize potential loss. Keep expensive gear to a minimum. Bring copies or take photos of important documents (passport and cards) to aid in replacement if they're lost or stolen. Back up photos and files frequently.

Beat the summer heat. If you wilt easily, choose a hotel with air-conditioning, start your day early, take a midday siesta, and resume your sightseeing later. Churches offer a cool haven (though dress modestly—no bare shoulders or shorts). Take frequent gelato breaks. Join the *passeggiata,* when locals stroll in the cool of the evening.

Guard your time and energy. Taking a taxi or Uber can be a good value if it saves you a long wait for a cheap bus or an exhausting walk across town. To avoid long lines, follow my crowd-beating tips, such as making advance reservations, or sightseeing early or late. Buy combo-tickets at less-visited sights to get quickly into popular sights.

Be flexible. Even if you have a well-planned itinerary, expect changes, strikes, closures, sore feet, bad weather, and so on. Your Plan B could turn out to be even better.

Attempt the language. Many Italians—especially in the tourist trade and in cities—speak English, but if you learn some Italian, even just a few pleasantries, you'll get more smiles and make more friends. Apps such as Google Translate work for on-the-go translation help, but you can get a head start by practicing the survival phrases near the end of this book.

Connect with the culture. Interacting with locals carbonates your experience. Enjoy the friendliness of the Italian people. Ask questions; most locals are happy to point you in their idea of the right direction. Set up your own quest for the best piazza, bell tower, or gelato. When an opportunity pops up, make it a habit to say "yes."

Italy...here you come!

VENICE

Venezia

Soak all day in this puddle of elegant decay. Venice is Europe's best-preserved big city. This car-free urban wonderland of a hundred islands—laced together by 400 bridges and 2,000 alleys—survives on the artificial respirator of tourism.

Born in a lagoon 1,500 years ago as a refuge from barbarians, Venice is overloaded with tourists and is slowly sinking (not because of the tourists). In the Middle Ages, the Venetians became Europe's clever middlemen for East-West trade and created a great trading empire. By smuggling in the bones of St. Mark (San Marco) in AD 828, Venice gained religious importance as well. With the discovery of America and new trading routes to the Orient, Venetian power ebbed. But as Venice fell, her appetite for decadence grew. Through the 17th and 18th centuries, Venice partied on the wealth accumulated through earlier centuries as a trading power.

Today, Venice is home to fewer than 51,000 people in its old city, down from about twice that number just three decades ago. While there are about 270,000 people in greater Venice (counting the mainland, not counting tourists), the old town has a small-town feel, and locals seem to know everyone.

Venice is expensive for residents as well as tourists because everything must be shipped in and hand-trucked to its final destination. I find that the best way to enjoy Venice is to succumb to its charms, accept that prices are higher than on the mainland, and blow through a little money. It's a unique place that's worth paying a premium to fully experience.

Escape the Rialto-San Marco tourist zone and savor the town early and late, without the hordes of vacationers day-tripping in

VENICE

from cruise ships and nearby beach resorts. A 10-minute walk from the madness puts you in an idyllic Venice that few tourists see.

PLANNING YOUR TIME

Venice is worth at least two nights and one busy day on even the speediest tour. Sleep in the old center to experience Venice at its best: early and late. On the night you arrive, walk or boat to the train station and then, aboard an empty vaporetto, take my self-guided Grand Canal Cruise to St. Mark's Square (it's less crowded and more romantic at night). The next day, do the major sights on St. Mark's Square (the square itself, Doge's Palace, and St. Mark's Basilica), enjoy the action at the Rialto Bridge and Rialto Market, see the Frari Church for art, and wander the back streets of the Dorsoduro district to the Accademia Bridge and back to St. Mark's Square. Enjoy an evening gondola ride and then a drink with the orchestras on St. Mark's Square. Remember that Venice's greatest sight is the city itself. It's a medieval cookie jar, and nobody's looking. Make time to simply wander.

VENICE

Orientation to Venice

The island city of Venice is shaped like a fish. Its major thorough-fares are canals. The Grand Canal winds through the middle of the fish, starting at the mouth where all the people and food enter, passing under the Rialto Bridge, and ending at St. Mark's Square (Piazza San Marco). Park your 21st-century perspective at the mouth and let Venice swallow you whole.

VENICE: A VERBAL MAP

Venice is a carless kaleidoscope of people, bridges, and odorless canals. It's made up of more than a hundred small islands—but for simplicity, I refer to the whole shebang as "the island."

Venice has six districts known as *sestieri:* San Marco (from St. Mark's Square to the Accademia Bridge), Castello (the area east of St. Mark's Square—the "tail" of the fish), Dorsoduro (the "belly," on the far side the Accademia Bridge), Cannaregio (between the train station and the Rialto Bridge), San Polo (west of the Rialto Bridge), and Santa Croce (the "eye" of the fish, across the canal from the train station).

The easiest way to navigate is by landmarks. Many street corners have a sign pointing you to *(per)* the nearest major landmark, such as San Marco, Accademia, Rialto, and Ferrovia (train station). Obedient visitors stick to the main thoroughfares as directed by these signs…and miss the charm of back-street Venice.

Beyond the city's core lie several other islands, including San Giorgio (with great views of Venice), Giudecca (more views), San Michele (old cemetery), Murano (famous for glass), Burano (lace-making), Torcello (old church), and Lido (with Venice's beach).

TOURIST INFORMATION

With this chapter, a free city map from your hotel, and the events schedule on the TI's website, there's little need to make an in-person visit to a Venice TI. That's fortunate, because although the city's TIs try to help, they're understaffed and have few materials to hand out. To check or confirm something, visit VeneziaUnica.it; this website can be more helpful than the actual TI office. Other useful websites are VisitMuve.it (city-run museums in Venice), UnOspiteDiVenezia.it/en (sights and events), VeniceExplorer.com (mapping), and VeniceForVisitors.com (general travel advice). If you must visit a TI, you'll find offices at St. Mark's Square (#71B, in the far-left corner with your back to the basilica), Marco Polo airport (arrivals area), Piazzale Roma (at the Autorimessa Comunale parking garage), and the train station (across from track 2).

Be wary of the travel agencies or special information services that masquerade as TIs but serve fancy hotels and tour companies. They're in the business of selling things you don't need.

Maps: Of all places, Venice demands a good map. Hotels give away freebies. TIs and some vaporetto ticket booths sell decent maps—but you can find a wider range at bookshops, newsstands, and postcard stands. Getting a map that shows all the tiny alleys may be the best money you spend in Venice. But know you'll still spend some time "exploring" (read: lost). Many just rely on Google Maps and do fine.

ARRIVAL IN VENICE

For a rundown on Venice's train station, bus station, airport, and cruise terminal, and tips for drivers, see the "Venice Connections" section later in this chapter.

HELPFUL HINTS

Sightseeing Tips: Venice offers plenty of sightseeing passes, but only a few are worth the money. For more on passes and other sightseeing advice, see page 59.

Day-Tripper Tax: Beginning in January 2023, Venice plans to charge day-trippers a tourism fee (ranging from €3 to €10) to enter the city center. Check the TI website for the latest.

Theft Alert: The dark, late-night streets of Venice are generally safe. Even so, pickpockets (often elegantly dressed) work all the extremely crowded areas: main streets, docks, and vaporetti. Be particularly careful at St. Mark's Basilica, near the Accademia or Rialto bridges (especially if you're preoccupied with taking photos), or on a tightly packed vaporetto.

A handy *polizia* station is on the right side of St. Mark's Square as you face the basilica (at #63, near Caffè Florian). To call the police, dial 112. The Venice TI handles complaints (www.veneziaunica.it, under "Contacts") about local crooks, including gondoliers, restaurants, and hotel rip-offs.

Medical Help: Venice's Santi Giovanni e Paolo hospital (+39 041 889 7908) is a 10-minute walk from both the Rialto and San Marco neighborhoods, located behind the big church of the same name on Fondamenta dei Mendicanti (toward Fondamente Nove). You can take vaporetto #4.1 from San Zaccaria, or #5.2 from the train station or Piazzale Roma, to the Ospedale stop. There's also a first-aid station staffed by English-speaking doctors on St. Mark's Square, on the right-hand side as you face the basilica (at #63 next to Caffè Florian—same address as *polizia* station, daily 8:00-20:00, +39 041 2960 784).

Behave in Venice: Remember that Venice is a community of about 50,000 people who welcome visitors but feel violated when tourists don't respect the city they love. The vast majority of visitors are day-trippers stampeding in, seeing the famous stuff, and stampeding out. Venetians ask that a few simple rules are followed: Dress decently, don't swim in the canals, don't litter, stay on the right as you walk, and treat things as if they are both historic and fragile...because they are.

Dress Modestly: When visiting St. Mark's Basilica or other major churches, men, women, and even children must cover their shoulders and knees. Remove hats when entering a church.

Picnics: Picnicking is illegal anywhere on St. Mark's Square, and offenders can be fined. The only place nearby for a legal picnic is in Giardinetti Reali, the small bench-filled park along the waterfront west of the Piazzetta near St. Mark's Square. Elsewhere in Venice, picnicking is no problem.

Bookstores: In keeping with its literary heritage, Venice has classy and inviting bookstores. The small **Studium,** a block behind St. Mark's Basilica, has a carefully chosen selection of new English books, including my guidebooks (Mon-Sat 9:30-19:30, shorter hours Sun, on Calle de la Canonica at #337—see map on page 61, +39 041 522 2382, www.libreriastudium.eu).

Used-bookstore lovers will appreciate the funky **Acqua**

VENICE

Venice

GHETTO

Canale de Cannaregio

CANNA

To Mestre & Mainland

GUGLIE BRIDGE

SAN LEONARDO

SAN GEREMIA

SAN MARCUOLA

Campo de Gheto Novo

SANTA LUCIA STATION (FERROVIA)

SCALZI

LISTA DI SPAGNA

Grand Canal

SAN ZAN DEGOLA

To Tronchetto & Mainland

SCALZI BRIDGE

SAN SIMEONE GRANDE

BEMBO

SAN GIACOMO

Campo S.Giacomo de l'Orio

SAN SIMEONE PICCOLO

GROCERY

SANTA CROCE

SAN

CALATRAVA BRIDGE

CA'AMAI

Campo San Stin

SAN

GARAGE

Piazzale Roma

SAN NICOLO DA TOLENTINO

SAN ROCCO

FRARI

Campo dei Frari

SAN POLO

PEOPLE MOVER

BUS STATION

TINTORETTO

SCUOLA SAN ROCCO

LARGA

MOMBOLI

SAONERI

To Stazione Marittima (Cruise Port) & Tronchetto (Parking)

RIO TERA DEI PENSIERI

FOND. DEL RIO NOVO

Campo San Rocco

SAN PANTALON

SAN TOMA

C. LARGA FOSCARI

SANTA MARGARITA

CA' FOSCARI

FONDAMENTA FOSCARINI

Campo Santa Margarita

R. TERA CANAL

CA' REZZONICO

PALAZZO GRASSI

C. CAR. SAL. S. SAM.

SANTA MARIA DEI CARMINI

FOND. S. SEBASTIAN

C. LARGA FOSCARI

Campo San Barnaba

SAN BARNABA

Grand Canal

CORFU

ACCADEMIA BRIDGE

SAN SEBASTIAN

SALIZADA SAN BASEGIO

C. LUNGA S. BARNABA

OGNISSANTI

TOLETTA

ACCADEMIA GALLERY

Campo San Basegio

SAN TROVASO

AGNESE

RIO TERA FOSCARINI

FONDAMENTA ZATTERE AL PONTE LONGO

DORSO

200 Meters
200 Yards

V Vaporetto Dock
T Traghetto Crossing
G Gondola Station
A Alilaguna Stop

N

Giudecca Canal

VENICE

Alta ("high water") bookstore, whose quirky owner Luigi has prepared for the next flood by displaying his wares in a selection of vessels, including bathtubs and a gondola. Look for the "book stairs" in his back garden (daily 9:00-19:30, large and classically disorganized selection includes prints of Venice, just beyond Campo Santa Maria Formosa on Lunga Santa Maria Formosa, Castello 5176—see map on page 95, +39 041 296 0841). For a solid selection of used books in English, visit **Libreria Marco Polo** on Campo Santa Margherita (Tue-Sat 11:00-13:00 & 15:00-19:00, closed Sun-Mon, Dorsoduro 2915, +39 041 822 4843).

Public Toilets: Handy pay WCs are near major landmarks, including St. Mark's Square (behind the Correr Museum and at the waterfront park, Giardinetti Reali), behind St. Mark's Basilica (just off Campo Santi Filippo e Giacomo), Rialto, and the Accademia Bridge. Or use free toilets at any museum you're visiting, or any tables-and-chairs café you're eating in.

Laundry: Across the Grand Canal from the train station is the coin-operated **Orange Self-Service Lavanderia** (daily 7:30-23:00, on Ramo de le Chioverete, Santa Croce 665a—see map on page 88, mobile +39 346 972 5446).

These laundry places are near St. Mark's Square (see page 88 for locations): Self-service **Effe Erre** is off Campo Santa Maria Formosa (daily 6:30-23:30, on Ruga Giuffa, Castello 4826, mobile +39 340 712 5290). **Lavanderia Gabriella** offers full-service laundry, a few streets north of St. Mark's Square (drop off Mon-Fri 8:30-12:30, closed Sat-Sun; pick up 2 hours later or next working day, on Rio Terà de le Colonne, San Marco 985, +39 041 522 1758, friendly Elisabetta).

Water: I carry a water bottle to refill at public fountains. Venetians pride themselves on having pure, safe, and tasty tap water piped in from the foothills of the Italian Alps. You can actually see the mountains from Venice's bell towers on crisp, clear winter days.

Pigeon Poop: If your head is bombed by a pigeon, resist the initial response to wipe it off immediately—it'll just smear into your hair. Wait until it dries, and it should flake off cleanly. But if the poop splatters on your clothes, wipe it off immediately to avoid a stain.

VENICE

Where to Find Venice's Best Views

- The soaring Campanile on St. Mark's Square
- The balcony of St. Mark's Basilica in the San Marco Museum
- Rialto Bridge, with a free, expansive view of the Grand Canal (and a cooling breeze)
- The luxury "mall" T Fondaco dei Tedeschi (just north of the Rialto Bridge) with great Grand Canal views
- Accademia Bridge, overlooking the Grand Canal and dome of La Salute Church
- The Church of San Giorgio Maggiore's bell tower, with views of Venice and all around the lagoon

GETTING AROUND VENICE

Venice is small. You can walk across it, from head to tail, in about an hour. Nearly all of your sightseeing is within a 20-minute walk of the Rialto Bridge or St. Mark's Square.

On Foot

The city's "streets" are narrow pedestrian walkways connecting its docks, squares, bridges, and courtyards. To navigate, look for signs on street corners pointing you to *(per)* the nearest major landmark. The first landmarks you'll get to know are San Marco (St. Mark's Square), Rialto (the bridge), Accademia (another bridge), Ferrovia (literally "railroad," meaning the train station), and Piazzale Roma (the bus station). Determine whether your destination is in the direction of a major, signposted landmark, then follow the signs through the maze.

As you get more comfortable with the city, dare to disobey these signs, avoid the posted routes, and make your own discoveries. While 80 percent of Venice is, in fact, not touristy, 80 percent of tourists never notice. Escape the crowds and explore on foot. Walk and walk to the far reaches of the town.

Don't worry about getting lost—in fact, get as lost as possible. When it comes time to find your way, just follow the arrows on building corners or simply ask a local, *"Dov'è San Marco?"* ("Where is St. Mark's?") Most Venetians speak some English. If you're lost, refer to a map, or pop into a hotel and ask for their business card—it probably comes with a map and a prominent "You are here."

Some helpful terminology: *Campo* means square, a *campiello* is a small square, *calle* (pronounced "KAH-lay" with an "L" sound) means "street," and *ponte* is a bridge. A *fondamenta* is the embankment along a canal or the lagoon. A *rio terà* is a street that was once a canal and has been filled in. A *sotoportego* is a covered passageway. *Salizzada* literally means a paved area (usually a wide street). The abbreviations S. and SS. mean "saint" and "saints," respectively. Don't get hung up on the exact spelling of street and square names, which may sometimes appear in Venetian dialect (which uses *de la*, *novo*, and *vechio*) and other times in standard Italian (which uses *della*, *nuovo*, and *vecchio*).

For centuries, Venice got along without any official street names or numbering. Navigating was by landmarks alone ("the fourth alley after the fruit stand closest to the canal"). But when Austria took over in 1798, it imposed the sometimes-confusing system that's still used today.

The Austrians picked a starting point in each *sestiere* (district) and assigned numbers to each house. In the San Marco *sestiere*, for example, numbering started at the Doge's Palace (San Marco 1) and kept going to the last house (San Marco 5562). To the ongoing chagrin of tourists, official addresses still contain just the district name and house number, but no street. That's fine for the postman, but for the sake of others, many businesses and individuals now add a street name.

By Vaporetto

Venice's public transit system, run by a company called ACTV, is a fleet of motorized bus-boats called vaporetti. They work like city buses except that they never get a flat, the stops are docks, and if you jump off between stops, you might drown. For the same prices, you can purchase tickets and passes at docks and from ACTV affiliate VèneziaUnica (ACTV—+39 041 2424, www. actv.it; VèneziaUnica—www. veneziaunica.it).

Tickets and Passes

Individual Vaporetto Tickets: A single ticket costs €7.50 (kids under 6 travel free). Tickets are good for 75 minutes of one-way travel; you can hop on and off at stops and change boats during that time. It's smart to keep your receipt (in case you're checked and your ticket is faulty).

Vaporetto Passes: Because single tickets are pricey, passes pay for themselves in a hurry. You can buy a pass for unlimited use of vaporetti: €21/24 hours, €30/48 hours, €40/72 hours, €60/7-day pass (the clock starts ticking the first time you use it). Think through your Venice itinerary before you step up to the ticket booth to pay for your first vaporetto trip. The 48-hour pass pays for itself with five rides (for example: to your hotel on your arrival, on a

Grand Canal joyride, into the lagoon and back, to the train station...and that spur-of-the-moment moonlight cruise). It's fun to be able to hop on and off spontaneously and avoid long ticket lines. Some smaller and outlying stops are unstaffed—another reason to buy a pass.

Travelers between ages 6-29 can get a 72-hour pass for €28 if they also buy a **Rolling Venice** discount card for €6 (see page 59).

Passes are also valid on some of ACTV's mainland buses, including bus #2 to Mestre (but not the #5 to the airport nor the airport buses run by ATVO, a separate company).

Buying and Validating Tickets and Passes: Purchase tickets and passes from the machines at most stops (English-language option, credit cards accepted), from ticket windows (at larger stops), or from the VèneziaUnica offices at the train station, bus station, and Tronchetto parking lot.

Before you board, validate your ticket or pass by touching it to the small white pad on the dock until you hear a pinging sound (you need to touch the pass each time you board a boat). The machine readout shows how long your ticket is valid—and inspectors do come by now and then to check tickets. If you're unable to purchase a ticket before boarding, seek out the conductor immediately to buy a single ticket (or risk a hefty fine).

Important Vaporetto Lines

For most travelers, only a few vaporetto lines matter.

Line #1 leaves every 10 minutes or so and goes up and down the Grand Canal, between the "mouth" of the fish at one end and St. Mark's Square at the other. Making every stop along the way, it takes 45 minutes to complete the full route.

Line #2 runs between Piazzale Roma (bus station) and San Marco/San Zaccaria via Giudecca (35 minutes); the companion **line #2/** goes from Piazzale Roma to Ferrovia (train station) and Rialto via the Grand Canal (10 minutes). From late May to mid-September, line #2 also runs an express route up and down the Grand Canal, between Piazzale Roma and San Marco/San Zaccaria (35 minutes).

Take time to study the maps at docks before you board. Some boats run on circular routes, in one direction only (for example, lines #5.1 and #5.2).

To clear up any confusion, ask a ticket seller or conductor for help (sometimes they're stationed on the dock to help confused tourists). Get a copy of the most current ACTV map and timetable (in English and Italian, download from www.actv.it, theoretically free at ticket booths but often unavailable), or consult the maps online. System maps are posted at stops. The easy-to-use **CheBateo?** app can help you figure out routes and schedules.

VENICE

Handy Vaporetti from San Zaccaria, near St. Mark's Square

Several vaporetti leave from the San Zaccaria docks, located 150 yards east of St. Mark's Square. The five docks are spaced about 70 yards apart, with seven different berths, lettered A to F. Check the big electronic board (next to the C/D dock), which indicates the departure time, line number, destination, and berth letter of upcoming vaporetti. Once you've figured out which boat you want, go to that berth and hop on.

Line #1: This vaporetto goes up the Grand Canal, making all the stops, including both San Marco stops, Rialto, Ferrovia (train station), and Piazzale Roma—but it does not go as far as Tronchetto (dock E). In the other direction, it goes from San Zaccaria to Arsenale and Giardini before ending on the Lido (dock F).

Line #2: This vaporetto zips over to San Giorgio Maggiore, the island church across from St. Mark's Square. From there, it continues on to stops on the island of Giudecca, the parking lot at Tronchetto, and then down the Grand Canal as far as Piazzale Roma (dock B). In summer, line #2 also runs up the Grand Canal to Rialto, Ferrovia, and Piazzale Roma (dock E).

Line #4.1: This boat goes to San Michele (cemetery) and Murano (45 minutes, dock D).

Line #7: This is the express boat to Murano (25 minutes, dock D).

Hilton Molino Stucky Shuttle Boat: This boat takes even non-guests to the Hilton Hotel on Giudecca, with its popular view bar (20-minute ride, 2-3/hour, dock B-1).

Lines #5.1 and **#5.2:** These are the *circulare* (cheer-koo-LAH-ray) lines, making a loop around the perimeter of the island, with a stop at the Lido—perfect if you just like riding boats. Line #5.1 goes counterclockwise, and #5.2 goes clockwise. Both run less

Boarding and Riding

Once you know which line you want, you need to find the right departure platform (many stops have more than one). At these larger stops, check the electronic departure board to see which boats are coming next, when, where they're going, and from which platform they leave (for example, "Line 2 to San Marco, from platform B"). At smaller stops without electronic displays, signs on each platform show the vaporetto lines that stop there and the direction they are headed. Once you find your platform, be aware frequently in the evenings (#5.1 leaves from dock F, #5.2 from dock C).

Alilaguna Shuttle Boat: This runs to and from the airport (dock B-1).

that other boats may also be leaving from the same platform. When the boat arrives, confirm the direction posted on the bow ("Line 2, San Marco"). To double-check, ask the conductor when you board ("San Marco?").

You'll notice at some big stops that there are two entries—one for tourists and one for locals (a reasonable way to protect locals from the frustrating mobs of visitors that flood their city in peak times). Sometimes boats arrive and can't accommodate everyone in line...leaving you to wait ten minutes until the next vaporetto.

Crowd-Beating Tips

For fun, take my self-guided Grand Canal Cruise. But be warned: Grand Canal vaporetti can be absolutely jam-packed, especially during the tourist rush hour (during mornings heading in from Piazzale Roma, and in evenings heading out to Piazzale Roma).

Is Venice Sinking?

Venice has battled rising water levels since the fifth century. But today, the water seems to be winning. Several factors, both natural and man-made, cause Venice to flood dozens of times a year—usually from October until late winter—a phenomenon called the *acqua alta.*

On my last trip I asked a Venetian how much the city is sinking. He said, "Less than the sea is rising." Venice sits atop sediments deposited at the ancient mouth of the Po River, which are still compacting and settling. Early industrial projects, such as offshore piers and the railroad bridge to the mainland, affected the sea floor and tidal cycles in ways that made the city more vulnerable to flooding. Twentieth-century industry worsened things by pumping massive amounts of groundwater out of the aquifer beneath the lagoon for nearly 50 years before the government stopped the practice in the 1970s. In the last century, Venice has sunk by about nine inches.

Meanwhile, the waters around Venice are rising, a phenomenon that's especially apparent in winter. The highest so far was in November of 1966, when a huge storm (the same one that famously flooded Florence) raised Venice's water level to more than six feet above the norm. The notorious *acqua alta* happens when an unusually high tide combines with strong sirocco winds and a storm. Although tides are minuscule in the Mediterranean, the narrow, shallow Adriatic Sea has about a three-foot tidal range. When a storm—an area of low pressure—travels over a body of water, it pulls the surface of the water up into a dome. As strong sirocco winds from Africa blow storms north up the Adriatic, they push this high water ahead of the front, causing a surging storm tide. Add to that the worldwide sea-level rise that's resulted from recent climate change (melting ice caps, thermal expansion of the water, more frequent and more powerful storms) and it makes a high sea that much higher.

If the *acqua alta* appears during your visit, you'll see the first

Riding at night, with nearly empty boats and chandelier-lit palace interiors viewable from the Grand Canal, can be a highlight of your Venetian experience.

By *Traghetto*

Only four bridges cross the Grand Canal, but *traghetti* (shuttle gondolas) ferry locals and in-the-know tourists across the Grand Canal puddles in the center of paved squares, pooling around the limestone grates at the square's lowest point. These grates cover cisterns that long held Venice's only source of drinking water. That's right: Surrounded by the lagoon and beset by constant flooding, this city had no natural source of fresh water. For centuries, residents carried water from the mainland with much effort and risk.

In the ninth century, they devised a way to collect rainwater by using paved, cleverly sloped squares as catchment systems, with limestone filters covering underground clay tubs. Venice's population grew markedly once citizens were able to access fresh water by simply dropping buckets down into these "wells." Hundreds of cisterns provided the city with drinking water up until 1884, when an aqueduct was built (paralleling the railroad bridge) to bring in water from nearby mountains. Now the wells are capped, the clay tubs are rotted out, and rain drains from squares into the lagoon—or up from it, as the case may be.

So, what is Venice doing about the flooding? After the 1966 flood, officials knew something had to be done, but it took about four decades to come up with a solution. In 2003, a consortium of engineering firms finally began construction on the MOSE Project. Named for the acronym of its Italian name, Modulo Sperimentale Elettromeccanico, it's also a nod to Moses and his (albeit temporary) mastery over the sea. But, in good Italian fashion, greedy government officials couldn't resist the opportunity for personal enrichment, and a corruption scandal stranded the entire project for years.

But finally, in 2020, the system had a promising trial. When high tides reached exceptional peaks, the retractable underwater gates (installed at the three inlets where the sea meets Venice's lagoon) successfully shut out the Adriatic. But with seas rising faster than engineers anticipated, how long MOSE can protect Venice's treasures is an open question.

at three additional locations (see the map on page 34). Just step in, hand the gondolier €2, and enjoy the ride—standing or sitting. Some *traghetti* are seasonal, some stop running as early as 12:30, and all stop by 18:00. *Traghetti* are not covered by any transit pass.

By Water Taxi

Venetian taxis, like speedboat limos, hang out at busy points along

Venice at a Glance

▲▲▲**St. Mark's Square** Venice's grand main square. See page 60.

▲▲▲**St. Mark's Basilica** Cathedral with mosaics, saint's bones, treasury, museum, and viewpoint of square. **Hours:** Mon-Sat 9:30-17:00, Sun 14:00-17:00 (Sun until 16:30 Nov-Easter). See page 62.

▲▲▲**Doge's Palace** Art-splashed palace of former rulers, with prison accessible through Bridge of Sighs. **Hours:** Daily 9:00-18:00, off-season until 17:00. See page 67.

▲▲▲**Rialto Bridge** Distinctive bridge spanning the Grand Canal, with a market nearby. **Hours:** Market—souvenir stalls open daily, produce market closed Sun, fish market closed Sun-Mon. See page 76.

▲▲**Correr Museum** Venetian history and art. **Hours:** Daily 10:00-19:00, Nov-March 10:30-17:00. See page 69.

▲▲**Accademia** Venice's top art museum. **Hours:** Tue-Sun 8:15-19:15, Mon until 14:00. See page 72.

▲▲**Peggy Guggenheim Collection** Popular display of 20th-century art. **Hours:** Wed-Mon 10:00-18:00, closed Tue. See page 74.

▲▲**Frari Church** Franciscan church featuring Renaissance masters. **Hours:** Mon-Sat 9:00-18:00, Sun from 13:00. See page 76.

▲▲**Scuola San Rocco** "Tintoretto's Sistine Chapel." **Hours:** Daily 9:30-17:30. See page 79.

▲**Ca' Rezzonico** Posh Grand Canal palazzo with 18th-century Venetian art. **Hours:** Wed-Mon 10:00-18:00, Nov-March until 17:00, closed Tue year-round. See page 75.

the Grand Canal. Prices are regulated and fixed by destination (for example, the 20-minute trip from the train station to San Marco costs €70). Despite regulation, prices can be soft; negotiate and settle on the price or rate before stepping in. For travelers with lots of luggage or small groups who can split the cost,

▲**Campanile** Dramatic bell tower on St. Mark's Square with elevator to the top. **Hours:** Daily roughly 9:30-20:45, shorter hours off-season. See page 70.

▲**Bridge of Sighs** Famous enclosed bridge, part of Doge's Palace, near St. Mark's Square. See page 70.

▲**La Salute Church** Striking church dedicated to the Virgin Mary. **Hours:** Daily 9:30-12:00 & 15:00-17:30. See page 74.

▲**Punta della Dogana** Museum of contemporary art. **Hours:** Wed-Mon 10:00-19:00, closed Tue. See page 75.

▲T **Fondaco dei Tedeschi View Terrace** Rooftop terrace atop luxury mall, with views over the Grand Canal. **Hours:** Daily 10:30-18:30, June-Aug until 20:15. See page 76.

Nearby Islands

▲**Burano** Sleepy island known for lacemaking and lace museum. **Hours:** Museum open Tue-Sun 10:00-16:00, closed Mon. See page 81.

▲**San Giorgio Maggiore** Island facing St. Mark's Square, featuring dreamy church and fine views back on Venice. **Hours:** Daily 9:00-19:00, Nov-March 8:30-18:00. See page 71.

▲**Murano** Island famous for glass factories and glassmaking museum. **Hours:** Glass Museum open daily 10:30-18:30, Nov-March until 16:30. See page 80.

▲**Torcello** Near-deserted island with old church, bell tower, and museum. **Hours:** Church open daily 10:30-17:30, Nov-Feb 10:00-17:00, museum closed Mon. See page 81.

taxi boat rides can be a worthwhile and time-saving convenience—and skipping across the lagoon in a classic wooden motorboat is a cool indulgence. For about €120 an hour, you can have a private, unguided taxi-boat tour. You may find more competitive rates if you prebook through the Consorzio Motoscafi water taxi association (prices good for groups of up to 4, one bag/person, extra passengers-€10 each, maximum 9 people, extra fees for late night and extra bags, +39 041 522 2303, www.motoscafivenezia.it). For info on taking a water taxi to/from the airport, see page 122.

VENICE

By Gondola

If you're interested in hiring a gondolier for your own private cruise, see page 82. But note that gondolas are not in business to be a floating Uber service. They only make loop tours.

Tours in Venice

Local guides and tour companies offer plenty of walking tours that cater to a variety of interests.

🎧 To sightsee on your own, download my series of free audio tours that illuminate some of Venice's top sights and neighborhoods (see the sidebar on page 26 for details).

Avventure Bellissime Venice Tours

This company offers several small-group, English-only tours, including a basic two-hour St. Mark's Square introduction that includes skip-the-line tickets to the basilica (€39, includes church entry, Mon-Sat at 11:00, 20 people maximum), an hour-long boat tour of the Grand Canal (€55, Mon-Sat at 10:00, 10 people maximum), and mainland excursions (RS%—10 percent discount on some tours, contact them before booking for a promo code; details at www.tours-italy.com, +39 041 970 499, info@tours-italy.com).

Alessandro's Classic Venice Bars Backstreets Tours

Alessandro Schezzini is a connoisseur of Venetian *bacari*—classic old bars serving wine and traditional *cicchetti* snacks. He organizes two-hour Venetian bar tours (€40/person, most nights at 17:30) that include sampling *cicchetti* with wines at three *bacari*. (If you think of this tour as a light dinner with a local friend, it's a particularly good value.) Tours depart almost daily in season when six or more sign up. They meet 50 yards north of the Rialto Bridge under the big clock on Campo San Giacomo. (Book via email, alessandro@schezzini.it, or by phone at 335-530-9024; www.schezzini.it.)

Venicescapes

Michael Broderick's private, themed tours of Venice are intellectually demanding and engrossing for history buffs. Michael, a passionate teacher, has spent 30 years living and studying in Venice. He's an instinctive "dot connector": His tours intertwine history, art, politics, economics, culture, and religion (various 4- to 6-hour itineraries, 2 people–€280-320 or the USD equivalent, €60/person after that, admissions and transport extra, +39 041 850 5742, mobile +39 349 479 7406, www.venicescapes.org, info@venicescapes. org).

Local Guides

Plenty of licensed, trained guides are available (figure on €75/hour with a 2-hour minimum). I've enjoyed working with the following guides and groups:

Walks Inside Venice is enthusiastic about teaching (€280/3 hours per group of up to 6, RS%; Roberta: mobile +39 347 253 0560; Sara: mobile +39 335 522 9714; www.walksinsidevenice. com, info@walksinsidevenice.com). Along with their four-hour "Grand Tour," they do Ghetto and Plague tours.

Elisabetta Morelli and **Corine Govi,** who run **2Guides-4Venice,** are informative and reliable (Elisabetta: mobile +39 328 753 5220, elisabettamorelli61@gmail.com; Corine: mobile +39 347 966 8346, corinegovi@gmail.com; www.2guides4venice.com).

Venice with a Guide, a co-op of eight good Venetian guides, offers a range of tours (€75/hour, www.venicewithaguide.com).

BestVeniceGuides.it offers a smartly organized online catalog of about 100 local guides, with information to help you pick the right guide for you. Note that Italy allows all licensed guides to lead tours anywhere in the country, so it behooves the thoughtful traveler to book a Venetian guide for the best Venetian experience (family-friendly guides, shared group tours available, most guides about €75/hour, www.bestveniceguides.it).

Grand Canal Cruise

Take a joyride and introduce yourself to Venice by boat, an experience worth ▲▲▲. Cruise the Canal Grande on vaporetto line #1 all the way to St. Mark's Square, starting at the train station (Ferrovia) or the bus station (Piazzale Roma, where you're more likely to find an empty seat). Consider topping it off with my self-guided tour of St. Mark's Basilica (later, under "Sights in Venice").

If it's your first trip down the Grand Canal, you might want to stow this book and just take it all in—Venice is a barrage on the senses that hardly needs narration. On the other hand, these notes give the cruise meaning and help orient you to this great city.

To help you enjoy the visual parade of canal wonders, the tour is organized by boat stop. I'll point out both what you can see from the current stop, and what to look forward to as you cruise to the next stop.

You can break up the tour by hopping on and off at various sights—but remember, a single-fare vaporetto ticket is good for just 75 minutes of one-way travel (passes let you hop on and off all day).

Which Boat? This tour is designed to be done on the slow boat #1—any other boat skips too many stops.

Tours: 🎧 Download my free Grand Canal Cruise audio tour.

Length of This Tour: Allow 45 minutes.

Seating Strategies: As the vaporetti can be jammed, strategize about where to sit—then, when the boat pulls up, make a beeline for your preference. You're more likely to find an empty seat if you catch the vaporetto at Piazzale Roma—the stop *before* Ferrovia (a five-minute walk away).

A few remaining older vaporetti have seats in the bow (in front of the captain's bridge), the perfect vantage point for spotting sights left, right, and forward. With a standard boat and normal crowds, I'd head for the open-air section in the stern and grab the middle seat. While views directly ahead are obliterated by the boat's cabin, you'll have a good view of my described sights on both sides of the boat. If it's not crowded, you can hang out in the middle (loading zone) and bop from side to side (especially easy after dark). Your worst option is sitting inside and trying to look out the window.

OVERVIEW

The Grand Canal is Venice's "Main Street." At more than two miles long, nearly 150 feet wide, and nearly 15 feet deep, it's the city's largest canal, lined with its most impressive palaces. It's the remnant of a river that once spilled from the mainland into the Adriatic. The sediment it carried formed barrier islands that cut Venice off from the sea, forming a lagoon.

Venice was built on the marshy islands of the former delta, sitting on wood pilings driven nearly 15 feet into the clay (alder was the preferred wood). About 25 miles of canals drain the city, dumping like streams into the Grand Canal. Technically, Venice has only three canals: Grand, Giudecca, and Cannaregio. The 45 small waterways that dump into the Grand Canal are referred to as rivers (e.g., Rio Novo).

Venice is a city of palaces, dating from the days when the city was the world's richest. The most lavish palaces formed a grand architectural cancan along the Grand Canal. Once frescoed in reds and blues, with black-and-white borders and gold-leaf trim, they made Venice a city of dazzling color. This cruise is the only way to truly appreciate the palaces, approaching them at water level, where their main entrances were located. Today, strict laws prohibit any changes in these buildings, so while landowners gnash their teeth, we can enjoy Europe's best-preserved medieval/Renaissance city—slowly rotting. Many of the grand buildings are now vacant. Others harbor chandeliered elegance above mossy, empty (often flooded) ground floors.

❷ SELF-GUIDED CRUISE

This tour starts at the Ferrovia vaporetto stop (at Santa Lucia train station). The #1 boat to San Marco generally leaves from dock E (far to the right).

❶ **Ferrovia:** This site has been the gateway into Venice since 1860, when the first train station was built. The Santa Lucia station, one of the few modern buildings in town, was
built in 1954. The "F.S."
logo above the entry stands
for "Ferrovie dello Stato,"
the Italian state railway
system. Consider that
before the causeway was
built in the mid-1800s,
Venice was an island with

no road or train access and no water system. With the causeway the city got a train line, an aqueduct, and a highway.

More than 20,000 people a day commute in from the mainland, making this the busiest part of Venice during rush hour. The nearby Calatrava Bridge, spanning the Grand Canal between the train station and Piazzale Roma upstream, was built in 2008 to alleviate some of the congestion.

❷ **Riva de Biasio:** Venice's main thoroughfare is busy with all kinds of boats: taxis, police boats, garbage boats, ambulances, construction cranes, and even brown-and-white UPS boats. Somehow they all manage to share the canal in relative peace.

About 25 yards past the Riva de Biasio stop, look left down the broad Cannaregio Canal to see what was the Jewish Ghetto. The twin, pale-pink, six-story "skyscrapers"—the tallest buildings you'll see at this end of the canal—are reminders of how densely populated the world's original ghetto was. Set aside as the local Jewish quarter in 1516, this area became extremely crowded. This

VENICE

Grand Canal

To Jewish Ghetto

STRADA

GUGLIE BRIDGE

SAN MARCUOLA

PALAZZO CORRER CONTARINI

Canale de Cannaregio

PALAZZO GRITTI

CASINÒ

PALAZZO VENDRAMIN CALERGI

SAN GEREMIA

LISTA DI SPAGNA

Grand

Canal

PALAZZO FLANGINI

② Riva de Biasio

③ San Marcuola

SANTA LUCIA TRAIN STATION (FERROVIA)

SCALZI

PALAZZO CALBO-CROTTA

SCALZI BRIDGE

PALAZZO MARCELLO

PALAZZO GIOVANELLI

TURKISH EXCHANGE

PAL. GRITTI

PALAZZO DONÀ BALBI

SAN ZAN DEGOLA

PALAZZO CA'TRON

① Ferrovia

SANTA   CROCE

SAN SIMEONE PICCOLO

SAN

CALATRAVA BRIDGE

PIAZZALE ROMA
& PEOPLE MOVER TO STAZIONE MARITTIMA & TRONCHETTO

FRARI

PALAZZO CAPPELLO-LAYARD

Vaporetto Stops

① Ferrovia
② Riva de Biasio
③ San Marcuola
④ San Stae
⑤ Ca' d'Oro
⑥ Rialto Mercato
⑦ Rialto
⑧ San Silvestro
⑨ Sant'Angelo
⑩ San Tomà
⑪ Ca' Rezzonico
⑫ Accademia
⑬ Santa Maria del Giglio
⑭ Salute
⑮ San Marco
⑯ San Zaccaria

Traghetto Stops

Ⓐ Traghetto Santa Sofia
Ⓑ Traghetto San Tomà
Ⓒ Traghetto Santa Maria del Giglio

SAN TOMÀ

PALAZZO BARBARIGO GIUSTINIAN

⑨

Ⓑ T Ⓐ

PALAZZO BALBI

⑩

PALAZZO MOCENIGO

FIRE STATION

CA' FOSCARI

PALAZZO VECCHIA

PALAZZO MORO LIN

PALAZZO GIUSTINIAN

CA' REZZONICO

Ⓐ

PALAZZO GRASSI

⑪

PALAZZO MALIPIERO-CAPPELLO

PALAZZO LOREDAN

PALAZZO FALIER

PALAZZO CONTARINI DEGLI SCRIGNI

PALAZZO GIUSTINIAN LOLIN

⑫

PALAZZO QUERINI

ACCADEMIA BRIDGE & GALLERY

PALAZZO BARBARO

PALAZZO BARBARIGO

DORSODURO

Giudecca Canal

To Zattere

VENICE

urban island developed into one of the most closely knit business and cultural quarters of all the Jewish communities in Italy, and gave us our word "ghetto" (from *geto*, the copper foundry located here).

❸ **San Marcuola:** At this stop, facing a tiny square just ahead, stands the unfinished Church of San Marcuola, one of only five churches fronting the Grand Canal. Centuries ago, this canal was a commercial drag of expensive real estate in high demand by wealthy merchants. About 20 yards ahead on the right (across the Grand Canal) stands the stately gray Turkish Exchange (Fondaco dei Turchi), one of the oldest houses in Ven-

ice. Its horseshoe arches and roofline of triangles and dingle balls are reminders of its Byzantine heritage. Turkish traders in turbans docked here, unloaded their goods into the warehouse on the bottom story, then went upstairs for a home-style meal and a place to sleep. Venice in the 1500s was very cosmopolitan, welcoming every religion and ethnicity, so long as they carried cash. (Today the building contains the city's Museum of Natural History—and Venice's only dinosaur skeleton.)

Just 100 yards ahead on the left (the tallest building with the red canopy), Venice's Casinò is housed in the palace where German composer Richard *(The Ring)* Wagner died in 1883. See his distinct, strong-jawed profile in the white plaque on the brick wall. In the 1700s, Venice was Europe's Vegas, with casinos and prostitutes everywhere. *Casinòs* ("little houses" in Venetian dialect) have long provided Italians with a handy escape from daily life. Today they're run by the state to keep Mafia influence at bay. Notice the fancy front porch, rolling out the red carpet for high rollers arriving by taxi or hotel boat. Across the canal, the plain brick 15th-century building was a granary. Now it's a grade school.

❹ **San Stae:** The San Stae Church sports a delightful Baroque facade. Opposite the San Stae stop is a little canal opening—on the second building to the right of that opening, look for the peeling plaster that once made up frescoes (you can barely distinguish the scant remains of little angels on the lower floors). Imagine the facades of the Grand Canal at their finest. Most of them would have been covered in frescoes by the best artists of the day. As colorful as the city is today, it's still only a faded, sepia-toned remnant of a long-gone era, a time of lavishly decorated, brilliantly colored palaces.

Just ahead (on the right, with blue posts) is the ornate white facade of Ca' Pesaro (which houses the International Gallery of Modern Art). "*Ca'*" is short for *casa* (house).

In this city of masks, notice how the rich marble facades along the Grand Canal mask what are generally just simple, no-nonsense brick buildings. Most merchants enjoyed showing off. However, being smart businessmen, they only decorated the sides of the buildings that would be seen and appreciated. But look back as you pass Ca' Pesaro. It's the only building you'll see with a fine side facade. Ahead (about 100 yards on the left) is Ca' d'Oro, with its glorious triple-decker medieval arcade (just before the next stop).

❺ Ca' d'Oro: The lacy Ca' d'Oro (House of Gold) is the best example of Venetian Gothic architecture on the canal. Although a

simple brick construction, its facade is one of the city's finest. Its three stories offer different variations on balcony design, topped with a spiny white roofline. Venetian Gothic mixes traditional Gothic (pointed arches and round medallions stamped with a four-leaf clover) with Byzantine styles (tall, narrow arches atop thin columns), filled in with Islamic frills. Like all the palaces, this was originally painted and gilded to make it even more glorious than it is now. Today the Ca' d'Oro is an art gallery.

Look at the Venetian chorus line of palaces in front of the boat. On the right is the arcade of the covered fish market, with the open-air produce market just beyond. It bustles in the morning but is quiet the rest of the day. This is a great scene to wander through—even though European Union hygiene standards have made it cleaner and less colorful than it once was.

Find the *traghetto* gondola ferrying shoppers—standing like Washington crossing the Delaware—back and forth. While once much more numerable, today only three *traghetto* cross-ings survive along the Grand Canal, each one marked by a classy low-key green-and-black sign. Piloting a *traghetto* isn't the normal day job of these gondoliers. As a public service, all gondoliers are obliged to row a *traghetto* a few days a month. Make a point to use them. At €2 a ride, *traghetti* offer the cheapest gondola ride in Venice (but at this price, don't expect them to sing to you).

❻ **Rialto Mercato:** This stop serves the busy market. The long, official-looking building at the stop is the Venice courthouse. Directly ahead (on the left), is the former trading center for German merchants, built in the 16th century. Later the central post office, it's now a T Fondaco dei Tedeschi, a luxury shopping mall with great rooftop views. Rising above it is the tip of the Campanile (bell tower), crowned by its golden-angel weathervane at St. Mark's Square, where this tour will end.

You'll cruise by some trendy and beautifully situated wine bars on the right, but look ahead as you round the corner and see the impressive Rialto Bridge come into view.

A major landmark, the Rialto Bridge is lined with shops and tourists. Constructed in 1588, it's the third bridge built on this spot. Until the 1850s, this was the only bridge crossing the Grand Canal. With a span of 160 feet and foundations stretching 650 feet on either side, the Rialto was an impressive engineering feat in its day. Earlier bridges here could open to let big ships in, but not this one. By the time it was complet-

ed in the 16th century, Venetian trading power was ebbing. After that, much of the Grand Canal was closed to shipping and became a canal of palaces.

When gondoliers pass under the fat arch of the Rialto Bridge, they take full advantage of its acoustics: *"Volare, oh, oh..."*

❼ **Rialto:** A separate town in the early days of Venice, Rialto has always been the commercial district, while San Marco was the religious and governmental center. Today, a winding street called the Mercerie connects the two, providing travelers with human traffic jams and a mesmerizing gauntlet of shopping temptations. This is one of the only stretches of the historic Grand Canal with landings upon which you can walk. Boats unloaded the city's basic necessities here: oil, wine, charcoal, iron. Today, the quay is lined with tourist-trap restaurants.

Venice's sleek, black, graceful gondolas are a symbol of the city. With about 500 gondoliers joyriding amid the churning vaporetti, there's a lot of congestion on the Grand Canal. Pay attention—this is where most of the gondola and vaporetto accidents take place. While the Rialto is the highlight of many gondola rides, gondoliers understandably prefer the quieter small canals. Watch your vaporetto driver curse the better-paid gondoliers.

Ahead 100 yards on the left, two gray-colored palaces stand side by side (City Hall and the mayor's office). Their horseshoe-shaped, arched windows are similar and their stories are the same height, lining up to create the effect of one long balcony.

❽ San Silvestro: We now enter a long stretch of important merchants' palaces, each with proud and different facades. Because ships couldn't navigate beyond the Rialto Bridge, the biggest palaces—with the major shipping needs—line this last stretch of the navigable Grand Canal.

Palaces like these were multifunctional: ground floor for the warehouse, offices and showrooms upstairs, and living quarters above, on the "noble floors" (with big windows to allow in maximum light). Servants lived and worked on the very top floors (with the smallest windows). For fire-safety reasons, kitchens were also located on the top floors. Peek into the noble floors to catch a glimpse of their still-glorious chandeliers of Murano glass.

The Palazzo Grimani (across from the San Silvestro dock) sports a heavy white Roman-style facade—a reminder that the Grimani family included a cardinal and had strong Roman connections.

The Palazzo Papadopoli, with the two obelisks on its roof (50 yards beyond the San Silvestro stop on the right, with the blue posts), is the very fancy Aman Hotel where George and Amal Clooney were married in 2014.

❾ Sant'Angelo: Notice how many buildings have a foundation of waterproof white stone *(pietra d'Istria)* upon which the bricks sit high and dry. Many canal-level floors are abandoned as the rising water level takes its toll.

The posts—historically painted gaily with the equivalent of family coats of arms—don't rot underwater. But the wood at the waterline, where it's exposed to oxygen, does. On the smallest canals, little "no motorboats" signs indicate that these canals are for gondolas only (no motorized craft, 5 kph speed limit, no wake).

❿ San Tomà: Fifty yards ahead, on the right side (with twin obelisks on the rooftop) stands Palazzo Balbi, the palace of an early-17th-century captain general of the sea. This palace, like so many in the city, flies three flags: Italy (green-white-red), the European Union (blue with ring of stars), and Venice (a lion on a field of red and gold). Today it houses the administrative headquarters of the regional government.

Just past the admiral's palace, look immediately to the right, down a side canal. On the right side of that canal, before the bridge, see the traffic light and the fire station (the 1930s Mussolini-era building with four arches hiding fireboats parked and ready to go).

The impressive Ca' Foscari, with a classic Venetian facade (on the corner, across from the fire station), dominates the bend in the canal. This is the main building of the University of Venice, which has about 25,000 students. Notice the elegant lamp on the corner—needed in the old days to light this intersection.

The grand, heavy, white Ca' Rezzonico, just before the stop of the same name, houses the Museum of 18th-Century Venice. Across the canal is the cleaner and leaner Palazzo Grassi, the last major palace built on the canal, erected in the late 1700s. It was

purchased by a French tycoon and now displays part of Punta della Dogana's contemporary art collection.

❶ Ca' Rezzonico: Up ahead, the Accademia Bridge leads over the Grand Canal to the Accademia Gallery (right side), filled with the best Venetian paintings. There was no bridge here until 1854, when a cast-iron one was built. It was replaced with this wooden bridge in 1933. While meant to be temporary, it still stands today, nearly a century later.

❷ Accademia: From here, look through the graceful bridge and way ahead to enjoy a classic view of La Salute Church, topped by a crown-shaped dome supported by scrolls. This Church of St. Mary of Good Health was built to ask God to deliver Venetians from the devastating plague of 1630 (which had killed about a third of the city's population).

The low, white building among greenery (100 yards ahead, on the right, between the Accademia Bridge and the church) is the Peggy Guggenheim Collection. The American heiress "retired" here, sprucing up a palace that had been abandoned in mid-construction. Peggy willed the city her fine collection of modern art.

Two doors past the Guggenheim, Palazzo Dario has a great set of characteristic funnel-shaped chimneys. These forced embers through a loop-the-loop channel until they were dead—required in the days when stone palaces were surrounded by humble wooden buildings, and a live spark could make a merchant's workforce homeless. Three doors later is the Salviati building, which once served as a glassworks. Its fine Art Nouveau mosaic, done in

the early 20th century, features Venice as a queen being appreciated by the big shots of society.

⓭ Santa Maria del Giglio: Back on the left stands the fancy Gritti Palace hotel. Hemingway and Woody Allen both stayed here.

Take a deep whiff of Venice. What's all this nonsense about stinky canals? All I smell is my shirt. By the way, how's your captain? Smooth dockings?

⓮ Salute: The huge La Salute Church towers overhead as if squirted from a can of Catholic Reddi-wip.

As the Grand Canal opens up into the lagoon, the last building on the right with the golden ball is the 17th-century Customs House, which now houses the Punta della Dogana contemporary art museum. Its two bronze Atlases hold a statue of Fortune riding the ball. Arriving ships stopped here to pay their tolls.

⓯ San Marco: Up ahead on the left, the green pointed tip of the Campanile marks St. Mark's Square, the political and religious center of Venice...and the final destination of this tour. You could get off at the San Marco stop and go straight to St. Mark's Square. But I'm staying on the boat for one more stop, just past St. Mark's Square (it's a quick walk back).

Survey the lagoon. Opposite St. Mark's Square, across the water, the ghostly white church with the pointy bell tower is San Giorgio Maggiore, with great views of Venice. Next to it is the residential island Giudecca, stretching from close to San Giorgio Maggiore past the Venice youth hostel (with a nice view, directly across) to the Hilton Hotel (good nighttime view, far right end of island).

Still on board? If you are, as we leave the San Marco stop look left and prepare for a drive-by view of St. Mark's Square. First comes the bold white facade of the old mint (in front of the bell tower) marked by a tiny cupola yet as sturdy as Fort Knox, where Venice's golden ducat, the "dollar" of the Venetian Republic, was made. Next door is the library, its facade just three windows wide. Then comes the city's ceremonial front door: twin columns topped by St. Theodore standing on a crocodile and the winged lion of St. Mark, who've welcomed visitors since the 15th century. Between the columns, catch a glimpse of two giant figures atop the Clock Tower—they've been whacking their clappers every hour since 1499. The domes of St. Mark's Basilica are soon eclipsed by the lacy facade of the Doge's Palace. Next you'll see many gondolas with their green breakwater buoys, the Bridge of Sighs (leading from the palace to the prison—check out the maximum-security bars), and finally the grand harborside promenade—the Riva.

Follow the Riva with your eye, past elegant hotels to the green area in the distance. This is the largest of Venice's few parks, which hosts the annual Biennale festival. Much farther in the distance is the Lido, the island with Venice's beach. Its sand and casinos are tempting, though given its car traffic, it lacks the medieval charm of Venice.

⓰ San Zaccaria: OK, you're at your last stop. Quick—muscle your way off this boat! (If you don't, you'll eventually end up at the Lido.)

At San Zaccaria, you're right in the thick of the action. A number of other vaporetti depart from here (see page 40). Otherwise, it's a short walk back along the Riva to St. Mark's Square. Ahoy!

Sights in Venice

Venice's greatest sight is the city itself. As well as seeing world-class museums and buildings, make time to wander narrow lanes, linger over a meal, or enjoy evening magic on St. Mark's Square. One of Venice's most delightful experiences—a gondola ride, worth ▲▲▲—is covered later, under "Experiences in Venice."

When you see a 🎧 in a listing, it means the sight is covered in a free audio tour (via my Rick Steves Audio Europe app—see page 26).

SIGHTSEEING STRATEGIES
Avoiding Lines and Crowds

Venice is inundated with cruise-ship passengers and tours from mainland hotels daily from 10:00 to about 16:00. Major sights are busiest in the late morning, making this a smart time to explore the back lanes. Sights that have crowd problems get even more packed when it rains.

Three sights are often plagued by long lines: Saint Mark's Basilica, the Doge's Palace, and the Campanile bell tower—and the only way to be sure to avoid a wait is to book a timed-entry ticket online in advance. You may also save time by booking ahead for the Accademia. For the rest of Venice's sights, you should be fine just dropping by at any time.

If you didn't buy ahead, and are confronted by a long line for the Doge's Palace, purchase your ticket at the Correr Museum across St. Mark's Square. And for the Campanile bell tower, remember that you can skip it entirely if you're going to the similar San Giorgio Maggiore bell tower—which actually offers a better view.

Sightseeing Passes

Venice offers a dizzying array of combo-tickets and sightseeing passes. Note that many of the most visit-worthy sights in town (the Accademia, Peggy Guggenheim Collection, Scuola San Rocco, Campanile, and St. Mark's Basilica—and its sights within that charge admission) are not covered by any pass.

Museum Pass: Busy sightseers may find value in this pass, which covers the Doge's Palace, Correr Museum, Ca' Rezzonico (Museum of 18th-Century Venice); Palazzo Mocenigo Costume Museum; Casa Goldoni (home of the Italian playwright); Ca' Pesaro (modern art); Museum of Natural History in the Santa Croce district; the Glass Museum on the island of Murano; and the Lace Museum on the island of Burano. At €35 (€18 for youth and seniors), this pass is an obvious value if you plan to see the Doge's Palace, Correr Museum, and one or two of the other covered museums. Buy it at any participating museum or via their websites (www.visitmuve.it).

Rolling Venice: If you're under 30, this €6 youth pass offers free admission and/or discounts at dozens of sights and shops, but its best deal is for transit. It lets you buy a 72-hour transit pass for a discounted €28 (sold at TIs, vaporetto ticket offices, and VèneziaUnica shops).

SAN MARCO DISTRICT

▲▲▲St. Mark's Square (Piazza San Marco)

This grand square is surrounded by splashy, historic buildings and sights: St. Mark's Basilica, the Doge's Palace, the Campanile bell tower, the Clock Tower, and the Correr Museum. The square is filled with music, lovers, pigeons, and tourists by day, and is your private rendezvous with the Venetian past late at night, when Europe's most magnificent dance floor is *the* romantic place to be.

For a slow and pricey evening thrill, invest €15 or so (including service and cover charge for the music) for a drink at one of the elegant cafés with the dueling orchestras (see "Cafés on St. Mark's Square" sidebar, later). For an unmatched experience that offers the best people-watching, it's worth the splurge.

For more on the square, the Clock Tower, the Campanile, and other sights on the square, download my free 🎧 St. Mark's Square audio tour.

Visiting the Square: St. Mark's Basilica dominates the square with its Eastern-style onion domes and glowing mosaics. Mark Twain said it looked like "a vast warty bug taking a meditative walk." (I say it looks like tiara-wearing ladybugs copulating.) To the right of the basilica is its 325-foot-tall Campanile. Behind the Campanile, you can catch a glimpse of the pale pink Doge's Palace. Lining the square are the former government offices *(procuratie)* that administered the Venetian empire's vast network of trading outposts, which stretched all the way to Turkey.

With your back to the church, survey one of Europe's great urban spaces, and the only square in Venice to merit the title "Piazza." Nearly two football fields long, it's surrounded by the offices of the republic. On the right are the "old offices" (16th-century Renaissance). At left are the "new offices" (17th-century High Renaissance). Napoleon called the piazza "the most beautiful drawing room in Europe," and added to the intimacy by building the final wing, opposite the basilica, that encloses the square.

The arcade ringing the square provides an elegant promenade—complete with drapes to provide relief from the sun.

Imagine this square full of water. That happens every so often at very high tides *(acqua alta)*, a reminder that Venice and the sea are intertwined. (Now, as one sinks and the other rises, they are more intertwined than ever.)

Watch out for pigeon speckle. Venetians don't like pigeons, but they do like seagulls—because they eat pigeons. In 2008, Venice outlawed the feeding of pigeons. But tourists—eager for a pigeon-clad photo op—still haven't gotten that message.

Campanile: The original Campanile (bell tower) was an observation tower and a marvel of medieval and Renaissance archi-

St. Mark's Square

Eateries & Entertainment
1. Caffè Florian
2. Gran Caffè Quadri
3. Gran Caffè Lavena
4. Gran Caffè Chioggia
5. Eden Bar
6. Caffè Aurora

Other
7. Il Merletto Lace Shop
8. Studium Bookstore

tecture until 1902, when it toppled into the center of the piazza. It had groaned ominously the night before, sending people scurrying from the cafés. The next morning...*crash!* The golden angel on top landed right at the basilica's front door, standing up.

The Campanile was rebuilt 10 years later complete with its golden archangel Gabriel, who always faces the breeze. You can ride an elevator to the top for one of the best views of Venice (though it can be crowded at peak times; see details later).

Clock Tower: Built during the Renaissance in 1496, the Clock Tower (Torre dell'Orologio) marks the entry to the main shopping drag, called the Mercerie (or "Marzarie," in Venetian dialect), which connects St. Mark's Square with the Rialto Bridge. From the piazza, you can see the bronze men (identified as Moors) swing their huge clappers at the top of each hour. In the 17th century, one of them knocked an unsuspecting worker off the top and to his death—probably the first ever killing by a robot. Notice one of the world's first "digital" clocks on the tower facing the square (with dramatic flips every five minutes).

You can go inside the Clock Tower with a prebooked 45-minute guided tour that takes you close to the clock's innards and out to a terrace with good views over the square and city rooftops (€13 combo-ticket includes Correr Museum—where the tour starts—as well as the National Archaeological Museum and the Monumental Rooms of the Biblioteca Marciana; reservations required; tours in English Mon at 11:00, Tue-Wed at 14:00, Fri and Sun at 11:00 and 14:00; no kids under age 6; +39 848 082 000, http:// torreorologio.visitmuve.it).

Piazzetta and Doge's Palace: The small square between the basilica and the water is the Piazzetta. This "Little Square" is framed by the Doge's Palace on the left, the library on the right, and the waterfront of the lagoon. In former days, the Piazzetta was closed to the public for a few hours a day so that government officials and bigwigs could gather in the sun to strike shady deals.

The pale pink Doge's Palace is the epitome of the style known as Venetian Gothic. Columns support traditional, pointed Gothic arches, but with a Venetian flair—they're curved to a point, ornamented with a trefoil (three-leaf clover), and topped with a round medallion of a quatrefoil (four-leaf clover). The pattern is found on buildings all over Venice and on the formerly Venetian-controlled Croatian coast, but nowhere else in the world (except Las Vegas).

The two large 12th-century columns near the water were (like so much else) looted from Constantinople. Mark's winged lion sits on top of one. The lion's body (nearly 15 feet long) predates the wings and is more than 2,000 years old. The other column holds St. Theodore (battling a crocodile), the former patron saint who was replaced by Mark. I guess stabbing crocs in the back isn't classy enough for an upwardly mobile world power. After public ridicule, criminals were executed by being hung from these columns in the hope that the public could learn its lessons vicariously.

▲▲▲St. Mark's Basilica (Basilica di San Marco)

Built in the 11th century to replace an earlier church, this basilica's distinctly Eastern-style architecture underlines Venice's connection with Byzantium (which protected it from the ambition of Charlemagne and his Holy Roman Empire). It's decorated with booty from returning sea captains—a kind of architectural Venetian trophy chest. The interior glows mysteriously with gold mosaics and colored marble. Since about AD 830, the saint's bones have been housed on this site. The San Marco Museum within holds the original bronze horses (copies of these overlook the square),

and a balcony offering a remarkable view over St. Mark's Square.

Cost and Hours: Basilica entry is €3, though if you reserve a timed-entry ticket online in advance (€6), you can skip the line. Once inside, you can add on any of three separate exhibits within the church (or buy ahead online): Treasury-€5, Golden Altar-piece-€5, and San Marco Museum-€7. Church and all exhibits open Mon-Sat 9:30-17:00, Sun 14:00-17:00 (Sun until 16:30 Nov-Easter), +39 041 270 8311, www.basilicasanmarco.it.

Reservations Recommended: There's almost always a long line to get into St. Mark's. By far the smartest workaround is to reserve an entry time online in advance, which lets you bypass the general admission line for a separate entrance. A limited number of line-skipping spots are available each day, so if you're visiting during busy times, book ahead by several days at least.

If you arrive without a reservation, you can head to the "line-skipping" entrance and scan the posted QR code. If there are time slots available—either immediately or for later that day—you can buy a ticket on your mobile phone on the spot.

For shorter lines and fewer crowds in general, visit early or late.

Prayers and Services: Worshippers may enter the church daily 8:00-19:30 using the Porta dei Fiori door on the north (left) side (Mass times are listed on the basilica website).

Baggage Check: The church will not let you in with a bag. On the north (left) side of the church, you'll find automated storage lockers (€3).

Photographers, Take Note: The interior is brilliantly lit Mon-Sat 11:30-12:45. After that, many of the mosaics are in shadow.

Tours: Free, hour-long English tours (heavy on the mosaics' religious symbolism) may be offered, typically at 11:00 (check website for current schedule). Audioguides (€5) are on sale as you enter.

🎧 Download my free St. Mark's Basilica audio tour.

⦿ Self-Guided Tour

Start outside in the square, far enough back to take in the whole facade. It's a riot of domes, columns, and statues, completely un-

VENICE

St. Mark's Basilica

To San Zaccaria

Not to Scale

MAIN ALTAR (MARK'S BONES BENEATH) — ❿

❽

❻ CENTRAL DOME ❼ — ❺

NORTH TRANSEPT

SOUTH TRANSEPT

CALLE DE LA CANONICA

TREASURY ❾

BAPTISTERY

ENTRY (WORSHIP ONLY)

C. RIZZA

BAG CHECK

SAN BASSO

Piazzetta dei Leoni

NARTHEX

NAVE ❸

❹

❶

ATRIUM

❷

❶❶

LIONS

SKIP-THE-LINE ENTRANCE

GENERAL ADMISSION ENTRANCE

To Doge's Palace

To Rialto

MARZARIA OROLOGIO

CLOCK TOWER

TOUR BEGINS

Piazza San Marco

To Campanile

❶ Mosaic of Mark's Relics
❷ Atrium Mosaic of Noah's Ark & the Great Flood
❸ Nave Mosaics
❹ Pentecost Mosaic
❺ Central Dome Ascension Mosaic
❻ Rood Screen
❼ Doge's Pulpit
❽ Nicopeia Icon
❾ Treasury
❿ Golden Altarpiece
⓫ Stairs up to Museum

like the towering Gothic churches of northern Europe or the heavy Baroque of much of the rest of Italy. Inside is a decor of mosaics, colored marbles, and oriental treasures that's rarely seen elsewhere. The Christian symbolism is unfamiliar to Western eyes, done in the style of Byzantine icons and even Islamic designs. Older than most of Europe's churches, St. Mark's feels like a remnant of a lost world.

The church is encrusted with materials looted from buildings throughout the Venetian empire. Their prize booty was the four bronze horses that adorn the balcony, stolen from Constantinople during the Fourth Crusade (these are copies); the atrium you're about to enter was added on to the church as their pedestal. Later, it was decorated with a mishmash of plundered columns. The architectural style of St. Mark's has been called "Early Ransack."

Now zero in on the details.

❶ Exterior—Mosaic of Mark's Relics: The mosaic over the far left door shows two men (in the center, with crooked staffs) entering the church bearing a coffin with the body of St. Mark.

Eight centuries after Mark's death, his holy body was in Muslim-occupied Alexandria, Egypt. In AD 829, two visiting Venetian merchants "rescued" the body from the "infidels" and spirited it away to Venice.

• *Enter the atrium of the basilica and find a place to view its ceiling mosaics. Start by finding a golden arch overhead with scenes of Noah's Ark. (Note that, depending on where the current entrance and exit are, you may have a better chance to study these fine atrium mosaics on your way out.)*

❷ Atrium Mosaic of Noah's Ark and the Great Flood: Of all the famous mosaics of St. Mark's, this Flood scene is one of the oldest (13th century) and finest. The scenes show Noah and his sons sawing logs to build the Ark. Below that are scenes of Noah putting all species of animals into the Ark, two by two. Then the Flood hits in full force, drowning the wicked. Noah sends out a dove twice to see whether there's any dry land where he can dock. He finds it, leaves the Ark with a gorgeous rainbow overhead, and offers a sacrifice of thanks to God.

• *Climb a few steps, and into the church. Just inside the door, step out of the flow and survey the church.*

❸ The Nave—Mosaics Above and Below: These golden mosaics are in the Byzantine style, though many were designed by art-

ists from the Italian Renaissance and later. The often-overlooked lower walls are covered with green-, yellow-, purple-, and rose-colored marble slabs, cut to expose the grain, and laid out in geometric patterns. Even the floor is mosaic, with mostly geometrical designs. It rolls like the sea. Venice is sinking and shifting, creating these cresting waves of stone.

• *Find the chandelier in the nave (in the shape of a cathedral space station), and run your eyes up the support chain to the dome above. This has one of the church's greatest mosaics.*

VENICE

❹ **Pentecost Mosaic:** In a golden heaven, the dove of the Holy Spirit shoots out a pinwheel of spiritual lasers, igniting tongues of fire on the heads of the 12 apostles below, giving them the ability to speak other languages without a Rick Steves phrase book. You'd think they'd be amazed, but their expressions are as solemn as...icons. One of the oldest mosaics in the church (c. 1125), it has distinct "Byzantine" features: a gold background and apostles with halos, solemn faces, almond eyes, delicate blessing hands, and rumpled robes, all facing forward.

• *Shuffle along with the crowds up to the center of the church.*

❺ **Central Dome Ascension Mosaic:** Here at the center of the church, notice the layout: the church has four equal arms, each topped with a dome, radiating out to form a Greek cross (+). The symmetrical floor plan symbolizes perfection, rather than the more common Latin cross of the Crucifixion (emphasizing man's sinfulness).

Now gape upward into the central dome, the very heart of the church. Christ—having lived his miraculous life and having been crucified for man's sins—ascends into the starry sky on a rainbow. In Byzantine churches, the window-lit dome represented heaven, while the dark church below represented earth—a microcosm of the hierarchical universe.

Under the Ascension Dome: Look around at the church's furnishings and imagine a service here. The ❻ **rood screen** (like the iconostasis in a Greek church), topped with 14 saints, separates the congregation from the high altar, heightening the "mystery" of the Mass. The ❼ **pulpit** (the purple one on the right) was reserved for the doge, who led prayers and made important announcements.

• *In the north transept (left of the altar), is an area usually reserved for prayer. The worshippers are facing a big stone canopy, which houses a small painting of the Virgin Mary.*

❽ **Nicopeia** (North Transept): Venetians then and now pray to a painted wooden icon of Mary and Baby Jesus known as Nicopeia, or Our Lady of Victory. For centuries, Nicopeia was venerated by the Byzantines, who asked Mary to protect them in battle. When Venetian Crusaders captured it, the icon came to protect Venice.

Additional Sights: The ❾ **Treasury** (Tesoro) and ❿ **Golden Altarpiece** (Pala d'Oro) are the easiest ways to see the glories of the Byzantine Empire outside of Istanbul or Ravenna. The treasury (may be closed for restoration) is a beautiful collection of chalices, reliquaries, and jewels, most of them stolen from Constantinople. As you view these treasures, remember that some are nearly 2,000 years old. Beneath the high altar lies the body of St. Mark ("Marce") and the Golden Altarpiece, made of 250 blue-backed enamels with religious scenes, all set in a gold frame and studded

VENICE

with 15 hefty rubies, 300 emeralds, 1,500 pearls, and assorted sapphires, amethysts, and topaz.

Upstairs, don't miss the wonderful ⓫ **San Marco Museum** (Museo di San Marco). It's well worth the price to see an up-close mosaic exhibition, more religious objects that once adorned the church, a fine view of the church interior from above, a view of the square from the balcony with bronze horses, and (inside, in their own room) the original horses. Signs at the back of the church, just before the exit, direct you to the museum entrance.

▲▲▲Doge's Palace (Palazzo Ducale)

The seat of the Venetian government and home of its ruling duke (doge), this was the most powerful half-acre in Europe for 400 years. The Doge's Palace was built to show off the power and wealth of the Republic. The doge lived with his family on the first floor up, near the halls of power. From his once-lavish (now sparse) quarters, you'll follow a one-way tour through the public rooms of the top floor, finishing with the Bridge of Sighs and the prison. The place is wallpapered with masterpieces by Veronese and Tintoretto.

Cost and Hours: €25 combo-ticket includes Correr Museum, €1 fee for online reservation (timed-entry), €13 for youth and seniors, also covered by Museum Pass; daily 9:00-18:00, off-season until 17:00, last entry one hour before closing; café, next to St. Mark's Basilica, just off St. Mark's Square, vaporetto stops: San Marco or San Zaccaria, +39 041 271 5911, http://palazzoducale. visitmuve.it.

Avoiding Lines: There are three lanes for entering the Doge's Palace: for those with a ticket or a pass, for those without a ticket, and for those booked on a Secret Itineraries tour. To enter directly through the turnstile without a wait, buy your ticket online in advance or from the uncrowded Correr Museum across the square.

Tours: The fine **Secret Itineraries Tour** follows the doge's footsteps through rooms not included in the general admission ticket. Though the tour skips the palace's main hall, you're wel-

VENICE

Doge's Palace

1 Doge's Apartments (1st floor)
2 Executive & Legislative Rooms (3rd floor)
3 Judicial Rooms & Armory Museum (3rd floor)
4 Hall of the Grand Council & Sala dello Scrutinio (3rd floor)
5 Café (courtyard level)

come to visit it afterward on your own. Three 75-minute English-language tours run each morning. Reserve ahead, as tours can fill up several weeks in advance—although you can try just showing up at the information desk (€28, includes Doge's Palace admission but not Correr Museum, €15 with combo-ticket; reserve at http://palazzoducale.visitmuve.it, €1 fee). Don't confuse this with the Doge's Hidden Treasures Tour, which isn't worth its cost.

The **audioguide** is dry but informative (€5, 1.5 hours).

Visiting the Doge's Palace: You'll see the restored facades from the **courtyard.** Notice a grand staircase (with nearly naked Moses and Paul Newman at the top). Even the most powerful visitors climbed this to meet the doge. This was the beginning of an architectural power trip.

In the **Senate Hall,** the 120 senators met, debated, and passed laws. Tintoretto's large *Triumph of Venice* on the ceiling (central painting, best viewed from the top) is an allegory of the city in all her glory. Lady Venice is up in heaven with the Greek gods, while barbaric lesser nations swirl up to give her gifts and tribute.

The **Armory**—a dazzling display originally assembled to intimidate potential adversaries—shows remnants of the military might that the empire employed to keep the East-West trade lines open (and the local economy booming).

The giant **Hall of the Grand Council** (175 feet by 80 feet, capacity 2,600) is where the entire nobility met to elect the senate and doge. It took a room this size to contain the grandeur of the Most Serene Republic. Ringing the top of the room are portraits of the first 76 doges (in chronological order). The one at the far end that's blacked out (in the left corner) is the notorious Doge Marin Falier, who opposed the will of the Grand Council in 1355. He was tried for treason, beheaded, and airbrushed from history.

On the wall over the doge's throne is Tintoretto's monster-piece, *Paradise,* the largest painted canvas in Venice. Christ and Mary are surrounded by a heavenly host of 500 saints. The painting leaves you feeling that you get to heaven not by being a good Christian, but by being a good Venetian.

Cross the covered **Bridge of Sighs** over the canal to the **prisons.** Circle the cells. Notice the carvings made by prisoners—from olden days up until the 1920s—on some of the stone windowsills of the cells, especially in the far corner of the building.

Cross back over the Bridge of Sighs, pausing to look through the marble-trellised windows at all of the tourists.

More Sights on the Square
▲▲Correr Museum (Museo Correr)

This uncrowded museum gives you a good overview of Venetian history and art. The doge memorabilia, armor, banners, statues (by Canova), and paintings (by the Bellini family and others) re-create the festive days of the Venetian Republic. And it's all accompanied—throughout the museum—by English descriptions and views of St. Mark's Square. But the Correr Museum has one more thing to offer, and that's a quiet refuge—an elegant Neoclassical space—in which to rise above St. Mark's Square when the piazza is too hot, too rainy, or too overrun with tourists.

Cost and Hours: €25 combo-ticket includes Doge's Palace, €13 for youth and seniors, also covered by Museum Pass; daily 10:00-19:00, Nov-March 10:30-17:00; free and mandatory bag check, elegant café, enter at far end of square directly opposite basilica, +39 041 240 5211, http://correr.visitmuve.it.

▲Campanile (Campanile di San Marco)

This dramatic bell tower replaced a shorter tower, part of the original fortress that guarded the entry of the Grand Canal. That tower crumbled into a pile of bricks in 1902, 800 years after it was built. Ride the elevator 325 feet to the top of the bell tower for one of the best views in Venice (especially at sunset). For an ear-shattering experience, be on top when the bells ring. The gilt-wooden statue of archangel Gabriel at the top always faces into the wind. Beat the crowds and enjoy the crisp morning air at 9:00 or the cool evening breeze at 18:00.

Cost and Hours: €10 on-site, where you'll wait in line; €12 timed-entry ticket lets you skip the line (buy online in advance or use the posted QR code at the entrance to book on the spot); daily roughly 9:30-20:45, shorter hours off-season; may close during bad weather, www.basilicasanmarco.it.

Behind St. Mark's Basilica
▲Bridge of Sighs

This much-photographed bridge connects the Doge's Palace with the prison. Travelers popularized this bridge in the Romantic 19th century. Supposedly, a condemned man would be led over this bridge on his way to the prison, take one last look at the glory of Venice, and sigh. Though overhyped, the Bridge of Sighs is undeniably tingle-worthy—especially after dark, when the crowds have dispersed and it's just you and floodlit Venice. In the middle of the day, however, being immersed in the pandemonium of global tourism (and selfie sticks) can be a fascinating experience in itself.

Getting There: The Bridge of Sighs is around the corner from the Doge's Palace. Walk toward the waterfront, turn left along the water, and look up the first canal on your left. You can walk across the bridge (from the inside) only by visiting the Doge's Palace.

Church of San Zaccaria

This historic church is home to a sometimes-waterlogged crypt, a Bellini altarpiece, a Tintoretto painting, and the final resting place of St. Zechariah, the father of John the Baptist.

Cost and Hours: Free, €3 to enter the crypt and choir chapel, €1 coin to light up Bellini's altarpiece; Mon-Sat 10:00-12:00 & 16:00-18:00, Sun 16:00-18:00 only; two canals behind St. Mark's Basilica.

ACROSS THE LAGOON FROM ST. MARK'S SQUARE

▲Island and Church of San Giorgio Maggiore

This is the dreamy church-topped island you can see from the waterfront by St. Mark's Square. The striking 16th-century church,

designed by Andrea Palladio with his trademark classical touch, features art by Tintoretto, a bell tower, and unforgettable views of Venice.

San Giorgio was the church of a Benedictine monastery, whose monks lived a simple lifestyle and cared for the poor. The church, with a facade like a Greek temple, feels so striking because it just doesn't fit with old-school Venice. Palladio made no concessions to the Byzantine legacy of Venice that you see across the water at the Doge's Palace. In keeping with Palladio's classical sensitivity, the interior decor is all in harmony (compared to the relative visual chaos of, say, the Frari Church). The monks hired Tintoretto (a common-man's painter) to create the Last Supper that hangs to the right of the altar and worked closely with him to hone the message that all are welcome—saints, servants, beggars, sinners—into the Christian faith.

The bell tower here has unobstructed views in all directions and is less crowded than the Campanile at St. Mark's.

Cost and Hours: Church—free, open daily 9:00-19:00, Nov-March 8:30-18:00; bell tower elevator—€8, runs daily 10:00-18:00 (in off-season, may close for lunch 13:00-14:00), does not run during Sun services; +39 041 522 7827.

Getting There: To reach the island from St. Mark's Square, take the one-stop, five-minute ride on vaporetto line #2 from San Zaccaria (runs every 12 minutes from dock B, direction: Piazzale Roma). Remember that one vaporetto ticket is good for 75 minutes of one-way travel, allowing for a quick and free visit here on the way to somewhere else.

Cafés on St. Mark's Square

In Venice's heyday, it was said that the freedoms a gentleman could experience here went far beyond what any true gentleman would actually care to indulge in. But one extravagance all could enjoy was the ritual of publicly consuming coffee: showing off with an affordable luxury, doing something trendy, while sharing the ideas of the Enlightenment.

Exotic coffee was made to order for the fancy café scene. Traders introduced coffee, called the "wine of Islam," from the Middle East (the plant is native to Ethiopia). The first coffeehouses opened in the 17th century, and by 1750 there were dozens of cafés lining Piazza San Marco and 200 operating in Venice.

Today, several fine old cafés survive and still line the square. Those with live music feature similar food, prices, and a three- to five-piece combo playing a selection of classical and pop hits, from Brahms to "Bésame Mucho."

You can wander around the square listening to the different orchestras, or take a seat at a café. At any place with live music, it's perfectly acceptable to nurse a cappuccino for an hour—you're paying for the music with the cover charge. Or you can sip your coffee at the bar at a nearly normal price. The prices are clearly posted. If you sit outside and get just an espresso (your cheapest option), expect to pay €12.50-€6.50 for the coffee and a €6 cover charge when the orchestra is playing (which is most of the day). Service is included (no need to tip).

DORSODURO DISTRICT
▲▲Accademia (Galleria dell'Accademia)

Venice's top art museum, packed with highlights of the Venetian Renaissance, features paintings by the Bellini family, Titian, Tintoretto, Veronese, Tiepolo, Giorgione, and Canaletto. It's just over the wooden Accademia Bridge from the San Marco action.

Cost and Hours: €12, €14 for timed-entry ticket that allows you to skip the line (buy online in advance); Tue-Sun 8:15-19:15, Mon until 14:00, last entry one hour before closing; dull audioguide-€6, vaporetto: Accademia, +39 041 524 3354, www.gallerieaccademia.it.

Visiting the Accademia: The Accademia offers a good overview of painters whose works you'll see all over town. Venetian art is underrated and, I think, misunderstood. It's nowhere near

For locations of the following cafés, see the "St. Mark's Square" map, earlier.

Caffè Florian (on the right as you face the church) is the most famous Venetian café and was one of the first places in Europe to serve coffee (daily 9:00-24:00, shorter hours in winter, www.caffeflorian.com). It was originally named "Triumphant Venice" (Venezia Trionfante). But under French occupation, in the early 19th century, that politically incorrect name was changed.

The Florian has been a popular spot for a discreet rendez-vous in Venice since 1720. Each room has a historic or artistic theme. For example the "Room of the Illustrious Men" (inside, far right) features portraits of great Venetians from Marco Polo to Titian. The outside tables are the main action, but do walk inside through the richly decorated old-time rooms where Casanova, Lord Byron, Charles Dickens, and Woody Allen have all paid too much for a drink. The café's orchestra—the most serious on the square—plays daily from 10:00 to 24:00. Each hour comes with a musical theme (operetta, Latin, Romantic, jazz, Venetian, and so on—you can ask for the program).

Gran Caffè Quadri, opposite the Florian and established in 1780, has another illustrious roster of famous clientele.

Gran Caffè Lavena, near the Clock Tower, is less storied—although it dates from 1750 and counts composer Richard Wagner as a former regular—so it's less intimidating than the more formal cafés here. It was the hangout of gondoliers and lantern bearers for local bigwigs. Drop in to check out its dazzling but politically incorrect chandelier.

Gran Caffè Chioggia, on the Piazzetta facing the Doge's Palace, has no cover and one or two musicians playing—usually a pianist (€7 cocktails, music from 10:30 to 23:00—jazz after 21:00).

Eden Bar and **Caffè Aurora** are less expensive and don't have live music.

as famous today as the work of the florescent Florentines, but—with historical slices of Venice, ravishing nudes, and very human Madonnas—it's livelier, more colorful, and simply more fun. The Venetian love of luxury shines through in this collection, which starts in the Middle Ages and runs to the 1700s. Look for grand canvases of colorful, spacious settings, peopled with happy locals in extravagant clothes having a great time.

Medieval highlights include elaborate altarpieces and golden-haloed Madonnas, all painted at a time when realism, depth of field, and emotion were considered beside the point. Medieval Venetians, with their close ties to the East, borrowed techniques such as gold-leafing, frontal poses, and "iconic" faces from the religious icons of Byzantium (modern-day Istanbul).

Among early masterpieces of the Renaissance is Mantegna's studly *St. George* (Room 4). As the Renaissance reaches its heights, so do the paintings, such as Titian's magnificent *Presentation of the Virgin* (Room 24). It's a religious scene, yes, but it's really just an excuse to display secular splendor (Titian was the most famous painter of his day—perhaps even more famous than Michelangelo). Veronese's sumptuous *Feast in the House of Levi* (Room 10), pictured above, also has an ostensibly religious theme (in the middle, find Jesus eating his final meal)—but it's outdone by the luxury and optimism of Renaissance Venice. Life was a good thing and beauty was to be enjoyed. (Veronese was hauled before the Inquisition for painting such a bawdy Last Supper...so he fine-tuned the title.)

End your tour in the largest room in the museum, Room 23. This giant hall is the upper half of an old Gothic church. The nave was divided under Napoleon's rule, and this became the fine arts academy—the Accademia.

▲▲Peggy Guggenheim Collection

The popular museum of far-out art, housed in the American heiress' former retirement palazzo, offers one of Europe's best reviews of the art of the first half of the 20th century. Stroll through styles represented by artists whom Peggy knew personally—Cubism (Picasso, Braque), Surrealism (Dalí, Ernst), Futurism (Boccioni), American Abstract Expressionism (Pollock), and a sprinkling of Klee, Calder, and Chagall.

Cost and Hours: €16; Wed-Mon 10:00-18:00, closed Tue; audioguide-€7, pricey café, 5-minute walk from the Accademia Bridge, vaporetto: Accademia or Salute, +39 041 240 5411, www.guggenheim-venice.it.

▲La Salute Church (Santa Maria della Salute)

This impressive church, a prime example of Venetian Baroque, was built and dedicated to the Virgin Mary by grateful survivors of the 1630 plague. Ornate and gleaming white, with a huge, crown-shaped dome, the landmark church dominates the skyline where the Grand

Canal meets the lagoon. A number of minor works by Titian and a Tintoretto are kept in the church's sacristy. The dome of La Salute, newly opened to visitors, makes for a breathtaking viewpoint.

Cost and Hours: Church-free, sacristy-€6, dome visit-€8—book ahead online; church open daily 9:00-12:00 & 15:00-17:30; sacristy open Tue 14:00-15:30 & 16:40-17:30, Wed-Sat 10:00-12:30 & 14:00-17:30, Sun 10:00-10:30 & 14:00-17:30, closed Mon; dome visits available Wed-Sun 10:00-17:00; 10-minute walk from Accademia Bridge, vaporetto: Salute, www.basilicasalutevenezia. it/la-basilica.

▲Punta della Dogana

Housed in the former Customs House at the end of the Grand Canal, this museum fea-tures cutting-edge 21st-century art in spacious rooms. This isn't Picasso and Matisse, or even Pol-lock and Warhol—those guys are ancient history. But if you're into newer contemporary artists, the museum is world class.

The displays change completely about every year, drawn from the museum's large collection—so large it also fills Palazzo Grassi, far-ther up the Grand Canal.

Cost and Hours: €20 (varies depending on exhibit); Wed-Mon 10:00-19:00, closed Tue, last entry one hour before closing; small café, +39 041-200-1057, www.palazzograssi.it.

Getting There: Punta della Dogana is near La Salute Church (vaporetto: Salute). Palazzo Grassi is a bit upstream, on the east side of the Grand Canal (vaporetto: San Samuele).

▲▲Ca' Rezzonico (Museum of 18th-Century Venice)

Venice in the 1700s was the playground for Europe's aristocrats, including the wealthy Rezzonico (ret-ZON-ee-koh) family, who owned this palace. Today, the Ca' Rezzonico (a.k.a. the Museo del Settecento Veneziano) contains furniture, decoration, and artwork from the period. This grand home on the Grand Canal is the best place in town to experience the luxurious, decadent spirit of Venice in the Settecento (the 1700s).

The first floor has palatial rooms decorated with period fur-niture and ceiling frescoes by G. B. Tiepolo. On the second floor, paintings by Canaletto, Guardi, G. D. Tiepolo, Longhi, and others bring the era to life. (The third-floor painting gallery—which is skippable—shows lots of flesh in lots of rooms.)

Cost and Hours: €10, €1 fee to reserve online; Wed-Mon

10:00-18:00, Nov-March until 17:00, closed Tue year-round; ticket office closes one hour before museum, audioguide-€4, café on the Grand Canal, vaporetto: Ca' Rezzonico, +39 041 241 0100, http://carezzonico.visitmuve.it.

SAN POLO DISTRICT
▲▲▲Rialto Bridge

One of the world's most famous bridges, this distinctive and dramatic stone structure crosses the Grand Canal with a single confi-

dent span. Designed in 1588 by architect Antonio da Ponte, it took only five years to complete. The arcades along the top of the bridge help reinforce the structure...and offer some enjoyable shopping diversions, as does the Rialto Market nearby (produce market closed Sun, fish market closed Sun-Mon).

▲T Fondaco dei Tedeschi View Terrace

In the Middle Ages, Venice was the world's trading center, hosting scores of nationalities, each with its own caravanserai-like center. The most famous, just off the Rialto Bridge, was once the home of Tedeschi (the Italian word for "German") traders. Later, the building served as the main post office of Venice before being purchased by a global conglomerate and turned into a luxury mall catering to travelers from China and cruise ships.

The mall's top-floor terrace offers a unique perspective over the roofs of Venice and an unforgettable view of the big bend in the Grand Canal. Four times an hour, 70 people are allowed onto the roof for 15 minutes. As you ride the red-carpet elevator to the top floor, notice how the old architectural bones of the structure survive.

Cost and Hours: The terrace is free but access requires a reservation (15-minute timeslots, book online at www.dfs.com/en/info/t-fondaco-rooftop-terrace; walk-ins are welcome if there's space, but no guarantees). Terrace open daily 10:30-18:30, June-Aug until 20:15; east side of Rialto Bridge, +39 041 314 2000.

▲▲Frari Church
(Basilica di Santa Maria Gloriosa dei Frari)

My favorite art experience in Venice is seeing art in the setting for which it was designed—as it is at the Frari Church. The Franciscan "Church of the Brothers" and the art that decorates it are warmed by the spirit of St. Francis. It features the work of three great Renaissance masters: Donatello, Giovanni Bellini, and Titian—each showing worshippers the glory of God in human terms.

Cost and Hours: €5; Mon-Thu 9:00-19:30, Fri until 23:00, Sat until 18:00, Sun 13:00-18:00, shorter hours off-season; modest dress recommended, on Campo dei Frari, near San Tomà vaporetto and *traghetto* stops, +39 041 272 8611, www.basilicadeifrari.it.

Tours: You can rent an audioguide for €2, or download my free ∩ Frari Church audio tour.

Visiting the Church: The church was built by the Franciscan order and consecrated in 1492. It's filled with fine tombs, as many great Venetians chose to be buried here. And its high-quality altarpieces make the church a kind of mini museum of sacred art. The Franciscan love of all of creation—Nature and Humanity—later inspired Renaissance painters to capture the beauty of the physical world and human emotions, showing worshippers the glory of God in human terms.

Enter the church and enjoy the view down the long nave toward the altar. The carved-marble choir, in the center of the nave,

allowed friars to hold smaller, more intimate services. As worshippers entered the church and looked down the long nave to the altar, they were greeted by Titian's glorious painted altarpiece—then, as now, framed by the arch of the choir entrance.

Glowing red and gold like a stained-glass window over the high altar, **Titian's** *Assumption of the Virgin* sets a tone of exuberant beauty. Titian the Venetian—a student of Bellini—painted steadily for 60 years (you'll see a lot of his art). As stunned apostles look up past the swirl of arms and legs, the complex composition of this painting draws you to the radiant face of the once-dying, now-triumphant Mary as she joins God in heaven. Titian died of the plague in 1576 and is buried in the sacristy of the Frari.

In **Donatello's wood statue of St. John the Baptist** (in the first chapel to the right of the high altar), the prophet of the desert—emaciated from his breakfast of bugs 'n' honey and dressed in animal skins—announces the coming of the Messiah. Donatello was a Florentine working at the dawn of the Renaissance.

Bellini's *Madonna and Child with Saints and Angels* painting (in the sacristy—the next room farther to the right) came later, done by a Venetian in a more Venetian style—soft focus without Donatello's harsh realism. While Renaissance humanism demanded Madonnas and saints that were accessible and human, Bellini

A Dying City?

Venice's population (fewer than 51,000 in the historic city) is half what it was just 30 years ago, and people are leaving at a rate of a thousand a year. Of those who stay, 25 percent are 65 or older.

Sad, yes, but imagine raising a family here: Apartments are small, high up, and expensive. Humidity and occasional flooding make basic maintenance a pain. Home-improvement projects require navigating miles of red tape, and you must follow regulations intended to preserve the historical ambience. Everything is expensive because it has to be shipped in from the mainland. You can easily get glass and tourist trinkets, but it's hard to find groceries or get your shoes fixed. Running basic errands involves lots of walking and stairs—imagine crossing over arched bridges while pushing a child in a stroller and carrying a day's worth of groceries.

With millions of visitors a year (150,000 a day at peak times), on any given day Venetians are likely outnumbered by tourists. Despite government efforts to subsidize rents and build cheap housing, the city is losing its residents. The economy itself is thriving, thanks to tourist dollars and rich foreigners buying second homes. But the culture is dying.

Greedy residents could sink Venice long before the sea swallows it up. Locals happily rent apartments to tourists a few times a month rather than affordably to local families, and shopkeepers sell trinkets to tourists before pots and pans to the local population. Even the most hopeful city planners worry that in a few decades Venice will not be a city at all, but a museum, a cultural theme park, a decaying Disneyland for adults.

places them in a physical setting so beautiful that it creates its own mood of serene holiness. The genius of Bellini, perhaps the greatest Venetian painter, is obvious in the pristine clarity, rich colors (notice Mary's clothing), believable depth, and reassuring calm of this three-paneled altarpiece.

Feel comfortable to discreetly freeload off passing tours. For many, these three pieces of art make a visit to the Accademia Gallery unnecessary (or they may whet your appetite for more). Before leaving, check out the Neoclassical pyramid-shaped Canova monument flanking the nave just inside the main entrance and (opposite that) the grandiose tomb of Titian. Compare the carved marble *Assumption* behind Titian's tombstone portrait with the painted original above the high altar.

▲▲Scuola San Rocco

Sometimes called "Tintoretto's Sistine Chapel," this lavish meeting hall (next to the Frari Church) has some 50 large, colorful Tintoretto paintings plastered to the walls and ceilings. The best paintings are upstairs in the grand Chapter Room and, especially, in an adjacent smaller room, with Tintoretto's *Crucifixion*. View the neck-breaking splendor with the mirrors available in the Chapter Room.

Cost and Hours: €10, daily 9:30-17:30, +39 041 523 4864, www.scuolagrandesanrocco.org.

VENICE'S LAGOON

With more time, venture to some nearby islands in Venice's lagoon. While still touristy, they offer an escape from the crowds, a chance to get out on a boat, and some enjoyable diversions for fans of glass-making, lace, and sunbathing.

Lagoon Tour

The islands of San Michele (cemetery), Murano (glass), Burano (lace), and Torcello (oldest church in Venice)—each worth ▲—make a good, varied, and long day trip that you can do on your own.

The Plan: You can travel to any of the four islands by vaporetto. Since single vaporetto tickets are only valid for 75 minutes of one-way travel, getting a vaporetto pass for a lagoon excursion makes more sense (for details on tickets and passes, see page 38). Confirm vaporetto times at www.actv.it.

Start your journey at the **Fondamente Nove** vaporetto stop, on Venice's north shore (the "back" of the fish). Fondamente Nove is a pleasant 15-minute walk from Rialto or St. Mark's. Alternatively, you could reach Fondamente Nove by vaporetto: From San Zaccaria (near St. Mark's), take the #4.1 (35 minutes). From the train or bus station, take #4.2 (30 minutes).

From Fondamente Nove, take the #4.1 or #4.2 vaporetto for Murano (about every 10 minutes). On the way, get off at the Cimitero stop on the island of San Michele to see the cemetery (6-minute ride). Continue on to Murano, arriving at the Murano-Colonna stop (3-minute ride). Sightsee Murano as you make your way to the Murano-Faro stop, where you board vaporetto #12 for the trip to Burano (30-40 minutes).

From Burano, you can side-trip to Torcello on the #9 vaporetto shuttle (4/hour, 5-minute ride). To return to Venice from Burano, take vaporetto #12 all the way back to Fondamente Nove (45 minutes). For a longer, more scenic return past even more lagoon

VENICE

islands, take the #14 from Burano to the San Zaccaria dock near St. Mark's Square (70 minutes).

Note that during summer, slightly faster express vaporetti go directly to Murano-Colonna (if you're OK with skipping the cemetery on San Michele): From San Zaccaria, catch the #7, or from the train/bus stations catch the #3.

San Michele (a.k.a. Cimitero): This island is the final resting place of Venetians and a few foreign VIPs, from poet Ezra Pound to composer Igor Stravinsky. It's also full of flowers, trees, scurrying lizards, and birdsong, and has an intriguing chapel (cemetery open daily 7:30-18:00, Oct-March until 16:30).

Murano: Famous for its glassmaking, this island is home to several glass factories and the Glass Museum. From the Colonna

vaporetto stop, skip the glass shops in front of you, walk to the right, and wander up the street along the canal, **Fondamenta dei Vetrai** (Glassmakers' Embankment). The Faro district of Murano, on the other side of the canal, is packed with factories *(fabriche)* and their furnaces *(fornaci)*. You'll pass dozens more **glass shops** along the canal. Early along this promenade, at #47, is the high-class **Venini** shop, with glass that's a cut above much of what else is on offer here, and with an interior showing off the ultimate in modern Venetian glass design (closed Sun). Murano's inviting ▲ **Glass Museum** (Museo del Vetro) traces the his-

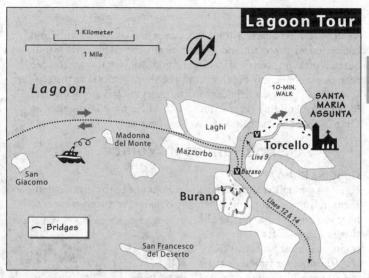

tory of this delicate art and is the best place to see real Murano glass (€10, covered by Museum Pass; daily 10:30-18:30, Nov-March until 16:30; +39 041 739 586, http://museovetro.visitmuve.it).

Burano: This island's claim to fame is lacemaking, and (along with countless lace shops) it offers a delightful pastel village alternative to big, bustling Venice. The tight **main drag** is packed with tourists and lined with shops, some of which sell Burano's locally produced white wine. Its **Lace Museum** (Museo del Merletto di Burano) shows the island's lace heritage (€5, covered by Museum Pass; Tue-Sun 10:00-16:00, closed Mon; +39 041 730 034, http://museomerletto.visitmuve.it). The museum also runs a lace shop, **Il Merletto,** just off St. Mark's Square (open daily, San Marco 95—see the map on page 61).

Torcello: The birthplace of Venice, this island is where the first mainland refugees settled, escaping the barbarian hordes. Yet today, it's the least-developed island (pop. 20) in the most natural state, marshy and shrub-covered. Come here to escape the crowds and relax—the island will not demand much of you. There are a few cafés with leafy outdoor seating, and those interested in church art can view **Santa Maria Assunta Church.** The oldest church in the Venetian lagoon (built in 639; reconstructed in 1008), it sports some impressive Venetian-Byzantine mosaics, a climbable **bell tower** (may be closed for renovation when you visit), and a modest **museum** of Roman sculpture and medieval sculpture and manuscripts (15-minute walk from the dock, church-€6, museum-€4; church open daily 10:30-17:30, Nov-Feb 10:00-17:00, museum closed Mon year-round; museum +39 041 730 761).

Lido Beach

Venice's nearest beach is the Lido, across the lagoon on an island connected to the mainland (which means car traffic). The sandy beach is pleasant, family-friendly, and good for swimming. You can rent an umbrella, buy beach gear at the shop, get food at the self-service café, or have a drink at the bar. Everything is affordable and in the same building (vaporetto: Lido S.M.E., walk 10 minutes on Gran Viale S. Maria Elisabetta to beach entry).

Experiences in Venice

Gondola Rides

Riding a gondola is simple, expensive, and one of the great experiences in Europe. Gondoliers hanging out all over town are eager to have you hop in for a ride. While this is a rip-off for some, it's a traditional must for romantics.

The price for a gondola starts at €80 for a 30-minute ride during the day. You can divide the cost—and the romance—among up to five people per boat, but only two get the love seat. Prices jump to €100 after 19:00—when it's most romantic and relaxing. Adding a singer and an accordionist will cost an additional €120. If you value budget over romance, you can save money by recruiting fellow travelers to split a gondola. Prices are standard and and set by the gondoliers' association. Routes are a loop, and gondoliers generally charge extra to drop you any place other than where you started.

Dozens of gondola stations *(servizio gondole)* are set up along canals all over town. Because your gondolier might offer narration or conversation during your ride, talk with several and choose one you like. You're welcome to review the map and discuss the route. Doing so is also a good way to see if you enjoy the gondolier's personality and language skills. Establish the price, route, and duration of the trip before boarding, enjoy your ride, and pay only when you're finished. While prices are pretty firm, you might find them softer during the day. Most gondoliers honor the official prices, but a few might try to scam you out of some extra euros, particularly by insisting on a tip. (While not required or even expected, if your gondolier does the full 35 minutes and entertains you en route, a 5-10 percent tip is appreciated; if he's surly or rushes through the trip, skip it.)

If you've hired musicians and want to hear a Venetian song *(un canto Veneziano)*, try requesting "Venezia La Luna e Tu." Asking to hear "O Sole Mio" (which comes from Naples) is like asking a Chicago lounge singer to sing "Swanee River."

Glide through nighttime Venice with your head on someone's shoulder. Follow the moon as it sails past otherwise unseen buildings. Silhouettes gaze down from bridges while window glitter spills onto the black water. You're anonymous in the city of masks, as the rhythmic thrust of your striped-shirted gondolier turns old crows into songbirds. This is extremely relaxing (and, I think, worth the extra cost to experience at night). Suggestion: Put the camera down and make it a point for you and your partner to enjoy a threesome with Venice. Women, beware...while gondoliers can be extremely charming, locals say that anyone who falls for one of these Venetian Romeos "has slices of ham over her eyes."

Gondola Alternatives: For cheap water thrills during the day, stick to a one-minute shuttle ride on a Grand Canal *traghetto*. At night, vaporetti are nearly empty, and it's a great time to cruise the Grand Canal on the slow boat #1 (labeled *N* after 23:30). Or hang out on a bridge along the gondola route and wave at fellow romantics.

Festivals

Venice's most famous festival is **Carnevale,** the celebration Americans call Mardi Gras (February; www.carnevale.venezia.it). In Carnevale's heyday—the 1600s and 1700s—you could do pretty much anything with anybody from any social class if you were wearing a mask. These days, tourists and Venetians—from kids to businessmen—gather for parades, parties, and masquerade balls. In drawing such big crowds, Carnevale has nearly been a victim of its own success, driving away many Venetians (who skip out on the craziness to go skiing in the Dolomites). Unless you're interested in joining the fun, any other day this time of year will be much less chaotic—and less expensive.

Every year, the city hosts the Venice **Biennale International al Art Exhibition,** a world-class contemporary fair alternating between art one year (the main event) and architecture the next (much smaller). The exhibition spreads over the Arsenale and Giardini Pubblici park. When the Biennale focuses on visual art, representatives from 80-plus nations offer the latest in contemporary art forms: video, digital art, performance art, and photography, along with painting and sculpture (take vaporetto #1 or, in summer, #2 to Giardini-Biennale; for details and an events calendar, see www.labiennale.org). The actual exhibition usually runs from April through November, but other events loosely connected with the Biennale—film, dance, theater—are held throughout the year (starting as early as February) in various venues on the island.

Shopping in Venice

Venice has more than its share of ticky-tacky souvenir stores hawking goofy knickknacks and knock-off glassware. But artisanal shops with genuine Murano glass, Burano lace, and Carnevale masks have a long history in the city, and the determined shopper can seek out the real thing. If you press beyond the crowded alleyways around San Marco, you'll discover many small, authentic boutiques and perhaps meet the designers behind the wares.

SHOPPING NEIGHBORHOODS

St. Mark's Square and Nearby: The streets closest to St. Mark's Square, and those along the Mercerie (the route between St. Mark's and the Rialto Bridge), are the most-trafficked, the highest-rent, and the highest-priced in town. This is where you'll see all of the big international names.

West of St. Mark's, toward the Accademia Bridge, is more elegant and exclusive, with high-fashion shops along Calle Vallaresso. As you get closer to the Accademia Bridge (around Campo Santo Stefano and Salizzada San Samuele), you'll find more characteristic and affordable textile shops, art boutiques, and galleries.

Dorsoduro: Across the Accademia Bridge, the area immediately around the Accademia and Peggy Guggenheim Collection is touristy but does have some worthwhile places selling glass art and jewelry. In the opposite direction, a 10-minute walk past the Accademia, is Campo San Barnaba, a lower-rent neighborhood that attracts innovative, less-established artisans; this is a great place to window-shop.

Rialto Bridge and Nearby: Right by the bridge, Venice's historic market area is a cancan of shopping opportunities. Many of the products here are edible, but there are lots of hole-in-the-wall jewelry and trinket stores on the bridge, under the arcades to the north, and on the Ruga (the street running from the Rialto toward Campo San Polo and the Frari Church). Near the Rialto end of this stretch is the luxury shopping mall T Fondaco dei Tedeschi.

VENETIAN GLASS

Some visitors feel that because they're in Venice, they ought to buy glass. Remember that you can buy fine glass back home, too (Venice stopped forbidding its glassblowers from leaving the republic a few centuries ago)—and under less time pressure.

Avoid the cheap glass you'll see in touristy shops: Most of it is imported from China or Mexico. Genuine, high-end Venetian glass comes with the signature of the artist etched directly into the glass, along with a number if it's a limited-edition piece (for example, 14/30—number 14 of a total of 30 pieces made).

Shops will ship your purchase home for you, but you're likely to pay as much or more for the shipping as you are for the item(s), and you may have to pay duty on larger purchases. Make sure the shop insures its merchandise *(assicurazione)*, or you're out of luck if it breaks.

If you're serious about glass, visit the island of Murano, its glass museum, and its many shops—you'll find greater variety on the island.

Nightlife in Venice

You must experience Venice after dark. The city is quieter at night, as many tour groups (not mine) stay in the cheaper hotels of Mestre on the mainland, and the masses of day-trippers return to their beach resorts and cruise ships.

Venice has a busy schedule of events, church concerts, festivals, and entertainment. Check at the TI or the TI's website (www. veneziaunica.it) for listings. The free monthly *Un Ospite di Venezi*a lists all the latest happenings in English (free at fancy hotels, or download a copy at www.unospitedivenezia.it).

Baroque Concerts

Venice is a city of the powdered-wig Baroque era. For about €30, you can take your pick of traditional Vivaldi concerts in churches throughout town. Homegrown Vivaldi is as ubiquitous here as Strauss is in Vienna and Mozart is in Salzburg. In fact, you'll find frilly young Vivaldis hawking concert tickets on many corners. Most shows start at 20:30 and generally last 1.5 hours. You'll see posters in hotels all over town (hotels sell tickets at face value).

Tickets for Baroque concerts in Venice can usually be bought the same day as the concert, so don't bother with websites that sell tickets with a surcharge. The general rule of thumb: Musicians in wigs and tights offer better spectacle; musicians in black-and-white suits are better performers.

The **Interpreti Veneziani orchestra,** considered the best group in town, generally performs 1.5-hour concerts nightly at 21:00 inside the sumptuous San Vidal Church (€36, church ticket booth open daily 9:30-21:00 or buy online, north end of Accademia Bridge, +39 041 277 0561, www.interpretiveneziani.com).

Other Performances

Venice's most famous theaters are **La Fenice** (grand old opera house, box office +39 041 2424), **Teatro Goldoni** (mostly Italian live theater), and **Teatro Fondamenta Nuove** (theater, music, and dance).

Musica a Palazzo is a unique evening of opera at a Venetian palace on the Grand Canal. You'll spend about 45 delightful minutes in each of three sumptuous rooms (about 2.25 hours total) as seven musicians (generally three instruments and four singers) perform. With these kinds of surroundings, and under Tiepolo frescoes, you'll be glad you dressed up. As there are only 70 seats, you must book by phone or online in advance, then pay cash at the door (€85, nightly at 20:30, Palazzo Barbarigo Minotto, Fondamenta Duodo o Barbarigo, vaporetto: Santa Maria del Giglio, San Marco 2504, mobile +39 340 971 7272, www.musicapalazzo.com).

St. Mark's Square

For tourists, St. Mark's Square is the highlight, with lantern light and live music echoing from the cafés. Just being here after dark is a thrill, as **dueling café orchestras** entertain. The ultimate Venetian music scene is at the venerable Caffè Florian. But Gran Caffè Chioggia (facing the Doge's Palace) doesn't charge extra for music and has good jazz nightly (see the sidebar on page 72). Every night, enthusiastic musicians play the same songs, creating the same irresistible magic. Hang out for free behind the tables (allowing you to move easily on to the next orchestra when the musicians take a break), or spring for a seat and enjoy a fun and gorgeously set concert. If you sit a while, expect to pay €15 and up (for a drink and the cover charge for music)—money well spent. Dancing on the square is free—and encouraged.

Several venerable cafés and bars on the square serve expensive drinks outside but cheap drinks inside at the bar. The scene in a bar like **Gran Caffè Lavena** (despite its questionable chandelier) can be great. You'll hear people talking about the famous **Harry's American Bar,** which sells overpriced food and American cocktails to dressy tourists near the San Marco-Vallaresso vaporetto stop. But it's a rip-off...and the last place Hemingway would drink today. It's far cheaper to get a drink at any of the hole-in-the-wall bars just off St. Mark's Square; you can get a bottle of beer or even prosecco-to-go in a plastic cup.

Wherever you end up, streetlamp halos, live music, floodlit history, and a ceiling of stars make St. Mark's magic at midnight.

Sleeping in Venice

I've listed rooms in these areas: St. Mark's bustle, the Rialto action, the quiet Dorsoduro area behind the Accademia art museum, and near the train station. For drivers, I've included a few hotels in Mestre, on the mainland.

Addresses: Hotels in Venice can be tricky to locate. Remember that Venice has six districts: San Marco, Castello, Cannaregio, San Polo, Santa Croce, and Dorsoduro. For much of its history, Venice has given addresses as simply the district name and a house number (such as "Castello 4647"). The Venice Explorer website (https://veniceexplorer.com/venice-map) works well for pinpointing addresses given this way (as well as conventional address).

To help your wayfinding, the listings below include the street name, district name, and house number (along with any useful landmarks).

Hotel Tips: I rank accommodations from $ budget to $$$$ splurge. For the best deal, contact my family-run places directly by phone or email. When you book direct, the owner avoids a commission and may be able to offer a discount. Book well in advance for peak season or if your trip coincides with a major holiday or festival (see the appendix).

As many hotels in central Venice are in historic buildings, rooms tend to be small and stairs are often plentiful. Unless noted, these listings do not have an elevator. For some travelers, short-term, Airbnb-type rentals can be a good alternative; search for places in my recommended hotel neighborhoods.

For more details on reservations, short-term rentals, and more, see the "Sleeping" section in the Practicalities chapter.

NEAR ST. MARK'S SQUARE

To get here from the train station or Piazzale Roma bus station, ride the slow vaporetto #1 to San Zaccaria; in summer you can ride the fast #2 (which also leaves from Tronchetto parking lot) to San Marco. If you take #1, consider using your ride to follow my tour of the Grand Canal (earlier in this chapter). To make sure your boat stops at your stop, confirm that your boat goes *"per"* your destination (for example, *"per San Zaccaria?"*).

East of St. Mark's Square

Located near the Bridge of Sighs, just off the Riva degli Schiavoni waterfront promenade, these places rub drainpipes with Venice's most palatial five-star hotels.

$$$$ Hotel Campiello, lacy and bright, was once part of a 19th-century convent. Ideally located 50 yards off the waterfront on a tiny square, its 16 rooms offer a tranquil, friendly refuge for

VENICE

Hotels & Restaurants near St. Mark's Square

Accommodations

1. Hotel Campiello
2. Hotel Fontana
3. To Hotel la Residenza
4. Locanda al Leon
5. Albergo Doni
6. Hotel Orion
7. Hotel al Piave
8. Locanda Silva
9. Corte Campana B&B
10. Hotel Flora
11. Hotel Bel Sito
12. Hotel Mercurio

VENICE

Eateries & Other

- ⑭ Ristorante Antica Sacrestia
- ⑮ Al Giardinetto da Severino Ristorante
- ⑯ Rossopomodoro Pizzeria
- ⑰ L'Ombra del Leone
- ⑱ Birreria Penasa
- ⑲ Aciugheta Pizzeria
- ⑳ Birreria Forst
- ㉑ Osteria alle Testiere
- ㉒ Gran Caffè Quadri (Bistro)
- ㉓ Gran Caffè Lavena (Gelato)
- ㉔ Todaro Gelato
- ㉕ Supermarket (3)
- ㉖ Laundry (2)

travelers who appreciate comfort and professional service (RS%, air-con, elevator, just steps from the San Zaccaria vaporetto stop, on Campiello del Vin at Castello 4647; +39 041 520 5764, www.hcampiello.it, campiello@hcampiello.it; family-run for four generations, currently by Thomas, Nicoletta, and Monica). They also rent three modern, upscale, and quiet family apartments for up to six people, under rustic timbers just steps away from the hotel.

$$$$ Hotel Fontana, two bridges behind St. Mark's Square, is a pleasant family-run place with 15 sparse but classic-feeling rooms overlooking a lively square (RS%, several rooms with terraces, family rooms, breakfast on terrace in good weather, air-con, elevator, closed Jan, on Campo San Provolo at Castello 4701, +39 041 522 0533, www.hotelfontana.it, info@hotelfontana.it, cousins Diego and Gabriele).

$$$$ Hotel la Residenza is a grand old palace facing a peaceful square. It has 16 rooms on three levels (with no elevator) and a huge, luxurious lounge. This is a good value for romantics—you'll feel like you're in the Doge's Palace after hours (2-night minimum on weekends, air-con; from the Riva degli Schiavone, go down Calle del Dose to Campo Bandiera e Moro at Castello 3608; +39 041 528 5315, www.venicelaresidenza.com, info@venicelaresidenza.com, Valentina).

$$$$ Locanda al Leon, which feels a little like a medieval tower house, is conscientiously run and rents 12 rooms just off Campo Santi Filippo e Giacomo (RS%, some view rooms, family rooms, air-con, one- and two-bedroom apartments, on Campo Santi Filippo e Giacomo at Castello 4270; +39 041 277 0393, www.hotelalleon.com, leon@hotelalleon.com, Giuliano and Marcella). They run two annexes: **B&B Ca' Marcella,** just down the street, has three newer, classy, and spacious rooms for the same rates (check in at main hotel); **Ca' San Marco,** overlooking a quiet canal, has six additional rooms.

$$ Albergo Doni, situated along a quiet canal, is dark and quiet. This time-warp—with creaky floors and 13 well-worn, once-classy rooms—is run by friendly Tessa and her two brothers, Barnaba and (now "retired") Italian stallion Nikos (RS%, cheaper rooms with shared bath, family rooms, ceiling fans, a few rooms have air-con, Wi-Fi in common areas, on Fondamenta del Vin at Castello 4656, +39 348 511 1007, albergodoni@hotmail.it). The hotel also has three nice overflow apartments (www.leoncinivenezia.it).

North of St. Mark's Square

$$$$ Hotel Orion rents 21 simple, welcoming, pricey rooms in the center of the action (you're paying a premium for the location). Steep stairs (there's no elevator) take you from the bustling street into a peaceful world high above (RS%, air-con; from San Zulian

Church it's just a few steps down Calle Spadaria, San Marco 700a; +39 041 522 3053, www.hotelorion.it, info@hotelorion.it).

$$$ Hotel al Piave, with 25 rooms above a bright, tight lobby and breakfast room, is comfortable and cheery, and you'll enjoy the neighborhood (RS%, family rooms, lots of narrow stairs, air-con, on Ruga Giuffa at Castello 4838, +39 041 528 5174, www. hotelalpiave.com, info@hotelalpiave.com; family-run by Mirella, Paolo, Ilaria, and Federico).

$$$ Locanda Casa Querini rents six bright, high-ceilinged rooms on a quiet square tucked away behind St. Mark's. You can enjoy your breakfast or a sunny happy-hour picnic sitting at their tables right on the sleepy little square (RS%, family rooms, in-room fridges, air-con, on Campo San Zaninovo/Giovanni Novo at Castello 4388, +39 041 241 1294, www.locandaquerini.com, info@ locandaquerini.com; Patrizia and Caterina).

$$$ Locanda Silva is a well-located hotel with a functional 1960s feel and a small terrace. It rents 23 simple rooms with small bathrooms (RS%, a few cheaper rooms with shared bathrooms, closed Dec-Jan, family rooms, air-con, lots of stairs, on Fonda-menta del Remedio at Castello 4423, +39 041 522 7643, www. locandasilva.it, info@locandasilva.it; Sandra and Katia).

$$ Corte Campana B&B, run by enthusiastic and helpful Riccardo and his Californian wife Grace, rents three quiet, spa-cious, characteristic rooms in a homey flat just behind St. Mark's Square. For one room, the private bath is down the hall (cash only, 2-3 night minimum, family rooms, air-con, elevator, on Calle del Remedio at Castello 4410, +39 041 523 3603, mobile +39 389 272 6500, www.cortecampana.com, info@cortecampana.com).

Near Campo Santa Maria Formosa

A bit farther north of the options listed above, these are in the quiet, somewhat less touristy Castello area, beyond the inviting Campo Santa Maria Formosa (for locations, see the map on page 95).

$$$ Locanda la Corte is perfumed with elegance without being snooty. Its 12 attractive, high-ceilinged, wood-beamed rooms—Venetian-style, done in earthy pastels—circle a small, sun-drenched courtyard and a ground-level restaurant (RS%, fam-ily rooms, air-con, on Calle Bressana at Castello 6317, +39 041 241 1300, www.locandalacorte.it, info@locandalacorte.it).

$$ Alloggi Barbaria, a good budget choice, rents eight sim-ple, characterless rooms on one floor around a bright but institu-tional-feeling common area. Beyond Campo San Zanipolo/Santi Giovanni e Paolo, it's a fair walk from the action, but in a pleas-ant residential neighborhood. The Ospedale vaporetto stop is two minutes away on foot, with no steps (RS%, family rooms, limited continental breakfast, air-con in summer, Wi-Fi in common areas, on Calle de le Capucine at Castello 6573, +39 041 522 2750, www. alloggibarbaria.it, info@alloggibarbaria.it, friendly Fausto). You can reach the Ospedale stop on vaporetto #5.2 from the train or bus stations, or via the Alilaguna blue line from the airport.

West of St. Mark's Square

These more expensive hotels are solid choices in a more elegant neighborhood.

$$$$ **Hotel Flora** sits buried in a sea of fancy designer boutiques and elegant hotels almost on the Grand Canal. It's formal, with uniformed staff and grand public spaces, yet the 40 rooms have a homey warmth and the garden oasis is a sanctuary for well-heeled, foot-weary guests (air-con, elevator, great family-size apartment, on Calle Bergamaschi at San Marco 2283a, +39 041 520 5844, www.hotelflora.it, info@hotelflora.it).

$$$$ **Hotel Bel Sito** offers pleasing Old World character, 34 smallish rooms, generous public spaces, a peaceful courtyard, a private water taxi dock, and a picturesque location facing a church on a small square between St. Mark's Square and the Accademia (RS%, some view rooms, air-con, elevator; near Santa Maria del Giglio vaporetto stop—line #1, on Campo Santa Maria Zobenigo/del Giglio at San Marco 2517; +39 041 522 3365, www. hotelbelsitovenezia.it, info@hotelbelsitovenezia.it, graceful Rossella).

$$$$ **Hotel Mercurio,** a lesser value a block from La Fenice Opera House, offers 29 peaceful, comfortable rooms (some view rooms, family rooms, air-con, lots of stairs, on Calle del Fruttariol at San Marco 1848, +39 041 522 0947, www.hotelmercurio.com, info@hotelmercurio.com).

NEAR THE RIALTO BRIDGE

These places are on opposite sides of the Grand Canal, within a short walk of the Rialto Bridge. Express vaporetto #2 brings you to the Rialto quickly from the train station, the Piazzale Roma bus station, and the parking-lot island of Tronchetto, but you'll need to take the "local" vaporetto #1 to reach the minor stops closer to the last two listings. To locate the following hotels, see the map on page 95.

$$$$ **Hotel al Ponte Antico,** in a restored 14th-century building, is exquisite, professional, and small. With nine plush rooms, a velvety royal living/breakfast room, and its own dock for water taxi arrivals, it's perfect for a romantic anniversary. Because its wonderful terrace overlooks the Grand Canal, Rialto Bridge, and market action, its rooms without a canal view may be a better value (air-con; 100 yards from Rialto Bridge on Calle dell'Aseo,

Cannaregio 5768, use Rialto vaporetto stop; +39 041 241 1944, www.alponteantico.com, info@alponteantico.com; Matteo makes you feel like royalty).

$$$ Pensione Guerrato, right above the colorful Rialto produce market and just two minutes from the Rialto Bridge, is run by friendly, creative, and hardworking Roberto, Piero, Monica, and Matilde. Their 800-year-old building—with 22 spacious, charming rooms—is simple, airy, and wonderfully characteristic. It's a great value considering the location and charm (RS%, cheaper rooms with shared bath, family rooms, air-con; take vaporetto #1 to Rialto Mercato stop to save walk over bridge—from the boat, go through the passageway, turn right onto Casaria, then take the second left to Calle drio la Scimia, San Polo 240a; +39 041 528 5927, www.hotelguerrato.com, info@hotelguerrato.com). My tour groups book this place for 60 nights each year. Sorry. The Guerrato also rents family apartments in the old center (great for groups of 4-8).

$$$ Hotel al Ponte Mocenigo is off the beaten path—a 10-minute walk northwest of the Rialto Bridge—but it's lovely and a great value. This 16th-century Venetian palazzo has a garden terrace and 15 comfy, beautifully appointed, and tranquil rooms (RS%, air-con; take vaporetto #1 to San Stae stop, then head inland along the right side of the church on Salizada San Stae to Santa Croce 1985; +39 041 524 4797, www.alpontemocenigo.com, info@alpontemocenigo.com, Sandro and Valter).

NEAR THE ACCADEMIA BRIDGE
In Dorsoduro

As you step over the Accademia Bridge, the commotion of touristy Venice is soon replaced by a sleepy village laced with canals. This quiet area, next to the best Venetian painting museum in town, is a 15-minute walk from the Rialto or St. Mark's Square. In summer, the fast vaporetto #2 to the Accademia stop is the typical way to get here from the train station, Piazzale Roma bus station, or St. Mark's Square. For hotels near the Zattere stop, vaporetto #5.1 or the Alilaguna boat from the airport are good options.

$$$$ Pensione Accademia fills the 17th-century Villa Maravege like a Bellini painting. Its 27 comfortable, elegant rooms gild the lily. You'll feel aristocratic gliding through its grand public spaces and lounging in its wistful, breezy gardens (family rooms, air-con, no elevator but most rooms on ground floor or one floor up, on Fondamenta Bollani at Dorsoduro 1058, +39 041 521 0188, www.pensioneaccademia.it, info@pensioneaccademia.it).

$$$$ Hotel la Calcina, the home of English writer John Ruskin in 1876, maintains a 19th-century formality. It comes with three-star comforts in a professional yet intimate package. Its 25

VENICE

VENICE

Hotels & Restaurants near the Rialto Bridge

Accommodations

1. Locanda la Corte
2. To Alloggi Barbaria
3. Hotel al Ponte Antico
4. Pensione Guerrato
5. Hotel al Ponte Mocenigo
6. Foresteria della Chiesa Valdese

---

18. Trattoria alla Madonna
19. Ristorante Vini da Pinto
20. Osteria al Ponte Storto
21. Trattoria Antiche Carampane
22. To Antica Birraria la Corte
23. Osteria alle Testiere

24. Osteria di Santa Marina
25. Peter Pan Kebabs & Pizza
26. Gelatoteca Suso
27. Supermarket (3)
28. Devil's Forest Pub
29. Inishark Pub

tasteful rooms are squeaky clean, with nice wood furniture, hardwood floors, and a peaceful waterside setting facing Giudecca Island (some view rooms, air-con, no elevator and lots of stairs, rooftop terrace, buffet breakfast outdoors in good weather on platform over lagoon, near Zattere vaporetto stop at south end of Rio de San Vio at Dorsoduro 780, +39 041 520 6466, www.lacalcina.com, info@lacalcina.com).

$$$$ **Hotel Galleria** has nine old-fashioned and velvety rooms, half with views of the Grand Canal. Some rooms are quite narrow, but you can open your window to watch boats pass by at any time. It's run with a family feel by Luciano and Lucio (one cheaper room with detached private bath, breakfast voucher for Foscarini café downstairs, ceiling fans; 30 yards from Accademia art museum, right near the bridge on Rio Terà A. Foscarini at Dorsoduro 878a; +39 041 523 2489, www.hotelgalleria.it, info@hotelgalleria.it).

$$$$ **Hotel Belle Arti,** with a stiff, serious staff, lacks personality but has a grand entry, an inviting garden terrace, and 67 heavily decorated rooms (air-con, elevator, 100 yards behind Accademia art museum on Rio Terà A. Foscarini at Dorsoduro 912a, +39 041 522 6230, www.hotelbellearti.com, info@hotelbellearti.com).

$$$$ **Don Orione Religious Guest House** is a big cultural center dedicated to the work of a local man who became a saint in modern times. With 80 rooms filling an old monastery, it feels cookie-cutter institutional (like a modern retreat center), but is also classy, clean, peaceful, and strictly run. It's beautifully located, comfortable, and supports a fine cause: Profits go to mission work in the developing world (family rooms, groups welcome, air-con, elevator, on Rio Terà A. Foscarini, Dorsoduro 909a, +39 041 522 4077, www.donorione-venezia.it, info@donorione-venezia.it).

$$$$ **Ca' San Trovaso** rents six pleasant rooms in a little three-floor, formerly residential building. The location is peaceful, on a small, out-of-the-way canal (RS%, some view rooms, breakfast voucher for nearby café, tiny roof terrace, apartments available with 3-night minimum; near Zattere vaporetto stop, off Fondamenta de le Romite at Dorsoduro 1350; +39 041 241 2215, mobile +39 349 125 3890, www.casantrovaso.com, info@casantrovaso.com, Anna and Alessandra).

$$ **Casa di Sara,** a colorfully decorated B&B, is hidden in a leafy courtyard in a humble back-street area overlooking a canal. Their four quiet rooms and tiny roof terrace offer the maximum in privacy (air-con, along Fondamenta de le Romite at Dorsoduro 1330, mobile +39 342 596 3563, www.casadisara.com, info@casadisara.com, Emanuele).

North of the Accademia Bridge

These places are between the Accademia Bridge and St. Mark's Square, near Campo Santo Stefano.

$$$$ Novecento Hotel rents nine plush rooms on three floors, complemented by a big, welcoming lounge, an elegant living room, and a small breakfast garden. This boutique hotel, with helpful staff, is nicely located in a quiet location (air-con, lots of stairs, on Calle del Dose, off Campo San Maurizio at San Marco 2684, +39 041 241 3765, www.novecento.biz, info@novecento.biz).

$$$$ Foresteria Levi, run by a foundation that promotes research on Venetian music, offers 32 quiet, institutional yet comfortable and spacious rooms—some are loft quads, a good deal for families (air-con, elevator, on Calle Giustinian at San Marco 2893, +39 041 277 0542, www.foresterialevi.it, info@foresterialevi.it). From the base of the Accademia Bridge, it's just over the tiny Ponte Giustinian.

$$$$ Domus Ciliota is a big, efficient, and sparkling-clean place—well-run, well-located, church-owned, and plainly furnished—with 30 dorm-like rooms and a peaceful courtyard. If you want comfort with no stress and don't need much character, this is a fine value. During the school year, half the rooms are used by students (air-con, elevator; just off Campo Santo Stefano at Calle delle Muneghe, San Marco 2976; +39 041 520 4888, www.ciliota.it, info@ciliota.it).

$$$ Hotel San Samuele rents 10 tidy rooms in an old residence near Campo Santo Stefano. Antique furniture and restored original floors give this place a homey feel. It's in a great locale, and the rooms with shared bath can be a good deal (RS%, no breakfast, fans, plenty of stairs, on Salizada San Samuele at San Marco 3358, +39 041 520 5165, www.hotelsansamuele.com, info@ hotelsansamuele.com, Judith).

ON THE MAINLAND, IN MESTRE

Drivers may want to stay on the mainland, in Mestre. It's easy to get between Mestre and Venice. From the big Mestre station, trains depart about every 10 minutes, zipping to Venice's Santa Lucia station in about 10 minutes.

$$ Hotel Tritone, a high-rise Best Western hotel with 60 rooms varying in decor from business to mod, has the most convenient location, facing Mestre's train station (air-con, elevator, pay parking; leaving the station, cross the street, turn right, and walk to the end of the block to find Viale Stazione 16, +39 041 538 3125, www.hoteltritonevenice.com, info@hoteltritonevenice.com).

$$ Hotel Paris is a few doors down from the station and worth considering if you can get a deal. It has 18 small, modern,

VENICE

Accommodations
1 Pensione Accademia
2 Hotel la Calcina
3 Hotel Galleria
4 Hotel Belle Arti
5 Don Orione Religious Guest House
6 Ca' San Trovaso
7 Casa di Sara
8 Novecento Hotel
9 Foresteria Levi
10 Domus Ciliota
11 Hotel San Samuele

Eateries
12 Bar Foscarini
13 Enoteca Cantine del Vino Già Schiavi
14 Al Vecio Marangon Ristorante
15 Nico Gelateria
16 Terrazza dei Nobili
17 Pizzeria Oke
18 Pizzeria alle Zattere

Hotels & Restaurants near Accademia Bridge

19 Ristoteca Oniga
20 Osteria Enoteca Ai Artisti
21 Pizzeria al Profeta
22 Enoteca e Trattoria la Bitta
23 Gelateria Il Doge
24 Campo Santa Margarita Eateries & Nightlife

25 Ristorante Lineadombra
26 Grocery (3)

Nightlife
27 Interpreti Veneziani Concerts
28 Musica a Palazzo

modestly stylish rooms (air-con, on-site parking, Via Venezia 11, +39 041 926 037, www.hotelparis.it, info@hotelparis.it).

Eating in Venice

The hard fact is that Venice is slowly becoming one big tourist attraction. As its population shrinks and the cost of business rises, eateries are forced to accommodate the changing market. To make matters worse, that market is increasingly day-trippers looking for low-end snacks and bar food like pizzas and sandwiches. In frustration, many of my favorite restauranteurs have sold in recent years, making it harder and harder to find places with both soul and ethics. For a special meal, Venetians (and savvy travelers) will venture far away from the center to distant corners of the lagoon.

Having said that, there are still good places, and (just like Disneyland) you have plenty of choices. The best values are no secret, so if you have your heart set on a particular place, make a reservation. Without a reservation, you may get lucky if you're at the door right when a place opens—but don't count on it. Eating early gives you fewer crowds and fewer Italians; eating later is more crowded and with fewer tourists. When considering prices, gird yourself for a 50 percent "charm tax"...you're eating in Venice! Enjoy.

EATING TIPS

Venetians often eat a snack—*cicchetti* or *panini*—while standing at a bar. (You'll usually pay more if you sit.) Unique to Venice, *cicchetti* bars specialize in finger foods and appetizers that combine to make a speedy and tasty meal. *Cicchetti* (the Venetian version of tapas) were designed as a quick meal for working people. The selection and ambience are best Monday through Saturday for lunch or early dinner (see "The Stand-Up Progressive Venetian Pub-Crawl Dinner" sidebar, later).

Sandwiches are sold fast and cheaply at bars everywhere (order a *panini*, *piadini*, or *tramezzini*). You can eat your sandwich at the bar or take it with you.

A favorite Italian tradition is the *aperitivo* (predinner drink). The dominant *aperitivo* among Venetians is the *spritz* (white wine, soda, and ice with a liquor of your choice). When you order, you'll be asked if you'd like your *spritz con Campari* (bitter) or *con Aperol* (sweeter).

NEAR THE RIALTO BRIDGE
North of the Bridge

These four places are serious restaurants located in Cannaregio. The first three are just steps off the Strada Nova, the main drag in the district; the last, Taverna al Remer, is closer to the Rialto Bridge. Consider reservations necessary at each.

$$$ Trattoria da Bepi, bright and paneled in knotty pine, feels like a classic, where Loris carries on his mother's passion for good, traditional Venetian cuisine and the freshest of ingredients. Like anywhere, be sure you understand the menu and your bill here. There's good seating inside and out (Fri-Wed 12:00-15:00 & 19:00-22:00, closed Thu; half a block off Campo Santi Apostoli on Salizada Pistor, Cannaregio 4550; +39 041 528 5031, www.dabepi. it).

$$ Trattoria Ca' d'Oro Alla Vedova is a venerable place respected for its traditional Venetian cuisine. It's compact yet romantic, with a tiny *cicchetti* bar at the door, where regulars sip and munch, and dressy tables in tight quarters beyond (Fri-Wed 11:00-14:30 & 18:30-22:30, closed Thu; from the Ca' d'Oro vaporetto stop, follow the small lane right across Strada Nova to Calle del Pistor, Cannaregio 3912; +39 041 528 5324).

$$$$ Vini da Gigio, a more expensive option, has a traditional Venetian menu and a classy but welcoming setting that's a pleasant mix of traditional and contemporary (Wed-Sun 12:00-14:30 & 19:00-22:30, closed Mon-Tue; 4 blocks from Ca' d'Oro vaporetto stop on Fondamenta San Felice, behind the church on Campo San Felice; Cannaregio 3628a, +39 041 528 5140, www. vinidagigio.com).

$$$$ Taverna al Remer hides out down a narrow alley with its own little courtyard on the Grand Canal, 100 meters from the Rialto Bridge. Their Venetian mixed-fish appetizer plate is a hit. You'll dine romantically by candlelight under brick vaults and old timbers, often with live mellow jazz serenading you. While Yuli, the owner, advertises "art food, drink, and charm," locals would call it fake charm for tourists (Wed-Mon 12:00-14:30 & 19:00-22:30, closed Tue; find it down the unmarked lane between Burger King and Bacaro Bar, near the Church of San Giovanni Crisostomo, Cannaregio 5701; +39 041 52 8789, https://tavernaremer.com).

East of the Rialto Bridge

The next few places hide away in the twisty lanes between the Rialto Bridge and Campo Santa Maria Formosa. Osteria da Alberto is a tad farther north of the others.

$$ Rosticceria Gislon is an institution in its neighborhood— a *tavola calda* (buffet line of cooked food) in a bright and practical diner setting with salads, fried mozzarella, pastas, seafood and more, all at good prices (from Campo San Bartolomeo, look for the neon green "Rosticceria" sign and head through the passageway to Calle de la Bissa, San Marco 5424a, +39 041 522 3569).

$$ Cicchetti near Campo San Bartolomeo: Three fun and

tiny *cicchetti* bars cluster within ten meters of each other (all are open daily). If the statue on Campo San Bartolomeo turned around, walked to the far right-hand corner, and explored the back lanes there, he'd find them in this order: **Osteria I Rusteghi** is more than your rough *cicchetti* bar. It's an *enoteca gastronomica*— a wine bar that pairs fine dishes with fine wines. It has a serious list of good wines by the glass and a jazzy interior on its own tiny, tranquil square (Corte dei Tentor 5513, +39 338 760 6034). Modern little **Bar SEPA** attracts a young crowd and sells good *cicchetti*, clearly priced. Push past the crowd of smokers at the door to find space at a stand-up barrel inside—no table seating here (on Calle della Bissa). **Bacarando Bar** is old school, with clearly marked and priced little dishes at the counter and two floors of table seating (Corte dell'Orso 5495).

$$ Osteria al Portego is a small and popular neighborhood eatery near Campo San Lio. Carlo serves good meals, bargain-priced house wine, and excellent €1-4 *cicchetti*—best enjoyed around 18:00 (picked over by 21:00). The *cicchetti* here can make a great meal, but consider sitting down for a dinner from their blackboard-fresh menu. Their six tables are reserved for those ordering from the menu; reserve ahead if you want a table (daily 11:30-15:00 & 17:30-22:00, on Calle de la Malvasia at Castello 6015, +39 041 522 9038, www.osteriaalportego.org, Federica). From Campo San Bartolomeo, continue over a bridge to Campo San Lio, turn left, and follow Calle Carminati straight 50 yards over another bridge.

$$ Osteria da Alberto, near Campo Santa Maria Novo, is one of my standbys, with locals at lunch and tourists at dinner. They offer excellent daily specials: seafood, pastas, and a good house wine in a woody and characteristic interior. It's smart to reserve at night—I'd request a table in front in "the first room" (daily 12:00-15:00 & 18:30-22:00; on Calle Larga Giacinto Gallina, midway between Campo Santi Apostoli and Campo San Zanipolo/Santi Giovanni e Paolo, and next to Ponte de la Panada bridge at Calle Larga Giacinto Gallina, Cannaregio 5401; +39 041 523 8153, www.osteriadaalberto.it, run by Graziano and Giovanni).

Rialto Market Area

The north end of the Rialto Bridge is thriving with places to eat and drink. As with market neighborhoods anywhere, you'll find lots of holes-in-the-wall with a line on the freshest of ingredients and catering to local shoppers needing a quick, affordable bite. This area is crowded by day, nearly empty early in the evening, and packed with young Venetians and tourists later.

My listings include a stretch of dark and rustic pubs serving *cicchetti* (Venetian tapas), a strip of trendy places fronting the Grand

Canal, a few little places on the market, and a couple of "normal" restaurants serving solid pasta, pizza, and *secondi*.

The *Cicchetti* Strip: Four Venetian Tapas Bars

The 100-yard-long stretch starting two blocks inland from the Rialto Market (along Sotoportego dei Do Mori and Calle de le Do Spade) has long been a favorite among Venetian *cicchetti* enthusiasts for its bar munchies, wine by the glass, and fun stand-up conviviality. These **$** places serve food all day, but the spread is best at around noon (generally open daily 12:00-15:00 & 18:00-20:00 or 21:00). Each place offers a fine bar-and-stools scene, and a couple can be treated like a restaurant—order from their rustic menu and grab a table. Scout these places in advance to help decide which ambience is right for the experience you have in mind. Then pick one, dig in, and drink up.

At each place, look for the list of snacks and wine by the glass at the bar or on the wall. For a simple €1 glass of house wine, ask for an *"ombra."* Better wine costs around €3, and *cicchetti* cost €2. They get unworkably crowded later in the evening.

Bar all'Arco is a bustling one-room joint serving mostly *crostini*—small open-faced sandwiches (Thu-Tue 10:00-14:30, closed Wed, Campo San Polo 436; Francesco, Anna, Matteo).

Cantina Do Mori serves a forest of little edibles on toothpicks and *francobolli* (a spicy selection of tiny, mayo-soaked sandwiches nicknamed "stamps"). Go here to be abused in a fine atmosphere—the frowns are part of the shtick—and be aware that prices can add up quickly (Mon-Sat 8:00-19:30, closed Sun, can be shoulder-to-shoulder, on Calle Do Mori at San Polo 430).

Osteria ai Storti, with a cool photo of the market in 1909, is more of a sit-down place (tables inside and on street). Study his cute little menu. Alessandro serves a selection of €2 fried little gut bombs and enjoys helping educate travelers (around corner from Cantina Do Mori on Calle San Matio, San Polo 819).

Cantina Do Spade is run by Francesco, who clearly lists the *cicchetti* (mostly deep fried) and wines of the day. It's also good for sit-down restaurant-style meals (30 yards from Osteria ai Storti down Calle de le Do Spade at San Polo 860, +39 041 521 0583).

The Bancogiro Stretch: Five Places Overlooking the Grand Canal

Just past the Rialto Bridge, between Campo San Giacomo and the Grand Canal, this strip of popular places in a recently renovated old building has some of the best canalside seating in Venice. I call this the "Bancogiro Stretch" (the restaurants front a former banking building called Bancogiro).

Each place has a unique character and formula. Unless otherwise noted, all are open daily and serve drinks, *cicchetti*, and some-

VENICE

The Stand-Up Progressive Venetian Pub-Crawl Dinner

A fine Venetian dinner is a pub crawl *(giro d'ombra)*—a tradition unique to Venice, where no cars means easy crawling. (*Giro*

means stroll, and *ombra*—slang for a glass of wine—means shade, from the old days when a portable wine bar scooted with the shadow of the Campanile bell tower across St. Mark's Square.)

Venice's residential back streets hide plenty of characteristic bars *(bacari)*, with countless trays of interesting toothpick munchies *(cicchetti)* and blackboards listing the wines that are uncorked and served by the glass. This is a great way to mingle and have fun with the Venetians. Bars don't stay open very late, and the *cicchetti* selection is best early, so go at lunch or start your evening by 18:00. Many bars are closed on Sunday. For a stress-free pub crawl, consider taking a tour with the charming Alessandro Schezzini (see page 46) or connect with one of the many "food tour guides" offering such Venetian pub crawls on one of the many online booking services.

The *Cicchetti* Experience

Cicchetti bars have a social stand-up zone and a cozy gaggle of tables where you can generally sit down with your *cicchetti* or order from a simple menu. In some of the more popular places, the crowds happily spill out into the street. Food generally costs the same whether you stand or sit. Bars are often clustered together, making the "pub crawl" approach very workable.

Look for a place that's more "bar" than "restaurant." Lately many are getting lazy and offering only little open-face sandwiches and fried items. I much prefer a wider selection with fewer gut-bombs and less bread. Make sure they have *cicchetti* on dis-

what pricey sit-down meals. While you can get a drink anytime, dinner is typically served only after 19:00 or 19:30. During meals, they charge more and limit table seating to those ordering full lunches or dinners; but between mealtimes you can enjoy a drink or a snack at fine prices. After dinner hours, the Bancogiro Stretch—especially in the surrounding alleys that house low-rent bars—becomes a youthful and trendy nightspot. Before or after dinner, this strip is one of the best places in town for a *spritz*.

Here's the rundown (in the order you'll reach them from the Rialto Bridge): **$$$ Bar Naranzaria** serves Italian dishes at the play. Bar-hopping Venetians enjoy an *aperitivo,* a before-dinner drink. Sip your drink and make the scene while standing at the bar. Next, order a *cicchetto* or two by pointing. Chill some more, while munching and sipping. Then order another one or two. Find a stool or table nearby where you can sit (but don't sit at tables with tablecloths—those are for diners). Pay when you're ready to leave. If you've crawled enough, most of my recommended bars make a fine one-stop, sit-down dinner.

What to Eat (and Drink)

While you can order a mixed *cicchetti* plate, Venetians prefer going one-by-one...sipping their wine and trying this...then give me one of those...and so on. Try deep-fried mozzarella cheese, gorgonzola, calamari, artichoke hearts, and anything ugly on a toothpick. Crostini (small, toasted bread with a topping) are popular, as are marinated seafood, olives, and prosciutto with melon. Meat and fish (*pesce;* PESH-ay) munchies can be expensive; veggies (*verdure*) are cheap, at about €3 for a meal-sized plate. In many places, there's a set price per food item (for example, €2). To get a plate of assorted appetizers for €8 (or more, depending on how hungry you are), ask for *"Un piatto classico di cicchetti misti da €8"* (oon pee-AH-toh KLAH-see-koh dee chee-KET-tee MEE-stee dah OH-toh eh-OO-roh). Bread sticks (*grissini*) are free for the asking.

  For drinks, start with an *aperitivo:* Order a Bellini, a *spritz con Aperol,* or a prosecco, and draw approving looks from the natives. Enjoy the house wines with the food. An *ombra* ("shadow") is a small glass of wine often offered with *cicchetti.* An *ombra rosso* (red) or *ombra bianco* (white), or a small beer (*birrino*), costs about €1. The house keg wine is cheap—€1 per glass, about €4 per liter. *Vin bon,* Venetian for fine wine, may run you from €2 to €6 per little glass. There are usually several fine wines uncorked and available by the glass. A good last drink is *fragolino,* the local sweet wine—*bianco* or *rosso.* It often comes with a little cookie (*biscotto*) for dipping.

best prices, open-faced sandwiches, and wines by the glass (closed Mon). **$$ Caffè Vergnano** is your cheapest option during mealtimes (pasta, salads, pizza, vegetarian dishes, and a busy microwave oven; long hours daily). **$$$ Osteria al Pesador** has a more extensive menu with a friendly staff serving local specialties (also seating upstairs; open daily). **$$$ Osteria Bancogiro** has a more sophisticated menu and the best reputation for dinner, a passion for the best cheese, and good *cicchetti* options at the bar. They offer fine dining upstairs (nice cheese plate, closed Mon, reservations smart, +39 041 523 2061, www.osteriabancogiro.it).

$ Al Mercà Bar ("At the Market"), a few steps away and off the canal, is a lively little nook with a happy crowd, where law-office workers have lunch and young locals gather in the evening for drinks (quality wine by the glass) and little snacks (€2 mini-sandwiches). The price list is clear, and the youthful crowd seems to enjoy connecting with curious tourists (stand at bar or in square—there are no tables and no interior, Mon-Sat 10:00-14:30 & 18:00-21:00, closed Sun, on Campo Bella Vienna, San Polo 213).

Restaurants near the Rialto Market

$$$ Trattoria alla Madonna is an old-school favorite frequented by retired locals who appreciate its traditional dishes (mostly seafood), formal waiters, white tablecloths, relaxing old-Venetian atmosphere, and fair prices. It's big and spacious for Venice, with high ceilings (inside dining only, lunch from 12:00, dinner from 19:00, closed Wed; on a quiet lane two blocks from the Rialto Bridge, Calle della Madonna, San Polo 594; +39 041 522 3824).

$$ Ristorante Vini da Pinto is a tourist-friendly eatery facing the fish market, with a large menu and relaxing outdoor seating and a dressy, spacious interior. Owner Giorgio visits the market each morning to select the day's best catch. Enjoy the lunch-only, fixed-price, three-course seafood meal for €18, including a pasta, seafood sampler plate, and veggies. Grander versions cost €25. Dinner à la carte can range from simple and inexpensive to a delightful splurge. Rick Steves readers receive a welcoming prosecco and a farewell *limoncello* and homemade cookie (daily 11:00-23:00, Campo de le Becarie, San Polo 367a, +39 041 522 4599). If dining outside, be careful to sit at a da Pinto table.

$$ Osteria al Ponte Storto, a little place on a quiet canalside corner a block off the main drag, is worth seeking out for its good-value fish dishes and peaceful location. Their small, hand-written menu changes with the daily specials. Rather than a romantic place, it feels like the corner favorite of the neighborhood (Mon-Sat 12:00-15:00 & 18:00-21:45, closed Sun, down Calle Bianca from San Aponal church, San Polo 1278, reservations smart, +39 041 528 2144).

Between the Rialto Bridge and Frari Church

$$$$ Trattoria Antiche Carampane is a dressy, family-run place with an open kitchen and a local following. They have a passion for fish (and make a point: no pizza) and serve traditional Venetian dishes with a fresh twist that change with the season. It's small—there are just 30 seats with six tables on the street (Tue-Sat 12:45-14:30 & 19:30-22:30, closed Sun-Mon, reservations necessary, Rio Tera delle Carampane, San Polo 1911, +39 041 524 0165, www.antichecarampane.com, Francesco).

VENICE

$$ Antica Birraria la Corte is an everyday eatery on the delightful Campo San Polo. Popular for its huge array of pizza—and smaller selection of hearty salads, pasta, and *secondi*—it fills the far side of this cozy, family-filled square. Although the interior is sprawling and modern, it's a joy to eat on the square, where metal tables teeter on the cobbles, the wind plays with the paper mats, and children run free (daily 12:00-15:00 & 18:00-22:30, on Campo San Polo at #2168, +39 041 275 0570).

NEAR ST. MARK'S SQUARE

Other than the first place, a more serious restaurant, the other eateries listed here are cheap-and-cheery options convenient to your sightseeing. For locations, see the map on page 88.

$$$$ Ristorante Antica Sacrestia is a classic restaurant where the owner, Pino, takes a hands-on approach to greeting guests. His staff serves creative fixed-price meals (€37, €52, or €80), a humdrum *menù del giorno*, and wonderful pizzas. You can also order à la carte; their antipasto spread looks like a lagoon aquarium spread out on a plate. My readers are welcome to a free *sgroppino* (lemon vodka after-dinner drink) upon request (Tue-Sun 11:30-15:00 & 18:00-23:00, closed Mon, behind San Zaninovo/Giovanni Novo Church on Calle Corona, Castello 4463, +39 041 523 0749, www.anticasacrestia.it). There's no wine by the glass. Order carefully. Pizza is your only budget escape.

$$$ Al Giardinetto da Severino Ristorante serves traditional Venetian fare (proudly no pizza) with a homey-dressy vibe and white-tablecloth elegance inside, and a big, peaceful garden filled with tables out back. The waitstaff works to provide a memorable and romantic dining experience, rare at this price (Fri-Wed 12:00-15:00 & 19:00-22:00, closed Thu, reservations smart, off Ruga Giuffa on Salizada Zorzi, Castello 4928, +39 041 528 5332, www.algiardinetto.it).

$$ Rossopomodoro Pizzeria is a big, fun, and practical pizzeria offering top quality, good prices, and a very handy location. They cook Naples-style pizzas in their wood oven and also offer a selection of hearty salads and pastas (long hours daily, Calle Larga San Marco 404, +39 041 243 8949).

$$$ L'Ombra del Leone is a big, modern, and classy bar (with attached restaurant), but its best feature is an elegant outdoor terrace right on the Grand Canal. Be sure to request the reasonably priced bar menu of salads and sandwiches (the restaurant menu is excellent but pricey). This spot is a hive of waterfront activity and popular with water taxi captains. Find the terrace at the very end of Calle Ridotto, past the Biennale archway (long hours daily, in Ca' Giustinian—the Biennale offices, behind San Moisè Church at Sestiere San Marco 1364, +39 041 241 3519).

Venetian Cuisine

Even more so than the rest of Italy, Venetian cuisine relies heavily on fish, shellfish, risotto, and polenta. Along with pizza and pasta, here are some typical foods you'll encounter. For more on Italian food, see the "Eating" section of the Practicalities chapter.

Sandwiches

Panini: Sandwiches made with rustic bread, filled with meat, vegetables, and cheese, served cold or toasted *(riscaldato).*

Piadini: Flatbread or wrap-like sandwiches.

Tramezzini: Crustless white sandwiches, served cold (various fillings, such as egg, tuna, or shrimp mixed with mayonnaise).

Antipasti (Appetizers)

Venetians start a meal with a light *antipasti* or some *cicchetti*—finger-food appetizers sold in many bars.

Antipasto di mare: Marinated mix of chilled fish and shellfish.

Asiago cheese: Cow's-milk cheese that's either *mezzano* (young, creamy) or *stravecchio* (aged, pungent).

Sarde in saor: Sardines marinated with onions.

Rice, Pasta, and Polenta

Bigoli in salsa: Long, fat, whole-wheat noodle in anchovy sauce.

Pasta alla buzzara: Pasta in a rich seafood-tomato sauce, generally with shrimp.

Pasta al pomodoro: Pasta in a simple tomato sauce.

Pasta al vongole: Pasta with clams.

Pasta e fagioli: Bean-and-pasta soup.

Polenta: Thick cornmeal porridge served soft or cut into firm slabs and grilled.

Risi e bisi: Rice and peas.

Risotto: Short-grain rice simmered in broth with seafood, meat, or veggies. *Risotto nero*—black risotto—is made with squid ink.

Frutti di Mare (Seafood)

Venetian fish are generally smaller than American salmon and trout (think sardines and anchovies). The weirder the seafood (eel, octopus, frogfish), the more local it is.

Baccalà: Preserved Atlantic salt cod that's rehydrated and served with polenta; also mixed with mayonnaise as a *cicchetti* topping, called *baccalà mantecato.*

Branzino: Sea bass, grilled and served whole.

Calamari: Squid, often cut into rings and deep-fried or marinated.

Cozze: Mussels, often steamed in an herb broth with tomato.

Gamberi: Shrimp—*gamberetti* are small, and *gamberoni* are large.

Moleche col pien: Fried soft-shell crabs.

Orata: Sea bream, a white fish.

Pesce fritto misto: Deep-fried seafood (often calamari and prawns).

Pesce spada: Swordfish.

Rombo: Turbot, a flatfish similar to flounder.

Rospo: Frogfish, a small fish that's often grilled.

Salmone: Salmon.

Seppia: Cuttlefish, a squid-like creature. *Nero di seppia* is the squid served in its own ink, often over spaghetti.

Sogliola: Sole, served poached or oven-roasted.

Vitello di mare: "Sea veal," like swordfish—firm, mild, and grilled.

Vongole: Clams, often steamed with fresh herbs and wine, or served as *spaghetti alle vongole*.

Zuppa di pesce: Seafood stew.

Dolci (Desserts)

Rather than order dessert in a restaurant, I like to stroll with a cup or cone of gelato from one of Venice's popular *gelaterie.* Cookies are also popular. The numerous varieties are due perhaps to Venice's position in trade (spices) and love of celebrations.

Bisse: Seahorse-shaped cookies.

Bussola: Ring-shaped cookies made for Easter.

Croccante: Toasted almond confection, similar to peanut brittle.

Fritole: Tiny doughnuts associated with Carnevale (Mardi Gras).

Pinza: Rustic cornmeal and wheat-flour cake filled with dried fruit; made for Epiphany, January 6.

Tiramisù: Spongy ladyfingers soaked in coffee and Marsala, layered with mascarpone cheese and bitter chocolate.

Cocktails and Local Wines

Amarone: Rich and intense red, made from dried Valpolicella grapes that yield a wine high in alcohol—often around 15 percent.

Bardolino: Beaujolais-like wine made from Valpolicella grapes.

Bellini: Cocktail of prosecco and white-peach puree (invented at the pricey Harry's American Bar near St. Mark's Square).

Fragolino: A sweet, slightly fizzy dessert wine made from a strawberry-flavored grape.

Prosecco: Sparkling white wine. Connoisseurs say the best hails from Valdobbiadene.

Recioto: Dessert wine made with dried, aged Valpolicella grapes.

Sgroppino: Traditional after-dinner drink of squeezed lemon juice, lemon gelato, and vodka.

Soave: Crisp, dry white wine, great with seafood.

Spritz: White wine and soda or prosecco mixed with Campari (bitter) or Aperol (sweeter), over ice.

Tiziano: Grape juice and prosecco.

Valpolicella: Light, dry, fruity red wine, often served as the *vino della casa* (house wine).

A Quick Lunch Behind St. Mark's Basilica

The best place for a reasonable value so close to the epicenter of tourism is a couple blocks behind the basilica on or near Campo Santi Filippo e Giacomo. As you enter the square from St. Mark's, on the left you'll first find Birreria Penasa and, a few steps beyond, Aciugheta; for Birreria Forst, continue a half-block beyond the square to Calle de le Rasse.

$ Birreria Penasa is a fast and practical place slamming out slate plates with cheap toasted sandwiches and beer. While you can sit and chose from the menu, I'd go inside to the bar and point to what looks good. Tables are set up like theater seating, so you can enjoy watching the parade of tourists shuffle by (daily 7:00-24:00, Campo Santi Filippo e Giacomo, +39 041 523 7202).

$$ Aciugheta Pizzeria is a handy place for lunch or a casual dinner with great outdoor and indoor seating. They take quality seriously when it comes to their pizzas and *cicchetti* (see the display under glass at the bar). Inside seating can be an oasis of quiet. And tables outside give you a great perch from the corner of the lively square (daily 12:00-24:00, Campo Santi Filippo e Giacomo, +39 041 522 4292).

$ Birreria Forst, halfway down Calle de le Rasse at #4540, serves busy local workers a selection of meaty sandwiches with tasty sauce on wheat bread, or made-to-order sandwiches. Order at the bar and grab a place at a rustic wooden table in their busy little dining room (daily 9:30-23:00, air-con, +39 041 523 0557).

Fine Dining North of St. Mark's Square, near Campo Santa Maria Formosa

Two Michelin-rated restaurants are near Campo Santa Maria Formosa. Each is romantic, expensive, requires a reservation, and is a rare and fine value for a gourmet experience.

$$$$ Osteria alle Testiere is my favorite dining splurge in Venice. Hugely respected, Luca and his staff are dedicated to quality, serving up creative, artfully presented market-fresh seafood (there's no meat on the menu), homemade pastas, and fine wine in what the chef calls a "Venetian Nouvelle" style. With only 22 seats, it's tight and homey, with the focus on food and service. They have daily specials, 10 wines by the glass, and one agenda: a great dining experience. This is a good spot to let loose and trust your host. They book up far in advance for lunch (12:00-15:00) and their two dinner seatings: 19:00 and 21:30 (reserve via email or website, plan on spending €75 for dinner, closed Sun-Mon; just off Campo Santa Maria Formosa at Calle del Mondo Novo, Castello 5801; +39 041 522 7220, www.osterialletestiere.it, info@osterialletestiere.it).

$$$$ Osteria di Santa Marina is the spot for a dressy meal among locals. It features creative gourmet Venetian cuisine, both traditional and innovative. More spacious than most Venetian places, the place has comfortable seating on the square and a fine dining room inside filled with character (€30 mains, €65 tasting *menu*; Tue-Sat 12:30-14:30 & 19:30-23:00, closed Sun-Mon; northwest of Campo Santa Maria Formosa near Campo Santa Marina, off Calle del Frutariol at Castello 5911; +39 041 528 5239). For location, see the "Hotels & Restaurants near the Rialto Bridge" map on page 95.

DORSODURO

The following recommendations are within a 10-minute walk of the Accademia Bridge (for locations, see the map on page 99). This area, called Dorsoduro, is great for restaurants and well worth the walk from the more touristy Rialto and San Marco areas. The first listings, near the Accademia, are best for lunch. The places in Zattere overlook the Giudecca Canal. Best for dinner are the restaurants near Campo San Barnaba. Last are a handful of pizzerias and *cicchetti* bars on Campo Santa Margarita. My top Dorsoduro listing, **Ristorante Lineadombra,** is described later in "Splurging on a Water (or Otherwise Great) View."

Near the Accademia Bridge

$$ Bar Foscarini, next to the Accademia Bridge and Galleria, offers edible pizzas and *panini* in a memorable Grand Canal-view setting. The food is forgettable and drinks are pricey. But you're paying a premium for this premium location. On each visit to Venice, I grab a pizza lunch here while I ponder the Grand Canal bustle. They also serve breakfast (daily 8:00-23:00, Nov-April until 20:30, on Rio Terà A. Foscarini at Dorsoduro 878c, +39 041 522 7281).

$ Enoteca Cantine del Vino Già Schiavi, with a wonderfully characteristic *cicchetti*-bar ambience, is much loved for its inexpensive *cicchetti*, sandwiches (order from list on board), and wine. You're welcome to enjoy your wine and finger food at the bar, in the back room surrounded by wine bottles, or out on the sidewalk (specify "*fuori*" to sit outside and they'll provide plastic cups; don't sit on the bridge). This is primarily a wine shop with great prices for bottles to go (Mon-Sat 8:30-20:30, closed Sun, 100 yards from Accademia art museum on San Trovaso canal; facing the Accademia, take a right and then a forced left at the canal to the second bridge—it's on Fondamenta Nani at Dorsoduro 992; +39 041 523 0034; they have no WC).

$$$ Al Vecio Marangon Ristorante glows like a dream come true on its corner tucked away about 100 yards west of the Accademia. This stylishly rustic restaurant serves *cicchetti*-style dishes and pastas within its picturesque interior (with extremely tight seating) or at a line of outdoor tables. Consider their splittable *piatto di cicchetti misti*, a sampler of sardines, octopus, codfish, and seafood salad. As they take no reservations, arrive early or be prepared to wait (daily 12:00-22:00, on Calle de la Toletta at Dorsoduro 1210, +39 041 277 8554).

Zattere

The far south side of Dorsoduro has the Fondamenta Zattere, a wide promenade along the Giudecca canal that has a special charm on warm summer evenings. I'd come here not for the food, but to dine on the canal. Each of these places has a big terrace literally on the water. And nearby is the popular **Nico Gelateria** (with floating seating on the canal).

$$$ Terrazza dei Nobili takes full advantage of the warm, romantic evening sun. They serve regional specialties (especially fish) and pizza at tolerable prices. The breezy and beautiful seaside seating comes with formal service and the rumble of vaporetti from the nearby stop (daily 12:00-24:00; at the Zattere vaporetto stop on the Fondamenta, Dorsoduro 924; +39 041 520 6895).

$$ Pizzeria Oke is playful, with casual tables on the embankment and a sprawling pizza-parlor interior. It's a hit with young Venetians for its fun atmosphere. While the energy and food are great, be careful to understand the bill—and be warned that dishes presented as free may end up on your check (daily 11:30-23:00, a couple hundred yards from the Zattere vaporetto stop on the Fondamenta, Dorsoduro 1414, +39 041 520 6601).

$$ Pizzeria alle Zattere, where you can enjoy your pizza on a floating dining barge, is next to the Zattere vaporetto stop (Wed-Mon 12:00-22:00, closed Tue, on the Fondamenta at Dorsoduro 791a, +39 041 520 4224).

On or near Campo San Barnaba

This small square is a delight—especially in the evening. As these places are within a few steps of each other—and the energy and atmosphere can vary—I like to survey the options before choosing a place for lunch. But, in the evening, you're smart to reserve in advance.

$$ Ristoteca Oniga has an eclectic yet cozy interior and great tables on the square. The menu has a few vegetarian and meat dishes but focuses on fresh fish and other sea creatures, highlighted by their specialty, *bucintoro*—a pan full of mussels, clams, prawns, calamari, and spaghetti—prepared for two at a premium price (daily 12:00-14:30 & 19:00-22:30, reservations smart, Campo San Barnaba, Dorsoduro 2852, +39 041 522 4410, www.oniga.it).

$$ Osteria Enoteca Ai Artisti serves well-presented quality dishes, with seating within its tight little wine-snob interior or at a few petite, romantic canal-side tables. They serve good wines by the glass. When reserving, make sure they know your preference— a table on the canal or inside (great pasta, cheese plates, and fish; Tue-Sat 12:45-14:30 & 19:00-22:00, closed Sun-Mon; Fondamenta de la Toletta, Dorsoduro 1169a, +39 041 523 8944, www. enotecaartisti.com, Vicenzo and chef Francesca).

$ Pizzeria al Profeta is a casual place popular with tourists for great pizza. Its sprawling interior seems to stoke conviviality, as does its leafy garden with spacious seating out back (daily 12:00-14:30 & 19:00-22:30; from Campo San Barnaba, it's a long walk down Calle Lunga San Barnaba to #2671; +39 041 523 7466, run by hard-working Simone).

$$ Enoteca e Trattoria la Bitta is dark and woody, with a homey bistro feel and tight indoor seating. They serve beautifully presented, traditional Venetian food with—proudly—no fish. Their helpful wait staff and handwritten daily menu are focused on local ingredients (including rabbit) and a "slow food" ethic. They do two dinner seatings (19:00 and 21:00) and require reservations (dinner only, closed Sun, just off Campo San Barnaba on Calle Lunga San Barnaba, Dorsoduro 2753a, +39 041 523 0531, Debora and Marcellino).

On Campo Santa Margarita

For a fresh, youthful neighborhood vibe away from the tourist crowds and cutesy Venice, hike out to Campo Santa Margarita, where you'll find a multigenerational, slice-of-life scene by day and a trendy college-bar scene after dark. The square is ringed by bakeries, pubs, pizzerias, and fruit stands offering options for everything from picnics to finer dining. If slumming, a picnic or takeout pizza on this square (with fine benches and trees) is great. The area gets a little sketchy late at night. For the best gelato on the square, find **Gelateria Il Doge.**

$$ Osteria alla Bifora, a former butcher shop, serves creative plates of mixed cold cuts in their candlelit woody interior and at tables on the square. While it's almost only cold platters, the presentation is elegant and pairs delightfully with their wine. For rustic *cicchetti* plates ranging from sardines, anchovies, and cod to platters of fine salamis and cheeses, this is a good choice with a fun-loving energy (daily 12:00-24:00, #2930, +39 041 523 6119, Franco and Mirella).

$$$ Osteria Do Torri, delightfully situated with tables overlooking the action, is your best bet for standard Venetian dishes on the square (daily, #3408, +39 041 522 0686).

$ Campo Santa Margarita's hole-in-the-wall *cicchetti* bars (on the square and just off it) serve drinks and *cicchetti* plates to local eaters with a contagious love of life.

SPLURGING ON A WATER (OR OTHERWISE GREAT) VIEW

$$$$ Ristorante Lineadombra, immediately behind La Salute Church, has commanding Giudecca Canal views from their big floating terrace and a spacious, modern, and dressy interior. This Michelin-rated place is a gourmet treat, with gorgeously presented dishes that are local and modern at the same time. Each dish is a memory, and even though plates are pricey, you are welcome to share. The appetizers especially are big and are happily served on two smaller plates. Reserve ahead and choose seating inside or on their terrace. Service is friendly yet professional (daily 12:00-15:00 & 19:00-22:00, closed Tue off-season; a short walk behind La Salute Church from the Salute vaporetto stop, Fondamenta Zattere, Dorsoduro 19; +39 041 241 1881, www.ristorantelineadombra. com).

$$$$ Ristorante Algiubagiò, on Fondamente Nove—handy to the docks for the islands of Murano and Burano—is a good place to eat as you look over the northern lagoon. The name joins the names of the four owners—Alberto, Giulio, Barbara, and Giovanna—who strive to impress visitors with quality, creative Venetian cuisine made with the best ingredients. Reserve a waterside table or sit in their classy cantina dining room (daily 12:00-15:00 & 19:00-22:30, between the two sets of vaporetto docks on Fondamente Nove, Cannaregio 5039—see map on page 95, +39 041 523 6084, www.algiubagio.net).

$$ Ristorante Pizzeria da Alvise, also on Fondamente Nove, is a popular place for traditional dishes and pizza with tables on a terrace with a lagoon view (Tue-Sun 12:00-14:00 & 19:00-22:00, closed Mon, Fondamente Nove 5045c—see map on page 95, +39 041 520 1515).

$$$$ Gran Caffè Quadri on Piazza San Marco is the place to go if you insist on dining fine on Venice's main square. Upstairs is their Michelin-star Quadri restaurant, but their **Quadrino** bistro, also dressy and a bit pretentious, shares the same kitchen, with a more traditional and accessible menu, and prices that won't completely ruin your appetite. While its 15 tables are all inside, the orchestra is just out the window (Wed-Sun 12:00-15:00 & 19:00-22:30, closed Mon-Tue, reservations smart, San Marco 121—see map on page 61, +39 041 522 2105, www.alajmo.it/grancaffe-quadri).

On Giudecca Island: A short vaporetto ride from San Marco or Dorsoduro takes you away from the crowds to the more peaceful and residential Giudecca Island. Between the Giudecca Palanca and Redentore stops, you'll find several canalside dining options. Stroll the embankment and take your pick. The friendly service at **$$ Bar La Palanca** attracts a happy crowd (lunch until 14:30, closed Sun, no dinner served, at Giudecca 448). **$$$ Osteria Ae Botti** is white-tablecloth fancy inside, but has a row of tables hugging the embankment outside (closed Tue, Giudecca 609). **$$ Trattoria Al Redentore** serves up average pizza and pasta, but arguably has the best Venice views (daily, Giudecca 205b).

PICNICS AND SWEETS
Picnicking

You're legally forbidden from picnicking anywhere on or near St. Mark's Square except for Giardinetti Reali, the waterfront park near the San Marco vaporetto docks. Though it's legal to eat outdoors elsewhere around town, you may be besieged by pigeons who are, in turn, besieged by aggressive seagulls.

Venice has one main produce market and several convenient supermarkets:

Outdoor Market near the Rialto Bridge: Assemble a fun picnic at the **fruit and vegetable market** that sprawls for a few blocks to the north of the Rialto Bridge (best Mon-Sat 8:00-13:00, liveliest in the morning, closed Sun). The adjacent **fish market** is wonderfully slimy (closed Sun-Mon). Side lanes in this area are speckled with fine hole-in-the-wall munchie bars, bakeries, and cheese shops. The recommended **Al Mercà Bar** is ideal for a few little sandwiches to go (see listing on page 95). The Rialto Mercato vaporetto stop is convenient to both.

Produce Stands: Many larger squares have a produce stand. To find the one nearest St. Mark's Square, face St. Mark's Basilica, then walk along its left side, heading east down Calle de la Canonica. Cross the bridge and turn left at Campo Santi Filippo e Giacomo.

Fast and Cheap Eats around Campo Santa Maria Formosa: The veggie stand on Campo Santa Maria Formosa is a fixture. And for *döner kebabs* and pizza to go, head down Calle Lunga Santa Maria Formosa to **$ Peter Pan** at #6249 (daily 11:30-23:00, Castello—see map on page 95).

Supermarket near St. Mark's Square: A handy **Co-op** supermarket is between St. Mark's and Campo Santa Maria Formosa, on the corner of Salizada San Lio and Calle del Mondo Novo at Castello 5817. It has a deli counter and a great selection of picnic supplies, including packaged salads and fresh sandwiches (daily 8:30-22:00).

Other Supermarkets: The largest supermarket in town is the **Co-op** at Piazzale Roma, next to the vaporetto stop at Santa Croce 505. It's an easy walk from the train station, as is a smaller **Co-op** on Campo San Felice (along the Strada Nova between the train station and Rialto area, Cannaregio 3660). There's a **Despar** grocery a few steps from San Zulian church (3-minute walk from St. Mark's at Calle al Ponte de la Guerra 514). Just beyond the Rialto vaporetto stop is another handy **Co-op** (facing the Grand Canal at Riva del Carbon 4173). All are open long hours daily.

In Dorsoduro, just around the corner from the Accademia, a tiny **Crai** grocery has all the basics and some takeaway food (daily, Rio Terrà Foscarini 879a). There are two **Conad** supermarkets on the Zattere embankment—at the west end, at #1492, by the San Basilio vaporetto stop, and on the east end, at #417, near the Santo Spirito vaporetto stop.

Good Gelato and Chocolate Spots

Venice isn't known for its quality gelato but you'll still find good *gelaterie* in every neighborhood, typically offering one-scoop cones for about €2 (€1 per extra scoop). The words *artigianale* or *produzione propria* indicate that a shop makes its own gelato, although sometimes from powder or paste bases (avoid brightly colored gelato or places that have overflowing tubs). The following places are all open long hours daily.

St. Mark's Side of the Rialto Bridge: A gourmet gelato shop, **Gelatoteca Suso,** serves delectable flavors in bowls you can eat (next to Campo San Bartolomeo on Calle de la Bissa, San Marco 5453a—see map on page 95).

St. Mark's Square: Both **Gran Caffè Lavena** at #134 and **Gelateria al Todaro** (on the corner of the Piazzetta at #3, near the water just under the crocodile-topped column) won't win any awards, but they are convenient if you want something to lick while enjoying the San Marco orchestras. For locations, see the map on page 88.

Near Campo Santa Maria Formosa: Cioccolateria Vizio-Virtù (Vice and Virtue) is a hit with chocolate lovers. Across from the recommended Osteria al Portego, it's a modern lab of deliciousness with fine gelato as a bonus (closed Mon, Calle del Forner, Castello 5988—see map on page 95).

Venice Connections

A two-mile-long causeway (with highway and train lines) connects Venice to the mainland. Mestre, the sprawling mainland section of Venice, has fewer crowds, cheaper hotels, and plenty of inexpensive parking lots, but zero charm. Don't stop in Mestre unless you're changing trains, parking your car, or sleeping there.

BY TRAIN

All trains to "Venice" stop at Venezia Mestre (on the mainland). Most continue on to **Santa Lucia Station** (a.k.a. Venezia S.L.) on the island of Venice itself. If your train only stops at Mestre, you'll need to buy a €1.40 Mestre-Santa Lucia ticket and validate it before hopping any nonexpress, regional train (with an R or RV prefix) for the short ride across the causeway to Venice (10/hour, 10 minutes).

The Santa Lucia train station plops you right into the old town on the Grand Canal, an easy vaporetto ride or fascinating 45-minute walk (with a number of bridges and steps) to St. Mark's Square.

The station has **baggage storage** (€19/24 hours, daily 6:00-23:00, no lockers, along track 1). Pay **WCs** are at track 1 and in the back of the big bar/cafeteria area inside the station (in front of track 3). You'll find the **TI** across from track 2. If the station TI is crowded when you arrive, visit the TI at St. Mark's Square instead.

If you need to confirm your departure plan, there are banks of user-friendly ticket machines all around the station (covering Italian destinations only). They take euros and credit cards, display schedules, and issue tickets.

Getting from the Train Station to Central Venice

The Ferrovia **vaporetto docks** are right outside the station's front door. There are five docks (A, B, C, D, and E), each serving different boats. Dock assignments can change with the season, so check the electronic signboards near the ticket windows to see which boats are leaving when and from which dock. Most tourists want the fast boats #2 or #2/ down the Grand Canal to Rialto (generally from dock B; #2/ goes only as far as Rialto; #2 continues to San Marco late May-mid-Sept) or the slow boat #1 down the Grand Canal, making every stop all the way to Rialto and San Marco (usually dock E).

Buy a ticket before you board—but before buying a single-ride ticket, consider getting a transit pass (see page 38). If ticket-window lines at the docks are too long, use the nearby self-service machines (English-language option, credit cards accepted) or buy from the TI inside the station. Find your dock and validate your ticket/pass by touching it to the circular pad; the gates will open to let you onto the dock. Because docks serve multiple lines, before

VENICE

Arrival in Venice

MAINLAND

Aeroporto — TERMINAL

BOATS & WATER TAXIS

MOVING SIDEWALK

MARCO POLO AIRPORT

To Padua & Treviso Airport

MESTRE TRAIN STATION

Lagoon

San Marco to:
Airport = 4 miles
Mestre = 5 miles
Lido = 2 miles

CAUSEWAY

SANTA LUCIA TRAIN STATION

Murano

Museo

Colonna

To Marghera

Grand Canal

San Michele

Guglie Bridge

Fondamente Nove

TRONCHETTO CAR PARK

Tronchetto

Rialto

VENICE

Marittima

PIAZZALE ROMA BUS STN

SAN MARCO

San Marco

San Zaccaria

CRUISE PORT

Zattere

Giudecca

Zitelle

SAN GIORGIO MAGGIORE

Lido (S.M.E.)

Lido

Beach

GRAN VIALE S. MARIA ELISABETTA

Rail
Bus
Alilaguna Boat
(Not all stops shown)
People Mover

1 Kilometer

1 Mile

you hop on the vaporetto, confirm with the conductor that this particular boat is going to your stop ("*per* Rialto?").

A **water taxi** from the train station to central Venice costs about €70-80 (the taxi dock is to the left of the vaporetto docks).

It's a pleasant 25-minute **walk** from the train station to hotels in the Rialto area (head over the big train-station bridge and follow *Rialto* signs).

Train Connections

Destinations in Italy: Padua (30 minutes, Trenitalia: 4/hour, Italo: about hourly), **Vicenza** (45 minutes, Trenitalia: 2/hour, Italo: 7/day), **Verona** (1.5-2 hours, Trenitalia: 2/hour, Italo: 7/day), **Ravenna** (1-2/hour, 3 hours, transfer in Ferrara or Bologna), **Florence** (Trenitalia: hourly direct, 2 hours, often crowded—reserve ahead; Italo: 7/day, 2 hours, reservations required), **Bolzano** (about hourly, 3 hours, transfer in Verona), **Milan** (Trenitalia: 1-2/hour, some direct, 2.5-3 hours; Italo: every 2 hours, 2.5 hours), **Cinque Terre/Monterosso** (at least hourly, 6 hours, 1-3 changes),

Rome (Trenitalia: hourly, 4 hours; direct night train, 7.5 hours, reserve ahead; Italo: 4/day, 4 hours, reservations required), **Naples** (Trenitalia: almost hourly, 5.5 hours, some change in Bologna or Rome, reserve ahead; Italo: 5/day, 5.5 hours, reservations required), **Brindisi** (8/day, 9 or more hours, change in Rome or Bologna).

International Destinations: **Interlaken** (4/day, 6 hours with 2 changes), **Munich** (1/day direct, 7 hours, more with change in Verona), **Innsbruck** (1/day direct, 5 hours, more with change in Verona), **Salzburg** (4/day, 6.5 hours with change in Villach), **Paris** (2/day, 11 hours, change in Turin), **Geneva** (1/day direct, more with change in Milan, 7-8 hours), **Vienna** (2/day direct, 8 hours; direct night train, 11 hours), **Ljubljana** (2/day, 5 hours, train to Trieste, then bus or train to Ljubljana). To Ljubljana, there's also a direct DRD bus from Mestre (1/day, 3 hours, www.drd.si) and a private shuttle service (www.goopti.com).

BY BUS

Venice's "bus station" is at **Piazzale Roma,** an open-air parking lot located at the head of the Grand Canal. The square itself is a jumble of different operators, platforms, and crosswalks over busy lanes of traffic. But bus stops are well signed.

The ticket windows for ACTV (including #5 to Marco Polo Airport) are in a building near the modern Calatrava Bridge and the vaporetto stop. The ATVO ticket office (express buses to Marco Polo and Treviso airports and to Padua) is at #497g in the big, white building, on the right side of the square as you face away from the canal (office open daily 7:00-20:00). There's a small TI located in the Autorimessa Comunale parking structure (across the street from the ACTV ticket windows and up the stairs next to the corner snack bar).

Piazzale Roma also has two big parking garages and the People Mover monorail (€1.50, links to the cruise port and then the parking-lot island of Tronchetto). A baggage-storage office is next to the monorail at #497m (€7/24 hours, daily 7:00-20:00, www.trasbagagli.it).

Getting from Piazzale Roma to Central Venice

Find the vaporetto docks (just left of the modern bridge) and take boat #1 down the Grand Canal to reach the Rialto, Accademia, or San Marco (St. Mark's Square) stops; the faster #2 and #2/ travel only as far as the Rialto (except in summer, when line #2 goes all the way to San Marco).

Electronic boards direct you to the dock you want. Before buying a single-ride vaporetto ticket, consider getting a transit pass (see page 38). If your hotel is near here or near the train station, you can get there on foot.

BY CAR

The freeway (monitored by speed cameras) dead-ends after crossing the causeway to Venice. At the end of the road you have two parking-garage choices: Tronchetto or Piazzale Roma. As you drive into the city, signboards with green and red lights indicate which lots are full.

Parking at Tronchetto

This big five-story garage is a bit farther out, but it's cheaper than the garages at Piazzale Roma, well connected by vaporetto, and with 3,000 spaces, most likely to have a spot (€3-5/hour, €22/24 hours, +39 041 520 7555, www.veniceparking.it).

From the garage, cross the street to the brick building and go right to the vaporetto dock (not well-signed, look for *ACTV*). At the dock, catch vaporetto #2 in one of two directions: via the Grand Canal as far as Piazzale Roma (10 minutes), where you can transfer to line #2/ (express to the train station and Rialto) or line #1 for other Grand Canal destinations; or via Giudecca to San Marco/San Zaccaria (30 minutes).

Don't be waylaid by aggressive water-taxi boatmen. They charge €100 to take you where the vaporetto will for €7.50. Also avoid travel agencies masquerading as TIs; deal only with the ticket booth at the vaporetto dock or the VèneziaUnica public transport office. If you're going to buy a local transit pass, do it now.

If you're staying near the bus or train station, you can take the €1.50 **People Mover** monorail, which brings you from Tronchetto to the bus bays at Piazzale Roma (3-minute trip, buy tickets with cash or credit card from machine). From there, it's a five-minute walk across the modern Calatrava Bridge to the train station.

Parking at Piazzale Roma

The two garages here are more convenient but more expensive and likelier to be full (but you can reserve ahead online). Both face the busy Piazzale Roma, where the road ends. The big white Autorimessa Comunale building is a city garage (at the end of the bridge before you get to the piazza, €26/24 hours, +39 041 272 7211, www.avmspa.it). In a back corner of the square is the private and much more expensive Garage San Marco (€45/24 hours, +39 041 523 2213, www.garagesanmarco.it). Avoid the Parcheggio Sant'Andrea (expensive short-term parking only).

BY PLANE
Marco Polo Airport

Venice's surprisingly large, modern airport is on the mainland shore of the lagoon, six miles north of the city (code: VCE, +39 041 260 9260, www.veniceairport.it). There's one sleek terminal, with a TI (daily 9:00-20:00), car-rental agencies, ATMs, a bank, and plenty of shops and eateries.

Getting Between the Airport and Venice

You can get between the airport and central Venice in any of four ways: by Alilaguna boat, water taxi, airport bus, or land taxi.

Type	Speed	Cost	Notes
Alilaguna boat	Slow	Moderate	No transfer
Water taxi	Fast	Expensive	No transfer
Airport bus to Piazzale Roma	Medium	Cheap	Transfer to vaporetto
Land taxi to Piazzale Roma	Medium	Moderate	Transfer to vaporetto

Alilaguna boats reach most of this chapter's recommended hotels very simply, with no changes. Hotels near the train station, however, are better served by the bus to Piazzale Roma.

Both Alilaguna boats and water taxis leave from the airport's boat dock, a 15-minute walk from the terminal. To get there, follow signs along a sleek series of (indoor) moving sidewalks.

When flying out of Venice, allow plenty of time to get to the airport. From your hotel to the airport can take two hours. Alilaguna boats are small and can fill up. In an emergency, you can always hop in a water taxi and get to the airport in 30 minutes.

Alilaguna Airport Boats

These boats make the scenic journey across the lagoon, shuttling passengers between the airport and the island of Venice (€15, €27 round-trip, €1 more if bought on boat, includes 1 suitcase and 1 piece of hand luggage, additional bags-€3 each, roughly 2/hour, 1-1.5-hour trip depending on destination). Alilaguna boats are not covered by city transit passes, but use the same docks and ticket windows as the regular vaporetti. You can buy Alilaguna tickets online for a slight discount, but it does not ensure a reservation as you must still exchange the voucher for a ticket (www.alilaguna.it or www.venicelink.com).

Three key Alilaguna lines reach St. Mark's Square. From the airport, the **orange line** *(linea arancio)* runs down the Grand Canal, reaching Guglie (handy for Cannaregio hotels, 45 minutes), Rialto (1 hour), and San Marco (1.25 hours). The **blue line** *(linea blu)* heads first to Fondamente Nove (40 minutes), then loops around to San Zaccaria and San Marco (about 1.5 hours) before continuing to Zattere and the cruise terminal (almost 2 hours). In high season, if it's running, the **red line** *(linea rossa)* runs to St. Mark's in just over an hour (may be suspended—check online). It circumnavigates Murano and then runs parallel to the blue line, ending at the cruise terminal.

For a full schedule, see www.alilaguna.it, visit the TI, call +39 041 240 1701, ask your hotelier, or scan the schedules posted at the docks.

From the Airport to Venice: Buy Alilaguna tickets at the information desk in the arrivals area or the ticket windows at the docks. Any ticket seller can tell you which line to catch to get to your destination. Blue- and orange-line boats from the airport run roughly twice an hour and go all day (until about midnight); red goes once an hour (may not be running when you visit, but typically runs 9:40-18:40; check online). Ask your hotelier (when you reserve your room) which stop in Venice is best.

From Venice to the Airport: Ask your hotelier which dock and which line is best. Blue-line boats start leaving Venice as early as 3:50 in the morning. Scope out the dock and buy your ticket in advance to avoid last-minute stress. Get there 10 minutes early to assure yourself a seat.

Water Taxis

Luxury taxi speedboats zip directly between the airport and the closest dock to your hotel, getting you within steps of your destination in about 30 minutes. The official price is €130 for up to four people; add €10 for every extra person (9-passenger limit). You may get a higher quote—politely talk it down. A taxi can be a smart investment for small groups and those with an early departure.

From the airport, arrange your ride at the water-taxi desk or with the boat captains at the dock. From Venice, book your taxi trip the day before your departure, either through your hotel or directly with the Consorzio Motoscafi water taxi association (Mon-Fri call +39 041 240 6712, Sat-Sun call +39 041 522 2303, www.motoscafivenezia.it).

Airport Shuttle Buses

Buses between the airport and Venice are fast, frequent, and cheap. They drop you at Venice's bus station, at the square called Piazzale Roma. From there, you can catch a vaporetto down the Grand Canal—convenient for hotels near the Rialto Bridge and St. Mark's Square. If you're staying near the train station, you can walk from Piazzale Roma to your hotel.

Two bus companies serve this route: ACTV and ATVO. ATVO buses take 20 minutes and go nonstop. ACTV buses make a few stops en route and take slightly longer (30 minutes), but you get a discount if you buy a Venice vaporetto pass at the same time (see page 38). The service is equally good (either bus: €8 one-way, €15 round-trip; ACTV bus with transit-pass discount: €6 one-way, €12 round-trip; runs about 5:00-24:00, 2/hour, drops to 1/hour early and late, check schedules at www.atvo.it or www.actv.it).

From the Airport to Venice: Buses leave from just outside the arrivals terminal. Buy tickets from the TI, the ticket desk in the terminal, the kiosk near baggage claim, or ticket machines. ATVO tickets are not valid on ACTV buses and vice versa. Double-check the destination; you want Piazzale Roma. If taking ACTV, you want bus #5.

From Venice to the Airport: At Piazzale Roma, buy your ticket from the ACTV windows (in the building by the bridge) or the ATVO office (at #497g) before heading out to the platforms (although sometimes an attendant sells tickets near the buses). The newsstand in the center of the lot also sells tickets.

Land Taxi or Private Minivan

It takes about 20 minutes to drive from the airport to Piazzale Roma or the cruise port. A **land taxi** can do the trip for about €50. To reserve a private minivan, contact **Treviso Car Service** (minivan—€60, seats up to 8; car—€50, seats up to 3; mobile +39 338 204 4390 or +39 333 411 2840, www.trevisocarservice.com).

Treviso Airport

Several budget airlines use Treviso Airport, 12 miles northwest of Venice (code: TSF, +39 042 231 5111, www.trevisoairport.it). The fastest option into Venice is on the **Barzi express bus,** which gets you to the Tronchetto parking lot (convenient if taking vaporetto line #2) in just 40 minutes (€12, buy tickets on board, every 1-2 hours, www.barziservice.com). From Tronchetto, hop on a vaporetto, or take the People Mover monorail to Piazzale Roma for €1.50. **ATVO buses** are a bit more frequent and drop you right at Piazzale Roma (saving you the People Mover ride), but take nearly twice as long (€12 one-way, €22 round-trip, about 2/hour, 70 minutes, www.atvo.it; buy tickets at the ATVO desk in the airport and stamp them on the bus). **Treviso Car Service** offers minivan service to Piazzale Roma (minivan—€75, seats up to 8; car—€65, seats up to 3; for contact info, see listing earlier).

BY CRUISE SHIP

As of 2022, large ships dock at the commercial Marghera port outside of Venice, or at ports in Trieste or Ravenna, and transfer passengers by bus to Venice's Stazione Marittima, at the west end of town. (Some smaller cruise ships dock directly at Stazione Marittima.) From Stazione Marittima, if it's running, the most direct way to reach St. Mark's Square is to take the Alilaguna **red line** (www.alilaguna.it). Otherwise, walk five minutes to the **People Mover** monorail for a three-minutes ride to Piazzale Roma, then hop on a **vaporetto.** Or, take an expensive **water taxi** ride (at least €70-80).

For more details, see my *Rick Steves Mediterranean Cruise Ports* guidebook.

NEAR VENICE

Padua • Vicenza • Verona

Venice is just one of many towns in the Italian region of Veneto (VEHN-eh-toh), but few visitors venture off the lagoon. That's a shame, as there's much to see within a very short hop of Venice. The trip from Venice westward to Milan is a route strewn with temptations: the Dolomite peaks, Italy's famous lakes, and—closer to Venice—the important and worthwhile towns of Padua, Vicenza, and Verona.

If you can't make it to all three, pick the one that interests you most. Art lovers will want to head to **Padua** to see Giotto's celebrated Scrovegni Chapel. History buffs should see **Verona**'s impressive Roman ruins. Verona is also the pick for star-crossed lovers retracing Romeo and Juliet's steps. Architecture fans could consider a quick stop in Palladio-designed **Vicenza,** located about halfway between Padua and Verona.

If you're Padua-bound, remember that you need to reserve ahead to see the Scrovegni Chapel. Don't bother visiting Vicenza on a Monday, when many of the top sights are closed; in Verona, the Roman Arena is open only in the afternoon on Mondays.

Spending a day at one of these towns as a side trip from Venice or town-hopping between Venice and Milan is exciting and efficient. Padua, Verona, and Vicenza are on the same train line. Connected by at least two trains per hour, they're easy to visit.

Train Tip: When day-tripping here, look on the Trenitalia schedule for economical RV trains, which are nearly as fast as the more expensive Freccia trains.

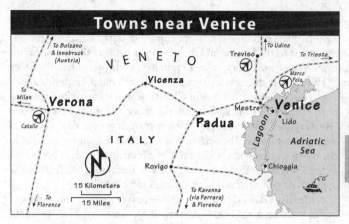

Towns near Venice

Padua

This easily appreciated city is a fine destination on its own and a convenient base for day trips all around the region. Nicknamed "the brain of Veneto," Padua (*Padova* in Italian) is home to the prestigious university (founded in 1222) that hosted Galileo, Copernicus, Dante, and Petrarch. Pilgrims know Padua as the home of the Basilica of St. Anthony, where the reverent assemble to touch his tomb and ogle his remarkably intact lower jaw, tongue, and vocal cords. And lovers of early Renaissance art come here to make a pilgrimage of their own: to gaze at the remarkable frescoes by Giotto in the Scrovegni Chapel. But despite the fact that Padua's museums and churches hold their own in Italy's artistic big league, its hotels are reasonably priced, and the city doesn't feel touristy. Padua's old town center is elegantly arcaded, filled with students, and sprinkled with surprises, including some of Italy's most inviting squares for lingering over an *aperitivo* as the sun slowly dips low in the sky.

From Padua, architecture fans can ride by train (20-30 minutes) to Vicenza and its celebrated Palladian buildings. And Venice is just a half-hour away in the other direction.

NEAR VENICE

PLANNING YOUR TIME: PADUA IN A DAY

Day-trippers can do a quick but enjoyable blitz of Padua—including a visit to the Scrovegni Chapel—in as little as six hours. Trains from Venice are cheap, take 30 minutes, and run frequently. Once in Padua, everything is a 10-minute walk or a quick tram ride apart.

To see Giotto's Scrovegni Chapel, you need to make a reservation; your entry time will dictate the order of your sightseeing (see "Reservations" on page 139). When planning your day, also consider these factors: The station has a reliable baggage-check desk; the open-air markets are vibrant in the morning; student life is best at the university late in the day; and the Basilica of St. Anthony is open all day, but the reliquary chapel closes midday.

Ideally, I'd do it this way: 9:00—market action and sightseeing in town center, 11:00—Basilica of St. Anthony, 13:00—lunch, 15:00—Scrovegni Chapel tour. Then, cap off your day with a *spritz* on the main square.

Orientation to Padua

Padua's main tourist sights lie on a north-south axis through the heart of the city, from the train station to Scrovegni Chapel to the market squares (the center of town) to the Basilica of St. Anthony. It's roughly a 10-minute walk between each of these sights, or about 30 minutes from end to end. Padua's wonderful single tram line makes lacing things together quick and easy (see "Getting Around Padua," later).

TOURIST INFORMATION

Padua has two TIs: in the **center** (in the alley behind Caffè Pedrocchi at Vicolo Cappellatto Pedrocchi 9, Mon-Sat 9:00-19:00, Sun 10:00-16:00) and at the **train station** (same hours, +39 049 520 7415, www.turismopadova.it). A seasonal TI kiosk sometimes sets up in the piazza in front of the **Basilica of St. Anthony.**

Sightseeing Card: The **Urbs Picta Card** includes entry to eight sights—including the recommended Scrovegni Chapel, Palazzo della Ragione, the Baptistery of the Duomo, and the Oratory of San Giorgio—plus unlimited tram rides (€28/48 hours, €35/72 hours; buy at either TI, the Scrovegni Chapel, or online at the chapel website, where you can make a chapel reservation—www.cappelladegliscrovegni.it).

ARRIVAL IN PADUA

By Train: The efficient station is a user-friendly shopping mall, including a Despar supermarket (long hours daily). Along track 1, on the far right as you face the tracks, are pay WCs and baggage storage (daily 6:30-20:00).

NEAR VENICE

Padua

To A-4
Autostrada
(Venice &
Verona)

TRAIN
STATION

Stazione

CITY
BUSES

BUSES TO
AIRPORT &
VENICE

VIA FRA
PAOLO SARPI

VIA GIOVANNI
VERDARA

S. DELLA ROTONDA

VIALE CODALUNGA

VIA B. CAIROLI

VIA N. TOMMASEO

VIA BEATO PELLEGRINO

VIA SAN PELLEGRINO

Piazza Alcide
de Gasperi

C. DEL POPOLO

V. FOSCOLO

V. DIEGO VALERI

VIA DELLA ROTONDA

VIA GIOTTO

VIA TRIESTE

Trieste

OLD CITY
WALLS

CARMINE
CHURCH

V. DEL CARMINE

GARIBALDI

**SCROVEGNI
CHAPEL**

See Padua Center detail map

VIA DEI SAVONAROLA

Piovego

Eremitani

PALAZZO
ZUCKERMANN

**CIVIC
MUSEUMS**
(SCROVEGNI
TICKETS)

Canale

VIA SAN PIETRO

V. CARLO LEONI

CORSO MILANO

VIA DANTE

V. SAN FERMO

CORSO

ERMITAGE
CHURCH

Piazza dell'
Insurrezione

V. VERDI

VIA SANTA LUCIA

S. NICOLÒ

V. PATRIARCATO

**MARKET
SQUARES**

PEDROCCHI
BLDG.

VIA CAVOUR

R. PONTI ROMANI

VIA ALTINATE

Piazza
Capitaniato

Piazza
Signori

Piazza
Frutta

Piazza
Cavour

Ponti
Romani

BAPTISTERY

PALAZZO
RAGIONE

Piazza
Erbe

UNIVERSITY
(PALAZZO BO)

VIA CESARE BATTISTI

V. DEI TADI

Piazza
Duomo

VIA MANIN

V. SONCIN

DUOMO

VIA DEI VESCOVADO

V. S. GREGORIO BARBARIGO

SOLFERINO

VIA ROMA

VIA TITO LIVIO

Piazza
Antenore

VIA DEL SANTO

VIA SAN FRANCESCO

VIA
SPERONI

MARSALA

Tito
Livio

**SAN
FRANCESCO**

VIA SANTA ROSA

S. MARIA
SERVI

RIVIERA TITO LIVIO

VIA GALILEO GALILEI

VIA SAN TOMASO

Piazza
del Castello

20 SETTEMBRE

Piazzetta
Palatucci

VIA SANTA
CHIARA

Piovego

V. SEMINARIO

VIA DEI ROGATI

VIA UMBERTO

RIVIERA RUZANTE

VIA RUDENA

Piazza
del
Santo

V. CESAROTTI

Canale

R. TISO CAMPOSAMPIERO

V. TORRESINO

Santo

**BASILICA OF
ST. ANTHONY**
See detail map

VIA DIMESSE

VIA ACQUETTE

Prato
della Valle

VIA BELLUDI

V. BRIOSCO

VIA ALBERTO

CAVALLETTO

**Prato
della Valle**

Botanic
Garden

200 Meters

200 Yards

To get downtown, simply hop on Padua's handy **tram** (for ticket info, see "Getting Around Padua," later). Leaving the station, the tram stop is 100 yards to the right at the foot of the bridge (direction: Capolinea Sud). Note that thieves like this tram when it comes to picking tourists' pockets. A **taxi** into town (a good option after dark) costs about €12-15.

By Bus: Buses arrive at platforms 100 yards east of the train station. Buses for Venice's Piazzale Roma and Marco Polo Airport use these platforms. (Buses directly in front of the station are in-city only.)

By Car: Padua has a smart park-and-ride system near each end of the tram line, providing cheap parking and convenient access to town using the tram. The north lot is at the Pontevigodarzere stop, the south lot at the Capolinea Guizza stop. At either lot, buy parking tickets from machines or at the nearby café (€1 for all day and free overnight).

For more costly parking closer to town, try **Padova Centro Park** (near the train station and the Scrovegni Chapel, €16/24 hours) or **Piazza Isaac Rabin** (near Prato della Valle, €18/24 hours).

HELPFUL HINTS

Pronunciation: You say Padua (PAD-joo-wah), they say Padova (PAH-doh-vah). The city's top sight, Scrovegni Chapel, is pronounced skroh-VEHN-yee.

Bookstore: Feltrinelli, with books in English, is one block from the main university building (daily 9:00-19:30, Via San Francesco 7, +39 199 151 173).

Launderette: Self-service **Lavami** is central, tiny, and modern with English instructions on flip cards (daily 7:00-21:15, Via Marsala 22 near intersection with Via dell'Arco, +39 049 876 4532).

Local Guide: Charming and helpful **Cristina Pernechèle** is a great teacher who is passionate about her hometown (€150/half-day, mobile +39 338 495 5453, cristina@pernechele.eu). If she's booked, she can suggest other good local guides.

GETTING AROUND PADUA

Ignore the city buses; pretend there is only the **tram** and rely on it. There's just one line, which efficiently and without stress connects everything you care about.

With an Urbs Picta Card (see "Sightseeing Card," earlier) you get unlimited tram use; just show the card upon request. Otherwise, pay onboard by tapping your contactless credit card at the reader at mid-tram, or buy tickets from shops inside the train station or from the low brown rectangular booth in front of the station (with machines and a staffed window) and validate on board. The

€1.30 single ticket is good for 75 minutes (€3.80 *biglietto giornaliero* good for one calendar day; departs every 8 minutes during the day Mon-Sat, every 20 minutes evenings and Sun). There are ticket machines at some stops, but they sell only single tickets and don't give change. The rubber-wheeled trams run on a single rail.

Before boarding, note the tram direction on posted schedules and above the front window (*Pontevigodarzere* is northbound, *Capolinea Sud* is southbound). Stops that matter to tourists include Stazione FS (train and bus stations), Eremitani (Scrovegni Chapel), Ponti Romani (old town center, market squares, university), Tito Livio (ghetto, old town center, Hotel Majestic Toscanelli), and Santo (Basilica of St. Anthony and neighborhood hotels).

Padua's **hop-on, hop-off tour buses** are not worth the time or money.

Sights in Padua

IN THE CENTER

Padua's two main sights, the Scrovegni Chapel and the Basilica of St. Anthony, are, respectively, at the north and south ends of the city center. But Padua's atmospheric, cobbled core—with bustling markets, vibrant student life, and inviting sun- and café-speckled piazzas—is its own ▲▲▲ attraction. You could simply stroll the area aimlessly or seek out some of the following spots.

▲▲Market Squares

The market squares **Piazza delle Erbe** and **Piazza della Frutta,** separated by the stately Palazzo della Ragione, are busy each

morning and all day Saturday (Mon-Fri roughly 8:00-13:00, Sat 8:00-19:00 but a bit quieter in the afternoon, closed Sun). Second only to the produce market in Italy's gastronomic capital of Bologna, this market has been renowned for centuries for its selection of fresh herbs, fruits, and vegetables. The presentation is an art in itself. As you wander, appreciate the local passion for good food: Residents can tell the month by the seasonal selections, and merchants share recipe tips with shoppers.

Don't miss the **indoor market** zone on the ground floor of the Palazzo della Ragione. Browsing through this H-shaped arcade—where you'll find butchers, *salumerie* (delicatessens), cheese shops, bakeries, and fishmongers—is a sensuous experience. For centuries, this was a market for luxury items (furs, fine fabrics, silver,

Padua Center

VIA DEI SAVONAROLA

Piovego

Canale

VIA SAN PIETRO

V. CARLO LEONI

VIA DANTE

Piazza dell' Insurrezione

CORSO MILANO

VIA DEI LIVELLO

VIA VERDI

VIA

VIA SANTA LUCIA

SAN NICOLÒ

V. PATRIARCATO

2

Piazza Capitaniato

LION

Piazza Signori

11

16

20

VIA BREDA

14

Piazza Frutta

12 23

BAPTISTERY

VIA MANIN

PALAZZO RAGIONE

STAIRS

VIA DEI TADI

Piazza Duomo

15

Piazza Erbe

S. CANZ.

8

V. SONCIN

DUOMO

7

VIA DEI VESCOVADO

VIA S. MARTIN E SOLFERINO

VIA S. FABBRI

1

VIA S. MART. SOLF.

VIA SPERONI

VIA S. GREGORIO BARBARIGO

22

V. ARCO

13

9

MARSALA

VIA SANTA ROSA

S. MARIA SERVI

VIA ROMA

VIA UMBERTO I

Piazza del Castello

20 SETTEMBRE

Piazzetta Palatucci

10

VIA

Piovego

VIA DEI ROGATI

Canale

P. TISO CAMPOSAMPIERO

V. A. ALEARDI

V. SEMINARIO

V. TORRESINO

VIA ANDREA MEMMO

19

VIA DIMESSE

VIA ROBERTO MARIN

VIA ACQUETTE

To Prato della Valle, Piazza Isaac Rabin Parking & A-13 Autostrada (Florence)

NEAR VENICE

Accommodations
1. Hotel Majestic Toscanelli
2. Albergo Verdi
3. Hotel Al Fagiano
4. Hotel Al Santo
5. Hotel Casa del Pellegrino

Eateries
6. Taverna Nane della Giulia
7. Osteria L'Anfora
8. Osteria dal Capo
9. Enotavola Pino
10. Enoteca Antonio Ferrari
11. La Lanterna
12. Bar dei Osei & La Folperia
13. Bar Corte Sconta
14. Bar All'Ombra della Piazza
15. Pastasuta & Cristina e Massimo
16. Gnam Gnam Gelato
17. Pizzeria Pago Pago
18. Pollodoro la Gastronomica
19. Portogallo Gelateria

Other
20. Grocery
21. Feltrinelli Bookstore
22. Launderette
23. Ai Due Cantini d'Oro (Old Pharmacy)

Note: Much of central Padua is pedestrian & bike-friendly

and gold—notice the decorative iron gates used to lock it up each evening). Then, the devastating 1797 fall of the Venetian Republic to the French marked the end of good times, and with no market for luxury items, the arcade was used to sell perishables—meat and cheese—out of the sun.

The Renaissance building with the flags overlooking Piazza delle Erbe is the Palazzo del Podestà. On the wing to the right, notice the 1930s-era panel celebrating Mussolini's pathetic little empire—Libya, Albania, Somalia, and Ethiopia. Immediately south of Piazza delle Erbe is the former Jewish quarter, a charming zone of arcaded lanes. Padua has some 15 miles of such lanes protected from sun and rain, giving the city an extra boost of elegance.

Students gather in these squares after the markets have closed, spilling out of colorful bars and cafés, drinks in hand (see sidebar). Bars and food stalls offer plenty of refreshments and fun food. Pizza by the slice is dirt-cheap.

On Piazza della Frutta, look for the recommended sandwich stand, **Bar dei Osei,** and a neighboring squid stand that sets up in the late afternoon (see "Eating in Padua," later). Just a few steps away from these is a classic old pharmacy that dates to 1841: The licorice-perfumed **Ai Due Cantini d'Oro,** which stocks retail items like it did before World War II, sells odd foods and specialty items for every dietary need (closed Mon, Piazza della Frutta 46).

▲Palazzo della Ragione

Looming over Padua's two big central market squares (Piazza delle Erbe and Piazza della Frutta), this grand 13th-century palazzo—commonly called *il Salone* (the great hall)—once held the medieval law courts.

Cost and Hours: €7; Tue-Sun 9:00-19:00, Nov-Jan until 18:00, closed Mon year-round; Ponti Romani tram stop, +39 049 820 5006, www.padovacultura.it.

Visiting the Palazzo: Facing the palazzo from Piazza delle Erbe, climb the grand staircase on the building's far right side, buy your ticket, and go to the loggia overlooking Piazza delle Erbe. Enjoy the view and the fine vaulting that was painted in the 1300s to celebrate the wealth of the independent Paduan city-state (one of many little states in "the land of a thousand bell towers" that ultimately formed Italy).

Step into the great hall and take it all in. This huge hall—265 feet by 90 feet—was at one time adorned with frescoes by Giotto and his workshop. After a fire in 1420 destroyed Giotto's work, the

Drinking a *Spritz* with the Student Crowd

Each early evening, before dinner, students enliven Padua by enjoying a convivial drink in their favorite places. Piazza dei Signori is trendier, with people of all ages, while the scene on Piazza delle Erbe is more bohemian and alternative. Or you could sit in front of the university, nurse your drink, and watch the graduates get roasted with their crazy gangs of friends.

The drink of choice is a *spritz,* an aperitif generally made with Campari (a red liqueur infused with bitter herbs), white wine or prosecco, and sparkling water, and garnished with a blood-orange wedge. Another version is a sweeter and lighter *spritz* made with Aperol (an orange-flavored liqueur), which has a lower alcohol content and is not as bitter as the heavier Campari *spritz.* Padovans brag that Aperol was created here in 1919.

Grab a table and be part of the scene. This is a classic opportunity to enjoy a real discussion with smart, English-speaking students who see tourists not as pests, but as interesting people from far away. For an instant conversation starter, ask about the current political situation in Italy, the right-wing party's policy on immigrants, or the cultural differences between Italy's North and South. A question they might ask you: "What the hell is the electoral college?"

walls were repainted with 333 frescoes depicting the signs of the zodiac, labors of the month, symbols representing characteristics of people born under each sign, and, finally, figures of the 12 apostles and favorite saints. Depicting a range of occupations, pursuits, and interests, the frescoes provide rare glimpses into contemporary European life in the early 15th century—from tanners stretching hides to aristocrats playing lawn tennis.

The enormous hull-shaped roof you see overhead was installed after the fire, and the partitions that once divided the space were removed, creating what was the largest vaulted room in 15th-century Europe.

As big as the hall is, it is almost dwarfed at one end by a gigantic, very anatomically correct wooden horse. It's said to be a copy of the bronze equestrian statue by Donatello that stands outside the Basilica of St. Anthony (see page 147).

At the other end of the hall, find the black "Stone of Shame," on which debtors sat in punishment during the Middle Ages.

St. Anthony reportedly introduced this public humiliation in 1230 as a compassionate alternative to prison. Instead of doing jail time, debtors sat upon this stone, surrendered their possessions, and denounced themselves publicly before being exiled from the city.

Also in the hall is a contemporary Foucault pendulum that demonstrates the rotation of the earth (well described in English).

Piazza dei Signori

Just a block away from Palazzo della Ragione, this square is a busy clothing market in the morning and the most popular gathering place in the evening for students out for a drink. The Palazzo del Capitanio closes off one end of the square, where a circa-1344 clock decorates a tower dedicated to its upkeep. It took three floors of the tower to house the clock mechanism, and the clock caretaker lived on the remaining two floors.

Sitting atop a column near the tower, the aggressive lion with unfurled wings, symbol of Venice and St. Mark, is a reminder that Padua was dominated by the Venetian Republic for nearly 400 years (1405-1797).

▲Caffè Pedrocchi

The white-columned, Neoclassical Pedrocchi building is much more than just a café on the ground floor. A complex of meeting rooms and entertainment venues, it stirs the Italian soul (or the patriotic Italian soul, at least). Built in 1831 during the period of Austrian rule, Caffè Pedrocchi was inaugurated for the fourth Italian Congress of Scientists, which convened during the mid-19th century to stir up nationalistic fervor as Italy

struggled to unite as a single country. In 1848, this symbol of patriotic hope was the target (no surprise) of those repressing a student uprising that was being plotted here. (For more on the story of Italy's unification, visit the upstairs Museum of the Risorgimento; see the next listing.)

Cost and Hours: Café interior free, daily 8:00-23:00, across from Via VIII Febbraio near Ponti Romani tram stop, +39 049 878 1231, www.caffepedrocchi.it.

Visiting the Café: Each of the café's three dining rooms is decorated and furnished in a different color (denoted by the hue of velvet on the chairs): red, white, or green—representing the colors of the Italian flag. In the outer, unheated **Sala Verde** (Green Room), people are welcome to sit and relax without ordering anything or having to pay. This is where Italian gentlemen read their newspapers and gather with friends to chat about the old days. In the **Sala Rossa** (Red Room), the clock over the bar is flanked by marble reliefs of morning and night, a reminder that, back in the 19th century, the room was open 24 hours a day. In the rooms on either side of the bar, maps of the hemispheres with south up top reflect the unconventional spirit of the place. In the **Sala Bianca** (White Room), where a student revolutionary in that ill-fated 1848 uprising was killed, you can see a bullet hole in the wall (framed in tarnished silver).

The menu offers teahouse fare, including sandwiches and ice-cream sundaes, a variety of breakfast combos, and the writer Stendhal's beloved *zabaglione,* a creamy custard made with Marsala wine. A shiny new bar in the center of the building has a pastry counter and serves sandwiches at outdoor tables. Remember that in Italy, you can order a basic coffee standing up at the bar of any place, no matter how fancy, and pay the same low, government-regulated price.

Museum of the Risorgimento
This small museum (above Caffè Pedrocchi) traces Padua's role in Italian history, from the downfall of the Venetian Republic (1797) to the founding of the Republic of Italy (1946). Exhibits include uniforms, medals, weaponry, old artillery, and fascist propaganda posters—but without English descriptions, this museum is of most interest to passionate students of Italian history.

Cost and Hours: €4; Tue-Sun 9:30-12:30 & 15:30-18:00, closed Mon; enter up staircase on the side of café farthest from Piazza Cavour, +39 049 878 1231.

▲University of Padua
The main building of this prestigious university, known as Palazzo Bo, is just down the street from Caffè Pedrocchi. Founded in 1222,

it's one of the first, greatest, and most progressive universities in Europe. Back when the Church controlled university curricula, a group of professors and students broke free from the University of Bologna to create this liberal school, which would be independent of Catholic constraints and accessible to people of other faiths.

A haven for free thought, the university attracted intellectuals from all over Europe, including the great astronomer Copernicus, who realized here that the universe didn't revolve around him. And Galileo—notorious for disagreeing with the Church's views on science—called his 18 years on the faculty here the best of his life.

Anyone can stroll through its two courtyards for free. Tours are given in English several times a day for a deeper look at Palazzo Bo and the famed Anatomy Theater.

Cost and Hours: Grounds—free, closed Sun; University and Anatomy Theater tour—€7 (English tours Mon-Sat generally at 12:00, 14:30, and 16:30, fewer tours off-season, no tours on Sun, maximum 25 people per tour); Via VIII Febbraio 7 (Ponti Romani tram stop), +39 049 827 3939, www.unipd.it/en/guidedtours. Confirm tour times and availability online or by phone, or stop by the ticket desk (in passage between two courtyards).

Visiting the Courtyards on Your Own: You can poke into two of the university's courtyards on any day but Sunday. Find the entrance on Via VIII Febbraio under the "Gymnasium" inscription (30 yards from Caffè Pedrocchi, facing City Hall). You'll pop into a 16th-century courtyard, the school's historic core. It's littered with the coats of arms of important faculty and leaders of the university over the ages. Classrooms, which open onto the square, are still used. Today, students gather here, surrounded by memories of illustrious alumni, including the first woman in the world to receive a university degree (in 1678).

A passageway leads from here to an adjacent second courtyard, dating from c. 1938 (the New Courtyard). The relief in Fascist style above the arches celebrates the fighting spirit of students of the Paduan *goliardia*—nowadays something akin to a fraternity—which got its start with the 1848 student revolt against Austrian occupation. Off this courtyard, notice the richly decorated stairway, frescoed in the 1930s with themes celebrating art, science, and the pursuit of knowledge.

The tiny Da Mario Bar, tucked into a corner of the second courtyard, displays photos and artifacts of *goliardia* rituals and university life (run by octogenerian Mario, famed for his strong spritzes, open Mon-Fri only).

University and Anatomy Theater Tour: Students give 45-minute tours of the university that include a look at Europe's first great Anatomy Theater (from 1595). Despite

Graduation Antics in Padua

With 60,000 students, Padua's university always seems to be hosting graduation ceremonies. There's a constant trickle of

happy grads and their friends and families celebrating the big event.

During the school year, every 20 minutes or so, a student steps into a formal room (upstairs, above the university courtyard) to officially meet with the leading professors of his or her faculty. When they're finished, the students are given a green laurel wreath. They pose for ceremonial group photos and family snapshots. It's a sweet scene. Then, craziness takes over.

The new graduates replace their somber clothing with raunchy outfits, as gangs of friends gather around them on Via VIII Febbraio, the street in front of the university. The roast begins. The gang rolls out a giant butcher-paper poster with a generally obscene caricature of the student and a litany of *This Is Your Life* photos and stories. The new grad, subject to various embarrassing pranks, reads the funny statements out loud. The poster is then taped to the university wall for all to see. (Find the plastic panels to the right of the main entry, facing Via VIII Febbraio. Graduation posters are allowed to stay there for 24 hours. The panels are emptied each morning, but by nighttime a new set of posters is affixed to the plastic shields.)

During the roast, the friends sing the catchy but obscene local university anthem, reminding their newly esteemed friend not to get too huffy: *Dottore, dottore, dottore del buso del cul. Vaffancul, vaffancul* (loosely translated: "Doctor, doctor. You're just a doctor of the a-hole...go f-off, go f-off"). After you've heard this song (with its fanfare and oom-pah-pah catchiness) and have seen all the good-natured fun, you can't stop singing it.

The crazy show is usually staged late in the afternoon. Outdoor café tables afford great seats to enjoy the spectacle.

the Church's strict ban on autopsies, more than 300 students would pack this theater to watch professors dissect human cadavers (the bodies of criminals from another town). This had to be done in a "don't ask, don't tell" kind of way, because the Roman Catholic Church only started allowing the teaching of anatomy through dissection in the late 1800s.

▲Baptistery of the Duomo (Battistero del Duomo)

This richly frescoed little building (next to Padua's skippable Duomo) was once the private chapel of Padua's ruling family, the Carraresi. In the 1370s, they hired Florentine artist Giusto de' Menabuoi to do a little interior redecoration. Later, in 1405, Venice conquered Padua and deposed the Carraresi; the building was turned into a baptistery, but the original decorations survived.

Cost and Hours: €4, Mon 13:30-18:00, Tue-Sun 10:00-13:30 & 14:00-18:00, on Piazza Duomo.

Visiting the Baptistery: The Carraresis intended their private chapel to be a family mausoleum, and accordingly summoned the artist Giusto to create a fresco cycle fitting to that purpose. Almighty Christ, the Pantocrator, is in majesty in the cupola, while approachable Mary and the multitude of saints and angels provide the devout with access to God. In the drum below are scenes from Genesis, including the creation of Eve, who is dramatically being pulled by God from Adam's side. From those scenes of Creation, a narrative cycle of Old and New Testament scenes spills across the walls. The four evangelists (Matthew, Mark, Luke, and John) with their books and symbols fill the corners. A vivid Crucifixion scene faces a gorgeous Annunciation. And the altar niche features a dim, blue-toned, literal Apocalypse from the book of Revelation.

The Baptistery was created 70 years after Giotto, and it seems relatively conservative compared to Giotto's Scrovegni Chapel. But even if tentative, Giusto clearly picked up some lessons from Giotto about vivid color, handling perspective, and creating fully formed human figures.

SCROVEGNI CHAPEL AND CIVIC MUSEUMS

Wallpapered with Giotto's beautifully preserved cycle of nearly 40 frescoes, the glorious Scrovegni Chapel holds scenes depicting the lives of Jesus and Mary. You must make reservations in advance to see the chapel. To protect the paintings from excess humidity, only 25 people are allowed in the chapel at a time. Every 20 minutes, a new group is admitted for a 15-minute video presentation in an anteroom, followed by 15 minutes in the chapel.

The chapel is within the Eremitani museum complex (at Piazza Eremitani 8), which also includes Padua's Civic Museums (collections of archaeological, medieval, and modern art). With a Scrovegni Chapel ticket you can also visit those museums.

Cost and Hours: €14, covers the Scrovegni Chapel and Civic Museums.

NEAR VENICE

Giotto di Bondone (c. 1267-1337)

Although details of his life are extremely sketchy, we know that the 12-year-old shepherd Giotto was discovered painting pictures of his father's sheep on rock slabs. He grew to become the wealthiest and most famous painter of his day. His achievement is especially remarkable because painters at that time weren't considered anything more than craftsmen—and weren't expected to be innovators.

After making a name for himself by painting frescoes of the life of St. Francis in Assisi, the Florentine tackled the Scrovegni Chapel (c. 1303-1305). At age 35, he was at the height of his powers. His scenes were more realistic and human than anything that had been done for a thousand years. Giotto didn't learn technique by dissecting corpses or studying the mathematics of 3-D perspective; he had innate talent. And his personality shines through in the humanity of his art.

The Scrovegni frescoes break ground by introducing nature—rocks, trees, animals—as a backdrop for religious scenes. Giotto's people, with their voluminous, deeply creased robes, are as sturdy and massive as Greek statues, throwbacks to the Byzantine icon art of the Middle Ages. But these figures exude stage presence. Their gestures are simple but expressive: A head tilted down says dejection, an arm flung out indicates grief, clasped hands indicate hope. Giotto created his figures not just by drawing outlines and filling them in with single colors; he filled the outlines in with subtle patchworks of lighter and darker shades, and in doing so pioneered modern modeling techniques. Giotto's storytelling style is straightforward, and anyone with knowledge of the episodes of Jesus' life can read the chapel like a comic book.

The Scrovegni represents a turning point in European art and culture—away from scenes of heaven and toward a more down-to-earth, human-centered view.

Reserve a timed-entry slot when you buy your ticket—see "Reservations," below. The **chapel** is open daily 9:00-19:00; the **museums** are open Tue-Sun 9:00-19:00, closed Mon. Special evening visits to the chapel are available in peak season (see below).

Information: +39 049 201 0020, www.cappelladegliscrovegni. it.

Reservations Required: To enter the chapel, you must make a reservation at least 24 hours in advance (same-day reservations are not possible). Demand is high, so reserve the day and time you want well in advance online (or by phone). Remember that you can get the Urbs Picta Card, which includes the Scrovegni plus other Padua sights and the tram. Buy the card from the chapel website and make your chapel reservation at the same time.

Unfortunate souls arriving in Padua without a Scrovegni reservation can sometimes buy a same-day ticket at the chapel ticket office, but don't count on it.

Evening Visit: Special 20-minute evening visits to the chapel are available for €8 (April-Oct daily 19:00-22:00). To book this online, choose "Giotto Under the Stars."

Helpful Hint: If you packed binoculars, bring them along for a better—and more comfortable—view of the uppermost frescoes.

Getting There: From either the town center or the train station, it's a 10-minute walk, or a quick tram ride to the Eremitani stop.

Getting In: The entrance to the chapel is through the Eremitani building, where you'll find the ticket office and the free and mandatory bag check. Though you're instructed to pick up your tickets at the ticket office one hour before your visit, in practice, 30 minutes is enough to weather any commotion at the desk. Present your confirmation number at the ticket desk, pick up your ticket, and check any bags or purses.

While waiting for your reserved time, read the chapel description below, since you'll only have a short time in the chapel itself.

From the ticket office, you'll be directed outside to a path to the chapel, passing some ruins of Roman Padua along the way. Be at the chapel doors at least five minutes before your scheduled visit. If you're even a minute late, you'll forfeit your time slot.

At your appointed time, you first enter an anteroom to watch an instructive 15-minute video (with English subtitles) and to establish humidity levels before continuing into the chapel. Although you have only a short visit inside the chapel, it's divine. You're inside a Giotto time capsule, looking back at an artist ahead of his time.

▲▲▲Scrovegni Chapel (Cappella degli Scrovegni)

Painted by Giotto and his assistants from 1303 to 1305, this work makes it clear: Europe was breaking out of the Middle Ages. A sign of the Renaissance to come, Giotto shifted the focus from heaven to earth, placing real people in real scenes, expressing real human emotions. These frescoes were radical for their 3-D nature, lively colors, light sources, emotion, and humanism.

The chapel was built out of guilt for white-collar crimes. Reginaldo degli Scrovegni charged sky-high interest rates at a time when the Church forbade the practice. He even caught the attention of Dante, who placed him in one of the levels of hell in his

Scrovegni Chapel

1 Joachim Driven from the Temple

2 Joachim Returns to the Sheepfold

3 Mary's Birth Announced to St. Anne

4 Birth of Jesus

5 Slaughter of the Innocents

6 Jesus Astounding the Scholars

7 Jesus Drives out the Money Changers

8 Last Supper

9 Betrayal of Christ

10 Jesus Beaten and Humiliated

11 Jesus Carrying the Cross

12 Lamentation (Deposition)

13 Last Judgment

Inferno. When Reginaldo died, the Church denied him a Christian burial. His son Enrico tried to buy forgiveness for his father's sins by building this superb chapel. After seeing Giotto's frescoes for the Franciscan monks of St. Anthony, Enrico knew he'd found the right artist to decorate the interior (and, he hoped, to save his father's soul). The Scrovegni residence once stood next to the chapel, but it was torn down in 1824.

Giotto's Frescoes: Giotto painted the entire chapel in 200 working days over two years, but you'll get only 15 minutes to see it.

As you enter the long, narrow chapel, look straight to the far end—the rear wall is covered with Giotto's big *Last Judgment.*

Christ in a bubble is flanked by crowds of saints and by scenes of heaven and hell. This is the final, climactic scene of the story told in the chapel's 38 panels—the three-generation history of Jesus, his mother Mary, and Mary's parents.

The story begins with Jesus' grandparents, on the long south wall (with the windows) in the upper-left corner. ❶ In the first frame, a priest scolds the man who will be Mary's father (Joachim, with the halo) and kicks him out of the temple for the sin of being childless. ❷ In the next panel to the right, Joachim returns dejectedly to his sheep farm. ❸ Meanwhile (next panel), his wife is in the bedroom, hearing the miraculous news that their prayers have been answered—she'll give birth to Mary, the mother of Jesus.

From this humble start, the story of Mary and Jesus spirals clockwise around the chapel, from top to bottom. The top row (both south and north walls) covers Mary's birth and life.

Jesus enters the picture in the middle row of the south (windowed) wall. ❹ The first frame shows his birth in a shedlike man-

ger. In the next frame, the Magi arrive and kneel to kiss his little toes. Then the child is presented in the tiny temple. Fearing danger, the family gets on a horse and flees to Egypt. ❺ Meanwhile, back home, all the baby boys are slaughtered in an attempt to prevent the coming of the Messiah (*Slaughter of the Innocents*).

Spinning clockwise to the opposite (north) wall, you see (in a badly damaged fresco) ❻ the child Jesus astounding scholars with his wisdom. Next, Jesus is baptized by John the Baptist. His first miracle, at a wedding, is turning jars of water into wine. Next, he raises a mummy-like Lazarus from the dead. Riding a donkey, he enters Jerusalem triumphantly. ❼ In the temple, he drives out the wicked money changers.

Turning again to the south wall (bottom row), we see scenes from Jesus' final days. ❽ In the first frame, he and his followers gather at a table for a Last Supper. Next, Jesus kneels humbly to wash their feet. ❾ He is betrayed with a kiss and arrested. Jesus is tried. ❿ Then he is beaten and humiliated.

⓫ Finally (north wall, bottom row), he is forced to carry his own cross, crucified, and prepared for burial, while his followers mourn (**⑫** *Lamentation*). Then he is resurrected and ascends to heaven, leaving his disciples to carry on.

⑬ The whole story concludes on the rear wall, where Jesus reigns at the Last Judgment. The long south wall (ground level) features the Virtues that lead to heaven, while the north wall has the (always more interesting) Vices. And all this unfolds beneath the blue, starry sky overhead on the ceiling.

Some panels deserve a closer look:

Joachim Returns to the Sheepfold (south wall, upper left, second panel): Though difficult to appreciate from ground level, this oft-reproduced scene is groundbreaking. Giotto—a former shepherd himself—uses nature as a stage, setting the scene in front of a backdrop of real-life mountains and adding down-home details like Joachim's jumping dog, frozen in midair.

Betrayal of Christ, a.k.a. *Il Bacio*, "The Kiss" (south wall, bottom row, center panel): Amid the crowded chaos of Jesus' arrest, Giotto skillfully creates a focus upon the central action, where Judas ensnares Jesus in his yellow robe (the color symbolizing envy), establishes meaningful eye contact, and kisses him.

Lamentation, a.k.a. *Deposition* (north wall, bottom row, middle): Jesus has been crucified, and his followers weep and wail over the lifeless body. John the Evangelist spreads his arms wide and shrieks, his cries echoed by anguished angels above. Each face is a study in grief. Giotto emphasizes these saints' human vulnerability.

Last Judgment (big west wall): Christ in the center is a glorious vision, but the real action is in hell (lower right). Satan is a Minotaur-headed ogre munching on sinners. Around him, demons give sinners their just desserts in a scene right out of Dante...who was Giotto's friend and fellow Florentine. Front and center is Enrico Scrovegni, in a violet robe (the color symbolizing penitence), donating the chapel to the Church in exchange for forgiveness of his father's sins.

Before the guard scoots you out, take a look at the actual altar. Though Enrico's father's tomb is lost, Enrico Scrovegni himself is in the tomb at the altar. The three statues are by Giovanni Pisano—Mary (in the center) supports Baby Jesus on her hip with a perfectly natural, maternal S-shape. She's flanked by anonymous deacons.

Nearby: Between the museum and the chapel are the scant remains of **Roman Padua**. The remnants are from the wall of an arena (with a reconstructed grand entry gate) and include nicely fitting pipes that once channeled water so that the arena could be flooded for special spectacles.

Civic Museums (Musei Civici agli Eremitani)

The former Augustinian monastery of the Eremitani friars now houses Padua's Civic Museums: archaeology on the ground floor and paintings upstairs in the Pinacoteca (all included with your Scrovegni Chapel ticket).

Archaeology Museum: Filling the ground floor around the monastery's courtyards is an impressive collection of ancient statues and artifacts—Egyptian, Venetian, and Roman. Sadly, there are no English descriptions.

Pinacoteca: The entire upper floor of the building is the home of the Pinacoteca (picture gallery). The collection has 13th- to 18th-century paintings by Titian, Tintoretto, Giorgione, Tiepolo, Veronese, Bellini, Canova, and other Veneto artists. But the highlight is the chance to study two masterpieces that affirm Giotto's greatness. The first is a remarkable **crucifix,** which originally hung in the Scrovegni Chapel between the Scrovegni family's private zone and the public's worshipping zone. If you kneel on the floor and look up, the body really pops. Nearby, and also by Giotto, is *L'Eterno Padre (The Eternal Father),* which originally occupied a high arch in the chapel. Both works, painted on wood, are fragile and kept here for conservation purposes. (If you can't locate these pieces, ask for *"La Croce di Giotto?"*—lah KROH-cheh dee JOH-toh.)

Rest of the Civic Museums: When it's open, the **multimedia room** in the basement (take the stairs down from the smaller cloister) contains several exhibits that give more meaning to the Scrovegni Chapel frescoes; there's also a 15-minute video in a small theater. Across the busy street is the **Palazzo Zuckermann,** with a commotion of applied and decorative arts (clothing, furniture, and ceramics) from the Venetian Republic (1600s and 1700s) and a collection of 19th-century coins and local Impressionist paintings.

THE BASILICA AND NEARBY
▲▲▲Basilica of St. Anthony (Basilica di Sant'Antonio)

Friar Anthony of Padua, "Christ's perfect follower and a tireless preacher of the Gospel," is buried here. Construction of this impressive Romanesque/Gothic church (with its Byzantine-style domes) started immediately after St. Anthony's death in 1231. As a mark of his universal appeal and importance in the medieval Church, he was sainted within a year of his death. Speedy. And for nearly 800 years, his remains and this glorious church have attracted pilgrims to Padua.

Cost and Hours: The **basilica** is free and open daily 6:15-19:00 (closes earlier off-season). The **Chapel of the Reliquaries** is

St. Anthony of Padua (1195-1231)

One of Christendom's most popular saints, Anthony is known as a powerful speaker, a miracle worker, and the finder of lost articles.

Born in Lisbon to a rich, well-connected family, Anthony disappointed his parents by choosing to dedicate his life to Christ. He left home at age 15, joined the learned Augustinian order, and was ordained as a priest. He lived contentedly with that order until a chance encounter with some Franciscans who stopped at his abbey while on their way to Morocco to preach the gospel. When news reached Anthony that his Franciscan friends had been martyred, he determined to follow their heroic path. He became a Franciscan and set off for Morocco, fully expecting to face martyrdom. He'd barely arrived when he became terribly ill and was forced to return to Portugal. On his journey home, a ferocious storm blew his ship off-course. He ended up in Italy, where he spent the rest of his life studying, meditating, and tending to the poor.

One day, he joined his fellow monks for an ordination service. The appointed speaker failed to show up, so Anthony was asked to say a few off-the-cuff words to the crowd. He started slowly, but, filled with the Spirit, he became more confident and amazed the audience with his eloquence. Up in Assisi, St. Francis heard about Anthony and sent him on a preaching tour through northern Italy and southern France. Anthony had a strong voice, knew several languages, had an encyclopedic knowledge of theology, and could speak spontaneously as the Spirit moved him. It's said that he even stood on the shores of the Adriatic Sea in Rimini and enticed a school of fish to listen. Anthony also was known as a prolific miracle worker.

Illness cut his life short at 36. Anthony said, "Happy is the man whose words issue from the Spirit and not from himself!"

also free and open daily 9:00-12:00 & 14:30-18:30. The nearest tram stop is Santo.

Information: +39 049 822 5652, www.santantonio.org. There's an information office just inside the cloister entrance, where you can rent a €3 audioguide to the basilica and buy tickets to the other basilica sights (see next).

Other Basilica Sights: A €7 combo-ticket gets you into a cluster of basilica museums—the Antonian Museum (basilica masterpieces), a Donatello exhibit, the Museum of Popular Devotion (votive offerings left by the faithful), the Oratory of San Giorgio, and the Scuola del Santo (the last two are on the piazza in front of the church). These sights are generally open Tue-Sun 9:00-13:00 & 14:00-18:00, closed Mon. Tickets are sold at the info desk at the cloisters and at the museum entries.

NEAR VENICE

Basilica of St. Anthony

- ❶ View of Basilica
- ❷ Nave
- ❸ St. Anthony's Tomb
- ❹ Chapel of Beato Luca
- ❺ Chapel of the Reliquaries
- ❻ Chapel of St. James
- ❼ Cloisters
- ❽ Oratory of San Giorgio & Scuola del Santo

Dress Code: A modest dress code is enforced.

Church Services: Mass is generally celebrated several times each morning (the last at 11:00), as well as at 17:00 and 18:00. Confirm the current schedule at the basilica's website.

Shops: There's a typical souvenir shop stocked with holy cards and religious statuaries and a more interesting *erboristeria* selling herbal remedies and a selection of botanical aperitivos.

⊘ Self-Guided Tour

❶ **View of Basilica:** Stand outside to view the basilica's red-brick facade. St. Anthony looks down and blesses all. He holds a book, a symbol of all the knowledge he had accumulated as a quiet monk before starting his preaching career.

A golden angel—the weathervane atop the spire—points her trumpet into the wind. Guarding the church is Donatello's life-size equestrian statue of the Venetian mercenary general, Gattamelata. Though it may look like any other man-on-a-horse statue, this life-size equestrian was the first such statue cast from bronze in a thousand years and became the model for subsequent equestrian statues of generals and kings for centuries to come.

The church is technically outside Italy. When you pass the banisters that mark its property line, you're passing into Vatican territory.

NEAR VENICE

• *Enter the basilica and grab a pew in the center of the nave. Let your eyes adjust.*

❷ **Nave:** Sit and appreciate the space. Gaze past the crowds and through the incense haze to Donatello's glorious crucifix rising from the altar, and realize that this is one of the most important pilgrimage sites in Christendom. Along with the crucifix, Donatello's bronze statues—Mary with Padua's six favorite saints—grace the high altar. Late in his career, the great Florentine sculptor spent more than a decade in Padua (1444-1455), creating the altar and Gattamelata.

• *Head to the left side of the nave to find the gleaming marble masterpiece that is the focus of the visiting pilgrims—the tomb of St. Anthony.*

❸ **St. Anthony's Tomb:** Pilgrims file slowly through this side chapel around the tomb, so focused on the saint that they hardly notice the nine fine mar-ble reliefs. (You can easily skirt around the side of this group for a closer look at each panel.) These Renaissance masterpieces were carved during the 16th century and show scenes and miracles from the life of the saint. As you enjoy each scene, notice the Renaissance mastery of realism and 3-D perspective and the intricate frames, which celebrate life with a burst of exuberance. Note also the vivid faces with their powerful emotions.

Stand in the corner for a moment, observing the passionate devotion that pilgrims and Paduans alike have for Anthony. Touching his tomb or kneeling in prayer, the faithful believe Anthony is their protector—a confidant and intercessor for the poor. And they believe he works miracles. Believers leave offerings, votives, and written prayers to ask for help or to give thanks for miracles they believe Anthony has performed. By putting their hands on his tomb while saying silent prayers, pilgrims show devotion to Anthony and feel the saint's presence.

Popular Anthony is the patron saint of dozens of things: orphans, pregnant women, infertile women, and glassblowers. Most pilgrims ask for his help in his role as the "finder of things"—from lost car keys to a life companion. You'll see dozens of photos posted on his tomb in prayer or as thanks, including many of fervently wished-for newborns.

Before leaving, pause to appreciate how the entire chapel is an integrated artistic wonder.

• *Leave the chapel and step into the oldest part of the church. This is the...*

❹ **Chapel of Beato Luca:** This chapel, decorated with beautiful frescoes by Giusto de' Menabuoi, is dedicated to Luca Belludi, a disciple of St. Anthony. The 13th-century altar preserves his remains. To the left of the altar, note the fine view of medieval Padua, with this church outside the wall (finished by 1300 and looking like it does today). Below the cityscape, in a circa-1380 fresco, Anthony on his cloud promises he'll watch over Padua.

• *Continue your circuit of the church by going behind the altar into the apse. You'll pass the Polish chapel with its ornate bronze gate and a painting of St. John Paul II (canonized in 2014). Next up is the often-crowded...*

❺ **Chapel of the Reliquaries:** The most prized relic is in the glass case at center stage—Anthony's tongue. When Anthony's remains were exhumed 32 years after his death (in 1263), his body had decayed to dust, but his tongue was found miraculously unspoiled and red in color. How appropriate for the great preacher who, full of the Spirit, couldn't stop talking about God.

Entering the chapel, join the parade of pilgrims working their way clockwise around the chapel and up the stairs. First, on the left, look for the red, triangular vestment in which Anthony's body was wrapped. Next is his rough-hewn wood coffin. Then, up the stairs, is his pillow—a comfy rock (chest level in first glass case). The center display case contains (top to bottom) the saint's lower jaw with all his teeth impressively intact (*il mento*, located about 8 feet high), his uncorrupted tongue (*lingua*, at about eye level), and, finally, his vocal chords (*apparato vocale*, at about waist level) discovered intact when his remains were examined in 1981. In the last display case, a fragment of the True Cross *(la croce)* is held in a precious cross-shaped reliquary. You'll also pass St. Anthony's holy, and holey, tunic *(tonaca)*. Pilgrims stop at a desk to pick up a small card with a tiny piece of blessed cloth that touched Anthony's tongue.

Above the relics, decorating the cornice, is the *Glorification of St. Anthony*. In this Baroque fantasy—made in 1691 of carved marble and stucco—a cloud of angels and giddy *putti* tumble to the left and right in jubilation as they play their Baroque-era musical instruments to celebrate Anthony's arrival in heaven.

• *Leaving this relic chapel, turn left to the **Chapel of Benediction.** Here, a priest is waiting to bless anyone who wishes to be blessed.*

Next, past the sacristy (where you can peek in at priests preparing for Mass), is a door leading to the cloisters. But before heading out, walk just beyond this passage to the...

❻ Chapel of St. James: Exactly opposite the tomb of St. Anthony, this chapel features an exquisite 14th-century fresco by Altichiero da Zevio. Study the vivid commotion around the Crucifixion, clearly inspired by Giotto (this was created 70 years after the Scrovegni Chapel). The faces are real—right off the streets of 14th-century Padua. From this chapel, look across the nave and appreciate how Anthony's massive tomb is so beautifully integrated into the church architecturally.

• *Next, exit out into the cloisters. From the right side of the nave as you face the altar, follow signs to* chiostro.

❼ Cloisters: Of the four cloisters at the basilica, you can wander in three. The main cloister is dominated by an exception-ally old **magnolia tree,** planted in 1810 (the magnolia was exotic for Europe when it was imported from America in 1760). Also in the cloister are the graves of the most illustrious Paduans, such as Gabriel Fallopius, the scientist who gave his name to his discovery, the Fallopian tube. When Napoleon decreed that graves should be moved out of cities, this once grave-covered courtyard was cleared of tombstones. But the bodies were left in the ground, perhaps contributing to the magnolia tree's fecundity. Today the tree remains an explosion of life.

In another cloister, you may be able to enter a **multimedia exhibit** about the life of St. Anthony and the Franciscan mission (free, a slow and evangelical 20 minutes).

In the next cloister over, you'll find the entrance to the Anto-nian Museum, a Donatello exhibit, and the Museum of Popular Devotion (all covered by combo-ticket). The latter is filled with vo-tives and folk art recounting miracles attributed to Anthony. The abbreviation *PGR* that you'll see on many votives stands for *per grazia ricevuta*—for answered prayers.

❽ Other Basilica Sights: The small but sumptuous **Oratory of San Giorgio** faces the little square in front of the basilica. Built as a mausoleum for the noble Lupi family, but now a consecrated church, the oratory is filled with vivid, circa-1370 frescoes showing scenes from the life of Christ and the patron saints of the Lupis: St. George, St. Lucia, and St. Catherine. Because many lovers credit St. Anthony with finding them their partners—and this is the closest place to St. Anthony where you can be married—it's popular for weddings.

Next door and upstairs is the skippable (and often closed) **Scuola del Santo** (a.k.a. La Scoletta), the former meeting hall of the Confraternity of Anthony. It has frescoes and paintings of the life of St. Anthony by various artists—including some by Titian.

Near the Basilica
Piazza Prato della Valle

This pleasant, 400-yard-long, oval piazza (150 yards southwest of the basilica, down Via Beato Luca Belludi) is actually an artificial island surrounded by a canal. Once the site of a Roman theater and later Anthony's preaching grounds, the grassy square is lively with fountains, walkways, and dozens of statues of Padua's eminent citizens. It's also an active **market** scene: fruit and vegetables (Mon-Fri morning); clothing, shoes, and household goods (Sat all day); and antiques (third Sun all day). This place is often busy with special events and festivals.

▲Botanic Garden (Orto Botanico)

Green thumbs, science fans, and anyone who wants a break from art or religious sights will appreciate this historic botanical garden, which contains the university's vast collection of rare plants. Founded in 1545 for the cultivation and study of medicinal plants, it's the world's oldest existing academic botanical garden. Because of the Venetian Republic's vast reach through trade and commerce, and the university's renown, exotic plants from all over the world made their way to Padua. It's believed that the first potato, sesame, lilac, and sunflower in Europe were planted in this city.

Cost and Hours: €10; Tue-Sun 10:00-19:00, closes earlier off-season, closed Mon, last entry one hour before closing; the garden's free app is best suited to plant and science buffs; entrance 150 yards south of Basilica of St. Anthony—with your back to the facade, take a hard left; Santo tram stop, +39 049 201 0222, www.ortobotanicopd.it.

Visiting the Garden: The botanical garden's original 16th-century square-within-a-circle configuration remains intact. Inside its circular wall, the garden is filled with elegant, geometrical plant beds. Wandering the paths, visitors can also admire a 340-year-old oriental plane tree, a magnolia that's only 10 years younger than the United States, and the garden's oldest specimen—a St. Peter's dwarf palm that was planted in 1585, and inspired Goethe to write his essay on the "Metamorphosis of Plants."

From the south end of the enclosed garden, find the path over a footbridge that leads to the striking and enormous **Biodiversity Garden.** The five greenhouse biomes take you on a journey through the world's major climate zones. Panels provide superb English descriptions of the environments and offer insight into how plant life has influenced the development of humankind—and vice versa.

Sleeping in Padua

Rooms in Padua's hotels are more spacious and a better value than those in Venice. I've listed hotels in the center and near the basilica. All are reachable from the station by tram; only Albergo Verdi is more than a five-minute walk from the nearest tram stop.

IN THE CENTER

$$ Hotel Majestic Toscanelli, an old-fashioned family-run hotel with 34 nicely furnished rooms, owns a perfect location right in the town center—buried in the characteristic ghetto with wonderful cobbled ambience. At night, this area is popular with noisy students; request a quiet room on the back side (RS%, some suites available, air-con, elevator, lounge bar, pay parking, Via dell'Arco 2, Tito Livio tram stop, +39 049 663 244, www.toscanelli.com, majestic@toscanelli.com, Mario Morosi and family). From the tram stop, follow the passageway next to #26, then jog left down Via Marsala and turn right on Via dell'Arco.

$ Albergo Verdi, an Ikea-esque little place, is crammed into an old building on a small back street beyond Piazza dei Signori. While public spaces are tight, the 14 rooms are simple and sufficient (air-con, tiny elevator, Via Dondi dall'Orologio 7, Ponti Romani tram stop, +39 049 836 4163, www.albergoverdipadova.it, info@albergoverdipadova.it). From Piazza dei Signori, walk through the arch under the clock tower and go to the far end of Piazza del Capitaniato; the hotel is on the side street to your right.

NEAR THE BASILICA OF ST. ANTHONY

Santo is the nearest tram stop for the following hotels.

$$ Hotel Al Fagiano feels like an art gallery with eclectic creative touches everywhere. They rent 37 bright and cheery rooms, each uniquely decorated with Rossella Fagiano's creations (RS%, air-con, elevator, pay parking, 50 yards from the Santo tram stop at Via Antonio Locatelli 45, +39 049 875 0073, www.alfagiano.com, info@alfagiano.com; Anita, Rossella, and Amato).

$ Hotel Al Santo, run with charm by Valentina and Antonio, offers 15 spacious rooms with essential comforts on two floors above their restaurant, a few steps from the basilica. Given the warm welcome and pleasant location, it's a fine value (family rooms, double-paned windows, quieter rooms off street, some rooms with basilica views, air-con, elevator, pay parking, Via del Santo 147, +39 049 875 2131, www.alsanto.it, alsanto@alsanto.it).

$ Hotel Casa del Pellegrino, with 147 spotless, cheap, bare rooms and straight pricing, is owned by the friars of St. Anthony. It's home to the pilgrims who come to pay homage to the saint in the basilica next door. Any visitor to Padua is welcome, making it popular with professors and students. Some rooms with basilica views also come with more noise—both from the street and, starting at 6:00 in the morning, the church bells; other rooms are in the hotel's modern wing (cheaper rooms with shared bath, family rooms, ask for a room off the street, breakfast extra, air-con, elevator, pay parking, Via Melchiorre Cesarotti 21, +39 049 823 9711, www.casadelpellegrino.com, info@casadelpellegrino.com).

Eating in Padua

The university population means cheap, good food abounds. My recommended restaurants are all centrally located in the historic core. You'd think there would be fine dining on the charming market squares, but they're dominated by takeout pizza, casual bars, and, after dark, students. La Lanterna, at the neighboring Piazza dei Signori, is the best on-square option—but they only offer functional Italian classics. The atmospheric ghetto neighborhood (just off the market squares) thrives after dark with a lively bar scene.

If you want a fun multistop meal of bar food capped with some fine gelato, string together my recommendations under "Cheap Eats and Bars with Tapas in the Center."

DINING NEAR THE CENTER

$$$ Taverna Nane della Giulia, warm and inviting, serves generous portions of well-made Venetian-style cuisine at fair prices (Wed-Sun 12:00-15:00 & 19:00-24:00, closed Mon-Tue, reservations recommended for dinner, Via Santa Sofia 1, +39 049 660 742).

$$ Osteria L'Anfora is a colorful if chaotic place serving classic dishes in an informal, fun-loving space. Don't be put off by the woody, ruffian decor, the squat toilet, and the fact that it's a popular hangout for a premeal drink. They take food seriously and serve it at good prices, and the fun energy and commotion add to the dining experience (meals served Mon-Sat 12:30-15:00 & 19:30-22:30, bar open 9:00-24:00, closed Sun, reservations smart for dinner, Via dei Soncin 13, +39 049 656 629).

$ Osteria dal Capo is a tight and jumbled little bistro with chandeliers and white tablecloths serving classic Veneto meat and fish dishes, home-cooking style (Mon-Sat 12:00-14:30 & 19:00-24:00, closed Sun, inside only, reserve for dinner, Via degli Obizzi 2, +39 049 663 105, www.osteriadalcapo.it).

$$ Enotavola Pino (*enotavola* means "wine table") is, in the front, a hip wine bar where owner/chef Pino offers scores of wines by the glass—each with a little plate of mortadella. The back is a bright fish-only restaurant with a busy, open kitchen and spacious seating. If you like the energy in the wine bar, you can order from the menu there, too (daily 12:30-14:30 & 19:30-23:00, Via dell'Arco 37, +39 049 876 2385).

$$$ Enoteca Antonio Ferrari is a top-end wine bar serving quality meat-and-cheese boards to a hungry local crowd. It's pricey but a good value and feels bright and youthful (daily, Via Umberto 1, +39 049 666 375).

CHEAP EATS AND BARS WITH TAPAS IN THE CENTER

$ Pizza on Piazza dei Signori: Though **La Lanterna** has a forgettable interior and a predictable menu of pizzas, pastas, and *secondi*, its prime location provides a rare-in-Padua chance to sit in a grand square under the stars, surrounded by great architecture. Locals know it as the first pizzeria in town (Fri-Wed 12:00-15:00 & 18:00-24:00, closed Thu, Piazza dei Signori 39, +39 049 660 770, www.lalanternapadova.it).

$ Squid, *Porchetta*, and *Spritz* on Piazza della Frutta: Just a simple sandwich place, **Bar dei Osei** has some of the best outdoor seats in town. While Paduans love their delicate *tramezzini*—white-bread sandwiches with crusts cut off, I'd choose their *porchetta*—savory roasted pork sandwiches. Wines are listed on the board (Mon-Sat 7:00-21:00, closed Sun, Piazza della Frutta 1, +39 049 875 9606). In the evenings, just a few feet away, **La Folperia squid stand** sells boiled and spiced plates of squid by weight—indicate small (€6) or big (€12) and request bread *(pane)*. Crowd your way up to the bar, and Massimiliano and Barbara will take care of you (Mon-Sat 17:00-20:30, closed Sun). Even with a plate of La Folperia seafood, you're welcome to grab a Bar dei Osei table and order a drink from the roaming server.

$ *Cicchetti* Bars Popular with Students: Surrounding Palazzo della Ragione you'll find lots of atmospheric bars jammed with students marked by the glowing orange glasses of *spritz*. These bars also serve little €1 and €2 bites (mostly fried gut bombs and enticing open-face sandwiches). While the tapas aren't advertised, the walls are scribbled with the various wines, vermouths, and cocktails for sale. Two classy holes-in-the-wall are particularly atmospheric (each about a block off the market squares): **Bar Corte Sconta** (across the street from the recommended Hotel Majestic Toscanelli, at Via dell'Arco 9) and **Bar All'Ombra della Piazza** (100 yards off Piazza della Frutta, down the tiny Via Pietro D'Abano at #16).

$ Pasta and Vegetarian on Piazza della Erbe: Pastasuta is a minimalist little pasta joint tucked away in the Palazzo della Ragione arcade (Piazza delle Erbe side). Choose your pasta and sauce combo or enjoy prepared options from their little *tavola fredda*. Seating is limited, but all of their dishes can be packed to go. Just say, *"Per portare via, per favore"* (Mon-Sat generally 9:00-15:00 & 17:00-20:00, closed Mon and Wed evenings and all day Sun). **Cristina e Massimo,** just a few doors down from Pastasuta, serves seasonal and creative vegetarian dishes, from fancy salads to muffins to tarts (Mon-Sat 7:00-20:00, closed Sun).

Gelato: For your best dessert in the market square area, enjoy a high-end gelato at **Gnam Gnam** (that means "yum yum") on Piazza dei Signori.

NEAR THE BASILICA OF ST. ANTHONY

$ Pizzeria Pago Pago dishes up wood-fired Neapolitan pizzas (a local favorite) and daily specials depending on what's in season. They also have good salads, non-pizza dishes, and beer on tap in a bright and high-energy dining area (Wed-Mon 12:00-14:00 & 19:00-24:00, closed Tue; 2 blocks from basilica, up Via del Santo and right onto Via Galileo Galilei to #59; +39 049 665 558, Gaetano and Modesto).

$ Pollodoro la Gastronomica, my pick of the takeout delis near the basilica, sells roast chicken, pastas, pizza, and veggies. They'll also make sandwiches (Wed-Mon 9:00-14:00, closed Tue, 100 yards from basilica at Via Belludi 34, +39 049 663 718).

Gelato: Portogallo Gelateria is considered the best gelateria in town, with amazing and creative flavors (Via Umberto 1).

Padua Connections

Unless otherwise specified, the following connections are for Trenitalia.

From Padua by Train to: Venice (4/hour, 30 minutes; Italo: about hourly, 30 minutes), **Vicenza** (at least 3/hour, fewer on weekends, 15-25 minutes), **Milan** (2-3/hour, 2-3 hours; Italo 7/day, 2 hours), **Verona** (3/hour, 40-90 minutes), **Florence** (10/day direct, 2 hours, require reservations; otherwise 3 or more hours with connections).

By Bus to: **Venice's Marco Polo Airport** (65 minutes, €8.50 from ticket windows, €10 on board, roughly hourly at :25 past the hour from 6:25 to 21:25, leaves from platform 11 at Padua's bus station, next to the train station; recheck times at www.fsbusitalia.it).

Vicenza

To many architects, Vicenza (vee-CHEHN-zah) is a pilgrimage site. Entire streets look like the back of a nickel. This is the city of Andrea Palladio (1508-1580), the 16th-century Renaissance architect who defined the Palladian style that is now so influential in countless British country homes. But as grandiose as Vicenza's Palladian facades may feel, there is little marble here because the city lacked the wealth to build with much more than painted wood and plaster.

If you're an architecture buff, Vicenza merits a quick day trip on any day but Monday, when major sights are closed. If you're packing light, it's an easy stop, located on the same train line as Padua, Verona, and Venice. However, there's no bag storage at the train station; though in a pinch, the TI is willing to store bags for you while you walk around town.

Tourist Information: The TI is next to the Olympic Theater at Piazza Matteotti 12 (daily 9:00-13:30 & 14:00-17:30, +39 0444 320 854, www.vicenzae.org). Ask for the free brochure on Palladio's buildings. Architecture fans appreciate the booklet titled *Vicenza and the Villas of Andrea Palladio.*

Arrival in Vicenza: From the **train station,** I'd head straight for the most distant sight, the Olympic Theater (with the TI next door) and then see other sights on the way back. Go straight out the train station's front door and use the crosswalk on the right side of the roundabout. From here, it's a five-minute walk straight ahead up wide Viale Roma to the Eurospar supermarket at the bottom of Corso Palladio; turn right through the gate, and then it's a good 10 minutes more down the Corso to the Olympic Theater.

A **taxi** from the station costs about €8. **Drivers** can park in one of the cheap parking lots (Parcheggio Bassano and Parcheggio Cricoli) and catch a free shuttle bus to the center.

Sights in Vicenza

Helpful bilingual signs in front of Palladio's buildings explain their history. Arrows around town point you to his major works.

Sightseeing Passes: All the sights mentioned (except the villas outside town) are covered by the **Vicenza Card** (€20, good for 8

Vicenza

(Map labels:) C. CANOVE; To A-4 & Padua; ARCHAEOLOGICAL & NATURAL HISTORY MUSEUM; OLYMPIC THEATER; PALAZZO LEONI MONTANARI; SANTA CORONA; River Bacchiglione; PEDEMURO SAN BIAGIO; GIACOMO ZANELLA; S. STEFANO; S. CORONA; Piazza Matteotti; SAN LORENZO; C. PORTI; SAN STEFANO; PINACOTECA; Piazza San Lorenzo; C. RIALE; PALLADIO; MORETTE; ORATORIO D. SERVI; S. FAUSTINO; GIURIOLO; VIA S. LORENZO; MOTTON SAN LORENZO; CORPENONS; FOGAZZARO; SAN MARCELLO; CORSO; BATTISTI; MONTE; CA VOUR; DO RODE; LOGGIA; Piazza Signori; COLUMNS; Piazza Biade; S. FRANCOLI; CONTRA D. SERVI; CABIANA; CONTRA DELLE BARCHE; Giardino Salvi; Piazzale del Castello; DUOMO; Piazza Érbe; BASILICA PALLADIANA; SAN PAOLO; River Retrone; To A-4 & Verona; Piazzale de Gasperi; Piazza Duomo; POST; PROTI; PASINI; To Villa Valmarana ai Noni & Villa Rotonda; SUPER-MKT.; VIA GORIZIA; VIALE ROMA; C. DELLA FASCINA; CARPAGNON; 200 Meters; 200 Yards; 200 yards to train station

days, sold at the TI and Palazzo Leoni Montanari Galleries). The **4 Museums Card** lets you choose any four sights (€15).

▲▲Olympic Theater (Teatro Olimpico)

Palladio's last work, one of his greatest, shouldn't be missed. This indoor theater is a wood-and-stucco festival of classical columns,

statues, and an oh-wow stage bursting with perspective tricks. When you step back outside, take another look at the town's main drag—named after Palladio. It's the same main street you saw on the stage of his theater.

Cost and Hours: €11; Tue-Sun 10:00-18:00 (9:00-17:00 in winter), closed Mon, very oc-
casionally closed when theater is in use; audioguide available, entrance to left of TI at Piazza Matteotti 11, info +39 0444 222 800, tickets +39 044 496 4380, www.teatrolimpicovicenza.it.

▲Church of Santa Corona (Chiesa di Santa Corona)

A block from the Olympic Theater, this "Church of the Holy Crown" was built in the 13th century to house a thorn from the Crown of Thorns, given to the bishop of Vicenza by the French king Louis IX. The church has two artistic highlights: Paolo Veronese's *Adoration of the Magi* (1573) and Giovanni Bellini's fine *Baptism of Christ* (c. 1502).

Cost and Hours: Free, Tue-Sun 10:00-18:00 (9:00-17:00 in winter), closed Mon, Contrà Santa Corona 2, +39 0444 323 644.

Archaeological and Natural History Museum (Museo Naturalistico Archeologico)

Located next door to the Church of Santa Corona, this museum's ground floor features Roman antiquities (mosaics, statues, and artifacts excavated from Rome's Baths of Caracalla, plus swords) and a barbarian warrior skeleton complete with sword and helmet. Prehistoric scraps are upstairs. Look for English description sheets near exhibit entryways throughout.

Cost and Hours: €5, Tue-Sun 9:00-17:00, closed Mon, Contrà Santa Corona 4, +39 0444 222 815, www.museicivicivicenza.it.

Palazzo Leoni Montanari Galleries (Gallerie di Palazzo Leoni Montanari)

Across the street from the Church of Santa Corona, this small museum is a palatial riot of Baroque, with cherub-cluttered ceilings jumbled like a preschool in heaven. A quick stroll shows off Venetian paintings and a floor of Russian icons.

Cost and Hours: €8.50, Tue-Sun 10:00-18:00, closed Mon, Contrà Santa Corona 25, +39 800 578 875, www.palazzomontanari.com.

Piazza dei Signori

Vicenza's main square has been the center of town ever since it was the site of the ancient Roman forum. The commanding **Basilica Palladiana,** with its 270-foot-tall, 13th-century tower, dominates the square. This was once the meeting place for local big shots. It was young Palladio's proposal to redo Vicenza's dilapidated Gothic palace of justice in the Neo-Greek style that established him as the city's favorite architect. The rest of Palladio's career was a one-man construction boom. The basilica hosts special exhibitions that sometimes involve a fee, but you can often pop in for a free look.

Villas on the Outskirts of Vicenza

Vicenza is surrounded by dreamy Venetian villas. When Venice's commercial trading empire receded in the 1500s, the city redirected its economic agenda to agribusiness, which led to the construction of lavish country villas, such as **Villa la Rotonda,** the inspi-

NEAR VENICE

ration for Thomas Jefferson's Monticello (www.villalarotonda.it), and **Villa Valmarana ai Nani** (www.villavalmarana.com). Located southeast of the town center, both houses are furnished with period pieces (closed Mon). Pick up the free brochure on Palladio's villas from the TI if you plan to visit.

Vicenza Connections

From Vicenza by Train to: Venice (Trenitalia: 2/hour, 45 minutes; Italo: 7/day, 45 minutes), **Padua** (at least 2/hour, 15-25 minutes), **Verona** (2/hour, 30-40 minutes), **Milan** (1-2/hour, 2 hours).

Verona

Romeo and Juliet made Verona a household word. Alas, a visit here has nothing to do with those two star-crossed lovers. You can pay

to visit the house that falsely claims to be Juliet's (with an almost believable balcony and a courtyard swarming with tour groups), join in the tradition of rubbing the breast of Juliet's statue to help find a lover (or to pick up the sweat of someone who can't), and even make a pilgrimage to what isn't "La Tomba di Giulietta."

Fiction aside, Verona has been an important crossroads for 2,000 years and is, therefore, packed with genuine history. R&J fans will take some solace in the fact that two real feuding families, the Montecchi and the Cappellos, were the models for Shakespeare's Montagues and Capulets. And, if R&J had existed and were alive today, they would still recognize much of their "hometown."

Verona's main attractions are its wealth of Roman ruins; the remnants of its 13th- and 14th-century political and cultural boom brought about by its leading family, the Scaligeri; its 21st-century, pedestrian-only ambience; and its world-class summer opera festival. After Venice's festival of tourism, the Veneto region's second city is a cool and welcome sip of pure Italy, where dumpsters are painted by schoolchildren as class projects and public spaces are primarily the domain of locals, not tourists. If you like Italy but don't need blockbuster sights, this town is a joy.

Orientation to Verona

Verona's old town fills an easy-to-defend bend in the River Adige. The vibrant and enjoyable core of Verona lies along Via Mazzini between Piazza Brà (pronounced "bra") and Piazza Erbe, Verona's market square since Roman times. Each evening the two main streets from Piazza Brà to Piazza Erbe, Via Mazzini and Corso Porta Borsari, are enlivened by a wonderful *passeggiata*...bustling with a slow and elegant parade of strollers. For a good day trip to Verona, take my self-guided walk, beginning with a visit to the Roman Arena.

NEAR VENICE

TOURIST INFORMATION

Verona's helpful TI is located inside Verona's City Hall (Palazzo Barbieri). The entrance is just off **Piazza Brà,** around the corner at Via Leoncino 61 (Mon-Sat 9:00-19:00, Sun 10:00-18:00, shorter hours off-season, +39 045 806 8680, www.turismoverona.eu). If you're staying the night, ask the TI about concerts.

Sightseeing Passes: The **Verona Card** covers city transportation and entry to all recommended Verona sights. The card can save day-trippers quite a bit if you're intent on blitzing the city's sights (€20/24 hours, €25/48 hours, sold at TI and at participating sights).

The €8 **Church Card,** sold at four churches that require admission (San Zeno, Duomo, Sant'Anastasia, and San Fermo, normally €4 each), pays for itself if you visit two (www.chieseverona.it).

Walking Tours: The TI organizes 90-minute tours in English (€12/person, April-Dec Sat-Sun at 11:00). Tours meet inside the TI and stroll all the way through the old town (confirm schedule, no reservation necessary).

ARRIVAL IN VERONA

By Train: Verona's main train station is called Verona Porta Nuova. In the main hall, you'll find pay WCs and a baggage-check office (daily 8:00-20:00). Buses and taxis are immediately outside.

Avoid the boring 20-minute walk from the station to the center. **Buses** are cheap, easy, and leave every few minutes (although taxis are smart after sundown). Buy a ticket from the tobacco shop inside the station or from machines at the bus bays (€1.30/90 minutes, €2 from on-board machine, €4 day pass valid until midnight, www.atv.verona.it). Leaving the station, angle right across the street to the bus stalls; helpful signs indicate which bus to take for your destination.

Buses for **Piazza Brà** (near the Roman Arena) and **San Fermo** (near the Ponte Navi bridge) depart from platform B1 (#11, #12, #13, #51, and #52 run Mon-Sat until 20:00; #90, #92, and #98 run

NEAR VENICE

Verona

<u>Accommodations</u>
1. Hotel Aurora
2. Albergo Mazzanti
3. Casa Coloniale
4. Protezione della Giovane
5. Hotel Milano
6. Hotel Giulietta e Romeo
7. Hotel Colomba d'Oro
8. To Pepita Lodge
9. Aparthotel Verona House

<u>Eateries & Other</u>
10. Darì Ristorante & Enoteca
11. Trattoria al Pompiere
12. Caffè Dante
13. Bottega del Vino
14. Ristorante Torcolo
15. Osteria Caffè Monte Baldo
16. La Piazzetta
17. Ristorante Sant'Eufemia
18. Osteria Sottoriva
19. Osteria del Bugiardo
20. Osteria la Mandorla
21. Pizzeria da Salvatore
22. Pizzeria Du de Cope
23. Döner Kebab Shop
24. Supermarket (2)
25. Salumeria Caliari & Salumeria Albertini
26. Gelateria Savoia
27. Gelateria Ponte Pietra
28. Launderette

200 Meters
200 Yards

NEAR VENICE

after 20:00 and all day Sun). For **Porta Borsari** (ancient city main gate), use platform D2 (#21, #22, #23, #24, #41, and #61 run Mon-Sat; #93, #94, and #95 run evenings and Sundays). If in doubt, confirm that your bus is headed to the city center by asking, *"Per il centro?"* (pehr eel CHEN-troh). Validate your ticket by stamping it in the machine on the bus.

If getting off at Piazza Brà, you'll see the can't-miss-it Roman Arena (bus stops in front of the big, yellow Neoclassical City Hall, where you'll find the TI—see earlier). You can catch return buses to the station from another bus stop on Piazza Brà, near the WCs.

Taxis pick up only at taxi stands (at Piazza Brà, Piazza Erbe, and the train station) and cost €10-12 for the quick ride between the train station and the center of town (€2 more on Sundays and after 22:00, €1/big bag).

By Car: The old town center (where nearly all my recommended hotels are located) is closed to traffic. Your hotel can get you permission to drive in—ask when you book. Otherwise your license plate will be photographed, and an expensive ticket might be waiting in the mail when you get home.

Drivers will find reasonably priced parking in well-marked lots and garages just outside the center. The underground **Cittadella garage,** at Piazza Cittadella (a block off Piazza Brà), is huge, convenient, and easy to find (€3/hour, €18/24 hours). The **Città di Nimes/Parking Stazione** lot is near the wall, a five-minute walk from the train station (€1.50/2 hours, €7/day). **Street parking** is limited to two hours and costs €1/hour (spaces marked with blue lines, buy ticket at a tobacco shop or ticket machine, place ticket on dashboard; some hotels can give you a free street-parking permit—ask).

By Plane: Verona's airport (known as Catullo or Verona-Villafranca) is 12 miles southwest of the city (code: VRN, +39 045 809 5666, www.aeroportoverona.it). Efficient **AeroBus** shuttles connect the airport with the train station (€6, valid for 75 minutes on AeroBus and city buses, buy tickets on board or at tobacco shop, 3/hour, 15 minutes).

HELPFUL HINTS

Sightseeing Schedules: Most sights (except churches) are closed on Monday mornings and typically open after lunchtime. The churches are closed Sun morning to sightseers.

Arena Opera Festival: From mid-June through early September, Verona's opera festival brings the city to life, with 15,000 music fans filling the Roman Arena for almost nightly performances (cheap upper-level seats—€30-40, day-of-show tickets often available). The city is packed and festive—restaurants have set seatings for dinner, and hotels jack up their prices.

Book tickets through the official box office (online at www. arena.it or call +39 +39 045 800 5151; during opera season, box office open daily 10:00-17:45, or until 21:00 on performance days; Via Dietro Anfiteatro 6B).

Laundry: The closest self-service **laundry** is a 20-minute walk from the Arena, over the Ponte Nevi bridge (daily 7:30-22:30, Via XX Settembre 92).

Private Guides: Three enthusiastic Verona guides give private tours of the town and region tailored to specific interests—villas, wine tasting, and so on. They are **Marina Menegoi** (€125/2 hours, €265/5 hours, mobile +39 328 958 1108, www. marinamenegoi.com, mmenegoi@gmail.com), **Valeria Biasi** (€150/2 hours, €375/5 hours, mobile +39 348 903 4238, www. veronatours.com, valeria@veronatours.com), and **Franklin Baumgarten** (€125/2 hours, €265/5 hours, mobile +39 347 566 6765, franklin_baumgarten@web.de).

Verona Walk

This walk covers the essential sights in the town core, starting at Piazza Brà and ending at the cathedral. Allow two hours (including the tower climb and some dawdling).

❶ Piazza Brà

If you're wondering about the name, it comes from the local dialect and means "big open space." A generation ago this piazza was noisy with cars. Now it's open and people friendly—it's become the community family room and natural festival grounds.

Grab a bench near the central **fountain** called "The Alps." This was a gift from Verona's sister city Munich, which is just over the mountains to the north. You'll see in the middle of the fountain the symbols of the two cities separated by the Alps, carved out of pink marble from this region. In general, Verona has a bit of an alpine feel; historically it was the place where people rested and prepared before crossing the mountains, and to this day it's the place where the main west-east, Milan-Venice train line meets the north-south line up to Bolzano, the Dolomites, and Austria.

The ancient **arena** looming over the piazza is a reminder that the city's history goes back to Roman times. On this walk, we'll meander across what was the ancient city, from the arena on this side to the theater across the river.

With the fall of Rome in the fifth century, Verona became a favored capital of barbarian kings. In the Middle Ages, noble families had to choose sides in the civil struggles between emperors (Ghibellines) and popes (Guelphs). During this time (1200s), the town bristled with several hundred San Gimignano-type towers, built by different families to symbolize their power. When the Scaligeri family rose to power here in the 14th century, they established stability on their terms and made the other noble families lop off their proud towers—only the Scaligeri were allowed to keep theirs. To add insult to injury, the Scaligeri paved the city's roads with bricks from the other families' toppled towers. But interfamily feuds made it impossible for the Scaligeri to maintain a stable government, and in 1405 the town essentially gave itself to Venice, which ruled Verona until Napoleon stopped by in 1796. During the 19th century, a tug-of-war between France and Austria actually divided the city for a time, with the river marking the border of each country's domain. Eventually Verona, like Venice, fell into Austrian hands.

Reminders of Austrian rule remain: The huge, yellow Neoclassical **City Hall** facing Piazza Brà (look for the flags) was built by the Austrians to serve as their 19th-century military headquarters (the TI is in this building; enter around the corner on Via Leoncino). Their former arsenal stands just across the river, and an Austrian fortress caps the hill looking over the city. But the big **equestrian statue** is of Italy's first king, Victor Emmanuel II, celebrating Italian independence and unity, which was won in the 1860s. The **statue of a modern soldier** striking a *David* pose, with a machine gun instead of a sling over his shoulder, honors Verona's war dead.

Apart from all its history, Piazza Brà is about strolling—the evening *passeggiata* is a kind of national sport in Italy. The broad, shiny sidewalk (named "Liston" after a Venetian promenade; note the fine, Venetian-style marble pavement slabs) was built by 17th-century Venetians, who made it big and wide so that promenading socialites could see and be seen in all their finery.

❷ Roman Arena

The Romans built this stadium outside their town walls, just as

NEAR VENICE

Verona Walk

1. Piazza Brà
2. Roman Arena
3. Devotional Column
4. Porta Borsari & Corso Porta Borsari
5. Enoteca Oreste dal Zovo
6. Piazza Erbe
7. House of Juliet
8. Piazza dei Signori
9. Tombs of the Scaligeri Family
10. Groceries (2)
11. Basilica of Sant'Anastasia
12. Ponte Pietra & River View
13. Duomo Complex

modern stadiums are usually located outside downtown districts. With 72 aisles, this elliptical, 466-by-400-foot amphitheater is the third largest in Italy (and it was originally 50 percent taller). Most of the stone you see is original. Dating from the first century AD, it looks great in its pink marble. Over the centuries, crowds of up to 25,000 spectators have cheered Roman gladiator battles, medieval executions, rock concerts, and modern plays, all taking advantage of the arena's famous acoustics. This is also where the popular opera festival is held every summer. Started in 1913, the festival has run continuously ever since, except for brief breaks during both World Wars, when the arena was used as a bomb shelter. While there's little to see inside except the impressive stonework, it's memorable to visit a Roman arena that is still a thriving concert venue. If you climb to the top, you'll enjoy great city views.

The gladiators posing with tourists out front are mostly from Albania and part of a local gang; they're notorious for overcharging for photos. While they're a nuisance, the police say it's better that they're scamming a living here than finding even more disreputable ways to get by.

Cost and Hours: €10, don't bother with the combo-ticket that includes the unimpressive Maffei Museum; Tue-Sun 8:30-19:30, Mon from 13:30, closes earlier—likely around 16:00—during summer opera season, last entry one hour before closing; WC near entry, +39 045 800 3204.

• *As you exit the arena, look to your right. Where the street splits you'll see the...*

❸ Devotional Column

In the Middle Ages, this column blessed a marketplace held here. Ten yards in front of it, a bronze plaque in the sidewalk shows the Roman city plan—a town of 20,000 placed strategically in the bend of the river, which provided protection on three sides. A wall enclosed the peninsula. The center of the grid was the forum, today's Piazza Erbe. (Look down Via Mazzini, the busy main pedestrian drag—the bell tower in the distance marks Piazza Erbe.)

• *After viewing the bronze plaque, turn with your back to the arena and head down Via Oberdan (bearing left at the fork). Continue a couple of blocks (passing a derelict fascist-era theater, the Astra, set back from the street on the left, at #13) until you see an ancient gate to your right.*

❹ Porta Borsari and Corso Porta Borsari

You're standing before the main entrance to Roman Verona; back then, this gate functioned as a tollbooth (*borsari* means purse, refer-ring to the collection of tolls that once took place here). Carved into the rock below the spiral, fluted columns (which parents nickname *"tortiglioni"*—a pasta kids can relate to), is a tribute to the emperor who restored this gate. Out-side the adjacent Caffè Rialto, the stone pillar on the curb is from a tomb: In Roman times, the roads outside the walls were lined with tombstones, be-cause burials were not allowed within the town itself. Turn around, look down Corso Cavour, and imagine it in Roman times, leading away from the city gate and lined with tombs. Step into the café. A glass panel in the floor shows the original Roman foundations and pavement stones.

Back outside, cross under the Roman gate and head into the ancient city. Walk down Corso Porta Borsari, the Roman main drag, toward what was the forum. Make it a scavenger hunt. As you walk, discover bits of the town's illustrious past—chips of Roman columns, medieval reliefs, fine old facades, fossils in marble—as well as its elegant present of fancy shops, in a setting that prioritiz-es pedestrians over cars. On the right, you'll pass the recommended Osteria del Bugiardo, a popular wine bar and a good place to take a break and hang out with Verona's young and trendy.

• *Between Corso Porta Borsari 13 and 15, detour right down Vicolo San Marco in Foro, following the* Pozzo dell'Amore *sign. Twenty yards ahead on your right, you'll find...*

❺ Enoteca Oreste dal Zovo

This funky wine and grappa bar has been run by Oreste like an old-style *enoteca* for decades. Browse and sample and clown around with Oreste. This historic *enoteca* was once the private chapel of the archbishop of Verona. Traces of the past hide between the bot-tles—ask Beverly (Oreste's Chicagoan wife) to tell you the story (wines by the glass with light snacks, Vicolo San Marco in Foro 7, +39 045 803 4369).

• *Return to Corso Porta Borsari and continue one block until you hit a big square.*

❻ Piazza Erbe

This bustling market square is a photographer's delight. Its pastel buildings corral the fountains, pigeons, and people who have congregated here since Roman times, when this was a forum. Notice the Venetian lion hovering above the square atop a column, reminding locals of the conquest of 1405. Wander into the market, to the fountain in the middle. A fountain has bubbled here for 2,000 years. The original Roman statue lost its head and arms. After a sculptor added a new head and arms, the statue became Verona's Madonna. She holds a small banner that reads, roughly, *"The city of Verona deserves respect and justice."* During medieval times, the stone canopy in the center of the square (past the fountain) held the scales where merchants measured the weight of goods they bought and sold, such as silk and wool.

If you were standing here in the Middle Ages, you would have been surrounded by proud noble-family towers. Medieval nobles showed off with towers. Renaissance nobles showed off with finely painted facades on their palaces. Find remnants of the 16th-century days when Verona was nicknamed "the painted city."

Locals like to start their evening with an *aperitivo* here. Each bar caters to a different market segment. Survey the scene and, if or when the time is right, choose the terrace that suits you and join in the ritual. It's simple: Grab a spot, adjust your seat for the best view, and order a *spritz* to drink (€4 with a plate of olives and chips).

• *At the far end of Piazza Erbe is a market column featuring St. Zeno, the patron of Verona, who looks at the crazy crowds flushing into the city's silly claim to touristic fame: the House of Juliet (100 yards down Via Cappello to #23, on the left—just follow the crowds). Side-trip there now (but watch your wallet—it's a pickpocket's haven).*

❼ House of Juliet

The tiny, admittedly romantic courtyard is a spectacle: Tourists from all over the world pose on the balcony, while those hoping for love wait their turn to polish Juliet's bronze breast. Residents marvel that each year, about 1,600 Japanese tour groups break their Venice-Milan ride for an hour-long stop in Verona just to see this courtyard (courtyard free, gates open roughly 8:30-19:30 or longer; €6 to enter nine-room "museum," open Tue-Sun 9:00-

19:00, closed Mon). It's fun to stand in the corner and observe the scene, knowing that all this commotion was started by a clever tour guide in the early 1970s as a way to attract visitors to Verona.

The courtyard walls are regularly filled with amorous graffiti that gets painted over just as regularly. The wall of padlocks is a gimmick enabling lovers to blow money in an attempt to prove that their hearts are thoroughly locked up. (The shop that sells the locks also sells pens to write on them.) The red mailbox is for love letters to Juliet. There's actually a Juliet Club that reviews these—and all the letters mailed from around the world to "Juliet, Verona, Italy." Each year, the club awards the author of the sweetest letter a free vacation to Verona.

Even those who milk their living out of this sight freely admit that no documentation has been discovered to prove the truth of the legend—but no documentation has disproved it either. The "museum," which displays art inspired by the love story, plus costumes and the bed from Franco Zeffirelli's film *Romeo and Juliet*, is certainly not worth the entry fee.

Was there ever a real Juliet Capulet? You just walked down Via Cappello, the street of the cap makers. Above the courtyard entry (looking out) is a coat of arms featuring a hat—representing a family that made hats and which would be named, logically, Capulet.

The public's interest in a fictional Romeo and Juliet—or at least Juliet—is a sign that there's a hunger for a Juliet in our world. Observing the mobs clamoring to polish her breast or blow kisses from her bogus balcony, I try to appreciate what she means to people, and to psychoanalyze what she provides to those who come to Verona specifically for this: the message that love will prevail. In love, you can lose, and still be a winner. Juliet is brave, tragic, honest, outspoken, timeless, and passionate. She's a mover and a shaker, a dreamer and a fighter. In a way, this is a pagan temple where the spirit of Juliet gives people something to believe in...or maybe it's just a bunch of baloney appreciated by a simple-minded crowd.

• *Return to Piazza Erbe. From the middle of the piazza, head right on Via della Costa and into the big square.*

❽ Piazza dei Signori

Literally the "Lords' Square," this is Verona's sitting room, quieter and more harmonious than Piazza Erbe. The buildings—which span five centuries—define the square and are all linked by arches. From one arch dangles a whale's rib. It was likely a souvenir brought home by a traveling merchant from a trip to the Orient, reminding the townspeople that there was a big world out there. The long portico on the left is inspired by a building in Florence: Brunelleschi's Hospital of the Innocents, considered the first Renaissance building.

Locals call the square Piazza Dante for the statue of the Italian poet **Dante Alighieri** that dominates it. Dante—always pensive, never smiling—seems to wonder why the tourists choose Juliet over him. Dante was expelled from Florence when that city sided with the pope (who didn't appreciate Dante's writing) and banished its greatest poet. Verona and its ruling Scaligeri family, however, were at odds with the pope (siding instead with the Holy Roman Emperor), and granted Dante asylum.

With the whale's rib behind you, you're facing the brick, crenellated, 14th-century Scaligeri residence. Behind Dante is the yellowish, 15th-century Venetian Renaissance-style Portico of the Counsel. At Dante's two o'clock is the 12th-century Romanesque Palazzo della Ragione.

Looking back the way you came, follow the white *toilette* signs into the courtyard of the **Palazzo della Ragione.** The impressive stairway is the only surviving Renaissance staircase in Verona. Within the palazzo you can visit the Gallery of Modern Art (skippable) and climb the 12th-century **Torre dei Lamberti** for a grand city view. The elevator saves you 243 steps—but you'll still need to walk up 46 more to get to the tower's first viewing platform (€6 ticket covers tower and Gallery of Modern Art, no individual tower tickets sold; Mon-Fri 10:00-18:00, Sat-Sun 11:00-19:00; ticket office next to staircase, +39 045 927 3027, www.torredeilamberti.it).

• *Exit the courtyard the way you entered and turn right, continuing downhill. Within a block, you'll find the...*

❾ Tombs of the Scaligeri Family

These exotic and veritable 14th-century Gothic tombs, with their fine, original, wrought-iron protective fencing, evoke the age when one family ruled Verona. The Scaligeri were to Verona what the Medici were to Florence. These were powerful people. They changed the law so that they could be buried within the town. They forbade the building of any noble family's new towers but their own. And, by building tombs atop pillars, they arranged to be looked up to, even in death.

• *Continue 15 yards to the next corner and take the first left on Vicolo Cavalletto. At the first corner, turn right along Corso Sant'Anastasia toward the big, unfinished brick facade of Verona's largest church. For a fragrant and potentially tasty diversion, pop into* ❿ *two classic grocery stores: Salumeria Caliari (at #33) and Salumeria Albertini (#41).*

⓫ Basilica of Sant'Anastasia (Basilica di Sant'Anastasia)

This church, the biggest in Verona, was built from the late 13th century through the 15th century. Although the facade was never finished (the builders ran out of steam), the interior was—and still is—brilliant. Step inside to see the delightful way this region's medieval churches were paint-ed. Note the grimacing hunchbacks holding basins of holy water on their backs (near main entrance at base of columns). And don't miss Pisanello's fresco of *St. George and the Princess of Trebizond* (1438; at the tip of the arch, high above chapel to right of altar). Once colorful, it has oxidized over time to its current monochrome state. For a closer look at its wonder-ful detail, check out the images on the monitor below the fresco. Ask for the English brochure, which describes the story of the church.

Cost and Hours: €4; Mon-Fri 10:00-18:00, Sat from 9:30, Sun 13:00-18:00, shorter hours in winter; www.chieseverona.it.

• *As you leave, from the steps make two quick lefts to walk along the right side of the church to Via Sottoriva. To the right, the Sottoriva ar-cade was once busy with colorful wine bars and* osterie, *some of which still exist (see "Eating in Verona," later). But for now, head to the left on Via Sottoriva. In a block, you'll reach a small riverfront area with stone benches that usually have a few modern-day Romeos and Juliets gazing at each other rather than at the view. Belly up to the river view.*

⓬ Ponte Pietra and River View

The white stones of the Ponte Pietra footbridge are from the origi-nal Roman bridge that stood here. After the bridge was bombed in World War II, the Veronese fished the marble chunks out of the river to rebuild it. From here, you can see across the river to the Roman Theater, built into the hillside behind the green hedge (see "Sights in Verona," later). Way above the theater (behind the cypress trees) is the fortress, Castello San Pietro. The nearby funicular can take you there.

The wide spot in the river here was called the "Millers' Widening," where boats stopped and unloaded grain to be milled. Water wheels once lined the river and powered medieval Verona, employing technology imported from the Holy Land by 10th-century Crusaders.

Continue up the river toward the bridge. Walk to its high point and enjoy the view.

• *From the bridge, look back 200 yards at the tall white spire...that's where you're heading. Walk back off the bridge, then turn right, keeping an eye on the left for the steeple of the...*

⓯ Duomo Complex (Complessa del Duomo)

Verona's duomo is more than a single building; it's a complex with the church, a baptistery, and the archaeological remains of much older churches. Early Christian basilicas have stood on this site at least as long ago as the fourth century. After a damaging earthquake in 1117, church fathers enlarged and patched things up, creating the duomo you see today.

Cost and Hours: €4, Mon-Fri 11:00-17:00, Sat until 15:30, Sun 13:30-17:30, shorter hours off-season, www.chieseverona.it.

Visiting the Church: Before entering, note the fine Romanesque double porch at the entry and the figural carvings on its facade.

Now step inside, ask for the leaflet that explains the church's highlights, and head to the last chapel on the left, with Titian's *Assumption of the Virgin* (c. 1530). Mary calmly rides a cloud—direction up—to the shock and bewilderment of the crowd below. Notice a handful of tombs embedded in the walls about 15 feet above floor level—an unusual feature. (Generally, tombs are found in the floor of the church or in crypts below.)

Now head up the aisle to the last door on the left (left of high altar), where you'll find the **ruins** of an older church. These are the 10th-century foundations of the Church of St. Elena, turned intriguingly into a modern-day chapel featuring exposed fourth-century mosaic floors from the Roman church that originally stood here.

From there, pass through the little open-air courtyard into the adjacent **baptistery,** with its clean Romanesque lines, hanging 14th-century crucifix, and fine octagonal font, carved from a single block of marble. Circle around it to identify the eight biblical scenes on its panels (go counterclockwise, starting with the panel just to the right of center): Annunciation; Visitation of Mary to Elizbeth and the Nativity, with animals licking Baby Jesus and giving him a barnyard welcome; announcement to shepherds of Jesus' birth, with their flock stacked on one side; the Three Kings giving their gifts to Baby Jesus; Herod commanding that all male infants be killed; Slaughter of the Innocents; flight into Egypt; and finally, facing the entry door, John the Baptist baptizing Christ.

Finally, after leaving the church, circle around its left side (as you face the main facade) to find the peaceful Romanesque **cloister** *(chiostro)*, with mosaics from a fifth-century Christian church exposed below the walk.

Sights in Verona

Several of Verona's main sights, including the Roman Arena, Church of Sant'Anastasia, and Duomo, are covered in my Verona Walk.

▲▲Evening *Passeggiata*

For me, the highlight of Verona is the *passeggiata* (stroll)—especially in the evening. Make a big circle from Piazza Brà through the old town on Via Mazzini (one of Europe's many "first" pedestrian-only streets) to the colorful Piazza Erbe, and then back down Corso Porta Borsari to Piazza Brà. This is a small town, where people know each other, and they're all out on parade. Like peacocks, the young and nubile spread their wings. The classy shop windows are integral to the *passeggiata* as, for many of the ladies, shopping is a sport. Their never-finished wardrobes are considered a work in progress, and this is when they gather ideas. If you're going to complement your stroll with a stop in a café or bar, the best plan is to enjoy a *spritz* drink—not on Piazza Brà, but on Piazza Erbe (the oldest and most elegant bars are on the end farthest from Juliet's balcony).

▲Castelvecchio Museum (Museo di Castelvecchio)

Verona's powerful Scaligeri family built this castle (c. 1356) as both a residence and a fortress. The huge, crenellated castle, located west of Piazza Brà and the Roman Arena, has two parts: the family palace and the quarters for their private army (separated, for the nervous family's security, by a fortified wall and an internal moat).

Today, it houses the city's enjoyable art museum, with an interesting but not overwhelming collection of sculpture and paintings from medieval times through the 18th century. An added bonus is access to the castle ramparts, with good city views.

Cost and Hours: €6, Tue-Sun 10:00-18:00, closed Mon, Corso Castelvecchio 2, +39 045 806 2611, www.museodicastelvecchio. comune.verona.it. Info sheets are available throughout, but the €4 audioguide is still worthwhile.

Visiting the Castle: From the ticket desk, you'll enter the ground-floor galleries, reserved for Romanesque and medieval sculptures from the Verona area. Religious statues were Verona's medieval forte, and some of the surprisingly expressive examples here, such as the Crucifixion ensemble in Room 4, still show signs of once-bright paint.

From the sculpture galleries, you'll cross to the next wing and head upstairs to walk through two floors of **paintings** from the 13th through 18th century. Paolo Veronese, the city's greatest artist, is represented, as are Mantegna, Titian, Tiepolo, Tintoretto, and others. Here in the residential part of the castle, several rooms show traces of decorative frescoes and walls painted with colorful geometric designs.

Before you exit, you'll also pass by a small armory collection. En route, watch for stairs that let you roam the **ramparts** with fine views of the city, river, and Ponte Scaligero. Kids (and kids at heart) enjoy scrambling across the delightfully crenellated parapets. Verona was an independent city-state from 1176 to 1387. Then came a long period of subjugation under other powers which, in more modern times, included the Austrians. From the ramparts you can see remnants of Austrian rule: the arsenal across the river and the castle atop the distant hill.

Nearby: Next to Castelvecchio, the picturesque red-brick bridge called **Ponte Scaligero**—fortified and crenellated, as if a continuation of the castle—is free, open to the public, and fun to stroll across. Destroyed by the Germans in World War II, it was rebuilt in the 1950s using many of its original bricks, which were dredged out of the river. Today it's a favorite for wedding-day photos.

OUTSIDE THE CITY CENTER
▲Basilica of San Zeno (Basilica di San Zeno)
This church, a 15-minute walk upriver beyond Castelvecchio, is dedicated to the patron saint of Verona, whose remains are bur-

ied in the crypt under the main altar. In addition to being a fine example of Italian Romanesque, the basilica features Mantegna's *San Zeno Triptych* (c. 1459) with its marvelous perspective, peaceful double-columned cloisters, and a set of 11th-century doors covered with 48 bronze panels. Nicknamed "the poor man's Bible," the panels illustrate episodes from St. Zeno's life and Old and New Testament stories—a sort of graphic novel for a medieval "reader." Facing the altar, on the walls of the right-side aisle, you can see frescoes painted on top of other frescoes and graffiti dating from the 1300s. These were done by people who fled into the church in times of war or flooding and scratched prayers into the walls. Druidic-looking runes are actually decorated letters typical of the Gothic period, like those in illuminated manuscripts.

Cost and Hours: €4; Mon-Sat 9:30-18:00, Sun from 13:00, shorter hours off-season; on Piazza San Zeno, www.chieseverona. it.

Roman Theater (Teatro Romano)

Dating from about the time of Christ, this ancient theater—located across the Roman Bridge, north of the city center—was discovered in the 19th century and restored. Admission includes the Roman Museum, located high in the building above the theater (reach it via elevator— start at the stage and walk up the middle set of stairs, then continue straight on the path through the bushes).

The museum displays a model of the theater, a small chapel, and Roman artifacts, including mosaic floors, busts and other statuary, clay and bronze votive figures, and architectural fragments. There's not much to see. Unless you've never seen a Roman ruin, I'd skip it.

Cost and Hours: €4.50; Tue-Sun 10:00-18:00, closed Mon, last entry one hour before closing; theater located across the river near Ponte Pietra footbridge, +39 045 800 0360. From mid-June through August, the theater stages Shakespeare plays—only a little more difficult to understand in Italian than in Elizabethan English.

Giusti Garden (Giardino Giusti)

You'll see this picturesque Renaissance-style garden capping the steep hilltop just across the Roman Bridge at the northern edge of the city. It's a little oasis with manicured box hedges, towering cypress trees, a maze, and a city view from the top of its hill. For most people, however, it's not worth the hike, time, or money.

Cost and Hours: €10, daily 10:00-19:00, until 18:00 in winter, across the river, beyond Ponte Nuovo, at Via Giardino Giusti 2, www.giardinogiusti. com.

Sleeping in Verona

Hotel prices soar from mid-June through early September (opera season), in early April (during the Vinitaly wine festival), and during big trade fairs or major holidays. Unless your goal is opera, consider coming outside the summer months. For hotel locations, see the "Verona" map, earlier.

NEAR PIAZZA ERBE

$$$ Hotel Aurora, at the corner of Piazza Erbe and Via Pelliciai, has friendly family management, attention to detail, a welcoming terrace with wonderful piazza views, and 18 straightforward rooms (family rooms, air-con, elevator, Piazzetta XIV Novembre 2, +39 045 594 717, www.hotelaurora.biz, info@hotelaurora.biz, Riccardo).

$$$ Albergo Mazzanti, tucked onto a quiet street behind Piazza Erbe, has a great central location. Its 16 classically furnished rooms, spread over two floors of an ancient building, are a good value (air-con, elevator, Mazzanti 6, +39 045 591 690, www. albergomazzanti.it, info@albergomazzanti.it).

$$ Casa Coloniale is just a stone's throw from Piazza Erbe. The four rooms all have balcony views and are simply but brightly furnished. Energetic owner Lucca runs the nearby Caffè Coloniale (Piazza Viviani Francesco 12), where breakfast is provided, along with B&B check-in after 15:00 (air-con, no elevator, Via Cairoli 6, +39 393 940 8687, mobile +39 337 472 737, www.casa-coloniale. com, info@casa-coloniale.com).

¢ Protezione della Giovane, run by an association that houses poor women, also rents rooms and dorm beds to female tourists (and their children, up to age 12 for boys). Buried deep in the old town and up several flights of stairs, this place offers 10 cheap beds in a clean, institutional, and peaceful setting (women only, no breakfast, 23:00 curfew, reception open 9:00-20:00, Wi-Fi in common areas, Via Pigna 7, +39 045 596 880, www.protezionedellagiovane. it, info@protezionedellagiovane.it).

NEAR PIAZZA BRÀ

You'll find several options in the quiet streets just off Piazza Brà. From the square, white or yellow signs point you to the hotels. Most of these are big, fairly impersonal business-class places. Albergo Arena and Pepita Lodge are a little farther out, but still within a short walk to Piazza Brà.

$$$$ Hotel Milano is an arty hotel with 56 rooms. The lobby and fancier rooms are tricked out in black and chrome. It has a wonderful terrace and hot tub overlooking the Roman Arena (air-con, elevator, pay parking in garage, Vicolo Tre Marchetti 11, +39 045 596 011, www.hotelmilano-vr.it, info@hotelmilano-vr.it).

$$$ Hotel Giulietta e Romeo is on a quiet side street 100 yards behind the Roman Arena. It's stylish and well-managed; 10 of its 37 ultra-modern rooms have balconies (air-con, elevator, loaner bikes, fitness room, pay parking in garage or ask for free street-parking permit, Vicolo Tre Marchetti 3, +39 045 800 3554, www.hotelgr.it, info@hotelgr.it).

$$$ Hotel Colomba d'Oro is a sprawling place with old-school elegance, renting 50 spacious rooms with Baroque flourishes. It has generous public spaces, including a peaceful courtyard, and overlooks a quiet and central street (air-con, elevator to every other floor, stairs between the rest, Via C. Cattaneo 10, +39 045 595 300, www.colombahotel.com, info@colombahotel.com).

$$$ Pepita Lodge is convenient for train travelers and a 10-minute walk from Piazza Brà. The artful and spacious rooms have a calm, contemporary, clean-lines vibe. Breakfast is provided across the street at a *pasticceria* (family rooms, air-con, elevator, pay parking, Corso Porta Nuova 103, reception at #99B, +39 045 800 1393, www.pepitalodge.it, info@pepitalodge.it).

$$ Aparthotel Verona House is a good option if you want hotel amenities and residential comfort. The 23 apartments are swanky and stylish (some can fit up to eight people). The bright, spacious breakfast room has great views onto Castelvecchio and doubles as an honor bar in the afternoon and evening (air-con, elevator, pay parking, loaner bikes, Stradone Provolo 3, +39 045 205 0366, www.veronahouse.com, info@hotels2go.it).

Eating in Verona

Every restaurant listed here is within a 10-minute walk of the others. They're mostly small and intimate and found along side streets. It's tempting to grab a table next to the *passeggiata* action along Piazza Brà, but you'll be sacrificing service, value, and quality for your view of the floodlit Roman Arena and Verona on parade (perhaps a fair trade-off). Restaurants on the piazza tend to charge a cover and service fee, making even pizza a pricey choice. For restaurant locations, see the Verona map, earlier.

FINE DINING

$$$$ Darì Ristorante & Enoteca, run by longtime Verona restaurateurs Corinna and Giuliano, has a lovely setting inside and out and beautifully presented food (Wed-Mon 12:00-15:00 & 18:30-22:30, closed Tue, Vicolo Cieco San Pietro Incarnario 5, +39 045 595 022, www.ristorantedari.com).

$$ Trattoria al Pompiere bustles with old-school waiters weaving among its tight tables and walls plastered with photos of big shots from the area. Marco and his gang serve regional classics as well as gourmet meat and cheese *antipasti* from their larger-than-life back counter. Reservations are wise (Mon-Sat 12:40-14:00 & 19:40-22:30, closed Sun; halfway between Piazza Erbe and Juliet's courtyard—head down narrow side street next to Via Cappello 8 to Vicolo Regina d'Ungheria 5; +39 045 803 0537, www.alpompiere. com).

$$$ Caffè Dante is a high-end place with a 19th-century pedigree and elegant service on the coziest and classiest square in town. You can enjoy a memorable meal of classic Veneto cuisine either at romantic tables on the square or inside. If you want to dress up and enjoy a slow, romantic, memorable meal, this can be a good value. The kitchen has limited hours, but the café is open throughout the day (Tue-Sun 12:00-15:00 & 18:00-23:00, closed Mon, closed Sun afternoon off-season; Piazza dei Signori 2, +39 045 800 0083, www.caffedante.it).

$$$ Bottega del Vino is pricey, venerable, and a bit pretentious. Under a high ceiling and walls of wine bottles, brisk, black-vested waiters match traditional dishes (polenta, duck, game) with glasses of fine wine. Choose from 50 open bottles. The waitstaff, ambience, and food have deep roots in local culture. I like their front room best. Reservations are smart for dinner (good daily specials, daily 11:00-23:00—kitchen closed 14:30-19:00, bar open later, off Via Mazzini at Via Scudo di Francia 3, +39 045 800 4535, www.bottegavini.it).

MODERATE RESTAURANTS

$$ Ristorante Torcolo, dressy but not stuffy, is a family restaurant, with mom (Paola) running the kitchen, and father and son (Roberto and Luca) supervising the dining room. Their accessible menu covers all the classics but with modern twists, and the wine list is extensive. Eat in their dining hall or on the courtyard outside (daily 12:30-14:30 & 19:00-22:30, dinner from 17:00 in opera season, just behind the Piazza Brà scene on a quiet street, Via Carlo Cattaneo 11, +39 045 803 3730).

The Wines of Verona

Wine connoisseurs love the high-quality wines of the Verona area. The hills to the east are covered with grapes to make Soave; to the north is Valpolicella country; and Bardolino comes from vineyards to the west.

Valpolicella grapes, which are used to make the fruity, red Valpolicella table wine (found everywhere), are also the basis for full-bodied red Amarone and the sweet dessert wine Recioto. To produce Amarone, grapes are partially dried *(passito)* before fermentation, then aged for a minimum of four years in oak casks, resulting in a rich, velvety, full-bodied red. Recioto, which in local dialect means "ears," uses only the grapes from the top of the cluster (so they sort of look like the "ears" of the cluster's "head"). Because these grapes get the most sun, they mature the fastest and have the highest concentration of sugar. Before pressing, the grapes are dried for months until all moisture has gone out; the wine is then aged for one to three years.

Bardolino, from the vineyards near Lake Garda, is a light, fruity wine, like a French Beaujolais. It's a perfect picnic wine.

Soave, one of Italy's best-known white wines, goes well with seafood and risotto dishes. The best are called "Soave Classico" and come from the heart of the region, near Soave Castle. Soave is sometimes aged in oak casks, giving it a mellow, rounded flavor.

Sample these and many others at the numerous *enoteche* (wine-tasting bars) or at any restaurant around town. In early April, Verona hosts Vinitaly, an important international convention of domestic and international wines. Vintners vie for prestigious awards for the past year's vintage. Hotels book up months in advance. Check with the TI and Vinitaly.com for details.

If you're visiting the area in the fall, consider a day trip to nearby Monteforte d'Alpone, east of Verona. The town hosts a fun, raucous wine festival in September—ask at the TI for more information on this and other regional wine festivals.

$$ Osteria Caffè Monte Baldo has cafè-style bites plus a full menu with dishes typical of Verona like *risotto all'Amarone* for two or *cacio e pepe alla veronese* (with truffles). Or just pop into this cozy, rustic spot for a drink and snack on some *tartine* (open daily 11:00-15:00 & 18:00-23:00, Via Rosa 12, +39 045 803 0579). Their sister eatery, **La Piazzetta,** offers a similar menu in a relaxed environment with terrace seating (daily 12:00-15:00 & 19:00-22:30, Corte San Giovanni in Foro 4/A, +39 045 591 099).

$$ Ristorante Sant'Eufemia, on a quiet side street near Piazza Erbe, offers excellent homemade pasta and typical Veronese cuisine at reasonable prices. The outdoor area, under twinkling fairy lights, is especially inviting (Tue-Sun 12:30-15:00 & 19:30-22:00, closed Mon, Corticella San Giovanni in Foro 7, +39 045 800 6865).

EATING IN OSTERIE (OLD BARS)

Wandering around the old town, you'll see plenty of Verona's thriving little watering holes. These traditional old bars focus more on wine than food, but most serve memorable and affordable plates. Menus are simple and rustic—sometimes just bar munchies and the daily pasta. Service is relaxed and the clientele is young and local. For drinks it's mostly wine or water—fine wines are served by the glass, with bottles open and prices listed on blackboards. (I saw one sign suggesting that patrons "don't drive too much to drink.")

$$ Osteria Sottoriva survives from an era when Verona's river served as the town thoroughfare, and business deals could be made over a glass of wine at rustic riverside eateries. Located in a fine old covered arcade (the portico of Via Sottoriva), with both cozy indoor and outdoor seating, Sottoriva serves simple Veneto fare that changes seasonally and with the owner's whim (daily 11:00-15:00 & 18:00-22:30—but open all day long in summer, closed Wed in winter, behind the Church of Sant'Anastasia at Via Sottoriva 9, +39 045 801 4323).

$ Osteria del Bugiardo is usually jammed with a happy crowd that spills out into the pedestrian-filled Corso Porta Borsari. They have a buffet of little sandwiches, can whip up a plate of top-quality cheeses, and serve a short list of pastas. They showcase their own Buglioni wines and are proud to tell you more about them (daily 11:00-24:00, in the old center at Corso Porta Borsari 17a, +39 045 591 869).

$$ Osteria la Mandorla hides behind its vintage *Vini—Liquori/Giovanni Zampieri* sign with a tiny bar and a few tables. It's been stoking conviviality with good wine since 1937. This place is passionate about organic wines, slow food, and craft beers. They don't serve much food—just some bar munchies and a nice *antipasti* plate. Locals go for horse's balls *(polpettine di cavallo)*, which are procured from the butcher down the street (daily 11:00-14:00 & 17:00-late except closed Mon for lunch, a few steps off Piazza Brà and next to Via Mazzini at Via Alberto Mario 23, +39 045 597 053). You're welcome to play foosball downstairs on what Italians call the *calcio balilla* ("the little boy soldiers of Mussolini").

PIZZA, CHEAP EATS, AND SWEETS

$ Pizzeria da Salvatore, Verona's first pizzeria, opened in 1963, when pizza was considered a foreign food...from Naples. They serve the best pizza in town, and a visit here offers a nice excuse to stroll across the river into a part of town with no tourists. It's family-friendly, not fancy or romantic, and you'll squeeze into a

NEAR VENICE

A Mobile Feast Through Verona

Verona is a great town to sample the *aperitivo* ritual. All over town, locals enjoy a refreshing *spritz,* ideally on Piazza Erbe between 18:00 and 20:00. Choose a nice perch, and then, for about €4, you'll get the drink of your choice and a few nibbles (olives and/or potato chips) and a chance to feel very local as you enjoy the *passeggiata* scene.

Consider this for a fun sampling of many dimensions of the Verona eating and socializing scene: Start with an *aperitivo* on **Piazza Erbe,** then walk across Ponte Nuovo to **Pizzeria da Salvatore** and enjoy the town's best pizza. If you have to wait for a table, have another *spritz* at the neighboring bar. Then stroll along the river to **Osteria Sottoriva,** and enjoy a little sampling of bar food with a glass of Amarone (wine to meditate with) under the old arcade. Finish by meandering through the old center back to Piazza Brà for a gelato at **Gelateria Savoia.** *Buon appetito!*

---

tight row of tiny tables, rubbing elbows with your neighbors. While it's not quite Naples, it's justifiably popular—come early, or plan to leave your name on the list and wait awhile (Tue-Sat 12:30-14:30 & 19:00-23:00, Sun 19:00-23:00 only, closed Mon, closed Sun in July, no reservations, across Ponte Nuovo to Piazza San Tomaso 6, +39 045 803 0366).

$ Pizzeria Du de Cope is a colorful, high-energy, informal place that buzzes with smartly attired young waiters and locals who keep coming back for the pizza (daily 12:00-14:30 & 19:00-23:00, flamboyant desserts, families welcome, no reservations, at Galleria Pelliciai 10, +39 045 595 562).

$ *Döner kebab* shops all over town serve hearty, cheap kebabs to munch on from a stool or to take out. *Piadine* (pita-bread) kebabs are worth the €5, and the super-sized kebabs can fill a couple on a very tight budget for a total of €8. The best kebabs, according to local assessments, are behind the Roman Arena at Via Leoncino 44. There's another good place on the other side of Piazza Brà at Via Teatro Filarmonico 6b. The benches in the center of Piazza Brà are handy for a scenic place to munch your cheap meal.

Groceries: The **PAM supermarket chain** has two locations (both generally open 8:00-21:00 with shorter hours on Sun). One is just outside the historic gate on Piazza Brà (exit Piazza Brà through the gate and take the first right to Via dei Mutilati 3). The other one is across the Adige River, beyond Ponte Vittoria (Via IV Novembre 6A). Near the Church of Sant'Anastasia are two classic grocery stores, **Salumeria Caliari** and **Salumeria Albertini** (as mentioned in the town walk, earlier).

Gelato: The venerable **Gelateria Savoia** has been in business since 1939. It's in an arcade just off Piazza Brà, marked by a crowd licking their specialty *semifreddo* of bitter-almond amaretto, cream, and cookie (just off Piazza Brà at Via Roma 1b). Near the foot of the Ponte Pietra bridge, **Gelateria Ponte Pietra** prides itself on using fine ingredients. Besides gelato, they serve Sicilian *granite* and milkshakes (Via Ponte Pietra 13).

Verona Connections

Every hour, at least two trains connect Verona with Venice, Padua, and Vicenza. Choose one of the cheaper regional trains (R or RV) instead of the faster Italo or Frecce express trains, which get you there slightly sooner but cost much more. Unless otherwise specified, the following connections are for Trenitalia.

From Verona by Train to: Venice (1.5-2 hours, Trenitalia: 2/hour, Italo: 7/day), **Padua** (2/hour, 40-80 minutes), **Vicenza** (2/hour, 30-60 minutes), **Florence** (about hourly, 1.5 hours direct or 2.5 hours with transfer in Bologna; Italo: 4/day, 1.5 hours), **Bologna** (hourly, 1.5 hours), **Milan** (2/hour, 1.5-2 hours; Italo: 7/day, 1.5 hours), **Rome** (at least hourly, 4-5 hours, often with transfer in Padua or Bologna, also 1 night train, 8 hours, with change in Padua; Italo: 4/day, 3.5 hours), and **Bolzano** (2/hour, 1.5 hours).

THE DOLOMITES

Bolzano • Castelrotto • Alpe di Siusi

Italy's dramatic rocky rooftop, the Dolomites, offers some of the best mountain thrills in Europe. The city of Bolzano—blending Austrian tidiness with an Italian love for life—is the gateway to the Dolomites. And the village of Castelrotto is a good home base for your exploration of Alpe di Siusi (Seiser Alm), Europe's largest alpine meadow. Dolomite, a sedimentary rock similar to limestone, gives these mountains their distinctive shape and color. The bold, light gray cliffs and spires flecked with snow, above green, flower-speckled meadows and beneath a blue sky, offer a powerful and memorable mountain experience.

A hard-fought history has left the region bicultural, with an emphasis on the German. In the mountains and closer to the border, most locals speak German first, and some wish they were still part of Austria. In the Middle Ages, as part of the Holy Roman Empire, the region faced north. Later, it was firmly in the Austrian Habsburg realm. By losing World War I, Austria's Südtirol (South Tirol) became Italy's Alto Adige. Mussolini did what he could to Italianize the region, including giving each town an Italian name. But even as recently as the 1990s, secessionist groups were agitating to reunify with Austria (see sidebar).

Today all signs and literature in the province of Alto Adige/Südtirol are in both Italian and German. Some include a third language, Ladin—an ancient Romance language still spoken in a few traditional areas. (I have listed both Italian and German, so the confusion caused by this guidebook will match that experienced in your travels.)

The Dolomites are well developed, and the region's most famous destinations suffer from après-ski fever. But in spite of all

The Dolomites

AUSTRIA

To Innsbruck
BRENNER PASS
A-22
Vipiteno/ Sterzing
ITALY
REIFENSTEIN CASTLE
Fortezza
SS-49
Brunico/ Bruneck
To Lienz & Salzburg
KLOSTER NEUSTIFT
Bressanone/ Brixen
Dobbiaco/ Toblach
Tre Cime
Ponte Gardena/ Waldbruck
SS-508
A-22
"CHIUSA/ KLAUSEN" EXIT
TRENTINO-ALTO ADIGE
SS-51
Castelrotto/ Kastelruth
Val Gardena
Ortisei/ St. Ulrich
Seceda
PASSO SELLA
PASSO GARDENA
Cortina d'Ampezzo
Lago Misurina
Oberbozen
Compatsch
Sella
Corvara
Bolzano/ Bozen
SS-12
Siusi/ Seis
Langkofel
SR-48
PASSO FALZAREGO
"NORD" EXIT
"SÜD" EXIT
See detail map
PASSO PORDOI
PASSO CAMPOLONGO
Pieve di Cadore
SS-241
ALPE DI SIUSI / SEISER ALM
Canazei
Vigo
Alleghe
To Trento & Verona
SR-48
Marmolada
A-22
Cavalese
10 Kilometers
10 Miles
SR-203
SS-51
To Belluno
To Venice

ITALY
Rome
200 Miles

N

DOLOMITES

the glamorous resorts and busy construction cranes, the regional color survives in a warm, blue-aproned, ruddy-faced, felt-hat-with-feathers way. There's yogurt and yodeling for breakfast. Culturally, as much as geographically, the area is reminiscent of Austria. In fact, the Austrian region of Tirol is named for a village that is now part of Italy.

PLANNING YOUR TIME

One night in the Dolomites will give you a feel for South Tirol's alpine culture. But it's best to stay at least two nights so you have at least one full day to hike. Pretty Castelrotto/Kastelruth is the best base for hiking in the spectacular Alpe di Siusi alpine meadow, but Italian-flavored Bolzano, down in the valley, is also in easy reach of the high-mountain lifts.

From either town, plan an early start up to Compatsch, the gateway to the high Alpe di Siusi/Seiser Alm meadow. Tenderfeet stroll and ride the lifts from there. For serious mountain thrills, do an all-day hike. And for an unforgettable memory, spend a night in a mountain hut. With a second day, do more hiking or spend time in Bolzano, where you can stroll the old town and visit Ötzi the Iceman at the excellent archaeology museum (best to get tickets a few days in advance, especially if you expect to visit on a rainy day). Seceda, above the town of Ortisei/St. Ulrich, is another very satisfying place for a day of alpine hiking.

Hiking season is mid-June through mid-October. The region is particularly crowded, booming, and blooming from mid-July through mid-September (but once you're out on the trails, you'll leave the crowds behind). It's packed with Italian vacationers in August. Spring is usually dead, with lifts shut down, huts closed, and the most exciting trails still under snow. Many hotels and restaurants close in April and November. By mid-May, most businesses reopen, some lifts start running (check dates at www.seiseralm. it), and—if you luck into good weather—a few rewarding hikes are already possible. Ski season (Dec-Easter) is busiest—and most expensive—of all.

Getting Around the Dolomites: This is a road-tripping paradise, but you can easily connect the dots on the region's good public-transit system. For details, see "Getting Around the Alpe di Siusi," later.

Bolzano

Willkommen to the Italian Tirol! If Bolzano (Bozen in German) weren't so sunny, you could be in Innsbruck. This enjoyable old city is the most convenient gateway to the Dolomites, especially if you're relying on public transportation. It's just the place to take a Tirolean stroll.

Bolzano feels like a happy castaway between the Germanic and Italian worlds. The people are warm and friendly, but organized. One person greets you in Italian, the next in German. But everyone can agree the city has a special verve, with lively shopping arcades, a food-and-flower market more bustling than anything you'll find north of the border in Austria, and a tidy main square with a backdrop of colorful churches and wooded foothills.

The town has only one museum worth entering, but it's world class, offering the chance to see Ötzi the Iceman—a 5,300-year-old Tirolean found frozen on a mountaintop—in the (shriveled, leathery) flesh. Beyond that, Bolzano is made for strolling, relaxing, and hiking in the nearby hills—and works well as a home base for venturing deeper into the mountains (though pretty Castelrotto is closer to the high-mountain lifts).

Orientation to Bolzano

Virtually everything I mention in Bolzano (pop. 107,000) is in the compact and strollable old town, which radiates out from the main square, Piazza Walther/Waltherplatz.

TOURIST INFORMATION

Bolzano's TI, just down the street from the train station, is helpful (Mon-Fri 9:00-19:00, Sat 9:30-18:00, Sun 10:00-15:00 except Nov-April closed Sun, Via Alto Adige/Südtiroler Strasse 60, +39 0471 307 000, www.bolzano-bozen.it).

Museum and Transit Cards: Busy sightseers might make use of the **Museumobil Card,** which covers most museums in South Tirol (including the archaeology museum, with its famous Iceman), plus local trains, buses, the Renon/Rittner cable car *(funivia/Seilbahn)* to Oberbozen, and more (€30/7 days, doesn't cover the gondola to or chairlifts on the Alpe di Siusi, available at the TI and transit offices, www.mobilcard.info). Some Bolzano hotels hand out free regional guest passes that cover essentially the same thing—check before shelling out for one. A transit-only version, the **Mobilcard,** covers the same trains, buses, and lifts (€15/1 day, €23/3 days, sold at TIs and transit offices).

Walking Tours: The TI offers a guided two-hour town walking tour in English on Fridays in season (€10, April-Oct at 10:30—confirm day and time in advance, departs from TI).

ARRIVAL IN BOLZANO

By Train: Bolzano has two train stations—you want *Bolzano,* not *Bolzano Süd.* WCs are in the underground passage by track 1, and luggage storage is just upstairs (see "Helpful Hints," next). To reach the **TI,** exit the station, turn left, and walk two long blocks. To get **downtown,** jog left through the park and go two blocks up the tree-lined Viale della Stazione/Bahnhofsallee to Piazza Walther/Waltherplatz and the start of my self-guided walk.

By Car: Some areas of Bolzano are ZTL zones (marked on signs with a red circle); avoid these or risk an automatic ticket. The most convenient parking lot for a short visit is the Piazza Walther garage, right under the main square (€3/hour, cheaper overnight; to find it, make your way to the train station, then drive up tree-lined Viale della Stazione/Bahnhofsallee, watching for the *Piazza Walther* entrance on your right). For longer stays or to save a few euros, try Parking Centro/Mitte, just south of the ring road and west of the train station—about a 10-minute walk from the main square (€1.80/hour, cheaper overnight, enter from Via Josef Mayr Nusser).

Ich bin ein Italiener

With the exception of Bolzano, where Italian has become the primary language, you'll hear mostly German in Dolomite villages. Overall, seven

in ten Italians living in South Tirol speak German as their mother tongue. Many are fair-skinned and blue-eyed and prefer dumplings and strudel to pasta and gelato. Most have a working knowledge of Italian, but they watch German-language TV, read newspapers *auf Deutsch*, listen to jaunty oompah music, and live in Tirolean-looking villages.

At the end of World War I, the region was ceded by Austria (loser) to Italy (winner). Mussolini suppressed Germanic cultural elements as part of his propaganda campaign to praise all things Italian. Many German speakers hoped that Hitler would "liberate" them from Italy, but Hitler's close alliance with Mussolini prevented that from happening. Instead, in June 1939, residents were given six months to make a hard choice: Move north to the Fatherland and become German citizens, or stay in their homeland *(Heimat)* under Italian rule. The majority (212,000 people, or 85 percent) decided to leave, but with the outbreak of World War II, only 75,000 actually moved.

After the war, German speakers were again disappointed when the Allies refused to grant them autonomy—or the chance to become Austrian citizens. Instead, the victors decided to stick with the prewar arrangement. The region rebuilt and the two linguistic groups patched things up, but for the remainder of the 20th century, German speakers were continually outvoted by the Italian-speaking majority in the regional government (comprising two provinces, Italian-speaking Trentino and German-speaking Alto Adige/Südtirol).

German speakers lobbied the national government for more control on the provincial (not regional) level, even turning to demonstrations and violence. Over the years, Rome has slowly and grudgingly granted increased local control. The country's 2001 constitution gave South Tirol a large measure of autonomy—similar to Sicily and Sardinia—though it's still officially tied to Trentino. Roads, water, electricity, communications, and schools are all under local control, including the Free University of Bozen-Bolzano, founded in 1998.

A good way to sum it all up: In many ways, the people of the Dolomites feel a closer bond with their Austrian ancestors than with their countrymen to the south. But when Italy plays Austria in a big soccer match, who do locals root for? Italy.

DOLOMITES

HELPFUL HINTS

Sleepy Sundays: This small, culturally conservative city is dead on Sunday (young locals add, "and the rest of the week, too").

Street Markets: Piazza delle Erbe/Obstplatz hosts an ancient and still-thriving open-air produce market (Mon-Sat all day, generally closed Sun). Wash your produce in the handy drinking fountain in the middle of the market. Another market (offering more variety, not just food) runs Saturday mornings on Piazza della Vittoria.

Baggage Storage: You can store bags at **Base Camp Dolomites,** at the train station by track 1 (daily 8:30-18:30, they also rent bikes, +39 0471 971 733, www.basecampdolomites.com).

Laundry: The self-service **Bolzano Lavanderia** is at Via Rosmini/Rosministrasse 39, southwest of the South Tirol Museum of Archaeology (daily 7:00-22:30, doors lock automatically at closing time, +39 0474 832 204).

Bike Rental: The city has a well-developed bike-trail system and a subsidized bike-sharing program. But visitors will find it easiest to rent a bike from **Base Camp Dolomites** at the station (see "Baggage Storage," above).

Bus InfoPoint: You can ask questions, get schedules, and buy tickets for buses and the Renon/Ritten cable car at the lime-green **SüdtirolMobil** office at the bus depot (Mon-Sat 7:00-19:20, Sun 8:00-13:40, pay WCs).

Bolzano Walk

This brief self-guided walk will help you get your bearings in central Bolzano.

• *Start the walk in...*

Piazza Walther/Waltherplatz: The statue in the center honors the square's namesake, Walther von der Vogelweide, a 12th-century politically incorrect German poet who courageously stood up to the pope in favor of the Holy Roman (German) Emperor. Walther's spunk against a far bigger power represents the Germanic pride of this region. The statue is made of marble quarried in the village of Laas, a little north of Bolzano.

When not hosting Bolzano's Christmas market, flower market (May Day), or Speck Fest (a spring ham festival), Piazza Walther/Waltherplatz is simply the town's living room. And locals care about it. It was the site of Italy's first McDonald's, which, in the early 1990s, became the first McDonald's to be shut down by locals protesting American fast food. Today the square is home to bustling cafés such as Café Walther, where (outside of meal times) you're welcome to nurse a local "Hugo" aperitif (see sidebar on page 199), "Venetian" *spritz*, or a pricier cocktail as long as you like.

• *Cross the street to the big church.*

The Cathedral: The cathedral's glazed-tile roof is typical of the Germanic world—a reminder that from the sixth century until 1919, when Italy said *benvenuti* to the Südtirol, German was the region's official language. The church was flattened in World War II (a common consequence of being located near a train station in 20th-century Europe).

Walk around to the right, to the Romanesque Lion's Gate entrance (at the far end), and step inside. The place feels Teutonic, rather than Italian, with a mostly Gothic interior that's broken at the front by an impressive Baroque tabernacle. Partway down the nave is a sandstone pulpit (c. 1500) with reliefs of the four Church fathers whose presence gave credibility to sermons preached here. Most of the art is by Bavarian artists.

• *Leaving the church, return to Piazza Walther/Waltherplatz and cross it diagonally, heading up the street to the right of the big Sparkasse bank building. Follow this for one block, to...*

Piazza del Grano/Kornplatz: Nine hundred years ago, this square was the center of urban life in Bolzano. The 12th-century castle of the Trentino prince-bishop was here—until a Tirolean rival destroyed it in 1277. The grain market was at one end of the square, and livestock at the other. The one freestanding building here (#12), the Casa della Pesa/Waaghaus, is the oldest structure in Bolzano. Until the late 18th century, this was the public weighing house—with the only officially calibrated scale in town. (You can catch a glimpse of the scale's appearance in an old fresco in the alley to the left of the building.)

• *Jog left into the alley with the scale fresco (above the archway at the end). You'll then pop out in the middle of...*

Via dei Portici/Laubengasse: In the 12th century, this was the only street in Bolzano. Step into the center (dodging bikes). Looking east and west, you see the width of the original town.

Turn left and stroll a bit, watching on the right for the frescoed, pointed arches of the old City Hall—the street's only Gothic building (at #30). Notice that the other buildings, with uniform

DOLOMITES

Bolzano

To Maretsch & Runkelstein Castles

CORSO DELLA LIBERTÀ

VIA DEI VANGA

Petrarcha Park

SOUTH TIROL MUSEUM OF ARCHAEOLOGY (ÖTZI THE ICEMAN)

VIA RAGGIO

16

Piazza della Vittoria

VICTORY MONUMENT

PONTE TALVERA

VIA MUSEO

WALK ENDS

19

VIA BATTISTI

NEW BOLZANO

MUSEO CIVICO

19

Piazza delle Erbe

11

VIA PETER MAYR

Talvera River

VIA CASSA DI RISPARMIO

VIA LEONARDO DA VINCI

Piazza Sernesi

VIA DELLA

VIALE VENEZIA

VIA SAN QUIRINO

FREE UNIVERSITY OF BOLZANO

POST

20

VIA ROSMINI

Piazza Domenicani

VIA OSPEDALE

6

DOMINICAN CHURCH

VIA CARDUCCI

VIA CAPP.

CHIESA DEI CAPPUCCINI

VIA MARCONI

Bike Path

Isarco/Eisack

To A-22 Autostrada "Bolzano Süd" Exit

Accommodations
1 Parkhotel Laurin
2 Hotel Greif
3 Stadt Hotel Città
4 Hotel Figl
5 Hotel Feichter
6 Kolpinghaus Bozen
7 Youth Hostel Bolzano

Eateries & Other
8 Franziskaner Stuben
9 Weisses Rössl
10 Batzen Häusl/Ca' de Bezzi

11 Hopfen & Co.
12 Paulaner Stuben
13 Humus
14 Enoteca Il Bacaro
15 Dai Carrettai
16 Drago D'Oro
17 Gul
18 Eccetera Gelato
19 Supermarket (4)
20 Launderette
21 Baggage Storage & Bike Rental

round arches, are all basically the same: Each had a storm cellar, cows out back, a ground-level shop, and living quarters upstairs. Bay windows were designed for maximum light—just right for clerks keeping track of accounts and for women doing their weaving. The arcades (*Lauben*, pictured at right), typical of Tirol, sheltered merchants

and their goods from both snow and sun. Narrow passages between shops lead to neighboring streets.

A bit farther along on the left, the only balcony marks the street's lone Baroque building—once the mercantile center (with a fine worth-a-look courtyard), now a skippable museum.

• *Continue to the end of the street, where you'll find a bustling market generally every day but Sunday.*

Piazza delle Erbe/Obstplatz: This square hosts an open-air produce market, liveliest in the morning. The historic market fountain gives Bolzano its only hint of the sea—a 17th-century statue of Neptune. Stroll around and see what's in season. All the breads, strudel, and hams *schmecken sehr gut.*

• *From the market, Via Museo/Museumstrasse leads straight ahead to the archaeology museum and Ötzi the Iceman.*

DOLOMITES

Sights in Bolzano

▲▲▲South Tirol Museum of Archaeology (Museo Archeologico dell'Alto Adige/Südtiroler Archäologiemuseum)

This excellent museum, which illuminates the prehistory of the region, boasts a unique attraction: the actual body of Ötzi the Iceman, who spent more than five millennia stuck in a glacier. With Ötzi as the centerpiece, the museum takes you on an intriguing journey through time, recounting the evolution of humanity—from the Paleolithic era to the Roman period and finally to the Middle Ages—in vivid detail. The interactive exhibit offers informative displays and models, and video recounts Ötzi's extraction and explains his personal effects. Everything's well described in English.

Cost and Hours: €13; Tue-Sun 10:00-18:00, closed Mon except July-Sept and Dec, €4 audioguide isn't essential; near the river at Via Museo/Museumstrasse 43, +39 0471 320 100, www.iceman.it.

Crowd-Beating Tips: If you're visiting in summer, it's smart to reserve an entry time in advance online, which lets you skip the line (can reserve only up to 3 days in advance). Capacity is limited, and ticket-buying lines can be long—sometimes up to three hours. It's busiest on rainy days in July and August, especially in the morning.

Background: Ötzi's frozen body was discovered high in the mountains on the Italian/Austrian border by a German couple in 1991. Police initially believed the corpse was a lost hiker, and Ötzi was chopped roughly out of the glacier, damaging his left side. But upon discovering his pre-Bronze Age hatchet, officials realized what they had found: a 5,300-year-old, nearly perfectly preserved man with clothing and gear in excellent condition for his age. Austria and Italy squabbled briefly over who would get him, but surveys showed that he was located 100 yards inside Italian territory. Tooth enamel studies have now shown that he did grow up on the Italian side. An Austrian journalist dubbed him Ötzi, after the Ötztal valley, where he was discovered.

Visiting the Museum: The permanent exhibit is smartly displayed on three floors (plus temporary exhibits on the top floor). First you'll learn about Ötzi's discovery, excavation, and preservation. Upstairs, you'll walk through displays of his incredibly well-preserved and fascinating clothing and gear, including a finely stitched two-color coat, his goat-hide loincloth, a fancy hat, shoes, a well-crafted hatchet, 14 arrows, a longbow, a dagger, and shreds of his rucksack (which held fire-making gadgets and a tree fungus used as a primitive antibiotic). And finally, you'll peek into a heavily fortified room to see Ötzi himself—still kept carefully frozen.

One floor up, exhibits focus on the Copper Age. The discovery of Ötzi helped researchers realize that the use of copper occurred in this region more than a millennium earlier than previously thought. There's also a complete medical workup of Ötzi, including an interactive flatscreen where you can zoom in on different parts of his body to see the layers of skin, muscle, and bone. And you'll learn how researchers have used modern forensic science techniques to better understand who Ötzi was and how he died. (Think of it as a very, very, very cold case.)

From all of this, scientists have formed a complete picture of the Iceman: In his mid-40s at the time of his death, Ötzi was 5 feet, 3 inches tall, with brown hair and brown eyes. He weighed about 110 pounds, was lactose intolerant, ate too much animal fat, and likely had trouble with his knees. And they've even determined the cause of death: an arrowhead buried in Ötzi's left shoulder. (Discoveries still make the news every few years—in 2018, for example, scientists were able to deduce what he'd eaten for his last meal.) At the end of the exhibit, you'll see an eerily lifelike reconstruction of how Ötzi may have looked when he was alive.

Dominican Church
(Chiesa dei Domenicani/Dominikanerkirche)

Art lovers can drop by this austere 13th-century Gothic church, part of a Dominican convent complex. You'll see surviving bits of

14th-century frescoes on the church's main walls, and massive octagonal pillars that divide the nave into three sections. The highlight, though, is the long and narrow side chapel of St. John (San Giovanni/St. Johannes; behind the modern altar and to the right). Frescoed in about 1329, the chapel

is evidence of how disruptive Giotto's figural innovations at Padua's Scrovegni Chapel were—and how quickly his style spread northward. Just 20 or so years after Giotto completed his fresco cycle in Padua, artists in Bolzano were already experimenting with the new naturalism, with barely a hint of Gothic linearity to be seen.

DOLOMITES

If it's open, peek through the door opposite the chapel entrance for a view of the convent's peaceful cloister.

Cost and Hours: Free, Mon-Sat 8:00-18:00, Sun from 12:00, on Piazza Domenicani, two blocks west of Piazza Walther/Waltherplatz.

Lift to Oberbozen and Renon/Ritten

The **Renon/Rittner cable car** (*funivia/Seilbahn*) whisks you over the hills from Bolzano to the resort village of Oberbozen on the high plateau of Renon/Ritten. The 12-minute cable-car ride itself is the main attraction, offering views of the town, surrounding mountains, made-for-yodeling farmsteads, and 18-wheelers downshifting along the expressway from Austria. It's no replacement for a trip to Castelrotto and the Alpe di Siusi, but you'll get a taste of the Alpine wonderland that lies above the valley floor—and this lift runs when many other do not. From Oberbozen, it's worth hopping on the narrow-gauge train to the village of Klobenstein/Collalbo for even better views (if you do, allow about two hours for the whole outing).

Cost and Hours: Cable-car—€10 round-trip, ticket machine (cash or cards) on ground floor to the left of the stairs, validate tickets in blue box next to machine or upstairs just before the gates; departures every 4 minutes year-round Mon-Sat 6:30-21:48, Sun from 7:10; every 12 minutes after 21:00 in low season; for info, visit www.ritten.com.

Getting There: The cable car's valley station is at Via Renon/Rittner Strasse 12, a five-block walk east of the Bolzano train station.

At the Top: Oberbozen (elevation 4,000 feet) is mostly a collection of resort hotels, most famous as the place where Sigmund Freud and his wife once celebrated their wedding anniversary. The TI is straight ahead from the cable-car station.

From Oberbozen, a narrow-gauge train makes a scenic 16-minute trip to **Klobenstein/Collalbo,** a larger and slightly less touristy village at 3,800 feet. From the train station, head left and follow signs to the center (5 minutes) for the TI, cafés, and restaurants (€3.50 one-way, €6 round-trip, €15 round-trip for both Oberbozen cable car and train, daily departures every 30 minutes—reduced to hourly early and after 19:00). The local TI has branches in both villages (www.ritten.com).

The lift station and narrow-gauge train depot have brochures suggesting short walks (as does the TI). More interesting than Oberbozen itself (though not a must-see) are the nearby **"earth pyramids"**—Bryce Canyon-like pinnacles that rise out of the ridge, created by eroding glacial debris dumped at the end of the last ice age. Some of these are visible from the Oberbozen cable car (on the right as you're riding up), but they're challenging to hike to; an easier-to-reach area is a 15-minute walk from Klobenstein. Another walk is the **Freudpromenade,** a fairly level, 1.5-hour stroll between Oberbozen and Klobenstein (you can take the train back).

New Bolzano (Nuova Bolzano)

Just across the river from the Museum of Archaeology, the fascist-style **Victory Monument** (Monumento alla Vittoria) glistens in white Zandobbio marble. It marks the beginning of the "new" city built by the fascist government in the 1920s to Italianize the otherwise Germanic-looking city. Indeed, you won't hear much German spoken in the shops and bars along the colonnaded Corso della Libertà—it feels a world away from the old town. A visit to New Bolzano comes with a delightful stroll over the river and the inviting, parklike Talvera promenade (described later).

In the basement of the arch-like structure, you'll find a small but well-done **exhibit** about the history of the monument itself, the Italianization of South Tirol, and the efforts of local people to keep their language, culture, and traditions alive (monument always viewable; exhibit free and open April-Sept Tue-Sun 11:00-13:00 & 14:00-17:00, Thu 15:00-21:00, shorter hours off-season, closed Mon year-round; good information in English, www.monumenttovictory.com).

The grand plans for this part of the city were never fully realized. But several blocks of buildings were constructed in a repetitive Modernist design, following the idea of imperial monumentalism trumpeting the dawn of a new era in Italy. Most of the structures were intended to house state institutions and highly desirable apartments for state employees. (A few blocks south on Piazza Tribunale, you can still find the somewhat faded image of Mussolini waving from one of the buildings.)

Bolzano Walks

Pick up the good map at the TI for scenic, accessible strolls that provide a different perspective on the region.

One popular option is the easy, shaded **Talvera promenade** just west of the Museum of Archaeology, following the river embankment north. This route has great people-watching in good weather, with views of vineyards and Maretsch Castle (Castello Mareccio/Burg Maretsch) to the right. In about 25 minutes, you'll reach the Bridge of St. Antonio, where you can cross (look for

DOLOMITES

Runkelstein signs), loop under onto the pedestrian path, and follow the river for another 15 minutes to the impressive **Runkelstein Castle** (Castel Roncolo/Schloss Runkelstein; be aware that the last 10 minutes are up a steep, unevenly cobbled path). Inside this 13th-century "illustrated manor" is an impressively large collection of secular medieval frescoes, with scenes from the everyday lives of knights and ladies (€8; Tue-Sun 10:00-18:00, until 17:00 off-season, closed Jan-Feb and Mon year-round; perched above the river north of town on Kaiser-Franz-Josef Weg, +39 0471 329 808, www.runkelstein.info).

To extend your hike, go back to the Bridge of St. Antonio and head up the hill about 45 minutes for the **St. Oswald** walk. This route takes you to the church of Santa Magdalena (with its 14th-century frescoes), offering great views back to the city.

Sleeping in Bolzano

All the places listed here are in the city center, within walking distance of the train and bus stations. Bolzano has no real high or low season; most hotels have the same rates all year.

$$$$ Parkhotel Laurin is a fancy Old World hotel near the train station, with 100 tastefully decorated rooms, marble bathrooms, a chic dining room and terrace, a small swimming pool (summer only), an extensive garden with dining options, and attentive staff. Frescoes throughout the grand lobby and atmospheric bar depict the legend of King Laurin (air-con, elevator, pay parking, Via Laurin/Laurinstrasse 4, +39 0471 311 000, www.laurin.it, info@laurin.it).

$$$$ Hotel Greif, a luxury boutique hotel, is right on Piazza Walther/Waltherplatz. Each of the 33 individually designed rooms makes you feel like you're in an avant-garde art installation (its website gives a room-by-room tour). It's not exactly cozy, but it is striking, and a stay here comes with one of my favorite breakfasts in Italy (family rooms, air-con, elevator, sauna, pay parking at Parking Walther under main square—enter hotel directly from level 1 of the garage or at Via della Rena/Raingasse 28, +39 0471 318 000, www.greif.it, info@greif.it).

$$$$ Stadt Hotel Città, a venerable old hotel with 99 modern, straightforward rooms and serving an uncommonly good breakfast, is ideally situated on Piazza Walther/Waltherplatz. The hotel's café spills out onto the piazza, offering a prime spot for people-watching (family rooms, air-con, elevator, pay parking at Parking Walther under main square—enter hotel directly from level 1 of the garage, Piazza Walther/Waltherplatz 21, +39 0471 180 0161, www.hotel-citta.com, info@hotel-citta.com). This place is an especially good value if you take advantage of their free-for-guests Wellness Center (Turkish bath, whirlpool, Finnish sauna, biosauna, massage by appointment)—a fine way to unwind.

$$$ Hotel Figl, warmly run by Anton and Helga Mayr, has 22 comfy, bright, good-value rooms. It's situated over a popular-with-locals café on a pedestrian square located a block from Piazza Walther/Waltherplatz (breakfast extra, air-con, elevator, pay parking at Parking Walther under main square—take the escalator to the square and walk a couple of minutes, Piazza del Grano/Kornplatz 9, +39 0471 978 412, www.figl.net, info@figl.net, include a phone number if you email).

$$ Hotel Feichter is a solid value: a well-priced, well-kept, family-run place with simple but sufficient amenities in a great location. Most of the 34 rooms are a little tight, but pleasantly renovated, and some share a communal terrace overlooking the rooftops of Bolzano. Papà Walter, Mamma Hedwig, Hannes, Irene, and Wolfi Feichter have run this homey hotel since 1969, and are a good source of local advice (family rooms, excellent breakfast, air-con, pay parking, elevator, ground-floor café serves lunch Mon-Fri 11:30-14:00; from station, walk up Via Laurin/Laurinstrasse, which becomes Via Grappoli/Weintraubengasse—hotel is on the right at #15; +39 0471 978 768, www.hotelfeichter.it, info@hotelfeichter.it). They also rent two nice apartments.

$$ Kolpinghaus Bozen, modern, clean, and church-run, has 50 rooms that feel like a renovated college dorm (doubles have two twin beds placed head to toe). Though institutional, it makes me feel thankful for no-nonsense budget rooms (weak air-con, elevator, pay laundry, pay parking, 4 blocks from Piazza Walther/Waltherplatz near Piazza Domenicani at Largo A. Kolping/Adolph-Kolping-Strasse 3, +39 0471 308 400, www.kolpingbozen.it, info@kolpingbozen.it). The line of people out front at lunchtime are waiting for their cafeteria to open (generally Mon-Fri 11:45-14:00, closed Sat-Sun).

¢Youth Hostel Bolzano is one of the most comfortable and inviting hostels I've seen in Italy. It has 17 four-bed rooms (each with two bunk beds and a full bathroom; fifth bed possible), one triple, and 10 delightful singles with bath. The bright, clean, modern rooms make it feel like a dorm in a fancy university (family discounts, no age limit, elevator, pay laundry, 9:00 checkout, 100 yards to the right as you leave the train station at Via Renon/Rittner Strasse 23; +39 0471 300 865, easy online reservations at www.ostello.bz, bolzano@ostello.bz).

Eating in Bolzano

All my recommendations are in the center of the old town. While nearly every local-style place serves a mix of German/Tirolean and Italian fare, I favor eating Tirolean here in Bozen. Many restaurants have no cover charge but put a basket of bread on the table; as in Austria, if you eat the bread, you'll be charged a small amount. Bolzano's restaurants tend to stay open all day, but at a few places the kitchen closes in the afternoon with only snacks available.

$$$ Franziskaner Stuben, with three spacious rooms, wide-plank wood floors, and genteel decor, spoils their customers with regional cuisine, fine wines, and attentive service (some outside tables, daily 11:00-14:30 & 18:00-22:00, Franziskanergasse/Via dei Francescani 7, +39 0471 976 183).

$$ Weisses Rössl ("White Pony") offers a spacious, traditional woody setting and a tasty mix of pasta and Tirolean food. This is a good spot for dining indoors among savvy locals (Mon-Fri 11:00-24:00, Sat 10:00-15:00, closed Sun, 2 blocks north of Piazza Municipio at Via Bottai/Bindergasse 6, +39 0471 973 267).

$$ Batzen Häusl/Ca' de Bezzi is Bolzano's oldest inn, with two Teutonic-feeling upper floors; by contrast, the patio and back room are refreshingly modern and untouristy. They make their own breads, pastas, and beer, and serve traditional Tirolean fare—stick-to-your-ribs grub (daily 9:00-late, Via Andreas Hofer/Andreas-Hofer-Strasse 30, +39 0471 050 950).

$$ Hopfen & Co. fills an 800-year-old house with happy eaters, drinkers, and the beer lover's favorite aroma: hops *(Hopfen)*. A tavern since the 1600s, it's a microbrewery today. This high-energy, boisterous place is packed with locals who come for its homemade beer, delicious Tirolean food, and reasonable prices (great salads, limited menu outside of mealtimes, daily 9:30-24:00, Piazza delle Erbe/Obstplatz 17, +39 0471 300 788).

$$ Paulaner Stuben is a restaurant-pizzeria-*Bierstube* serving good food (more Italian than German) and a favorite Bavarian beer. It has good outside seating and a take-me-to-Munich interior (Mon-Sat 11:00-24:00, closed Sun, Via Argentieri/Silbergasse 16—or use back entrance at Via dei Portici/Laubengasse 51, +39 0471 980 407).

$$ Humus is a trendy eatery packed with locals enjoying a hearty mix of Italian and Middle Eastern dishes. With an emphasis on organic food, this place feels fresh, lively, and inviting (Mon-Sat 8:00-20:00, closed Sun, Via Argentieri/Silbergasse 16D, +39 0471 971 961).

Drinks and Light Food: $ Enoteca Il Bacaro, a hole-in-the-wall wine bar, is an intriguing spot for a glass of wine and bar snacks amid locals. Wines available by the glass are listed on the

Tirolean Cuisine

During your visit to the Dolomites, take a break from Italian-style pizzas and pastas to sample some of the region's traditional cui-

sine...with a distinctly Austrian flavor. For simplicity, I've generally listed Italian names here, though local menus are in both Italian and German (and usually also English).

Wurst and sauerkraut are the Tirolean clichés. More adventurous eaters seek out *speck,* a raw (prosciutto-style) ham smoked for five months then thinly sliced and served as an antipasto or in sandwiches. *Canederli*—large dumplings with bits of *speck,* liver, spinach, beets, or cheese—are often served in broth, or with butter and cheese. (Never cut a dumpling with a knife—it'll destroy the chef.) *Merenda* is a platter of cured meats and hard cheeses. Pastas aren't an integral part of the local cuisine, but you will see *mezzelune*—half-moon-shaped ravioli.

The stars of Tirolean cuisine are the hearty meat dishes—which, unlike traditional Italian main courses, are nearly always served with side dishes of doughy dumplings or vegetables and potatoes. Try *stinco di maiale* (roasted pork shank, usually garnished with potatoes) and *crauti rossi* (a sweetish sauerkraut made from red cabbage). *Carrè affumicato* is pork shank that is first smoked, then boiled. *Selvaggina,* or wild game, comes in the form of *capriolo* (fawn), *cervo* (venison), or *camoscio* (chamois/antelope). Game is eaten smoked and thinly sliced in antipasti; in meat sauce *(ragù)* with fresh pasta or as ravioli stuffing; or in entrées, as tender chunks grilled or roasted in a rich sauce *(spezzatino)*.

For dessert, strudel is everywhere, filled with the harvest from this region's renowned apple orchards. Cakes and pies are loaded with other locally grown fruits, raisins, and nuts. *Kaiserschmarrn* is an interesting alternative: a thick, fluffy, caramelized pancake that's pulled apart into pieces, usually prepared with raisins and topped with powdered sugar and red currant jam.

Bier (birra) is king in South Tirol (the best-known brand, Forst, is brewed in nearby Merano), but the wines of the area are well matched to the local fare. *Magdalener* is a light, dry red made from Schiava grapes. *Lagrein scuro* is a full-bodied red, dry and fruity, similar to a cabernet sauvignon or merlot. *Gewürztraminer* is a dry white wine with a spicy fruit flavor. For a local aperitif, try the popular and refreshing Hugo, made with sparkling wine, elderflower syrup (stir your drink), sparkling water, and a sprig of mint. For something stronger, try grappa made from Williams pears (and served with a wedge of fresh pear), or *grappa nocino*—a darker, sweeter brew similar to Jägermeister. *Guten Appetit und Prost!*

DOLOMITES

blackboard (Mon-Fri 8:00-14:00 & 17:00-21:00, Sat 8:00-14:00, closed Sun; located a half-block east of Hopfen & Co. on a hidden alley off Via Argentieri/Silbergasse 17, look for *vino/Wein* sign next to fountain on south side of street and enter courtyard; +39 0471 971 421). **$ Dai Carrettai** is a popular bar where locals meet after work over a glass of wine—the crowd spills out onto the street. Browse the array of toothpick snacks at the counter, or order a bruschetta from the menu (also serves hot lunches, Mon-Fri 7:00-14:00 & 16:30-21:00, Sat 7:00-14:00, closed Sun, Via Dr. Streiter/Dr.-Streiter-Gasse 20b, +39 0471 970 558).

International Food: $ Drago D'Oro is a good and affordable Chinese restaurant on a pleasant old-town lane, with plenty of shaded seating out back (Mon 11:30-15:00, Tue-Sun 11:30-15:00 & 18:00-23:00, Via Roggia/Rauschertorgasse 7a, +39 0471 977 621). **$$ Gul** has Indian-Pakistani standards (Mon-Sat 12:00-14:30 & 18:00-23:00, closed Sun, at Via Dr. Streiter/Dr.-Streiter-Gasse 2, +39 0471 970 518). Both are takeout-friendly, as are several small pizzerias in the same area.

Gelato: At the tip of a city block less than five minutes from Piazza Walther/Waltherplatz is **Eccetera,** a tiny gelato counter with no seating, just excellent (and excellently priced) gelato. They often have more flavors available than what's right under your nose—check the sign overhead for today's selection (daily, Via Grappoli/Weintraubengasse 23).

Picnics: Assemble the ingredients at the **Piazza delle Erbe/Obstplatz** market and dine in the park along the Talvera River (the leafy green area with benches past the museum). Bakeries up and down Via del Bottai/Grappoli sell a tempting variety of takeaway sandwiches. Or visit one of the four **Despar supermarkets:** The largest is just before the museum at Via Museo/Museumstrasse 39 (daily 9:00-19:00). Another is a little more centrally located at the end of the Galleria Greif arcade (enter arcade from Piazza Walther/Waltherplatz by Hotel Greif and walk to far end—the supermarket is downstairs; same hours as the big store but closes Sun at 13:00). Smaller branches are on Piazza delle Erbe/Obstplatz and at Via Bottai/Bindergasse 29 (both open Mon-Sat 8:30-19:30, closed Sun).

Bolzano Connections

Most trains from Bolzano are operated by Trenitalia (departures marked *R* or *RV* on schedules), but some long-distance trains on the Innsbruck-Bolzano-Verona line are run by the German or Austrian railways—DB/ÖBB for short (trains marked *Eurocity, EC,* or *Trenord*). Tickets for either are sold through Trenitalia (machines in stations or via the Trenitalia app).

From Bolzano by Train to: Milan (about hourly, 4 hours, change in Verona; one fast Freccia train is direct), **Verona** (2/hour, 1.5 hours, take the regional/"R" trains—avoid fast trains that take the same time for double the cost), **Venice** (about hourly, 3.5 hours, change in Verona), **Florence** (every 1-2 hours, 5 hours, change in Verona and/or Bologna), **Innsbruck** (1/hour, 2.5 hours, some regional connections change in Brennero), **Vienna** (4/day, 7 hours, change in Innsbruck), **Salzburg** (at least hourly, 4 hours, change in Brennero/Brenner, Innsbruck, and/or Rosenheim), **Munich** (called "Monaco" in Italy, 5/day direct, 4 hours).

By Bus: Bus #170 connects Bolzano with the gondola to **Compatsch** (putting you at the gateway to all the Alpe di Siusi hikes in about an hour) and the town of **Castelrotto** (direction: Kastelruth/Castelrotto, 2/hour Mon-Sat, hourly on Sun, last departure at 20:12—may run until later in summer, free schedule at bus station, €4 each way, buy tickets from machine or counter at bus depot InfoPoint, +39 0471 220 880, www.suedtirolmobil.info).

The bus leaves from Bolzano's bus station (just north of the train station) and then winds high into the mountains. For the Alpe di Siusi, ask the driver to let you off at the "Bergbahn" station (Seiser Alm Bahn gondola, 40 minutes from Bolzano), then ascend to Compatsch. Otherwise, stay on the bus another 10 minutes to reach the center of Castelrotto.

Castelrotto

Castelrotto (altitude: 3,475 feet, Kastelruth in German) is the ideal home base for a day of hiking on the Alpe di Siusi/Seiser Alm or Seceda. Stay at least two nights. Relax on the traffic-free main square, surrounded by a mountain backdrop and a thousand years of history, with an oversized (and hyperactive) bell tower above you. You'll feel almost lost in another world. Easy bus and cable-car connections bring you up to trails on the Alpe di Siusi and down to Bolzano.

With a population of around 2,300, Castelrotto is a combination of real town, ski resort, and administrative center for surrounding villages. Tourism has become increasingly important here; while farming occupied most of the population in the 1960s, it's a small

DOLOMITES

part of the economy nowadays. Castelrotto's good lodging and ser-vices help make your stay trouble-free. Though I've used the town's Italian name, life here goes on almost entirely in German. (Fewer than 5 percent of Castelrotto's residents are native Italian speakers.)

Orientation to Castelrotto

TOURIST INFORMATION

The helpful TI is on the main square, facing the church (Mon-Sat 8:30-12:00 & 15:00-18:00, closed afternoons in Nov and some-times April, closed Sun except July-Aug 9:00-12:00, +39 0471 706 333, www.castelrotto.info). If you plan to hike, pick up the TI's free "Hiking Area" pictorial map, which includes estimated walk-ing times and trail numbers. For longer hikes, 1:25,000 maps are worthwhile.

If visiting the TI, pop upstairs for a minute to see the free **Trachten Museum,** where traditional costumes are displayed be-side paintings and photos of the same styles worn by locals in cen-turies past (no English descriptions, hours similar to TI).

Transit Deals: If you're sleeping anywhere in the Castelrotto and Alpe di Siusi area, you'll get a free **Südtirol Guest Pass** (ask at hotel check-in). It covers local buses between Castelrotto and Bolzano and the base of the Seiser Alm Bahn gondola (but not the Seiser Alm gondola itself, and no other lifts or buses to or on the Seiser Alm). It doesn't cover anything above the gondola base (at Seis/Siusi).

The TI also sells the pricey **Combi Card** transit pass, which only makes sense if you're here several days and/or take at least three round-trip rides on the Seiser Alm Bahn gondola.

HELPFUL HINTS

Spring and Fall Closures: The periods between ski season and hiking season (April-mid-May and Nov) are quiet, with lifts closed for maintenance and most hotels and restaurants shut-tered.

Business Hours: Shops in Castelrotto close between 12:30 and 15:30—a good time for a long lunch, a hike in the hills...or a siesta.

Launderette: There's none in the area.

Recreation: A heated outdoor **swimming pool** with alpine views and nearby tennis courts is in the hamlet of Telfen, between Castelrotto and Seis/Siusi (mid-May-mid-Sept 9:00-21:00, +39 0471 705 090). You can **rent a horse** at Unter-Lanzinerhof in Telfen (+39 339 868 6868, www.reiterhof-oberlanzin.com, Karin speaks some English). For more excitement, tandem **paragliding** flights—you and the pilot—depart from the Alpe

Castelrotto

100 Meters
100 Yards

CALVARY HILL STROLL

To San Michele, Val Gardena & Sella Pass

SP-64

HOTEL VILLA KASTELRUTH

CHURCH

Main Square BELL TOWER

WC

(Underground) P

BANDSTAND

MENDEL HAUS

BUS STN.

To 9

KASTELRUTHER SPATZEN-LADEN

PANIDERSTR.

WEGSCHEID

TIOSLERWEG

MARINZEN CHAIRLIFT

POST

To Pool, Alpe di Siusi, Siusi Village (Cable Car to Alpe di Siusi) & Bolzano via SS-12

SP-64

To 8 & St. Valentin Church

DOLOMITES

Accommodations
1 Hotel Cavallino d'Oro
2 Hotel/Rest. zum Turm
3 Hotel zum Wolf
4 Residence Trocker
5 Pension Lantschner

Eateries & Other
6 Saalstuben Restaurant
7 Zur Alten Schmiede Pizzeria
8 To Ristorante Liftstüberl
9 To Pizzeria Sporthütte
10 Hotel Schgaguler Bar
11 Supermarket (2)

di Siusi and land either there or in Castelrotto (+39 335 603 6400, www.tandem-paragliding.com, Ruben). You can rent **skis and snowboards** at both the bottom and top stations of the Alpe di Siusi lift.

Annual Events: The **Oswald-von-Wolkenstein Riding Tournament,** held on a spring weekend (between mid-May and mid-June), features medieval-style equestrian tournament games, followed by a feast (www.ovwritt.com). The town also holds **religious processions** with locals dressed in traditional costumes, usually on the Sunday after Corpus Christi; on the feast day of the village protectors, Sts. Peter and Paul (nearest Sunday to June 29); and on the local Thanksgiving (first

Sun in Oct). On the night following **Ascension,** the church's big bell intermittently clangs for an hour beginning at 3:30 (at 4:00, townsfolk gather in the square to begin a long procession marking the area's suffering during plague times.) In mid-October, the town is packed for the **Kastelruther Spatzenfest,** a concert weekend for the local musical heartthrobs, the Kastelruther Spatzen.

ARRIVAL IN CASTELROTTO

The **bus station** *(Busbahnhof)* is 100 yards below the town's main square. It's unstaffed, but there's a shelter with timetables and a ticket machine (cash only). Free WCs are in a building at the tip of the bus loop. Take the stairs (by the tiny elevator) to get to the main square and TI.

Drivers can park in one of the two underground parking lots: The Zentrum garage is near the bus station, and the other is on Wolkensteinstrasse, next to the recommended Saalstuben Restaurant (€1.80/hour, €20/day, cash only). My recommended hotels have free parking (ask for details when you book).

Coming from the south, drivers exit the expressway at *Bolzano Nord.* Coming from Innsbruck and points north, exit (earlier than you would expect) at *Chiusa/Klausen* and continue five miles toward Bolzano along the secondary road (SS-12) before crossing the river (signed *Waidbruck/Ponte Gardena*) and following signs for *Kastelruth/Castelrotto.*

Castelrotto Walk

Castelrotto is a great place to sleep but has only a little sightseeing of its own—the surrounding mountains and hikes are the attractions here. This quick self-guided walk will get you oriented and trace the town's history.

• *Start in the...*

Main Square (Krausplatz): This square is named for the noble family who ruled the town from 1550 to 1800. Their palace, now the City Hall, overlooks the square and sports the Kraus family coat of arms.

Castelrotto puts its square to use. A farmers market takes place here on Friday mornings in the summer, and a clothing/craft market fills the square most Thursday mornings. Before and after Sunday Mass, the square is crowded with villagers and farmers (who fill the church) dressed in traditional clothing. The main Mass (Sat at 20:00 and Sun at 10:00) is in German.

• *A landmark in the square is the...*

Bell Tower: At 250 feet, the freestanding bell tower dominates the town. It was once attached to a church, which burned down in 1753. While the bell tower was quickly rebuilt, the gutted church was torn down, and the church you see today was constructed farther back, enlarging the square.

When you feel the pride that the locals have in their tower—which symbolizes their town—you'll better understand why Italy has been called "the land of a thousand bell towers." The bells of Castelrotto, which are a big part of the town experience, ring on the hour from 6:00 until 22:00. While sleepy tourists may wonder why the bells clang so very early in the morning, locals who grew up with the chimes find them comforting. The beloved bells mark the hours, summon people to work and to Mass, announce festivals, and warn when storms threaten. In the days when people used to believe that thunder was the devil approaching, the bells called everyone to pray. (Townspeople thought the bells' sound cleared the clouds.)

Bells ring big at 7:00, noon, and 19:00. The biggest of the eight bells (7,500 pounds) peals only on special days. When the bells ring at 15:00 on Friday, it commemorates Christ's sacrifice at the supposed hour of his death—a little bit of Good Friday every Friday. The colorful poles in front of the church (yellow-and-white for the Vatican, red-and-white for Tirol) fly flags on festival days. The towering maypole, a Bavarian tradition, was a gift from Castelrotto's sister city in Bavaria.

• *Also on the square is the...*

Church: Before entering, notice the plaque on the exterior. This commemorative inscription honors the tiny community's WWI dead—*Fraktion Dorf* means from the village itself, and the other sections list soldiers from the surrounding hamlets. Stepping into the church, you're surrounded by harmonious art from about 1850. The church is dedicated to Sts. Peter and Paul, and the paintings that flank the high altar show how each was martyred (crucifixion and beheading). The pews (and smart matching confessionals) are carved of walnut wood.

• *Back outside, belly up to the...*

Fountain: Opposite the church, Castelrotto's fountain dates from 1884. St. Florian, the protector against fires, keeps an eye on it today as he did when villagers (and their horses) first came here for a drink of water.

• *With your back to the church and the fountain on your left, walk a half-block down the lane to see the finely frescoed...*

DOLOMITES

Mendel Haus: This house, with its traditional facade, contains a woodcarving shop. Its frescoes (from 1886) include many symbolic figures, as well as an emblem of a carpenter above the door—a relic from the days when images, rather than address numbers, identified the house. Notice St. Florian again; this time, he's pouring water on a small painting of this very house engulfed in flames. Inside Mendel Haus are fine carvings, a reminder that this region—especially nearby Val Gardena—is famous for its woodwork. You'll also see many witches, folk figures that date back to when this area was the Salem of this corner of Europe. Women who didn't fit society's mold—including midwives, healers, and redheads—were sometimes burned as witches.

• *Continue downhill to the left of Mendel Haus, then before the underpass, climb the stairs on your right. At the top of the stairs, turn left on Dolomiten Strasse. In 50 yards, on the left at #21, is a shop dedicated to Castelrotto's big hometown heroes.*

Kastelruther Spatzen-Laden: The ABBA of the Alps, the folk-singing group Kastelruther Spatzen (literally "sparrows") is a gang of local boys who put Castelrotto on the map in the 1980s. They have a huge following here and throughout the German-speaking world. Though he's now in his early 60s, the lead singer, Norbert Rier, remains a Germanic heartthrob. You'll see his face on ads all over town—in the recommended Saalstuben Restaurant, suggesting what to order for dessert, or in the Co-op supermarket, reminding you to drink lots of Tirolean milk. The group's feel-good folk-pop style—an alpine version of German *Schlager* music—is popular with the kind of conservative, working-class Germans who like to vacation in South Tirol. (Younger, more progressive Germans cringe at this stuff, with its nationalistic overtones.) At a big festival in Castelrotto on the second weekend in October, the band puts on a hometown concert, filling this place with fans from as far away as the Alsace and the Netherlands. They also hold an open-air concert here in June and a Christmas concert.

Browse the store, which is part souvenir shop and part insignia and apparel outlet. Downstairs is a sprawling, folksy museum slathered with gifts, awards, and gold records (€2 museum entry, refunded with €5 purchase in the shop, Mon-Fri 9:30-12:00 & 15:00-18:00, Sat 9:30-12:00, closed Sun).

• *Leaving the shop, cross the street for a...*

Fine Mountain View of the Schlern: This bold limestone outcropping—so typical of the Dolomites—is a symbol of the

DOLOMITES

The Dramatic Dolomites

The Dolomites have been called the most beautiful mountains on earth, and certainly they are among the most dramatic.

They differ from the rest of the Alps because of their dominant rock type, dolomite, which forms sheer vertical walls of white, gray, and pink that rise abruptly from green valleys and meadows. Many parts of the mountains (including the Alpe di Siusi/Seiser Alm) are protected as regional or national parks, where development is restricted. Still, rail lines, roads, good bus routes, and innumerable lifts make this group of mountains very accessible.

Once dubbed the "Pale Mountains" or the "Venetian Alps," this mountain range was named after French mineralogist Dolomieu, who in the late 1700s first described the rock type responsible for the region's light-colored bluffs and peaks.

These sedimentary rocks (similar to limestone) were formed in warm tropical seas during the Triassic Period (about 250 million years ago). The marine sediments, along with the fossilized remains of coral reefs and other animals, were buried, hardened, and later scooped upward along with the rest of the Alps by the tectonic-plate action of Africa slowly smashing into Europe. Today, marine fossils are found atop the region's highest peaks, including the skyscraping, nearly 11,000-foot-high Marmolada.

During World War I, the front line between the Italian and Austro-Hungarian forces ran through these mountains, and many paths were cut into the range for military use. Today mountaineers can still follow these networks of metal rungs, cables, and ladders (called *via ferrata*). One famous wartime trail is the "Strada delle Gallerie," near Rovereto, which passes through 52 tunnels (*gallerie*).

A paradise for hikers, cyclists, and climbers in summer, the Dolomites are even better known as a top skiing destination. A popular winter activity for intrepid skiers is the "Sella Ronda"—circling the Sella massif using a system of lifts and 28 miles of ski runs. The 1956 Winter Olympics in Cortina d'Ampezzo brought the Dolomites to the world's attention, and the 2026 Winter Olympics (shared between Cortina and Milan) are set to do it all over again.

Whether you experience the Dolomites with your hand on a walking stick, a ski pole, or an *aperitivo* while mountain-gazing from a café, it's easy to enjoy this spectacular region.

Südtirol. Witches are said to live there, and many locals climb it yearly (it's an easy—if long—walk up the back side).

Look left—the street points to a ridge in the distance. That's Puflatsch (a high meadow with a popular trail called the "Trail of the Witches"—see "Activities in the Alpe di Siusi," later).

• *Continue up the hill 50 yards, cross left, pass the little parking lot square, and find two stones marking the top of a cobbled pedestrian lane that leads downhill back into town. Look up at the top of the bell tower. Ahead stands the elegant...*

Hotel zum Wolf Facade: This was painted by the same artist who did the Mendel Haus. St. Florian is still pouring water on burning houses and locals are busy enjoying the local wine.

As you head left, uphill back to the town square, enjoy windows filled with traditional Südtirol formal wear—delightful dirndls. You'll pass an old hotel, which, by the looks of its street sign, must be called The Golden Pony (*Cavallino d'Oro* or *Goldenes Rössl*). Ahead of you is the inviting sound of a refreshing drink from the town fountain.

• *Our walk is over. Ahead (through a white arch just to the right of the TI) are two big pictorial maps showing the region in summer and in ski season, as well as a modern café with ice cream and a nice terrace. The arch that's closer to the church leads up to Calvary Hill for a fine little loop walk, described next.*

Activities in Castelrotto

Calvary Hill (Kalvarienberg) Stroll

For an easy stroll to Castelrotto's finest postcard views—the giant bell tower with a dramatic alpine backdrop—take a 15-minute mini hike around the town's hill, Kalvarienberg/Calvario (Calvary). Originally, this was the site of the ancient Roman fortress, and later the fortified home of the medieval lord. One lane circles the hill while another spirals to the top past seven little chapels, each depicting a scene from Christ's Passion and culminating in the Crucifixion.

Facing the church, take the road under the arch to the left, and then follow signs to *Kofelrunde* (to go around the hill) or *Kofelka-pelle* (to get directly to the top). The light is best late in the day, and the stroll is also great after dark—romantically lit and under the stars. (The lead singer of the Kastelruther Spatzen enjoyed his first kiss right here.) For a longer walk back into town, take the

Friedensweg (Peace Trail) from the top of the hill. This 30-minute forest walk is decorated with peace-themed artwork by local elementary students.

Marinzen Lift

The little Marinzen chairlift trundles you up above town in two-person seats to the Marinzenhütte café (at 4,875 feet), which has a playground and animal park for kids (open when the lift runs). The views from the top are nothing special, but several hikes leave from here—and as you ride back down, you'll enjoy pleasant panoramas over Castelrotto. Or skip the return ride—it's a sce-

nic one-hour hike back down; to extend the walk, detour to St. Valentin church, described next. While the chairlift doesn't compare with going up to the Alpe di Siusi, it's still a nice activity. Catch it right in town, up the lane behind the Co-op/Konsum-Markt supermarket.

Cost and Hours: €9 one-way, €14 round-trip, daily late May-Oct 9:00-17:00, until 17:30 July-Aug, slow and scenic 22 minutes each way, closed off-season and rainy mornings, +39 0471 707 160, www.marinzen.com.

Hillside Walk to St. Valentin Church

On a clear summer evening, my favorite post-dinner activity is the gentle 40-minute walk above town to the picture-perfect St. Valentin Church, perched on a hillside high above Seis/Siusi. Although the church is rarely open, on the way there you'll enjoy uninterrupted views of the stern Schlern, the smell of hay (and cows), and the distinct clang of Castelrotto's church bell.

From Castelrotto's town center, walk uphill along Marinzen-weg, passing the driveway to Ristorante Liftstüberl. Stay on the road until you reach a signpost for *St. Valentin* and *Seis*. Follow the path (and signs to *Seis*) past a few farmhouses to a well-kept shrine to the Virgin Mary. Just after the shrine, take the path to the right and into the grass (on the #7 trail). Crossing a road, you'll head down a paved driveway and take the far-left fork between a barn and a white building (marked *za Oberzonn*) to find the church standing proudly under the mighty Schlern.

From the church you can either retrace your steps back to Castelrotto (my preference), walk another 15 minutes steeply downhill to Seis/Siusi and catch a bus back to Castelrotto (#3, #3a, or #170; last departure around 20:45), or split the difference and head more gently downhill to the main road to catch the bus back.

This walk can be combined with a walk down from the top of the Marinzen chairlift, but it's a steep descent to the church. Instead I'd walk down toward Castelrotto until the path leaves the forested hillside, then head left to follow the gentle, mostly level walk toward the church.

NEAR CASTELROTTO
Pflegerhof Herb Farm

On a narrow country road a little outside the nearby town of Seis/ Siusi, you'll find an organic farm that grows dozens of varieties of herbs. Walk among the scent-filled, fully labeled beds and browse the wide variety of herbal products in the shop. To reach the farm from Castelrotto, drive through Seis/Siusi, pass the turnoff for the cable car on your left, and after about a half-mile, turn right following *St. Oswald* and *Pflegerhof* signs.

Cost and Hours: Free, Mon-Sat 10:00-18:00, Sept-March until 17:00, closed Sun year-round, St. Oswald 24, +39 0471 706 771, www.pflegerhof.com.

Nightlife in and near Castelrotto

In summer, traditionally costumed groups offer free band concerts on Thursday evenings at the bandstand near the bus station (usually at 21:00 and kicked off with a procession from the main square).

For a more contemporary scene, the recommended **Zur Alten Schmiede Pizzeria** in Castelrotto is a fun spot that's open late. **Hotel Schgaguler** in Castelrotto has a fancy bar, and **Sasso's**, on Schlernstrasse in the nearby town of Seis/Siusi, is a trendy wine bar. A popular hangout for the younger crowd in Seis/Siusi is **Santners** (the only dance club in the area), at the Seiser Alm Bahn station. If you're here on the weekend, the "Nightliner" version of bus #170 can bring you home in the wee hours (Fri-Sat roughly hourly 20:40-2:40, schedules at www.silbernagl.it).

Sleeping in and near Castelrotto

Castelrotto has the largest selection of accommodations and is the only truly convenient option for those traveling in this region by public transport. If you've come to hike on the Alpe di Siusi, you could also stay in one of the hotels there (in or around Compatsch)—I've listed two less expensive options—and even a mountain hut.

Dozens of farmhouses in the area also offer accommodations;

I've listed a few that are willing to accept guests for two or three nights (the typical American stay here).

Dollar-sign ratings are based on the price of a double room in June or September. Rates skyrocket in July, August, and around Christmas. Accommodations often close in November and from April to mid-May.

If sleeping in this area, you're entitled to the **Südtirol Guest Pass**—a free pass for many local buses (described earlier, under "Tourist Information"). Be sure to ask your hotelier for one.

IN CASTELROTTO VILLAGE

These listings are within 300 yards of the bus station. The first three are in the traffic-free area of the old town; hotel guests are allowed to drive in to park. All have free parking.

$$$ Hotel Cavallino d'Oro (in German, **Goldenes Rössl**), right on the main square, is plush and inviting, with the best Tirolean character in town. The entire place is dappled with artistic, woodsy touches—painted doors, carved wood, and canopy beds in many rooms—and historical photos. If you love antiques and a chance to fancy yourself a weary medieval traveler, this 700-year-old hotel is the place for you. The honesty bar in the front lounge and cozy game room beyond the stairway make rainy days less of a disappointment. The reception desk is generally unstaffed; check in at Hotel Villa Kastelruth, a short walk away at Plattenstrasse 9—see "Castelrotto" map (elevator, free self-service laundry, closed late March-mid-May and mid-Oct-Nov, Krausplatz 1, +39 0471 706 337, www.cavallino.it, info@cavallino.it). What had once been the hotel's wine cellar is now a Roman steam bath and Finnish sauna (free for guests, great after a hike, can book an hour for exclusive use before 14:00)—complete with heated tile seats, and a solarium for tanning.

$$ Hotel zum Turm (in Italian, **Albergo alla Torre**) is comfortable, cozy, and warmly run by Gabi and Günther. The 15 rooms are woody and modern. If you're staying at least three nights, the €15/person half-board option is a great value (family rooms, elevator, free passes for Marinzen chairlift, closed April-mid-May and mid-Oct-Nov, Kofelgasse 8, +39 0471 706 349, www.zumturm.com, info@zumturm.com). From Castelrotto's main square, walk (or drive) through the upper of the two archways. If coming on a Wednesday, let them know your arrival time in advance.

$$ Hotel zum Wolf (in Italian, **al Lupo**) is pure Tirolean, with all the comforts in 23 neat-as-a-pin rooms, most with balconies (elevator, coin-op laundry, closed April-late May and Nov-mid-Dec, a block below main square at Wolkensteinstrasse 5, +39 0471 706 332, www.hotelwolf.it, info@hotelwolf.it, Malknecht family).

$$ Residence Trocker is run by the Moser family, who rent

11 great rooms in a place that's solid yet warm-wood cozy. While perhaps less welcoming than some other places listed here, this compound is beautifully laid out—with a café-bar (a popular, often-smoky local hangout), garden, sauna, steam bath, roof deck with hot tub, and coin-op laundry (family rooms, apartments available, elevator, closed Nov, Föstlweg 3, +39 0471 705 200, www. residencetrocker.com, garni@residencetrocker.com, Stefan). If arriving on Sunday (the family's day off), be sure to let them know in advance what time you'll arrive.

$ **Pension Lantschner** is family-run and a good budget value. Its 10 rooms—on the two upper floors of a large traditional house—are a little smaller, simpler, and older than at my other listings, but all are comfortable and have balconies with views (Kleinmichlweg 8, +39 0471 706 025, www.garni-lantschner.com, info@garni-lantschner.com).

FARM STAYS NEAR CASTELROTTO

Dozens of working farms around Castelrotto take in visitors, mostly in apartments with a kitchen and a minimum stay of five to seven nights (the TI has a complete list). A few farms also accept guests for short stays—even one night—and serve breakfast. Expect rustic doubles with bath for about €70-90. Staying in these places is practical only if you have a car. Consider the following (all $): **Goldrainerhof** (a 10-minute uphill trudge from Castelrotto, Tioslerweg 10, +39 0471 706 100, www.goldrainerhof.com); **Tonderhof** (a fruit farm in a dramatic hillside setting along the road down to Waidbruck/Ponte Gardena, Tisens 25, +39 0741 706 733, www.tonderhof.com) and their neighbor, **Schiedhof** (Tisens 23, +39 345 583 7278, www.schiedhof.it); and **Formsunhof** (along the road up to Alpe di Siusi, before the checkpoint, 4-night minimum stay, St. Valentin 12, +39 0471 706 015, www.formsunhof.com).

ON THE ALPE DI SIUSI/SEISER ALM, NEAR THE HIKING TRAILS

There are more than two dozen hotels up on the Alpe di Siusi, most in Compatsch (where the gondola from Seis/Siusi arrives) but some farther into the park. Most are quite expensive, four- and five-star affairs, with doubles from €200 and up in July and August. The two hotels listed here cost less—because Compatsch and the park entrance are a 10-minute uphill walk away. These are most practical for drivers (though they can reached by the Seiser Alm Bahn gondola and bus #10). Half-board is wise here, as there's nowhere else to eat dinner (except other hotels). The main advantage: Staying here, you can hike all day without concern for catching the last gondola down. Serious hikers should consider staying at the park's high-altitude mountain huts (mentioned under "Activities on the Alpe di Siusi," later).

$$$ Hotel Schmung is along the road and has fine, recently renovated rooms (most with balconies). During the day, the Seiser Alm Bahn gondolas float through the air just outside the front balconies (dinner available, free sauna, closed mid-April-May and Nov-mid-Dec, Compatsch 12, +39 0471 727 943, www.schmung. com, info@schmung.com).

$$ Hotel Seelaus is a friendly, mellow, family-run, creekside place a little off the road to Compatsch. Most of its 30 rooms have been smartly renovated with a modern look, but the hotel still has an Austrian feel (family rooms, half-board pricing; free wellness area with sauna, hydro-massage, and minipool; closed mid-April-mid-May and mid-Oct-early Dec, Compatsch 8, +39 0471 727 954, www.hotelseelaus.it, info@hotelseelaus.it, Roberto). Roberto offers free rides from the bus or cable-car station, and affordable transfers to/from Bolzano—arrange in advance.

Eating in Castelrotto

$$$ Hotel zum Turm's restaurant tries hard to up the culinary bar in town, focusing on locally sourced ingredients and serving good, meaty fare—including venison—and inventive vegetarian options. You can sit in the humdrum breakfast room, the cozy and very traditional *Stube,* or out on the oasis of a back terrace. The service is a bit Germanic (read: formal) but still welcoming (salad bar, Thu-Tue 12:00-13:45 & 18:00-20:45, closed Wed, closed April-mid-May and late Oct-Nov, +39 0471 706 349, www.zumturm.com).

$$$ Saalstuben Restaurant is a good choice for Tirolean cuisine that's classic (including lots of grilled meats) yet elevated, with modern presentation and a few creative twists. The interior is cozy, while the outdoor terrace—a few steps below the main road through town—is cheery and breezy (Fri-Wed 11:30-14:00 & 18:00-21:00, may also open Thu in July-Aug, Wolkensteinstrasse 12, +39 0471 707 394, www.saalstuben.com).

$$ Zur Alten Schmiede Pizzeria is a great place to enjoy an evening drinking Forst, the local beer, and playing darts. They offer a wide range of nothing-fancy grub—pizzas, pastas, meaty dishes, and *wurst* meals (Tue-Sun 12:00-14:00 & 17:30-21:00, pizza until 23:00, closed Mon, outdoor seating, near bus station entrance at Paniderstrasse 7, +39 0471 707 390).

$$ Ristorante Liftstüberl is a good bet on a nice day if you'd like to eat in nature rather than in town. It's a charming local favorite offering good traditional dishes and three-course dinners for less than €20. The classic woody interior is nothing special, but the picnic benches come with sweeping views, and there's a mini playground for the kids. Find it in a meadow about a 10-minute, gently uphill walk south of town (Mon-Sat 9:00-23:00, closed Sun, Marinzenweg 35, +39 0471 706 804).

$$ Pizzeria Sporthütte, with gingham curtains and a log-cabin vibe, offers good wood-fired pizzas, a salad bar, and daily Tirolean specials. It's about a 10-minute walk from the center (including a bit uphill), but worth it for the view from the outdoor tables (Tioslerweg 3, +39 0471 706 465).

Picnics: Castelrotto has two supermarkets in the center, both with a decent selection of useful items beyond groceries. **Eurospar** is the handiest, at the town's main intersection (Mon-Sat 8:00-19:00, closed Sun except in high season, on Wolkensteinstrasse). The **Co-op/Konsum-Markt** has the best selection of locally produced food and a hardware section where you can pick up a bell for your cow—no joke (Mon-Sat 7:30-12:30 & 15:00-19:00, closed Sun, Paniderstrasse 24).

Castelrotto Connections

Get bus schedules at the TI, or check Suedtirolmobil.info or Silbernagl.it.

From Castelrotto by Bus to: Seiser Alm Bahn gondola station (#3 and #3a, frequent departures—see "Alpe di Siusi/Getting There," later), **Bolzano** (#170, 2/hour Mon-Sat, hourly Sun, 50 minutes, last departure at 20:00 most of the year, covered by Südtirol Guest Pass; if you're connecting to a train in Bolzano, give yourself about 10 minutes to get to your platform at the train station). From Bolzano, you can easily connect to **Verona, Venice, Innsbruck, Munich,** and beyond.

Alpe di Siusi

This grassy mountain plateau above the village of Seis/Siusi (the next over from Castelrotto) is the largest high meadow—and summer pastureland—in the Alps.

It's a premier hiking and skiing area, and also home to hundreds of cows every summer. Undulating rather than flat, broken by rushing streams, and dappled with shapely evergreens, what makes the Alpe di Siusi/Seiser Alm really spectacular are the views of the surrounding

Dolomite peaks. Well-kept huts, trails, and lifts make hiking here a joy. It's family-friendly, with lots of playgrounds.

The cows munching away in this vast pasture all summer after a winter huddled in Castelrotto produce two million gallons of milk annually, much of which is sent to Bolzano to make cheese. After tourism, dairy is the leading industry here.

To enjoy the Alpe di Siusi, you'll need a full day and decent weather. Arrive in Compatsch (the main entry point) as early as you can, then hike (or bike) as much as you please. Bring a picnic (or buy lunch at a high mountain hut), and aim to wrap up the day in midafternoon—many upper lifts close at 17:00, and thunder-clouds tend to gather even on days that start out sunny.

The hiking season runs roughly from mid-June through mid-October (though if the weather's good, you can hit some of the trails as early as mid-May). The trails are pretty dead in April, early May, and November. For a fragrant festival of wildflowers suited to growing at 6,000 feet, come in June.

With additional time, you can explore more of the park or overnight in one of the mountain huts as a base for more remote and challenging hikes. You're more than a mile high here, so take it easy and give yourself frequent breaks to catch your breath.

Get to know the park's mountains by sight. The jagged peaks called **Langkofel** (Sassolungo, "Long Stone") and **Plattkofel** (Sasso Piatto, "Flat Stone") together form an "M" at the far end of the Alpe di Siusi—providing a storybook Dolomite backdrop. The dark, eerie saddle between them fires the imagination. To the right, and closer to Compatsch, the outcropping called the **Schlern** (Sciliar in Italian) is a long, flat ridge that ends in spooky crags boldly staring into the summer haze. The Schlern's Santner Peak, looking like a devilish *Winged Victory*, gave ancient peoples enough willies to spawn legends of supernatural forces. The Schlern witch, today's tourist-brochure mascot, was the cause of many a broom-riding medieval townswoman's fiery death.

Compatsch provides great views of the Schlern, but only a truncated look at Langkofel and Plattkofel. For better views, gain some altitude on a lift, or hop the bus (or hike) toward **Saltria**, at the far end of the Alpe di Siusi. (Because Saltria sits down in a val-ley, the views are even better from the road just above it, near the hut called Rauchhütte.)

GETTING THERE

By Car: The winding, six-mile road up to Compatsch starts be-tween Castelrotto and Seis/Siusi (at San Valentino). To keep the meadow serene, it's closed to cars during the day (9:00-17:00), unless you're staying in one of the hotels in the park. (The road is unblocked, but you'll likely be stopped by roving traffic moni-

DOLOMITES

Alpe di Siusi

Langkofel
10,436

Sella
10,341

PLATTKOFEL
9,695

Sella
Pass
7,349

To Cortina
d'Ampezzo

FLORIAN

Selva Gardena/
Wolkenstein

Monte
Pana

Saltria
5,544

Santa
Cristina

RAUCHHÜTTE

Ⓑ #11
Ⓑ #10 & 11

To
Seceda

SS-242

MONT
SÈUC

SONNE/
SOLE

ENGELRAST/
PUFLATSCH BERG
7,139

A l p e   d i

①

PANORAMA

PUFLATSCH

Compatsch
6,048

Ⓑ P
#10 & 11

HOTEL
SEELAUS

St. Ulrich/
Ortisei

ARNIKA
6,762

②

DIBAITA
6,952

HOTEL
SCHMUNG

P

Val Gardena
Grödnertal

MARINZEN
4,895

SP-64

Road closed
daily
9:00-17:00

CHECK-
POINT

MARINZEN

St.
Valentin

SP-64

To Ponte Gardena / Waidbruck,
& Autostrada A-22
Chiusa/Klausen
Exit

Castelrotto/
Kastelruth
3,475

Ⓑ
#3, 4,
10 & 170

SP-24

To A-22
Autostrada

● Town	•••• Chair Lift
════ Road	Gondola
---- Trail	▲ Mtn. Hut
	(Hütte/Rifugio)

Note: This 3-D view looks southeast & is not to scale. Elevations in feet

Marmolada
10,965

PLATTKOFEL
7,544

WILLIAMS
6,890

ZALLINGER
6,683

DIALER
KIRCHL
7,037

Tierser Alpl
8,006

MAHLKNECHT
6,739

Siusi

PANORAMA
6,600

SALTNER
Dairy Farm
"TSCHAPIT"
6,004

SCHLERNHAUS
7,544

Pez
8,400

SPITZBÜHL
6,348

Schlern

SPITZBÜHL

SEISER ALM BAHN
(CABINOVIA)

#3, 4 &
170 Ⓑ
Siusi/Seis
3,287

→ To A-22 Autostrada
Bolzano Nord
Exit

DOLOMITES

Hikes
❶ Compatsch to Rauschhütte (& Saltria)
❷ "Trail of the Witches"
❸ Panorama to Zallingerhütte & Florian Chairlift
❹ High Route to Zallingerhütte
❺ Schlern Summit

tors—be ready to show your hotel reservation confirmation.) But if you're an early riser, there's no reason not to drive up if you can arrive at the checkpoint before 9:00. (You can drive back down at any time.) Compatsch has a huge parking lot (€19/day—the same price as one round-trip cable-car ticket, so groups of at least two save by driving).

By Bus from Bolzano or Castelrotto to the Gondola near Seis/Siusi: Regular buses from Bolzano and Castelrotto link to the bottom of the gondola that whisks visitors from Seis/Siusi to the Alpe di Siusi. Buses #3 and #3a run from Castelrotto (4/hour July-Aug in morning and afternoon peak times, otherwise 2/hour; 10 minutes, €1.50 ticket valid for the whole day, use machine, if no machine pay driver, covered by Südtirol Guest Pass). Be sure to check your bus's direction before boarding (or ask the driver)—you want buses to the Seiser Alm Bahn. These buses stop directly at the gondola station. Some buses, including #170 to/from Bolzano (see page 201), stop on the main road just below the station—a steep five-minute hike up.

By Gondola from Seis/Siusi: The Seiser Alm Bahn gondola (in Italian, Cabinovia Alpe di Siusi) runs hikers and skiers up to Compatsch (mid-May-early Nov daily 8:00-18:00, mid-June-mid-Sept until 19:00, closed most of Nov and mid-April-late May, runs continuously during open hours, 15-minute ride to the top, €13.50 one-way, €20 round-trip, +39 0471 704 270, www.seiseralmbahn. it). You can reach the valley station either by car (free outdoor parking and pay garage parking) or by bus (see earlier). The lower cable-car station is a slick mini shopping mall, with lots of outdoor outfitters and a tempting local-products store.

By Bus from Castelrotto: Bus #10 runs from Castelrotto all the way to Compatsch. It costs the same as the more memorable—and environmentally friendly—gondola, takes the same amount of time, and runs less frequently. The only advantage to the bus: It runs in some shoulder season periods when the gondola doesn't, and in high season leaves Compatsch 10 minutes after the gondola stops running—useful if you're a little late getting back to Compatsch (9 buses/day mid-June-mid-Oct, 20 minutes, fewer mid-May-mid-June and late Oct, www.silbernagl.it). Round-trip gondola tickets aren't good on the bus (or vice versa). Note that the Südtirol Guest Pass does not cover this bus (or other buses that run above Seis/Siusi).

Transit Passes: For short-time visitors, most passes don't make sense. If you're here for three or more days, the Combi Card pass covering the Seiser Alm Bahn gondola and area buses can be worthwhile. Consider the Seiser Alm Card Gold pass only if you're staying for a week. Ask at a TI or your hotel for details.

Missed the Last Gondola Down? If you don't make the last gondola off the meadow, you can walk about 2.5 hours to Castel-rotto (via St. Valentin) or about 2 hours to Seis for buses to Bol-zano—or call a taxi (about €35 to Castelrotto; the "Hiking Area" map/brochure has numbers for taxi services—call one for the Seiser Alm).

GETTING AROUND THE ALPE DI SIUSI

For a helpful journey planner and downloadable timetables for buses, see Suedtirolmobil.info and Silbernagl.it. For gondolas, cable cars, and chairlifts, see SeiserAlm.it.

Shuttle Buses: The plateau is essentially car-free, except for guests staying at a few hotels inside the park. The #11 shuttle bus takes visitors to and from key points along the tiny road between Compatsch—the gateway to the Alpe di Siusi—and Saltria, at the foot of the postcard-dramatic Kofel/Sasso peaks and the base of the Florian lift (2-3/hour mid-June-mid-Oct, fewer mid-May-mid-June and in late Oct, runs about 8:30-18:40—but double-check before heading out, 15 minutes from Compatsch to Saltria, €2.50, not covered by Südtirol Guest Pass, buy ticket at vending machines at the station or pay driver, www.silbernagl.it). At the end of the day, buses back from Saltria can be jam-packed, and may be too full to pick up passengers between Saltria and Compatsch. Bus #14 serves some hotels on the meadow but isn't helpful for points in this chapter.

Gondolas and Chairlifts: Five upper lifts (marked on maps) are worth the €8-14 per ride to get you into the higher and more scenic hiking areas expeditiously (or back to the shuttle buses quickly). The Puflatsch lift takes credit cards, but as of my last visit, the others are cash only. Keep in mind that the upper lifts stop running fairly early (typically at about 17:00; the Seiser Alm Bahn gondola from Compatsch down into the valley runs until 18:00 most of the year—and until 19:00 in high season). Check schedules locally and plan your day accordingly.

Orientation to Compatsch

Compatsch (about 6,000 feet), at the entrance to Alpe di Siusi, isn't quite a "village," but rather a collection of hotels and visitor services. The upper station of the Seiser Alm Bahn gondola has WCs and a few shops and eateries, but most services cluster around a parking lot about five minutes away (including the TI, ATMs, restaurants, bike rental, small grocery store, and shops; from the top of the gondola, it's to the right).

Make a point to stop by the **Compatsch TI,** which sells maps and has the latest on snow conditions and trail openings. If consid-ering a demanding hike, review your plan here. If you're not sure where to start, let them suggest a day plan that takes into account your hiking ability, time constraints, and the weather (Mon-Sat 8:15-12:30, closed Sun, +39 0471 727 904, www.seiseralm.it).

HELPFUL HINTS

Trekking-Pole Rental: Most of the hikes here have at least some bits with uneven or gravely footing—poles can be nice to have along (rentals-€4-5/day, used poles often available to buy for about €15-20, at nearly every sport shop on either end of the Seiser Alm Bahn gondola).

Bike Rental: Two shops offer standard, performance, and e-bikes, along with helmets, maps, and trail advice, and have roughly similar prices (standard bike-€28-38/day; performance or e-bike-€48-62/day). **Sporthaus Fill** is by the cable-car station (+39 0471 729 063, www.sporthausfill.com) and **Sport Hans** is across from the parking lot (+39 0471 727 824, www.sporthans.com, Hans and son Samuel). There's a world of tiny paved and gravel lanes to pedal. Pick up a map of suggested routes and consider the ones I describe later. Rentable baby buggies are popular for those with toddlers.

Groceries: Onkel Eugen's, a tiny store across from the parking lot, has necessities (open early June-mid-Oct and Dec-Easter 9:00-17:30).

Horse-Drawn Carriage Rides: These are available next to the TI (May-Oct 9:00-16:00, €30 for 30 minutes in a one-horse carriage, price depends on size of carriage).

Activities in the Alpe di Siusi

HIKING

Easy meadow walks abound on the Alpe di Siusi, giving novice hikers classic Dolomite views from manicured trails. Experienced hikers should consider the tougher, more exciting treks. Before attempting a hike, call or stop by the TI to confirm lift schedules and check your understanding of the time and skills required. As always, when hiking in the mountains, assume weather can change quickly, and pack accordingly (wear good shoes and carry water and an extra layer).

Meadow walks, for flower lovers and strollers, are pretty—but for advanced hikers, they can be boring. Chairlifts are springboards for more dramatic and demanding hikes. Upper lifts generally close at 17:00.

Trails are very well marked with wooden signposts pointing to mountain huts (*Hütte* in German, *rifugi* in Italian), which offer food and, often, beds. The number on the arrow is the number of the trail; the number near the destination name is the approximate time in minutes. In theory, the trail numbers are keyed into local maps. In practice, trail numbers on signs don't always match the numbers shown on maps. Instead, navigate by knowing your huts, which are clearly labeled on all signage and maps. (When asked for directions, most locals will know the trail by the huts it connects rather than its number.) For simple hikes, you can basically string together three or four names off the free pictorial map in the "Hiking Area" brochure. For anything more serious, invest in a good 1:25,000 map from the TI. The Alpe di Siusi website (www. seiseralm.it) has more information (click on "Active/Summer/Hiking").

Low-Exertion Excursions: Besides hiking, there are fun ways to bask in the high-alpine beauty with minimum huffing and puffing. From the two lift stations near Compatsch you could ride the Puflatsch and/or Panorama lifts up on a round-trip ticket, look at the views, enjoy a restaurant meal or picnic at the top, and simply ride back down. You could also ride the #11 shuttle bus from Compatsch to Saltria (or walk there, described later) and take a round-trip ride on the Florian chairlift before riding back to Compatsch.

Shoulder-Season Strategies: The Seiser Alm Bahn gondola up to Compatsch starts running in mid-May, but upper lifts begin operating a few weeks later; there's a similar gap at the end of the season (mid-Oct-early Nov). But even during these shoulder seasons, the Alpe di Siusi can still be worth visiting (and busy with hikers) in good weather. Many of the hikes listed here are doable without a lift—but only if you're willing to hike to the trailhead (most realistic for the "Trail of the Witches" and the Panorama-to-Zallingerhütte route). Get local advice about snow levels and which hikes are possible. The simplest option is to hike trail #30 or ride bus #11 along the valley floor between Compatsch and Saltria, enjoying the views along the way.

Easy Hikes
▲Compatsch to Rauschhütte (and Saltria)
Bus #11 connects Compatsch to Saltria (at the far end of Alpe di Siusi, tucked under Langkofel and Plattkofel) in about 15 minutes—zipping past some impressive scenery en route. For a very easy, mostly level walk, follow this same route by foot, in about one hour one-way (returning on the bus) or 1.5 hours round-trip (using trail #30, which parallels the route). To begin, leave the top gon-

DOLOMITES

dola station via the stairs to the road that leads under the view terrace to the TI. From the TI, follow the road for a few minutes (with the gondola station behind and to your right) to the modern wood chapel, then follow signs pointing off the road to the #30 trail.

The last stretch—into Saltria—is steeply downhill and has less impressive views; consider going only as far as **Rauchhütte** (a charming old hut serving good food, spectacular views, closed Wed, www.rauchhuette.com), located where the road starts to switchback down. Bus #11 stops at various points along this route (including Rauchhütte and Ritschhütte)—making it easy to do as much or as little of this by foot as you like. (Saltria is not a good destination on its own: It's a steep walk below Rauchhütte and has hotels, trailheads, and a bus stop, but no shops.)

▲▲▲The "Trail of the Witches"

This three-hour loop trail—past the legendary stone "witches' benches" *(Hexenbänke)*—is popular with first-time visitors and can be crowded in peak season. You'll enjoy ever-changing views as you get a handy 360-degree panorama of the peaks and valleys that ring the Alpe di Siusi. It's mostly downhill, with a few brief uphill stretches.

From the top of the Seiser Alm Bahn gondola, ride the Puflatsch gondola (or chairlift, depending on weather) up to Puflatsch Berg (6,952 feet). A two-minute walk above the lift, an engraved map at the Engelrast ("Angel's Rest") observation point identifies the surrounding mountains. The counterclockwise hike follows *PU/Puflatsch* signs around the rim of the Puflatsch plateau. First you'll have Langkofel and Plattkofel on your right as you hike gently but steadily uphill. Eventually you'll hit a little cross overlooking the valley village of Ortisei/St. Ulrich (far below in Val Gardena), then hook left and trace the dramatic rim of the plateau. Soon tiny Castelrotto pops into view, then you'll pass Arnikahütte (with a café), and finally you'll head back toward the Schlern. At Arnika, you can either hike steeply back up to the Engelrast/Puflatsch Berg lift, or—better and easier—keep going downhill all the way into Compatsch, with fine valley views the entire time.

Note: If you're here when the upper lifts aren't running (or even in the early evening, assuming you're staying in Compatsch or have a car for returning to the valley after the main lift stops running), this is your most realistic and rewarding option. But be ready for a very steep 30-minute uphill hike to the top of the Puflatsch lift to begin the hike.

Top Alpe di Siusi Hikes at a Glance

Reminder: Unless you're sleeping up on the Alpe di Siusi/Seiser Alm, be sure to time your hikes with the gondola's last-ride-down time in mind (19:00 in mid-June-mid-Sept, otherwise 18:00).

▲▲▲"Trail of the Witches" Moderately easy.
Round-trip time from Compatsch: 3 hours, more with stop for lunch.
Lift: Puflatsch (one-way, up).
Notable huts: Engelrast, Arnika, Diabaita.
Add-on option: Panorama meadow stroll for different views.

▲▲▲Panorama to Zallingerhütte and Florian Lift
Moderately difficult.
Round-trip time from Compatsch: 5-6 hours, including a stop for lunch.
Lifts: Panorama up (or walk up), Florian down (last ride down at 17:00, or 17:30 mid-July-early Sept).
Notable huts: Almrosen, Mahlknecht, Zallinger, Williams.
Add-on options: Dialer Kirchl (20 minutes extra) or high-route option to the Florian lift via the Dialer. Kirchl and Plattkofelhütte (adds 2 hours and another notch in difficulty).

▲▲▲Schlern Summit Challenging.
Round-trip time from Compatsch: 8 hours, including a stop for lunch.
Lifts: Spitzbühl (round-trip; last ride down at 17:00).
Notable huts: Schlernhaus, Saltner.
Add-on options: Overnight in Schlernhaus or Tierserl Alpl hut (2 hours away, along the ridge).

▲▲Panorama Meadow Stroll Easy.
Round-trip time from Compatsch: 1 hour, or linger longer.
Lifts: Panorama round-trip (or walk up and/or down).
Notable huts: Panorama.
Add-on option: Skip lift down and/or up, or amble down from Panorama to Rauschhütte to take the road back to Compatsch on foot or by bus.

▲Compatsch to Rauchhütte Easy.
Round-trip time from Compatsch: 1.5 hours, 1 hour if returning by bus.
Lifts: None, but bus #11 lets you skip the walk back to Compatsch.
Notable huts: Ritsch, Rauch.
Add-on option: Continue down to Saltria to ride the Florian lift up to Williamshütte for close-up views of the Langkofel and Plattkofel.

DOLOMITES

Moderate Hikes
▲▲▲Panorama to Zallingerhütte and Florian Chairlift

This walk on well-marked trails is a great introduction to the Alpe di Siusi. While it starts and ends at about the same altitude, it includes plenty of ups and downs. It comes with fine vistas, changes of scenery (meadows, woods, and high valleys), fun stops along the way, and lifts up and down on each end. Though signs rate it at three hours without stops, allow five or six hours (including the lift from Compatsch, lift down to Saltria, and bus back to Compatsch) so you'll have time to dawdle, yodel, and eat.

Start by riding the Panorama chairlift from its base near Compatsch (the Panorama lift is on your right as you walk down the gravel path from the Seiser Alm Bahn's terrace). From the Panorama hut (6,600 feet), find the signpost pointing toward trail #2, and follow it across the meadow to the paved road, and then join trail #7. You'll pass the rustic Edelweisshütte (snacks only), and the Almrosenhütte (hot food); after about 1.5 hours total you'll reach the Mahlknechthütte (6,739 feet, hot food and plenty of outside seating).

From the Mahlknechthütte, you'll cross two streams (one on stepping stones, another by bridge). Shortly after the bridge, you hit the highest point of the walk, just below a small wooden church (Dialer Kirchl, 7,037 feet) that makes a good picnic spot. Continuing on trail #7 from just below the church, you'll go gently through woods, mostly downhill, for another hour and a quarter to Zallingerhütte (6,683 feet). From here it's a serious 10-minute climb to Williamshütte (6,890 feet, full restaurant), where you catch the Florian chairlift (€11.50 one-way) to Saltria and the shuttle-bus stop (return to Compatsch on bus #11).

High Route to Zallingerhütte: For a more thrilling, demanding version of the previous hike—longer by two hours—branch off at the wooden church (Dialer Kirchl) following trail #4B and then the high #4 ridge trail, with commanding views both left and right, to the Plattkofelhütte/Rifugio Sasso Piatto hut (7,544 feet, excellent lunches, +39 0462 601 721). Then descend steeply to Zallingerhütte and Williamshütte (6,890 feet). No special experience or gear is needed for this trail, and it richly rewards those who take it.

Serious hikers can hike a steep and satisfying hour from the Plattkofelhütte to the peak of the Plattkofel/Sasso Piatto.

Challenging Hikes
▲▲▲Schlern Summit

For a serious 12-mile hike—with a possible overnight in a traditional mountain refuge (generally open mid-June-Sept)—consider hiking to the summit of Schlern (Sciliar). This route, which takes about eight hours round-trip (including lunch) from Compatsch, is popular with hardy hikers; some call it the best hike in the region.

Start at the Spitzbühl chairlift, a 20-minute walk below Compatsch (5,659 feet, free parking, Castelrotto-Compatsch bus stops here), which brings you up to 6,348 feet. Trail #5 takes you through a high meadow, down to the Saltner dairy farm (6,004 feet—you want the Saltner dairy farm at Tschapit, not the one near Zallingerhütte), across a stream, and steeply up the Schlern mountain. About three hours into your hike, you'll meet trail #1 and walk across the rocky tabletop plateau of Schlern to the **Schlernhaus** mountain "hut," really a simple restaurant and 120-bed hostel (7,544 feet, called "Rifugio Bolzano" in Italian). From this dramatic setting, you can enjoy a meal and get a great view of the Rosengarten range. Hike 20 more minutes up the nearby peak (Monte Pez, 8,400 feet), where you'll find a lofty meadow, cows in the summer, and the region's ultimate 360-degree alpine panorama. Unless you're staying overnight, hike back the way you came.

Overnight Option: To do the Schlern summit hike as an overnight, either sleep at the ¢ **Schlernhaus** (bunks and private rooms, open early June-mid-Oct, coin-op shower, summer only +39 0471 612 024, off-season +39 0471 724 094, can reserve by email before hut opens in June, www.schlernhaus.it, info@schlernhaus.it) or walk two hours farther along the Schlern to the hut at ¢ **Tierser Alpl**, at 8,006 feet (bunks and private rooms, open June-late Oct, +39 0471 727 958, mobile +39 333 654 6865, www.tierseralpl.com, info@tierseralpl.com). From Tierser Alpl, you can descend to Saltria or Compatsch by any of several different scenic routes.

TRAIL RUNNING

The Running Park Seiser Alm includes 46 miles of signed running trails in the meadow. The clean air and high mountain altitude attract many international runners/masochists. During a one-day, scenic half-marathon on the first Sunday of July, they invite the public to run with them...or at least try. Contact the Compatsch TI for trail info and maps, or go to www.seiseralm.it and click on "Active/Summer/Running."

BIKING

Bikes are easy to rent (including electric ones—see "Helpful Hints," earlier), welcome on many lifts for free or a small fee, and permitted on many of the trails and lanes in Alpe di Siusi. The Compatsch TI has a good information flier that lists the best routes. You can also go to www.seiseralm.it and click on "Active/Summer/Biking." Get local advice to confirm difficulty levels and your plan before starting any ride; the TI hands out helpful bike-route cards. Those with a bike don't need to worry as much about lifts shutting down early.

For a fairly easy, 2.5-hour ride that gives you the same scenic thrills as the Panorama to Zallingerhütte and Florian Lift hike recommended earlier, try this: Start from Compatsch (6,048 feet), bike or ride the lift to Panorama (6,600 feet), and take road #7, which runs generally uphill to Goldknopf and then follows a series of hills and dips to Mahlknechthütte (6,739 feet). Then take road #8 downhill to Saltria (5,544 feet) and back to Compatsch (6,048 feet). About 60 percent is paved and 40 percent is gravel lanes.

More Sights in the Dolomites

▲▲▲Alpe di Seceda

In good weather, hiking among the serrated formations at Seceda is among the most dramatic experiences in the Dolomites. These are the striking peaks that you can see, from a distance, on some of the Alpe di Siusi's most impressive hikes.

From Castelrotto, it's a short ride on bus #172 (or a 20-minute drive) northeast, up the Val Gardena/Grödner Tal, to the town of Ortisei/St. Ulrich. From the Seceda parking garage at the top of town, cable cars whisk you up to the edge of a thrilling cliff with unforgettable ridge walks and jaw-dropping views. A ski area in winter, Seceda is a meadow in summer, with lots of enticing trails. The obvious, easy choice is to simply hike straight out along the ridge toward the otherworldly, dragon's-teeth peaks that jab sharply into the sky. From there, you can circle back to the cable car, or follow any of several scenic paths farther down into the meadow. (The rounded formations at Pieralongia are a satisfying extension.) As at the Alpe di Siusi, a variety of smaller lifts make it easier to traverse the meadow (and skip some demanding uphill stretches), so come up with a plan based on your time and stamina, and with an eye on when various lifts stop running. For details, see Seceda.it.

▲▲Mountain Drive from Venice to Bolzano

Between Venice and Bolzano, most drivers just take the expressway through Verona. But going across the mountains gives you the definitive Dolomite experience. You'll take the Venice-Belluno autostrada, then this route: Belluno-Cortina-Pordoi Pass-Val di Fassa-Bolzano (about 125 miles). If you aren't traveling in summer, check road conditions before you depart (call +39 0471 200 198, in Italian or German only).

▲▲Short Dolomite Loop Drive

You could spend a day from Bolzano or Castelrotto driving a loop over the scenic Sella Pass (Sellajoch, Passo di Sella)—it's about 70 miles on windy roads, so allow four hours. Note that on certain summer days, traffic on the pass may be limited to buses and bikes. Confirm the route is open to drivers by talking to a local TI or your hotelier before heading out.

Going clockwise, you drive first through a long valley, the Grödner Tal/Val Gardena, which is famous for its skiing and hiking resorts, traditional Ladin culture (notice the trilingual road signs), and woodcarvers (the woodcarving company ANRI is from the town of St. Cristina). You'll first reach the large town of Ortisei/St. Ulrich, with base stations for two different cable cars. One heads up to the Alpe di Siusi, and the other to Seceda (described earlier).

An hour beyond Ortisei/St. Ulrich, you'll reach Sella Pass (7,349 feet). After a series of tight hairpin turns a half-mile or so over the pass, you'll see some benches and cars. Pull over and watch the rock climbers. Over the pass is the town of Canazei, with nice ambience and altitude (4,642 feet).

If you'd like to take a ridge hike, hop the gondola that runs from Canazei to a hillside shelf called Pecol; from there a cable car runs up to Col dei Rossi Belvedere. From the top cable-car station you can hike the Viel del Pan trail past Rifugio Belvedere and Rifugio Fredarola along an easy but breathtaking ridge to Rifugio Viel del Pan. This three-hour round-trip hike has views of the highest mountain in the Dolomites—the Marmolada—and the Dolo-mighty Sella range.

From Canazei, you can either follow very twisty roads (via St. Zyprian and Tiers) back to Castelrotto, or take the easier and slightly faster route via Welschnofen and Birchabruck back to Bolzano and the main valley highway.

Bus Option: It's possible to experience the Sella Pass without a car by riding a bus from Castelrotto via Ortisei/St. Ulrich and Plan to the base of the Col dei Rossi cable car (about 2 hours one-way). Get details at the TI.

Brixen (Bressanone)

This charming small city (pop. 20,000), on the highway between Bolzano and Innsbruck, is a worthwhile pit stop (park at garage P2 and take the pedestrian underpass into the old town; the main square is a 5-minute stroll away). With an illustrious history of powerful bishops—and a sleepy present—Brixen feels like a charming, mini Bolzano with a bit more Germanic character. It has a sprawling, traffic-free old town; a big main square with two stately churches (connected by a fine cloister); arcaded shopping streets; and plenty of al fresco cafés and restaurants. Explore the lanes beyond the main square to find a beautiful waterside walking and biking path.

Near Brixen: More impressive than any sight in Brixen itself, the **Kloster Neustift** (Abbazia di Novacella)—just two miles north—is an Augustinian monastery complex that's open to the public. The centerpiece is a basilica with the region's most glorious Bavarian-style Baroque interior—slathered with decadent white and pink stucco, frilly curlicues, twisty columns, and pudgy winged babies everywhere. While a quick stroll through the grounds and a look at the church interior is plenty satisfying, you can also take a guided tour or try the monk-made wines in the *enoteca* (+39 0472 836 189, www.kloster-neustift.it).

▲Reifenstein Castle (Castel Tasso)

Reifenstein Castle, with one of my favorite castle interiors in Europe, is just off the highway at the town of Sterzing/Vipiteno.

While easy for drivers, it's not worth the trouble for those without wheels—it's unique and interesting but only open for a few tours a day. The castle is privately owned and has not been developed for tourism (no gift shop, no café—and no photos). Its layout and decor have changed little since the 15th century, when it passed into the hands of the Teutonic Knights. Since 1813, a branch of the noble Thurn and Taxis family has owned the castle. The current heads of the family have chosen to keep the castle just as it was when they spent summer vacations here in the 1940s as children. On your tour, you'll see most of the building, including bedrooms with original wall paneling and decorations, a real dungeon, wooden boxes knights slept in, and a medieval kitchen with a roof that is black with centuries of soot.

Cost and Hours: €8 for required downloadable audio tour; May-early Nov Sun-Fri 10:30-12:30 & 14:00-16:00, until 17:00

mid-July-early Sept, closed Sat year-round; +39 339 264 3752; www.sterzing-ratschings.com, choose "Activities/Sightseeing."

Getting There: By car, the castle is about 45 minutes from Bolzano, Castelrotto, and Innsbruck. Exit the Innsbruck-Bolzano expressway at Sterzing/Vipiteno (just on the Italian side of the Brenner Pass and Austrian/Italian border), and carefully follow brown *Reifenstein* signs. Park at the base of the castle's rock (in the spot right off the road from the bridge) and hike up the castle drive (10 minutes). Of the two castles here, Reifenstein is the one to the west of the expressway.

▲High-Alpine Route Between Como and the Dolomites

Between the Dolomites and Lake Como, the scenic high road (SS-38, via Meran and Bormio) is about 1.5 hours slower than the expressway through Verona. The high point is the incredible 9,045-foot Stelvio Pass (Passo dello Stelvio/Stilfser Joch), which makes the extra time worthwhile, at least for thrill-seeking drivers (the 48 hairpin curves on the Alto Adige side are not for the faint of heart). The pass is generally open June-October, but can close in bad weather (check road conditions before venturing out). The pass also closes to vehicles except bikes one Saturday in August or September. On the way, you can stop for a meal in the cute, untouristed little town of Glorenza/Glurns (45 minutes west of touristy Meran, www.glurns.eu). Glorenza/Glurns still lives within its square wall on the Adige River, with a church bell tower that has a thing about ringing, typical Tirolean arcaded streets, and real farms rather than tourist boutiques.

DOLOMITES

THE LAKES

Lake Como • Varenna • Bellagio • Lake Maggiore

Commune with nature where Italy is joined to the Alps, in the lovely Italian lakes district. In this land of lakes, the million-euro question is: Which one? For the best mix of accessibility, scenery, and offbeatness, Lake Como is my choice—and I stay in the village of Varenna. The town of Bellagio on the same lake is a good second choice. And Lake Maggiore is a suitable backup. Enjoying either place, you'll get a complete dose of Italian-lakes wonder and aristocratic old-days romance.

You could spend a busy day side-tripping from Milan (about one hour away by train) to either lake, do some island- and villa-hopping, and be home in time for dinner. But the lakes are an ideal place to slow down and take a break from your busy vacation. Settle in here, and bustling Milan doesn't even exist. Now it's your turn to be *chiuso per restauro* (closed for restoration). If relaxation's not on your agenda, the lakes shouldn't be either.

Lake Como

Lake Como (Lago di Como)—lined with elegant 19th-century villas, crowned by snowcapped mountains, and busy with boats carrying cars and passengers—is a good place to take a break from the intensity and turnstile culture of central Italy. It seems like half the travelers you'll meet have tossed their itineraries into the lake and are actually relaxing.

Lake Como is Milan's quick getaway, and the sleepy mid-lake village of Varenna is the handiest base of operations. With good

The Lakes

To Bern
To Luzern
To St. Moritz
To Pontresina
Chiavenna

SWITZERLAND

Domodossola
Locarno
Bellinzona

TICINO

Lake Maggiore

Lugano
Lake Como
Colico
To Tirano & St. Moritz

Menaggio
Varenna

Mt. Mottarone
Lake Lugano
Bellagio

See Central Lake Como detail map

Stresa

Orta
Arona
Como
Lecco

Lake Orta

LOMBARDY

Bergamo
To Brescia & Venice

PIEDMONT
Gallarate
Saronno

Malpensa
Monza
Orio al Serio

ITALY

To Turin
Novara

Milan
Linate
To Venice

Rail
High Speed Rail
Bus
Boat

To Genoa & Cinque Terre

15 Kilometers
15 Miles

To Florence

LAKES

connections to other mid-lake towns (and Milan), Varenna is my favorite home base for exploring the lake. While Varenna has a village vibe, beautiful Bellagio has earned its ritzy allure and feels a bit more like a resort. Menaggio has a fine town square and a youth hostel for budget travelers.

The hazy, lazy lake's only serious industry is tourism. In fact, every day lots of lakeside residents commute to work in Lugano, just across the border in Switzerland, for a good paycheck. The lake's isolation and flat economy have left it pretty much the way the 19th-century Romantic poets described it: heaven on earth.

PLANNING YOUR TIME

Even though there are no essential activities, plan for at least two nights so you'll have an uninterrupted day to see how slow you can get your pulse. Spend some time exploring your home base town, take my self-guided ferry tour to view the scenery (with visits to the lake's two main villas), and hop off the boat to poke around towns you're not staying in. With additional time, visit more lakeside villas or go for a hike.

Lake Como Boat Schedule Literacy

Boats
Traghetto/autotraghetto: Car and passenger ferry
Servizio rapido/SR: Hydrofoil (pricier, faster, enclosed)
Battello: Slow passenger-only boat going all the way to Como
Navetta: Shuttle serving mid-lake only

Schedules
Feriali/Fer.: Monday-Saturday
Festivi/Fest.: Sundays and holidays
Ogni giorno/Gior.: Daily
Partenze da: Departing from

Lake Como is also workable as a day trip from Milan. Take a morning train to Varenna, ride the boat to Lenno (and tour Villa Balbianello), then take a boat to Villa Carlotta to tour the gardens. From there, head either to Bellagio or back to Varenna to linger and explore (or, with more time and energy, see a little of both) before taking the train back to Milan from Varenna. Start early to pack everything in; otherwise, you'll have to be more selective (with time to see just one of the villas).

GETTING TO LAKE COMO

From any destination covered in this book, you'll reach Lake Como via Milan. The quickest, easiest, and cheapest way to get from Milan to any mid-lake town is to take the train to Varenna. From Varenna you can hop on a boat to Bellagio or Menaggio. Alternatively, you can go by train from Milan to the town of Como, switching there to a boat or bus.

By Train via Varenna: Trains leave Milano Centrale station for Varenna at :20 past most hours (1 hour direct). Leaving Milan, sit on the left for maximum lake-view beauty. Get off at Varenna-Esino-Perledo. (Train schedules list just Varenna or Varenna-Esino, but *Varenna-Esino-Perledo* is what you'll see at the platform.) Trains stop only briefly—be ready to hop out. The platform you'll step onto (with double yellow lines) is very narrow here.

By Train and Boat via Como: For a less convenient, slower, but more scenic trip, you can get to Varenna or Bellagio from Milan via the town of Como. Trains take you from Milano Centrale station to Como's main station, Como S. Giovanni (1-2/hour, 40 minutes). From the station in Como, it's a 10-minute walk to the dock, where you catch either the speedy hydrofoil or the leisurely *battello* (slow boat—great for enjoying the scenery) for the ride up the lake to Varenna, Bellagio, or Menaggio. Boats leave Como about every 2 hours (*battello:* €11.60, 2.5 hours, last departure

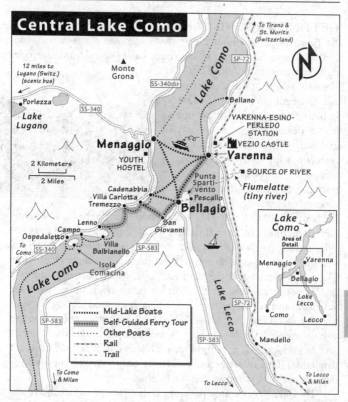

Central Lake Como

about 15:20; hydrofoil: €16.20, 1 hour, last departure about 19:00, fewer on Sun, www.navigazionelaghi.it). There are also buses from Como to Bellagio and Menaggio (see pages 250 and 262).

By Plane from Milan's Airports: Head first to Milan's Centrale train station, using the Malpensa Express train from Malpensa Airport, an airport express bus from Linate Airport, or any of the buses from Bergamo's Orio al Serio Airport (see "Milan Connections" at the end of the next chapter). Then transfer to a Varenna-bound train (see earlier).

By Taxi: Taxis between Varenna and Milan or its airports can be worth it for the convenience. **Marco Barili** (and his wife Nelly) don't charge extra for baggage or early/late departures (€170 for up to 4 people, €220 for 5-8 people in a minivan, +39 0341 815 061, +39 348 550 0787, taxi.varenna@tiscali.it).

By Car: Some of the expressways between Milan and the lakes have shifted to an automated toll system that takes a photo of each license plate and sends a bill to the owner. When picking up a rental car, check how this will be handled so that you don't get hit with late-payment fees (more info at http://apl.pedemontana.com).

GETTING AROUND LAKE COMO

By Boat: Boats go about every 30-45 minutes between Varenna, Bellagio, and Menaggio (€4.60/hop, cash only, 15-minute ride, daily approximately 7:00-22:30).

Because these mid-lake trips are frequent and the schedule is hard to read, I just show up, buy a ticket for the next boat, and wait. Always ask which slip *(pontile)* your boat will leave from—it's not posted, and each port has two docks, for car ferries and for passenger-only boats (boat info: +39 031 579 211, www.navigazionelaghi.it). On sunny days, long lines can form at ticket booths; don't dillydally, and consider buying your tickets in advance at a quieter time. The one-day €15 mid-lake pass makes sense if you take four or more rides—unlikely (pass does not cover fast hydrofoils, which cost a bit more).

If you're making more complex plans, pick up a free **boat schedule** and ask for help to decipher it. It's a good idea to ask your hotelier to review your possible connections before you set out so you can pace your day smartly. You'll find the schedule at hotels and boat docks. Confusingly, you have to check several different timetables (for car ferries and passenger-only boats) to know all the departures; for key terms, see the sidebar.

By Car: With scarce parking, traffic jams, and expensive car ferries, Lake Como is no place to drive. While it's possible to drive around the lake, it's not a scenic loop: The road is narrow, congested, and lined with privacy-seeking walls, hedges, and tall fences. If you do have a car, park it in Varenna's big underground garage, and use the boat to get around. Parking in Bellagio is more difficult than in Varenna.

While you can rent cars in Bellagio, for most travelers, it's best to take the train to Milan and pick up a car there, either at the central train station or at one of Milan's three airports.

Varenna

This well-manicured village of 800 people offers the best of all lake worlds. Easily accessible by train, on the less-driven side of the lake, Varenna has a romantic promenade, a tiny harbor, steep and narrow stepped lanes, and some scenic sights (a ruined castle and two villas). It's just the right place to savor a lakeside cappuccino or *aperitivo*. There's wonderfully little to do here, and it's very quiet at night...unless you're here during one of the hundred-or-so annual American wedding parties. The *passerella* (lakeside promenade, well lit and inviting after dark) is adorned with caryatid lovers pressing silently against each other in the shadows. Varenna is a popular destination with my readers and European vacationers—book well in advance for high season (May-Oct). From November to mid-March,

Varenna practically shuts down: Hotels close for the winter, and restaurants and shops reduce their hours.

Orientation to Varenna

TOURIST INFORMATION

The TI is near the **main square** (Wed-Mon 10:00-13:00 & 14:00-17:00, closed Tue, weekends only off-season, just past the bank at Via IV Novembre 7, +39 0341 830 367, www.varennaturismo.com). The Tivano travel agency, located in the **train station,** also operates as a TI (see "Helpful Hints"). At either (or your hotel), pick up a town map and lake info.

LAKES

ARRIVAL IN VARENNA

Varenna is small, and pretty much everything is within a 15-minute walk.

By Train: From Varenna's train station, follow the blue-painted pedestrian lane down to the main road. If you're heading for the ferry to Bellagio, go straight to the water and turn left; otherwise, turn left along Via Corrado Venini, the main road, and keep rolling uphill into town (a 15-minute walk from the station). If you have a bag with wheels, use the high road rather than the lakeside promenade, which ends in stairs and cobbles.

A **taxi** from the station costs about €10. Reliable Marco Barili (or his wife Nelly) can meet you at the train station if you know your exact arrival time. Look for a flashing sign with your name (+39 0341 815 061, +39 348 550 0787, taxi.varenna@tiscali.it).

By Boat: The boat docks are close to the train station and a 10-minute stroll north of Varenna's main square and old town.

By Car: Don't even try to park on the streets of Varenna; the few spots are mostly reserved for residents. The easiest parking option is the multilevel garage at the south end of town, across from the entrance to Villa Monastero (€2/hour, 6:00-22:00, otherwise €1/hour, €20/24 hours).

Parking at Varenna's train station is free overnight, but you'll

Varenna

VARENNA-ESINO-PERLEDO TRAIN STATION

To Tirano

I VIAGGI DEL TIVANO

Torento Esino

Steep Trail

Wooded

To Colico & 15

WALK BEGINS

(SP-72)

VIA PER VEZIO

BANK

VIA CORRADO VENINI (MAIN ROAD)

PASSARELLA STARTS

CAR FERRY DOCK

Lido (Beach)

WC

TICKETS

PASSENGER-ONLY BOAT DOCK

PASSERELLA

Lake

Passerella (Lakeside Promenade)

To Menaggio

To Bellagio & Como

LAKES

Accommodations
1 Hotel du Lac
2 Villa Cipressi
3 Hotel Royal Victoria & Barilott Bar
4 To Villa Monti
5 Albergo Milano, Casa Rossa & Ristorante la Vista
6 Albergo/Ristorante del Sole
7 Hotel Montecodeno
8 Albergo Beretta

Eateries & Other
9 Ristorante il Cavatappi
10 Osteria Quatro Pass
11 Varenna Monamour

pay from 8:00 to 23:00 most of the year (€1.70/hour, €15/day, use coins or credit card at machine in center of lot and put ticket on dashboard).

HELPFUL HINTS

Travel Agency: Varenna's travel agency, **I Viaggi del Tivano,** is conveniently located in the train station and acts as an informal TI (daily 9:30-13:00 & 14:00-18:30; good place to pick

⑫ Vecchia Varenna Ristorante

⑬ Ristorante al Prato

⑭ Varenna Caffè Bistrot, Bar il Molo & Nilus Bar

⑮ To Ristorante il Caminetto & Cooking Class

⑯ Pub l'Orso

⑰ Albergo/Ristorante Olivedo

⑱ Gelateria Riva & La Passerella

⑲ Café III Binario

⑳ Pizza e Sifizzi

㉑ Grocery (2)

㉒ Laundry (3)

up boat schedules, +39 0341 814 009, www.tivanotours.com, helpful Cristina, Martina, and Beatrice). They also offer baggage storage (€5/day).

Laundry: Lavanderia Pensa Barbara can wash and dry your laundry in 24 hours with morning drop-off (priced by weight, no self-service, Mon-Fri 9:00-12:00 & 15:00-19:00, Sat 9:00-12:00, closed Sun, Via Venini 31, +39 340 466 2977). A self-service machine is tucked in the back of the little "Il Bottaio" shopping gallery facing the old harbor (you'll pay for laundry plus a €1 entry voucher every time you go in/out, voucher covers WC or can be used toward food or drinks at nearby Bar il Molo, daily 8:00-24:00). Another self-service option is just off the main square, between the recommended Albergo del Sole and the post office ("change" machine dispenses only tokens, Bar Il Molo can break bills for you, daily 24 hours, Contrada del Prato 10).

Nightlife? None. Here your time is better spent taking a lakeside stroll and watching the moonlight dance on the water.

Varenna Walk

Since you came here to relax, this short self-guided walk gives you just the town basics.

• *Begin by standing in the little piazza next to the…*

Bridge Just Below Train Station: This main bridge spans the tiny Esino River, which divides two communities: Perledo (which sprawls up the hill—notice the church spire high above) and the old fishing town of Varenna (huddled around its harbor). The train station, called Varenna-Esino-Perledo, gives due respect to both, as well as to the village of Esino, eight miles higher in the hills.

Go down the tree-lined promenade on the right (north) side of the river. You'll run into the entrance to the town's public beach—the lido (small fee to enter)—and then cross the cute pedestrian bridge to the small square, which hosts a little market on Wednesday mornings.

The yellow inn facing the boat docks, Hotel Olivedo, has greeted ferry travelers since the late 19th century and is named for the olive groves you can see growing halfway up the hill. Locals claim this is the farthest north that olives grow in Europe.

• *Across from Hotel Olivedo is Varenna's…*

Ferry Landing: When the train came to Varenna in 1892, this dock became the main link to Milan and the world for the other "mid-lake" communities of Bellagio and Menaggio. From this viewpoint, you can almost see how Lake Como is shaped like a man. The head is the north end (to the right, up by the Swiss Alps). Varenna is the left hip (to the east). Menaggio, across the lake, is the right hip (to the west). And Bellagio (hiding behind the smaller wooded hill to your left) is the crotch—or, more poetically, Punta Spartivento ("Point That Divides the Wind"). In a more colorful description, a traditional poem says, "Lake Como is a man, with Colico the head, Lecco and Como the feet, and Bellagio the testicles." (In the regional dialect, this rhymes—ask a native to say it for you.)

Across the lake, the farthest high ridges mark the border of

Switzerland. This region's longtime poverty shaped the local character. Many still remember that the Varenna side of the lake was the poorest, because those on the Menaggio side controlled the lucrative cigarette-smuggling business over the Swiss border. Today, the entire region is thriving—thanks to tourism (and the many Italians who commute across the border to jobs in Switzerland).

• *Walk past the ferry dock and a small playground. Just beyond is Varenna's shoreline walk, called the...*

Passerella: A generation ago, Varenna built this elegant lakeside promenade, which connects the ferry docks with the old town

center. Strolling this lane, you'll come to a tiny, two-dinghy, concrete breakwater of a villa. Lake Como is lined with swanky 19th-century villas; their front doors face the lake to welcome visitors arriving by boat. At this point, the modern *passerella* cuts between this villa's water gate and its private harbor. Just around the bend, enjoy a good Varenna town view. These buildings are stringently protected by preservation laws; you can't even change the color of your villa's paint.

Just over the hump (which allows boats into a covered moorage), look back and up at another typical old villa—with a private *passerella*, a lovely veil of wisteria, and a prime lake-view terrace. Many of these villas are owned by the region's "impoverished nobility." Raised with no need to work, eventually they found themselves unable to pay for the upkeep of their sprawling houses. Some of these villas have now been bought by the region's nouveau riche.

• *At the community harbor, walk to the end of the pier for a town overview, then continue under the old-time arcades—with chestnut beams and a fishing heritage going back to the 1600s—toward the multihued homes facing the harbor.*

Varenna Harborfront: There are no streets in the old town—just the characteristic stepped lanes called *contrade*. Varenna was

originally a fishing community. Even today, old-timers enjoy Lake Como's counterpart to Norwegian lutefisk: *missoltino*, air-dried and salted lake "sardines."

Imagine this harbor 200 years ago: The Il Bottaio gallery is named for

LAKES

the coopers who once worked here fitting chestnut and oak staves into barrels. Stoneworkers were busy carving the black marble that was quarried just above town. Fishermen dragged boats onto the sloping beach and unloaded their goods onto carts for horses to carry up Contrada dei Cavalli (named for those horses, with gentler, more horse-friendly steps than other lanes) to the market square above. The little stone harbor dates from about 1600. Today, the fishing boats are just for recreation.

At the south end of the harbor, belly up to the banister of Bar il Molo's upper terrace for a colorful town view. Another traditional ditty goes, "If you love Lake Como, you know Bellagio is the pearl...but Varenna is the diamond."

• *Continue straight, leaving the harbor. A lane curves around Hotel du Lac, where you can check out its fine lakeside terrace (it welcomes even nonguests for drinks—try the afternoon happy hour—and has an amazing view). Then climb the stairs opposite the hotel on the lane called Contrada Oscura to...*

Piazza San Giorgio: Varenna's town square, historically the market square, faces what for centuries has been the lakeside highway. In earlier eras it was busy with traders and pilgrims.

The sycamore, or plane, trees, groomed to provide shade, are planted to make a V for Varenna. The street plan survives from Roman times, when gutters flowed down to the lake. The little church on the lake side of the square is the baptistery. Dating from the ninth century, it's one of the oldest churches on the lake (but rarely open).

The Hotel Royal Victoria, also on the main square, recalls the 1839 visit of Queen Victoria, who registered herself as the Countess of Clare in an attempt to remain anonymous.

Church of San Giorgio (Chiesa di San Giorgio): Varenna is an understandably popular spot for weddings—rice often litters the church's front pavement. The main church was built in the 1200s. Imagine being a 13th-century wayfarer and coming upon the fresco of St. Christopher, patron saint of travelers, on the church's facade. With a backpack at his feet, just like you, he welcomes all to step inside.

You'll find a Romanesque interior with a few humble, centuries-old bits of carving and frescoes. The black floor and chapels are made from local marble. On the right, a beautifully carved walnut confessional is ornamented with symbols reminding worshippers that in death, all are equal. And the fresco on the back wall, dating from the same century as Dante's *Inferno* (the 14th), makes the horrors of hell all too clear.

• *Leaving the church, turn left to find the TI and, in the same building, the Ornithology and Natural Science Museum, with a small collection of stuffed birds and other wildlife (small fee).*

Lake and Garden View from Villa Monastero: Finish your walk a hundred yards farther down the street (past the Villa Cipressi). Across from the big parking garage, step through the door of the Villa Monastero and up to the balcony overlooking the garden and the lake: Here you can savor an ultimate Lake Como view.

Lake Como is lined with aristocratic 19th-century villas. In the Romantic Age, a villa came with a charming lakeside kiosk and an extravagant garden. People loved exotic trees, and here—at the latitude of Boston—they could grow palms and oranges. A promenade through this mix of gardens and architecture was enjoyed as an art form.

Your tour is over, and now you have options. You can pay to explore the Villa Monastero gardens, or catch the steep trail nearby up to Vezio Castle (both described next). Or you can return to the square and head downhill to enjoy the Varenna waterfront. Either of the lanes flanking the Hotel Royal Victoria go down to the humble beach, and farther along, lanes go to the café-lined harborfront.

Sights and Activities in Varenna

▲Hike to Vezio Castle (Castello di Vezio)

A steep and stony trail leads to Varenna's ruined hilltop castle, located in the peaceful, traffic-free, one-chapel hamlet of Vezio. It was built on the remains of an ancient Roman fort that was part of a defense system spanning the entire lake. In the sixth century, after the fall of Rome, the barbarian Longobards settled here and needed a fortress on this strategic spot. Today, the castle itself is barren—a courtyard protecting an empty tower, where you can cross a drawbridge and climb 60 steps to earn 360 degrees of Lake Como panoramas.

Cost and Hours: €5, Mon-Fri 10:00-18:00, Sat-Sun until 19:00, June-Aug stays open one hour later, March and Oct closes one hour earlier, closed Nov-Feb and in bad weather, +39 333 448 5975, www.castellodivezio.it.

Visiting the Castle: To get to the castle, hike up Via per Vezio, the small road near Hotel Montecodeno (figure on a 30-minute steep climb one-way). Arriving in Vezio, follow *castello* signs. Beyond the church square you'll reach the castle and its bar (with drinks, light food, and WCs), which serves as the ticket desk.

Once inside the grounds, the views are the main attraction: Follow the little loop trail on the lake side of the castle for vistas down on Varenna's rooftops and the adjacent lakefront community of Pino.

Falconry Shows: The castle hosts low-key falconry shows (free, about an hour), usually around 14:00—but days and times vary, so check the website or call in the morning for times.

Hiking Back Down: Leaving the castle grounds you'll see a sign indicating two ways back to Varenna. You can hike back the way you came or make a loop by continuing down to the east end of Varenna, on a steeper, narrower, less-manicured trail. To do that, from the castle gate turn right and follow signs for *Varenna Scabium* and *Sentiero del Viandante.* You'll wander past some backyards and scenic tennis courts, then gradually descend, popping out at the parking garage for the Hotel Eremo Gaudio. From here, head down to the right to walk back into Varenna, passing the entrances for both Villa Cipressi and Villa Monastero on your way to the main square.

Villa Gardens

Two separate manicured lakeside gardens sit next door to each other just a short distance from Varenna's main square. While the villas and gardens elsewhere on the lake are more magnificent (see "More Sights on Lake Como," later), these are a good option if you're staying around Varenna.

Villa Cipressi: The small but lush terraces of Villa Cipressi stretch to the nearby Hotel Royal Victoria. The gardens were principally built between 1400 and 1800, and have been carefully restored and embellished. The lakeside climate is amenable to species not otherwise common in northern Italy. Look for agaves, myrtles, and a rare California cypress (€8, €15 combo-ticket includes Villa Monastero gardens but not museum, QR codes on trees and shrubs link to descriptions on website, daily 10:00-sunset, closed Nov-Feb, can close for private events—check website, www.hotelvillacipressi.it).

Villa Monastero: Just beyond Villa Cipressi are the more interesting grounds of Villa Monastero, which also admits visitors into the former residence of the De Marchi family. Now a museum filled with overly ornate furnishings from the late 1800s, it offers the handiest look inside one of the old villas that line the lakeshore. The gardens feature cypress and oak trees, several varieties of palms, a collection of English roses, a citrus garden, and a wisteria garden that is delightful when in bloom (gardens-€8, gardens and museum-€10; €15 combo-ticket covers gardens here and at Villa Cipressi but not museum; gardens open April-Sept daily 9:30-19:30, March and Oct 10:00-17:00, mostly closed Nov-Feb; museum open same times but shorter hours off-season; garden bar serves snacks, +39 0341 295 450, www.villamonastero.eu).

LAKES

Swimming

There are three spots to swim in Varenna: the free little beach behind the Hotel Royal Victoria off Piazza San Giorgio, the central lakefront area by Nilus Bar, and the lido (best-equipped for swimmers). Just north of the ferry dock, it's a wide concrete slab with sand and a swimming area off an old boat ramp. It has showers, bathrooms, a restaurant, a bar, and lounge chairs and umbrellas for rent (small entry fee, +39 0341 815 3700). Swimming by the ferry dock is strictly forbidden for safety reasons.

Boat Tours (or Rent Your Own)

You can explore the lake either by taking a boat tour with a captain who narrates the views as you skirt elegant villas and the homes of famous neighbors (1-3 hours, 6-10 people on a fast boat) or by renting your own boat (with a 40-hp engine, no license required). It's not realistic to stop anywhere, so you'll just putter around the mid-lake region trying to stay out of the ferry's path.

Taxi Boat Varenna organizes hour-long central-lake tours (€40/person), plus a 2.5-hour version that adds a stop at Villa Balbianello (€70/person, price includes villa entry and one-hour tour). They also offer hour-long romantic private tours (€220 for up to 6 people) and a three-hour tour. Book directly on the website (mid-March-mid-Nov only, +39 349 229 0953, www.taxiboatvarenna. com). A similar company works out of Bellagio.

Lake Como Boat, for those who want to be their own skipper, rents motorboats (from €80/hour, up to 6 people) and zero-horsepower kayaks (€10/hour). You'll find them at the harbor in front of the Bar il Molo (+39 342 997 1937, https://lakecomoboat.eu).

Varenna Rent a Boat is a more serious boat-rental shop with a fleet just beyond the ferry dock. Roberto's a mechanic, so you know things are in good shape, and his boats come with GPS systems, so he always knows where you are (from €80/hour, +39 338 140 7424, www.varennarentaboat.com).

Full-Day Boat and Villas Tour: Lake Como For You, run by Laura and her creative team, has a selection of guided activities. For a well-organized and very experiential day, consider their "Central Lake Boat, Food, and Villas Tour" (runs most mornings at 10:30 from Varenna). You'll load into a van to visit an old mill for an olive oil tasting, take a guided walk through Varenna with an included lunch, hop in a boat for an hour-long tour of the lake, see Villa Balbianello with a local guide, and finish in Bellagio with a walk through the botanical gardens at Villa Melzi. This leaves you in Bellagio at about 17:00, free for the evening and a convenient ferry ride away from your Varenna starting point (€255, RS%—use code "ricksteves," +39 349 560 0603, www.lakecomoforyou.com).

Hiking

Wayfarers' Path: The best three-hour hike from Varenna is along the Wayfarers' Path that links Bellano and Varenna. Take the train (or boat) to Bellano and hike steeply up and then along the hill and back into Varenna on the well-marked trail. (Get details from your hotel or the TI.)

Fiumelatte: The town of Fiumelatte, about a half-mile south of Varenna, was named for its "milky river." Promoted as the shortest river in Italy (at 800 feet), it runs—like the area's tourist industry—only from April through September (though even then it may be dry, depending on the weather). The *Sorgente del Fiumelatte* brochure, available at Varenna's TI, lays out a walk from Varenna to the Fiumelatte, then to a castle, and back. It's a 30-minute hike to the source *(sorgente)* of the river (at Varenna's monastery—take the high road, drop into the tranquil and evocative cemetery, and climb steps to the wooded trail leading to the peaceful and refreshing cave from which the river spouts).

Cooking Class

Charming chef Moreno of the recommended Ristorante il Caminetto picks you up in Varenna, zips you 10 minutes up the mountain to his restaurant, and then shows you some basics of Italian cooking. Gathered around a big table with a dozen or so other English-speaking travelers, you'll learn how to make fresh pasta and regional specialties. Demonstrations cover three recipes and last about five hours, including time to *mangiare* (€77 includes transfers from and back to Varenna, lesson, recipes, and lunch complete with wine, cookies, and coffee; Mon, Tue, Thu, and Fri; 10:00 pickup from Varenna ferry landing or parking garage, return by 16:00; reservations required—best by email, +39 0341 815 225, www.ilcaminettoonline.com, info@ilcaminettoonline.com).

Sleeping in Varenna

Reservations are tight in August, snug May through October, and wide open most of the rest of the year. Many places close in winter.

$$$$ Hotel du Lac, filling a refined and modernized 19th-century villa, is classy and dignified. From its exclusive private perch on the point, it offers a quiet lakefront breakfast terrace; genteel public spaces; a friendly, professional staff; and 16 delightful rooms—all but three with lake views (air-con, some rooms with elevator access, pay parking, Via del Prestino 11, +39 0341 830 238, www.albergodulac.com, info@albergodulac.com, Valeria).

$$$$ Villa Cipressi is a sprawling, centuries-old lakeside mansion with 31 rooms (some in a courtyard annex) that have a sophisticated simplicity. The villa sits in a huge, quiet, terraced garden that nonguests pay to see. Its elegant but understated public spaces are often busy with wedding parties. Guests can use their free shuttle service to and from the train station or ferry dock between 9:00 and 16:00 (RS%, some view rooms, family rooms, streetside rooms can be noisy, air-con, elevator in main building, pay parking, Via IV Novembre 22, +39 0341 830 113, www.hotelvillacipressi.it, info@hotelvillacipressi.it).

$$$$ Hotel Royal Victoria, a central splurge facing the main square, has a classic, grand-hotel lobby, an inviting terrace with a swimming pool just above the lake, two restaurants, and 43 richly furnished rooms with modern amenities (RS%, some view rooms, air-con, elevator, pay parking, Piazza San Giorgio 2, +39 0341 815 111, www.royalvictoria.com, info@royalvictoria.com).

$$$$ Villa Monti has six apartments (most with lake views, two with balconies) perched along Via Roma. Each is styled with a modern coziness, sleek kitchenette, and beautiful artwork. The pool is petite but has impeccable views and lots of deck chairs along a terraced garden (family rooms, air-con, no breakfast, check-in 14:00-18:00 or by appointment, Via Roma 9, tel. 0341 831 138, www.visitvarenna.com, villamonti@visitvarenna.com).

$$$$ Albergo Milano, right in the old town, is graciously run by Egidio and his Swiss wife, Bettina. Fusing the best of Italy with the best of Switzerland, this well-run, romantic hotel has eight comfortable rooms with extravagant views, balconies, and big terraces (air-con and/or ceiling fans, no elevator; from the station, take main road to town and turn right at steep alley where sidewalk and guardrail break; Via XX Settembre 35, +39 0341 830 298, www.varenna.net, reservations@varenna.net). This place whispers *luna di miele*—honeymoon (see website for honeymoon deal). Nearby is **$$$ Casa Rossa,** an annex with five comfortable rooms (breakfast served at main hotel); they also have apartments that work well for families in Villa Gina, near the train station. Their recommended Ristorante la Vista is worth considering for dinner.

$$$ Albergo del Sole rents eight simple, comfortable rooms (with partial-lake or piazza views) above a restaurant right on the town square, which can be lively at night. It's run by fun-loving Francesco and Gaetano (family rooms, air-con, hardwood floors, shiny bathrooms, elevator, Piazza San Giorgio 17, +39 0341 157 0408, www.solevarenna.altervista.org, albergo.sole@virgilio.it).

$$ Hotel Montecodeno, with 11 decent rooms and no views, is a functional concrete box along the main road, next to the northern trailhead to Vezio Castle. It's a five-minute walk from the train station and ferries (RS%, air-con, no elevator, attached restaurant, Via Venini 146, +39 0341 830 123, +39 331 640 0473, www.hotelmontecodeno.com, info@hotelmontecodeno.com).

$$ Albergo Beretta, on the main road a block below the station, has 10 small, basic rooms, several with balconies (and street noise). Second-floor rooms are quietest. Above a coffee shop that doubles as the reception, it feels dated and lacks lakeside glamour but is a decent budget option (elevator, pay parking nearby, Via per Esino 1, +39 0341 830 132, www.albergo-beretta.hoteldirect. it, hotelberetta@iol.it, Barbara).

Eating in Varenna

Lavarello, a lake whitefish, is popular on menus. For something more adventurous, consider *missoltino,* which are salted little fish often served with pasta or local-style polenta (buckwheat is mixed in with the corn). *Pizzocchere* is a regional pasta dish made with buckwheat noodles, boiled potatoes, greens, and lots of melty cheese—a carb lover's dream. As with Varenna's hotels, many of these restaurants close off-season.

FINE DINING

$$$ Ristorante la Vista, at Albergo Milano, feels like a private hotel restaurant but also welcomes nonguests. On a balmy evening, its terrace overlooking the town and the lake is hard to beat. Egidio (or Egi—pronounced "edgy") and his staff give traditional cuisine a creative twist, and his selection is great for foodies with discerning tastes. While you can order à la carte, I'd go with his €45 three-course fixed-price dinner (Mon and Wed-Sun 19:00-22:00, closed Tue; serves lunch on summer weekends; reservations required, Via XX Settembre 35, +39 0341 830 298, www.varenna.net).

$$ Ristorante il Cavatappi serves honest, unpretentious dishes grounded in classic Italian cuisine. It's a classy little place on a quiet lane, with only seven tables, so the cook-and-waiter team can connect personally with diners. It's both elegant and intimate with tight and convivial seating under a single vault and three tables outside on the stony lane. The chef is vegetarian, so there's always a good veggie course (lunch Thu-Sun 12:00-14:00, dinner Thu-Tue 18:30-21:00, closed Wed and Dec-Feb, reserve for dinner, Via XX Settembre 10, +39 0341 815 349, www.cavatappivarenna.it).

$$$ Osteria Quatro Pass is a welcoming bistro known for its homemade pasta, lake fish, and meat. It offers 20 candlelit tables under picturesque vaults, plus sidewalk seating. Its fun energy lets you know that it's a popular spot (daily 12:00-14:00 & 18:30-22:00, closed Mon-Wed in winter, Via XX Settembre 20, +39 0341 815 091, Chiara serves while her husband Giuseppe cooks).

$$ Varenna Monamour's split-level interior, done up with stone and beams, feels sleek but casual. Its menu has a nouvelle-cuisine flair, and the restaurant prides itself on specializing not in lake fish but in seafood (Wed-Mon 12:00-14:30 & 18:00-22:00, closed Tue and mid-Nov-Feb, Contrada Scoscesa 7, +39 0341 814 016, www.varennamonamour.it).

$$ Vecchia Varenna Ristorante, the only classy restaurant right on the water, is under the old stone arcade in the center of town. Its creative menu offers a fine value, and the food seems to taste even better if you sit on the terrace. Chef Luca takes no reservations (Tue-Sun 12:30-14:00 & 19:30-21:30, closed Mon, Contrada Scoscesa 14, +39 0341 830 793).

$$$ Ristorante al Prato, tucked onto a quiet square a block off the harbor, does regional specialties and international dishes with local ingredients and influences. Chef Giulio's joy of cooking shows through in the meals, and good-natured owner Giovanni enjoys interacting with the guests (daily 12:00-14:00 & 19:00-21:00, Piazza del Prato 6, +39 348 712 4389).

FAST FOOD WITH A LAKE VIEW

Beautifully situated along the waterfront in Varenna's old section are three simple eateries: **Varenna Caffè Bistrot, Bar il Molo,** and **Nilus Bar.** All are crowd-pleasers for their great lakefront seating and ideal for lingering over affordable food in a stunning setting. Each serves salads, sandwiches, pizzas, and pastas for around €10 and cocktails between meals. All are open daily; Il Molo and Varenna Caffè Bistrot are also open at 9:00 for breakfast. While Il Molo and Nilus have nicer terraces, the food at Varenna Caffè Bistrot is a bit more serious.

EATING SIMPLY WITHOUT A LAKE VIEW

$$ Ristorante del Sole is an old-school place facing the town square that feels like it was here before tourism. It serves respectable, well-priced meals and Neapolitan-style pizzas. This family-friendly restaurant provides a fun atmosphere, a cozy, walled-in garden in back, and tables on the square. Try their hearty *pizzoc-chere*—buckwheat pasta with melted cheese, potatoes, and greens (daily 12:00-22:00, takes afternoon break off-season, Piazza San Giorgio 17, +39 0341 815 218, www.solevarenna.altervista.org; Francesco and Gaetano).

$ Barilott is a bar/tobacco shop that's also a lively place for breakfast, a *panino*, or a glass of wine (daily 7:00-20:00, next to Hotel Royal Victoria at Via IV Novembre 6, +39 0341 815 045, Claudia and Fabrizio).

High Above Town: $$$ Ristorante il Caminetto is a homey, backwoods mountain trattoria in Gittana, a tiny town in the hills above Varenna. Getting there entails a curvy 10-minute drive (they'll pick you up for free at 19:00 or 19:30 at the ferry dock or the parking garage and bring you home after dinner). Moreno and Rossella take pride in their specialties, including grilled meats

LAKES

and risotto with porcini mushrooms and apples. They serve 22 diners a night and that's it. Plan on the €32 three-course fixed-price meal and spending the evening—you won't regret it (open Thu-Tue 19:30-21:30, Sat-Sun also 12:30-14:30, closed Wed, reservations mandatory to confirm pickup from Varenna—best by email, Viale Progresso 4, +39 0341 815 225, www.ilcaminettoonline.com, info@ilcaminettoonline.com).

OTHER EATERIES

By the Ferry Dock: $$ Pub l'Orso, filling a renovated former joiner's workshop, is a fun bar that serves cheap salads and sandwiches (at the ferry dock, behind Hotel Olivedo). **$$$ Hotel Olivedo,** a fine old hotel facing the ferry dock, serves diners in a classic Grand Tour hall.

At the Train Station: $ Café III Binario is both charming and classy, offering fresh salads, homemade pizza, sandwiches, pasta, pastries, and €8-10 set breakfasts. Enjoy your food on their terrace or take it to go (daily 6:00-21:00).

Takeaway Pizza: $ Pizza e Sfizzi, just off the main square, dishes up straightforward pizzas, and burgers too (Via Venini 7).

Gelato: Side-by-side places by the ferry dock compete with good gelato and pillows on the adjacent stone steps. At **Gelateria Riva,** Duilio prepares his gelato fresh every day. Try his *nocciola* (hazelnut) before making your choice (daily 11:00-19:00, later in summer). A few doors down, Giulia at **La Passerella** makes tasty gelato and refreshing fruit sorbets. Also on the menu is an enticing array of pastries and sweets (daily 10:00-20:00, later in summer).

Scenic *Aperitivo*: The Hotel du Lac has the most beautiful lakeside setting in town. Anyone is welcome to enjoy its garden or terrace, which literally hangs over the lake, for a happy hour *aperitivo* (daily 15:00-19:00). A €10 *spritz* or glass of wine comes with a plate of meat and cheese. They also have wine tasting on the menu.

Picnics: A few mom-and-pop stores around the main square have all you need for a tasty balcony or breakwater picnic. The *salumeria* sells meat and cheese, and makes sandwiches; try their homemade salami (Tue-Sat 8:30-12:30 & 16:00-19:00, Sun-Mon 8:30-12:30 only, longer in summer, Via IV Novembre 2). The **grocery store** just north of the main square, by the pharmacy, stocks fresh fruits, veggies, and a few essentials (Tue-Sat 8:30-19:00, Sun-Mon until 12:30, shorter hours off-season, Via Venini 6). There's also a **bakery** at Via IV Novembre 4.

Breakfast in Varenna: For a leisurely start to your day on the lakefront, Varenna Caffè Bistrot and Bar il Molo each have a breakfast menu. (They get up and running at about 9:00.) Hotel Royal Victoria offers a buffet breakfast with eye-popping views to nonguests for about €20 (check with reception that morning for

availability). If you're catching an early train, Café III Binario offers a good breakfast right at the station. To feel as though you're
staying in a boutique guesthouse (with an amazing view terrace
overlooking the lake), break your fast at Albergo Milano, which
offers visitors the same fine breakfast it serves its guests (€15, you
must reserve the night before).

Varenna Connections

BY TRAIN

Confirm train times at the station or at Trenitalia.com. Tickets for
most destinations are easily purchased with the Trenitalia app. At
the station, you can buy tickets for regional destinations (as far as
Milan) from a machine. For Milan, it will ask you to choose between two routes—you can select the default. Stamp your ticket in
the yellow machine at the station before boarding.

The I Viaggi del Tivano travel agency at the station can offer
a helping hand and also sells tickets for anything more distant (see
"Helpful Hints," above). Don't cut it too close, in case there's a line.

Varenna to Milan: Trains from Varenna to Milano Centrale
take about an hour and leave at :35 past most hours.

Varenna to Stresa (on Lake Maggiore): You'll have to take the
train back to Milano Centrale, then connect from there to Stresa
(3-4 hours).

Varenna to Lugano (Switzerland): Catch the ferry to Menaggio and then the #C12 bus (about hourly, 1 hour, €7, www.
asfautolinee.it). From the Menaggio ferry dock, the nearest #C12
bus stop is 5 minutes away at Via Como 9—or walk 10 minutes
north to Piazza Roma, where the bus originates (buy tickets at
newsstands, bus terminal, or with a small surcharge from drivers).

Varenna to St. Moritz (Switzerland): Take the train from Varenna to Tirano (1.5 hours), where you'll change to the train over
the scenic Bernina Pass to St. Moritz (another 2.5 hours, 5 connec-
tions/day). A slightly quicker, but less dramatic route is to take the
train to Chiavenna (changing in Colico), then transfer to a bus over
the Maloja Pass to St. Moritz (5-6/day, 3.5 hours total). For times,
see www.sbb.ch; for tickets, stop by the I Viaggi del Tivano travel
agency (see "Helpful Hints," earlier). With an early start, you can
make St. Moritz a day trip, going out via Tirano and back via Chiavenna. For more about St. Moritz and the Bernina Pass, consider
my guidebook *Rick Steves Switzerland*.

Bellagio

The self-proclaimed "Pearl of the Lake" is a classy combination of tidiness and Old World elegance. If you don't mind that "tramp in a palace" feeling, it's a fine place to shop for ties and umbrellas while surrounding yourself with the more adventurous posh travelers. Heavy curtains between the harborfront arcades create welcome shade and keep visitors and their poodles from sweating. Thriving yet still cute, Bellagio is a much more substantial town than Varenna.

Orientation to Bellagio

TOURIST INFORMATION

The TI is at the top of town, on the square by the church (daily 9:30-17:00, shorter hours Nov-March, Piazza della Chiesa 14, +39 031 951 555, www.bellagiolakecomo.com). The TI has free brochures for several walking tours, varying from one to three hours. They also hand out a map that shows hikes with a range of difficulty and duration.

ARRIVAL IN BELLAGIO

By Boat: Frequent ferries sail to Bellagio from Varenna, Como, and other points along the lake. Bellagio has two docks a couple hundred yards apart. One serves passenger-only boats (along the Como-Colico route); the other is for car ferries from Varenna, Menaggio, and Cadenabbia. When you depart, be sure you're at the right dock—ask when you buy your ticket. For details on boat schedules, see "Getting Around Lake Como" near the beginning of this chapter.

By Car: You can drive to Bellagio via Como or Lecco, or bring your wheels over on one of the ferries, but having a car here makes little sense. The center of town is a no-traffic "ZTL" zone from 10:00 to 18:30, and parking on the perimeter is difficult. Look for pay-to-park spaces marked with blue lines (use pay-and-display machines—€1.50/hour 8:00-23:00, free overnight). There's a large lot on Via Valassina, near the town cemetery, a 10-minute walk above the car ferry dock.

By Bus: Hourly buses from Como use a stop near the car ferry dock (drivers sell tickets).

Bellagio

Accommodations

1. Hotel Florence
2. Hotel/Rist./Snack Bar Metropole
3. Hotel Bellagio
4. Hotel Centrale
5. Il Borgo Apartments

Eateries & Other

6. The Florence Ristorante
7. Trattoria San Giacomo
8. Bilacus Ristorante & Aperitivo Et Al
9. Ristorante Terrazza Barchetta & Ristorante Formi e Gusto
10. La Fontana Ristorante Pizzeria & Antichi Sapori
11. To Alle Darsene di Loppia
12. To La Punta Ristorante
13. Torre del Borgo
14. Vecchio Borgo
15. Daisy's Bar
16. Enoteca Cava Turacciolo
17. Gelateria del Borgo
18. Grocery
19. Launderette
20. Bellagio Water Limousines
21. To Bellagio Water Sports

LAKES

HELPFUL HINTS

Laundry: La Lavandera is handy (open 24 hours, Salita Carlo Grandi 21, +39 031 952 092). You can pass the time at the fun Angelo DiVino wine bar across the way.

Music Festival: The Bellagio and Lake Como Festival, with orchestral, chamber music, and jazz performances around the Lake Como area, takes place every summer (www.bellagiofestival.com).

Sights and Activities in Bellagio

Strolling

Bellagio was built below a medieval fortress that capped its hill (today's Villa Serbelloni Park). The town's chic image was stoked by the Rockefellers (who purchased Villa Serbelloni in 1927) and by John F. Kennedy (who visited in 1961).

The harborfront is mostly fancy shops and cafés designed for visitors. Café Rossi, with a 1905 interior, faces the ferry dock. While Johnnie Walker and jewelry sell best at lake level, the natives shop up the hill.

Explore the steep-stepped lanes rising from the harborfront. Piazza della Chiesa, near the top of town, has an 11th-century church that's worth a look. It's dedicated to Saint James and has a dark, typically Romanesque interior with small windows, a marble pulpit carved with symbols of the four evangelists, and a golden altarpiece under glittering mosaics (pick up the English handout that describes its art).

North of Town: The de facto capital of the mid-lake region, Bellagio is located where the two legs of the lake split off to the south. For an easy break in a park with a great view, wander right on out to the crotch. Meander behind the rich-and-famous Hotel Villa Serbelloni, and walk 10 minutes up a concrete alley to **Punta Spartivento** ("Point That Divides the Wind"). You'll pop out to find a Renoir atmosphere complete with an inviting bar-restaurant (see "Eating in Bellagio," later), a tiny harbor, and a chance to sit on a park bench and gaze north past Menaggio, Varenna, and the end of the lake to the Swiss Alps.

South of Town: For another stroll, head south from the car-ferry dock down the tree-shaded promenade. Ten minutes later, you'll pass the town's "beach." The Lido di Bellagio is actually a terrace with sand and rentable lounge chairs, a youthful cocktail bar, a concrete pool, and a swimming platform in the lake. Just beyond the lido is **Villa Melzi Gardens** (€8, daily 10:00-19:00, www.giardinidivillamelzi.it). While the villa is not open to the public, the gardens are. Visitors enjoy a long and lovely lakeside promenade with exotic plants, flowers, and trees (all labeled—pick up the botanical guide at the entry) and Neoclassical sculpture that was assembled by the vice president of Napoleon's Italian Republic in the early 19th century. Although not as elaborate as some of the lake's finer gardens, it offers a pleasant, tree-shaded lakefront stroll. Gaze across the lake at the Villa Carlotta (straight over, surrounded by greenery—described later, under "More Sights on Lake Como") and imagine the time when aristocrats tried to outdo each other (and showcase their wealth) by creating unique and immense horticulture collections.

At the far end of the garden you can exit at the tiny harbor of Loppia, where you'll be tempted by the recommended Alle Darsene di Loppia restaurant. About 15 minutes farther south, you'll reach San Giovanni, with a pebbly public beach (no showers).

Villa Serbelloni Park

This park (accessible only with guided tour) overlooks the town. The villa itself, owned by the Rockefeller Foundation, is not open to the public. The gardens sprawl over 50 acres, covering nearly all of Bellagio's promontory.

Cost and Hours: €10, required 90-minute tour Tue-Sun at 11:00 and 15:30; no tours Mon, Nov-mid-March, or when rainy; first two-thirds of walk is uphill, show up at the TI (in the medieval tower on Piazza della Chiesa) 15 minutes before tour time to buy tickets, confirm time with TI, +39 031 951 555, www.bellagiolakecomo.com.

Boating and Water Sports

Bellagio Water Limousines, with a small stand adjacent to the slow boat/hydrofoil dock, is run by Australian Jennine and Italian Luca, who offer tours and private service in their shiny mahogany Venetian water taxi. Consider their one-hour mid-lake tour (€50, most days) or their 2.5-hour mid-lake tour with a stop at Villa del Balbianello (€72, RS%, check blackboard for day's offerings or call +39 338 524 4914, www.bellagiowaterlimousines.com, bellagiowaterlimousines@gmail.com).

Bellagio Water Sports is where Michele offers 90-minute kayaking tours (€64-70, RS%, most days at 9:00 and 11:30, weather dependent). He's a 15-minute hike over a hill and down on Pescallo Bay near Hotel la Pergola at Via Sfondrati 1, +39 340 394 9375, www.bellagiowatersports.com, info@bellagiowatersports.com).

Sleeping in Bellagio

This is a "boom or bust" lake resort, with high-season prices straight through from May to September, plus a brief shoulder season (with discounted prices) in April and from October to November. Bellagio closes down almost completely from December to February and is only half-open in March.

$$$$ Hotel Florence has a prime lakefront setting in the center of town. The 160-year-old place, run by the German Ketzlar family, features 30 rooms, hardwood floors, bold earth tones with splashes of bright colors, and a rich touch of Old World elegance (RS%, some rooms with view and balcony, air-con, elevator, Piazza Mazzini 46, +39 031 950 342, www.hotelflorencebellagio.it, info@ hotelflorencebellagio.it).

$$$$ Hotel Metropole, dominating Bellagio's waterfront between the ferry docks, is a grand old place with plush public spaces. Its tranquil rooms have classic flair and all the comforts. All 42 rooms have lake views, either side or full (family rooms, air-con, elevator, enormous roof terrace, Piazza Mazzini 1, +39 031 950 409, www.albergometropole.it, info@albergometropole.it).

$$$ Hotel Bellagio is stylish but unpretentious, with 28 airy rooms and parquet floors (some with balconies, most with views). The rooftop deck has sun chairs, and the basement gym is small but mighty (air-con, elevator, pay parking, Salita Grandi 6, +39 031 952 202, www.hotelbellagio.it, info@hotelbellagio.it).

$$$ Hotel Centrale, managed with pride and care by Giacomo Borelli, warmly welcomes its guests into a true-blue family operation: Signore Borelli's two sons help out, his mama painted the art, and grandpa crafted much of the Art Deco-era furniture. Look for old family photos near the stairwell. The 17 bright, comfortable rooms lack views, but the public spaces are generous, including the balcony terrace (air-con, elevator, Salita Plinio 7, +39 031 951 940, www.hc-bellagio.com, info@hc-bellagio.com).

$$ Il Borgo Apartments offers seven efficient, spacious units in the old center. Equipped with kitchenettes, these are a great deal for families or small groups. Easygoing Flavio and son David are available for check-in daily 13:00-16:00 or by appointment (RS%, no breakfast, air-con, elevator, Salita Plinio 4, +39 338 193 5559, www.borgoresidence.it, info@borgoresidence.it).

Eating in Bellagio

As with Bellagio's hotels, many of these restaurants close off-season (generally December through February or March). Two places associated with hotels serve food on the lakefront in the town center (the Florence and Hotel Metropole's Terrazzo Ristorante). The service won't make you smile, and the price will dent your wallet. But the setting will be unforgettable. Rather than eat on the lakefront, I'd hang out there with a drink and find a better-value restaurant at a higher altitude.

IN THE OLD TOWN, WITHOUT LAKE VIEWS

$$ Trattoria San Giacomo is a high-energy place with traditional North Italian cuisine, such as *riso e filetto di pesce* (rice and perch fillet in butter and sage), and seasonal specials. It offers fun seating on a steep, cobbled lane or tight seating inside (Wed-Mon 12:00-14:30 & 19:00-21:30, closed Tue, Salita Serbelloni 45, +39 031 950 329, www.trattoriabellagio.it).

$$ Bilacus Ristorante, across the street, has a brighter, more open dining room, a fine garden terrace, an emphasis on wine (including some top-quality vintages by the glass), and a menu of traditional Italian dishes (Tue-Sun 12:00-14:30 & 19:00-21:30, closed Mon, Salita Serbelloni 32, +39 031 950 480, www.bilacusbellagio.it). Aurelio is happy to give those with this book a complimentary vin santo and biscotti for dessert.

$$$ Ristorante Terrazza Barchetta, set on a terrace with no lake view and bedecked with summery colors, puts a creative twist on regional favorites such as lake fish, but is a little pricey (Wed-Sun 12:00-14:30 & 19:00-22:15, closed Tue, Salita Mella 13, +39 031 951 389, www.ristorantebarchetta.com). Its simpler and less-expensive sister, Ristoro Formi e Gusto, is downstairs (described next).

$$ Ristorante Formi e Gusto serves quality, fairly priced pizza and pasta, with simple indoor and outdoor seating (daily 12:00-22:30, Salita Mella 13, +39 031 951 389).

$$ La Fontana Ristorante Pizzeria, near the top of the old center, serves classic Italian dishes at tight interior tables and on a nice terrace (go up Salita Monastero to Via Centrale 7, +39 031 950 283).

$$ Antichi Sapori, next door, is another good alternative—a favorite for salads, pizza, and pasta with a warm and cozy interior and a fine terrace (daily 11:30-22:00, Via Centrale 5, +39 031 950 431, Julia and Nico).

GOURMET SPLURGE SOUTH OF TOWN

$$$$ Alle Darsene di Loppia, the kind of place you'd expect jetsetters to dress up for, is a romantic gourmet restaurant serving beautifully presented Mediterranean cuisine. Consider their seared scallops and their tasting menu. It's a 15-minute walk south of town (through the exquisite Villa Melzi Gardens—worth paying for if dining here to avoid the walk along the street). While seating indoors is OK, dining out on a historic little harbor under their

LAKES

pergolato is more memorable (Tue-Sun 12:00-14:30 & 19:00-21:30, closed Mon, on the far side of the Villa Melzi Gardens at Via Melzi D'Eril in Loppia, +39 031 952 069, www.ristorantedarsenediloppia. com).

OTHER OPTIONS

Dining North of Town: $$ La Punta Ristorante is a good bet for a lakeside meal a 10-minute walk north at the dramatic Punta Spartivento. Set in a peaceful park, this family-run, white-table-cloth place has reasonable prices and very fresh fish (daily 12:00-22:00, +39 031 951 888, www.ristorantelapunta.it).

Breakfast: If your hotel or B&B doesn't provide breakfast, several cafés clustered near Piazza della Chiesa offer either full breakfast menus or à la carte options at tourist pricing: Pick from Torre del Borgo, Vecchio Borgo, and Daisy's Bar.

Wine Tasting: $$ Enoteca Cava Turacciolo is a classy-for-a-troll vaulted stone cellar wine bar. This fun-loving place run by Norberto and Rosy is great for a last drink before catching your ferry, or a simple meat-cheese-wine meal. They offer my readers a €19 taste of three regional wines with a sampling of cheeses, meats, and breads (Thu-Tue 11:00-24:00, closed Wed, Salita Genazzini 3, +39 031 950 975, www.cavaturacciolo.it).

$$$ Aperitivo Et Al, slick and jazzy, is a trendier wine bar; it also offers mixed *salumi* and *formaggi* plates and light lunches paired with the right wine. Alessandro serves a great selection of wines by the glass (daily 11:00-24:00, Salita Serbelloni 34, +39 031 951 523).

Gelato: It's easy to find a cone or sundae at places along the waterfront, but residents agree that these aren't the best *gelaterie* in town. Instead, climb up a couple of blocks to **Gelateria del Borgo** near the church (daily 10:00-22:00, Via Garibaldi 46, +39 031 950 755, Stefania and Gianfranco).

Picnics: You'll find benches at the park, along the waterfront in town, lining the promenade south of town, and a 10-minute walk north in the lovely park at the tip of the peninsula (Punta Spartivento). **Butti Macelleria e Salumeria,** on the upper street near Gelateria del Borgo, makes sandwiches and sells a few pre-pared foods (daily 8:00-19:00, closed Mon off-season, Via Garibaldi 42, +39 031 950 333).

More Sights on Lake Como

For the best one-day look at Lake Como, take my self-guided ferry tour to get your bearings, and hop off at the towns and villas of your choice. The two main villas worth considering (described after the tour) are Villa Carlotta—with a sterile, museum-like interior and gorgeous, sprawling gardens—and Villa del Balbianello, a bit harder to reach but with a more striking setting, gardens that are more architectural than botanical, and a fascinating tour of the lived-in interior. If you have time, visit both—they're complementary. In this section, I also describe two other lake towns—Menaggio and Como—plus how to side-trip to Lugano in Switzerland.

▲▲Self-Guided Ferry Tour

The best simple day out is to take the *battello navetta* (slow passenger ferry) on the 50-minute run from Varenna-Bellagio-Villa Carlotta-Tremezzo-Lenno

(€9.20 without stops, or buy the €15 one-day pass and make it hop-on, hop-off; departs Varenna about hourly starting at 9:20, confirm times locally; for more information, see page 234). Then come back the same way, hopping off at any sights that interest you: Lenno (to see Villa del Balbianello), Villa Carlotta, and/or Bellagio. This commentary describes what you'll see along the way, leaving from Varenna, though it's doable from Bellagio too.

Leaving Varenna: Looking back at Varenna from the lake, you'll see Vezio Castle rising above the town, with new Varenna on the left (bigger buildings and modern ferry dock) and old Varenna on the right (tighter, more colorful buildings). The big development

high on the hillside is an ugly example of cronyism (without the mayor involved, this would never have happened). Under the castle is a grove of olives—reputedly the northernmost ones grown in Italy. Because the lake is protected from the north wind, exotic flowers grow well in the lake's many fine gardens.

To the right of Varenna's castle are the town cemetery, a lift up to Hotel Eremo Gaudio (a former hermitage), and a spurt of water gushing out of the mountain just above lake level. This is the tiny Fiumelatte, Italy's shortest river.

• *On your way across to Bellagio, take a look around.*

Mid-Lake: The Swiss Alps rise to the north. Directly across the lake from Varenna is Menaggio, and just over the ridge from there is Lugano and the "Swiss Riviera." The winds alternate between north and south. In preindustrial times, traders harnessed the wind to sail up and down the lake. Notice the V-shaped, fjord-like terrain. Lake Como is glacier-cut. And, at more than 1,200 feet deep, it's one of Europe's deepest lakes. You'll cruise past the Punta Spartivento, the bulbous point that literally "splits the wind" and where the two "legs" of the lake join (Lake Lecco is on the left/east, and Lake Como on the right).

• *Before long, you'll be...*

Approaching Bellagio: Survey the park at Punta Spartiven-to—it's a pleasant walk from town. Bellagio has three times the number of hotel rooms as Va-renna, as you can see upon approach. The town, with its strip of swanky hotels, is bookended by Grand Hotel Villa Serbelloni (five stars) on the left, dominating the lakefront, and the sprawling Grand Hotel Bretagne (four stars) on the right. In the 19th century, aristocratic Rus-

sians hung out in the Serbelloni, and well-heeled English chose the Bretagne. These days, the Serbelloni is the second-most luxurious hotel on the lake after Villa d'Este, while Bretagne is mired in a long renovation project.

• *Leaving Bellagio, you'll pass Villa Melzi and its gardens, then the tiny harbor at Loppia. About half the boats make a stop at **San Giovanni**, a small, nondescript lakefront community just down the shore from Bellagio. Whether your boat stops here or not, soon you'll head across the lake for a stop at...*

Villa Carlotta: Because of lake taxes and high maintenance costs, owners of once-elite villas have been forced to turn them into hotels or to open their doors to the paying public. Since 1927, this has been an example of the latter. One of the finest properties on the lake, Villa Carlotta has some good Neoclassical sculpture (including works by Canova) and one of the lake's lushest gardens (see listing below).

• *The shortest hop on this route (you could walk it in less than 10 minutes) takes you along to the town of...*

Tremezzo: As you leave the dock at Villa Carlotta, notice the Grand Hotel Tremezzo, with its striking Liberty Style (Art Nouveau) facade and swimming pool floating on the lake. Above the town is a villa built in the 19th-century Romantic Age to resemble a medieval castle (next to the stub of a real one).

After the Tremezzo stop—and just before the Tremezzo church—you'll see a public park with a fountain and balustrade. When the road separated this land from its villa, its owners gave it to the community. Here the lake is dotted by a string of old villas with elegant landings and gated boathouses. Built in the days before motors, they are now too small for most modern lake boats.

Lenno: This pleasant resort town has a long, arcing bay sheltering lots of little docks, and a generously shaded promenade.

It's decision time: To see the recommended Villa del Balbianello, hop off here and turn to the next page. Return boats depart hourly; check the schedule before you set off. This is the end of the line for some boats, which turn around here and head back the way you came—on these, if you don't plan to see the villa, you can just stay put. Other boats continue south to Como, and you'll need to get off and wait for the next return boat.

▲Villa Carlotta

This is the best of Lake Como's famed villas for flower gardens—especially in spring, when the many camellias, azaleas, and rhododendrons are in bloom. For gardeners, it's worth ▲▲▲. I see the lakes as a break from Italy's art, but if you need a culture fix, Villa Carlotta also offers an elegant Neoclassical interior with a sculpture gallery, including works by Antonio Canova.

Cost and Hours: €12 includes villa/museum and gardens, daily 9:00-19:00, last ticket sold at 18:00, museum closes at 18:30, closed Nov-mid-March, +39 034 440 405, www.villacarlotta.it.

Getting There: Villa Carlotta, at the southern end of the town of Tremezzo, has its own dock (served by the slow *battello* passenger boats). It's also less than a 10-minute walk from the more frequently served Tremezzo and Cadenabbia docks. You can also use bus #C10 to zip along the lakefront; it stops here on its way between Como and Menaggio (1-2/hour, pay driver, www.asfautolinee.it, bus stop to the right as you exit Villa Carlotta).

Visiting the Villa: When buying your ticket, pick up the map that identifies the rooms in the house and the major plant groups in the gardens. Inside, there's a café and a designated picnic area.

From the entrance, hike up the grand staircase and enter the **villa** itself. The main floor is filled with Neoclassical sculpture, including Antonio Canova's *Maddalena Penitente* and *Palamede* and works by his students (look for the impressive replica of Canova's famous *Love and Psyche Reclining*). There are also pieces by the great Danish sculptor Bertel Thorvaldsen. On the next floor up are generally well-presented special exhibits, and on the top floor are painstakingly appointed period rooms with elegant Empire Style (early 19th-century French) furniture.

Then explore the main attraction, the **gardens,** which sprawl in both directions from the villa. To the south (toward Tremezzo) is the classical Old Garden. To the north, things get more interesting: pretty camellias, luscious azaleas, a maze of rhododendrons, a bamboo garden, and the gasp-worthy Valley of the Ferns—a lush jungle gorge with a river coursing through it.

▲▲Villa del Balbianello

The dreamiest villa on the lake perches on a romantic promontory near Lenno, overlooking Lake Como and facing Bellagio. Built at the end of the 18th century on the remains of an old Franciscan church, today the villa reflects the exotic vision of its last owner, explorer and mountaineer Guido Monzino, who died in 1988— leaving his villa and everything in it to the state. It's well worth paying extra to tour the interior to get to know Monzino, who

led the first Italian expedition to climb Mount Everest in 1973. But the real masterpiece here is the terraced garden and elegant loggia, where the land fits the architecture and landscaping in a lovely way.

Cost and Hours: Garden only–€11, garden with villa tour–€22, Thu-Sun and Tue 10:00-18:00, closed Mon and Wed and mid-Nov-mid-March, last entry to garden one hour before closing, +39 034 456 110, www.visitfai.it.

Tours: The only way inside the villa is with an English tour. Limited to 15 people per tour, these depart at least hourly (more frequently with demand); the first tour is usually at 11:00 and the last at 16:30.

Getting There: It's at the end of a hilly point next to the town of Lenno. From the Lenno ferry dock, turn left and stroll around to the far end of the harbor (about 10 minutes). Here, you can either pay for a **speedboat shuttle** (+39 333 410 3854, www.taxiboat.net) or carry on by foot. If you choose to **walk,** continue past the boat dock and through the gate marked *Villa Balbianello,* where two options are clearly signposted in kilometers: a 20-minute, 1-kilometer (half-mile) hike (including some up and down), or a more challenging 45-minute, 2.5-kilometer (about 1 mile) huff over the top.

Visiting the Villa: Your visit includes two parts: the villa and the gardens. If walking from the boat and back (taking the shorter 20-minute path), allow a leisurely three hours total for the walk and garden/villa visit.

Poke around the **gardens** while waiting for your villa tour to begin. On the Bellagio-facing side, you'll find a tranquil terrace with sweeping lake views. Along the path, notice the circular stone shed. Originally used for refrigeration (they used ice

from the mountains to keep things cool), today this shed houses the tomb of Guido Monzino. On the opposite side of the point, you'll find a terrace in front of the original Franciscan church (now a gift shop selling overpriced drinks). A WC is nearby, and just down the steps is the dock for the speedboat return to Lenno.

The 50-minute tour of the **villa** is as fascinating as its larger-than-life former owner. You'll tour the loggia (with a library and a study), then spend the rest of the time seeing 18 of the main building's 25 rooms. While finely decorated, these feel cozy, lived-in, and not too extravagant. Each one gives you a bit more insight into Monzino—from his personal living quarters, to his extensive collection of prehistoric artifacts from around the world, to the top-floor museum of his expeditions, with memorabilia from his North Pole and Mount Everest adventures. You'll see secret passages, learn why his furniture came with handles, and find out what's hiding behind the faux bookcase.

Menaggio

Menaggio—the third of the "big three" mid-lake towns (along with Varenna and Bellagio)—has a little more urban bulk than its

neighbors. Budget travelers stay in the youth hostel here, and day visitors are charmed by Menaggio's lovely main square and lakefront park. Since many find Lake Como too dirty for swimming, consider spending time in Menaggio's outdoor public pool

(look for the *lido*). Several good hikes start here, too. (Just a few decades ago, cigarette smugglers used these trails at night to sneak back into Italy from Switzerland with their tax-free booty.) The **TI** (and its website) has detailed suggestions for walkers and mountain bikers (Piazza Garibaldi 3, +39 034 432 924, www.menaggio.com).

Sleeping in Menaggio: ¢ **La Primula Youth Hostel** is a classic, old-school hostel, offering sailing lessons, Italian-language courses, cooking classes, kayak and bike rentals, and a great location on the lake, a two-minute walk south of the ferry dock (Via IV Novembre 106, +39 034 432 356, www.lakecomohostel.com, info@ lakecomohostel.com).

Menaggio Connections: Both car ferries and passenger-only boats connect Menaggio frequently to Varenna and Bellagio. Bus #C10 also runs along the lakeshore here (1-2/hour, pay driver), linking Menaggio to Villa Carlotta and Villa del Balbianiello, and to **Como town** in about an hour. Menaggio is also a springboard for visiting Switzerland—remember to bring your passport. Bus #C12 goes to **Lugano** (€7, nearly hourly, 1 hour, www.asfautolinee. it). In summer, the yellow Palm Express bus runs once daily to **St. Moritz** (2.5 hours, reservations required, www.postauto.ch).

Make sure to check which of the several bus stops in Menaggio your bus leaves from. Near the ferry dock, Como- and villa-bound #C10 buses stop at the Hotel Menaggio stop, while the #C12 Lugano bus stops at Via Como 9. You can also catch these buses at their terminus, the bus garage at Piazza Roma. The Palm Express departs from yet another stop at Hotel Bellavista, near Piazza Garibaldi.

Como Town

On the southwest tip of the lake, Como has a good, traffic-free old town, an interesting Gothic/Renaissance cathedral, a cable car up to a mountaintop viewpoint, and a pleasant lakefront with a promenade (TI at Via Giocondo Albertolli 7, +39 031 269 712, www.lakecomo.is). It's an easy 10-minute walk from the boat dock to the train station (trains to Milan depart about twice per hour, 40 minutes). For details on boats connecting Como to Bellagio and Varenna, see page 234.

All-Day Lugano Side Trip

From Varenna or Bellagio, you can make a loop that lets you nip into Switzerland to see the elegant lake resort of Lugano, pass through the town of Como, and cruise a good part of Lake Como. Here's a good day plan (times are approximate—confirm schedules locally): about 9:30—ferry to Menaggio (15 minutes from Varenna); 10:30—bus to Lugano (1 hour, bring your passport); 11:30—explore Lugano; 16:00—train to Como (45 minutes); 17:00/18:00/19:00—fast hydrofoil from Como to Varenna (1 hour). For more information on Lugano, see www.ricksteves.com/lugano.

Lake Maggiore

Lake Maggiore is ringed by mountains, snowcapped in spring and fall, and lined with resort towns such as Stresa. Although Lake Maggiore lacks the cozy charm of Lake Como, it does have a fun sight—three little islands, two with exotic gardens and lovely villas built by the Borromeo family.

Through many generations since 1630, the Borromeos lovingly turned their islands into magical retreats, with elaborate villas and fragrant gardens. Isola Bella has a palace and terraced garden; Isola Madre has a villa and a more casual English-style garden. The Borromeos, who made their money from trade and banking, enjoyed the arts—from paintings (hung in lavish abundance throughout the palace and villa) to plays (performed in an open-air theater on Isola Bella) and marionette shows (you'll see the puppets that once performed here).

The third island, Isola Superiore (a.k.a. Isola dei Pescatori), is small, serene, and residential. The town of Stresa, a characterless resort, is the departure point for exploring all three of Lake Maggiore's garden islands.

Tourists flock here in May and June, when flowers are in bloom, and in September. Concerts held in scenic settings draw music lovers, particularly during the summer Stresa Festival (www.stresafestival.eu). For fewer crowds, visit in April, July, August (when Italians prefer the Mediterranean beaches), or October. In winter, the snow-covered mountains (with resorts a 1.5-hour drive away) attract skiers.

PLANNING YOUR TIME

This region is best visited on a sunny day, when the mountains are clear, the lake is calm, and the heat of the sun brings out the scent of the blossoms. The two top islands for sightseeing are Isola Bella and Isola Madre (if tight on time, focus on Isola Bella). Isola Superiore has no sights but is a peaceful place for lunch. You can stay the night in Stresa, but a day trip is sufficient for most. My suggested plan: Walk from the Stresa train station 10 minutes downhill to the boat dock, and catch a boat to Isola Madre. Work your way back to Isola Superiore for a lazy lunch, and then go on to Isola Bella for the afternoon, before returning to Stresa and back to Milan.

Day Trip from Milan: Catch a one-hour, early regional train from Milan to the town of Stresa. These generally leave Milano Centrale station at 7:25, 8:25, and 9:25. (There is also an express at 8:20; it saves 10 minutes but costs twice as much.)

GETTING TO THE ISLANDS

Boats link the islands to Stresa, running about twice hourly (Stresa to Isola Bella, 10 minutes; Isola Superiore, 15 minutes; Isola Madre, 40 minutes). *Important:* Buy boat tickets at the ticket window in the gallery of the yellow dock building (with the arches), signposted *Navigazione Lago Maggiore*. Don't be fooled by private taxi-boat drivers, dressed in sailor outfits, who may accost you on the promenade or in front of a booth labeled *Biglietteria*. They'll try to talk you into paying way too much for private tours on their smaller boats.

For maximum flexibility, buy a **"free circulation" ticket,** which allows you to get off at multiple stops of your choice (€10.70 includes Bella and Superiore, €13.70 Bella and Madre, €18.40 all three islands, €22.20 for the islands and Villa Taranto). Just going to Isola Bella costs €7.30 round-trip. A visitor tax of €0.50 per island is included in the price you pay, but not in the prices posted at the window.

Boats run daily April through September, starting at 7:00 (8:15 on Sun). The map on page 265 shows most of the route: Stresa, Carciano/Lido (most boats skip this stop), Isola Bella, and Isola Superiore. From Isola Superiore, boats continue to Baveno (another lakeside town), Isola Madre, and then across the lake to Pallanza and Villa Taranto. Off-season, the boats cover a shorter route (boat info: +39 0322 233 200, www.navigazionelaghi.it).

STRESA

The town of Stresa—which means "thin stretch"—was named for the original strip of fishermen's huts that lined the shore. Today, grand old hotels run along that same shore. Don't linger in Stresa—it's just a functional springboard for the islands and gardens.

Arrival in Stresa: Upon arrival in Stresa, jot down your return options (regional trains to Milano Centrale leave every two hours until about 21:00). To get downtown, exit right from the station and take your first left (by the underpass, on Viale Duchessa di Genova). This takes you straight down to the lake; once you're there, the boat dock is about four blocks to your right along the promenade. At the dock, the helpful **TI** is in the same arched building as the ticket window (TI daily 10:00-12:30 & 14:30-18:30, Nov-mid-March closed Sat afternoon and all day Sun, Piazza Marconi 16, +39 032 331 308, www.stresaturismo.it). Taxis charge a fixed rate of €11 from the station to the dock.

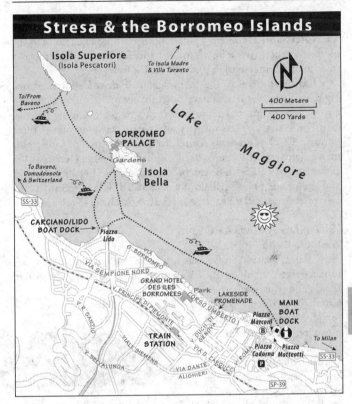

Stresa & the Borromeo Islands

Visiting Stresa: The **old town**—basically a traffic-free touristy shopping mall—is just a few blocks deep, stretching inland from the main boat dock. Stresa's stately 19th-century lakeside hotels date back to the days when this town was on the Grand Tour circuit.

In any Romantic Age resort like Stresa, hotels had names designed to appeal to Victorian aristocrats...like Regina Palace (rather than Palazzo), Astoria, Bristol, and Victoria.

The **Grand Hotel des Iles Borromées** was the first (built in 1862). In 1918, 19-year-old Ernest Hemingway—wounded in Slovenia while driving an ambulance for the Italian Red Cross—was taken to this hotel, which served, like its regal neighbors, as an infirmary during World War I. Hemingway returned to the same hotel in 1948, stayed in the same room (#205, now called the "Hemingway suite"—you can stay there for a couple thousand dollars a night), and signed the guest book as "an old client." Another "old client" was Winston Churchill, who honeymooned here.

Sleeping in Stresa: I prefer to stay in other towns, but Stresa has a few options: **$$$ Hotel Milan** Speranza au Lac is a big, group-oriented hotel facing the boat dock (www.milansperanza.it); **$$ Hotel Saini Meublè** is a small, homey, affordable choice in the old town center (www.hotelsaini.it); and **$$ Hotel Moderno** is a midsize, midrange option in the old town (www.hms.it).

Eating in Stresa: The main square, Piazza Cadorna, is one big tourist trap, yet it does have a certain charm. (At night, it seems anyone who claims to be a musician can get a gig singing for diners.) For a (slightly) less touristy alternative, seek out one of these options: **$$ Osteria degli Amici,** tucked away under a vine trellis on a quieter square a couple of blocks beyond Piazza Cadorna (Via Bolongaro 31); **$$$ La Botte,** off the main street between the port and the square (Via Garibaldi 8); or **$$$$ Il Clandestino,** a fancier, romantic, modern splurge specializing in fish (Via Rosmini 5).

ISLANDS AND GARDENS
▲▲Isola Bella

This island, nearest Stresa, has a formal garden and a fancy Baroque palace. Looking like a stepped pyramid from the water, the island was named by Charles Borromeo (sponsor of Milan's Duomo) for his wife, Isabella. The island itself is touristy, with a gauntlet of souvenir stands and a corral of restaurants. A few back streets provide

evidence that people actually live here. While the Borromeo family now lives in Milan, they spend a few weeks on Isola Bella each summer (when their blue-and-red family flag flies from the top of the garden). There's no entry fee to just disembark at the island, but there's not much to do aside from visiting the palace and garden.

Cost and Hours: Palace and garden—€20, €28 combo-ticket includes Isola Madre, daily 10:00-18:30, Oct until 18:00, mid-March-mid-April open Fri-Sun only, closed Nov-mid-March, last entry one hour before closing, +39 0323 933 478, www.isoleborromee.it.

Tours: A fine €4 audioguide describes the palace, which also has posted English descriptions. A €1.50 booklet explains the gardens.

Eating: Several restaurants cluster between the boat docks and the villa. Picnicking is not allowed in the garden, but you can picnic in the pebbly park at the point of the island, beyond the villa (free and open to the public).

Visiting the Island: There are two docks on this island, one for each direction, with a WC nearby. It's just a few steps from the boat to the hulking villa (turn left from the dock). Once inside,

LAKES

your visit is a one-way tour, starting with the palace and finishing with the garden. (There's no way to see the garden without the palace.)

In the lavishly decorated Baroque **palace,** stairs lead up under stucco crests of Italy's top families (balls signify the Medici, bees mean the Barberini, and a unicorn symbolizes the Borromeos' motto: Humility). You'll loop through the picture gallery, containing 130 beautifully restored 16th-century paintings from the Borromeo family's private collection, hung wall-to-ceiling in several cramped rooms. Then you'll get a peek at the canopied bedchambers and ogle the ornate throne room. Continue through the dining room, with a portrait of the first Borromeo, and into a richly stuccoed grand hall, with an 80-foot-high dome and featuring an 18th-century model of the villa, including a grand water entry that never materialized.

Next comes the music room, the site of the 1935 Stresa Conference, in which Mussolini met with British and French diplomats in a united attempt to scare Germany out of starting World War II. Look for a copy of the treaty with Mussolini's signature on the wall next to the exit. Unfortunately, the "Stresa Front" soon fizzled, when Mussolini attacked Ethiopia and joined forces with Hitler.

Napoleon's bedroom comes with an engraving that depicts his 1797 visit (Napoleon is on a bench with his wife and sister enjoying festivities in his honor). Continue through several more opulent halls, many of which display souvenirs and gifts that the Borromeo family picked up over the generations.

Downstairs, many of the famous Borromeo marionettes are on display. (A larger collection is on Isola Madre.) The 18th-century, multiroom grotto, decorated from ceiling to floor with shell motifs and black-and-white stones, still serves its original function of providing a cool refuge from Italy's heat. The dreamy marble statues are by Gaetano Monti, a student of Antonio Canova. Climbing out of the basement, look up at the unique, cantilevered, spiral stairs; they're from a 16th-century fortress that predates this building.

Pass through the mirrored corridor and follow the route through more rooms until you come to the ornate hall of 16th-century Flemish tapestries. This leads to the finale of this island visit: the beautiful **garden,** complete with Chinese white peacocks, which give it an exotic splash. (Before continuing to the garden, consider heading up the stairs near the WC to stroll through Elisa's Greenhouse, named for Napoleon's sister and home to tropical plants.)

From the palace, head straight up the stairs into the main part of the garden. Baroque—which is exactly what you see here—is all about controlling nature. The centerpiece is a pyramid-shaped outdoor grotto, crowned by the Borromeo family unicorn. Up the stairs and behind this fanciful structure is a vast terrace with views over the lower gardens and Stresa. Back downstairs, follow the signs (hidden in the bushes) to the café and bookshop, which anchor the far points of the island, to see the terraces behind the "pyramid." Finally, follow *exit* signs to pop out a side gate at the top of a twisty, stepped lane back through town to the boat docks.

▲Isola Superiore

This sleepy island, also called Isola dei Pescatori, is residential—though only a handful of inhabitants remain—and was never owned by the Borromeo family.

It has a few good fish restaurants, ample pizza-by-the-slice takeout joints, picnic benches, views, and, blissfully, nothing much to do—all under arbors of wisteria. Simply stroll the narrow, cobbled lanes, or relax at the long, skinny, pebbly park/ beach at the tip of the island. A delight for photographers and painters, the island is never really crowded, except at lunchtime.

▲Isola Madre

Don't come to this island unless you intend to tour the sight, because that's all there is: an interesting furnished villa (with a few sparse English descriptions) and a lovely garden filled with exotic birds and plants. Garden lovers can invest a few euros in a booklet about the plantings.

Cost and Hours: Villa and garden-€17, €28 combo-ticket includes Isola Bella, same hours and contact details as Isola Bella.

Visitor Services: A WC is next to the chapel. You'll also find a café/bookshop (selling basic sandwiches) just outside the villa. While eating is best on Isola Superiore, Isola Madre has one real restaurant, **$$$ La Piratera Ristorante Bar,** which owns a big, beautiful terrace over the lake. You'll run into this immediately after leaving the villa/garden complex (good-value fixed-price tourist meal, daily 8:00-18:00, sit-down meals 12:00-15:30, simple sandwiches and slices of pizza to-go anytime, picnic at the rocky beach a minute's walk from the restaurant, just to your right as you exit the gardens, +39 0323 31171).

Visiting the Island: Visiting is a one-way affair. From the boat dock, walk up the stairs to the ticket desk for the villa. Then, once through the gate, take the level path to the right to loop around the gardens and end at the villa (*ingresso al giardino* signs). Or, if you're in a rush, take the stairs to the left instead to go straight to the villa.

First you'll circle all the way around the **gardens.** Eight gardeners (with the help of water continually pumped from the lake) keep this English-style garden paradise lush. It's a joy, even for those bored by flowers and foliage. You'll see trees from around the world, and an exotic bird menagerie with golden and silver pheasants and Chinese peacocks. (You'll see and hear them roaming wild; also look for the bird cages partway up the main staircase to the villa, on the left.)

In front of the villa, a once-magnificent **Himalayan cypress tree** paints your world a streaky green. The 150-year-old tree, knocked down by a tornado in 2006 but successfully saved, is an attraction in its own right, with steel guy-wires now anchoring it firmly in place.

The 16th-century **villa** is the first of the Borromeo palaces, dating from the Renaissance. A century older than the Isola Bella villa, it's dark and somber. The clever angled hinges keep the doors from flapping in the lake breeze. The family's huge collection of dolls, marionettes, and exquisite 17th-century marionette theater sets—painted by a La Scala opera set designer—fills several rooms. A corner room is painted to take you into an 18th-century Venetian Rococo sitting room under a floral greenhouse.

Some of the garden's best flowers are in view immediately after leaving the villa. Walk down the stairs to the terrace in front of the chapel, with WCs tucked around the left side. Stairs lead directly down to the boat dock from here. Or you can loop past the villa to exit at the far end, just above La Piratera restaurant. From there, you can walk through the shop to reach a terrace path that leads you back to the boat dock.

Villa Taranto Botanical Gardens

Garden lovers will enjoy this large landscaped park, located on the mainland across the lake from Stresa. Although it's the most sprawling garden in the area, and enjoyable for a stroll in a park, it's a bit underwhelming. The gardens are a Scotsman's labor of love. Starting in the 1930s, Neil McEacharn created this garden of delights—bringing in thousands of plants from all over the world—and here he stays, in the small mausoleum. The park's highlight is a terraced garden with a series of cascading pools. Villa Taranto is directly across the street from the boat dock.

Cost and Hours: €12, daily 9:00-19:00, March until 18:00,

LAKES

Oct until 17:30, closed Nov-Feb, last entry one hour before closing, +39 0323 404 555, www.villataranto.it.

Getting There: By boat, it's two stops (about 15 minutes) past Isola Madre—50 minutes from Stresa. On the way, you'll pass a scenic promontory speckled with villas. Note that only about half of the lake boats stop here, which means an hour between return departures—check schedules carefully.

MILAN

Milano

For every church in Rome, there's a bank in Milan. Italy's second city and the capital of the Lombardy region, Milan is a hardworking, style-conscious, time-is-money city of 1.4 million. A melting pot of people and history, Milan may get its industriousness from its medieval rulers, the Teutonic Lombards, or from its years under Austrian rule. Either way, Milan is modern Italy's center of fashion, industry, banking, television, publishing, and conventions. It's also a major university town, a train hub, home to one of the world's leading opera houses, and host to two football (soccer) teams and the nearby Monza Formula One racetrack.

Milan can't compare with Florence and Rome as a center of Renaissance and religious art, although it does boast Michelangelo's last pietà sculpture (in Sforza Castle), Leonardo da Vinci's *Last Supper,* and the Gothic spires of the Duomo. Many of the city's unique and noteworthy sights date from more recent centuries, such as the Galleria Vittorio Emanuele II arcade, the La Scala opera house, and the modern architecture at Porta Nuova.

Founded by the Romans as Mediolanum ("the place in the middle"), by the fourth century AD Milan was the capital of the western half of the Roman Empire. It was the namesake of Constantine's Edict of Milan legalizing Christianity, and home of St. Ambrose, a powerful early Christian bishop.

After some barbarian darkness, medieval Milan became a successful mercantile city, eventually rising to regional prominence under the Visconti and Sforza families. The mammoth cathedral, or Duomo, is a testament to the city's wealth and ambition. By the time of the Renaissance, Milan was nicknamed "the New Athens" and was enough of a cultural center for Leonardo da Vinci to call

MILAN

it home. Then came 400 years of foreign domination (under Spain, Austria, France, more Austria). Milan was a focal point of the 1848 revolution against Austria and helped lead Italy to full unification in 1870. The impressive Galleria Vittorio Emanuele II and the interior of the La Scala opera house reflect the wealth and sophistication of turn-of-the-20th-century Milan.

Mussolini left a heavy fascist touch on the architecture here (such as the central train station). His excesses also led to the WWII bombing of Milan. But the city rose again. The 1959 Pirelli Tower (the skinny skyscraper in front of the station), while a trendsetter in its day, now seems quaint considering Milan's glassy new high-rise developments. Today, Milan is people-friendly, with a good transit system and inviting pedestrian zones.

Many tourists come to Italy for the past. But Milan is today's Italy. In this city of refined tastes, window displays are gorgeous, cigarettes are chic, and even the cheese comes gift-wrapped. Yet, thankfully, Milan is no more expensive for tourists than any other Italian city.

For pleasant excursions nearby, consider visiting Lake Como or Lake Maggiore—both are about an hour from Milan by train (see the previous chapter).

PLANNING YOUR TIME

Milan isn't as charming as Venice or Florence, but it's still a vibrant and vital piece of the Italian puzzle. With two nights and a full day,

you can gain an appreciation for the city and see a few major sights. Tour the Duomo, hit any art you like (reserve ahead to see *The Last Supper*), browse elegant shops and the Galleria Vittorio Emanuele II, or see an opera. Alternatively, spend some of your time in the Porta Nuova district to catch the 21st-century spirit. To maximize your time in Milan, use the Metro to get around.

For those with a round-trip flight into Milan: I'd recommend starting your journey softly by going first to Lake Como (one-hour train ride to Varenna). Then, with jet lag under control, dive into Milan.

Monday is a terrible sightseeing day, since many museums are closed (including *The Last Supper* and the cathedral's museum). August is oppressively hot and muggy, and locals who can vacate do, leaving the city quiet. Those visiting in August find that the nightlife is sleepy, and many shops and restaurants are closed.

A Three-Hour Tour: If you're just changing trains at Milan's Centrale station (as, sooner or later, you probably will), consider catching a later train and taking this blitz tour: Check your bag at the station, ride the subway to the Duomo, peruse the square, explore the cathedral's rooftop terraces and interior, drop into the Duomo Museum, have a scenic coffee in the Galleria Vittorio Emanuele II, maybe see a museum (most are within a 10-minute walk of the main square), and return by subway to the station. A practical way to make the most of this quick visit is to use my free ∩ Milan's Duomo neighborhood audio tour—see page 26.

MILAN

Rome vs. Milan: A Classic Squabble

In Italy, the North and South bicker about each other, hurling barbs, quips, and generalizations. All the classic North/South traits can be applied to Milan (the business capital) and Rome (the government and religious capital). Italians like to say that people come to Milan to sin, and they go to Rome to ask for forgiveness.

The Milanesi say the Romans are lazy. Government jobs in Rome come with short hours—made even shorter by multiple coffee breaks, three-hour lunches, chats with colleagues, and phone calls to friends and relatives. Milanesi contend that "Roma *ladrona*" (Rome, the big thief) is a parasite that lives off the taxes of people up North. There's still a strong Milan-based movement promoting secession.

Romans, meanwhile, dismiss the Milanesi as uptight workaholics with nothing else to live for—gray like their foggy city. But Romans do admit that in Milan, job opportunities are better and based on merit. And the Milanesi grudgingly concede the Romans have a gift for enjoying life.

While Rome is more of a family city, Milan is the place for

Orientation to Milan

TOURIST INFORMATION

A small InfoPoint across from the Duomo hands out free maps and events listings; it's off the forecourt of the Palazzo Reale, to the left if your back is to the Duomo (daily 10:00-18:00, +39 02 8845 5555, www.yesmilano.it). If you can get a map from your hotel, there's little reason to come here.

ARRIVAL IN MILAN

For arrival by plane, see "Milan Connections" at the end of this chapter.

By Train

Visitors disembark at one of three major train stations: Milano Centrale, Porta Garibaldi, or Cadorna. Centrale handles most Trenitalia and Italo trains as well as airport buses. Some trains, both international and domestic, arrive at Porta Garibaldi. Both high-powered singles on the career fast track. Milanese yuppies mix with each other...not the city's longtime residents. Milan is seen as wary of foreigners and inward-looking, and Rome as fun-loving, tolerant, and friendly. In Milan, bureaucracy (such as social services) works logically and efficiently, while in Rome, accom-

plishing even small chores can be exasperating. Everything in Rome—from finding a babysitter to buying a car—is done through friends.

Milanesi find Romans vulgar. The Roman dialect is considered one of the coarsest in the country. Much as they try, Milanesi just can't say "Damn your dead relatives" quite as effectively as the Romans. Still, Milanesi enjoy Roman comedians and love to imitate the accent.

The Milanesi feel that Rome is dirty and Roman traffic nerve-wracking. But despite the craziness, Rome maintains a genuine village feel. People share family news with their neighborhood grocer. Milan lacks people-friendly piazzas, and entertainment comes at a high price. But in Rome, *la dolce vita* is as close as the nearest square, and a full moon is enjoyed by all.

Centrale and Cadorna are terminals for express trains from Malpensa Airport.

Milano Centrale

This huge, sternly decorated, fascist-built (in 1931) train station is a sight in itself. Notice how the monumental halls and art make you feel small—emphasizing that a powerful state is a good thing. In the front lobby, heroic people celebrate "modern" transportation (find the round medallions high above, just below the skylights—circa-1930 ships, trains, and cars) opposite reliefs depicting old-fashioned sailboats and horse carts.

Moving walkways link the station's three main levels: platforms on top, shopping below on a small mezzanine, and most services below that at ground level (including pay WCs, ATMs, and a food court). For baggage check *(deposito bagagli)*, taxis, or buses to Linate Airport, head toward the ground-level exit marked *Piazza Luigi di Savoia*. For buses to Malpensa Airport, head to the exit marked *Piazza IV Novembre*. Outside the station's front entrance, under the atrium, are car-rental offices. Escalators lead down to a fourth, basement level with the Metro entrance and a few shops, including a Sapori & Dintorni supermarket (daily).

To **buy domestic train tickets,** follow the blue *Biglietti* signs and use the Trenitalia or Italo machines. For international tickets or complicated questions, join the line at the Trenitalia ticket office on the ground floor. There's also an Italo office on the ground floor. For quick questions, you might use the Italo and Trenitalia info booths by the tracks.

Getting to the Center: "Centrale" is a misnomer—the Duomo is a 35-minute walk away. But it's a straight shot on the **Metro** (8 minutes). Buy a ticket from the machines or at a kiosk, follow signs for yellow line 3 (direction: San Donato), and go four stops to the Duomo stop. You'll surface facing the cathedral.

Taxis to the center are a good value for two or more people or if you don't want to lug bags on the Metro (€12-15, departing taxis are to the left of the train station).

Milano Porta Garibaldi

Some trains, both domestic and international, use Porta Garibaldi station, also north of the city center. This smaller, well-organized station is on Metro green line 2, two stops from Milano Centrale, and purple line 5.

Milano Cadorna

You're most likely to use this commuter-rail station if you take the Malpensa Express airport train, which stops at track 1. The Cadorna Metro station—with a direct connection to the Duomo on Metro red line 1—is directly out front.

By Car

Leonardo never drove in Milan. Smart guy. Driving downtown is bad enough to make the €30/day fee for a garage a blessing. And there's a €5 congestion fee on weekdays if you drive in the city center ("Area C"). Do Milan (and Lake Como) before or after you rent your car, not while you've got it, and use the park-and-ride lots at suburban Metro stations such as Cascina Gobba. These are shown on the official Metro map, and full details are at www.atm.it (select English, then "Travel with ATM," then "Cars").

HELPFUL HINTS

Theft Alert: Be on guard. Milan's thieves target tourists, especially at the Centrale train station, getting in and out of the subway, and around the Duomo. They can be dressed as tourists, businessmen, or beggars, or they can be gangs of too-young-to-arrest children. Watch out for ragged people carrying newspapers and cardboard—they'll thrust these at you as a distraction while they pick your pocket. If you're ripped off and plan to file an insurance claim, fill out a report with the police (main Questura police station, Via Fatebenefratelli 11, Metro: Turati, open daily 24 hours, +39 02 62261).

Medical Help: Here are two medical clinics with emergency care facilities (both closed Sat-Sun): the **International Health Center** in Galleria Strasburgo (also does dentistry, between Via Durini and Corso Europa, at #3, third floor, Metro: San Babila, +39 02 7634 0720, www.ihc.it), and the **American International Medical Center** at Via Mercalli 11 (Metro: Missori or Crocetta, call for appointment, +39 02 5831 9808, http://www.aimclinic.it/www.aimclinic.it).

Bookstores: The handiest major bookstore is **La Feltrinelli,** under the Galleria Vittorio Emanuele II (daily, Metro: Duomo). The **American Bookstore** is at Via Manfredo Camperio 16, near Sforza Castle (closed Sun, Metro: Cairoli, +39 02 878 920).

Laundry: A self-service *lavanderia* is at Via A. Tadino 6, in a pleasant neighborhood near Metro: Porta Venezia, four stops on the red line from the Duomo. It's staffed, and they'll help (Mon-Sat 8:30-12:30 & 14:30-18:30, Sun 15:00-18:00, +39 349 314 2939).

Events and Entertainment: HelloMilano.it, WantedinMilan.com, and YesMilano.it are decent websites for info on what's happening in the city.

Soccer: For a dose of Europe's soccer mania (which many believe provides a necessary testosterone vent to keep Europe out of a third big war), catch a match while you're here. A.C. Milan and Inter Milan are the ferociously competitive home teams. Both teams play in the 85,000-seat **Meazza Stadium** (a.k.a. San Siro) most Sunday afternoons from September to June (ride Metro purple line 5 to San Siro Stadio, bring passport for security checks, www.acmilan.com or www.inter.it).

MILAN

GETTING AROUND MILAN

By Public Transit: Compared to Rome or Naples, it's a pleasure to use Milan's public transit system, called ATM (www.atm.it, English journey planner on website, "ATM Point" info desk at the Duomo Metro station).

The clean, spacious, fast, and easy **Metro** zips you nearly anywhere you may want to go, and trams and city buses fill in the gaps. The handiest Metro line for a quick visit is the yellow line 3, which connects Centrale station to the Duomo. The other lines are red (1), green (2), and purple (5). It's helpful to know the name of the end station in the direction you're traveling. The Metro shuts down at about midnight, but many trams continue until 1:00 or 2:00.

With 100 miles of track, Milan's classic, century-old yellow

Milan Metro

LINE 5 PURPLE
LINE 3 YELLOW
LINE 1 RED

Bignami
Comasina
Sesto FS
Zara

Buses and trains to Malpensa airport; buses to Linate & Bergamo airports

CENTRAL TRAIN STATION
Centrale F.S.

Not to scale & not all lines or stations shown

Isola
Sondrio
PORTA GARIBALDI TRAIN STN.
Gioia
Lambrate FS

Monumentale
Cenisio
Garibaldi FS
PORTA NUOVA
Loreto
To Cologno Nord & Gessate

To San Siro
Gerusalemme
Moscova
Repubblica
Lima

BRERA GALLERY
Turati
Porta Venezia

SFORZA CASTLE
Lanza
Montenapoleone

To Rho, QT8, Lotto, Molino Dorino & Bisceglie
GALLERIA
DUOMO
Palestro

Cadorna
Conciliazione
Cairoli
Cordusio
Duomo
San Babila

LAST SUPPER
Sant' Ambrogio
SANT' AMBROGIO
CENTRAL MILAN
Missori

Sant' Agostino
Crocetta

Porta Genova FS
NAVIGLIO GRANDE

METRO LINES
—— LINE 1 (RED)
—— LINE 2 (GREEN)
--- LINE 3 (YELLOW)
-·- LINE 5 (PURPLE)

Assago & Abbiategrasso
LINE 2 GREEN

S. Donato
LINE 3 YELLOW

MILAN

trams are both efficient and atmospheric, but tram signage is poor, and stop announcements are hard to hear. Maps of the tram lines are posted in Metro stations—or use the online journey planner.

A **single ticket,** valid for 90 minutes, can be used for one ride, including transfers, on the Metro, bus, or tram (€2; sold at machines in subway stations—select "M1-M3" ticket—and at newsstands, tobacco shops, and shops with *ATM* sticker in window). Other ticket options include a **24-hour pass** (€7) and a **3-day pass** (€12). At Metro turnstiles, tickets must be run through the machines when you enter and again when you leave the system. On buses and trams, you only validate once, upon entry (including if you are transferring or using a pass)—machines are at the front and rear.

By Taxi: Small groups go cheap and fast by taxi (drop charge—€3.40, €1.12/kilometer; €5.60 drop charge on Sun and holidays, €6.70 from 21:00 to 6:00 in the morning). You don't flag down cabs here; call, or walk to a taxi stand. Handy stands are at Piazza del Duomo and in front of Sforza Castle. Hotels and restaurants are also happy to call one for you (+39 02 8585 or +39 02 6969). The **FreeNow** app (www.free-now.com) lets you summon and pay for a taxi. **Uber** Black and UberLux also operate in Milan.

By Bike: Public BikeMi stations are generally near Metro stations. Download the BikeMi app to see available bikes and parking spots (subscription is €4.50/day, €9/week; first 30 minutes free, then €0.50/30 minutes up to 2 hours, after that €2/hour, www.bikemi.com).

Tours in Milan

🎧 To sightsee on your own, download my free Milan's Duomo Neighborhood audio tour.

Local Guides

Lorenza Scorti is a hardworking young guide who knows her city's history and how to teach it. She also enjoys leading Lake Como day trips (€180/3 hours, same price for individuals or groups, evenings OK, +39 347 735 1346, lorenza.scorti@libero.it). **Sara Cerri** is another good licensed local guide who enjoys passing on her knowledge (€240/3 hours, then €40/hour, +39 380 433 3019, www.walkingtourmilan.it). At **Bella Milano Tours,** smart and fun-loving Valeria Andreoli and Mirella Maestri lead a variety of themed tours (highlights tour—€60/hour, €180/half-day, +39 338 301 2220, www.bellamilanotours.com).

Walking and Bus Tours with *The Last Supper*

If you can't get a reservation for *The Last Supper,* consider joining a walking or bus tour that includes a guided visit to Leonardo's masterpiece. These tours (usually 3 hours, about €65-100) also take you to top sights such as the Duomo, Galleria Vittorio Emanuele II, La Scala Opera House, and Sforza Castle. Ideally book at least a week in advance, but it's worth a try at the last minute, too.

For the best experience, I'd book a walking tour with **Veditalia** (www.veditalia.com) or **City Wonders** (www.citywonders.com). Both have good guides and solid reputations. **Get Your Guide** (www.getyourguide.com) is another worthwhile option. The bus-and-walking tours are less satisfying, but you can try **Autostradale** ("Look Mi" tour, offices in passage at far end of Piazza del Duomo and in front of Sforza Castle, +39 02 8058 1354,

MILAN

Central Milan

ARCO DELLA PACE

Piazza Sempione

ARENA

VIA LEGNANO

To Malpensa Airport & Como

Parco Sempione

BRANCA TOWER

TRIENNALE DI MILANO

PALAZZO DELL'ARTE

VIALE MOLIERE

FORO

See Milan Hotels & Restaurants detail map

VIA GADIO

FORO

Lanza M

VIA BUONAPARTE

SFORZA CASTLE

ENTRANCE TO MUSEUM OF ANCIENT ART

Piazza Castello

MICHELANGELO'S PIETÀ

ZANI VIAGGI TOURS

To Fiera di Milano Trade Fair

V. 20 SETTEMBRE

VIA VICENZO MONTI

AUTOSTRADALE TOUR OFFICE

Cairoli M

Largo Cairoli

CADORNA STATION

M *Cadorna*

BUONAPARTE

TEATRO DAL VERME

AMERICAN BOOKSTORE

VIA G. PUCCINI

VIA CAMPERIO

VIA GIOVANNI BOCCACCIO

VIA GIOVANNI MURO

VIA MERAVIGLI

LAST SUPPER

S. MARIA D. GRAZIE

T #16

PALAZZO LITTA

CORSO MAGENTA

T #16

SAN MAURIZIO

BORSA

V. S. GIOVANNI SUL MURO

❶

CORSO MAGENTA

V. CARADOSSO

To Leonardo's Horse & Meazza Stadium

PALAZZO DELLE STELLINE

❺

VIA GIOSUE CARDUCCI

VIA SANT' AGNESE

ARCHAEOLOGICAL MUSEUM

VIA NIRONE

VIA LUINI

VIA BRISA

Piazza degli Affari

THE FINGER

VIA BOSCHETI

V. SAN VITTORE

OSPEDALE S. GIUSEPPE

VIA TERRAGGIO

VIA SANT'ORSOLA

❷

S. VITTORE AL CORPO

LEONARDO DA VINCI NATIONAL SCIENCE & TECHNOLOGY MUSEUM

M *Sant' Ambrogio*

BASILICA DI S. AMBROGIO

UNIVERSITÀ CATTOLICA

V. L. NECCHI

VIA SANTA MARTA

V. CAPPUCCIO

PUSTERLA DI S. AMBROGIO

VIA LANZONE

V. CAM

VIA CORENTI

❹

❸

VIA STAMPA

VIA SAN VITO

VIA OLONA

AUSONIO

EDMONDO DE AMICIS

VIA SAN

M *Sant'Agostino*

VIA C. DA SESTO

VIA ARIBERTO

S. VINCENZO

VIA CALOGERO

VIA MORA

S. LORENZO

VIALE PAPINIANO

CORSO GENOVA

V. SIMONETTA

V. MOLINO D. ARMI

V. CONI ZUGNA

To Naviglio Grande District

To Porta Garibaldi, Eataly & Porta Nuova District

To Porta Nuova

To Centrale Station

VIA PALERMO

Largo Treves

6

S. SIMPLICIANO

VIA MONTEBELLO

V. TURATI

V. MARCO DE

MANIN

Turati

Giardini Pubblici

CORSO GARIBALDI

VIA SOLEFERINO

S. MARCO

VIA FATEBENEFRATELLI

VIA DELL'ANNUNCIATA

MARCHI

V. PALESTRO

VIA PONTACCIO

VIA FIORI CHIARI

CORSO DI PORTA NUOVA

VIA MARINA

RISORGIMENTO MUSEUM

VIA MERCATO

BRERA GALLERY

S. MARIA D. CARMINE

V. CARMINE

VIA BRERA

VIA BORGONUOVO

VIA GIARDINI

VIA MANZONI

VIA DELLA SPIGA

PALAZZO SCOTTI

VIA SANTO SPIRITO

BAGATTI VALSECCHI MUSEUM

V. SACCHI

PALAZZO MONTE DI PIETA

VIA MONTE PIETA

Montenapoleone

VIA SAN'T ANDREA

VIA DELL'ORSO

VIA GESU

V. CUSANI

V. LAURO

POLDI PEZZOLI MUSEUM

VIA MONTENAPOLEONE

VIA MONTE NAPOLEONE (HIGH-FASHION SHOPS)

EX SEMINARIO

V. BROLETTO

See Milan Duomo Area detail map

V. VERDI

PALAZZO BELGIOIOSO

LA SCALA

GALLERIE D'ITALIA

Piazza Meda

CORSO VENEZIA

V. DANTE

OPERA MUSEUM

Piazza della Scala

VIA AGNELLO

CORSO MATTEOTTI

San Babila

GALLERIA V. EMANUELE II

VIA SAN PAOLO

Cordusio

Piazza Cordusio

LA RINASCENTE DEP'T STORE

CORSO VITT EMANUELE II

POST

Piazza dei Mercanti

V. POSTA

V. BOCCHETTO

VIA ARMORARI

Duomo

Piazza del Duomo

VIA OREFICI

DUOMO

Piazza Beccaria

CORSO EUROPA

VIA DURINI

PINACOTECA AMBROSIANA

T #2

T #16

PATTARI

Piazza Fontana

VIA SAN MAURILIO

SAN SATIRO

MUSEO DEL NOVECENTO

PALAZZO REALE

DUOMO MUSEUM

LARGA

V. TORINO

Piazza Diaz

VIA LAGRETTO

Piazza S. Stefano

VIA NERINO

B #73

VIA MAZZINI

VIA SIGNORA

VIA FRANCESCO SFORZA

Missori

VIA SANT ANTONIO

VELASCA TOWER

VIA SAN BARNABA

V. AMEDEI

VIA DI PORTA ROMANA

VIA SAN BARNABA

N

ITALIA

VIA SANT'EUFEMIA

CORSO ITALIA

200 Meters

200 Yards

V. S. SOFIA

VIA CROCEFISSO

MILAN

Accommodations & Eateries

1. Antica Locanda Leonardo
2. B&B Hotel Milano Sant'Ambrogio
3. Hotel Ariston
4. Ostello Bello
5. Boccondivino
6. Ristornate Rigolo

www.autostradaleviaggi.it) or **Zani Viaggi** (office disguised as a "tourist information" point, Largo Caroli 18 at corner of Foro Buonaparte and Via Cusani, near Sforza Castle, +39 02 867 131, www.zaniviaggi.com).

Hop-On, Hop-Off Option: Zani Viaggi also operates **CitySightseeing Milano** hop-on, hop-off buses (look for the red buses—easiest at Duomo and La Scala, €24/all day, €28/48 hours, buy on board, recorded commentary, www.city-sightseeing.it). With the 48-hour bus ticket, you can pay an additional €41 for a *Last Supper* reservation—exorbitant but worth considering if you're desperate (April-Oct Sun and Thu only).

Sights in Milan

Milan's core sights—the Duomo, Duomo Museum, and Galleria Vittorio Emanuele II—cluster at the heart of town. Also in the Duomo area are the Piazza della Scala and La Scala Opera House.

The city's other main sights—Basilica di Sant'Ambrogio, Sforza Castle, and Brera Art Gallery—are scattered farther afield, but walkably so. *The Last Supper* is a tram or Metro ride away.

MILAN DUOMO

The city's centerpiece (Duomo di Milano), worth ▲▲▲, is the third-largest church in Europe (after St. Peter's Basilica in Rome and the cathedral in Sevilla). At 525 by 300 feet, the place is immense, with more than 2,000 statues inside (and another thousand outside) and 52 100-foot-tall, sequoia-size pillars representing the weeks of the year and the liturgical calendar. If you do two laps, you've done your daily walk. The church was built to hold 40,000 worshippers—the entire population of Milan when construction began.

A visit here has several elements. First, take in the overwhelming exterior from various angles, admiring its remarkable bulk and many spires and statues. Then go inside to see the church's vast nave, stained glass, historic tombs, basement archaeological area, and a quirky, one-of-a-kind statue of a flayed man. A visit to the adjacent Duomo Museum lets you see the church's statues and details up close. Finally, take an elevator ride (or long stair climb) up to the Duomo rooftop for city views and a stroll through a forest of jagged church spires.

Cost: Cathedral-€5, museum-€5, rooftops by elevator-€15.

Milan Duomo Area

POLDI PEZZOLI
MUSEUM

VIA VERDI

VIA ALESSANDRO MANZONI

To
Main Train
Station

EVENING
BOX OFFICE

LA
SCALA

PALAZZO
BELGIOIOSO

GALLERIE
D'ITALIA

*Piazza
della Scala*

OPERA
MUSEUM

LEONARDO
STATUE

*Piazza
Meda*

V. CLERICI

VIA S. MARGHERITA

PALAZZO
MARINO

SAN
FEDELE

BORSALINO
HAT SHOP

VIA S. RADEGONDA

VIA AGNELLO

VIA SAN PAOLO

To
Via Dante &
Sforza Castle

BULL MOSAIC

GALLERIA
VITTORIO EMANUELE II

BAR
CAMPARINO

PALAZZO
DELLA
RAGIONE

*Piazza del
Mercanti*

LA RINASCENTE
DEP'T STORE

CORSO
V. EMANUELE II

Ⓜ *Duomo*

STAIRS TO
DUOMO ROOF

DUOMO

ELEVATORS
TO/FROM
DUOMO ROOF

PATTARI

VICTOR
EMMANUEL II
STATUE

*Piazza del
Duomo*

Ⓜ *Duomo*

Ⓣ *#16*

**MUSEO DEL
NOVECENTO**

DUOMO
MUSEUM

ⓘ

*Piazza
Fontana*

V. HUGO

OREFICI

To
Pinoteca
Ambrosiana

#2 Ⓣ

VIA TORINO

VIA SPERONARI

VIA MAZZINI

VIA CAPP.

V. MARCONI

VIA PALAZZO REALE

PALAZZO
REALE

SAN
SATIRO

*Piazza
Diaz*

VIA LARGA

V. GONZAGA

Ⓑ *#73*

200 Meters

200 Yards

MILAN

The archaeological area (which you access from inside the church)
is free with any ticket. Of the various combo-tickets, the best is the
€20 Duomo Pass Lift, which includes the cathedral, rooftop terraces by elevator, archaeological area, and Duomo Museum.

Hours: Cathedral, archaeological area, and rooftop open daily
9:00-19:00; Duomo Museum Tue-Sun 10:00-19:00, closed Mon;
last entry one hour before closing.

Information: Church +39 02 7202 3375, museum +39 02 3616
9351, www.duomomilano.it.

Buying Tickets and Avoiding Lines: Timed-entry tickets,

Milan at a Glance

▲▲▲**Duomo** Milan's showpiece cathedral, with an amazing ▲▲ roof you can walk on and an archaeological area below. **Hours:** Daily 9:00-19:00. See page 282.

▲▲**Duomo Museum** Church art and original sculptures from Milan's cathedral. **Hours:** Tue-Sun 10:00-19:00, closed Mon. See page 291.

▲▲**Galleria Vittorio Emanuele II** Glass-domed arcade on the main square, perfect for window shopping and people-watching anytime. See page 295.

▲▲**Pinacoteca Ambrosiana** Oldest museum in Milan, with works by Raphael, Leonardo, Botticelli, Titian, and Caravaggio. **Hours:** Tue-Sun 10:00-18:00, closed Mon. See page 301.

▲▲**Basilica di Sant'Ambrogio** Historic, art-packed church dating to early Roman times. **Hours:** Mon-Sat 10:00-12:30 & 14:30-18:00, Sun 15:00-17:00. See page 304.

▲▲*The Last Supper* Leonardo da Vinci's masterpiece, displayed in the Church of Santa Maria delle Grazie (reservation required). **Hours:** Tue-Sat 8:15-18:45 (last entry), Sun from 14:00, closed Mon. See page 306.

▲▲**Brera Art Gallery** World-class collection of Italian paintings (13th-20th century), including Raphael, Caravaggio, Piero della Francesca, and the Bellinis. **Hours:** Tue-Sun 8:30-19:15, closed Mon. See page 309.

▲▲**Sforza Castle** Milan's castle, highlighted by an unfinished Michelangelo pietà. **Hours:** Museum—Tue-Sun 10:00-17:30, closed Mon; grounds—daily 7:00-19:30. See page 311.

▲▲**Porta Nuova** Sleek, futuristic neighborhood of condo towers and shopping mall boulevards. See page 314.

▲**La Scala Opera House and Museum** The world's most presti-

MILAN

bought in advance online, are the simplest way to avoid lines. To purchase tickets on-site, look for the ticket center with info office on the south side of the cathedral (across from the Duomo's right transept at #14a). Pick a number and wait. Lines can be very long and slow, but you can minimize the wait by using a machine or arriving very early or late. Security lines can also be long. You can gious opera house. **Hours:** Museum daily 9:00-17:30. See page 298.

▲**Piazza del Duomo** Milan's main square, full of energy, history, and pickpockets. See page 294.

▲**Museo del Novecento** Milan's 20th-century art collection, housed in the fascist-era City Hall. **Hours:** Tue-Sun 9:30-19:30 (Thu until 22:30), closed Mon. See page 296.

▲**Piazza dei Mercanti** The evocative medieval heart of the city. See page 297.

▲**Gallerie d'Italia** Three adjacent palaces filled with 19th- and 20th-century Italian art. **Hours:** Tue-Sun 9:30-19:30, Thu until 22:30, closed Mon. See page 300.

▲**Church of San Maurizio** The "Sistine Chapel of Lombardy," gorgeously frescoed by Bernardino Luini, a follower of Leonardo. **Hours:** Wed-Sun 10:00-17:30, closed Mon-Tue. See page 303.

▲**Leonardo da Vinci National Science and Technology Museum** Leonardo's designs illustrated in wooden models, plus a vast collection of historical and technological bric-a-brac and machines. **Hours:** Tue-Fri 9:30-17:00, Sat-Sun until 18:30, closed Mon. See page 305.

▲**Risorgimento Museum** Italy's rocky road to unification on one floor. **Hours:** Tue-Sun 10:00-17:30, closed Mon. See page 310.

▲**Naviglio Grande** Milan's old canal port—once a working-class zone, now an atmospheric nightspot for dinner or drinks. See page 316.

▲**Monumental Cemetery** Final resting spot with tombs showcasing expressive art styles from 1870 to 1930. **Hours:** Tue-Sun 8:00-18:00, closed Mon. See page 317.

MILAN

avoid the church security line by doing the rooftop first and descending from there directly into the church.

Dress Code: Modest dress is required to visit the church. Keep shoulders and knees covered, and don't wear sports T-shirts or shorts. They sell a gauzy modesty gown for €2.50—if you're improperly dressed, it'll get you in (and, I think, actually make you look sexier).

Tours: An €8 audioguide for the church and museum is available at a kiosk inside the church's main door (no rentals Sun). This guide, which uses a standard earbud jack, is very helpful at the museum and is not available there.

◐ Self-Guided Tour

Exterior

Stand facing the main facade. The Duomo is huge and angular, with prickly spires topped with statues. The style, Flamboyant Gothic, means "flame-like," and the church seems to flicker toward heaven with flames of stone. The facade is divided by six vertical buttresses, all done in pink-white marble. The dozens of statues, pinnacles, and pointed-arch windows on the facade are just a fraction of the many adornments on this architecturally rich structure.

For more than 2,000 years, this spot has been the spiritual heart of Milan: In 2014, archaeologists probing for ancient Roman ruins beneath the Duomo discovered the remains of what might be a temple to the goddess Minerva. A church has stood on this site since the days of the ancient Romans and St. Ambrose (4th century), but construction of the building we see today began in 1386. Back then, the dukes of Milan wanted to impress their counterparts in Germany, France, and the Vatican with this massive cathedral. They chose the trendy Gothic style coming out of France, and stuck with it even after Renaissance-style domes came into vogue elsewhere in Italy. The cathedral was built not from ordinary stone but from expensive marble, top to bottom. Pink Candoglia marble was rafted in from a quarry about 60 miles away, across Lake Maggiore and down a canal to a port at the cathedral—a journey that took about a week. Construction continued from 1386 to 1810, with final touches added as late as 1965.

The statues on the lower level of the facade—full of energy and movement—are early Baroque, from about 1600. Of the five bronze doors, the center one is biggest. Made in 1907 in the Liberty Style (Italian Art Nouveau), it features the Joy and Sorrow of the Virgin Mary. Sad scenes are on the left, joyful ones on the right, and on top is the coronation of Mary in heaven by Jesus, with all the saints and angels looking on. (High above that is what looks like the Statue of Liberty, dating from the 1820s—decades before Frédéric-Auguste Bartholdi designed the one Americans know and love. Hmmm.)

Topping the church (you may have to back up to see it) is its tallest spire. It rises up from the center of the Duomo to display a large golden statue of the Madonna of the Nativity, to whom the church is dedicated.

A Closer Look: Along the right side of the church are interesting views from every angle: the horizontal line of the long build-

ing, the verticals of the spires, and the diagonals of the flying buttresses supporting the roof. Get close to the facade's right corner to
appreciate the many intricate details: a nude Atlas holding up the
corner buttress, robed saints, relief panels of Bible scenes, and tiny
faces—angry, smiling, happy, sad.

Stroll a little farther down the right to see the range of statues, from placid saints to thrashing nudes. These statues were made
between the 14th and 20th centuries by sculptors from all over Europe. There are hundreds of them—each different. Midway up are
the fanciful gargoyles (96 in total) that functioned as drain spouts.
Look way up to see the statues on the tips of the spires...they seem
so relaxed, like they're just hanging out, waiting for their big day.

The back end of the church is the oldest part, with the earliest stones, laid in the late 1300s. The sun-in-rose window was the
proud symbol of the city's leading Visconti family. It's flanked by
the angel telling Mary she's going to bear the Messiah. (Just outside, behind the church at Piazza Duomo 20, is a shrine to the leading religion of the 21st century: soccer. The Football Team store is
filled with colorful vestments and relics of local soccer saints.)

Inside the Church

Nave: It's the fourth-longest nave in Christendom, stretching more
than 500 feet from the entrance to the stained-glass rose window

at the far end. The apse at the
far end was started in 1385. The
wall behind you wasn't finished
until 1520. The style is Gothic,
a rarity in Italy. Fifty-two tree-
size **pillars** rise to support a
ribbed, pointed-arch ceiling,
and the church is lit by glorious stained glass. At the far end,
marking the altar, is a small tab-

ernacle of a dome atop columns—a bit of an anomaly in a Gothic
church (more on that later). Notice the little red light on the cross
high above the altar. This marks where a nail from the cross of Jesus
is kept. This relic was brought to Milan by St. Helen (Emperor
Constantine's mother) in the fourth century, when Milan was the
capital of the western Roman Empire. It's on display for three days
a year (in mid-September).

Notice the two pillars flanking the main door—each is made
from a single stone. Now, facing the altar, look high to the right,
in the rear corner of the church, and find a tiny pinhole of white
light. This is designed to shine a 10-inch sunbeam at noon onto the
bronze line that runs across the floor, indicating where we are on
the zodiac calendar.

MILAN

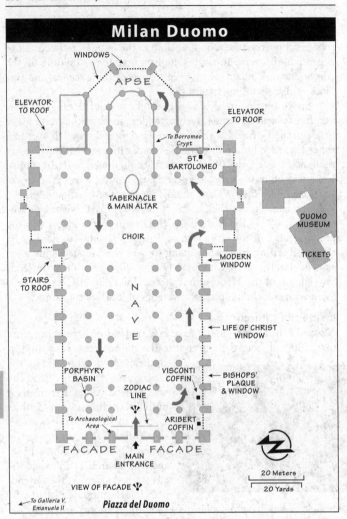

Milan Duomo

WINDOWS

APSE

ELEVATOR
TO ROOF

ELEVATOR
TO ROOF

To Borromeo
Crypt

ST.
BARTOLOMEO

DUOMO
MUSEUM

TABERNACLE
& MAIN ALTAR

TICKETS

CHOIR

MODERN
WINDOW

STAIRS
TO ROOF

N
A
V
E

LIFE OF CHRIST
WINDOW

PORPHYRY
BASIN

VISCONTI
COFFIN

BISHOPS'
PLAQUE
& WINDOW

ZODIAC
LINE

To Archaeological
Area

ARIBERT
COFFIN

FACADE   FACADE

MAIN
ENTRANCE

20 Meters

20 Yards

VIEW OF FACADE

To Galleria V.
Emanuele II

Piazza del Duomo

MILAN

This 600-year-old church is filled with history. It represents the continuous line of bishops who have presided over Milan, stretching back to the days of St. Ambrose (c. 340-397).

• *Before wandering deeper into the church, head to the end of the...*

Right Aisle: The first recess along the right wall has the 1,000-year-old gray, stone coffin of **Archbishop Aribert,** a formidable figure in 11th-century Milan. A couple of steps farther along, you'll see a red coffin atop columns belonging to the noble **Visconti** family who commissioned this church.

The third bay has a plaque where you can trace the uninterrupted rule of 144 local archbishops back to AD 51. Check out the **stained-glass window** above the plaque. Find familiar scenes along the window's bottom level: Cain killing Abel, the Flood, and the drunkenness of Noah. The brilliant and expensive colored glass (stained, not painted) is from the 15th century. Bought by wealthy families seeking the Church's favor, the windows face south to get the most light. The windows' purpose was to teach the illiterate masses the way to salvation through stories from the Old Testament and the life of Jesus. Many of the windows are more modern—from the 16th to the 20th century—and are generally made of dimmer, cheaper painted glass. Many are replacements for ones destroyed by the concussion of WWII bombs that fell nearby.

The **fifth window** dates from 1470, "just" 85 years after the first stone of the cathedral was laid. The window shows the story of Jesus, from Annunciation to Crucifixion. In the bottom window, as the angel Gabriel tells Mary the news, the Holy Spirit (in the form of a dove) enters Mary's window and world.

The **seventh window** is from the 1980s. Bright and bold, it celebrates two local cardinals (whose tombs and bodies are behind glass). The memorials to Cardinal Ferrari (below the window) and Cardinal Schuster (in the next bay), who heroically helped the Milanese out of their post-WWII blues, are a reminder that this great church is more than a tourist attraction—it's a living part of Milan.

• *Now take a few steps back into the nave for a view of the...*

Main Altar: The altar area is anchored by the domed tabernacle atop columns. This houses the receptacle that holds the Eucharist. Flanking the tabernacle are two silver statues of famous bishops. On the left is **St. Ambrose,** the influential fourth-century bishop who put Milan on the map and became the city's patron saint. The other is **St. Charles Borromeo,** the bishop who transformed the Duomo in the 16th century. Charles had inherited a cathedral that was barely half-finished. He reenergized the project and commissioned the tabernacle. Above are four 16th-century pipe organs.

While the rest of the church is Gothic, the altar is Baroque— a dramatic stage-like setting in the style of the Vatican in the 1570s. Borromeo was a great champion of the Catholic Church, and this powerful style was a statement to counter the threat posed by the Protestant Reformation. Look up above the altar into the round dome that rises 215 feet from an octagonal base. **Napoleon** crowned himself king of Italy under this dome in 1805. It was Napoleon who sped up construction, so that in 1810—finally—the church was essentially completed.

• *Before moving on, look to the rear, up at the ceiling, and see the fancy "carved" tracery on the ceiling's ribs. Nope, that's painted. It looks expensive, but paint is more affordable than carved stone. Now continue up the right aisle and walk through the south (right) transept. On the far wall, find the bald statue.*

St. Bartolomeo Statue: This is a grotesque 16th-century statue of St. Bartolomeo, an apostle and first-century martyr skinned alive by the Romans. Examine the details (face, hands, feet) of the poor guy. He piously holds a Bible in one hand and wears his own skin like a robe. Carved by a student of Leonardo da Vinci, this is a study in human anatomy learned by dissection, forbidden by the Church at the time. Read the sculptor's proud Latin inscription on the base: "I was not made by Praxiteles"—the classical master of beautiful nudes—"but by Marco d'Agrate."

• *Walk toward the altar, checking out the fine 16th-century inlaid-marble floor. The black marble (quarried from Lake Como) is harder and more durable, while the lighter colors (white from Lake Maggiore, pink from Verona) look and feel more worn. At the altar, bear right around the corner 15 steps. You'll see a door marked Scurolo di S. Carlo (often closed). This leads down to the...*

Crypt of St. Charles Borromeo: Steps lead under the altar to the tomb of St. Charles Borromeo (1538-1584), the economic power behind the church. You can still see Charles' withered body inside the rock-crystal coffin. Charles was bishop of Milan, and the second-most important hometown saint after St. Ambrose. Tarnished silver reliefs around the ceiling show scenes from Charles' life.

• *Now resurface and continue around the apse, looking up at the...*

Windows: The apse is lit by three huge windows, all 19th-century painted copies. The originals, destroyed in Napoleonic times, were made of precious stained glass. Each window has 12 panels and 12 rows, creating 144 separate scenes.

• *From the apse, head back through the church toward the main entrance (today's exit). Near the entrance stands a large basin of expensive purple porphyry. Made by Borromeo's favorite architect, Pellegrini, it was used to baptize infants. Before leaving the church, find the entrance and stairs that lead down to the...*

Archaeological Area: The church's "basement" is a maze of ruined brick foundations of earlier churches that stood here long before the present one. Milan has been an important center of Christianity since its beginning. In Roman times, Mediolanum's streets were 10 feet below today's level. The stones and mosaics you see, the pavement you walk on, and the artifacts in the glass case date from the time of the Edict of Milan (AD 313) when Emperor Constantine, ruling from this city, made Christianity legal in the Roman Empire. All are well described in English.

The highlight here is the scant remains of the eight-sided **Paleo-Christian Baptistery of San Giovanni.** It stands alongside the remains of a little church. Back then, since you couldn't enter the church until you were baptized (which didn't happen until age 18), churches had a little baptistery just outside for the unbaptized.

This humble baptistery was where St. Ambrose was baptized. Ambrose went on to become bishop here, and to mentor a randy and rebellious Roman named Augustine. On this spot in AD 387, Ambrose baptized the 31-year-old **Augustine of Hippo,** who later became one of Christianity's (and the world's) most influential thinkers, philosophers, and writers. And the rest—like this tour—is history.

More Duomo Sights

For information on tickets and opening times for these sights, see the cost and hours for the Duomo, earlier.

▲▲Duomo Museum (Museo del Duomo)

This museum, to the right of the Duomo in the Palazzo Reale, fills in the rest of the story of Milan's cathedral and lets you see its original art and treasures up close. The collection is much more meaningful with the audioguide (€8; available only inside cathedral).

Visiting the Museum: Just after the ticket taker, notice (on the wall to your right) the original **inlaid-marble floor** of the Duomo. The black (from Lake Como) marble is harder. Go ahead, wear down the white a little more.

Now follow the roughly chronological one-way route. Among the early treasures of the cathedral is a 900-year-old, Byzantine-style **crucifix.** Made of copper gilded with real gold and nailed onto wood, it was part of the tomb of the archbishop of Milan. A copy is in today's cathedral.

You'll pass a big, wooden model of the church (we'll get a better look at this later, on the way out). Then you'll step through a long room with paintings, chalices, glass monstrances, and lifelike reliquary busts of Sts. Charles, Sebastian, and Thecla.

Look for the big, 600-year-old statue of **St. George.** While it makes George look like a modern inflatable toy, it's among the cathedral's oldest statues. It once stood on the front (and first constructed) spire of the Duomo. Some think this is the face of Duke Visconti—the man who started the cathedral. The museum is filled with statues and spires like this, carved of *marmo di Candoglia*—marble from Candoglia. The duke's family gave the entire Candoglia quarry (near Stresa) to the church for all the marble it would ever need.

You'll pop into a long room filled with more statues. On your left, gaze into the eyes of the big, gilded bust of **God the Father.** Made of wood, wrapped in copper, and gilded in the early 1400s, this giant head covered the keystone connecting the tallest arches directly above the high altar of the Duomo.

MILAN

Continue into a narrow room lined with grotesque **gargoyles**. When attached to the cathedral, they served two purposes: to scare away evil spirits and to spew rainwater away from the building.

Twist through several more rooms of 14th- and 15th-century statues big and small that embellished the church's many spires. In one long, brick-walled hall, watch on the left for **St. Paul the Hermit,** who got close to God by living in the desert. While wearing only a simple robe, he's filled with inner richness. The intent is for pilgrims to commune with him and feel at peace (but I couldn't stop thinking of the Cowardly Lion—"Put 'em up! Put 'em up!").

Ten steps beyond Paul, look for the 15th-century dandy with the rolled-up contract in his hand. That's Visconti's descendant, Galeazzo Sforza, and if it weren't for him, the church facade might still be brick as bare as the walls of this room. The contract he holds makes it official—the church now owns the marble quarry (and it makes money on it to this day).

In the next room, study the brilliantly gilded and dynamic statue *God the Father* (1554). Five steps farther is a sumptuous Flanders-style **tapestry,** woven of silk, silver, and gold in 1468. Half a millennium ago, this hung from the high altar. In true Flemish style, it weaves vivid details of everyday life into the theology. It tells the story of the Crucifixion by showing three scenes at once. Note the exquisite detail, down to the tears on Mary's cheeks.

Next you'll step through a stunning room with 360 degrees of gorgeous **stained glass** from the 12th to 15th century, telling the easily recognizable stories of the Creation, the Tower of Babel, and David and Goliath. Take a close look at details that used to be too far above the cathedral floor to be seen clearly—again, designed for God's eyes only.

Farther on, you'll reach a display of **terra-cotta panels** juxtaposed with large **monochrome paintings** (1628) by Giovanni Battista Crespi. After Crespi finished the paintings, they were translated into terra-cotta, and finally sculpted in marble to decorate the doorways of the cathedral. Study Crespi's *Creation of Eve (Creazione di Eva)* and its terra-cotta twin. This served as the model for the marble statue that still stands above the center door on the church's west portal (1643). You'll pass a few more of these scenes, then hook into a room with the original, stone-carved, swirling *Dancing Angels,* which decorated the ceiling over the door.

• *Follow the one-way route to see the final exhibits.*

After passing several big tapestries, and a big warehouse where statues and their terra-cotta models are stacked on shelves stretching up to the ceiling, you'll reach the *Frame of the Madonnina* (1773). Standing like a Picasso is the original iron frame for the statue of the Virgin Mary that still crowns the cathedral's tallest spire. In 1967, a steel replacement was made for the 33 pieces of gilded copper bolted to the frame. The carved-wood face of Mary (in the corner) is the original mold for Mary's cathedral-crowning copper face.

Soon you'll get a better look at that **wooden model** of the Duomo. This is the actual model used in the 16th century by the architects and engineers to build the church. This version of the facade wasn't built, and other rejected facades line the walls.

On your way out, you'll pass models for the Duomo's doors. And stepping outside, as your eyes adjust to the sunlight, you'll see the grand church itself—looking so glorious thanks to the many centuries of hard work you've just learned about.

▲▲Duomo Rooftop

Strolling between the frilly spires of the cathedral rooftop terraces is the most memorable part of a Duomo visit. You can climb the stairs or take the elevators. (The stairs save you €5 but don't really bypass any line. The stairs and elevators are at both transepts, but which ones are open varies—look for signs.) Touring the roof first before entering the church lets you avoid a second security line.

Once up there, you'll loop around the rooftop, wandering through a fancy forest of spires with great views of the city, the square, and—on clear days—the crisp and jagged Alps to the north. And, 330 feet above everything, La Madonnina overlooks it all. This 15-foot-tall gilded Virgin Mary is a symbol of the city.

Visiting the Rooftop: As you emerge from the stairs or lift, you first walk along the **lower side-terrace.** You'll enjoy close-ups of fanciful gargoyles, statue-topped spires, and ever-changing views of the rows of flying buttresses (which, on this lavishly ornamented Gothic church, are both decorative and functional).

Take a moment to appreciate the detail. Keep in mind that the stairs you climbed were designed not for the public but for workers. The exquisite figures carved in stone around you—every face and every glower all different—were unseen by the public for over 400 years. They were all carved as a gift to God.

Next you climb a richly carved staircase to the sloping **rooftop**—directly above the nave. As you wander among the spires, pick any one and appreciate its details. At the **spires'** base is the marble "fence" that surrounds the entire rooftop, with its pointed arches topped with pinnacles, which themselves are mostly crowned with crosses. Each spire is supported by blocks of Candoglia marble, with its pink-white-green-blue hues (which blend into gray).

On the next level up, the spires have vertical ribs and saints in cages. Continuing up, they get more ornate, with flamboyant flames that flicker upward toward still more saints posing beneath church-like awnings. Finally, the spire tapers into a slender point, topped with a lifelike **saint** who gazes out over the city. The church has 135 spires—all similar, yet each different. No wonder it took 600 years to carve it all.

At the **counter-facade** (the back side of the church's false-front facade), find a few 20th-century details that are among the last things done. To the left (as you face toward the Piazza del Duomo), find carved reliefs with boxing scenes. Just above and to the right of the boxing scenes is a relief of carved foliage. The proud-looking face (from the 1930s) peering out from the leaves is none other than the WWII dictator Benito Mussolini.

Before leaving, check out the great **views** of the city. To the east, you can peer down into the Piazza del Duomo, 20 stories below.

To the south of the Duomo is the red-brick, octagonal, statue-topped bell tower of San Gottardo Church, built in the 1300s by the same Visconti family that began the Duomo. The hard-to-miss Velasca Tower (Torre Velasca) is a top-heavy skyscraper from the 1950s (modeled on medieval watchtowers such as those at the Sforza Castle), which became a symbol of Milan's rise from the ashes of World War II.

Looking north, there's a skyline of a dozen-plus skyscrapers. At the far right of the group is the 32-story Pirelli Tower, a slender rectangle with tapering sides, which proclaimed Italy's postwar "economic miracle." The UniCredit Tower (from 2011), with its 750-foot-high rocket-like spire, is Italy's tallest building, and represents Milan's future. (This marks the Porta Nuova neighborhood, described later and worth a visit.)

As you leave, a single staircase takes you to the ground floor inside the church, where you can continue out or—if you have a ticket—enter the church.

AROUND THE DUOMO
▲Piazza del Duomo

Stand in the center of Milan's main square and take in the scene. Before you rises the massive, prickly facade of Milan's cathedral, the Duomo. The huge equestrian **statue** in the center of the piazza is Victor Emmanuel II, the first king of Italy. He's looking at the grand **Galleria** named for him. The words above the triumphal arch entrance read: "To Victor Emmanuel II, from the people of

Milan." This grand square is ground zero for public events, marches, and spectacles in Milan.

To the right of the Duomo are the twin fascist buildings of the Arengario Palace. Mussolini made grandiose speeches from the balcony on the left. Study the build-

ings' relief panels, which tell—with fascist melodrama—the history of Milan. Today the left palace houses a museum of 20th-century art (described later).

Directly to the right of the Duomo is the historic ducal palace, the Palazzo Reale, which now houses the **Duomo Museum** (described earlier). The palace was redone in the Neoclassical style by Empress Maria Theresa in the late 1700s, when Milan was ruled by the Austrian Habsburgs.

Behind the Victor Emmanuel II statue (opposite the cathedral, about a block beyond the square), hiding in a small courtyard, is **Piazza dei Mercanti,** the center of medieval Milan (described later).

And all around you in Piazza del Duomo is a classic European scene and a local gathering point. Professionals scurry, fashion-forward kids loiter, and young thieves peruse.

MILAN

▲▲Galleria Vittorio Emanuele II

This breathtaking four-story glass-domed arcade, next to Piazza del Duomo, is a symbol of Milan. The iron-and-glass shopping

mall (built during the age of Eiffel and the heady days of Italian unification) showcased a new, modern era. It was the first building in town to have electric lighting, and since its inception it's been an elegant and popular meeting place. (Sadly, its designer, Giuseppe Mengoni, fell off a scaffold and died the day before the gallery opened.) Here, in this covered piazza, you can turn an expensive cup of coffee into a good value by enjoying some of Europe's best people-watching.

The venerable **Bar Camparino** (at the Galleria's Piazza del Duomo entry), with a period interior surviving from the 1870s, is the former haunt of famous opera composer Giuseppe Verdi and conductor Arturo Toscanini, who used to stop by after their performances at La Scala. It's a fine place to enjoy a drink and people-watch (€4 for an espresso is a great deal to take a seat, relax, and enjoy the view, or pay €1.30 at the bar just to experience the scene). The café is named after the Campari family (its first owners), originators of the famous red Campari bitter. You can enjoy a Campari or a Campari *spritz* at this unforgettable perch for €15 (daily 9:30-23:00, closed Aug, Piazza Duomo 21, +39 02 8646 4435).

Wander around the Galleria. Its art celebrates the establishment of Italy as an independent country. Around the central dome,

patriotic mosaics symbolize the four major continents (sorry, Australia). The mosaic floor is also patriotic. The white cross in the center is part of the king's coat of arms. The she-wolf with Romulus and Remus (on the south side—facing Rome) honors the city that, since 1870, has been the national capital. On the west side (facing Torino, the provisional capital of Italy from 1861 to 1865), you'll find that city's symbol: a *torino* (little bull). For good luck, locals step on his irresistible little testicles. Two local girls explained to me that it works better if you spin—two times, and it must be clockwise. Find the poor little bull and observe for a few minutes...it's a cute scene. With so much spinning, the mosaic is replaced every few years.

Luxury shops have had outlets here from the beginning. Along with Gucci, Louis Vuitton, and Prada, you'll find Borsalino (at the end near Piazza della Scala), which has been selling hats here since the gallery opened in 1877.

If you cut through the Galleria to the other side, you'll pop out at Piazza della Scala, with its famous opera house and the Gallerie d'Italia—all described later. (While you may be tempted to walk the Highline Galleria, which hangs among the Galleria Vittorio Emanuele II rooftops, it's not worth the time or money.)

▲Museo del Novecento

Northern Italy's contributions to 20th-century *(novecento)* art fill one of the twin buildings of the Arengario Palace, Mussolini's fascist-era City Hall. In this nicely laid-out museum, you'll work your way up the escalators and through the decades, and enjoy a fine panoramic view over Piazza del Duomo through grand arches. The museum sprinkles in a few works by international masters like Picasso, Braque, and Klee to put local art in context.

Cost and Hours: €5; Tue-Sun 9:30-19:30 (Thu until

22:30), closed Mon; last entry one hour before closing, facing Piazza del Duomo at Via Marconi 1, +39 02 8844 4072, www. museodelnovecento.org.

Visiting the Museum: Spiral up the entry ramp, pausing to gaze into the eyes of Italian workers in Giuseppe Pellizza da Volpedo's *The Fourth Estate*. This painting, from 1901, was a bold manifesto of a new era and sets the tone for the revolutionary spirit of the museum.

The second floor introduces Italy's Futurists, who followed trends in Europe as the 1900s began. Artists like Umberto Boccioni and Gino Severini evolved from placid painters of realistic portraits to bold sculptors of swirling forms, capturing a changing world in high-tech motion.

Next, you'll see highlights from the 1920s up to around World War II, including innovative portraiture and experiments with abstraction and geometric form. A few works bring out artists' struggle to navigate the shifting, oppressive ideologies of the fascist years. In Alberto Savinio's *Jour de Reception* four birds strut, like politicians, on a seaside terrace.

The heady postwar years brought a turn toward abstract art. One of the most striking of these works is a sadly misguided celebration of Maoist China by Mario Schifano, created amid the student uprisings of 1968. The museum ends with a race through mostly conceptual work from the remaining decades of the century.

▲Piazza dei Mercanti

This small square, the center of political power in 13th-century Milan, hides one block off Piazza del Duomo (directly opposite the cathedral). A strangely peaceful place today, it offers a fine smattering of historic architecture that escaped the bombs of World War II.

The arcaded, red-brick building that dominates the center of the square was the City Hall (Palazzo della Ragione); its arcades once housed the market hall. Overlooking the wellhead in the middle of the square is a balcony with coats of arms—this is where new laws were announced. Eventually two big families—Visconti and Sforza—took power, Medici-style, in Milan; the snake is their symbol. Running the show in Renaissance times, these dynasties shaped much of the city we see today, including the Duomo and the fortress. In 1454, the Sforza family made peace with Venice while enjoying a friendship with the Medici in Florence (who taught them how to become successful bankers). This ushered in a time of stability and peace, when the region's major city-states were run by banking families and money was freed up for the Renaissance generation to make art, not war.

This square also held the Palace of Justice (the 16th-century courthouse with the clock tower), the market (not food, but crafts: leather, gold, and iron goods), the bank, the city's first university, and its prison.

ON PIAZZA DELLA SCALA

To reach these sights, cut through the Galleria Vittorio Emanuele II from Piazza del Duomo.

Piazza della Scala

This smart little traffic-free square, between the Galleria and the opera house, is dominated by a statue of Leonardo da Vinci. The statue (from 1870) is a reminder that Leonardo spent his best 20 years in Milan, where he found well-paid, steady work. He was the brainy darling of the Sforza family (who dominated Milan as the Medici family dominated Florence). Under the great Renaissance genius stand four of his greatest "Leonardeschi." (He apprenticed a sizable group of followers.) The reliefs show his various contributions as a painter, architect, and engineer. Leonardo, wearing his hydro-engineer hat, reengineered Milan's canal system, complete with locks. (Until the 1920s, Milan was one of Italy's major ports, with canals connecting the city to the Po River and Lake Maggiore. For more on this footnote of Milan's history, read about the Naviglio Grande on page 316.)

The statue of Leonardo is looking at a plain but famous Neoclassical building, arguably the world's most prestigious opera house (described next).

▲La Scala Opera House and Museum

Milan's famous Teatro alla Scala opened in 1778 with an opera by Antonio Salieri (Mozart's wannabe rival). Today, opera buffs can get a glimpse of the theater and tour the adjacent museum's extensive collection, featuring Verdi's top hat, Rossini's eyeglasses, Toscanini's baton, Fettuccini's pesto, original scores, diorama stage sets, busts, portraits, and death masks of great composers and musicians. For true devotees, La Scala is the Mecca of the religion of opera.

Cost and Hours: €10, online booking encouraged, daily 9:00-

17:30, Piazza della Scala, +39 02 8879 7473, www.teatroallascala. org.

Visiting the Museum: The main reason to visit the museum is the opportunity to peek into the theater (on many mornings you'll see the orchestra practicing). The stage is as big as the seating area on the ground floor. (You can see the towering stage box from Piazza della Scala across the street.) A renovation corrected acoustical problems caused by WWII bombing and subsequent reconstruction. The royal box is just below your vantage point, in the center rear. Take in the ornate red-velvet seats, white-and-gold trim, huge stage and orchestra pit, and massive chandelier made of Bohemian crystal.

The museum itself is a handful of small rooms with low-tech displays. Room 1 has antique musical instruments—some are familiar-looking keyboards and guitars, some are strange and weirdly shaped. Room 2 takes you to the roots of opera in *commedia dell'arte*—those humorous plays of outsize characters and elaborate costumes, like clever harlequins and buffoonish doctors in masks. Room 3 features Liszt's grand piano, still in playing condition.

Room 4's paintings lead you through opera's heyday in Milan. There's a street scene of La Scala in 1852, with fancy carriages and well-dressed ladies and gents. Find portraits of great opera composers like portly Rossini, sideburned Donizetti, and thick-bearded Verdi (flanked by his three loves: two wives and a piano). In the glass case are miniature portraits of famous opera composers and singers, as well as Napoleon's sword. Pass through Room 5 and into Room 6, with a glass case holding a snip of Mozart's hair and a cast of Chopin's slender hand. (The stairs lead up to temporary exhibits.)

Room 7 features many of opera's all-stars. In the glass case is a snip of Verdi's hair, scores by Verdi and Puccini, and batons of the great conductor (and music director of La Scala) Toscanini, who's practically a saint in this town. The room's portraits bring opera into the modern age. There's the great composer Puccini, whose accessible operas seem to unfold like realistic plays that just happen to be sung. The great early-20th-century tenor Enrico Caruso brought sophisticated Italian opera to barbaric lands like America. There are portraits of renowned sopranos (and world-class divas) Maria Callas and Renata Tebaldi.

Performances in the Opera House

The show goes on at the world-famous La Scala Opera House, which also hosts ballet and classical concerts. There are performances every month except August, and showtime is usually at 20:00 (for information, check online or call Scala Infotel Service, daily 12:00-18:00, +39 02 7200 3744). On the opening night of an opera, a dress code is enforced for men (suit and tie).

Advance Booking: Seats sell out quickly. Online tickets go on sale two months before performances (www.teatroallascala.org).

Same-Day Tickets: On performance days, 140 sky-high, restricted-view, peanut-gallery tickets are offered at a low price (generally €10-15) at the box office (located down the left side of the theater toward the back on Via Filodrammatici, and marked with *Biglietteria Serale* sign). It's a bit complicated: Show up at 13:00 with an official ID (driver's license or passport) to put your name on a list (one ticket per person; for popular shows people start lining up long before, weekends tend to be busiest), then return at 17:30 for the roll call. You must be present when your name is called to receive a voucher, which you'll then show at the window to purchase your ticket before the performance. Any remaining tickets are sold at a 25 percent discount two hours before showtime online and one hour before showtime at the box office. For details, visit www.teatroallascala.org, then click on "Box Office," then "Tickets and Prices."

▲Gallerie d'Italia

This museum shows exquisite work by 19th- and 20th-century Italian painters and sculptors. It fills three adjacent buildings on Piazza della Scala; the collection was built by a bank that once occupied part of this space. The bank building's architecture is early-20th-century Tiffany-like Historicism, with a hint of Art Nouveau; it's connected to two impressive palazzos that boast the nicest Neoclassical interiors I've seen in Milan.

Cost and Hours: €5, more during special exhibits, free first Sun of the month; open Tue-Sun 9:30-19:30, Thu until 22:30, closed Mon, last entry one hour before closing; audioguide-€1, across from La Scala Opera House at Piazza della Scala 6, www.gallerieditalia.com.

Visiting the Museum: Enter through the bank building facing Piazza della Scala and take the red-velvet stairs to the basement to pick up an audioguide (also downstairs is a bag check, WCs, and the original bank vault, which now stores racks and racks of paintings not on display).

Back upstairs, head into the main atrium of the bank, and consider the special exhibits displayed there. Then, to tackle the permanent art collection in chronological order, head to the far end of the complex and work your way back (follow signs for *Palazzo*

Anguissola Antona Traversi and *Palazzo Brentani*). You'll go through the café back into the Neoclassical palaces, where you'll trace the one-way route through the "Da Canova a Boccioni" exhibit, including marble reliefs by the Neoclassical sculptor Antonio Canova and Romantic paintings by Francesco Hayez. Upstairs, you'll see dramatic and thrilling scenes from the unification of Italy, as well as beautiful landscapes and cityscapes, especially of Milan. (An entire room is devoted to depictions of the now-trendy Naviglio Grande canal area in its workaday prime.)

On your way back to the bank building and the rest of the exhibit, take a moment to poke around the courtyard to find the *officina di restituzioni alle gallerie*—a lab where you can watch art restorers at work. Rejoining the permanent exhibit, you'll see paintings from the late 19th and early 20th centuries: Romantic landscapes; hyperrealistic, time-travel scenes of folk life; and Impressionism. Finally, you'll catch up to the art of the late 20th century, tucked between old bank-teller windows.

WEST OF THE DUOMO

These sights are listed roughly in the order you'll reach them as you travel west from Piazza del Duomo. The first one is just a few short blocks from the cathedral, while the last is just over a mile away.

▲▲Pinacoteca Ambrosiana

This oldest museum in Milan was inaugurated in 1618 to house Cardinal Federico Borromeo's painting collection. It began as a teaching academy, which explains its many replicas of famous works of art. Highlights include original paintings by Botticelli, Caravaggio, and Titian—and, most important, a huge-scale sketch by Raphael and a rare oil painting by Leonardo da Vinci.

Cost and Hours: €15, open Tue-Sun 10:00-18:00, closed Mon, last entry one hour before closing, audioguide-€4, near Piazza del Duomo at Piazza Pio XI 2, Metro: Duomo or Cordusio, +39 02 806 921, www.ambrosiana.eu.

Visiting the Museum: Pick up the map locating the rooms and major works I highlight below, and rent the audioguide (covers both permanent and special exhibits). Then head upstairs to begin your visit.

Raphael's Cartoon (Room 5): Filling an entire wall, this drawing served as an outline for Raphael's famous *School of Athens* fresco at the Vatican Museums. (A cartoon—*cartone* in Italian—is a full-size sketch that's used to transfer a design to another surface.) First, watch the five-minute video introduction. While the Vatican's much-adored fresco is attributed entirely to Raphael, it was painted mostly by his students. But this *cartone* was wholly sketched by the hand of Raphael. To transfer the fresco design to the wall, his assistants riddled this cartoon with pinpricks along the outlines of the figures, stuck it to the wall of the pope's study, and then applied a colored powder. (Where the master cared more about the detail, you'll see more pinpricks.) When they removed the *cartone*, the figures' shapes were marked on the wall, and completing the fresco was a lot like filling in a coloring book.

Jan Brueghel (Room 7): As Cardinal Borromeo was a friend of Jan Brueghel, this entire room is filled with delightful works by the artist and other Flemish masters. Study the wonderful detail in Brueghel's *Allegory of Fire* and *Allegory of Water*. The Flemish paintings are extremely detailed—many are painted on copper to heighten the effect—and offer an insight into the psyche of the age. If the cardinal were asked why he enjoyed paintings that celebrated the secular life, he'd likely say, "Secular themes are God's book of nature."

Leonardo Hall (Room 24): During his productive Milan years, Leonardo painted (oil on wood) *Portrait of a Musician*—as delicate, mysterious, and thought-provoking as the *Mona Lisa*. (This is the only one of his paintings that remains in Milan.) The large fresco filling the far wall—with Christ receiving the crown of thorns—is by Bernardino Luini, one of Leonardo's disciples. But I find the big replica painting of *The Last Supper* most interesting. When the cardinal realized that Leonardo's marvelous frescoed original was fading, he commissioned Andrea Bianchi to paint on canvas a careful copy to be displayed here for posterity. Today, this copy gives a rare chance to appreciate the original colorful richness of the now-faded masterpiece.

The Pinacoteca's 17th-century **library** (not to be confused with the separate Biblioteca Ambrosiana, in the same building) hosts a revolving display of Leonardo sketches and notes. These are from the precious Codex Atlanticus, with more than a thousand busy pages done by Leonardo for his own reference, giving us a peek into his amazing mind. On any given day about a dozen pages are on display, with English descriptions.

Piazza degli Affari and a Towering Middle Finger

This square and monument mark the center of Milan's financial district. The bold fascist buildings in the neighborhood were built in the 1930s under Mussolini. Italy's major stock exchange, the Borsa, faces the square. Stand in the center and appreciate the contemporary take on ancient aesthetics (you're standing atop the city's ancient Roman theater). Find the stern statues (at the top of the facade) representing various labors and occupations and celebrating the nobility of workers—typical whistle-while-you-work fascist themes.

Now notice the equally bold modern statue in the center. After a 2009 contest to find the most appropriate sculpture to grace the financial district, this was the winner. With Italy's continuing financial problems, here we see how "the 99 percent" feel when they stand before symbols of corporate power. (Notice how the finger is oriented—it's the 1 percent, and not the 99 percent, who's flipping the bird.) The 36-foot-tall Carrara marble digit was made by Maurizio Cattelan, the most famous—or, at least, most controversial—Italian sculptor of our age. *L.O.V.E.,* as the statue is titled, was temporary at first. But locals liked it, and, by popular demand, it's now permanent.

▲Church of San Maurizio (San Maurizio al Monastero Maggiore)

This church, part of a ninth-century convent built into a surviving bit of Milan's ancient Roman wall, dates from around 1500.

Despite its simple facade, it's a hit with art lovers for its amazing cycle of Bernardino Luini frescoes. Stepping into this church is like stepping into the Sistine Chapel of Lombardy.

Cost and Hours: Free; Wed-Sun 10:00-17:30, closed Mon-Tue; Corso Magenta 15 at the Monastero Maggiore, Metro: Cadorna or Cairoli, +39 02 8844 5208, www. museoarcheologicomilano.it.

Visiting the Church: Bernardino Luini (1480-1532), a follower of Leonardo, was also inspired by his contemporaries Michelangelo and Raphael. Sit in a pew and take in the art, which has the movement and force of Michelangelo and the grace and calm beauty of Leonardo.

Maurizio, the patron saint of this church, was a third-century Roman soldier who persecuted Christians, then converted, and eventually worked to stop those same persecutions. He's the guy standing on the pedestal in the upper right, wearing a bright yellow cape. The nobleman who paid for the art is to the left of the altar, kneeling and cloaked in black and white. His daughter, who joined the convent here and was treated as a queen (as nuns with noble connections were), is to the right. And all around are martyrs—identified by their palm fronds.

The adjacent **Hall of Nuns** (Aula delle Monache), a walled-off area behind the altar, is where cloistered sisters could worship apart from the general congregation. Fine Luini frescoes appear above and around the wooden crucifix. The Annunciation scene at

MILAN

the corners of the arch features a cute Baby Jesus zooming down from heaven (see Mary, on the right, ready to catch him). The organ dates from 1554, and the venue, with its fine acoustics, is popular for concerts with period instruments. Explore the pictorial Bible that lines the walls behind the wooden seats of the choir. Luini's landscapes were groundbreaking in the 16th century. Leonardo incorporated landscapes into his paintings, but Luini was among the first to make landscape the main subject of the painting.

Nearby: You'll exit the Hall of Nuns into the lobby of the adjacent **Archaeological Museum,** where you can pay €5 to see part of the ancient city wall and a third-century Roman tower.

▲▲Basilica di Sant'Ambrogio

One of Milan's top religious, artistic, and historic sights, this church was first built on top of an early Christian martyr's cemetery by St. Ambrose around AD 380, when Milan had become the capital of the fading (and Christian) western Roman Empire.

Cost and Hours: Free, Mon-Sat 10:00-12:30 & 14:30-18:00, Sun 15:00-17:00, modest attire required, Piazza Sant'Ambrogio 15, Metro: Sant'Ambrogio, +39 02 8645 0895, www.basilicasantambrogio.it.

Visiting the Church: Ambrose was a local bishop and one of the great fathers of the early Church. Besides his writings, he's remembered for converting and baptizing St. Augustine of Hippo, who himself became another great Church father. The original fourth-century church was later (in the 12th century) rebuilt in the Romanesque style you see today.

As you step "inside" from the street, you emerge into an arcaded **atrium**—standard in many churches back when people weren't allowed to actually enter the church until they were baptized. The unbaptized waited here during Mass. The courtyard is textbook Romanesque, with playful capitals engraved with fanciful animals. Inset into the wall (right side, above the pagan sarcophagi) are stone markers of Christian tombs—a reminder that this church, like St. Peter's at the Vatican, is built upon an ancient Roman cemetery.

From the atrium, marvel at the elegant 12th-century **facade,** or west portal. It's typical Lombard medieval style. The local bishop would bless crowds from its upper loggia. As two different monastic communities shared the church and were divided in their theology, there were also two different bell towers.

Step into the **nave** and grab a pew. The mosaic in the apse features Christ Pantocrator ("All Powerful") in the company of Milanese saints. Around you are pillars with Romanesque capitals and surviving fragments of the 12th-century frescoes that once covered the church.

The 12th-century **pulpit** sits atop a Christian sarcophagus dating from the year 400. Study its late Roman and early Christian iconography—on the side facing the altar, Apollo on his chariot morphs into Jesus on a chariot. You can see the moment when Jesus gave the Old Testament (the first five books, anyway) to his apostles.

The precious, ninth-century golden **altar** has four ancient porphyry columns under an elegant Romanesque 12th-century canopy. The entire ensemble was taken to the Vatican during World War II to avoid destruction. That was smart—the apse took a direct hit in 1943. A 13th-century mosaic was destroyed; today we see a reconstruction.

Step into the **crypt,** under the altar, to see the skeletal bodies of three people: Ambrose (in the middle, highest) and two earlier Christian martyrs whose tombs he visited before building the church.

Nearby: For a little bonus after visiting the church, consider this: The **Benedictine monastery** next to the church is now Cattolica University. With its stately colonnaded courtyards designed by Renaissance architect Donato Bramante, it's a nice place to study. It's fun to poke around and imagine being a student here.

MILAN

▲Leonardo da Vinci National Science and Technology Museum (Museo Nazionale della Scienza e Tecnica "Leonardo da Vinci")

The spirit of Leonardo lives here (a 10-minute walk from his *Last Supper*). Most tourists focus on the hall of Leonardo—the core of the museum—where wooden models illustrate his designs. But the rest of this immense collection of industrial cleverness is fascinating in its own right. There are exhibits on space exploration, mining, and radio and television (with some original Marconi radios); old musical instruments, computers, and telephones; chunks of the first transatlantic cable; and interactive science workshops. Out back are several more buildings containing antique locomotives and a 150-foot-long submarine from 1957. Ask for an English museum map from the ticket desk—you'll need it. On weekends, this museum is very popular with families, so come early or be prepared to wait in line.

Cost and Hours: €10; Tue-Fri 9:30-17:00, Sat-Sun until 18:30, closed Mon; Via San Vittore 21, Metro: Sant'Ambrogio; +39 02 485 551, www.museoscienza.org.

▲▲Leonardo da Vinci's *Last Supper* (L'Ultima Cena/Cenacolo Vinciano)

Decorating the former dining hall *(cenacolo)* of the Church of Santa Maria delle Grazie, this remarkable, exactingly crafted fresco is one of the ultimate masterpieces of the Renaissance. Reservations are mandatory and should be booked weeks in advance.

Cost and Hours: Entry–€15, entry with guided tour–€23 (tour times listed on website); Tue-Sat 8:15-18:45, Sun from 14:00, closed Mon, arrive at ticket counter 30 minutes before your timed entry; Piazza Santa Maria delle Grazie 2; +39 02 9280 0360, http://cenacolovinciano.org.

Reservations: Timed-entry reservations can be made online or by phone—but they can sell out in minutes. The museum divides the year into three-month spans and opens reservations during the month preceding each span; for example, bookings for May through July open in April. Check the website to find out when tickets for your dates will go on sale. For peak season tickets, be ready to book the moment they're released (Milan time).

To book **online,** go to http://cenacolovinciano.vivaticket.it (you'll have to create an account to book tickets). A calendar shows available time slots for the coming months.

Booking by **phone** lets you get help from a real person but doesn't give you any advantage in getting tickets, and the number is often busy—you may have to call several times to get through (+39 02 9280 0360, office open Mon-Sat 8:00-18:30, closed Sun; select 2 for an English-speaking operator).

Third-Party Tour Option: If you can't get a reservation, you can book a pricier (€65-100) walking or bus tour with an outside vendor that includes a guided visit to *The Last Supper*. Reserve at least a week ahead (see page 279).

Last-Minute Tickets: Occasionally, slots free up on short notice (a day or two ahead) due to cancellations. Just check the website for up-to-date availability—going in person is a waste of time.

Getting There: The Church of Santa Maria delle Grazie is a seven-minute walk from Metro: Conciliazione. From the track, follow signs for *Cenacolo*. You'll walk four blocks. After the first bend you'll see the fine red-brick facade of the church ahead. Or take tram #16 from the Duomo (direction: San Siro or Piazzale Segesta), which drops you off in front of the church. When leaving, cross the street to catch the tram back to the Duomo.

Getting In: Stow your bag (free, required), pick up your ticket, and consider renting the audioguide if it's available. Your time will be called 15 minutes before, and you'll enter the waiting room. Use this time to study up. At your appointed time, the doors open and your group enters. No stress, no crowds, beautifully organized...it's a peaceful and inspiring experience. There's a fine WC at the exit.

Audioguide: If it's available, the €3.50 audioguide is very helpful. Its spiel fills every second of the time you're in the room—a short intro (#100) and then tracks 1 through 5—for the entire 15 minutes you're inside. You can start listening in the waiting room while studying the reproduction of *The Last Supper*.

Background: Milan's leading family, the Sforzas, hired Leonardo to decorate the dining hall of the Dominican monastery that adjoins the church (the Dominican order traditionally placed a Last Supper on one end of their refectories, and a Crucifixion at the other). Leonardo worked on the project from about 1494 until 1498. This gift was essentially a bribe to the monks so that the Sforzas could place their family tomb in the church. Ultimately, the French drove the Sforzas out of Milan, they were never buried here, and the Dominicans got a great fresco for nothing.

Deterioration began within six years of *The Last Supper*'s completion because Leonardo painted on the wall in layers, as he would on a canvas, instead of applying pigment to wet plaster in the usual fresco technique. (Examining the extremely close-up photos in the waiting room lets you see how the paint is simply flaking off.) The church was bombed in World War II, but—miraculously, it seems—the wall holding *The Last Supper* remained standing. A 21-year restoration project (completed in 1999) peeled away 500 years of touch-ups, leaving Leonardo's masterpiece faint but vibrant.

Visiting *The Last Supper*: To minimize damage from humidity, only 30 tourists are allowed in every 15 minutes for exactly 15 minutes. While you wait, read the history of the masterpiece or listen to the audioguide. As your appointed time nears, you'll be herded between several rooms to dehumidify, while doors close behind you and open up slowly in front of you.

And then the last door opens, you take a step, you look right, and...there it is. In a big, vacant, whitewashed room, you'll see

MILAN

faded pastels and not a crisp edge. The feet under the table look like negatives. But the composition is dreamy—Leonardo captures the psychological drama as the Lord says, "One of you will betray me," and the apostles huddle in stressed-out groups of three, wondering, "Lord, is it I?" Some are scandalized. Others want more information. Simon (on the far right) gestures as if to ask a question that has no answer. In this agitated atmosphere, only Judas (fourth from left and the only one with his face in shadow)—clutching his 30 pieces of silver and looking pretty guilty—is not shocked.

The circle meant life and harmony to Leonardo. Deep into a study of how life emanates in circles—like ripples on a pool hit by a pebble—Leonardo positioned the 13 characters in a semicircle. Jesus is in the center, from whence the spiritual force of God emanates, or ripples out.

The room depicted in the painting seems like an architectural extension of the monks' dining hall. The disciples form an apse, with Jesus as the altar—in keeping with the Eucharist. Jesus anticipates his sacrifice, his face sad, all-knowing, and accepting. His feet even foreshadow his death by crucifixion. Had the door, which was cut out in 1652, not been added, you'd see how Leonardo placed Jesus' feet atop each other, ready for the nail.

The perspective is mathematically correct, with Jesus' head as the vanishing point where the converging sight lines meet. In fact, restorers found a tiny nail hole in Jesus' left eye, which anchored the strings Leonardo used to establish these lines. The table is cheated out to show the meal. Notice the exquisite lighting. The walls are lined with tapestries (as they would have been), and the one on the right is brighter in order to fit the actual lighting in the refectory (which has windows on the left). With the extremely natural effect of the light and the drama of the faces, Leonardo created a masterpiece.

The monks ate at three tables just like the one Leonardo painted, with a carefully ironed tablecloth also just like the one painted. The monks ate in silence, communicating with hand gestures (notice the ballet of hand gestures in Leonardo's composition).

Save a minute or two for the fresco of the Crucifixion on the opposite wall, which provides an instructive contrast. This is done in the traditional fresco technique—less soul and subtlety but much better preserved. It needed to be done quickly (as the plaster dried) and was finished in three months (compared to over three years for *The Last Supper*). For a good look at the contrasting styles, find the faded image of the Sforza duchess in the lower-right corner. She was added to the scene by Leonardo using the same technique he used in *The Last Supper*.

Before stepping out, from the back of the room look one last time at Leonardo's masterpiece and imagine this room filled with three more tables and 60 monks immersed in devotion and with no idea that 500 years later travelers would be dropping by to appreciate the art decorating their hall.

The adjacent **Church of Santa Maria delle Grazie** survived World War II unscathed and is worth a quick look (free). Its fine Gothic arches lead to a Renaissance Bramante-designed dome. The Dominican monks frescoed in black and white on each pilaster were the first monks to eat under Leonardo's *Last Supper*.

NORTH OF THE DUOMO
▲▲Brera Art Gallery (Pinacoteca di Brera)

Milan's top collection of Italian paintings (13th-20th century) is world class, but it can't top those in Rome or Florence. Established

in 1809 to house Napoleon's looted art, it fills the first floor above a prestigious art college. You'll dodge scruffy starving artists...and wonder if there's a 21st-century Leonardo in your midst.

Cost and Hours: €15, advance timed-entry ticket may be required—check ahead online, free first Sun of month; Tue-Sun 8:30-19:15, closed Mon, last entry one hour before closing; helpful audioguide-€5, free lockers, Via Brera 28, Metro: Lanza or Montenapoleone, +39 02 722 631, www.pinacotecabrera. org.

Visiting the Museum: Enter the grand courtyard of a former monastery, where you'll be greeted by the nude *Napoleon with Tinkerbell* (by Antonio Canova), then climb the stairway, following signs to *Pinacoteca*. Pick up a map of the museum's masterpieces, some of which I've highlighted below. To get the most out of your visit, invest in the audioguide. You'll follow a clockwise, chronological route through the huge collection. Take time to read the English descriptions, many of which are absolutely poetic. Here are the highlights:

Next to the information desk peek through the window to see the 300-year-old library, then pop into the chapel (on the left) frescoed by a follower of Giotto in the 1300s. After the turnstile, enjoy the setup in the short entry hall.

Before Antonio Canova's big marble statue of naked Napoleon, head left into the dark, narrow blue hall to see Andrea Mantegna's iconic foreshortened Christ (and others by the influential early Renaissance master). Room 8 features more Mantegna, and bright and vivid paintings by the Bellini brothers from around

1500. Room 9 is for the big canvases by 16th-century Venetian masters (like Tintoretto and Paolo Veronese).

Past the towering marble statue of Napoleon, Room 15 holds four paintings by Vincenzo Campi, offering slices of local Milan life from 1591.

Then you reach the restoration lab, which offers a chance to peek in on the hard work of keeping these paintings looking so good.

Room 22 sparkles with High Gothic art. Carlo Crivelli, a contemporary of Leonardo, employed Renaissance technique while clinging to the mystique of the Gothic Age (that's why I like him so much). And Gentile da Fabriano hints at the realism of the coming Renaissance (check out the lifelike flowers and realistic, bright gold paint—he used real gold powder).

Room 26 is nicknamed "The Golden Room" for its Renaissance masterpieces from the early 16th century by Raphael *(The Marriage of the Virgin),* Piero della Francesca *(Madonna and Child with Saints),* and Donato Bramante.

In Room 28 don't miss the gritty-yet-intimate realism of Caravaggio's *Supper at Emmaus.* Room 31 features Rubens (and other Dutch and Flemish works). And Room 35 is dedicated to "postcard" art from the 18th-century Grand Tour days (like Venice-scapes by Canaletto and Francesco Guardi).

Finally, in Room 37 you come to 19th-century Romanticism, and in Room 38 three patriotic paintings, including *The Kiss* by Francesco Hayez, which evoke the spirit of Italy's fight for independence, the Risorgimento.

▲Risorgimento Museum

With a quick swing through this quiet one-floor museum, you'll get an idea of the interesting story of Italy's rocky road to unity: from Napoleon (1796) to the victory in Rome (1870). You'll see paintings, uniforms, monuments, a city model, and other artifacts. Thoughtful English descriptions help make this a meaningful look at this important period of Italian history.

Cost and Hours: Free; Tue-Sun 10:00-17:30, closed Mon; just around the block from Brera Art Gallery at Via Borgonuovo 23, Metro: Montenapoleone, +39 02 8846 4176, www.museodelrisorgimento.mi.it.

Poldi Pezzoli Museum

This classy house of art features Italian paintings of the 15th through 18th century, old weaponry, and lots of interesting decorative arts, such as a roomful of old sundials and compasses. It's all on view in a sumptuous 19th-century residence.

Cost and Hours: €14; Wed-Mon 10:00-13:00 & 14:00-18:00,

closed Tue; audioguide–€3, Via Manzoni 12, Metro: Montenapoleone, +39 02 794 889, www.museopoldipezzoli.it.

Bagatti Valsecchi Museum

This unique 19th-century collection of Italian Renaissance furnishings was assembled by two aristocratic brothers who spent a wad turning their home into a Renaissance mansion.

Cost and Hours: €12, includes audioguide; Wed-Fri 13:00-17:45, Sat-Sun 10:00-17:45, closed Mon-Tue; Via Gesù 5, Metro: Montenapoleone, +39 02 7600 6132, www.museobagattivalsecchi. org.

SFORZA CASTLE AND NEARBY
▲▲Sforza Castle (Castello Sforzesco)

The castle of Milan tells the story of the city in brick. Today it features a vast courtyard, a sprawling museum, and—most important—a chance to see Michelangelo's final, unfinished pietà.

Cost and Hours: €5, or €10 when there's an exhibit on; museum open Tue-Sun 10:00-17:30, closed Mon; two counters sell the same ticket covering everything here; castle grounds open daily 7:00-19:30; WCs and free/mandatory lockers downstairs from ticket counter, Metro: Cairoli or Lanza, +39 02 8846 3700, www.milanocastello.it.

Background: Built in the late 1300s as a military fortress, Sforza Castle guarded the gate to the city wall and defended Milan from enemies "within and without." It was beefed up by the Sforza duke in 1450 in anticipation of a Venetian attack. Later, the Sforza family made it their residence, building their Renaissance palace into the fortress. It was even home to their in-house genius, Leonardo. (When he applied for a position with the Sforza family, he did so as a military engineer and contributed to the design of the ramparts.) During the time of foreign rule (16th-19th century), it was a barracks for occupying Spanish, French, and Austrian soldiers. Today it houses an array of museums, but I'd concentrate on the Michelangelo pietà and the Museum of Ancient Art.

◐ Self-Guided Tour: This tour begins outside the fortress (on the Piazza Castello side), then focuses on the highlights inside.

The Fortress: The **gate** facing the city center stands above a ditch that was once filled with water. A relief celebrates Umberto I, the second king of Italy. Above that, a statue of St. Ambrose, the patron of Milan (and a local bishop in the fourth century), oversees the action. Notice the diagram a few steps away that shows how the city was encircled first by a crude medieval wall, and then by a state-of-the-art 16th-century wall—of which this castle was a key element. It's apparent from the enormity of these walls that Milan was a strategic prize. Today, the walls are gone, giving the city two circular boulevards.

This immense brick fortress—exhausting at first sight—can only be described as heavy. Its three huge courtyards originally functioned as military parade grounds but today host concerts and welcome the public. (The holes in the walls were for scaffolding during the construction.)

• *As you enter the main courtyard, look to your left to see the restored hospital building that houses the...*

Museo Pietà Rondanini (Michelangelo): This is a rare opportunity to enjoy a Michelangelo statue with no crowds, beautifully displayed in a room that dates from the same era as the artwork—the mid-1500s. Michelangelo died while still working on this piece, his fourth pietà—a representation of a dead Christ with a sorrowful Virgin Mary. While unfinished and seemingly a mishmash of corrections and reworks, it's a thought-provoking work by a genius at nearly 90 years of age, who knows he's fast approaching the end of his life. The symbolism is of life and of death: Jesus returning to his mother, as two bodies seem to become one.

Michelangelo's more famous pietà at the Vatican (carved when he was in his 20s) features a beautiful, young, and astonished Mary. Here, Mary is older and wiser. Perhaps Mary is now better able to accept death as part of life...as is Michelangelo. The pietà at the Vatican is simple and clear, showing two different people: the mother holding her dead son. Contemplating the *Pietà Rondanini,* you wonder who's supporting whom. It's confused and complex, each figure seeming to both need and support the other.

This unfinished statue shows the genius of Michelangelo midway through a major rework—Christ's head is cut out of Mary's right shoulder, and an earlier arm is still just hanging there. Above Mary's right ear, you can see the remains of a previous face (eye, brow, and hairline).

And there's a certain power to this rawness. Walk around the back to see the strain in Mary's back (and Michelangelo's rough chisel work) as she struggles to support her son. The sculpture's elongated form hints at the Mannerist style that would follow.

Facing the pietà is a bronze life-size head, based on a death mask made at the artist's passing in 1564. Imagine him working on his pietà—still vibrant and seeking.

• *From the pietà, return to the big courtyard and head for the little draw-bridge (on the left, directly across from where you entered the complex). As you cross, look into the moat on the right at the stone balls—not shot from a cannon but hurled by a catapult. Gunpowder amped up military power during the Renaissance. The fortifications you see here have thicker walls, to be cannon-resistant, and round turrets, so cannonballs would more likely glance off without causing damage. Pass through to find (on the right) the entrance to the...*

Museum of Ancient Art (Museo d'Arte Antica): This sprawling collection fills the old Sforza family palace with interesting medieval armor, furniture, early Lombard art, and much more.

In the first room, among ancient sarcophagi (with early Christian themes), stands a fine 14th-century **equestrian statue**—a memorial to Bernabò Visconti. Of the four virtues, he selected only two (strength and justice) to stand beside his anatomically correct horse, opting out of love and patience.

Farther along, the room of **tapestries** is dominated by a big embroidery of St. Ambrose defeating the heretical Arians. While that was a fourth-century struggle, 12 centuries later, he was summoned back in spirit to deal with Protestants, in support of Archbishop Borromeo. With St. Peter's Basilica behind him, a Borromeo-like Ambrose stands tall and strong as a Counter-Reformation leader in defense of the Roman Church. The room is lined with 16th-century Flemish tapestries, which were easy to pack up quickly as the nobility traveled. These were typical of those used to warm chilly stone palaces.

Next, you'll come to the **Sala delle Asse.** The Visconti family, who grew rich making silk in the Lake Como region, had their ballroom painted by Leonardo and his followers. Plastered over for centuries, this room was restored around 1900. Not much sparkle survives, but you can appreciate the intricate canopy woven with branches and rope in complicated knots—the work of Leonardo himself, in 1498.

From here, you'll pass through rooms filled with weapons and armor from the 16th and 17th centuries.

• *At this point, you're free to go. But if you have a larger-than-average attention span, follow signs upstairs to the Decorative Arts Museum, then the Painting Gallery (Pinacoteca), and finally the Musical Instruments Museum. When you're done, consider popping out the back door of the fortress and taking a break in the lush Sempione Park.*

Sempione Park (Parco Sempione) and Arco della Pace

This is Milan's equivalent of Central Park. With its circa-1900 English-style gardens, free Liberty Style aquarium, views of the triumphal arch, and sprawling family-friendly grounds, this park is particularly popular on weekends.

A 15-minute walk through the park, on the left, is the erector-set **Branca Tower** (Torre Branca), built for an exposition in the 1930s. For a commanding city view, you can ride an elevator as high as the Mary that crowns the Duomo (€6, best in daylight, erratic hours, closed when windy).

Next to the tower is the excellent **Triennale di Milano,** a design museum with changing exhibits that celebrate one of this city's fortes (www.triennale.org).

At the far end of the park is the monumental **Arco della Pace.** Originally an arch of triumph, it comes with Nike, goddess of victory, commanding a six-horse chariot. It was built facing Paris to welcome Napoleon's rule and to celebrate the ideals of the French Revolution, destined to lift Italy into the modern age. When the locals learned Napoleon was just another megalomaniac, they turned the horses around, their tails facing France. Today the arch is ringed by the circular Piazza Sempione, with a wonderful community vibe. It's a local favorite for its bars and *aperitivo* scene.

Via Dante

This grand pedestrian boulevard and popular shopping street leads from Sforza Castle toward the town center and the Duomo. Via Dante was carved out of a medieval tangle of streets to celebrate Italian unification (c. 1870) and make Milan a worthy metropolis. Consequently, all the facades lining it are relatively new. Enjoy strolling this beautiful people zone, where you'll hear the whir of bikes and the lilting melodies of accordion players instead of traffic noise. Photo exhibits are frequently displayed up and down the street. In front of Sforza Castle, a commanding statue of Giuseppe Garibaldi, a hero of the unification movement, looks down one of Europe's longest pedestrian zones. From here you can walk to the Duomo and beyond (about 1.5 miles), appreciating Italian design both in shop windows and on smartly clothed Milanese.

AWAY FROM THE CENTER
▲▲Porta Nuova: The New Milan

A little north of downtown, by the Porta Garibaldi train station, a sparkling forest of glassy office and condominium towers has risen around a parklike, pedestrian-only urban-renewal district called Porta Nuova. Milan is Italy's center of design, architecture, and urban planning, so it's not surprising that civic leaders have worked to decentralize the Duomo-centric city by reenvisioning this once run-down neighborhood, neglected since its WWII bombing. An hour spent wandering this sleek, successful cityscape does more to expand your understanding of Milan (and Italy) than any other time you could spend here.

Visiting Porta Nuova: For help orienting yourself in this district, see the "Greater Milan" map on page 272.

Ride the Metro to Garibaldi FS, and exit following *Corso Como* signs. Rocketing skyward before you in a group of contemporary office towers is the tallest structure in Italy, the **UniCredit Building** (750 feet high). Follow the curved road to reach the complex upon which that building sits. Ride the escalators up to the main square, called...

Piazza Gae Aulenti: Enjoy this lively public hub, with its delightful **pond** that transforms from shallow reflecting pool to dancing fountains throughout the day. In the center you'll see **glass "horns."** Find their visual echo under the passageway to the right: brass horns that allow people to gossip from one level to the next—a reminder that piazzas have always enabled people to connect with one another.

Many locals refer to this area simply as "Garibaldi." Essentially an outdoor mall (with multinationals renting space), it's a fun place to search for views of the Alps or to sate your hunger in the fancy downstairs food court, where you might also enjoy browsing at **Esselunga,** a full-size Italian supermarket with a complete range of local products (daily).

Continue your stroll beyond the piazza toward the building with the wooden facade. On your left in the Isola (Island) neigh-

borhood, you'll see two condominium towers bushy with trees (800 of them plus about 20,000 other plants) called the **Vertical Forest.** Named the best tall building in Europe (designed by the Italian architect Stefano Boeri), these twin towers take "green" to a new level. The trees balance the pollution created by the towers' residents and contribute to a cooler atmosphere.

"Growing" from the towers' base is a little park called the **Library of Trees.** Laid out in a network of geometric patterns and paths, it serves as pedestrian zone, play area, and event venue. People can commune with each other and the more than 135,000 plants and trees living in this field of greens. Sustainability, workability, livability, lowered energy consumption, and innovation are key goals here.

MILAN

Next, follow the Passerella Gioia signposts past the wooden building to a pedestrian bridge. Cross the bridge to Piazza Alvar Aalto and the Varesine district. In front of you, a cluster of jagged, balconied towers mix condominium residences with ground-floor shops and eateries. Walk just beyond to see an urban park flanked by shorter condos and a series of commercial buildings nicknamed Diamantini (Little Diamonds). This name is a nod to the massive, laminated glass Diamond Tower high-rise at the end of the development. Affectionately called Il Diamantone (The Big Diamond) for its irregular angles, the 31-story tower also earned an energy-efficiency award.

Now retrace your steps back over the bridge and marvel at this sparkling, futuristic neighborhood from the opposite angle.

Corso Como and Porta Garibaldi: Back at the main square (Piazza Gae Aulenti), depart past the golden gossip horns down Via V. Capelli. Bear left on Corso Como and head to the 16th-century gate called Porta Garibaldi, once part of the city walls. Corso Como, while an old street, is trendy, high-end, and pedestrianized—popular for its *aperitivo* and cocktail bars and stylish shops. At #10 is 10 Corso Como, a fashion boutique with a café that's worth a quick look.

Immediately left of Porta Garibaldi is **Eataly.** This contemporary marketplace (now found throughout Italy—and the world) has turned the former Teatro Smeraldo into a gourmet megastore. It's overwhelming but oddly enchanting, with its overpriced Italian market goods and restaurants serving all the major food groups—pasta, meats, vegetables, chocolate, and, of course, gelato (daily 8:30-23:00, Piazza XXV Aprile 10, Metro: Moscova, www.eataly.net).

Beyond Porta Garibaldi stretches Corso Garibaldi, for more lively Milanese pedestrian and shopping action.

▲Naviglio Grande (Canal District)

Milan, although far from any major lake or river, has a sizable port, literally called the "Big Canal." Since 1170, boats have been able to sail from Milan to the Mediterranean via the Ticino River (which flows into the Po River on its way to the Adriatic Sea). Five hundred years ago, Leonardo helped design a modern lock system. During the booming Industrial Age in the 19th century—and especially with the flurry of construction after Italian unification—ships used the canals to bring in the marble and stone needed to make Milan the great city it is today. In fact, centuries ago, one canal (filled in during the 1930s) let barges unload stone right at the building site of the great cathedral. In the 1950s, landlocked Milan was the seventh-biggest port in Italy, as its canals aided in rebuilding the bombed-out city.

Today, disused train tracks parallel the canal, old warehouse buildings recall the area's working-class heritage, and former workers' tenements—once squalid and undesirable—are being renovated. The once-rough area now dubbed Milan's "Little Venice" is trendy, traffic-free, and thriving with inviting bars and eateries. Come here for dinner or a late-afternoon drink (for recommendations, see "Eating in Milan," later).

Getting There: Ride the Metro (or tram #2) to Porta Genova, exit following signs to *Via Casale*, and walk the length of Via Casale one block directly to the canal. Most bars and restaurants are to the left, on both sides of the canal. (See the map on page 272.)

▲Monumental Cemetery (Il Cimitero Monumentale)

Europe's most artistic and dreamy cemetery experience, this grand place was built just after unification to provide a suitable final rest-ing spot for the city's "famous and well-deserving men." Any cemetery can be evocative, but this one—with its super-emotional portrayals of the deceased and their heavenly escorts (in art styles c. 1870-1930)—is in a class by itself. It's a vast garden art gallery of proud busts and grim reapers, heartbroken angels and weeping widows, too-young soldiers and countless old smiles, frozen on yellowed black-and-white photos.

Cost and Hours: Free, Tue-Sun 8:00-18:00, closed Mon, pick up map at the entrance gate, ride Metro purple line 5 to Monumentale, +39 02 8846 5706, https://monumentale. comune.milano.it.

Leonardo's Horse

The largest equestrian monument in the world is a reconstruction of a model created in 1482 by Leonardo da Vinci for the Sforza family. The clay prototype was destroyed in 1499 by invading French forces, who used it for target practice. In 1982, American Renaissance-art collector Charles Dent decided to build the 15-ton, 24-foot-long statue from Leonardo's design, planning to present it to the Italians in homage to Leonardo's genius. Unfortunately, Dent died before the project could be completed. In 1997, American sculptor Nina Akamu created a new clay model that became the template for the final statue; it was unveiled in 1999.

Getting There: The statue (free to view) is at a horse racetrack on the western outskirts of town—ride Metro purple line 5 to San Siro Ippodromo.

Shoah Memorial of Milan (Memoriale della Shoah Milano)

Near Milano Centrale station, this "place of memory and meeting" is a poignant reminder that the Holocaust did not spare Italy's Jews. From 1943 to 1945 the Nazis used the underground track 21 at the station (designed for transferring postal carriages) to secretly gather and ship out trainloads of Jews. Once full, boxcars—designed for animals but jammed with 60 people—would roll north, destined for distant concentration camps. With rare surviving boxcars and a series of exhibits, the memorial confronts the theme "Indifference is violence," recalling how populations often choose not to know when evil is in their midst. It's fascinating and emotional; the only English you'll find is in the explanatory brochure that comes with your ticket.

Cost and Hours: €10, down the right side of Milano Centrale station at Piazza Safra 1, Sat-Thu 10:00-16:00, closed Fri, +39 02 282 0975, www.memorialeshoah.it).

Shopping in Milan

For locations, see the map on page 322.

High Fashion in the Quadrilateral

For world-class window shopping, visit the Quadrilateral, an elegant high-fashion shopping area around Via Montenapoleone, northeast of La Scala Opera House. This was the original Beverly Hills of Milan. In the 1920s, the top fashion shops moved in, and today it remains *the* place for designer labels. In this land where fur is still prized, the people-watching is as entertaining as the window shopping. Notice also the exclusive penthouse apartments with roof gardens high above the scene. Via Montenapoleone and the pedestrianized Via della Spiga are the best streets.

Whether you're gawking or shopping, here's the best route: From Piazza della Scala, walk up Via Alessandro Manzoni to the Metro stop at Montenapoleone, browse down Via Montenapoleone, and cut left on Via Santo Spirito (lined with grand aristocratic palazzos—peek into the courtyard at #7). Across the street, step into the elegant courtyard at #10 to check out the café sitters and their poodles. Continue to the end of Via Santo Spirito, then turn right to window shop down traffic-free Via della Spiga. After a few short blocks, turn right on Via Sant'Andrea and then left, back onto Montenapoleone, which leads you through a final gauntlet of temptations to Corso Giacomo Matteotti, near the Piazza San Babila. Then (for less-expensive shopping thrills), walk back to the Duomo down the pedestrian-only Corso Vittorio Emanuele II.

Shops near the Duomo

For a (slightly) more reasonably priced shopping excursion, step into **La Rinascente**—one of Europe's classic department stores. (It's around the left side as you face the front of the Duomo.) Simply riding the escalator up and up gives a fun overview of Italian design and marketing. The seventh floor is a top-end food circus with recommended restaurants, terrace views of the Duomo, and a public WC. The store's name translates roughly as "the place reborn" and fits its history. In an earlier life, this was a fine Art Nouveau-style building—until it burned down in 1918. Rebuilt, it was bombed in World War II and rebuilt once again (Sun-Thu 10:00-21:00, Fri-Sat until 22:00, has a VAT refund office, faces north side of the Duomo on Piazza del Duomo).

Sleeping in Milan

My recommended hotels are all within a few minutes' walk of a fairly central Metro station. With Milan's fine subway system, you can get anywhere in town in a flash. To save money, search for a deal at a basic chain hotel (such as Ibis) near an outlying Metro stop.

Hotel prices in Milan rise and fall with the convention schedule. In March, April, September, and October, the city can be completely jammed by conventions, and hotel prices go sky-high (see www.fieramilano.it for convention schedule).

Summer is usually wide open, with soft or discounted prices, though many hotels close in August for vacation. Hotels cater more to business travelers than to tourists, so prices and availability are a little better on Fridays and Saturdays.

NEAR THE DUOMO

The Duomo area is thick with people-watching, reasonably priced eateries, and major sights, but hotel prices are high.

$$$$ Hotel Spadari boasts an Art Deco-inspired lobby designed by the Milanese artist Giò Pomodoro ("Joe Tomato" in English). The 40 cool-blue rooms have billowing drapes, big paintings, and designer doors. Breakfast is sumptuous, and the Duomo is two blocks away (RS%, air-con, elevator, Via Spadari 11, +39 02 7200 2371, www.spadarihotel.com, reservation@spadarihotel.com).

$$$$ Hotel Gran Duca di York, three blocks from the Duomo, is on a stark street of banks and public buildings. Set in a former priory-run school attended by the then-future Pope Pius X, it has comfy and spacious public areas, delightfully helpful staff, and 33 modern and bright rooms (air-con, elevator, Via Moneta 1, Metro: Cordusio or Duomo, +39 02 874 863, www.ducadiyork.com, info@ducadiyork.com).

BETWEEN LA SCALA AND SFORZA CASTLE

These slightly less-central places are close to the Via Dante and Via Brera shopping and restaurant scenes.

$$$$ Antica Locanda dei Mercanti offers 15 rooms in an 18th-century palazzo an easy 10-minute walk from the Duomo. While each room has its own personality (some have kitchenettes and four have small terraces), all have a fresh-flower vibe that embraces old and new—a nice change for businesslike Milan (RS%—use code "RSMILANO," air-con, elevator, Via San Tomaso 6, reception on first floor, Metro: Cairoli or Cordusio, +39 02 805 4080, www.locanda.it, locanda@locanda.it, Alex and Eri).

$$$$ Hotel Cusani prides itself on service and has 92 classy, classic, and bright rooms and ample space to lounge (air-con, elevator, family rooms, pay parking; Via Cusani 13, Metro: Cairoli, +39 028 5601, www.gruppouna.it, hotel.cusani@unahotels.it).

$$$$ Hotel Star, a bit more down-to-earth, rents 30 rooms with striking, gaudy artwork over the bed. Ask if you want a quieter interior room (air-con, elevator, Via dei Bossi 5, Metro: Cordusio, +39 02 801 501, www.hotelstar.it, hotelstar@hotelstar.it, Cristina).

NEAR THE LAST SUPPER

These two hotels are farther from the action in a sleepy, mostly residential zone, but the prices are lower. For locations (about a 15-minute walk or quick tram or Metro ride west of the Duomo), see the map on page 280.

$$$ Antica Locanda Leonardo, just down the street from *The Last Supper,* has a romantic, Old World vibe, antique furnishings, and a spacious breakfast room. Each of its 24 uniquely decorated rooms faces either a courtyard (cheaper, some street noise) or a tranquil garden (some rooms with garden balcony, air-con, elevator, Corso Magenta 78, +39 02 4801 4197, www.anticalocandaleonardo.com, info@anticalocandaleonardo.com). From the Duomo area, you can ride tram #16 to the Santa Maria delle Grazie stop, or take the Metro to either Cadorna or Concili-azione and walk five minutes.

$ B&B Hotel Milano Sant'Ambrogio, part of a chain of budget hotels, has 94 efficient, cookie-cutter rooms and a siz-able fourth-floor terrace. Quieter rooms in the back have frosted windows because of the school next door—to respect students' privacy (breakfast extra, air-con, elevator, Via degli Olivetani 4, Metro: S. Ambrogio, +39 02 4810 1089, www.hotel-bb.com, mi.santambrogio@hotelbb.com).

NEAR BASILICA DI SANT'AMBROGIO

These places are a 10-minute walk east of the basilica. See the map on page 280 for locations.

$$$ Hotel Ariston, with uniformed porters, offers 56 con-temporary rooms, some with commanding views, on 10 floors of a high-rise building. It's practical rather than charming, and a solid option (air-con, elevator, Largo del Carrobbio 2, Metro: Duomo, +39 02 7200 0556, www.aristonhotel.com, info@aristonhotel.com).

Hostel: ¢ Ostello Bello sits along a skinny lane and is brim-ming with youthful and young-at-heart travelers. It has quirky decor and is generous, considering its value price, with nearly nightly activities and a welcome drink. The multiuse entry room is the reception, dining area, bar, lounge, and entertainment venue rolled into one. They also have a bigger ("grande") location by Mi-lano Centrale train station (private rooms available, air-con, eleva-tor, game room, laundry, terraces; Via Medici 4, Metro: Duomo or Missori, +39 02 3658 2720, www.ostellobello.com, booking@ostellobello.com).

NEAR MILANO CENTRALE TRAIN STATION

The train station neighborhood is more practical than characteris-tic. Its hotels are utilitarian business-class places with prices that bounce all over depending on the convention schedule. You'll find more shady characters than shady trees in the parks, and lots of in-ternational eateries and massage parlors as you head away from the immediate vicinity of the station. But it's convenient to trains, the Metro, and airport shuttles, and if you hit it outside of convention times, the prices are hard to beat.

On Via Napo Torriani: This street, a five-minute walk from the station, is lined with midrange hotels (exit the station, head straight across the square, then veer left onto Via Napo Torriani).

$$ Hotel Garda has 55 straightforward rooms (RS%—email first to get a promo code, then book on their website; breakfast extra, air-con, elevator, Via Napo Torriani 21, +39 02 6698 2576, www.hotelgardamilan.com, info@hotelgardamilan.com). **$$ Hotel Berna** feels classically European with an old-school lobby, uniformed bell-

Milan Hotels & Restaurants

MILAN

Map labels:
To Porta Nuova · Parco Sempione · VIA SOLE · CORSO GARIBALDI · VIA PONTACCIO · VIA · FORO BUONAPARTE · Lanza M · VIA MERCATO · VIA FIORI CHIARI · S. MARIA D. CARMINE · VIA BRERA · SFORZA CASTLE · ENTRY TO MUSEUM OF ANCIENT ART · V. SACCHI · VIA VETERO · V. CARMINE · MICHAELANGELO'S PIETÀ · Piazza Castello · V. CUSANI · VIA DELL'ORSO · VIA LAURO · Cairoli M · Largo Cairoli · VIA ROVELLO · V. BROLETTO · V. BOSSI · FORO BUONAPARTE · TEATRO DAL VERME · VIA PUCCINI · V. TOMASSO · VIA DANTE · V. CLERICI · PALAZZO LITTA · ⊤ #16 · V. SAN GIOVANNI MURO · V. CAMPERIO · CORSO MAGENTA · SAN MAURIZIO · VIA MERAVIGLI · V. S. MARIA · BORSA · THE FINGER · Cordusio M · Piazza Cordusio · ARCHAEOLOGICAL MUSEUM · V. BRISA · Piazza degli Affari · POST · Piazza dei Mercanti · VIA NIRONE · VIA LUINI · V. BORROMEI · V. S. M. FULC. · VIA POSTA · VIA ARMORARI · CANTU · OREFICI · VIA BOCCHETTO · V. MONETA · VIA SANT'ORSOLA · VIA S. MARIA · HUGO · #2 ⊤ · SPADARI · PINACOTECA AMBROSIANA · VIA SPERONARI · VIA TORINO · SAN SATIRO · VIA S. MAURILIO · To Naviglio Grande District & · V. ARCIM

Accommodations

1. Hotel Spadari, Peck & Ciacco Gelato
2. Hotel Gran Duca di York
3. Antica Locanda dei Mercanti
4. Hotel Cusani
5. Hotel Star
6. To Centrale Station Area Hotels

Eateries

7. Trattoria Milanese
8. Ristorante Giacomo Arengario
9. Ristorante Spazio Niko Romito
10. Ristorante Galleria
11. Casa Lodi
12. Giacomo Caffè
13. Elevator to La Rinascente Dep't Store Eateries
14. La Vecchia Latteria Vegetarian
15. Pizzeria Piz
16. Princi & Rosticceria Fontana
17. Luini Panzerotti & other takeout joints

18 Trafilata

19 Salad House

20 Ciciarà Trattoria & Al Confini del Gusto

21 Velavevodetto

22 Cantina Piemontese

23 Colibrì Café Bar

24 Trattoria Burla Gio

25 Motoplex City Lounge

26 Bar Brera & Via Brera Eateries

27 Via Fiori Chiari Eateries

28 To Naviglio Grande Eateries

29 Bar Camparino

hops, and 116 rooms (air-con, elevator, Via Napo Torriani 18, +39 02 677 311, www.hotelberna.com).

Closest to Station: These options are in the same block of buildings just in front and to the left of the station.

$$$ Hotel Aosta is IKEA-esque, practical, tidy, and convenient. Some of the 63 business-class rooms have views onto the piazza, as does the breakfast room (air-con, elevator, Piazza Duca d'Aosta 16, +39 02 669 1951, www.minihotel.it, aosta@minihotel.it).

Hostel: ¢ Ostello Bello Grande has converted what was a business-class hotel into a hostel with hipster flair. Worth considering even if you're not a hosteler, it comes with an inviting rooftop terrace and a shared kitchen (private rooms available, breakfast extra, air-con, elevator, laundry, Via Lepetit 33, +39 02 670 5921, www.ostellobello.com, booking.lepetit@ostellobello.com). With the tracks to your back, leave the station to the left, cross the taxi stand, and then cross the road. The hostel is around the corner from Ristorante Giglio Rosso.

NEAR MALPENSA AIRPORT

$$$$ Sheraton Milan Malpensa Airport Hotel is adjacent to Terminal 1—from the lobby, it's just a five-minute walk to airport security (+39 02 23351, www.marriott.com). Or try **$ Best Western Cavalieri della Corona,** with big rooms and a restaurant (airport shuttle-€3, 2/hour; +39 0331 730 350, www.cavalieridellacorona.com).

Eating in Milan

You'll find delightful eateries all over town, and except right around the Duomo, most are more for locals than for tourists. A wonderful Milanese tradition is the happy hour *aperitivo*—a selection of appetizers offered free with a drink (see sidebar).

Fine Dining Options: Several of my listings lend themselves to a romantic, dressy, fine-dining splurge (€50-100/person with wine). All serve Milanese or Italian cuisine. For contact info, see the listings below. In gourmet-logical order, they are: **Ristorante Giacomo Arengario** (pleasingly pretentious, best view of Duomo and Piazza Duomo, seating inside and out); **Ristorante Rigolo** (classy, venerable, old-school favorite of Milan's journalists, in the Brera neighborhood, indoor only); **Cantina Piemontese** (top quality, focus on Piedmont cuisine and Barolo wine, inside and out); **Trattoria Milanese** (old Milan class, a celebration of tradition, indoor); **Ristorante Spazio Niko Romito** (Michelin-star chef, fancy food by his student chefs, no view, indoor); **Boccondivino** (festive, one high price for six courses featuring cured meats, pastas and fresh cheeses, all with paired wine, indoor); and **Ristorante Galleria** (authentic food, formal waitstaff, in the elegant Galleria Vittorio Emanuele II).

Milanese Cuisine: Two signature dishes in Milan are *risotto alla Milanese* and *ossobuco*. The risotto is flavored with saffron, which gives it an intense yellow color. The subtle flavor of the saffron pairs nicely with the veal shanks of *ossobuco* (meaning "marrow" or, literally, "hole in the bone" shank). The prized marrow, extracted with special little forks, is considered the best part of the meal. Another dish named after the city is *cotoletta alla Milanese*, a thin, breaded veal cutlet fried in clarified butter (don't say this too loud, but it's schnitzel). Some places have supersized it and call it *orecchio di elefante*, an "elephant's ear" (large enough to share).

NEAR THE DUOMO
Restaurants with Class

$$$ Trattoria Milanese, family-run and passionately Milanese, is an elegant time warp. On a back street, it has an enthusiastic clientele and a classic energy, with a curt and professional waitstaff. Expect great food and an old-fashioned Milanese ambience (Mon-Sat 12:00-14:30 & 19:00-22:30, closed Sun and mid-July-Aug, reservations recommended, air-con, Via Santa Marta 11, behind the Pinacoteca Ambrosiana, +39 02 8645 1991).

$$$$ Ristorante Giacomo Arengario is a dressy splurge perched on the top floor of the towers overlooking Piazza Duomo and the cathedral. Its indoor seating almost feels like outdoors, and its terrace has the best views possible of the Duomo. The decor is romantic 1930s, the cuisine is classic Milanese (with signature pastas and fish), and its reputation among locals is stellar (open daily 12:00-23:00, Via Marconi 1, +39 02 7209 3814, https://giacomomilano.com).

$$$ Ristorante Spazio Niko Romito is a sleek and romantic little place offering one of the best fine dining values in town. Run by three-star Michelin chef Niko Romito, this is where many of his students get experience (6-course tasting menu €60, Tue-Sat 12:30-14:30 & 19:30-22:00, in the Mercato del Duomo food hall, fourth floor—next to Galleria Vittorio Emanuele II, above La Feltrinelli bookstore, Piazza del Duomo 1, +39 02 878 400, www.spazionikoromito.com).

$$$ Ristorante Galleria would be my choice for a meal in the Galleria Vittorio Emanuele II. They serve classic Milanese dishes and pizza in a dressy setting. While the food is just OK, the service is good and the setting and people-watching unforgettable (daily 12:00-23:00, #75 at the La Scala end of the gallery, +39 02 8646 4912).

MILAN

Simpler Dining

$$ Casa Lodi brings the cuisine and wine of rural Lombardy into the big city with an honest celebration of the area's traditions and ingredients. The menu includes salads, pastas, and the house specialty, risotto (12:00-22:00, closed Mon for dinner, Via Cappellari 3, +39 02 897 77217). Each evening they put out a quality *aperitivo* buffet to go with your glass of wine or *spritz* (until 20:00).

$$$ Peck is a pricey, aristocratic gourmet deli, *rosticceria,* and pastry/gelato shop. Even if all you can afford is the aroma, peek in. Check out the classic circa-1930 salami slicer by the stairway, and glance into the assembly-line kitchen in back. They serve delectable fancy food to go for a superb picnic dinner mostly by weight—an *etto* is 100 grams; 250 grams equals about a half-pound. There are also a few tables inside, where waiters serve light bites to elegantly dressed customers (Mon 15:00-20:00, Tue-Sat 9:00-20:00, closed Sun, Via Spadari 9, +39 02 802 31644, www.peck.it).

Gelato: Two doors down from Peck, **Ciacco Gelato** serves purist gelato with "the fewest ingredients possible." I like their *fior di latte* (Mon-Sat 9:00-21:00, Sun 14:00-20:00, Via Spadari 13).

Trendy Eateries with a Duomo View: The seventh floor of **La Rinascente** department store, alongside the Duomo, has a crowded and upscale food court offering everything from sandwiches to sushi. Three of its many eateries share a sunny outdoor terrace—the reason to venture up here—with commanding views of the cathedral's rooftop: **$$$ Obicà** is a swanky "mozzarella bar" offering this heavenly cheese in salads, on pizzas, or on splittable €23 antipasti plates, accompanied by *salumi,* tapenades, and vegetables. **$$$$ Ristorante Maio** has pricey full-meal service. And **$$$$ Il Bar,** living-room cozy with cushy divans and low coffee tables, serves light meals (sandwiches, salads, pasta), coffee, desserts, and cocktails (all three open daily until 24:00; during or after store hours, use the elevator on Via S. Radegonda to zip directly to the seventh floor).

Cheaper Eats and Takeout

$$ Giacomo Caffè hides out next to the Duomo Museum entry, with tables inside and out, on a quiet courtyard. It's a classy fixture that locals and guides rely on for a pleasant lunch of salads and sandwiches, or for a coffee break—the chef is famous for his pastries (daily 8:00-19:30, in Palazzo Reale at Piazza Duomo 12, +39 02 890 96698).

$$ La Vecchia Latteria Vegetarian, with a 50-year history, is a homey hole-in-the-wall that serves a good vegetarian lunch. This busy joint—with tight seating in front and behind the kitchen—serves soup, salads, pastas, and veggie entrées at affordable prices. Their *il misto forno* is an assortment of soufflés, quiches, and roasted

Milan's *Aperitivo* Culture

Many locals like to precede dinner with an *aperitivo*—a buffet of finger foods offered free with a drink during happy hour. (While Campari made its debut in Milan, a simple glass of *vino bianco* or prosecco, the Italian champagne, is just as popular.) At about 18:00, keep an eye out for bars filling their counters with inviting baskets of munchies, served free with these drinks. A cheap drink can actually become a light meal. Locals joke you can make your *aperitivo* an *apericena* (*cena* means dinner) for the cost of a cocktail. This *aperitivo* custom is common throughout Italy but especially prized by the Milanesi—who invented it.

While lots of places pull out *aperitivo* nibbles, some do a more generous job than others with their buffet. It's hard to recommend a particular bar, but certain neighborhoods hum with hardworking and competitive *aperitivo* bars each early evening (17:30 to 21:00). Three of the best are **Piazza Sempione, Via Brera,** and canalside at **Naviglio Grande.** Near the Duomo, **Casa Lodi** is known for its buffet (recommended above, daily 18:00-20:00).

and sautéed veggies (Mon-Sat 12:00-16:00, closed Sun, off Via Torino at Via dell'Unione 6, Metro: Missori, +39 02 874 401). Their rare old-time squat toilet is truly unforgettable.

$ Pizzeria Piz serves very basic pizzas with evangelical fervor to a young crowd. It's a cheap and rustic joint with lots of tables spilling out onto a traffic-free lane that wraps around a little church just off busy Via Torino. They serve just three pizzas—*margherita* (tomato sauce and cheese), *marinara* (no cheese), and a "daily surprise." They don't take reservations (daily 12:00-15:00 & 19:00-23:00, under Church of San Sebastiano at Via Torino 34, +39 02 8645 3482).

$ Princi is popular for its enticing wall of fresh-baked breads, focaccia (and a famous focaccia pizza), and luscious pastries. They sell rustic sandwiches all day, and at lunch they have a *tavola calda* with various €8-12 plates of the day (12:00-15:00 only). You can do two half-courses for the cost of the more expensive one—if the dishes lend themselves to splitting (daily 7:00-20:00; off Via Torino, a block southwest of Piazza del Duomo at Via Speronari 6; +39 02 874 797). If Princi is too slick and crowded for your mood, across the street at #5 is the quiet, old-fashioned **Rosticceria Fontana,** with an inviting *tavola calda*, featuring tasty traditional plates by weight, with humble stools nearby.

$ Street Food: Luini Panzerotti, a wildly popular local institution, is a bakery that serves up €3 warm mini calzones (*panzerotti)* stuffed with mozzarella, tomatoes, ham, or whatever you like.

MILAN

Don't overlook the *dolci* half of the menu (Mon-Sat 10:00-20:00, closed Sun and Aug, Via S. Radegonda 16, +39 02 8646 1917). From the back of the Duomo, head north and look for the lines out front. Order from the menus posted on the wall. Traditionally, Milanesi munch their hot little meals on the benches of nearby Piazza San Fedele (just to the right as you leave).

Panzerotti can be mobbed with tourists, and locals complain that quality has gone downhill. Several good competitors are close by, including **Antica Pizza Fritta,** which serves fried calzones (around the block directly behind Panzerotti). And across the street is another local hit, **Cioccolati Italiani,** for chocoholics in search of something over the top.

UNIVERSITY DISTRICT

These places are a few blocks from the Duomo—far enough to be much less touristy but within easy walking distance. It's a local vibe, nearly traffic-free, and invigorated by a university crowd. I've listed some cheap and cheery places for a fast lunch, as well as a couple of romantic options for a memorable dinner. To get here, start from Via Palazzo Reale (next to the Duomo Museum), go one long block, and then angle left onto Via Santa Tecla. The Santo Stefano church is a block beyond that.

Via Santa Tecla Fast Lunch Joints: This small, traffic-free lane is made-to-order for a sightseer's fast and cheap lunch. These two little spots have indoor and outdoor seating and are open daily 12:00-16:00: **$ Trafilata,** which lets you design your own pasta (just pick your noodle and topping, at #4, kid-friendly), and **$ Salad House** (with a good selection of healthy salads, at #3).

Facing Santo Stefano Church: Two fine lunch places are side-by-side at Piazza Santo Stefano #8. **$$$ Ciciarà Trattoria** is a traditional restaurant specializing in free-range meats; notice the blackboard tracking what's left for the day (lunch 12:30-14:30, dinner 20:00-22:30, closed Sun evening and Mon, reserve for dinner, +39 02 8417 8681, www.ciciara.it). **$ Al Confini del Gusto** is a simple and hardworking place serving sandwiches, crêpes, and four plates of the day (on display under glass just inside, +39 02 3296 1814). It's lunch-only here on a covered outdoor terrace facing the church.

$$ Velavevodetto, which means "I told you so," is a Roman institution, now with this branch in Milan. It's quiet and dressy with friendly service, and it does *carciofi alla giudìa* (artichokes) expertly. Dining is inside only, surrounded by walls of wine bottles (daily from 12:15 and 19:15, Via Festa del Perdono 1, +39 02 9286 3557).

$$$$ Cantina Piemontese features the meaty cuisine and famously full-bodied wines of the Piedmont region. The food, while honest and simple, is almost gourmet, with top-quality ingredients. The dining room is romantic with a homey elegance, and the terrace feels like a garden (daily from 12:30 and 19:30, Via Laghetto 2, reservations smart, +39 02 784 618, www.cantina-piemontese. it). They print a new menu daily and offer an extensive list of fine wines by the glass.

$ Colibrì Café Bar is a casual, stay-awhile student favorite for drinks and snacks (and a couple of main dishes chalked on a board)—it has a great vibe inside and out (daily until late, Via Laghetto 9, +39 349 401 6961).

NEAR VIA DANTE

These places are a short walk from the Duomo area and convenient to many hotels.

$$$ Boccondivino, a fun-loving place with no menu, is as much a party as a restaurant. There's one option: You enjoy six courses for €75, each with a different wine designed to match. A constant parade of food carts rolls through the happy dining room, keeping all entertained and happily fed. Fabrizio is the master of ceremonies making sure English speakers understand what's being served: lots of quality meats and cheeses, pâté, pasta, and a token vegetable course—all "designed to maximize your cholesterol." You may share a bigger table; it's yours for the evening. The name is a play on words: a divine mouthful or a mouthful of wine (nightly from 19:30, reservations necessary, Via Carducci 17—see the map on page 280, +39 02 866 040, www.boccondivino.com).

$$ Trattoria Burla Gio, homey and traditional as can be, caters to locals with €15 lunch specials and a fancier dinner menu. Paolo and Gisella carry on the 50-year family tradition with a passion for home cooking and Milanese traditions like their *cotoletta alla Milanese* (the local veal cutlet). For the best ambience, climb upstairs into a red-and-white-tablecloth time-warp dining hall (just off Via San Giovanni at Via Meravigli 18, +39 02 805 7096).

$$ Motoplex City Lounge is more than a Vespa showroom: It's also a café that's popular with locals and the business-suit set (Mon-Fri 8:00-18:00, Sat from 12:00, closed Sun, Via Broletto 13).

ON OR NEAR VIA BRERA

The Brera neighborhood, near the famed art gallery of the same name (and surrounding the Church of St. Carmine), is laced with narrow, inviting pedestrian streets. Make an evening of your visit by having an *aperitivo* with snacks at one of the many bars lining the traffic-free stretch of Via Brera (most serve munchies with drinks from about 17:00 or 18:00 until 21:00). Afterward, stroll along restaurant row on **Via Fiori Chiari** and Via Brera, or duck into the semicircular lane of Via Madonnina to survey the sidewalk cafés as you pass fortune tellers, artists, and knockoff handbag vendors.

Bars along via Brera compete for the local art students with inexpensive sandwiches, pastas, and salads. The cheapest (while not the best) is **$ Bar Brera,** which also has a lively *aperitivo* happy hour (drinks and a buffet of hearty snacks start at 18:00; open daily 7:00-late, Via Brera 23, +39 02 877 091).

$$$$ Ristorante Rigolo boasts a professional waitstaff and beautifully presented dishes. The menu has two lists: classics and seasonal specials. Discerning locals choose from four themed rooms: Photography, Painting, Satire, and "Rigolettore"—the library (Tue-Sun 12:15-14:00 & 19:30-22:00, closed Mon, reservations smart, Via Solferino 11 at the corner of Largo Treves—see "Central Milan" map, +39 02 8646 3220, www.ristoranterigolo.it).

NAVIGLIO GRANDE (CANAL DISTRICT)

Consider ending your day at the former port of Milan. This district bustles with memorable and affordable bars and restaurants and a great people scene (see listing on page 316). In addition to endless *aperitivo* spreads and traditional trattorias, there are some more creative choices, too: Greek fare, artisanal microbrews (for example, at #44 along the canal), and "Brazilian sushi." Come here for the fun energy—not for a quiet, romantic meal. (Note that addresses along the canal are even numbers on one side, odd on the other.)

Getting There: Ride the Metro or tram #2 to Porta Genova and walk down pedestrianized Via Casale, which dead-ends a block away at the canal. Walk halfway across the metal bridge and survey the scene. The street you just walked has plenty of cheap options. Most of the action—and all of my other recommendations—are to the left, on or near the canal. Do a reconnaissance stroll before settling in somewhere: Walk down the left bank of the canal to the bridge with cars, then go back on the other side.

Here are a few good options to consider:

$$ Luca e Andrea is artsy-rustic, lively, and serves typical Milanese and Lombard meals. Enjoy the conviviality indoors or people-watch as you dine outdoors canalside (daily 12:00-22:00, Alzaia Naviglio Grande 34, near the arched bridge, no reservations, +39 02 5810 1142).

$$ L'Altro Luca e Andrea, the sister of Luca e Andrea, is a few doors away. With a little less magic and a little more practicality, it's bigger and a bit less rustic, with less wine and lots more canalside tables. A happy checked-tablecloth diner, it has a very small, basic Italian menu and no pretense (daily 12:00-22:30, Naviglio Grande 24, +39 02 8941 5771).

$$ Iter—a block or so from the canal scene—is funky and

cool with clever, eclectic decor that mirrors its mishmash culinary style. While lunch consists of basic Italian fare, the dinner menu rotates through the cuisine of a different country every six months. Cocktails are a specialty here (daily 9:00-24:00; 20 yards from the curved bridge with the zigzag design—go away from canal on Via Argelati to Via Mario Fusetti 1; +39 02 3599 9589).

$ Pizzeria Spaghetteria la Magolfa, down a side street, feels like a neighborhood hangout, offering good, cheap salads, pastas, and pizzas. While you're 200 yards from the canal scene, this is your best old-school budget bet. Sit inside, on a veranda, or at a table on the street. For €20, two people can enjoy hearty pizzas and a good bottle of wine (daily 12:00-15:00 & 18:00-24:00, go to the end of Via Fusetti to Via Magolfa 15, +39 02 832 1696).

Orso Bianco Gelateria, on your way back to the Metro or tram, is the place for "artisanal" gelato. Their *nocciola*—or hazelnut—is *buonissimo* (Via Casale 7, on your right as you walk back to the Metro, +39 02 973 6848).

SUPERMARKETS

Esselunga, in the food zone downstairs from Piazza Gae Aulenti at the Porta Nuova development (described under "Sights in Milan," earlier), is large, right by the Garibaldi train and Metro station, and has a good deli section with ready-to-go meals (Mon-Sat 7:30-22:00, Sun 8:00-20:00, Viale Luigi Sturzo 13). The smaller **Sapori & Dintorni** in the basement of Milano Centrale station is also handy (daily 7:00-20:00).

Milan Connections

BY TRAIN

Unless otherwise specified, the following connections are for Trenitalia.

From Milano Centrale to: Venice (1-2/hour, some direct, 2.5-3 hours; Italo: every 2 hours, 2.5 hours), **Florence** (hourly, 2 hours; Italo: 1-2/hour), **Rome** (1-3/hour, 3.5 hours; Italo: 1-2/hour), **Monterosso** (5-6/day direct, 3 hours, more with changes), **La Spezia** (9/day direct, 3 hours, more with changes), **Varenna** (about hourly, 1 hour), **Stresa** (about hourly; 50-minute fast train costs much more than 65-minute slow train), **Como** (2/hour, 45 minutes), **Naples** (2/hour, 5 hours; Italo: 1-2/hour), **Lugano** (1-2/hour, 75 minutes), **Zürich** (every 2 hours direct, 3 hours), **St. Moritz** (5/day with change in Tirano, 5 hours, or slightly faster by train to Chiavenna and then bus), **Munich** (8 hours, change in Zürich); **Nice** (5/day, 5 hours, change in Ventimiglia), **Paris** (2/day direct, 7 hours, more with changes).

Train Connections from Milan

MILAN

From Milano Porta Garibaldi to: Naples (night train, 11 hours), **Munich** (night train, 12 hours), **Vienna** (night train, 12 hours), **Paris** (French TGV trains, 3/day, 7 hours).

BY PLANE
Malpensa Airport
Most international flights land at Terminal 1 of the manageable Malpensa Airport (code: MXP), 28 miles northwest of Milan. Low-cost EU flights use Terminal 2 (buses connect the two). Airport info: +39 02 5858 0080, www.milanairports.com.

Trains between Malpensa and Milan: The Malpensa Express train is usually the most sensible option (+39 02 7249 4494, www.malpensaexpress.it). Trains stop at underground stations at Terminals 1 and 2 (both stations have ticket offices and ticket machines). There are two lines: Malpensa-Milano Cadorna and Malpensa-Milano Centrale. For either, the ride costs €13 one-way (€20 round-trip). Both run from very early to late (about 5:00-23:00).

If you are leaving from (or going to) downtown or most other points in the city, take the **Cadorna** line, which is quicker, runs more often and later, and drops you at a convenient downtown Metro station (2/hour, 40 minutes).

If you are heading to the area around Milano Centrale station, or connecting by train to other destinations, take the **Centrale** line (2/hour, 50 minutes).

When **leaving Milan** to go *to* the airport, at Milano Centrale, trains usually leave from tracks 1 and 2, which are hidden behind tracks 3 and 4 and poorly signed. Cadorna is a little easier to deal with; trains usually depart from track 1.

By Shuttle Bus: Three bus companies run between Malpensa Airport and Milano Centrale train station, offering virtually identical, competing services. They each charge about €10 for the one-hour trip (buy ticket from driver) and depart from the same places: in front of Terminal 2 at the airport (outside exit 4), and from Piazza IV Novembre on the west side of Milano Centrale station (with your back to the tracks, exit to the right). They also pick up and drop off at the airport's Terminal 1. Buses leave about every 20 minutes daily, from very early until just after midnight (Malpensa Shuttle +39 02-5858-3185, www.malpensashuttle. it; Autostradale +39 02 3008 9000, www.autostradale.it; and Terravision, www.terravision.eu).

By Taxi: Taxis into Milan cost a fixed rate of €95; avoid hustlers in airport halls (catch taxis outside exit 8). Considering how far the city is from the airport and how good the train and bus services are, Milan is the last place I'd take an airport taxi.

Linate Airport

Most intra-European flights land at Linate (code: LIN, www. milanairports.com), five miles east of Milan. Eventually the Metro's new line 4 will link Linate with the city. For now, you can get to downtown Milan by bus or taxi.

By Bus: Public bus #73 connects Linate to the Duomo in about 50 minutes (covered by €2 public transit ticket, departs every 10 minutes, less frequently evenings and Sun). If you're heading from town to the airport, look for the #73 bus stop a couple of blocks south of the Duomo, on Via Maurizio Gonzaga.

Private companies also run shuttles between Linate and Milano Centrale train station (handy only if you're catching a train; €5, roughly hourly, 30 minutes, www.airportbusexpress.it). At Milano Centrale, buses for Linate leave from the east side of the station (Piazza Luigi di Savoia).

By Taxi: Taxis between Linate and the Duomo cost about €30.

Bergamo (Orio al Serio) Airport

Some budget airlines use Bergamo Airport—about 30 miles from Milan—as their Milan hub (code: BGY, +39 035 326 323,

MILAN

www.milanbergamoairport.it). At least three bus companies ply the route between the east side of Milano Centrale train station (Piazza Luigi di Savoia) and Orio al Serio (about €10, 5/hour, 1 hour): Autostradale (www.airportbusexpress.it), Terravision (www.terravision.eu), and the Orio Shuttle (www.orioshuttle.com).

THE CINQUE TERRE

Monterosso al Mare • Vernazza • Corniglia • Manarola • Riomaggiore

Tucked between Genoa and Pisa, in a mountainous and seductive corner of the Italian Riviera, lies the Cinque Terre (CHINK-weh TAY-reh)—five villages carving a good life out of difficult terrain. With a traffic-free charm—a happy result of natural isolation—the Cinque Terre offers a rugged alternative to the beachy Riviera resorts nearby.

Each village fills a ravine with a lazy hive of human activity. Calloused locals and sunburned travelers enjoy the area's unique mix of Italian culture and nature. There isn't a Fiat or museum in sight—just sun, sea, sand (well, pebbles), and wine. Choose a home base according to just how cut off you'd like to be from the outer world: resorty Monterosso, cover-girl Vernazza, hilltop Corniglia, photogenic Manarola, or amiable Riomaggiore.

This breathtakingly scenic six-mile stretch of coast was first described in medieval times as the "five lands" *(cinque terre).* Tiny communities grew up in the shadows of castles, which doubled as lookouts for pirate raids. As the threat of pirates faded, the villages prospered, catching fish and cultivating grapes. Until the advent of tourism, the towns remained isolated. Even today, each village comes with its own traditions, a distinct dialect, and a proud heritage. Other Italians think of locals here as "mountain people by the sea."

The Cinque Terre

To A-12 Autostrada
(Brugnato Exit)

To Genoa
A-12

SP-1

To La Spezia & Pisa

To A-12 Autostrada
(Carrodano Exit)

SP-566

To Sestri Levante,
Santa Margherita,
Bonassola & Genoa

Beverino

2 Kilometers

2 Miles

Pignone

Pian di Barca

SP-1

Levanto   SP-370

To New Town
(Fegina)

To Monterosso's
Old Town   SP-38

SP-1

Monterosso
al Mare

SP-63

To La Spezia
& A-12

SANDY
BEACH

Vernazza

Corniglia

SP-51

Volastra

Punta
Mesco

CORNIGLIA STATION

Ligurian

Manarola

VIA
LITORANEA

To La Spezia
& A-12

Sea

Riomaggiore

SP-370

To Porto Venere

The Cinque Terre is now a national park (founded in 1999), where all can enjoy the villages, hiking, swimming, boat rides, and evening romance of one of God's great gifts to tourism. While the region is well discovered and can get jam-packed, I've never seen happier, more relaxed tourists.

In this chapter, I cover general tips for your visit to the Cinque Terre, then describe the five towns in order from north to south—from Monterosso to Riomaggiore.

PLANNING YOUR TIME

The ideal stay in the Cinque Terre is two or three full days; at the least, give yourself two nights and an uninterrupted day.

The villages are connected by trains, boats, and trails. There's no checklist of sights or experiences—just a hike, the towns themselves, and your fondest vacation desires. Read this chapter in advance to piece together your best visit, mixing hiking, swimming, trains, and boat rides.

Cinque Terre in Two Days: You could spend one day hiking between towns (taking a boat or train part of the way, or as the return trip). Spend a second day visiting any towns you've yet to see, comparing main streets, beaches, and focaccia.

Here's a sample day: If you're based in Monterosso, take a morning train to Corniglia, hike to Vernazza for lunch (where you

The Cinque Terre at a Glance

▲▲**Monterosso al Mare** Resorty, relatively level, and spread out along the coast, with a charming old town, a modern new town, and the Cinque Terre's best beaches, swimming, and nightlife. It has the most restaurants and the most comfortable hotels. See page 356.

▲▲▲**Vernazza** The region's gem, dramatically crowned with a ruined castle above and a lively harborfront cradling a natural harbor below. See page 373.

▲**Corniglia** Quiet hilltop village known for its cooler temperatures (it's the only one without a harbor), fewer tourists, and a tradition of fine wines. See page 393.

▲▲**Manarola** Hiking-focused waterfront village wrapped in vineyards and dotted with a picturesque mix of shops and cliff-climbing houses. See page 398.

▲▲**Riomaggiore** The most workaday of the five villages, with nightlife, too. See page 408.

Near the Cinque Terre

The Riviera towns north and south of the Cinque Terre make for fun, easy side trips—and some are workable home bases. See the next chapter for more on Levanto, Sestri Levante, Santa Margherita Ligure, and Portofino (all to the north), and Porto Venere and transit-hub La Spezia (to the south).

could explore the town, hike to the grand view cemetery, or cool off at the beach), then catch the boat back to Monterosso to stroll the beach promenade. And that's only one day out of dozens of memorable Cinque Terre combinations you can dream up.

On any evening, linger over dinner, enjoy live music at a low-key club (or opera singers in Vernazza), try a wine tasting, or follow one of my self-guided town walks. At sunset, take a glass of your favorite beverage out to the breakwater to watch the sun slip into the Mediterranean.

With More Time: Frequent trains make day trips along the coast easy (though seeing Portofino is more relaxed if you overnight in Santa Margherita Ligure). A day trip to Levanto is a snap (by train, boat, or a hike from Monterosso) and a side excursion from Levanto to Bonassola and Framura is fun. For double the beaches, visit Sestri Levante. South of the Cinque Terre, reach lovely Porto Venere by boat, or by train and bus via La Spezia.

Day-Tripping to the Cinque Terre: Speed demons could store their baggage, take a hike in the morning, have a waterfront lunch, laze on a beach in the afternoon, and leave by evening to somewhere back in the real world. But be warned: The Cinque Terre is inundated with cruise-ship groups doing the same thing. The best way to enjoy the Cinque Terre is to be here before and after the daily day-trip deluge. (Ironically, some travelers decide against an overnight because they've heard the Cinque Terre is crowded—then day-trip in, only experiencing it with those terrible crowds.) The charm of the region survives—early and late.

When to Go: May, June, September, and early October are ideal times (though May is a popular time for tour groups), with more pleasant hiking weather and lower prices than the local vacation months of July and August. If you do come in July or August, book further ahead, and get up early to enjoy the trails before the heat of the day—perhaps even before breakfast. April weekends can be very busy: Easter and the public holidays of Liberation Day (April 25) and Labor Day (May 1) bring crowds of Italians, prices shoot up, and restaurants fill. Weekdays are quieter at any time of year.

Flexible and open-minded travelers can enjoy a trip in March or late October, perhaps even late February or early November, but should plan for chilly weather, fewer or no boats, and shuttered shops, restaurants, and hotels (many close from November to mid-March). The midwinter months are really dead.

Orientation to the Cinque Terre

TOURIST AND PARK INFORMATION

Each town's train station has a Cinque Terre national park information office, which doubles as an all-purpose town TI and gift shop. They can answer questions about trails (including conditions and closures), shuttle bus schedules, and so on. You can also call the park's main phone number (+39 0187 762 600) or visit their useful website, ParcoNazionale5terre.it.

A blog worth a look is CinqueTerreInsider.com, written by resident American expat Amy Inman; it's filled with practicalities for visitors to this always-in-flux region.

ARRIVAL IN THE CINQUE TERRE

By Train: The five towns of the Cinque Terre are on a milk-run line, with trains coming through about twice an hour on their way between La Spezia and points north. Fast long-distance trains usually speed right through the Cinque Terre without stopping, although a few serve Monterosso and let you get there directly from Milan or Pisa. Otherwise, expect to connect to a local train at La

Spezia's Centrale station (if coming from the south) or at Genoa, Sestri Levante, or Levanto (from the north).

For details on riding the train between Cinque Terre towns, see "Getting Around the Cinque Terre," later; for information on arrival in each town, see each "Arrival" section. For outbound trains, see "Monterosso Connections" on page 372 and "La Spezia Connections" on page 457.

By Car (Not Recommended): Don't bring a car to the Cinque Terre; you won't need it. Given the narrow roads and parking headaches, the only Cinque Terre town I'd drive to is Monterosso (and then only if my hotel had parking). Each town has a remote and often congested little parking lot (a shuttle-bus ride up the hill), but for your own good, park your car in a larger town nearby and take the train in: It's safer, cheaper, faster, and smarter. Parking is easy in Levanto or La Spezia (La Spezia has a fine modern underground garage at the station; see the next chapter). A rare exception is if you're lodging in the hills above one of the Cinque Terre towns, in which case driving might be less hassle than lugging bags up from a train station (ask your hotelier for advice).

HELPFUL HINTS

Pickpocket Alert: At peak times, the Cinque Terre can be notoriously crowded, and pickpockets (often teens in groups of three or four, frequently dressed as tourists), aggressively and expertly work the most congested areas. Be on guard, especially in train stations, on platforms, and while you're on trains, particularly when getting on or off with a crush of people. Wear a money belt, and keep your things zipped up and buttoned down.

Money: You'll find ATMs and banks throughout the region. Use ATMs attached to actual banks. Shops earn a commission by hosting rip-off ATMs on their premises.

Markets: Market days perk up the Cinque Terre and nearby towns from around 8:00 to 13:00 on Tuesday in Vernazza, Wednesday in Levanto, Thursday in Monterosso, Friday in Santa Margherita Ligure, and Saturday in Sestri Levante.

Booking Services: Arbaspàa, based in Manarola, sets up wine tastings, cooking classes, fishing trips, and more (www.arbaspaa.com; see page 404). **Cinque Terre Riviera,** based in Vernazza, books rooms and apartments throughout the region, Vernazza opera tickets, cooking classes, and more (www.cinqueterreriviera.com; see page 376). **BeautifuLiguria,** run by Anna Merulla, offers various excursions (www.beautifuliguria.com).

Local Guides: Two knowledgeable guides, both a delight to be with, are **Andrea Bordigoni** (€130/half-day, €230/day, +39

Events in the Cinque Terre

Use this list to find and join a festival—or to avoid crowds. For more festival information and to confirm dates, check LaMiaLiguria.it. Food festivals in particular are subject to change.

Easter and Easter Monday	Popular time to visit the Cinque Terre. As it's extremely crowded, book long in advance.
April 25	Italian Liberation Day. Avoid this day, as locals literally shut down the trails.
May 1	Labor Day. Day-trippers pack the five towns.
May (3rd Sunday)	Monterosso: Lemon Festival
June (3rd Sunday)	Monterosso: Anchovy Festival
June 23	Monterosso and Vernazza: Feast of Corpus Domini (procession on carpet of flowers)
June 24	Riomaggiore and Monterosso: Feast day of St. John the Baptist (procession and fireworks, floating candles on the sea; big fire on Monterosso's old-town beach the day before)
June 29	Corniglia: Feast day of Sts. Peter and Paul
July 20	Vernazza: Feast day of patron St. Margaret, with fireworks
Aug (1st Sunday)	Vernazza: Feast of Nostra Signora di Reggio (hike up to Madonna di Reggio sanctuary for food and church procession)
Aug 10	Manarola: Feast day of patron St. Lawrence
Aug 15	Feast of the Assumption (Ferragosto)
Sept 8	Monterosso: Feast of Madonna di Fegina (luminarias and procession up to hilltop sanctuary)

393 133 9409, bordigo@inwind.it) and **Marco Brizzi** (€125/half-day, €210/day, +39 328 694 2847, marco_brizzi@yahoo.it).

Nightlife: There's not much in this sleepy region, though Monterosso and Riomaggiore have lively late-night bars. For a little high culture, consider Wednesday or Friday evening opera music in Vernazza (see the Vernazza section).

Rainy Day Activities: Explore the towns, taking trains to connect them; splurge for a tasty meal; or nurse a coffee or drink at a harborfront café while watching the roiling waves.

Baggage Storage and Delivery: You can pay to store bags at or near the train stations in Monterosso and Riomaggiore. Near the Cinque Terre, you can store bags in Santa Margherita Ligure and in La Spezia. See specifics per destination.

To transfer luggage from the station to your accommodations, call ahead and arrange with **Roberto Pecunia;** he's based in Riomaggiore but works in any of the towns (+39 370 375 7972, www.robytransport5terre.com).

Taxi: These traffic-free towns are set up for train access, but there are a few cases, like group airport transfers, where a taxi makes sense. **Cinqueterre Taxi,** based in Levanto, covers all five towns (Matteo +39 334 776 1946, Christian +39 347 652 0837, www.cinqueterretaxi.com). The pricey **5 Terre Transfer** is in Riomaggiore (Luciana +39 339 130 1183, Marzio +39 340 356 5268, www.5terretransfer.com).

GETTING AROUND THE CINQUE TERRE

Trains are the cheapest, fastest, and most frequent way to connect towns within the Cinque Terre. But don't get stuck in a train rut: In calm weather, **boats** connect the towns nearly as frequently—and more scenically.

By Train

By train, the five towns are just a few minutes apart.

Tickets: A train ride between any two Cinque Terre towns costs €5—steep for such a short trip, as the price includes a park fee (from November to March there's no fee and tickets cost €2.10.) You must buy a new **individual ticket** for every train ride. You can buy tickets online or with the Trenitalia app (www.trenitalia.com), at ticket machines (at each station), at Cinque Terre park desks, or at staffed ticket windows in Mon-

terosso, Levanto, and La Spezia. Don't wait to buy a ticket at the last minute: Ticket machines can be broken, and there can be very long lines at the window.

The **Cinque Terre Treno Card** (€18.20/day, described later, under "Hiking the Cinque Terre") can be worthwhile even if you don't hike, as it allows you to catch trains at the last minute without ticket concerns. It pays for itself if you take four rides in one day, but its value comes more from convenience than economy (https://card.parconazionale5terre.it).

Trains are covered by the Eurail Pass, but unless you have days to waste, it doesn't make sense to use up a valuable travel day here.

Using Tickets and Cards: Your ticket (or park card) must be validated before you board. These days, many train tickets are pre-validated and you don't need to do anything. This includes tickets

Swimming and Kayaking in the Cinque Terre

Every coastal town has a beach—or, at least, a rocky place to **swim.** Monterosso has the Cinque Terre's biggest and sandiest beach, with umbrellas and beach-use fees (but any stretch of beach without umbrellas is free). Vernazza's main beach and new beach are tiny—better for sunning than swimming (some people swim in the deep water off the breakwater). Manarola and Riomaggiore have the worst beaches (no sand), but Manarola offers the best deep-water swimming. Levanto, just a few minutes' train ride past Monterosso, has big and broad beaches, with even better ones an easy bike ride away, in Bonassola and Framura. And Sestri Levante, farther north, has two beautiful beaches.

Pack your swim gear. Several beaches have showers. Don't tote your white hotel towels; most hotels will provide beach towels (sometimes for a fee). Underwater sightseeing is full of fish. Sea urchins line the rocks, and sometimes jellyfish wash up on the pebbles (water shoes and goggles sold in local shops). If no one is swimming, it's likely because of stinging jellyfish. Ask, *"Medusa?"*

You can rent **kayaks** or **boats** in Monterosso and Riomaggiore. While experienced boaters have a blast here, if you're not comfortable navigating a tippy kayak, this is not a good place to learn.

bought online or with the Trenitalia app, and tickets that list a specific train time. Other tickets and passes are "open," and you must validate them by stamping them in one of the green-and-white machines located on train platforms and in station passages. If you're not sure what to do, ask when you buy your ticket or card. Conductors here are notorious for levying stiff fines on tourists riding with an unstamped ticket.

Station Helpers: Red-vested track-side staff can answer your train-related questions. But be aware they are also there to keep crowds at bay as trains approach...and to nail travelers without tickets (they get a cut of the fines they levy).

Schedules: In peak season, trains connecting the five towns generally run two to three times hourly in each direction, but the frequency declines after about 20:00.

Since the train is the Cinque Terre's lifeline, shops, hotels, and restaurants often post the current schedule, and many hand out paper copies. Study the key to know which departures are only for weekdays, Sundays, and so on. Make a note of the departure time of the train you want to take and ideally its train number and final destination, as that's how the station monitors identify departing trains.

Printed schedules also tell you which towns any given train will stop in. Some trains skip lesser stations (particularly Vernazza, Corniglia, and Manarola).

At the Station: As you enter, look for monitors that display a list of upcoming departures, listed by time, train number, and final destination (they do not show intermediate stops). They also show if a train is late—*in ritardo*—and by how many minutes; *SOPP* means "cancelled." Note your platform number *(binario)*. On the platform, digital displays reconfirm the train's final destination and usually show a list of intermediate stops. Confirm that the train will stop where you want on this display, or check the yellow "Partenze" posters.

Northbound trains (using the tracks closest to the water) are going to Levanto, Sestri Levante, or Genova; southbound trains (using tracks on the mountain side) are headed for La Spezia.

Getting Off: Know your stop. As the train leaves the town previous to your destination, go to the door and get ready to slip out before the mobs flood in at your stop. If it's crowded, you may need to be assertive. Say *"permesso"* (per-MEH-soh) and push on through. Note that stations are small and trains are long—you might have to get off deep in a tunnel, especially in Vernazza and Riomaggiore. If this happens, just head toward daylight. Also, train doors don't open automatically—you may have to open the door yourself (push the green button, twist the black handle, or lift up the red one).

By Boat

From late March through October, a daily boat service connects Monterosso, Vernazza, Manarola, Riomaggiore, Porto Venere, and beyond. Though they can be very crowded, these boats provide a scenic way to get from town to town (operated by Consorzio 5 Terre Golfo dei Poeti, +39 0187 732 987, www.navigazionegolfodeipoeti. it).

Because the boats nose in and tourists disembark over little more than a plank, even just a small chop can cancel some or all of the stops.

Tickets: The ticket price depends on the length of the boat ride (€7 for a short hop; up to €20 for a five-town, one-way ride with stops). An all-day Cinque Terre pass costs €30; if you add Porto Venere, it's €37, plus an optional €5 extra for a 40-minute

Crowd-Beating Tips

Italy's slice of traffic-free Riviera has been discovered, frustrating both locals and conscientious visitors. The most dramatic influx is created by groups—whether day-tripping tours or mobs of cruise-ship sightseers. Avoid the worst of the log-jams by following these tips:

Time your visit. July, August, and spring holiday weekends (Easter, Liberation Day on April 25, and Labor Day on May 1) are the busiest times of the year. Weekends are more crowded than weekdays. Late spring (aside from holidays) and early fall generally have fewer crowds and cooler temperatures for hiking (although it can be too cold to swim).

Make the most of early and late hours. Take advantage of the cool, relaxed, and quiet mornings and evenings. Starting a hike at 8:00 or at 16:00 or 17:00 is a joy; dining after 18:00 is a delight. Cruisers and day-trippers start pouring into the Cinque Terre around 10:00 and typically head out by 17:00. Those midday hours are your time to hit the beach, or find a hike away from the main trails. At midday, the main coastal trail is a hot human traffic jam. Beyond the busy coastal trail, there are plenty of hikes where you'll scarcely see another tourist.

Sleep in the Cinque Terre—not nearby. Levanto and La Spezia are close and well-connected by train, making them popular home bases. But it's easier to enjoy the Cinque Terre early and late—when it's quiet and cool—if you're sleeping here.

Be careful on crowded train platforms. At peak times, be cautious, stay well behind the yellow line, and be alert for pickpockets. Spread out to less crowded areas to wait.

Hire your own boat. If the regularly scheduled boats are jammed, consider hiring your own boat to zip you to the next town. Captains hang out at each town's harbor, offering one-way transfers to other towns, hour-long cruises, and more.

scenic ride around three small islands near Porto Venere (2/day). Buy tickets at the little stands at each town's harbor.

Schedules: Boat schedules are posted online and at docks, harbor bars, Cinque Terre park offices, and hotels. Boats depart Monterosso about hourly (9:30-17:00), stopping at the Cinque Terre towns (except Corniglia, the hill town) and ending up about 90 minutes later in Porto Venere. In the other direction, boats depart Porto Venere toward Monterosso about hourly (8:30-17:00). In high season, a few boats per day extend the route from Monterosso north to Levanto, and from Porto Venere east to La Spezia.

Private Boats: To escape the crowds—or for a scenic splurge—hire a captain to ferry you between towns. For example, at the harbor in Vernazza, you can pay around €50 to hop to any other Cinque Terre town. Split the cost among a few fellow travelers, and you have an affordable water taxi. For a memorable and relaxing time on the water, groups can hire a captain for a coastal tour, swimming excursion to a hidden cove, or a fishing trip. Or take a sunset *aperitivo* cruise (per-person charge). See the specific listing in each town.

By Shuttle Bus

ATC shuttle buses (which locals call *pulmino*) connect each Cinque Terre town with its closest parking lot and various points in the hills (but they don't connect the five towns to each other). The one you're most likely to use runs between Corniglia's train station and its hilltop town center. Rides cost €1.50 (€2.50 from driver), and are covered by the Cinque Terre park card (described in next section). Buy tickets and get bus schedules at park info offices or TIs, or check times posted at bus stops (also online at www.atcesercizio.it). As you board, it's smart to tell the driver where you want to go. Departures often coordinate with train arrival times.

Some shuttles go beyond the parking lots and high into the hills—often terminating at the town's sanctuary church. To soak in the scenery, you can ride up and hike down. This works particularly well from Manarola and Vernazza. Or you can ride both ways (50 minutes round-trip, covered by one ticket).

Hiking the Cinque Terre

The five Cinque Terre towns are connected directly by a main coastal trail, and indirectly by a web of trails higher up. Unfortunately, the two southern sections of the main coastal trail have been closed for the last few years due to falling rocks (Corniglia to Manarola, and Manarola to Riomaggiore). The two longer, northern sections remain open (Monterosso to Vernazza, and Vernazza to Corniglia).

With so many day-trippers blitzing in with the same hiking agenda, go early or late if you want to enjoy either of the open coastal sections. At any time of day, consider the paths that run higher up and farther inland. They are less crowded, free to use, and just as scenic. The single best high-country hike is from Manarola to Corniglia via Volastra, and you can take a shuttle bus to avoid its steepest climb (described below).

Cinque Terre Park Cards: Visitors hiking on the main coastal trail must buy a park card. Cards are not needed to hike on higher

Cinque Terre Hikes at a Glance

Hikes can be done in either direction. Get local advice before you set out. I've omitted trails closed as of this printing.

Main Coastal Trail

▲▲▲**Vernazza-Monterosso** Challenging but dramatic 2-hour hike, including long stretches of steep steps above Monterosso. See page 349.

▲▲▲**Corniglia-Vernazza** Most scenic and rewarding segment (1.5 hours) of the main coastal trail, with fine views, significant elevation changes, and moderately challenging stretches on uneven stone steps. See page 350.

Above the Main Coastal Trail

▲▲**Manarola-Corniglia via Volastra** Demanding but gorgeous 2.5-hour hike through vineyards high over the coast; made much easier and shorter if you take the shuttle bus from Manarola to Volastra. Park card not required for hike, though it covers the cheap bus ride. See page 350.

trails. Cards can be purchased online, or at train stations, TIs, and trailheads (http://card.parconazionale5terre.it). Some area hotels sell discounted park cards to guests—ask.

The **Cinque Terre Trekking Card** costs €7.50 for one day of hiking or €14.50 for two days (covers trails, free use of WCs, park Wi-Fi, and ATC shuttle buses, but not trains).

The **Cinque Terre Treno Card** covers what the Trekking Card does, but also includes local trains connecting all Cinque Terre towns, plus Levanto and La Spezia (€18.20/1 day, €33/2 days, €47/3 days, less off-season, validate card at train station by punching it in the machine, expires at midnight).

Navigation: Park offices hand out a map showing each trail and its number ("SVA" indicates the main coastal trail). Maps aren't essential for the basic coastal path. But for the more challenging routes higher up, you'll want either the park map or one of the commercial maps on sale at park offices for about €5. Trails are usually marked with red and white paint, and often with arrows, trail numbers, and destination names. The word for "path" is *sentiero*.

Hiking Conditions: While the main coastal trail can get strenuous, it's doable for any fit hiker...and the scenery is worth

▲▲Madonna di Reggio Sanctuary Hike Easy 30-minute downhill hike from the sanctuary above Vernazza, best reached by shuttle bus. See page 364.

High Route between Porto Venere and Levanto Remote, cliff-capping 22-mile trail (AV5T) high above the main coastal trail and sanctuary trails, best for well-equipped, hardy hikers.

Extending the Coastal Trail
To the North

▲Monterosso-Levanto A 3.5-hour hike over Punta Mesco; a notch more challenging and longer than other coastal trail segments. See page 352.

▲Levanto-Bonassola Promenade Level 30-minute walk that cuts through mountains (largely through tunnels) to connect Levanto to the beach town of Bonassola; fine by foot but better by bike. See page 352.

To the South

▲Riomaggiore-Porto Venere Very demanding, 6-hour trek high into the hills, ending at picturesque Porto Venere.

the sweat. But the trails are narrow and rocky, and come with lots of steep, challenging steps. Don't overestimate your abilities. I get many emails from readers who say the trails were tougher than they'd expected. The rocks and metal grates can be slippery in the rain. Flip-flops are not allowed. Pace yourself. For less ambitious walkers, there are great short walks around each town (see below).

Preparation and Safety: Before embarking on the more difficult hikes, get advice from one of the national park offices (located at each train station), or from Cinque Terre Trekking in Manarola (see page 404). The park maintains a map online that shows if trails are open and color-codes them by difficulty—closed *(chiuso)* trails are in black (www.pn5t.it/mappe, then select "Mappa"). Sturdy footwear, a phone for emergencies, plenty of water and snacks, sunscreen (and/or a hat), and a good map are essential.

When to Go: The coastal trail can be extremely crowded and very hot at midday. For the best light, coolest temperatures, and fewer crowds, start your hike early (by 8:00) or late (around 16:00 or 17:00). Before setting out for an evening hike, find out when the

CINQUE TERRE

CINQUE TERRE

sun will set, and leave plenty of time to arrive at your destination before dark; there's no lighting on the trails.

Shuttle Buses: ATC shuttle buses can make the going easier, connecting coastal villages to trailheads higher up. Locals know all the options—and shuttle bus schedules—so ask around. But be aware that shuttles heading into the high country run only in summer, and just once or twice a day. If frustrated with bus schedules, try the local taxis.

Guided Hikes and Excursions: Your park card includes guided hikes and other local excursions (such as town walking tours), which take place almost daily in the summer months. These are announced on the park website (www.parconazionale5terre.it, under "Agenda" or "Initiatives and Events").

Cinque Terre Hikes

SP-38

TRAIL #AV5T
"THE RED TRAIL"

2 Kilometers

2 Miles

SP-63

MADONNA
DI REGGIO
315 m

Vernazza

San
Bernardino

MADONNA
DELLE GRAZIE
350 m   SP-51

CORNIGLIA-
VERNAZZA

Corniglia

MADONNA
DELLE SALUTE

CANTINA
SOCIALE
WINE

TRAIL #AV5T
"THE RED TRAIL"

MANAROLA-
CORNIGLIA
VIA VOLASTRA

B
Volastra

Manarola

RIOMAGGIORE-
PORTO VENERE

Riomaggiore

To
Porto Venere

NOSTRA SIGNORA
DI MONTENERO
340 m   SP-51

To
La Spezia

CINQUE TERRE

TOP THREE HIKES

These three hikes each give the quintessential Cinque Terre hiking experience. The first two are part of the main coastal trail (and require the national park card); the third takes you much higher (and is free).

Main Coastal Trail

▲▲▲Vernazza-Monterosso (2 hours, 2 miles)

The scenic up-and-down-a-lot trek from Vernazza to Monterosso is both challenging and rewarding. The trail is narrow, steep, and crumbly in spots, with a lot of steps but easy to follow. The views just out of Vernazza, looking back at the town, are spectacular. From there you'll gradually ascend to 550 feet, passing some scenic waterfalls populated by croaking frogs. As you approach Monterosso, you'll descend steeply through vineyards—on very deep, knee-testing stairs—and eventually follow a rivulet to the sea. The last stretch is along a pleasant, paved pathway clinging to the cliff. You'll pop out right at Monterosso's refreshing old-town beach.

▲▲▲Corniglia-Vernazza (1.5 hours, 2 miles)

The hike from Corniglia to Vernazza—the wildest and greenest section of the coast—is very rewarding but very hilly. From the Corniglia train station, zigzag up to the town (via the steep stairs, the longer road, or the shuttle bus). From Corniglia, you'll reach the trailhead on the main road, past Villa Cecio. You'll hike through vineyards toward Vernazza. After about 10 minutes, you'll see a faded sign for Guvano beach, far beneath you (formerly a nude beach—now closed). The scenic trail continues through lots of fragrant and flowery vegetation into Vernazza. If you need a break before reaching Vernazza, stop at Bar la Torre, with a strip of amazingly scenic and delightfully shady tables perched high above the town.

Above the Main Coastal Trail
▲▲Manarola-Corniglia via Volastra (2.5 hours, 4 miles)

This challenging hike from Manarola leads up to the village of Volastra, then north through high-altitude vineyard terraces, and steeply down through a forest to Corniglia. You can shave the two steepest miles off this route by taking the ATC shuttle bus from Manarola up to Volastra (about hourly, 15-minute trip).

If you'd rather hike up to Volastra, you have two options: The more established trail #506 cuts up through the valley. For a more scenic but rougher alternate, take steeper trail #502, which follows the ridge at the top of Manarola's vineyards, with wonderful sea views. One way to access trail #502 is to begin with the vineyard hike on my self-guided walk for Manarola (page 402); partway along this walk, where you reach the wooden religious scenes scampering up the hillside, take a sharp right and walk uphill, following signs for *Panoramico Volastra (Corniglia)*.

Tiny **Volastra,** perched between Manarola and Corniglia,

hosts lots of Germans and Italians in the summer. Its church (Madonna delle Salute) is the sanctuary church for Manarola (as well as the shuttle bus stop). A 20-minute detour from Volastra, in the neighboring hamlet of Groppo, is Cantina Sociale, a cooperative winery open to the public (wine tastings, www.cantinacinqueterre.com).

When you're ready to head on to Corniglia, make your way to the Volastra church and look for *Corniglia* signs. From the front door of the church, directly across the piazza, find the trailhead (marked by an iron cross) for trail #586 to Case Pianca.

Here begins one of the region's finest paths, tightroping along the walled edges of vineyard terraces, with spectacular bird's-eye views over the entire Cinque Terre. You'll cut up and down the terraces a bit—just keep following the red-and-white markings and arrows. After passing a little village (and following signs through someone's seaview backyard), the trail enters a forest and begins its sharp, rocky descent into Corniglia. (To skip the descent, backtrack to Volastra and return by shuttle bus to Manarola.) High above Corniglia, you'll reach a fork, where you turn left to proceed downhill on trail #587 to Corniglia.

OTHER CINQUE TERRE WALKS AND HIKES

Beyond the three I've highlighted above, there are dozens of satisfying walks in the Cinque Terre at all levels of difficulty. None of the walks described below requires a park card.

Walks in the Villages

For each Cinque Terre town, I include a **self-guided walk** to help you explore the town (anytime, day or night). My Manarola walk brings you up above town on an easy, rewarding stroll through vineyards with stunning views. In Monterosso, I describe the short huff up to the town's hilltop convent and cemetery. Vernazza's evocative cemetery is also a fairly quick climb from town.

Sanctuary Trails and Other Inland Walks

Each of the five towns has its own chapel or church dedicated to the Virgin Mary, hovering in the hills a mile or two above town and accessible by a long, steep hike (quiet and uncrowded). These sanctuaries were a place of refuge for each village in the age of pirate attacks.

Villagers feel deeply connected to these spiritual retreats, where they remember lost relatives and feel part of a timeless community. In two cases (at Volastra and San Bernardino) the sanctuary church is also the focal point of a small hamlet. In most towns, the shuttle bus can take you from the town center to the sanctuary—you could ride up and hike down (described with each town's coverage next). You can also hike crosswise from one sanctuary to the next (these routes are shown on the park trail map).

Although the flat coastal path between Manarola and Riomaggiore (the Via dell'Amore) remains closed, a steep, challenging route over the bluffs between the two towns is open (trail #531, taking about an hour).

High Route Between Porto Venere and Levanto

Far above the coastal trails, and higher than the sanctuaries, is the 22-mile AV5T trail (*alta via 5 Terre*, also labeled "the red trail"), offering sky-high views over the Cinque Terre seafront. It's cool, uncrowded, and at the top of the world. The park rates the trail itself as of medium difficulty, but getting up to it (at 2,000 feet) is a demanding climb. This trail continues all the way down to Porto Venere in the south and far beyond the Cinque Terre to the north.

EXTENDING THE COASTAL TRAIL

The coastal trail (SVA) continues north of Monterosso and south of Riomaggiore. These stretches are just as scenic and do not require a park card.

To the North

▲Monterosso-Levanto (3.5 hours, 4 miles)

This strenuous, rugged, and wild hike on the coastal trail (SVA) will take you all the way to Levanto. Wear good shoes and bring lots of water.

Starting from Monterosso, look for signs for the coastal trail at the west end of the new town, and head steeply up. You'll hike up and over Punta Mesco, the bluff that separates the two towns. The first stretch, out of Monterosso, is almost entirely big steps; the rest is mostly a gradual up-and-down.

For a short scenic detour, look for trail #591 not far out of Monterosso. This brief jog leads to the ruined chapel of Sant'Antonio.

To begin the hike in Levanto, see page 421.

Alternate Route: You can enjoy a higher hike by skipping the steepest stretch and riding one of Monterosso's shuttle buses to Colle di Gritta (and Hotel Monterosso Alto). From there, follow trail #591 along the ridge and down to Colle di Bagari, where several trails intersect. You can follow trail #571c from here or go a little lower to #571—both head down to trail SVA and Levanto. Or, to make your hike a loop that returns directly to Monterosso, continue from Colle di Bagari along trail #591 to trail SVA, and drop steeply into Monterosso.

▲Levanto-Bonassola (30 minutes)

For an easy excursion, take the train to Levanto, then stroll (or better yet, bike) the level, rails-to-trails promenade to the beach town

Cruise Ship Travelers: Please Avoid Excursions to the Cinque Terre

There are two Cinque Terres: when the cruise groups are inundating it and when they are not. Huge ships stop in La Spezia, Genoa, or even Livorno, and offer guided excursions to the five towns, dumping literally thousands of travelers on the Cinque Terre, which doesn't have the infrastructure for huge crowds.

When the cruise ships are in, Cinque Terre trains and platforms are dangerously overcrowded, the trails become almost impassable, and the towns' tiny main lanes are clogged. Sure, cruise travelers can cross the Cinque Terre off their bucket list. But nobody arriving with a cruise ship horde can experience much of the Cinque Terre. And locals do not like cruise groups.

Please, visit on your own. Don't try to experience the villages and fragile trails of the Cinque Terre as part of a cruise ship mob. (If you're visiting Italy by cruise, do a cruise excursion to Pisa and Lucca instead—they can handle the crowds. Or for a seaside experience, consider Porto Venere, or ride the train up to Sestri Levante or Santa Margherita Ligure—all covered in the next chapter.) I love cruising. And I love the Cinque Terre. But in my opinion, they just don't mix.

of Bonassola. With a bike, you can continue further on, to Framura (see the next chapter).

To the South
▲Riomaggiore-Porto Venere (6 hours, 8 miles)
For this challenging trek (which has some scary spots if you don't like heights), you'll hike south from Riomaggiore on trail SVA—or on the steep shortcut trail #593—up to the town sanctuary (Madonna di Montenero). Then you'll continue up to Colle del Telegrafo, where you join the high AV5T trail that leads all the way down to Porto Venere. Partway along, the town of Campiglia has a little bar/restaurant (and buses to La Spezia).

Sleeping in the Cinque Terre

Part of the pleasure of planning a trip to the Cinque Terre is settling on which town to stay in.

Vernazza, the salty essence of the Cinque Terre, is my top choice for a home base. Its summer opera series has beefed up its nightlife. But if you think too many people have my book, you'll get fewer crowds and better value for your money in other towns.

Monterosso is a good choice for sun-worshipping beach lovers, those who prefer the ease of a real hotel, and those interested in youthful nightlife.

Manarola, charming and not overrun, draws serious hikers and sophisticated Europeans. The town has a good range of professional-feeling small accommodations (and a youth hostel), but fewer dining and evening options.

Riomaggiore, the second-largest Cinque Terre town, has the cheapest beds and rivals Monterosso for nightlife.

Corniglia, on a hilltop (no harbor), attracts hermits, anarchists, wine lovers, and mountain goats. It also has a hostel.

Many accommodations in the Cinque Terre (especially in Vernazza) are **private rooms for rent** *(affittacamere).* The typical offer is a nicely done-up bedroom with private bath or a comfortable apartment with a small kitchen. You get a key and come and go as you like, rarely seeing your landlord, who lives elsewhere and may manage five or ten such rooms. Expect thin walls (pack earplugs). Plan on paying cash. If you must cancel an *affittacamere* reservation, do it as early as possible—since people renting rooms usually don't take deposits, they lose money if you don't show up.

Breakfast: Breakfast is not included at most *affittacamere* and other simple accommodations. Locals don't make much of breakfast anyway: The basic, very Italian approach is to drop by a neighborhood bar for a cappuccino and a *cornetto* (croissant) or a piece of focaccia. Some pricier places include breakfast, but this often consists of a few paltry items (packaged croissants, yogurt, instant coffee) in a minifridge in your room.

Air-Conditioning: While air-conditioning is essential in the summer elsewhere in Italy, in the breezy Cinque Terre you can generally manage fine without it.

Eating in the Cinque Terre

Hanging out at a seaview restaurant while sampling local treats could become one of your favorite Cinque Terre memories.

Fresh anchovies (*acciughe;* ah-CHOO-gay)—ideally served the day they're caught—are a staple protein here. If you've always hated preserved anchovies (the slimy, salty kind), try them fresh here. These little fish (typically 3 to 5 inches long) are prepared in a dizzying variety of ways: marinated, salted, drenched in lemon juice, butterflied and deep-fried (sometimes with a tasty garlic/vinegar sauce called *giada*), and so on. A favorite way to prepare fresh anchovies is baked in a casserole, layered whole with potatoes, tomatoes, white wine, oil, and herbs. To try this, look on menus for *tegame alla vernazzana* (*tegame* means "skillet").

Seafood is plentiful. You'll often see *muscoli ripieni* (stuffed mussels) on menus. And, while antipasto means cheese and salami in Tuscany, here you'll get *an-*

tipasti frutti di mare (or simply *antipasti misti*): a plate of mixed "fruits of the sea." Many restaurants are proud of their *frutti di mare*—it's how they show off—and it's a fine way to start a meal. For two diners, splitting one of these and a pasta dish can be plenty.

This region is the birthplace of pesto. Basil, which loves the temperate Ligurian climate, is ground with cheese (half *parmigiano* and half pecorino), garlic, olive oil, and pine nuts, and then poured over pasta. You'll see it on gnocchi or on pasta designed specifically for pesto to cling to: *trenette* (ruffled on one side) or *trofie* (short, dense twists). Many also like pesto lasagna, made with white sauce.

Pansotti are ravioli with ricotta and a mixture of greens, often served with a walnut sauce *(salsa di noci)*...delightful and filling.

Focaccia—pillowy, flat, salty, olive-oily bread—also originates here in Liguria. The baker roughs up the dough with finger holes, sprinkles it with salt water, then bakes it. Focaccia comes plain or with onions, sage, or olives, and is a local favorite for a snack on the beach. Bakeries sell it in rounds or slices by weight (a portion is about 100 grams, or *un etto*).

Farinata, a humble flatbread snack sold at pizza and focaccia places, is made from chickpea flour, water, oil, and pepper and baked on a copper tray in a wood-burning stove. It's dense, filling, and less flavorful than focaccia.

The region also loves its locally grown lemons. Lemon liqueur here is called *limoncino*—it's the same as what's called *limoncello* in southern Italy.

Vino delle Cinque Terre, while not one of Italy's top wines, flows cheap and easy throughout the region. It's white—crisp, refreshing, and great with seafood. It's defined as a blend, predominantly using the bosco grape, grown only here. Local wine has become more sophisticated and appreciated, and plenty of wine bars offer tasting experiences.

A sweet but potent dessert wine, the local *sciacchetrà* (shah-keh-TRAH) is worth a try (18 percent alcohol, often served with dunkable cookies). Like the German *Eiswein*, it's sweet because it's made from near-raisins; 10 kilos of grapes make only 1.5 liters of

CINQUE TERRE

sciacchetrà. The word means roughly "crush and pull"—crush lots of grapes, pull out the best wine.

Monterosso al Mare

Monterosso al Mare—the only Cinque Terre town with some flat land—has two parts: A new town (called Fegina) with a parking lot, train station, and TI;

and an old town *(centro storico)* which cradles Old World charm in its small, crooked lanes. In the old town, you'll find hole-in-the-wall shops, rustic pastel townscapes, and a new generation of creative small business owners eager to keep their visitors happy. A handy pedestrian tunnel connects the old with the new.

This is a resort town with a few cars and lots of hotels, rentable beach umbrellas, and crowds. Strolling the waterfront promenade, you can pick out each of the Cinque Terre towns decorating the coast. After dark, they sparkle. Monterosso is the most enjoyable of the five for backpackers or the young-at-heart wanting to connect with others looking for a little nightlife.

Orientation to Monterosso

TOURIST INFORMATION

The TI, called Proloco Monterosso, is on the street below the train station (daily 9:00-19:00, mostly closed Nov-March, baggage storage, exit station and go left a few doors to Via Fegina 38, +39 0187 817 506, www.prolocomonterosso.it).

ARRIVAL IN MONTEROSSO

By Train: The station is in the new town. Upstairs within the station you'll find a Cinque Terre park office (daily 8:30-19:00, shorter hours off-season) and train ticket windows (daily 6:00-20:00).

The bar along platform 1 (serving salads, sandwiches, and drinks) overlooks both the tracks and the beach, and is a handy place with a cool breeze to hang out while waiting for a train to pull in. As many trains run late, this can turn a frustration into a blessing.

To reach most of my recommended new town hotels, turn right from the station. To get to the old town, turn left from the station, follow the seafront promenade, then duck through the tunnel just before the point—it's a scenic, flat 10-minute stroll.

Taxis usually wait outside the train station, but if not, you can call one (€10 from station to old town, +39 335 616 5842, +39 335 616 5845, or +39 335 628 0933). ATC **shuttle buses** also go to the old town and are cheaper, but only run about once an hour and don't take luggage.

By Car: Monterosso is 30 minutes off the freeway (exit: Carrodano-Levanto). About three miles above Monterosso, there's an intersection where you must choose either *Monterosso Centro Storico* (old part of town) or *Monterosso Fegina* (new town and beachfront parking). Know where you want to go, because you can't drive directly between the new town and old center (the tunnel is closed to most cars). Most drivers should choose the Fegina fork, but get directions from your hotelier.

Parking is easy (except July-Aug and weekends in June) in the new town in the huge beachfront guarded lot (€25/24 hours). In the old town, you'll find the Loreto parking garage on Via Roma, from which it's a 10-minute downhill walk to the main square (€2.50/hour, €25/24 hours).

HELPFUL HINTS

Market: Every Thursday morning (8:00-13:00), trucks pull into the old town and fill the public area by the beach with stalls selling produce and more.

Baggage Storage: The **TI** will store bags (€5-8/day—but confirm closing time).

Pharmacy: You'll find one at Via Fegina 42, next to the train station (Mon-Fri, closed Sat-Sun, +39 0187 818 391).

Laundry: For full-service, same-day laundry in the new town, try **Wash and Dry Lavarapido.** They'll pick up at your hotel, or you can drop it at their shop. The owners speak little English, so ask your hotelier to arrange the details (daily 8:00-19:00, Via Molinelli 17, +39 339 484 0940, Lucia and Ivano). In the old town, head uphill to **Luètu Lavanderia,** by the post office (daily 8:00-18:00, Via Roma 86, +39 0187 765 354).

Massage: Physiotherapist **Giorgio Moggia** gives good massages at your hotel or his in-home studio (€70/hour, +39 339 314 6127, giomogg@tin.it).

CINQUE TERRE

Monterosso Walks

These self-guided walks will introduce you to Monterosso. The first one, focusing on the mostly level town center, takes about 30 minutes. For the second one, you'll summit the adjacent hill—allow an hour or so.

MONTEROSSO HARBOR AND TOWN WALK

• *Let's begin with an easy sweep of the sights: Hike out from the dock in the old town and stand atop the concrete breakwater. (If you're arriving by boat, you'll disembark here.)*

Breakwater

From this point you can survey Monterosso's old town (straight ahead) and new town (stretching to the left, with train station and parking lot). Notice the bluff that separates old and new, and imagine how much harder your commute would be if the narrow road tethering these two towns were somehow cut off. It happened in the spring of 2013, when the wall below the hill-topping Capuchin church gave way in a landslide. For a time, the only way to connect the two halves of town by car was to drive six miles around; on foot, you had to hike up and over this hill. (The little fort halfway up the hill, which dates from 1550, is now a fancy restaurant, with a private home upstairs.)

Looking to the right, you can see all *cinque* of the *terre* from one spot: Vernazza, Corniglia (above the shore), Manarola, and a few buildings of Riomaggiore beyond that.

These days, the harbor hosts more paddleboats than fishing boats. Erosion is a major problem. The partial breakwater—the row of giant rocks in the middle of the harbor—is designed to save the beach from washing away. While old-timers remember a vast beach, their grandchildren truck in sand each spring to give tourists something to bask on. (The Nazis liked the Cinque Terre, too—find two of their bomb-hardened bunkers embedded in the bluff. During World War II, nearby La Spezia was an important Axis naval base, and Monterosso was bombed while the Germans were here.)

The fancy four-star Hotel Porto Roca (the pink building high on the hill, on the far right of the harbor) marks the trail to Vernazza. High above, you see an example of the costly roads built in the 1980s to connect the Cinque Terre towns with the freeway over the hills.

The two prominent capes (Punta di Montenero to the right, and Punta Mesco to the left) define the Cinque Terre region. The closer Punta Mesco is part of a protected marine sanctuary and home to a rare sea grass that provides an ideal home for fish eggs.

Buoys keep fishing boats away. The cape was once a quarry, providing employment to locals who chipped out the stones used to build the local towns (the greenish stones making up part of the breakwater are from there).

On the far end of the new town, marking the best free beach around, you can just see the statue named *Il Gigante* (hard to spot because it blends in with the gray rock). It's 45 feet tall and once held a trident. While it looks as if it were hewn from the rocky cliff, it's actually made of reinforced concrete and dates from the beginning of the 20th century, when it supported a dance terrace for a *fin de siècle* villa. A violent storm left the giant holding nothing but memories of Monterosso's glamorous age.

• *From the breakwater, walk toward the old town (noticing the big drainage tunnels opening onto the beach—critical to avoid flooding during big rainstorms) and under the train tracks. Then venture right into the square and find the statue of a dandy holding what looks like a box cutter (behind the big playground).*

Piazza Garibaldi

The statue honors Giuseppe Garibaldi, the dashing firebrand revolutionary who, in the 1860s, helped unite the people of Italy into a modern nation. Facing Garibaldi, with your back to the sea, you'll see (on your right) the orange City Hall (with the European Union flag beside the Italian one).

Just under the bell tower (with your back to the sea, it's on your left), a set of covered arcades facing the sea is where the old-timers hang out (they see all and know all). The crenellated bell tower marks the church. This was originally the tower of a fortified gate that protected the town back in the days when they hid out of view of marauding pirates.

• *Go to church.*

Church of St. John the Baptist (Chiesa di San Giovanni Battista)

First, walk along the side the church. Near the second side door, find the high-water mark *(altezza massima)* from an October 1966 flood—which also famously devastated Florence. Nearby, a second (higher) plaque commemorates the 2011 flood.

Now hook left, around the church—and appreciate its striped main facade. Alternating white marble from Carrara and green marble from Punta Mesco, the stripes get narrower the higher they go, creating the illusion that the church is taller than it really is. The church is typical of the region's Gothic style. Note the lacy, stone rose window above the entrance—considered one of the finest in northern Italy. It's as delicate as crochet work, with 18 slender columns (creating the petals of the rose).

CINQUE TERRE

Monterosso al Mare

Accommodations
1. Hotel Villa Steno
2. Il Giardino Incantato
3. Hotel Pasquale
4. Buranco Agriturismo
5. Locanda il Maestrale
6. Hotel la Colonnina
7. Albergo Marina
8. Manuel's Guesthouse
9. L'Antica Terrazza & Gastronomia "San Martino"
10. Albergo al Carugio
11. La Villa degli Argentieri
12. To Hotel Villa Adriana
13. Hotel la Spiaggia & Bar Giò
14. A Cà du Gigante
15. Hotel Punta Mesco
16. Raffaella Viviani Rooms

Eateries & Nightlife
17. Ristorante Belvedere
18. Il Casello
19. L'Ancora della Tortuga & Torre Aurora
20. Via Venti & Bakery
21. L'Osteria & Emy's Way
22. Ristorante al Pozzo
23. Ciak
24. La Smorfia & Pasticceria Laura
25. Miky
26. La Cantina di Miky
27. Il Frantoio Focacceria
28. Il Massimo della Focaccia

CINQUE TERRE

Step inside for more Ligurian Gothic: original marble columns and capitals with pointed arches to match. The octagonal baptismal font (in the back of the church) was carved from Carrara marble in 1359. Imagine the job getting that from the quarries, about 40 miles away. The fine Baroque altar was crafted with various marbles from around Italy in the 1700s. The church itself dates from 1307—the proud inscription on the left-middle column reads "MilloCCCVII."

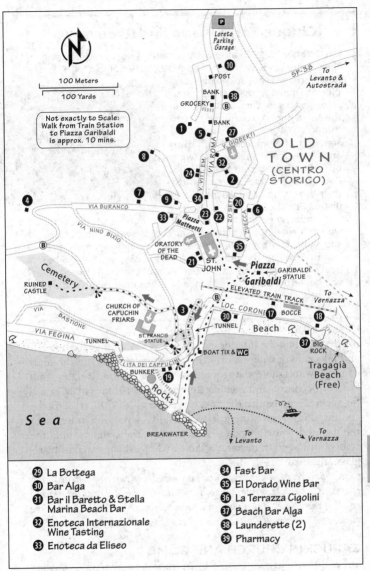

N

100 Meters
100 Yards

Not exactly to Scale:
Walk from Train Station
to Piazza Garibaldi
is approx. 10 mins.

29 La Bottega
30 Bar Alga
31 Bar il Baretto & Stella
   Marina Beach Bar
32 Enoteca Internazionale
   Wine Tasting
33 Enoteca da Eliseo

34 Fast Bar
35 El Dorado Wine Bar
36 La Terrazza Cigolini
37 Beach Bar Alga
38 Launderette (2)
39 Pharmacy

CINQUE TERRE

• *Leaving the church, turn left and go to church again.*

Oratory of the Dead (Oratorio dei Neri)

During the Counter-Reformation, the Catholic Church offset the rising influence of Protestantism by creating brotherhoods of good works. These religious Rotary clubs were called "confraternities." Monterosso had two, nicknamed White and Black. This building is the oratory of the Black group, whose mission—as the maca-

Cinque Terre Flood and Recovery

On October 25, 2011, after a dry summer, a heavy rainstorm hit the Cinque Terre. Within four hours, 22 inches of rain fell. Flash floods rushed down the hillsides, picking up mud, rocks, trees, furniture, and even cars and buses in their raging, destructive path through the streets down to the sea. Part of Monterosso's old town and Vernazza's main drag were buried under a dozen feet of mud. Four villagers from Vernazza lost their lives. One body washed up in distant France.

Today, the Cinque Terre is back to normal. Most visitors wouldn't even notice that in the affected areas of Monterosso and Vernazza, everything is new: stoves, tables, chairs, and plates. Strolling through these towns today, you'll hear the peaceful sound of streams under most of the main streets. As you do, appreciate the resilience of the human spirit (and the importance of good drainage).

---

bre decor filling the interior indicates—was to arrange for funerals and take care of widows, orphans, the shipwrecked, and the souls of those who ignore the request for a €1 donation. It dates from the 16th century, and membership has passed from father to son for generations. Notice the fine, carved pews (c. 1700, with toothy smiling skulls reminding us that mortality is nothing to fear) and the haunted-house chandeliers. Look up at the ceiling to find the symbol of the confraternity: a skull-and-crossbones and an hourglass...death awaits us all.

• *On that cheery note, if you're in a lazy mood, you can end your walking tour here to enjoy strolling, shopping, gelato-licking, a day at the beach... or all of the above. But if you're up for a hike, face out to sea, look to the right, and imagine the view from the top of that hill. Now...go see it.*

CAPUCHIN CHURCH AND CLIMB

The hill that separates the old town from the new rewards anyone who climbs up with a peaceful church, a cemetery in the clouds, and a panoramic view.

• *From the old town's beachfront, find the brick steps squeezed between Hotel Pasquale and its restaurant, and start climbing. The lane is signed* Salita dei Cappuccini, *but in the local dialect it's called* Zii di Frati, *or...*

Switchbacks of the Friars

Follow the yellow brick road (OK, it's not yellow...but I couldn't help singing as I skipped skyward). Several switchbacks up, above the seaside castle, detour left to the statue of St. Francis and a wolf taking in a grand view. Enjoy an opportunity to see all five of the Cinque Terre towns. Then backtrack 20 yards to the switchback and continue uphill. (Continuing straight on from St. Francis would drop you down into the new town.)

• *When you reach a gate marked* Convento e Chiesa Cappuccini, *you have arrived at the...*

Church of the Capuchin Friars

Walk through the gate and up the stairs into the church courtyard. The former monastery is now manned by a single caretaker friar. (If you meet Father Renato, take a moment to speak with him—he's a joyful soul who loves to connect.) Before stepping inside, notice the church's striped Romanesque facade. It's all fake. Tap it—no marble, just cheap 18th-century stucco. Go inside and sit in the rear pew. The high altarpiece painting of St. Francis can be rolled up on special days to reveal a statue of Mary standing behind it.

The fine painting of the **Crucifixion (on the left)** recalls how, when Jesus died, the earth went dark. Notice the eclipsed sun in the painting, just to the right of the cross.

• *Leave and turn left through another gate to hike 100 yards uphill to the cemetery filling the ruined castle at the top of the hill. Reaching the cemetery's gate, look back and enjoy the view over the town.*

Cemetery in the Ruined Castle

In the Dark Ages, the village huddled behind this castle. As the threat of pirates passed, it slowly expanded to the waterfront. Notice the town view from here—no sea. You're looking at the oldest part of Monterosso, tucked behind the hill, out of view of 13th-century pirates.

Respectfully explore the cemetery. Ponder the black-and-white photos of grandparents past. Read the headstones: Q.R.P. is *Qui Riposa in Pace* (i.e., R.I.P.). Rich families had their own little tomb buildings. The fresh flowers show how much people treasure this place.

Climb to the very summit—the castle's keep, or place of last refuge. Priests are buried in a line of graves closest to the sea, but facing inland, looking toward the town's holy sanctuary high on the hillside (above the road, with its triangular steeple just peeking above the trees). Each Cinque Terre town has a lofty sanctuary, dedicated to Mary and dear to the village hearts.

• *Your tour is over—any trail leads you back into town.*

CINQUE TERRE

Experiences in Monterosso

Hikes from Monterosso

For a relatively easy in-town hike, take a rewarding climb up to the **hilltop cemetery** between the old and the new towns (described above).

The most popular hike from Monterosso is to **Vernazza** on the main coastal trail; you'll need a park card (sold at the trailhead or at park offices). The hike to **Levanto** is free, either over the Punta Mesco bluff on the main SVA trail, or on another route where you first take the bus up to Colle di Gritta—which makes most of the rest of the hike downhill.

Another option is path #509 between Monterosso and its **Madonna di Soviore sanctuary** (you could take the shuttle bus up and walk down). From Soviore, you could hike to Vernazza's **Madonna di Reggio sanctuary,** following a mostly level trail (#591) to Termine, then down to Madonna di Reggio (on #582), and then, if you wish, steeply downhill into Vernazza (on #508). Allow 2.5 hours to Vernazza on this route if you start with the shuttle bus to Soviore. (For more on these hikes, see "Hiking the Cinque Terre," earlier.)

Beaches

Monterosso's **new town** has easily the Cinque Terre's best—and most crowded—beach (immediately in front of the train station). Most of the beach is technically private, where (at Stella Marina) you'll pay €35 to rent two chairs and an umbrella for the day (prices get soft in the afternoon). Light lunches are served by beach cafés to sunbathers at their lounge chairs. Various outfits along here rent kayaks and stand-up paddleboards (look for signs at the west end of the beach—near the parking lot—or ask around). If there are no umbrellas on a stretch of beach, it's public (free), so you can spread out a towel anywhere. There's a free beach at the far west end, near the Gigante statue; others are marked on the "Monterosso al Mare" map, earlier.

The **old town** also has its own predominantly private beach; rent umbrellas, chairs, kayaks, and paddleboats from Beach Bar Alga (run by Stefano, €35 for two including showers, changing room, WC, two lounge chairs, and an umbrella), which is also a scenic spot for a drink. Tucked just beyond the private beach—under the Il Casello restaurant at the east end of town—is the free public beach called Tragagià, which is gravelly and generally less crowded (showers). The bocce ball court (next to Il Casello) is busy with older men enjoying their favorite pastime.

Wine Tasting

Buranco Agriturismo is one of the largest producers of wines in the Cinque Terre, and in the afternoon (from 15:00-18:00) they welcome visitors to tastings on their expansive terrace overlooking the vineyards. You'll try some of their wines, plus grappa (firewater) and *limoncino*, while snacking on bruschetta, olives, and the like (about €40/person). Another option is "wine trekking," where you get a picnic basket and audioguide and set off on a walk around the grounds (€50/couple, call or email to arrange). At mealtimes, you can taste their wines over lunch or dinner—see "Eating in Monterosso," later (follow Via Buranco uphill to path, 10 minutes above town, also rents rooms, +39 349 434 8046, www.burancocinqueterre.it, info@buranco.it, Mary).

Enoteca Internazionale is a good place in town to sample local wines. Mario, Susanna, and Valentina are very knowledgeable and serve a selection of five wines for €20 (his bruschetta makes a fine light meal as you're sipping, open daily until late, Via Roma 62, +39 0187 817 278, www.enotecainternazionale.com).

Boat Rides

In addition to the regularly scheduled big boats (see page 343), you can hire your own captain for transfers to other towns or for a lazy sightseeing cruise (if the water's calm).

Stefano has a six-person boat, the *Matilde* (about €100/hour, two hours is enough for a quick spin and a swimming stop; 5-hour trips to Porto Venere and offshore islands possible; +39 333 821 2007, www.matildenavigazione.com, info@matildenavigazione.com).

Fish & Chill offers five-hour daytime excursions on a cushy boat that carries nine (departs about 10:30, €150/person). Expect snorkeling, village visits, and a buffet lunch onboard. They also do sunset tours and private groups (+39 340 834 7834, www.cinqueterreboat.com, 5terretourfishandchill@gmail.com, Diego and Silvia).

Sea Breeze Boat Tours arranges day and *aperitivo* sunset tours and will shuttle you to any of the coastal towns. They also run tours from Levanto (€85-140/person, +39 328 824 6889 or +39 338 809 9278, www.seabreezeboattours.com, info@seabreezeboattours.com, Matteo and Federica).

Nightlife in Monterosso

Although I've listed these establishments for their nightlife, they work any time of day for a drink and spot to relax.

Enoteca da Eliseo, my favorite wine bar in town, comes with operatic ambience. Eliseo and his wife, Mary, love music and wine. Taste by the glass *(bicchiere)*, or select a fine bottle from their shop shelf, then enjoy the wine, a few included nibbles, and views of the village action from their cozy tables. Eliseo stocks more than a hundred varieties of grappa (Wed-Mon 10:00-23:00, closed Tue, Piazza Matteotti 3, a block inland behind church, +39 0187 817 308).

Fast Bar is super basic, but it's the best bar in town for young travelers and night owls. Customers mix travel tales with big, cold beers, and the crowd (and the rock 'n' roll) gets noisier as the night rolls on. Come here to watch sports on TV all day (cheap *panini*, pizza, salads, and other light meals usually served until midnight, open 7:00-late, in the old town at Via Roma 13, +39 0187 819 278; Alex, Francesco, and Stefano).

La Cantina di Miky, in the new town just beyond the train station, is a trendy bar-restaurant with an extensive cocktail and grappa menu. The seating is in three zones: overlooking the beach, in the garden, or in the cellar. Try the fun "five villages" wine tasting. This is the best place in town for top-end Italian microbrews (Thu-Tue until late, closed Wed, Via Fegina 90, +39 0187 802 525). It's also recommended for dining (see listing under "Eating in Monterosso," later).

El Dorado Wine Bar is the local old-town nighttime hangout. Set on a small piazza, it offers music, drinks, pizza, and people-watching late into the night (Piazza Garibaldi 22, daily 10:00-2:00 in the morning, +39 331 475 9611).

Beach Bars: On a balmy evening, enjoy a memorable drink with a view of swimmers, sunbathers, and the languid Ligurian Sea. In the new town, try **La Terrazza Cigolini,** overlooking the beach by the big rock. In the old town, **Beach Bar Alga** has an island ambience (all outside, daily until 20:00, Stefano).

Sleeping in Monterosso

Monterosso, the most beach-resorty of the five Cinque Terre towns, offers maximum comfort and ease. Rooms in Monterosso are a better value than similar rooms in crowded Vernazza, and the proprietors tend to be more genuine and welcoming.

IN THE OLD TOWN

$$$$ Hotel Villa Steno is lovingly managed and features great view balconies, panoramic gardens and a roof terrace with sun beds, air-conditioning, and the friendly help of Matteo and his wife, Carla. Of their 16 rooms, 14 have view balconies (RS%, family rooms, hearty buffet breakfast, elevator, laundry service, ask about pay parking when you reserve, hike up to their panoramic terrace, cooking classes, Via Roma 109, +39 0187 817 028 or +39 0187 818 336, www.villasteno.com, steno@pasini.com). It's a 15-minute climb (or €10 taxi ride) from the train station to the top of the old town. My readers get a free Cinque Terre info packet and a glass of local wine when they check in—ask for it.

$$$$ Il Giardino Incantato ("The Enchanted Garden") is a charming, comfortable four-room B&B with impressive attention to detail in a tastefully renovated 16th-century Ligurian home in the heart of the old town. It's run by kind and eager-to-please Fausto and Mariapia and their gregarious staff. Sip their homemade *limoncino* at *aperitivo* time, and have breakfast under lemon trees in their delightful hidden garden, illuminated with candles in the evening (air-con, free minibar and tea-and-coffee service, laundry service, Via Mazzini 18, +39 0187 818 315, mobile +39 333 264 9252, www.ilgiardinoincantato.net, giardino_incantato@libero.it).

$$$$ Hotel Pasquale is modern and comfortable with 15 seaview rooms (nine with balconies), run by the same family as Hotel Villa Steno (listed earlier). Located right on the harbor, it's just a few steps from the beach, boat dock, and tunnel to the new town. While there is some train noise, the soundtrack is mostly a lullaby of waves. Marco's photographs decorate the breakfast room (RS%, family room, air-con, elevator, laundry service, cooking demonstrations, closed Nov-Feb, Via Fegina 4, +39 0187 817 550 or +39 0187 817 477, www.hotelpasquale.it, pasquale@pasini.com, welcoming Felicita and Marco). Felicita also rents several well-equipped apartments in the center of the old town.

$$$$ Buranco Agriturismo, a 10-minute hike above the old town, has wonderful gardens and views over a hidden valley draped with vineyards and lemon groves. Along with their recommended restaurant and wine and olive-oil production, they offer three rooms and three apartments, with breakfast served on a covered terrace. It's a rare opportunity to stay in a farmhouse but still be able to get to town on foot (air-con, free parking, +39 349 434 8046, www.burancocinqueterre.it, info@buranco.it, informally run by Loredana, Mary, and Irene).

$$$ Locanda il Maestrale rents six stylish rooms in a sophisticated and peaceful little inn. Although renovated with all the modern comforts and thoughtful details, it retains centuries-old character under frescoed ceilings. Its peaceful sun terrace overlooking the old town and Via Roma action is a delight. Guests enjoy complimentary drinks and snacks each afternoon (air-con, Via Roma 37, +39 0187 817 013, mobile +39 338 4530 531, www.locandamaestrale.net, maestrale@monterossonet.com, Stefania and Giovanni).

$$$ Hotel la Colonnina has 22 big rooms, all but one with a private terrace. The generous and meticulously cared-for public spaces include a cozy garden and an inviting shared seaview terrace with sun beds. It's buried in the town's fragrant and sleepy back streets (family rooms, air-con, fridges, elevator, a block inland from main square at Via Zuecca 6, +39 0187 817 439, www. lacolonninacinqueterre.it, info@lacolonninacinqueterre.it, Cristina).

$$$ Albergo Marina, run by enthusiastic husband-and-wife team Marina and Eraldo, has 23 pleasant rooms and a garden with lemon trees. They serve a good breakfast, provide lots of little extras, and offer a fine value (RS%, family rooms, elevator, air-con, fridges, kayak and snorkel equipment, Via Buranco 40, +39 0187 817 613, www.hotelmarina5terre.com, marina@hotelmarina5terre. com).

$$$ Manuel's Guesthouse, perched high above the town among terraces, is a garden getaway run by Lorenzo and his father, Giovanni. They have six big, artfully decorated rooms and a grand view. After climbing the killer stairs from the town center, their killer terrace is hard to leave—especially after a few drinks (cash only, air-con, up about 100 steps behind church—you can ask Lorenzo to carry your bags up the hill, Via San Martino 39, +39 333 439 0809, www.manuelsguesthouse.com, manuelsguesthouse@ libero.it).

$$ L'Antica Terrazza rents four tight, classy rooms right in town. With a pretty terrace overlooking the pedestrian street, Raffaella and Jon offer a good deal (RS%, one single has private bath down the hall, air-con, Vicolo San Martino 1, +39 347 132 6213, www.anticaterrazza.com, post@anticaterrazza.com).

$$ Albergo al Carugio has nine practical rooms in a big apartment-style building with a small patio at the top of the old town. It's quiet, comfy, and a fine budget value; one room has a private terrace (RS%, no breakfast, air-con, fridges, Via Roma 100, +39 0187 817 453, mobile +39 328 847 6276, www.alcarugio.it, info@alcarugio.it, conscientiously run by kindly Andrea).

IN THE NEW TOWN

$$$$ La Villa degli Argentieri offers 11 spacious rooms, six with balconies, from a choice position at the quiet end of the new town's beachfront street. From the front rooms you'll get a peek-a-boo look (through trees) at the water, but the inviting rooftop breakfast terrace has panoramic views (air-con, elevator, Via Fegina 120, +39 0187 916 295, www. villaargentieri.it, info@villaargentieri.it).

$$$$ Hotel Villa Adriana is big, contemporary, and bright, set on a church-owned estate with a peaceful garden, a pool, free parking (reserve ahead), and a no-stress style. They rent 55 sterile rooms—most with terraces, a few with sea views (family rooms, air-con, elevator, free loaner bikes, affordable dinners, Via IV Novembre 23, +39 0187 818 109, www.villaadriana.info, info@ villaadriana.info).

$$$$ Hotel la Spiaggia, facing the beach, is a venerable place with 19 rooms (half with sea views) and a quiet garden retreat (air-con, elevator, free parking—reserve in advance, Via Lungomare 96, +39 0187 817 567, www.laspiaggiahotel.it, laspiaggiahotel@gmail.com, Maria). They also rent four pricey, ultra-mod rooms in a small building on the seafront promenade.

$$$$ A Cà du Gigante, despite its name, is a tiny yet chic refuge with nine rooms, most on the ground floor. About 100 yards from the beach (and surrounded by blocky apartments), the interior is tastefully done with upscale comfort in mind (air-con, limited pay parking—reserve ahead, Via IV Novembre 11, +39 0187 817 401, www.ilgigantecinqueterre.it, gigante@ilgigantecinqueterre.it, Claudia).

$$$ Hotel Punta Mesco is a tidy, well-run little haven renting 17 quiet, casual rooms at a good price. While none have views, 10 rooms have small terraces backed up to the building next door (family room, air-con, parking, Via Molinelli 35, +39 0187 817 495, www.hotelpuntamesco.it, info@hotelpuntamesco.it, Roberto, Diego, and Manuel).

$$ Raffaella Viviani rents five basic, dated, but affordable rooms up a single flight of stairs from the beachfront road. Three rooms face the sea (two with small balconies); two have terraces overlooking a little garden (big family rooms, cash only, no breakfast, air-con, Via Fegina 84, +39 329 336 9577, www.affittacamerevivianiraffaella.it, lella-v71@hotmail.it).

Eating in Monterosso

WITH A SEA VIEW

$$ Ristorante Belvedere, big and sprawling, serves good-value meals indoors or outdoors on the harborfront. Their huge €52 *anfora belvedere*—mixed seafood stew dumped dramatically at the table from a pottery amphora into your bowl—can easily be split among up to four diners. Another fishy treat, their €20 *misto mare* plate, nearly makes an entire meal for two. Mussel fans will enjoy the *tagliolini della casa*. It's energetically run by Federico and Roberto (Wed-Mon 12:00-14:30 & 18:00-22:00, closed Tue, on the harbor in the old town, +39 0187 817 033).

$$ Il Casello offers outdoor terrace seating only, on a little bluff overlooking the old town beach when the weather's nice. It's a pleasant spot for pasta, seafood, or a drink (daily 12:00-22:00, +39 333 492 7629, Bacco and Gianfranco).

$$$ L'Ancora della Tortuga is a top option in Monterosso for seaview elegance, with gorgeous outdoor seating high on a bluff and a white-tablecloth-and-candles interior fit for an admiral. Drop by to choose and reserve a table for later. Consider their €40 tasting *menu* (Tue-Sun 12:30-15:30 & 18:30-21:30, closed Mon

CINQUE TERRE

and when stormy; at the tip of the point between the old and new towns—just outside the tunnel; +39 0187 800 065, mobile +39 333 240 7956, Silvia and Giamba).

$$$$ Torre Aurora is a top-end, fancy restaurant with no indoor seating. You'll dine outside (wrapped in a blanket if it's cold) around the medieval tower with commanding views of approaching pirates while enjoying simple yet creative dishes. Reservations are smart (daily from 12:30 in good weather, +39 366 145 3702, www.torreauroracinqueterre.com, Elia). They serve cocktails outside of mealtime.

IN THE OLD TOWN

$$$$ Via Venti is a quiet little trattoria, hidden on a traffic-free street deep in the heart of the old town, where chef Ilaria and her husband Michele create and serve imaginative seafood dishes. Eat indoors or out; you'll be tempted by their delicate and savory gnocchi with crab, tender ravioli stuffed with fresh fish, and pear-and-pecorino pasta (Fri-Wed 12:00-14:30 & 18:30-22:30, closed Thu, Via XX Settembre 32, +39 0187 818 347).

$$$ Buranco Agriturismo, just 10 minutes' walk uphill from the old town, feels like another world. You'll eat on a heated, roofed-over terrace, overlooking their beautiful grounds and forested hillsides. Chef Giovanni is proud of his shrimp risotto, spaghetti with anchovies, and sophisticated fish and meat courses; they serve their own wines (air-con, free parking, reservations wise, also has rooms, +39 349 434 8046, www.burancocinqueterre.it, Mary).

$ Gastronomia "San Martino," warmly run by hard-working Moreno and Sabrina, is a tiny, humble combination of takeaway and sit-down café with surprisingly affordable, quality dishes. Belly up to the glass case and see what's cooking today, then eat at one of the few tables—inside or out on a pleasant street—or find a driftwood log for a feast-to-go. You're welcome to create your own €15 mixed plate by pointing to whatever appeals (Tue-Sun 12:00-15:00 & 18:00-21:30, closed Mon, next to recommended L'Antica Terrazza hotel at Vicolo San Martino 3, +39 346 109 7338).

$$ L'Osteria is a delightful little family-run place serving "cuisine with passion" at wonderful prices. Alessandro thoughtfully explains your options and Elisa is understandably proud of her cakes. Their Possa wine, from vineyards close to the sea, is the oyster of local wines, or maybe it's just the Ligurian music the family is sure to play (Tue-Sun lunch served 12:00-14:30, evening seatings at 19:00 and 21:00, closed Mon, Via Vittorio Emanuele 5, +39 0187 819 224). It's a cozy scene inside with a few tables outside in the shadow of the church.

$$$ Ristorante al Pozzo is a favorite among locals. It's family-run, with good old-fashioned quality, as Gino (with his long white beard) cooks, and his engaging English-speaking son, Manuel, serves. They have one of the best wine lists in town, serve only homemade pasta, and are known for their raw fish and wonderful seafood *antipasti misti*, which you can check out in a case near the entrance (Fri-Wed 12:00-15:00 & 18:30-22:30, closed Thu, Via Roma 24, +39 0187 817 575).

$$$ Ciak, high-energy and tightly packed—inside and out— is a local institution with reliably good food and (sometimes) a bit of an attitude. Stroll a couple of paces past the outdoor tables up Via Roma to see what Signore Ciak (who wears his Popeye cap in the kitchen) has on the stove (Thu-Tue 12:00-15:00 & 18:00-22:30, closed Wed, Piazza Don Minzoni 6, +39 0187 817 014, www.ristoranteciak.net).

$ La Smorfia—a local favorite—cooks up good pizza in a sloppy setting that somehow seems to say, "Great pizza enjoyed here." Their large pizzas can feed three (Wed-Mon 11:00-24:00, closed Tue, Via Vittorio Emanuele 73, +39 0187 818 395).

IN THE NEW TOWN

$$$$ Miky is packed with a well-dressed clientele who know their seafood. For elegantly presented, top-quality food that celebrates local ingredients and traditions, it's worth the steep prices. It's a proud family operation—Miky (dad), Simonetta (mom), charming Sara (daughter, who greets guests)—and the attentive waitstaff all work hard. Their "pizza pasta" is served in a bowl topped with a thin pizza crust dome to contain the flavor, then flambéed at your table. Many of the wines on their fine list are available by the glass if you ask. Their mixed dessert sampler plate, *dolce misto*, serves two and is a fitting capper (Wed-Mon 12:00-15:00 & 19:00-23:00, closed Tue, reservations wise, in the new town 100 yards from train station at Via Fegina 104, +39 0187 817 608, www.ristorantemiky.it).

$$$ La Cantina di Miky, a few doors down from the station, serves artfully crafted Ligurian specialties that follow in Miky's family tradition of quality. Run by son Manuel—and Christine from New Jersey—it's more youthful and informal (but reservations are still wise—sit downstairs, in the garden, or on the promenade overlooking the sea). The €23 anchovy tasting plate is an education in the many ways to prepare this local specialty (creative desserts, large selection of Italian microbrews, Thu-Tue 12:00-15:00 & 19:00-22:00, closed Wed, Via Fegina 90, +39 0187 802 525). This place doubles as a cocktail bar in the evenings.

LIGHT MEALS, TAKEOUT FOOD, AND BREAKFAST

In the Old Town: Lots of shops sell pizza and focaccia to eat in or take out for an easy picnic on the beach or trail. At **$ Il Frantoio**

Focacceria, Simone makes tasty pizza and focaccia (Fri-Wed 9:00-14:00 & 16:30-20:00, closed Thu, just off Via Roma at Via Gioberti 1). **$ Emy's Way** offers pasta, thick-crust pizza, and deep-fried seafood in to-go cones (daily 12:00-22:00, along the skinny street next to the church, +39 331 788 1088, Emiliano).

In the New Town: For a quick bite right under the train station (or to take over to the beach), try **$ Il Massimo della Focaccia** for its quiche-like tortes, sandwiches, focaccia pizzas, and desserts. There are benches just in front—a good bet for a light meal with a sea view (Thu-Tue 9:00-19:00, closed Wed, Via Fegina 50). **La Bottega** is Monterosso's largest grocery store, a smart minimart with fresh produce, *antipasti,* deli items, and other picnic fare. They'll make you a sandwich: Select a bread and filling, and pay by weight (Mon-Sat 8:00-13:00 & 16:30-19:00, closed Sun, Via Molinelli 9).

Breakfast: Although most hotels include breakfast in the room rate, a handful leave you to your own devices. In the **old town,** for breakfast on the beach, try **Bar Alga** (from 8:00 when the weather's nice). For the freshest bakery items, follow your nose to **Pasticceria Laura,** serving coffee and pastries every morning from 7:00 (Via Vittorio Emanuele 59). There's a **bakery** at Via XX Settembre 26, next to the recommended Via Venti restaurant.

In the **new town,** these places (on Via Fegina, near Hotel la Spiaggia) serve something akin to breakfast starting at 8:00: **Bar Giò** (bacon and eggs), **Bar il Baretto** (bacon and eggs), and **Stella Marina Beach Bar** (croissants and yogurt—served down on the beach). Your best bet here might be a picnic breakfast from the tiny, nearby *alimentari*/supermarket at Via Fegina 116. They open at 8:00, and have a good selection of cheeses, breads, pastries, and fruit.

Monterosso Connections

Of the five Cinque Terre towns, Monterosso has the most direct train connections with towns outside the Cinque Terre.

From Monterosso by Train to: Levanto (3-4/hour, 5 minutes), **Sestri Levante** (at least hourly, 30-40 minutes, most trains to Genoa stop here), **Santa Margherita Ligure** (at least hourly, 50-60 minutes, often with a change in Sestri Levante), **Genoa** (at least hourly, 1.5 hours, often with 1 change; change trains here for destinations in France), **Milan** (5-6/day direct, 3 hours, more with changes), **Venice** (at least hourly, 6 hours, 1-3 changes, simplest to change in Milan), **La Spezia** (2-3/hour, 15-30 minutes), **Pisa** (at least hourly, 1-1.5 hours, most change in La Spezia), **Rome** (every 1-2 hours, 4.5 hours, change in La Spezia).

Vernazza

With the closest thing to a natural harbor—overseen by a ruined castle, a stout stone church, and a pastel canyon of fisherfolk homes—Vernazza is the jewel of the Cinque Terre. Only the regular noisy slurping up of the train by the mountain reminds you of the modern world.

The action is at the harbor, where you'll find outdoor eateries ringing a humble piazza, a restaurant hanging on the edge of the castle, and a breakwater with a promenade, corralled by a natural amphitheater of terraced hills.

Proud of their Vernazzan heritage, the town's 500 residents like to brag: "Vernazza is locally owned. Portofino has sold out." Fearing change, keep-Vernazza-small proponents stopped the construction of a major road into the town and region. Families are tight and go back centuries; you'll notice certain surnames (such as Basso and Moggia) everywhere. In the winter, the population shrinks, as many people return to more-comfortable big-city apartments to spend the money they earned during the tourist season.

During the day in season the tiny harborfront and one main street are clogged with gawking group excursions. But early and late, Vernazza is the cool and content domain of locals...and travelers who are lucky enough to call the town home for a couple of nights.

Join (or sit on a bench and watch) the locals devoting their leisure time to taking part in the *passeggiata*—strolling lazily together up and down the main street, doing *vasche* (laps). Explore the characteristic alleys called *caruggi*. Learn—and live—the phrase *"la vita pigra di Vernazza"* (the lazy life of Vernazza).

Orientation to Vernazza

TOURIST INFORMATION

There's a park office at the train station (daily 8:30-19:30, shorter hours off-season). WCs are just down the platform.

ARRIVAL IN VERNAZZA

By Train: Vernazza's station is only about three train cars long, but the trains themselves are much longer, so most cars come to a stop

Vernazza

CINQUE TERRE

Accommodations

1. La Malà & La Marina Rooms
2. Cinque Terre Vacation
3. Nicolina Rooms Reception & Ristorante Pizzeria Vulnetia
4. Monica Lercari Rooms
5. Francamaria Reception & Albergo Barbara Rooms
6. Vernazza Rentals
7. Vernazza Rooms Reception
8. Rosa Vitali Rooms
9. Maria Capellini Rooms (2)
10. Martina Callo Rooms, Capitano Rooms Reception & Trattoria del Capitano
11. Rooms Francesca Reception (Enoteca Sciacchetrà)
12. Ivo Basso Rooms
13. Eva's Rooms & Trattoria da Sandro
14. Manuela Moggia Rooms
15. Casa Cato
16. Giuliano Basso Rooms
17. Camere Fontanavecchia
18. La Rosa dei Venti

To Madonna di Reggio Sanctuary

To P & Coastal Road

B

B

WALK ENDS
21

VIA BRIGATE PARTIGIANE

Cemetery

LAUNDERETTE

POST

18

33

BANK & ATM

17

VIA GAVINO

Little "River"

34

CITY HALL

WORLD WARS MONUMENT

VIA S. FRAN.

"Millstone Square"

TUNNEL

14

VIA DEL SANTO

TRAIN PLATFORM

TRAIN STATION

7

16

31

11 6 29

22

ATM

VIA   ROMA

12

13

30

15

35

SANTA MARTA CHAPEL

23

VIA MARCANTONIO CARATTINO

TUNNEL

2

Cliffs

32

Trail to Corniglia

CINQUE TERRE

19 Gianni Franzi Reception/Ristorante
20 Gianni Franzi Rooms

Eateries & Other
21 Il Pirata delle Cinque Terre Café
22 Blue Marlin Bar
23 Lunch Box
24 Ananasso Bar
25 Ristorante Luca
26 Gambero Rosso
27 Ristorante Belforte

28 Ristorante al Castello
29 Antica Osteria il Baretto
30 Pizzeria da Ercole
31 Gelateria (3)
32 Bar la Torre
33 Cantina Cheo Wine Tasting
34 Cinque Sensi Wine Tasting
35 Cinque Terre Riviera Agency (Room Rental; Bag Storage; Opera Tickets)

in a long, dimly lit tunnel. Get out anyway, and walk through the tunnel—heading for the light—to reach the station. From there the main street flows through town right down to the harbor. If you're sleeping here, many locals who rent rooms will meet you at the station and walk you to your place (call ahead to tell them which train you're on).

By Car: Don't drive in Vernazza; the roads to town are in bad shape, and parking is mostly residents-only. If you're coming from the north, park in Levanto. If arriving from the south, park in La Spezia. From either town, hop on the train. (If you must drive here, leave your car at Parking Vernassoa, about a half-mile uphill from the top end of town; €15/day, free shuttle.)

HELPFUL HINTS

Market: Vernazza's skimpy business community is augmented Tuesday mornings (8:00-13:00), when a meager gang of cars and trucks pulls into town for a tailgate market.

Baggage Storage: You can store your bags at the Cinque Terre Riviera agency on Via Roma (€5/bag, daily 9:30-18:30—see listing below).

Pharmacy: There's a little *farmacia* on the main drag, a few blocks up from the water (Via Roma 2, +39 0187 812 396).

Laundry: A small self-serve launderette is at the top of town next to the post office (Via Gavino 32, daily 8:00-20:00).

Booking Agency: Cinque Terre Riviera, run by Miriana, books vacation rentals in the Cinque Terre towns and La Spezia. They also store bags, sell tickets for Vernazza's summer opera, and can arrange transportation, cooking classes, and weddings (Via Roma 24, +39 351 785 8879, www.cinqueterreriviera. com, info@cinqueterreriviera.com).

Massage: Kate Allen offers a relaxing fusion of aromatic/Swedish/holistic massage and reflexology in her studio in the center across from the pharmacy (+39 0187 812 537, +39 333 568 4653, www.vernazzamassage5terre.com, katarinaallen@ hotmail.com).

Vernazza Walk

This self-guided walk gives you a quick overview of the town and starts out on its breakwater.

• *From the train station, just walk downhill and all the way out onto the breakwater. (Ropes are put up to protect gawky tourists from dangerous waves.) Find a comfortable and safe place to sit and get to know Vernazza.*

The Town

The earliest references call the town "Fortress Vernazza." Its towers, fortified walls, and hillside terracing date mostly from the 12th through 15th century. Vernazza allied itself with the Republic of Genoa, a maritime power of the day. In the 12th century, the **big yellow central building** facing the harbor was a site where Genoese warships were built.

In the Middle Ages, there was no beach or square. The water went right up to the buildings, where boats would tie up, Venetian-style. Imagine what Vernazza looked like in those days, when it was the biggest and richest of the Cinque Terre towns. The harborside buildings had a water gate (facing today's square) and a front door on the higher inland side. There was no pastel plaster—just fine stonework (traces of which survive above Trattoria del Capitano). The town, hiding behind its little bluff, was camouflaged by its gray stonework—certainly not gaily painted, lest it attract the eyes of marauding pirates. But apart from the added paint and plaster, the general shape and size of the town has changed little in five centuries. Survey the windows and notice inhabitants quietly gazing back. (At least they did before Airbnb changed the economic environment of touristy towns like Vernazza, driving prices up and locals away from the most charming spots.)

Vernazza has two halves. *Sciuiu* (Vernazzan dialect for "flowery") is the sunny side on the left (with your back to the sea), and *luvegu* (dank) is the shady side on the right. Houses below the castle were connected by an interior arcade—ideal for fleeing attacks.

The "Ligurian pastel" colors of the buildings are regulated by the regional government's commissioner of good taste. The square before you is known for some of the area's finest restaurants.

While the town has 1,500 residents in summer, only 500 stay here through the winter. Vernazza has accommodations for about that many tourists.

Above Town

The small, **round tower** above the red building is another part of the city fortifications, recalling the town's importance in the Middle Ages. Back then, Genoa's enemies (rival maritime republics, especially Pisa) were Vernazza's enemies too. That tower recalls a time when the town was fortified by a stone wall.

CINQUE TERRE

Vineyards fill the mountainside beyond the town. Notice the many terraces. For six centuries, the economy was based on wine and olive oil. Then came the 1980s—and the tourists. Locals turned to tourism to make a living, and stopped tending the land and vineyards.

Although many locals still maintain their small plots and proudly serve their family wines, the patchwork of vineyards is atomized and complex because of inheritance traditions. Historically, families divided their land among their children. Parents wanted each child to receive good land, though some lots were "kissed by the sun" while others were shady. Lots were split into increasingly tiny, unviable pieces, and many were eventually abandoned. The vineyards once stretched as high as you can see, but since fewer people sweat in the fields these days, the most distant terraces have gone wild again.

Church, School, and City Hall

Vernazza's Ligurian Gothic **church,** built with black stones quarried from Punta Mesco (the distant point between Monterosso and Levanto), dates from 1318. Note the gray stone (on the left) that marks the church's 16th-century expansion. The gray and red house above the spire is the **elementary school** (about 25 children attend). Older students go to the "big city," La Spezia. The red building on the hill to the right of the schoolhouse, a former monastery, is now the **City Hall.** Vernazza and neighboring Corniglia function as one community. Through most of the 1990s, the local government was Communist. In 1999, residents elected a coalition of many parties working to rise above ideologies and simply make Vernazza a better place. That practical notion of government continues here today.

Finally, on the top of the hill, with the best view of all, is the **town cemetery.** It's only fair that hardworking Vernazzans—who spend their lives climbing up and down and up and down and up and down the hillsides that hem in their little town—are rewarded with a world-class view from their eternal resting place.

• *Look high on your right to the castle.*

Castle (Castello Doria)

The castle, which is now just stones and a grassy park with super views, still guards the town (€2, daily 10:00-20:00, Nov-March weekends only; from the harbor, take the stairs by Trattoria Gianni and follow *Ristorante al Castello* signs—the tower is a few steps beyond). This was the town's watchtower back in pirate days.

The squat tower below the castle, overlooking the water, Ristorante Belforte, is a great spot for a glass of wine or a meal. From the breakwater, you could follow the rope to the restaurant and pop inside, past an actual submarine door. A photo of a major storm showing the entire tower under a wave (not uncommon in the winter) hangs near the bar.

Harbor

In a moderate storm, you'd get soaked where you're sitting, as waves routinely crash over the *molo* (**breakwater,** built in 1972).

Waves can rearrange the huge rocks—depositing them from the breakwater onto the piazza and its benches. Freak waves have even washed away tourists squinting excitedly into their cameras. (I've seen it happen.) In 2007, an American woman was swept away and killed by a rogue wave.

The old **train line** (across the harbor) was constructed in 1874 to tie together a newly united Italy, linking Turin and Genoa with Rome. (The line now in use, hidden in a tunnel at this point, was built in the 1920s.) The yellow building alongside the tracks was Vernazza's **first train station.** Along the wall behind the tracks, you can see the four bricked-up alcoves where people once waited for trains. The wonderful concrete **sunbathing** strip (and place for late-night privacy) laid below the tracks along the rocks makes for a fun little stroll. (Buoys along the shoreline establish a boat-free swimming zone.)

Vernazza's **fishing fleet** is down to just a few boats with net spools, but Vernazzans are still more likely to own a boat than a car. Boats are moored on buoys, except in winter or when the red storm flag indicates rough seas (see the pole at the start of the breakwater). When the red flag flies, boat owners are permitted to pull them up onto the square—which is usually reserved for restaurant tables. In the 1970s, tiny Vernazza had one of Italy's top water polo teams, and the harbor was their "pool." Later, when the league required a real pool, Vernazza dropped out.

• *Stroll from the breakwater to the harbor square. Look for a small historic stone just before the narrow stairway on the right.*

Harbor Square (Piazza Marconi)

Vernazza, with the Cinque Terre's only natural harbor, was once the sole place boats could pick up the fine local wine. The two-foot-high square **stone** at the foot of the stairs is marked *Sasso del Sego* (stone of tallow). Workers crushed animal flesh and fat in its basin to make tallow, which drained out from the tiny hole below. The tallow was then used to waterproof boats or wine barrels.

Stonework is the soul of the region. Take some time to appreciate the medieval stonework and chestnut timbers of the restaurant interiors facing the harbor. From here steps lead to your right up to the castle.

Towns along this coast were designed as what's called a "Ligurian Palazzata"—an interlinked series of buildings intended to provide protection from seaborne attacks. Vernazza's harborfront retains its thousand-year-old "stockade" of buildings, connected with tiny and easy-to-defend staircases leading from the vulnerable harbor higher into the community.

• *Cross to the church side of the harbor, and peek into the tiny street leading away from the water with its commotion of arches. Vernazza's most characteristic* **side streets** *(caruggi) lead up from here. Another narrow set of stairs marks the beginning of the trail that leads up, up, up to the quintessential view of Vernazza—and, eventually, on to Monterosso (my favorite two-hour hike in the region).*

Vernazza's Church

Vernazza's harborfront **church** sits on the tiny piazza, decorated with a river-rock mosaic. This popular hangout spot is where the town's older ladies soak up the last bit of sun, and kids enjoy a level patch for playing ball. The church, nestled awkwardly into the rocks, is unusual for its east-facing (rather than the standard west-facing) entryway. With relative peace and prosperity in the 16th century, the townspeople doubled the size of their church, extending it west over what was the little piazza that faced it.

Enter under a statue of St. Margaret, patron saint of Vernazza, and climb the steps into the nave. The space was originally dark (with just the upper slit windows) before the bigger gothic windows were added with the 16th-century expansion. The lighter pillars in the back mark the extension. Three historic portable crosses hanging on the walls are carried through town during religious processions. These are replicas of crosses that (locals like to believe) Vernazzan ships once carried on crusades to the Holy Land.

• *Now walk back across the harbor square and head left into town. On the main drag, continue uphill to...*

Vernazza's "Main Street"

You're now strolling through Vernazza's "commercial center": souvenir shops, wine shops, the Blue Marlin Bar (a good nightspot), and so on. You'll walk by a *gelateria*, bakery, pharmacy, grocery, and another *gelateria*. There are plenty of fun and cheap food-to-go options here. The small stone chapel with iron grillwork over the window (on the right) is the tiny **Chapel of Santa Marta**, where Mass is celebrated on special

Sundays. While it's easy to get distracted by all the tourists, try to see through them to notice locals going about their business.

• *Pause just before the train tracks.*

Vernazza is built around this one street, which is basically a lid over the stream in its ravine. During torrential rainstorms, the surrounding hills act like a funnel, directing flash-flood waters and mudslides right through the middle of town. That's precisely what happened in the devastating flood of October 25, 2011. Four townspeople lost their lives. Imagine this street, from here to the harbor, buried under 13 feet of mud. Every shop, restaurant, and hotel on the main drag had to be rewired, replumbed, and re-equipped.

The second set of train tracks (nearer the harbor) has been renovated to lessen disruptive noise. At the base of the stairs a handy monitor displays up-to-the-minute schedules for arriving and departing trains (including any running late—*ritardo*). The walls under the tracks serve as a sort of community information center. Just above the tracks (to the right), the town provides limited space for political advertising (but only during the weeks leading up to an election).

• *Hike a few steps under and above the tracks to the little square.*

"Millstone Square"

The **millstones** set on the square are a reminder that Vernazza's water mill was once powered by the town stream (which runs underground here; you've been walking over it since leaving the harbor area). You can still see the tiny "river" if you follow this road up a few steps. Until the 1950s, the river ran openly through the center of town. Old-timers recall the days before the breakwater, when the river cascaded down, charming bridges spanned the ravine, and the surf sent waves rolling up Vernazza's main drag.

Corralling this stream under the modern street, and forcing it to take a hard turn here, contributed to the damage caused by the 2011 flood. As a result, Swiss engineers redesigned the drainage system, so any future floods will be less destructive. Nets installed above the town now protect it from landslides.

On the wall ahead, at the bend in the road, notice the **World Wars Monument**—dedicated to those killed in World Wars I and II. Not a family in Vernazza was spared. Listed on the left are soldiers who died *(morti in combattimento)* in World War I; on the right is the WWII section. Some were deported to *Germania;* others—labeled *Part* (for *partigiani,* or partisans)—were killed while fighting against Mussolini.

The **path to Corniglia** begins from here (behind and above the monument). Even if you don't plan to hike its entire length, you don't have to go far to find fine views over Vernazza's stony peninsula.

• *To see a more workaday part of Vernazza, head a couple of minutes uphill from here to the...*

Top of Town

First you'll pass the **ambulance barn** (on the left, at #7, with big brown garage doors and a *croce verde Vernazza* sign), where a group of volunteers is always on call for a dash to the hospital, 40 minutes away in La Spezia. Farther up, you'll come to a functional strip of modern apartment blocks facing the river. In this practical zone—the only place in town that allows cars—are a bank, the post office, a launderette, and the popular bar/café called Il Pirata delle Cinque Terre. A parking lot fills the square called **Fontana Vecchia,** named for an "old fountain" that's so old, it's long gone. Shuttle buses run from here to hamlets and sanctuaries in the hills above. (Check the schedule post if you want to enjoy the scenic shuttle bus up to the sanctuary and hike back into town—described below.)

Looming over this neighborhood is a terraced hill capped by the town cemetery (a 20-minute steep hike from here) and, a 30-minute climb beyond that, the town's Madonna di Reggio sanctuary.

Experiences in Vernazza

Hikes from Vernazza

For a rundown of ambitious hikes from Vernazza—including the main coastal trail to Corniglia and to Monterosso—see page 349. The following shorter alternatives closer to town offer classic photo

CINQUE TERRE

ops. They are steeply, but briefly, uphill (about 10 minutes to the best views and park ticket checkpoints).

For the best light in the morning, follow the trail **toward Corniglia;** you'll twist up through vineyards to earn great views down over the stony back side of Vernazza's peninsula, with its round castle tower poking up and a Monterosso backdrop. The best views are from just before the national park ticket checkpoint. If you need a rewarding rest up here, Bar la Torre offers drinks with a grand view.

The trail **toward Monterosso** has the best light in the evening. From the harbor, you'll hike up through the steep and narrow alleys before popping out on the trail above town. Follow this around the bluff, enjoying better and better views of Vernazza's tidy pastel harbor. The views are fine before the ticket booth, but even better after—if you don't want to buy a Cinque Terre park card, you can hike up here in the evening, after the park officially closes (typically around 19:00).

Hike to the Cemetery: To hike up to Vernazza's sweet little **cemetery,** find the steep lane from the ravine at the top of town. From here, it's a 20-minute hike to the top. You'll find a peaceful world of lovingly tended family graves with stunning views over the Cinque Terre. Imagine the entire village sadly trudging up here during funerals. The cemetery is peaceful and evocative at sunset, when the fading light touches each crypt.

▲▲Madonna di Reggio Shuttle Bus Joyride and/or Hike

For a cheap and scenic joyride (50 minutes, €1.50), and a chance to chat about the region with the friendly drivers, ride the ATC shuttle bus, which loops about four times a day from the top of Vernazza to sanctuaries and hamlets high in the hills and back again (for times, check schedule posted at the bus stop, ask at the TI, or check online at www.atcesercizio.it). Look for the bus serving Madonna di Reggio and Fornacchi. Stay on for the full loop back to Vernazza, or get off at Madonna di Reggio and return downhill on foot.

Joyride: The bus ride is absolutely stunning, though it can be crowded. As you ride, you'll see tiny hamlets and hillside terraces that go back a thousand years. You'll switchback past chestnut trees, which historically provided wood for fuel and lumber, and chestnuts, which were ground to make a kind of flour in a land with no grain.

Hiking Down from Madonna di Reggio: For a delightful and easy (if steep) half-hour hike into Vernazza, ask the driver to let you out at the stop for Vernazza's sanctuary, Madonna di Reggio.

First, walk two minutes below the bus stop to the sanctuary, which dates from 1248 and has a Romanesque facade. Inside the church, interesting votives (little ships and paintings of ships in angry seas given as tokens of thanks) fill the rear corner—gifts from sailors who survived storms and soldiers who survived wars. A volunteer staffs the church selling coffee, water, and snacks.

From here signs direct you to trail #508—the historic original trail down to Vernazza. You'll be walking on thousand-year-old cobbles through abandoned olive groves and past the Stations of the Cross, which have inspired generations of processions trudging up from Vernazza. You may see a parked *trenino*, one of about 40 monorail mini-trains in the area that help farmers get their grapes from distant fields to their trucks.

You'll descend through the cemetery, then either take the stairs down to the train station, or continue to the left down the lane to the square called Fontana Vecchia, where you caught the shuttle bus.

Beaches

The harbor's sandy cove has sunning rocks and showers by the breakwater. The sunbathing lane directly under the church has a shower. A ladder on the seaside of the breakwater aids deep-water swimmers.

Boat Rides

In addition to the regularly scheduled big boats that depart from Vernazza's harbor (see page 343), hiring your own boat can be handy for intertown transport. It's also a great way to escape the crowds and get a different angle on Cinque Terre splendor. From Vernazza, figure around €50 one-way to sail to the other towns (for up to six passengers in an outboard). Or hire a boat for a one-hour sightseeing cruise of the entire Cinque Terre (about €150); one popular stop is the tiny *acqua pendente* (waterfall) cove between Vernazza and Monterosso, which locals call their *laguna blu*.

Some boat captains offer evening *aperitivo* cruises on a per-person basis. At Vernazza's breakwater you'll find **Nord Est,** run by Vincenzo (with help from Cesare), the best-established option (+39 338 700 0436, www.nordest-vernazza.it). **Vernazza Water Taxi,** run by Pietro, is another choice (+39 338 911 3869, www.vernazzawatertaxi.it).

Wine Tasting

Cantina Cheo, above the train station near the top of town, invites you in for afternoon tastings of its own wines—grown on the nearby hillside (€5, more for private tours, April-mid-Oct daily 14:30-18:30, closed off-season, Via Brigate Partigiane 1, +39 333 959 4758, www.cheo.it). Cinque Sensi, behind the train station, offers an assortment of wines with snacks (€15-25, Via Roma 71, daily 12:00-24:00, +39 338 766 7423).

Nightlife in Vernazza

A Little Taste of Opera

In summer, a pair of talented opera singers comes to Vernazza once or twice a week to perform with piano accompaniment in the town's small oratory, a medieval building with fine acoustics (just up the steps from the church). Performances begin at 19:00 and last just over an hour—strategically timed to squeeze between a late-afternoon aperitivo on the harbor and a 20:30 dinner reservation (€25, June-mid-Oct Wed and Fri, April-May Fri only, book tickets at Cinque Terre Riviera office on the main street—see "Helpful Hints," earlier).

The Bar Scene

Vernazza's nightlife centers on the bars on its waterfront piazza and generally shuts down pretty early (nightspots are required to close by midnight). The **Blue Marlin Bar** dominates the scene with a mix of locals and tourists, good drinks, and an open piano. If you play piano, you're welcome to join in. **Ananasso Bar** offers early-evening happy-hour fun and cocktails (*aperitivi*) that both locals and visitors enjoy. Its harborfront tables get the last sunshine of the day. For more on these bars, see their listings under "Eating in Vernazza," later.

Sleeping in Vernazza

Vernazza lacks any real hotels, and almost all of my listings are *affittacamere* (private rooms for rent). I favor hosts who rent multiple rooms and have a proven track record of good communication (they speak just enough English, have email, and are reliable). Airbnb is really big in Vernazza.

Most places accept only cash, promise free Wi-Fi (often spotty), and don't include breakfast unless noted. Some have killer views, and some come with lots of stairs. Expect noise at night: Trains tearing through, church bells (7:00-22:00), crashing waves, delivery vans in the upper town. Come to think of it, just pack earplugs.

Some places have all their beds in one building; others have rooms scattered all over town. Some have an informal reception desk (often at a restaurant or other business) where you can check in. Others have no reception at all. The Vernazza map in this book shows only the places that have a fixed address or reception office; if I mention "reception," you'll check in there.

If you overnight here, communicate your arrival time to your host and get clear instructions on where to meet and pick up the keys. They'll usually offer to meet you at the train station if they know when you're coming.

ROOMS FOR RENT (AFFITTACAMERE)

The **Cinque Terre Riviera** agency, based in Vernazza, rents rooms here and throughout the region (see page 376).

Scattered Through the Town Center
More Expensive, with More Amenities

$$$$ **La Malà** is the town's jet-setter pad. Four crisp, pristine white rooms boast fancy hotel-type extras and a shared seaview terrace. It's a climb—way up to the top of town—but they'll carry your bags to and from the station. Book early; this place fills up quickly (includes breakfast at a bar, family rooms, air-con, +39 334 287 5718, www.lamala.it, info@lamala.it, charming Giamba and his mama, Armanda). They also rent two rooms at the simpler $ **"Armanda's Room"** nearby—a great value, since you get Giamba's attention to detail and amenities without paying for a big view (includes simple breakfast, air-con, www.armanda.it).

$$$$ **Cinque Terre Vacation** rents two luxury apartments (one- and two-bedroom, sleeping up to 6) that overlook the sea and town from private, spacious terraces. The light-filled, airy units come with sea breezes and a crashing-waves soundtrack. The apartments can be connected for even larger groups (air-con, fully equipped kitchens, 2-night minimum, climb steps up to Via Carattino 12 or Via Mazzini 17, +39 345 363 6118, www. cinqueterrevacation.com, ruth@cinqueterrevacation.com, run by helpful American-Italian Ruth and her family).

$$$ **Nicolina Rooms** consists of five rooms and two apartments in three different buildings. Two cheaper rooms are in the center over the pharmacy, up a few steep steps; another, pricier studio with a terrace is on a twisty lane above the harbor; and four more rooms are in a building beyond the church, with great views and church bells (all include breakfast, Piazza Marconi 29—check in at Pizzeria Vulnetia, +39 0187 821 193, +39 333 842 6879, www. camerenicolina.it, info@camerenicolina.it).

$$$ **La Marina Rooms** is run by hardworking Cristian, who speaks English and happily carries bags to and from the station. He rents a single, two doubles, and two apartments, all well-tended, airy, and renovated, most high above the main street, and most with

sea views and air-con (+39 338 476 7472, www.lamarinarooms. com, mapcri@yahoo.it).

$$$ Monica Lercari rents several rooms with modern comforts, including one (more expensive) perched at the top of town with a seaview terrace (air-con, +39 0187 812 296, mobile +39 320 025 4515, monimarimax@gmail.com). Monica and her husband, Massimo, run the recommended Ristorante al Castello.

Simpler, Good-Value Places

$$ Francamaria and her husband Andrea rent 10 sharp, comfortable, and creatively renovated rooms near the harbor square, with relatively few stairs (family rooms, air-con, reception desk on the ground floor at Piazza Marconi 30, +39 328 711 9728, www. francamaria.com, francamariareservation@gmail.com). They also rent a room in Manarola.

$$ Vernazza Rentals offers several rooms, including a spacious and classy room on the harbor square, and a *molto* chic split-level apartment on a quiet side street (reception at Via Roma 27, +39 339 834 2486, mobile +39 338 117 6814, www.vernazzarentals. com, info@vernazzarentals.com).

$$ Vernazza Rooms, run by Massimo, rents 14 rooms: Four are above the Blue Marlin Bar looking down on the main street, and seven are a steep climb higher up, just under the City Hall (big family apartments, a few with air-con and others with fans, fridges in all rooms, arrange check-in time in advance and meet your host at Via del Santo 9, +39 351 918 3164, www.vernazzarooms.com, info@vernazzarooms.com).

$$ Lovely Rosa Vitali rents a four-person apartment with a kitchen; it's across from the pharmacy overlooking the main street—and beyond the worst of the train noise (ring bell at Via Visconti 10—just before the tobacco shop near Piazza Marconi, +39 340 267 5009, www.rosacamere.it, rosa.vitali@libero.it).

$$ Maria Capellini rents two simple, clean rooms that face each other across the harbor. One is at ground level just steps from the beach, with a view; the other looks over a skinny street (fridge, fans, +39 347 441 3695, www.mariacapellini.com, mariacapellini@ hotmail.it, kindly Maria and Giacomo, and son Gianni).

$$ Martina Callo's four old-fashioned, spartan rooms overlook the harbor square; they're up plenty of steps near the silent-at-night church tower. Two rooms have a sea view and cost more (family room, air-con in most rooms, ring bell at Piazza Marconi 26, +39 0187 812 365, mobile +39 329 435 5344, www.roomartina. it, roomartina@roomartina.it, Martina and her father, Giuseppe).

$$ Albergo Barbara rents eight tidy, Ikea-chic top-floor rooms overlooking the square with an attic communal lounge. Most have small windows and small views; view rooms are more

CINQUE TERRE

expensive. It's a good value in a nice location, run by Alessio and Alberto (cheaper rooms with shared bathroom, lots of stairs, reserve online with credit card but pay cash, Piazza Marconi 30, +39 0187 812 398, www.albergobarbara.it, info@albergobarbara.it).

$ Rooms Francesca offers one tidy room with sea views and air-con, and a two-bedroom apartment with fans. Both hide out in the steep streets just below City Hall (check in at Enoteca Sciacchetrà at Via Roma 19, +39 0187 821 112, mobile +39 339 191 2962, www.5terre-vernazza.it, moggia.franco@libero.it; Francesca and Franco).

$ Ivo Basso rents two tight but well-appointed rooms several flights of stairs above the main street (air-con, Via Roma 6, +39 333 477 5521, www.ivocamere.com, post@ivocamere.com).

More Options

If my recommendations above are full, try these:

$$ Capitano Rooms (3 rooms and 1 apartment several flights of stairs above main drag, fans; ask for Julia, Paolo, Edoardo, or Barbara at Trattoria del Capitano restaurant on main square at Piazza Marconi 21, +39 0187 812 201, www.tavernavernazza.com, info@tavernavernazza.com); **$$ Eva's Rooms** (a single and a double on the main street, air-con, train noise, 2-night minimum, +39 334 798 6500 or +39 331 153 2035, www.evasrooms.it, evasrooms@yahoo.it, Rebecca and Maurizia); **$$$ Manuela Moggia** (3 apartments and 2 rooms, behind train station at Via Gavino 22 and on main square, +39 0187 812 397, mobile +39 333 413 6374, www.manuela-vernazza.com, info@manuela-vernazza.com).

In the Inland Part of Town

Above the Train Station: $$$$ Casa Cato offers five modern, tight but well-outfitted rooms, three with private balconies and two with a shared balcony, all overlooking the sea and town (RS%, air-con, fridge, expect some train noise, +39 334 123 8579, www.casacatocinqueterre.com, info@casacatocinqueterre.com, Lisa). They also rent an apartment in the center of town.

$$ Giuliano Basso's four carefully crafted, well-appointed rooms form a cozy little compound with a common lounge and view terrace, straddling a ravine among orange trees. Giuliano—the town's last stone-layer—proudly built the place himself. To reach this quiet retreat on the green hillside just above town and the train station, you'll climb partway up the Corniglia footpath (2 rooms have air-con, more train noise than others; follow the main road up above the station, take the ramp up toward Corniglia just before Pensione Sorriso, follow the path, and watch for a sharp left turn—or ask Giuliano to meet you at the station; +39 333 341 4792, www.cameregiuliano.com, giuliano@cdh.it).

In the Ravine at the Top of Town: These practical options are a five-minute, gently uphill stroll behind the train station. While this functional zone is less atmospheric, it is easy to access (with fewer steep stairs). There's no train or church-bell noise—the constant soundtrack is Vernazza's gurgling river—but there can be traffic noise.

$$ Camere Fontanavecchia, run by Annamaria, is the best choice here, with eight bright and cheery rooms (three with terraces) overlooking the ravine and its rushing river (Via Gavino 15, +39 333 454 9371, www.cinqueterrecamere.com, m.annamaria@libero.it). She also rents an apartment.

$ La Rosa dei Venti ("The Compass Rose"), run by Giuliana Basso, houses three airy, good-value rooms in her childhood home, on the third floor of an apartment building (call to arrange meeting time, air-con, Via Gavino 19, mobile +39 333 762 4679, www.larosadeiventi-vernazza.it, info@larosadeiventi-vernazza.it).

GUESTHOUSE (PENSIONE)

$$$ Gianni Franzi, who owns a busy restaurant on the harbor square, runs the closest thing to a hotel in Vernazza. His 24 small rooms are in three buildings a hundred tight, winding stairs above the harbor square. Some rooms are funky and decorated à la shipwreck, with tiny balconies and grand sea views. The comfy, newer rooms lack views. All guests have access to a super-scenic cliff-hanging garden and panoramic terrace (where breakfast is served in season). Pick up your keys at the restaurant, but on Wednesday, when the restaurant is closed, call ahead to make other arrangements (RS%, closed Jan-Feb, Piazza Marconi 1, +39 0187 812 228, mobile +39 393 9008 155, www.giannifranzi.it, info@giannifranzi.it, Emanuele and Simona).

Eating in Vernazza

BREAKFAST

B&Bs in Vernazza provide B but no B. That's kind of a blessing, as Vernazza has plenty of options, from full bacon and eggs (Blue Marlin and Capitano), to fresh pastries from a Sicilian bakery (Il Pirata), to coffee and a sweet roll on the harborfront (Ananasso), to any number of bakeries selling sweet and savory options to go. Here are your main options from the top of town to the harbor (in that order). Most of these places are also recommended in my lunch and dinner listings.

$ Il Pirata delle Cinque Terre, located in the workaday zone at the parking lot at the top of town, is playful, efficient, comfortable, and serves tasty breakfast bruschetta, frittatas, and an array of fresh pastries. The fun service of the dynamic duo Gianluca and

Massimo (hardworking Sicilian twins, a.k.a. the Cannoli
brothers) makes up for the lack
of a view. They pride themselves
on not serving bacon and eggs,
since "this is Italy." While the
atmosphere feels more like suburban Milan, it has charisma
(Fri-Wed 7:00-24:00, closed
Thu, also serves lunch and din-
ner—see later, Via Gavino 36, +39 0187 812 047).

$$ Blue Marlin Bar (midtown, just below the train station)
serves a good array of clearly priced à la carte breakfast items (Ital-
ian breakfast from 7:00, eggs and bacon 8:30-11:30). If you're
awaiting a train and the platform isn't crowded, it's pleasant to have
a seat at Blue Marlin's outdoor seating with a drink in view of the
tracks (Thu-Tue 7:00-23:00, closed Wed).

$ Lunch Box is the hardworking new kid on the block, with
lots of hot options and a fun little perch for a couple of tables over-
looking the main drag (daily 7:00-22:00, also serves lunch and din-
ner—see later, Via Roma 34, +39 338 908 2841, Stefano).

$$ Trattoria del Capitano offers outdoor seating on the harbor, as well as cozy spots inside the restaurant and a full menu
(Wed-Mon 8:00-22:00, closed Tue, on Piazza Marconi, +39 0187
812 201, hardworking Paolo and Barbara speak English).

$$ Ananasso Bar has a youthful energy, a great location right
on the harbor, and a skimpy Italian breakfast menu (toasted *panini*,
pastries, Muesli with yogurt, and cappuccino). You can eat a bit
cheaper at the bar (you're welcome to picnic on the nearby bench or
seawall rocks with a Mediterranean view) or enjoy the best-situated
tables in town (Fri-Wed 8:00-late, closed Thu, on Piazza Marconi).

Picnic Breakfast: Drop by one of Vernazza's many little bak-
eries, focaccia shops, or grocery stores to assemble a breakfast to eat
on the breakwater. Top it off with a coffee in a nearby bar.

LUNCH AND DINNER

Vernazza's restaurants work hard to win your business. Wander
around at about 20:00 and compare the ambience. If you dine in
Vernazza but are staying in another town, check train schedules
before sitting down to eat, as evening trains run less frequently,
with gaps in the schedule. To get an outdoor table on summer
weekends, reserve ahead. Harborside restaurants and bars are easy-
going. You're welcome to grab a cup of coffee or glass of wine and
disappear somewhere on the breakwater, returning your glass when
you're done.

CINQUE TERRE

Harborside

$$$ Gianni Franzi is an old standby for well-prepared seafood and pastas. Emanuele, Lorenzo, and their crew provide steady, reliable, and friendly service. The outdoor seating is partially tucked under an arcade, while the indoor setting is big, open, and classy. The *cucina tipica Vernazza* page of their menu showcases local specialties (Thu-Tue 12:00-15:00 & 19:00-22:00, closed Wed, +39 0187 812 228).

$$ Trattoria del Capitano feels unpretentious and serves a short menu of straightforward local dishes, including *spaghetti allo scoglio*—pasta entangled with various types of seafood (for hours and location, see "Breakfast," earlier).

$$$ Ristorante Pizzeria Vulnetia has a nautical, jovial atmosphere and is proud of its locally sourced ingredients. Unlike the others, it also dishes up thin-crust pizzas—making this a good choice for a group with differing tastes, those on a budget, and families (Tue-Sun 12:00-22:00, closed Mon, Piazza Marconi 29, +39 0187 821 193, Tullio and Federica).

$$$ Ristorante Luca serves seafood dishes at a roofed-over circle of tables right on the breakwater—a memorable spot (Sat-Thu 11:30-22:00, closed Fri, +39 0187 812 113, Luca and Andrea).

$$$$ Gambero Rosso rounds out the options on the harbor. Long the top restaurant in town, today it's lost its edge (it was sold to a big-city restaurateur who runs it from afar). Still, it's reliably good, and has a fine interior and great outdoor tables (Fri-Wed 12:00-15:00 & 19:00-22:00, closed Thu and Dec-Feb, Piazza Marconi 7, +39 0187 812 265).

Above the Harbor, by the Castle

$$$$ Ristorante Belforte is a cut above the rest, serving a fine blend of traditional and creative cuisine, fishy *spaghetti alla Bruno*, *trofie al pesto* (hand-rolled noodles with pesto), and classic *antipasto misto di pesce*—an assortment of fish on five small plates (€25/person; 2-person minimum). Enter from the breakwater; a rope leads up stairs to a web of tables embedded in four levels of the old castle. While their indoor seating is great, for the ultimate seaside perch, reserve a table on the *terrazza con vista* (view terrace) or request the "lovers' table" on its own little terrace. Most of Belforte's seating is outdoors—if the weather's bad, the interior can get crowded. Late in the evening, Andrea cranks up the fun (Wed-Mon 12:00-15:00 & 19:00-22:00, closed Tue and Nov-March, +39 0187 812 222, Michela).

$$$ Ristorante al Castello is a homey seafood restaurant on a covered terrace just below the castle, with commanding views out to sea (to reward your climb). It's run by gracious, English-speaking Monica and her husband Massimo, who are proud of their €30 mixed grilled-fish plate (which two or even three can split) and their *trofie al pesto*. Reserve one of the dozen romantic cliffside seaview tables for two—some of the tables snake around the castle, where you'll feel like you're eating all alone with the Mediterranean. Monica offers a free *sciacchetrà* or *limoncello* with biscotti with this book by request (Thu-Tue 12:00-15:00 & 19:00-22:00, closed Wed and Nov-April, +39 0187 812 296).

Near the Train Station
These places have no harbor ambience but are pleasing and slightly cheaper.

$$ Trattoria da Sandro, on the main drag, mixes quality Genovese and Ligurian cuisine with friendly service and can be a peaceful alternative to the harborside scene. The family proudly maintains its cultural traditions and dishes up award-winning stuffed mussels (Wed-Mon 12:00-15:30 & 18:30-22:00, closed Tue, Via Roma 62, +39 0187 812 223, Argentina and Alessandro).

$$ Antica Osteria il Baretto is another solid bet for homey, reasonably priced traditional cuisine, run by Simone and Jenny. As it's off the harbor and less glitzy than the others, it's favored by locals who prefer less noisy English while they eat great homemade fare. Sitting deep in their interior can be a tranquil escape (Tue-Sun 12:00-22:00, closed Mon, indoor and outdoor seating in summer, Via Roma 31, +39 0187 812 381).

Other Eating Options
$$ Blue Marlin Bar, on the main street, busts out of the Vernazzan cuisine rut with a short, creative menu of more casual dishes (pizzas, salads). It's a good choice if you want to grab something basic rather than dine (for more details and hours, see "Breakfast," earlier).

$$ Il Pirata delle Cinque Terre, a huge hit for breakfast, also attracts travelers for lunch and dinner. While you're eating facing a parking lot, the food, service, and energy are great. And many are charmed by the Cannoli twins, who entertain while they serve. The menu (pastas and salads) is aimed squarely at American tourists' taste buds (lunch from 12:00, reserve ahead for dinner from 18:00, good cannoli and Sicilian slushies, at the top of town; for more details and contact info, see "Breakfast," earlier). The self-serve laundry is next door for those who like to multitask.

$ Lunch Box serves *panini*, salads, and fresh fruit juices from a clever and flexible menu. Assemble your own salad (or juice) from a long list of ingredients (for hours and location, see "Breakfast," earlier).

$ Pizzeria da Ercole dishes out pies cheap and fast on simple tables right in the busy center of town (or to take away). More tables are in a humble little secret terrace hiding in the back, where tour guides go to escape their groups (daily, Via Visconti 34, +39 338 771 3844).

Pizzerias, Sandwiches, and Groceries: Vernazza's main-street eateries offer a fine range of quick meals. Several bakeries and creative little takeaway joints sell sandwiches and pizza by the slice. **Pino's grocery store** at Via Visconti 19 makes inexpensive sandwiches to order (daily 8:00-13:00 & 17:00-19:30 except closed Sun evening). There's a **Coop** grocery at Via Roma 39 (next to the Blue Marlin Bar).

Gelato: The town has plenty of good gelato shops. On the harbor, the aptly named **Gelateria Il Porticciolo** ("Marina") uses fresh ingredients to create intense flavors (try their *cannella*—cinnamon, or *nocciola*—hazelnut). **Gelateria Vernazza,** near the top of the main street, takes its gelato seriously, occasionally flirting with creative ingredients (soy) and flavors (*riso*—rice, and ricotta and fig). **Gelateria Amore Mio** (midtown) used to be Gelateria Stalin, founded in 1968 by a pastry chef with that unfortunate name; now it's run by his niece Sonia and nephew Francesco, with great people-watching tables.

Corniglia

If you think of the Cinque Terre as the Beatles, Corniglia is Ringo. This tiny, sleepy town is the only one of the five not directly on the water. According to legend, the town was originally settled by a Roman farmer who named it for his mother, Cornelia (which is how Corniglia is pronounced). Locals claim that its ancient residents produced a wine so widely exported that vases have

been found at Pompeii stamped with the town name. Wine remains Corniglia's lifeblood today. Sample some when you're in town.

Less visited than the other Cinque Terre towns, Corniglia has fewer tourists, cooler temperatures, a laid-back main square, a few restaurants, a windy overlook on its promontory, and plenty of private rooms for rent. You don't go to Corniglia for the beach: Its once fine beach below the station has washed away. From the town center, signs for *al mare* or *Marina* point to where a stepped path leads steeply down to sunning rocks.

CINQUE TERRE

Corniglia

To Vernazza

200 Meters
200 Yards

Trail to Vernazza

SUNNING ROCKS

VIA ALLA MARINA

VIA FIESCHI

VIA ALLA STAZIONE

LOC. CANALE
VIA SERRA

LOC. CHIOSO

385 STEPS

VIA LARDARINA

To Manarola

"CIAPPÀ" SQUARE & BUS STOP

LARGO TARAGIO

ORATORY

SANTA MARIA BELVEDERE

Ligurian Sea

TRAIN STATION

❶ Villa Cecio Rooms
❷ Il Carugio Rooms & Butiega Gastronomia
❸ Pan e Vin Bar (Ricci Rooms Check-In)
❹ Corniglia Hostel
❺ Ristorante il Buongustaio
❻ Osteria Mananan & Enoteca il Pirùn
❼ La Posada Ristorante
❽ Gelateria

Orientation to Corniglia

Hill-capping Corniglia is connected with its train station far below by a long set of stairs, and much easier, by a hardworking little shuttle bus. Its reliable schedule is posted both at the station and in the town. Because of the steep distance between the town and its station, and the lack of a boat dock, Corniglia is inconvenient as a home base for town-hopping.

Tourist Information: A park information office is down at the train station (daily 8:30-18:30, shorter hours off-season). At busy times, there may also be a kiosk up in town on Ciappà square.

Hiking: From Corniglia, you can hike on the coastal trail to **Vernazza**. Also consider the challenging but rewarding "high road" to **Manarola via Volastra**. For details, see "Hiking the Cinque Terre" on page 345.

ARRIVAL IN CORNIGLIA

By Train: From the station far below town, a footpath zigzags up 385 steps (and nearly that many switchbacks) to the town in about 20 minutes. If you'd rather not walk, hop on the tiny ATC shuttle that connects the station with Corniglia's Ciappà

CINQUE TERRE

square, the starting point of my short self-guided walk (€1.50, buy tickets at park office—or €2.50 from driver, covered by park passes; departs about every 15 minutes from 8:00-20:00, get in line promptly as buses fill quickly).

If leaving Corniglia by train, either walk down or review the shuttle schedule to plan your return to the station.

By Car: Only residents can park on the main road between the recommended Villa Cecio and the point where the steep switch-back staircase meets the road. Beyond that area, anyone can park for a fee. All parking areas are within an easy and fairly level walk from the town center.

Corniglia Walk

We'll explore this tiny town—population 240—and end at a scenic viewpoint. This self-guided walk might take 30 minutes or more... but only if you let yourself browse, sample the wine, or lick a gelato cone.

• *Begin at the upper shuttle bus stop, on...*

Ciappà Square

The gateway to this community is Ciappà square, with the bus stop, an ATM, old wine press, and sometimes a TI kiosk in summer. The Cinque Terre's designation as a national park sparked a revitalization of the town.

• *Look for the arrow pointing to the* centro. *Stroll along Via Fieschi, the spine of Corniglia. In the fall, the smell of grapes (on their way to becoming wine) wafts from busy cellars. Along this main street, you'll see...*

Corniglia's Enticing Shops

As you enter Via Fieschi, a trio of neighboring gelato shops jockeys for your business. My favorite is the last one you come to (at #74, on the right), **Alberto's Gelateria** (open late). Before ordering, get a free taste of Alberto's *miele di Corniglia*, made from local honey; he and Cristina are also proud of their basil flavor. Their lemon slush *(granita)* takes pucker to new heights.

Farther along, located in a cool cantina on the left, **Enoteca il Pirùn** is named for a type of oddly shaped old-fashioned wine pitcher designed to aerate the wine and give the alcohol more kick as you squirt it into your mouth (Via Fieschi 115). Try some local wines (small tastes generally free, €3/glass). If you order wine to drink from the *pirùn*, Mario will give you a bib. While this is a practicality (rookies tend to dribble), it also makes a nice souvenir.

Farther along, **Butiega Gastronomia** (#142) is an old-fashioned grocery store/deli where Simone sells organic local special-ties (daily 8:00-20:00). For picnickers, they offer made-to-order ham-and-cheese sandwiches and a fun *antipasti misti* (priced by weight). He also prepares pesto and other specialties daily in the shop's tiny kitchen. You'll find good places to picnic farther along on this walk.

• *Following Via Fieschi, you'll end up at the mellow...*

Main Square (Largo Taragio)

On the main square, tables from two bars and a trattoria spill around a WWI memorial and the town's old well. It once piped in natural spring water from the hillside to locals living without plumbing. What looks like a church is the **Oratory of Santa Caterina.** (An oratory is a kind of spiritual clubhouse for a service group doing social work in the name of the Catholic Church.) Up the stairs and behind the oratory, you'll find a terrace that children have made into a soccer field. The stone benches and viewpoint make this a peaceful place for a picnic (less crowded than the end-of-town viewpoint, described next).

Opposite the oratory, notice how steps lead steeply down Via alla Marina, taking you in 5 minutes to sunning rocks and a small deck (with a shower and treacherous entry into the water).

• *From the square, continue up Via Fieschi to the...*

End-of-Town Viewpoint

The Santa Maria Belvedere, named for a church that once stood here, marks the scenic end of Corniglia. This is a super picnic spot. From here, look high to the west (right), where the village and sanctuary of San Bernardino straddle a ridge (accessible by shuttle bus or a long uphill hike from Vernazza). Way down below are the local swimming hole and huge sunning rocks.

Sleeping in Corniglia

Because Corniglia has no harbor, its mostly humble accommodations are almost never full.

$$ Villa Cecio (pronounced "chay-choh"), sits atop the old-time Ristorante Cecio (with great views). They offer eight freshly decorated, well-priced, sizeable rooms on the quiet outskirts of town. Most rooms have postcard views, and three have terraces—worth requesting when you book. All rooms share a big rooftop view terrace (breakfast extra, four rooms have air-con, on main road toward Vernazza at Via Serra 58—keep going 200 yards beyond Ciappà square and you'll find it on the right, +39 0187 812 043, mobile +39 351 566 3661, www.cecio5terre.com, cecio5terre@gmail.com, Cristina and Valentina). They also rent eight more rooms in an annex on the square where the bus stops.

$$ Il Carugio has six modern, fresh, sunny rooms, and a communal rooftop terrace with a commanding view of the coast. Five of the rooms have a kitchen (2-night minimum, family rooms, air-con, no breakfast, free parking, free self-serve laundry, +39 0187 812 293, mobile +39 339 228 3803 or +39 338 112 6504, www. ilcarugiodicorniglia.com, info@ilcarugiodicorniglia.com, Lidia and Giulia). They also have four more rooms, with breakfast included, in another building.

$ Cristiana Ricci rents three small, clean, and peaceful rooms—one with a terrace and sweeping view—just inland from the bus stop (family rooms, check in and breakfast at Pan e Vin bar at Via Fieschi 123, +39 338 937 6547, www.corniglia-room. com, cri_affittacamere@virgilio.it). She also rents three big, modern apartments.

¢ Corniglia Hostel, the town's former schoolhouse, rents 24 beds in a yellow municipal building up some steps from the square where the bus stops (find the entrance at the back of the building). Despite its institutional atmosphere, the hostel's prices, central location, and bright, clean rooms ensure its popularity. Its hotelesque double rooms are open to anyone (breakfast extra, office open 15:00-20:00, free lockers when office closed, air-con, self-serve laundry, Via alla Stazione 3, +39 0187 812 559, www. ostellocorniglia.com, ostellocorniglia@gmail.com, Alessandro).

Eating in Corniglia

A typical array of pizzerias, *focaccerie*, and *alimentari* (grocery stores) line the narrow main drag. I've highlighted a few places for a quick bite on my self-guided walk, earlier.

For a full, sit-down meal, consider one of these restaurants.

$$$ Ristorante il Buongustaio is a good bet for dinner on the square. Daniela and the Guelfi family pride themselves in serving *cucina casalinga* (home cooking) and good seafood pasta and risotto (nice tables on the main square as well as in a big indoor dining room, daily 12:00-21:15, Via Fieschi 164, +39 0187 821 424).

$$ Osteria Mananan—between the Ciappà bus stop and the main square at Via Fieschi 117—has earned a good reputation with tasty dishes and a small, stony, elegant interior (Wed-Mon 12:30-14:30 & 19:00-22:30, closed Tue, no outdoor seating, +39 0187 821 166, Agostino).

$$ Enoteca il Pirùn, on Via Fieschi, has a small restaurant above the wine bar, where Mario serves typical local dishes (Fri-Wed 12:00-16:00 & 19:00-23:30, closed Thu, +39 0187 812 315).

$$ La Posada Ristorante serves seafood in a tree-shaded garden overlooking the sea and in a modern interior. It's at the top of the stairs that lead down to the station, just outside the old center (daily 12:00-16:00 & 19:00-23:00, +39 333 454 2113).

CINQUE TERRE

Manarola

Mellow Manarola fills a ravine, bookended by its wild little harbor to the west and a diminutive hilltop church square inland to the east. Manarola is exceptional for being unexceptional: While Vernazza is prettier, Monterosso glitzier, Riomaggiore bigger, and Corniglia more rustic, Manarola hits a fine balance, giving it the "just right" combination of Cinque Terre qualities. Perhaps that's why it's a favorite among savvy Europeans seeking a relatively untrampled home base. The touristy zone squeezed between the cement-encased train tracks and the harbor can be stressfully congested, but head just a few steps uphill and you can breathe again.

Manarola, whose hillsides are blanketed with vineyards, also provides the easiest access to the Cinque Terre's remarkable dry-stone terraces. The trail ringing the town's cemetery, on the peninsula north of the main harbor, affords some of the most strikingly beautiful town views anywhere in the region. Follow my gentle self-guided stroll from the harbor up through town, then through vineyards, to this stunning Mediterranean viewpoint.

Orientation to Manarola

TOURIST INFORMATION

The TI/national park information office is in the train station (daily 8:30-19:30, shorter hours off-season).

ARRIVAL IN MANAROLA

By Train: From the station, to reach the town, you'll walk through a 200-yard-long tunnel that's lined with interesting photos. (During WWII air raids, these tunnels provided refuge and a safe place for rattled villagers to sleep.) To reach the busy harbor—with touristy restaurants, boat dock, and the start of my self-guided walk, head left (downhill) when you come out of the tunnel.

The ATC **shuttle bus** runs from near the old waterwheel (halfway up Manarola's main street), stopping first at the parking lots above town, and then going all the way up to Volastra (about 2/hour except for afternoon breaks).

By Car: If you're overnighting here, ask your hotelier for parking advice. Park your car in one of the two pay lots just before town, then walk down the road to the church; from there, it's an easy downhill walk to the main piazza, train-station tunnel, and harbor (the start of my self-guided walk), or you can wait for the shuttle bus.

Manarola Walk

From the harbor, this 45-minute self-guided walk shows you the town and surrounding vineyards and ends at a fantastic viewpoint.
• *Start down at the waterfront. Belly up to the wooden banister overlooking the rocky harbor, between the two restaurants.*

Harbor

Manarola is tiny and picturesque, a tumble of buildings bunny-hopping down its ravine to the fun-loving waterfront. The **breakwater**—which attempts to make this jagged harbor a bit less dangerous—was built (with reject marble from Carrara) just over a decade ago. Notice how the I-beam crane launches boats (which must be pulled ashore when bad weather is expected, to avoid being smashed or swept away).

Facing the water, look up to the right, at the hillside Punta Bonfiglio **cemetery** and park. The trail running around the base of the point—where this walk ends—offers magnificent views back on this part of town. If you see a crowd, it's Instagram devotees who travel here from around the world (mostly Asia) to take and post their selfies.

The town's **swimming hole** is just below you. Manarola has no sand but offers the best deep-water swimming in the area. The first "beach" has a shower, ladder, and wonderful rocks. The second has tougher access and no shower but feels more remote and pristine (follow the paved path toward Corniglia, just around the point).
• *Go inland up the town's main drag. You'll climb a concrete ramp lined by classic **photos** and quotes from Manarola's history. The ramp leads to Manarola's "new" square, which covers the train tracks, and is called...*

Piazza Capellini

Built in 2004, this square is an all-around great idea, giving the town a safe, fun zone for kids. Locals living near the tracks also enjoy a little less train noise. The mosaic in the middle of the square depicts the varieties of local fish in colorful enamel.
• *Go down the stairs at the upper end of the square. On your right, notice the tunnel that leads to Manarola's train station (and the closed Via dell'Amore trailhead). Head up...*

Via Discovolo

Manarola's main street twists up through town, lined by modest

Manarola

To Corniglia,
(trail closed)

To Volastra
(Panoramico
trail)

50 Meters
50 Yards

SWIMMING

Punta
Bonfiglio WC   Cemetery

Manarola
Vineyard Trail

WALK
ENDS   VIA **13** DEI GIOVANNI

14

BEST
VIEW

*Piazza
Capellini*

SWIMMING
& SHOWER

"MAIN STREET"

9

VIA BELVEDERE

5

11

**WALK
BEGINS**

VIA BIROLL

12

V. BELVEDERE

V. BALURADO

VIA

BOAT
DOCK   VIA DI MEZZO

7

To
Vernazza

VIA
PELVEDERE

*Piazza
Castello*

BREAKWATER

BOAT
DOCK

*Piazzetta
Eugenio Montale*

To
Riomaggiore

*Ligurian
Sea*

CINQUE TERRE

shops and filled with pooped hikers. About 100 yards up, just before the road bends sharply right, watch (on the right) for a **waterwheel.** One possible origin of the town's name is that it's local
dialect for "big wheel." A waterwheel like this once powered local
industry. As you continue up (all the way to the church), you'll
still hear the rushing waters of Manarola's stream. Like those in
Riomaggiore, Monterosso, and Vernazza, Manarola's rivulet was
covered over after World War II. Before that time, romantic bridges arched over its ravine. You can peek below the concrete street in
several places to see the stream surging below your feet.

Across the street from the waterwheel and a bit farther up,
notice the **Cinque Terre Trekking** shop on your left, which outfits

To Volastra
(car, shuttle bus)

To Volastra
(Official
trail)

VIA LITORANEA

SP-370

TUNNEL

To **8**

P

P

CANTINE
BURASCA
WINE BAR

15

6

4

WATER-
WHEEL

VIA DISCOVOLO

Manarola
Vineyard Trail
Entrance

BELL
TOWER

POST

B

16

1

ORATORY

SAN LORENZO
CHURCH

DISCOVOLO

10

ROLLANDI

RESIDENTIAL
ZONE

2

3

B

Piazza
Papa Innocenzo IV

PEDESTRIAN TUNNEL

TRAIN STATION

Via dell'Amore ♥
(trail closed)

To Riomaggiore

Accommodations
1. La Torretta Rooms
2. B&B Da Baranin
3. Aria di Mare Rooms
4. Albergo Ca' d'Andrean
5. Hotel Marina Piccola
6. Da Paulin Rooms
7. 5 Terre Pelagos
8. To Hotel il Saraceno

Eateries & Other
9. Ristorante da Aristide &
   Bar Caffè da Aristide
10. Trattoria dal Billy
11. Trattoria il Porticciolo &
    Sorbetteria 5 Terre Gelateria
12. Cafè il Porticciolo
13. Nessun Dorma
14. Grocery
15. Cinque Terre Trekking
16. Shuttle Bus to Parking Lot
    & Volastra

CINQUE TERRE

hikers with both information and gear (for details, see "Hikes from Manarola," later).

Around the corner is the **Cantine Burasca** wine bar. With fine outdoor-only seating, it's a good place for a little wine tasting (closed in bad weather, Via Discovolo 86, +39 339 807 1261).

• *Keep climbing until you come to the square at the...*

Top of Manarola

The square is faced by a church, an oratory—now a religious and community meeting place—and a bell tower (with a WWI memorial etched in it), which served as a watchtower when pirates raided the town (the cupola was added once the attacks ceased). To the right of the oratory, a stepped lane leads to the town's sizable, less-touristy residential zone.

Check out the **church.** The Parish Church of St. Lawrence (San Lorenzo) dates from "MCCCXXXVIII" (1338). Step inside to see two altarpiece paint-ings from the unnamed Master of the Cinque Terre, the only painter of any note from this re-gion (left wall and above main altar). While the style is Gothic, the work dates from the time of Michelangelo, long after Flor-ence had entered the Renais-sance. Note the humble painted stone ceiling, which replaced the wooden original in the 1800s. It features Lawrence, patron saint of the Cinque Terre, with his grill, the symbol of his martyrdom (he was roasted on it).

• *With the bell tower on your left, head about 20 yards back down the main street below the church and find a wooden railing on the right, just before the Cantine Burasca wine bar, signposted as* trail #502C. *It marks the start of a delightful stroll around the high side of town and back to the seafront. This is the beginning of the...*

Manarola Vineyard Trail

Don't miss this fun, short walk. Simply follow the wooden railing, enjoying lemon groves and great views. Along the path, which is largely flat, you'll get a close-up look at the region's famous dry-stone walls and finely crafted vineyards (with dried-heather thatch-es to protect the grapes from southwest winds). Smell the rosemary. Study the structure of the town, and pick out the scant remains of an old fort. Notice the S-shape of the main road—once a riv-erbed—that flows through town. The town's roofs are tradition-ally made of locally quarried slate and held down by rocks during windstorms.

Halfway along the lip of the ravine, a path marked *Panorami-co Volastra (Corniglia)* leads steeply up into the vineyards (a chal-lenging route that leads to the tiny hamlet of Volastra and then to Corniglia—described on page 350).

Stay on the level path, passing a variety of simple wooden reli-gious scenes, the work of local resident Mario Andreoli. Before his father died, Mario promised him he'd replace the old cross on the family's vineyard. Mario has been adding figures ever since. On re-ligious holidays, everything's lit up: the Nativity, the Last Supper, the Crucifixion, the Resurrection, and more. Some of the scenes are left up year-round. (You can see more of his figures across the ravine, gathered together in a little open patch between buildings.)

CINQUE TERRE

High above, notice ancient terraces that line the terrain like a topographic map.

• *Continue on the trail as it winds down to the cemetery (sometimes closed, but at least stop by the gate for a peek inside).*

Cemetery

Ever since Napoleon—who was king of Italy in the early 1800s—decreed that cemeteries were health risks, Cinque Terre's burial spots have been located out-

side the towns. The result: The dearly departed generally get first-class sea views. Each cemetery—with evocative photos and finely carved Carrara marble memorial reliefs—is worth a look. Manarola's is a little lower down and easier to walk to than the others.

In cemeteries like these, the real estate is similar to that for the living: The wealthy get their own piece of land (a **grave**), regular people get the equivalent of a condo (with their remains parked in a niche called a **loculus**), and the poor and forgotten end up tossed in a communal **ossuary.** Because of the tight space, spots are rented and a person's remains are allowed to stay only as long as their loved ones care enough to pay the rent. (No rent means you end up in the ossuary, making room for the newly dead with family willing to pay.) Traditionally, locals make weekly visits to loved ones here, often bringing flowers. The rolling stepladder makes access to top-floor loculi easy.

• *From the cemetery follow the steep and narrow stairs (through the green gate immediately below the cemetery) and walk out onto the bluff.*

Punta Bonfiglio

This point offers some of the most commanding **views** of the entire region. To find the best vantage point, walk out toward the water through a park (playground, drinking water, WC, and picnic benches). An inviting and recommended bar, **Nessun Dorma,** fills a long narrow terrace with people enjoying the vista.

Your Manarola finale is the bench at the tip of the point. (It's often congested with travelers taking photos from this point for their Instagram bucket lists.) Pause and take in the view.

• *From here steps go down and the path winds scenically back to the harbor, where we started.*

CINQUE TERRE

Experiences in Manarola

Hikes from Manarola

The coastal trail from Manarola—leading to **Corniglia** in one direction and to **Riomaggiore** in the other (the famous Via dell'Amore)—has been closed for years due to landslides. But you can still enjoy hiking from here. One of my favorite easy hikes is the **vineyards trail** outlined just above in my "Manarola Walk."

For a longer hike, consider taking the **high route to Corniglia via Volastra** (much easier if you ride the shuttle bus up to Volastra). For details, see "Hiking the Cinque Terre" on page 345.

Hiking Gear and Tips: A wonderful resource for hikers, **Cinque Terre Trekking** is near the top of the main street (halfway up to the church). Christine (from Minnesota) and Nicola are generous with hiking advice, and fill their shop with all the gear you may need: boots, clothes, walking sticks, maps, and more. If you're serious about hiking, stop in here to confirm your plans and to gear up (daily 11:00-13:00 & 14:00-19:00, shorter hours off-season, Via Discovolo 108, +39 0187 920 834, www.cinqueterretrekking.com, info@cinqueterretrekking.com).

Pesto Making

Entrepreneurial Simone at the Nessun Dorma cantina (perched next to the cemetery at the most scenic edge of Manarola) leads a pesto-making workshop for up to 30 people at 10:30, followed by lunch at noon. The setting is unforgettable, making pesto in the place of its origin is exciting, and you get to eat what you make plus a *tagliere* plate of cold cuts (€60/person, includes wine, no class on Tue, reserve ahead at www.nessundormacinqueterre.com or call +39 340 888 4133, class cancelled in bad weather).

Tours

Arbaspàa arranges vineyard wine tastings, cooking classes (6-person minimum), fishing trips, paragliding, rock climbing, and more (see website for options and book in advance, www.arbaspaa.com; or visit office at Via Discovolo 204, daily 9:00-19:00, +39 0187 760 083).

Boat Rides

To get to the dock and the boats that connect Manarola with the other Cinque Terre towns, find the steps to the left of the harbor view—they lead down to the ticket kiosk. Continue around the left side of the cliff (as you're facing the water) to catch the boats.

CINQUE TERRE

Sleeping in Manarola

Manarola has some of the most appealing, well-run accommodations in the region (rivaling Monterosso's). Like the others, it also has plenty of private rooms (Airbnb has consumed the market). If you need breakfast, the recommended Bar Caffè da Aristide is your best choice. Otherwise grab a coffee and croissant along the main drag.

IN THE RESIDENTIAL ZONE ABOVE THE CHURCH

This area is a 10-minute steeply uphill hike from the train station—just huff up the main drag to the church. All are within a five-minute walk from there.

$$$$ La Torretta offers 16 trendy, upscale rooms (most with private deck) that cater to an elite clientele. Probably the most elegant retreat in the region, this peaceful refuge has all the comforts for those happy to pay, including a communal hot tub with a view. Guests enjoy a complimentary snack and glass of prosecco on arrival, an ample breakfast buffet, and stocked minibars. Each chic room is distinct (top-end family suite, book several months in advance, closed Dec-March; on Piazza della Chiesa beside the bell tower at Vico Volto 20, +39 0187 920 327, www.torrettas.com, torretta@cdh.it, Gabriele).

$$$ B&B Da Baranin, with eight good rooms and one apartment, is a bit too pricey but has sleek modern style and a nice breakfast terrace (family rooms, air-con, Via Aldo Rollandi 29, +39 0187 920 595, www.baranin.com, info@baranin.com).

$$ Aria di Mare Rooms rents four sunny, tidy, well-equipped rooms and two apartments a few steps beyond Trattoria dal Billy at the very top of town. While it's a steep hike up (high above the tourists), this is an excellent value. Three rooms and the two apartments have spacious terraces, and all can enjoy the knockout views from lounge chairs in the front yard (RS% with 4-night stay, no breakfast but tea/coffee service in room, air-con, up the stairs at Via Aldo Rollandi 149, +39 349 058 4155, www.ariadimare.info, info@ariadimare.info, Maurizio; ask at Billy's if no one's home).

ON OR NEAR THE MAIN STREET

These options line up along (or near) the main street, between the harbor and the church. While in a less atmospheric area than those near the church, they're closer to the station—and therefore a bit handier for those packing heavy.

$$$ Albergo Ca' d'Andrean is quiet, comfortable, and chic. It has 10 big, sunny, tranquil rooms, with lots of tile. Public spaces artfully display family artifacts, and the cool garden oasis comes complete with lemon trees. If you don't mind stairs, consider one

CINQUE TERRE

of their pricier top-floor rooms, with great terrace views (breakfast extra, air-con, up the hill at Via Discovolo 101, +39 0187 920 040, www.cadandrean.it, info@cadandrean.it, Simone, Ariana, and Nicola).

$$$ Hotel Marina Piccola offers 12 simple, stylish rooms near the bustle of the square on the water (some with sea views). Though low on character, it's well run and handy to the harbor area (breakfast extra, air-con, Via Birolli 120, +39 0187 920 770, www. hotelmarinapiccola.com, info@hotelmarinapiccola.com, Jessica and Micaela).

$$ Da Paulin, run by charming Donatella (who makes a mean *limoncello*) and Eraldo (the town's retired policeman), has three surprisingly modern, fresh, well-equipped, hotelesque rooms with a large and inviting common living room. They also rent three apartments (with fans). This fine value is at the bend in the main street, a five-minute hike above the train tracks (breakfast extra, air-con, Via Discovolo 126, +39 334 389 4764, www.dapaulin.it, prenotazioni@dapaulin.it).

$$ 5 Terre Pelagos has eight pastel, shabby-chic rooms in two buildings. Four are at Via Belvedere 58, an awkward building down a side lane. Built into the side of the mountain, the common room has a caveman ambience, but some rooms come with view terraces. The other rooms are more steeply uphill near the church, at Via dei Mulini 26—confirm which building you are in when you book (air-con, +39 335 122 6490, www.5terrepelagos.com, info@5terrepelagos.com, Edoardo).

HIGH ABOVE MANAROLA, IN VOLASTRA

$$ Hotel il Saraceno, with seven spacious, utilitarian rooms, is a deal for drivers. Located above Manarola in the tiny town of Volastra (chock-full of vacationing Germans and Italians in summer), it's serene, clean, and right by the shuttle bus to Manarola (includes breakfast, free parking, air-con, +39 0187 760 081, www. thesaraceno.com, hotel@thesaraceno.com, friendly Antonella).

Eating in Manarola

Touristy restaurants are concentrated between Piazza Capellini and the harbor. For finer dining, consider one of the following choices.

$$ Ristorante da Aristide, right on Piazza Capellini, is run by three generations of hardworking women and offers a trendy atmosphere and a pleasant outdoor setting, with a view of budding soccer stars rather than harborfront glitz. Consider the €45 three-course meal with wine (Fri-Wed 12:00-15:00 & 19:00-22:00, closed Thu, Via Discovolo 290—you run right into it from the train tunnel, +39 0187 920 000).

$$ Bar Caffè da Aristide, next door along the street, is a busy and modern little place with reasonable prices. They have indoor and streetside seating, a lighter menu of pasta and salads (see daily specials on blackboard), and breakfast (Fri-Wed 8:00-11:30 & 12:00-18:00, closed Thu, same address and phone number; charming Elena, Mamma Monica, and Nonna Grazia).

$$$ Trattoria dal Billy, the most memorable restaurant in town, is in the residential zone high above the touristy action. It's worth the climb for Edoardo and chef Enrico's homemade black pasta with seafood and squid ink, green pasta with artichokes, and homemade desserts. Their antipasto misto di mare comes with a dazzling array of seafood treats—each one perfectly executed. Billy's outdoor terraces offer commanding views over Manarola, while across the street an elegant, glassy dining room is carved into the rock. Either setting is perfect for a romantic candlelight meal. Reservations are a must (Fri-Wed 12:00-15:00 & 18:00-22:00, closed Thu, Via Aldo Rollandi 122, +39 0187 920 628, www.trattoriabilly. com).

The Scorza family works hard at **$$ Trattoria il Porticciolo** (Thu-Tue 12:00-15:00 & 19:00-21:30, closed Wed, Via Birolli 92, +39 0187 920 083) and at their contemporary **cafè,** cheap and fast, across the way.

DRINKS AND LIGHT MEALS WITH A VIEW

$$ Nessun Dorma is dramatically perched under the cemetery and above the harbor, facing the classic view of Manarola. Simone and his staff serve no pizza or pasta, but keep the masses happy with bruschetta, cold cuts, salads, and tempting cocktails. This place has become inundated with Instagram influencers and scenesters, so there can be long lines waiting for a table (no reservations). It's named for a Puccini aria made famous by Pavarotti, whose face graces the menu (Wed-Mon 12:00-21:00, closed Tue, Localita Punta Bonfiglio, +39 340 888 4133, www.nessundormacinqueterre.com). Simone runs a morning pesto-making class that culminates in a scenic lunch just before opening time—perhaps the most peaceful (and educational) way to enjoy this beautiful spot (described earlier, under "Experiences in Manarola").

QUICK BITES AND TAKEOUT

Via Discovolo, the main street climbing up through town from Piazza Capellini to the church, has several shops selling focaccia, pizza by the slice, and fried goodies that are fine for a quick lunch. Buy picnic supplies at the **Coop grocery** at #224 (daily 7:30-13:00 & 17:00-20:00). **Bar Caffè da Aristide** is the busiest for breakfast. And the most enticing *gelateria* in town is **Sorbetteria 5 Terre Gelateria** (below the piazza, toward the harbor).

CINQUE TERRE

Riomaggiore

The second-largest of the five towns, Riomaggiore is more real and laid-back than its neighbors. The main drag, while traffic-free, feels more urban than "village." Despite Riomaggiore's worka-day soul, the views back on its harbor from the breakwater—especially at sunset—are some of the region's prettiest. Surround-ing the harbor is a fascinating tangle of pastel homes leaning on each other like drunken sailors.

Orientation to Riomaggiore

TOURIST INFORMATION

The **national park office** and InfoPoint is in the striped building adjacent to the station (daily 8:30-19:30, shorter hours off-season).

ARRIVAL IN RIOMAGGIORE

By Train: Riomaggiore's train station is in the next ravine over from the village, separated from the town center by a bluff. To get to the center quickly, take the pedestrian tunnel that parallels the rail tunnel. You'll exit at the bottom of Via Colombo; most recom-mended accommodations are a short hike up this steep main drag. If you're staying near the top of town, you can catch the sporadic shuttle bus at the bottom of Via Colombo and ride it partway up.

If you're not in a hurry or carrying luggage, take the scenic route around the bluff into town, which gives you a better feel for life here—see my "Riomaggiore Walk," later.

By Car: Day-trippers park at the two-story pay-and-display lot above town (€5/hour, €35/day). If you're staying overnight, your hotel may have parking.

HELPFUL HINTS

Baggage Storage: You can check your bag at the casually run *de-posito bagagli* office—it's behind the café/bar that's straight ahead as you exit the station (daily 9:00-12:30 & 14:00-19:00—confirm times, closed in winter).

Services: There are three public pay WCs in town: at the station and at the top and bottom of Via Colombo.

Laundry: A self-service launderette is on the main street (daily in summer 8:00-23:00, shorter hours off-season, Via Colombo 107).

Riomaggiore Walk

Here's an easy self-guided walk that loops up and over, taking the long and scenic way from the station into town. You'll enjoy some fine views and get to know the town before strolling down the main street to the harbor.

• *Start at the train station. (If you arrive by boat, cross beneath the tracks and take a left, then hike through the tunnel along the tracks to reach the station.)*

Climb to the Top of Town

With your back to the sea and station, look left and notice the stairs climbing up just past the station building. These lead to the easy (but closed) trail to Manarola, the **Via dell'Amore.**

Now hike up Via Telemaco Signorini (next to Bar Stazione). Listen to the paved-over creek under your feet. Where the road hairpins right, see the waterfall (and turtles in the cage). Farther along is a close-up look at dry-stone rockery work. You'll cross over the train tracks, passing the top of a concrete elevator tower. Just beyond the elevator, you'll arrive at a fine **viewpoint,** with spectacular sea views and a few benches.

• *When you're ready to move on, hook left around the bluff; rounding the bend, ignore the steps marked* marina seacoast *(which lead to the harbor). Look on your left for the stairway marked* Salita Castello, *across from house #179. If you're up for a steep side trip, climb a few flights of stairs to the...*

Riomaggiore Castle

The castle, a hulk at the top of the hill, is usually shut up tight, but it's sometimes used for cultural events. You'll find great sea views from benches in front, and the tiny church of San Rocco (built for plague victims, and therefore outside of the town walls).

• *Descend the way you came up.*

Town Views and Church of San Giovanni Battista (St. John the Baptist)

Continuing along the smooth and level lane, you'll go by the **City Hall** (with flags) and several decaying **murals** by Silvio Benedetto. These glorify the region's nameless workers—grape pickers, fishermen, and everyone who built the nearly 300 million cubic feet of mortarless, dry-stone walls that run throughout the Cinque Terre. These walls give the region its characteristic terracing for vineyards and olive groves. Unfortunately, the murals are not aging well.

CINQUE TERRE

WATERFALL

VIA TELEMACO SIGNORINI

To Manarola
(trail closed)

Via dell'Amore
(trail closed)

Cliffs

13

18

TRAIN
STATION

WALK
BEGINS

14

National
Park Shop

ELEVATOR

SAN
ROCCO V. PECUNIA

CASTLE

CITY
HALL

Ligurian Sea

PEDESTRIAN
TUNNEL

VIA TELEMACO SIGNORINI

VIA SANT'ANTONIO

PUNTA

VIA

B

7
Piazza
Vignaioli **12** **15**

6

WC
(UNDER
TUNNEL)

Cliffs

20

1

16

BOAT
DOCK

VIA SAN GIACOMO

Harbor

BREAKWATER

BOAT
TICKETS

Accommodations
1. Alla Marina Rooms; Enoteca & Ristorante Dau Cila
2. Casato Bapò
3. Il BoMa Rooms
4. La Dolce Vita Rooms
5. Edi's Rooms

Eateries & Other
6. Rio Bistrot
7. Trattoria la Grotta
8. Bar Centrale & Gelateria
9. Primo Piatto & Vertical Lounge Bar
10. Il Pescato Cucinato
11. Tutti Fritti
12. Alimentari Franca
13. Bar Stazione
14. Bar & Vini A Piè de Mà
15. La Zorza Café & Bar O'Netto
16. La Conchiglia Café/Bar
17. Grocery (2)
18. Bag Storage
19. Launderette
20. Diving Center 5 Terre

You'll next reach a piazza and the gray stone San Giovanni church. Pause here at the big **terrace** to enjoy the views over town, perhaps with lots of local kids (schools are close by). The town is named after its large *(maggiore)* river *(rio)*, now covered by the main street, as in the other Cinque Terre towns. The river carved the canyon now filled by the town's pastel high-rises. The romantic arched bridges that once connected the two sides have been replaced by a practical modern road. Other than that, the town is beautifully preserved.

The **church,** while rebuilt in 1870, was first established in 1340. It's dedicated to St. John the Baptist, the patron saint of Genoa, the maritime republic that once dominated the region.

• *Continue straight past the church and along the narrow lane leading down to the town's main street, and hang a right on...*

Via Colombo

This street has the town's shops and services. Heading downhill, the big covered terrace on the right belongs to the recommended **Bar Centrale,** a popular hangout for international visitors day or night.

As you round the bend to the left, notice the old-timey pharmacy just above (on the right, with a good bakery underneath). On your left, at #199, peek into the **Il Pescato Cucinato** shop, where Laura fries up her husband Edoardo's fresh catch; grab a paper cone of deep-fried seafood as a snack. Where the road bends sharply right, notice the bench on your left (just before La Zorza Café)—the hangout for the town's old-timers, who keep a running commentary on the steady flow of people. Straight ahead, you can already see where this street will dead-end. The last shop on the left, **Alimentari Franca** (at #251), is a well-stocked grocery where you can gather the makings for a perfect picnic out on the harbor.

Where Via Colombo dead-ends, look right to see the tunnel leading back to the station. Look left to see two sets of stairs. Climb the "up" stairs to a parklike **square** (Piazza Vignaioli) built over the train tracks, which provides the children of the town a bit of level land on which to kick their soccer balls and to learn to ride a bike. The murals above, marking the town's middle school, celebrate the great-grandparents of these very children—the salt-of-the-earth locals who earned a humble living before the age of tourism. Riomaggiorians are proud that they are the only Cinque Terre town with their own middle school *(scuola media)*—in the other towns, kids start commuting to school much earlier.

• *Now take the "down" stairs to the...*

Harbor

In this most picturesque corner of Riomaggiore, a tight cluster of buildings huddles nervously around a tiny square and harbor. Because Riomaggiore lacks the naturally protected harbor of Vernazza, when bad weather is expected, fishermen pull their boats up to the safety of the little square. This is quite an operation, so it's a team effort—the signal goes out, and anyone with a boat of their own helps move the whole fleet. Sometimes the fishermen are busy beaching their boats even on a bright, sunny day—an indication that they know something you don't.

A couple of recommended restaurants—with high prices and memorable seating—look down over the action. Head past them and up the walkway along the left side of the harbor, and enjoy the **views** back at the town's colorful pastel buildings, with the craggy coastline of the Cinque Terre just beyond. The best views are from up top, at the edge of the bluff. Below you, the breakwater (made of reject marble blocks from the famous nearby quarries of Carrara) curves out to sea, providing a bit of protection for the harbor.

These rocks are popular with sunbathers by day and romantics and photographers at sunset.

For a peek at Riomaggiore's beach, continue around the bluff on this trail toward Punta di Montenero, the cape that defines the southern end of the Cinque Terre. As you walk, you'll pass the rugged boat landing and eventually run into Riomaggiore's uncomfortably rocky but still inviting beach *(spiaggia)*. Ponder how Europeans manage to look relaxed when lounging on football-sized "pebbles."

Experiences in Riomaggiore

Hikes from Riomaggiore

For an **easy walk** along the lip of the one-time river ravine, take **Via di Loca,** which veers off Via Colombo at the top of town (directly across from the stairs at the upper end of Via Colombo). This leads in just a few minutes to the town playground *(parco giochi)*, benches, neighborhood pea patches, and pleasant views over town (especially at sunset). There's also a steep staircase from here

up to the town cemetery; from there, an even steeper trail runs all the way up to the town's 14th-century **Nostra Signora di Montenero sanctuary,** high above the town.

For an easier climb to the sanctuary, opt for the **scenic one-hour trail** that rises from the top of town. Take the main road inland until you see signs at the roundabout at the end of Via Santuario; or ride the shuttle bus 12 minutes from the town center to the sanctuary trail, then walk uphill another 20 minutes (great picnic spot up top).

Beach

Riomaggiore's rugged and tiny "beach" is rocky, but it's clean and peaceful. It's just around the bluff from the harbor, past the boat landing—to find it, see the end of my self-guided walk, above. There's a shower here in the summer, and another closer to town by the boat landing—where many enjoy sunning on and jumping from the rocks.

Kayaks and Water Sports

Diving Center 5 Terre rents kayaks as well as snorkeling and scuba equipment; they also lead guided dives of the protected marine waters nearby (open only in good weather, underground office in the passage leading to the harbor—down the stairs and under the tracks, Via San Giacomo, +39 0187 920 011, www.5terrediving.it).

Nightlife in Riomaggiore

With a youthful spirit and lively evening bustle, Riomaggiore has an enjoyable night scene. Stroll the main drag, scope out these listings (serving €6-8 cocktails), and find the one that appeals. Several of these places have full menus if you want to eat.

Bar Centrale, run by sociable Ivo, Alberto, and the gang, offers "nightlife" any time of day—it's a magnet for tourists. Ivo, who lived in the Bay Area, fills his bar with San Franciscan rock and a fun-loving vibe; it feels a little like the village's living room (great mojitos, daily 7:30-late, Via Colombo 144).

Bar & Vini A Piè de Mà, above the train station at the now closed Via dell'Amore trailhead, has piles of charm, frequent music, and stays open until 23:00 from June through September.

More Bars and Cafés: Near the bottom of Via Colombo, facing each other, are the noisy **La Zorza Café** (appealing to international tourists with thumping music and freestyle bartender) and the classier **Bar O'Netto** (geared more for young locals, with a mellower vibe and nice outdoor seating). Higher up on Via Colombo (at #76), **Vertical Lounge Bar** has a lively and loose ambience, light food (a good *aperitivo* buffet at happy-hour time), and a fine people-watching perch near the top of the promenade zone. And at sunset, you can't beat **La Conchiglia**—the simple café/bar (closed Wed) on the bluff overlooking the harbor—a perfect location for watching the sun disappear into the Ligurian Sea and the lights of Monterosso twinkling on the horizon.

Sleeping in Riomaggiore

Riomaggiore has few hotels worth your time; I recommend staying in one of the town's many private rooms for rent. Breakfast is normally on your own.

$$$ Alla Marina is Riomaggiore's best value, renting a half-dozen rooms and apartments—most with sea views—at the top of one of the tall, skinny buildings that rise up from the harbor. The furnishings are a combination of modern and nautical, and friendly brothers Sandro and Andrea take pride in running a tight ship (RS%, breakfast extra, pay parking, office open 9:00-18:00, Via San Giacomo 61—ask about the easier back-door entrance, +39 328 013 4077, www.allamarina.com, info@allamarina.com). They also rent several other rooms in Riomaggiore and Manarola.

$$$ Casato Bapò has three airy, spacious rooms with unobstructed views at the top of town near the Church of San Giovanni.

They're on the fourth floor, but accessible via the public elevator nearby (Via Pecunia 116, +39 340 705 6723, www.casatobapo.com, casatobapo@gmail.com, Sabrina).

$$ Il BoMa—named for the owners, American Maddy and her Italian husband, Bombetta, has three old-fashioned rooms along the main drag (one cheaper room with private bath down the hall, air-con, up three flights at Via Colombo 99, +39 0187 920 395, mobile +39 320 074 8826, www.ilboma5terre.com, info@ilboma5terre.com). They also rent two nearby apartments.

$$ La Dolce Vita offers six modern, good-value rooms on the main drag, plus two apartments elsewhere in town (some with air-con, open daily 9:30-19:30—if they're closed, they're full; Via Colombo 167, +39 331 903 6704, agonatal@libero.it, helpful Giacomo and Simone).

$$ Edi manages three rooms and an apartment. You pay extra for views (most rooms with air-con, reception at Via Colombo 12, +39 320 111 7074, www.appartamenticinqueterre.net, edi-vesigna@iol.it).

$ Amy Inman (an American expat who runs the Cinque Terre Insider blog) and her Italian husband, Francesco, offer an apartment and three private rooms (RS%, cash only, air-con, +39 329 572 0138—WhatsApp messages welcomed, www.riomaggioreservations.wordpress.com, info@riomaggioreservations.com).

Eating in Riomaggiore

ON THE HARBOR

Harborfront dining comes with slightly higher prices, a dressy ambience, and glorious views.

$$$$ Enoteca & Ristorante Dau Cila (pronounced "dow CHEE-lah") is decked out like a black-and-white movie set in an old boat shed with extra tables outside on a rustic deck over dinghies. Try their €25 seafood antipasto plate and listen to the waves lapping at the harbor below (daily 12:30-15:00 & 19:30-22:30, Via San Giacomo 65, +39 0187 760 032, Luca).

$$$$ Rio Bistrot, small and intimate at the top of the harbor, jazzes up its Ligurian cuisine with international influences. You can order à la carte from the short but well-designed menu, or try their €40-60 tasting menus (daily 12:30-16:00 & 19:00-22:00, Via San Giacomo 46, +39 0187 920 616, Manuel).

ON THE MAIN STREET, VIA COLOMBO

$$$ Trattoria la Grotta, right in the town center (with no view), has a passion for anchovies and mussels. You'll enjoy reliably good food surrounded by historical photos and wonderful stonework in a dramatic, dressy, cave-like setting (reservations smart, Thu-Tue

12:00-14:30 & 18:00-22:30, closed Wed, Via Colombo 247, +39 0187 920 187, mobile +39 346 260 8709, www.lagrottariomaggiore. it).

$$ Bar Centrale is a casual, family-friendly place for hamburgers, salads, and pesto. They also have a *gelateria* on site (long hours daily, see listing earlier, under "Nightlife in Riomaggiore").

Light Meals: Various handy carryout eateries along the main drag offer good lunches or snacks. **$ Primo Piatto,** at the top of town, offers takeaway handmade pastas and sauces, cooked to order on the spot. It's cheap and delicious (Wed-Mon 10:30-19:30 or later, closed Tue, Via Colombo 72, Roberta). For deep-fried seafood in a paper cone, **$ Il Pescato Cucinato** is where Edoardo fishes and his wife, Laura, fries (chalkboard out front explains what's fresh, daily 11:30-20:30, near the bottom of Via Colombo at #199). A few doors away, **$ Tutti Fritti** serves only freshly fried nibbles, including fish (daily 10:00-21:00, Via Colombo 161, Andrea and Isabella).

Picnics: Groceries and delis lining Via Colombo sell food to-go for a picnic at the harbor or beach. **Co-op** grocery stores have the best prices (at #122 and #205, closed Sun). For a more appetizing selection and good service, head to **Alimentari Franca,** on the main street by the train-station tunnel (daily 8:00-20:00, shorter hours off-season, Via Colombo 251).

Breakfast: Most of my recommended accommodations don't serve breakfast—and those that do often simply leave a coffee kettle and some basic continental breakfast fixings in your room. For eggs or a good croissant-and-espresso fix, drop by **Bar Centrale** (described earlier); or **Bar Stazione,** at the train station.

NEAR THE TRAIN STATION

$$ Bar & Vini A Piè de Mà, at the trailhead on the Manarola end of town, is good for a scenic light bite or quiet drink at night. The bar, with great outdoor seating, is self-service: Head into the bar to place your order, then bring it out to your preferred perch (Wed-Mon 11:00-21:00, June-Sept until 23:00, closed Tue and off-season). Enjoy a meal on its dramatically situated terrace for an indelible Cinque Terre memory.

CINQUE TERRE

RIVIERA TOWNS

Levanto • Sestri Levante • Santa Margherita Ligure •
Portofino • Porto Venere • La Spezia

The Cinque Terre is tops, but there's much more to the Italian Riviera. To the north of the Cinque Terre is a trio of beach towns: Levanto, the northern gateway to the Cinque Terre; Sestri Levante, stunningly situated on a narrow peninsula flanked by two beaches; and Santa Margherita Ligure, a thriving city with an active waterfront and easy connections to yacht-happy Portofino. At the south end of the Cinque Terre is the pretty resort of Porto Venere and the region's workaday transit hub, La Spezia.

The best of these towns—the high-end yin to the Cinque Terre's ramshackle yang—can be user-friendly home bases for day trips along the Riviera coast. But they are also worth visiting in their own right. After exploring the villages and trails of the Cinque Terre, these Riviera towns feel like a return to civilization.

Riviera hotels aren't necessarily cheaper than the Cinque Terre, but they are more likely to have space. High season here is roughly May through September, peaking in July and August. Some hotels close in winter.

Home Bases: Levanto, Sestri Levante, and Santa Margherita Ligure are practical home bases for those who want modern hotels with predictable resort amenities, and for drivers wanting to park at their hotel and side-trip to the Cinque Terre by train.

Levanto—just minutes north of Monterosso by train—is the handiest. Sestri Levante is a bit farther away with a little less train service. Santa Margherita Ligure is the most distant and often requires a transfer to the Cinque Terre, but the town compensates by being the most appealing—and it gives you easy access to posh Portofino. Porto Venere is better as a day trip, and La Spezia is more functional than appealing, although either can serve in a pinch.

Riviera Towns at a Glance

North of the Cinque Terre

▲**Levanto** Town popular with surfers and families for its long beach; just one stop by train from the Cinque Terre. It offers an easy, level hike (or bike ride) to the sleepy villages of **Bonassola** and **Framura**. See page 419.

▲**Sestri Levante** Charming town on a peninsula flanked by two crescent beaches. See page 429.

▲▲**Santa Margherita Ligure** Easygoing old-school resort town with just enough urban bustle, a handful of sights, and proximity to Portofino. See page 433.

▲**Portofino** Yacht-harbor resort with grand scenery, an easy hop (by boat, bus, or on foot) from Santa Margherita Ligure. See page 444.

South of the Cinque Terre

▲▲**Porto Venere** Enchanting seafront village perfect for a scenic day trip (by boat or bus). See page 451.

La Spezia Beachless transportation hub, with trains and boats to the Cinque Terre and buses and boats to Porto Venere. See page 454.

Keep in mind that you'll be competing with other day-trippers for space on prime midday trains to and from the Cinque Terre. Turn this problem into an advantage: Enjoy your home-base town during the day, then head into the Cinque Terre in the late afternoon for untrampled charm, a romantic dinner, and a late train back.

North of the Cinque Terre

When most people imagine the "Italian Riviera," they're thinking of the shimmering resort towns north of the Cinque Terre. Stately Old World hotels loom over crowded pebble beaches with rentable umbrellas. Fastidiously landscaped parks and promenades are jammed with more Italian visitors than American tourists. These towns are perfect for day-tripping—or even an overnight.

RIVIERA TOWNS

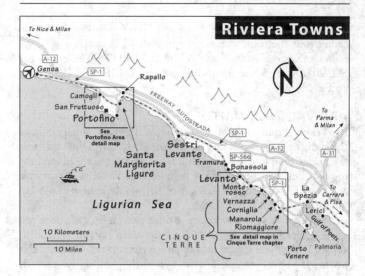

Riviera Towns

To Nice & Milan

A-12
Genoa
SP-1
Rapallo
Camogli
San Fruttuoso
Portofino
See Portofino Area detail map
Santa Margherita Ligure
Sestri Levante
Framura
Bonassola
Levanto
Monterosso
Vernazza
Corniglia
Manarola
Riomaggiore
See detail map in Cinque Terre chapter
CINQUE TERRE
La Spezia
Lerici
Porto Venere
Palmaria
Gulf of Poets
To Carrara & Pisa
To Parma & Milan
SP-1
SP-566
A-12
A-31
FREEWAY AUTOSTRADA

Ligurian Sea

10 Kilometers
10 Miles

Levanto

Graced with a long, sandy beach, Levanto (LEH-vahn-toh) is packed in summer and popular with families, surfers, and beach bums. The rest of the year, it's just a small, sleepy town with kids playing in the square and locals whizzing around on bicycles. Although not as charming as the Cinque Terre, Levanto is just a short train ride away and enjoys fewer crowds and more varied hotel and dining options, including budget-friendly family rooms and affordable apartments with kitchenettes. From Levanto, you can bike or stroll on a delightful, level path to the uncrowded beach villages of Bonassola and Framura, or spend a half-day on the no-wimps-allowed hike to Monterosso.

Orientation to Levanto

Levanto (pop. 5,200) faces the sea along a broad, curving beach. Much of the "new" town, closer to the train station, is actually old and full of character, with quaint pedestrian shopping streets like Via Garibaldi and handsome 19th-century villas close to the waterfront. The sleepy, twisty old town—bisected by a modern street—is tucked up against the adjacent hill.

Tourist Information: A Cinque Terre National Park info center is at the train station. The helpful TI is in the new town, at Piazza Cavour 1 (daily 9:00-13:00 & 15:00-18:00 except closed Sun afternoon, shorter hours off-season, +39 0187 808 125, www.visitlevanto.it).

ARRIVAL IN LEVANTO

By Train: From the train station (no baggage storage), head through the parking lot and down the stairs, turn right, and cross the bridge onto Corso Roma. The beach is straight ahead, and the town center, with most of my recommended hotels, restaurants, and the TI, is to your left. You can walk from the station to most of my listings in about 10 minutes.

By Car: If your hotel doesn't offer parking—or if you're not sleeping here—the lots surrounding the **train station** are affordable (€24/day) and handy for hopping a train to the Cinque Terre towns. If you're heading for the beach, the parking lot there is handy but more expensive.

HELPFUL HINTS

Markets: Levanto's modern covered *mercato*, which sells produce and fish, is on Via XXV Aprile, between the train station and the beach (daily 7:30-13:00). On Wednesday morning, an **open-air market** with clothes, shoes, and housewares sets up along the beach.

Laundry: A **self-service launderette** stuffed with snack-and-drink vending machines is at Piazza Staglieno 38, facing an inviting park (daily 24 hours, +39 338 701 6341). A larger self-service place is at Via Garibaldi 32 (daily 8:00-22:00, same phone).

Sports Rentals: Right on the beach, **Rosa dei Venti** rents kayaks, canoes, surfboards, and windsurfing equipment (+39 329 451 1981, https://rosadeiventiboattours.com, Marco).

Bike Rental: Relatively flat Levanto, with light traffic, is a great bike town—and the ride to nearby Bonassola and Framura is easy and delightful. Regular bikes cost €10/day at both **Cicli Raso** (daily 9:30-12:30 & 15:00-19:00, closed Sun Nov-April, Via Garibaldi 63, +39 0187 802 511, www.cicliraso.com) and the **Sensafreni Bike Shop,** convenient to the beach boardwalk (daily 9:00-13:00 & 16:00-20:00, Piazza del Popolo 1, +39 0187 807 128).

Electric Bike Tours: Get a helpful boost on the hills with **Ebikein,** which offers a variety of guided tours on electric bikes. Options include a three-hour Levanto-Monterosso sunset tour (€59) and a four-hour trek to sanctuaries above the Cinque Terre towns (€65; +39 334 190 0496, https://ebikein-cinqueterre.it).

Boat Tours: Its base is in Monterosso, but **Sea Breeze** will pick you up in Levanto for full-day or *aperitivo* sunset tours. See page 365.

Sights in Levanto

Beach

Levanto's beach hides below a parking lot and promenade that's elevated above the sand—look for underpasses or stairs along its length. There are pretty boardwalks up on the elevated promenade and down along the beachfront. As you face the harbor, the boat dock is to your far left, and the diving center is to your far right.

In summer, three parts of the beach are free: both sides of the boat dock, and near Piazza Mazzini. The rest of the beach is broken up into private sections that you pay to enter. Pay beaches come with comfy lounge chairs, bar service, showers, and someone keeping an eye on your things while you swim. Shop around to find the best price (about €25/chair, less in the afternoon). You can always stroll along the beach, even through the private sections— just don't sit down. Off-season, roughly October through May, the entire beach is free, and you can lay your towel anywhere you like. Ask your hotel for towels; most have beach towels to loan or rent.

The city's seaside pool is privately run and is for serious lap swimmers only. Check with your hotel; they may have entry passes.

Old Town

The old town spills down from the Church of Sant'Andrea (c. 1212), with Piazza del Popolo at its heart. Until a few decades ago, the town's open-air market was held at the 13th-century loggia (covered set of archways) in the square. The modern, elevated street is the old rail line (built in the 1870s and replaced by the current, higher route in 1970).

Explore the back streets (including Via Guani), the oratory of San Giacomo, and the old clock tower. Levanto was once an important harbor of the Republic of Genoa (the second biggest harbor after Genoa itself); from here, shipments of olive oil, wine, and the coveted red marble called *rosso levanto* set sail. You can still discover traces of ancient warehouses and the dockland area around Piazza del Popolo.

▲Hike to Monterosso

This 3.5-hour hike from Levanto to Monterosso is strenuous at the beginning and end but easier in the middle (for details, see page 352). To begin in Levanto, start on Piazza del Popolo, and head up-hill to the striped Church of Sant'Andrea. From the church court-yard, follow the sign to the *castello* (a private residence), go under

RIVIERA TOWNS

Levanto

CONVENT OF
SANTA
ANNUNCIATA

SALITA SAN FRANCESCO

Road to
Bonassola

STRADA PROVINCIALE FRAMURA-LEVANTO SS-332

Path to
Bonassola
& Framura

1

Ghiararo River

10

CORSO ROMA

P

Piazza
Mazzini

NEW
TOWN

VIA VAREGO

Free
Beach

PASSEGGIATA DEL MARE

VIA MAZZINI

CORSO ITALIA

VIA ZOPPI

VIA CONCIA

19

VIA JAC. LEVANTO

16

POST

SARAGONI
TOWN
HALL
Piazza
Cavour

VIA VINZONI

P

13

i

Piazzetta
Marina

VIA CAIROLI

3

23

VIA DANTE

25

21

VIA DANTE

VIA GUANI

6

Piazza
Staglieno

17

SAN
GIACOMO

PEDESTRIAN
UNDERPASSES

ELEVATED ROAD

24

26

LOGGIA

11

*Ligurian
Sea*

POOL
(PRIVATE)

Piazza
Colombo

VIA D. GRILLO

Piazza
del Popolo

Piazza della
Areneta

14

9

Free
Beach

VIA GUERANO SEMENZA

STRADA DEL CASTELLO

OLD
TOWN

MATTALANA

22

VIA

Boats to
Cinque Terre

CASTLE

WALL

SANT
ANDREA

4

BREAKWATER

Free
Beach

VIA SEMENZA

VIA MESCO

Trail to
Monterosso

TRAIN STATION

To Monterosso
& Autostrada A-12
(Carrodano exit)

SS-332

VIA CANZIO

ELEVATED TRAIN LINE

ROMA

VIA VIVIANI

CORSO

SALITA SAN FRAN.

VIA XXV APRILE

VIA GARIBALDI

7

2

VIA GALLI

COVERED MARKET

5

VIA TERRARO

VIA TERRARO

18

VIA MARTITI DELLA LIBERTA

VIA GALLI

24

15

CLOCK TOWER

N

200 Meters

200 Yards

VIA DELL' OROLOGICO

8

VIA PREALBA

12

STRADA PREALBA

SAN NIC.

To P

20

CAMP-GROUND

Accommodations

1 Villa Margherita
2 Hotel Carla
3 Hotel Primavera
4 Piè del Castello
5 Oasi Hotel
6 Hotel Garden
7 A Durmì
8 Villa Clelia B&B
9 La Rosa dei Venti
10 A Due Passi dal Mare
11 La Loggia Guesthouse & Restaurant
12 Ostello Ospitalia del Mare

Eateries & Other

13 Ristorante L'Oasi
14 Osteria Tumelin
15 Da Rino
16 Ristorante Moresco
17 Gattabriga
18 Taverna Garibaldi & Bike Rental
19 La Picea
20 Pizzeria L'Igea
21 Bar Macaja & Focacceria il Falcone
22 Enoteca La Compera
23 Supermarket
24 Launderette (2)
25 Canoe & Kayak Rental
26 Bike Rental

RIVIERA TOWNS

the stone arch, and continue uphill. From here, take trail SVA (following signs toward *Punta Mesco,* the rugged tip of the peninsula), then drop steeply down into Monterosso. (If you have knee issues, consider starting in Monterosso instead.)

▲Hike or Bike to Bonassola (and Framura)

Tucked along the main train line on a cove north of Levanto, the small beach resort of Bonassola (boh-nah-SOH-lah, pop. 950) is a

peaceful little eddy. As far as Riviera beach resorts go, this is a jewel. With a low-key vibe, a tidy grid street plan that feels almost French, and a picturesque dark-sand beach hemmed in by jagged bluffs, Bonassola is a fine alternative to the region's other beaches. And the next best thing to a beach day in Bonassola is getting there: A level, easy, rails-to-trails path cuts through the mountain from Levanto—enjoyable by foot, but even better by bike.

Levanto to Bonassola: Local **trains** run between Levanto and Bonassola (hourly, 3 minutes, confirm your train will stop in Bonassola). But I'd rather take the **promenade.** At the northern end of Levanto's beachfront road/parking lot, you'll find a level, roughly 1.5-mile path neatly divided into bike and pedestrian lanes. Most of the route is through well-lit former train tunnels, with brief breaks overlooking the sea (and hikes down to secluded beaches). The walk takes about 30 minutes, with long stretches through cool tunnels; by bike, it's less than 10 minutes. The promenade runs along the original rail line that linked Italy in the 1870s. Think of the effort of building it, and how much it meant for the newly unified country. The last trains chugged along the historic tracks in 1970, when the current rail line opened.

Visiting Bonassola: The town itself—with manicured promenades and piazzas—is worth exploring. **$$ Caffè delle Rose,** facing the town's elevated road (at Via Fratelli Rezzano 22), has good gelato, food, and drinks. Several *foccacerie* and other eateries cluster at the far end of town.

The beach is separated from the town center by the elevated road (shared by bicyclists, walkers, and a parking lot). The inviting **beach** has mostly private sections, with a few free public areas.

For a scenic **walk/hike,** head to the far (north) end of the beach, where a promenade snakes along the base of the cliff (with rocky perches for sunbathing and swimming). For higher views, find the stairs near the flagpole, and follow the steps up on the right side of the yellow church. Popping out at the top, turn left along the scenic, private road as it curls around the top of the bay, with great views back on the town and beach; the path ends at the blocky little Madonnina della Punta chapel.

Bonassola to Framura (best for bicyclists): From Bonassola, the promenade continues another 1.5 miles to the town of **Framura**—a settlement made up of five medieval hamlets that rise from the seafront to the hilltop (pop. 750). Because this part of the route is almost entirely through tunnels, it's boring for walkers—but quick for bikers. The trail ends overlooking Framura's rocky little harbor and near its train station.

Visiting Framura: Park and lock your bike at the trailhead, take the stairs (or elevator) down to the small-boat harbor, cross under the train tracks through the boat-shed archway, walk through the big tunnel, and you'll emerge near the station. The welcoming **TI** at the Framura station has maps and advice (+39 0187 160 0577, www.framuraturismo.it).

At the station, the tunnel to platforms 2 and 3 also leads to the start of the scenic Via del Mare path, with a basic café at the trailhead. This easy promenade takes you north along a cliff face in 10 minutes to two small, pristine gravel beaches that are free and uncrowded.

Hikers can walk the panoramic but steep trail that connects Framura's five hamlets, which are sprinkled with medieval watchtowers, churches, and washhouses. To avoid the uphill climb, ride the summer shuttle to any of the five towns and walk down (shuttles run hourly, timed to the arrival of trains from the Cinque Terre).

Sleeping in Levanto

$$$ Villa Margherita, in a 1906 Art Nouveau building, is across the river and a bit uphill (about a 10-minute walk from the town center or train station), but the shaded view gardens, 12 characteristic colorfully tiled rooms, and tranquility are worth the walk (family rooms, deluxe apartment, air-con, elevator one flight up from street level, free parking, Via Trento e Trieste 31, +39 0187 807 212, mobile +39 328 842 6934, www.villamargherita.net, info@villamargherita.net, Paola).

$$$ Hotel Carla faces a school in a quiet residential zone, about 10 minutes from the beach and the station. Its 30 rooms come with surprising contemporary style—most have balconies, and all are decorated in soothing, neutral colors (RS%, family rooms, air-con, elevator, free loaner bikes, Via Galli 3, +39 0187 808 275, mobile +39 351 52 3388, www.carlahotel.com, info@carlahotel.com, Laura).

$$$ Hotel Primavera is homey and family-run, with 17 colorful rooms—10 with balconies (but no views)—just a block from the beach (family rooms, request a quiet room off the street, includes hearty breakfast buffet, air-con, pay private parking, Via Cairoli 5, +39 0187 808 023, www.primaverahotel.com, info@primaverahotel.com; friendly Carlo, cheerful Daniela, and daughters Giuditta and Gloria).

$$$ Piè del Castello is just above the campground, right on the Levanto-Monterosso trail. Andrea and his wife Tiziana rent three double rooms, each with a patio and access to a sprawling garden with views of the ancient city wall and the Church of Sant'Andrea. Hikers will appreciate the location and Andrea's knowledge of area trails (includes breakfast, air-con, fridge, ping-pong table, free parking, Via Guido Semenza 2, +39 366 1467 7886, www.piedelcastello.com, info@piedelcastello.com).

$$$ Oasi Hotel, well-run by Silvia, has 14 rooms in a cozy small hotel behind the market hall. Some rooms have balconies, others have direct access to the garden, and a few have neither but are larger—request your choice when you reserve (RS%, air-con, elevator, pay parking, Via Terraro, +39 0187 807 356, www.oasihotel.eu, info@oasihotel.eu).

$$ Hotel Garden offers 17 functional, businesslike, modern rooms (all with balconies but no views) on the first floor of an apartment building. Its value is its proximity to the beach—just across the street (a more expensive fifth-floor room has sea views and a terrace, closed Nov-mid-March, air-con, elevator, free off-site parking, loaner bikes, Corso Italia 6, +39 0187 808 173, www.nuovogarden.com, info@nuovogarden.com, Davide and Damiano).

$$ A Durmì is a happy little guesthouse owned by lovely Graziella, Gianni, and their two daughters, Elisa and Chiara. Their sunny patios, green leafy gardens, six immaculate beach bungalow-type rooms, and five sunlit apartments make this a welcoming place to stay (breakfast extra, family rooms, air-con, bar, pay parking, Via D. Viviani 12, +39 0187 800 823, mobile +39 342 805 3135, www.adurmi.it, info@adurmi.it).

$$ Villa Clelia B&B offers six basic rooms (named for the winds—*scirocco, maestrale,* and so on) with minifridges and terraces. The rooms surround a garden courtyard just a short walk up from the sea (in-room breakfast, air-con, pay parking, free loaner bikes; with the old town's loggia on your left, it's straight ahead at Piazza da Passano 1; +39 329 379 4859, www.villaclelia.it, info@

villaclelia.it). They also rent apartments in the center that economically sleep up to five.

$ La Rosa dei Venti is an *affittacamere* just a couple of blocks from the beach, in the old town. Enthusiastic Rosanna and her son Marco rent six old-fashioned rooms with dark hardwood floors, comfy rugs, and glittery seashore decor (air-con, parking, from Piazza del Popolo take the lane next to Osteria Tumelin to Via della Compera, +39 0187 808 165, Marco's mobile +39 328 742 8268, www.larosadeiventilevanto.com, info@larosadeiventilevanto.com).

$ A Due Passi dal Mare is along the town's main road, a five-minute walk from the beach or the train station. Friendly Francesca and husband Maurizio rent four crisp, quiet, ground-floor rooms in a large villa built by her grandfather in the 1920s, with access to a small back garden (free on-site parking, closed Jan-Feb, Corso Roma 37, +39 0187 809 177, mobile +39 338 960 1537, www.a2passidalmare.com, info@a2passidalmare.com).

$ La Loggia has eight cozy, older, and cheap rooms, perched above the old loggia on Piazza del Popolo (request balcony, quieter rooms in back, two basic side-by-side apartments great for families of 4-8, lots of stairs, air-con, free parking, reception open 9:00-23:00, Piazza del Popolo 7, +39 0187 808 107, mobile +39 335 641 7701, www.loggialevanto.com, laloggialaloggia@gmail.com, Alessandro). They also have a recommended restaurant.

Hostel: A budget gem run by the city tourist association, **¢ Ostello Ospitalia del Mare** has 70 basic beds, airy rooms, an elevator, and a terrace in a well-renovated medieval palazzo a few steps from the old town (all ages, dorms with private bath, private rooms, breakfast available, self-service laundry, no curfew or lockout; may close Nov-March, Via San Nicolò 1, +39 0187 802 562, www.ospitalialevanto.com, info@ospitalialevanto.com).

Eating in Levanto

$$$$ Ristorante L'Oasi—spacious, bright, and with a garden feel right on the main square—is family run, with Claudio in the kitchen and Lella supervising the dining room. This is a polished setting for enjoying seafood, including fresh tuna tartare, marinated anchovies, and grilled swordfish. If you really want to treat yourself, order a whole fish baked under salt (daily 12:30-14:30 & 19:30-22:30, closed Wed Sept-June, Piazza Cavour, +39 0187 800 856).

$$$ Osteria Tumelin has a dressy ambience in its elegant dining room, a casual covered terrace out front, and a wide selection of fresh seafood. Reservations are smart on weekends or to dine outside. Check out the aquarium containing giant lobster and moray eels in the corner dining room (daily 12:00-14:30 & 19:00-

22:30, closed Thu, Via D. Grillo 32, across the square from the loggia, +39 0187 808 379, www.tumelin.it).

$$$ Da Rino, a small trattoria on a quiet pedestrian lane, dishes up seafood, meat, and homemade Ligurian specialties. Consider the grilled *totani* (squid), *pansotti con salsa di noci* (ravioli with walnut sauce), and *trofie al pesto* (pasta with pesto sauce). Dine indoors or at one of the outdoor tables (Wed-Mon 18:30-22:00, closed Tue, Via Garibaldi 10, +39 0187 813 475).

$$ Ristorante la Loggia, a Levanto standby, has been dishing up classic Ligurian cuisine for more than 50 years. Choose between the homey, wood-paneled dining room with nooks and crannies or the little terrace overlooking the square (daily 12:30-14:00 & 19:00-22:00, closed Wed and Nov-Feb, Piazza del Popolo 7, +39 0187 808 107). They also rent rooms (see previous section).

$$ Ristorante Moresco serves large portions of pasta and seafood at reasonable prices in a vaulted, candlelit room decorated with Moorish-style frescoes (Tue-Sun 12:00-14:00 & 19:00-21:00, closed Mon, reservations appreciated, Via Jacopo 24, +39 0187 807 253, Roberto and Francesca).

$$ Gattabriga hides out on a back lane behind Piazza del Popolo with a contemporary look; an updated and well-priced menu of pastas, seafood, and meats; and friendly service (Tue-Sun 19:00-21:30, closed Mon, Via Guani 47, +39 366 527 3582).

$$ Taverna Garibaldi, a comfy good-value place on the town's most characteristic street, serves focaccia with various toppings, made-to-order *farinata* (savory chickpea crêpes), salads, and more than 30 types of pizza (Fri-Wed 19:00-22:00, closed Thu, Via Garibaldi 57, +39 0187 808 098).

$$ La Picea offers creative wood-fired pizzas (check out the oven) and a large selection of beers—eat in or take out (Tue-Sun 12:00-14:30 & 18:30-23:00, closed Mon, just off Piazza Cavour at Via della Concia 18, +39 0187 802 063, mobile +39 392 958 3294).

$$ Pizzeria L'Igea, usually packed with locals, is tucked just inside the Campeggio Acquadolce campground, 50 yards past the hostel. It's a favorite among locals who know you don't have to be a camper to enjoy freshly made, budget-conscious pizza and pasta in their bright dining hall. Their specialty is *gattafin*—deep-fried herb-stuffed ravioli. Come early or be prepared to wait, even for takeout (daily 12:00-14:30 & 18:45-22:30, Via Guido Semenza 5, +39 0187 807 293).

$-$$ Bar Macaja, decorated in shabby chic beach style, is a tiny place with a big happy vibe. Stop in for a continental breakfast, espresso or a drink, *panini*, and local seafood—including anchovies prepared six ways (daily 7:00-23:00, just up from the beach at Via Cairoli 25, +39 349 844 8424).

$ Enoteca La Compera is a wine bar where you can try two wines and an *aperitivo* for €12. It offers a quiet respite on a hidden courtyard below the church in the old town (Thu-Tue 17:00-23:00, closed Wed, follow the red-brick road—under the stone arch—to Piazza della Compera 3, +39 334 712 8517).

Picnics and Bites on the Go: *Focaccerie, rosticcerie,* and delis with takeout pasta abound on Via Dante Alighieri. **$ Focacceria il Falcone** has a great selection of focaccia with different toppings, plus big salads (daily 9:30-22:00, shorter hours off-season, Via Cairoli 19, +39 0187 807 370). For more picnic options, try the *mercato* (see "Helpful Hints," earlier) or visit **Crai,** a good supermarket just off Piazza Cavour (daily 8:00-20:00 except Sun closed 13:00-15:00, Vicolo San Rocco 5). For a shaded setting, lay out your spread on a bench in the grassy park at triangular Piazza Staglieno. Another fine picnic spot is Piazza Cristoforo Colombo, located east of the swimming pool, with benches and sea views.

Levanto Connections

Trains run frequently from Levanto to the Cinque Terre towns (5 minutes to Monterosso). A slower, more scenic, infrequent option is the **boat,** which stops at every Cinque Terre town (except Corniglia) before heading to Porto Venere (3/day in high season, price depends on distance traveled—or get a €37 all-day hop-on, hop-off ticket; only one return boat daily stops at Levanto, at about 18:50; get latest boat schedule and price sheet at TI or boat dock or check website, +39 0187 732 987, www.navigazionegolfodeipoeti.it).

Sestri Levante

Sestri Levante (SEH-stree leh-VAHN-teh) is squeezed as skinny as a hot dog between its two beaches. The pedestrian-friendly Via XXV Aprile, which runs down the middle of the peninsula, is lined with shops that sell takeout pizza, pastries, and beach paraphernalia.

Hans Christian Andersen enjoyed his visit here in the mid-1800s, writing, "What a fabulous evening I spent in Sestri Levante!" One of the bays—Baia delle Favole—is named in his honor (*favole* means "fairy tale"). The small mermaid curled on the edge of the fountain behind the TI is another nod to the beloved Danish storyteller.

RIVIERA TOWNS

Orientation to Sestri Levante

Sestri Levante (pop. 18,000) is dominated by its big, dull modern town in front of the train station. But don't be discouraged—the old-town peninsula, a 10-minute walk away, has charm to spare.

Tourist Information: It's at Corso Colombo 50, on the ground floor of Palazzo Fascie, the town's cultural center (daily 9:00-13:00 & 14:00-17:00, shorter hours off-season, +39 0185 478 530, www.sestri-levante.net). They can tell you about the summer bike-sharing program (€8/5 hours) and direct you to the trail (south of town) for a 1.5-hour hike (each way) to the scenic Punta Manara promontory.

Arrival in Sestri Levante: To reach the enjoyable pedestrian zone, the old-town peninsula, and beaches, follow the "Stroll the Town" advice below.

Baggage Storage: The tobacco store in the train station stores bags.

Market Day: It's on Saturday at Piazza Aldo Moro (8:00-13:00).

Laundry: A self-service launderette is in the urban zone southeast of the train station (daily 8:30-20:30, Via Costantino Raffo 8, +39 389 101 1454).

Sights in Sestri Levante

Stroll the Town

For a get-acquainted walk, head straight out from the train station and across the piazza to go down the arcaded Viale Roma until it dead ends at the leafy city park. Go left two blocks to the roundabout, and then take the second exit onto Corso Colombo (just past the Bermuda Bar). This main drag will take you to the TI before turning into the pedestrianized Via XXV Aprile. This street, running the length of the peninsula, is lively with shops, eateries, and delightful pastel facades. When you reach Piazza Matteotti, dominated by a large white Renaissance-era church, you're at the narrow waist of the isthmus, with beaches to the right (pay) and left (free). If you continue up the lane to the left of the church, you'll pass a scenic amphitheater, then the evocative arches of a ruined chapel (bombed during World War II and left as a memorial). A few minutes farther on, past a stony Romanesque church, the road winds to the right to Grand Hotel dei Castelli. The rocky, forested bluff at the end of the town's peninsula is the huge private backyard of this fancy hotel.

Beaches

These are named after the bays *(baie)* that they border. The less scenic, bigger beach, **Baia delle Favole,** is divided up much of the

Sestri Levante

To Rapallo & Santa Margherita Ligure

To Santa Margherita Ligure

TRAIN STATION

Piazza Caduti

To Santa Margherita Ligure & Portofino

To Cinque Terre

Ligurian Sea

VIA OLIVE

LUNGO. G. DESCALZO

VIALE MAZZINI

V. ROMA

VIA ERALDO

To Levanto & Cinque Terre

Piazza Italia

VIA NAZIONALE

To

Baia delle Favole

Beaches

Giardini Ventre

V. XX SETT.

VIALE V. VENETO

V. TERESA G. COLOMBO

Piazza Sant' Antonio

Piazza Sant'

To A-12 Freeway

Piazza Repubblica

VIA FASCIE

PROMENADE & BIKE PATH

V. R. MAGENZA

V. XXV

V. DANTE

APRILE

Piazza Aldo Moro

VIA DELLA CHIUSA

BOAT DOCK

VIA PILADE QUEROLO

VICO CORO

VIA POZZETTO

Piazza Matteotti

V. PENISOLA

V. PORTI

VIA CAPPUCCINI

(Private)

GRAND HOTEL DEI CASTELLI

FREE BEACH

Baia del Silenzio

RUINED CHAPEL

ROMANESQUE CHURCH

200 Meters

200 Yards

To Punta Manara

Accommodations
1 Hotel Helvetia & Citto Beach Bar
2 Hotel Celeste
3 Hotel Genova
4 Albergo Marina

Eateries & Other
5 L'Osteria Mattana
6 Polpo Mario & Ristorante La Mainola
7 Pelagica
8 Ice Cream's Angels
9 Supermarket
10 To Laundrette

year (May-Sept) into sections that you must pay to enter. Fees, up to €30 per day in August, generally include chairs, umbrellas, and fewer crowds. There are several small free sections: at the ends and in the middle (look for *libere* signs, and ask *"Gratis?"* to make sure that it's free). For less expensive sections of beach (where you can rent a chair for about €8-10), ask for *spiaggia libera attrezzata* (spee-AH-jah LEE-behr-ah ah-treh-ZAHT-tah). The usual beach-town activities are clustered along this *baia:* boat rentals, sailing lessons, and bocce courts.

The town's other beach, **Baia del Silenzio,** is picturesque, narrow, virtually all free, and jam-packed, providing a good chance to see Italian families at play. There isn't much more to do here than unroll a beach towel and join in. Because of the bay's small size and the currents, the water gets warmer here than at **Baia delle Favole.** At the far end of Baia del Silenzio (under recommended Hotel Helvetia) is the **$$ Citto Beach Bar,** which offers front-row

RIVIERA TOWNS

seats with bay views (summer until very late, spring and fall until sunset, sandwiches and salads at lunchtime only, Gilberto).

Sleeping in Sestri Levante

Hotels Genova and Celeste are the closest to the station. Either is an easy roll with wheeled luggage.

$$$$ Hotel Helvetia, overlooking Baia del Silenzio, feels posh and romantic, with 21 plush rooms, a large sun terrace with a heated, cliff-hanging swimming pool, and a peaceful garden atmosphere. With doubles renting for €400-plus in peak season, it's a big but enticing splurge (family rooms, air-con, elevator, valet parking, closed Nov-March, Via Cappuccini 43, +39 0185 41175, www.hotelhelvetia.it, helvetia@hotelhelvetia.it, Alex).

$$$ Hotel Celeste, a dream for beach lovers, rests along the waterfront. Its 39 rooms are modern, crisp, and pricey, but you're paying for the sea breeze (family rooms, air-con, elevator, attached beachside bar/breakfast terrace, Lungomare Descalzo 14, +39 0185 485 005, www.hotelceleste.com, info@hotelceleste.com, Franco).

$$ Hotel Genova, well-run by the Bertoni family, is a ship-shape hotel with 19 shiny-clean, modern, and cheery rooms (three with sea views), a sunny lounge, rooftop sundeck, and a good location just two blocks from Baia delle Favole (ask for quieter room in back, family rooms, air-con, elevator, pay parking, Viale Mazzini 126, +39 0185 41057, www.hotelgenovasestrilevante.com, info@ hotelgenovasestrilevante.com, Stefano). They also book apartments in a nearby palazzo (www.appartamentisestrilevante.com).

$$ Albergo Marina's friendly Magda and her brother Santo rent 23 peaceful, clean, good-value rooms painted in sea-foam green. Though the hotel is located on a busy boulevard in the more urban part of town, rooms face a quiet back courtyard and it's a short walk to the beach and train station (family rooms, air-con, elevator, free self-service laundry, pool table, closed Nov-Easter, Via Fascie 100, +39 0185 487 332, www.marinahotel.it, marinahotel@ marinahotel.it).

Eating in Sestri Levante

Via XXV Aprile abounds with pastry shops, bakeries selling take-out pizza by the slice, and other edibles. For picnics, stop by a supermarket on your way from the train station; you'll pass a Carrefour Express at Viale Roma 25 (open daily). For a sit-down meal, try one of the places below.

$$ L'Osteria Mattana has long, shared tables in two white-tiled dining rooms (one in front and the other past the wood oven and brazier). Daily specials—most featuring seafood—are listed on chalkboard menus (lunch Sat-Sun only 12:30-14:30, dinner daily 19:30-22:30, closed Mon, Via XXV Aprile 34, +39 0185 457 633, Marco).

$$$ Polpo Mario has its own boat that brings in fresh fish each day. This is the place to try *polpo* (octopus), either spicy *(alla diavola)* or as *ragù di polpo* tossed with spaghetti. For an appetizer, the *acciughe al limone*—fresh anchovies cured in lemon—might just change your mind about this humble fish (Tue-Sun 12:00-15:00 & 19:00-23:00, closed Mon, reservations smart, Via XXV Aprile 163, +39 0185 480 203, www.polpomario.com).

$$$ Pelagica, a contemporary restaurant with a choice spot overlooking the Baia delle Favole, focuses on seafood, from anchovies to fried squid to traditional fish soup. Their rooftop terrace doubles as a cocktail lounge in the evening (kitchen daily 12:00-14:15 & 19:00-22:15, closed Wed, Via Pilade Queirolo 7, +39 393 882 0255).

$$ Ristorante La Mainolla offers pizzas, big salads, focaccia sandwiches, and reasonably priced pastas near Piazza Matteotti (daily 12:00-16:00 & 19:00-22:00, Via XXV Aprile 187, +39 0185 42792).

Gelato: Tourists flock to **Ice Cream's Angels,** flamboyantly set at the intersection of Via XXV Aprile and Via della Chiusa. Riccardo and Elena artfully load up your cone and top it with a dollop of Nutella chocolate-hazelnut cream (daily until late in summer).

Sestri Levante Connections

From Sestri Levante by Train to: Levanto (at least hourly, 15-30 minutes), **Monterosso** (at least hourly, 30-40 minutes), **other Cinque Terre towns** (nearly hourly direct, more with a change in Levanto or Monterosso), **Santa Margherita Ligure** (2/hour, 20-25 minutes).

Boats depart to the Cinque Terre, Porto Venere, Santa Margherita Ligure, Portofino, and San Fruttuoso from the dock *(molo)* on the peninsula (Easter-Oct, +39 0185 284 670, www.traghettiportofino.it).

Santa Margherita Ligure

If you need the Riviera of movie stars, park your yacht at Portofino. Or you can settle down with more elbow room in nearby and more personable Santa Margherita Ligure (SAHN-tah mar-geh-REE-tah lee-GOO-reh), one hour by train from the Cinque Terre. While Portofino's velour allure is tarnished by a nonstop traffic jam in peak season, Santa Margherita Ligure tumbles easily downhill from its train station. The town has a fun Old World resort character and a breezy harborfront with a beach promenade. With its nice big-city vitality, it feels bustling and lived-in, even off-season.

Orientation to Santa Margherita Ligure

On a quick day trip to Santa Margherita Ligure, walk the beach promenade and see the old town center before catching the bus or boat to Portofino to discover what all the fuss is about. With more time, Santa Margherita Ligure (pop. 10,200) makes a fine overnight stop or a home base for visiting Portofino or the Cinque Terre.

Tourist Information: The TI is as central as can be, in a green harborside kiosk at the city traffic hub, Piazza Vittorio Veneto (daily 9:30-13:00 & 15:00-17:00, shorter hours off-season, +39 0185 28 74 85, www.livesanta.it). They sell tickets for bus #782 to Portofino, which stops at the curb in front.

ARRIVAL IN SANTA MARGHERITA LIGURE

By Train: The bar/café (at the end of track 1) stores bags (small fee) and sells bus, train, and sightseeing-boat tickets. Bus #782 to Portofino leaves from in front of the station.

To get from the station to the city center, take the stairs marked *Mare* (sea) down to the harbor; or turn right and head more gently down Via Roma, which leads to the town center, the TI, the start of my town walk, and recommended hotels (about 10 minutes away on foot).

By Car: Ask your hotelier about parking; some have free spots. Otherwise, try a private pay lot such as the Garage Europa *autopark* next to the post office (Via Roma 38). An hourly pay-and-display lot is by the harbor, in front of the fish market. Parking is generally free where there are white lines (though there may be a time limit); blue lines mean you pay.

HELPFUL HINTS

Market: A market sets up on Fridays on Corso Matteotti (8:00-13:00).

Laundry: There's none in town.

Bike Rental: City and ebikes are available to rent by the day from **Ciclomania**, which puts together guided day trips to nearby destinations, too (Mon-Sat 8:30-12:30 & 15:30-19:00, closed

Sun, Via Luigi Bozzo 22, +39 0185 283 530, www.ciclomania-liguria.it, Mimmo).

Scooter Rental: Head to **GM Rent,** which also has little Smart cars in its fleet (daily 9:00-13:00 & 15:00-19:00, Via XXV Aprile 11, +39 329 406 6274, www.gmrent.it, Francesco).

Taxi: Taxis wait outside the train station and TI and charge €15 for a ride anywhere in town, €25 to Paraggi beach, and €35 to Portofino (+39 0185 286 508).

Driver: Helpful taxi driver **Alessandro,** who has both cars and minivans, offers airport transfers to Genoa, Milan, Florence, and Nice. He is also available for local excursions, including day trips to the Cinque Terre (+39 338 860 2349, www.alessandrotaxi.com, alessandrotaxi@yahoo.it).

Santa Margherita Ligure Walk

Get your bearings with this self-guided walk, starting on Piazza Caprera, the square facing the exuberant Baroque facade of the Basilica of Santa Margherita.

Basilica of Santa Margherita

The town's main church is textbook Italian Baroque (free, daily 7:30-12:00 & 15:00-18:30). Its 18th-century facade hides a 17th-century interior slathered with art and dripping with chandeliers. The altar is typical of 17th-century Ligurian altars—shaped like a boat, with lots of shelf space for candles, flowers, and relics. Its centerpiece is a much-venerated statue of Our Lady of the Rose that's adorned this altar since 1756.

Baroque is theater...and this altar is stagecraft. After the Vatican II decrees of the 1960s, priests began to face their flocks instead of the old altars. For this reason, all over the Catholic world, modern tables serving as post-Vatican II altars stand in front of earlier altars, like the one here, that are no longer the center of attention during Mass.

Wander the church and its chapels, noticing the inlaid-marble floors and sparkling glass chandeliers. As you marvel at the richness, remember that the region's aristocrats amassed wealth from trade from the 11th to the 15th century. When Constantinople fell to the Turks in 1453, free trade in the Mediterranean stopped, and Genovese traders became bankers—making even more money. A popular saying of the day was, "Silver is born in America, lives

Santa Margherita Ligure

Accommodations
- ❶ To Villa Anita
- ❷ Hotel Laurin
- ❸ Ma Hotel
- ❹ Hotel Jolanda
- ❺ Hotel Tigullio et de Milan
- ❻ Hotel Sant'Andrea
- ❼ Sabini Rentals
- ❽ Albergo Annabella

Eateries & Other
- ❾ Angolo 48
- ❿ Vineria Machiavello
- ⓫ Da Pezzi
- ⓬ La Cambusa
- ⓭ Il Vernissage Lounge Bar
- ⓮ Pizzeria il Delfino
- ⓯ Pizzeria Cavaliere
- ⓰ Simonetti Gelateria
- ⓱ Gelateria Centrale
- ⓲ Seghezzo Grocery
- ⓳ Supermarket
- ⓴ Fruttivendolo "Milanese"
- ㉑ Bike Rental
- ㉒ Scooter & Smart Car Rental

RIVIERA TOWNS

in Spain, and dies in Genoa." Bankers here served Spain's 17th-century royalty and aristocracy, and their accrued wealth paid for the art you see here.

Piazza Caprera

Each day this square hosts a few farmers selling their produce. On the corner of Via Cavour, just next to the basilica, don't miss

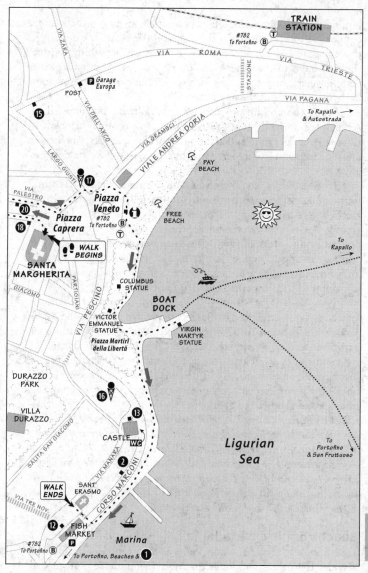

Seghezzo, a venerable luxury grocery store that's a feast for the eyes. If you don't go in, at least admire the window displays.

• *Now side-trip up the town's main corridor of retail commerce, Via Palestro and Via Cavour. You'll go two blocks up to Piazza Mazzini and back.*

Main Shopping Streets

Via Cavour and Via Palestro are parallel streets divided by very tall, narrow buildings. As you head up Via Cavour (on the left, by Seghezzo grocery) check out the shops on the right: The buildings that separate Via Cavour from Via Palestro are so skinny you see right through to the other side. The mix of fine boutiques, wine bars, jewelers, and casual restaurants hints at the elite—but not flashy—ambience of the town.

Study the building facades as you walk. It's not unusual to see painted garlands gently hanging below a roofline or colorful ribbons over doorways and arches. Like a blank canvas, the houses are bedecked and embroidered in attractive styles. No two look just alike.

In two blocks, you'll emerge onto a square, Piazza Mazzini, with enough elbow room to study the pastel house fronts. These facades were painted and decorated in the characteristic Ligurian trompe-l'oeil style from the turn of the last century. Every building presents some sort of illusion—the decorators went so far as to add painted-on upper windows, shutters, and window frames. Ligurians were practical: It was much less expensive to hire a painter than a sculptor to add decorative detail to these houses.

Now do a U-turn onto Via Palestro to return to where we started (staying straight past the recommended **Angolo 48** restaurant on the corner). At #34 (on the left), you'll pass a traditional *panificio* (bakery) where you can say, *"Vorrei un etto di focaccia"* to treat yourself to about a quarter-pound of the region's famed bread. Just beyond, on the right at #13, **Fruttivendolo "Milanese"** is just one of the many greengrocers in town selling an array of tempting produce and glass-jarred delicacies.

• *Back on Piazza Caprera, turn left and walk away from the church one block to busy Largo Antonio Giusti. Next to the cinema (across the street), a penguin marks the recommended* **Gelateria Centrale.** *Head right to Piazza Vittorio Veneto, with its busy roundabout and little park on the harbor. In the park facing the roundabout you'll find the TI (which sells bus tickets) and a bus stop for Portofino. Use the crosswalks to negotiate the busy intersection and reach the promenade.*

Beachfront Promenade

Take a look to the left, along Viale Andrea Doria. The sidewalk is wider than the street, reflecting how visitors have promenaded here, under pastel facades, for more than a century. Now turn right and walk into the waterfront park.

At the midpoint of the park is a Christopher Columbus statue. He was born "Cristoforo Colombo" in 1451 in Genoa, near here, and first sailed on Genovese boats along this Ligurian coast. Next comes a statue of King Victor Emmanuel II, always ready to brandish his sword and create Italy.

• *Head out on the little pier with the white statue facing out to sea.*

View from the Pier

From here, standing with the "Santa Margherita Virgin Martyr" statue, you can take in all of Santa Margherita Ligure—from the villas dotting the hills, to the castle built in the 16th century to defend against pirates, to the exclusive hotels. Tourist boats to Portofino, the Cinque Terre, and beyond depart from this pier.

• *Continue along the waterfront on Corso Marconi.*

Harbor and Fish Market

On the right, notice the trendy, recommended **Il Vernissage Lounge Bar** with tables up at the base of the castle (with WCs down below). Continuing around the corner from the castle (closed to visitors), walk along the harbor. The region's largest fishing fleet—20 boats—ties up here. The fishing industry survives, dragnetting octopus, shrimp, and miscellaneous "blue fish." (Anchovies are no longer fished from here but from nearby Sestri Levante.) The **fish market** (Mercato del Pesca, across the street, inside the rust-colored building with arches and columns) wiggles weekdays from about 16:00 until 20:00 or so—depending on who's catching what and when. It's a cool scene as fishermen take bins of freshly caught fish directly to waiting customers.

• *Climb the narrow brick stairs just to the right of the fish market to a delightful little square. Find the characteristic, black-and-white pebble mosaic and relax on the benches to enjoy harbor views. Facing the square is the little...*

Oratory of Sant'Erasmo

This pastel-hued building is named for St. Erasmus, the protector of sailors, as indicated by the stone-mosaic medallion of a ship decorating the little plaza in front. This building is an "oratory," where a brotherhood of faithful men who did anonymous good deeds congregated and worshipped. While rarely open, do check. The interior is decorated with ships and paintings of storms that local seafarers survived—thanks to St. Erasmus. The huge crosses standing in the nave are carried through town on special religious holidays.

• *Your walk is over. For a little extra exercise to see a pleasant park, climb the long stairs from here up to the Church of San Giacomo (with an interior similar to the Basilica of Santa Margherita) and Durazzo Park.*

Sights in Santa Margherita Ligure

In addition to the sights listed here, consider a side-trip to one of Italy's most beautiful and famous little Mediterranean resorts, Portofino (see page 444). It's just a couple miles down the coast and easy to visit from Santa Margherita Ligure.

RIVIERA TOWNS

Durazzo Park (Parco di Villa Durazzo)

This park is a delight, with a breezy café (seasonal), a carefully coiffed Italian garden, and an intentionally wild "English garden" below (free, daily 9:00-19:00, July-Aug until 20:00, closes earlier off-season, WC near café). The Italian garden is famous for its varied collection of palm trees and an extensive collection of camellias. It's OK to feed the large turtles in the central pond (they like bits of fish or meat).

The park is dominated by **Villa Durazzo.** It's not worth touring for most, but take the time to admire its remarkable pebble courtyard, carpeted in a fleur-de-lis pattern of white and gray stone—a Ligurian specialty (€5.50 to enter and view its Murano glass chandeliers and stucco and majolica decor, open daily 9:30-13:00 & 14:00-18:00, concerts held here in summer, www.villadurazzo.it).

Beaches (Spiagge)

The handiest free beaches are just below the train station toward the boat dock. But the best beaches are on the road to Portofino.

These beaches are a 20-minute walk from downtown, or you can take bus #782 from the train station or from in front of the TI at Piazza Veneto. For locations, see the map on page 445.

The beach on the south side of **Grand Hotel Miramare** offers a relaxing experience and is good for kids. Also nice is **Minaglia,** with rentable sunbeds and kayaks. My favorite, **Giò e Rino** (just before the Covo di Nord Est night club), has sunbeds for rent and a fun, youthful crowd.

Paraggi, a small, sandy beach halfway to Portofino (and an easy stop on the bus #782 route), is better than any of the close-in Santa Margherita Ligure beaches, but it's pricey (as much as €60/day in July and Aug)—and it can be packed with sun worshippers from Portofino (where there's no beach—only rocks). There's more than one *bagni* establishment here, so choose the one that most appeals. Off-season, the entire beach is all yours and free of charge. A narrow patch of sand smack-dab in the middle of Paraggi beach is free year-round.

Fishing

To combine the art of fishing with the beauty of the Portofino promontory from the water, arrange a trip with Luca. His boat is equipped for *tonnara di Camogli:* the region's old tuna-fishing trap system (€110/2 people or €180/4 people for 4 hours, 4 peo-

Rise of a Resort: The History of Santa Margherita Ligure

This town, like the entire region (from the border of France to La Spezia), was once ruled by the Republic of Genoa. In the 16th century, when Arab pirates from North Africa plagued the entire coastal area, Genoa built castles in the towns and lookout towers in the neighboring hills.

At the time, Santa Margherita Ligure was two bickering towns—each with its own bay. In 1800, Napoleon came along, took over the Republic of Genoa, and turned the rival towns into one city—naming it Porto Napoleone. When Napoleon fell in 1815, the town stayed united and took the name of the patron saint of its leading church, Santa Margherita.

In 1850, residents set to work creating a Riviera resort. They imported palm trees from North Africa and paved a fine beach promenade. Santa Margherita Ligure (and the surrounding area) was studded with fancy villas built by the aristocracy of Genoa. English, Russian, and German aristocrats discovered the town in the 19th century. Mass tourism only hit in the last generation. Even with the increased crowds, the town decided to stay chic and kept huge developments out. Its neighbor, Rapallo, chose the extreme opposite—giving the Italian language a new word for uncontrolled growth ruining a once-cute town: *rapallizzazione*.

ple max; trip includes light snacks, snorkel masks, and stops for snorkeling and swimming; morning, afternoon, and night trips can be arranged, +39 340 242 6483, www.portofinofishing.com, portofinofishing@gmail.com).

Sleeping in Santa Margherita Ligure

Except for Villa Anita, all the hotels listed here are within a 10-minute walk of the train station.

$$$$ Villa Anita is an elegant-yet-homey family hotel run by Daniela and her son, Sandro. They rent 12 tidy rooms—nearly all with terraces—overlooking a peaceful residential neighborhood a five-minute uphill walk from the seaside boulevard (air-con, family rooms, playground, small gym, small heated pool and sauna, loaner bikes, scooter and boat rentals, pay parking, closed in winter, Viale Minerva 25, +39 0185 286 543, www.hotelvillaanita.com, info@ hotelvillaanita.com).

$$$$ Hotel Laurin, nestled up against castle ruins, offers 44 slick, modern, and pricey rooms looking onto the sea. All double rooms face the harbor and have terraces; on the rooftop sundeck, there's a small pool (RS%, air-con, elevator, gym, limited pay parking—request when you reserve, just past the castle at Corso Marconi 3, +39 0185 289 971, www.laurinhotel.it, info@laurinhotel.it, Tiziana).

$$$ Ma Hotel is a crystal-chandelier-classy boutique hotel with a fresh, modern flair. Although it sits along a busy street, its 11 stylish and spacious rooms are at the back of the building (air-con, patio, free minibar, Via XXV Aprile 18, +39 0185 280 224, www.mahotel.it, info@mahotel.it, Matteo).

$$$ Pastine Hotels is a small chain of three well-run hotels that combine solid service, sumptuous public spaces, and pleasant rooms. The two main branches are around the corner from each other, an easy walk from the station: **Hotel Jolanda** has a lavish lobby and regal colors, and its 49 pleasant rooms have soothing decor (RS%, air-con, elevator, free use of small weight room and hot tub, pay dry sauna, valet parking, Via Luisito Costa 6, +39 0185 287 512, www.hoteljolanda.it, info@hoteljolanda.it); **Hotel Tigullio et de Milan** is smaller and tidier, with 36 updated rooms. The superior rooms are especially nice, but even most standard doubles come with a terrace—specify when you book. The rooftop sun terrace offers sunbeds, a bar, and hot tub in the summer (RS%, air-con, elevator, valet parking, Via Rainusso 3, +39 0185 287 455, www.hoteltigullio.eu, info@hoteltigullio.eu). The newest branch, the boutique-like **Hotel Sant'Andrea,** has 11 rooms just above Piazza Mazzini, with a patio and whirlpool for guests (RS%, air-con, valet parking, Via Belvedere 10, +39 0185 293 487, www.hotelsantandrea.net, info@hotelsantandrea.net).

$$ Sabini Rentals, in a bland but central residential zone, offers three straightforward rooms and one apartment with a tiny corner kitchen (RS%, family rooms, 2-night minimum, cash only, breakfast on request, laundry service, Via Belvedere 31, +39 338 902 7582, www.sabinirentals.com, info@sabinirentals.com, Cristina and Giancarlo).

$ Albergo Annabella has 11 well-kept rooms, six of which are old-style budget throwbacks with sinks in the room and shared bath (no breakfast, air-con, Via Costasecca 10, +39 0185 286 531, www.albergoannabella.it, info@albergoannabella.it, Annabella speaks just enough English).

Eating in Santa Margherita Ligure

In the City Center

$$$ Angolo 48, run by savvy Elisa and Valentina, serves well-presented and reasonably priced Genovese and Ligurian dishes. This cozy locale is popular: Either arrive right when they open or make a reservation. There's great seating both on the square and inside. Try their handmade *pansotti* in walnut sauce (lunch Sat-Sun only 12:00-13:45, dinner Tue-Sun 18:30-22:00, closed Mon, Via Palestro 48, +39 0185 286 650).

$$ Vineria Machiavello feels more urban Tuscan than seaside Ligurian. This well-stocked *enoteca* (wine shop) offers tastings and full bottles, but also serves a short menu of well-priced dishes at a few humble tables tucked between the wine racks (Wed-Mon 10:00-14:00 & 17:30-24:00, closed Tue, in the heart of the pedestrian zone at Via Cavour 17, +39 0185 286 122).

$ Da Pezzi, with a cheap cafeteria-style atmosphere, is packed with locals at midday and at night. They're standing at the bar munching *farinata* (crêpes made from chickpeas, available Oct-May 18:00-20:00) or enjoying pesto and fresh fish in the dining room. Consider the deli counter with its Genovese picnic ingredients (Sun-Fri 10:00-14:00 & 18:00-21:00, table service after 12:00 and 18:15, closed Sat, Via Cavour 21, +39 0185 285 303, Giancarlo and Giobatta).

On the Waterfront

All along the harbor side of Via Tommaso Bottaro, south of the marina, you'll find restaurants, pizzerias, and bars serving food with a nautical view.

$$$ La Cambusa, perched above the fish market, is popular for its seafood. While the food is forgettable, the view from its harborside terrace is not. In cooler weather, the terrace is covered and heated. Diners receive a free glass of *sciacchetrà* (dessert wine) and biscotti with this book (daily 12:00-15:00 & 19:00-23:00 except closed Thu Oct-June, Via Tommaso Bottaro 1, +39 0185 287 410).

At **$$ Il Vernissage Lounge Bar,** you can nurse your drink with a million-dollar view. There are 20 wines by the glass, plus cocktails and *spritzes,* which come with a nice plate of finger food (daily 18:00-late, Sun from 11:00, Salita al Castello 8, +39 349 220 5846, Sandro).

Budget Options

$$ Pizzeria il Delfino serves thin, big, wood-fired pizzas in a rustic, fun local scene, with a few quiet tables outside and tight inside seating under nautical bric-a-brac (cash only, daily 12:00-15:00 & 18:00-23:00 except closed Tue lunch, Via Cavour 29, +39 0185 286 488). For cheaper takeout pizza and kebabs, head for **Pizzeria Cavaliere,** on the way to the station (open daily, Via Roma 16).

Gelato: Along the waterfront, try **Simonetti**—especially their chocolate-truffle *tartufato* (under the castle at Piazza Martiri della Libertà 48). **Gelateria Centrale,** just off Piazza Veneto near the cinema, serves up *pinguino* (penguin) cones, your choice of gelato dipped in chocolate (Largo Antonio Giusti 14).

Groceries: Classy **Seghezzo** is a gorgeous luxury grocery, deli, and wine shop. It's great for a meal to go—ask them to *riscaldare* (heat up) their white *lasagne al pesto* or dish up their special *carpaccio di polpo*—thinly sliced octopus (Thu-Tue 7:30-13:00 & 15:30-20:00, closed Wed off-season, near the church on Via Cavour, +39 0185 287 172, www.seghezzo.com). Cheaper and less romantic, the **Co-op** grocery is a fine place to stock up (daily 8:00-13:30 & 15:30-19:30 except Sun from 8:30, Corso Giacomo Matteotti 9).

Santa Margherita Ligure Connections

To reach the **Cinque Terre** towns (beyond Monterosso), you'll usually have to change in Sestri Levante, Levanto, or Monterosso.

From Santa Margherita Ligure by Train to: Sestri Levante (2/hour, 20-25 minutes), **Monterosso** (at least hourly, 50-60 minutes, often with a change in Sestri Levante), **La Spezia** (nearly hourly direct, 55-65 minutes), **Pisa** (5/day direct, 2 hours, more with transfer), **Florence** (4 hours, transfer in La Spezia or Pisa), **Milan** (9/day direct, 2 hours, more with transfer in Genoa), **Ventimiglia**/French border (almost hourly, 3.5 hours, change in Genoa), **Venice** (5-7 hours, 1-2 changes).

By Boat to the Cinque Terre: Tour boats make various trips to Vernazza, Porto Venere, and other ports nearly every day. Pick up a schedule of departures and excursion options from the TI, visit the ticket shack on the dock, call +39 0185 284 670, or check www.traghettiportofino.it.

Portofino

Santa Margherita Ligure, with its aristocratic architecture, hints at old wealth. But nearby Portofino (por-toh-FEE-noh; pop. 500)—

with its sleek jewelry shops, art galleries, and haute couture boutiques filling a humble village shell—has the sheen of new money. It's the kind of place where the sailing masts are taller than the houses and church steeples. But the picture-perfect harbor, classic Italian architecture, and wooded peninsula turn posh Portofino into an appealing destination. Just a couple of miles down the coast, it's a fun, easy day trip from Santa Margherita Ligure.

Planning Your Time: In summer, my favorite Portofino plan is to visit in the late afternoon. Leave Santa Margherita Ligure by bus at about 16:30, get off at Paraggi beach, and hike 30 minutes over the bluff into Portofino. Explore the town, splurge for a drink on the harborfront, or get a takeout fruity sundae (*paciugo;* pah-CHOO-goh) and sit by the water. Then return by bus to Santa Margherita Ligure for dinner (confirm late departures). If you plan to do longer hikes around Portofino, come earlier in the day.

Tourist Information: The Portofino TI is tucked under an arch between the harbor and the bus stop (Wed-Mon 10:00-13:00 & 14:00-18:00, closed Tue, Via Roma 35, +39 0185 215 037, www. comune.portofino.genova.it).

GETTING TO PORTOFINO

You can reach Portofino from Santa Margherita Ligure by bus or boat, or on foot. For a fun combination, go one way by bus and on foot from Paraggi, and the other way by boat. (I wouldn't suggest biking it, because of the blind corners.)

By Bus: Catch bus #782 from Santa Margherita Ligure's train station, TI, or bus stops along the harbor (€3 one-way or €5 round-trip, €1 more if bought from driver, 4/hour, 20 minutes, www.amt. genova.it). Buy tickets at the train station bar, the green ticket machine outside the TI, or any newsstand, tobacco shop, or shop that displays a *Biglietti Bus* sign. If you're at the TI, grab a bus schedule to plan your return (last bus around 24:00 in summer).

By Taxi: A taxi ride from Santa Margherita Ligure costs around €35 to Portofino or €25 to Paraggi beach (more at night). Taxi stands in Santa Margherita Ligure are at the train station and at the curb in front of the TI.

By Boat: The boat makes the 15-minute trip with more class and scenery—and without the traffic jams. The dock in Santa Margherita Ligure juts out from the waterfront park at Piazza Martiri della Libertà, near the TI (€8 one-way, €14 round-trip; hourly departures May-Sept daily 10:15-16:15, fewer in April and Oct, no boats off-season; purchase tickets at the dock, +39 0185 284 670, www.traghettiportofino.it).

If you arrive in Portofino by boat but will be busing back, follow the narrow lanes up from the harbor to the bus stop in Piazza della Libertà (ticket machine and tobacco store there sell tickets).

On Foot: To hike from Santa Margherita Ligure to Portofino, you have two options: You can follow the sidewalk along (and sometimes hanging over) the sea (1 hour, 2.5 miles)—although traffic can be noisy, and in places, the footpath disappears. Or, if you're hardy and ambitious, you can take a quieter two-hour hike by leaving Santa Margherita Ligure at Via Maragliano, then following the Ligurian-symbol trail markers (keep a close eye out for red-and-white stripes). This hike takes you high into the hills. Keep left after Cappelletta delle Gave. Several blocks past a castle, you'll drop down into Paraggi beach, where you'll take the Portofino trail (described next) the rest of the way.

Bus-and-Hike Option: For a short—but rewarding—30-minute hike into Portofino, ride bus #782 from Santa Margherita Ligure to Paraggi beach (tell the driver you want to get off there—you can't miss the inlet bay with a sandy beach). At the Portofino end of the beach, look for the *Parco di Portofino* sign to find the steps that begin the hilly, paved trail marked *Pedonale per Portofino* high above the road. There's a fair amount of up and down, but it's all well-paved and scenic. After Paraggi, you'll curl around another bay—with the famously top-end Hotel Splendido hovering on the hill above—before snaking your way to Portofino (you'll pop out at a yellow-and-gray church labeled *Divo Martino*).

Off-season, you can easily **reverse the bus-and-hike option**—by hiking from Portofino to Paraggi (taking the *Pedonale per Paraggi* trail near the Divo Martino church), then busing from the beach to Santa Margherita Ligure—but this works only when crowds are light; on busy days, return buses fill up in Portofino and won't stop in Paraggi.

Sights in Portofino

▲▲Self-Guided Visual Tour from the Harbor

Stand or sit on the angled boat launch where Piazza Martiri dell'Olivetta meets the harbor (or nurse an overpriced cocktail at the nearby café tables) and get oriented to Portofino. It's one of the Mediterranean's most beautiful and famous little resorts.

Scanning the narrow pastel houses around the harbor, notice the painted-on details. You may also see laundry hanging out to dry—a surprising reminder that, while Ferragamo and Prada may reside on street level, actual villagers still live upstairs.

Now look out to the well-protected natural harbor—which has held substantial strategic value ever since the Romans first founded a town here. Since then, it has been appreciated by everyone from Napoleon to the Nazis.

A new flock of fans arrived in the 1950s, when *National Geographic* ran a beautiful article on the idyllic port. Locals claim that's when the Hollywood elite took note. Liz Taylor and Richard Burton came here annually (as did Liz Taylor and Eddie Fisher). During one famous party, Rex Harrison dropped his Oscar into the bay (it was recovered). Ava Gardner came down from her villa each evening for a drink—sporting her famous fur coat. Greta Garbo loved to swim naked in the harbor, not knowing (or caring) that half the town was watching. Truman Capote also called Portofino home. But VIPs were also here a century earlier. Friedrich Nietzsche famously wrote about philosophizing with the mythical prophet Zarathustra on the path between Portofino and Santa Margherita Ligure.

Today, the celebrity cachet lives on. When you tell locals you're going to Portofino, they say, "Maybe you'll see George and Amal Clooney!" Count the yachts and the tall-masted sailboats and imagine who might be on them.

Now scan the panorama on the hillside in front of you. On the left is **Castello Brown,** an actual medieval castle built by the Genovese in the 16th century to protect this strategic harbor. It later became a private mansion, and today it is primarily an event space featuring lush gardens and sweeping viewpoints (€5; daily July-Aug 10:00-20:00, March-June until 19:00, shorter hours in fall and winter, +39 375 791 8926, www.castellobrown.com).

Panning right, you'll see the **Church and Castle of San Giorgio,** with its popular two-way viewpoint terrace, looking down over the port and out over the ocean. This is an easy option for a picnic with grand views. Boats back to Portofino, or on to the San Fruttuoso Abbey, depart from the harbor below this church. The Museo del Parco (described next) is also along this embankment.

Now look back toward town. A tidy grid of narrow cobbled

RIVIERA TOWNS

streets angles gently uphill to the modern part of town, around Piazza della Libertà (with bus stop and taxi stand). These streets—where budget takeaway eateries and grocery stores are mixed in with swanky shops—are a good place to hunt for picnic fare. Up on the right is the striped church of San Martino, marking the well-manicured, enjoyable 30-minute trail to Paraggi beach.

Museo del Parco

For an artsy break, walk around the harbor to the right, where you can stroll around a park littered with 148 contemporary sculptures by mostly Italian artists, including a few top names (€5, open Wed-Mon 10:00-13:30 & 15:00-20:00 in summer; closed Tue, off-season, and in bad weather).

Hikes

The TIs in Portofino and Santa Margherita Ligure can outline your options. For even more detail, look at ParcoPortofino.com, a helpful website with sample itineraries. Here are several options easily doable from Portofino itself.

Lighthouse Hike: A paved stone path winds up and down

to the lighthouse *(faro)* at the scenic point beyond the Church and Castle of San Giorgio. Start your climb on little Salita San Giorgio—it's tucked between the Delfino and Tripoli restaurants on the harborfront. Spend a few minutes enjoying the views on the church terrace (and if it's open, duck into the flower-bedecked cemetery behind the church). Rejoin the path signed *al Faro* to continue up. Walls and hedges block views at some points, but in the end, you'll be rewarded with the open sea—and a lounge/bar (open May-Sept, 25-minute walk). Consider popping into the medieval Castello Brown on the way up or down.

Paraggi Beach Hike: You can stroll the hilly pedestrian promenade through the trees from Portofino to Paraggi beach—
if you're lucky, you might see a wild boar en route (30 minutes, path starts to the right of striped Divo Martino church just above the harborfront piazza, and ends at ritzy Paraggi beach, where bus #782 stops on its way back to Santa Margherita Ligure—though in peak season, the bus may be full and won't stop). For more details see "Bike-and-Hike Option" under "Getting to Portofino," earlier.

San Fruttuoso Hike: Another option is to hike out to San Fruttuoso, with its abbey and underwater Christ statue—see next.

NEAR PORTOFINO
San Fruttuoso

Farther out on the peninsula, this tiny settlement around a sheltered cove is accessible only by foot or boat. It's a lazy place to relax on a nice day: You'll find a small pebbly beach (half private, half free), a handful of restaurants, hiking trails, and a couple of offbeat sights. Aside from a caretaker, no one actually lives here.

A **Benedictine abbey** at the water's edge was established at San Fruttuoso in the 10th century and abandoned in the 15th century. The well-preserved building has been turned into a museum. Medievalists and archeologists will enjoy its exhibits, which are well-described in English. You'll see the tiny cloister, tombs of the Doria family (longtime patrons of the abbey), and a simple church (€8; June-mid-Sept 10:00-17:45, shorter hours off-season and closed Mon in winter; +39 0185 772 703, www.abbaziadisanfruttuoso.it).

Aside from the abbey, many are drawn here to see the statue of **Christ of the Abyss** *(Cristo degli Abissi)*—60 feet underwater, offshore from the abbey, in a specially protected marine area. The

RIVIERA TOWNS

statue was placed there in 1954 for the divine protection of the region's divers. In summer, for a few euros, boats on the beach can take you out to a spot above the statue, where you can look down to just barely see the arms of Jesus-outstretched, reaching upward. Some people bring goggles and dive in for a better view. A copy of the statue is in the abbey church (no entry fee required).

The private section of the **beach** has sunbeds (€17/day), showers, and towel and kayak rentals. It can fill up in summer (reserve at +39 328 450 5521 or email bagnisanfruttuoso@gmail.it; www.bagnisanfruttuoso.it).

Getting There by Boat: The same boats that link Santa Margherita Ligure and Portofino continue on another 30 minutes to San Fruttuoso (€12.50 one-way, €19 round-trip from Santa Margherita Ligure, allows stop at Portofino). A different company's boats link San Fruttuoso to Camogli, north of the peninsula (€10, +39 0185 772 091, schedule at www.golfoparadiso.it). From Camogli, it's easy to take the train back to Santa Margherita Ligure.

Getting There by Foot: The three-mile trail from Portofino to San Fruttuoso is steep at the beginning and end, rising about 1,000 feet (allow up to 2.5 hours—pick up the trailhead at the inland-most point of Portofino town, past Piazza della Libertà and the *carabinieri* station).

Portofino Peninsula Grand Tour

For a one-day grand tour of the Portofino peninsula, enthusiastic walkers can follow this plan: Take an early boat or bus from Santa Margherita Ligure to Portofino, have a quick look at the town, and then hike 2.5 hours to San Fruttuoso. Reserve a spot in advance at the private beach (bring your swimsuit). You'll have the rest of the afternoon to enjoy the beach, visit the abbey, eat, and perhaps see the *Cristo*. To finish your tour, take the 30-minute ferry to Camogli (last boat at 18:00 in June, 19:00 in July/Aug, www.golfoparadiso.it) where you can catch a train for the short ride back to Santa Margherita Ligure (2/hour, 5 minutes, station is 10 minutes on foot from the ferry port). Confirm these times locally before starting out.

EATING IN PORTOFINO

Bring a picnic if you want to eat affordably in this beautiful village. Fancy restaurants ring the harbor, but the quality often doesn't match the high prices. I'd rather dine in Santa Margherita Ligure. There are a few glitzy cafés and bakeries in the back streets, but you won't find any bargains.

If you do eat in Portofino, **$$$$ Ristorante lo Stella,** just a few steps from the boat dock, has well-prepared dishes and portholes in the bathrooms (+39 0185 269 007). **$$$$ Taverna del**

Marinaio, across the harbor, has a prime location to soak up the last of the day's sun, tables under arcades, and a small, cozy, classy interior (+39 0185 269 103). And **$$$$ Puny,** at the top of the harborfront square, is a famous splurge (reserve ahead, +39 0185 269 037, https://punyportofino.it). There are several *gelaterie*, including **Calata 32,** opposite the boat dock.

South of the Cinque Terre

South of the Cinque Terre is the nothing-special city of La Spezia, a handy transit hub with excellent train connections. And near La Spezia is a gem—the resort town of Porto Venere, worthy of a day trip from the Cinque Terre (by direct boat, or by train and bus via La Spezia).

Porto Venere

The enchanting village of Porto Venere (POR-toh VEH-neh-reh) hides just around the bay from La Spezia. Comparably scenic to the Cinque Terre towns—but with a bit of glitz and a darker history—Porto Venere clings to a rocky, fortress-crowned promontory. A rainbow of tall, skinny pastel facades rises from its inviting harborfront promenade.

Little Porto Venere is light on sights, but it's a breeze to reach by boat from the Cinque Terre and fun to explore: The higher you go, the better the views. Rather than the open sea, Porto Venere faces the beautiful Gulf of La Spezia—more romantically known as the Gulf of Poets—where Lord Byron was said to have gone for a hardy swim despite rough seas and local warnings to the contrary. (He survived...at least for a little while longer.) Scanning the bay, you'll see the outskirts of muscular La Spezia, the often-snow-covered peaks of the Apuan Alps, the resort town of Lerici, and—across a narrow strait—the rugged island of Palmaria.

GETTING TO PORTO VENERE

By Boat: Porto Venere is an easy day trip from the Cinque Terre towns by **boat** (late April-mid-Oct, 1.5 hours from Monterosso,

€20 one-way, €37 day pass allows hopping on and off, +39 0187 732 987, see schedule at www.navigazionegolfodeipoeti.it).

By Train and Bus: The budget route to Porto Venere is by train to La Spezia and then by city **bus #P or #11 to Porto Venere.** The bus stop closest to the La Spezia Centrale train station is about a 15-minute walk away, on Via Nicolo Fieschi, the extension of Viale Garibaldi (see the "La Spezia" map in the next section for location—stops are marked "Fermata ATC"; 2/hour, 30 minutes, €2.50 each way; buy ticket at tobacco shop or newsstand in train station; www.atcesercizio.it). You could take the boat one way and the bus back (or vice versa), giving you a chance to explore La Spezia as well.

By Car: For **drivers,** parking is challenging. In peak season, shuttle buses connect the parking lot just outside Porto Venere to the harborside square. Otherwise, test your luck with the pay spots on the seaside.

VISITING PORTO VENERE

Tourist Information: The TI (Pro Loco Porto Venere) fills an old guard tower at the top of the main square (daily 10:00-12:00, also

Thu-Sun 15:00-17:00, shorter hours off-season, Piazza Bastreri 7, +39 0187 790 691, www.portovenere.com).

The town is essentially two streets deep: the harborfront promenade and the main street (Via Capellini), a block uphill. A complete loop around Porto Venere includes both of these streets and a moderately steep hike up to the town's two main churches and fortress for the views. You can see everything in just a few hours; add more time for lunch or lingering.

Along the **harborfront,** seafood restaurants enjoy a Technicolor backdrop and boat captains try to talk you into a 40-minute excursion around Palmaria and two other nearby islands. But all the action is on **Via Capellini** (just through the big arch from the TI—or hike up any of the narrow stepped lanes from the harbor). Skinny and shaded, Via Capellini has a mix of restaurants, focaccia-and-pizza takeaway stands, local shops, and boutiques selling gourmet gifty edibles and gaudy beachwear.

At the west end of the promenade and Via Capellini, the town and its fortifications come to a point at the late-13th-century **Church of San Pietro,** with Gothic features and a black-and-white-striped interior typical of this region. Climb the stairs to the roof terrace for fine views in both directions (including the "Grotta Byron" sea cave).

More viewpoints line the walk from here up the stairs to the town's other big church, **San Lorenzo.** With a dark and brood-

ing Romanesque interior, this church—like much of Porto Venere—was built by the Genovese to establish a strategic foothold at the entrance to the bay in the 12th century.

From in front of the church, more steps lead up to the town's fortress, **Castello Doria.** A hulking shell, it's not worth the money to go inside, but a hike up to the terrace out front is rewarded with striking panoramas.

From the castle, head back into town; to make this walk a loop, bear left to follow the very steeply stepped lane that runs just inside the crenellated wall back down to the TI.

Hardy **hikers** enjoy the five-hour (or more) hike to Riomaggiore, the nearest Cinque Terre town. Get details on this and other hikes at the TI; for more on hiking the Cinque Terre, see page 345.

EATING IN PORTO VENERE

On the harbor, take your pick of views and menus (seafood/pizza) for a meal along "Restaurant Row" in a memorable setting next to colorful bobbing boats.

For better values and more variety, stroll one block inland to Via Capellini. For a sit-down meal along here, try **$$ Ristorante Portivene,** serving local dishes with modern flair at reasonable prices (reservations smart, closed Mon, at #94, +39 0187 792 722). Better yet, browse the fun selection of takeaway shops (selling pizza slices, bruschetta, focaccia, and top-notch deli items) to put together a picnic to enjoy by the port. **$ Anciùa** (at #40) assembles *panini* to order with interesting ingredients; they also have fresh fried anchovies and other Ligurian street food.

La Spezia

While it's the next train stop south of the fanciful Cinque Terre, the working city of La Spezia (lah SPEH-tsee-ah; pop. 93,000) feels like "reality Italy." Useful as a transit point, La Spezia is slim on sights and has no beaches, but its pleasant center is filled with Liberty-style buildings (Italian Art Nouveau). You'll change trains here if traveling between the Cinque Terre and points farther south in Italy, and you'll see at least a bit of La Spezia if you use the bus to daytrip to Porto Venere—or if you arrive on one of the big cruise ships that funnel groups into the Cinque Terre. Italians know La Spezia as their country's main naval base, and residents of the Cinque Terre come here to shop or visit the dentist.

ORIENTATION TO LA SPEZIA

Arrival in La Spezia: Get off at the La Spezia Centrale train station—not the suburban La Spezia Migliarina station, where some trains terminate. Along track 1 is a Cinque Terre **National Park information desk,** which sells park tickets (see page 345) and acts as a TI (daily 8:00-19:00, shorter hours off-season, www.parconazionale5terre.it). You'll also find an office selling tickets for the Cinque Terre boats, a tobacco store, and a newsstand (handy if you need a ticket for the bus to Porto Venere). The city TI is a 10-minute walk away.

For **drivers** who want to leave a car in La Spezia then head to the Cinque Terre by train, the easiest parking is under the train station, at the modern Park Centro Stazione (enter from Via Fiume or Via Paleocapa, €30/day, www.mobpark.eu). There are cheaper lots a bus ride away.

Baggage Storage: It's expensive, but day-trippers can store bags about 350 yards from the station—a three-minute walk—at the **Stow and Go** *deposito bagagli* at Via XX Settembre 209 (open

La Spezia

Eateries & Other
5 Antica Trattoria Sevieri
6 Locanda del Mercato & Avis Car Rental
7 All'Inferno dal 1905
8 La Pia Centenaria
9 Covered Market
10 Launderette & Baggage Storage
11 Porto Venere Bus Stop
12 Baggage Storage

Accommodations
1 Hotel Firenze e Continentale
2 Via Chiodo Luxury Rooms
3 Casa Danè (2)
4 L'Arca di Noè B&B

24/7, self-serve lockers in 3 sizes, €18/day). The **World Services** shop at Via Fiume 115 offers cheaper storage close to the station, but with more limited hours.

Laundry: The handy **Mezzora** self-service **launderette** is just steps from the train station, down the street from Stow and Go (daily 8:30-20:30, Sun from 9:00, Via Fiume 95).

Car Rental: You won't need a car in the Cinque Terre region, but you may want one before or after your visit. La Spezia is the most convenient place to pick up or drop off a car near the Cinque Terre. **Avis** is closest to the train station (10 minutes on foot, closed Sat-Sun, Via Fratelli Rosselli 76, +39 0187 770 270). Hertz and Europcar are located in Viale San Bartolomeo, a short taxi ride away.

VISITING LA SPEZIA

The city center is a 10-minute walk downhill from the station, and the waterfront is another 10 minutes beyond that. Leave the station, turn left, and walk a long downhill block (on Via Pietro Paleocapa) to the big roundabout (Piazza Saint Bon). A nice pedestrian street starts on the other side of the roundabout, first called **Via Fiume** and, lower down, **Via del Prione.** You can continue on this street all the way to the harborfront gardens.

On your way you'll pass the **TI** at Via del Prione 228 (daily 9:00-12:30 and 15:00-19:00, shorter hours off-season, +39 0187 026 152, http://www.myspezia.it/). The side streets leading off to the right are worth exploring, such as Via Fratelli Rosselli, which leads to recommended restaurants and La Spezia's atmospheric covered market. Next to the TI is the nearly deserted **Museo Amedeo Lia,** a grab bag of Italian art and archeology up to the 18th century, including some minor works by Venetian masters (€8, Tue-Sun 10:00-18:00, closed Mon, +39 0187-731-100, http://museolia.spezianet.it).

NEAR LA SPEZIA: CARRARA

Carrara, a 35-minute drive from La Spezia, is an easy stop for drivers connecting La Spezia and points south. It's home to the world's most famous marble quarries, where Michelangelo chose the marble for his masterpieces. Carrara's Marble Museum (Museo Civico del Marmo) traces the story of marble-cutting here from pre-Roman times until today (closed Mon, Viale XX Settembre 85, +39 0585 845 746).

SLEEPING IN LA SPEZIA

Stay in the Cinque Terre if you can. La Spezia is a functional home base if there's no room elsewhere or if you've got a car to park.

$$ Hotel Firenze e Continentale, 100 yards from the train station, is a big, good-value, nicely modernized hotel with 70 rooms and lofty common spaces (RS%—request by email, air-con, elevator, pay parking—reserve ahead, Via Pietro Paleocapa 7, +39 0187 713 210, www.hotelfirenzecontinentale.it, info@ hotelfirenzecontinentale.it).

$$ Via Chiodo Luxury Rooms, with nine elegant, bright white rooms on the second floor of a large downtown building, is a soothing retreat near the harbor and close to the public gardens—though if you're coming from the train station, you'll probably want a taxi (air-con, elevator, no parking, Via Chiodo 13, +39 0187 22 607, see "Via Chiodo Luxury Rooms" at www. costaestate.it, info@costaestate.it).

$$ Casa Danè offers 10 chic rooms with comfy linens and orange trees outside the door, plus 20 more rooms inside the train station, in former train conductor barracks. Some rooms overlook the tracks but good windows reduce the noise (RS%—use code "RICK2023," family rooms, air-con, Via Paleocapa 4, +39 338 535 3103, www.casadane.it, reception@casadane.it, Paolo).

$ L'Arca di Noè B&B, at the top of the pedestrian zone a five-minute walk from the station, has three bright, artsy, affordable rooms, all with private bath (air-con, homey communal kitchen, Via Fiume 39, mobile +39 320 485 2434, montialex74@gmail.com, Alessandra).

EATING IN LA SPEZIA

These eateries are on and around the pedestrian zone, within a 10-minute walk of the train station.

$$$ Antica Trattoria Sevieri is an elegant place across from the covered market, featuring fresh fish and superb seafood pastas and risotto. Alessandro, the chef/owner, will help you pick from the catch of the day and choose the cooking method (vegetarian and meat dishes too, Mon-Sat 12:00-15:00 & 19:00-24:00, closed Sun, Via della Canonica 13, +39 0187 751 1776).

$$ Locanda del Mercato has white tablecloths, formal service, and Ligurian specialties that you can savor inside or out (Wed-Mon 11:30-15:30 & 18:30-23:30, closed Tue, Via Fratelli Rosselli 88, +39 0187 732 651).

$ All'Inferno dal 1905, a small, busy, less-expensive restaurant with a laid-back atmosphere, serves traditional chickpea soup *(mesciua)*, linguine with mussels, and homemade pesto. Look for the red door in the narrow cross-street of Piazza Cavour (Mon-Sat 12:15-14:30 & 19:30-22:30, closed Sun, +39 0187 29458, Via L. Costa 3).

$ La Pia Centenaria draws local crowds to its takeaway counter for its specialty—*farinata* (€2-5 chickpea pancakes, eaten plain or with savory toppings). They also sell focaccia and pizza by the slice and have a separate, simple, sit-down section with table service (Mon-Sat 11:00-15:00 & 17:00-22:00, closed Sun, Via Magenta 12, +39 0187 739 999, www.lapia.it).

LA SPEZIA CONNECTIONS

Trains leave at least twice hourly for the **Cinque Terre towns** (direction: Levanto or Sestri Levante). A few express trains (headed to Genoa or Milan) stop only at Monterosso. Other connections from La Spezia include **Pisa** (at least hourly, 50-80 minutes), **Florence** (5/day direct, 2.5 hours, or nearly hourly with change in Pisa), **Rome** (8/day direct, 3-4 hours, more with change in Pisa), **Milan** (about every 2 hours direct, 3.5 hours), and **Venice** (6 hours, change in Milan or Florence).

It's also possible to go by **boat** to the Cinque Terre, Porto Venere, and outer islands from the La Spezia dock (www. navigazionegolfodeipoeti.it). The boat office in the train station sells tickets.

FLORENCE

Firenze

Florence, the home of the Renaissance and birthplace of our modern world, has the best Renaissance art in Europe. In a single day, you could look Michelangelo's *David* in the eyes, fall under the seductive sway of Botticelli's *Birth of Venus,* and climb the modern world's first dome, which still dominates the skyline.

Get your bearings with a Renaissance walk. Florentine art goes beyond paintings and statues—enjoy the food, fashion, and street markets. You can lick Italy's best gelato while enjoying some of Europe's best people-watching.

PLANNING YOUR TIME

Florence deserves at least one well-organized day: see the Accademia *(David),* tour the Uffizi Gallery (Renaissance art), visit the Duomo Museum (original bronze Baptistery doors) or the underrated Bargello (best statues), and do my "Renaissance Walk" (described later in this chapter; to avoid heat and crowds, do this walk in the morning or late afternoon). Art lovers will want to chisel out another day of their itinerary for the many other Florentine cultural treasures. Shoppers and ice-cream lovers may need to do the same.

Use my strategies to avoid wasting hours in long lines. This is especially true for peak season (April-Oct), holidays and weekends, and for the big attractions—the Uffizi, Accademia, and Duomo complex. Make reservations well in advance for the first two (see "Advance Reservations and Sightseeing Passes," page 482).

Florence Overview

Orientation to Florence

The highlights of Florence lie on the north bank of the Arno River. The main historical sights cluster around the venerable dome of the cathedral (Duomo). Everything is within a 20-minute walk of the train station, cathedral, or Ponte Vecchio (Old Bridge). The less famous but more characteristic Oltrarno area (south bank) is just over the bridge.

Though small, Florence is intense. Prepare for scorching summer heat, crowded narrow lanes and sidewalks, slick pickpockets, few WCs, steep prices, and long lines. But also prepare to celebrate the city that boldly led Europe out of the Middle Ages and into our humanistic modern world.

FLORENCE: A VERBAL MAP

For a big and touristy city, Florence (pop. 380,000) is remarkably compact and easy to navigate. Here's a neighborhood-by-neighborhood rundown:

Historic Core: The Duomo—with its iconic, towering dome—is the visual, geographical, and historical center of Florence. A 10-minute walk away is the Palazzo Vecchio (City Hall), with its skyscraping medieval spire. Connecting these two landmarks is the north-south pedestrian street called Via dei Calzai-uoli. This central axis—Duomo to the Palazzo Vecchio to the Arno River—is the spine for Florentine sightseeing and the route of my self-guided Renaissance Walk. To the west of this axis is a glitzy shopping zone, and to the east is a characteristic web of narrow lanes.

Accademia/San Lorenzo (North of the Duomo): From the Duomo, Via Cavour runs north, bisecting the neighborhood. To the east lie the Accademia and the Museum of San Marco. The western part clusters around the Basilica of San Lorenzo, with its Medici Chapels. The area near San Lorenzo teems with tourists: There are the vendor stalls of San Lorenzo Market, the lively Mercato Centrale, and many hotels and trattorias.

Train Station/Santa Maria Novella (West of the Duomo): The area near the train station and Church of Santa Maria Novella has inexpensive hotels and characteristic eateries. Closer to the river (near Palazzo Strozzi) is a posh shopping zone.

Santa Croce (East of the Duomo): A 10-minute walk east from the Palazzo Vecchio leads to the Church of Santa Croce. Along the way is the Bargello sculpture museum. This neighbor-hood is congested with tourists by day and students partying by night. But the area stretching north and west from Santa Croce is increasingly authentic and workaday, offering a glimpse at untour-isty Florence.

Oltrarno (South of the River): Literally the "Other Side of the Arno River," this neighborhood reveals a Florence from a time before tourism. Many artisans still have workshops here and open their doors to passing visitors. The Oltrarno starts just across Ponte Vecchio (jammed with tourists and tackiness) and stretches south to the giant Pitti Palace and surrounding gardens (Boboli and Bardini). To the west is the rough-but-bohemian Piazza di Santo Spirito (with its namesake church) and the lavishly frescoed Brancacci Chapel. To the east of Pitti, perched high on the hill, is Piazzale Michelangelo, with Florence's most popular viewpoint. Tucked between there and the river is the little San Niccolò neigh-borhood, with its lively bars and eateries.

TOURIST INFORMATION

The city TI's main branch is across the square from the **train sta-tion** (Mon-Sat 9:00-19:00, Sun until 14:00; at the back corner of the Church of Santa Maria Novella at Piazza della Stazione 4; +39 055 212 245, www.feelflorence.it). Museum hours in Florence are constantly changing. Check the TI's website or stop by and pick up a current timetable as you confirm your sightseeing plans.

A less crowded TI (covering both the city and the greater province of Florence) is a couple of blocks **north of the Duomo,**

Florence

See Heart of Florence detail map

PORTA AL PRATO TRAIN STN.

To Airport & A-1 Autostrada (Firenze Nord exit)

V. FRATELLI ROSSELLI

V. FRATELLI ROSSELLI

VIA IL PRATO

VIA DELLA SCALA

SAN JACOPO DI RIPOLI

EPISCOPALE AMERICANA DI ST. JAMES

CASA DI RIPOSO D. BEATA

VIA LUIGI ALAMANNI

PALAZZO DEGLI AFFARI

Piazza del Crocifisso

Piazza del Valfonda

Piazza Adua

CENACOLO DI FULIGNO

SANTA MARIA NOVELLA TRAIN STATION

WC

BUS STN.

#12

SANTA MARIA NOVELLA

VIA DELLA SCALA

VIA NAZIONALE

VIA FAENZA

PALAZZO DEI CARTELLONI

Piazza della Stazione

Piazza dell'Unità Italiana

PERFUMERY

VIA PALAZZUOLO

TEATRO COMUNALE

CORSO ITALIA

LUNGARNO AMERIGO VESPUCCI

SAN LUCIA SUL PRATO

OGNISSANTI

Piazza d'Ognissanti

V. PANZANI

VIA DEI BANCHI

Piazza di Santa Maria Novella

B

VIA DEL SOLE

VIA DEL FOSSI

RUCELLAI PALACE

STROZZI PALACE

VIA DEI TORNABUONI

Arno River

LUNG. SANTA ROSA

VIA PISANA

TABERNACLE

PORTA SANTA ROSA

PONTE AMERIGO VESPUCCI

L. AMERIGO VESPUCCI

BORGO OGNISSANTI

VIA PORCELLANA

VIA VIGNA NUOVA

VIA DEL PARIONE

Piazza Goldoni

PALAZZO CORSINI

SANTA TRÍNITA

L. CORSINI

BORGO

PORTA SAN FREDIANO

Piazza d. Verzaia

VIA SANT'ONOFRIO

LUNGARNO

SODERINI

PONTE ALLA CARRAIA

Piazza Nazaro Sauro

L. GUICCIARDINI

PONTE SANTA TRÍNITA

Piazza de' Frescobaldi

ACCIAIUOLI

Cimitero Israelitico

VIA ALIARDI

Piazza de' Nerti

BORGO SAN FREDIANO

Piazza di Cestello

VIA S. SPIRITO

B. SAN JACOPO

CITY WALLS

V. CAMALDOLI

Piazza del Carmine

Piazza T. Tasso

BRANCACCI CHAPEL

SANTA MARIA DEL CARMINE

O L T R A R N O

B. SAN MARTINO

SANTO SPIRITO

Pza d. Passera

Piazza di Santa Felicità

VIA DELLA CHIESA

VIA DEI SERRAGLI

Piazza di Santo Spirito

VIA D. PRESTO

VIA MAGGIO

D. GUICCIARDINI

GROTTO

BACCHUS

VIA DEL CAMPUCCIO

Giardino Torrigiani

PAL. DE COSIMO RIDOLFI

Piazza di San Felice

Piazza de' Pitti

PITTI PALACE

VIA ROMANA

Hotels & Eateries outside the Center
❶ Locanda de' Ciompi
❷ Ristorante Natalino
❸ Caffè del Verone

Tour Company
❹ Florencetown Tours

Giardino di Analena

AMPHI-THEATER

GARDENS ENTRANCE

Boboli Gardens

FONTANA D. NETTUNO

VIA DEI SERRAGLI

FONTANA DELL'OCEANO

CITY WALLS

PORTA ROMANA

GARDENS ENTRANCE

ART INSTITUTE

Piazzale della Porta Romana

To A-1 Autostrada (Firenze Impruneta exit) & Siena via Superstrada

FLORENCE

just past the Medici-Riccardi Palace (Mon-Fri 9:00-13:00, closed Sat-Sun, Via Cavour 1 red, +39 055 290 832). There's also a TI booth at the **airport.**

At any TI, you can pick up a city map. For goings-on around town, ask for a copy of *The Florentine* newspaper, which has great articles with cultural insights (in English, published monthly and updated online every other Thu at www.theflorentine.net).

ARRIVAL IN FLORENCE

For a rundown on Florence's train, bus, and tram stations; airport; cruise ship arrival at the Livorno port; and information for drivers; see the "Florence Connections" section at the end of this chapter.

HELPFUL HINTS

Sightseeing Tips: Everyone—and I mean everyone—visiting Florence wants to see the **Uffizi** and the **Accademia,** and climb the Duomo's **dome.**
It's flat out stupid to attempt a visit to any of these without a reservation. The process for making reservations is clearly explained under "Sights in Florence," later.

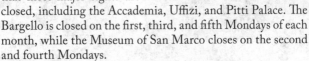

Closed Days: If you're in Florene on a Monday, note that most major sights are closed, including the Accademia, Uffizi, and Pitti Palace. The Bargello is closed on the first, third, and fifth Mondays of each month, while the Museum of San Marco closes on the second and fourth Mondays.

Theft Alert: Florence has hardworking gangs of thieves who hang out near the train station, the station's underpass (especially where the tunnel surfaces), around Mercato Centrale, and at major sights. American tourists are considered easy targets. Some thieves even dress like tourists to fool you. Any crowded bus likely holds at least one thief.

Medical Help: Medical Service Firenze provides 24/7 phone consults; they also do house calls in English or will see you at their walk-in clinic (clinic closed Sun—check website for hours, Via Roma 4, between the Duomo and Piazza della Repubblica, +39 055 475 411, www.medicalservice.firenze.it). The TI has a list of English-speaking doctors.

There are 24-hour **pharmacies** at the train station and near Palazzo Vecchio (at Via dei Calzaiuoli 7).

Visiting Churches: Modest dress is required in some churches, including the Duomo, Santa Maria Novella, Santa Croce,

Santa Maria del Carmine/Brancacci Chapel, and the Medici Chapels. Be respectful of worshippers and the paintings; don't use a flash. Many churches, though not the biggies I mention, close from 12:00 or 12:30 until 15:00 or 16:00.

Chill Out: Schedule several breaks into your sightseeing when you can sit, pause, cool off, and refresh yourself with a gelato or coffee. Carry a water bottle to refill at Florence's twist-the-handle public fountains (around the corner from the "Piglet" at Mercato Nuovo, or in front of the Pitti Palace). Try the *fontanello* (dispenser of free cold water) on Piazza della Signoria, behind the statue of Neptune (on the left side of the Palazzo Vecchio).

Addresses: Florence has a confusing system for street addresses, with "red" numbers for businesses and "black" (sometimes blue) numbers for residences. Street signs are indeed red or black (though usually faded and hard to read); in print, addresses are indicated with "r" (as in Via Cavour 2r) or "n" (for black—*nero,* as in Via Cavour 25n). Red and black numbers are interspersed together on the same street; each set goes in roughly consecutive order, but their numbers bear no connection with each other.

Bookstores: For a good selection of brand-name guidebooks (including mine), try these: **Paperback Exchange** has the widest selection of English books, new and used (Mon-Sat 10:00-19:00, closed Sun, just south of the Duomo on Via delle Oche 4 red). **RED** (stands for "Read, Eat, Dream"), a flagship store for the Feltrinelli chain (the Italian Barnes & Noble) with a café and restaurant, has a small selection of English books (daily 9:00-20:00, on Piazza della Repubblica).

WCs: Public restrooms are scarce. Use them when you can, in any café or museum you patronize. Pay public WCs are typically €1. Convenient locations include: at the Baptistery ticket office (near the Duomo); near the entrance to the Church of Santa Maria Novella; inside the train station (near track 5 and in the food court); just down the street from Piazza Santa Croce (at Borgo Santa Croce 29 red); on Piazza Santo Spirito; and up near Piazzale Michelangelo.

Laundry: The **Wash & Dry Lavarapido** chain offers long hours and efficient, self-service launderettes at several locations (generally daily 7:30-23:00). These locations are close to recommended hotels: Via del Sole 29 red and Via della Scala 52 red (this location is a Speed Queen, between train station and river), and Via Ghibellina 143 red (Palazzo Vecchio). On the Oltrarno side, there's one at Via dei Serragli 87 red (Santo Spirito area).

Bike Rental: I don't recommend biking in the city as it's so jam-packed with pedestrians. But if you must, **Florence by Bike** rents two-wheelers of all sizes (€12/day and up depending on type of bike, includes bike lock and helmet; Mon-Sat 9:00-13:00 & 15:30-19:30, Sun until 15:00, closed Sun Nov-March; a 15-minute walk north of the Duomo at Via San Zanobi 54 red, +39 055 488 992, www.florencebybike.it).

Travel Agencies: Travel agencies can be helpful for getting both domestic and international tickets and reservations. Convenient travel agencies in the town center are **Intertravel Viaggi** (Mon-Fri 9:00-12:00 & 14:00-17:00, closed Sat-Sun, south of Piazza della Repubblica at Via de Lamberti 39 red, +39 055 280 706) and **Florentour** (Mon-Fri 9:30-13:30, closed Sat-Sun, Via dei Servi 23 red, a block off the Duomo, +39 055 292 237). For locations of both, see the map on page 490.

GETTING AROUND FLORENCE

I organize my sightseeing geographically and do it all on foot. I think of Florence as a Renaissance treadmill—it requires a lot of walking. You likely won't need public transit, except maybe to head up to Piazzale Michelangelo and San Miniato Church for the view. For major bus and tram stop locations, see the map on page 490.

By Bus

The city's full-size buses don't cover the old center well (the whole area around the Duomo is off-limits to motorized traffic). Pick up a map of transit routes at the bus station; you'll also find routes online (www.at-bus.it/it/orari).

Buy bus tickets at tobacco shops *(tabacchi)*, newsstands, or tram stops (€1.50/90 minutes). Be sure to validate your ticket in the machine on board (or risk a steep fine). Do this as you board, otherwise you're cheating. Inspectors fine even innocent-looking tourists €50. You can sometimes buy a ticket on board, but you'll pay more and may need exact change. Follow general bus etiquette: Board at front or rear doors, exit out the center.

Of the many bus lines, I find these to be of most value for seeing outlying sights:

Bus **#12** goes from near Piazza d'Ognissanti, over the Carraia bridge to Porta Romana, then up to San Miniato Church and Piazzale Michelangelo (3/hour). Bus **#13** makes the return trip down the hill.

Fun little **minibuses** (many of them electric—*elettrico*) wind through the tangled old center of town and up and down the river—just €1.50 gets you a 1.5-hour joyride.

These buses, which run every 10 minutes from 7:00 to 21:00 (less frequent on Sun), are popular with sore-footed sightseers and eccentric local seniors. The minibuses also connect many major parking lots with the historic center (buy tickets from machines at lots).

Bus **#C1** stops behind the Palazzo Vecchio and Piazza Santa Croce, then heads north, passing near San Marco and the Accademia before heading up to Piazza Libertà. On its southbound route, this bus also stops near the train station, the Basilica of San Lorenzo, and the Duomo.

Bus **#C2**, if operating, twists through the congested old center from the train station, passing near Piazza della Repubblica and Piazza della Signoria to Piazza Beccaria.

Bus **#C3** goes up and down the Arno River, with stops near Piazza Santa Croce, Ponte Vecchio, the Carraia bridge to the Oltrarno (including the Pitti Palace), and beyond.

Bus **#C4** goes from near the Duomo to the train station, crosses the Carraia bridge, and cruises through the Oltrarno (passing the Pitti Palace) before heading into the San Niccolò neighborhood.

By Tram

The T1 and T2 tram lines are cheap, easy, and frequent. For travelers, they're generally most useful for service between the airport (T2) or the big park-and-ride lots at Villa Costanza (T1) near the town of Scandicci to the train station (€1.50, 25 minutes; www. gestramvia.com). See "Florence Connections" at the end of this chapter for more details.

By Taxi

The minimum cost for a taxi ride is about €7 (more after 22:00 and on Sun); rides in the center of town should be charged as tariff #1. The flat rate for the airport is €22 plus €1 per bag if the driver puts them in the trunk (also more on nights and weekends). Taxi fares and supplements (e.g., €2 extra to call a cab rather than hail one) are clearly explained on signs in each taxi. Look for an official, regulated cab (white; marked with *Taxi/Comune di Firenze,* red fleur-de-lis, and one of the official phone numbers: 4390 or 4242). Before getting in a cab at a stand or on the street, ask for an approximate cost (*"Più o meno, quanto costa?"* pew oh MEH-noh, KWAHN-toh KOH-stah). If you can't get a straight answer or the price is outrageous, wait for the next one. It can be hard to find a cab on the street, but they stop and sometimes wait in taxi ranks near the major tourist sights (marked by orange *Taxi* signs). To call one, dial +39 055 4390 or +39 055 4242 (or ask your waiter or hotelier to call for you). Uber does not operate in Florence.

Tours in Florence

For extra insight with a personal touch, consider the tour companies and individual Florentine guides listed here. Many tour companies (such as Florencetown) offer regularly scheduled group tours that anyone can sign up for. This is usually the cheapest option for individual travelers. But families and small groups can book a private guide for a similar price (since rates are hourly for any size of group).

Some tour companies offer bus excursions that go out to smaller towns in the Tuscan countryside. The most popular day trips are Siena, San Gimignano, Pisa, and into Chianti country for wine tasting. To see Florence itself, it's clearly best on foot.

♩ To sightsee on your own, download my **free audio tours** that illuminate some of Florence's top sights and neighborhoods (see page 26).

Walking Tours
Artviva

Artviva offers an intriguing variety of tours (guided by native English speakers). Popular choices include their small-group overview tour ("Original Florence" 3-hour town walk); and private tours, including "Florence in One Glorious Day," which combines the town walk and tours of the Uffizi and Accademia (6 hours total). They also have standalone Uffizi and Accademia tours, cooking classes, art classes, food tours, tours around Tuscany and to the Cinque Terre, and more (RS%—10 percent discount with this book, use the password "reader"; +39 055 264 5033, www.artviva.com).

Florencetown

This company offers English-language tours and experiences on foot or by bike. Their most popular offerings are "Walk and Talk Florence" (€35, 2.5 hours, April-Oct daily at 10:00 and 15:00, basic stops including the Oltrarno) and "I Bike Florence" (€39; 3 hours on one-speed bike, 15-stop blitz of town's top sights, helmets optional; in bad weather it goes as a walking tour). They also offer cooking classes and wine tours. Their booking office is at Piazza Mentana (see "Florence" map in this chapter); they also have a "Tourist Point" kiosk on Piazza della Repubblica, under the arches at the corner with Via Pellicceria (RS%, +39 055 281 103, www.florencetown.com).

Florentia

Top-notch private walking tours—geared for thoughtful, well-heeled travelers with longer-than-average attention spans—are led by Florentine scholars. The tours range from introductory city walks and museum visits to in-depth thematic walks, such as the

Oltrarno, Jewish Florence, or the Medici dynasty; they also offer family-oriented tours (€250 and up, includes planning assistance by email, www.florentia.net).

Context Florence

This scholarly group of graduate students and professors leads small-group or private "walking seminars," such as a 3.5-hour study of Michelangelo's work and influence and a two-hour evening orientation stroll. See their website for pricing and other innovative offerings: Medici walk, family tours, private fresco workshop, and more (www.contexttravel.com).

Walks Inside Florence

Two art historians—Paola Barubiani and Francesco Calanca—and their 15 partners provide quality private tours at a discounted rate for my readers (RS%—€200/group for three-hour intro tour, up to 6 people). Their "Florence in a Day" tour gives you the essentials in four hours (€265/group, up to 6 people, museum admissions extra—they make the reservations so there's no waiting in line). Other offerings are described on their website (e.g. shopping tour featuring select artisans, guided evening walk, and cruise excursions from the port of Livorno; +39 333 483 1431, www. walksinsideflorence.it).

Exclusive Connection

This smart, high-end, and well-connected agency offers an impressive list of services in Florence and around Italy, including specialized tours and museum bookings. Both Lucia Montuschi and Cora Ferroni have a passion for history, art, and culture, and love sharing it with visitors (+39 055 200 1586, www.exclusiveconnection.it).

Food Tours of Florence

Most tour companies (including Florencetown) offer food tours, as do countless food lovers who simply offer their services on various online-booking sites. Typically, tours last 3-4 hours and make 5-6 stops as you walk, munch, and learn with small groups of 6-8 people (a natural limit since hole-in-the-wall bakeries and wine bars are tiny). I enjoy Toni Mazzaglia's **Taste Florence Food Tours.** A native of North Carolina, Toni's been in Florence for 20 years, and does a fine tour in and around the Mercato Centrale ($109, RS%, most days at 10:00, 4 hours, 6 stops, www.tasteflorence.com).

Local Guides

Vanessa Garau is an enthusiastic young guide with good connections in the Oltrarno and an infectious love of Florence (half-day private tours for €180, +39 349 133 6894, garau.vanessa@gmail. com).

    Alessandra Marchetti, a Florentine who has lived in the US,

Florence at a Glance

▲▲▲**Accademia** Michelangelo's *David* and powerful (unfinished) *Prisoners.* Reserve ahead. **Hours:** Tue-Sun 9:00-19:00, closed Mon, may stay open later in peak season. See page 488.

▲▲▲**Uffizi Gallery** Greatest collection of Italian paintings anywhere. Reserve well in advance. **Hours:** Tue-Sun 8:15-18:30, closed Mon, may stay open later in peak season. See page 497.

▲▲▲**Bargello** Underappreciated sculpture museum (Michelangelo, Donatello, Medici treasures). **Hours:** Daily 8:15-14:00; may close on second and fourth Sun and first, third, and fifth Mon of each month. See page 503.

▲▲▲**Duomo Museum** Freshly renovated cathedral museum with the finest in Florentine sculpture. **Hours:** Daily 9:00-19:45, closed first Tue of each month. See page 486.

▲▲▲**Pitti Palace** Several museums in lavish palace plus sprawling Boboli and Bardini Gardens. **Hours:** Palatine Gallery, Royal Apartments, Treasury, Museum of Costume and Fashion, and Gallery of Modern Art open Tue-Sun 8:15-18:50, closed Mon; Boboli and Bardini Gardens, and Porcelain Museum open daily June-Aug 8:15-19:00, April-May and Sept-Oct until 18:30, Nov-March until 16:30; closed first and last Mon of each month. See page 506.

▲▲**Duomo** Gothic cathedral with colorful facade and the first dome built since ancient Roman times. **Hours:** Mon-Sat 10:15-16:45, closed Sun. See page 484.

▲▲**Museum of San Marco** Best collection anywhere of artwork by the early Renaissance master Fra Angelico. **Hours:** Mon-Fri 8:15-14:00, Sat until 17:00, closed Sun; also closed second and fourth Mon of each month. See page 493.

▲▲**Medici Chapels** Tombs of Florence's great ruling family, designed and carved by Michelangelo. **Hours:** Sat-Mon 8:15-13:50, Wed-Fri 13:15-18:50; closed Tue and first, third, and fifth Sun of each month. See page 494.

▲▲**Palazzo Vecchio** Fortified palace, once the home of the Medici family, wallpapered with history. **Hours:** Museum and excavations open daily 9:00-19:00 except Thu until 14:00; shorter hours off-season; shorter hours for tower. See page 501.

▲▲**Galileo Science Museum** Fascinating old clocks, telescopes, maps, and three of Galileo's fingers. **Hours:** Daily 9:30-18:00 except Tue until 13:00. See page 503.

▲▲**Santa Croce Church** Precious art, tombs of famous Florentines, and Brunelleschi's Pazzi Chapel in 14th-century church. **Hours:** Mon-Sat 9:30-17:30, Sun from 12:30. See page 504.

▲▲**Church of Santa Maria Novella** Thirteenth-century Dominican church with Masaccio's famous 3-D painting. **Hours:** Mon-Thu and Sat 10:00-17:00, Fri from 11:00, Sun from 13:00. See page 505.

▲▲**Brancacci Chapel** Works of Masaccio, early Renaissance master who reinvented perspective. **Hours:** Fri-Sat and Mon 10:00-17:00, Sun from 13:00, closed Tue-Thu. See page 507.

▲▲**San Miniato Church** Sumptuous Renaissance chapel and sacristy showing scenes of St. Benedict. **Hours:** Daily 9:30-13:00 & 15:00-19:00, closed sporadically for special occasions. See page 510.

▲**Climbing the Duomo's Dome** Grand view into the cathedral, close-up of dome architecture, and, after 463 steps, a glorious city vista. Reservations required. **Hours:** Mon-Fri 8:15-19:30, Sat until 17:15, Sun 12:45-16:30. See page 485.

▲**Campanile** Bell tower with views similar to Duomo's, 50 fewer steps, and shorter lines. **Hours:** Daily 8:15-19:45. See page 485.

▲**Baptistery** Bronze doors fit to be the gates of paradise. **Hours:** Doors always viewable; interior open daily 9:00-19:45. See page 486.

▲**Piazza Santissima Annunziata** Lovely square epitomizing Renaissance harmony, with Brunelleschi's Hospital of the Innocents, considered the first Renaissance building. See page 492.

▲**Medici-Riccardi Palace** Lorenzo the Magnificent's home, with fine art, frescoed ceilings, and Gozzoli's lovely Chapel of the Magi. **Hours:** Thu-Tue 9:00-19:00, closed Wed. See page 495.

▲**Ponte Vecchio** Famous bridge lined with gold and silver shops. See page 502.

▲**Piazzale Michelangelo** Hilltop square with stunning view of Duomo and Florence, with San Miniato Church just uphill. See page 507.

FLORENCE

gives private walking tours of Florence and driving tours of Tuscany. Her passion is Michelangelo (from €60-85/hour, +39 347 386 9839, www.tuscanydriverguide.com, alessandramarchettitours@gmail.com).

Paola Migliorini and her partners offer museum tours, city walking tours, family tours, private cooking classes, wine tours, and Tuscan excursions by van—you can tailor tours as you like (€65/hour without car, €70/hour in a van for up to 8 passengers, minimum 3 hours, +39 347 657 2611, www.florencetour.com). They also do cruise excursions from the port of Livorno (€600/up to 4 people, €680/up to 6, €780/up to 8).

Elena Fulceri, specializing in art, history, and secret corners and gardens, is a delightful and engaging guide. She organizes tailor-made private tours, has good Oltrarno artisan connections, and enjoys family tours (from €60/hour for 2 people, +39 347 942 2054, www.florencewithflair.com).

Renaissance Walk

This great and rich city is easily covered on foot. We'll start with the soaring church dome that stands as the proud symbol of the Renaissance spirit; just opposite, you'll find the Baptistery doors that opened the Renaissance. We'll then stroll down the city's pedestrian-only main street to the Palazzo Vecchio and the Arno River. Along the way, we'll pass elegant stores, lively eateries, and the parade of people that make up Florence today. For more details on many of the stops on this walk, see the individual listings under "Sights in Florence," later.

Length of This Walk: The walk is less than a mile long. Allow two hours, including a visit to the interior of the Baptistery.

Tours: ⋂ Download my free Renaissance Walk audio tour and I'll personally give you this tour.

Services: Pay WCs are at the ticket office opposite the Baptistery. Keep an eye out for public twist-the-handle fountains along this route where you can refill your water bottle.

Background: The Renaissance—the "rebirth" of Greek and Roman culture that swept across Europe—started around 1400 and lasted about 150 years. In politics, the Renaissance meant democracy; in science, a renewed interest in exploring nature. The general mood was optimistic and "humanistic," with a confidence in the power of the individual.

Renaissance art was a return to the realism and balance of

Greek and Roman sculpture and architecture. Domes and round arches replaced Gothic spires and pointed arches. In painting and sculpture, Renaissance artists strove for realism. Merging art and science, they used mathematics, the laws of perspective, and direct observation of nature.

This was not an anti-Christian movement. Artists saw themselves as an extension of God's creative powers. The Church even supported the Renaissance and commissioned many of its greatest works.

After 1,000 years of waiting, the embers of Europe's classical heritage burst into flames right here in Florence.

● SELF-GUIDED WALK

• *The Duomo, the cathedral with the distinctive red dome, is the center of Florence and the orientation point for this walk. If you ever get lost, home's the dome. Stroll around the piazza in front of the cathedral (the Duomo) and take in the sights. To the right of the Duomo rises its skyscraping bell tower (the Campanile) with its Renaissance statues. In front of the church is the Baptistery, an octagonal, green-and-white stone building that's bigger than many churches.*

❶ The Duomo

Florence's massive cathedral is the city's geographical and spiritual heart. Its dome, visible from all over the city, inspired Florentines to do great things.

The church was begun in 1296, in the Gothic style. After generations of work, it was still unfinished. The facade was little more than bare brick, and it stood that way until it was completed in 1870 in the "Neo"-Gothic style. Its "retro" look captures the feel of the original medieval facade, with green, white, and pink marble sheets that cover the brick construction. You'll see Gothic (pointed) arches and three stories decorated with mosaics and statues. This over-the-top facade is adored by many, while others call it "the cathedral in pajamas." The Duomo is dedicated to the Virgin Mary. Find her statue right in the center—above the main doorway but below the round window.

We won't go inside the church on this tour. It has a cavernous, bare interior with a few noteworthy sights. Entry is free, but there's often a long wait unless you buy a pass that allows you to enter through the crypt.

• *Now turn to the church's bell tower, to the right.*

Renaissance Walk

To Accademia (David) & San Marco
To San Lorenzo
To Train Station
DUOMO COMPLEX TICKETS
WC
VIA DE' CERRETANI
Piazza di San Giovanni
BAPTISTERY
SANTA MARIA MAGGIORE
VIA PECORI
WALK BEGINS
MAIN ENTRANCE
DOME ENTRANCE
DUOMO
CRYPT ENTRANCE
DUOMO MUSEUM
Piazza del Duomo
EDOARDO GELATO
DUOMO COMPLEX TICKETS
LOGGIA DEL BIGALLO
CANONICA
VIA DELL' ORIUOLO
VIA DE' VECCHIETTI
VIA CORSI
TOSINGHI
BRUNELLESCHI
VIA ROMA
MEDICI
VIA DELL'OCHE
BONIZZI
OPERA DEL DUOMO STUDIO
S. MARIA DE' RICCI
Piazza della Repubblica
VIA D. STROZZI
SPEZIALI
VIA DEI CALZAIUOLI
STUDIO
VIA DEL CORSO
CERCHI
CASA DI DANTE
PRESTO
PROCONSOLO
ST. GEORGE
V. D. ANSELMI
SASSETTI
POST
ORSAN-MICHELE
VIA PELLICCERIA
LAMBERTI
CALIMALA
ORSAN
VIA TAVOLINI
PERCHÉ NO! GELATO
VIA D. ALIGHIERI
S. MARIA
LA BADIA
BARGELLO MUSEUM
CIMATORI
ST. MARK
VIA DELLA CONDOTTA
VIA DEI MAGAZZINI
VIA DELL' ANGUILLARA
VIA PORTA ROSSA
DAVANZATI PALACE
MERCATO NUOVO
IL PORCELLINO
ROMAN CITY PLAN
Piazza della Signoria
COSIMO I
GUCCI MUSEUM
Piazza San Firenze
To Santa Croce
VIA DELLE TERME
V. VACC.
ARMA
NEPTUNE
WC
GONDI
BORGO DE' GRECI
B. S. APOSTOLI
VIA POR SANTA MARIA
LOGGIA DEI LANZI
Piazza de' Salt.
PALAZZO VECCHIO
VIA LEONI
LAMB.
S. STEFANO
BARONCELLI
NINNA
LORENZO
Piazza del Grano
VIA DEI NERI
PONTE VECCHIO
GIRO.
VASARI CORRIDOR
UFFIZI GALLERY
MICHEL-ANGELO
EXIT
CASTELLANI
CASTELLO
WALK ENDS
GALILEO
GALILEO SCIENCE MUSEUM
Piazza dei Guidicci
SAPONAI
LUNG. GEN. DIAZ
Piazza Mentana
Arno River
To Pitti Palace

100 Meters
100 Yards

1. The Duomo
2. Campanile
3. View of the Dome
4. Baptistery – North Doors
5. Baptistery – East Doors (Gates of Paradise)
6. Via dei Calzaiuoli
7. Piazza della Repubblica
8. Orsanmichele Church
9. Piazza della Signoria
10. Loggia dei Lanzi
11. Savonarola Plaque
12. Uffizi Courtyard Statues
13. Arno River
14. Ponte Vecchio

FLORENCE

❷ Campanile (Giotto's Tower)

The 270-foot bell tower was begun in the 1300s by the great painter Giotto. As a forerunner of the Renaissance genius, Giotto excelled in many artistic fields, just as Michelangelo would do two centuries later. In his day, Giotto was called the ugliest man to ever walk the streets of Florence, but he designed what many call the most beautiful bell tower in all of Europe.

You can climb the Campanile for great views. It doesn't require a reservation, just the Duomo's Giotto Pass (see page 485 for information about climbing the tower).

• *Now take in the Duomo's star attraction: the dome. The best viewing spot is just to the right of the facade, from the corner of the pedestrian-only Via dei Calzaiuoli.*

❸ View of Brunelleschi's Dome

Though construction of the church began in 1296, by the 1400s there still was no suitable roof. (For a century, the old cathedral remained inside the new so people could still go to Mass.) City fathers intended to top the new church with a dome, but the technology to span the 140-foot-wide hole had yet to be invented. *Non c'è problema.* The brash Florentines knew that someday someone would come along who could handle the challenge. That man was Filippo Brunelleschi.

Brunelleschi had a plan. He would cap the church's octagonal hole-in-the-roof with a round Roman-style dome. It would be a tall, self-supporting dome as grand as that of the ancient Pantheon—which he had studied.

Brunelleschi used a dome within a dome. What you see is the outer shell, covered in terra-cotta tile. The inner dome is thicker and provides much of the structural support. The grand white skeletal ribs connect at the top, supporting each other in a way similar to a pointed arch. Hidden between them are interlocking bricks, laid in a herringbone pattern. Rather than being stacked horizontally, like traditional brickwork, the alternating vertical bricks act as "bookends." The dome grew upward like an igloo, supporting itself as it proceeded from the base. When the ribs reached the top, Brunelleschi arched them in and fixed them in place with a decorative, nonstructural architectural cherry on top—the lantern. His dome, built in only 16 years, was the largest since ancient Rome's Pantheon.

FLORENCE

When completed in 1436, Brunelleschi's dome was the wonder of the age. It became the model for many domes to follow, from St. Peter's Basilica in Rome to the US Capitol. Michelangelo, setting out to construct the dome of St. Peter's, drew inspiration from the dome of Florence. He said, "I'll make its sister...bigger, but not more beautiful."

You can climb the dome for Florence's best views, but it requires a reservation and the Duomo's Brunelleschi pass (for details, see page 484).

• *Next up, the Baptistery. Step into the zone between the Duomo and the Baptistery that local tour guides call the "Piazza of Paradise."*

Baptistery and Ghiberti's Bronze Doors

Built in the 11th century, atop Roman foundations, this is Florence's oldest surviving buildings—a thousand years old. The Baptistery is known for its doors. Andrea Pisano created the oldest set (from the 1330s, on the south side). The most famous ones are the East Doors, which face the cathedral, but let's start with the North Doors—around to the right, where tourists go in—which may be even more important. (Note that the original doors are in the Duomo Museum and well worth seeing.)

❹ **North Doors:** Some say that these doors actually started the Renaissance. It was the year 1401, and Florence was holding a competition to find the best artist to make some doors for the Baptistery entrance. All the greats entered the contest, including Donatello and Brunelleschi. The winner was relatively unknown 24-year-old Lorenzo Ghiberti. Take a moment to appreciate the composition—impressive—but no background. On the left, eight feet up in the center with the turban, is the young artist Ghiberti.

For the next 25 years, he worked on these North Doors.

• *Now return to the more famous doors facing the church—and see progress made in 25 years.*

❺ **East Doors** (Gates of Paradise): Ghiberti's bronze panels for these doors added a whole new dimension to art—depth. Michelangelo said these doors were fit to be the "Gates of Paradise." Here we see how the Renaissance masters merged art and science.

Realism was in, and Renaissance artists used math, illusion, and dissection
to create it.

Inside the Baptistery: The spacious interior, topped with an octagonal dome, features a fine example of
pre-Renaissance mosaic art (1200s-
1300s) in the Byzantine style. Workers
from St. Mark's in Venice came here
to make the remarkable ceiling mosaics (of Venetian glass) in the late 1200s.

• *Now head south, down the busy pedestrian-only street that runs from here toward the Arno River.*

❻ Via dei Calzaiuoli

Via dei Calzaiuoli (kahlts-ay-WOH-lee), the former "street of the
stocking makers," was part of the ancient Roman grid plan that
became Florence. Around the year 1400, as the Renaissance was
blooming, this street connected the religious center (where we are
now) with the political center (where we're heading), a five-minute
walk away.

Since most vehicles were banned a few years back, this street
has been transformed into a pleasant place to stroll, people-watch,
window-shop, and wonder why American cities can't become more
pedestrian friendly.

• *Continue down Via dei Calzaiuoli. Two blocks down from the Baptistery, turn right on Via degli Speziali toward the triumphal arch that
marks...*

❼ Piazza della Repubblica

This large square sits on the site of the original Roman Forum. The
lone column that still stands here—nicknamed the "belly button of
Florence"—once marked the intersection of the two main Roman

roads (Via Corso and Via
Roma). If you look at a
map of Florence today, you
can make out the ghost of
Rome in its streets: a rectangular grid-plan city center surrounded by a circular city wall.

In the 1860s, the
square got its magnificent

triumphal arch. It celebrated the unification of Italy. In fact, from 1865 to 1870, Florence became the capital of the newly united nation of Italy.

Venerable cafés and stores line the square. During the 19th century, intellectuals met in cafés here. Gilli, on the northeast corner, is a favorite for its grand atmosphere and tasty sweets (cheap if you stand at the bar, expensive to sit down). The much-loved drink called Negroni (gin, vermouth, bitter Campari, and a slice of orange) was named for a local count who popularized it here.

• *Return to the main street and continue walking toward the river. A block farther, at the intersection with Via Orsanmichele, is the...*

❽ Orsanmichele Church

Originally, this was an open loggia (covered porch) with a huge grain warehouse upstairs. Then, as you can see, the arches of the loggia were artfully filled in (14th century) to make walls, and the building gained a new purpose—as a church.

The 14 niches in the exterior walls feature remarkable-in-their-day statues paid for by the city's rising middle class of merchants and their 21 guilds. Florence in 1400 was a republic, a government working for the interests not of a king, but of these guilds, which commissioned statues as PR gestures.

• *Circle the church exterior counterclockwise to enjoy the statues. Start on the church's right side (along Via Orsanmichele).*

In the third niche is **Nanni di Banco's** *Quattro Santi Coronati* (c. 1415-1417). These four early Christians were sculptors martyred by the Roman emperor Diocletian because they refused to sculpt pagan gods. They seem to be contemplating the consequences of the fatal decision they're about to make.

Just to the right of Banco's saints is **Donatello's** *St. George:* He's alert, perched on the edge of his niche, scanning the horizon for dragons and announcing the new age with its new outlook. His knitted brow shows there's a drama unfolding. Sure, he's anxious, but he's also self-assured. Comparing this Renaissance-style *St. George* to *Quattro Santi Coronati,* you can psychoanalyze the heady changes underway. This is humanism.

The back side of the church has three statues worth a look. *St. Matthew,* patron of bankers, and *St. Stephen,* patron of wool merchants (both by Ghiberti), are a reminder that banking and textiles were mainstays of the Florentine economy—and wealthy enough to actually pay for bronze statues rather than marble. Nanni di

Banco's *St. Eligius*, patron of metalworkers, shows workers shoeing a horse.

Around the corner, the first niche features **Donatello's** *St. Mark* (1411-1413). The evangelist cradles his gospel in his strong, veined hand and gazes out, resting his weight on the right leg while bending the left. Though subtle, St. Mark's twisting *contrapposto* pose was the first seen since antiquity. Eighty years after young Donatello carved this statue, a teenage Michelangelo Buonarroti stood here and marveled.

• *Continue down the mall 50 more yards, to the huge and historic square...*

❾ Piazza della Signoria

What a view! This piazza—the main civic center of Florence—is dominated by the massive stone facade of the Palazzo Vecchio, with

a tower that reaches for the sky. The square is dotted with statues. The stately Uffizi Gallery is nearby, and the marble greatness of old Florence litters the cobbles. Piazza della Signoria, with the feel of an open-air museum of statuary, still vibrates with the echoes of the city's past—executions, riots, and great celebrations. There's even Roman history: Look for the **chart** showing the ancient city (20 steps into the square on the right). Today, it's a tourist's world with pigeons, selfie sticks, horse buggies, and tired spouses.

Before you towers the **Palazzo Vecchio,** the "old palace" and palatial Town Hall of the Medici—a fortress designed to contain riches and survive the many riots that went with local politics. The windows are just beyond the reach of angry stones, and the tower was a handy lookout post. Capping the tip of the tower is a lion weathervane. (Locals like to say "when the lion pees in the river, it's going to rain.) Justice was doled out sternly on this square. Until 1873, Michelangelo's *David* stood where you see the replica today. Step through the front door into the Palazzo Vecchio's courtyard (free). This palace was Florence's symbol of civic power. You're surrounded by art for art's sake—a cherub playing with a dolphin frivolously marks the courtyard's center, and ornate stuccoes and frescoes decorate the walls and columns. Such luxury represented a big change 500 years ago.

For more on the palazzo and climbing its tower, see page 501.

• *Back outside, check out the arcade of three arches filled with statues.*

❿ Loggia dei Lanzi

This loggia, once a forum for public debate, was perfect for a city that prided itself on its democratic traditions. But later, when the Medici figured that good art was more desirable than free speech, it was turned into an outdoor sculpture gallery.

Two statues in the front deserve a closer look. At the right end of the loggia, *The Rape of the Sabine Women* (c. 1583)—with its pulse-quickening rhythm of muscles—is from the restless Mannerist period. The sculptor, Giambologna, proved his mastery of the medium by sculpting three entangled bodies from one piece of marble.

Benvenuto Cellini's *Perseus* (1545-1553), the loggia's most noteworthy piece, shows the Greek hero who decapitated the snake-headed Medusa. Cellini, a notorious braggart, placed his name prominently across the sash on the front and amazingly, included a secret self-portrait on the back of Perseus' head: His locks form the beard while the helmet frames the bushy brow and eyes.

• *Cross the square to Bartolomeo Ammanati's big* **fountain of Neptune.** *Near it, the guy on the horse is Cosimo I, the post–Renaissance Medici who commissioned the Uffizi. Find the round marble plaque on the ground 10 steps in front of the fountain.*

⓫ Savonarola Plaque

In the 1490s the Medici family was briefly thrown from power by an austere and charismatic monk named Savonarola, who made Florence a constitutional republic. He organized huge rallies lit by roaring bonfires here on the square where he preached. The devout brought their rich "vanities" (such as paintings, musical instruments, and playing cards) and threw them into the flames.

But not everyone wanted a return to the medieval past. Encouraged by the pope, the Florentines fought back and arrested Savonarola. For two days, they tortured him, and finally, on the very spot where Savonarola's followers had built bonfires of vanities, the monk was burned, ending his theocracy. Then—after 18 years in exile—the Medici returned to power and the Renaissance picked up where it left off.

• *Stay cool, we have 200 yards to go. Follow the gaze of the fake David into the courtyard of the two-tone horseshoe-shaped building.*

⓬ Uffizi Courtyard Statues

The top floor of this building, known as the *uffizi* (offices) during Medici days, is filled with the greatest collection of Florentine
painting anywhere. It's one of Europe's top four or five art galleries
(see page 497 for what you'll find inside).

The courtyard is watched over by 19th-century statues of the
great figures of the Renaissance: artists (Michelangelo, Giotto,
Donatello, Leonardo), philosophers (Machiavelli), scientists (Galileo), poets (Dante and Petrarch), explorers (Vespucci), and the
great patron of the Renaissance—Lorenzo "the Magnificent" de'
Medici.

• *At the far end of the courtyard, pause at the* ⓭ *Arno River, with a
magnificent view of the Ponte Vecchio, where we'll finish this walk.*

⓮ Ponte Vecchio

Since ancient times, a bridge has stood at this narrow spot in the
Arno. When a flood washed away the old wooden bridge, this one

was built in 1345, and is
now called the Ponte Vec-
chio (Old Bridge).

In times past, the
bridge's shops were inhabited by butchers and hide
tanners—a natural fit,
because they could empty
their waste into the river
below. In the 1500s, the
Medici booted them out and installed gold- and silversmiths who
tempt visitors to this day. Fittingly, a famous goldsmith is honored
with a fine bust at the central point of the bridge—the sculptor
Benvenuto *("Perseus")* Cellini.

Looking upstream and down, you have timeless views of the
city. The neighborhood across the river, known as the Oltrarno, is
more rustic and working-class. The other bridges are all modern
replacements.

The Ponte Vecchio is a romantic spot in the evening. Street
musicians play and lovers hold hands. The city of Florence—born
in Roman times, flourishing in the medieval age, and blossoming
in the Renaissance—remains a vibrant cultural capital.

• *From the Duomo to the Arno, we've taken in sights from Florence's
medieval roots and Renaissance greats. After this introduction, several
of the finest museums in Europe await your discovery—or perhaps it's
time for a nice espresso or gelato. Enjoy.*

FLORENCE

Sights in Florence

For general tips on sightseeing, see the Practicalities chapter. Remember to check the Florence TI's website, www.feelflorence.it, for up-to-date hours for sights. Many museums have erratic hours (for example, closing on alternating Sundays and Mondays), and Florence—more than most cities—has a tendency to change these hours from season to season.

Avoid Free-Entry Crowds: For most of the year, state museums are free on the first Sunday of each month (no reservations are available). In Florence, this includes the Uffizi Gallery, Accademia (Michelangelo's *David*), Pitti Palace and gardens, and the Bargello. Free days are actually bad news—they attract crowds, especially at the Uffizi and Accademia. Make a point to avoid these days.

ADVANCE RESERVATIONS AND SIGHTSEEING PASSES

While mobs of visitors line up for (literally) hours throughout the year to ogle *David* in the Accademia, tour the Uffizi Gallery, and climb the Duomo's dome, the rest of the city is easy without reservations.

Consider reservations mandatory for the **Uffizi** and **Accademia.** For the **Duomo complex** (cathedral, cathedral crypt, dome, Baptistery, Campanile, and Duomo Museum), the easy answer is to enjoy the complex from the outside and only go into the magnificent museum (with one of three Duomo passes—described later—which you can generally buy at the entrance with no serious line). To climb the Duomo's dome, you'll need a pass and a reservation.

Uffizi and Accademia Tickets: To book your timed-entry tickets in advance for both museums, simply go to the **official website** at www.b-ticket.com/b-Ticket/uffizi and follow the prompts.

If there's no availability at this site, you can try **for-profit vendors** such as Florence.net or Tickitaly.com, which may have time slots available, though you'll pay about €5 more per ticket. Various private companies—including those listed on page 468—sell tours that include a reserved museum entry. If you're booking a private guide well in advance, they are often happy to obtain tickets and reservations for your tour with them.

If you show up in Florence without reservations, **Opera Your Preview** is a handy little ticket office that can book for you in-person what most will just do online (Uffizi and Accademia only, €4/

museum extra, daily 10:00-17:45, 50 yards before Ponte Vecchio on Via Por Santa Maria, www.operayourpreview.com).

The ticket office at the **Orsanmichele Church** is another place to make reservations for the Uffizi and Accademia (Mon-Sat 9:00-16:00, closed Sun).

Uffizi/Pitti Palace/Boboli Gardens Combo-Ticket: This pass, officially called "PassePartout," is valid for five consecutive days and offers admission to these sights at a €12 savings (€38 March-Oct, €18 Nov-Feb, requires Uffizi reservation). Purchase the pass in advance at www.b-ticket.com/b-Ticket/uffizi.

Duomo Complex Tickets: See the next section.

THE DUOMO COMPLEX

Florence's most distinctive monuments—the Duomo (cathedral), Baptistery, and Campanile—are gathered around the pedestrian-only Piazza del Duomo. Just behind the Duomo, the excellent Duomo Museum holds many of the original treasures from these monuments. The Duomo complex also includes the crypt beneath the cathedral and the dome climb.

Duomo Complex Tickets: Three passes (named for the artists Ghiberti, Giotto, and Brunelleschi) cover the various Duomo sights. The cathedral itself is free to enter, but has extremely long lines to get in. The only way to avoid these lines is to buy one of the passes: They all include the cathedral's crypt, which has a separate entrance into the church with short lines.

The Duomo's dome climb can only be done with a reservation, which you get when you buy the Brunelleschi Pass. The Campanile, the Baptistery, and the Duomo Museum—the most important of these sights—never have long lines but require a pass (which you can easily buy at the Duomo Museum door).

The easiest approach: View everything from the outside and only go into the Duomo Museum. For anything more than that, sort through these three passes (each good for 3 days):

FLORENCE

Ghiberti Pass: €15; includes entrance to the cathedral via the crypt (shorter line, near the Campanile), the crypt in the church, the Baptistery, and the Duomo Museum (no timed reservations required, just establish the first day).

Giotto Pass: €20; includes everything in the Ghiberti Pass plus the Campanile (having this pass is the only way to go up the tower).

Brunelleschi Pass: €30; includes everything in the Giotto Pass, plus a timed entry to climb the Duomo's dome (this is the only way to climb the dome). You'll choose your time slot when you buy the pass.

Booking in Advance: To arrive in Florence with your Duomo complex pass already in hand, book online at www.museumflorence.com. You'll get a bar code that you can print out or download to your phone to show at each automated entry.

Ticket Offices: While it's easy to book your pass online, passes are also sold at three offices near the cathedral. The main ticket office faces the Campanile entrance (at #14 on the square, staffed counter; daily 8:00-19:00). There are also ticket counters in the Duomo Museum lobby and opposite the Baptistery (at #7). Some offices also have self-service machines (cash and credit card).

🎧 The Duomo, dome, Campanile, and Baptistery are also covered on my free Renaissance Walk audio tour.

▲▲Duomo (Cattedrale di Santa Maria del Fiore)

Florence's Gothic cathedral has the third-longest nave in Christendom. The church's noisy Neo-Gothic facade (from the 1870s) is covered with pink, green, and white Tuscan marble. The cathedral's claim to artistic fame is Brunelleschi's magnificent dome—the first Renaissance dome and *the* model for domes to follow. While viewing the Duomo from the outside is well worth ▲▲, the massive but empty-feeling interior is lucky to rate ▲—it doesn't justify the massive crowds that line up to get inside. Much of the church's great art is housed in the Duomo Museum behind the church.

Cost and Hours: Free to enter the cathedral, Duomo complex pass required for crypt; open Mon-Sat 10:15-16:45, closed Sun; open hours sometimes change due to religious functions, modest dress code enforced, +39 055 230 2885, www.museumflorence.com.

Mass: The church is open to all for Mass: English Mass on Sun at 17:00 and old-school Latin Mass with Gregorian chants on Sun at 10:30.

▲Climbing the Duomo's Dome

For a grand view into the cathedral from the base of the dome, a chance to see Brunelleschi's "dome-within-a-dome" construction, and a glorious Florence view from the top, climb 463 steps up the dome. The claustrophobic one-way route takes you up narrow, steep staircases and walkways to the top—but it's well worth the climb.

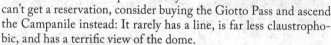

Cost and Hours: Covered by the Brunelleschi Pass (see earlier); Mon-Fri 8:15-19:30, Sat until 17:15, Sun 12:45-16:30.

Reservations: You must reserve your dome-climb entry when you purchase your pass. If possible, visit at sunset for a romantic experience. If you can't get a reservation, consider buying the Giotto Pass and ascend the Campanile instead: It rarely has a line, is far less claustrophobic, and has a terrific view of the dome.

Getting In: Enter the dome climb from the north side of the church (get in line about 15 minutes before your reservation time).

Climbing the Dome: While waiting to enter at your reserved time, spend a few minutes studying the side-entrance door, called the Porta della Mandorla ("Almond Door"). Just above the delicately carved doorframe is a colorful Annunciation mosaic by Nanni di Banco, and above that, in a sculpted almond-shaped frame, the Madonna is borne up to heaven by angels. If you look up from here you'll see an empty pedestal atop the transept. Michelangelo's *David* was originally destined to adorn one of these.

The climb is long but there are small landings where you can pull over and take a breather. Halfway up, you'll stroll on the walkway high above the altar where you can get a close-up of Vasari's *Last Judgment* ceiling (especially the ghoulish lower portion, filled with scenes of eternal torment) and a vertigo-inducing view of the nave. After a few tight, winding staircases and a steep final climb, you'll pop out of the hatch on the crowded terrace with a grand city view.

▲Campanile (Giotto's Tower)

The 270-foot bell tower has 50-some fewer steps than the Duomo's dome (but that's still 414 steps—no elevator); offers a faster, less-intense climb (with typically short lines); and

FLORENCE

has a view of that magnificent dome to boot. On the way up, there are several intermediate levels where you can catch your breath and enjoy ever-higher views. The stairs narrow as you go, creating a mosh-pit bottleneck near the very top—but the views are worth the hassle. While the viewpoints are enclosed by cage-like bars, the gaps are big enough to snap great photos.

Cost and Hours: Covered by the Giotto Pass (see earlier); daily 8:15-19:45, last entry 40 minutes before closing.

▲Baptistery

Michelangelo said the bronze doors of this octagonal building facing the Duomo were fit to be the Gates of Paradise. Check out the gleaming copies of Lorenzo Ghiberti's bronze doors (the originals are in the Duomo Museum). Making a breakthrough in perspective, Ghiberti used mathematical laws to create the illusion of receding distance on a basically flat surface.

The doors on the north side of the building (around to the right from the Gates of Paradise) were designed by Ghiberti when he was younger; he'd won the honor and opportunity by beating Brunelleschi in a competition (the rivals' original entries are in the Bargello).

Inside, sit and savor the medieval mosaic ceiling, where it's always Judgment Day and Jesus is giving the ultimate thumbs-up or thumbs-down.

Cost and Hours: Covered by all three Duomo passes (see earlier); interior generally open daily 9:00-19:45. The (facsimile) bronze doors on the exterior are always viewable.

▲▲▲Duomo Museum (Museo dell'Opera del Duomo)

The often-overlooked but superbly presented cathedral museum is filled with some of the best sculpture of the Renaissance, including a late Michelangelo *Pietà* and statues from the original Baptistery facade. Remarkably, it's almost never crowded. It also holds Brunelleschi's models for his dome, Donatello's emaciated *Mary Magdalene* and playful choir loft, and Ghiberti's original bronze Gates of Paradise doors with all the panels (the ones on the Baptistery's doors today are copies).

Cost and Hours: Covered by all three Duomo passes (see earlier); daily 9:00-19:45, closed first Tue of each month, last entry one hour before closing; one of the few museums in Florence open every Mon; behind the church at Via del Proconsolo 9, +39 055 230 2885, www. museumflorence.com.

Visiting the Museum: Begin with the model of the Duomo's facade circa 1500, the era of Michelangelo (Room 4). Notice that only the lower third is faced with marble and statues; the rest was only bare brick. Church construction began in 1296, but after an initial burst of energy, petered out. The facade was meant to be a glorious showcase of great statues set into niches.

Now enter the **Hall of Paradise** (Sala del Paradiso, Room 6). On one wall, this room re-creates that lower third of the facade we saw on the model. The opposite wall re-creates the Baptistery facade. Both buildings were a showcase of the greatest art of Florence from roughly 1300 to 1600.

Start with the Duomo wall. Peruse the various statues, done by many different artists from different eras, and consider the church's long evolution. The Duomo began life in early medieval times as a humble church overshadowed by the more prestigious Baptistery. By the 1200s, the church wasn't big enough to contain the exuberant spirit of a city growing rich from the wool trade and banking. So Florence set out to rebuild it, intending to make the finest church of the age.

Facing the facade of the church, as they did in the Middle Ages, are the famous doors of the Baptistery. Here's your chance to study the original panels. The oldest doors on the left are by Pisano (South Doors, c. 1330-1336). The original competition doors on the right are the first ones done by Ghiberti (North Doors, 1403-1424). And in the center are the Gates of Paradise by Ghiberti (East Doors, 1425-1452, see diagram on the next page).

These bronze "Gates of Paradise" revolutionized the way Renaissance people saw the world around them. They tell several Old Testament stories using perspective and realism as never before. Ghiberti poured his energy and creativity into these panels. That's him in the center of the door frame, atop the second row of panels—the head on the left with the shiny male-pattern baldness.

Armed with new rules of perspective, Ghiberti rendered reality with a mathematical precision revolutionary for the time. To understand how these advances made visual space feel more real than ever before, take a closer look at the space created by the arches in the **Jacob and Esau panel** (left side, third from the top). At the center is the so-called vanishing point on the distant horizon, where all the arches and floor tiles converge. Those closest to us, at the bottom of the panel, are big and clearly defined. Distant figures are smaller, fuzzier, and higher up. Ghiberti has placed us as part of this casual crowd of holy people—some with their backs to us—

Ghiberti's "Gates of Paradise"

Adam & Eve

Noah

Jacob & Esau

Moses — Ghiberti's Head

David

Cain & Abel

Abraham & Issac

Joseph & Benjamin

Joshua

Solomon & the Queen of Sheba

Not to Scale: Doors are 17' high x 10' wide

milling around an arcade. Suddenly the world has acquired a whole new dimension—depth.

Also on the ground floor are rooms dedicated to the museum's most famous statues. Donatello's **Mary Magdalene** (Santa Maria Maddalena, c. 1455), carved from white poplar and originally painted with realistic colors, is a Renaissance work of intense devotion (Room 8). The aging Michelangelo (1475-1564) designed his own tomb, with a **Pietà** (1547-1555) as the centerpiece (Room 10). Three mourners tend the broken body of the crucified Christ. We see Mary, his mother (the shadowy figure on our right); Mary Magdalene (on the left); and Nicodemus, the converted Pharisee, whose face is that of Michelangelo himself.

Upstairs, the first floor displays original **statues and panels** from the bell tower's third story, where copies stand today, two marble **choir lofts** (*cantorie;* by Lucca della Robbia and Donatello) that once sat above the sacristy doors of the Duomo, and **Brunelleschi's model** of the dome. Don't miss the Terrazza Brunelleschiana on the third floor—an **outdoor terrace** with an up-close, rooftop view of the Duomo.

NORTH OF THE DUOMO
▲▲▲Accademia (Galleria dell'Accademia)

This museum houses Michelangelo's *David*, the consummate Renaissance statue of the buff, biblical shepherd boy ready to take on the giant. This six-ton, 17-foot-tall symbol of divine victory over evil represents a new century and a whole new Renaissance outlook. This is the age of Columbus and classicism, Galileo and Gutenberg, Luther and Leonardo—of Florence and the Renaissance.

The Accademia also contains some of the master's other works, including his powerful (unfinished) *Prisoners* and *St. Matthew,* as well as a *Pietà* (possibly by one of his disciples). You'll also see some mildly interesting pre-Renaissance and Renaissance paintings, including a couple of Botticellis, the plaster model of Giambologna's *Rape of the Sabine Women,* and a musical instrument collection with one of the very first-ever pianos (the pianoforte was invented here in Florence).

Cost and Hours: €12, additional €4 for recommended reservation; Tue-Sun 9:00-19:00, closed Mon, may stay open later in peak season; audioguide-€6, Via Ricasoli 60, +39 055 294 883; reservations: www.b-ticket.com/b-Ticket/uffizi, info: www.galleriaaccademiafirenze.it/en.

Visiting the Museum: In 1501, Michelangelo Buonarroti, a 26-year-old Florentine, was commissioned to carve a large-scale work for the Duomo. He was given a block of marble that other sculptors had rejected as too tall, shallow, and flawed to be of any value. But Michelangelo picked up his hammer and chisel, knocked a knot off what became *David*'s heart, and started to work.

The statue captures David as he's sizing up his enemy. He stands relaxed but alert, leaning on one leg in a classical pose known as *contrapposto.* In his powerful left hand, he fondles the handle of the sling, ready to fling a stone at the giant. His gaze is steady—searching with intense concentration, but also with extreme confidence. Michelangelo has caught the precise moment when David is saying to himself, "I can take this guy."

David is a symbol of Renaissance optimism. He's no brute. He's a civilized, thinking individual who can grapple with and overcome problems. He needs no armor, only his God-given physical strength and wits. Look at his right hand, with the raised veins and strong, relaxed fingers—many complained that it was too big and overdeveloped. But this is the hand of a man with the strength of God on his side. No mere boy could slay the giant. But David, powered by God, could...and did.

Renaissance Florentines could identify with *David.* Like him, they considered themselves God-blessed underdogs fighting their

Heart of Florence

VIA GUELFA

Tram T-2 to Airport

To Fortezza da Basso

CONSERVATORIO DI FULIGNO

PALAZZO DEGLI AFFARI

V. VALFONDA

VIA CENNINI

VIA ALAMANNI

VIA PIAGGETO

Piazza Adua

CENACOLO DI FULIGNO

SAN LORENZO MARKET

VIA NAZIONALE

VIA TADDEA

VIA S. ZANOBI

Piazza del Mercato Centrale

MERCATO CENTRALE

FAENZA

VIA DELL'ARIENTO

SANTA MARIA NOVELLA TRAIN STATION

Valfonda Line T1

VIA FIUME

B #1 & 6 (to San Marco) & 7 (from Fiesole)

BORGO LA NOCE

Alamanni-Stazione Line T1 & T2

B #7 (to Fiesole)

Largo Alinari

PALAZZO DEI CARTELLONI

S. ANTONINO

Piazza di San Lorenzo

BORGO S. LORENZO

BUS STATION

VIA S. CATERINA DI SIENA

Piazza della Stazione

#12, 23, C2 & C4

Piazza dell'Unità Italiana

Piazza Madonna

V. DEI MELARANCIO

S. AMARINO

MEDICI CHAPELS

SAN LORENZO

VIA DELLA SCALA

SANTA MARIA NOVELLA

Unità Line T2

PEDESTRIAN UNDERPASS TO TRAIN STN.

LAURENTIAN MEDICI LIBRARY

VIA DEL GIGLIO

V. DEI CONTI

ZANNETTI

BORGO

VIA DE' CANACCI

VIA DELLA SCALA

VIA BENEDETTA

VIA PALAZZUOLO

SANTA MARIA NOVELLA PERFUMERY

VIA D'AVELLI

VIA PANZANI

VIA DELL'ALLORO

Piazza di Santa Maria Novella

VIA DEI BANCHI

VIA DE' CERRETANI

Piazza di San Giovanni

OGNISSANTI

VIA DELLA PORCELLANA

VIA DI PAOLINO

LOGGIA DI SAN PAOLO

VIA D. BELLE DONNE

TREBBIO

RONDINELLI

ANTINORI

SANTA MARIA MAGGIORE

VIA PECORI

Piazza d'Ognissanti

BORGO OGNISSANTI

VIA DEL FOSSI

VIA DEL SOLE

VIA DEL MORO

SAN GAETANO

GIAC.

VIA CORSI

Y. DE' VECCHIETTI

PESCIONI

BRUNELLESCHI

ROMA

TOSINGHI

Piazza della Repubblica

LUNGARNO VESPUCCI

VIA DELLA SPADA

VIA DE' FEDERIGHI

RUCELLAI PALACE

VIA DE' TORNABUONI

VIA D. STROZZI

SASSETTI

LA RINASCENTE DEPT. STORE

PONTE ALLA CARRAIA

VIA DELLA VIGNA NUOVA

Piazza Carlo Goldoni

VIA DEL PARIONE

PURGATORIO

INFERNO

PALAZZO STROZZI

V. D. ANSELMI

ODEON CINEMA

POST

Piazza de' Davanzati

MONALDA

PELLICCERIA

CALIMALA

INTER-TRAVEL

PALAZZO CORSINI

SANTA TRINITÀ

LUNGARNO CORSINI

PARIONCINO

Piazza di Santa Trinità

V. DELLE TERME

PALAZZO DAVANZATI

VIA PORTA ROSSA

MERCATO NUOVO

B #12

Arno River

FERRAGAMO MUSEUM

BORGO SS. APOSTOLI

LUNGARNO ACCIAIUOLI

BOMBARDE

MANETTO

Piazza de' Salt.

LAMB

VIA POR S. MARIA

ARMA

Piazza Nazaro Sauro

LUNGARNO GUICCIARDINI

PONTE S. TRINITÀ

FLORENCE

VIA SERRAGLI

VIA SANTO SPIRITO

GEPPI

VIA MAFFIA

COVERELLI

VIA DE' SERRAGLI

VIA S. AGOSTINO

VIA MAGGIO

VIA S. MARTINO

VIA DELLE CALDAIE

Piazza de' Frescobaldi

PONTE VECCHIO

S. Stefano

VASARI CORRIDOR

To Brancacci Chapel

OLTRARNO

SANTO SPIRITO

BORGO SAN JACOPO

SAN JACOPO

SPRONE

V. D. RAMAGLI ANTI

Piazza della Passera

To Pitti Palace

Piazza di Santo Spirito

Piazza di Santa Felicità

Piazza di Santa Maria Soprarno

city-state rivals. In a deeper sense, they were civilized Renaissance people slaying the ugly giant of medieval superstition, pessimism, and oppression.

▲Piazza Santissima Annunziata

The most Renaissance square in Florence is tucked just a block behind the Accademia. It's like an urban cloister (the image of the ideal city) from the 15th century, with three fine buildings—a convent church, a hospital, and an orphanage—ringing a fine equestrian statue of Ferdinand, a Medici grand duke of the then-independent state of Tuscany. Stand in the center and slowly spin, imagining being here in 1500 as you survey the only Renaissance square in Florence, with the towering Duomo down the street.

The 15th-century **Santissima Annunziata church** (with its patronage attribution to the Pucci brothers: Alexander and Roberto) is worth a peek. The welcoming cloister has early-16th-century frescoes by Andrea del Sarto, and the church's interior is slathered in Baroque—rare in Florence.

Filippo Brunelleschi's **Hospital of the Innocents** (Ospedale degli Innocenti), built in the 1420s, is considered the first Renaissance building. Its graceful arches and columns, with each set of columns forming a square, embody the quintessence of Renaissance harmony and typified the new aesthetic of calm balance and symmetry. It's ornamented with terra-cotta medallions by Luca della Robbia—each showing a different way to wrap an infant (swaddled—meant to help babies grow straight, and practiced in Italy until about a century ago). Terra-cotta—made of glazed and painted clay—was a combination of painting and sculpture, durable and economic. For three generations, the Della Robbia family guarded the secret recipe and made their name by bringing this affordable art medium to Florence.

With its mission to care for the least among society (parentless or unwanted children), this hospital was also an important symbol of the increasingly humanistic and humanitarian outlook of Renaissance Florence. For four centuries (until 1875), orphans would be left at the "wheel of the innocents" (the small, barred window at the far left of the porch).

The **Museum of the Innocents** fills the hospital. A fine exhibit tells the story of these infants with artifacts that help you imagine what it was like living here. It also houses some fine art, including several iconic glazed terra-cotta medallions by the Della Robbia family (€8, Wed-Mon 11:00-18:00, closed Tue, audioguide-€3, +39 055 203 7301, www.museodeglinnocenti.it).

Eating: $$ Caffè del Verone, on the museum's top terrace, offers a nice, peaceful break with rooftop views.

▲▲Museum of San Marco (Museo di San Marco)

One block north of the Accademia, this 15th-century monastery houses the greatest collection anywhere of frescoes and paintings by the early Renaissance master Fra Angelico. The ground floor features the monk's paintings, along with works by Fra Bartolomeo.

Upstairs are 43 cells decorated by Fra Angelico and his assistants. While the monk/painter was trained in the medieval religious style, he also learned and adopted Renaissance techniques and sensibilities, producing works that blended Christian symbols and Renaissance realism. Don't miss the cell of Savonarola, the charismatic monk who rode in from the Christian right, threw out the Medici, turned Florence into a theocracy, sponsored "bonfires of the vanities" (burning books, paintings, and so on), and was finally burned himself when Florence decided to change channels.

Cost and Hours: €8; Mon-Fri 8:15-14:00, Sat until 17:00, closed Sun; also closed second and fourth Mon of each month; reservations possible but unnecessary, on Piazza San Marco, +39 055 238 8608.

Basilica of San Lorenzo

The Basilica of San Lorenzo—on the site of the first Christian church in Florence—was built outside the Roman walls and consecrated in AD 393, then rebuilt in the early 1400s. That's when Filippo Brunelleschi was hired to replace a Romanesque church that stood here. Brunelleschi designed the building, and Donatello worked on the bronze pulpits inside (among other things). Adjacent to the church is a cloister where you can visit the crypt (with the tombs of Cosimo the Elder and Donatello) and the Laurentian Medici Library, designed by Michelangelo. (The

FLORENCE

famed Medici Chapels, with Michelangelo's tomb sculptures, are part of the church complex but have a separate ticket; see next listing.)

Cost and Hours: €9 for the church and crypt, buy ticket just inside cloister to the left of the facade; €4 for library only (purchase upstairs); church and crypt open Mon-Sat 9:30-17:30, closed Sun, shorter hours off-season; library Mon-Fri 10:00-13:30, closed Sat-Sun; Piazza di San Lorenzo, +39 055 214 042, basilica: www.sanlorenzofirenze.it, library: www.bmlonline.it.

▲▲Medici Chapels (Cappelle Medicee)

The burial site of the ruling Medici family in the Basilica of San Lorenzo includes the dusky crypt; the big, domed Chapel of Princes; and the magnificent New Sacristy, featuring architecture, tombs, and statues almost entirely by Michelangelo. The Medici made their money in textiles and banking, and patronized a dream team of Renaissance artists that put Florence on the cultural map. Michelangelo, who spent his teen years living with the Medici, was commissioned to create the family's final tribute.

Cost and Hours: €9; Sat-Mon 8:15-13:50, Wed-Fri 13:15-18:50; closed Tue and first, third, and fifth Sun of each month; reservations possible but unnecessary, audioguide-€6, modest dress required, +39 055 294 886, www.bargellomusei.beniculturali.it.

▲San Lorenzo Market

Florence's vast open-air market sprawls in the streets between the Duomo and the train station, with the highest concentration in the streets ringing Mercato Centrale (daily 9:00-19:00). More popular with tourists than locals, it's a hodgepodge of vendors selling T-shirts, scarves, cheap souvenirs, and leather goods of varying quality. At stalls or shops, prices are soft—don't be shy about bargaining.

▲Mercato Centrale (Central Market)

Florence's giant iron-and-glass-covered central market was constructed around 1865 as part of the city remake during the unification of Italy, when Florence was, for a few years, the capital of the newly formed country. Stand back and see it as an Industrial Age triumph...a temple of commerce and good food. Then step in and explore the fragrant and picturesque wonderland of produce.

Downstairs, you'll see parts of the cow (and bull) you'd never dream of eating (no, that's not a turkey neck), enjoy free samples, watch pasta being made, and have your pick of plenty of fun eateries sloshing out cheap and tasty pasta to locals (Mon-Fri 7:00-14:00, Sat until 17:00, closed Sun).

Upstairs, the restored glass roof and steel rafters soar over a modern and extremely touristy food court (daily 10:00-24:00). For eating ideas downstairs, upstairs, and around the market, see "Eating in Florence," later.

▲Medici-Riccardi Palace (Palazzo Medici-Riccardi)

Lorenzo the Magnificent's home is worth a look for its art. The tiny Chapel of the Magi contains colorful Renaissance gems such as

The Journey of the Magi frescoes by Benozzo Gozzoli. The former library has a Baroque ceiling fresco by Luca Giordano, a prolific artist from Naples known as "Fast Luke" *(Luca fa presto)* for his speedy workmanship. While the Medici originally occupied this 1444 house, in the 1700s it became home to the Riccardi family, who added the Baroque flourishes.

Cost and Hours: €10, Thu-Tue 9:00-19:00, closed Wed; ticket entrance is off the central courtyard, enter from Via Cavour 3 or sometimes from Via de' Ginori 2; +39 055 276 0552, www.palazzomediciriccardi.it.

BETWEEN THE DUOMO AND PIAZZA DELLA SIGNORIA

▲Orsanmichele Church

In the ninth century, this loggia (covered courtyard) was a market used for selling grain (stored upstairs). Later, it was enclosed to make a church. Focus on the exterior, with its dynamic, statue-filled niches, some with accompanying symbols from the guilds that sponsored the art. For more on the statues, see page 478.

The interior (open only two days a week) has a glorious Gothic tabernacle (1359), which houses the painted wooden panel that depicts *Madonna delle Grazie* (1346). The iron bars spanning the vaults were the Italian Gothic answer to the French Gothic external buttresses. The rectangular holes in the piers were once grain chutes that connected to the upper floors. The museum upstairs displays most of the original statues from the niches outside the building, including ones by Ghiberti, Donatello, Brunelleschi, and others.

Cost and Hours: €4, includes museum; Tue and Sat 10:30-

FLORENCE

18:00, closed Sun-Mon and Wed-Fri; ticket office open Mon-Sat 9:00-16:00, closed Sun, books concert tickets (see next) as well as Uffizi and Accademia tickets; www.bargellomusei.beniculturali.it.

Evening Concerts: You can give special thanks if you're in town when the church is hosting an evening concert (tickets sold on day of concert from door facing Via dei Calzaiuoli or, on Sun, from the doorway opposite the church entrance).

▲Mercato Nuovo (a.k.a. the Straw Market)

This market loggia is how Orsanmichele looked before it became a church. Originally a silk-and-straw market, Mercato Nuovo still functions as a rustic yet touristy market (at the intersection of Via Calimala and Via Porta Rossa; daily 9:00-18:30). Notice the circled X in the center, marking the spot where people landed after being hoisted up to the top and dropped as punishment for bankruptcy (easiest to find when the market is closed and the vendors disappear). You'll also find *Il Porcellino* (a statue of a wild boar nicknamed "The Piglet"), which people rub and give coins to ensure their return to Florence. This new copy, while only a few years old, already has a polished snout. At the back corner, a wagon sells tripe (cow innards) sandwiches—a local favorite.

▲Piazza della Repubblica

Lined with venerable cafés and high-fashion stores, this square has been the center of Florence for millennia. In Roman times, it was a fort at the intersection of the two main roads (marked today by the square's lone column). In 1571, Cosimo I de' Medici had the area walled in and made into the Jewish ghetto. If you venture outside the piazza, you get a sense of what the old neighborhood was like— a tangle of narrow, winding lanes dotted with medieval towers. In the late 19th century, the area was razed to create this spacious square, with a huge triumphal arch celebrating the unification of Italy.

Today, people sip drinks at outdoor cafes, shop at the local La Rinascente department store, or enjoy a reasonably priced coffee on the store's rooftop terrace, with great Duomo and city views.

For more about Piazza della Repubblica, see the "Renaissance Walk," earlier.

▲Palazzo Davanzati

This five-story, late-medieval tower house offers a rare look at a noble dwelling built in the 14th century. Like other buildings of the age, the exterior is festooned with 14th-century horse-tethering rings made from iron, torch holders, and poles upon which to hang tapestries and fly flags. Inside, though the furnishings are pretty sparse, you'll see richly painted walls, a long chute that functioned as a well, plenty of fireplaces, a lace display, and even an indoor "outhouse." You can borrow English descriptions in each room.

Cost and Hours: €6; Tue-Thu 8:45-13:30, Fri-Sun 13:45-18:30; closed Mon and first, third, and fifth Sun of each month; reservations possible but unnecessary; Via Porta Rossa 13, +39 055 238 8610, www.bargellomusei.beniculturali.it.

ON AND NEAR PIAZZA DELLA SIGNORIA
▲▲▲Uffizi Gallery

This greatest collection of Italian paintings anywhere features works by Giotto, Leonardo, Raphael, Caravaggio, Titian, and Mi-

chelangelo, and a roomful of Botticellis, including the *Birth of Venus*. Start with Giotto's early stabs at Renaissance-style realism, then move on through the 3-D experimentation of the early 1400s to the real thing rendered by the likes of Botticelli and Leonardo. Finish off with Michelangelo and Raphael. Because only 600 visitors are allowed inside the building at any one time, there's generally a very long wait. The good news: no Vatican-style mob scenes inside. The museum is nowhere near as big as it is great.

Cost and Hours: €20 plus €4 for recommended timed-entry reservation, cheaper in winter, covered by €38 Uffizi/Pitti Palace/Boboli Gardens "PassePartout" combo-ticket; open Tue-Sun 8:15-18:30, closed Mon, may stay open later in peak season, last entry one hour before closing; audioguide-€6, +39 055 294 883, reservations: www.b-ticket.com/b-Ticket/uffizi, info: www.uffizi.it.

Reservations Required: To skip the notoriously long ticket-buying lines, book your Uffizi entrance in advance online. You'll be emailed a voucher that you'll swap for an actual ticket 15 minutes before your visit at the reservation ticket office (across the courtyard from the museum entrance).

When to Go: While ridiculous, if you don't have a reservation, try going 90 minutes before closing and see the museum in a rush.

Getting In: If you arrive with a **reservation**, go first to the courtyard door #3 to pick up your ticket (labeled *Reservation Ticket Office*). There you exchange your email voucher/confirmation number for a ticket. Tickets are available for pickup 15 minutes before your appointed time. Then, with ticket in hand, walk briskly across

Uffizi Gallery Overview

Not to Scale

To Duomo

Piazza della Signoria

DAVID COPY

PALAZZO VECCHIO

LOGGIA BELOW

BELVEDERE TERRACE

VIA DELLA NINNA

To Santa Croce

CAFÉ

STATUES OF FAMOUS FLORENTINES LINE THE COURTYARD

ELEVATOR

GRANDUCALE STAIRS UP FROM ENTRY & **WC**

LANZI STAIRS DOWN TO WC & EXIT

NORTHERN ART

TOUR BEGINS

GIOTTO & EARLY REN.

EXIT RAMP

3

1 →

ENTRANCES

MICHELANGELO

2 →

BOTTICELLI

BUONTALENTI STAIRS DOWN TO FIRST FLOOR & EXIT →

W E S T   C O R R I D O R

Piazza degli Uffizi (Courtyard)

E A S T   C O R R I D O R

VIA DI CASTELLANI

LEONARDO

VENUS DE' MEDICI

UNDERPASS

Piazza dei Giudici

VIEW OF PONTE VECCHIO →

SCULPTURE HALL

LUPA ■

■ DORIFORO

GALILEO SCIENCE MUSEUM

UNDERPASS

To Ponte Vecchio

LUNGARNO   DE'MEDICI

1 Reservation Entrance

2 Main Entrance & Same-Day Reservations

3 Reservation Ticket Office

Arno River

the courtyard to door #1. Get in the queue for "individuals," not "groups."

To **buy a ticket on the spot,** line up with everyone else at door #2, marked *Main Entrance.*

Renovation: The Uffizi recently completed a reorganization; pick up a map as you enter for the latest (some locations may vary from this tour).

Tours: The 2.5-hour audioguide costs €6. Or download my free Uffizi Gallery audio tour.

Visiting the Museum: The Uffizi is U-shaped, running around an exterior courtyard. The artwork we'll see is up four long flights of stairs, on the top floor. The east wing contains Florentine paintings from medieval to Renaissance times. At the far end, you pass through a short hallway filled with the kind of ancient sculpture that inspired the Renaissance. The west wing has the Renaissance biggies—Leonardo, Michelangelo, and Raphael. Downstairs there are many more rooms of art, showing how the Florentine Renaissance morphed into Mannerism (Parmigianino), spread to Venice (Titian), and inspired the Baroque (Caravaggio).

Medieval (1200-1400): Three similar-looking Madonna-and-Bambinos—all painted within a few decades of each other, in about the year 1300—show baby steps in the march to Renaissance realism (Room 4). Duccio's piece is the most medieval and two-dimensional. There's no background, and the angels are just stacked one on top of the other, floating in the golden atmosphere. Cimabue mixes the iconic Byzantine style with budding Italian realism. Giotto creates a space and fills it. Like a set designer, he builds a three-dimensional "stage"—the canopied throne—then peoples it with real beings. The throne has angels in front, prophets behind, and a canopy over the top. But the real triumph here is Mary herself—big and monumental, like a Roman statue. Beneath her robe, she has a real live body, with knees and breasts that stick out at us. This three-dimensionality was revolutionary in its day, a taste of the Renaissance a century before it began.

Early Renaissance (mid-1400s): In the 1400s, painters worked out the problems of painting realistically, using mathematics to create the illusion of three-dimensionality. Paolo Uccello's colorful Battle of San Romano is not so much a piece of art as an exercise in perspective (Room 9). The fallen horses and soldiers are experiments in "foreshortening"—creating the illusion of distance. Some of the figures are definitely A-plus material, like the fallen gray horse in the center. But some are more like B-minus work—the fallen soldier at the far right would be child-size if he stood up. Uccello almost literally went crazy trying to master the three dimensions (thank God he was born before Einstein discovered one more).

We don't need the wispy halo over the head of Fra Filippo's **Madonna and Child with Two Angels** to tell us she's holy—she radiates sweetness and light from her divine face (Room 9). Lippi painted idealized beauty, but his models were real flesh-and-blood human beings. You could look through all the thousands of paintings from the Middle Ages and not find anything so human as the mischievous face of one of Lippi's little angel boys.

In medieval times, only saints and angels were worthy of being painted. In the humanistic Renaissance, however, even nonreligious folk like the husband and wife **Federico da Montefeltro and Battista Sforza** had their features preserved for posterity, in this case by Piero della Francesca (Room 9). Renaissance artists discovered the beauty in ordinary people and painted them, literally, warts and all.

The Renaissance (1450-1500): Florence in 1450 was in a Firenz-y of activity. There was a can-do spirit of optimism in the air, led by prosperous merchants and bankers and a strong middle class. Lorenzo de' Medici, head of the powerful Medici family, epitomized this new humanistic spirit. He gathered Florence's best and brightest around him for evening wine and discussions of great ideas. One of this circle was the painter Botticelli.

The Botticelli rooms (11-12) are filled with masterpieces and classical fleshiness. Botticelli's *Spring* is the Renaissance in its first bloom, its "springtime" of innocence. Madonna is out, Venus is in. This is a return to the pre-Christian pagan world of classical Greece, where things of the flesh are not sinful. Botticelli emphasizes pristine beauty over gritty realism. The lines of the bodies have pleasing, S-like curves. The faces are idealized but have real human features. There's a look of thoughtfulness and even melancholy in the faces—as though everyone knows that the innocence of spring will not last forever.

Birth of Venus is a masterpiece of Western art. This is the purest expression of Renaissance beauty. Venus' naked body is not sensual, but innocent. Botticelli thought that physical beauty was a way of appreciating God.

Classical Sculpture: If the Renaissance was the foundation of the modern world, the foundation of the Renaissance was classical sculpture. Sculptors, painters, and poets alike turned for inspiration to these ancient Greek and Roman works as the epitome of balance, 3-D perspective, human anatomy, and beauty.

In the Tribune Room, the highlight is the *Venus de' Medici* (first century BC), a Roman copy of the lost original by the great Greek sculptor Praxiteles. Balanced, harmonious, and serene, the statue embodies the attributes of Greece's "Golden Age," when balance was admired in every aspect of life.

The **sculpture hall** has 2,000-year-old Roman copies of 2,500-year-old Greek originals. The most impressive is the male nude, **Doriforo** ("spear carrier"), a Roman copy of the Greek original by Polykleitos. The purple statue in the center of the hall—headless and limbless—is the Roman **"she-wolf"** (Lupa, c. AD 120), the animal that raised Rome's legendary founders.

High Renaissance (1500-1550): A scientist, architect, engineer, musician, and painter, Leonardo da Vinci (1452-1519) was a true Renaissance Man. He worked at his own pace rather than to please an employer, so he often left works unfinished.

In the *Annunciation*, the angel Gabriel has walked up to Mary, and now kneels on one knee like an ambassador, saluting her (Room 35). See how relaxed his other hand is, draped over his knee. Mary, who's been reading, looks up with a gesture of surprise and curiosity. Leonardo constructs a beautifully landscaped "stage" and puts his characters in it. He's taken a miraculous event—an angel appearing out of the blue—and presented it in a very human way.

Leonardo's human insight is even more apparent in this unfinished *Adoration of the Magi*. The poor kings are amazed at the Christ Child—even afraid of him. This work is as agitated as the *Annunciation* is calm, giving us an idea of Leonardo's range.

Don't miss Michelangelo's **Holy Family** (a.k.a *Doni Tondo*, Room 38), the only completed easel painting by the greatest sculptor in history. Florentine painters were sculptors with brushes; this shows it. Instead of a painting, it's more like three clusters of statues with some clothes painted on.

Michelangelo was a Florentine—in fact, he was like an adopted son of the Medici, who recognized his talent—but much of his greatest work was done in Rome as part of the pope's face-lift of the city. We can see here some of the techniques he used on the Sistine Chapel ceiling that revolutionized painting—monumental figures; dramatic angles (looking up Mary's nose); accentuated, rippling muscles; and bright, clashing colors.

Nearby is Raphael's Madonna of the Goldfinch, in which the artist brings Mary and bambino down from heaven and into the real world of trees, water, and sky. The two halves of the painting balance perfectly. Draw a line down the middle, through Mary's nose and down through her knee. John the Baptist on the left is balanced by Jesus on the right. Even the trees in the background balance each other, left and right. These things help create the subconscious feelings of balance and order that reinforce the atmosphere of maternal security in this domestic scene—pure Renaissance.

More Art on the Lower Floor: For those willing to linger longer, the first floor is worth a look. It features work from after the Renaissance: Mannerism (such as Parmigianino), Venetian (Titian), Baroque (Caravaggio), and finally Flemish and Dutch (Rubens and Rembrandt). Before you head down, you may want to take advantage of the second floor's fine café, open-air terrace, and WC. To reach the first floor, retrace your steps to the staircase between the Leonardo da Vinci and Michelangelo galleries and head down.

▲▲Palazzo Vecchio

This castle-like fortress with the 300-foot spire dominates Florence's main square. In Renaissance times, it was the Town Hall, where citizens pioneered the once-radical notion of self-rule. Its official name—Palazzo della Signoria—refers to the elected members of the city council. In 1540, the tyrant Cosimo I made the building his personal palace, redecorating the interior in lavish style. Today the building functions once again as the Town Hall.

Entry to the ground-floor Michelozzo courtyard, with its arcade of intricately carved columns, is free, so even if you don't go upstairs to the museum, you can step inside and feel the essence of the Medici. There's also a fine little exhibit of scenes from old Florence (ground level in adjacent ticketing courtyard). Paying customers can see Cosimo's (fairly) lavish royal apartments, decorated with (fairly) top-notch paintings and statues by Michelangelo and Donatello. The highlight is the Grand Hall (Salone dei Cinquecento), a 13,000-square-foot hall lined with huge frescoes and interesting statues.

Across from the Palazzo, facing the square, is the **Loggia dei Lanzi,** where Renaissance Florentines once debated the issues of the day; a collection of Medici-approved sculptures now stand (or writhe) under its canopy, including Cellini's bronze *Perseus*.

Cost and Hours: Michelozzo courtyard-free, museum and tower climb (418 steps)-€12.50 each, excavations-€4. Museum and excavations open daily 9:00-19:00 except Thu until 14:00, may stay open later in peak season; tower keeps shorter hours (last entry one hour before closing) and closed in bad weather; last tickets for all sights sold one hour before closing; videoguide-€5, Piazza della Signoria, +39 055 276 8224, http://biglettimusei.comune.fi.it.

▲Ponte Vecchio

Florence's most famous bridge has long been lined with shops. Originally these were butcher shops that used the river as a handy disposal system. Then, when the powerful and princely Medici built the Vasari Corridor over the bridge, the stinky meat market was replaced by more elegant gold-and-silver shops (some of which remain here to this day). The corridor, an elevated passageway above the bridge, was built so the Medici could com-

mute comfortably between their Pitti Palace home and their Palazzo Vecchio offices (corridor may be closed for renovation when you visit). A statue of Benvenuto Cellini, the master goldsmith of the Renaissance, stands in the center of the bridge, ignored by the flood of tacky tourism.

▲▲Galileo Science Museum (Museo Galilei)

When we think of the Florentine Renaissance, we think of visual arts: painting, mosaics, architecture, and sculpture. But when the

visual arts declined in the 1600s (abused and co-opted by political powers), music and science flourished in Florence. The first opera was written here. And Florence hosted many scientific breakthroughs, as you'll see in this fascinating collection of Renaissance and later clocks, telescopes, maps, and ingenious gadgets. Trace the technical innovations as modern science emerges from 1000 to 1900. Some of the most talked-about bottles in Florence are the ones here that contain Galileo's fingers. Exhibits include various tools for gauging the world, from a compass and thermometer to Galileo's telescopes. Other displays delve into pumps, medicine, and chemistry. It's friendly, comfortably cool, never crowded, and just a block east of the Uffizi on the Arno River.

Cost and Hours: €10, daily 9:30-18:00 except Tue until 13:00, Piazza dei Giudici 1, +39 055 265 311, www.museogalileo.it.

EAST OF PIAZZA DELLA SIGNORIA

▲▲▲Bargello (Museo Nazionale del Bargello)

This underappreciated sculpture museum is in a former police station-turned-prison that looks like a mini-Palazzo Vecchio. The

Renaissance began with sculpture and you can see the birth of this revolution of 3-D in the Bargello. It's a small, uncrowded museum and a pleasant break from the intensity of the rest of Florence. You'll see 150 years of great statues, spanning the history of Florence's heyday.

Highlights include Donatello's very influential, painfully beautiful *David* (the first male nude to be sculpted in a thousand years), multiple works by Michelangelo, and rooms of Medici treasures. Moody Donatello, who embraced realism with his lifelike statues, set the personal and artistic style for many Renaissance artists to follow. The best pieces are in the ground-floor room at the foot of the outdoor staircase (with fine works by Michelangelo, Cellini, and Giambologna) and in the "Donatello room" directly above (including his two different *David*s, plus Ghiberti and Brunelleschi's dueling competition entries for the Baptistery doors—and yet another *David* by Verrocchio).

Cost and Hours: €9; usually daily 8:15-14:00—later for special exhibits; may close on second and fourth Sun and first, third, and fifth Mon of each month; last entry 50 minutes before closing; reservations possible but unnecessary, audioguide-€6; Via del Proconsolo 4, +39 055 238 8606, www.bargellomusei.beniculturali.it.

▲▲Santa Croce Church

This 14th-century Franciscan church, decorated with centuries of precious art, holds the tombs of great Florentines. The loud 19th-century Victorian Gothic facade faces a huge square ringed with tempting shops and littered with tired tourists. Escape into the church and admire its sheer height and spaciousness. Your ticket includes the Pazzi Chapel and a small museum; the complex also houses a leather school.

Cost and Hours: Church—€8; Mon-Sat 9:30-17:30, Sun from 12:30; multimedia guide-€4, modest dress required, 10-minute walk east of the Palazzo Vecchio along Borgo de' Greci, +39 055 246 6105, www.santacroceopera.it. Leather school—free, use entry at the back of the church; Mon-Sat 10:00-18:00, closed Sun; https://leatherschool.biz.

Visiting the Church: On the left wall (as you face the altar) is the tomb of **Galileo Galilei** (1564-1642), the Pisan who lived his last years under house arrest near Florence. His crime? Defying the Church by saying that the earth revolved around the sun. His heretical remains were only allowed in the church long after his death.

Directly opposite (on the right wall) is the tomb of **Michelangelo Buonarroti** (1475-1564). Santa Croce was Michelangelo's childhood church, as he grew up a block west of here. Farther up the nave is the tomb of **Niccolò Machiavelli** (1469-1527), a champion of democratic Florence and author of *The Prince*, a how-to manual on hardball politics—which later Medici rulers found instructive.

The first chapel to the right of the main altar features the famous *Death of St. Francis* fresco by Giotto. With simple but eloquent gestures, Francis' brothers bid him a sad farewell. The Sacristy has Cimabue's impressive *Crucifixion* (before 1288), a survivor of the devastating flood of 1966.

Exit the church nave between the Rossini and Machiavelli tombs to enter a delightful cloister. On the left is the small Brunelleschi-designed Pazzi Chapel, whose unity and harmony of design captures the Renaissance in miniature. Straight ahead is the church museum, with several rooms of paintings, statues, and altarpieces.

Around the back of the church is the **leather school,** founded after World War II to give war orphans a trade. It became the first shop in what is now a popular leather district. You can watch the leatherworking in action and browse the (very expensive) finished products for sale.

▲Casa Buonarroti (Michelangelo's House)

A property once owned by Michelangelo, this house was built after the artist's death by his grandnephew "Michelangelo the Younger," who turned it into a little museum honoring his famous relative. The highlights—Michelangelo's first sculptures and some sketches—are not must-sees in art-heavy Florence, but are appreciated by Michelangelo lovers. The place where Michelangelo actually grew up is only a few blocks from here, at 10 Via de' Bentaccordi.

Cost and Hours: €8, Wed-Mon 10:00-16:30, closed Tue, Via Ghibellina 70, +39 055 241 752, www.casabuonarroti.it.

NEAR THE TRAIN STATION
▲▲Church of Santa Maria Novella

This 13th-century Dominican church is rich in art. Along with crucifixes by Giotto and Brunelleschi, it contains the textbook example of the early Renaissance mastery of perspective: *The Trinity* by Masaccio. The exquisite chapels trace art in Florence from medieval times to early Baroque. The outside of the church features a dash of Romanesque (horizontal stripes), Gothic (pointed arches),

Renaissance (geometric shapes), and Baroque (scrolls). Step in and look down the 330-foot nave for a 14th-century optical illusion.

Next to the church are the cloisters and the **museum,** located in the old Dominican convent of Santa Maria Novella. The museum's highlight is the breathtaking Spanish Chapel, with walls covered by a series of frescoes by Andrea di Bonaiuto.

Cost and Hours: Church and museum—€7.50; Mon-Thu and

Sat 10:00-17:00, Fri from 11:00, Sun from 13:00; multimedia guide-€3, modest dress required; main entrance on Piazza Santa Maria Novella across from the train station; +39 055 219 257, www.smn.it.

THE OLTRARNO (SOUTH OF THE ARNO RIVER)
▲▲▲Pitti Palace

The imposing Pitti Palace, several blocks southwest of Ponte Vecchio, has many separate museums and two gardens. The main reason to visit is to see the Palatine Gallery, which houses a fine painting collection that picks up where the Uffizi leaves off, with High Renaissance. Lovers of Raphael's Madonnas and Titian's portraits will find some of the world's best of each. If it's a nice day, take a stroll in the Boboli Gardens, a rare and inviting patch of extensive green space within old Florence.

Cost and Hours: The €16 **Pitti Palace** ticket covers the Palatine Gallery, Royal Apartments, Treasury of the Grand Dukes (silver museum), Museum of Costume and Fashion, and Gallery of Modern Art; open Tue-Sun 8:15-18:50, closed Mon, last entry one hour before closing. The €10 **Boboli Garden** ticket covers the Boboli and Bardini Gardens as well as the Porcelain Museum located in the garden; open daily June-Aug 8:15-19:00, April-May and Sept-Oct until 18:30, Nov-March until 16:30; closed first and last Mon of each month, last entry one hour before closing. An €8 audioguide explains the sprawling palace (+39 055 238 8614, www.uffizi.it).

Visiting the Museum: In the Palatine Gallery you'll walk through one palatial room after another, with walls sagging with masterpieces by 16th- and 17th-century masters, including Titian and Raphael. The Pitti's Raphael collection is the second-biggest anywhere—the Vatican beats it by one. Use the information folders in each room to help find the featured paintings.

The collection is all on one floor. To see the highlights, walk straight down the spine through a dozen or so rooms. After the Palatine Gallery, the route flows naturally into the even more lavish rooms of the Royal Apartments. These 14 rooms (of which only a few are open at any one time) are where Florence's aristocrats lived in the 18th and 19th centuries. Each room features the style of a particular time period. Here, you get a real feel for the splendor of the dukes' world.

The rest of Pitti Palace is skippable, unless the various sights match your interests: the **Gallery of Modern Art** (second floor; Romantic, Neoclassical, and Impressionist works by 19th- and 20th-century Tuscan painters), **Treasury of the Grand Dukes** (ground and mezzanine floors; Medici treasures from jeweled crucifixes to gilded ostrich eggs), **Museum of Costume and Fashion, Porcelain Museum,** and **Boboli and Bardini gardens** (behind the palace; enter from Pitti Palace courtyard—be prepared to climb uphill).

▲▲Brancacci Chapel (Capella Brancacci)

In the Brancacci Chapel, Masaccio created a world in paint that looked like the world we inhabit. For the first time in a thousand years, Man and Nature were frozen for inspection. Masaccio's painting techniques were copied by many Renaissance artists, and his people—sturdy, intelligent, and dignified, with expressions of understated astonishment—helped shape Renaissance men and women's own self-images.

Half of the chapel's frescoes are by Masaccio, and half by either Masolino or Filippino Lippi, who completed the chapel more than 50 years later. Although Masaccio is the star, the panels by his colleagues provide a good contrast in styles.

Cost and Hours: €10; Fri-Sat and Mon 10:00-17:00, Sun from 13:00, closed Tue-Thu, reservations required; videoguide-€3, knees and shoulders must be covered, in Church of Santa Maria del Carmine on Piazza del Carmine; to reserve call +39 055 276 8224 or +39 055 276 8558, or email cappellabrancacci@musefirenze.it; www.musefirenze.it.

▲Piazzale Michelangelo

Overlooking the city from across the river (look for the huge bronze statue of *David*), this square has a superb view of Florence and the stunning dome of the Duomo. It's worth the 25-minute hike, taxi, or bus ride.

An inviting café (open seasonally) with great views is just below the overlook. The best photos are taken from the street immediately below the overlook. After dark, the square is packed with school kids licking ice cream and each other. About 200 yards beyond all the tour groups and teenagers is the stark, beautiful, crowd-free, Romanesque San Miniato Church (next listing). A WC is located just off the road, halfway between the two sights.

Getting There (and Back): While you can catch bus #12 (from

Accommodations
1 Hotel Silla
2 Hotel Annalena

Eateries
3 Burro & Acciughe Fish Restaurant, Trattoria dell'Orto & Ristorante Il Guscio
4 Antico Ristoro di' Cambi
5 Trattoria Sabatino
6 To Santarosa Bistrot
7 Il Rifrullo & Il Gelato di Filo
8 Antica Mescita San Niccolò & Boccadarno
9 Zeb Wine Bar

Nightlife & Other
10 Zoe Nightclub
11 Abraham Clet Gallery

near Piazza d'Ognissanti, can be a long ride) or a taxi up to the piazza, the walk up from the Oltrarno neighborhood of San Niccolò is popular—especially in the early evening—and not that challenging (see the map on page 509).

Start at the intersection of Via San Niccolò and Via San Miniato, just below Porta San Miniato (scope out the restaurants and bars here, as you'll circle back to this spot in about an hour if you walk down). Point yourself uphill, head through the old gate, and continue until you reach a broad, terraced hill-climb to the left. Up

Oltrarno, South of the Arno River

Piazza della Repubblica

LAMBERTI

ROSSA

V. POR S. MARIA

Piazza della Signoria

PALAZZO VECCHIO

V. POR S. MARIA

LAMB.

V. LAMB

UFFIZI GALLERY

VASARI CORRIDOR

Piazza di Santa Maria Soprarno

GALILEO SCIENCE MUSEUM

V. DEI LEONI

OSTERIA

VINEGRIA

VIA DEI NERI

VAGELLA

L. GEN. DIAZ

CAST.

LUNGARNO

COSTA D. SAN GIORGIO

COSTA SCAR.

VIA DE' BARDI

TORRIGIANI

SAN GIORGIO

PALAZZO DE' MOZZI

PORTA SAN GIORGIO

FORTE DI BELVEDERE

Bardini Gardens

CITY WALLS

VIA DI BELVEDERE

Niccolò

V. DI SAN LEONARDO

BARGELLO MUSEUM

V. D. VIGNA VECCHIA

V. DELL'ANGUILLARA

BORGO DE' GRECI

Piazza Santa Croce

B. S. CROCE

CORSO DEI TINTORI

MALENCHINI

CASA BUONARROTI

VIA GHIBELLINA

VIALE PEPI

BORGO ALLEGRI

SANTA CROCE

PAZZI CHAPEL

V. DI SAN GIUSEPPE

ANTONIO MAG.

LUNGARNO DELLE GRAZIE

L. D. ZECCA VECCHIA

PONTE ALLE GRAZIE

Arno River

Piazza Demidoff

V. RENAI

VIA S. NIC.

LUNGARNO SERRISTORI

10

1

11

8

9

7

PORTA SAN MINIATO

V. SAN NICCOLÒ

Piazzale G. Poggi

TORRE SAN NICCOLÒ

PESCAIA DI SAN NICCOLÒ

VIA DE' BASTIONI

VIALE POGGI

Piazzale Michelangelo

PIAZZALE MICHELANGELO HILL CLIMB

V. DEL MONTE ALLE CROCE

PIAZZALE MICHELANGELO

VIALE GALILEO GALILEI

SAN SALVATORE AL MONTE

To A-1 Autostrada (Firenze Sud exit)

SAN MINIATO

N

300 Meters

300 Yards

Cimitero delle Porte Sante

---

top, Piazzale Michelangelo will be to your left, and San Miniato Church to your right.

When you're ready to leave, the hike down is quick and enjoyable (or take bus #13). You can retrace your steps, or you can turn this walk into a loop: From the parking lot, take the ramp leading down toward Ponte Vecchio (near the replica *David*). At the bottom of the ramp, cross the street and continue down the pathway. You'll cross one more street, then zigzag downhill toward the river. You are descending on the so-called Poggi ramps, developed in the late 19th century as a string of staircases, fountains, and grottos that embellishes (and stabilizes) the hillside. When you draw even with the big tower (Porta San Niccolò), turn left onto Via San Niccolò and make your way back to the group of lively cafés and restaurants where you started (for recommendations, see page 540).

▲▲San Miniato Church

According to legend, the martyred St. Minias—this church's namesake—was beheaded on the banks of the Arno in AD 250.

He picked up his head and walked here (this was before the #12 bus), where he died and was buried in what became the first Christian cemetery in Florence. In the 11th century, this church was built to house Minias' remains.

The church's green-and-white marble facade (12th century) is classic Florentine Romanesque, one of the oldest in town. Inside you'll find some wonderful 3-D paintings, a plush ceiling of glazed terra-cotta panels by Luca della Robbia, and an exquisite Renaissance chapel (on the left side of the nave). The highlight for me is the brilliantly preserved art in the sacristy (upstairs to right of altar, in the room on right) showing scenes from the life of St. Benedict (circa 1350, by a follower of Giotto). Drop €2 into the electronic panel in the corner to light the room for five minutes. The evening vesper service with the monks chanting in Latin offers a meditative worship experience—a peaceful way to end your visit.

Cost and Hours: Free, daily 9:30-13:00 & 15:00-19:00, closed sporadically for special occasions, +39 055 234 2731, www.sanminiatoalmonte.it.

Getting There: It's about 200 yards above Piazzale Michelangelo. Follow the walking directions in the Piazzale Michelangelo listing earlier, or take bus #12 to the San Miniato al Monte stop (hop off and hike up the grand staircase); bus #13 takes you back down the hill.

Gregorian Chants: These are held Mon-Sat at 18:00 and 18:30, and Sun at 17:30—but as the schedule is subject to change, double-check with any TI, the church's website, or call ahead.

Shopping in Florence

Florence may be one of Europe's best shopping towns—it's been known for its sense of style since the Medici days. Smaller stores are generally open about 9:00-13:00 and 15:30-19:30, usually closed on Sunday, often closed on Monday (or at least Monday morning), and sometimes closed for a couple of weeks around August 15. Bigger stores have similar hours, without the afternoon break.

For authentic, locally produced wares, look for shops displaying the *Esercizi Storici Fiorentini* seal, with a picture of the Palazzo Vecchio's tower. At these city-endorsed "Historical Florentine Ventures," you may pay a premium, but quality is assured (for a list of shops, see www.esercizistoricifiorentini.it).

Department Stores

Department store chains include the upscale **La Rinascente** (daily 10:00-20:30, on Piazza della Repubblica); and **OVS,** a discount clothing chain (daily 10:00-19:30, near train station at intersection of Via Panzani and Via del Giglio).

Best Shopping Areas

San Lorenzo Market: The market stalls between the Basilica of San Lorenzo and Mercato Centrale are no secret—this is ground zero for tourists seeking cheap, cut-rate souvenirs, lower-end leather, clothing, T-shirts, and handbags. It's a fun area to browse and bargain (just hang onto your wallet—this is pickpocket central). You'll find many of the stalls in the narrow streets around Mercato Centrale (daily 9:00-19:00, closed Mon in winter).

Upscale Boutique Streets: The entire area between the river and the cathedral is busy with inviting boutiques that show off ritzy Italian fashions. The highest concentration of shops is along Via dei Calzaiuoli, Via de' Tornabuoni, and the streets in between (particularly around Piazza della Repubblica). For a fun and productive shopping stroll, trace a triangle from Via del Parione, Via della Vigna Nuova, and Via de' Tornabuoni. You'll get a good look at high fashion, one-of-a-kind boutiques, craft workshops, and collectibles.

Borgo Santi Apostoli: This narrow street, just one short block up from Ponte Vecchio, hosts boutiques, designer handbag shops, antique and art stores, and jewelers.

Via Pietrapiana and Borgo La Croce (Oltrarno): To get off the beaten path, head to the Oltrarno neighborhood, just a short walk across the river. You'll find small artisan shops with handmade furniture, jewelry, leather shoes, and pottery. In unassuming workshops, craftsmen breathe new life into antique pieces and artworks using age-old techniques. Walk about 10 minutes northeast of Santa Croce, to the axis formed by Via Pietrapiana, Borgo La Croce, and Via Gioberti. This authentic-feeling area isn't about artsy souvenirs, but about getting a glimpse at what Florentines buy for day-to-day life.

FLORENCE

Sleeping in Florence

Most of my recommended hotels are grouped in central Florence. If arriving by train, you can either walk (usually around 10-20 minutes) or take a taxi (roughly €7-10) to reach most of my recommended accommodations. For some travelers, short-term, Airbnb-type rentals can be a good alternative; search for places in my recommended hotel neighborhoods.

Book any accommodations well in advance, especially if you'll be traveling during peak season or if your trip coincides with a major holiday or festival (see the appendix). Note, though, that Florence can be busy any time of year.

Beware of Bugs: Florence is notorious for its mosquitoes. If your hotel lacks air-conditioning, request a fan and don't open your windows, especially at night. Many hotels furnish a small plug-in bulb *(zanzariere)*—usually set in the ashtray—that helps keep the bloodsuckers at bay. If not, you can purchase one cheaply at any pharmacy.

NEAR THE DUOMO

$$$$ Palazzo Niccolini al Duomo, one of five elite Historic Residence Hotels in Florence, is run by the Niccolini di Camugliano family. The lounge (where tea and pastries are offered every afternoon) is palatial, but the six rooms and seven suites, while splendid, vary in size and are only worth the splurge for an up-close Duomo view. If you have the money and want a Florentine palace to call home, this can be a good bet (RS%, family rooms, elevator, air-con, pay parking—reserve ahead, Via dei Servi 2, +39 055 282 412, www.niccolinidomepalace.com, info@niccolinidomepalace.com).

$$$$ Hotel Duomo's 24 rooms are modern and comfortable enough, but you're paying for the location and the views—the Duomo looms like a monster outside the hotel's windows. If staying here, you might as well spring the extra €20 or so for a "classic" room with a view (RS%, air-con, historic elevator, Piazza del Duomo 1, fourth floor, +39 055 219 922, www.hotelduomofirenze.it, info@hotelduomofirenze.it, Paolo, Gilvaneide, and Federico).

$$$ Soggiorno Battistero rents seven simple yet pristine rooms, most with great views, overlooking the Baptistery and the Duomo square. Request a view or a quieter room in the back when you book, but keep in mind there's always some noise in the city center. It's a minimalist place with no public spaces or full-time reception, but the location is great (RS%—use code "Rick_Steves_Discount," air-con, elevator, Piazza San Giovanni 1, third floor, +39 055 295 143, www.soggiornobattistero.it, info@soggiornobattistero.it, Francesco).

$$$ Residenza Giotto B&B offers a well-priced chance to

stay on Florence's upscale shopping drag, Via Roma. Occupying the top floor of a 19th-century building, this place has six bright rooms (three with Duomo views) and a terrace with knockout views of the Duomo's tower. Reception is generally open Mon-Sat 9:00-17:00 and Sun 9:00-13:00; let them know your arrival time in advance (RS%, air-con, elevator, Via Roma 6, +39 055 214 593, www.residenzagiotto.it, info@residenzagiotto.it).

$$ La Residenza del Proconsolo B&B has six older-feeling rooms a minute from the Duomo (three rooms have Duomo views). The place lacks public spaces, but the rooms are quite large and nice—perfect for eating breakfast, which is served in your room (extra cost for slightly larger "deluxe" with view, air-con, no elevator, Via del Proconsolo 18 black, +39 055 264 5657, www.proconsolo.com, info@proconsolo.com, Susie).

NORTH OF THE DUOMO
Near the Accademia
$$$$ Hotel Morandi alla Crocetta, a former convent, envelops you in a 16th-century cocoon. Located on a quiet street with 12 rooms, its period furnishings, squeaky clean parquet floors, and original frescoes (in the chapel bedroom) take you back a few centuries and up a few social classes. A few rooms come with lovely patios (family rooms, air-con, elevator, pay parking, a block off Piazza Santissima Annunziata at Via Laura 50, +39 055 234 4748, www.hotelmorandi.it, welcome@hotelmorandi.it, well-run by Rachele, Maurizio, Rolando, and Cristiano).

$$$ Residenza dei Pucci rents 13 pleasant rooms (each one different) spread over three floors (with no elevator). The appealing decor, a mix of traditional fabrics and aristocratic furniture, makes this place feel upscale for the price range (RS%—use code "RICK," family rooms, no breakfast, confirm reception hours when you book, air-con, Via dei Pucci 9, +39 350 074 7676, www.residenzadeipucci.com, info@residenzadeipucci.com, Gaia and Pietro).

North of Mercato Centrale
After dark, this neighborhood can feel a little deserted, but I've never heard of anyone running into harm here. It's a short walk from the train station and a stroll to all the sightseeing action. While workaday, it's practical, with plenty of good budget restaurants and markets nearby.

$$$ Relais & Maison Grand Tour has eight cozy, eclectic, and thoughtfully appointed rooms on a nondescript street between the train station and the Accademia. The spacious suites and one three-bedroom apartment come with a garden ambience. Friendly Ulrike, from Germany, takes good care of her guests (RS%, family suites; includes breakfast voucher for the corner bar, for "green"

Florence Hotels

Near the Duomo

❶ Palazzo Niccolini al Duomo
❷ Hotel Duomo
❸ Soggiorno Battistero
❹ Residenza Giotto B&B
❺ La Residenza del Proconsolo B&B

North of the Duomo

❻ Hotel Morandi alla Crocetta
❼ Residenza dei Pucci
❽ Relais & Maison Grand Tour
❾ Galileo Hotel
❿ Hotel Il Bargellino
⓫ Casa Rabatti
⓬ Hotel Centrale
⓭ Hotel Accademia
⓮ Hotel Lorena

East of the Duomo

⓯ Residenza il Villino
⓰ Haggi's Residence
⓱ To Locanda de' Ciompi
⓲ Hotel Dalí
⓳ Suore Oblate dell' Assunzione

South of the Duomo

⓴ In Piazza della Signoria B&B
㉑ Hotel Pendini
㉒ Hotel Maxim Axial
㉓ B&B Il Bargello
㉔ Hotel Davanzati
㉕ Hotel Torre Guelfa
㉖ Relais Ufizzi
㉗ Hotel Alessandra

Near Santa Maria Novella

㉘ Bellevue House, Palazzo Riblet & Hotel Margaret

FLORENCE

FLORENCE

rate, ask to skip breakfast and cleanings; air-con, Via Santa Reparata 21, +39 055 399 5223, www.florencegrandtour.com, info@florencegrandtour.com).

$$$ Galileo Hotel, located on a busy street, is a comfortable, old-school business hotel with 31 rooms and dated bathrooms (RS%, family rooms, quadruple-paned windows shut out street noise, air-con, elevator, Via Nazionale 22a, +39 055 496 645, www.galileohotel.it, info@galileohotel.it).

$$ Hotel Il Bargellino, run by Bostonian Carmel and her Italian husband Pino, is a good-value place with an old-time convivial atmosphere. In a residential neighborhood within walking distance of the center, the 10 summery rooms are decorated with funky antiques and Pino's modern paintings. Guests enjoy relaxing and chatting on the big, breezy, momentum-slowing terrace adorned with plants and lemon shrubs (RS%, cheaper rooms with shared bath, no breakfast served but espresso machine available in rooms, some rooms have air-con, north of the train station at Via Guelfa 87, +39 055 238 2658, www.ilbargellino.com, carmel@ilbargellino.com).

$ Casa Rabatti, a great option for budget travelers, rents four simple and clean rooms (RS%, cheaper rooms with shared bath, family rooms, cash only but secure reservation with credit card, no breakfast, air-con, communal kitchen, 5 blocks from station at Via San Zanobi 48 black, +39 338 153 4159, www.casarabatti.it, info@casarabatti.it). Sergio also rents two modern **$$ apartments** with kitchenettes and access to a tranquil garden—ideal for longer stays.

Near the Medici Chapels

The mostly pedestrianized Via Faenza is the spine of this neighborhood, with lots of tourist services.

$$$$ Hotel Centrale is indeed central, just a short walk from the Duomo. The 35 spacious but overpriced rooms—with a tasteful mix of old and new decor—are over a businesslike conference center (air-con, elevator, Via dei Conti 3, check in at big front desk on ground floor, +39 055 215 761, www.hotelcentralefirenze.it, info@hotelcentralefirenze.it, Roberto).

$$$$ Hotel Accademia has 18 quiet rooms on a pedestrianized street in a convenient location. The modern, sizeable rooms cluster around a sunny courtyard (RS%, family rooms, air-con, no elevator, Via Faenza 7, +39 055 290 993, www.hotelaccademiafirenze.com, info@hotelaccademiafirenze.com, Tea and Francesca).

$ Hotel Lorena, just across from the Medici Chapels, has 19 simple, well-worn rooms (six with shared bathrooms) and a tiny lobby. Though it feels a little like a youth hostel, it's well located, inexpensive, and run with care by the Galli family (air-con, elevator from first floor, Via Faenza 1, +39 055 282 785, www.hotellorena. com, info@hotellorena.com).

EAST OF THE DUOMO

While convenient to the sights and offering a good value, these places are mostly along nondescript urban streets, lacking the grit, charm, or glitz of some of my other recommended neighborhoods.

$$$ Residenza il Villino has 10 charming rooms and a picturesque, peaceful little courtyard. As it's in a "little villa" (as the name implies) set back from the street, this is a quiet refuge from the bustle of Florence (RS%, family rooms, air-con, parking available, just north of Via degli Alfani at Via della Pergola 53, +39 055 200 1116, www.ilvillino.it, info@ilvillino.it, friendly Barbara).

$$$ Haggi's Residence, once a convent and today part of the owner's extensive home, is a classy B&B, with five chic, romantic, and spacious rooms, antique furnishings, and historic architectural touches (RS%, family room, air-con, closed Dec-Feb, Via della Pergola 42, +39 351 818 7488, www.pergola42.com, info@ pergola42.com, suave Alex).

$$ Locanda de' Ciompi, overlooking the inviting Piazza dei Ciompi in a lively neighborhood, is just right for travelers who want to feel like a part of the town. Mira and Francesco have five attractive rooms that are tidy, lovingly maintained, and a good value (RS%, cheaper room with private bath across the hall, includes breakfast at nearby bar, air-con, 8 blocks behind the Duomo at Via Pietrapiana 28 black—see "Florence" map on page 462, +39 055 263 8034, https://locandadeciompi.it, info@locandadeciompi.it).

$$ Hotel Dalí has 10 cheery, worn rooms in a nice location for a great price. Samanta and Marco, who run this guesthouse with a charming passion and idealism, are a delight to know (request one of the quiet and spacious rooms facing the courtyard when you book, cheaper rooms with shared bath available, nearby apartments sleep 2-6 people, no breakfast, fans but no air-con, elevator, free parking, 2 blocks behind the Duomo at Via dell'Oriuolo 17 on the second floor, +39 055 216 680, www.hoteldali.com, hoteldaliflorence@gmail.com).

$$ Suore Oblate dell' Assunzione, run by the Oblate Sisters of the Assumption, is an institutional 42-room hotel in a Renaissance building with a dreamy garden, great public spaces, appropriately simple rooms, and a quiet, prayerful ambience (family rooms, single beds only, air-con, elevator, Borgo Pinti 15, +39 055 234 6291, www.oblate.it, info@oblate.it).

SOUTH OF THE DUOMO
Between the Duomo and Piazza della Signoria

Buried in the narrow, characteristic lanes in the very heart of town, these are the most central of my accommodation recommendations (and therefore a little overpriced). While this location is worth the extra cost for many, nearly every hotel in this chapter can be considered central given Florence's walkable, essentially traffic-free core.

$$$$ In Piazza della Signoria B&B, in a stellar location overlooking Piazza della Signoria, is peaceful, refined, and homey. The service is friendly and efficient. The nine rooms are beautifully decorated; the priciest ones have genuine views of the square (from other rooms, views are peekaboo). Guests enjoy socializing at the big, shared breakfast table (RS%, 2 family apartments, air-con, tiny elevator, Via dei Magazzini 2, +39 055 239 9546, mobile +39 348 321 0565, www.inpiazzadellasignoria.com, info@inpiazzadellasignoria.com).

$$$$ Hotel Pendini, with three stars and 44 plush, flowery rooms, fills the top floor of a grand building overlooking Piazza della Repubblica. This place just feels classy; walking into the lobby is like stepping back in time. While pricey, this level of elegance makes it a good value for those looking to indulge (RS%, "deluxe" rooms come with square view and after-hours liveliness, family rooms, air-con, elevator, near the arch at Via Strozzi 2, +39 055 211 170, www.hotelpendini.it, info@hotelpendini.it).

$$$ Hotel Maxim Axial, well run by the Maoli family since 1981, has 39 straightforward rooms spread over three floors in a good location on the main pedestrian drag. Its painting-lined halls and cozy lounge have old Florentine charm. More expensive "comfort" and "deluxe" rooms are renovated and worth the splurge, but budget travelers can choose an "economy" room on the fourth floor—which is a walk-up from the third floor (RS%—use code "RICK," family rooms, reception on third floor, air-con, elevator, Via dei Calzaiuoli 11, +39 055 217 474, www.hotelmaximaxial.com, info@hotelmaximaxial.com, Chiara).

$$ B&B Il Bargello is a home away from home, run by friendly and helpful Canadian expat Gabriella. Hike up three long flights (no elevator) to reach six traditional rooms. Gabriella offers a cozy living room, a communal kitchenette, and an inviting rooftop terrace with close-up views of Florence's towers (RS%, fully equipped apartment across the hall sleeps up to six with one bathroom; air-con, 20 yards off Via Proconsolo at Via de' Pandolfini 33 black, +39 055 215 330, mobile +39 339 175 3110, www.firenze-bedandbreakfast.it, info@firenze-bedandbreakfast.it).

Near Ponte Vecchio

This sleepy zone is handy to several sights and some fine shopping streets, though it's accordingly pricey and lacks a neighborhood feel of its own.

$$$$ Hotel Davanzati, bright and shiny with artistic

touches, has 26 cheerful rooms with all the comforts. The place is a family affair, thoughtfully run by friendly Tommaso, Riccardo, and their father Fabrizio, who offer tea time, drinks, and snacks each evening at their intimate happy hour, plus lots of other extras (RS%, family rooms, free on-demand videos—including my travel shows about Italy—on your room TV, air-con, 20 steep steps to the elevator, handy room fridges, next to Piazza Davanzati at Via Porta Rossa 5—easy to miss so watch for low-profile sign above the door, +39 055 286 666, www.hoteldavanzati.it, info@hoteldavanzati.it).

$$$$ Hotel Torre Guelfa has grand public spaces and is topped by a fun medieval tower with a panoramic rooftop terrace (72 stairs take you up—

and back 720 years). Its 31 pricey rooms vary wildly in size and furnishings, but most come with the noise of the city center. Room 315, with a private terrace, is worth reserving several months in advance (RS%, family rooms, air-con, elevator, a couple of blocks northwest of Ponte Vecchio, Borgo SS. Apostoli 8, +39 055 239 6338, www.hoteltorreguelfa.com, info@hoteltorreguelfa.com, Niccolo).

$$$$ Relais Uffizi is a modern, upscale hotel offering 15 classy rooms tucked away down a tiny alley off Piazza della Signoria. The cocktail lounge has a huge window overlooking the action in the piazza—a unique view (family rooms, air-con, elevator; official address is Chiasso del Buco 16—from the square, go down tiny Chiasso de Baroncelli lane—right of the loggia—and after 50 yards turn right through the arch and look for entrance on your right; +39 055 267 6239, www.relaisuffizi.it, info@relaisuffizi.it).

$$$ Hotel Alessandra is a tranquil and sprawling place, occupying part of a 16th-century building with 30 big, old-school rooms with modern bathrooms and a tiny Arno-view terrace (family rooms, air-con, 30 steps to the elevator, Borgo SS. Apostoli 17, +39 055 283 438, www.hotelalessandra.com, info@hotelalessandra.com; Anna, son Andrea, and spunky Monti). Their annex across the street, **Residenza Alessandra,** is more contemporary and a good option for families or small groups (apartments sleep up to 4 people).

NEAR SANTA MARIA NOVELLA

These fine, charming little budget options are around the corner from Santa Maria Novella, near the train station.

$$ Bellevue House is a third-floor oasis of tranquility, with

Oltrarno Hotels & Restaurants

Accommodations
1. Hotel Palazzo Guadagni
2. Hotel la Scaletta
3. Casa Santo Nome di Gesù
4. Soggiorno Alessandra
5. Foresteria Valdese di Firenze
6. Ostello Santa Monaca

Eateries
7. Signorvino
8. Golden View Firenze & La Forneria Firenze Wine Bar/Bakery
9. Osteria Ponte Vecchio
10. Tamerò
11. Trattoria Casalinga
12. Gusta Osteria

six spacious, old-fashioned rooms flanking a long, mellow-yellow lobby. It's a peaceful home away from home, thoughtfully run by the Michel family (RS%, family rooms, no breakfast, air-con, elevator, Via della Scala 21, +39 055 260 8932, www.bellevuehouse. it, info@bellevuehouse.it; Luciano, Susan, and Alessandro). On a lower floor, their other property, **$$ Palazzo Riblet,** offers three upscale rooms (one with a private terrace) with frescoes and elegant furnishings (+39 055 260 8932, www.palazzoriblet.it, info@ palazzoriblet.it).

$$ Hotel Margaret offers seven tidy, simple rooms but no public lounge or breakfast (RS%, some cheaper rooms with shower

13 Gusta Pizza

14 Trattoria Sant'Agostino

15 O Munaciello Pizzeria

16 Il Santo Bevitore Ristorante & Enoteca il Santino Gastronomia

17 Trattoria 4 Leoni

18 Le Volpi e l'Uva

19 Gelateria la Carraia

<u>Nightlife & Other</u>

20 Archea Brewery

21 Volume Bar

22 Pop Café

23 Gosh

24 NOF

25 Supermarket

26 In Tavola Cooking School

but toilet down the hall, air-con, Via della Scala 25, +39 055 210 138, www.hotel-margaret.it, info@hotel-margaret.it; Francesco and Graziano).

THE OLTRARNO

$$$$ Hotel Palazzo Guadagni, perched high above Piazza Santo Spirito, is a romantic, Grand Tour retreat from modern Florence. The 15 refined rooms are spacious, with antique furnishings and frescoes. While the ample, chandeliered public spaces are pleasant, the highlight is the panoramic wrap-around loggia/terrace with comfy, stay-awhile seating and lovely views (family rooms, air-con, elevator, Piazza Santo Spirito 9, +39 055 265 8376, www. palazzoguadagni.com, info@palazzoguadagni.com).

$$$$ Hotel la Scaletta has 36 pricey, sleek rooms hiding in a convoluted floor plan. Their fabulous rooftop terrace overlooks the Boboli Gardens and is a nice place for a drink (RS% when you pay with cash, family rooms, breakfast extra, air-con, elevator, Via de' Guicciardini 13, +39 055 283 028, www.hotellascaletta.it, info@ hotellascaletta.it, Sara).

$$$ Hotel Silla is a classic three-star hotel with 36 cheery rooms. Rooms with river views are modern and sleek, while rooms along the back are more spacious and classic. The breezy terrace faces the Arno River, overlooking a small park near the San Niccolò neighborhood. There's free coffee and tea for guests in the late afternoon. The surroundings can be a bit noisy (RS%—use promo code "RICK," air-con, elevator, self-service washing machine, Via dei Renai 5, for location see map on page 509, +39 055 234 2888, www.hotelsilla.it, hotelsilla@hotelsilla.it; Laura, Chiara, Massimo, Ravin, Stefano, and Salvo).

$$ Hotel Annalena, on the third floor of a faded palazzo, is a bit tatty with small bathrooms, but it's in a quiet location near the Pitti Palace. Many of its 19 tidy rooms (some with terraces) overlook a private park next door (family rooms, bar/lounge, air-con, no elevator, laundry service, opposite the side entrance to the Boboli Gardens at Via Romana 34, for location see map on page 509, +39 055 222 402, www.annalenahotel.com, reception@annalenahotel. com).

$$ Casa Santo Nome di Gesù is a grand convent whose sisters—Franciscan Missionaries of Mary—are thankful to rent 24 simple but spacious rooms to tourists. Staying in this 15th-century palace, you'll be immersed in the tranquil atmosphere created by a huge, peaceful garden, generous and prayerful public spaces, and smiling nuns. It's a good value and understandably popular—it's best to reserve a couple of months in advance (family rooms, air-con, elevator, memorable breakfast room, Piazza del Carmine 21, +39 055 213 856, www.fmmfirenze.it, info@fmmfirenze.it).

$ Soggiorno Alessandra has four bright and comfy rooms, all with en suite bathrooms. Because of its double-paned windows, you'll hardly notice the traffic noise (family rooms, includes basic breakfast in room, air-con, no elevator; there's no formal reception, so let them know what time you'll arrive; just past the Carraia Bridge at Via Borgo San Frediano 6, +39 055 290 424, www. soggiornoalessandra.it, info@soggiornoalessandra.it, Alessandra).

$ Foresteria Valdese di Firenze, with 40 clean and functional rooms, is located in a 17th-century palace overlooking a beautiful garden courtyard. The complex also houses the Instituto Gould, which helps socially disadvantaged kids, and proceeds raised from renting rooms help fund that important work (extra for quieter garden rooms, air-con, elevator reaches most rooms, family rooms, breakfast extra, Via dei Serragli 49, +39 055 212 576, www.firenzeforesteria.it, info@firenzeforesteria.it). The reception desk closes at lunchtime—confirm hours before you arrive. After-hours check-in is possible with advance notice.

Hostel: ¢ Ostello Santa Monaca is a well-run, institutional-feeling hostel a long block east of the Brancacci Chapel. As clean as its guests, it attracts a young backpacking crowd (2:00 in the morning curfew, air-con, bike rental, pay laundry, Via Santa Monaca 6, +39 055 268 338, www.ostellosantamonaca.com, info@ostellosantamonaca.com).

Eating in Florence

The old center of Florence is dominated by tourism. Locals still keep restaurants busy at lunch, but with the city's many Airbnb guests and city-center traffic restrictions, the hometown clientele tends to retreat away from downtown in the evening. This makes it tough to find a "nontouristy" place for dinner. Still, the competition is fierce, and you'll find plenty of fine options and good values even in the tourist zone. For the best experience and better quality meals, hike to places further out and across the river in the Oltrarno.

EATING TIPS

The sightseer's reality is to eat a quick and simple lunch and spend more time and money at a well-chosen and more memorable restaurant for dinner. Keep lunch fast and simple at one of Florence's countless sandwich shops and stands, pizzerias, or self-service cafeterias.

You'll find a unique range of sandwich options. In addition to the basic *panino* (usually on a baguette), crostini (open-faced, toasted baguette), and *semel* (big, puffy roll), you'll see places advertising *schiaccata* (sandwich made with a "squashed," focaccia-like bread). Florence is also peppered with carts selling tripe sandwiches—a prized local specialty.

Picnicking is easy. You can picnic your way through Mercato Centrale, near the Basilica of San Lorenzo. You'll also find good *supermercati* throughout the city. I like the classy Sapori & Dintorni markets (run by Conad), with branches near the Duomo (Borgo San Lorenzo 15 red) and just over Ponte Vecchio in the Oltrarno (Via de Bardi 45). Carrefour Express is another handy grocery chain (there's one around the corner from the Duomo Museum at Via dell'Oriuolo 66).

Reservations Recommended: Florence is so crowded that

reservations are smart for any serious dinner. Most restauranteurs speak English and are used to tourists. It's quick and easy to call ahead and book a table. Without reservations, have dinner early or very late.

MERCATO CENTRALE AND NEARBY
In Mercato Centrale

Florence's Industrial Age steel-and-glass Mercato Centrale (Central Market) is a fun-to-explore edible wonderland of vendors selling meat, fish, produce, and other staples to a mostly local clientele, plus some lunch-only food counters.

$ Ground Floor: The market zone, with lots of raw ingredients and a few humble food counters, is open only through lunchtime (Mon-Fri 7:00-14:00, Sat until 17:00, closed Sun). Buy a picnic of fresh mozzarella cheese, olives, fruit, and crunchy bread to munch on the steps of the nearby Basilica of San Lorenzo. Merchants are often happy to give samples. The fancy deli, **Perini,** is famous for its quality products and enticing displays. The adjacent **Pasta Perini** stand is good for a quick bowl of pasta. For a simple sit-down meal, head for the venerable **Nerbone in the Market.** It's generally mobbed by shoppers and workers who crowd up to the bar to grab inexpensive plates, then find a stool at cramped shared tables nearby (lunch menu served Mon-Sat 12:00-14:00, cash only, on the side closest to the Basilica of San Lorenzo). Its less-famous sisters, nearby, have better seating and fewer crowds.

$$ Upstairs: The upper floor is a touristy and jam-packed food court (daily 10:00-24:00) with counters selling pizza, pasta, fish, meat, *salumi, lampredotto,* wine, and so on. Buy what you like at any counter and grab a table (drinks will be brought to your table). Even if you're not eating, it's fun to explore the many options. While the food court can be a zoo at lunch, it's often more relaxed at dinnertime.

Near Mercato Centrale

A huge array of eateries is within a couple of blocks of the market. Each has its own distinct vibe, so scout around to find your favorite.

$ Casa del Vino, Florence's oldest operating wine shop, is a crowded little bar offering an unforgettable stand-up lunch experience with a selection of wine by the glass from 20 different bottles (prices are chalked onto each opened bottle behind the cashier). Owner Gianni, a sommelier whose family has run the Casa for 70 years, is a class act. Pair a glass of wine with a sandwich, crostini, or €7 "Tuscany appetizer plate" of meat and cheese for a great little lunch. During busy times, it's a mob scene—you'll munch and sip standing outside amongst workers on a lunch break. But early or late you can actually connect with Gianni (Mon-Thu 10:00-15:30,

Fri-Sat until 20:00; closed Sun year-round, Sat in summer, and Aug; Via dell'Ariento 16 red, +39 055 215 609).

$$ Pepò, a colorful and charmingly unpretentious space, is tucked just around the corner from the touristy glitz on Piazza del Mercato Centrale. The short menu offers simple but well-prepared Florentine classics such as *ribollita* and *pollo alla cacciatora*—chicken cacciatore (daily 12:00-14:30 & 19:00-22:30, Via Rosina 4 red, +39 055 283 259).

$$$ Trattoria da Garibaldi is a big, practical place serving traditional Tuscan dishes and pizzas with a sprawling interior and delightful tables on the square (daily 11:00-23:00, Piazza del Mercato Centrale 38 red, +39 055 212 267).

$$ Trattoria Sergio Gozzi is your classic neighborhood lunch-only place, serving hearty, traditional Florentine fare to market-goers since 1915—long before the tourist crush of today. The handwritten menu is limited and changes daily, and service can be hectic, but it's understandably a local favorite (Mon-Sat 12:00-15:00, closed Sun, Piazza di San Lorenzo 8, +39 055 281 941).

$$ Trattoria la Burrasca is a rustic time-warp, where a dozen rickety tables cluster under a single vault. Elio and his staff offer a traditional menu featuring fine steak and good-value seasonal specials—both Sicilian and Tuscan (Tue-Sat 12:00-15:00 & 19:00-22:30, closed Sun-Mon, Via Panicale 6, north corner of Mercato Centrale, +39 055 215 827).

$ Simbiosi Organic Pizza and Lovely Food is a happy little pizzeria under a medieval vault with a young crew, open fire, and healthy, organic energy (daily 18:30-23:00, good salads, craft beer, Via de' Ginori 56 red, +39 055 064 0115). Their similarly named pasta sister is next door at #58.

$$ Trattoria lo Stracotto is an inviting eatery with a modern interior and good outdoor seating, where you'll enjoy good-value, standard Tuscan dishes in the shadow of the Medici Chapels (daily 12:00-15:00 & 18:00-22:30, Piazza di Madonna degli Aldobrandini 17, +39 055 230 2062, Francesco).

$$$ Ristorante Cafaggi fills a bright yet low-energy space on a drab street between the Accademia and Mercato Centrale. With a vaguely 1950s vibe, the place emphasizes their generations-old passion for Florentine food, serving up *ribollita* (hearty Tuscan soup), osso buco, and tripe. It's been family-run since 1922 (Mon-Sat 12:30-15:00 & 19:00-22:00, closed Sun and several weeks in Aug, Via Guelfa 35 red, +39 055 294 989).

$$$ Trattoria la Gratella, near my recommended hotels north of the center, serves solid Tuscan cuisine to a mostly local crowd. The crowded front room gives way to a sprawling interior and an outdoor courtyard, full of diners grilling their own *bistecca*

Florence Restaurants

Piazza della Indipendenza

300 Meters
300 Yards

To Fortezza da Basso

PALAZZO DEI CONGRESSI

CONSERVATORIO DI FULIGNO **10**

VIA VALFONDA
VIA LUIGI ALAMANNI

PALAZZO DEGLI AFFARI

VIA CENNINI

CENACOLO DI FULIGNO

VIA GUELFA

VIA SAN ZANOBI

Piazza Adua

VIA NAZIONALE

VIA FAENZA

VIA DELL'ARIENTO

V. CHIARA PANICALE

VIA TADDEA

36

6

MERCATO CENTRALE **1**

Piazza del Mercato Centrale **3**

4

SANTA MARIA NOVELLA TRAIN STATION

Largo Alinari

VIA FIUME

VIA DEGLI AVELLI

PALAZZO DEI CARTELLONI

VIA S. ANTONINO

2

BORGO LA NOCE

VIA STURA

Piazza di San Lorenzo **5**

BUS STATION **B**

Piazza della Stazione

V. FAMINO

MEDICI CHAPELS

Piazza Madonna

SAN LORENZO

Piazza dell'Unità Italiana

V. DEI MELARANCIO

8

VIA DE' CONTI

VIA DE' ZANNETTI

VIA DELL'GIGLIO

V. DELL'ALLORO

Laurentian Medici Library

VIA DELLA SCALA

VIA DE' CANACCI
BENEDETTA
VIA PALAZZUOLO

MAIN TOURIST INFO **i**

SANTA MARIA NOVELLA

VIA PANZANI

24

37

SAN LORENZO

WC

33

SANTA MARIA NOVELLA PERFUMERY

Piazza di Santa Maria Novella

VIA D. BELLE DONNE

VIA DEI BANCHI

VIA DE' CERRETANI

Piazza di S. Gio.

BAPTISTERY

TREBBIO
RONDINELLI

SANTA MARIA MAGGIORE

OGNISSANTI **31**

LOGGIA DI SAN PAOLO

ANTINORI

VIA DEI FOSSI

VIA DEL SOLE

SAN GAETANO

VIA PECORI

12

LOGGIA DI BIGALLO

TOSINGHI

BRUNELLESCHI

VIA DE' PORCELLANA
VIA DI PAOLINO

GIAC.

VIA CORSI

VIA DE' VECCHIETTI

ROMA

MEDICI

BORGO OGNISSANTI

35

VIA DEL MORO
VIA DELLA SPADA
VIA DE' FEDERIGHI

14

PESCIONI

VIA D. STROZZI

Piazza della Repubblica

34

Rucellai Palace

32

STROZZI PALACE

V. D. ANSELMI

ORSAN-MICHELE

Piazza Carlo Goldoni

VIA DELLA VIGNA NUOVA

INFERNO

MONALDA

SASSETTI

POST

CALIMALA

PONTE ALLA CARRAIA

VIA DEL PARIONE

PALAZZO CORSINI

PARIONCINO
PURGATORIO

Piazza de' Davanzati

VIA PELLICCERIA

MERCATO NUOVO

SANTA TRINITÀ

Piazza di Santa Trinita

VIA PORTA ROSSA

17

Lungarno Vespucci

Piazza Nazaro Sauro

LUNGARNO CORSINI

DAVANZATI PALACE

DELLE TERME

VIA POR S. MARIA

16

Arno River

LUNGARNO GUICCIARDINI

Piazza de' Frescobaldi

PONTE S. TRINITÀ

BORGO S. S. APOSTOLI

LUNGARNO ACCIAIUOLI

18

LAMBERTESCA

Piazza de' Salt.

SAN STEFANO

BORGO SAN FREDIANO

To Brancacci Chapel

PONTE VECCHIO

22

SAN JACOPO

BORGO SAN JACOPO

OLTRARNO

SANTO SPIRITO

VIA MAGGIO

Piazza della Passera

To Pitti Palace

Gelaterie

38 Gelateria Carabè
39 Edoardo
40 Perchè No!
41 Gelateria de' Neri

FLORENCE

1. Mercato Centrale Eateries
2. Casa del Vino
3. Pepò
4. Trattoria da Garibaldi
5. Trattoria Sergio Gozzi
6. Trattoria la Burrasca
7. Simbiosi Organic Pizza & Lovely Food
8. Trattoria lo Stracotto
9. Ristorante Cafaggi
10. Trattoria la Gratella
11. Enoteca Coquinarius
12. Self-Service Ristorante Leonardo
13. EATaly
14. Procacci
15. Rosalia Salad Gourmet
16. Ristorante Pizzeria Il Bargello
17. Rivoire Café
18. Ristorante Toto
19. Osteria Vini e Vecchi Sapori
20. Cantinetta dei Verrazzano
21. I Fratellini
22. 'Ino Sandwich Shop/Wine Bar
23. Da' Vinattieri
24. Shake Café (3)
25. La Mescita Fiaschetteria
26. Pasticceria Robiglio
27. To Trattoria Cucchietta & Antica Trattoria da Tito
28. Ristorante del Fagioli
29. Ristorante Boccadama
30. Via dei Neri Sandwich Mosh Pit
31. Trattoria Sostanza-Troia
32. Trattoria Marione
33. Trattoria "da Giorgio"
34. Caffè Tosca & Nino
35. Sesto Bar
36. Mostodolce Craft Brewery
37. Groceries (3)

FLORENCE

alla fiorentina on mini barbeques at the table (daily 12:00-15:00 & 19:00-23:00, Via Guelfa 81 red, +39 055 211 292).

AROUND THE DUOMO

$$ Enoteca Coquinarius feels as welcoming as someone's cool and spacious living room or library. It's a relaxed, hip place with a slow-food ethic, tasty salads and pastas, and a nice selection of wines by the glass (daily 12:00-15:30 & 19:00-22:30, a few steps from the Duomo workshop at Via delle Oche 11 red, +39 055 230 2153).

$$$ Ristorante Natalino is worth the short walk for a memorable dinner. It's a family-run fixture in its neighborhood with outdoor seating on a characteristic corner. The place is known for its homemade pasta, *bistecca alla fiorentina*, and classic Tuscan dishes (daily 12:00-14:30 & 19:00-22:30, Borgo degli Albizi 17 red, for location see the "Florence" map on page 462, +39 055 289 404).

$ Self-Service Ristorante Leonardo is a quick, cheap, air-conditioned, and handy cafeteria just a block from the Duomo. While it's no-frills and stuck in the 1970s, the food is better than many table-service eateries in this part of town. Stefano and Luciano run the place with enthusiasm and free pitchers of tap water (lots of vegetables, daily 11:45-14:45 & 18:45-21:45, upstairs at Via Pecori 11, +39 055 284 446).

$$ EATaly, a slick, modern space a half-block from the Duomo, is an outpost of a chain of foodie mini malls located in big Italian cities (as well as in a few major US cities). Along with a grocery store for top-end Italian ingredients, plenty of edible gifts, and kitchen gadgets, it has a bright, modern dining area in the back serving pastas, pizzas, salads, and *secondi* to tourists (daily 10:00-22:30, Via de' Martelli 22 red, +39 055 015 3601).

$$$ Procacci, right on Florence's most genteel boutique-browsing street, is upscale and posh. This wine-and-cocktail bar, with a swanky, 1885 atmosphere, specializes in pungent truffle-scented ingredients: cheap mini panini and €20 sampler plates of *salumi* and cheeses. They have a small lunch menu of pasta, salads, and sandwiches. There's no dinner menu, but their tiny sandwiches are always available. Paired with an €8 glass of wine, a bite here makes an elegant light meal (daily 10:00-21:00, Via Tornabuoni 64 red, +39 055 211 656).

$ Rosalia Salad Gourmet is a quick, build-your-own-salad spot behind the Duomo. Eat in or take out a salad bowl, veggie wrap, smoothie, or fresh fruit juice (daily 8:00-20:00, Via dei Servi 37, +39 320 706 9331).

ON OR NEAR PIAZZA DELLA SIGNORIA

Piazza della Signoria, the scenic square facing the Palazzo Vecchio, is ringed by beautifully situated yet touristy eateries serving over-

priced, forgettable food with an unforgettable view.

$$$ Ristorante Pizzeria il Bargello is a good choice if you want to eat outdoors on Florence's main square with a view of the Palazzo Vecchio. It's a happy, family-run place with good salads, pastas, and pizzas (Tue-Sun 11:30-22:30, closed Mon, Piazza della Signoria 4 red, +39 055 214 071, Mimmo).

$$$ Rivoire Café is famous for its fancy desserts and thick hot chocolate (€7). A bowl of pasta or a salad—when enjoyed at the best view tables on the square—can be a worthwhile experience. Their delightful bar is perfectly affordable, and drinks often come with fine *aperitivo* munchies (daily 8:00-24:00, +39 055 214 412).

$$ Ristorante Toto is a simple, fun, traditional eatery with a spacious dining hall serving classic Tuscan plates at decent prices. The focus is on steak, homemade pasta, and pizza (Thu-Tue 12:00-15:00 & 19:00-22:00, closed Wed, indoor seating only, tucked away two blocks from the Ponte Vecchio at Borgo SS. Apostoli 6 red, +39 055 212 096).

$$ Osteria Vini e Vecchi Sapori is a colorful eatery—tight, tiny, and with attitude. They serve Tuscan food—like *pappardelle* with duck—from a fun, accessible menu of delicious pastas and *secondi*. For dessert, Tommaso promises a free Vin Santo and *cantucci* for readers with this book (Mon-Sat seatings at 12:30, 14:00, 19:30, and 21:30; closed Sun, call ahead to reserve; Via dei Magazzini 3 red, +39 055 293 045, run by Mario while wife Rosanna cooks and son Tommaso serves).

Favorite Sandwiches near Piazza della Signoria

$$ Cantinetta dei Verrazzano is an elegant wine bar serving delightful sandwich plates. Their *selezione Verrazzano* is a plate of four little crostini featuring breads, cheeses, and meats from the Chianti region. The *tagliere di focacce*, a sampler of mini focaccia sandwiches, is also fun. Add a glass of Chianti to either of these dishes to make a fine, light meal. Office workers pop in for a quick lunch, and it's traditional to share tables. You can eat cheaper at the bar (or at the tiny stools facing it). Simply step to the back and point to a hot *focacce* sandwich, order a drink at the bar, and enjoy the action while you munch (Mon-Sat 8:00-15:30, closed Sun, no reservations, off Via dei Calzaiuoli, at Via dei Tavolini 18 red, +39 055 268 590).

FLORENCE

Florentine and Tuscan Cuisine

In general, Tuscan cuisine is hearty, simple food: grilled meats, high-quality seasonal vegetables, fresh herbs, prized olive oil, and rustic bread. If a dish ends with *"alla toscana"* or *"alla fiorentina,"* it's cooked in the Tuscan or Florentine style—usually a preparation highlighting local products. In addition to specialty dishes, most restaurants also serve pasta and pizza, veal cutlets, and salad (for more on Italian cuisine, see page 1162).

There's nothing wrong with your Tuscan bread—it's supposed to taste like that. *Pane alla toscana* is unsalted and nearly flavorless (from the days when salt's preservative powers made it more valuable than gold). Italians drench it in olive oil and sprinkle it with salt, or use it to scoop up sauce.

Antipasti (Appetizers)

Bruschetta: Toasted bread brushed with olive oil and rubbed with garlic, topped with chopped tomato, mushrooms, or whatever else sounds good.

Crostini: Toasted bread rounds topped with meat or vegetable pastes. *Alla toscana* generally means with chicken liver pâté.

Panzanella: Simple summer salad, made of day-old bread, chopped tomatoes, onion, and basil, tossed in a light vinaigrette.

Pecorino cheese: Fresh *(fresco)* or aged *(stagionato),* from ewe's milk.

Porcini mushrooms: Used as a topping on bruschetta; also served marinated or stewed.

Salumi: Cold cuts, usually air- or salt-dried pork. Popular kinds include prosciutto (air-cured ham hock), pancetta (cured pork belly), *lardo* (cured pork lard), and *finocchiona* (fennel salami). For a list of other *salumi,* see page 1173.

Tagliere: Selection of cold cuts and/or cheeses served on a wooden platter.

Primo Piatto (First Course)

Carabaccia: Onion soup.

Pappa al pomodoro: Thick stew of tomatoes, olive oil, and bread.

Pappardelle al sugo di lepre: Rich wild-hare sauce over long, broad noodles.

Pici al ragù: Fat, spaghetti-like, hand-rolled pasta served with a meat-tomato sauce.

Ribollita: "Reboiled" soup, traditionally made with leftovers including white beans *(fagioli),* seasonal vegetables, and olive oil, with layers of day-old Tuscan bread.

Zuppa alla volterrana: Volterra-style soup, similar to *ribollita* but with fresh bread.

Secondo Piatto (Second Course)

Arrosto misto: Assortment of roasted meats, sometimes served on a skewer *(spiedino).*

Bistecca alla fiorentina: Thick T-bone steak, generally grilled very rare and lightly seasoned (often sold by weight—per *etto,* or 100 grams). The best—and most expensive—is from the white Chianina cattle you'll see grazing throughout Tuscany.

Cinghiale: Wild boar, served grilled; in soups, stews, and pasta; or made into many varieties of sausage and *salumi.*

Fegatelli: Liver meatballs.

Game birds: Squab (*piccione*), pheasant (*fagiano*), and guinea hen (*faraona*) are popular.

Trippa alla fiorentina: Tripe and vegetables sautéed in tomato sauce, sometimes baked with parmesan. *Trippa* (and the similar *lampredotto*) are popular in sandwiches.

Dolci (Desserts)

Cantucci: Florentines love to end a meal by dipping this crunchy almond cookie in Vin Santo wine (described below). These are commonly misnamed "biscotti" by Americans.

Gelato: The Florentines claim they invented Italian-style ice cream. Rather than order dessert in a restaurant, I like to stroll with a gelato. For more on gelato, see page 1175; for tips on enjoying it here, see page 535.

Panforte: Dense, clove-and-cinnamon-spiced cake from Siena.

Local Wines

Many Tuscan wines are made with sangiovese ("blood of Jupiter") grapes. But the characteristics of the soil, temperature, and exposure make each wine unique to its area.

Brunello di Montalcino: One of Italy's best reds, this full-bodied wine comes from the slopes of Montalcino, south of Siena. Smooth and dry, it pairs well with hearty, meaty food.

Chianti: This red hails from the Chianti region (20 miles south of Florence). Varieties range from cheap, acidic basket-bottles of table wine (called *fiaschi*) to the hearty Chianti Classico.

Rosso di Montalcino: This cheaper, younger "baby Brunello," also made in Montalcino, lacks Brunello's depth of flavor and complexity—but it's still a great wine at a bargain price.

Super Tuscans: This newer wine blends traditional grapes with locally grown non-Italian grapes (such as cabernet or merlot).

Vernaccia di San Gimignano: This medium-dry white goes well with pasta and salad. Trebbiano and vermentino are two other local white grapes.

Vino Nobile di Montepulciano: This high-quality, ruby red, dry wine pairs well with meat, especially chicken.

Vin Santo: Sweet and syrupy, this "holy" dessert wine is often served with a cookie for dipping.

FLORENCE

$ I Fratellini is a literal hole-in-the-wall stand-up joint where the "little brothers" have served peasants two dozen types of sandwiches and a fine selection of wine at great prices (see list on wall) since 1875. Join the local crowd to order, then sit on a nearby curb to eat, placing your glass on the wall rack as you leave. Be adventurous with the menu (order by number: perhaps #22, cured lard aged in Carrara marble; or #19, spicy boar salami). It's worth ordering the most expensive wine they're selling by the glass (daily 12:00-18:00, open later on weekends, 20 yards in front of Orsanmichele Church on Via dei Cimatori, +39 055 239 6096).

$ 'Ino Sandwich Shop/Wine Bar is a mod little spot (on a back alley between the Uffizi and Ponte Vecchio) where Alessandro and his staff serve creative sandwiches and glasses of their house wine. You'll munch your meal while perched on a tiny, uncomfortable stool—and be glad you did. The sandwiches—arguably the best and among the most expensive in town—are easily splittable (daily 12:00-16:00, immediately behind Uffizi Gallery courtyard on Ponte Vecchio side, at Via dei Georgofili 7 red, +39 055 214 154).

$ Tripe Sandwiches in Dante's Neighborhood: Another literal hole-in-the-wall with a tiny bar next door, **Da' Vinattieri** sells traditional *schiaccata* sandwiches, plus *trippa* (tripe) and *lampredotto* (stomach). While it's a hit with locals, ordering here takes an adventurous spirit (daily 11:30-19:00, next to Casa di Dante at Via Santa Margherita 4 red, +39 392 734 5773). The best place to enjoy your sandwich while people-watching is nearby on Piazza della Signoria.

NEAR THE ACCADEMIA

There are piles of cheap and practical eateries (serving pizza, sandwiches, and salads to eat in or take out) on the boring streets near *David*. Hungry tourists looking for a quick lunch can survey a line of economical options a block away on Piazza di San Marco and around the corner from that along Via Cavour. If picnicking, head over to the traffic-free Piazza Santissima Annunziata—the first Renaissance square in Florence, with a fountain for washing fruit and plenty of stony places to sit.

$ Shake Café, great for a quick and healthy lunch, is a modern salad bar on busy Via Cavour with spacious and inviting courtyard seating. Along with tasty salads, the menu includes veggie bowls, wraps, smoothies, and fancy juices (daily 7:00-19:00, Via Cavour 67 red). Other handy Shake locations are on Piazza Santa Maria Novella and between the Duomo and Bargello at Via del Corso 28.

$ La Mescita Fiaschetteria is a characteristic hole-in-the-wall where, since 1919, locals have been enjoying a simple menu of pastas, traditional Tuscan soups, and the daily *secondi* with tasty, cheap house wine. The place can either be mobbed by students or a peaceful time warp, depending on when you stop by. Mirco and Alessio are gregarious to the point of being a bit pushy...order carefully and check your bill. They serve a nice Vin Santo and *cantucci* dessert (daily 11:30-15:30, Via degli Alfani 70 red, +39 338 992 2640).

$$ Pasticceria Robiglio is a classy local fixture with a stately and calm dining area and a few shaded tables on the sidewalk. They have a small lunch-only menu of salads and daily pasta and *secondi* specials. It's good any time for a coffee and one of their pretty pastries—famous among Florentines (café open daily 7:30-20:00, lunch served 12:00-16:00, a block toward the Duomo off Piazza Santissima Annunziata at Via dei Servi 112 red, +39 055 212 784).

Memorable Dining North of the Center

These places are away from the tourists and offer perhaps the most authentic of all. The first is a 10-minute taxi ride north of the center, and the second is just a few blocks' walk from *David.*

$$$ Trattoria Cucchietta is your chance for a modern, totally local dining experience. It's a hard-working family affair with a youthful and passionate team and a small, enticing menu filled with creative Tuscan temptations. Venturing out here, you risk having the best meal of your trip (Mon-Sat 12:00-14:30 & 19:30-22:30, closed Sun, reservations strongly recommended, 10-minute taxi ride north of the center at Via Firenzuola 15 red, +39 055 578 889, http://cucchietta.it).

$$$ Antica Trattoria da Tito, a 10-minute hike from the Accademia along Via San Gallo, is a fun-loving food party. Come here for a memorable meal with a local crowd and smart-aleck service inspired by the lovable boss, Bobo. The food is hearty and rustic, the ingredients are fresh, and there's lots of wine and no pretense. It's a noisy playground of Tuscan cuisine. Their €18 *antipasti* sampler plate (cold cuts, cheeses, a few veggies, and bruschetta) is plenty for two. Dinner is served in four seatings: 19:30 (more sanity), 20:30, 21:30, and 22:15 (less sanity; daily 12:30-15:00 & 19:00-23:00, reservations recommended, Via San Gallo 112 red, +39 055 472 475, http//trattoriadatito.business.site).

BETWEEN THE PALAZZO VECCHIO AND SANTA CROCE CHURCH

$$ Ristorante del Fagioli is an enthusiastically run eatery where you can sense the heritage, from the wood-paneled dining room to the daily specials chalked on a board. Maurizio commands the kitchen while family members Antonio and Simone keep the throngs of loyal customers returning. The cuisine: home-style bread-soups, hearty steaks, and other Florentine classics. Don't worry—while *fagioli* means "beans," that's the family name, not the extent of the menu (Mon-Fri 12:30-14:30 & 19:30-22:30, closed Sat-Sun, cash only, reserve for dinner, a block north of the Alle Grazie bridge at Corso dei Tintori 47 red, +39 055 244 285).

$$$ Ristorante Boccadama is a fun place with great tables on Piazza di Santa Croce. The menu focuses on meat and traditional dishes. For dessert, Giorgio and Marco offer a free Vin Santo and *cantucci* to readers with this book (daily 12:00-23:00 & 18:00-23:00, Piazza Santa Croce 25 red, +39 055 243 640).

$ The Via dei Neri Sandwich Mosh Pit: Via dei Neri has become a human traffic jam of people munching hearty and cheap sandwiches in the street. These low-end sandwich shops are the trend all over town, but the craze originated here at #65, **All'Antico Vinaio.** Just walking down this street—a sandwich ghetto—is an experience.

NEAR THE CHURCH OF SANTA MARIA NOVELLA

$$$ Trattoria Sostanza-Troia, characteristic and well established, is famous for its steaks and its *pollo al burro* (chicken in butter). Whirling ceiling fans and walls strewn with old photos evoke earlier times, while the artichoke pie *(tortino di carciofi)* and Max (who insists on no changes) reminds locals of Grandma's cooking. Crowded, with just eight shared tables, a small menu, and grumpy service, the place feels like a simple bistro. Reservations are essential for their two dinner seatings: 19:30 and 21:00 (cash only, open Mon-Sat, closed Sun, lunch served 12:30-14:00, Via del Porcellana 25 red, +39 055 212 691).

$$ Trattoria Marione serves home-cooked-style meals to a mixed group of tourists and Florentines crowding very tight tables beneath hanging ham hocks. The ambience is happy and a bit frantic—no reservations, so arrive early. You come here for the character...not for fine cuisine (daily 12:00-16:00 & 19:00-23:00, Via della Spada 27 red, +39 055 214 756).

$$ Trattoria "da Giorgio" is a rustic family-style diner on a sketchy street serving up simple home cooking to happy locals and tourists alike. Their €15 three-course lunch fixed-price meal, including a drink, is a great value (€20 at dinner). This place is completely without pretense—head here for a taste of working-class Florence (no reservations, Mon-Sat 12:00-14:30 & 19:00-22:00, closed Sun, Via Palazzuolo 100 red, +39 055 284 302, Silvano).

$ Shake Café, another outpost of this handy chain, is a healthy salad bar with seating on Piazza Santa Maria Novella. It's good for a quick lunch, with a menu of veggie bowls, wraps, smoothies, and juices (daily 7:00-20:00, two blocks in front of the train station at Via degli Avelli 2 red).

Gelato

Italy's ice cream is famed—and many believe the best is in Florence. But beware of scams at touristy joints on busy streets that turn a simple request for a cone into a €10 "tourist special" rip-off. To avoid this, survey the size options and specify what you want—for example, *un cono da tre euro* (a €3 cone). A rule of thumb: Stay away from places with heaping mounds of brightly (artificially) colored gelato. For more gelato tips, see the "Eating" section of the Practicalities chapter. The following places are a cut above the norm and open long hours daily.

Near the Accademia: A Sicilian choice on a tourist thoroughfare, **Gelateria Carabè** is particularly famous for its pistachio and its luscious *granite*—Italian ices made with fresh fruit. A *cremolata* is a *granita* with a dollop of gelato (almond and pistachio work well together). From the Accademia, it's a block toward the Duomo (at Via Ricasoli 60 red).

Near the Duomo: A favorite, **Edoardo** features organic ingredients and tasty handmade cones (facing the southwest corner of the Duomo at Piazza del Duomo 45 red).

Near Orsanmichele Church: This shop's name, **Perchè No!,** translates to "Why not!"—good advice when it comes to gelato. It feels touristy but serves one of the widest range of flavors around, and the quality's top notch (just off the busy main pedestrian drag, Via dei Calzaiuoli, at Via dei Tavolini 19).

Near the Church of Santa Croce: Florentines flock to **Gelateria de' Neri,** with an enticingly wide array of flavors (Via dei Neri 9 red).

Just Across the Carraia Bridge: On the Oltrarno side of the bridge, **Gelateria la Carraia** is a hit with locals (Piazza Nazario Sauro 25 red—see the map on page 520).

HIDDEN ROOFTOP CAFÉ TERRACES

If you're willing to pay extra to enjoy a drink surrounded by splendid Florentine views, head to one of these rooftop terraces:

$$ Caffè Tosca & Nino is on the rooftop of La Rinascente department store overlooking Piazza della Repubblica. While the place is a tight and plain little perch, its handful of tables comes with commanding views of the Duomo, which looms gloriously on the horizon (daily 9:00-24:00; coffee drinks, pastas, salads, and light bites; +39 055 493 3468).

$$$$ Sesto is a dressy bar and restaurant designed for dressy people on a partially covered terrace atop the luxurious Westin Hotel. While their Mediterranean cuisine and cocktails are pricey, it all comes with amazing city views. To turn your spendy drink into a light dinner, come during their *aperitivo* happy hour (18:00-21:00) when, for €30, your drink includes a little gourmet buffet of six tapas, giving you something to nibble as you enjoy the sunset (daily 12:00-24:00, reservations required, Piazza Ognissanti 3, +39 055 27151, www.sestoonarno.com).

$$ Caffè del Verone is perched on the rooftop terrace of the Hospital of the Innocents on Piazza Santissima Annunziata. It offers a nice, peaceful atmosphere for a coffee break with rooftop view (no ticket required, just catch the elevator by the museum entrance, Wed-Mon 16:00-20:00, open later on weekends, closed Tue, Piazza Santissima Annunziata 13, for location see the "Florence" map on page 462, +39 345 167 8267).

THE OLTRARNO

In general, dining in the Oltrarno, south of the Arno River, offers a more authentic experience. While it's just a few minutes' walk beyond Ponte Vecchio, this area sees far fewer tourists than the other side of the river. You may even find that Florentines outnumber tourists.

Dining or Drinking with a Ponte Vecchio View

For locations, see the "Oltrarno Hotels and Restaurants" map on page 520.

$$$ Signorvino is a bright and modern *enoteca* (wine shop) with a simple restaurant that has a rare terrace literally over the Arno River, with Ponte Vecchio views. Though it lacks historic charm with its stark-white IKEA vibe, it's a fun-loving place with a passion for quality Italian ingredients. They serve regional dishes and plates of fine meats and cheeses to pair with a wonderful array of wines by the glass, allowing you to drink and eat your way merrily across Italy (food served 12:00-22:30, call to reserve for river-view seating, Via dei Bardi 46 red, +39 055 286 258, www.signorvino.com).

$$$$ Golden View Firenze is two-in-one: a classy restaurant and a simpler wine bar/bakery, both overlooking the Ponte Vecchio and Arno River. The restaurant's white, minimalist interior is a dramatic contrast to atmospheric old Florence. Reservations for window tables are essential. Mixing their fine wine and river views makes for a wonderful evening (long hours daily, 50 yards east of Ponte Vecchio at Via dei Bardi 58, +39 055 214 502, https://goldenview.it, run by Paolo and Tommaso). Tommaso's new venture, **La Forneria Firenze,** is a combo wine bar/bakery with gourmet focaccia. The philosophy here is that top-quality fundamentals like bread, cheese, meat, and wine can amount to fine dining, especially if it comes with a view of the Ponte Vecchio.

$ Osteria Ponte Vecchio is a tiny place—little more than a bar—serving basic drinks, panini, pasta, and microwaved snacks with a couple of amazing tables on the river (daily 10:00-23:00, off-season until 20:00, a block downstream from Ponte Vecchio at Via Borgo San Jacopo 16 red, Giacomo).

On or near Piazza di Santo Spirito

Piazza di Santo Spirito is a thriving neighborhood square in the heart of the Oltrarno, with a collection of fun **$$** eateries and rustic bars. Several bars offer *aperitivo* buffets with their drinks during happy hour (generally 18:00-20:00). For locations, see the map on page 520. Later in the evening, the area becomes a club scene, filled with foreign students and young locals.

$$ Tamerò is an artsy pasta bar—a kind of "ruin pub" in an old auto mechanic's shop—serving Sardinian-Tuscan dishes (daily 12:00-late, Piazza Santo Spirito 11 red, +39 055 282 596).

$$ Trattoria Casalinga was here long before any of the others. It's an inexpensive standby with bustling aproned waiters. Florentines (who enjoy the tripe and tongue) and tourists (who opt for *ribollita*, anything with ragù sauce, and easier to swallow Tuscan favorites) both pack the place and leave full and happy. Their street-side tables are fun, but the old-time trattoria action is inside (Mon-Sat 12:00-14:30 & 19:00-22:00, closed Sun and Aug, just off Piazza di Santo Spirito, near the church at Via de' Michelozzi 9 red, +39 055 218 624, www.trattorialacasalinga.it, Andrea and Paolo).

$$ Gusta Osteria, just around the corner from the piazza, serves big salads and predictable Tuscan fare at playful, cozy indoor seating or at outdoor tables (Tue-Sun 12:00-23:00, closed Mon, Via de' Michelozzi 13 red, +39 055 285 033).

$ Gusta Pizza is a jam-packed, touristy, cheap, sloppy, and fun neighborhood pizzeria (Tue-Sun 11:30-15:30 & 19:00-23:30, closed Mon, two blocks off Piazza di Santo Spirito at Via Maggio 46 red, +39 055 285 068).

$$ Trattoria Sant'Agostino, a block away from the Piazza di Santo Spirito action, is charming and more relaxed with comfortable seating. It's a good place for local favorites, soups, and the Roman noodle dish *pici cacio e pepe* (daily 12:00-23:00, Via Sant'Agostino 23 red, +39 055 281 995).

$ O Munaciello Pizzeria is where Italian kids dream of going on their birthday. Named after a ghost of Neapolitan folklore, it's a kitschy, sprawling, family-friendly festival of happy eating. The menu is fun, there's a youthful energy, and the Naples-style pizza is a hit (daily 12:30-15:00 & 19:00-24:00, Via Maffia 31 red, +39 055 287 198).

Night Spots: Piazza di Santo Spirito is lined with popular bars and restaurants. **Volume** caters to a younger crowd with a living-room atmosphere (daily 8:30-24:00, Piazza di Santo Spirito 5 red). On the opposite side of the square, **Pop Café** feels trendy, though it's plastic-plate simple (daily 8:00-late, Piazza di Santo Spirito 18). A bit farther from the square, **Gosh** bar mixes up craft cocktails and herb-infused drinks with flair (daily until 24:00, Via Santo Spirito 46 red). **NOF** is a late-night hangout with live music ranging from rock to jazz (Mon-Sat 18:30-late, Borgo San Frediano 17 red).

Beyond Piazza del Carmine, away from Tourists

While Piazza di Santo Spirito is well known by tourists, a short walk beyond it gets you completely away from the tourist scene. These neighboring restaurants (on quiet Via dell'Orto, each with sidewalk tables) are worth the five-minute walk beyond Piazza del Carmine. For locations, see the "Oltrarno, South of the Arno River" map on page 509.

$$$ Burro & Acciughe Fish Restaurant ("butter and anchovies") is a minimalist place packed with locals enjoying fresh seafood. With just 35 seats in a long, narrow setting, it oozes quality (Tue-Sun 19:30-24:00, closed Mon, Via dell'Orto 35 red, +39 055 045 7286).

$$ Trattoria dell'Orto is a classic Florentine trattoria filled with Florentines enjoying steaks, grilled dishes, and quintessential local fare. It has a boisterous vibe and an inviting covered outdoor terrace in back (Wed-Mon 12:00-15:00 & 19:30-23:30, closed Tue, Via dell'Orto 35a, +39 055 224 148).

$$$ Ristorante il Guscio is another very local place with a more romantic feel, an enticing menu, and quality wine (Mon-Sat 12:00-15:00 & 19:30-23:00, closed Sun, Via dell'Orto 49, +39 055 224 421).

Dining near the Oltrarno

These trendy spots are closer to the river and more formal. Reservations are a good idea in the evening. For locations see the map on page 520.

$$$ Il Santo Bevitore Ristorante, lit like a Rembrandt

painting and unusually spacious, serves creative, modern Tuscan cuisine at dressy tables. They're enthusiastic about matching quality produce from the area with the right wine (daily 12:30-14:30 & 19:30-23:00, good wine list by the glass or bottle, acoustics can make it noisy inside, Via di Santo Spirito 64 red, +39 055 211 264, www.ilsantobevitore.com).

$$ Enoteca il Santino Gastronomia, Il Santo Bevitore's tiny wine bar next door, feels like the perfect after-work hangout for foodies who'd like a glass of wine and a light bite. Tight, cozy, and atmospheric, it can be impossibly intimidating if you're shy, so come early before the crowds. There's a prominent bar, where you can assemble an €8-12 *tagliere* of local cheeses and *salumi*. They also have a few affordable hot dishes. The food and the wine are locally sourced from small producers (daily 12:30-23:00, Via di Santo Spirito 60 red, no reservations, +39 055 230 2820).

$$$ Trattoria 4 Leoni creates the quintessential Oltrarno dinner scene, and is understandably popular with tourists. The Tuscan-style food is made with an innovative twist and an appreciation for vegetables. Their steak and *fiocchetti* pasta are big hits. You'll enjoy the fun energy and characteristic seating, both outside on the colorful square and inside (daily 12:00-24:00; midway between Ponte Vecchio and Piazza di Santo Spirito, on Piazza della Passera at Via de' Vellutini 1; +39 055 218 562, www.4leoni.com).

$$$ Antico Ristoro di' Cambi is thick with Tuscan traditions, rustic touches, T-bone steaks, and a bustling beer-hall energy. The glass case filled with red chunks of Chianina beef makes clear the house specialty (for the famous *bistecca alla fiorentina* it's €50/kilo). Before you order, they'll show you the cut and tell you the weight (1.2 kilos is the typical serving for two; 800 grams is the smallest two can split). Unless you insist otherwise, the steak comes nearly uncooked (as it's air-dried for 21 days, it's not really raw, just very tasty and tender). Sit inside the convivial woody interior or outside on the square (Mon-Sat 12:00-14:30 & 18:00-22:30, closed Sun, Via Sant'Onofrio 1 red, one block south of Ponte Amerigo Vespucci, see map on page 509, +39 055 217 134, www.anticoristorodicambi.it, run by Stefano).

Casual Oltrarno Neighborhood Eateries

$$ Le Volpi e l'Uva, a wine bar just steps from Ponte Vecchio, has a limited menu of *affettati* (cold cuts), cheese, and *crostone* (hearty bruschetta)—a nice spot for a light lunch (Mon-Sat 12:00-21:00, closed Sun, 65 yards south of Ponte Vecchio—walk through Piazza Santa Felicità to Piazza dei Rossi 1, +39 055 239 8132).

$ Trattoria Sabatino, the farthest away of my Oltrarno listings (and not touristy), is a spacious, brightly lit mess hall. It's changed little since it opened in 1956. It's disturbingly cheap,

FLORENCE

Cooking Classes

Below are a few of your many choices. Do some homework online and book well ahead.

In Tavola: This cooking school in the heart of the Oltrarno features trained, English-speaking Italian chefs who quickly demonstrate each step before setting you loose. You'll work in a functional kitchen, then sit down to eat in the cozy wine cellar (**RS%,** classes range from €55-129/person, ideally book well ahead but you can try calling last-minute, between the Pitti Palace and Brancacci Chapel at Via dei Velluti 20 red, +39 055 217 672, www.intavola. org, Fabrizio).

Artviva: The Artviva walking-tour company offers a wide range of hands-on cooking, pasta, and pastry classes, as well as unique foodie experiences such as truffle hunting (from €60/person, see listing on page 468).

Florencetown: This walking-tour company offers a five-hour experience that starts with a trip to Mercato Centrale, then settles in to their kitchen for a cooking lesson (from €99/person, also 3-hour pizza- and gelato-making class for €69/person, see listing on page 468).

with family character and a simple menu—a super place to watch locals munch, especially since you'll likely be sharing a table. It's a 15-minute walk from Ponte Vecchio (Mon-Fri 12:00-14:30 & 19:15-22:00, closed Sat-Sun, no reservations, just outside Porta San Frediano, Via Pisana 2 red, see map on page 509, +39 055 225 955, little English spoken).

$$ Santarosa Bistrot is part of a city government project to redevelop the public gardens along the city wall and the river. It's a trendy, youthful, and family-friendly spot. The creative and modern menu has a dash of Naples. Offerings include salads, pastas, bar food, and cocktails (Tue-Sun 10:00-18:00, closed Mon, fills a garden just behind Trattoria Sabatino at Lungarno di Santa Rosa, see map on page 509, +39 055 230 9057).

San Niccolò Neighborhood

The charming little Via San Niccolò—just over Ponte alle Grazie—is the heart of the San Niccolò neighborhood and a fun place to get away from the tourist mobs (for locations, see the map on page 509).

This is groovy Italy, with a convivial neighborhood pizzeria, happening little restaurants, trendy cocktail bars, and a good *gelateria* (**Il Gelato di Filo,** at Via San Miniato 5 red). Street-art lovers enjoy popping into the gallery of **Abraham Clet,** the artist who stealthily and humorously alters street signs around town (daily 10:30-19:30, 50 meters from my recommended eateries at Via dell'Olmo 8 red). For those looking to dine, several good eateries anchor the square:

$$ Il Rifrullo, creatively run by Filippo and his young and hard-working team, is a rollicking cocktail bar with a sprawling, breezy terrace out back. They serve a fun lunch *menu* and delightful gourmet platters of cold cuts *(tagliere)* any time of day (daily until late, Via San Niccolò 55 red, +39 055 234 2621).

$$ Antica Mescita San Niccolò, with traditional decor but a modern approach, feels like the grandkids took over Nonno's trattoria. Technically a wine bar, they also serve up Tuscan standbys (like soups and stews). There's delightful seating outside and in (daily 12:00-23:00, Via San Niccolò 60 red, +39 055 234 2836).

$$ Boccadarno, next door at #56 red, is run by brother-and-sister team Gerardo and Carlotta. The service is friendly, and the menu is all about fish. Eat in the light, bright interior or at an outdoor table (Tue-Sat 18:00-23:30, closed Sun, +39 055 386 0860).

$$$ Zeb is tight and mod, and Michelin rated for its gourmet plates. A minimalist wine-bar/deli, it's just one long counter with two dozen seats. Although the name stands for *zuppe e bolliti* ("soup and boiled meats"), they dish up all types of well-executed and elegantly presented Italian dishes. Portions are large and fun to share, served up by charming Mama Guiseppina and her son Alberto (Mon-Tue and Thu-Sat 12:00-15:30 & 19:30-22:30, closed Sun and Wed, reservations recommended, Via San Miniato 2 red, +39 055 234 2864, www.zebgastronomia.com).

Nightlife: To rub elbows with the locals, head toward tiny Piazza Demidoff (cross the bridge east of Ponte Vecchio and turn left, about a 10-minute walk). **Zoe** has outdoor seating (opens Mon-Sat at 9:00, Sun at 18:00, Via dei Renai 13 red+39 055 243 111).

Florence Connections

Florence is Tuscany's transportation hub, with fine train, bus, and plane connections to virtually anywhere in Italy. The city has several train stations, a bus station (next to the main train station), and an airport (and Pisa's airport is nearby). Livorno, on the coast west of Florence, is a major cruise-ship port.

BY TRAIN

Florence's main train station is called **Santa Maria Novella** (*Firenze S.M.N.* on schedules and signs). Florence also has two suburban train stations: **Firenze Rifredi** and **Firenze Campo di Marte**.

FLORENCE

Some trains don't stop at the main station—confirm that you're heading for S.M.N., or you may overshoot the city. (The other stations are a short taxi ride from the center.)

As at any busy train station, be on guard: Don't trust "porters" who want to help you find your train or carry your bags (they're not official), and politely decline offers of help using the ticket machines by anyone other than uniformed staff. For general information on train travel in Italy—including ticket-buying options—see the Practicalities chapter.

Santa Maria Novella Station

To orient yourself to the station, stand with your back to the tracks. Look left to see the green cross of a 24-hour pharmacy *(farmacia)* and the exit to the taxi queue. Baggage storage *(deposito bagagli)* is also to the left, halfway down track 16 (long hours daily, passport required). Fast-food outlets are along track 16. Directly ahead of you is the main hall *(salone biglietti)*, where you can buy train and bus tickets. Pay WCs are to the right, near the head of track 5.

To reach the **TI**, walk away from the tracks and exit the station; it's straight across the square, 100 yards away, by the stone church.

Buying Tickets: For travel within Italy, it's quick and easy to buy tickets online; with the Trenitalia app, you can even purchase them minutes before the train departs. If you buy tickets at the station, take advantage of the ticket *(biglietti)* machines that display schedules and issue tickets. For most international tickets, you'll need to go to a Trenitalia ticket window (in the main hall).

For Trenitalia information, use window #18 or #19 (take a number). For Italo tickets and information, use window #10 or #11, or visit their main office, opposite track 5, near the exit.

To buy city bus tickets, head to the bus station next door (and ask for a transit map while you're there).

Eating: $ VyTA, across from track 13, has good sandwiches, snacks, and pastries. **$ Tentazioni Café,** near track 5, offers drinks, salads, and other goodies. A Carrefour Express, next to the bus station, is the closest supermarket (daily until 21:00).

Services: Feltrinelli has English-language books and magazines and a café (across from track 14) while a modern **shopping gallery** with clothing stores and another café is down the escalator, across from tracks 11-12.

Getting to the Duomo and City Center

The Duomo and town center are to your left (with your back to the tracks). Out the doorway to the left, you'll find city buses and the taxi stand. **Taxis** cost about €8 to the Duomo. **Buses** generally don't cover the center well and probably aren't the best way

Greater Florence

to reach your hotel (walking could be faster). To **walk** into town (10-15 minutes), exit the station straight ahead (with your back to the tracks), through the main hall, and head straight across the square outside (toward the Church of Santa Maria Novella). On the far side of the square, keep left and head down the main Via dei Panzani, which leads directly to the Duomo.

Train Connections

The following connections are for Trenitalia unless noted.

From Florence by Train to: Pisa (2/hour, 45-75 minutes), **Lucca** (2/hour, 1.5 hours), **Siena** (direct trains hourly, 1.5 hours; bus is better because Siena's train station is far from the center), **Camucia-Cortona** (hourly, 1.5 hours), **Livorno** (hourly, 1.5 hours, some change in Pisa), **La Spezia** (for the Cinque Terre, 5/day direct, 2.5 hours, otherwise nearly hourly with change in Pisa), **Milan** (hourly, 2 hours; Italo: 2/hour, 2 hours), **Venice** (hourly, 2-3 hours, may transfer in Bologna, often crowded—reserve ahead;

FLORENCE

Italo: 4/day, 2 hours, reservations required), **Assisi** (7/day direct, 2-3 hours), **Orvieto** (hourly, 2 hours, some with change in Campo di Marte or Rifredi Station), **Rome** (2-3/hour, 1.5 hours, most require seat reservations; Italo: 2/hour, 1.5 hours), **Naples** (at least hourly, 3 hours; Italo: hourly, 3 hours).

BY BUS

The bus station, operated by **Autolinee Toscane,** is 50 yards southwest of the train station, near the T1 tram stop. Its hard-to-find entrance is located just off the main square, on Via Santa Caterina da Siena; pedestrians enter through the same portal the buses do. The station is little more than a big, old-school lot with numbered stalls, a ticket office, and a snack bar. Schedules for regional trips are posted, and monitors show imminent departures. It's best to buy tickets in the station or at machines, as they aren't always sold aboard the bus. Bus info: +39 800 373 760 (daily 6:30-20:00), www.at-bus.it.

Getting to the Train Station and City Center: Exit the station through the main door and turn left along the busy street. The train station is on your left, while downtown Florence is straight ahead and a bit to the right.

Bus Connections

From Florence by Bus to: San Gimignano (hourly, fewer on Sun, 1.5-2 hours, change in Poggibonsi), **Siena** (roughly 2/hour—fewer off-season, 1.5-hour *rapida/via superstrada* buses are fastest, avoid the slower *ordinaria* buses, in Siena get off at Piazza Gramsci or Via Tozzi, www.tiemmespa.it), **Volterra** (4/day Mon-Sat, 1/day Sun, 2 hours, change in Colle di Val d'Elsa; or faster train to Pontedera-Casciana Terme and then transfer to bus #500 to Volterra, 7/day, fewer on Sun, 1.5 hours), **Montepulciano** (1-2/day, 2 hours, LFI bus, www.lfi.it; or train to Chiusi, then bus to Montepulciano).

BY PRIVATE CAR

Zipping to nearby towns by private car service can be a comfortable option. Florence-based **Transfer Chauffeur Service** has a fleet of modern vehicles with drivers who can whisk you through the Tuscan countryside for around the same price as a cab (+39 338 862 3129, www.transfercs.com, welcome@transfercs.com, Marco). **Prestige Rent** also has friendly, English-speaking drivers and offers similar services (office at Via della Saggina 98, +39 055 286 059, www.prestigerent.com, usa@prestigerent.com, Saverio).

BY CAR

Renting a car at the Florence airport, with easy access to the autostrada, is the best option. There's also a rental office located on the

T1 tram line (Sansovino stop) that's far enough from the historic core to make driving out of the city doable.

Don't even attempt driving into the city center. The autostrada has several exits for Florence. Get off at the *Nord, Scandicci, Impruneta,* or *Sud* exits and follow signs toward—but not into—the *Centro.* Park on the outskirts—see the next section—and take a bus, tram, or taxi in.

Florence's traffic-reduction system is complicated and confusing even to locals. Every car passing into the "limited traffic zone" (*Zona Traffico Limitato,* or *ZTL*) is photographed; those without a permit can expect a €100 ticket in the mail. If you have a reservation at a hotel within the ZTL area—and it has parking—ask in advance if they can get you permission to enter town.

Another potentially expensive mistake drivers make in Florence is using the lanes designated for buses only (usually marked with yellow stripes). Driving in these lanes can also result in a ticket in the mail. Pay careful attention to signs.

Parking in Florence

The city center is ringed with big, efficient parking lots (signposted with a big *P*). From these, you can ride into the center (via taxi, bus, or possibly tram). Check www.fipark.com for details on parking lots, availability, and prices. From the freeway, follow the signs to *Centro,* then *Stadio,* then *P.*

The huge park-and-ride lot called Villa Costanza, just outside the town of Scandicci (south of Florence), has its own dedicated freeway off-ramp (just north of Impruneta) and is the terminus for the T1 tram line that zips smart drivers downtown (€1.50, departing every five minutes). Just look for it as you approach Florence on the autostrada (see the "Greater Florence" map on page 543).

BY PLANE

Amerigo Vespucci Airport, also called Peretola Airport, is about five miles northwest of the city (code: FLR, www.aeroporto. firenze.it). On the ground floor, you'll find a TI, café, and ATMs.

Getting Between the Airport and City Center

The **T2 tram** (to the left as you exit the arrivals hall) runs every five minutes from the airport to near the train station (Alamanni Stazione, across from the station) and Piazza dell'Unità (one stop beyond the station, slightly closer to downtown) in about 20 minutes (runs 5:00-24:00, €1.50, buy ticket from machine on platform, cash or credit card, validate onboard, good for 90 minutes and transferable to bus lines, www.gestramvia.com).

Shuttle buses (to the far right as you exit the arrivals hall) connect the airport with Florence's train and bus stations (2/hour until 22:00, 1/hour until 00:30, 30 minutes, runs 5:00-00:30, €6 one-way—buy ticket on board, €10 round-trip—buy ticket inside airport). If you're changing to a different intercity bus in Florence (for instance, one bound for Siena), stay on the bus through the first stop (at the train station); it will continue on to the bus station nearby.

Official **taxi** companies have fixed rates for the 20- to 30-minute ride between the airport and downtown: €22 during the day (6:00-22:00), €25.30 at night, and €24 on Sunday. Be sure to use an official taxi (white, marked with *Taxi/Comune di Firenze* and a red fleur-de-lis).

The airport's **rental-car** offices share one big parking lot at Via Palagio degli Spini that's a three-minute drive away (shuttle bus departs directly outside the arrivals door).

BY CRUISE SHIP

Cruise ships dock in the coastal town of **Livorno,** about 60 miles west of Florence. The most seamless way to reach Florence from the port is to catch a transfer-only shuttle-bus; they guarantee you'll make it back to your ship in plenty of time (+39 058 6188 8623, www.tuscanybus.com). On your own, you can take a train to Florence (hourly, 1.5 hours). Taxis are pricey, but sharing a minibus taxi with other cruisers can bring the round-trip cost down. For more details, see my *Rick Steves Mediterranean Cruise Ports* guidebook.

PISA & LUCCA

The two Tuscan towns of Pisa and Lucca, near Florence and each other, make for easy day trips. But both cities deserve more than a touristy quickie. If you can, take the time to savor Pisa's rich architectural heritage and to bask in Lucca's ambiance.

The Leaning Tower of Pisa is one of the most iconic images in the world. It's touristy but worth a visit. Many travelers are surprised to see that the famous tower is only a small part of a gleaming white architectural complex—featuring a massive cathedral and baptistery—that dominates the grand green square called the Field of Miracles. The rest of the city is virtually tourist-free and merits a wander for its rich history, architecture, and student vibe.

Lucca, contained within its fine Renaissance wall, lacks any blockbuster sights but has a charm that causes many connoisseurs of Italy to claim it as a favorite stop. The town's garden-topped city wall is perfect for a laid-back bike ride—the single must-do activity in this pleasant getaway.

The two towns are about 25 minutes apart by train and 50 minutes by bus (for side-tripping between Pisa and Lucca, see the "Connections" sections later). Each is about 1.5 hours (or less) by train from Florence and well served by excellent highways.

Using public transportation, you could day-trip from Florence to both cities. But with more time, stay overnight in Lucca. Take the train to Pisa in the morning, do your sightseeing, catch the bus or train to Lucca late in the afternoon, enjoy the evening scene, and stay the night. Sightsee Lucca the next day, then move on to your next destination by train.

Pisa

Famous for its tipsy Tower, Pisa ("PEE-zah") is much more than its iconic landmark. This thriving midsize city has a wealth of history and architectural treasures, an unexpectedly fun-to-explore arcaded core, and a prestigious university. The Tower and its companion buildings at the Field of Miracles are undoubtedly a must-see. But beyond that tourist-clogged zone, Pisa feels

like a real-world antidote to all that Tuscan cutesiness...a humbler version of Florence.

Centuries ago, Pisa was a major power—rivaling Venice and Genoa for control of the seas. City leaders erected an ensemble of Pisan Romanesque landmarks—the Duomo, Baptistery, and Tower—that float regally on the best lawn in Italy. It's no surprise that Piazza del Duomo is now better known as the Campo dei Miracoli (Field of Miracles), for the grandness of the undertaking.

After its port silted up, Pisa was left high and dry, and eventually entered a period of steady decline...leaving those grand landmarks as reminders of its past glory.

PLANNING YOUR TIME

For most visitors, Pisa is a touristy quickie—seeing the Tower, visiting the square, and wandering through the Duomo. But it's a shame to skip the rest of the city. Considering Pisa's historic importance and the ambience created by its rich architectural heritage and vibrant student population, the city deserves at least a half-day visit.

To ascend the Tower, it's smartest to book a time in advance online at OPAPisa.it. Otherwise, go straight to the ticket office upon arrival to snag an appointment—usually for a couple of hours later, especially in summer. If you'll be seeing both the town and the Field of Miracles, plan on a six-hour stop. If just blitzing the Field of Miracles, three hours is the minimum.

Orientation to Pisa

Pisa is manageable, with about 100,000 people. The city is framed on the north by the Field of Miracles (with the Leaning Tower) and on the south by Pisa Centrale train station. The Arno River flows east to west, bisecting the city. The two main streets for tourists and shoppers are Via Santa Maria (running south from the Tower) and Corso Italia/Borgo Stretto (running north from the station). A thousand years ago, the city was a fortified burg on the north side of the river between those two main streets.

TOURIST INFORMATION

The main TI is located on the Field of Miracles, next to the Duomo's ticket office at the Museum of the Sinopias (daily 10:00-18:00, Nov-Feb until 16:00, Piazza Duomo 7, +39 050 550 100, www. turismo.pisa.it). It sells bus tickets and offers videoguide walking tours of the main sights and the city center (€5-8). For those doing Pisa as a stopover, the TI offers baggage storage (€4). In summer, there may be another TI in the town center, on Piazza XX Settembre (near the loggia, just south of the Arno).

ARRIVAL IN PISA
By Train

Most trains (and visitors) arrive at Pisa Centrale station, about a mile south of the Tower and Field of Miracles. Some trains, particularly those from Lucca or La Spezia, also stop at the smaller Pisa San Rossore station, an easy walk (less than 10 minutes) from the Tower.

Pisa Centrale Station: This station has a baggage-check desk—look for *deposito bagagli*, at the far-right end of platform 1 (with the tracks at your back).

To get to the Field of Miracles, you can **walk** (30 minutes direct, one hour if you follow my self-guided walk), take a **taxi** (€10, +39 050 541 600, taxi stand at station), or go by **bus** (which can be plagued by pickpockets).

Bus **LAM Rossa** (also marked *L/R*) stops in front of the station (to the right when you exit; bus stop at the corner). It runs about

every 10 minutes to Piazza Manin, in front of the Field of Miracles (15-minute ride, stop: Torre, buy €1.50 ticket at machine or from any tobacco shop before boarding).

If you need to return to the train station from the Tower, catch bus LAM Rossa across from the BNL bank, on the opposite side of the street from where you got off (buy ticket from machine at bus stop). You'll find taxi stands 30 yards from the Tower and in front of the BNL bank on Piazza Manin. Or see if your departing

Pisa

See Field of Miracles detail map

To Autostrada
& P Pietrasantina

VIALE CASCINE
To San Rossore Station
Largo Griffi
P Piazza dei Miracoli
To Lucca
Piazza Manin
Tower
To Centrale Station
WALL WALK
LEANING TOWER
CAMPOSANTO
BAPT.
DUOMO
PORTA NUOVA
FIELD OF MIRACLES
DUOMO MUSEUM
TICKETS
WALK ENDS
Piazza Arch.

GARIBALDI ARENA

VIA CONTESSA MATILDE
VIA LUIGI BIANCHI
To Lucca & Market
OLD CITY WALLS
V. CARDINALE MAFFI
PORTA A LUCCA
V. CAPPONI

VIA BONANNO PISANO
VIA DON GAETANO BOSCHI
GRAND HOTEL
VIA SAN GIUSEPPE
Piazza San Caterina
Piazza Martiri della Libertà

VIA NICOLA PISANO
VIA PAOLO SAVI
VIA PERNA
VIA RISORGIMENTO
VIA ROMA
VIA SANTA MARIA
VIA VOLTA
VIA DEI MILLE
VIA FAGGIOLA
VIA MARTIRI
VIA SAN LORENZO
SANTO STEFANO
VIA G. CARDUCCI
BORGO STRETTO

N

Piazza Cavalotti
Piazza Cavalieri
SAN SISTO
SAN FREDIANO
Piazza S. Fred.
Piazza Dante
Piazza Carrara
VIA PAOLI
VIA TAVO.
V. CAV.
Piazza delle Vettovaglie
S. FRANCESCO
V. MERC.
VIA PALESTRO
Piazza Garibaldi

VIA ENRICO FERMI
VIA TRIESTE
VIA TRENTO
VIA VOLTURNO
LUNGARNO PACINOTTI
PONTE DI MEZZO
To Nazionale di San Matteo
LUNG. GALILEI

SANTA MARIA DELLA SPINA
LUNGARNO GAMBACORTI
LUNGARNO MEDICEO
LUNG. LOGGIA
VIA SAN MARTINO
VIA CECI

PONTE SOLFERINO
Arno River
LUNGARNO SIMONELLA
LUNGARNO SONNINO
VIA SAN PAOLO
V. A. MARIO
V. GIUSEPPE MAZZINI
NUNZIATINA
CORSO ITALIA

V. NICOLA PISANO
VIA FRANCESCO CRISPI
VIA MANZONI
NICOLA PISANO STATUE
VIA CARMINE
CHURCH OF CARMINE

VIA FRANCESCO NIOSI
VIA LAVAGNA
VIA NINO BIXIO
Piazza San Antonio
HARING MURAL
VIA F. TURATI
VIA BENEDETTO CROCE

OLD CITY WALLS
VIA CESARE BATTISTI
BUS STATION
Piazza Vittorio Emanuele II
VIALE BONAINI

200 Meters
200 Yards

WALK BEGINS
To Field of Miracles
Piazza d. Stazione
VIA ALESSANDRA DELLA SPINA

PISA CENTRALE TRAIN STATION

Pisa Key

<u>Accommodations</u>
- **1** Relais dei Mercanti
- **2** Hotel Royal Victoria
- **3** Hotel Pisa Tower
- **4** Casa San Tommaso
- **5** Hotel Helvetia
- **6** Hotel Alessandro della Spina
- **7** Stazione22

<u>Eateries & Other</u>
- **8** Ristorante-Pizzeria La Torre
- **9** Pizzeria al Bagno di Nerone

- **10** La Vineria di Piazza & Produce Market
- **11** Antica Trattoria il Campano
- **12** Osteria dei Cavalieri
- **13** Caffetteria BetsaBea
- **14** Il Montino Pizzeria
- **15** Orzo Bruno Brewpub
- **16** La Mescita
- **17** La Bottega del Gelato
- **18** De' Coltelli Gelato & Caffè dell'Ussero
- **19** Supermarket

train also stops at San Rossore station (see next)—saving you the trip back to Pisa Centrale.

Pisa San Rossore Station: This little suburban train station is just a four-block walk (less than 10 minutes) to the Tower. On arrival, exit the underpass at platform 2L, and follow the exit signs to *Torre Pendente*. Once out of the station area, turn left and follow brown *Torre Pendente* signs on Via Andrea Pisano, heading for the Baptistery's dome.

By Car

Pisa has several restricted driving areas that are monitored by camera and marked by "*ZTL*" signs (you could get a ticket by mail). For a quick visit, there are two pay lots just west of the tower (both around €2/hour): **Parcheggio di Piazza dei Miracoli** lot (enter from Via Giovanni Battista Niccolini) and **Tower Parking** (enter from Via Andrea Pisano). Or try the free, big **Pietrasantina parking lot** (which you'll share with lots of tour buses). To find it, exit the autostrada at *Pisa Nord* and follow signs to *Pisa* (on the left), then *Bus Parking*.

At the center of the lot is a high-roofed bus stop where you can catch the LAM Rossa **bus** to Piazza Manin at the gate of the Field of Miracles (€1.50 at the parking lot's cafeteria; bus continues to Pisa Centrale station if you'd like to follow my self-guided walk to the Field of Miracles). Or you can **walk** to the Tower in about 15 minutes: From the newspaper/souvenir kiosk at the east end of the lot, turn right onto the curving road. Follow the blue signs indicating a pedestrian path and brown signs pointing to the Leaning Tower. You'll cross train tracks on the left, then continue to the right.

By Plane

For details on Pisa's Galileo Galilei Airport, see "Pisa Connections," later.

HELPFUL HINTS

Markets: An open-air produce market attracts picnickers to Piazza delle Vettovaglie, one block north of the Arno River near Ponte di Mezzo, and nearby Piazza Sant'Uomobuono (Mon-Sat 8:00-13:00, closed Sun). A street market—with more practical goods than food—bustles on Wednesday and Saturday mornings between Via del Brennero and Via Paparrelli (8:00-13:00, just outside of wall, about 6 blocks east of the Tower). A small flea market pops up in Via San Martino every Wednesday and Saturday morning.

Supermarket: Just to the northwest of the Field of Miracles entrance, **Carrefour Express** has everything you need. It sells quick lunch items and has a coffee bar and picnic area, Wi-Fi, and a clean WC free for customers (daily 10:00-18:00, Largo Cocco Griffi).

Local Guides: For tours of Pisa as well as the surrounding countryside, try **Dottore Vincenzo Riolo** (€150/3 hours, +39 338 211 2939, www.pisatour.it, info@pisatour.it) or **Martina Manfredi** (€140/3 hours, +39 328 898 2927, www.tuscanyatheart.it, info@tuscanyatheart.it).

Pisa Walk

A leisurely one-hour self-guided stroll from Pisa Centrale train station to the Tower is a great way to get acquainted with the more subtle virtues of this fine city. Because the hordes that descend daily on the Tower rarely bother with the rest of the town, you'll find most of Pisa to be delightfully untouristy—a student-filled, classy, Old World town with an Arno-scape much like its upstream rival, Florence.

• *Exit Pisa Centrale and walk straight ahead (north, under the fascist marble arcade) up Viale Antonio Gramsci to the circular square called...*

Piazza Vittorio Emanuele II

The Allies considered Pisa to be strategically important in World War II, and both the train station and its main bridge were targeted for bombing. Forty percent of this district was destroyed. The piazza has been rebuilt, and now this generous public space with grass and benches is actually a lid for an underground parking lot. The circular pink building in the middle of the square, on the right, is La Bottega del Parco, a shop that sells Tuscan products and offers light meals.

At the top of the square, on the left (by the modern gray tower with the Credito Artigiano bank), find the little piazza with a colorful bar/café that faces a mural, called *Tuttomondo (Whole Wide World)*, painted by American artist **Keith Haring.** The mural, which decorates the back of a church that was bombed and rebuilt in the 1950s, is worth studying. It's a celebration of diversity, chaos, and the liveliness of our world, vibrating with energy. Enjoy the symbolism: the cross of people, three races connected like nesting dolls holding a heart. The message of tolerance is as timely today as it was when this mural was completed in 1989. Haring (who died of AIDS in 1990) brought New York City street art into the mainstream.

• *Head back to the middle of the big square and take the first left. This is Pisa's main drag.*

Corso Italia

As you leave Piazza Vittorio Emanuele II, look to the right (on the wall of the bar on the corner, under the gallery) and orient yourself with the circa-1960 wall map of Pisa with a steam train. Then follow the pedestrianized Corso Italia straight north for several blocks, toward the river. This is Pisa's main shopping street for locals, not tourists. Students hang out and stroll here—you'll see plenty of cheap department stores and youthful fashions.

A few blocks up, in front of the Church of Santa Maria del Carmine (on the right, at #88), meet **Nicola Pisano.** He and his son, Giovanni (who worked in the 13th century), represented the pinnacle of Gothic art and inspired Michelangelo. Although they were from the south, their work in their adopted town earned them the name "Pisano" (from Pisa).

Continuing on Corso Italia, just before the river, you run into a stately **loggia.** Like much of the city, this was built under Medici (Florentine) rule—and it resembles the markets you'll still find in Florence. But remember that before Florence ruled Pisa, this city was an independent and strong maritime republic.

• *At the Arno River, cross to the middle of the bridge.*

Ponte di Mezzo

This modern bridge, the site of Pisa's first bridge and therefore its birthplace, marks the center of Pisa. In the Middle Ages, Ponte di Mezzo (like Florence's Ponte Vecchio) was lined with shops. It's been destroyed several times by floods...and in 1943 by British and American bombers. Enjoy the view from the center of the bridge of the elegant mansions that line the riverbank, recalling Pisa's days of trading glory—the cityscape feels a bit like Venice's Grand Canal.

Looking downstream (to the left), notice the red-brick building on the right bank (the former silk merchants' quarters) that looks like it's about to slide into the river. Pisa sits on shifting delta sand, making construction tricky. The entire town leans.

• *Cross the bridge to...*

Piazza Garibaldi

This square is named for the charismatic leader of the Risorgimento, the unification movement that led to Italian independence in

1861. Knowing Pisa was strongly nationalist (and gave many of its sons to the national struggle), a wounded Garibaldi came here to be nursed back to health. Find his statue and study the left side of the bronze relief at the base of the statue to see him docking in Pisa and receiving a warm and caring welcome.

For a gelato break, stop by **La Bottega del Gelato,** right on this square and most Pisans' sentimental favorite. Or, head about 100 yards downstream (to the left on Lungarno Pacinotti as you come off the bridge) to **De' Coltelli** (at #23), which scoops up organic, artisanal gelato with unusual and vibrant flavors. Just beyond that, in the slouching red building (at #28), step into **Caffè dell'Ussero.** This venerable café has long been a hangout of both politicians...and the students bent on overthrowing them.

• *Back on Piazza Garibaldi, continue north up the elegantly arcaded street called...*

Borgo Stretto

Welcome to Pisa's other main shopping street—this one higher-end. On the right, the Church of St. Michael, with its fine Pisan Romanesque facade, was likely built upon a Roman temple.

From here, look farther up the street and notice how it undulates like a flowing river. In the sixth century BC, Pisa was born when two parallel rivers were connected by canals. This street echoes the flow of one of those canals.

• *Just past the church, pause to appreciate the Renaissance arcades (loggias) in every direction. Then detour left onto Via delle Colonne, and walk one block down to...*

Piazza delle Vettovaglie

Pisa's historic market square, Piazza delle Vettovaglie, is lively by day and sketchy by night. Its Renaissance loggia has hosted the fish-and-vegetable market for generations. Stalls are set up in this piazza in the morning and stay open later in the neighboring piazza to the west (Piazza Sant'Uomobuono). You could cobble together a picnic from the sandwich shops and fruit-and-veggie stalls ringing these squares, or enjoy lunch at the recommended **La Vineria di Piazza** trattoria (under the arcades of Piazza delle Vettovaglie).

• *Return to Borgo Stretto and continue north another 100 yards, passing a modern apartment development on the right at Largo Ciro Menotti, an example of 1960s city design that followed WWII bombings. Standing out front is a statue of native son Galileo Galilei, erected in early 2020.*

Carry on for a couple more short blocks, and turn left on nondescript Via Ulisse Dini (immediately at the arcade's end, just before the pharmacy). This leads in a few short blocks to Pisa's historic core, the square called...

Piazza dei Cavalieri (Knights' Square)

For Pisans, this square is a place of lost glory. It feels sad, nostalgic...the only piazza I've seen in Italy without a bar or café. The

square (site of the market, or forum, in ancient Roman times) long hosted the head of a proud and independent Pisan government. A Palazzo Vecchio-like capitol stood here during Pisa's glory days when the city was a big maritime power in a league with Genoa and Amalfi.

Then came a couple of centuries of Florentine rule. Walk to the statue in front of the curved building. **Cosimo I,** a Medici who ruled the Grand Duchy of Tuscany (and Pisa), appears noble but reminds Pisans of those dark

times. Cosimo asserted Florentine rule by turning this square into a Florentine military base. The Pisan palace became the late-Renaissance Florentine military school you see here today.

From here, take Via Corsica (to the left of the clock tower). The humble, stony, 11th-century **Church of San Sisto,** ahead on the left, is worth a quick look. This was the standard Romanesque style that predated the more lavish Pisan Romanesque style of the Field of Miracles structures: simple bricks, assorted reused columns—some of them ancient Roman, a delightful assortment of capitals, heavy walls, and tiny windows. Its 11th-century facade was once covered with plaster and colorfully painted. You can see

the remains of the Eastern-flavored ceramic bowls across the top
that once shined in the sun like gems.

• *Follow Via Corsica as it turns into Via dei Mille, then turn right
after the little parklike square on Via Santa Maria, which leads north,
becoming a touristy can-can of eateries, and finally ends at the Field of
Miracles and the Tower. (Consider the Grand Hotel Duomo the border
between tolerable touristy restaurants and terrible touristy restaurants
nearer the Leaning Tower.)*

Sights in Pisa

THE BEST OF THE FIELD OF MIRACLES

Imagine arriving in Pisa as a sailor in the 12th century, when the
river came to just outside the walls surrounding this square, the
church here was one of the biggest in the world, and this ensemble
in gleaming white marble was the most impressive space in Christendom. Calling it the Field of Miracles (Campo dei Miracoli)
would not have been hyperbole.

Scattered across a golf-course-green lawn are five grand buildings: the cathedral (or Duomo), its bell tower (the Leaning Tower),
the Baptistery, the hospital (today's Museum of the Sinopias), and
the Camposanto Cemetery. Each building has a simple ground
floor and rows of delicate columns and arches that form open-air
arcades, giving the Campo a pleasant visual unity.

The style is called Pisan Romanesque. Unlike traditional Romanesque, with its heavy fortress-like feel, Pisan Romanesque is
light and elegant. At ground level, most of the structures have simple half-columns and arches. On the upper levels, you'll see a little
of everything—tight rows of thin columns; pointed Gothic gables
and prickly spires; Byzantine mosaics and horseshoe arches; and
geometric designs (such as diamonds) and striped, colored marbles
inspired by mosques in Muslim lands.

Architecturally, the Campo is unique and exotic. Traditionally, its buildings marked the main events of every Pisan's life: chris-
tened in the Baptistery, married in the Duomo, called to celebrate
by the bells in the tower, healed in the hospital, and buried in the
Camposanto Cemetery.

Lining this field of artistic pearls are dozens of people who
have simultaneously had the same bright idea: posing for a photo
as though they're propping up the Leaning Tower. Although the
smooth green carpet looks like the ideal picnic spot—and many
people are doing just that—officially, lounging on this lawn can
result in a €25 fine.

▲▲▲Leaning Tower

A 15-foot lean from the vertical makes the Leaning Tower one of

Pisa's Field of Miracles

To Autostrada & P Pietrasantina

VIALE CASCINE

To San Rossore Station

Largo Cocco Griffi

VIA CONTESSA MATILDE

WALL WALK

Jewish Cemetery

Piazza dei Miracoli

TACKY SOUVENIR STANDS

BAPTISTERY

PORTA S. MARIA

CAMPOSANTO CEMETERY

WC

OLD CITY WALLS

LEANING TOWER

VIA C. P. MAFFI

VIA A. PISANO

Piazza Manin

Grassy Lawn

DUOMO

Piazza del Duomo

DUOMO MUSEUM

Piazza Archivescovado

Tower

MUSEUM OF THE SINOPIAS

VIA BONANINO PISANO

VIA ROMA

VIA SANTA MARIA

To rest of town & Centrale Station

VIA TASSI

100 Meters
100 Yards

- ❶ Ticket Offices (2)
- ❷ Baggage Check
- ❸ Bus to Centrale Station
- ❹ Bus to Lucca
- ❺ Bus Ticket Machine

Europe's most recognizable images. You can see it for free—it's always viewable, and worth ▲▲▲ simply to ogle from the outside—or you can pay to climb nearly 300 stairs to the top.

The off-kilter Tower parallels Pisa's history. It was started in the late 12th century, when Pisa was at its peak: one of the world's richest, most powerful, and most sophisticated cities. Pisans had built their huge cathedral to reflect their city's superpower status, and the cathedral's bell tower—the Leaning Tower—was the perfect complement. But as Pisa's power declined, the Tower reclined, and both have required a great deal of effort to prop up. Modern engineering has stabilized the Tower, so you can admire it in all its cockeyed glory.

Cost and Hours: €20 (or €27 for combo-ticket covering all Field of Miracles sights), kids under age 8 not allowed, generally April-Sept daily 9:00-20:00, until 22:00 during busy times, Oct and late March until 19:00, early March until 18:00, Nov-Feb 10:00-17:00, ticket office opens 30 minutes early, reservations smart, www.opapisa.it/en.

Getting In: Entry to the Tower is by a timed ticket good for a 30-minute visit. Every 15 minutes, 50 people can clamber up the 294 tilting steps to the top. Children ages 8-18 must stay with an adult at all times.

Reservations: Online bookings are accepted no earlier than

Field of Miracles Tickets

Pisa's combo-ticket scheme is designed to get you into its neglected secondary sights: the Baptistery, Camposanto Cemetery, Duomo Museum, and Museum of the Sinopias (fresco patterns). Any of those sights costs €7 individually, but the €10 combo-ticket covers all the Field of Miracle sights (except the Tower climb).

It's free to enter the Duomo, but you either need a voucher with an appointed time, or you can get in anytime if you have any other ticket (the €7 or €10 version). The Tower by itself costs €20 (€27 includes the Tower plus all the other sights).

You can get the Duomo voucher and any of these tickets from either ticket office on the Field of Miracles: One is behind the Leaning Tower and the other is at the Museum of the Sinopias (near the TI, less crowded). It's also possible to buy tickets in advance online at OPAPisa.it (no sooner than 20 days ahead of your visit; Duomo voucher not available online).

And what about entering the **Tower?** Is it worth that hefty price tag—and a likely wait to enter? It's a minor thrill to clomp up those twisty stairs, and the view from the top is enjoyable. But Pisa isn't particularly scenic, and it's a lot of expense and hassle for a view. Unless climbing the Tower is what you came to do, the real thrill comes from seeing it from the outside.

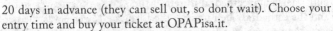

20 days in advance (they can sell out, so don't wait). Choose your entry time and buy your ticket at OPAPisa.it.

To reserve in person, go to either **ticket office:** behind the Tower on the left (in the yellow building) or (less crowded) at the Museum of the Sinopias.

Planning Your Time: In summer, for same-day entry, you'll likely wait 2-3 hours before going up (see the rest of the monuments and grab lunch while waiting).

With a reservation, arrive at least 15 minutes ahead of your entry time or you may not be allowed in. It's busiest between 12:00 and 15:00. If you come after 18:00 there's generally no line at all... on my last visit, I was the only one climbing the Tower at 19:00.

Baggage Check: You can't take anything up the Tower other than your phone or camera. Day-bag-size lockers are available at the ticket office next to the Tower—show your ticket to check your bag. You may check your bag 15 minutes before your reservation time and must pick it up immediately after your Tower visit.

Leaning Tower

BUILT 1350-1372
BUILT 1272-1284
BUILT 1173-1185

200' TALL

8TH (BELFRY)
7TH
6TH
5TH
4TH
3RD
2ND
1ST STORY

Mamma Mia!

STAIRS

55' DIAMETER

13' "SALA DEL PESCE"

MARBLE COLUMNS FORMING CIRCULAR ARCADE AROUND EACH LEVEL

HOLLOW CYLINDRICAL STRUCTURAL CORE OF LIMESTONE BRICKS

15' OFF VERTICAL 5 DEGREE ANGLE

GROUND LEVEL

NORTH SIDE

15' HOLES DRILLED IN 1990s

FOUNDATION LEVEL

MARSHY, UNSTABLE SOIL

SOUTH SIDE

Caution: The railings are skinny, the steps are slanted, there are no handrails, and rain makes the marble slippery—all in all, it's more dizzying than you might expect. Anyone with balance issues of any sort should think twice before ascending.

The Tower and Its Story

Rising up alongside the cathedral, the Tower is nearly 200 feet tall and 55 feet wide, weighing 14,000 tons and currently leaning at a five-degree angle (15 feet off the vertical axis). It started to lean almost immediately after construction began (it would take two centuries to finish the structure). Count the eight stories— a simple base, six stories of columns (forming arcades), and a belfry on top. The inner structural core is a hollow cylinder built of limestone bricks, faced with white marble. The thin columns of the open-air arcades make the heavy Tower seem light and graceful.

The Building of the Tower: The Tower was built over two centuries by at least three architects. You can see how the successive architects tried to correct the leaning problem—once halfway up (after the fourth story), once at the belfry on the top.

The first stones were laid in 1173, probably under the direction of the architect Bonanno Pisano (who also designed the Duomo's bronze back door). Five years later, just as the base and the first arcade were finished, someone said, "Is it just me, or does that look crooked?" The heavy Tower—resting on a very shallow 13-foot foundation—was sinking on the south side into the marshy, multilayered, unstable soil. (Actually, all of the Campo's buildings tilt somewhat.) The builders carried on anyway, until they'd finished four stories (the base, plus three arcade floors). Then, construction suddenly halted—no one knows why—and for a century the Tower sat half-finished and visibly leaning.

Around 1272, the next architect, Giovanni di Simone, tried to correct the problem by angling the next three stories backward, in the opposite direction of the lean. The project then again sat mysteriously idle for nearly another century. Finally, Tommaso Pisano put the belfry on the top (c. 1350-1372), also kinking it to overcome the leaning.

Man Versus Gravity: In an effort to stop the Tower's slow-motion fall, well-intentioned engineers in 1838 pumped out groundwater around it. But they only further destabilized the Tower, causing its lean rate to increase to a millimeter per year.

As well as gravity, erosion threatens the Tower. Since its construction, 135 of the Tower's 180 marble columns have had to be replaced. Stone decay, deposits of lime and calcium phosphate, accumulations of dirt and moss, cracking from the stress of the lean—all of these are factors in its decline.

It got so bad that in 1990 the Tower was closed for repairs, and $30 million was spent cleaning it and trying to stabilize it. Engineers dried the soil with pipes containing liquid nitrogen, anchored the Tower to the ground with steel cables, and buried 600 tons of lead on the north side as a counterweight (not visible)—all with little success. The breakthrough came when they drilled 15-foot-long holes in the ground on the north side and sucked out 60 tons of soil, allowing the Tower to sink on the north side and straighten out its lean by about six inches.

All the work to shore up, straighten, and clean the Tower has probably turned the clock back a few centuries.

▲▲Duomo (Cathedral)

The huge Pisan Romanesque cathedral, with its carved pulpit by Giovanni Pisano, is artistically more important than its more famous bell tower. Budget some sightseeing time for the church's artistic and historic treasures.

Cost and Hours: Free. If you have a ticket for any Field of Miracles sight, you can walk right in; otherwise, pick up a voucher with an entry time at either ticket office (voucher not available in advance online; see the "Field of Miracles Tickets" sidebar, earlier). Hours vary (check ahead), but the interior always opens at 10:00, after morning Mass; it closes April-Sept at 20:00, Oct at 19:00, Nov-Feb at 17:00 (also 13:00-14:00), March at 18:00.

Dress Code: Shorts are OK as long as they're not too short, and shoulders should be covered (although it's not really enforced).

❍ Self-Guided Tour

The Duomo is the centerpiece of the Field of Miracles' complex of religious buildings. Begun in 1063, it was financed by a galley-load of booty ransacked that year from the Muslim-held capital of Palermo, Sicily. The architect Buschetto created the frilly Pisan Romanesque style that set the tone for the Baptistery and Tower that followed. In the 1150s, the architect Rainaldo added the impressive main-entrance facade.

Exterior View: The lower half of the church is simple Roman-esque, with blind arches. The upper half has four rows of columns that form arcades. Stripes of black-and-white marble, mosaics, stone inlay, and even recycled Roman tomb-stones complete the decoration.

• *Enter the church at the west facade, opposite the Baptistery.*

Nave: The 320-foot nave was designed to be the longest in Christendom when it was built. It's modeled on a traditional Roman basilica, with 68 Corinthian columns of granite (most shipped from Elba and Corsica in 1063) dividing the space into five aisles. But the striped marble and arches-on-columns give the nave an exotic, almost mosque-like feel.

• *Walk up the nave, almost to the transept. Hanging from the ceiling of the central nave is...*

Galileo's Lamp: The bronze incense burner is said to be the one (actually, this is a replacement of the original) that caught the teenage Galileo's attention one day in church. According to legend, someone left a church door open, and a gust of wind set the lamp swinging. Galileo timed the swings and realized that the burner swung back and forth in the same amount of time regardless of how wide the arc. This pendulum motion was a constant that allowed Galileo to measure our ever-changing universe.

• *High up in the apse (behind the altar) is the...*

Apse Mosaic: The mosaic (c. 1300, partly done by the great artist Cimabue) shows Christ Pantocrator ("All Powerful") between Mary and St. John the Evangelist. The Pantocrator image of Christ is standard fare among Eastern Orthodox Christians—that is, the "Byzantine" people who were Pisa's partners in trade.

Dome: Look up into the dome. Because this church is dedicated to Mary—the patron and protector of the city—you'll see the Assumption of Mary. As the heavens open, and rings of saints and angels spiral upward, a hazy God greets Mary (in red). Beneath the dome is an inlaid-marble, Cosmati-style mosaic floor. The modern (and therefore controversial) marble altar and pulpit were carved by a Florentine artist in 2002.

• *Next to Galileo's Lamp, you'll find...*

Giovanni Pisano's Pulpit (1301-1311): The 15-foot-tall, octagonal pulpit by Giovanni Pisano (c. 1240-1319) is the last, biggest, and most complex of the four pulpits created by the Pisano father-and-son team. Four hundred intricately sculpted figures smother the pulpit. The creamy-white Carrara marble has the look and feel of carved French ivories, which the Pisanos loved. At the base, lions roar and crouch over their prey, symbolizing how Christ (the lion) triumphs over Satan (the horse, as in the Four Horsemen of the Apocalypse).

Four of the pulpit's support "columns" are statues. The central "column" features three graceful ladies representing Faith, Hope, and Charity. Around the top of the pulpit, Christ's life unfolds in a series of panels. Since the panels are curved and unframed, you "read" Christ's life in a continuous scroll.

• *Find the following two sights in the right (south) transept.*

St. Ranieri's Body: In a glass-lined casket on the altar lies the skeleton of Pisa's patron saint, encased in silver at his head, with his hair shirt covering his body.

• *Look on the wall to the left to find...*

Emperor Henry VII's Tomb: Pause at the tomb of Holy Roman Emperor Henry VII, whose untimely death plunged Pisa into its centuries-long decline. Henry lies sleeping, arms folded, his head turned to the side, resting on a soft pillow. This German king (c. 1275-1313) invaded Italy and was welcomed by Pisans as a non-partisan leader who could bring peace to Italy's warring Guelphs and Ghibellines. In 1312, he was crowned emperor by the pope in Rome. He was preparing to polish off the last opposition when he caught a fever and died.

• *Exit the church, turn left, and walk around to its back end (facing the Tower), where you'll find (under a canopy) the...*

Bronze Doors of St. Ranieri (Porta San Ranieri): Designed by Bonanno Pisano (c. 1186)—who is thought by some historians to have been the Tower's first architect—the doors have 24 panels that show Christ's story using the same simple, skinny figures found in Byzantine icons. (The originals are housed in the Duomo Museum.)

THE REST OF THE FIELD OF MIRACLES

The Leaning Tower nearly steals the show from the massive cathedral, which muscles out the other sights. But don't neglect the rest of the Field of Miracles: the Baptistery, Camposanto Cemetery, Museum of the Sinopias, and Duomo Museum. To do all of these sights takes about two hours. Start with the Baptistery, located in front of the Duomo's facade, and then head for

Camposanto Cemetery, on the north side of the Field of Miracles. With sufficient interest and time, you can visit the Museum of the Sinopias, across the street from the Baptistery entrance. The Duomo Museum, behind the Tower, makes a good segue from a visit to the Duomo.

Cost and Hours: €7 for one sight, €10 for all of the sights. All four sights share the same schedule: daily April-Sept 9:00-20:00, Oct 9:00-19:00, Nov-Feb 10:00-17:00, March 9:00-18:00.

▲Baptistery

Pisa's Baptistery is Italy's biggest. It's interesting for its pulpit and interior ambience, and especially great for its acoustics.

Visiting the Baptistery: The building is 180 feet tall—John the Baptist on top is almost eye-to-eye with the tourists looking out from the nearly 200-foot Leaning Tower. Notice that the Baptistery leans about 1.5 feet to the north, toward the Tower (which leans 15 feet to the south). The building (begun in 1153) is modeled on the circular-domed Church of the Holy Sepulchre in Jerusalem, seen by Pisan Crusaders who occupied Jerusalem in 1099.

From the **outside,** you see three distinct sections, which reflect the changing tastes of the years spent building it: simple Romanesque blind arches at the base (1153) and ornate Gothic spires and pointed arches in the middle (1250). The roofing looks mismatched, but was intentionally designed with red clay tiles on the seaward side and lead tiles (more prestigious but prone to corrosion) on the sheltered east side. The statues of the midsection are by Nicola Pisano (c. 1220-1278, Giovanni's father), who sculpted the pulpit inside.

Inside, it's simple, spacious, and baptized with light. Tall arches atop thin columns once again echo the Campo's architectural theme of arches above blank spaces. The columns encircle just a few pieces of religious furniture.

In the center sits the beautiful marble **octagonal font** (1246). A statue of the first Baptist, John the Baptist, stretches out his hand and says, "Welcome to my Baptistery." The font contains plenty of space for baptizing adults by immersion (the medieval custom), plus four wells for dunking babies.

Baptismal fonts—where sinners symbolically die and are reborn—are traditionally octagons. The shape suggests a cross (symbolizing Christ's death), and the eight sides represent the eighth day of Christ's ordeal, when he was resurrected. The font's sides, carved with inlaid multicolored marble, feature circle-in-a-square patterns, indicating the interlocking of heaven and earth. The circles are studded with interesting faces, both human and animal. Behind the font, the altar features similar inlaid-marble work.

On your left is the **pulpit** created by Nicola Pisano. It's the first authenticated (signed) work by the "Giotto of sculpture," working in what came to be called the Renaissance style. The freestanding sculpture has classical columns, realistic people and animals, and 3-D effects in the carved panels.

The 15-foot-tall, hexagonal pulpit is the earliest (1260) and simplest of the four pulpits by the Pisano father-and-son team. Nicola, born in southern Italy, settled in Pisa, where he found steady work. Ten-year-old Giovanni learned the art of pulpit-making here at the feet of his father.

The speaker's platform stands on columns that rest on the backs of animals, representing Christianity's triumph over paganism. The white Carrara-marble panels are framed by dark rose-colored marble, making a pleasant contrast. Make a sound in here and it echoes for a good 10 seconds. A priest standing at the baptismal font could sing three tones within those 10 seconds—"Ave Maria"—and make a chord, singing haunting harmonies with himself. Today, a security guard sings every 30 minutes (on the hour and half-hour), starting when the doors open in the morning.

You can climb 75 steps to the interior **gallery** (midway up) for an impressive view back down on the baptismal font. Try to be here when the guard sings.

▲Camposanto Cemetery

Until people started getting excited about the Leaning Tower around 1900, the big attraction in Pisa was its dreamy and exquisite cemetery, the Camposanto (built 1278-1465). Highlights are the building's cloistered interior courtyard, some ancient sarcophagi, and the large 14th-century fresco, *The Triumph of Death*.

Visiting the Cemetery: The delightful open-air **courtyard** is surrounded by an arcade with intricately carved tracery in the arches. The courtyard's grass grows on special dirt shipped here by returning 12th-century Crusaders from Jerusalem's Mount Calvary, where Christ was crucified. If you couldn't be buried in the Holy Land, you could be buried in dirt from the Holy Land.

Displayed in the arcade are dozens of ancient Roman **sarcophagi.** These coffins, which originally held dead Romans, were reused by medieval big shots. In anticipation of death, a wealthy Pisan would shop around, choose a good sarcophagus, and chip his message into it. When he died, his marble box was placed with the others around the exterior of the cathedral. Great sculptors such as Nicola and Giovanni Pisano passed them daily, gaining inspiration.

After decorating these corridors for 600 years, the frescoes of Camposanto Cemetery were badly damaged in World War II. They've been under restoration ever since. Along these walls, you'll see the ones that have been returned to their original position, including the masterpiece *Triumph of Death.* This 1,000-square-foot fresco (c. 1340, by a 14th-century master) captures late-medieval Europe's concern with death in a fascinating composition.

In the lower left, a parade of wealthy (finely dressed) and powerful (some with crowns) hedonists are riding gaily through the countryside when they come across a hermit-monk who blocks their path and shows them three corpses in coffins. Confronted with death, they each react differently—a woman puts her hand thoughtfully to her chin, a man holds his nose against the stench, while a horse leans in for a better whiff. Above them, a monk scours the Bible for the meaning of death.

Elsewhere, young people gather in a garden to play music (symbolizing earthly pleasure), oblivious to the death around them.

This is just one of four big frescoes: Next to *The Triumph of Death* are *The Last Judgment,* the extremely graphic *Hell,* and *The Pious Life* (a handbook for avoiding hell). A posted information plaque near each fresco describes the intense scenes.

Museum of the Sinopias (Museo delle Sinopie)
Housed in a 13th-century hospital, this museum features the original preliminary sketches (sinopias) for the Camposanto's frescoes. If you loved *The Triumph of Death* and others in the Camposanto, or if you're interested in fresco technique, this museum is worthwhile.

Whether or not you pay to go in, you can watch two free videos in the entry: a 15-minute story of the Tower, its tilt, and its fix.

Once inside the turnstile, the stars of this museum are the sinopias: sketches made in red paint directly on the wall, designed to guide the making of the final colored fresco. The master always did the sinopia himself. It was a way for him (and for those who paid for the work) to see exactly how the scene would look in its designated spot. If it wasn't quite right, the master changed a detail here and there. When satisfied with the design, the master and his team covered the sinopia with a thin layer of plaster and, while it was still wet, quickly filled in the color and details, producing the final frescoes (now on display at the Camposanto). These sinopias—never meant to be seen—were uncovered by the bombing and restoration of the Camposanto and brought here.

Duomo Museum (Museo dell'Opera del Duomo)
Near the Tower is the entrance to the Duomo Museum, which houses many of the original statues and much of the artwork that

once adorned the Campo's buildings (where copies stand today), notably the statues by Nicola and Giovanni Pisano. You'll circle through a modern space with two manageable floors of well-presented artifacts, all described in English.

Starting on the ground floor, you'll see the Duomo's original 12th-century bronze doors of St. Ranieri, designed by Bonanno Pisano, with scenes from the life of Jesus. You'll continue past weather-worn stone statues (from the Pisanos) and a row of carved human heads in boxes, which used to surround the base of the cathedral. Upstairs you'll see fine inlaid woodwork that once graced the choir stalls of the sacristy, treasures of the cathedral, and illuminated manuscripts. Be sure to step out to the upper gallery (with a café) for some fresh air and views of the Tower and the Duomo beyond.

Sleeping in Pisa

NORTH OF THE RIVER, NEAR THE TOWER

$$$ Relais dei Mercanti is tucked away in the historic core of the city, on a lively square that throbs on Friday and Saturday. The six rooms are bright, modern, and well appointed, with shiny marble floors and bathrooms (air-con, Piazza Sant'Omobono 16, +39 050 520 2135, www.relaisdeimercanti.it, relaisdeimercanti@gmail. com).

$$ Hotel Royal Victoria is like sleeping in a museum. Overlooking the Arno River, it's been run by the Piegaja family since 1837. Its 38 creaky, antique-filled rooms with bygone plumbing and chipped plaster may not be for everybody, but the elegant ambience is ideal for romantics. The location—midway between the Tower and Pisa Centrale train station—is the most atmospheric of my listings, though it faces a busy riverfront road (RS%, family rooms, air-con in most rooms, elevator, tight pay parking garage, lush communal terrace, Lungarno Pacinotti 12, +39 050 940 111, www.royalvictoria.it, post@royalvictoria.it).

$$ Hotel Pisa Tower has 12 rooms overlooking the noisy, souvenir-stand square just outside the gate to the Field of Miracles, along a busy street. But the prices are reasonable, and the proximity to the Tower is enticing (breakfast extra, family rooms, air-con, pay parking, Piazza Manin 9, +39 050 550 146, www.hotelpisatower. com, info@hotelpisatower.com).

$ Casa San Tommaso has 22 classic-feeling, homey rooms on a quiet back lane about a five-minute walk from the Tower (air-con, Via San Tommaso 13, +39 050 830 782, www.santommasopisa. com, info@santommasopisa.com, Giuliano).

$ Hotel Helvetia, a friendly, no-frills, clean, and quiet inn just 100 yards from the Tower, rents 29 economical rooms over four floors. Ask them to show you the "biggest cactus in Tuscany" in their garden courtyard...it really is (cheaper rooms with shared bath, family suites, no breakfast, ceiling fans, no elevator, Via Don G. Boschi 31, +39 050 553 084, www.pensionehelvetiapisa.com, helvetiapisatower@gmail.com, Micaele and Sandra).

SOUTH OF THE RIVER, NEAR THE TRAIN STATION

This zone is far less atmospheric than the zone near the Tower—with a lot of concrete, congestion, and loitering.

$$ Hotel Alessandro della Spina, run by Pio and family, has 16 elegant and colorful rooms, each named after a flower (air-con, elevator, pay parking, an eight-minute walk from the train station at Via Alessandro della Spina 5, +39 050 502 777, www.hoteldellaspina.it, info@hoteldellaspina.it, Louisa).

$ Stazione22 is a tidy B&B just across the piazza from the train station, perfect for a quick overnight or if your luggage is heavy. Friendly Alessandra tends her four budget rooms with a youthful warmth (some street noise, family room, breakfast extra at nearby bar, air-con, elevator, Piazza della Stazione 22, +39 327 857 5259, stazione22@gmail.com).

Eating in Pisa

A QUICK LUNCH CLOSE TO THE TOWER

The Via Santa Maria tourist strip is pedestrianized and lined with touristy eateries. From the Tower, walk past Grand Hotel Duomo to avoid the worst of the tourist traps. From there on you can find a decent (if overpriced) sandwich, pizza, or salad at any number of places. Of these, **$$ Ristorante-Pizzeria La Torre** (Via Santa Maria 86) has a good reputation.

$$ Pizzeria al Bagno di Nerone, a short walk from the Tower, is particularly popular with students. Belly up to the bar and grab a slice to go, or sit in their small dining room for a whole pie. Try the *cecina,* a crêpe-like chickpea flatbread (Wed-Mon 12:00-14:30 & 17:45-22:30, closed Tue, Largo Carlo Fedeli 26, +39 050 551 085).

REAL MEALS DEEPER IN THE TOWN CENTER

These places are within about a 10-to-15-minute walk from the Tower, near the river. Unless you're in a huge rush, it's well worth the extra walk for a better-quality, better-value, more memorable meal in this area.

$$ La Vineria di Piazza is a quintessential little Tuscan trattoria tucked under the arcades of Piazza delle Vettovaglie. The menu changes with the seasons, and their wine selection is high quality. Sit in the elegantly simple interior or out at tables facing the market (lunch daily 12:00-15:00, dinner Wed-Sat 20:00-23:00, Piazza delle Vettovaglie 14, +39 050 520 7846).

$$$ Antica Trattoria il Campano, just off the market square, has a typically Tuscan menu and a candlelit, stay-awhile atmosphere. The ground floor, surrounded by wine bottles, is cozier, while the upstairs—with high wood-beam ceilings—is classier (nightly 19:30-22:45, open Sat-Sun for lunch in high season, Via Cavalca 19, +39 050 580 585, Giovanna).

$$$ Osteria dei Cavalieri, on a quiet back street just off Piazza dei Cavalieri (and a bit closer to the Tower than the other listings here), seems pleasantly oblivious to the tourists and students that abound in nearby streets. The ambience is classic yet relaxed and warm, and the short menu of artfully presented local dishes—some with modern flair—is fun to explore (Mon-Tue and Thu-Sat 12:00-15:30 & 19:30-22:20, Wed 19:30-22:20 only, closed Sun, Via San Frediano 16, +39 050 580 858).

$ Caffetteria BetsaBea is basic and handy for takeaway meals, has good seating on the square, whips up hearty and creative salads—which you design with their interactive menu—and is popular for its *aperitivo* happy hour (Mon-Sat 8:00-18:30, closed Sun, Piazza San Frediano 6).

$ Il Montino is a rambunctious favorite for tasty, no-frills pizza. Tucked behind a church in a grubby corner deep in the old center, it has a loyal following among students. Enjoy full pies in the *nuovo rustico* interior or out on the alley (Mon-Sat 11:30-15:00 & 17:30-22:30, closed Sun, Vicolo del Monte 1, +39 050 598 695).

$$ Orzo Bruno—*il birrificio artigiano* ("the artisan brewpub")—is a lively, rollicking brew hall filled with Pisans of all ages enjoying rock, jazz, and blues, with seven different microbrews (including a rotating tap) and a simple menu of sandwiches and cold cuts (nightly 19:00-late, a block off Borgo Stretto at Via Case Dipinte 6, +39 050 578 802).

$$ La Mescita, just off the market square, serves up pasta and meat dishes in a jazz-inspired, artsy interior (daily 12:30-14:30 & 19:30-23:00, Via Domenico Cavalca 2, +39 050 314 4680).

Pisa Connections

Pisa has excellent connections by train, bus, or car. The busy airport (popular with discount airlines) is practically downtown.

Side-Tripping to (or from) Lucca: Pisa and Lucca are well connected by train and by bus (both options are around €4), making a half-day side trip from one town to the other particularly easy.

The **train** takes about half as long as the bus—but getting between the Centrale train station and the Field of Miracles is time-consuming. Here's a time-saving tip: Check if your train also stops

Pisa & Lucca Area

CINQUE TERRE
MARBLE QUARRIES
20 Kilometers
20 Miles
High-speed Rail
Other Rail
Bus
To Bologna, Ravenna, Milan & Venice
Carrara
Massa
Monte-catini
Pistoia
La Spezia
Viareggio
Lucca
Vespucci / Peretola
Fiesole
Florence
PISA SAN ROSSORE STN.
Ponte-dera
Empoli
Pisa
Ligurian Sea
Livorno
Galileo
San Gimignano
Poggibonsi
Arezzo
TUSCANY
Saline di Volterra
Colle di Val d'Elsa
Cecina
Volterra
Siena
To Rome
To Rome

at the Pisa San Rossore station, less than a 10-minute walk from the Field of Miracles. From the tacky souvenir zone just outside the gate, cross the busy street and continue straight ahead along Via Andrea Pisano. After two blocks, you'll see the gray gateway to the train station on your right.

A handy **bus** connects the Field of Miracles with Lucca's Piazzale Giuseppe Verdi in about 45-55 minutes (runs about hourly Mon-Sat, fewer on Sun, www.at-bus.it). To find the bus stops, from the Baptistery end of the Field of Miracles, walk straight out the gate to the edge of the souvenir-stand square. Along the busy road, the bus stop to Lucca is on the corner on your right. Buy tickets at the machine that's kitty-corner across the street (see "Pisa's Field of Miracles" map on page 557). You can also catch this bus at Pisa Centrale train station.

From Pisa Centrale Station by Train to: Florence (2/hour, 45-75 minutes), **Livorno** (2/hour, 20 minutes), **Rome** (1-2/hour, 3 hours, some change in Florence), **La Spezia** (at least hourly, 50-80 minutes), **Monterosso** (hourly, 1-1.5 hours), **Siena** (2/hour, 1.5 hours, some change at Empoli), **Lucca** (1-2/hour, 30 minutes, many also stop at Pisa San Rossore station).

By Car: The drive between Pisa and Florence is that rare case where the regular highway (free, more direct, and at least as fast) is a better deal than the autostrada.

By Plane: Pisa's handy **Galileo Galilei Airport**—just two miles from the train station—handles both international and domestic flights (code: PSA, +39 050 849 300, www.pisa-airport. com). The Pisa Mover train offers an easy connection to Pisa Centrale train station, where you can catch the LAM Rossa bus—see "Arrival in Pisa," earlier—to the Leaning Tower (€5, daily 6:00-24:00, 5-minute trip, www.pisa-mover.com). You can taxi into town for about €10.

Pisa's airport is handy for other towns as well: To reach **Lucca, Florence,** the **Cinque Terre,** or other destinations in Italy, take the Pisa Mover to Pisa Centrale train station and connect from there. There may be direct bus connections from Pisa Airport directly to Florence's Santa Maria Novella train station—check online or ask around.

Lucca

Surrounded by well-preserved ramparts, layered with history, alternately quaint and urbane, Lucca charms its visitors. The city is a paradox. Though it hasn't been involved in a war since 1430, it is Italy's most impressive fortress city, encircled by a perfectly intact wall. Most cities tear down their walls to make way for modern traffic, but Lucca's effectively keeps out both traffic and,

it seems, the stress of the modern world. Locals are very protective of their wall, which they enjoy like a community roof garden.

Lucca has no single monumental sight to attract tourists—it's simply a uniquely human and undamaged, never-bombed city. Romanesque churches and shady piazzas filled with soccer-playing children seem to be around every corner. Even its touristic center—the mostly traffic-free old town—feels more local than touristy (aside from a few cruise excursions from nearby Livorno that pass through each day). Simply put, Lucca has elegance and plenty of reasons to be proud.

PLANNING YOUR TIME

Lucca is easy to enjoy. With a day in town, start with my self-guided Lucca Walk and spend the afternoon biking (or strolling) atop the wall, popping in on whatever other sights interest you, and browsing. Music lovers enjoy the evening Puccini concert. The busy sightseer can consider visiting Pisa's Field of Miracles (with the Leaning Tower), an easy half-day side trip away by train (to Pisa San Rossore station in under 30 minutes) or bus (from downtown Lucca to the Leaning Tower in under an hour).

Lucca

200 Meters
200 Yards

PISA & LUCCA

To Piazzale Don Franco Baroni

V. MAT-

VIA DELLE TAGLIATE TERZA

VIALE CARLO DEL PRETE

TUNNEL UNDER RAMPARTS

RAMPARTS

Parlatucci

PORTA SAN DONATO

PASSAGGIATA DELLE MURA

SAN FREDIANO

Piazza S. Agostino

PALAZZO PFANNER

15

VIA PELLERIA

PANIFICIO

VIA DELLE STUFA

V. ASILI

V. BATTISTI

13

Piazzale San Donato

VIA COLOMBAIA

SAN GIORGIO

16

TOMMASO

V. LORETO

V. DEL MORO

3

VIA FILLUNGO

VIA

TEGNINI

SANTA GIUSTINA

19

V. DEL POZZO

V. DE BUIA

CLOCK TOWER

PALAZZO MANSI

V. TORO

PUCCINI'S HOUSE

21

18

VIA SAN

VIA POGGIO

CALDERIA

22

SAN MICHELE

VIA PAOLINO

Piazzale Giuseppe Verdi

B Bus to Pisa

VAIBUS TICKETS

PAOLINO

24

Piazza San Michele

V. ROMA

V. GALLI TASSI

VIA BURLAMACCHI

VITTORIO EMANUELE II

V. CENAMI

V. BATTISTERO

PORTA VITTORIO EMANUELE/ PORTA SANT'ANNA

VIA DEL PALLONE

Citadella

VIA DEI TABACCHI

Piazza Napoleone

17

VIA LUPORINI

CITTADELLA

P

SAN ROMANO

12

Piazza d. Giglio

SAN GIOVANNI

SAN PAOLINO BASTION

4

VIA DELLA CASERMA

VITTORIO VENETO

CORSO GARIBALDI

7

PASSAGGIATA DELLE MURA

VIA FRANCESCO CARRARA

V. NIERI

GIOSUE

CARDUCCI

VIA EUROPA

P Carducci

P

PORTA SAN PIETRO

V. REPUBBLICA

VIA

VIALE

To Autostrada

V. CAMILLO CAVOUR

To 10

Accommodations

1 A Palazzo Busdraghi
2 La Romea B&B
3 La Bohème B&B
4 Relais Inn Lucca
5 Palazzo Dipinto
6 Hotel la Luna
7 Albergo San Martino & Hotel Diana Reception

8 To Hotel San Marco
9 Hotel Rex
10 To Hotel Moderno

Eateries & Other

11 Canuleia Trattoria
12 Ristorante Giglio
13 Osteria dal Manzo
14 Il Mecenate

VIALE AGOSTINO MARTI

↑ To ⑧

PORTA SAN JACOPO

SAN MARTINO BASTION

TEUCCI

Piazzale Martiri della Libertà

PORTA SANTA MARIA

Piazza Santa Maria

VIA BUIAMONTI

VIA MICHELE ROSI

P

PORTA BORGHI ⑳

⑳

CAVALLERUZZA

VIA FILLUNGO

①

VIA DELL' ANFITEATRO

Piazza dell' Anfiteatro

⑥

⑪

VIA ANTONIO MORDINI

GUINIGI TOWER

VIA SANT'ANDREA

②

VIC. 'ALTOPASCIO

VIA SANTA CROCE

Piazza San Martino

POST

CATHEDRAL MUSEUM

VIA DUOMO

SAN MARTINO CATHEDRAL

V. VALLISNERI

⑳

VIA DEL FOSSO

⑭

SAN FRANCESCO

P

VIA DELLA QUARQUONIA

VILLA GUINIGI

VIA BRUNERO PAOLI

VIA SANTA CHIARA

VIA SAN NICOLAO

VIA DEL FOSSO

PORTA SAN GERVASIO

V. DELL'ANGELO CUSTODE

VIA ELISA

PORTA ELISA

V. CROCE

V. ROSA

SS. TRINITÀ

Botanical Garden

V. GIARDINO BOTANICO

PASSAGGIATA DELLE MURA

VIALE GUGLIELMO MARCONI

PASSAGGIATA DELLE MURA

V. FOSSO

RAMPARTS

SAN COLOMBANO BASTION

㉓

VIALE GIUSEPPE GIUSTI

VIA FABIO FILZI

VIALE GIACOMO PACINI

VIA CANTORE

VIA D. PUB MACELLI

MARGHERITA

①

VIA G. MAZZINI

⑨

㉕

VIA B. CAIROLI

TRAIN STATION

Ramparts Walk/Bike Path ------
Bike Rental 🚲

⑮ La Bottega di Anna & Leo
⑯ Osteria Via San Giorgio
⑰ Il Cuore Enogastronomia
⑱ Pizzeria da Felice
⑲ Trattoria da Leo
⑳ Porta dei Borghi Bars
㉑ Caffè del Mercato

㉒ De' Coltelli Gelateria, Alice Pizza & Grocery
㉓ Caffetteria San Colombano
㉔ Launderette
㉕ Tourist Center Lucca (Bag Storage, Bikes)
㉖ Italian Cuisine in Lucca (Cooking School)

Orientation to Lucca

Lucca (population 87,000, with roughly 10,000 living within the town walls) is big enough to be engaging but small enough to be manageable. Everything of interest to a visitor is within the 2.5-mile-long city wall; it takes just 20 minutes to walk from one end of the old town to the other. The train station sits south of the wall (just beyond the cathedral), and the bus to and from Pisa stops just inside the western tip. My self-guided walk traces the main thoroughfares through town; venturing beyond these streets, you realize Lucca is bigger than it first seems, but its back streets are very sleepy. While the core of the town is based on an old Roman grid street plan, the surrounding areas—especially near the circular footprint of the amphitheater—are more confusing. This, combined with tall houses and a lack of consistent signage, makes Lucca easy to get lost in. Pick up the town map at your hotel and use it.

TOURIST INFORMATION

Lucca's helpful main TI is on Piazzale Giuseppe Verdi (daily 9:30-18:30, Nov-March until 16:30, WC, +39 0583 583 150, www.turismo.lucca.it). A smaller TI is close to the train station (to the right along the busy road, on Piazza Curtatone; Tue-Sat 9:30-13:30, Tue and Thu also 14:30-17:30, closed Sun-Mon, +39 0583 442 213).

ARRIVAL IN LUCCA

By Train: Lucca's little station sits just outside its walls, to the south. Bag storage is available at the Tourist Center Lucca shop on the square in front of the station (see "Helpful Hints" for details). To reach the city center from the train station, walk toward the walls and head left, to the entry at Porta San Pietro. Or, if you don't mind steps, go straight ahead and follow the path through the moat-like park to go up and over the wall. Taxis wait out front; otherwise, try calling +39 0583 1745 or +39 0583 164 6464; a ride from the station to Piazza dell'Anfiteatro costs about €8.

By Bus: Buses from Pisa, Viareggio, and nearby villages arrive just inside the walls, at the western end of town on Piazzale Giuseppe Verdi (near the TI).

By Car: Don't drive within the walls: Much of the center of Lucca is a limited traffic zone (€90 fine). You'll know when you're about to enter it when you see the letters "ZTL" painted on the road.

If you don't mind paying extra for proximity to the sights, consider **Parking Citadella,** just inside the walls (but outside the ZTL zone) in the southwestern part of town (€1.50/hour).

For longer stays, it's cheaper to park outside the city walls. Parking is always free in **Piazzale Don Franco Baroni,** a 10-minute walk north of the walls. Two pay lots are also nearby: **Parking Carducci,** southwest of town (this is the first lot you hit after leaving the autostrada) and **Parking Parlatucci,** to the northwest. Or park outside the gates near the train station or on the boulevard surrounding the city (pay and display). Overnight parking (20:00-8:00) on city streets and in city lots outside the walls is usually free; check with your hotelier to be sure. For more on parking in Lucca, see www.parcheggilucca.it.

HELPFUL HINTS

Markets: Lucca's atmospheric markets are worth visiting. On the third weekend of the month, one of the largest **antique markets** in Italy sprawls in the blocks between Piazza Antelminelli and Piazza San Giovanni (8:00-19:00). The last weekend of the month, local artisans sell **arts and crafts** around town, mainly near the cathedral (8:00-19:00). At the **general market,** held Wednesdays and Saturdays on Piazza Don Franco Baroni, you'll find produce and household goods (8:30-13:00).

Shops and Museums Alert: City-run museums are often closed Sunday and/or Monday. Most shops close Sunday and Monday mornings.

Puccini Concerts: San Giovanni Church hosts themed one-hour concerts featuring a pianist and singers performing works by hometown composer Giacomo Puccini (€25 at the door, €20 in advance—buy tickets at the venue, the TI, or possibly your hotel; April-Oct nightly at 19:00, Thu-Sat off-season, www.puccinielasualucca.com).

Festivals: The Lucca Classica festival offers lots of free concerts (four days in early May, www.luccaclassica.it). On September 13 and 14, the city celebrates Volto Santo ("Holy Face"), with a procession of the treasured local crucifix and a fair in Piazza Antelminelli.

Baggage Storage: Train travelers can store bags at **Tourist Center Lucca,** on the left side of the square at #203 as you exit the train station (€5/day, also rents bikes, daily 9:00-19:00, Nov-March until 18:00). If arriving by bus at the other end of town, ask at the TI if there are any options.

Laundry: The self-service **Lavanderia la Perfetta** is near the west end of town, between Piazza San Michele and the TI (daily 7:00-22:30, Via Galli Tassi 12).

Bike Rental: A one-hour rental (ID required) gives you time for two leisurely loops around the ramparts. Several places with identical prices cluster around Piazza Santa Maria (€4/first hour, then €2/hour, €16/all day, most shops also rent tandem bikes and bike carts, helmets available on request, daily about 9:00-19:00 or until sunset). Try these easygoing shops: **Antonio Poli** (Piazza Santa Maria 42, +39 0583 493 787, Cristiana) and, right next to it, **Cicli Bizzarri** (Piazza Santa Maria 32, +39 0583 496 682, Australian Dely). At the south end, at Porta San Pietro, you'll find **Chronò** (Corso Garibaldi 93, +39 0583 490 591, www.chronobikes. com). At the train station, **Tourist Center Lucca** is good.

Taxi: A taxi from Lucca to Pisa's Leaning Tower costs €45. Drivers are also available for transfers (€80 to Pisa airport) or for half- and full-day unguided tours (up to 8 people, +39 0583 1745 or +39 0583 164 6464, www.luccataxi.it).

Cooking Class: Gianluca Pardini runs a cooking school called **Italian Cuisine in Lucca,** where you can learn to prepare and then eat a four-course Tuscan meal (€70-100/person depending on group size, 3-hour lesson plus time to dine, includes wine, reserve at least 2 days in advance, Via della Zecca 37, +39 347 678 7447, www.italiancuisine.it, info@italiancuisine.it).

Tours in Lucca

Walking Tours

The TI offers two-hour guided city walks in English and Italian, departing from the office on Piazzale Giuseppe Verdi (€10, plus €3 to enter cathedral at the end, daily April-Oct at 14:00, weekends only in winter, +39 0583 583 150). On summer weekends, they run a slightly different tour in the mornings that includes the cathedral (€15, meet at Piazza San Michele). For either tour, confirm the latest schedule and book at the TI.

The **Andante...ma con Brio Music tour** celebrates Lucca's musical heritage with a music-loving local guide, visits to the Teatro del Giglio and the Puccini Museum, and musical clips along the way (€15 includes theater and museum entry, smart to book ahead, mid-April-Oct Sat at 11:00, 2.5 hours, in Italian and English, meet at Teatro del Giglio, turislucca@turislucca.com, +39 0583 342 404).

Tuscany Like a Local offers three-hour, casual, youthful, stream-of-consciousness rambles through town with stops in small bars or delis. These small-group tours are English-only and led by proud locals who love sharing Lucchese culture—past and present (basic food tour—€65, at 10:00; "bike and bites" tour—€85, at 14:00; *aperitivo* walk—€71, at 17:30; RS%—15 percent discount if you book direct by email, www.tuscanylocaltours.com, info@tuscanylocaltours.com, Chiara and Luca).

Local Guide

Gabriele Calabrese knows and shares his hometown well. He was a big help in creating the Lucca Walk in this chapter, and with his guidance you'll go even deeper into the city (€130/3 hours, by foot or bike, +39 0583 342 404, mobile +39 347 788 0667, www.turislucca.com, turislucca@turislucca.com).

Lucca Walk

This hour-long self-guided walk (not counting time at the sights) connects Lucca's main points of interest by way of its most entertaining streets.

• *Start right in the heart of things, at Lucca's main square. For the classic view of the circular square, stand at the east end of the oval at #29.*

❶ Piazza dell'Anfiteatro

The architectural ghost of a Roman amphitheater can be felt in the delightful Piazza dell'Anfiteatro. With the fall of Rome, the the-

ater (which seated 10,000 and sat just outside the original rectangular city walls) was gradually cannibalized for its stones and inhabited by people living in a mishmash of huts. The huts were cleared away at the end of the 19th century to better show off the town's illustrious past and make one purely secular square (every other square is dominated by a church) for the town market. The modern street level is nine feet above the original arena floor. Today, the square is a circle of touristy shops, galleries, mediocre restaurants, and inviting al fresco cafés.

Leave the amphitheater through the arch at #29. Once on the other side, turn back, look up to study the exterior of the Roman amphitheater, and notice how medieval scavengers transformed it.

Now turn left and begin circling counterclockwise along Via Anfiteatro. For the next 100 yards or so, study the stonework and see how medieval buildings filled the ancient arches. As you approach the bigger cross street, at #2 on the left is the tempting Pizzicheria la Grotta *salumi* shop—worth popping into for a peek

Lucca Walk

To 🅿

V. MATTEUCCI

Piazzale Martiri della Libertà

VIALE CARLO DEL PRETE

PORTA SANTA MARIA

Piazza Santa Maria

🅿

N

200 Meters

200 Yards

TUNNEL UNDER RAMPARTS

RAMPARTS

PASSAGGIATA DELLE MURA

VIA DELLE STUA

SAN FREDIANO

Piazza dell' Anfiteatro

VIA FILLUNGO

VIA DELL' ANFITEATRO

🚲

1 WALK BEGINS 👣

2

Piazza S. Agostino

PALAZZO PFANNER

VIA BATTISTI

PANIFICIO

V. PELLERIA

VIA

SAN

VIA GIORGIO

CADERIA

VIA DEL FOSSO

3

ANTONIO MORDINI

GUINIGI TOWER

V. COLOMBAIA

VIA LORETO

VIA ASILI

TOMMASO

TEGNINI

VIA SANTA GIUSTINA

TOWER HOUSE

VIA FILLUNGO

VIA SANT'ANDREA

V. DELL'ANGELO CUSTODE

PALAZZO MANSI

V. TORO

Piazza Citadella

PUCCINI'S HOUSE

VIA POGGIO

SAN MICHELE

CLOCK TOWER

VIA SAN PAOLINO

5

Piazza San Michele

VIC. 'ALTOPASCIO

To Plazza Verdi

VIA BURLAMACCHI

4

VIA SANTA CROCE

V. CROCE

SAN PAOLINO

VIA CENAMI

BOOKSTORE

VIA VITTORIO EMANUELE II

V. BATTISTERO

V. ROSA

V. GIARD

VIA DEI TABACCHI

Piazza Napoleone

6

SAN GIOVANNI

WALK ENDS

V. VALLISNERI

V. CALLIASSI

SAN ROMANO

7

Piazza d. Giglio

VIA DUOMO

9 CATHEDRAL MUSEUM

CITADELLA

VIA VITTORIO VENETO

VIA DELLA CASERMA

CORSO GARIBALDI

8

Piazza San Martino

SAN MARTINO CATHEDRAL

V. FOSSO

PASSAGGIATA DELLA MURA

VIA FRANCESCO CARRARA

RAMPARTS

VIALE GIOSUE CARDUCCI

To Porta Vittorio Emanuele

V. REPUBBLICA

PORTA SAN PIETRO

VIA MARGHERITA

VIA MAZZINI

ℹ

🚲

VIA B. CAIROLI

V. CAMILLO CAVOUR

🚲

TRAIN STATION

VIA NOTTOLINI

VIA GIOVANNI GUIDICCIONI

1 Piazza dell'Anfiteatro
2 Church of San Frediano
3 Via Fillungo Shops
4 Piazza San Michele
5 Via San Paolino

6 Piazza Napoleone & Piazza del Giglio
7 San Giovanni Church
8 San Martino Cathedral
9 Cathedral Museum

at local specialties. Then you reach the busy shopping street, Via Fillungo.

• *Turn left and walk a block down Via Fillungo. On the left, at #126, check out Zizzi (with a busy loom, weaving totally Italian scarves). Then go right and cross a little square to the big church with a fine mosaic facade.*

❷ Church of San Frediano

This impressive church was built in 1112 by the pope to one-up Lucca's bishop and his spiffy cathedral (which we'll see later on this

walk). Lucca was the first Mediterranean stop on the pilgrim route from northern Europe, and the pope wanted to remind pilgrims that the action, the glory, and the papacy awaited them in Rome. Therefore, he had the church made "Roman-esque." The pure marble facade frames an early Christian Roman-style mosaic of Christ with his 12 apostles. Inside (€3, daily 9:30-17:00), there's a notable piece of art in each corner: a 12th-century baptistery showing the story of Moses; St. Zita's body, put there in 1278; a particularly serene Virgin Mary, depicted at the moment she gets the news that she'll bring the Messiah into the world; and a painting on wood of the *Assumption of the Virgin* (c. 1510), with Doubting Thomas receiving Mary's red belt as she ascends so he'll doubt no more.

• *Leaving the church, head straight back through the little square, and turn right to peruse the many...*

❸ Via Fillungo Shops

Lucca's best street to stroll connects the town's two busiest squares: Piazza dell'Anfiteatro (which we just left) and Piazza San Michele. Along the way, you'll get a taste of Lucca's rich past, including several elegant, century-old storefronts.

Head down the street. On the left, you'll pass Piazza degli Scapellini, with market stalls and another entrance into Piazza dell'Anfiteatro.

As you stroll, notice how many of the original storefront paintings, reliefs, and mosaics survive—even if today's shopkeeper sells something entirely different. Observe the warm and convivial small-town vibe on the street. Notice also the powerful heritage of shops named for the families that have run them for many generations, the creative new energy brought by small entrepreneurs, and the aggressive inroads big chain stores are making in this tender urban econo-system.

At #92 (left) a shop sells an array of beers from nearby micro-breweries. Since 2007, vino-centric Italy has enjoyed a trendy and youthful microbrew industry.

A few blocks farther, at #97 (right), is the classic old **Carli Jewelry Store.** Signore Carli is the 12th generation of jewelers from his family to work on this spot. (He still has a once-state-of-the-art 17th-century safe in the back.) The Carli storefront has kept its T-shaped arrangement, which lets it close up tight as a canned ham. After hours, all you see from the street is a wooden T in the wall, and during opening hours it unfolds with a fine old-time display. This design dates from when the merchant sold his goods in front, did his work in the back, and lived upstairs.

Judging from its historic sign, **"Intimo"** (#56, on the left) was once an underwear shop. It now sells truffles and generally offers samples of little treats with truffle oil.

At the corner with Via Buia, #67 is a surviving five-story **tower house.** At one time, nearly every corner in Lucca sported its own tower. The stubby stones that still stick out once supported wooden staircases (there were no interior connections between floors). So many towers cast shadows over this part of town that this cross street is called "Dark Street" (Via Buia).

Look left down Via Sant'Andrea for a peek at the town's tallest tower, Guinigi, in the distance—capped by its characteristic mini oak-tree forest. You can pay to climb up for the view (see "More Sights in Lucca," later).

The shop at #65 (right) sports a beautiful, Liberty-style *Profumaria Venus* sign. For over a century, its sexy reliefs (dating from the time of Puccini) have stirred Lucchesi menfolk to buy their woman a fragrant gift. Today the storefront is protected as a historic landmark—and, fittingly, a new perfume shop recently took up residence here.

Farther down, at #45, you'll see two more good examples of tower houses. On the left is the 14th-century **Clock Tower** (Torre delle Ore, #26), which has a hand-wound Swiss clock that clanged four times an hour from 1754 until it died for good a few years back (€4 to climb the 207 wooden steps for the view and to see the nonfunctioning mechanism; closed Nov-mid-March).

A bit farther along, on the left, is the striking 13th-century facade of a **Pisan Romanesque church.**

The intersection of Via Fillungo and Via Roma/Via Santa Croce marks the center of town, where the two original Roman roads crossed. The big old palace you're facing (on the right)—with the heavy grates on the windows and the benches built into its stony facade—is the **In Mondadori bookstore.** While the interior is worth a peek, the benches out front are even more interesting: They're the town hangout, where old-timers sit to swap gossip.

• *Turn right down Via Roma, studying the people warming those stone benches along the way. You'll pop out at...*

❹ Piazza San Michele

This square has been the center of town since Roman times, when it was the forum. It's dominated by the **Church of San Michele.** Circle around to the church's main door. Towering above the fancy Pisan Romanesque facade, the archangel Michael stands ready to flap his wings (which he actually did on special occasions with the help of crude but awe-inspiring-in-its-day mechanical assistance from behind). Perched above many of the columns are the faces of a dozen or so heroes in the Italian independence and unification movement: Victor Emmanuel II (with a crown, above the short red column on the right, second level up), the Count of Cavour (next to Victor, above the column with black zigzags), and—hey, look—there's Giuseppe Mazzini (on the far left, fourth from the end).

The square is surrounded by an architectural hodgepodge. The circa-1495 loggia (to the right as you face the church) was the first Renaissance building in town. There's a late-19th-century interior in Buccellato Taddeucci, a 130-year-old pastry shop (#34, behind the church, next to its tower). The left section of the BNL bank (#5, facing the church facade) sports an Art Nouveau facade that celebrates both Amerigo Vespucci and Cristoforo Colombo. This was the original facade of the Bertolli shipping company—famed among Italian Americans as the shipping company their grandparents sailed with to reach America.

If the church is open, pop in. A fine 12th-century wooden crucifix hangs above the high altar, which shows off the body of St. Davino, sporting the scallop shells that identify him as a pilgrim. Nearby is an exquisite painting, *The Four Saints,* by Filippino Lippi (a student of the Florentine master Sandro Botticelli). You may notice curious little doodles on the pillars, scratched into the marble back in the 12th century.

• *From here, continue out of the square (opposite from where you entered) to take a little detour down...*

❺ Via San Paolino

This bustling street—which eventually goes all the way to Piazzale Guiseppe Verdi (with the TI and bus to Pisa)—is another fine shopping drag. Along here, a wide variety of storefronts cater not just to tourists but also to locals.

One block down this street, in the little square called **Piazza Citadella** (on the right), a statue of Giacomo Puccini (1858-1924) sits genteelly on a chair, holding court. The great composer of operas was born in the house down the little alley over his left shoulder (now the well-presented Puccini's House museum, worth a visit for music lovers—see "More Sights in Lucca," later).

• *Feel free to browse your way as far down this street as you like, but eventually return to Piazza San Michele to continue the walk to Lucca's cathedral. Facing the church facade, turn right and go down Via Vittorio Veneto (with the loggia on your left) to the vast, café-lined pair of squares...*

❻ Piazza Napoleone and Piazza del Giglio

The first of these two squares is named for the French despot who was the first outsider to take over Lucca. The dominant building on the right was the seat of government for the independent Republic of Lucca from 1369 to 1799—the year Napoleon came and messed everything up. Caffé Ninci, on the left (with some nice tables for people-watching), has been caffeinating locals since 1925 and serves what's considered to be the best coffee in town.

Cross diagonally through this square into the smaller **Piazza del Giglio,** dominated by the Giglio Theater. Like a mini La Scala, this has long been the number-one theater (of seven) in the highly cultured city of Puccini.

• *Continue to the left, along the big orange building, up Via del Duomo. After a block, you'll see...*

❼ San Giovanni Church

This first cathedral of Lucca is interesting only for its archaeological finds. The entire floor of the 12th-century church has been excavated in recent decades, revealing layers of Roman houses, ancient hot tubs that date back to the time of Christ, early churches, and theological graffiti. Sporadic English translations help you understand what you're looking at. As you climb under the church's present-day floor and wander the lanes of Roman Lucca, remember that the entire city sits on similar ruins. Ascend the 190 steps of the church's campanile (bell tower) for a panoramic view (but not quite as good as the one from the Guinigi Tower).

Cost and Hours: €4 includes tower climb, €10 combo-ticket also includes cathedral, its bell tower, and Cathedral Museum; daily 10:00-18:00, shorter hours Nov-Feb. For info on the Puccini concerts held at the church, see "Helpful Hints," earlier.

• *Continuing past San Giovanni, you'll be face-to-face with...*

❽ San Martino Cathedral

This cathedral—the main church of the Republic of Lucca and worth ▲—was begun in the 11th century and became an enter-

taining mix of architectural and artistic styles. It's also home to the exquisite 15th-century tomb of Ilaria del Carretto, who married into the wealthy Guinigi family.

Cost and Hours: €3, tower climb-€3, €10 combo-ticket includes both plus Cathedral Museum and San Giovanni Church; Mon-Sat 10:00-18:00, Sun from 12:00, Nov-Feb until 17:00; Piazza San Martino, www.cattedralelucca.it. There's a WC under the bell tower.

Visiting the Cathedral: The cathedral's elaborate Pisan Romanesque **facade** features Christian teaching scenes, animals, and candy-cane-striped columns. The horseback figure (over the two right arches) is St. Martin, a Roman military officer from Hungary who, by offering his cloak to a beggar, came to more fully understand the beauty of Christian compassion.

The **interior**—bigger than it seems from outside—features brightly frescoed Gothic arches, Renaissance paintings, and stained glass from the 19th century. On the left side of the nave, a small, elaborate, birdcage-like temple contains the wooden crucifix—much revered by locals—called **Volto Santo.** It's said to have been sculpted by Nicodemus in Jerusalem and set afloat in an unmanned boat that landed on the coast of Tuscany, from where wild oxen miraculously carried it to Lucca in 782.

On the right side of the nave, just before the transept, the sacristy houses the enchanting **memorial tomb** of Ilaria del Carretto by Jacopo della Quercia (1407). This young bride of silk baron Paolo Guinigi is so realistically realized that the statue was nicknamed "Sleeping Beauty." Her nose is partially worn off because of a long-standing tradition of lonely young ladies rubbing it for luck in finding a boyfriend.

As you head for the church's exit, stop by the third painting from the end (on the left)—*The Last Supper* by Jacopo Tintoretto. This is a typical Baroque spectacle, with the drama of the event emphasized as if it's theater. Notice the actors on the stage and how the mother, giving her child his "first supper" in the foreground, connects with us, inviting us to be present.

• *There's one more sight to consider, but it's extra credit. As you face the cathedral facade, on the little square to the left is the entrance to the...*

❾ Cathedral Museum (Museo della Cattedrale)

This beautifully presented museum houses original paintings, sculptures, and vestments from the cathedral and other Lucca churches. Pass through a room with illuminated manuscripts on your way to the ticket desk, then follow the one-way route up and down through the collection. You'll see church paintings and sculptures, silver ecclesiastical gear, and a big cutaway model of the cathedral (€4, €10 combo-ticket includes cathedral, its bell tower, and San Giovanni Church; daily 10:00-18:00, shorter hours Nov-Feb; audioguide-€5, left of the cathedral on Piazza Antelminelli).

• *Our walk is finished. From here, it's just a short stroll south to the city wall—and a bike-rental office, if you want to take a spin. Otherwise, simply explore the city...lose yourself in Lucca.*

More Sights in Lucca

Lucca Ramparts (and Bike Ride)

Lucca's most remarkable feature, its Renaissance wall, is also its most enjoyable attraction, worth ▲▲—especially when circled on a rental bike. Stretching for 2.5 miles, this is an ideal place to come for an overview of the city by foot or bike.

Lucca has had a protective wall for 2,000 years. You can read three walls into today's map: the first rectangular Roman wall, the later medieval wall (nearly the size of today's), and the 16th-century Renaissance ramparts that still survive.

With the advent of cannons, thin medieval walls were suddenly vulnerable. A new design—the same one that stands today—was state-of-the-art when it was built (1550-1650). Much of the old medieval wall (look for the old stones) was incorporated into the

Renaissance wall (with uniform bricks). The new wall was squat: a 100-foot-wide mound of dirt faced with bricks, engineered to absorb a cannonball pummeling. The townspeople cleared a wide no-man's-land around the town, exposing any attackers from a distance. Eleven heart-shaped bastions (now inviting picnic areas) were designed to minimize exposure to cannonballs and to maximize defense capabilities. The ramparts were armed with 130 cannons.

The town invested a third of its income for more than a century to construct the wall, and—since it kept away the Florentines and nasty Pisans—it was considered a fine investment. In fact, nobody ever bothered to try to attack the wall. Locals say that the only time it actually defended the city was during an 1812 flood of the Serchio River, when the gates were sandbagged and the ramparts kept out the high water.

If exploring the wall, you can venture into its tunnels and interior at either San Paolino Bastion or San Martino Bastion.

Today, the ramparts seem made to order for a leisurely, wonderfully smooth bike ride (20-30 minutes, bike-rental options listed earlier, under "Helpful Hints"). There are also several handy places to get up on the wall. Note that the best people-watching—and slowest pedaling—is during *passeggiata* time, just before dinner, when it seems that all of Lucca is doing slow laps around its beloved wall.

Guinigi Tower (Torre Guinigi)

Many Tuscan towns have towers, but none is quite like the Guinigi family's. Up 227 steps is a small garden with fragrant trees, surrounded by fine views over the city's rooftops. You'll head up wide stone stairs, then huff up twisty metal ones through the hollow brick tower.

Cost and Hours: €5, erratic hours but typically June-Sept daily 10:00-19:30, until later on weekends, mid-March-May until 18:30, winter until 16:00, Via Sant'Andrea 41.

Puccini's House

This modern, well-presented museum fills the home where Giacomo Puccini grew up. It's well worth a visit for opera enthusiasts...but mostly lost on anybody else. Buy your ticket at the shop/office on the square, then buzz to be let in. In period-furnished apartments—including the room where Puccini was born—you'll see lots of artifacts, including the Steinway piano where he did much of his composing, and original compositions and manuscripts. Don't miss the small staircase up to the garret (storage room up above the house), where a stage set from *La Bohème* evokes the composer's greatest work.

Cost and Hours: €9; daily 9:30-19:30; April until 18:30; Oct Wed-Mon until 18:30, closed Tue; Nov-March shorter hours and closed Tue; Corte San Lorenzo 9, +39 0583 584 028, www.puccinimuseum.it.

Sleeping in Lucca

BOUTIQUE B&BS WITHIN THE WALLS

$$ A Palazzo Busdraghi has eight comfortable, pastel-colored rooms with modern baths (some with whirlpool tubs) in a tastefully converted 13th-century palace tucked inside a courtyard. Sweet Marta (with help from Ingrid and Veronica) hustles to keep guests happy and bakes tasty cakes for breakfast. It's conveniently located on busy Via Fillungo, so it comes with some traffic rumbles and occasional weekend-revelry noise (family room, air-con, pay parking, Via Fillungo 170, +39 0583 950 856, www.apalazzobusdraghi.it, info@apalazzobusdraghi.it).

$$ La Romea B&B, in an air-conditioned, restored, 14th-century palazzo near Guinigi Tower, feels like a royal splurge. Its five rooms are lavishly decorated in handsome colors and surround a big, plush lounge with stately Venetian-style mosaic-linoleum floors (RS%, family rooms, Vicolo delle Ventaglie 2, +39 0583 464 175, www.laromea.com, info@laromea.com, Gaia and Giulio).

$$ La Bohème B&B has a cozy yet elegant ambience, offering seven large rooms, each named for a Puccini opera. Chandeliers, 1920s-vintage tile floors, and tasteful antiques add to the charm (RS%, family room, air-con, pay parking, one floor up at Via del Moro 2, +39 0583 462 404, www.boheme.it, info@boheme.it, Laura).

$$ Relais Inn Lucca takes up a stately palazzo near Piazza Napoleone. Their nine rooms are chic and modern, and run with youthful enthusiasm by Alessandra (air-con, elevator, pay parking, Corso Garibaldi 19, +39 0583 464 218, www.relaisinnlucca.it, info@relaisinnlucca.it).

SLEEPING MORE FORGETTABLY WITHIN THE WALLS

$$$$ Palazzo Dipinto is your "design hotel with class" option, buried deep in the heart of the old town, just a few steps from Puccini's House. It has less character (and fewer quirks) than the B&Bs, but the stylish lobby and 22 rooms provide predictable comfort (family rooms, air-con, elevator, pay parking—book ahead, Piazza del Palazzo Dipinto 27, +39 0583 582 873, www.palazzodipinto.com, info@palazzodipinto.com).

$$$ Hotel la Luna has 29 rooms in a great location in the heart of the city. Rooms are split between two adjacent buildings just off the main shopping street. Rooms in the main, historical building are larger and classier, with old wood-beam ceilings (and, in some, original frescoes), while the modern building feels newer and has an elevator but less personality (RS%, family rooms, air-con, pay parking, Via Fillungo at Corte Compagni 12, +39 0583 493 634, www.hotellaluna.it, info@hotellaluna.it).

$$ Albergo San Martino and **$ Hotel Diana** are two hotels run from the same reception—both friendly and conveniently located for train travelers. The main hotel has 12 art-adorned rooms, a nice lounge, and a cheery curbside breakfast terrace, plus six newer, slightly cheaper rooms in an annex. Hotel Diana is the budget choice, with nine fresh, affordable rooms with a colorful Italian-modern design flair (both hotels: skip breakfast to save a few euros, call ahead—reception not open 24 hours, family rooms, air-con, tight parking—free with this book if you book direct, bikes available, reception at Via della Dogana 9, +39 0583 469 181, www.albergosanmartino.it, info@albergosanmartino.it, Andrea and Fabrizio).

OUTSIDE THE WALLS

$$$ Hotel San Marco, a 10-minute walk outside the Porta Santa Maria or Porta San Jacopo, is a postmodern place with a peaceful garden and pool. Its 42 rooms are sleek, with all the comforts, and its easy location makes it a good choice for drivers (air-con in summer, elevator, bike rental, free parking, taxi from station—€13, Via San Marco 368, +39 0583 495 010, www.hotelsanmarcolucca.it, info@hotelsanmarcolucca.com, proud Francesco).

$$ Hotel Rex rents 25 dated but lovingly maintained rooms in a practical contemporary building on the train station square. While in the modern world, this family-friendly place is just 200 yards away from the old town and offers a good value. Ask for a slightly quieter room at the back (family rooms, children's play area and toys, air-con, elevator, free parking, a few steps from the train station at Piazza Ricasoli 19, +39 0583 955 443, www.hotelrexlucca.com, info@hotelrexlucca.com, Elisabetta and Valentina).

$ Hotel Moderno is indeed modern, with 12 rooms tastefully decorated. Although it's in a strange location, backing up to the train tracks, the rooms are quiet, and it offers class unusual for this price range (RS%, family rooms, air-con, Via Vincenzo Civitali 38—turn left out of train station and go over stair-heavy bridge across tracks, +39 0583 570 819, www.albergomodernolucca.com, info@albergomodernolucca.com, Stefano).

Eating in Lucca

FINE AND ROMANTIC DINING

$$ Canuleia Trattoria is run by enthusiastic Matteo (the chef) and Eleonora (head waiter), who make everything fresh in their small kitchen. You can eat tasty Tuscan cuisine in a tight, dressy, and romantic little dining room or outside on the garden courtyard. Reserve for dinner (Tue-Sun 12:30-14:00 & 19:30-22:00, closed Mon, Via Canuleia 14, +39 0583 467 470, www.canuleiatrattoria. it).

$$$$ Ristorante Giglio is a venerable old dining hall where the spirit of Puccini lives on and local families enjoy special oc-

casions under a big chandelier. The short but thoughtful menu features a fusion of traditional Tuscan and creative international gastronomy. Though pricier than most of my listings, this is a big step up in dining experience. Consider their tasting menus (€80/six courses, €100/eight courses) to best appreciate how they've earned a Michelin star (reserve ahead, impressive wine list, Wed-Mon 12:15-14:30 & 19:15-22:15, closed Tue, Piazza del Giglio 2, +39 0583 494 058, www.ristorantegiglio.com).

$$$ Osteria dal Manzo feels both classy and inviting. Gentlemanly Antonio warmly welcomes diners with a concise and enticing menu of elegantly simple, seasonal cuisine. There are typically five items for each of three courses—two meat, two fish, and one vegetarian (Mon-Sat 19:30-23:00, Sun 12:30-14:30, Via Cesare Battisti 28, +39 0583 490 649).

$$$ Il Mecenate faces a tranquil, picturesque canal at the eastern edge of the tourist's Lucca, a five-minute walk beyond the main zone. The traditional dishes are beautifully executed; this is a good place to try meat-filled *tordelli* pasta, *garmugia* (vegetable soup), and *testaroli*, an ancient bread-like pasta tossed with pesto (book ahead and dress up a bit, Wed-Mon 12:00-14:30 & 19:30-22:30, closed Tue, Via del Fosso 94, +39 0583 511 861, www. ristorantemecenate.it).

CHARMING AND RUSTIC DINING

$$ La Bottega di Anna & Leo, run by Claudio and Lidia (and named for their children), is a pastel and lovable little eatery with a simple menu and a passion for quality. They have tight seating inside and a few charming tables facing the side of the Church of San Frediano (erratic hours but typically Tue-Sat 12:00-14:30 & 19:00-22:30, Sun 12:00-14:30, closed Mon, reservations smart, Via San Frediano 16, +39 393 577 9910 or +39 393 530 2512, www. labottegadiannaeleo.it).

$$ Osteria Via San Giorgio, where Daniela cooks and her brother Piero serves, is a cheery family eatery that satisfies both fish and meat lovers. The indoor seating is tight and convivial, the outdoor courtyard is cheery in summer, and the house wine is high quality (Tue-Sun 12:00-16:00 & 18:30-23:00, closed Mon, Via San Giorgio 26, +39 0583 953 233).

$$ Il Cuore Enogastronomia is a cozy blend of restaurant and deli—if you like your meal you can buy more to take home. Browse their cases of prepared dishes and order some to take away, or sit in the dining room for homemade pasta, big salads, pizza, meats, and desserts (Tue-Sat 10:30-22:00, Sun lunch only, closed Mon, closed Jan-Feb, Via del Battistero 4, +39 0583 493 196, enthusiastic Anna takes good care of diners).

$ Pizzeria da Felice is a mom-and-pop hole-in-the-wall takeout pizza joint. Grab an *etto* of *cecina* (garbanzo-bean crepes) or a slice of freshly baked pizza and a short glass of wine. From September through April, they're known for their *castagnaccio*, a cake made with roasted chestnuts and ricotta (daily 10:00-20:30 except closed Sun Jan-Aug and closed 2 weeks in Aug, Via Buia 12, +39 0583 494 986).

$$ Trattoria da Leo packs in chatty locals for characteristic home cooking in a high-energy, diner-type atmosphere. Sit in the rollicking interior, or out on a tight, atmospheric lane (Mon-Sat 12:00-15:00 & 19:30-22:30, Sun 12:00-15:00, Via Tegrimi 1, +39 0583 492 236).

SNACKS, GELATO, AND HAPPY-HOUR *APERITIVO* BARS

Aperitivi near Porta dei Borghi: This gate at the end of Via Fillungo (and the little square just beyond it) is a great area for characteristic bars serving free and tasty buffets with any drink during their *aperitivo* time. These places are popular with young locals and are a perfect spot to relax after cycling the wall (near Piazza Santa Maria bike rentals).

Vinarkia, a characteristic wine bar, is popular for its *aperitivo* buffet from 18:30 to 20:00 (closed Mon, Via Fillungo 188, +39 0583 152 5357, Alekos).

Specialties in Lucca

Lucca has some tasty specialties worth seeking out. *Ceci* (CHEH-chee), also called *cecina* (cheh-CHEE-nah), makes an ideal cheap snack any time of day. This crepe-like garbanzo-bean flatbread is sold in pizza shops and is best accompanied by a nip of red wine. *Farro*, a grain (spelt) dating back to ancient Roman cuisine, shows up in restaurants in soups or as a creamy rice-like dish *(risotto di farro)*.

Tordelli, the Lucchesi version of *tortelli*, is homemade ravioli. It's traditionally stuffed with meat and served with more meat sauce, but chefs creatively pair cheeses and vegetables, too.

Lardo di Colonnata—a specialty from the Carrara marble region—is *salumi* made with cured lard and rosemary, sliced thin, and served as an antipasto.

Lucca has excellent olive oil that appears in many dishes and soups, such as *garmugia* (a bounty of spring vegetables).

Meat, not fish, is the star at most restaurants, especially steak, which is listed on menus as *filetto di manzo* (filet), *tagliata di manzo* (thin slices of grilled tenderloin), or the king of steaks, *bistecca alla fiorentina*. Order *al sangue* (rare), *medio* (medium rare), *cotto* (medium), or *ben cotto* (well). Anything more than *al sangue* is considered a travesty for steak connoisseurs. *Ravellino* is a thin cut of beef that's deep-fried, then pan-fried again later to heat it up.

That said, you'll find more seafood on Lucca menus than in many other parts of Tuscany—after all, you're just a 30-minute drive from the sea.

Note that steaks (as well as fish) are often sold by weight, noted on menus as *s.q.* (according to quantity ordered) or *l'etto* (cost per 100 grams—250 grams is about an 8-ounce steak).

For something sweet, bakeries sell *buccellato*, bread dotted with raisins, lightly flavored with anise, and often shaped like a wreath. It's sold only in large quantities, but luckily it stays good for a few days (and it also pairs well with Vin Santo—fortified Tuscan dessert wine). An old proverb says, "Coming to Lucca without eating the *buccellato* is like not having come at all." *Buon appetito!*

De Cervesia is a craft beer pub, with three microbrews on rotating taps (and one English-style pull) and dozens by the bottle (Tue-Sun 17:00-22:00, closed Mon, Via Michele Rosi 20—look for big *Italian Craft Beer* signs, +39 0583 492 620, Matteo).

Ciclo DiVino, across the street, is a wine bar with a bike-shop theme and enticing snacks (Mon-Fri 16:00-22:00, Sat-Sun from 11:00, Via Michele Rosi 7, +39 0583 471 869).

Aperitivi on **Piazza San Michele: Caffè del Mercato,** on the other side of the old town and catering to an older clientele, has good *aperitivo* snacks nightly from 18:00 to 20:00 (facing church at Piazza San Michele 17, +39 0583 494 127).

Gelato: Just off Piazza San Michele, **De' Coltelli** has some of my favorite gelato in Italy. It's proudly Sicilian-style (with Arab roots), and many of their flavors rotate with the season. Sample with a spirit of adventure and then have fun ordering: The salted caramel is a standout, and their granita takes the slushy to new heights (Sun-Thu 11:00-20:00, Fri-Sat until 21:00, Via San Paolino 10, Valentina).

Pizza: Two doors away from De' Coltelli, **Alice Pizza** offers good pizza by the slice (Tue-Sun 10:00-20:30, closed Mon, Via San Paolino 22, +39 0583 572 712).

Refreshments on the Wall: Caffetteria San Colombano is a handy pit stop for bikers and walkers on the city wall. This place is slick with bite-sized snacks and cappuccinos, perfect for a take-away meal on top of the wall (overpriced at the table). If you're not feeling too wobbly already from biking, try a *caffè corretto* (espresso with your choice of Sambuca, rum, or grappa) or a *Biadina*, a bit-tersweet liqueur served with pine nuts. The fancier sit-down restau-rant serves pasta and big salads with a view (daily 9:00-late, near top of ramp at San Colombano Bastion, +39 0583 464 641).

Groceries: Pam is a small, central market just off Piazza San Michele (Mon-Sat 8:00-22:00, Sun 9:00-20:00, Via San Paolino 16).

Lucca Connections

Even if you have a car, I'd opt for the much faster and cheaper train or bus to reach the Leaning Tower. For more on day-tripping to Pisa, see page 569.

From Lucca by Train to: Florence (2/hour, 1.5 hours), **Pisa** (1-2/hour, 30 minutes; if going directly to Leaning Tower, hop off at Pisa San Rossore station; to reach Pisa Airport, change to the tram at Centrale station), **Livorno** (about hourly, 1-1.5 hours, transfer at Pisa Centrale), **Milan** (2/hour except Sun, 4-5 hours, transfer in Florence), **Rome** (1/hour except Sun, 3-4 hours, change in Florence), **Cinque Terre** (hourly, about 2 hours, transfer in Vi-areggio and La Spezia).

From Lucca by Bus: Autolinee Toscane (AT) runs handy, di-rect routes from Lucca's Piazzale Giuseppe Verdi, at the west end of the old town (near the main TI). This is handiest to **Pisa;** the ones noted as going via "S.M. Guidice" (green on schedules) are about 10 minutes faster than the ones marked "Ripafratta" (black)—but both will take you right to the Field of Miracles and Leaning Tower (€3.50, continues to Centrale station, Mon-Sat about hourly, fewer on Sun, 45-55 minutes). Bus #DD runs to **Florence** (stops at Stazione Leopolda, west of the center; your bus ticket also covers the connecting tram to downtown); this bus can also drop you at **Florence Airport** (Peretola stop—request from driver; €7.60, Mon-Sat nearly hourly, less on Sun, 1.25 hours to airport, 1.5 hours total to downtown Florence). Before boarding, buy tickets at the bus ticket office on Piazzale Giuseppe Verdi (Mon-Sat 6:00-20:00, Sun 8:00-19:45; schedule info but no tickets at www.at-bus.it).

SIENA

Siena was medieval Florence's archrival. And while Florence ultimately won the battle for political and economic superiority, Siena still competes for the tourists. Sure, Florence has the heavyweight sights. But Siena seems to be every Italy connoisseur's favorite town.

Situated atop three hills, Siena qualifies as Italy's ultimate "hill town." Its thriving historic center, with movie-set lanes cascading every which way, offers Italy's best medieval city experience. Most people visit Siena, just 35 miles south of Florence, as a day trip, but it's best experienced at twilight. While Florence has the blockbuster museums, Siena has an easy-to-enjoy soul: Courtyards sport flower-decked wells, alleys dead-end at rooftop views, and today, even with all the tourists, a strong local spirit pervades.

For those who dream of a Fiat-free Italy, Siena is a haven. Pedestrians rule in the old center of town, as the only drivers allowed are residents and cabbies. Nurse a drink on the stunning main square, Il Campo. Wander narrow streets, tether an imaginary horse to the old metal rings, be stirred by colorful flags. Take time to savor the first European city to eliminate automobile traffic from its main square (1966) and then, just to be silly, wonder what would happen if they did it in your hometown.

PLANNING YOUR TIME

On a quick trip, consider spending two nights in Siena (or three nights with a whole-day side trip into Florence). Whatever you do, be sure to enjoy a sleepy medieval evening in Siena. The next morning, you can see the city's major sights in half a day.

Orientation to Siena

Siena lounges atop a ridge, stretching its three legs out from Il Campo. This pedestrianized main square is the historic meeting point of Siena's neighborhoods.

Just about everything is within a 10-minute walk of the square. Navigate by three major landmarks (Il Campo, Duomo, and Basilica of San Domenico), following the excellent system of street-corner signs. The typical visitor sticks to the Il Campo-San Domenico axis. But make it a point to stray from this main artery to find a corner of town to yourself. Sienese streets go in anything but a straight line, so it's easy to get lost—but equally easy to get found.

Siena's individual attractions come in two main clusters: Il Campo (Civic Museum and City Tower) and the cathedral (Duomo Museum, with its surprise viewpoint; and Santa Maria della Scala, a hospital-turned-museum, just across the street). Roughly between them is the Pinacoteca, for medieval art lovers. Check off some or all these sights, and then you're free to wander.

TOURIST INFORMATION

The TI is right on Il Campo (daily 9:00-18:00, Il Campo 7, +39 0577 292 222, www.terresiena.it). At busy times, there may be other TI outposts near the Duomo and at Piazza Gramsci, where some buses arrive.

ARRIVAL IN SIENA
By Train

Siena's small train station is at the base of the hill, on the edge of town. It has a bar/tobacco shop, an Autolinee Toscane intercity bus office (Mon-Fri 7:15-19:30, Sat until 17:45, Sun 9:00-12:15 & 14:30-18:30), and a newsstand (which sells tickets for other buses, including city buses). A shopping mall with a supermarket is across the plaza facing the station. WCs are on track 1, past the pharmacy.

Getting from the Train Station to the City Center: To reach central Siena, you can ride a long series of escalators (free, slow); hop a city bus (cheap, somewhat faster); or take a taxi (fastest and most expensive). For two or more traveling together, the **taxi** is your best value (€10 to the center, taxi stand just outside station, +39 0577 49222).

By Escalator or City Bus: To reach either the bus or the escalators, head for the shopping mall across the square (far left corner as you leave—look for the bull's-eye). The first of a series of **escalators** climbs through the mall up into the town. From the top of the escalators, it's a 20-minute walk to the town center: Turn left,

Greater Siena

To Florence (Direct Route)
Siena Nord Exit
To Florence via Castellina & Chianti Region
To Monteriggione, Poggibonsi & Florence
To Florence via Gaiole, Radda
SS-222
SR-2
VIA CASSIA
VIA BANDELLI
VIA FIORENTINA
SCIAVO
VIA CAVOUR
SP-408
SUPERSTRADA FREEWAY
Aquacalda Exit
TRAIN STATION SOME BUSES STOP HERE, TOO
CAMPING
ESCALATOR
VIA MAZZINI
STRADA DELL'ASCARELLO
PORTA CAMOLLIA
P
PORTA OVILE
VIALE PIETRO TOSELLI
STRADA DI VALDIPUGNA
FORTEZZA & P
STRADA DI PESCAIA
B
PIAZZA GRAMSCI (MAIN BUS STOP)
STADIO & P
IL★ CAMPO
See detail maps
PORTA PISPINI
VIA PIEVE BOZZONE
PORTA SAN MARCO
CITY WALLS
P
PORTA ROMANA
VIA ARETINA
STRADA CASONE
PORTA TUFI
VIA PICCOLOMINI
N
Siena Ovest Exit
STRADA MASSETANA ROMANA
1/2 Kilometer
1/2 Mile
Siena Sud Exit
SS-223
SR-2
To A-1 Autostrada, Assisi, Rome & SP-438
SP-46
Siena Exit
To San Galgano
MADONNA BELLA FARM
SS-223
VIA CASSIA
SS-73
SP-46
SR-2
SS-223
To Grosseto
To Ville di Corsano
To Buonconvento, Pienza & Montepulciano

SIENA

walk about five minutes to the Porta Camollia gate, then follow Via Camollia into town.

To ride the **city bus,** head to the bus stop below the mall (catch the down elevator from inside the mall's first glass door, on immediate right). All buses (big and small) go to Piazza del Sale or Piazza Gramsci (within a block of each other—see "By Bus," below). Buy your €1.50 bus ticket from the train station newsstand or at the machines by the bus stop; before boarding, confirm that the bus is going to the center—ask *"Centro?"* (CHEHN-troh).

Returning to the Train Station from the City Center: Catch

Visiting Tuscany

It's a joy to downshift to the more peaceful pace of Italy's small cities...and even smaller hill towns. I've covered my favorites in this book.

Siena, Pisa, and Lucca are in a category of their own, with more artistic and historic sights. **Siena** is the ultimate (and biggest) hill town, with an unrivaled spirit any visitor can enjoy. Like a medieval stage set, its pedestrian-friendly old town is surrounded by its fortified wall. Siena's stunning main square—the gently tilted red-brick Campo—is the city's proud centerpiece. As Tuscany's hub, Siena is well connected by bus to Florence (also handy by train) and the surrounding hill towns.

Pisa's iconic Leaning Tower draws flocks of tourists, but this midsize city also offers plenty of history and beautiful architecture, along with a thriving student scene. Lesser-known and smaller, charming **Lucca** is a "flat hill town" with winding streets ringed by a well-preserved Renaissance wall, perfect for circling on a bike. Both lie an hour or so west of Florence and are easily reached by train or bus.

But how in Dante's name does one choose from among Tuscany's hundreds of small hill towns? The one(s) you visit will depend on your interests, time, and mode of transportation.

Volterra—with its rustic vitality—is a beautifully preserved jewel. Its out-of-the-way location keeps this town from being trampled by tourist crowds, and its Etruscan history makes for compelling sightseeing. With 14 surviving medieval towers, walled **San Gimignano** is a classic. But because it's easy to visit from Florence—about 1.5 hours by bus—midday crowds can overwhelm its charms (it's an evocative delight early and late in the day). Both Volterra and San Gimignano work best for drivers but can be reached by public transportation.

South of Siena, in the region I call the "Heart of Tuscany," drivers have their pick of hill towns. Ridge-hugging **Montepulciano**'s medieval cityscape resembles a miniature Florence. With several historic wine cellars and easy access to wine country, it attracts wine aficionados, as does **Montalcino,** itself a happy gauntlet of wine shops and art galleries. Fans of architecture and urban design appreciate little **Pienza**'s well-planned streets and squares. All three towns are covered in the Heart of Tuscany chapter.

Getting Around Tuscany

By Bus or Train: Buses are often the only public-transportation choice to get between small hill towns. Train stations are likely to be in the valley below the town center, connected by a local bus.

By Car: Exploring Tuscany and its hill towns by car can be a great experience. Wait to pick up your car until the last sizable town you visit (or at the nearest airport to avoid big-city traffic), and carry a good, detailed road map in addition to a mapping app. Freeways (such as the toll autostrada and the non-toll *su-*

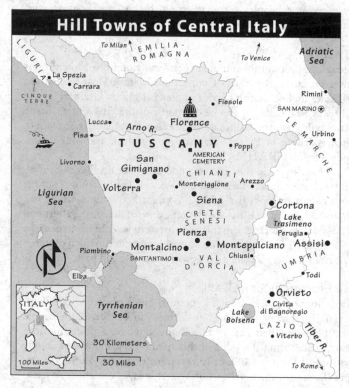

Hill Towns of Central Italy

LIGURIA — To Milan — EMILIA-ROMAGNA — To Venice — Adriatic Sea

La Spezia
Carrara
CINQUE TERRE
Rimini
SAN MARINO ✪
Fiesole
Lucca
Pisa
Florence
Arno R.
Urbino
LE MARCHE
TUSCANY
Poppi
Livorno
San Gimignano
AMERICAN CEMETERY
CHIANTI
Arezzo
Ligurian Sea
Volterra
Monteriggione
Siena
Cortona
CRETE SENESI
Lake Trasimeno
Perugia
Pienza
Montepulciano
Assisi
Piombino
Montalcino
Chiusi
UMBRIA
SANT'ANTIMO ■
VAL D'ORCIA
Elba
Todi
Orvieto
Tyrrhenian Sea
Civita di Bagnoregio
Lake Bolsena
LAZIO
Tiber R.
ITALY
Viterbo
100 Miles
30 Kilometers
30 Miles
To Rome

perstrada) are the fastest way to connect two points, but smaller roads, including the super-scenic SS-222, connecting Florence and Siena, are more rewarding.

Some towns don't allow visitors to drive or park in the city center. Be alert for "ZTL" (*Zona Traffico Limitato*) signs, indicating no cars allowed. Leave your car outside the walls and walk into town. Lots are usually free and plentiful outside city walls (and sometimes linked to the town center by elevators or escalators). For more driving and parking tips, see the Practicalities chapter.

Sleeping in Rural Tuscany and Beyond

For a relaxing break from big-city Italy, settle down in an *agriturismo*—a farmhouse that rents out rooms to travelers (usually for a minimum of a week in high season). These rural B&Bs—almost by definition in the middle of nowhere—provide a good home base from which to find the magic of Italy's hill towns. Many provide memorable meals from locally sourced ingredients. I've listed several good options in the following four chapters. For more information, see *"Agriturismi"* in the Practicalities chapter.

a small shuttle bus directly to the station from Piazza del Sale, or take a big city bus from Piazza Gramsci. Look for *Ferrovia* or *Stazione* on schedules and marked on the bus, and confirm with the driver that the bus is going to the *stazione* (staht-see-OH-nay).

By Bus

Siena is a pleasant 90-minute express bus ride from Florence (for more on buses, see "Siena Connections," later). Most buses from Florence and other cities arrive in Siena at Piazza Gramsci (or the adjacent Via Tozzi), a few blocks north of the city center. (Some buses only go to the train station; others go first to the train station, then continue to Piazza Gramsci—to confirm, ask your driver, "pee-aht-sah GRAHM-shee?")

Downstairs, in the concrete underpass beneath Piazza Gramsci, you'll find ticket offices and pay WCs. If day-tripping, confirm your departure from timetables posted at the platform where you disembark or at the ticket counters downstairs. Late-afternoon buses back to Florence can fill up, so arrive at least 15 minutes early.

From Piazza Gramsci, it's an easy walk into the town center— just head in the opposite direction of the tree-filled park.

By Florence-Siena Taxi

Taxis make the trip from Florence to Siena—hotel to hotel—in about an hour for around €140. (Prices can be soft. Ask a couple of cabbies for their best price. Clearly agree on a price from the start.) If debating the value of this splurge, consider that a couple will spend roughly €40 for two taxi transfers and two train tickets, and the luxury of a hotel-to-hotel cab ride saves you about an hour.

By Car

Siena is not a good place to drive. Park in a big lot or garage and walk into town. For more on where to park legally—and how to avoid a big fine by driving into the restricted "ZTL" zone—see "Driving" in the Practicalities chapter.

Drivers coming from the autostrada take the *Siena Ovest* exit and follow signs for *Centro*, then *Stadio* (stadium). The soccer-ball signs take you to the **stadium lot** (Parcheggio Stadio, pay when you leave) near Piazza Gramsci and the huge, bare-brick Basilica of San Domenico. The **Fortezza lot** is also nearby.

Another good option is the underground **Santa Caterina garage** (you'll see signs on the way to the stadium lot). From the garage, hike 150 yards uphill through a gate to an escalator on the right, which carries you up into the city. Take a left at the top onto Siena's main street.

If you're staying in the south end of town, try the **Il Campo** lot, near Porta Tufi.

Yet another option is the **Leonardo garage,** near the Porta Camollia; they offer a "valet" service where they'll meet you at the garage, drive you into town with your bags, then park your car for you (€25/day, arrange in advance, Via Bettino Ricasoli 29, +39 389 577 5886, www.parcheggiosiena.it).

You can park for **free** in the lot west of the Fortezza, in white-striped spots south of the Fortezza, and overnight in most city lots (20:00-8:00).

HELPFUL HINTS

Combo-Tickets: Siena often experiments with different combo-tickets. The Opa Si Pass covers the Duomo-related sights (see "Duomo and Related Sights," later); the other pass offers various combinations of city sights, including the Civic Museum, City Tower, Santa Maria della Scala, and Pinacoteca (see listing for City Hall and Civic Museum, later).

Market: Every Wednesday morning a market of clothes, knick-knacks, and food sprawls between the Fortezza and Piazza Gramsci along Viale Cesare Maccari and the adjacent Viale XXV Aprile.

Bookstores: For books and magazines in English, try **Libreria Senese** (daily, Via di Città 62) and the **Feltrinelli** bookstore (closed Sun, Via Banchi di Sopra 52).

Cooking Classes: At **Fonte Giusta Cooking School,** you'll prepare a meal under the instruction of a local chef—and then eat it (€80-120, 2-3 hours, Via Camollia 78, call +39 0577 40506 or email info@trattoriafontegiusta.com for schedule and details, www.scuoladicucinafontegiusta.com).

Laundry: Try **Lavanderia San Pietro** (daily 8:00-21:00, not far from the Duomo at Via San Pietro 70) or **Lavanderia Waterland** (daily 7:00-21:00, north of Il Campo near Porta San Francesco at Via dei Rossi 94).

Tours in Siena

🎧 To sightsee on your own, download my free Siena City Walk audio tour.

LOCAL GUIDES

Federica Olla leads walking tours of Siena with a knack for creative teaching (€55/hour, minimum 2 hours, +39 338 133 9525, www.ollaeventi.com, info@ollaeventi.com).

Anna Piperato, an expert on Palio culture, leads walking tours in Siena—including a visit to her *contrada,* Lupa—and environs (€60/hour, special treat for Rick Steves readers, +39 333 682 9336, www.sienaitalytours.com, anna@sienaitalytours.com).

Siena

100 Meters
100 Yards

To Freeway to Florence

To Porta Camollia & Escalator to Train Station

VIA CAMOLLIA

ISTRICE

VIALE AMANDO DIAZ

V. LUIGI CADORNA

VIALE RINALDO FRANCI

GIARDINI LA LIZZA

La Lizza

VIALE CESARE BATTISTI

VIALE VITTORIO VENETO

VIALE CESARE MACCARI

SOTTOPASSAGGIO LA LIZZA

Piazza Gramsci

V. FEDERICO TOZZI

VIALE DELLO STADIO

P

VIALE 25 APRILE

FORTEZZA

STADIO

P

DRAGO

VIALE VITTORIO VENETO

VIALE DEI MILLE

VIALE CURTATONE

V. DEL PARADISO

VIA D.

VIALE TRENTO

VIA ENRICO TOTI

VIALE TRIESTE

VIA GINO FROBCHELLI

Piazza San Domenico

V. CAMPOREGIO

VIALE FILIPPO CORRIDONI

VIA ARTURO PANNILUNGHI

VIA BRUNO BONCI

WC

SAN DOMENICO

STA. CATERINA

VIC. DEL

Fonte Branda

VIA 24 MAGGIO

VIA MONTICCHIELLO

VIA 24 MAGGIO

VIA

PORTA FONTEBRANDA

SELVA

NOTE: MUCH OF CENTRAL SIENA IS A PEDESTRIAN ZONE

VIA ESTERNA DI FONTEBRANDA

ANCIENT CITY WALLS

VIA DI VALLEPIATTA

VIA FRANCIOSA

V. DEL

SAN SEB.

STRADA DELLE GROTTE

SANTA MARIA DELLA SCALA (MUSEUM)

PANTERA

Piazzetta delle Due Porte

VIA

PIANO MANTELLINI

SIENA

1 Piazza Gramsci Bus Stop (Tickets Underground)
2 Libreria Senese Bookstore
3 Feltrinelli Bookstore
4 Tuscan Wine School
5 Launderette (2)
6 Train Station Shuttle Bus

SIENA

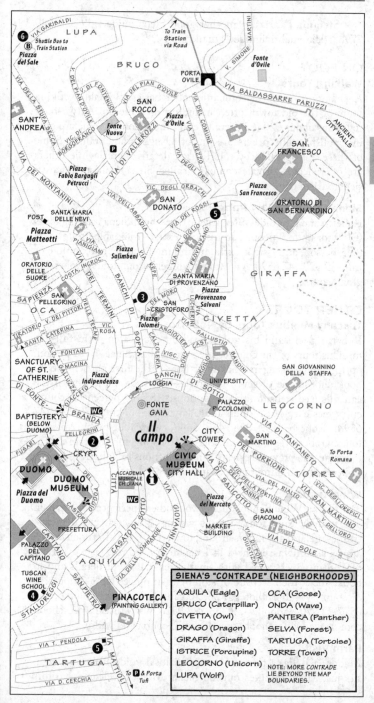

Stefania Fabrizi is another good Siena guide (+39 338 640 7796, stefaniafabriziguide@gmail.com).

ON FOOT
Walking Tours

A changing lineup of companies offer basic, affordable walking tours of the old town, often including the Duomo. A two-hour tour runs about €20 (€5 extra to enter the Duomo); some are only in English, while others are in both English and Italian. Some of these are operated by the TI (get details there), while others are offered by a private company called Siena Tourism (https://sienatourism.com).

Siena City Walks by Roberto

Roberto and his guides offer private three-hour Siena walking tours (€180 for up to 8 people, admissions extra) or joinable group tours (€45/person, admissions extra, minimum 4 people; book online or call +39 320 147 6590, www.toursbyroberto.com, toursbyroberto@gmail.com).

OTHER TOURS
Tuscany Minibus Tours by Roberto

Roberto Bechi and his guides lead off-the-beaten-path, full-day minibus tours of the countryside surrounding Siena (€110/person, up to eight passengers, pickup at hotel). The first participants to book choose one of seven itineraries—then others join until the van fills (see website for tour options, RS%-10 percent discount, entry fees extra; also offers multiday tours, booking +39 320 147 6590, Roberto +39 328 425 5648, www.toursbyroberto.com, toursbyroberto@gmail.com). See later listing for Roberto's farm tours; he also provides private van connections to Volterra—see the Volterra & San Gimignano chapter.

Wine Tasting

The Tuscan Wine School offers two foodie experiences in English. The midday **food tour** features tastings (focaccia, cured meats, truffles, gelato) at vendors around town (€60); the afternoon **wine-appreciation classes,** held in a classroom, let you taste a variety of Tuscan wines paired with small bites (€45). For details and to book, check their website or stop by their office (RS%-20 percent discount, Via di Stalloreggi 26, 30 yards from Hotel Duomo, +39 0577 221 704, mobile +39 333 722 9716, www.tuscanwineschool.com, tuscanwineschool@gmail.com, Georgia and Milo).

Farm Visit

Madonna Bella, a farm co-owned by local guide Roberto Bechi, sits just a few minutes outside Siena. Monica welcomes visitors

Siena at a Glance

▲▲▲**Il Campo** Best square in Italy. See page 604.

▲▲▲**Duomo** Art-packed cathedral with mosaic floors and statues by Michelangelo and Bernini. **Hours:** Mon-Sat 10:00-19:00, Sun 13:30-17:30, Nov-March closes daily at 17:00. See page 616.

▲▲**Civic Museum** City museum in City Hall with Sienese frescoes, the *Effects of Good and Bad Government*. **Hours:** Daily 10:00-19:00, Nov-Feb until 18:00. See page 612.

▲▲**Duomo Museum** Siena's best museum, with cathedral art (Duccio's *Maestá*) and sweeping Tuscan views. **Hours:** Same hours as Duomo. See page 619.

▲**City Tower** Siena's 330-foot tower climb. **Hours:** Daily 10:00-19:00, Nov-Feb until 16:00. See page 613.

▲**Pinacoteca** Fine Sienese paintings. **Hours:** Mon and Fri-Sun 8:30-13:30, Tue-Thu 14:00-19:00, closed two Sun a month. See page 614.

▲**Baptistery of San Giovanni** Cave-like building with baptismal font decorated by Ghiberti and Donatello. **Hours:** Same hours as Duomo. See page 621.

▲**Santa Maria della Scala** Museum with much of the original Fountain of Joy, Byzantine reliquaries, and vibrant frescoes. **Hours:** Daily 10:00-19:00, Thu until 22:00; mid-Oct-mid-March Mon and Wed-Fri until 17:00, Sat-Sun until 19:00, closed Tue. See page 622.

▲**Sanctuary of St. Catherine** Home of St. Catherine. **Hours:** Daily 9:00-18:00, chapel closes 12:30-15:00. See page 623.

SIENA

to stop in, enjoy the views, visit the farm, take part in wine and olive-oil tastings, and learn how olive oil and pasta are made. Book ahead to enjoy a food/wine pairing that anyone would consider an abundant lunch. They also offer cooking classes and can arrange a taxi from and to central Siena for about €15 each way (Strada del Tesoro 25—just outside Siena on road SP-46, +39 393 858 2981, www.madonnabella.com).

Siena City Walk

This short self-guided walk laces together Siena's most important sights. If you do the walk without entering the sights, it works great at night when the city is peaceful.

🎧 This walk is also available as a free Rick Steves audio tour.

• *Start in the center of the main square, Il Campo, standing just below the fountain.*

SIENA

❶ Il Campo

This square is the heart of Siena, both geographically and metaphorically—and it's worth ▲▲▲. First laid out in the 12th century, today Il Campo (officially the Piazza del Campo) is the only town square I've seen where people stretch out as if at the beach. However, if you start eating—well, now you're "picnicking," which is not allowed—you could be fined. At the flat end of its clamshell shape is City Hall, where you can tour the Civic Museum and climb the City Tower. From there the square fans out as if to create an amphitheater. All eyes are on Il Campo twice each summer, when it hosts the famous Palio horse races (see sidebar on page 610).

Originally, this area was just a field *(campo)* outside the city walls (which encircled the cathedral). Bits of those original walls, which curved against today's square, can be seen above the pharmacy (the black and white stones, third story up, to the right as you face City Hall). In the 1200s, with the advent of the Sienese republic, the city expanded. Il Campo became its marketplace and the historic junction of Siena's various competing *contrade* (neighborhood districts). The square and its buildings are the color of the soil on which they stand—a color known to artists and Crayola users as "burnt sienna."

City Hall (Palazzo Pubblico), with its looming tower, dominates the square. In medieval Siena, this was the center of the city, and the whole focus of Il Campo still flows down to it.

Siena Walk

SIENA

1. Il Campo
2. Fountain of Joy
3. Chigi-Saracini Palace
4. Quattro Cantoni
5. Piazza del Duomo & Duomo
6. Unfinished Church
7. Supporting an Oversized Church
8. Piazza Indipendenza
9. Loggia della Mercanzia
10. Banchi di Sopra & Banchi di Sotto
11. Piazza Salimbeni

The **City Tower** was built around 1340. At 330 feet, it's one of Italy's tallest secular towers. Medieval Siena was a proud republic, and this tower stands like an exclamation point—an architectural declaration of independence from papacy and empire. The tower's Italian nickname, Torre del Mangia, comes from a hedonistic bell ringer who consumed his earnings like a glutton consumes food. (His chewed-up statue is just inside City Hall's courtyard, to the left as you enter.)

The open **chapel** at the base of the tower was built as thanks to the Virgin Mary for ending the Black Death of 1348 (after it killed more than a third of the population). Siena rededicated itself to the Virgin in 2022, to implore her help in weathering another plague—Covid-19. These days, the chapel is where Palio contestants are blessed (and where EMTs stand by during the race).

You can visit the Civic Museum inside City Hall and climb the tower (see page 612).

• *Now turn around and take a closer look at the fountain in the top center of the square.*

❷ Fountain of Joy (Fonte Gaia)

This fountain—a copy of an early-15th-century work by Jacopo della Quercia—marks the square's high point. The joy is all about how the Sienese republic blessed its people with water. Find Lady Justice with her scales and sword (right of center), overseeing the free distribution of water to all. The Fountain of Joy still reminds locals that life in Siena is good. The relief panel on the far left shows God creating Adam by helping him to his feet. It's said that this reclining Adam (carved a century before Michelangelo's day) influenced Michelangelo when he painted his Sistine Chapel ceiling. The fountain's original statuary is exhibited at Santa Maria della Scala (see page 622).

• *Leave Il Campo uphill on the widest ramp (with your back to the tower, it's at 10 o'clock). After a few steps you reach Via di Città. Turn left and walk 100 yards uphill toward the imposing white palace with brick crenellations on top.*

Halfway to the palace, at the first corner, notice small plaques on the first level of the building facades—these mark the boundary of a neighborhood, or *contrada.* If the flags are flying, they reinforce the point. You are stepping from the *contrada* of the Forest (Selva) into the *contrada* of the Eagle (Aquila).

Notice also the once mighty and foreboding medieval **tower**

house (on the Il Campo side). Towers once soared all around town, but they're now truncated and no longer add to the skyline—look for their bases as you walk the city.

• *On the left, you reach the big curving facade of the…*

❸ Chigi-Saracini Palace (Palazzo Chigi-Saracini)

This old fortified noble palace is today home to a prestigious music academy, the Accademia Musicale Chigiana. If open, step into the courtyard with its photogenic well (powerful medieval families enjoyed direct connections to the city's underground network of aqueducts). The walls of the loggia are decorated with the busts of Chigi-Saracini patriarchs, and the vaults are painted in the Grotesque style popular during the Renaissance. What look like pigeonholes in the other walls are actually for scaffolding, for both construction and ongoing maintenance.

Head into the shop/café, which sprawls into a mild museum with old musical instruments, portraits of classical composers, pictures of old Siena, and a chance to watch classical concert videos. In July and August, students may be presenting concerts around town—ask (www.chigiana.it).

• *Walk uphill to the next major intersection.*

❹ Quattro Cantoni

The intersection known as Quattro Cantoni (Four Corners) offers a delightful perch from which to study the city. The modern column (from 1996) with a Carrara marble she-wolf marks one of the three hills on which the city is built. You are still in the Eagle district (see the fountain and the corner plaque)—but beware. Just one block up the street, a ready-to-pounce panther—from the rival neighboring district—awaits.

Only the very rich could afford stone residences. The fancy facades here hide their economical brick construction behind a stucco veneer. The stone tower on this corner had only one door—30 feet above street level and reached by ladder, which could be pulled up as necessary. Within a few doors, you'll find a classy bar, an elegant grocery store, and a *gelateria*.

Take a little side trip, venturing up Via San Pietro. Interesting stops (mostly on the left) include the window with Palio video clips playing (at #1), Simon and Paula's art shop with delightful Palio and *contrade* knickknacks (#5), a weaver's shop (#7), the recommended La Vecchia Latteria *gelateria* (on the right, at #10), an art gallery (#11), and four enticing little osterias. At the end of the block you'll reach the best medieval art collection in town, the **Pinacoteca** (for a self-guided tour of its interior, see page 614).

• *Return to the Four Corners and carry on straight up Via del Capitano, passing another massive Chigi family palace (on the left, at #1). Up next, at the end of the street, is the...*

❺ Piazza del Duomo and the Duomo

The pair of she-wolves atop columns flanking the cathedral's facade says it all: The church was built and paid for not by the pope but by the people and the republic of Siena.

This 13th-century Gothic cathedral, with its striped bell tower—Siena's ultimate tribute to the Virgin Mary—is heaped with statues, plastered with frescoes, and paved with art.

The current structure dates back to 1215, with the major decoration done during Siena's heyday (1250-1350). The lower story, by Giovanni Pisano (who worked from 1284 to 1297), features remnants of the fading Romanesque style (round arches over the doors), topped with the pointed arches of the new Gothic style that was seeping in from France. The upper half, in full-blown frilly Gothic, was designed and built a century later.

The six-story bell tower (c. 1315) looks even taller, thanks to an optical illusion: The white marble stripes get narrower toward the top, making the upper part seem farther away.

The interior is a Renaissance riot of striped columns, remarkably intricate inlaid-marble floors, a Michelangelo statue, evocative Bernini sculptures, and the amazing Piccolomini Library. (If you want to enter now, you'll need a ticket—the ticket office moves around, but it's most likely around the left side of the Duomo's entrance; for a self-guided tour of the interior, see page 616.

Facing the cathedral is **Santa Maria della Scala,** a huge building that housed pilgrims and, until the 1990s, was used as a hospital. Its labyrinthine 12th-century cellars—carved from sandstone and finished with brick—go down several floors and, during medieval times, stored supplies for the hospital upstairs. Today, the exhibit-filled hospital and cellars can be a welcome refuge from the hot streets (for more on this sight, see page 622).

• *Walk along the right side of the church toward its rear end. This is part of what was once intended to be an extension of the Duomo.*

❻ Unfinished Church

Grand as Siena's cathedral is, it's actually the rump of a failed vision. After rival republic Florence began its grand cathedral (1296), proud Siena planned to build an even bigger one, the biggest in all Christendom.

Look at the unfinished wall with see-through windows (circa 1330). Just imagine the audacity of this vision: Today's cathedral would have been just a transept. Worshippers would have entered the church through the unfinished wall. (Look way up at the highest part of the wall. That viewpoint is accessible from inside the Duomo Museum.) Some of the nave's dark-green-and-white-striped columns were built, but the space between them is now partially filled in with brick. White stones in the pavement mark where a row of pillars would have been.

But this grand vision underestimated the complexity of constructing such a building without enough land. That, coupled with the devastating effects of the 1348 plague, killed the city's ability and will to finish the project. Many Sienese saw the Black Death as a sign from God, punishing them for their pride. They canceled their plans and humbly faded into the background of Tuscan history.

• *On your left is the entrance to the* **Duomo Museum**, *housing the church's art (see page 619). To continue our walk, exit the piazza through the doorway in the wall abutting the back end of the church. After a few steps, pause at the top of the marble stairs leading down.*

❼ Supporting an Oversized Church

From here you can see how the church sticks out, high above the lower street level. Because there wasn't enough flat ground, builders propped up the overhanging edge with the church's subterranean features—the Crypt and Baptistery. (Both are worth entering and included in the Opa Si Pass; see page 615.)

• *Descend the stairs, nicknamed* "*The Steps of St. Catherine*," *as she would have climbed them each day on her walk from home to the Santa Maria della Scala Hospital where she worked. Below the Baptistery, jog right, then immediately left, through a tunnel down Via di Diacceto. Just ahead, pause on the bridge (originally a drawbridge) to enjoy a beautiful view (to the left) of the towering brick Dominican church in the distance. Then continue straight up the lane until you reach the next big square.*

❽ Piazza Indipendenza

This square celebrates the creation of a unified Italy (1861) with a 19th-century loggia sporting busts of the first two Italian kings. Stacking history on history, the neo-Renaissance loggia is backed by a Gothic palace and an older medieval tower.

• *Head right, downhill one block (on Via delle Terme), back to the grand Via di Città, and take a few steps to the left to see another, fancier loggia.*

❾ Loggia della Mercanzia

This Gothic-Renaissance loggia was built about 1420 as a kind of headquarters for the union of merchants. Siena's nobility purchased

Siena's *Contrade* and the Palio

Siena's 17 historic neighborhoods, or *contrade*—each with a parish church, well or fountain, and square—still play an active role in the life of the city. Each is represented by a mascot (porcupine, unicorn, wolf, etc.) and unique colors worn proudly by residents.

Contrada pride is evident year-round in Siena's parades and colorful banners, lamps, and wall plaques. If you hear the thunder of distant drumming, run to it for some medieval action—there's a good chance it'll feature flag throwers. Buy a scarf in *contrada* colors, and join in the merriment of these lively neighborhood festivals. (But be careful where you wear them...you don't want to stumble naively into a rival *contrada*'s celebration.)

Contrade rivalries are most visible twice a year—on July 2 and August 16—during the city's world-famous horse race, the **Palio di Siena.** Ten of the 17 neighborhoods compete (chosen by rotation and lot), hurling themselves with medieval abandon into several days of trial races and traditional revelry. Jockeys—usually from out of town—are considered hired guns, no better than mercenaries. Locals boast about which *contrada* will win...and lose. Betting on the outcome is strictly forbidden...officially. Despite the shady behind-the-scenes dealing, on the big day the horses are taken into their *contrada*'s church to be blessed. ("Go and return victorious," says the priest.) It's considered a sign of luck if a horse leaves droppings in the church.

On the evening of the race, Il Campo is stuffed to the brim with locals and tourists. Dirt is brought in and packed down to create the track's surface, while mattresses pad the walls of sur-

the loggia, and eventually it became the clubhouse of the local elites. To this day, it's a private, ritzy, and notoriously out-of-step-with-the-times men's club. The "Gli Uniti" above the door is a "let's stick together" declaration.

• *Next to the loggia, steep steps lead down to Il Campo, but we'll go left and uphill on Via Banchi di Sopra. Pause at the fork in the road, which separates...*

SIENA

rounding buildings. The most treacherous spots are the sharp corners, where many a rider has bitten the dust.

Picture the scene: Ten snorting horses and their nervous riders line up near the pharmacy (on the west side of the square) to await the starting signal. Then they race like crazy while spectators wave the scarves of their neighborhoods.

Every possible vantage point and perch is packed with people straining to see the action. One lap around the course is about a quarter of a mile; three laps make a full circuit. In this no-holds-barred race—which lasts just over a minute—a horse can win even without its rider (jockeys ride precariously without saddles and often fall off the horses' sweaty backs).

When the winner crosses the line, 1/17th of Siena—the prevailing neighborhood—goes berserk. Winners receive a *palio* (banner)—painted by a Sienese artist in July and an international artist in August, and always featuring the Virgin Mary (the race is dedicated to her). But the true prizes are proving that your *contrada* is *numero uno,* and mocking your losing rivals.

All over town, sketches and posters depict the Palio. This is not some folkloric event—it's a real medieval moment. If you're packed onto the square with 15,000 people, all hungry for victory, you may not see much, but you'll feel it. Bleacher and balcony seats are expensive, but it's free to join the masses in the square. Go with an empty bladder (as there are no WCs) and be prepared to surrender any sense of personal space.

While the actual Palio packs the city, you can more easily see the horse-race trials—called *prove*—on any of the three days before the main event (usually at 9:00 and after 19:00, bleacher seats may be available; the calmest, most accessible *prova* is the final one—9:00 on the morning of the race—since nobody wants to risk injury so close to the real thing). Good sources for more information include IlPalio.org and ComitatoAmiciDelPalio.it.

❿ Banchi di Sopra and Banchi di Sotto

These main drags are named "upper row of banks" and "lower row of banks." They were once lined with market tables *(banchi),* and vendors paid rent to the city for a table's position along the street. If the owner of a *banco* neglected to pay up, thugs came along and literally broke *(rotto)* his table. It is from this practice—*banco rotto,* broken table—that we get the English word "bankrupt."

In medieval times, these streets were part of the Via Francigena, the main thoroughfare (busy with pilgrims, merchants, and crusaders) linking Rome with northern Europe. Today, strollers—out each evening for their *passeggiata*—fill Via Banchi di Sopra. Join the crowd, strolling past Siena's finest shops.

A block or so farther up the street, **Piazza Tolomei** faces the imposing Tolomei family palace (now an imposing bank). This is a center for the Owl *contrada*. The column in the square, topped by the she-wolf, marks another of Siena's three hills.

• *Continue on Banchi di Sopra to Piazza Salimbeni. This gets my vote for Siena's finest stretch of palaces.*

⓫ Piazza Salimbeni

Piazza Salimbeni is dominated by Monte dei Paschi, the head office of a bank founded in 1472. It's amazing to think this bank has been in business on this square for over 500 years. Originally Monte dei Paschi was a kind of community bank for common people. The statue in the center of the square honors Sallustio Antonio Bandini, a reformer who helped develop a system that let people secure firm title to their land.

Directly across from Piazza Salimbeni, the steep little lane called Costa dell'Incrociata leads straight (down and then up) to the Basilica of San Domenico (it's worth the hike; see page 623). Also nearby (behind the cute green newsstand) is the most elegant grocery store in town, Consorzio Agrario di Siena (see page 623).

• *With this walk under your belt, you've got the lay of the land. The city is ready for further exploration—the sights associated with City Hall and the Duomo are all just a few minutes away. Enjoy delving deeper into Siena.*

Sights in Siena

IL CAMPO AND NEARBY

The gorgeous red-brick square known as Il Campo—worth ▲▲▲—is the best in Italy (for more on the square itself, see page 604). It's also home to City Hall (with the Civic Museum and City Tower) and other sights.

▲▲City Hall (Palazzo Pubblico) and Civic Museum (Museo Civico)

Siena's fine Gothic City Hall is still the seat of city government. With its proud tower, this building symbolizes a republic independent from the pope and the Holy Roman Emperor. It also represents a rising secular society, one that appeared first in Tuscany in late medieval times, then spread throughout Europe as humanism took hold during the Renaissance.

City Hall has a fine and manageable museum on its top floor. You'll see the large assembly hall where democracy was forged, adorned with some of Siena's most historic frescoes. There's memorabilia from the birth of the nation of Italy. The highlight is a room of medieval-era frescoes depicting fascinating examples of governance—good and bad. (Note that these frescoes are undergoing an extensive renovation and may be covered up.) Strolling the halls, you'll get a glimpse into the city-as-utopia, when this proud town understandably considered itself the vanguard of Western civilization.

Cost and Hours: Museum-€10 by itself (cheaper if frescoes are covered), or €15 with City Tower; also covered by other combotickets that include Santa Maria della Scala and/or the Pinacoteca (up to €25 for everything); look for small ticket window straight ahead as you enter City Hall courtyard; open daily 10:00-19:00, Nov-Feb until 18:00, last entry 45 minutes before closing; +39 0577 292 232, www.comune.siena.it.

Visiting the Museum: Start in the Sala del Risorgimento, with dramatic scenes of the 19th-century unification of Italy. Make your way to the chapel, where the city's governors and bureaucrats prayed, then enter the Sala del Mappamondo. On one end of the room is the beautiful *Maestà* (*Enthroned Virgin*, 1315), by Siena's great Simone Martini (c. 1280-1344). This is a groundbreaking work. It's Siena's first fresco showing a Madonna not in a faraway, gold-leaf heaven, but under the blue sky of a real space that we inhabit.

On the opposite end of the room is the famous *Equestrian Portrait of Guidoriccio da Fogliano* (1330; traditionally attributed to Simone Martini), which depicts a mercenary commander surveying the siege fort, with the catapult that helped Siena win.

Next is the Sala della Pace, where the Council of Nine, who ruled Siena from 1287 to 1355, met. They were surrounded by a fascinating fresco series showing the *Effects of Good and Bad Government*, by Ambrogio Lorenzetti (1337-1340). (Unfortunately, these frescoes may be covered for restoration during your visit.)

Notice the better-preserved fresco (on the long wall to the right) depicting the beneficial effects of good government. Compare the whistle-while-you-work happiness against the crime, devastation, and societal mayhem of a community ruled by politicians with more typical values.

You can cap your visit by climbing the **stairs to a grand view** of the city and its surroundings. (For a less impressive view, you could skip the stairs and simply peek behind the curtains in the Sala della Pace.)

▲City Tower (Torre del Mangia)

The tower's nearly 400 steps get pretty skinny at the top, but the reward is a grand view. For more on the tower, see page 606.

Cost and Hours: €10, €15 combo-ticket with Civic Museum, also included in various combo-tickets with Santa Maria della Scala and/or the Pinacoteca, daily 10:00-19:00, Nov-Feb until 16:00, closed in rain, last entry one hour before closing, free and mandatory bag check.

SIENA

Crowd Alert: Admission is limited to 50 people at a time. Wait at the bottom of the stairs for the green *Avanti* light. Try to avoid midday crowds (up to an hour wait at peak times).

▲Pinacoteca

If you're into medieval art, you should enjoy this quiet, uncrowded, colorful museum—though it has no spectacular highlights. The museum (officially the Pinacoteca Nazionale di Siena) walks you through Siena's art chronologically, from the 12th through the 16th century, when a revolution in realism was percolating in Tuscany.

Cost and Hours: €8, Mon and Fri-Sun 8:30-13:30, Tue-Thu 14:00-19:00, closed two Sundays a month; from Il Campo, walk out Via di Città and go left on Via San Pietro to #29; +39 0577 281 161, www.pinacotecanazionale.siena.it.

Visiting the Museum: In general, the collection lets you follow the evolution of painting styles from Byzantine to Gothic, then to International Gothic, and finally to Renaissance.

Long after Florentine art went realistic, the Sienese embraced a timeless, otherworldly style glittering with lots of gold. But Sienese art features more than just paintings. In this city of proud craftsmen, the gilding and carpentry of the frames almost compete with the actual paintings. The exquisite attention to detail gives a glimpse into the wealth of the 13th and 14th centuries, Siena's golden age. The woven silk and gold clothing you'll see was worn by the very people who once walked these halls, when this was a private mansion (appreciate the colonnaded courtyard).

The core of the collection is on the second floor, in Rooms 1-19. Works by Duccio di Buoninsegna (who created the *Maestà* in the Duomo Museum) feature groundbreaking innovations that are subtle: less gold-leaf background, fewer gold creases in robes, translucent garments, inlaid-marble thrones, and a more human Mary and Jesus. Notice that the Madonna-and-Bambino pose is eerily identical in each version.

In *St. Augustine of Siena*, Duccio's assistant Simone Martini portrays the saint's life in realistic Sienese streets, buildings, and landscapes. In each panel, the saint pops out at the oddest (difficult to draw) angles to save the day. (Simone Martini also did the *Maestà* and possibly the Guidoriccio frescoes in the Civic Museum.)

Also look for religious works by the hometown Lorenzetti brothers (Ambrogio is best known for the secular masterpiece *Effects of Good and Bad Government,* in the Civic Museum).

Two famous small wooden panels, *Città sul Mare (City by the Sea)* and *Castello in Riva al Lago (Castle on the Lakeshore),* feature a strange, medieval-landscape Cubism. Notice the weird, melancholic light that captures the sense of the Dark Ages.

Several colorful rooms on the first floor are dedicated to Domenico Beccafumi (1486-1551), who designed many of the Duomo's inlaid pavement panels. With strong bodies, twisting poses, and dramatic gestures, Beccafumi's works epitomize the Mannerist style of the High Renaissance.

DUOMO AND RELATED SIGHTS

Siena's monumental cathedral complex encompasses the Duomo, Duomo Museum (and its panoramic terrace), Baptistery, and Crypt.

Ticket Options and Hours

The Duomo's various sights are covered by a confusing variety of tickets. Here are your basic choices:

Duomo Interior (including the Piccolomini Library): €5 most of the year; €8 when floor panels are uncovered (typically July and mid-Aug-mid-Oct).

Opa Si Pass: €13; €15 when floor panels are uncovered. Covers Duomo interior, Duomo Museum (with original Duomo art, plus a fantastic viewpoint over Siena), the Crypt (frescoes), and the Baptistery (with a fine baptismal font).

Porta del Cielo ("Gate of Heaven") Pass: €20, covers everything in the Opa Si Pass and adds an escorted visit up to the cathedral's dome and rooftop (described later). It's wise to reserve this pass—see "Crowd-Beating Tips," below.

Hours: The Duomo is open Mon-Sat 10:00-19:00, Sun 13:30-17:30; Nov-March daily until 17:00. The associated sights keep similar hours (but if arriving late in the day, confirm closing times to plan your visit strategically). The Porta del Cielo roof visits are offered daily, Nov-March on weekends only with some closures.

Information: +39 0577 286 300, www.operaduomo.siena.it.

Getting Tickets: As of this writing, the ticket office for Duomo sights is on the left side of the Duomo, as you face it. However, ticket options and sales points get reconfigured frequently. Expect changes, and when in doubt, ask uniformed staff for help.

Crowd-Beating Tips: Crowds peak midmorning in high season; early, late, or lunchtime visits can be less busy. If you anticipate crowds, you can prebook at www.operaduomo.siena.it (€2 booking fee/ticket; click "Booking Online" to be redirected to official ticket-booking site). Prebook Porta del Cielo cathedral roof visits; slots fill up.

▲▲▲Duomo (Duomo di Siena)

Siena's 13th-century cathedral and striped bell tower are one of the most illustrious examples of Romanesque-Gothic style in Italy.

This ornate but surprisingly secular shrine to the Virgin Mary is slathered with colorful art inside and out, from inlaid-marble floors to stained-glass windows. The cathedral's interior showcases the work of the greatest sculptors of successive eras—Pisano, Donatello, Michelangelo, and Bernini—and the Piccolomini Library features a series of 15th-century frescoes chronicling the adventures of Siena's philanderer-turned-pope, Aeneas Piccolomini.

Cost and Hours: See "Ticket Options and Hours," earlier.

Dress Code: Modest dress is required, but stylish paper ponchos are provided for the inappropriately clothed.

Church Services: Worshippers attending Mass can enter the church free; use the entrance on the right side of the building, set farther back from the main one (Mon-Sat at 10:00; Sun at 8:00, 11:00, 12:15, and 18:30). When the fragile floor panels are uncovered in July and mid-Aug–mid-Oct, Mass is held elsewhere or in a side chapel.

Tours: There may be a downloadable app or a rentable audioguide (ask on-site)—but the information covered here is plenty for a casual visit.

❷ Self-Guided Tour: Grab a spot on a stone bench opposite the entry to take in this architectural festival of green, white, pink, and gold. The Duomo sits atop Siena's highest point, with one of the most extravagant facades in all of Europe. Like a medieval altarpiece, the facade is divided into sections, each frame filled with patriarchs and prophets, studded with roaring gargoyles, and topped with prickly pinnacles (for more about the facade, see page 608).

• *Step inside, putting yourself in the mindset of a pilgrim as you take in this trove of religious art.*

Nave: The heads of 171 popes—who reigned from the time of St. Peter to the 12th century—peer down from above, looking over the fine inlaid art on the floor. With a forest of striped columns, a

SIENA

coffered dome, a large stained-glass window at the far end (it's a copy—the original is viewable up close in the Duomo Museum), and an art gallery's worth of early Renaissance art, this is one busy interior. If you look closely at the popes, you'll see the same four faces repeated over and over.

For almost two centuries (1373-1547), 40 artists paved the marble floor with scenes from the Old Testament, allegories, and intricate patterns. The series starts near the entrance with histori-cal allegories; the larger, more elaborate scenes surrounding the altar are mostly stories from the Old Testament. Many of the floor panels are roped off and covered to prevent further wear and tear. But typically in July and from mid-August through October, the cathedral uncovers them and holds Mass elsewhere. The second pavement panel from the entrance depicts Siena as a she-wolf. The proud city of Siena is the center of the Italian universe, orbited by such lesser lights as Roma, Florentia (Florence), and Pisa.

The fourth pavement panel from the entrance is the Fortune Panel, with Lady Luck (lower right) arriving on earth, where she teeters back and forth on a ball and a tipsy boat. The lesson? For-tune is an unstable foundation for life. On the right wall hangs a dim **painting of St. Catherine** (fourth from entrance). Siena's homegrown saint had a vision in which she mystically married Christ.

• *On the opposite wall is a marble altarpiece decorated with statues.*

Piccolomini Altar: This was commissioned by the Sienese-born Pope Pius III (born Francesco Piccolomini) but was never used. The altar is most interesting for its statues: one by Michel-angelo and three by his students. Michelangelo was originally contracted to do 15 statues, but another sculptor had started the marble blocks, and Michelangelo's heart was never in the project. He personally finished the figure of St. Paul (lower right, clearly more interesting than the bland, bored saints above him).

• *Now grab a seat under the dome. The dome sits on a 12-sided base, but its "coffered" ceiling is a painted illusion.*

Duccio's Stained-Glass Rose Window: At the far end of the church, high up above the altar, is the rose window, a kaleidoscope of colors and intricate designs. The window is dedicated to the Vir-gin Mary, as is the church and the city itself. This is a copy of the original window made about 1287-1290 (described on page 620).

• *Closer to you, on the left side of the nave, is a stone podium sitting atop columns. This is...*

Pisano's Pulpit: The octagonal Carrara marble pulpit (1268) rests on the backs of lions, symbols of Christianity triumphant. Like the lions, the Church eats its catch (devouring paganism) and nurses its cubs. The seven relief panels tell the life of Christ in rich detail. The pulpit is the work of Nicola Pisano (c. 1220-1278), the

"Giotto of sculpture," whose revival of classical forms (columns, sarcophagus-like relief panels) signaled the coming Renaissance. His son Giovanni (c. 1240-1319) carved many of the panels, mixing his dad's classicism and realism with the decorative detail and curvy lines of French Gothic.

• *A few steps to the left of the pulpit (in the left transept), find a panel in the floor, the...*

Slaughter of the Innocents Pavement Panel: Herod (left), sitting enthroned amid Renaissance arches, orders the massacre of all babies to prevent the coming of the promised Messiah. It's a chaotic scene of angry soldiers, grieving mothers, and dead babies, reminding locals that a republic ruled by a tyrant will always experience misery.

• *Nearby in the left transept is a small chapel with a well-known statue.*

Donatello's St. John the Baptist: The rugged saint in his famous rags stands in a quiet chapel. Donatello, the aging Florentine sculptor, whose style was now considered passé in Florence, came here to build bronze doors for the church (similar to Ghiberti's in Florence). Donatello didn't complete the door project, but he did finish this bronze statue (1457).

• *Cross the church. Directly opposite find the Chigi Chapel (with its ironwork entrance), also known as the...*

Chapel of the *Madonna del Voto*: To understand why Bernini is considered the greatest Baroque sculptor, step into this sumptuous chapel (designed in the early 1660s for Fabio Chigi, a.k.a. Pope Alexander VII). Move up to the altar and look back at the **two Bernini statues** that frame the doorway: Mary Magdalene in a state of spiritual ecstasy and St. Jerome playing the crucifix like a violinist lost in heavenly music.

The painting over the altar is the *Madonna del Voto*, a Madonna and Child adorned with a real crown of gold and jewels (painted by a Sienese master in the mid-13th century). In typical medieval fashion, the scene is set in the golden light of heaven. Mary has the almond eyes, long fingers, and golden folds in her robe that are found in orthodox icons of the time. Still, this Mary tilts her head and looks out sympathetically, ready to listen to the prayers of the faithful. This is the Mary to whom the Palio is dedicated, dear to the hearts of the Sienese.

In thanks, they give **offerings** of silver hearts and medallions, many of which now hang on the walls to the right and left as you exit the chapel.

• *Cross back to the other side of the church. Next to the altar, look for the door to the...*

Piccolomini Library: Brilliantly frescoed, the library captures the exuberant, optimistic spirit of the 1400s, when humanism and the Renaissance were born. The never-restored frescoes look nearly as vivid now as the day they were finished 550 years ago. The painter Pinturicchio (c. 1454-1513) was hired to celebrate the life of one of Siena's hometown boys—a man many call "the first humanist," Aeneas Piccolomini (1405-1464), who became Pope Pius II. (Pius II fans can visit his birthplace, Pienza—which was named for him—described in the Heart of Tuscany chapter.) Each of the 10 scenes is framed with an arch, as if Pinturicchio were opening a window onto the spacious 3-D world we inhabit.

The library also contains intricately decorated, illuminated music scores and a statue (a Roman copy of a Greek original) of the Three Graces, who almost seem to dance to the beat. The oddly huge sheepskin sheets of music are from the days before individual hymnals—they had to be big so that many singers could read the music from a distance. Appreciate the fine painted decorations on the music—the gold-leaf highlights, the blue tones from expensive ultramarine (made from precious lapis lazuli), and the miniature figures. All of this exquisite detail was lovingly crafted by Benedictine monks for the glory of God.

• *Our tour is finished. But to truly appreciate the grandeur of the Duomo, exit the church and make a U-turn to the left, walking alongside the church to Piazza Jacopo della Quercia. Had the massive church Siena envisioned been built, the nave would be where the piazza is today. Look through the unfinished entrance facade, note blue sky where the stained-glass windows would have been, and ponder the struggles, triumphs, and failures of the human spirit. (For more on the unfinished church, see page 608.)*

▲▲Duomo Museum and Viewpoint (Museo dell'Opera e Panorama)

Siena's most enjoyable museum, housing the cathedral's art, is located in the skeleton of the Duomo's grand but unfinished extension (to the right as you face the cathedral's main facade). Stand eye-to-eye with the saints and angels who once languished, unknown, in the church's upper reaches (where copies are found today).

Cost and Hours: See "Ticket Options and Hours," earlier.

➲ **Self-Guided Tour:** Start on the ground floor, which houses the church's original statues, mainly from the facade and exterior. After descending a few steps, turn your back on the hall of statues and wrought-iron gate. You're now face-to-face with **Donatello's** *Madonna and Child* (c. 1458). In this round, carved relief, a slender and tender Mary gazes down at her chubby-cheeked baby. Her sad eyes say that she knows the eventual fate of her son.

At the opposite end of the room is **Duccio's Stained-Glass Window** (c. 1287-1290). This splendid original window was installed for centuries above and behind the Duomo's altar. Now the church has a copy, and art lovers can enjoy a close-up look at this masterpiece. The rose window—20 feet across—is dedicated (like the church and the city itself) to the Virgin Mary.

The work is by Siena's most famous artist, Duccio di Buoninsegna (c. 1255-1319). Duccio combined elements from rigid Byzantine icons (Mary's almond-shaped bubble, called a *mandorla*, and the full-frontal saints that flank her) with a budding sense of 3-D realism (the throne turned at a three-quarter angle to simulate depth, with angels behind).

Upstairs awaits a private audience with Duccio's *Maestà* (*Enthroned Virgin*, 1311). The panels in this room were once part of the Duomo's main altarpiece. Grab a seat and study one of the great pieces of medieval art. Although the former altarpiece was disassembled (and the frame was lost), most of the pieces are displayed here, with the front side (*Maestà*, with Mary and saints; pronounced my-STAH) at one end of the room and the back side (26 Passion panels) at the other.

Maestà was revolutionary for the time in its sheer size and opulence, and in Duccio's budding realism, which broke standard conventions. Duccio, at the height of his powers, used every innovative arrow in his quiver. He replaced the standard gold-leaf background (symbolizing heaven) with a gold, intricately patterned curtain draped over the throne. Mary's blue robe opens to reveal her body, and the curve of her knee suggests real anatomy beneath the robe. Baby Jesus wears a delicately transparent garment. Their faces are modeled with light—a patchwork of bright flesh and shadowy valleys, as if lit from the left (a technique Duccio likely learned from his contemporary Giotto during a visit to Florence).

The Passion of Christ: The flip side of the altarpiece featured these 26 smaller panels showing colorful scenes from the Passion of Christ.

• *Our museum tour is done, but the finale of your visit—to the top of the unfinished Duomo facade—is yet to come. After corkscrewing up 140 narrow steps, you'll reach the...*

Panorama del Facciatone: Standing on the wall from this high point in the city, you're rewarded with a stunning view of Siena...and an interesting perspective. Look toward the Duomo

and remember this: To
outdo Florence, Siena had
planned to enlarge this cathedral by turning it into a
transept and constructing
an enormous nave. You're
standing on top of what
would have been the new
entrance facade. Columns
would have stood where

you see the rows of white stones in the pavement below. Had the
church been completed, you'd be looking straight down the nave
toward the altar.

▲Baptistery of San Giovanni (Battistero di San Giovanni)

This richly adorned and quietly tucked-away cave of art is worth a
look for its cool tranquility and exquisite art, including an ornately
painted vaulted ceiling. The highlight is the baptismal font created
in the 1420s by a host of early Renaissance all-stars from marble,
bronze, and enamel. The overall design was by Jacopo ("Fountain
of Joy") della Quercia. On the base, the first bronze panel you encounter was done by Lorenzo ("Gates of Paradise") Ghiberti. To
the right, the tiny bronze statues of Lady Faith and (farther right)
the Angel of Hope were done by the great Donatello. Also on the
right side, Donatello made the bronze panel depicting John the
Baptist's severed head being brought in on a platter, set in a 3-D
banquet hall of receding arches. With this font, we're witnessing
the start of the Renaissance.

Cost and Hours: See "Ticket Options and Hours," earlier;
located at the back end of the Duomo, all the way down the stairs.

Crypt (Cripta)

The cathedral "crypt" is archaeologically important. The site of a
small 12th-century Romanesque church, it was filled in with dirt
a century after its creation to provide a foundation for the huge
church that sits atop it today. Recently excavated (with modern
metal supports from the 1990s), the several rediscovered rooms
show off what are likely the oldest frescoes in town (well described
in English).

Cost and Hours: See "Ticket Options and Hours," earlier;
located at the back end of the Duomo, partway down the stairs.

Porto del Cielo ("Gate of Heaven") Cathedral Roof Visit

To make a 30-minute escorted (but not guided) visit to the dome's
cupola and roof, buy the Porto del Cielo combo-ticket (reservation
recommended; see "Ticket Options and Hours," earlier). You'll
climb 79 steps to see restored rooms with impressive inlaid floors

and get a close-up look at the cupola. You'll also walk briefly outside on the rooftop for a breathtaking view.

Other Cathedral-Area Sights
▲Santa Maria della Scala

This museum, opposite the Duomo, operated for centuries as a hospital, foundling home (orphanage), and pilgrim lodging. Many of those activities are visible in the 15th-century frescoes of its main hall, the Pellegrinaio. Today, the hospital and its cellars are filled with fascinating exhibits (well described in English).

Cost and Hours: €9; various combo-tickets also include Civic Museum, City Tower, and/or Pinacoteca; daily 10:00-19:00, Thu until 22:00; mid-Oct-mid-March Mon and Wed-Fri 10:00-17:00, Sat-Sun until 19:00, closed Tue; on Piazza del Duomo opposite the cathedral, +39 0577 534 571, www.santamariadellascala.com.

Visiting the Museum: It's easy to get lost in this gigantic complex, so stay focused on the main attractions—the fancily frescoed Pellegrinaio Hall (ground floor) and the Fountain of Joy statues (one floor down). Then explore the lower floors.

From the entrance, turn right to enter what was until the 1970s Siena's main hospital. Enter the first room on your right, the **Sacristy,** which displays some powerful relics preserved in golden and silver reliquaries. You may see a drop of Jesus' blood in a vial *(sangue di Christo),* a nail from Jesus' cross *(sacro chiodo),* a piece of the Virgin's robe *(beata Vergine),* and lots of saints' bones. They're encased in reliquaries that befit the preciousness of these sacred bits and saintly pieces. Some of the oldest are Byzantine reliquaries made of gold, silver, and precious stones.

Continue down the hallway (browsing exhibits in side rooms) until you reach the sumptuously frescoed **Pellegrinaio Hall.** This was a reception hall for visiting pilgrims before being converted into a hospital room, lined with beds for the sick. The frescoes (mostly by Domenico di Bartolo, c. 1440) show medieval Siena's innovative health care and social welfare system in action.

Now head downstairs, following signs to *Fonte Gaia.* These are the original statues from the **Fountain of Joy** (Fonte Gaia), Siena's landmark fountain on Il Campo. Jacopo della Quercia's early-15th-century masterpiece began crumbling, so in the 19th century, it was dismantled and plaster casts were made. (These casts formed the replica that graces Il Campo today.) Here you'll see the badly eroded original statues and relief panels, paired alongside their casts (labeled *"calco"*).

In the second basement, under the groin vaults of the **Archaeological Museum** (Museo Archeologico), you're alone with piles of ancient stuff, from Bronze Age axes to Roman pottery. The highlight is a group of Etruscan artifacts excavated from tombs dating from the seventh to second century before Christ—the Etruscan heyday. You'll see their coins, figurines, and terra-cotta funeral urns for ashes (often designed with a standard body but a personalized head). The sarcophagi show the deceased

reclining atop the lid, a reminder of their lofty social status.

SAN DOMENICO AREA
Basilica of San Domenico (Basilica di San Domenico)
This huge brick church is worth a quick look. Spacious and plain (except for the colorful flags of the city's 17 *contrade*), the Gothic interior fits the austere philosophy of the Dominicans and invites meditation on the thoughts and deeds of St. Catherine. Halfway up the nave on the right, find a copper bust of St. Catherine (for four centuries it contained her skull), a small case housing her thumb, and her little flagellation whip. In the chapel, surrounded with candles, you'll see Catherine's head (a clay mask around her skull with her actual teeth showing through) atop the altar.

Cost and Hours: Free, daily 7:00-18:30, shorter hours off-season, www.basilicacateriniana.com.

▲Sanctuary of St. Catherine (Santuario di Santa Caterina)
Step into the cool and peaceful site of Catherine's home. Siena remembers its favorite hometown gal, a simple, unschooled but mystically devout soul who helped convince the pope to return to Rome from France, where the papacy had moved in 1309. Pilgrims have visited this place since 1464, and architects and artists have greatly embellished what was probably once a humble home (her family worked as wool dyers). You'll see paintings throughout showing scenes from her life.

Cost and Hours: Free, daily 9:00-18:00 but chapel closes 12:30-15:00, a few downhill blocks toward the center from San Domenico—follow signs to *Santuario di Santa Caterina*—at Costa di Sant'Antonio 6, +39 0577 288 175.

Sleeping in Siena

Finding a room in Siena is tough during Easter or the Palio (July 2 and Aug 16). Many hotels won't take reservations until the end of May for the Palio, and even then they might require a four-night stay. If tranquility is important to you, ask for a room that's off the street, or consider staying outside the center.

BIGGER HOTELS IN THE CENTER

$$$ Pensione Palazzo Ravizza is elegant, friendly, and beautifully appointed, with 40 rooms and an aristocratic feel. Guests enjoy a peaceful garden set on a dramatic bluff, along with a Steinway in the upper lounge (RS%, family rooms, rooms in back overlook countryside, air-con, elevator, free parking, Via Piano dei Mantellini 34, +39 0577 280 462, www.palazzoravizza.it, bureau@palazzoravizza.it).

$$$ Hotel Palazzetto Rosso is a boutique hotel that fills a stunningly restored, 13th-century, red tower house down a side street from the main drag. The French owners have adorned the nine rooms with modern, colorful, minimalist style for a quirky combination of new and old (lavish "design" suites, no air-con but innovative floor-cooling system, elevator, Via dei Rossi 38, +39 0577 236 197, www.palazzettorosso.com, info@palazzettorosso.com).

$$$ Hotel Duomo is dated but well located, with 20 spacious but overpriced rooms (many with Duomo views—request when booking) and a picnic-friendly roof terrace (family rooms, air-con, elevator with some stairs, expensive pay parking; Via di Stalloreggi 38, +39 0577 289 088, www.hotelduomo.it, booking@hotelduomo.it, Alessandro).

B&BS IN THE CENTER

$$ Antica Residenza Cicogna is a seven-room guesthouse with a homey elegance and an ideal location. It's warmly run by charming Elisa (who named this family property for her grandmother) and her friend Ilaria, who set out biscotti, Vin Santo, and tea for their guests in the afternoon. With artfully frescoed walls and ceilings, this is remarkably genteel for the price (air-con, no elevator, Via delle Terme 76, +39 0577 285 613, mobile +39 347 007 2888, www.anticaresidenzacicogna.it, info@anticaresidenzacicogna.it).

$$ Palazzo Masi B&B, run by friendly Alizzardo and Daniela, is just below Il Campo. They rent six pleasant, spacious, antique-furnished rooms with shared common areas on the second and third floors of a restored 13th-century building (RS%—use code "RICK," cheaper rooms with shared bath, no elevator; breakfast provided on Il Campo; from City Hall, walk 50 yards down Casato di Sotto to #29; +39 349 600 9155, www.palazzomasi.com, info@palazzomasi.it).

$$ Il Giardino di Pantaneto, down a less-touristed street not far from Il Campo, rents 12 fresh, smartly designed rooms—many with views over a garden for slightly higher prices (family rooms, air-con, elevator, Via Pantaneto 77, +39 0577 574 910, mobile +39 335 630 6949, www.ilgiardinodipantaneto.com, info@ilgiardinodipantaneto.com).

$$ B&B Palazzo Bruchi, a bit farther down the same street, is another charming spot with four rooms overlooking a fine little courtyard, garden, and the countryside (air-con, Via Pantaneto 105, +39 351 927 7340, www.palazzobruchi.it, booking@palazzobruchi.it).

$$ B&B Alle Due Porte is a charming little establishment renting three big rooms with sweet furniture under medieval beams. The shared breakfast room is delightful (air-con, Via di Stalloreggi 51, +39 351 835 1819, www.sienatur.it, alledueportesiena@gmail.com, Mariangela).

$$ Siena Gallery B&B, run by kindhearted Elisabetta and Fabio, is tucked onto the fourth floor of a relatively modern building, offering four contemporary-yet-simple rooms (air-con, elevator, Via Banchi di Sopra 31, enter at Galleria Odeon—look for green pharmacy sign, +39 334 3997 8694, www.sienagallery.it, info@sienagallery.it).

$$ I Terzi di Siena, run by the same family as Siena Gallery B&B, houses six rooms in an 11th-century building. It's absent an elevator but full of humble charm and noteworthy views (air-con, Via dei Termini 13, +39 339 669 9143, www.terzidisiena.it, info@terzidisiena.it).

$ Le Camerine di Silvia, a romantic hideaway perched near a grassy olive grove, rents five simple rooms in a converted 16th-century building. A small terrace with fruit trees and a private hedged garden lends itself to contemplation (cash only, view room on request, breakfast on request, fans, free parking nearby, Via Bastianini 1—ring bell marked "Conti," +39 338 761 5052 or +39 339 123 7687, www.lecamerinedisilvia.com, info@lecamerinedisilvia.com, Conti family).

SIMPLE PLACES IN THE CENTER

$$ Piccolo Hotel Etruria, with 20 rooms, is well located, very close to Il Campo (RS%, family rooms, breakfast extra, air-con May-Oct only, elevator, at Via delle Donzelle 3, +39 0577 288 088, www.hoteletruria.com, info@hoteletruria.com, friendly Leopoldo and Lucrezia). They also rent apartments nearby.

$ Albergo Tre Donzelle, run by the same family as Piccolo Hotel Etruria, has 20 homey rooms that may be the best value in the center. Il Campo, a block away, is your terrace (RS%, cheaper rooms with shared bath, family rooms, breakfast extra, fans, no elevator; with your back to the tower, head away from Il Campo toward 2 o'clock to Via delle Donzelle 5; +39 0577 270 390, www.tredonzelle.com, info@tredonzelle.com).

SIENA

SIENA

Siena Hotels & Restaurants

To Porta Camollia, Escalator to Train Station & 35

100 Meters
100 Yards

VIALE CESARE BATTISTI
VIALE VITTORIO VENETO
V. LUIGI CADORNA
VIALE AMANDO DIAZ
ISTRICE
VIA CAMOLLIA
GIARDINI LA LIZZA
VIALE RINALDO FRANCI
La Lizza
VIALE CESARE MACCARI
SOTTOPASSAGGIO LA LIZZA
Piazza Gramsci
VIALE DELLO STADIO
V. FEDERICO TOZZI

FORTEZZA

VIALE 25 APRILE

STADIO

DRAGO

VIALE VITTORIO VENETO
VIALE TRENTO
VIALE TRIESTE
VIA ENRICO TOTI
VIALE FILIPPO CORRIDONI
VIA ARTURO PANNILUNGHI
VIA GINO FRUSCHELLI
VIA BRUNO BONCI
VIA 24 MAGGIO
VIA MONTICCHIELLO
VIALE DEI MILLE
VIALE CURTATONE
V. DEL PARADISO
VIA D.

15

Piazza San Domenico

WC

V. CAMPOREGIO

18

STA CATERINA

SAN DOMENICO

Fonte Branda

VIA

16

PORTA FONTEBRANDA

SELVA

VIA ESTERNA DI FONTEBRANDA
ANCIENT CITY WALLS

NOTE: MUCH OF CENTRAL SIENA IS A PEDESTRIAN ZONE

VIA DI VALLEPIATTA
VIA FRANCIOSA
V. DEL

SAN SEB.

SANTA MARIA DELLA SCALA (MUSEUM)

PANTERA

Piazzetta delle Due Porte

Eateries & Nightlife

20 Osteria le Logge
21 Osteria la Sosta di Violante
22 Grotta Santa Caterina da Bagoga
23 Compagnia dei Vinattieri
24 Trattoria Papei
25 Ostaria il Carroccio
26 La Taverna di Cecco
27 Trattoria la Torre
28 Osteria del Gatto
29 Osteria il Grattacielo
30 Il Bandierino
31 Bar il Palio
32 Gelateria Costarella

33 Bar Paninoteca San Paolo
34 Key Largo Bar & Salumeria il Cencio
35 To Osteria il Vinaio & Trattoria Fonte Giusta
36 Consorzio Agrario di Siena
37 Antica Pizzicheria al Palazzo della Chigiana
38 Nannini Pastry Shop (2)
39 La Vecchia Latteria Gelato
40 Grom Gelato
41 Venchi Gelato
42 Il Camerlengo Gelato
43 The Tea Room
44 Morbidi

1
8
11
28
VIA PIAN MANTELLINI

Accommodations

1. Pensione Palazzo Ravizza
2. Hotel Palazzetto Rosso
3. Hotel Duomo
4. Antica Residenza Cicogna
5. Palazzo Masi B&B
6. Il Giardino di Pantaneto
7. B&B Palazzo Bruchi
8. B&B Alle Due Porte
9. Siena Gallery B&B
10. I Terzi di Siena
11. To Le Camerine di Silvia
12. Piccolo Hotel Etruria
13. Albergo Tre Donzelle
14. Hotel Cannon d'Oro
15. Hotel Chiusarelli
16. Hotel Villa Elda
17. Albergo Bernini
18. Alma Domus
19. Hotel Minerva

$ Hotel Cannon d'Oro, a few blocks up Banchi di Sopra, is a bland, labyrinthine slumbermill renting 30 institutional rooms (RS%, family rooms, fans, elevator with some stairs, Via dei Montanini 28, +39 0577 44321, www.cannondoro.com, info@cannondoro.com, Tommaso and Rodrigo).

NEAR BASILICA OF SAN DOMENICO

$$$ Hotel Chiusarelli, with a mix of 48 classic and modern rooms in a beautiful, frescoed Neoclassical villa, is just outside the medieval town center on a busy street—ask for a quieter room in back when you reserve (RS%, family rooms, air-con, limited free parking, across from San Domenico at Viale Curtatone 15, +39 0577 280 562, www.chiusarelli.com, info@chiusarelli.com).

$$$ Hotel Villa Elda rents 11 bright and light rooms in a recently renovated villa. It's classy, stately, and run with a stylish charm (view rooms extra, air-con, no elevator, garden and view terrace, closed Nov-March, Viale Ventiquattro Maggio 10, +39 0577 247 927, www.villaeldasiena.it, info@villaeldasiena.it).

$$ Albergo Bernini makes you part of a Sienese family in a modest, clean home with 10 traditional rooms. Giovanni, charming wife Daniela, and their daughters welcome you to their spectacular view terrace—a great spot for a glass of wine or a picnic (cheaper rooms with shared bath, family rooms, breakfast extra, fans, on the main Il Campo-San Domenico drag at Via della Sapienza 15, +39 0577 289 047, mobile +39 339 112 4113, www.albergobernini.com, info@albergobernini.com).

$ Alma Domus is a church-run hotel and a great value, featuring 49 tidy, streamlined rooms with quaint balconies, some fantastic views (ask for a room *con vista*), stately public rooms, and a pleasant atmosphere—though nearby church bells can be a drawback (family rooms, air-con, elevator; from San Domenico, walk downhill toward the view with the church on your right, turn left down Via Camporegio, make a U-turn down the brick steps to Via Camporegio 37; +39 0577 44177, www.hotelalmadomus.it, info@hotelalmadomus.it, Luigi).

FARTHER FROM THE CENTER

$$ Hotel Minerva is your big, impersonal, plain, efficient option. It's got zero personality and mediocre views, but offers predictable business-class comfort in its 56 rooms. It works best for those with cars—its pay parking is reasonable, and it's a 15-minute walk from the action (RS%, view rooms extra, air-con, elevator, just inside Porta Ovile at the north end of town at Via Garibaldi 72, +39 0577 284 474, www.albergominerva.it, info@albergominerva.it).

Eating in Siena

Sienese restaurants are a great value by Florence, Venice, or Rome standards. For pasta, a good option is *pici* (PEE-chee), a thick Sienese spaghetti that seems to be at the top of every menu. Reservations are wise for dinner.

IN THE OLD TOWN
Fine Dining

$$$$ Osteria le Logge caters to a fancy crowd and offers pricey Tuscan favorites with a gourmet twist, made with seasonal local ingredients. Inside you'll enjoy a gorgeous living-room setting, and outside there's fine seating on a pedestrian street. I find dining inside on the ground floor most romantic (Mon-Sat 12:00-15:00 & 19:00-23:00, closed Sun, two blocks off Il Campo at Via del Porrione 33, +39 0577 48013, www.osterialelogge.it, Mirko).

$$ Osteria la Sosta di Violante, beyond the tourist zone, is the best fine-dining value of my listings. You'll share this dreamy little spot with smart locals. For over 20 years, chefs Duccio and Enrico have offered artfully executed food with no pretense—they make sure diners feel right at home. Order with a sense of adventure. Diners with this book cap their meal with complimentary Vin Santo and *contucci* (great indoor and outdoor seating, Mon-Sat 12:30-15:00 & 19:00-23:00, closed Sun, walk down Via Banchi di Sotto to Via Pantaneto 115, +39 0577 43774).

$$$ Grotta Santa Caterina da Bagoga, tucked down a less-touristed lane below Il Campo, offers an all-around memorable experience. The cook (whose nickname, Bagoga, means "apricot" in the dialect of his native Montalcino) cultivates a menu that's traditional yet creative. The shareable *misto Bagoga* mixed-appetizer plate kicks off the meal nicely. The cave-like interior oozes with atmosphere; there are also some benches lining the stony lane outside (Tue-Sat 12:00-15:00 & 19:00-22:00, Sun 12:00-15:00 only, closed Mon, Via della Galluzza 26, +39 0577 282 208, www.ristorantebagoga.it).

$$$ Compagnia dei Vinattieri, a good bet for wine lovers, serves Tuscan dishes with a creative touch. In this dressy and sedate place, you can enjoy a romantic meal under graceful brick arches. The menu is small and accessible. Owner Marco is happy to take you down to the marvelous wine cellar (leave this book on the table for a complimentary *aperitivo* or *digestivo*, daily 12:30-15:00 & 19:30-23:00, Via delle Terme 79, +39 0577 236 568, www.vinattieri.net).

Traditional and Rustic Places

$$ Trattoria Papei is a sprawling place with festive outdoor seat-

SIENA

Gelato, Tea, and Cocktails in Siena

Evenings are a wonderful time to be out and about in Siena, after the tour groups have left for the day. Join the evening *passeggiata* (peak strolling time is 19:00) along Banchi di Sopra with gelato in hand.

Gelato: There's always a good gelato place nearby (all open daily, generally until late). A good locally owned option is **La Vecchia Latteria** (a 5-minute walk from Il Campo at Via di San Pietro 10). Two chains have outposts in Siena: **Grom** (across from Nannini at Banchi di Sopra 13) and **Venchi** (across from the Loggia della Mercanzia at Via di Città 28). For gelato on Il Campo, drop by the *bar gelateria* **Il Camerlengo** (at #6, just to the right of City Hall, with a handy WC).

Tea: The Tea Room is an artful ensemble of stone vaults, cozy furniture, lovingly presented pastries, and a long list of fine teas. Hiding out behind City Hall, it offers a tranquil escape (Tue-Sun 17:00-24:00, closed Mon, 200 yards below Il Campo, from the car park banister at the far end of Piazza del Mercato, look down and to the left, at Porta Giustizia 11, +39 0577 222 753).

***Aperitivo* Happy Hour:** As elsewhere in Italy, you'll find bars all over town attracting an early evening crowd by offering an *aperitivo*—a free buffet of snacks that's included with the purchase of a drink. For many, this happy-hour special (usually nightly 18:00-20:00) can make a light dinner. Some good ones to consider are: **Morbidi,** a trendy and youthful cocktail bar (closed Sun, Via Banchi di Sopra 75); the classic *caffè/pasticceria* **Nannini** (Via Banchi di Sopra 24, also a branch at Piazza Matteotti 15); and **Bar il Palio,** for cocktails and light bites on Il Campo (described below).

ing under a big tent and a high-energy interior. It has a casual, rollicking family atmosphere and friendly servers dishing out generous portions of rib-stickin' Tuscan specialties and grilled meats (daily 12:00-15:00 & 19:00-22:30, on the market square behind City Hall at Piazza del Mercato 6, +39 0577 280 894; Amedeo and Eduardo).

$$ Osteria il Carroccio, artsy and convivial, seats guests in a characteristic but tight dining room. They serve traditional "slow food" with innovative flair at affordable prices. To maintain their quality, they have only 35 seats and don't turn the tables—reserve ahead. They give complimentary Vin Santo and *contucci* with this book (Thu-Tue 12:15-15:00 & 19:15-22:00, closed Wed, Casato di Sotto 32, +39 0577 41165).

$$ La Taverna di Cecco is a cozy, comfortable little eatery on a quiet back lane where grandma Olga cooks, and earnest Luca and Gianni serve. The place settings feel like nana's finest, and the few tables outside are inviting as well. They offer a simple menu of traditional Sienese favorites along with hearty salads (daily 12:00-16:00 & 19:00-23:00, Via Cecco Angiolieri 19, +39 0577 288 518).

$$ Trattoria la Torre is an unfussy family-run *casalinga* (home-cooking) place, popular for its homemade pasta. Its open kitchen and 10 tables are packed under one medieval brick arch. Service is brisk and casual—the only menu is posted outside because they like to explain your options individually—and the food is simple but good. Though located just under the City Tower, it feels more like a local hangout than a tourist trap (Fri-Wed 12:00-15:00 & 19:00-22:00, closed Thu, steps below Il Campo at Via di Salicotto 7, +39 0577 287 548, Marco).

$ Osteria del Gatto is a classic neighborhood fixture thriving with townspeople and powered by a passion for good Sienese cuisine. Friendly Marco Coradeschi and his staff cook and serve daily specials with attitude. As it's so small and popular, it can get loud (Mon-Sat 12:30-15:00 & 19:30-22:00, closed Sun, 10-minute walk from Il Campo at Via San Marco 8, look for *La Vecchia Osteria* sign, +39 0577 287 133).

$ Osteria il Grattacielo is a funky hole-in-the-wall with a tight yet homey interior and three big tables under a tunnel-like arch outside. Luca, who's clearly found his niche in life, has no menu and just one solid house wine. You'll eat what he's cooking. Lunch is a mixed plate from the bar (be bold and point) or pasta (€10, includes wine). Dinner is three courses—antipasto bar, pasta, and a *secondi*—€20 for Rick Steves readers; €3 extra adds a Vin Santo-and-cookies finale (Mon-Sat 12:00-15:00 & 19:30-21:30, Sun 12:00-15:00 only, Via dei Pontani 8, +39 331 742 2835).

ON IL CAMPO

If you choose to dine on perhaps the finest town square in Italy, you'll pay a premium, meet waiters who don't need to hustle, and eat mediocre food. And yet, I recommend it. Survey the scene during your sightseeing day and reserve a table at the place that suits you. (All places listed are open daily for long hours.)

Dining and Drinks on the Square

$$$ Il Bandierino, with an angled view of City Hall, has solid food and no cover but a 20 percent service charge (Piazza del Campo 64, +39 0577 275 894).

$$$ Bar il Palio is the best bar on

Il Campo for a before- or after-dinner drink: It has straightforward prices, no cover, and a fine view (Piazza del Campo 47, +39 0577 282 055).

Drinks or Snacks Overlooking Il Campo

These places (all open daily until late) have skinny balconies with benches overlooking the main square for their customers.

$ Gelateria Costarella, on the corner of Via di Città and Costarella dei Barbieri, is a modern cocktail/gelato bar with a great little balcony over Il Campo—which is open to anyone ordering off their pricier menu (Via di Città 33).

$ Bar Paninoteca San Paolo has a youthful English-pub ambience and a row of stools overlooking the square. They have dozens of hearty sandwiches, big salads, and several beers on tap—it's not traditional Italian, but it's quick, filling, and available all day (order and pay at the counter, under the arch on Vicolo di San Paolo, +39 0577 226 622).

$ Key Largo Bar has a nondescript interior, but two long, upper-story benches in the corner offer a wonderful secret perch. Buy your drink or snack at the bar, climb upstairs, and open the ancient door (no cover and no extra charge to sit on the balcony). Enjoy stretching out, and try to imagine how, during the Palio, three layers of spectators cram into this space—notice the iron railing used to plaster the top row of sardines up against the wall. Suddenly you're picturing Palio ponies zipping wildly around the square's notoriously dangerous corner (closed Mon, on the corner at Via Rinaldini 17, +39 0577 236 339).

$ Salumeria il Cencio is a simple rustic sandwich shop with a tiny balcony upstairs (enter through back), where, for the takeout price, you can munch your humble meal (daily, near Key Largo Bar at the corner of Il Campo and Via del Porrione, +39 0577 283 007).

DINING WITH LOCALS, AWAY FROM THE CENTER

A pleasant 15-minute stroll north of Il Campo, Via Camollia—a continuation of the chic Via Banchi di Sopra and Via dei Montanini shopping streets—offers good eating options.

$$ Osteria il Vinaio—also called **Bobbe e Davide** for its owners—is my favorite in this area, at #167. Festooned with neighborhood memorabilia on the walls, it's an informal place—bright and fun—offering simple dishes at good prices from an inviting menu (Mon-Sat 19:00-22:00, closed Sun, +39 0577 49615).

$$ Trattoria Fonte Giusta, at #102, is a big, family-friendly eatery known for its grilled meat dishes (plenty of streetside tables, daily 12:00-23:00, +39 0577 40506).

EATING CHEAPLY IN THE CENTER

Consorzio Agrario di Siena gourmet market is a great place to assemble a cheap yet top-quality meal (salad and smoothie bar at the front, bakery/pizzeria at the back). Take a stool at the excellent pizzeria in the rear, or find a spot on the big comfy stone bench across the way on Piazza Salimbeni (Mon-Sat 8:00-20:00, Sun from 9:30, just off Piazza Matteotti, facing Piazza Salimbeni at Via Pianigiani 9).

DESSERTS AND TREATS

Siena's claim to caloric fame is its panforte, a rich, chewy concoction of nuts, honey, and candied fruits that impresses even fruitcake haters. There are a few varieties: *Margherita,* dusted in powdered sugar, is fruitier, while *panpepato* has a spicy, peppery crust. Locals also enjoy chewy, super-sweet, white macaroon-and-almond cookies called *ricciarelli*.

Nannini is the top-end, classic café and pastry shop every grandmother has fond memories of. It's ideally located in the center of the evening strolling scene a few blocks off Il Campo. For a special dessert or a sweet treat any time of day, stop by. The local specialties are around back at the far end of the bar (Mon-Sat 7:30-21:00, Sun until 19:00, *aperitivo* happy hour 18:00 until closing, Banchi di Sopra 24). There's also a branch at Piazza Matteotti 15.

Siena Connections

Siena has sparse train connections but is a handy hub for buses to the hill towns. For most, Florence is the gateway to Siena. The bus and train take about the same amount of time, but Siena's bus station is more convenient and central than its train station.

BY TRAIN

Siena's train station is at the edge of town. For details on getting between the town center and the station, see page 594.

From Siena by Train to: Florence (direct trains hourly, 1.5 hours), **Pisa** (2/hour, 1.5 hours, most change at Empoli), **Lucca** (approximately hourly, requires change either in Florence or in Pisa and Empoli, 2.5-3 hours), **Assisi** (10/day, about 4 hours, most involve 2 changes, bus is faster), **Rome** (1-2/hour, 3-4 hours, 1 change), **Orvieto** (12/day, 2.5 hours, change in Chiusi). Train info: Trenitalia.com.

BY BUS

Siena's intercity buses are operated by two companies. For each one, buses may use the handy-to-downtown stop at Piazza Gramsci (sometimes labeled *Via Tozzi* on schedules), or they may stop at the more distant train station (when possible, opt for Piazza Gramsci). The fastest buses are marked *rapida*.

Autolinee Toscane (AT) Buses: This company serves destinations throughout Tuscany (for timetables, see www.at-bus.it). Buy tickets at an Autolinee Toscane office, either inside the train station or in the underground passageway beneath Piazza Gramsci—look for stairwells, or take the elevator near the bus stops. You can also buy tickets from machines. Destinations include **Florence** (roughly 2/hour—fewer off-season, take the 1.5-hour *rapida/via superstrada* bus—*ordinaria* buses take longer; tickets available at tobacco shops/*tabacchi*; generally leaves from Piazza Gramsci as well as train station), **San Gimignano** (8/day direct, on Sun must change in Poggibonsi, 1.5 hours, from Piazza Gramsci), **Volterra** (4/day Mon-Sat, no buses on Sun, 2 hours, change in Colle di Val d'Elsa, leaves from Piazza Gramsci), **Montepulciano** (6-7/day, none on Sun, 1.5 hours, from train station), **Pienza** (6/day, none on Sun, 1.5 hours, from train station), **Montalcino** (6/day Mon-Sat, 4/day Sun, 1.5 hours, from train station or Piazza del Sale).

Flixbus Buses: This company serves destinations beyond Tuscany. Tickets can only be booked on their website (https://global.flixbus.com; you'll be emailed a QR code that you'll show as you board). Destinations include **Rome** (13/day, 3 hours, arrives at Rome's Tiburtina station on Metro line B with easy connections to the central Termini train station), **Naples** (6/day direct, 5.5 hours, one overnight bus), **Milan** (6-8/day direct, 5-7 hours, arrives at Milan's Lampugnano Metro station for the red line 1), **Assisi** (3/day direct, 2 hours, departs from Siena train station). To reach the town center of **Pisa**, the train is better (described earlier).

VOLTERRA & SAN GIMIGNANO

This fine duo of hill towns—perhaps Italy's most underrated and most overrated, respectively—sits just a half-hour drive apart in the middle of the triangle formed by Florence, Siena, and Pisa. San Gimignano is the region's glamour girl, getting all the fawning attention from passing tour buses. And a quick stroll through its core, in the shadows of its 14 surviving medieval towers, is a delight. But once you've seen it, you've seen it...and that's when you head for Volterra. Volterra isn't as eye-catching as San Gimignano, but it has unmistakable authenticity and surprising depth, richly rewarding travelers adventurous enough to break out of the San Gimignano rut. With its many engaging museums, Volterra offers the best sightseeing of all of Italy's small hill towns.

GETTING THERE

These towns work best for drivers, who can easily reach both in one go. Volterra is farther off the main Florence-Siena road, but it's near the main coastal highway connecting the north (Pisa, Lucca, and Cinque Terre) and south (Montalcino/Montepulciano and Rome). It's a little more than an hour's drive from Pisa or Florence.

If you're relying on public transportation, both towns are reachable—to a point. Visiting either one by bus from Florence or Siena requires a longer-than-it-should-be trek, often with a change (in Colle di Val d'Elsa for Volterra, in Poggibonsi for San Gimignano). Volterra can also be reached by a train-and-bus combination from La Spezia, Pisa, or Florence (transfer to a bus in Pontedera). See each town's "Connections" section for details.

San Gimignano is better connected, but Volterra merits the additional effort. Note that while these towns are only about a

Volterra & San Gimignano Area

30-minute drive apart, they're poorly connected to each other by public transit.

PLANNING YOUR TIME

Volterra and San Gimignano are a handy yin-and-yang pair. Ideally, you'll overnight in one town and visit the other either as a side trip or en route. Sleeping in Volterra lets you really settle into a charming burg with good restaurants, but it forces you to visit San Gimignano during the day, when it's busiest. Sleeping in San Gimignano lets you enjoy that gorgeous town when it's relatively quiet, but some visitors find it *too* quiet. Ultimately I'd aim to sleep in Volterra, and try to visit San Gimignano as early or late in the day as is practical to avoid crowds. Those with a car may choose to stay in the countryside between the two, visiting Volterra during the day and dining in San Gimignano at night.

Volterra

Encircled by impressive walls and topped with a grand fortress, Volterra perches high above the rich farmland surrounding it. More than 2,000 years ago, Volterra was an important Etruscan city, and much larger than we see today. Greek-trained Etruscan artists worked here, leaving a significant stash of art, particularly cinerary urns. Eventually Volterra was absorbed into the Roman Empire, and for centuries it was an independent city-state. Volterra fought bitterly against the Florentines, but like many Tuscan towns, it lost in the end and was given a Medici fortress atop the city to "protect" its citizens.

Unlike other famous towns in Tuscany, Volterra feels neither cutesy nor touristy...but real, vibrant, and almost oblivious to the allure of the tourist dollar. Millennia past its prime, Volterra seems to have settled into a well-worn groove; locals are resistant to change. At a town meeting about whether to run high-speed internet cable to the town, a local grumbled, "The Etruscans didn't need it—why do we?" This stubbornness helps make Volterra a refreshing change of pace from its more aggressively commercial neighbors. Volterra also boasts some interesting sights, from an ancient Roman theater, to a finely decorated Pisan Romanesque cathedral, to an excellent museum of Etruscan artifacts. And most evenings, charming Annie and Claudia give a delightful, one-hour guided town walk sure to help you appreciate their city (see "Tours in Volterra," later). All in all, Volterra is my favorite small town in Tuscany.

Orientation to Volterra

Compact and walkable, Volterra (pop. 10,000—6,000 inside the old wall) stretches out from the pleasant Piazza dei Priori to the old city gates and beyond. Be ready for some steep walking: While the spine of the city from the main square to the Etruscan Museum is fairly level, nearly everything else involves a climb.

TOURIST INFORMATION

The helpful TI is on the main square, at Piazza dei Priori 20 (daily 10:00-13:00 & 14:00-18:00, shorter hours off-season, +39 0588 87257, www.volterratur.it). They have bus schedules, a city map, and plenty of suggestions to keep you busy. Check the TI website for details on frequent summer festivals and concerts. Ignore the private travel agency, disguised as a TI, in the opposite corner of the piazza.

ARRIVAL IN VOLTERRA

By Public Transport: Buses stop at Piazza Martiri della Libertà in the town center. Train travelers can reach the town with a short bus ride from Pontedera, which has the nearest train station.

By Car: From Pisa, take the highway known as FI-PI-LI (for "Firenze-Pisa-Livorno") in the direction of Florence, exiting at

Pontedera to follow the scenic country road SR-439 toward Ponsacco and on to Volterra. From Florence, leave the city to the south to reach SR-2 toward Siena. Exit just past Poggibonsi onto SR-68 toward Colle di Val d'Elsa, passing the road to San Gimignano on the way to Volterra.

Don't drive into the town center; it's prohibited except for locals (and you'll get a huge fine). It's easiest to simply wind to the top where the road ends at Piazza Martiri della Libertà. (Halfway up the hill, there's a confusing hard right—don't take it; keep going straight uphill under the wall.) Immediately before the Piazza Martiri bus roundabout is the entry to *Parcheggio La Dogana* **underground garage** (€2/hour, €15/day, keep ticket and pay as you leave) that's within a few blocks of nearly all my recommended hotels and sights.

If the main garage is full, the police may direct you to other pay **lots** that ring the town walls (try the handy-but-small lot facing the Roman Theater and Porta Fiorentina gate). You can also pay to park outside the walls in any street spot marked with blue lines. Behind town, a lot named Docciola is free, but it requires a steep climb from the Porta di Docciola gate up into town.

If you're staying in town, check with your hotel about the best parking options.

HELPFUL HINTS

Volterra Card: This €15 card covers all the main sights—except for the Palazzo Viti (valid 72 hours, buy at TI or any covered sight). If traveling with kids, ask about the family card, an especially good deal (€24 for 1-2 adults and kids under 18).

Market Day: The market is on Saturday morning near the Roman Theater (8:00-13:00; Nov-March it moves to Piazza dei Priori). The TI hands out a list of other market days in the area.

Laundry: The handy self-service **Lavanderia Azzurra** is just off the main square (daily 7:00-22:00, Via Roma 7, +39 0588 80030). Their next-door dry-cleaning shop also provides wash-and-dry services that usually take about 24 hours (closed Sun).

Tours in Volterra

▲▲Guided Volterra Walk

Annie Adair and her colleague Claudia Meucci offer a great one-hour, English-only introductory walking tour of Volterra for €10. The walk touches on Volterra's Etruscan, Roman, and medieval history, as well as the contemporary cultural scene (daily April-Oct, rain or shine Mon, Wed, and Fri at 12:30, Tue, Thu, Sat, and Sun at 18:00; meet in front of alabaster shop on Piazza Martiri della Libertà, no need to reserve; www.volterrawalkingtour.com or www.tuscantour.com, info@volterrawalkingtour.com). There's no better way to spend €10 and one hour in this city. I mean it. Don't miss this beautiful experience.

Local Guides

American **Annie Adair** is an excellent guide for private, in-depth tours of Volterra (€180/half-day). Her husband **Francesco,** an easy-going sommelier and wine critic, and his team lead a Wine Tasting 101 crash course in sampling Tuscan wines (€60/hour per group, plus cost of wine). Annie and Francesco also offer excursions to a honey farm, alabaster quarry, and winery, or a more wine-focused trip to Montalcino or the heart of Chianti (about €450/day for 2-4 people, larger groups possible, +39 347 143 5004, www.tuscantour.com, info@tuscantour.com).

Sights in Volterra

I've linked these sights with handy walking directions.
• *Begin at the Etruscan Arch at the bottom of Via Porta all'Arco (about 4 blocks below the main square, Piazza dei Priori).*

▲Etruscan Arch (Porta all'Arco)

Volterra's renowned Etruscan arch was built of massive stones in the fourth century BC. The original city wall was four miles around—twice the size of today's wall.

Imagine: This city had 20,000 people four centuries before Christ. Volterra was a key trading center and one of 12 leading towns in the confederation of Etruria. The three seriously eroded heads, dating from the first century BC, show what happens when you leave something outside for 2,000 years. The newer stones are part of the 13th-century city wall, which incorporated parts of the much older Etruscan wall.

A plaque just outside remembers June 30, 1944. That night, Nazi forces were planning to blow up the arch to slow the Allied advance. To save their treasured landmark, Volterrans ripped up the stones that pave Via Porta all'Arco, plugged up the gate, and managed to convince the Nazi commander that there was no need to blow up the arch. Today, all the paving stones are back in their places, and like silent heroes, they welcome you through the oldest standing gate into Volterra. Locals claim this as the oldest surviving rounded arch of the Etruscan age; some experts believe this is where the Romans got the idea for using a keystone in their arches.

• *Go through the arch and head up Via Porta all'Arco, which I like to call...*

"Artisan Lane" (Via Porta all'Arco)

This steep and atmospheric lane is lined with interesting shops featuring the work of artisans and producers. Because of its alabaster heritage, Volterra developed a tradition of craftsmanship and artistry, and today you'll find a rich variety of handiwork (shops generally open Mon-Sat 10:00-13:00 & 16:00-19:00, closed Sun).

From the Etruscan Arch, browse your way up the hill, checking out these shops and items (listed from bottom to top): alabaster shop (#45); book bindery and papery (#26); jewelry (#25); etchings (#23); and bronze work (#6).

• *Reaching the top of Via Porta all'Arco, turn left and walk a few steps into Volterra's main square, Piazza dei Priori. It's dominated by the...*

Palazzo dei Priori

Volterra's City Hall, built about 1200, claims to be the oldest of any Tuscan city-state. It clearly inspired the more famous Palazzo Vecchio in Florence. Town halls like this are emblematic of the era of powerful city-states. They were architectural exclamation points declaring that, around here, no pope or emperor called the shots. Towns such as Volterra were truly city-states—proudly independent and relatively democratic. They had their own armies, taxes, and even weights and measures. Notice the horizontal "cane" cut into the City Hall wall (10 yards to the right of the door). For a thousand years, this square hosted a market, and the "cane" was the local yardstick.

Cost and Hours: €8, includes council chambers and tower climb, daily 9:00-19:00, Nov-mid-March until 16:30, tower closed in bad weather.

• *As you face the City Hall, find the little back door in the black-and-white striped wall (to the right), which leads into Volterra's cathedral.*

Duomo

This church is not as elaborate as its cousin in Pisa, but it is a beautiful example of the Pisan Romanesque style. The simple 13th-century facade conceals a more intricate interior (rebuilt in the late 16th and 19th centuries), with a central nave flanked by monolithic stucco columns painted to imitate pink granite and topped by a gilded, coffered ceiling. Just past the pulpit on the right (at the Rosary Chapel), check out the *Annunciation,* painted in 1497 by Mariotto Albertinelli and Fra Bartolomeo (both were students of Fra Angelico). The two, friends since childhood, delicately give worshippers a way to see Mary "conceived by the Holy Spirit." Note the vibrant colors, exaggerated perspective, and Mary's *contrapposto* pose—all attributes of the Renaissance.

Cost and Hours: €7 includes the Duomo, baptistery, and skippable old hospital where you buy your ticket, Mon-Sat 10:00-18:00, Sun from 13:30, shorter hours off-season.

• *Exit the cathedral through its "front" door and go right, circling all the way around the block to return to Piazza dei Priori. Exit the far end of the square; after one short block, you're standing at the head (on the left) of...*

▲Via Matteotti

The town's main drag, named after the popular Socialist leader Giacomo Matteotti (killed by the fascists in 1924), provides a good cultural scavenger hunt.

At #1, on the left, is a typical **Italian bank security door.** (Step in and say, "Beam me up, Scotty.") Back outside, stand at the corner and look up and all around. Find the medieval griffin torch-holder—symbol of Volterra, looking down Via Matteotti—and imagine it holding a flaming torch. The pharmacy kitty-corner sports the symbol of its medieval guild. Across the street from the bank, #2 is the base of what was a San Gimignano-style **fortified Tuscan tower.** Look up and imagine heavy beams cantilevered out, supporting extra wooden rooms and balconies crowding out over the street. Throughout Tuscany, today's stark and stony old building fronts once supported a tangle of wooden extensions.

As you head down Via Matteotti, notice how the doors show centuries of refitting work. Doors that once led to these extra rooms are now partially bricked up to make windows. Contemplate urban density in the 14th century, before the plague thinned out the population. Be careful: A **wild boar** (a local delicacy) awaits you at #10.

At #12, on the right, notice the line of doorbells: This typical **palace,** once the home of a single rich family, is now occupied by many middle-class families. After the social revolution in the 18th century and the rise of the middle class, former palaces were

Accommodations

1. Hotel San Lino
2. Hotel Volterra In
3. Hotel La Locanda
4. Albergo Nazionale
5. Albergo Etruria
6. To Park Hotel Le Fonti
7. La Primavera B&B
8. To Hotel Foresteria, Chiostro delle Monache Hostel & Trattoria da Badò

Eateries & Nightlife

9. Ristorante Enoteca del Duca
10. La Carabaccia
11. Ristorante il Sacco Fiorentino
12. La Vecchia Lira
13. Ristorante Ombra della Sera
14. Pizzeria La Mangiatoia
15. Pizzeria Ombra della Sera
16. Supermarket
17. L'Isola del Gusto Gelato
18. Antica Velathri Cafè

condominium-ized. Even so, the original family still lives here—apartment #1 is the home of Count Guidi.

On the right at #16, pop into the **alabaster showroom.** Alabaster, quarried nearby, has long been a big industry here. Volterra alabaster—softer and more translucent than marble—was sliced thin to serve as windows for Italy's medieval churches.

At #19, the recommended **La Vecchia Lira** is a lively restaurant. The **Bar L'Incontro** across the street is a favorite for breakfast

Volterra

100 Meters
100 Yards

VIA PORTA DIANA

PORTA FIORENTINA

VIA D'ANNUNZIO

SEMINARIO VESCOVILE SANT'ANDREA

V. VITTORIO VENETO

VIALE DEI FILOSOFI

VIA GUARNACCI

SAN MICHELE

VIA DI SOTTO

PORTA DI DOCCIOLA

CITY WALLS

VIA FONTE

S. AGOSTINO

V. ORTI DI

VIA PORTA MARCOLI

PORTA MARCOLI

VIA GRAMSCI

Piazza XX Settembre

SANT' AGOSTINO

ETRUSCAN MUSEUM

SAN PIETRO

VIA DI CASTELLO

Archaeological Park

ROCCA NUOVA

MEDICI FORTRESS

VIA DON MINZONI

PORTA A SELCI

To San Gimignano, Siena &

GARIBALDI

V. CARDUCCI

To 6

VOLTERRA & SAN GIMIGNANO

Other

19 Alab'Arte Alabaster Showroom
20 Alab'Arte Alabaster Workshop
21 "Artisan Lane"

22 La Vena di Vino Wine Tasting
23 Launderette
24 Guided Walk Meeting Point

and pastries; in the summer, they sell homemade gelato, while in the winter they make chocolates. In the evening, it's a bustling local spot for a drink.

Across the way, side-trip 10 steps up Vicolo delle Prigioni to the fun **Panificio Rosetti** bakery. They're happy to sell small quantities if you want to try the local *Cantuccini* (almond biscotti) or another treat.

Continue on Via Matteotti to the end of the block. Notice the bit of **Etruscan wall** artfully used to display more alabaster art (at #51).

Locals gather early each evening at **Osteria dei Poeti** (#57) for some of the best cocktails in town (served with free munchies). The cinema is across the street. Movies in Italy are rarely in their original language; Italians are used to getting their movies dubbed into Italian. To bring some culture to this little town, they also show live broadcasts of operas and concerts (advertised in the window).

Another **Tuscan tower** on the corner (#66) marks the end of the street. This noble house had a ground floor with no interior access to the safe upper floors. Rope ladders were used to get upstairs. The tiny door was wide enough to let in your skinny friends...but definitely not anyone wearing armor and carrying big weapons.

Across the little square stands the ancient **Church of St. Michael.** After long years of barbarian chaos, the Germanic Langobards moved in from the north in the sixth century and asserted law and order in places like Volterra. That generally included building a Christian church over the old Roman forum to symbolically claim and tame the center of town. The church standing here today is Romanesque, dating from the 12th century.

Around the right side, find the crude little guy and the smiling octopus under its eaves—they've been making faces at the passing crowds for 800 years.

• *When you reach the little* piazzetta *with a Romanesque church, turn left down Via dei Sarti. Our next stop—Palazzo Viti—is halfway down the block. But if you want to linger on the square for a bit, drop in for a glass of wine at* **Enoteca Scali** *(at Via Guarnacci 3), where friendly Massimo and Patrizia sell a vast selection of wines and local delicacies in an inviting atmosphere.*

▲Palazzo Viti

Palazzo Viti takes you behind the rustic, heavy stone walls of the city to see how the wealthy lived—in this case, rich from the 19th-century alabaster trade. This time warp is popular with Italian movie directors. With 12 rooms on one floor open to the public, Palazzo Viti feels remarkably lived in—because it is. Behind the ropes you'll see intimate family photos. You may well find Signora Viti herself selling admission tickets.

Cost and Hours: €5, Mon-Fri 10:30-17:00, Sat-Sun 10:00-17:30, by appointment only Nov-March, ask for an English brochure, Via dei Sarti 41, +39 0588 84047, www.palazzoviti.it, info@palazzoviti.it.

Visiting the Palazzo: The elegant interior is compact and well described. You'll climb up a stately staircase, buy your ticket, and head into the grand ballroom. From here, you'll tour the blue-hued dining room (with slice-of-life Chinese scenes painted on rice paper); the salon of battles (with warfare paintings on the walls); and the long hall of temporary exhibits. Looping back, you'll see the porcelain hall (decorated with priceless plates) and the inviting library (notice the delicate lamp with a finely carved lampshade).

The Brachettone Salon is named for the local artist responsible for the small sketch of near-nudes hanging just left of the door into the next room. Brachettone (from *brache,* "pants") is the nickname for the hometown 16th-century artist Daniele da Volterra, who owns the dubious distinction of having painted all those wispy loincloths over the genitalia of Michelangelo's figures in the *Last Judgment* at the Sistine Chapel. (In this drawing, notice a similar aversion to showing the full monty... though everything-but is fair game.) On the table, notice the family wedding photo with Pope John Paul II presiding. In the red room, a portrait of

Giuseppe Viti (looking like Pavarotti) hangs next to the exit door. He's the man who purchased the place in 1850. Your visit ends with bedrooms and a dressing room.

Your Palazzo Viti ticket sometimes gets you a fine little cheese, *salumi,* and wine tasting, typically in high season. As you leave the palace, climb down into the cool cellar (used as a disco on some weekends), where you can pop into a Roman cistern, marvel at an Etruscan well, and enjoy a friendly sit-down snack.

• *A block past Palazzo Viti, also on Via dei Sarti, is the...*

Pinacoteca and Alabaster Museum (Pinacoteca e Ecomuseo dell'Alabastro)

The Pinacoteca fills a 15th-century palace with fine paintings that feel more Florentine than Sienese—a reminder of whose domain this town was in. You'll see a stunning altarpiece by Taddeo di Bartolo, once displayed in the original residence. You'll also find roomfuls of gilded altarpieces and saintly statues, as well as a trio of striking High Renaissance altar paintings by Signorelli, Fiorentino, and Ghirlandaio.

The adjoining Alabaster Museum gives a fascinating overview of the local alabaster industry, past and present.

Cost and Hours: €8, daily 9:00-19:00, Nov-mid-March until 16:30, Via dei Sarti 1, +39 0588 87580.

• *Exiting the building, circle right along the side of the museum into the tunnel-like Passo del Gualduccio passage; then turn right and walk along the wall, enjoying views of the...*

Roman Theater (Teatro Romano)

With the fine aerial view from the city wall promenade, there's no reason to pay to enter this well-preserved, first-century theater

(although it is covered by the Volterra Card). The 13th-century wall that you're standing on divided the theater from the town center...so, naturally, the theater became the town dump. Over time, the theater was forgotten—covered in the garbage of Volterra. It was rediscovered in the 1950s and excavated.

The stage wall (immediately in front of the theater seats) was standard Roman design—with three levels from which actors would appear: one level for mortals, one for heroes, and the top one for gods. Parts of two levels still stand. Gods leaped out onto the third level for the last time around the third century AD, which is when the town began to use the theater stones to build fancy baths instead. You can see the scant remains of the baths behind the theater, including the little round sauna in the far corner with brick supports that raise the heated floor.

From this vantage point, you can trace Volterra's vast Etruscan wall. Find the church in the distance, on the left, and notice the stones just below. They are from the Etruscan wall that followed the ridge into the valley and defined Volterra in the fourth century BC.

• *From the theater viewpoint, continue along the wall downhill to the T-intersection (the old gate, Porta Fiorentina, with fine wooden medieval doors, is on your left). Turn right, making your way uphill on Via Guarnacci, which becomes Via Matteotti. A block up Via Matteotti, you can't miss the wide, pedestrianized shopping street called Via Gramsci. Follow this up to Piazza XX Settembre, walk through that leafy square, and continue uphill on Via Don Minzoni. At #18, you'll find an...*

▲Alabaster Showroom and Workshop

For a fun peek into the art of alabaster, visit the Alab'Arte show-

room, featuring the work of Roberto Chiti and Giorgio Finazzo. Lighting shows off the translucent quality of the stone and the expertise of these artists, who are delighted to share their work with visitors. If they're not in the showroom, the duo might be found at their nearby workshop (just down the narrow lane, Via Porta Marcoli, which runs next to the Etruscan Museum), where everything—including Roberto and Giorgio—is covered in a fine white dust. This is not a touristy guided visit, but something far more special: the chance to see busy artisans practicing their craft.

Cost and Hours: Free, showroom—daily 10:00-13:00 & 15:00-19:00, closes at 17:30 in off-season, closed Nov-Feb, Via Don Minzoni 18; workshop—Mon-Sat 10:00-12:30 & 15:00-19:00, closed Sun, if showroom is closed ask in the workshop, Via Orti Sant'Agostino 28, www.alabarte.com.

• *Next pay a visit to the...*

▲▲Etruscan Museum (Museo Etrusco Guarnacci)

Filled top to bottom with rare Etruscan artifacts, this museum—founded in 1732 (one of Italy's first public museums and among the oldest in Europe)—makes it easy to appreciate how advanced this pre-Roman culture was.

Cost and Hours: €8, daily 9:00-19:00, Nov-mid-March 10:00-16:30, Via Don Minzoni 15, +39 0588 86347, www.volterratur.it/en/poi/guarnacci-etruscan-museum.

Visiting the Museum: To see the exhibits in chronological order, take the elevator or stairs to the top floor and make your way down. Otherwise, start on the ground floor with some beautiful Etruscan urns and an inviting public garden out back.

The ground-floor collection starts with an introduction to the Etruscans and the history of the excavations carried out in this area. Filling the rest of the ground floor is a vast collection of stone Etruscan **cinerary urns** (seventh-first century BC). Etruscan urns have two parts: The box on the bottom contained the cremated remains (with elaborately carved panels), while the lid was decorated with a sculpture of the deceased. The carved bas-relief scenes and motifs decorating the urns are a prized catalog of Etruscan life and activities.

First pay attention to the people on top. While contemporaries of the Greeks, the Etruscans were more libertine. Their religion was less demanding, and their women were a respected part of both the social and public spheres. Women and men alike are depicted lounging on Etruscan urns. While they seem to be just hanging out, the lounging dead were actually offering the gods a banquet—in order to gain the Etruscan equivalent of salvation. Etruscans really did lounge like this in front of a table, but this banquet had eternal consequences. The dearly departed are often depicted holding blank wax tablets (symbolizing blank new lives in the next world). Men hold containers that would generally be used at banquets, including libation cups for offering wine to the gods. The women are finely dressed, sometimes holding a pomegranate (symbolizing fertility) or a mirror. Look at the faces and imagine the lives they lived.

Now tune into the reliefs carved into the fronts of the boxes. The motifs vary widely, from floral patterns to mystical animals (such as a Starbucks-like mermaid) to parades of magistrates. Some show journeys on horseback—appropriate for someone leaving this world and entering the next. Some show the fabled horseback-and-carriage ride to the underworld, where the dead are greeted by Charun, an underworld demon, with his hammer and pointy ears.

While the finer urns are carved of alabaster, most are made of limestone. Originally they were colorfully painted. Many lids are mismatched—casualties of reckless 18th- and 19th-century archaeological digs.

Head upstairs to the **first floor.** You'll enter a room with a circular mosaic in the floor (a Roman original, found in Volterra and transplanted here). To the left of the stairs, explore more Etruscan treasures in a series of rooms filled with urns depicting Greek myths and the voyage of Ulysses. A large room displays statues and inscriptions from the city's Roman Theater.

To the right of the stairs, fans of Alberto Giacometti will be amazed at how the tall, skinny figure called *The Evening Shadow* (*L'Ombra della Sera,* third century BC) looks just like the modern Swiss sculptor's work—but 2,500 years older. This is an example of the ex-voto bronze statues that the Etruscans created in thanks to the gods. With his supremely lanky frame, distinctive wavy hairdo, and inscrutable smirk, this Etruscan lad captures the illusion of a shadow stretching long, late in the day. Admire the sheer artistry and modernity of the statue.

The museum's other top piece is the *Urn of the Spouses* (*Urna degli Sposi,* first century BC). It's unique for various reasons, including its material (it's in terra-cotta—relatively rare for these urns) and its depiction of two people rather than one. Looking at this elderly couple, it's easy to imagine the long life they spent together and their desire to pass eternity lounging with each other at a banquet for the gods.

Other highlights include locally produced black-glazed pottery and painted kraters (vases with handles used for mixing water and wine), ex-voto water-bearer statues, bronze hand mirrors, exquisite golden jewelry that would still be fashionable today, a battle helmet ominously dented at the left temple, and hundreds of ancient coins.

The **top floor** features pieces from the Bronze Age and the early Etruscan period, including some impressive jewelry, the first examples of Etruscan writing, and the funeral dowry (artifacts that the dead would pack along and be buried with) of a warrior with his impressive helmet and remarkable double-spouted military flask for wine and water. Don't miss the re-created tomb, with several neatly aligned urns, a shattered eggshell, and more funeral dowries—including mirrors, coins, hardware for vases, votive statues, pots, pans, and jewelry.

• *After your museum visit, duck across the street to the...*

▲La Vena di Vino Wine Tasting

La Vena di Vino, just across from the Etruscan Museum, is a fun *enoteca* where Bruno and Lucio have devoted themselves to the won-

ders of wine and share it with a fun-loving passion. Each day they open six or eight bottles, serve your choice by the glass, and pair it with characteristic munchies amid unusual decor (the place is strewn with bras). Hang out here with the local characters. According to Bruno, a Brunello is just right with wild

boar and a Super Tuscan is perfect for meditation. Volterra can be quiet late at night, but this place is full of action (Wed-Mon 11:30-24:00, closed Tue, Nov-Feb open Fri-Sat only, Via Don Minzoni 30, +39 0588 81491, www.lavenadivino.com).

• *Volterra's final sight is perched atop the hill just above the wine bar. Climb up one of the lanes nearby, then walk (to the right) along the formidable wall to find the park.*

Medici Fortress and Archaeological Park (Fortezza Medicea and Parco Archeologico)

The archaeological park marks what was the acropolis of Volterra from 1500 BC until AD 1472, when Florence conquered the

pesky city. The Florentines burned Volterra's political and historic center, turning it into a grassy commons and building the adjacent Medici Fortress. The old fortress—a symbol of Florentine dominance—now keeps people in rather than out. It's a

maximum-security prison housing only about 120 special prisoners.

Under the Etruscan Sun
(c. 900 BC-AD 1)

Around 550 BC—just before the golden age of Greece—the Etruscan people of central Italy had their own golden age. Though their origins are unclear, the Etruscans' mix of Greek-style art with Roman-style customs helped lay a civilized foundation for the rise of the Roman Empire. As you travel through Italy—particularly in Tuscany (from "Etruscan")—you'll find traces of this long-lost people.

Etruscan tombs and artifacts are still being discovered, often by farmers in the countryside.

The Etruscans were established in central Italy by the early seventh century BC, when a number of settlements sprouted up in sparsely populated Tuscany and Umbria, including today's hill towns of Cortona, Chiusi, and Volterra. Possibly immigrants from Turkey, but more likely local farmers who moved to the city, they became sailors, traders, and craftsmen, and welcomed new ideas from Greece.

More technologically advanced than their neighbors, the Etruscans mined iron ore, smelting and exporting it around the Mediterranean. They drained and irrigated large tracts of land, creating the fertile farmland of central Italy's breadbasket. With their disciplined army, warships, merchant vessels, and (from the Greek perspective) pirate galleys, they ruled central Italy and the major ports along the Tyrrhenian Sea. For nearly two centuries (c. 700-500 BC), much of Italy lived in peace and prosperity under the Etruscan sun.

Judging from the frescoes and many luxury items that have survived, the Etruscans enjoyed the good life: They look healthy and vibrant as they play flutes, dance with birds, or play party games. Etruscan artists celebrated individual people, showing their wrinkles, crooked noses, silly smiles, and funny haircuts.

Scholars today have deciphered the Etruscans' Greek-style alphabet and some individual words, but they have yet to fully understand their language, which is unlike any other in Europe. Much of what we know of the Etruscans comes from their tombs. The tomb was a home in the hereafter, complete with the deceased's belongings. The urn might have a statue on the lid of the deceased at a banquet—lying across a dining couch, spooning with his wife, smiles on their faces, living the good life for all eternity.

Seven decades of wars with the Greeks (545-474 BC) disrupted their trade routes and drained the Etruscan League, just as a new Mediterranean power was emerging: Rome. In 509 BC, the Romans overthrew their Etruscan king, and Rome expanded, capturing Etruscan cities one by one (the last in 264 BC). Etruscan resisters were killed, the survivors intermarried with Romans, and their kids grew up speaking Latin. By Julius Caesar's time, the only remnants of Etruscan culture were its priests, who be-

The Etruscan Empire

Bologna
Ravenna
Adriatic Sea
Appenine Mountains
La Spezia
Florence ■ Fiesole
Arno R.
Pisa
Ligurian Sea
ETRUSCAN
Volterra (M)
Siena
Cortona (M)
Perugia
Murlo (M)
Chiusi (M)
Lake Trasimeno
Populonia
EMPIRE
■ Vetulonia
Orvieto (M)
■ Roselle
Bolsena
Elba
Lake Bolsena
Tyrrhenian Sea
Vulci
Tiber R.
Tarquinia ■
Veio
Cerveteri ■
Rome (M)

■ Etruscan Cities
● Modern Cities
(M) Etruscan Museum
— - Border of Tuscany

ITALY
100 Miles

came Rome's professional soothsayers. Interestingly, the Etruscan prophets had foreseen their own demise, having predicted that Etruscan civilization would last 10 centuries.

But Etruscan culture lived on in Roman religion (pantheon of gods, household gods, and divination rituals), art (realism), lifestyle (the banquet), and in a taste for Greek styles—the mix that became our "Western civilization."

Etruscan Sights in Italy

Rome: Traces of original Etruscan engineering projects (e.g., Circus Maximus), Vatican Museum artifacts, and Villa Giulia Museum, with the famous "husband and wife sarcophagus."

Orvieto: Archaeological Museum (coins, dinnerware, and a sarcophagus), necropolis, and underground tunnels and caves.

Volterra: Etruscan gate (Porta all'Arco, from fourth century BC) and Etruscan Museum (urns, pottery, and devotional figures).

The park sprawling next to the fortress (toward the town center) is a rare, grassy meadow at the top of a rustic hill town—a favorite place for locals to relax and picnic on a sunny day. Nearby are the scant remains of the acropolis, which can be viewed through the fence for free, or entered for a fee. Of more interest to antiquities enthusiasts is the acropolis' first-century Roman cistern. You can descend 40 tight spiral steps to stand in a chamber that once held about 250,000 gallons of water, enough to provide for more than a thousand people. While not huge, it provides a good look at Roman engineering and reminds you just how important a supply of water was to the survival of a hill town.

Cost and Hours: Park—free, open until 20:00 in peak of summer, shorter hours off-season; acropolis and cistern—€8, daily 10:30-17:30, shorter hours off-season.

Evening Scene

Passeggiata: As they have for generations, Volterrans young and old stroll during the cool of the early evening. The main cruising is along Via Gramsci and Via Matteotti to the main square, Piazza dei Priori.

Aperitivo: Each evening several bars put out little buffet spreads free with a drink to attract a crowd. Bars popular for their *aperitivo* include VolaTerra (Via Turazza 5, next to City Hall), L'Incontro (Via Matteotti 19), and Bar dei Poeti (across from the cinema, Via Matteotti 57). And the gang at La Vena di Vino (described under "Sights in Volterra") always seems ready for a good time.

Antica Velathri Cafè: Venture just a bit off the beaten path, between Piazza XX Settembre and the park, to Antica Velathri Cafè for a drink in the evening (or a light meal any time of the day). Pietro makes creative cocktails and good conversation while his mama makes the pastries (Tue-Sun 9:30-24:00, closed Mon, Via Ormanni 3, +39 0588 190 0121).

Sleeping in Volterra

Volterra has plenty of places offering a good night's sleep at a fair price. Lodgings outside the old town are generally a bit cheaper (and easier for drivers). But keep in mind that some of these places involve not just walking, but steep walking.

INSIDE THE OLD TOWN

$$$ Hotel San Lino fills a former convent with 40 modern rooms, all named for the nuns who lived in them. It's at the sleepy lower end of town—close to the Porta San Francesco gate, and about a five-minute uphill walk to the main drag. Although it's within the town walls, it doesn't feel like it: The hotel has a fine swimming pool and view terrace and is the only in-town option that's convenient for drivers, who can reserve pay parking in advance (RS%, family rooms, air-con, elevator, closed Nov-Feb, Via San Lino 26, +39 0588 85250, www.hotelsanlino.com, info@hotelsanlino.com).

$$$ Hotel Volterra In is fresh, tasteful, and in a central yet quiet location. Marco rents 10 bright and spacious rooms with thoughtful, upscale touches and a hearty buffet breakfast (RS%, air-con, elevator, Via Porta all'Arco 41, +39 0588 86820, www.hotelvolterrain.it, info@hotelvolterrain.it).

$$ Hotel La Locanda feels stately and old-fashioned. This well-located place (just inside Porta Fiorentina, near the Roman

Theater and parking lot) rents 18 rooms with flowery decor and modern comforts (RS%, family rooms, air-con, elevator, Via Guarnacci 24, +39 058 881 547, www.hotel-lalocanda.com, staff@hotel-lalocanda.com, Irina, Oksana, and Monica).

$$ Albergo Nazionale, with 36 big and overpriced rooms, is popular with school groups, and steps from the bus stop. It's a nicely located last resort if you have your heart set on sleeping in the old town (RS%, family rooms, elevator, Via dei Marchesi 11, +39 058 807 0681, www.allegroitalia.it, infonazionale@allegroitalia.it).

$ Albergo Etruria is a family-run hotel on Volterra's main drag. They offer a good location, a peaceful rooftop garden, and 19 frilly rooms (RS%, family rooms, air-con, Via Matteotti 32, +39 0588 87377, www.albergoetruria.it, info@albergoetruria.it, Paola, Daniele, and Sveva).

JUST OUTSIDE THE OLD TOWN

These accommodations are within a 5- to 20-minute walk of the city walls.

$$$ Park Hotel Le Fonti, a dull and steep 15-minute walk downhill from Porta all'Arco, can't decide whether it's a business hotel or a resort. The spacious, imposing building, old and stately, has 64 modern, comfortable rooms, half with views. While generally overpriced, it can be a good value if you manage to snag a deal. In addition to the swimming pool, guests can use its small spa (pay more for a view or a balcony, elevator, on-site restaurant, wine bar, free parking, Via di Fontecorrenti 2, +39 0588 85219, www.parkhotellefonti.com, info@parkhotellefonti.com).

$ La Primavera B&B feels like a British B&B transplanted to Tuscany. It's a great value just a few minutes' walk outside Porta Fiorentina (near the Roman Theater). Silvia rents five charming, neat-as-a-pin rooms that share a cutesy-country lounge. The house is set back from the road in a pleasant courtyard and with a garden to lounge in. With free parking and a short walk to the old town, this is a handy option for drivers (RS%, fans but no air-con, closed Nov-Feb, Via Porta Diana 15, +39 0588 87295, mobile +39 328 865 0390, www.affittacamere-laprimavera.com, info@affittacamere-laprimavera.com).

$ Hotel Foresteria, near Chiostro delle Monache (see next) and run by the same organization, has 35 big, utilitarian, new-feeling rooms with decent prices but the same location woes as the hostel; it's worth considering for a family with a car and a tight budget (family rooms, air-con, elevator, restaurant, free parking, Borgo San Lazzaro, +39 0588 80050, www.foresteriavolterra.com, info@foresteriavolterra.com).

¢ Chiostro delle Monache, Volterra's youth hostel, fills a wing of the restored Convent of San Girolamo. It's modern, spacious, and very institutional, with lots of services and a tranquil cloister. Unfortunately, it's about a 20-minute hike from town, in a boring area near deserted hospital buildings (private rooms available and include breakfast, family rooms, reception closed 13:00-15:00 and after 19:00, elevator, restaurant, free parking, kids' playroom; Via dell Teatro 4, look for hospital sign from main Volterra-San Gimi-gnano road; +39 0588 86613, www.chiostrodellemonache.com, info@chiostrodellemonache.it).

IN THE COUNTRYSIDE NEAR VOLTERRA

Charming farmhouse accommodations dot the countryside sur-rounding Volterra, and for drivers, these can be a good value and a fun experience. Some properties offer swimming pools, cooking classes, and more. For locations, see the map on page 636.

$$ Podere Marcampo is an *agriturismo* set in the dramatic landscape surrounding Volterra. Run by Genuino (owner of the recommended Ristorante Enoteca del Duca), his wife Ivana, and their English-speaking daughter Claudia, this peaceful spot has three dark but well-appointed rooms and three apartments, plus a swimming pool with panoramic views. Genuino and Claudia produce their Sangiovese and award-winning Merlot on site; you can tour where the wine is made and then sample it in their view tasting room. Cooking classes are available for guests and non-guests (breakfast included for Rick Steves readers, air-con, free self-service laundry, about two miles north of Volterra on the road to Pisa, +39 0588 85393, Claudia's mobile +39 328 174 4605, www.poderemarcampo.com, info@agriturismo-marcampo.com).

$$ **Agriturismo il Mulinaccio** is a welcoming, family-friendly farm about a five-minute drive down a dirt road outside Volterra. Hardworking Alessio and his family rent four spacious apartments and four bed-and-breakfast rooms, all with a cozy style. They also offer dinner, truffle hunts, cooking classes, wine tastings, and a spa/wellness center (air-con, pool, Via Vicinale di Pretenzano 49, +39 338 149 8432, www.agriturismoilmulinaccio.it, info@agriturismoilmulinaccio.it).

$$ **Agriturismo Santa Vittoria** sits on the top of a hill, with commanding views into the Volterra countryside. Their four bright apartments, decorated with funky art, have access to a cliffside pool. The popular restaurant serves up hearty dishes from their farm, served at view tables. Call ahead to confirm they are open (week-long stays preferred in summer, breakfast extra, Localita Molino d'Era, hotel +39 348 561 3670, restaurant +39 348 561 3670, www.agriturismosantavittoria.com, info@agriturismosantavittoria.com, Katuscia).

Eating in Volterra

Menus feature a Volterran take on regional dishes. *Zuppa alla Volterrana* is a fresh vegetable-and-bread soup. *Torta di ceci*, also known as *cecina*, is a savory crêpe-like garbanzo-bean flatbread that's served at pizzerias. Those with more adventurous palates dive into *trippa* (tripe stew, the traditional breakfast of the alabaster carvers). *Fegatelli* are meatballs made with liver.

$$$$ **Ristorante Enoteca del Duca,** serving well-presented and creative Tuscan cuisine, offers the best elegant meal in town. You can dine under a medieval arch with walls lined with wine bottles, in a sedate, high-ceilinged dining room (with an Etruscan statuette at each table), in their little *enoteca* (wine cellar), or in their terraced garden in summer. The friendly staff take good care of diners. The fine wine list includes Genuino and Claudia's own highly regarded Merlot and Sangiovese. The spacious seating, dressy clientele, and calm atmosphere make this a good choice for a romantic splurge. Their €70 food-sampler fixed-price meal comes with a free glass of wine for diners with this book (Wed-Mon 12:30-14:45 & 19:30-21:45, closed Tue, reservations smart, near City Hall at Via di Castello 2, +39 0588 81510, www.enoteca-delduca-ristorante.it).

$$ **La Carabaccia** is unique: It feels like a local family invited you over for a dinner of classic Tuscan comfort food that's rarely seen on restaurant menus. They serve only two pastas and two *secondi* on any given day (listed on the chalkboard by the door), in addition to quality cheese and cold-cut plates. Committed to tradition, on Fridays they serve only fish. They also have fun,

family-friendly outdoor seating on a traffic-free piazza (Tue-Sat 12:30-14:30 & 19:30-22:00, Sun 12:30-14:30, closed Mon, reservations smart, Piazza XX Settembre 4, +39 0588 86239, Patrizia and daughters Sara and Ilaria).

$$ Ristorante il Sacco Fiorentino is a family-run local favorite for traditional cuisine and seasonal specials. While mostly indoors, the restaurant has a few nice tables on a peaceful street (Thu-Tue 12:00-15:00 & 19:00-22:00, closed Wed, Via Giusto Turazza 13, +39 0588 88537, Cristina).

$$ Trattoria da Badò, a 10-minute hike out of town, is popular with a local crowd for its *cucina tipica Volterrana*. Giacomo and family offer a rustic atmosphere and serve food with no pretense— "the way you wish your mamma cooks." Reserve before you go, as it's often full, especially on weekends (Thu-Tue 12:30-14:30 & 19:30-22:00, closed Wed, Borgo San Lazzero 9—along the main road toward San Gimignano, near the turnoff for the old hospital, +39 0588 80402, www.trattoriadabado.com).

$$ La Vecchia Lira, bright and cheery, is a classy eatery that's a hit with locals looking for fresh fare and a focus on gluten-free and vegetarian options (Fri-Wed 12:00-14:30 & 19:00-22:00, closed Thu, Via Matteotti 19, +39 0588 86180, Massimo).

$$ Ristorante Ombra della Sera is another good fine-dining option for elegant Tuscan cuisine and truffle dishes. While they have a dressy interior, I'd eat here to be on the street and part of the *passeggiata* action (Tue-Sun 12:00-15:00 & 19:00-22:00, closed Mon and mid-Nov-mid-March, Via Gramsci 70, +39 0588 86663, Massimo and Cinzia).

$$ Pizzeria La Mangiatoia is a fun and convivial place with a Tuscan-cowboy interior and picnic tables outside amid a family-friendly street scene. Enjoy pizzas, huge salads, and kebabs at a table or to go (Thu-Tue 11:00-23:00, closed Wed, Via Gramsci 35, +39 0588 85695).

$ Pizzeria Ombra della Sera dishes out what local kids consider the best pizza in town (Tue-Sun 12:00-15:00 & 19:00-22:00, closed Mon and mid-Nov-mid-March, Via Guarnacci 16, +39 0588 85274).

Picnic: You can assemble a picnic at the few grocery stores around town and eat in the breezy archaeological park. The most convenient supermarket is **Punto Simply** at Via Gramsci 12 (Mon-Sat 7:30-13:00 & 16:00-20:00, Sun 8:30-13:00).

Gelato: Of the many ice-cream shops in the center, I've

found **L'Isola del Gusto** to be reliably high quality, with flavors limited to what's in season (daily, closed Nov-Feb, Via Gramsci 3, cheery Giorgia will make you feel happy).

Volterra Connections

By Bus: In Volterra, buses come and go from Piazza Martiri della Libertà (buy tickets at the tobacco shop right on the piazza or on board). Most connections are through Colle di Val d'Elsa ("koh-leh" for short), a workaday town in the valley (4/day Mon-Sat, 1/day Sun, 50 minutes); for Pisa, you'll change in Pontedera or Saline di Volterra. Ask at the TI for schedules or check www.at-bus.it.

From Volterra, you can ride the bus to these destinations: **Florence** (4/day Mon-Sat, 1/day Sun, 2 hours, change in Colle di Val d'Elsa), **Siena** (4/day Mon-Sat, no buses on Sun, 2 hours, change in Colle di Val d'Elsa), **San Gimignano** (4/day Mon-Sat, 1/day Sun, 2 hours, change in Colle di Val d'Elsa, one connection also requires change in Poggibonsi), **Pisa** (9/day, fewer on Sun, 2 hours, change in Pontedera).

By Train: The nearest train station is in Saline di Volterra, a 15-minute bus ride away (7/day, 2/day Sun); however, trains from Saline run only to the coast, not to the major bus destinations listed here. It's better to take a bus from Volterra to Pontedera (8/day, 1 on Sun, 1.5 hours), where you can catch a train to **Florence, Pisa,** or **La Spezia** (convenient for the Cinque Terre).

By Private Transfer: For those with more money than time, or for travel on tricky Sundays and holidays, a private transfer to or from Volterra is the most efficient option. **Roberto Bechi** and his drivers can take up to eight people in their comfortable vans (€165 to Siena, €185 to Florence, for reservations call +39 320 147 6590 or Roberto's mobile +39 328 425 5648, www.toursbyroberto.com, toursbyroberto@gmail.com.

San Gimignano

The epitome of a Tuscan hill town, with 14 medieval towers still standing (out of an original 72), San Gimignano (sahn jee-meen-YAH-noh) is a perfectly preserved tourist trap. There are no important interiors to sightsee, and the town feels greedy and packed with crass commercialism. The locals seem spoiled by the easy money of tourism, and most of the rustic is faux. But San Gimignano is so easy to reach and so visually striking that it remains a good stop, especially if you can sidestep some of the hordes. The town is an ideal place to go against the touristic flow—arrive late in the day, enjoy it at twilight, then take off in the morning before the deluge begins. (Or day-trip here from Volterra—a 30-minute drive away—and visit early or late.)

In the 13th century—back in the days of Romeo and Juliet—feuding noble families ran the hill towns. They'd periodically battle things out from the protection of their respective family towers. Pointy skylines like San Gimignano's were the norm in medieval Tuscany.

San Gimignano's cuisine is mostly what you might find in Siena—typical Tuscan home cooking. *Cinghiale* (cheen-gee-AH-lay, boar) is served in almost every way: stews, soups, cutlets, and, my favorite, *salumi*. The area is well known for producing some of the best saffron in Italy; you'll find the spice for sale in shops and as a flavoring in meals at finer restaurants. Although Tuscany is normally a red-wine region, the most famous Tuscan white wine comes from here: the inexpensive, light, and fruity Vernaccia di San Gimignano.

Orientation to San Gimignano

While the basic ▲▲▲ sight here is the town of San Gimignano itself (pop. 7,800, just 2,000 of whom live within the walls), there are a few worthwhile stops. The wall circles an amazingly preserved stony town, once on the Via Francigena pilgrimage route to Rome. The road, which cuts through the middle of San Gimignano, is named for St. Matthew in the north of town (Via San Matteo) and St. John in the south (Via San Giovanni). The town is centered on two delightful squares—Piazza del Duomo and Piazza della Cisterna—where you find the town well, City Hall, and cathedral (along with most of the tourists).

TOURIST INFORMATION
The helpful TI, in the old center on Piazza del Duomo, sells bus tickets to Siena and Florence (daily 10:00-13:00 & 15:00-19:00,

VOLTERRA & SAN GIMIGNANO

San Gimignano

Accommodations
1. Hotel l'Antico Pozzo
2. Le Undici Lune
3. Locanda il Pino
4. Hotel la Cisterna
5. Palazzo al Torrione
6. Terra d'Ombra & Le Vecchie Mura Ristorante
7. To Locanda dei Logi
8. To Podere Ponte a Nappo

Eateries & Other
9. Dulcis in Fundo Ristorante
10. Trattoria Chiribiri
11. Locanda di Sant'Agostino
12. Supermarket
13. Gelateria Dondoli

Nov-Feb 10:00-13:00 & 14:00-18:00, +39 0577 940 008, www.
sangimignano.com). They offer occasional countryside tours and a
guided city tour (€15, April-Oct Mon, Wed, Fri-Sat at 11:00 and
16:00, Sun at 11:00).

ARRIVAL IN SAN GIMIGNANO

The **bus** stops at the main town gate, Porta San Giovanni. There's
no baggage storage in town.

You can't **drive** within the walled town; drive past the *"ZTL"*
red circle and you'll get socked with a big fine. Three numbered
pay lots are a short walk outside the walls (and connected to town
by a shuttle bus in summer; see below): The handiest is Parcheggio Montemaggio (P2), at the bottom of town near the bus stop,
just outside Porta San Giovanni (€2/hour, €15/day). Least expensive but a steeper walk into town is the lot below the roundabout
and Co-op supermarket, Parcheggio Giubileo (P1; €1.50/hour,
€6/day). And at the north end of town, by Porta San Jacopo, is
Parcheggio Bagnaia (P3/P4, €2/hour, €15/day). Note that some
lots—including the one directly in front of Co-op and the one just
outside Porta San Matteo—are designated for locals and have a
one-hour limit for tourists.

HELPFUL HINTS

Market Day: Thursday is market day on Piazza del Duomo and
Piazza delle Erbe (8:00-13:00), but for local merchants, every
day is a sales frenzy.

Services: A public WC is just off Piazza della Cisterna; you'll also
find WCs at the Rocca fortress, near San Bartolo church, just
outside Porta San Matteo, and at the Parcheggio Bagnaia
parking lot.

Shuttle Bus: A little electric shuttle bus does its laps about hourly
all day from Porta San Giovanni to Piazza della Cisterna to
Porta San Matteo. Route #1 runs back and forth through
town; route #2—which runs only in summer—connects the
parking lots to the town center (€1.20 one-way). When pedestrian congestion in the town center is greatest (Sat afternoons,
all day Sun, and May-Sept), the bus runs along the road skirt-
ing the outside of town.

San Gimignano Walk

This quick self-guided walking tour takes you across town, from the
bus stop at Porta San Giovanni through the town's main squares to
the Duomo, and on to the Sant'Agostino Church.

• *Start at the Porta San Giovanni gate at the bottom (south) end of*
town.

Porta San Giovanni

San Gimignano lies about 25 miles from both Siena and Florence, a day's trek for pilgrims en route to those cities, and on a naturally fortified hilltop that encouraged settlement. The town's walls were built in the 13th century, and gates like this helped regulate who came and went. Today, modern posts keep out all but service and emergency vehicles. The small square just outside the gate features a memorial to the town's WWII dead. Follow the pilgrims' route (and flood of modern tourists) through the gate and up the main drag.

About 100 yards up, where the street widens, look right to see a pilgrims' shelter (12th century, Pisan Romanesque). The eight-pointed Maltese cross on the facade of the church indicates that it was built by the Knights of Malta, whose early mission (before they became Crusaders) was to provide care for sick and poor pilgrims. It was one of 11 such shelters in town. Today, only the wall of the shelter remains, and the surviving interior of the church houses yet one more shop selling gifty edibles.

• *Carry on past all manner of shops, up to the top of Via San Giovanni. Look up at the formidable inner wall, built 200 years before today's outer wall. Just beyond that is the central Piazza della Cisterna. Sit on the steps of the well.*

Piazza della Cisterna

The piazza is named for the cistern that is served by the old well standing in the center of this square. A clever system of pipes drained rainwater from the nearby rooftops into the underground cistern. This square has been the center of the town since the ninth century. Turn in a slow circle and observe the commotion of rustic yet proud facades crowding in a tight huddle around the well. Imagine this square in pilgrimage times, lined by inns and taverns for the town's guests. Now finger the grooves in the lip of the well and imagine generations of women and children fetching water. Each Thursday morning, the square fills with a market—as it has for more than a thousand years.

• *Notice San Gimignano's famous towers.*

The Towers

Of the original 72 towers, only 14 survive (and one can be climbed—at the City Hall). Some of the original towers were just empty, chimney-like structures built to boost noble egos, while others were actually the forts of wealthy families.

Before effective city walls were developed, rich people needed to fortify and protect their homes themselves. These towers provided a handy refuge when ruffians and rival city-states were sacking the town. If under attack, tower owners would set fire to the external wooden staircase, leaving the sole entrance unreachable a story up; inside, fleeing nobles pulled up behind them the ladders that connected each level, leaving invaders no way to reach the stronghold at the tower's top. These towers became a standard part of medieval skylines. Even after town walls were built, the towers continued to rise—now to fortify noble families feuding within a town (Montague and Capulet-style).

In the 14th century, San Gimignano's good times turned very bad. At the start of that century, about 13,000 people lived within the walls. But in 1348, a six-month plague decimated the population, leaving the once-mighty town with barely 4,000 survivors. Once fiercely independent, now crushed and demoralized, San Gimignano came under Florence's control and was forced to tear down most of its towers. (The Banca CR Firenze building occupies the remains of one such toppled tower.) And, to add insult to injury, Florence redirected the vital trade route away from San Gimignano. The town never recovered, and poverty left it in an architectural time warp. That well-preserved 14th-century cityscape, ironically, is responsible for the town's prosperity today.

• *From the well, walk 30 yards uphill to the adjoining square with the cathedral.*

Piazza del Duomo

Stand at the base of the stairs in front of the church. Since before there was gelato, people have lounged on these steps. Take a 360-degree spin clockwise: The cathedral's 12th-century facade is plain-Jane Romanesque—finished even though it doesn't look it. To the right, the two Salvucci Towers date from the 13th century. (Locals claim that the architect who designed New York City's Twin Towers was inspired by these). The towers are empty shells, built by the wealthy Salvucci family simply to show off. At that time, no one was allowed a vanity tower higher than the City Hall's 170 feet. So the Salvuccis built two 130-foot towers—totaling 260 feet of stony ego trip.

The stubby tower next to the Salvucci Towers is the Merchant's Tower. Imagine this in use: ground-floor shop, warehouse upstairs (see the functional shipping door), living quarters, and finally the kitchen on the top (for fire-safety reasons). The holes in the walls held beams that supported wooden balconies and exterior staircases. The tower has heavy stone on the first floor, then cheaper and lighter brick for the upper stories.

Opposite the church stands the first City Hall, with its 170-foot tower, nicknamed "the bad news tower." While the church got to ring its bells in good times, these bells were for battles and fires. The tower's arched public space hosted a textile market back when cloth was the foundation of San Gimignano's booming economy.

Next is the super-size "new" City Hall with its 200-foot tower (the only one in town open to the public; for visiting info, see the Civic Museum and Tower listing, later). The climbing lion is the symbol of the city. The coats of arms of the city's leading families have been ripped down or disfigured. In medieval times locals would have blamed witches or ghosts. For the last two centuries, they've blamed Napoleon instead.

Between the City Hall and the cathedral, a statue of St. Gimignano presides over all the hubbub. The fourth-century bishop protected the village from rampaging barbarians—and is now the city's patron saint. (To enter the cathedral, walk under that statue.)
• *You'll also see the...*

Duomo (Duomo di San Gimignano/La Collegiata)

The nave of San Gimignano's Romanesque cathedral is lined with frescoes that tell the stories of the Bible—Old Testament on the left and New Testament on the right. Painted by masters of the 14th-century Sienese school, the frescoes are a classic use of teaching through art, with parallel themes aligned: Creation faces the Annunciation, the birth of Adam is opposite the Nativity, and—farther forward—the suffering of Job faces the agony of Jesus. Many scenes are portrayed with a 14th-century "slice of life" setting to help lay townspeople relate to Jesus.

To the right of the altar, the St. Fina Chapel honors the devout, 13th-century local girl who brought forth many miracles on her death. Her tomb is beautifully frescoed with scenes from her life by Domenico Ghirlandaio (famed as Michelangelo's teacher). The altar sits atop Fina's skeleton, and its centerpiece is a reliquary that contains her skull (€5, includes dry audioguide; April-Oct Mon-Fri 10:00-19:30, Sat until 17:00, Sun 12:30-19:30; shorter

VOLTERRA & SAN GIMIGNANO

hours off-season; buy ticket and enter from courtyard around left side, www.duomosangimignano.it).

• *From the church, hike uphill (passing the church on your left) following signs to* Rocca e Parco di Montestaffoli. *Keep walking until you enter a peaceful hilltop park and olive grove, set within the shell of a 14th-century fortress the Medici of Florence built to protect this town from Siena.*

Hilltop Views at the Rocca

On the far side, 33 steps take you to the top of a little tower (free) for the best views of San Gimignano's skyline; the far end of town and the Sant'Agostino Church (where this walk ends); and a commanding 360-degree view of the Tuscan countryside. San Gimignano is surrounded by olives, grapes, cypress trees, and—in the Middle Ages—lots of wild dangers. Back then, farmers lived inside the walls and were thankful for the protection.

• *Return to the bottom of Piazza del Duomo, turn left, and continue your walk, cutting under the double arch (from the town's first wall).*

In around 1200, this wall defined the end of town. The **Church of San Bartolo** stood just outside the wall (on the right). The Maltese cross over the door indicates that it likely served as a hostel for pilgrims. As you continue down Via San Matteo, notice that the crowds have dropped by at least half. Enjoy the breathing room as you pass a fascinating array of stone facades from the 13th and 14th centuries—now a happy cancan of wine shops and galleries.

• *Reaching the gateway at the end of town, follow signs to the right to find...*

Sant'Agostino Church

This tranquil church, at the far end of town (built by the Augustinians who arrived in 1260), has fewer crowds and more soul. Behind the altar, a lovely fresco cycle by Benozzo Gozzoli (who painted the exquisite Chapel of the Magi in the Medici-Riccardi Palace in Florence) tells of the life of St. Augustine, a North African monk who preached simplicity (pay a few coins for light). The kind, English-speaking friars (often from Britain and the US) are happy to tell you about the frescoes and their way of life. Pace the peaceful cloister before heading back into the tourist mobs (free, April-Oct daily 10:00-12:00 & 15:00-19:00, shorter hours off-season; Sunday Mass in English at 11:00).

Sights in San Gimignano

▲Civic Museum and Tower (Musei Civici and Torre Grossa)

This small, entertaining museum, consisting of three unfurnished rooms, is inside the City Hall (Palazzo Comunale). The main reason to visit is to scale the tower, which offers sweeping views over San Gimignano and the countryside.

Cost and Hours: €9 includes museum and tower; daily 10:00-19:30, Oct-March 11:00-17:30, Piazza del Duomo, +39 0577 990 312, www.sangimignanomusei.it.

Visiting the Museum: You'll enter the complex through a delightful stony courtyard (to the left as you face the Duomo). Climb up to the loggia to buy your ticket.

The main room (across from the ticket desk), called the **Sala del Consiglio** (a.k.a. Dante Hall, recalling his visit in 1300), is covered in festive frescoes, including the *Maestà* by Lippo Memmi (from 1317). This virtual copy of Simone Martini's *Maestà* in Siena proves that Memmi didn't have quite the same talent as his famous brother-in-law. The art gives you a peek at how people dressed, lived, worked, and warred back in the 14th century.

Upstairs, the **Pinacoteca** displays a classy little painting collection of mostly altarpieces. The highlight is a 1422 altarpiece by Taddeo di Bartolo honoring St. Gimignano (far end of last room). You can see the saint, with the town—bristling with towers—in his hands, surrounded by events from his life.

Before going back downstairs, be sure to stop by the **Mayor's Room** (Camera del Podestà, across the stairwell from the Pinacoteca). Frescoed in 1310, it offers an intimate and candid peek into the 14th century. As you enter, look right up in the corner to find a young man ready to experience the world. He hits his parents up for a bag of money and is on his way. Suddenly (above the window), he's in trouble, entrapped by two prostitutes, who lead him into a tent where he loses his money, is turned out, and is beaten. Above the door, from left to right, you see a parade of better choices: marriage, the cradle of love, the bride led to the groom's house, and newlyweds bathing together and retiring hap-

pily to their bed.

The highlight for most visitors is a chance to climb the **Tower** (entrance halfway down the stairs from the Pinacoteca). The city's tallest tower, 200 feet and 218 steps up, rewards those who climb it with a commanding view. See if you can count the town's 14 towers. It's a sturdy, modern staircase most of the way, but the last stretch is a steep, ladder-like climb.

▲Campatelli Tower House (Torre e Casa Campatelli)

The Campatelli family, wealthy landowners from Florence, bought an age-old tower and adjacent properties in the 19th century and turned them into a palatial residence. They lived here until 2005, when the last of the family donated it to a nonprofit organization that protects heritage buildings and gardens, which opened it to the public. The house contains family belongings and tells the story of upper-class life in Tuscany, but the highlights are an audiovisual presentation on the history of the city and the chance to peer up through the tower, with a cutaway staircase and floor, to see how the towers in San Gimignano were built.

Cost and Hours: €7, Tue-Sun 10:30-19:00, closed Mon, shorter hours Oct-Feb, Via San Giovanni 15, +39 0577 941 419, www.fondoambiente.it/luoghi/beni-fai.

San Gimignano 1300

Artists and brothers Michelangelo and Raffaello Rubino share an interesting attraction in their workshop: a painstakingly rendered 1:100 scale clay model of San Gimignano at the turn of the 14th century. Step through a shop selling their art to enjoy the model. You can see the 72 original "tower houses," and marvel at how unchanged the street plan remains today. You'll peek into cross-sections of buildings, view scenes of medieval life both within and outside the city walls, and watch a video about the making of the model.

Cost and Hours: Free, donations appreciated, daily 10:00-18:00, Dec-April until 17:00, on a quiet street a block over from the main square at Via Costarella 3, +39 327 439 5965, www.sangimignano1300.com.

Sleeping in San Gimignano

Although the town is a zoo during the daytime, locals outnumber tourists when evening comes, and San Gimignano becomes mellow and enjoyable.

NEAR PORTA SAN MATTEO, AT THE QUIET END OF TOWN

If arriving by bus, save yourself a crosstown walk to these accommodations by asking for the Porta San Matteo stop. Drivers can park at the less-crowded Bagnaia lots (P3 and P4), and walk around to Porta San Matteo.

$$$ Hotel l'Antico Pozzo is an elegantly restored, 15th-century townhouse with 18 tranquil, comfortable rooms, a peaceful interior courtyard terrace, and an elite air (RS%—use code RICK, family rooms, air-con, elevator, Via San Matteo 87, +39 0577 942 014, www.anticopozzo.com, info@anticopozzo.com; Emanuele, Elisabetta, and Mariangela).

$$ Le Undici Lune ("The 11 Moons") is situated in a tight but characteristic circa-1300 townhouse with steep stairs at the tranquil end of town. Its seven rooms are colorfully decorated (air-con, Via Mainardi 9, +39 328 053 5922, https://leundicilunesangimignano.it, info@leundicilune.it, Vincenzo).

$ Locanda il Pino has just seven rooms and a big living room. It's plain but clean and quiet. Run by English-speaking Elena and her family, it sits above their elegant restaurant just inside Porta San Matteo (fans, Via Cellolese 4, +39 0577 907 003, www.locandailpino.it, locandailpino@gmail.com).

NEAR THE MAIN SQUARE, AT THE BUSY END OF TOWN

$$ Hotel la Cisterna, right on Piazza della Cisterna, feels old and stately. Its 48 rooms range from old-fashioned to more modern. It's worth paying extra for the contemporary rooms with panoramic views (RS%, family rooms, air-con, elevator, good restaurant with great view, closed Jan-Feb, Piazza della Cisterna 23, +39 0577 940 328, www.hotelcisterna.it, info@hotelcisterna.it, Alessio and Paola).

$$ Palazzo al Torrione, on an untrampled side street just inside Porta San Giovanni, is quiet and handy. Their 10 modern rooms, some with countryside views and terraces, are spacious and tastefully appointed (RS%, family rooms, breakfast extra, air-con, inside and left of gate at Via Berignano 76; +39 0577 940 375, www.palazzoaltorrione.com, info@palazzoaltorrione.com, Vanna).

$ Terra d'Ombra offers three good rooms above the recommended Le Vecchie Mura Ristorante, along a rustic lane just below the main square (no breakfast, air-con, Via Piandornella 15, +39 366 106 0631, www.terradombra.net, terradombra2022@gmail.com, Bagnai family).

IN THE COUNTRYSIDE

$$$$ Locanda dei Logi, in the tiny *borgo* of San Donato—eight minutes from San Gimignano—houses six ultramodern luxury rooms within a cluster of medieval buildings. Each room is elegantly designed, and all look out over the property's vineyard. Wine lovers can combine an overnight and a tasting of their top-notch wines in their cantina (wine tastings available by appointment, lunch and dinner on request, air-con, plunge pool, Localita San Donato 1, +39 392 506 8229, www.locandadeilogi.it, info@locandadeilogi.it).

VOLTERRA & SAN GIMIGNANO

$$ Podere Ponte a Nappo, run by enterprising Carla Rossi and her English-speaking sons Francesco and Andrea, has six basic rooms and two apartments in a kid-friendly farmhouse boasting fine San Gimignano views. Located a mile below town, it can be reached by foot in about 20 minutes if you don't have a car. A picnic dinner lounging on their comfy garden furniture next to the big swimming pool as the sun sets is good Tuscan living (RS%—use code "RickSteves," onsite restaurant and cooking classes, air-con, free parking, +39 0577 907 282, mobile +39 349 882 1565, www. accommodation-sangimignano.com, info@rossicarla.it). About 100 yards below the monument square at Porta San Giovanni, find tiny Via Baccanella/Via Vecchia and drive downhill. They also rent a dozen rooms and apartments on the main square in town.

Eating in San Gimignano

My first two listings cling to quiet, rustic lanes overlooking the Tuscan hills; the rest are buried deep in the old center.

$$$ Dulcis in Fundo Ristorante, small and family-run, proudly serves modest portions of "revisited" Tuscan cuisine (with a modern twist and gourmet presentation) in a jazzy ambience. This enlightened place uses top-quality ingredients, many of which come from their own farm (Thu-Tue 12:30-14:30 & 19:15-21:45, closed Wed and Nov-Feb, Vicolo degli Innocenti 21, +39 0577 941 919, Cristina).

$$ Le Vecchie Mura Ristorante is welcoming, with good service, great prices, tasty if unexceptional home cooking, and the ultimate view. It's romantic indoors or out. They have a dressy, modern interior where you can dine with a view of the busy stainless-steel kitchen under rustic vaults, but the main reason to come is for the incredible cliffside garden terrace. To reserve a cliffside table, call or drop by: Ask for "front view" (open only for dinner 18:00-22:00 and lunch some weekends, closed Tue, reservations smart, Via Piandornella 15, +39 0577 940 270, Bagnai family).

$ Trattoria Chiribiri, just inside Porta San Giovanni, serves homemade pastas and desserts at good prices. While its petite size and tight seating make it hot in the summer, it's a good budget option—and as such, it's in all the guidebooks (daily 11:00-23:00, Piazza della Madonna 1, +39 0577 941 948, Roberto and Maurizio).

$ Locanda di Sant'Agostino spills out onto the peaceful square, facing Sant'Agostino Church. It's homey and cheerful, serving lunch and dinner daily—big portions of basic food in a restful setting. Dripping with wheat stalks and atmosphere on the inside, it has shady on-the-square seating outside (Thu-Tue 11:00-16:00 & 18:30-23:00, closed Wed, closed Jan-Feb, Piazza Sant'Agostino 15, +39 0577 943 141, Genziana and sons).

Near Porta San Matteo: Just inside Porta San Matteo is a variety of handy and inviting good-value restaurants, bars, cafés, and gelato shops.

Picnics: The big, modern **Co-op supermarket** sells all you need for a nice spread (Mon-Sat 8:00-20:00, closed Sun, at parking lot below Porta San Giovanni). Or browse the little shops guarded by boar heads within the town walls; they sell pricey boar meat *(cinghiale)*. Pick up 100 grams (about a quarter pound) of boar, cheese, bread, and wine and enjoy a picnic in the garden at the Rocca or the park outside Porta San Giovanni.

Gelato: To cap the evening and sweeten your late-night city stroll, stop by **Gelateria Dondoli** on Piazza della Cisterna (at #4, daily 9:00-23:00, until 19:00 in winter, +39 0577 942 244, Dondoli family). Charismatic Sergio also offers hands-on gelato-making classes in his kitchen down the street (www.gelateriadondoli.com).

San Gimignano Connections

Bus tickets are sold at the bar just inside the town gate or at the TI. Many connections require a change at Poggibonsi (poh-jee-BOHN-see), which has the nearest train station. Note that the bus connection to Volterra is four times as long as the drive; if you're desperate to get there faster, you can pay about €70 for a taxi.

From San Gimignano by Bus to: Florence (hourly, fewer on Sun, 1.5-2 hours, change in Poggibonsi), **Siena** (8/day direct, on Sun must change in Poggibonsi, 1.5 hours), **Volterra** (4/day Mon-Sat; 1/day Sun—in the late afternoon and usually crowded—with no return to San Gimignano; 2 hours, change in Colle di Val d'Elsa, one connection also requires change in Poggibonsi).

By Car: San Gimignano is an easy 45-minute drive from Florence (take the A-1 exit marked *Firenze Imprugneta*, then a right past tollbooth following *Siena per 4 corsie* sign; exit the freeway at *Poggibonsi Nord*). From San Gimignano, it's a scenic and windy half-hour drive to Volterra.

THE HEART OF TUSCANY

Montepulciano • Pienza • Montalcino • Heart of Tuscany Drive

If your Tuscan dreams feature vibrant neon-green fields rolling to infinity, punctuated by snaking, cypress-lined driveways; humble but beautiful (and steep) hill towns; and world-class wines to make a connoisseur weep, set your sights on the heart of this region.

An hour south of Siena, this slice of splendor—which specializes in views and wine—is a highlight, particularly for drivers. With an astonishing diversity of towns, villages, abbeys, wineries, countryside restaurants, and accommodations—all set within jaw-dropping scenery—this subregion of Tuscany is a fine place to abandon your itinerary and just slow down.

Even though the area's towns sometimes seem little more than a rack upon which to hang the vine-draped hills, each one has its own endearing personality. The biggest and most interesting, Montepulciano, boasts a medieval cityscape wearing a Renaissance coat, wine cellars that plunge deep into the cliffs it sits upon, and a classic town square. Pienza is a sure-of-itself, planned Renaissance town that gave the world a pope. And mellow Montalcino is (even more than most towns around here) all about its wine: the famous Brunello di Montalcino.

PLANNING YOUR TIME

As this compact region is hemmed in by Italy's two main north-south thoroughfares—the A-1 expressway and SR-2 highway—even those with a few hours to spare can get an enticing taste. But ideally, spend two nights and three full days.

Montepulciano is the most all-around engaging town; it's the best choice for those without a car (though connections can still be tricky). With easy access to the vineyards, Montalcino makes sense for wine pilgrims. For drivers who'd like to home-base in the countryside, I've listed several *agriturismi* and other rural accommodations.

The Heart of Tuscany in Three Days

Here's a smart plan, assuming you're coming from Siena. (If coming from the south, do it in reverse.)

Day 1: On your way south from Siena, make a winery stop north of Montalcino before settling into Montepulciano (or your countryside accommodation).

Day 2: Follow my Heart of Tuscany Drive, including a sightseeing-and-gelato stop in Pienza. Have dinner in Montepulciano, or in the nearby countryside.

Day 3: Your day is free to enjoy and sightsee Montepulciano, or drive to countryside attractions. You could head to your next destination this afternoon, or spend a third night.

GETTING AROUND THE HEART OF TUSCANY

By Car: This area is ideal by car. Distances are short, and it's easy to mix-and-match sights.

Navigate by town names and use a good map or a mapping app to keep you on track. Be aware that GPS will usually take you on the most direct route—not always the most scenic. Some sights and wineries are on tiny back lanes, marked only with easy-to-miss, low-profile signs. Many of the small towns in this area are designated as "ZTL" (limited-traffic zone)—off-limits to nonlocal traffic. Make it a habit to park at the lot just outside town and walk in. White lines indicate free parking; blue lines indicate paid parking (pay and display the ticket on your windshield); and yellow lines are only for locals.

By Public Transportation: While you can reach many of this chapter's sights by public buses, connections are slow, infrequent, and often require a transfer. Taxis can help connect the dots more efficiently. Montepulciano is the best home base for those without a car (though it's still not entirely convenient).

TOURS IN TUSCANY

A good local guide can help you take full advantage of everything this area has to offer. One with a car can save you lots of time and stress.

Antonella Piredda is smart, well organized, and enjoyably opinionated (from €60/hour, 3-hour minimum, she can join you in your car or hire a driver for extra, mobile +39 347 456 5150, www. antonellapiredda.com, antonella.piredda@live.it).

Roberto Bechi runs all-day minibus tours with a passion for local culture, hands-on experiences, and offbeat sights. The price is reasonable, since he assembles groups of up to eight people to share the experience...and the cost (see website for tour options, RS%-10 percent discount, full-day minibus tours-€100/person, mobile +39 320 147 6590, www.toursbyroberto.com, toursbyroberto@gmail. com). For more on Roberto's tours, see page 602.

COUNTRYSIDE ACCOMMODATIONS

A beautiful way to more fully experience this area is to sleep in a farmhouse B&B. For locations, see the "Heart of Tuscany" map. Many of these are working farms (a prerequisite to be officially called an *agriturismo*) and give a great sense of rural family life. Others are just lovely homes in the countryside. The beautiful common denominator about these listings is the wonderful people you'll meet as your hosts.

Near Pienza

On the outskirts of untouristy **Castelmuzio** (five miles north of

Heart of Tuscany at a Glance

▲▲▲**Montepulciano** Hill town with grand vistas, wonderful wine cellars, and a medieval soul that corrals the essence of Tuscany within its walls. See page 676.

▲▲▲**Heart of Tuscany Drive** An unforgettable day lacing together the views, villages, and rural attractions of this region (including both Montepulciano and Pienza). See page 710.

▲▲**Pienza** Unique, pint-sized planned Renaissance town that's amazingly well preserved, very touristy, and relatively unhilly. See page 692.

▲▲**Montalcino** Touristy "Brunello-ville" wine capital that still exudes a stony charm; aside from the wine, it feels like a second-rate repeat of Montepulciano. See page 700.

▲▲**Sleeping at an *Agriturismo* or Countryside B&B** The best way to experience rural Tuscany: rustic, rural accommodations ranging from fragrant working farms to luxurious retreats. Most are run by families dedicated to making sure their cows and their guests are both well-fed. See page 673.

▲**La Foce Gardens** Delightful, unique gardens with gorgeous plantings, engaging history, and fine panoramas. See page 714.

▲**Bagno Vignoni** Quirky little spa town that's simply fun to check out, whether you take a dip or not. See page 715.

Pienza), **$$$$ La Moscadella** (a.k.a. The Isabella Experience), is a luxurious countryside oasis run by Isabella and her team. It comes with 12 impeccably decorated rooms and a two-bedroom cottage, plus a gourmet-quality restaurant (also open to non-guests—see page 699). Isabella excels at creating vivid cultural experiences, from pasta-rolling classes to olive oil tastings. This is an excellent value for those seeking a beautifully curated Tuscan experience (weeklong stays preferred but may be flexible, air-con, elevator, swimming pool, +39 0577 665 516, mobile +39 338 740 9245, www.theisabellaexperience.com, info@theisabellaexperience.com).

Isabella rents two other properties nearby, in the village of Castelmuzio: **$$$ Le Casine di Castello,** a townhouse with two units, and **$$$$ Casa Moricciani,** a swanky villa with dreamy views and a garden terrace. She also works closely with Agriturismo Cretaiole (see below). For Isabella's help navigating your options, call or email her.

$$$ Agriturismo Cretaiole is rustic yet comfortable and idyllically set, perched on a ledge in an olive grove just outside of Pienza. Three generations of the farming Moricciani family—Luciano, Carlo, and Nicco—enjoy hosting travelers here. They even let their guests pick from the vegetable garden. The one-week minimum stay (Sat to Sat) facilitates a community feeling among the 20 or so guests and includes a variety of hands-on activities, from farm tours to olive oil tastings to pasta-making classes (some coordinated via the Isabella Experience, described earlier; no air-con, swimming pool, or breakfast; shorter stays may be possible off-season, +39 0577 665 516 or +39 338 740 9245, www.cretaiole. it, info@cretaiole.it).

$$$ Fonte Bertusi, a classy and artistic guesthouse between Pienza and Cretaiole, is nicely run by young couple Manuela and Andrea, Andrea's artist-father Edoardo, and their attention-starved cats. The eight apartments mix rustic decor with avant-garde creations. The setting is sublime, with a grand sunset-view terrace, a communal barbecue and outdoor kitchen, and a swimming pool (laundry service, outside Pienza toward San Quirico d'Orcia on the right—just after the turnoff for "Il Fonte," +39 0578 748 077, Manuela's mobile +39 339 655 5648, www.fontebertusi.it, info@ fontebertusi.it).

Near Montepulciano

$$$$ Relais Ortaglia, run by Americans Sandy, Phil (who was a Disney animator), and dog Cooper, rents five pricey rooms in a converted 17th-century farmhouse on the outskirts of Montepulciano. While preserving a rustic ambience, they offer modern amenities such as an infinity pool, activities (cooking classes), and a free bottle of prosecco for my readers. Well-organized Sandy keeps guests busy with her favorite experiences in the area (includes breakfast, 2-night minimum, air-con, mobile +39 391 163 9887, www.relaisortaglia.com, tuscany@ortaglia.it). Leaving Montepulciano on the main road toward Pienza, watch for the easy-to-miss brown *Ortaglia* sign on the left, just a half-mile past the San Biagio church turnoff.

$$ La Bruciata is a family-friendly *agriturismo* charmingly tucked into the countryside a five-minute drive outside Montepulciano (on the way to Pienza). Can-do Laura and several generations of her family produce wine and olive oil and rent several tasteful, modern rooms that share a peaceful yard with a swimming pool. From April through October, they prefer one-week stays (pay air-con, farm-fresh meals, cooking classes, Via del Termine 9, +39 0578 757 704, mobile +39 339 781 5106, www.agriturismolabruciata.it, info@agriturismolabruciata.it). Leaving Montepulciano toward Pienza, turn off on the left for *Poggiano*, then carefully track brown *La Bruciata* signs (on gravel roads).

$$$ B&B Palazzolo La Foce lets you sleep aristocratically in a small villa just below the La Foce Gardens, south of Montepulciano. Its seven colorful rooms share a welcoming lounge and breakfast area with a giant fireplace, and an outdoor swimming pool with glorious Tuscan views. All the rooms bask in fine panoramas (air-con, Strada della Vittoria 61—but check in at gardens' main entrance to get specific directions to your room, villas also available, +39 0578 69101, www.lafoce.com, info@lafoce.com, Origo family).

Near Montalcino

$$ La Crociona, an *agriturismo* farm and working vineyard, rents seven fully equipped and simple apartments with dated furnishings. Fiorella Vannoni and Roberto and Barbara Nannetti offer cooking classes and tastes of the Brunello wine grown and bottled on the premises (reception open 9:00-13:00 & 14:30-19:30, no air-con, breakfast extra, laundry service, pool, hot tub, fitness room, La Croce 15, +39 0577 847 133, www.lacrociona.com, info@lacrociona.com). The farm is about two miles south of Montalcino on the road to the Sant'Antimo Abbey; don't turn off at the first entrance to the village of La Croce—wait for the second one, following signs to *Tenuta Crocedimezzo e Crociona*. A good restaurant is next door.

Montepulciano

Curving its way along a ridge, Montepulciano (mohn-teh-puhl-CHAH-noh) delights visitors with *vino*, views, and—perhaps more than any other large town in this area—a sense of being a real, bustling community rather than just a tourist depot.

Alternately under Sienese and Florentine rule, the city still retains its medieval *contrade* (districts), each with a mascot and flag. The neighborhoods compete the last Sunday of August in the Bravio delle Botti, where teams of men push large wine casks uphill from Piazza Marzocco to Piazza Grande, all hoping to win a banner and bragging rights. The entire last week of August is a festival:

Each *contrada* arranges musical entertainment and serves food at outdoor eateries, along with generous tastings of the local *vino*.

The city is a collage of architectural styles, but the elegant San Biagio Church, just outside the city walls at the base of the hill, is its best Renaissance building. Most visitors ignore the architecture and focus more on the city's other creative accomplishment, the tasty Vino Nobile di Montepulciano red wine.

Montepulciano is a great starting and ending point for my scenic loop drive through the Heart of Tuscany, described later in this chapter.

Orientation to Montepulciano

Commercial action in Montepulciano centers in the lower town, mostly along Via di Gracciano nel Corso (nicknamed "Corso"). This stretch begins at the town gate called Porta al Prato (near the TI, bus station, and some parking) and winds slowly up, up, up through town—narrated by my self-guided walk. Strolling here, you'll find eateries, gift shops, and tourist traps. The back streets are worth exploring. The main square, at the top of town (up a steep switchback lane from the Corso), is Piazza Grande. Standing proudly above all the touristy sales energy, the square has a noble, Florentine feel.

TOURIST INFORMATION

The helpful TI is hidden below the Porta al Prato city gate, in the small P1 parking lot (Mon-Sat 9:00-13:00 & 14:00-19:00, Sun 9:00-13:00, sells train tickets, Piazza Don Minzoni, +39 0578 757 341, www.prolocomontepulciano.it). A TI branch inside the Palazzo Comunale sells tickets to climb its tower and has a good map of wine producers in the Vino Nobile di Montepulciano area (daily 10:00-18:00).

The office on the main square that looks like a TI, near the well, is actually the privately run Valdichiana Living tour agency. They provide wine-road maps, wine tours in the city, minibus winery tours farther afield, and cooking classes and other culinary experiences (Mon-Fri 10:00-13:30 & 14:30-18:00, shorter Sat hours, Sun 10:00-13:00, Piazza Grande 7, +39 0578 717 484, www. valdichianaliving.it).

ARRIVAL IN MONTEPULCIANO

Whether you arrive by car or bus, ease your climb to the top of town by riding the shuttle bus. For details, see "Helpful Hints," later.

By Car: Well-signed pay-and-display parking lots ring the city center (marked with blue lines). Some free street parking is mixed in (marked with white lines)—look around before you park, and keep an eye out for time limits.

To start your visit by following my self-guided walk (up the length of the Corso to the main square), park at the north end of town, near the Porta al Prato gate. Around here, the handiest lots are P1 (in front of the TI, with some free spaces) and the unnumbered lot just above, directly in front of the stone gate. If these are full, try lots P2, P4, or P5 (all near the bus station).

For quicker access to the main square up top, use one of the parking lots at the top end of town: Approaching Montepulciano, follow signs for *centro storico*, *duomo*, and *Piazza Grande*, and use the Fortezza or San Donato lots (flanking the fortress).

Avoid "ZTL" no-traffic zone (signs marked with a red circle). If you're sleeping in town, your hotelier can give you a permit to park within the walls; be sure to get very specific instructions before you arrive.

By Bus: Buses leave passengers at the bus station on Piazza Nenni, downhill from the Poggiofanti Gardens. From the station, cross the street and head inside the gritty orange-brick structure burrowed into the hillside, where there's an elevator. Ride to level 1, walk straight down the corridor (following signs for *centro storico*), and ride a second elevator (to a different level 1 and the Poggiofanti Gardens); walk to the end of this park and hook left to find the Porta al Prato gate. If the elevator isn't working, take the stairs, or hop on the shuttle bus (see "Helpful Hints," next).

HELPFUL HINTS

Market Day: It's on Thursday morning (8:00-13:00), near the bus station.

Services: There's no official **baggage storage,** but the TI below the Porta al Prato gate might let you leave bags with them if they have space. Public **WCs** are located at the TI, to the left of Palazzo Comunale, and at the Sant'Agostino Church.

Shuttle Buses: To avoid the hike up through town to Piazza

Montepulciano

Accommodations
1. La Locanda di San Francesco & E Lucevan le Stelle Wine Bar
2. Palazzo del Mercante
3. Mueblè il Riccio
4. Albergo Duomo
5. Vicolo dell'Oste B&B
6. Camere Bellavista

Eateries
7. Ost. dell'Acquacheta
8. Osteria del Conte
9. Le Pentolaccia
10. Ai Quattro Venti
11. La Schiaccia dell'Opio
12. Sgarbi Gelato Natura
13. To La Grotta

Other
14. Copper Shop
15. Copper Workshop
16. Contucci Cantina
17. De' Ricci Cantine
18. Cantina della Talosa
19. Launderette
20. Valdichiana Living Tours

Ⓑ Local Shuttle Bus

HEART OF TUSCANY

Grande, hop on the orange shuttle bus. It departs about every 30 minutes from the parking lot near the bus station and from the lane leading to the Porta al Prato gate, just above the TI (€1.20, buy tickets at bus station or tobacco shop). Some buses also go to San Biagio Church—confirm with the driver.

Laundry: An elegant self-service launderette, **Lavabenincasa,** is at the top of town at Via del Paolino 2, just around the corner from the recommended Camere Bellavista (daily 8:00-22:00, +39 0578 717 544).

Taxis: Two English-speaking taxi drivers operate in Montepulciano. Call +39 330 732 723 for short trips within town (€10 for rides up or down hill); to reach other towns, call +39 348 733 5343.

Montepulciano Walk

This two-part self-guided walk traces the spine of the town from its main entrance up to its hilltop seat of power. Part 1 begins at the big gate at the bottom of town, Porta al Prato (near the TI and several parking lots); Part 2 focuses on the square at the very top of town and the nearby streets. Part 1 is steeply uphill; to skip straight to the more level part of town (and Part 2), ride the shuttle bus up, or park at one of the lots near the Fortezza. (When you're done there, you can still do Part 1—backwards—on the way back down.)

PART 1: UP THE CORSO

This guided stroll takes you up through Montepulciano's commercial (and touristy) gamut from the bottom of town to the top. While the street is lined mostly with gift shops, you'll pass a few relics of an earlier age.

Begin in front of the imposing **Porta al Prato,** one of the many stout city gates that once fortified this highly strategic town. Walk directly through the Porta al Prato, looking up to see the slot where the portcullis (heavily fortified gate) could slide down to seal things off. Notice that there are two gates, enabling defenders to trap would-be invaders in a no-man's-land where they could be doused with hot tar. Besides having a drop-down portcullis, each gate also had a hinged door—effectively putting four barriers between the town and its enemies.

Pass through the gate and head a block uphill to reach the **Colonna del Marzocco.** This column, topped with a lion holding the Medici shield, is a reminder that Montepulciano existed under the auspices of Florence—but only for part of its history.

The column is also the starting point for Montepulciano's masochistic tradition, the **Bravio delle Botti,** held on the last Sunday of August, in which each local *contrada* (neighborhood) selects its two stoutest young men to roll a 180-pound barrel up the hill through town. If the vertical climb through town wears you out, be glad you're only toting a daypack. Do you see colorful flags lining the street? If so, you'll notice you're in the Gracciano *contrada*, symbolized by the green, black, and yellow lion. Notice how the flags change with the neighborhood as you continue through town.

A few steps up, on the right (at #91, with stylized lion heads), is one of the many fine noble palaces that front Montepulciano's main strip. The town is fortunate to be graced with so many bold and noble *palazzi*—Florentine nobility favored Montepulciano as a breezy and relaxed place for a secondary residence. The higher you go in Montepulciano, the closer you are to the town center...and the fancier the mansions.

Farther up on the right, at #73 (Palazzo Bucelli), take a moment to examine the **Etruscan and Roman fragments** embedded in the wall, left here by a 19th-century antiques dealer. You can quickly distinguish which pieces came from the Romans and those belonging to the earlier Etruscans by their alphabets: The "backwards" Etruscan letters (they read from right to left) resemble Greek. Many of the fragments show a circle flanked by a pair of inward-facing semicircular designs. This symbol represents the libation cup used for drinking at an Etruscan banquet.

At the top of the block, just after the recommended Sgarbi Gelato Natura shop, is the **Church of Sant'Agostino.** Its late-Gothic facade features a terra-cotta sculpture group by the architect Michelozzo, a favorite of the Medicis in Florence. The interior is a clean, serene, white-and-beige space.

Hike up a few more steps, then take a breather to look back and see the **clock tower** in the middle of the street. The bell ringer at the top takes the form of the character Pulcinella, one of the wild and carefree revelers familiar from Italy's commedia dell'arte theatrical tradition.

Continuing up, **Caseificio Cugusi** (at #29) has been selling pecorino cheese in Montepulciano for 50 years. Drop into their shop for some picnic supplies, and consider a trip to their dairy farm just outside of town (see "On the Outskirts," later in this chapter). At the *alimentari* on the right (at #23), notice the classic old sign advertising milk, butter, margarine, and olive and canola oil. Keep on going (imagine pushing a barrel now), and bear right with the street under another sturdy **gateway**—indicating that this city grew in concentric circles. Passing through the gate, you'll run into a loggia (with the Florentine Medici seal—a shield with balls).

Facing the loggia, veer left and keep on going. As you huff and puff, notice (on your right, and later on both sides) the steep, narrow, often-covered lanes called *vicolo* ("little street"). You're getting a peek at the higgledy-piggledy medieval Montepulciano. Only when the rationality of Renaissance aesthetics took hold was the main street realigned, becoming symmetrical and pretty. Beneath its fancy suit, though, Montepulciano remains a rugged Gothic city.

Again, notice the fine and ever-bulkier palaces. On the left, a tiny courtyard makes it easier to appreciate the grandiosity of the next palace. By the way, the stone scrolls under the window are a design element called a "kneeling window"—created by Michelangelo and a popular decorative element in High Renaissance and Mannerist architecture. You'll see kneeling windows all over town.

Just after is a fine spot for a coffee break (on the left, at #27): **Caffè Poliziano,** the town's most venerable watering hole (from 1868). Step inside to soak in the genteel atmosphere, with a busy espresso machine, loaner newspapers on long sticks, and a little terrace with spectacular views.

A bit farther up, on the right, notice the precipitous **Vicolo dello Sdrucciolo**—literally "slippery lane." Any *vicolo* on the right can be used as a steep shortcut to the upper part of town, while those on the left generally lead to fine vistas. Many of these side lanes are spanned by brick arches, allowing centuries-old buildings to lean on each other for support rather than toppling over—a fitting metaphor for the tight-knit communities that vitalize small Italian towns.

Continuing up, notice more kneeling windows. The next church on the left, the Jesuit **Church of Gesù,** is worth a look. Its interior is elliptical in shape and full of 3-D illusions (the side chapels and the cupola are all painted on flat surfaces).

Soon the street levels out—enjoy this nice, lazy, easy stretch, with interesting shops and artisan workshops (such as the mosaics studio at #14, on the right). A few short blocks farther, across from #64, a lane leads to a charming terrace with a commanding view of the Tuscan countryside.

The Mazzetti **copper shop** (#64, marked *Rameria Mazzetti*) is crammed full of decorative and practical items. The production of hand-hammered copper vessels like these is a dying art. This shop displays pieces by Cesare, who makes them in his **workshop** just up the street.

With your back to the trees, continue steeply uphill to the main square. At the bend just before the square, the Contucci family loves to introduce travelers to Montepulciano's fine wines at the

Contucci Cantina (described later). Visit Contucci now, or head up to the square for Part 2 of this walk.

Either way, Montepulciano's main square is just ahead. You made it!

PART 2: PIAZZA GRANDE AND NEARBY

This pleasant, lively piazza is surrounded by a grab bag of architectural sights. The medieval **Palazzo Comunale,** or Town Hall, resembles Florence's Palazzo Vecchio—yet another reminder that Florence dominated Montepulciano in the 15th and 16th centuries. The crenellations along the roof were never intended to hide soldiers—they just symbolize power. The big, square central tower makes it clear that the city is keeping an eye out in all directions.

Take a moment to survey the square, where the town's four great powers stare each other down. Face the Palazzo Comunale, and keep turning to the right. You'll see the one-time building of the courts, behind the well (Palazzo del Capitano); the noble Palazzo Tarugi, a Renaissance-arcaded confection (with a public loggia at ground level and a private loggia—now enclosed—directly above); and the aristocratic Palazzo Contucci, with its 16th-century Renaissance facade. (The Contucci family still lives in their palace, producing and selling their own wine.) Continuing your spin, you see the unfinished Duomo looking glumly on, wishing the city hadn't run out of money for its facade.

A cistern system fed by rainwater draining from the roofs of surrounding palaces supplied the fine **well** in the corner. Check out its 19th-century pulleys, the grilles to keep animals from contaminating the water supply, and its decorative top: the Medici coat of arms flanked by lions (representing Florence) dwarfing griffins (representing Montepulciano).

Climbing the Town Hall's **tower** rewards you with a wind-blown but commanding panorama from the terrace below the clock (tower open daily May-Oct 10:00-18:00, closed in winter). To ascend, enter the Palazzo Comunale and buy your ticket at the TI on the main floor. You can pay to go just as far as the terrace, at the base of the tower (€2.50, 71 stairs, or ride the elevator halfway up); or pay more to go all the way to the top, twisting up extremely narrow brick steps past the antiquated bell-ringing mechanism (€5, 76 additional stairs). If you don't mind the claustrophobic climb, it's

The Beauty of Tuscany's Geology (and Vice Versa)

While tourists have romanticized notions of the "Tuscan" land-scape, there are a surprisingly wide variety of land forms in the region. Never having been crushed by a glacier, Tuscany is anything but flat. Its hills and mountains are made up of different substances, each suited to very different types of cultivation.

The Chianti region (between Florence and Siena) is rough and rocky, with an inhospitable soil that challenges grape vines to survive while coaxing them to produce excellent wine grapes.

South of Siena, the soil switches from rock to clay, silt, and sand. The region called the Crete Senesi is the perfectly described "Sienese Clay Hills." Looking out from a breezy viewpoint, you can easily visualize how these clay hills were once at the bottom of the sea floor. The soil here is perfect for truffles and for vast fields of wheat, sun-yellow rapeseed (for canola oil), and peri-

worth paying extra to reach the very top, from where you can see all the way to Pienza (look just to the right of San Biagio Church).

The street to the left as you face the tower leads to the **Fortez-za,** built on a distant ledge at the very edge of town to safeguard the rulers keeping an eye on their townspeople.

To the Church of San Francesco and Views: From the main square, a short, mostly level walk leads to a fine viewpoint. You could head straight down the wide street to the right as you face the tower. But for a more interesting look at Montepulciano behind its pretty Renaissance facades, go down **Via Talosa,** the narrow lane between the two palaces in the far-left corner of the square. Pause at the recommended Mueblè il Riccio B&B (with a fine courtyard—peek inside) and look high up across the street to see how centuries of structures have been stitched together, sometimes gracelessly. Across the street is the recommended Cantina della Talosa wine cellar—imagine the wine caves below your feet.

Follow this lane as it bends left, and eventually you'll pop out just below the main square, a few doors from the recommended De' Ricci Cantine wine cellar. Turn right and head down toward the church. Just before #21 (on the left), look for a red-and-gold symbol over a door with the name *Talosa.* This marks the home of one of Montepulciano's *contrade,* or neighborhoods; birth and odically fava beans (to add nitrogen to the soil). In the spring and summer, the Crete Senesi is blanketed with brightly colorful crops and flowers, but by the fall, after the harvest, it's brown, dusty, and desolate. Within the Crete Senesi, you can distinguish two types of hills shaped by erosion: smooth, rounded *biancane* and pointy, jagged *calanchi*.

The area around Montepulciano and Montalcino is more varied, with rocky protuberances that break up the undulating clay hills and provide a suitable home for wine grapes. Even farther south is the Val d'Orcia. This valley of the Orcia River is similar to the Crete Senesi, but has fewer rocks and jagged *calanchi*. Montepulciano sits in a unique position between the Val d'Orcia and the much flatter Val di Chiana (through which Italy's main north-south expressway runs).

You'll see many hot springs in this part of Tuscany, as well as town names with the word Terme (for "spa" or "hot spring") or Bagno ("bath"). These generally occur where clay meets rock: Water moving through the clay encounters a barrier and gets trapped. A byproduct of these mineral springs is the limestone called travertine, explaining the quarries you may see around spa towns.

death announcements for the *contrada* are posted on the board next to the door.

Across the street and a few steps farther (on the right), you hit a **viewpoint**. From here, it's easy to appreciate Montepulciano's highly strategic position. The ancient town sitting on this high ridge was surrounded by powerful forces—everything you see in this direction was part of the Papal States, ruled from Rome. In the distance is Lake Trasimeno, once a notorious swampland that made it even harder to invade this town.

Continue a few steps downhill, then uphill, into the big parking lot in front of the **Church of San Francesco.** Head out to the overlook for a totally different view: the rolling hills that belonged to Siena. And keep in mind that Montepulciano itself belonged to Florence. For the first half of the 16th century, those three formidable powers—Florence, Siena, and Rome (the papacy)—vied to control this small area. You can also see Montepulciano's most impressive church, San Biagio—well worth a visit for drivers or hikers.

From here, you can head back up to the main square, or drop into one of my recommended cantinas to spelunk their wine cellars.

Sights and Experiences in Montepulciano

For me, Montepulciano's best "experiences" have long been personal: dropping in on Adamo, the winemaker at Contucci Cantina, and Cesare, the coppersmith at Ramaio Cesare. Adamo has now retired, and Cesare will likely retire soon. But today a new generation of winemakers, craftspeople, and cheesemongers are keeping Montepulciano's artisan traditions alive. Take some time to seek them out and make your own connections.

▲▲Contucci Cantina

Montepulciano's most popular attraction isn't made of stone—it's the famous wine, Vino Nobile. This robust red can be tasted in any

of the cantinas lining Via Ricci and Via di Gracciano nel Corso, but the cantina in the basement of Palazzo Contucci is both historic and fun. The palace's enoteca faces the square, but I prefer the actual cellars, down the lane on the right, where you'll meet the Contucci family and their staff. Andrea and Ginevra Contucci love to share their family's products with the public. They usually have a few bottles open for you to sample. If you're lucky, you may even meet the famous Adamo, who recently retired after making wine here for almost 60 years.

After sipping a little wine, explore the palace basement, with its 13th-century vaults. Originally part of the town's wall, these chambers have been filled since the 1500s with huge barrels of wine.

Cost and Hours: Free drop-in tasting, free cellar tour upon request, daily 11:00-18:00, shorter hours off-season, Piazza Grande 13, +39 0578 757 006, www.contucci.it.

▲Ramaio Cesare

Cesare the coppersmith is an institution in Montepulciano, carrying on his father's and grandfather's trade by hammering into existence an immense selection of copper objects in his cavernous **workshop.** Cesare (CHEH-zah-ray) greets guests with a torrent of cheerful Italian and photos of his work—including the copper top of the Duomo in Siena and the piece he designed and personally delivered to Pope Benedict. Just smile and nod, pick up what you can from gestures, and appreciate this rare opportunity to meet a true local character.

Peruse his tools: a giant Road Runner-style anvil, wooden hammers, and stencils dating from 1857 that have been passed down from his grandfather and father. Next door, he has assembled a fine museum with items he and his relatives have made, as well as pieces from his personal collection. Cesare's justifiable pride in his vocation evokes the hardworking, highly skilled craft guilds that once dominated small-town Italy.

Cost and Hours: Demonstration and museum are free, Cesare is generally in his workshop Mon-Sat 9:00-12:30 & 14:30-18:30, closed Sun, 50 yards steeply downhill from the Contucci Cantina at Via del Teatro 4, +39 0578 758 753, www.rameria.com. If Cesare's not there, stop by his delightful **shop** on the main drag and ask about his availability, a block below at Corso #64—look for *Rameria Mazzetti,* open long hours daily.

Duomo

This church's unfinished facade—rough stonework left waiting for the final marble veneer—is not that unusual. Many Tuscan churches

were built just to the point where they had a functional interior, and then, for various practical reasons, the facades were left unfinished. But step inside, where, amid the fairly austere interior, you'll be rewarded with some fine art. A beautiful blue-and-white, glazed-terra-cotta *Altar of the Lilies* by Andrea della Robbia is behind the baptismal font (on the left as you enter). The high altar, with a top like a pine forest, features a luminous, late-Gothic Assumption triptych by the Sienese artist Taddeo di Bartolo. Showing Mary in her dreamy eternal sleep as she ascends to be crowned by Jesus, it illustrates how Siena clung to the Gothic aesthetic—elaborate gold leaf and lacy pointed arches—to show heavenly grandeur.

Cost and Hours: Free, daily 8:30-18:30.

▲De' Ricci Cantine

The most impressive wine cellars in Montepulciano sit below the Palazzo Ricci, just a few steps off the main square (toward the Church of San Francesco). Enter through the unassuming door and find your way down, down, down a spiral staircase—with rounded steps designed to go easy on fragile noble feet, and lined with rings held in place by tiny, finely crafted wrought-iron goat heads. You'll wind up in the dramatic cellars, with gigantic barrels under even more gigantic vaults—several stories high. As you go deeper and deeper into the cellars, high up, natural stone seems to take over the brick. At the deepest point, you can peer into the atmospheric Etruscan cave, where a warren of corridors spins off from a filled-in well. Finally you emerge in the shop, where you're welcome to taste a few wines (with some local cheese). Don't miss their delightful dessert wine, vin santo.

Cost and Hours: First three tastings-free, two additional premium tastes-€5, €12-35 bottles, affordable shipping, daily 10:30-18:30, enter Palazzo Ricci at Via Ricci 11—look for signs for *Cantine de' Ricci*, +39 0578 757 166, www.cantinadericci.it, Enrico.

Cantina della Talosa

This historic cellar, which goes down and down to an Etruscan tomb at the bottom, ages a well-respected wine. With a passion and love of their craft, Andrea and Cristian Pepi give enthusiastic tours and tastings. While you can drop by for a free sample, it's also possible to call ahead to book a complete tour and tasting (€20, including five wines to taste and light food).

Cost and Hours: Free tasting, daily March-Oct 10:30-19:00, shorter hours off-season, a block off Piazza Grande at Via Talosa 8, +39 0578 757 929, www.talosa.it.

ON THE OUTSKIRTS

▲San Biagio Church (Chiesa de San Biagio)

The church is just west of town, at the base of Montepulciano's hill, down a picturesque cypress-lined driveway. Often called the "Temple of San Biagio" because of its Greek-cross style, this church—designed by Antonio da Sangallo the Elder and built of locally quarried travertine—feels like Renaissance perfection. If the church is empty, experiment worshipfully with the marvelous acoustics. Consider a picnic or snooze on the grass in back, with fine vistas over the Chiana Valley. The recommended La Grotta restaurant is across the street from the church.

Cost and Hours: €3.50, includes 20-minute audioguide; Mon-Sat 10:00-18:00, Sun from 11:30, shorter hours in winter; www.tempiosanbiagio.it.

Cugusi Dairy Farm (Caseificio Cugusi)

Perched scenically in the hills outside Montepulciano, this family-run dairy farm has been crafting fine pecorino cheeses for more than 50 years. Sisters Giovanna and Silvana welcome picnickers to assemble a custom basket of cheeses, meats, and wines before settling in under a shaded pergola with views over the countryside (April-Oct daily 8:00-19:30, shorter hours off-season; at Via della Boccia 8, look for signed turn-off from SP-146, a 10-minute drive from Montepulciano—for location, see the "Heart

of Tuscany Drive" map on page 711; +39 0578 757 558, www.
caseificiocugusi.it).

Sleeping in Montepulciano

$$$$ La Locanda di San Francesco is overpriced but luxurious,
with four stylish view rooms over a classy wine bar on a quiet square
at Montepulciano's summit (air-con, free parking nearby, Piazza
San Francesco 5, +39 0578 758 725, www.locandasanfrancesco.it,
info@locandasanfrancesco.it, Luca).

$$$ Palazzo del Mercante, steps away from the Piazza
Grande, offers six updated and neatly-appointed rooms with
modern bathrooms (Via Ricci 14, +39 057 844 0591, www.
palazzodelmercante.it, info@palazzodelmercante.it).

$$ Mueblè il Riccio ("The Hedgehog") is medieval-elegant,
with 10 spotless rooms and an inviting roof terrace. Five are newer
"superior" rooms with grand views across the Tuscan valleys (family rooms with lofts, breakfast extra, air-con, limited free parking—request when you reserve, a block below the main square at
Via Talosa 21, +39 0578 757 713, www.ilriccio.net, info@ilriccio.
net, friendly Gió and Ivana speak English). In summer, charming
Gió and his son Iacopo give tours of the countryside in one of their
classic Italian cars (€80/hour).

$$ Albergo Duomo is big, with 13 tattered rooms (with small
bathrooms) and a comfortable lounge downstairs. Though the place
lacks personality, it's in a handy location just a few steps from the
main square at the very top of town, with free private parking near-
by (RS%, elevator, air-con in some rooms, Via di San Donato 14,
+39 0578 757 473, www.albergoduomo.it, info@albergoduomo.it,
Simone).

$$ Vicolo dell'Oste B&B, just off the main drag halfway up
through town, has five family-friendly modern rooms. Some are
like tiny apartments (RS%, includes breakfast at nearby café, on
Via dell'Oste 1—an alley leading right off the main drag just after
Caffè Poliziano and opposite the *farmacia* at #47, +39 0578 758
393, www.vicolodelloste.it, info@vicolodelloste.it, Luisa and Giuseppe).

$ Camere Bellavista, owned by the same people who run
Palazzo del Mercante across the street, has 10 tidy rooms that
make you feel like you're at grandma's. True to its name, the rooms
have fine views—though some are better than others. Room 6 has
a view terrace worth reserving; there's also one economy room
without a view (small breakfast delivered to room, lots of stairs
with no elevator, reception not always staffed—call before arriving,
Via Ricci 25, +39 338 229 1964, mobile +39 347 823 2314, www.

HEART OF TUSCANY

camerebellavista.it, info@camerebellavista.it, Gabriella and Alessio speak just enough English).

Eating in Montepulciano

Unless otherwise noted, these places are all open for lunch (about 12:30-14:30) and again for dinner (about 19:30-22:00).

$$$ Osteria dell'Acquacheta is a carnivore's dream come true, beloved among locals for its beef steaks. Its long, narrow room is jammed with shared tables and tight, family-style seating, with an open fire in back and a big hunk of red beef lying on the counter like a corpse on a gurney. Giulio and his wife, Chiara, run a fun-loving but tight ship—posing with slabs of red meat yet embracing decades of trattoria tradition (you'll get one glass

to use alternately for wine and water). Steaks are sold by weight. Typically, two people split a 1.6-kilo steak (that's 3.5 pounds; the smallest they'll cook is 1.2 kilos). They also serve hearty pastas and salads, other meaty plates, and a fine house wine (possible to bring your own wine for a tiny corkage fee, reservations required by phone; seatings generally at 12:30, 14:30, 19:30, and 21:30 only; closed Tue and unpredictably on other days; Via del Teatro 22, +39 0578 717 086, www.acquacheta.eu).

$$ Osteria del Conte, an attractive but humble family-run bistro, offers cooking like your Italian mom's. While the interior is very simple, they also have outdoor tables on a stony street at the top of the historic center (closed Mon, Via San Donato 19, +39 0578 756 062).

$$ Le Pentolaccia is a small, family-run restaurant about two-thirds of the way up the main drag. With both indoor and outdoor seating, they make tasty traditional Tuscan dishes as well as daily fish specials. Cristiana serves, and husband-and-wife team Jacobo and Alessia stir up a storm in the kitchen (Fri-Wed 12:00-15:00 & 19:00-22:00, closed Thu, Corso 86, +39 0578 757 582).

$$ Ai Quattro Venti is right on Piazza Grande, with a simple dining room and outdoor tables on the square. It offers reasonable portions of unfussy Tuscan food in an unpretentious setting. Try the organic house olive oil and wine (closed Thu, next to City Hall on Piazza Grande, +39 0578 717 231, Chiara).

Wine Bar/Bistro: With a terrace on a tranquil square in front of the Church of San Francesco, **$$ E Lucevan le Stelle** (part of La Locanda di San Francesco) is a fine place to nurse a glass of local wine (also pastas, salads, and soups; daily 12:00-24:00, closed Nov-Easter, may close when things are quiet, Piazza San Francesco 5, +39 0578 758 725, Luca).

Sandwiches to Go: $ La Schiaccia dell'Opio, at one of the hairpin turns near the top of town, is a takeout shop offering pricey but delicious made-to-order sandwiches on *schiaccia*—crispy, savory flatbread hot out of the oven (daily 11:00-15:00 & 16:30-21:00, lunch only off-season, Via dell'Opio nel Corso 45, +39 0578 778 861).

Gelato: For the best gelato in town, look for **Sgarbi Gelato Natura,** near the bottom of the main drag. Owner Nicola makes his gelato fresh every morning, using locally sourced ingredients from producers he knows personally (daily 11:00-20:00, open later in summer, Corso 50; also runs Buon Gusto in Pienza).

Just Outside Montepulciano: Facing San Biagio Church (at the base of Montepulciano's hill, and described earlier), **$$$ La Grotta** has an excellent reputation for elevated Tuscan cuisine in a sophisticated, dressy setting. Reservations are recommended (Thu-Tue 12:30-14:15 & 19:30-22:00, closed Wed, Via di San Biagio 15, +39 0578 757 479, www.lagrottamontepulciano.it).

Near Montepulciano: Skim this chapter for recommendations, and consider combining dinner with a scenic joyride. Good choices include **Ristorante Daria** in Monticchiello (page 717) and **The Isabella Experience**'s dinners near Castelmuzio (page 699).

Montepulciano Connections

Get bus schedules at the TI or the bus station on Piazza Pietro Nenni, which seems to double as the town hangout, with a lively bar and locals chatting inside. In fact, there's no real ticket window—buy your tickets at the bar. Check www.at-bus.it for schedules.

By Bus to: Florence (1/day departs in the wee hours, 2/week additional departures a bit later in the morning, 2 hours, LFI bus, www.lfi.it; or take a bus to Chiusi to catch a train—see below), **Siena** (6-7/day, none on Sun, 1.5 hours, also possible to change here for Florence express bus), **Pienza** (8/day, 30 minutes), **Montalcino** (3-4/day, none Sun, change in Torrenieri, 1 hour; or consider a taxi—see below).

By Train: Trains are impractical here; the Montepulciano train station is served only by milk-run trains and a 15-minute taxi/bus ride to town. Instead consider connecting through the town of **Chiusi.** Its convenient train station is on the main Florence-Rome rail line and linked to Montepulciano by an hourly 50-minute bus ride.

Taxi Alternatives: As the **Montalcino** bus connection is infrequent and complicated, consider hiring a taxi (about €70; see contact info under "Helpful Hints," earlier).

Pienza

HEART OF TUSCANY

Set on a crest and surrounded by green, rolling hills, the small town of Pienza packs a lot of Renaissance punch. In the 1400s, locally born Pope Pius II of the Piccolomini family decided to remodel his birthplace into a city fit for a pope, in the style that was all the rage: Renaissance. Propelled by papal clout, the town of Corsignano was transformed—in only five years' time—into a jewel of Renaissance architecture. It was renamed Pienza, after Pope Pius.

Pienza's architectural focal point is its main square, Piazza Pio II, surrounded by the Duomo and the pope's family residence, Palazzo Piccolomini. While Piazza Pio II is Pienza's pride and joy, the entire town—a mix of old stonework, potted plants, and grand views—is fun to explore, especially with a camera or sketchpad in hand. You can walk every lane in the tiny town in well under an hour. Pienza is situated on a relatively flat plateau rather than the steep pinnacle of more dramatic towns like Montepulciano and Montalcino. (This is a plus for visitors with limited mobility, who find basically level Pienza easy to explore.)

Tourists flood Pienza on weekends and in peak season, and authentic local shops are outnumbered by boutiques selling gifty packages of pecorino cheese and local wine. Restaurants here tend to be more expensive and less reliable than alternatives in the nearby countryside. For these reasons, Pienza is made to order as a stretch-your-legs break to enjoy the townscape and panoramas, but it's not ideal for lingering overnight (though some excellent options exist just outside town; see "Countryside Accommodations," earlier). For the best experience, visit late in the day, after the day-trippers have dispersed.

Nearly every shop sells the town's specialty: pecorino, a pungent sheep's cheese (you'll smell it before you see it) that's sometimes infused with other ingredients, such as truffles or cayenne pepper. Look on menus for warm pecorino *(al forno* or *alla griglia),* often topped with honey and pine nuts or pears and served with bread. Along with a glass of local wine, this just might lead you to a new understanding of *la dolce vita.*

Orientation to Pienza

Tourist Information: The TI is 10 yards up the street from Piazza Pio II, inside the skippable Diocesan Museum (Wed-Mon 10:00-18:30, shorter hours off-season, closed Tue year-round, Corso il Rossellino 30, +39 0578 749 905). Ignore the *Informaturista* kiosk just outside the gate—it's a private travel agency.

Arrival in Pienza: If **driving,** read signs carefully—some parking spots are reserved for locals, others require the use of a cardboard clock, and others are pay-and-display. Parking is tight, so if you don't see anything quickly, head for the large pay lot at Piazza del Mercato near Largo Roma outside the old town: As you approach town and reach the "ZTL" cul-de-sac (marked with a red circle) in front of the town gate, head up the left side of town and look for the parking turnoff on the left (closed Fri morning during market). **Buses** drop you just a couple of blocks from the town's main entrance.

Helpful Hints: The TI and most sights are **closed on Tuesdays.** On Friday mornings, a **market** fills Piazza del Mercato, the main parking lot just outside the town walls. A public **WC,** marked *gabinetti pubblici,* is on the right as you face the town gate from outside on Piazza Dante Alighieri (down the lane next to the faux TI).

Sights in Pienza

I've connected Pienza's main sights with walking directions, which can serve as a handy little orientation to the town. You could do this stroll in 30 minutes; entering some of the sights could extend your visit to a few hours.

• *Begin in the little park just in front of the town (near the main roundabout and bus stop), called Piazza Dante Alighieri. Facing the town, go through the big, ornamental gateway on the right (which was destroyed in World War II, and rebuilt in 1955) and head up the main street...*

Corso il Rossellino

This main drag—named for Bernardo Rossellino (1409-1464), the Renaissance architect who redesigned Pienza according to Pius' orders—is jammed with touristy boutiques. While you won't find great values, these shops are (like Pienza) cute and convenient.

As you stroll this street, step into one of the many **cheese-and-salami shops.** Take a deep whiff and survey the racks of pecorino cheese, made from sheep's milk. There are three broad categories of pecorino: *fresco* (young, soft, and mild), *medio* (medium), and *stagionato* (hard, crumbly, and pungent). Consider stocking up at one of these shops for a pricey but memorable picnic; some shops may be willing to give you a free sample. *Finocchiona* is salami with fennel seeds. This was first popularized by wine traders, because fennel seeds make wine taste better. To this day, Italians use the word *infinocchiare* ("fennel-ize") to mean "to trick."

Farther along, watch for the **Church of San Francesco** on the right. It's the only important building in town that dates from before the Pius II extreme makeover. Its humble facade, simple nave, wood-beamed ceiling, bits of 14th-century frescoes, and tranquil adjacent cloister have a charm that's particularly peaceful in the 21st century. But this gloomy medieval style was exactly what Pius wanted to get away from.

· Continuing one more block, you'll pop out at Pienza's showcase square...

▲Piazza Pio II

Pienza's small main piazza gets high marks from architecture highbrows for its elegance and artistic unity. One day, Pope Pius II (who was born here) was traveling nearby with Leon Battista Alberti, one of the great architectural pioneers of the Renaissance. Proud to show off his hometown, Pius brought Alberti here...but, seeing it through the eyes of his esteemed companion, he

was filled with embarrassment rather than pride at its primitive architectural style. Pius decided this just wouldn't do, and commissioned Alberti's student Bernardo Rossellino to remake the town into a Renaissance masterpiece.

Rossellino designed the piazza and surrounding buildings to form an "outdoor room." Everything is perfectly planned and plotted. Do a clockwise spin to check out the buildings that face the

Pope Pius II

Pope Pius II (Enea Silvio Bartolomeo Piccolomini, 1405-1464) was born into one of the most powerful families in Siena. He had an illustrious career as a diplomat, traveled far and wide (fathering two illegitimate children, in Switzerland and Scotland), and gained a reputation for his erotic writings (*The Tale of Two Lovers*). Upon donning the frock, Piccolomini went from ordination to the papacy in just 11 years—a stunning pace spurred, no doubt, by his esteemed lineage. Owing to his educated and worldly upbringing, upon ascending to the papacy Piccolomini chose a name that was not religious, but literary: the ancient poet Virgil first used the term "pious" to describe his hero, Aeneus. One of the most enlightened popes of his time, Pius embraced the burgeoning Renaissance and set out to remake his hometown in pure Renaissance style. At the time, Christian Europe was facing the prospect of an Ottoman invasion, and Pius rallied Europeans around their common heritage and shared goals. In that respect, Pius was the first prominent figure to suggest the bold notion of a united Europe. (The pope's dramatic life is immortalized in the Piccolomini Library frescoes in Siena's duomo; see page 619.)

square, starting with the **Duomo** (which we'll visit soon). High up on the facade is one of many examples you'll spot around town of the Piccolomini family crest: five half-moons, advertising the number of crusades that his family funded.

To the right of the Duomo is the **Piccolomini family palace,** now a tourable museum. Notice that the grid lines in the square's pavement continue all the way up the sides of this building, creating a Renaissance cube. Upon closer inspection, you can see that the windows at the far end of the building are a bit narrower—creating an optical illusion that the palace is longer than it actually is.

Looking farther right, you'll see **City Hall** (Palazzo Comunale), with a Renaissance facade and a fine loggia (to match the square) but a 13th-century bell tower that's shorter than the church's tower. That's unusual here in civic-minded Tuscany, where municipal towers usually trumpet the importance of town over Church.

Looking up the lane to the left of City Hall, notice the cantilevered upper floors of the characteristic old houses—a reminder that, while Pienza appears Renaissance on the surface, much of that sheen was added later to fit Pius' vision. Turning right again, see the **Bishop's Palace,** also called the Borgia Palace (now housing the TI and the skippable Diocesan Museum). Pius envisioned his remade hometown as a sort of "summer Vatican," where an entourage of VIPs would spend time—and each one needed their own palace. The Borgia clan, who built this palace, produced one of the most controversial popes of that age, Alexander VI, who ascended to the papacy a few decades after Pius II.

Finally, between the Bishop's Palace and the Duomo, a lane leads to the best **view terrace** in town.

• *Before going there, now's the time to tour whichever of the square's sights interest you:*

Duomo

The cathedral's classic, symmetrical Renaissance facade (1462) dominates Piazza Pio II. The interior, bathed in light, is an illu-

minating encapsulation of Pius II's architectural philosophy (free, generally daily 8:00-13:00 & 14:30-19:00).

Pius envisioned this church as an antidote to dark, claustrophobic medieval churches, like the Church of San Francesco we saw earlier. Instead, this was to be a "house of glass," representing the cultural enlightenment that came with the Renaissance. As you walk to the end of the church, notice the cracks in the apse walls and floor, and get seasick behind the main altar. The church's cliff-hanging position bathes the interior in light, but the building also feels as though it could break in half if you jumped up and down.

▲Palazzo Piccolomini

This palace, the home of Pius II and the Piccolomini family (until 1962), is not quite the interesting slice of 15th-century aristocratic life that it could be (I'd like to know more about the pope's toilet). But this is still the best small-town palace experience I've found in Tuscany. (It famously starred as the Capulets' home in Franco Zeffirelli's 1968 Academy Award-winning *Romeo and Juliet*.) You can peek inside the door for free to check out the well-preserved courtyard. In Renaissance times, most buildings were covered with elaborate paintings like those you'll see here.

Cost and Hours: €7; Wed-Mon 10:00-12:30 & 14:00-18:00, until 16:00 off-season, closed Tue year-round; Piazza Pio II 2, +39 0577 286 300, www.palazzopiccolominipienza.it.

• *When you're done sightseeing, head up the little lane to the left of the church facade. This takes you out to a grand pedestrian-only...*

HEART OF TUSCANY

View Terrace

Stroll this panoramic promenade to the end, taking in views over the Tuscan countryside and, in the distance, Monte Amiata, the largest mountain in southern Tuscany. Retrace your steps and exit the viewpoint down the first alley, Via del'Amore—the original Lover's Lane—which leads back to the main drag, Corso il Rossellino.

• *Turn right and stroll along this street one block, then turn left up Via Sant' Andrea. Soon you'll run into* **Via delle Case Nuove,** *a charming row of homes with staggered doorways. These "new houses" (as the street's name means) were built by the pope to house the poor. Just to the left (as you face these houses) is Pienza's "destination" gelateria, the recommended* **Buon Gusto.**

JUST OUTSIDE PIENZA
Corsignano Parish Church (Pieve di Corsignano)

This classic Romanesque parish church *(pieve),* hugging the slope just below Pienza, is a reminder of a much earlier, rougher, simpler time (before Pope Pius II).

This was one of the medieval pilgrimage stops on the Via Francigena. The round, eighth-century watchtower guards the squat, 11th-century church, whose unusual exterior iconography is from an age when the pagan roots of early Christianity were vivid and unmistakable—especially here, deep in the countryside. The church is decorated not with saints and angels, but with geometric and flowery motifs as well as mysterious creatures. Inside, near the entrance on the right, look for the font that was used to baptize the infant who would grow up to be Pope Pius II.

Getting There: On foot from Pienza, it's a steep 10-minute downhill walk (as you exit Pienza into the main park, look to your left for *pieve di Corsignano* signs). Drivers loop around the far end of town (as described on my Heart of Tuscany drive, later); just before the road bends sharply left and twists downhill, watch for the *pieve di Corsignano* signs on the right (free parking).

Eating in and near Pienza

IN PIENZA

$$$ La Bandita Townhouse Caffè offers a break from Tuscan rusticity, focusing instead on tempting modern Italian cuisine (such as spring pea soup or spicy Chianina beef tartare). Diners watch the chef work in his open kitchen (dinner nightly 19:30-22:00, lunch Tue-Sun 12:30-15:00, indoor/outdoor seating, Corso il Rossellino 111, easier to enter around the corner on Via Sant'Andrea, +39 0578 749 005).

$$ Trattoria Latte di Luna, with outdoor tables filling a delightful little square, is the more traditional choice. While the food can be hit or miss, locals swear by their specialty, roast suckling pig *(maialino da latte arrosto)*. Run by friendly Roberto with Delfina in the kitchen, the dining room features an ancient well and sits on top of Etruscan tunnels (Wed-Mon 10:30-17:00, closed Tue, at the far end of town at Via San Carlo 2, +39 0578 748 606).

Quick Lunch: For something cheap, characteristic, and fast, just grab a tasty **$ *porchetta* sandwich** at the little no-name shop 30 yards off the main square (at Corso il Rossellino 81) and munch it under the loggia or at the viewpoint (daily 8:00-20:00).

Gelato: Quality ingredients are on the menu at **Buon Gusto.** Nicola creates fun original flavors, such as carrot-ginger, creamy basil, or kiwi-spinach. They also do fresh-pressed juices and smoothies (daily 12:00-19:00, open later in summer, closed Nov-March, Via delle Case Nuove 26, +39 335 704 9165). Nicola also runs Sgarbi Gelato Natura in Montepulciano.

Cocktails with Nibbles: Pienza isn't much for nightlife, but for a cocktail in a local-feeling setting, drop in at **Idyllium**—a hip cocktail bar serving creative herb-infused drinks, light food, and outdoor seating facing grand Tuscan splendor (daily 11:00-late, shorter hours off-season; from the main square, go down the little lane to the right of the church to Via Gozzante 67; +39 0578 748 176).

NEAR PIENZA

Despite having more than its share of tourists, Pienza suffers from a lack of quality restaurants. These options are all within about a 15-minute drive and offer a more memorable meal you'll find in town. To locate Castelmuzio, see the "Heart of Tuscany" map on page 673.

Just Outside Castelmuzio: For an excellent meal—perhaps combined with a memorable activity—consider dinner at the fine **$$$** restaurant at **La Moscadella,** run by The Isabella Experience (recommended in "Countryside Accommodations," earlier in this chapter). A limited number of tables are available to nonguests who book ahead. Chef Giancarlo prepares classic, always-delicious Tuscan meals, occasionally with a modern spin. You can dine in the rustic yet elegant glassed-in veranda or out on the pebbly terrace—both have views. Call or email ahead to check the schedule of activities (such as pasta-making and wine/olive oil tasting) or to reserve one of the limited tables (reservations required, restaurant open Fri-Wed, closed Thu, veggie and gluten-free options available, +39 0577 665 516, mobile +39 338 740 9245).

In Castelmuzio: To escape Pienza's tourist crowds, drive about 15 minutes to the remote village of Castelmuzio. The hamlet's lone restaurant, **$$ Locanda di Casalmustia,** is a cozy and typically uncrowded spot serving good local cuisine. Choose between sitting out on the stony lane or in a cute fresco-ceilinged dining room. While not quite a destination restaurant, it's a good excuse to explore an untrampled hill town and enjoy sweeping views of the countryside (Tue-Sun 8:00-22:00, closed Mon, in the heart of the town at Piazza della Pieve 3, +39 0577 665 166).

In Monticchiello: In the opposite direction but about the same distance away is the excellent **Ristorante Daria** (see "Eating in Monticchiello," later in this chapter; for location see the "Heart of Tuscany Drive" map on page 711).

Pienza Connections

Bus tickets are sold at the bar/café (marked *Il Caffè,* closed Tue) just outside Pienza's town gate (or pay a little extra and buy tickets from the driver). Buses leave from a few blocks up the street, directly in front of the town entrance. Montepulciano is the nearest transportation hub.

From Pienza by Bus to: Siena (6/day, none on Sun, 1.5 hours), **Montepulciano** (8/day, 30 minutes), **Montalcino** (3-4/day, none Sun, change in Torrenieri, 1 hour). Bus info: www.at-bus.it.

Montalcino

On a hill overlooking vineyards and valleys, Montalcino is famous for its delicious and pricey Brunello di Montalcino red wines. It's a pleasant, low-impact town crawling with wine-loving tourists and has a smattering of classy shops, but little sightseeing. Everyone touring this area seems to be relaxed and in an easy groove...as if enjoying a little wine buzz.

While today it's all about the wine, Montalcino (mohn-tahl-CHEE-noh) has an incredibly long history: Human settlement here dates back to the Etruscan period. It's possible that Neolithic humans were here long before that. That's because Montalcino has a unique setting, with protective caves

Montalcino

Accommodations
1. Hotel Dei Capitani
2. B&B da Idolina
3. Albergo Giardino

Eateries & Other
4. Re di Macchia
5. Taverna del Grappolo Blu

6. Ristorante-Pizzeria San Giorgio
7. Pizza al Taglio
8. Supermarket

Wine Bars
9. Caffè Fiaschetteria Italiana
10. Enoteca di Piazza
11. Enoteca la Fortezza di Montalcino

HEART OF TUSCANY

and a freshwater spring high atop a rocky pinnacle—a highly desirable position for early settlers. For much of its long history, Montalcino was a veritable fortress, perched high overlooking the valley below and its Via Francigena pilgrim route.

Flash forward to the Middle Ages, when Montalcino was considered Siena's biggest ally. Originally aligned with Florence, the town switched sides after the Sienese beat up Florence in the Battle of Montaperti in 1260. The Sienese persuaded the Montalcinesi to join their side by forcing them to collect corpses and sleep one night in the bloody, Florentine-strewn battlefield. Later, the Montalcinesi took in Sienese refugees. To this day, in gratitude for their support, the Sienese invite the Montalcinesi to lead the parade that kicks off Siena's Palio celebrations.

Montalcino prospered under Siena, but like its ally, it waned after the Medici family took control of the region. The village became a humble place. Then, in the late 19th century, the Biondi Santi family created a fine, dark red wine, calling it "the brunette" (Brunello). Today's affluence is due to the town's much-sought-after wine. (For more on this wine, see the "Wines in the Region" sidebar later in this chapter). Montalcino provides a handy springboard for exploring the surrounding wine region.

Orientation to Montalcino

Sitting atop a hill amidst a sea of vineyards, Montalcino is surrounded by walls and dominated by its Fortezza (a.k.a. "La Rocca"). From here, roads lead down into the two main squares: Piazza Garibaldi and Piazza del Popolo.

Tourist Information: The TI, just off Piazza Garibaldi in the Old City Hall, is good for a map, but not much else (daily 10:00-13:30 & 14:00-18:30, +39 337 142 2762).

Arrival in Montalcino: For a short visit here by **car,** drivers should head to the pay lot in Piazzale Fortezza. Skirt around the fortress, take the first right (just past a little park), and follow signs to *parking* and *Fortezza* (€1.50/hour, free 20:00-8:00). Or, if you don't mind a short climb, park for free below the fortress: At the roundabout with the ugly statue, take the small downhill lane into the big lower parking lot (blue lines mean that you have to pay, but the lower-level unmarked spots are always free). If these lots are full, follow the town's western wall toward the Madonna del Soccorso church and a long pay lot.

The **bus** stop is on Piazza Cavour, a little park about 300 yards from the town center. From here, simply follow the main drag, Via Mazzini, straight up into town. While Montalcino has no official baggage storage, a few shops may be willing to hold on to one or two bags on a short-term basis; ask at the TI.

Helpful Hints: Friday is **market** day (7:00-13:00) on Viale della Libertà, near the Fortezza.

Sights and Experiences in Montalcino

Piazza del Popolo

All roads in tiny Montalcino lead to the main square, Piazza del Popolo ("People's Square").

The **Old City Hall** was the fortified seat of government. It's decorated by the coats of arms of judges who, in the interest of fairness, were from outside of town. Like Siena, Montalcino was a republic in the Middle Ages. When Florentines took Siena in 1555, Siena's ruling class retreated here and held out for four more years. The Medici coat of arms (with the six balls, or pills) dominates the others. The one-handed **clock** was the norm until 200 years ago.

For five centuries, the large arcaded **loggia** (on your left as you face the clock tower) hosted the town market.

For some wine-centric whimsy, go up around the right side of the Old City Hall and find a series of **plaques** (each designed by a different artist), which show off the annual rating of the Brunello harvest from two to five stars—important, as wine is the lifeblood of the local economy. And, of course, it's fun to simply observe the *passeggiata*—these days mostly a parade of tourists here for the wine.

Back on the square, in front of the clock tower, notice the grand café. Since 1888, **Caffè Fiaschetteria Italiana** has been *the* elegant place to enjoy a drink. Its founder, inspired by Caffè Florian in Venice, brought fine coffee to this humble town of woodcutters. It's now both a café and a wine bar.

Montalcino Museums (Musei di Montalcino)

While technically several museums in one, and surprisingly big and modern for this little town, Montalcino's **L'Oro di Montalcino** ranks only as a decent bad-weather activity. The cellar features two exhibits: one on prehistoric times, and a multimedia experience on the famed Brunello di Montalcino and its winemakers. The ground, first, and second floors hold medieval and modern art collections, with an emphasis on Gothic sacred art (with works from Montalcino's heyday, the 13th to 16th century). The ground floor is best, with a large collection of crucifixes and the museum's highlights, a glazed terra-cotta altarpiece and a statue of St. Sebastian, both by Andrea della Robbia.

Cost and Hours: €10, includes entry to Sant'Agostino Church,

HEART OF TUSCANY

daily 10:30-19:00, Via Ricasoli 31, to the right of Sant'Agostino Church, +39 0577 286 300, www.orodimontalcino.it.

Fortezza

This 14th-century fort, built under Sienese rule, is now little more than an empty shell (with a popular wine bar—see below). It was built to defend against catapults and arrows, but the cannon was invented shortly thereafter. You can still see pockmarks from cannonballs fired here in 1553 on the outer wall (facing away from the town), but the fort withstood the attack. You're welcome to enter the big, open courtyard (with WCs out the far end), or just enjoy a picnic in the park surrounding the fort, but if you want to climb the ramparts for a panoramic view, you'll have to pay.

Cost and Hours: €4, enter though wine bar, daily 9:00-20:00, off-season 10:00-18:00.

Wine Bars in Town

If you won't make it to the wineries outside Montalcino, simply visit a wine bar in town, where you can comfortably taste a variety of vintages before stumbling safely back to your hotel. This is also a great strategy for Sundays, when many countryside wineries are closed.

Caffè Fiaschetteria Italiana, a touristy café/wine bar, was founded by Ferruccio Biondi Santi, the creator of the famous Brunello wine. The wine library in the back of the café boasts many local choices. A meeting place since 1888, this grand café also serves light lunches (Brunellos by the glass, light snacks and plates; same prices inside, outside, or in back room; daily 7:30-23:00, shorter hours off-season; Piazza del Popolo 6, +39 0577 849 043).

Enoteca di Piazza—part of a chain of wine shops with mechanical dispensers—is a fun way to efficiently taste a variety of different wines in a forgettable setting. Here's how it works: A "drink card" (like a debit card) keeps track of the samples you take, for which you'll pay from €1 to €9 apiece. They stock 100 different wines, including some whites—rare in this town. Their small restaurant across the street lets you enjoy your new purchase with local dishes (daily 9:00-20:00, near Piazza del Popolo at Via Matteotti 43, +39 0577 848 104, www.enotecadipiazza.com).

Enoteca la Fortezza di Montalcino offers a chance to taste top-end wines by the glass, each with an English explanation. Spoil yourself with Brunello in the cozy *enoteca* or at an outdoor table in the fortress courtyard (tastings start at €18 for 3 wines and go up from there; small menu and sampler plates of cheeses and *salumi;* daily 9:00-20:00, until 18:00 Nov-March; inside the Fortezza, +39 0577 849 211).

WINERIES NEAR MONTALCINO

The countryside around Montalcino is littered with wineries, some of which offer tastings. As Brunello is the poshest of Italian wines, these wineries feel a bit upscale, and most require an advance reservation. It's a simple process (just call or email to arrange a time), and they'll delight in showing you around. Tours generally last 45-60 minutes, cost at least €15 per person, and conclude with a tasting of three or four wines. The Montalcino TI can give you a list of more than 150 regional wineries. Or check with the vintners' consortium (+39 0577 848 246, www.consorziobrunellodimontalcino.it). Many wineries are closed on Sunday, so check before heading out. For locations of the wineries listed below, see the "Heart of Tuscany" map, near the beginning of the chapter.

If you lack a car (or don't want to drive), you can take a tour on the **Brunello Wine Bus,** which laces together visits to four wineries, with a lunch break in the middle, either on your own in Montalcino or at a farmhouse for an extra fee (€190, RS% with this book; tours run March-Nov Tue and Thu only; departs at 10:00, returns at 19:00; tours leave from their office, or they will pick you up within 3 miles of Montalcino; half-day tours available Tue and Thu-Sat for €95; Via Circonvallazione 3, +39 0577 846 021, www. winetravelsforyou.com, info@winetravelsforyou.com).

If you're paying for a wine tasting, you aren't obligated to buy. But if a winery is doing a small tasting just for you, they're hoping you'll buy a bottle or two.

South of Montalcino
Tornesi

This charmingly low-key, family-run winery is a short drive outside of Montalcino, perched on a grand view terrace overlooking the famous Biondi Santi winery (where Brunello was invented). Maurizio, Elisa, and Valentina offer tours and tastings in this scenic setting. They enjoy explaining how their logo—the cuckoo *(kuku-la)* bird—was inspired by their chatty grandfather (€18 for 3 tastes plus tour, €40 tasting includes lunch, €20-40 bottles; closed Sun, reserve ahead, mobile +39 349 093 2167, www.brunellotornesi.it,

Wines in the Region

This region has two well-respected red wines, each centered on a specific town: Montepulciano is known for its Vino Nobile, while Montalcino is famous for its Brunello. In each wine, the predominant grape is a clone of sangiovese (Tuscany's main red wine grape).

Vino Nobile di Montepulciano ("noble wine of Montepulciano") is a high-quality, dry ruby red, made mostly with the Prugnolo Gentile variety of sangiovese (70 percent), plus other varieties including Mammolo (30 percent). Aged two years (or three for a *riserva*)—one year of which must be in oak casks—it pairs well with meat, especially roasted lamb with rosemary, rabbit or boar ragù over pasta, grilled portobello mushrooms, and local cheeses like pecorino. Several large wineries produce and age their Vino Nobile in the sprawling cellars beneath the town of Montepulciano. Three of these are fun and easy to tour (see "Sights and Experiences in Montepulciano" on page 686). The oldest red wine in Tuscany, Vino Nobile has been produced since the late 1500s.

Brunello di Montalcino ("the little brown one of Montalcino"—named for the color of the grapes be-

degustazionicasatornesi@gmail.com). Leaving Montalcino, at the main roundabout, go uphill toward *Grosetto*, then watch for the brown *Benducce* sign on the left (just before the road bends right). Tornesi is a short drive down this gravel road, on the left.

Mastrojanni

Perched high above the Romanesque Sant'Antimo Abbey, overlooking sprawling vineyards, this winery (owned by the Illy coffee company) is big and glitzy—yet doesn't feel as corporate or soulless as some of the bigger players (€30-50 for tour and tasting, €17-36 bottles; daily 10:00-16:30, reserve ahead; Podere Loreto e San Pio, +39 0577 835 681, www.mastrojanni.com, visite@mastrojanni.com). To reach it, head up into the town of Castelnuovo dell'Abate (just above Sant'Antimo Abbey), bear left at the Bassomondo restaurant, and continue up along the gravel road (enjoying vineyard and abbey views).

Ciacci Piccolomini d'Aragona

This well-respected, family-run vineyard has a classy tasting room/*enoteca* and an outdoor view terrace. If you're just dropping in, belly up to the wine bar for a few free tastes. Or reserve ahead fore harvest) is even more highly regarded and ranks among Italy's finest and most expensive wines. Made from 100 percent Sangiovese Grosso (a.k.a. Brunello) grapes, it's smooth, dry, and aged for a minimum of two years in wood casks, plus an additional four months in the bottle. *Riserva* wines are aged an additional year. Brunello is designed to cellar for 10 years or longer—but who can wait?

It pairs well with the local cuisine, but the perfect match is the fine Chianina beef. *Buon appetito!*

Today, there are around 240 mostly small producers of Brunello in the Montalcino region; I've recommended just a few, which I find fun and accessible. A simpler option is to sample a few different wines at one of the good wine bars in Montalcino (see page 704).

You'll also see Rosso di Montalcino (a younger version of Brunello), which is aged for one year. This "poor man's Brunello" is very good, at half the price.

for a more formal tasting of top-quality wines (€15 tasting, €40 tasting plus tour of cellar, €10-25 bottles; April-Oct Mon-Sat 10:00-18:00, closed Nov-March and Sun year-round; down a back lane near Sant'Antimo Abbey—head toward Castelnuovo dell'Abate but go right before entering that town, following signs toward *Sant'Angelo in Colle*, +39 0577 835 616, www.ciaccipiccolomini.com, visite@ciaccipiccolomini.com).

Castello Banfi-Poggio alle Mura

Much bigger and glossier than the other recommended wineries, Banfi is one of the largest producers in the area. Despite its size, the estate is charming, set in a castle located in a picturesque corner southwest of Sant'Antimo. This is a good option for Sundays, when other places are closed, or for a spontaneous drop-in tasting at the winery's *enoteca* (tastings start at €24; daily 10:00-19:30, shorter hours off-season; expensive tours available on request, +39 055 877 500, www.castellobanfiilborgo.com, hospitality@banfi.it). You'll find Banfi about 20 minutes south of Montalcino; follow SP-14 to Borgo Santa Rita and cut back north, following signs to *Poggio alle Mura*.

North of Montalcino
Altesino
Elegant and stately, Altesino owns perhaps the most stunning location of all, just off the back road connecting Montalcino north to Buonconvento. You'll twist up on cypress-lined gravel lanes to this perch, which looks out over an expanse of vineyards with Montalcino hovering on the horizon (€15 for tour and basic tasting; daily 10:00-17:00, shorter hours off-season; reserve ahead, Loc. Altesino 54, +39 0577 806 208, www.altesino.it, info@altesino.it). You'll find the turnoff for Altesino along the back road (SP-45) between Montalcino and Buonconvento.

Santa Giulia
On the outskirts of Torrenieri, this is a quintessential family-run winery, with an emphasis on quality over quantity (only 30,000 bottles a year). They also pro-duce excellent olive oil, prosciutto, and salami. Less picturesque and much more rustic than the other wineries listed here, a tour at Santa Giulia is a Back Door experience. Call or email in advance to reserve a "Zero Kilometer" lunchtime tasting, with farm-fresh cold cuts, cheese, and bruschetta for €25; add pasta and dessert for €20 more (€15 for 3 tastes and tour, 2-person minimum, €15-34 bottles; Mon-Sat 10:00-17:00, closed Sun; Loc. Santa Giulia 48, +39 0577 834 270, www.santagiuliamontalcino.it, info@santagiuliamontalcino.it).

From Torrenieri's main intersection, follow the brown *Via Francigena* signs. After crossing the train tracks and a bridge, watch on the left and follow signs for *Sta. Giulia;* you'll take gravel roads through farm fields to the winery.

Sleeping in Montalcino

$$$ **Hotel Dei Capitani,** at the end of town near the bus station, has plush public spaces, an inviting summertime pool, and a cliffside terrace offering plenty of reasons to lounge. About half of the 29 basic rooms come with vast Tuscan views and are worth pay-

ing a bit extra for (no balconies, request a view room when you reserve); the nonview rooms are bigger but face a somewhat noisy street (RS%, air-con, elevator, limited free parking—first come, first served, Via Lapini 6, +39 0577 847 227, www.deicapitani.it, info@deicapitani.it).

$ B&B da Idolina has four good rooms above an antique shop on the main street (check-in 15:00-19:00—call if arriving later, parking available, Via Mazzini 65, check in at the antique shop, +39 0577 849 212, www.idolina1946.com, fulvia.soda@gmail.com, Fulvia).

$ Albergo Giardino has nine big, modern-minimalist rooms in a convenient location near the bus stop (RS%, air-con, free parking, Piazza Cavour 4, +39 0577 848 257, mobile +39 371 426 1838, www.albergoilgiardino.it, info@albergoilgiardino.it).

Eating in Montalcino

$$ Re di Macchia is an invitingly intimate restaurant where Antonio serves up the big, hearty portions of Tuscan fare that Roberta cooks. Look for their seasonal menu and a fine Montalcino wine list (reservations strongly recommended, Fri-Wed 12:00-14:00 & 19:00-21:00, closed Thu, Via Soccorso Saloni 21, +39 0577 846 116).

$$ Taverna del Grappolo Blu, tucked in a cellar down a picturesque staircase off the main drag, is serious about its wine, game, homemade pasta, and vegetarian options (reservations smart, daily 12:00-15:00 & 19:00-22:00, a few steps off Via Mazzini at Scale di Via Moglio 1, +39 0577 847 150, www.grappoloblu.it, friendly Luciano).

$$ Ristorante-Pizzeria San Giorgio is a homey trattoria/pizzeria with traditional decor and reasonable prices. It's great for families and a reliable choice for a simple meal (daily 12:00-15:00 & 19:00-22:30, Via Soccorso Saloni 10, +39 0577 848 507, Mara).

Quick Bite: The **$** *pizza al taglio* shop, right on Piazza del Popolo at #11, has both pizza slices and sandwiches that they can heat up for you—ask for *scalda* (daily 10:30-21:30).

Picnic: Gather ingredients at the **Co-op supermarket** on Via Sant'Agostino (Mon-Sat 8:30-13:00 & 16:00-20:00, closed Sun, near Sant'Agostino Church), then enjoy your feast up at the Madonna del Soccorso Church, with vast territorial views.

Montalcino Connections

Montalcino is well connected to Siena; other bus connections are inconvenient but generally workable. Montalcino's bus stop is on Piazza Cavour, within the town walls. Bus tickets are sold at the bar on Piazza Cavour, at the TI, and at some tobacco shops, but not on board. Check schedules at the TI, at the bus station, or online (at www.at-bus.it). The nearest train station is a 30-minute bus ride away, in Buonconvento.

From Montalcino by Bus: For long-distance journeys, you'll always start out on bus #114, which goes to **Siena** (6/day Mon-Sat, 4/day Sun, 1.5 hours). En route, this bus goes through Torrenieri (change for **Pienza** or **Montepulciano,** 3-4/day, none on Sun); from Torrenieri it's 25 minutes to Pienza, 45 minutes to Montepulciano, then **Buonconvento** (where you can catch a train to **Florence**). You can also reach Florence by riding the bus to Siena, then taking the train. Since the Montepulciano bus connection is sporadic, consider hiring a taxi (about €70 one-way).

Heart of Tuscany Drive

VAL D'ORCIA LOOP

If you have just one day to connect the ultimate Tuscan towns and views, this is the loop I'd stitch together with a driving tour. In addition to larger towns (Montepulciano, Pienza) and smaller ones (Bagno Vignoni, Rocca d'Orcia), this loop drive, worth ▲▲▲, gives you a good look at the area called the Val d'Orcia (val DOR-chah), boasting some of the best scenery in Italy. The Val d'Orcia is manicured and feels manmade—shaped by gen-

erations of hardworking farmers. Most of this journey is through velvety, gentle, rolling hillsides generously draped with vivid-green crops in the springtime, and a parched moonscape in the late summer and fall. Hilltop villas and hill towns big and small recede to the horizon. This almost otherworldly smoothness constitutes many travelers' notions of Tuscan perfection.

Planning Your Drive: If you're in a rush and don't linger in any of the towns, you could do this drive in a couple of hours. To hit the sights, explore the towns, and linger over a meal or a glass of wine, spread it out over an entire day. (You could even splice in a side trip to a Brunello winery for a tasting.) I've started and ended the clockwise loop in Montepulciano, but you could just as easily start and end in Pienza. If gardens are your thing, do this loop when La Foce Gardens are open.

Heart of Tuscany Drive

To Montepulciano Train Stn.

To Castelmuzio & Siena

CUGUSI DAIRY FARM

SAN BIAGIO CHURCH

SP-17

SP-71

SP-146

DRIVING TOUR BEGINS & ENDS

Montepulciano

SP-146

To Torrenieri & Siena

SP-146

Pienza

SP-146

CORSIGNANO CHURCH

SP-18

❹

SR-2

San Quirico d'Orcia

To Montalcino & Siena

SR-2

SPEDALETTO CASTLE

SP-88

Monticchiello

SP-88

Chianciano Terme

SP-146

❶

To Chiusi & A-1 Autostrada to Orvieto & Rome

Bagno ❷ **Vignoni**

SP-18

SP-53

LA FOCE GARDENS

❸

Rocca d'Orcia

Castiglione d'Orcia

SR-2 (Via Cassia)

V A L   D '   O R C I A

Orcia River

SS-323

To Montalcino & Sant'Antimo

To Monte Amiata (in distance)

SR-2

To Orvieto & Rome

Note: Driving route width exaggerated for clarity

5 Kilometers

5 Miles

HEART OF TUSCANY

Eateries

❶ Dopolavoro La Foce
❷ Osteria del Leone & Il Loggiato
❸ La Cisterna nel Borgo
❹ Ristorante Daria

From Montepulciano to Bagno Vignoni (via La Foce)

Before leaving Montepulciano, consider dropping by the showpiece Renaissance **San Biagio Church,** which sits at the base of the town (watch for its long, level, tree-lined driveway exactly where you leave Montepulciano on the road toward Pienza—see "Sights and Experiences in Montepulciano," earlier in this chapter).

To begin our loop, drive south, at first following signs to *Chianciano Terme* and *Chiusi.* Just 1 kilometer south of Montepulciano, watch on the right for the turnoff to *Castelluccio* and *Monticchiello.* Turn off here and zip along a pastoral back road for 5 kilometers. Pass the turnoff for Monticchiello on your right, and carry on straight ahead as the road continues uphill and becomes gravel. Grinding your way up, watch on your right for the jagged Tuscan cliffs called *calanchi.* You'll pop out at the T-intersection in front of the entrance to the **La Foce Gardens** (from this intersection, parking and reception are 50 yards to the left—look for *Loc. La Foce;* learn more about the gardens later in this chapter).

From La Foce, head downhill tracking signs toward *Siena* and *Roma.* After a few hundred yards, watch on the left for the big gravel parking lot of the recommended **Dopolavoro La Foce** restaurant (across the street). From this lot, you have a fine view of one of the iconic cypress-lined driveways of Tuscany.

Continue downhill along this road for about 5 kilometers, through pristine farm fields, until you reach a major intersection, where you'll turn right toward *Pienza* and *Siena* (on SP-53). Immersed in spectacular scenery, you'll twist between giant cypresses for about 10 kilometers. This road parallels the region's namesake **Orcia River** ("Val d'Orcia" means "Orcia River Valley").

Take a moment to simply appreciate your surroundings. You're surrounded by clay hills—once the floor of a prehistoric sea—that are ideal for cereal crops. Grains alternate every few years with a crop of fava beans, which help reintroduce nitrogen to the soil. It seems that every grassy hilltop is capped with a family farmhouse. Partway along this road, you'll pass a turnoff (on the right) offering a speedy shortcut to Pienza, just 8 stunning kilometers away. But there's so much more to see; I'd rather carry on with our loop.

The tower looming on the hill ahead of you is Rocca d'Orcia's Tentennano Castle (described later). Nearing the end of the road, you'll pass (on the left) the front door of an old farmhouse with oddly formidable crenellated towers, like a little castle in the field. This is **Spedaletto Castle,** built during the 12th century as a hospice for pilgrims walking the Via Francigena to Rome. Today it serves a similar purpose, as an *agriturismi,* housing wayfarers like you.

When you reach a T-intersection with the main SR-2 highway, turn left (toward *Roma*), then immediately take the exit for **Bagno Vignoni.** To explore this fascinating medieval spa town—with its main square filled with a thermal-spring-fed pool—see "Heart of Tuscany Sights," in the next section. To see the empty fortress at **Rocca d'Orcia,** stay on the SR-2 highway just 1 kilometer past Bagno Vignoni, then watch for the next turnoff.

From Bagno Vignoni to Pienza (with Detours to Brunello Wineries and Tuscan Views)

From Bagno Vignoni, head north on SR-2 (toward *San Quirico d'Orcia* and *Siena*). After just 4 kilometers, in San Quirico d'Orcia, turn off onto the SP-146 road to Pienza, also marked for *Chiusi, Chianciano Terme,* and *Montepulciano.*

But before heading down that road, consider a few potential detours: First, if you won't have time to delve deeply into Brunello wine country, now is a good time to side-trip to your choice of

Brunello wineries; those I've recommended on page 705 are all within about a 20- to 25-minute drive of San Quirico. Read the descriptions, take your pick, and call ahead to reserve a tour and tasting. Most of the places I list don't allow drop-ins. Another option is to zip into the town of **Montalcino** itself—an easy and well-signed 15-minute drive from San Quirico—and taste some local vintages at a wine bar there.

Back on the SP-146 road from San Quirico to Pienza, you enjoy one of the region's most postcard-worthy stretches—with grand panoramas in both directions, including two more quintessential Tuscan scenes: the **Chapel of Madonna di Vitaleta** (after 2 kilometers, on the right); and a classic **farmhouse with trees,** just before Pienza (about 9 kilometers after San Quirico, on the left).

Finally you'll pull into **Pienza,** where you can park and tour the town using the information earlier in this chapter.

From Pienza to Montepulciano (via Monticchiello)

If you're in a hurry or losing sunlight, just hop back on the main SP-146 road for the 12-kilometer straight shot back to Montepulciano (enjoying some pullouts on the left with fine views of the town). But I prefer this longer, even more dramatic route, via the fortified village of Monticchiello.

From the traffic circle at the entry to Pienza's town center, instead of heading for Montepulciano, follow the road that runs along the left side of town (marked *Amiata* and *Monticchiello*—as you face Pienza, you'll continue straight when the main road bends left). This road loops around behind and below the far end of the village, where you can consider a brief detour to see Pienza's oldest church: Turn off on the right at the brown sign for *Pieve di Corsigiano* and drive a few hundred yards to **Corsignano Parish Church** (described on page 698).

Continuing on the main road past that turnoff, you'll drop steeply down into the valley, feeling as if you're sinking into a lavish painting. Dead ahead is **Monte Amiata,** the tallest mountain in Tuscany. Meanwhile, don't forget to savor the similarly stellar views of Pienza in your rearview mirror. After 5 kilometers, look on the left for the turnoff to Monticchiello (brown sign). From here, carry on for 4 kilometers—watching on the left for fine vistas of Pienza and for another classic twisty cypress-lined road—to the pleasant town of **Monticchiello.** This town, with an excellent recommended restaurant (Daria) and a compact, fortified townscape worth exploring, is a good place to stretch your legs; see more in the next section.

From Monticchiello, there are two routes back to Montepulciano: For the shorter route (6 kilometers), partly on gravel roads, drive all the way to the base of the Monticchiello old town, then turn right. For the longer route (10 kilometers), which stays on paved roads but circles back the way our loop started, turn off for Montepulciano at the main intersection, in the flat part of town that's lower down.

HEART OF TUSCANY SIGHTS

Below are the main sights you'll pass on my Heart of Tuscany driving route. Two of the main stops—the towns of Montepulciano and Pienza—are covered earlier in this chapter.

▲La Foce Gardens

One of the finest gardens in Tuscany, La Foce (lah FOH-cheh) caps a hill with geometrical Italian gardens and rugged English

gardens that flow seamlessly into the Tuscan countryside. The gardens were a labor of love for Iris Origo, an English-born, Italian-bred aristocrat who left her mark on this area and wrote evocatively about her time here. The gardens—which are worth a pilgrimage for garden lovers—can be visited only with a guided tour, and only three days a week (Wed, Thu, Sun) and some holidays.

Cost and Hours: €10; 45-minute tours offered April-Oct Wed at 15:00, 16:00, 17:00, and 18:00; Thu, Sun, and holidays at 11:30, 15:00, and 16:30—can be closed for private events, so check online in advance; private tours available, no tours in winter, ticket office opens 15 minutes before tour time, +39 0578 69101, www. lafoce.com.

Getting There: La Foce sits in the hills above the busy town of Chianciano Terme. You can avoid SP-146 from Montepulciano through Chianciano (heavy traffic, poor signage) by following a more scenic route through the countryside (described at the start of my Heart of Tuscany Drive).

Eating and Sleeping near La Foce: Near the gardens, the Origo family runs a memorably charming roadside restaurant, **$$ Dopolavoro La Foce** ("After Work"). Once the quitting-time hangout for local farmers, today its interior is country-chic. The menu offers basic sandwiches or pasta and meat (featuring elegant hamburgers). The garden terrace out back is a chirpy delight, and the parking lot across the busy road offers one of the best vantage points on that perfect Tuscan road (Tue-Sun 12:30-21:30, closed Mon and Nov-March, Strada della Vittoria 90, +39 0578 754 025, run with flair by Asia). Also nearby is their remote, restful B&B (described on page 676).

▲Bagno Vignoni

Thanks to the unique geology of this part of Tuscany (see sidebar), several natural hot springs bubble up between the wineries and hill towns. And the town of Bagno Vignoni (BAHN-yoh veen-YOH-nee)—with a quirky history, a pleasant-to-stroll street plan punctuated with steamy canals, and various places to take a dip—is the most accessible and enjoyable to explore. If you'd like to recuperate from your sightseeing and wine tasting by soaking in the thermal baths, bring your swimsuit.

Getting There: Bagno Vignoni is well signed, just off the main SR-2 highway linking Siena to Rome (5 kilometers south of San Quirico d'Orcia). Park in the free lot (just past the Adler Spa Resort Thermae) or in the pay lot by the big roundabout and walk into town, taking the left fork (in front of Hotel Le Terme).

Bagno Vignoni Town Walk: Emerging into the main square, walk under the covered loggia and look out over the aptly named **Piazza delle Sorgenti** ("Square of the Sources"), filled with a vast pool. Natural spring water bubbles up at the far end at temperatures around 125 degrees Fahrenheit. Known since Roman times, these hot springs were harnessed for their medicinal properties in the Middle Ages.

You're not allowed to wade or swim in this main pool today, but an easy stroll through town shows you other facets of these healing waters. Turn right and circle the pool, then turn left down Via delle Sorgenti. Listen for the water that gushes under your feet, as it leaves the pool and heads for its big plunge over the cliff. You'll emerge at an open zone with the cliff-capping **ruins** of medieval mills and cisterns that once made full use of Bagno Vignoni's main resource. Here you'll also have a chance to dip your toes or fingers into streams of now-tepid water. At the canals' end, the water plunges down into the gorge carved by the Orcia River.

Taking the Waters: The modern **Piscina Val di Sole** bath complex, inside Hotel Posta Marcucci, is simple but sophisticated. It's a serene spot to soak (in water ranging from 80 to 105 degrees Fahrenheit) while taking in soaring views of Rocca d'Orcia across the valley (€33, towel rental and lockers available; daily 9:30-18:00,

Fri-Sat also 21:00-24:00; +39 0577 887 112, www.postamarcucci.it).

Eating in Bagno Vignoni: The town's class act is **$$$ Osteria del Leone,** on the cheery little *piazzetta* just behind the loggia, with charming tables out on the square. Inside it's dull and modern, with a fine interior garden (closed Mon, Via dei Mulini 3, +39 0577 887 300, www.osteriadelleone.it). For something a bit more affordable and casual, drop by the nearby **$$ Il Loggiato,** with stony indoor seating or outdoor tables (closed Thu, Via delle Sorgenti 36, +39 0577 139 0723).

Rocca d'Orcia

The fortress looming over Rocca d'Orcia (ROH-kah DOR-chah) perches high above the main SR-2 highway. Likely inhabited and fortified since Etruscan times, this strategic hilltop was a seat of great regional power in the 12th century. During this time, Rocca d'Orcia was one of a chain of forts that watched over pilgrims walking the Via Francigena to Rome.

Today the **Rocca di Tentennano** fortress—an empty shell of a castle with modern steel stairs and a grand 360-degree panorama at its top—looks stark and abandoned. It seems to dare you to pay €3 to take the very steep hike up from the parking lots below (May-Sept daily 10:30-13:30 & 16:30-18:30, shorter hours off-season; mobile +39 392 003 3028 or +39 333 986 0788).

Eating in Rocca d'Orcia: It's worth the effort to reach rustic **$$ La Cisterna nel Borgo.** Marta and Fede serve up simple but beautifully prepared dishes that mingle big Tuscan flavors and flourishes gathered from Marta's travels. The cavelike interior has character, but try to get an outdoor table, facing the namesake cistern on an enchanting, ivy-draped piazza where old ladies chat and stray dogs and cats beg for scraps (Tue-Fri 12:00-14:00 & 19:00-22:00, Sat-Sun 19:00-22:00 only, closed Mon and unpredictably at other times—call ahead; Borgo Mestro 37, tel. 0577-887-280, www.cisternanelborgo.com). Dining here comes with a hike: Park at the lot below Rocca di Tentennano, hike up past the castle entrance, then keep going as the road crests the hill and twists downhill into the village.

▲Monticchiello

This 200-person fortified village clings to the high ground in the countryside just south of Pienza and Montepulciano. While not quite "undiscovered," Monticchiello is relatively untrampled, and feels like a real place where you can get in touch with authentic Tuscan village life.

Eating in Monticchiello: At the warm and classy **$$$ Ristorante Daria,** you'll enjoy seasonal, traditional Tuscan dishes presented with flair in a modern setting. It's in the heart of the stony hill town amid sumptuous scenery. Reservations are wise (Thu-Tue 12:15-14:30 & 19:15-22:00, closed Wed, Via San Luigi 3, +39 0578 755 170, www.ristorantedaria.it). Arriving in Monticchiello, walk through the town's gate, head about 50 yards straight up the hill, and bear right.

ASSISI

Assisi is famous for its hometown boy, St. Francis, who made very, very good. While Francis the saint is interesting, Francesco Bernardone the man is even more so, and mementos of his days in Assisi are everywhere—where he was baptized, a shirt he wore, a hill he prayed on, and a church where a vision changed his life.

Around the year 1200, this simple friar from Assisi countered the decadence of Church government and society in general with a powerful message of nonmaterialism and a "slow down and smell God's roses" lifestyle. Like Jesus, Francis taught by example, living without worldly goods and aiming to love all creation. A huge monastic order grew out of his teachings, which were gradually embraced (some would say co-opted) by the Church. Christianity's most popular saint and its purest example of simplicity is now glorified in beautiful churches, along with his female counterpart, St. Clare. In 1939, Italy made Francis one of its patron saints; in 2013, the newly elected pope took his name.

Francis' message of love, simplicity, and sensitivity to the environment has a broad and timeless appeal. But every pilgrimage site inevitably gets commercialized, and Francis' legacy is now Assisi's basic industry. In summer, this Umbrian town bursts with flash-in-the-pan Francis fans and Franciscan knickknacks. Those able to see past the glow-in-the-dark rosaries and bobble-head friars can have a "travel on purpose" experience. Even a block or two off the congested main drag, you'll find pockets of serenity that, it's easy to imagine, must have made Francis feel at peace.

Assisi Area

To Valfabbrica
To Gualdo Tadino
To Tordibetto
ASSISI
See detail maps
SS-147
ROCCA MAGGIORE
To Bastia Umbria
BASILICA OF ST. FRANCIS
BUS STOP & P
Piazza Matteotti
VIA SANTUARIO
P
BUS STOP
Piazza Unità d'Italia
P B
BUS STOP
Largo Properzio
To Perugia & Florence
LAUNDERETTE
VIA ASSISI
PATH
HERMITAGE
TRAIN STATION
SAN DAMIANO
SS-75
Mount Subasio
BUS STOP
TO SIENA & UPPER TOWN
EXIT
SS-147
BASILICA OF SANTA MARIA DEGLI ANGELI
FREEWAY
To La Mandrie di San Paolo Agriturismo
1 Kilometer
1 Mile
N
To Spello & Foligno

PLANNING YOUR TIME

Assisi is worth a day and a night. Its walled old town has a half-day of sightseeing and another half-day of wonder. The essential sight is the Basilica of St. Francis. For a good visit, take my self-guided Assisi Walk, going from the top of town to the basilica at the bottom, and my Basilica of St. Francis Tour. With more time, wander the back streets and linger on the main square, Piazza del Comune.

Most visitors are day-trippers. While the town's a zoo by day, it's a delight at night. Assisi after dark is closer to a place Francis could call home. But for most visitors, two nights is more than you really need.

Orientation to Assisi

Crowned by a ruined castle, Assisi spills downhill to its famous Basilica of St. Francis. The town is beautifully preserved and rich in history. A 5.5-magnitude earthquake in 1997 did more damage to the tourist industry than to the town's buildings. Fortunately, tourists—whether art lovers, pilgrims, or both— have returned, drawn by Assisi's special allure.

The city stretches across a ridge that rises from a flat plain. The Basilica of St. Francis sits at the low end of town; Piazza Matteotti (bus stop and parking lot) is at the high end; and the main square, Piazza del Comune, lies in between. The main drag (called Via San Francesco for most of its course) runs from Piazza del Comune to the basilica. Capping the hill above the town is the ruined castle, called the Rocca Maggiore, and rising above that is Mount Subasio. The town is smaller than its fame might lead you to think: Walking uphill from the basilica to Piazza Matteotti takes 30 minutes, while the downhill journey takes about 15 minutes. Some Francis sights lie outside the city walls, in the flat area beneath the ridge (the modern part of town, called Santa Maria degli Angeli) and in the hills above.

TOURIST INFORMATION

The TI is in the center of the old town on Piazza del Comune (daily 9:00-19:00, above the Roman Forum museum, +39 075 813 8680, www.visit-assisi.it). There's also a branch (with shorter hours) down in the valley, across the street from the big piazza in front of the Basilica of Santa Maria degli Angeli.

The **Assisi Card,** available to overnight guests, offers discounts on area sights, parking, and taxis.

ARRIVAL IN ASSISI

By Train: The train station is about two miles below Assisi, in Santa Maria degli Angeli. There is no official baggage storage, but the newsstand on the main floor will hold bags for a small charge. There's no baggage storage in the old town.

Assisi Link city **buses** labeled *Centro/San Francesco* (line #C) connect the station with the hilltop old town. Buses usually leave twice hourly from the bus stop immediately to your left as you exit the station (daily 5:30-23:00, schedule posted at stop, 15-minute ride; buy tickets at the newsstand inside the train station for €1.30, or on board the bus for €2, validate ticket at yellow box as you board, operated by Busitalia). The bus may be awaiting the arrival of your train. If so, don't dawdle or you may miss it.

On the way up into town, the bus makes three stops: **Piazza Unità d'Italia** (near Porta San Pietro, below the Basilica of St. Francis), **Largo Properzio** (just outside Porta Nuova), and finally up top at **Piazza Matteotti.** The middle stop, Largo Properzio, is best for hotels in the center—just walk uphill and through the gateway and take the straight, mostly level street (past the Basilica of St. Clare) about 10 minutes to the main square.

Returning from the old town to the train station, buses reverse the route, leaving Piazza Matteotti twice hourly, driving down through town to the train station (then proceeding to the Basilica of Santa Maria degli Angeli).

Taxis from the train station to the old town cost about €15, with extra charges for luggage, night service, additional people... and sometimes just for being a tourist. When departing the old town, you'll find taxi stands at Piazza Giovanni Paolo II, the Basilica of St. Francis, the Basilica of St. Clare, and Piazza del Comune (or have your hotel call for you, +39 075 813 100). Expect to pay a minimum of €10 for any ride.

By Bus: Buses from Siena generally arrive at the stop next to the Basilica of Santa Maria degli Angeli, near the train station (see earlier for directions from the station into town). Most other intercity buses arrive at the base of the old town.

By Car: Drivers can follow *parcheggi* signs to several handy parking lots. Piazza Matteotti's wonderful underground parking garage is at the top of the town and comes with bits of ancient Rome in the walls. Another big lot, Parcheggio Giovanni Paolo II, is at the bottom end of town, 200 yards below the Basilica of St. Francis (next to the Piazza Unità d'Italia bus stop). At Parcheggio Porta Nuova, at the south end of town, an escalator delivers you to Porta Nuova near St. Clare's. The lots vary in price (about €1.30/hour, €12/day), but overnight guests get a discount with the Assisi Card. For day-trippers, the best plan is to park at Piazza Matteotti, follow my self-guided town walk, tour the Basilica of St. Francis, and then either catch a bus back to Piazza Matteotti or simply wander back up through town to your car.

ASSISI

HELPFUL HINTS

Best Shopping: Tacky knickknack vendors line the streets leading to the Basilica of St. Francis. For better shops (with local handicrafts), head to Via San Rufino and Corso Mazzini (both just off Piazza del Comune; some shops described on page 732). A Saturday-morning market fills Via Borgo San Pietro (along the bottom edge of town).

Festivals: Assisi hosts several annual festivals commemorating St. Francis and life in the Middle Ages. The springtime medieval **Festa di Calendimaggio** features costume parades, concerts, and competitions among Assisi's rival neighborhoods (www.calendimaggiodiassisi.it). The **Settimana Francescana** commemorates the beginning of the end of Francis' life, when he made his way for the last time to the Porziuncola Chapel (Sept 28). This week-long celebration culminates on October 4 in the **Festa di San Francesco,** which marks his death with religious processions, special church services, and an arts, crafts, and folklore fair.

Laundry: **Lavanderia Lemon 2** is out of the way in the lower

1 Lower Basilica Entrance & Basilica Info Office
2 Upper Basilica Entrance
3 Pinacoteca (Art Museum)
4 To Le Mandrie di San Paolo Agriturismo
5 Locanda del Podestà Restaurant
6 Le Terrazze di Properzio

town, a five-minute walk from the Basilica of Santa Maria degli Angeli (daily 8:00-23:00, Via Giovanni Becchetti 38, +39 393 332 2229).

Travel Agencies: You can purchase train, bus, and plane tickets at **Agenzia Viaggi Stoppini,** centrally located between Piazza del Comune and the Basilica of St. Clare. Manager Fabrizio is patient with tourists' needs (Mon-Sat 9:30-12:30 and some afternoons, closed Sun, also offers day trips to nearby towns,

Corso Mazzini 31, +39 075 812 597, www.viaggistoppiniassisi. it).

Local Guides: Giuseppe Karabotis is a good licensed guide (€130/3 hours, €260/6 hours, mobile +39 328 867 0567, iokarabot@libero.it). **Daniela Moretti** is a hardworking guide from Perugia who knows Assisi and all of Umbria (€120/half-day, €240/day, mobile +39 335 829 9984, www.danyguide. com, danyguide@hotmail.com). If they're busy, they can recommend other guides.

GETTING AROUND ASSISI

Most visitors need only their feet to get everywhere in Assisi, except to the lower town—with the train station and Basilica of Santa Maria degli Angeli—which can be reached by bus on Assisi Link line #C (see directions earlier, under "Arrival in Assisi").

Within the old town, minibuses #A and #B run every 20-40 minutes, linking the lower end (near the Basilica of St. Francis) with the middle (Piazza del Comune) and the top (Piazza Matteotti). While it's only a 15-minute stroll from the upper end to the lower, the climb back up can have you looking for a lift. Hop on a bus marked *Piazza Matteotti* if you're exhausted after your Basilica of St. Francis visit and need a sweat-free five-minute return to the top of the old town. Before boarding, confirm the destination (catch the bus below the basilica, just outside the Porta San Francesco).

You can buy a bus ticket (good on any city bus) at a newsstand or tobacco shop for €1.30, or get a ticket from the driver for €2. After you've stamped your ticket on board, it's valid for 90 minutes.

Assisi Walk

There's much more to Assisi than just St. Francis and what the blitz tour groups see. This self-guided walk, worth ▲▲, covers the town from top to bottom, starting near Piazza Matteotti. To reach the piazza, ride the bus from the train station (or from Piazza Giovanni Paolo II) to the last stop; drive up (and park in the underground lot); or hike 10 minutes uphill from Piazza del Comune.

🎧 Download my free Assisi Town Walk audio tour.

• *Start 50 yards beyond Piazza Matteotti at the busy intersection (opposite the big palazzo with the small balcony, where a small road angles downhill—see map).*

❶ Roman Amphitheater (Anfiteatro Romano)

This lane, named Via Anfiteatro Romano, skirts the cozy neighborhood built around the site of a long-gone Roman amphitheater—a reminder that Assisi was once an important Roman town. Circle to the right along the curved lane that marks the amphitheater's footprint. Imagine how colorful the town laundry basin (on the right) must have been in previous generations, when the women of Assisi gathered here to do their wash. Just beyond, above another small rectangular basin, are the coats of arms of Assisi's leading families.

A few steps farther, leave the amphitheater, hiking up the stairs on the right to the top of the hill, for an overhead view of the ancient oval. The Roman stones have long been absorbed into the medieval architecture. It was Roman tradition to locate the amphitheater outside of town, which this used to be. While the amphitheater dates from the first century AD, the buildings filling it today were built in the 13th and 14th centuries. Notice the town's carefully maintained complexion: When redoing a roof, locals will mix old and new tiles.

• *Continue on, peeking out the last window on your right before heading to the top of the staircase to enjoy the even grander fortress view in the distance.*

❷ Fortress View

Rocca Minore ("little fortress"), to the right, gives the town's young lovers a little privacy. Rocca Maggiore ("big fortress"), to the far left, offers fine views for those willing to make the ascent (described later, under "More Sights in Assisi"). It provided townsfolk a refuge in times of attack. A quarry underneath the Rocca Maggiore was a handy source for Assisi's characteristic pink limestone.

• *Follow Via Porta Perlici downhill into town (toward Hotel la Rocca). Enjoy the higgledy-piggledy architecture (this neighborhood has some of the most photogenic back lanes in town).*

Fifty yards down, to the left of the arched gate, find the wall containing an **aqueduct** that dates from Roman times. It still brings water from a mountain spring into the city (push the brass tap for a taste). After another 50 yards, turn left through a medieval town gate (with Hotel la Rocca on your right). Just after the hotel, you'll pass under a second gate dating from Roman times. Follow Via Porta Perlici a few atmospheric blocks downhill until you hit a fine square facing a big church.

❸ Cathedral of San Rufino
(Cattedrale San Rufino)

Trick question: Who's Assisi's patron saint? While Francis is one of Italy's patron saints, Rufino (the town's first bishop, martyred and buried here in the third

century) is Assisi's. This cathedral (seat of the local bishop)—worth ▲▲—is 11th-century Romanesque with a Neoclassical interior, and dedicated to Rufino. Although it has what is considered one of the best and purest Romanesque facades in all of Umbria, the big triangular top (just a decorative wall) was added in Gothic times. Inside you can see the 11th-century font where Francis and Clare were baptized, and traces of earlier Roman construction.

Assisi Walk

Cost and Hours: Cathedral—free, daily 7:00-19:00, +39 075 812 283; museum—€3.50, Thu-Tue 10:00-13:00 & 15:00-18:00, closed Wed, shorter hours off-season and Sun, www.assisimuseodiocesano.it.

Visiting the Church: Before going in, study the facade—a jungle of beasts emphasizing how the church was a refuge and sanctuary in a scary world. Notice the lions at the base of the facade, flanking each door. One is eating a Christian martyr, reminding worshippers of the courage of early Christians. Here, as in other medieval Assisi churches, worshippers absorbed pre-Christian themes and symbols into their world.

Enter the church. While the front of the church is an unremarkable mix of 17th- and 18th-century Baroque and Neoclassical, the rear (near where you enter) has several points of interest. Notice the two fine statues at the bases of the first pillars: *St. Francis* and *St. Clare* (by Giovanni Dupré, 1888).

In the church's back-right corner is an old baptismal font (sur-

❶	Roman Amphitheater
❷	Fortress View
❸	Cathedral of San Rufino
❹	Medieval Architecture
❺	Basilica of St. Clare
❻	Umbrian View
❼	Arches & Artisans
❽	Piazza del Comune
❾	Church of Santo Stefano
❿	To Via San Francesco

rounded by a semicircular black iron grate). In about 1181, a baby boy was baptized in this font. His parents were upwardly mobile Francophiles who called him Francesco ("Frenchy"). In 1194, a nobleman baptized his daughter Clare here. Eighteen years later, their paths crossed in this same church, when Clare attended a class and became mesmerized by the teacher—Francis. Traditionally, the children of Assisi are still baptized here.

In the nave, the striking glass panels in the floor reveal foundations preserved from the ninth-century church that once stood here. You're walking on history. After the 1997 earthquake, structural inspectors checked the church from ceiling to floor. When they looked under the paving stones, they discovered graves (until Napoleon decreed otherwise, it was common practice to bury people in churches). Underneath that level, they found Roman foundations and some animal bones (suggesting the possibility of animal sacrifice). There might have been a Roman temple here; churches were often built upon temple ruins. Stand at the back of the church

St. Francis of Assisi (1181-1226)

In 1202, young Francesco Bernardone donned armor and rode out to battle the Perugians (residents of Umbria's capital city). The battle went badly, and Francis was captured and imprisoned for a year. He returned a changed man. He avoided friends and his father's lucrative business and spent more and more time outside the city walls fasting, praying, and searching for something.

In 1206, a vision changed his life, culminating in a dramatic confrontation. He stripped naked before the town leaders, threw his clothes at his father—turning his back on the comfortable material life—and declared his loyalty to God alone.

Idealistic young men flocked to Francis, and they wandered Italy like troubadours, spreading the joy of the Gospel to rich and poor. Francis became a cult figure, attracting huge crowds. They'd never seen anything like it—sermons preached outdoors, in the local language (not Church Latin), making God accessible to all. Francis' new order of monks was also extremely unmaterialistic, extolling poverty and simplicity. Despite their radicalism, the order eventually gained the pope's approval and spread through the world. Francis, who died in Assisi at the age of 44, left a legacy of humanism, equality, and love of nature that would eventually flower in the Renaissance.

In Francis' Sandal Steps

1. Baptized in Assisi's **Cathedral of San Rufino.**
2. Raised in the family home just off Piazza del Comune (now the **Chiesa Nuova**).
3. Heard call to "rebuild church" in **San Damiano.** (The crucifix of the church is now in the **Basilica of St. Clare.**)
4. Settled and established his order of monks at the **Porziuncola Chapel** (inside today's Basilica of Santa Maria degli Angeli).
5. Met Clare. (Her tomb and possessions are at the **Basilica of St. Clare.**)
6. Received the pope's blessing for his order (1223 document in the reliquary chapel at the **Basilica of St. Francis**).
7. Had many visions and was associated with miracles during his life (depicted in **Giotto's frescoes** in the Basilica of St. Francis' upper level).
8. Died at the **Porziuncola,** his body later interred beneath the **Basilica of St. Francis.**

facing the altar, and look left to the Roman cistern that collected rainwater (just beyond the great stone archway, next to where you entered). Take the three steps down and marvel at the fine stonework and Roman engineering. In the Middle Ages, this was the town's emergency water source when under attack.

Diocesan Museum and Crypt: Underneath the church, incorporated into the Roman ruins and columns, are the foundations of an earlier Church of San Rufino, now the crypt and a fine little museum. When it's open, you can go below to see the saint's sarcophagus (third century) and the cathedral's art from centuries past (down the stairs, near the baptismal font, well-described in English).

• *Leaving the church, walk to the end of the square and take a sharp left (at the recommended Pizza al Taglio da Andrea, on Via Dono Doni). After 20 yards, take a right and go all the way down the stairway to see some...*

❹ Medieval Architecture

At the bottom of the stairs, notice the pink limestone pavement, part of the surviving medieval town. The arches built over doorways indicate that the buildings date from the 12th through the 14th century, when Assisi was booming. Italian cities such as Assisi—thriving on the north-south trade between northern Europe and Rome—were in the process of inventing free-market capitalism, dabbling in democratic self-rule, and creating the modern urban lifestyle. The vaults you see that turn lanes into tunnels are reminders of medieval urban expansion—creating more living space (mostly 15th century). While the population grew, people wanted to live within the town's protective walls. Medieval Assisi had several times the population density of modern Assisi.

Notice the blooming balconies; Assisi holds a flower competition each June.

• *From the bottom of the stairs, head to the left and continue downhill. When you arrive at a street, turn left, going slightly uphill for a long block, then take the low road (right) at the Y, and head down Via Sermei. Continue down to the big church. Walk right, under the three massive buttresses, to Piazza Santa Chiara and the front of the church.*

❺ Basilica of St. Clare (Basilica di Santa Chiara)

Dedicated to the founder of the Order of the Poor Clares, this Umbrian Gothic church—worth ▲▲—is simple, in keeping with the order's dedication to a life of contemplation. In Clare's lifetime, the order was located in the humble Church of San Damiano, in the valley below, but after Clare's death, they needed a bigger and more glorious building. The church was built in 1265, and the huge buttresses were added in the next century.

ASSISI

St. Clare (1194-1253)

The 18-year-old rich girl of Assisi fell in love with Francis' message, and made secret arrangements to meet him. The night of Palm Sunday, 1212, she slipped out of her father's mansion in town and escaped to the valley below. A procession of friars with torches met her and took her to (what is today) the Basilica of Santa Maria degli Angeli. There, Francis cut her hair, clothed her in a simple brown tunic, and welcomed her into a life of voluntary poverty. Clare's father begged, ordered, and physically threatened her to return, but she would not budge.

Clare was joined by other women who banded together as the Poor Clares. She spent the next 40 years of her life within the confines of the convent of San Damiano: barefoot, vegetarian, and largely silent. Her regimen of prayer, meditation, and simple manual labor—especially knitting—impressed commoners and popes, leading to her canonization almost immediately after her death. St. Clare is often depicted carrying a monstrance (a little temple holding the Eucharist wafer).

Cost and Hours: Free, daily 9:00-12:00 & 14:00-19:00, until 18:00 in winter, +39 075 812 216, www.assisisantachiara.it.

Visiting the Basilica: The interior's fine frescoes were whitewashed in Baroque times. The battered remains of one on the left show how the fresco surface was hacked up so whitewash would stick. Imagine all the pristine frescoes hiding behind the whitewash (here and all over Europe).

On the right is the door to the Chapel of the Crucifix of San Damiano, with the simple wooden crucifix that changed Francis' life. In 1206, an emaciated, soul-searching, stark-raving Francis knelt before this crucifix of a living Christ (then located in the Church of San Damiano) and asked for guidance. According to legend, the crucifix spoke: "Go and rebuild my Church, which you can see has fallen into ruin." Francis followed the call.

Back in the nave, stairs lead

down to the tomb of St. Clare. Her tomb—discovered in about 1850—is at the far right end of the richly ornamented neo-Gothic crypt (the image is fiberglass; her actual bones lie underneath). As you circulate with the crowd of pilgrims, notice the paintings on the walls depicting spiritual lessons from Clare's life and death. At the opposite end of the crypt (near the stairs as you exit, well described in English) are important relics: the saint's robes, hair (in a silver box), and an enormous tunic she made—along with relics of St. Francis (including a bloodstained stocking he wore after receiving the stigmata). The attached cloistered community of the Poor Clares has flourished for 700 years.

• *Leave the church and belly up to the viewpoint at the edge of the square for a...*

❻ Umbrian View

On the left is the convent of St. Clare (global headquarters of all the Poor Clares). Below you lies the olive grove of the Poor Clares, which has been there since the 13th century. In the distance is a grand Umbrian view. Assisi overlooks the richest and biggest valley in hilly and mountainous Umbria. Called the "green heart of Italy," Umbria is the country's geographical center and Italy's only landlocked region. Enjoy the various shades of green: silver green (olives) and emerald green (grape vines) on the valley floor, and deep green on the hillsides (evergreen oak trees). The valleys are dotted by small family farms, many of which rent rooms as *agriturismi*.

Across the valley to the far right (and over the Tiber River), the rival town Perugia, where Francis was imprisoned, sits on its own hill.

Assisi's lower town, called Santa Maria degli Angeli, grew up with the coming of the railway in the 19th century. The church with the grayish-blue dome is the Basilica of Santa Maria degli Angeli (described later), the cradle of the Franciscan order. A popular pilgrimage site today, it marks the place where St. Francis lived, worked, and died.

By the way, many Spanish-speaking Franciscans established missions in California. Three grew into major cities: Los Angeles (named after this church), San Francisco (named after St. Francis), and Santa Clara (named after St. Clare).

• *From the church square, step out into Via Santa Chiara.*

❼ Arches and Artisans

Look left and right to find three old town gates, which illustrate how the city has grown (in concentric circles) since antiquity. First, look to the left, uphill on Via Santa Chiara, the high road. This first arch marks the site of the original Roman wall. In Roman days, this was the extent of Assisi. Now look right, beyond the church.

This old gate over the road dates from 1265, as the town expanded during the boom years and the city wall was pushed outward. Farther on, you can just make out the crenellations of the third gate: the Porta Nuova. Built in 1316, this "New Gate" marks the final expansion of Assisi, before its centuries of slow decline.

Walk uphill along Via Santa Chiara (which becomes Corso Mazzini) to the city's main square. As you pass under the arch you enter what was Roman Assisi—the city that Francis knew. The street is lined with interesting shops selling traditional embroidery, religious souvenirs, and gifty edibles. The shops on Corso Mazzini, on the stretch between the gate and Piazza del Comune, show off many local crafts. As you browse, watch for the following shops:

Galleria d'Arte Perna (on the left, #20b) sells the medieval fantasy townscapes of Paolo Grimaldi, a local painter who runs this shop with his brother, Alessandro.

A helpful **travel agency** is across the street and a few steps up (at #31, Agenzia Viaggi Stoppini; see "Helpful Hints," earlier).

Next, **d'Olivo** at #23 sells olive-wood carvings. It's said that St. Francis made the first Nativity scene to help humanize and, therefore, teach the Christmas message. That's why you'll see so many crèches in Assisi. (Even today, nearby villages are enthusiastic about their "living" manger scenes, and Italians everywhere enjoy setting up elaborate crèches in churches for Christmas.)

At #14A (also on the left) is a bakery, **Bar Sensi,** selling the traditional raisin-and-apple strudel called *rocciata* (roh-CHAH-tah, big enough to share).

Farther along on the left (on the corner at #2A) is **Antichita il Duomo,** selling religious art, manger scenes, Christmas ornaments, and Crucifixion figurines. Across the street at #5A is Galleria del Corso, displaying finely embroidered linens and baby clothes.

And on the square (at #34, on the right), the recommended **La Bottega dei Sapori** is worth a visit for edible and drinkable souvenirs.

• *You've walked up what was, in ancient times, the main drag into town. Ahead of you, the six fluted Corinthian columns of the Temple of Minerva marked the forum, today's...*

❽ Piazza del Comune

Sit at the fountain on the piazza for a few minutes of people-watching—don't you just love Italy? Within a few hundred yards of this square, on either side, were the medieval walls. Imagine the commotion of 5,000 people confined within these walls. No wonder St. Francis needed an escape for some peace and quiet.

Today, while the municipality of Assisi has a population of 25,000, only 1,000 people live in the old town: Many who left damaged homes after the 1997 earthquake decided to stay in the modern city below. This is one reason for the old town's plethora of tourist shops (and few services for residents like supermarkets or hardware stores).

• *Head over to the temple on the square.*

Temple of Minerva/Christian Church: Assisi has always been a spiritual center. The Romans went to great lengths to make this first-century BC Temple of Minerva a centerpiece of their city. Notice the columns that cut into the stairway. It was a tight fit here on the hilltop. In ancient times, the stairs went down—about twice as far as they do now—to the main drag, which has gradually been filled in over time. The Church of Santa Maria sopra ("over") Minerva was added in the 9th century. The bell tower is from the 13th century.

Pop inside the temple/church (free, daily 8:00-19:00, shorter hours in winter). Today's interior is 17th-century Baroque. Walk to the front. Flanking the altar to the back are the original Roman temple floor stones. You can even see the drains for the bloody sacrifices that took place here. Behind the statues of Peter and Paul, the original Roman embankment peeks through.

As you exit the church, look to the right, next to the door of the **bell tower.** The shapes set into the wall are the medieval city standards for the market that used to take place here. The large shapes are building materials, bricks, and roof tiles. The metal bars were the official measuring sticks for goods sold by length, a measurement that could change from city to city.

• *Across the square next to #11, step into the 16th-century frescoed vaults of the...*

Loggia of the Palazzo del Comune: Notice the Italian flair for fine design. Even this little loggia features decorative art (in the Grotesque style—named for the fanciful paintings of bizarre creatures found on unfinished lower-level walls at Nero's Golden House in Rome). This scene was indisputably painted after 1492. How do they know? Because it features turkeys—first seen in Europe after Columbus returned from the Americas with his ship full of exotic souvenirs. The turkeys painted here may have been that bird's European debut.

• *At the end of the square is the TI, and to its left—a few steps down Via Portica—is the entrance to the Roman Forum (beneath the square; described later, under "More Sights in Assisi").*

But we'll instead exit the square to the right of the TI and hike up Via San Paolo. After 150 yards (across from #24), a sign on the left directs you down a stepped lane to the...

❾ Church of Santo Stefano (Chiesa di Santo Stefano)

Surrounded by cypress, fig, and walnut trees, Santo Stefano—which used to be outside the town walls in the days of St. Francis—is a delightful bit of offbeat Assisi (free, daily 8:30-20:00, shorter hours off-season). Legend has it that Santo Stefano's bells miraculously rang on October 3, 1226, the day St. Francis died. Step inside. This is the typical rural Italian Romanesque church—no architect, just built by simple stonemasons who put together the most basic design. Hundreds of years later, it still stands.

• *The lane zigzags down to Via San Francesco. When you reach the narrow lane, go left (downhill). Then, emerging at the wider street, turn right and walk under the arch toward the Basilica of St. Francis. To trace the rest of our route, see the "Assisi" map on page 723.*

❿ Via San Francesco

This main drag leads from the town to the basilica holding the body of St. Francis. Francis was a big deal even in his own day. He was made a saint in 1228—the same year that the basilica's foundations were laid—and his body was moved here by 1230. Assisi was a big-time pilgrimage center, and this street was its booming hub. The arch marks the end of what was Assisi in St. Francis' day. Notice the fine medieval balcony immediately past the arch (on the left).

About 30 yards farther down (on the left), find the **fountain** where medieval pilgrims might have cooled themselves. The hospice next door was built in 1237 to house pilgrims. Notice the three surviving faces of its fresco: Jesus, Francis, and Clare.

Farther down on the left, across from #12A, is the **Oratorio dei Pellegrini,** dating from the 1450s. A brotherhood ran a hostel here for travelers passing through to pay homage to St. Francis. The chapel is open to the public and offers a richly frescoed 14th-century space designed to inspire pilgrims—perfect for any traveler to pause and contemplate the saint's message.

From here, the road continues a few more short blocks downhill to the Basilica of St. Francis. Just before the basilica is a three-floor museum about Capuchin missionaries' work in the Amazon region since 1909 (**Museo Missionario Indios,** on the left at #19). Depending on your feelings about missionaries in the developing world, this may be of interest—with exhibits on ethnography, flora and fauna, and Franciscan theology.

• *Continuing on, you'll reach Assisi's main sight, the Basilica of St.*

ASSISI

Francis. For the start of my self-guided tour, walk downhill to the basilica's lower courtyard.

Basilica of St. Francis Tour

The Basilica of St. Francis (Basilica di San Francesco), worth ▲▲▲, is one of the artistic and religious highlights of Europe.

It stands where, in 1226, St. Francis was buried (with the outcasts he had stood by) outside of his town on the "Hill of the Damned"—now called the "Hill of Paradise." The basilica is frescoed from top to bottom with scenes by the leading artists of the day: Cimabue, Giotto, Simone Martini, and Pietro Lorenzetti. A 13th-century historian wrote, "No more exquisite monument to the Lord has been built."

From a distance, you see the huge arcades "supporting" the basilica. These were 15th-century quarters for the monks. The arcades that line the square and lead to the church housed medieval pilgrims.

ORIENTATION

Cost and Hours: The complex is free to enter, with different hours for various parts. The **lower basilica and tomb** are open to tourists daily 6:00-19:00 (shorter hours on Wed and in winter). In practice, the basilica remains open for worship and discreet sightseers an hour later. Within the lower basilica, the **reliquary chapel** opens at 9:00 but is often closed Sat-Sun (and occasionally for religious services). The **upper basilica** is open daily 8:30-18:45 (until 17:45 in winter). And the skippable **treasury/museum** is open Mon-Tue and Thu-Sat 9:30-18:00, closed Wed, shorter hours Sun and off-season.

Dress Code: Modest dress is required to enter the church—no above-the-knee skirts or shorts and no sleeveless tops for men, women, or children.

Information: +39 075 819 0170, www.sanfrancescoassisi.org. Call or check the website for details on upcoming events at the basilica. A handy information office is in the arcade of the lower courtyard—on the right as you face the church (daily 9:00-19:30).

Tours: Videoguides loaded with a one-hour tour are available at

ASSISI

the information office under the arcade in the courtyard of the lower basilica (€6, €10/2 people).

🎧 Download my free Basilica of St. Francis audio tour.

Bookstore: The church bookshop is in the inner courtyard behind the upper and lower basilica. It sells an excellent guidebook, *The Basilica of Saint Francis: A Spiritual Pilgrimage* (€3, by Goulet, McInally, and Wood); I used this book, and a tour with Brother Michael, as sources for this self-guided tour.

Church Services: To worship here, consider joining the Franciscan brothers for Mass in *Italiano* (Mon-Sat in the lower basilica at 7:15, 10:00, 11:00, and 18:00; Sun in the lower basilica at 7:30, 9:00, 17:00, and 18:30; Sun in the upper basilica at 10:30 and 12:00). On Sundays in summer (Easter-Oct), there's an English Mass in the upper basilica at 9:00. Additional English and sung Masses don't follow a set schedule. Call the basilica to find out when English-speaking pilgrimage groups or choirs have reserved Masses, and attend with them (+39 075 819 0170).

OVERVIEW

The Basilica of St. Francis, a theological work of genius, can be difficult for the 21st-century tourist/pilgrim to appreciate.

Since the basilica is the reason that most people visit Assisi, and the message of St. Francis has even the least devout sightseers blessing the town Vespas, I've designed this self-guided tour with an emphasis on the place's theology (rather than art history).

A disclaimer before we start: Just as Francis used many biblical legends to help teach the Christian message, legends from the life of Francis were told in later ages to teach the same message. Are they true? In general, probably not. Are they in keeping with Francis' message? Yes. Do I share legends here as if they are historic? Sure.

The church has three parts: the upper basilica, the lower basilica, and the saint's tomb (below the lower basilica). We'll tour the complex from the bottom up. To get oriented, head down the ramp from the grassy lawn and stand in the big plaza that stretches in front of the lower entrance. While empty today, centuries ago this main piazza was cluttered with pilgrim services and the medieval equivalent of souvenir shops. As you face the church, the information office is under the arcade to your right, and the WCs are just behind that. (Go before you enter, as there aren't any WCs inside the basilica.)

⊙ SELF-GUIDED TOUR

Enter through the grand doorway of the lower basilica. Just inside, decorating the top of the first arch, look up and see ❶ **St. Francis,** who greets you with a Latin inscription. Sounding a bit like John Wayne, he says the equivalent of, "Slow down and be joyful, pilgrim. You've reached the Hill of Paradise. And, if you're observant and thoughtful, this church will knock your spiritual socks off."

· *Start with the tomb. To get there, turn left into the nave. Midway down, follow the signs and take the stairs to the tomb downstairs.*

❷ The Tomb

The saint's remains are above the altar in the stone box with the iron ties. In medieval times, pilgrims came to Assisi because St. Francis was buried here. Holy relics were the "ruby slippers" of medieval Europe. Relics gave you power—they answered your prayers and won your wars—and ultimately helped you get back to your eternal Kansas. Assisi made no bones about promoting the saint's relics but hid his tomb for obvious reasons of security. His body was buried secretly while the basilica was under construction, and over the next 600 years, the exact location was forgotten. When the tomb was to be opened to the public in 1818, it took more than a month to find his actual remains.

Francis' four closest friends and first followers are memorialized in the corners of the room. Near the entrance, notice the small copper box behind the metal grille. This contains the remains of Francis' rich Roman patron, Jacopa dei Settesoli. She traveled to see him on his deathbed but was turned away because she was female. Francis waived the rule and welcomed "Brother Jacopa" to his side. These five tombs—in the Franciscan spirit of being with your friends—were added in the 19th century.

The candles you see are the only real candles in the church (others are electric). Pilgrims pay a coin, pick up a candle, and place it in the small box on the side. The friars will light it later.

· *Climb back up to the lower nave.*

Lower Basilica

Appropriately Franciscan—subdued and Romanesque—this nave is frescoed with parallel scenes from the lives of Christ (right) and Francis (left), connected by a ceiling of stars. The Passion of Christ and the Compassion of Francis lead to the altar built over Francis' tomb. After the church was built and decorated, side chapels were erected to provide mausoleums for the rich families that patronized

ASSISI

Basilica of St. Francis—Lower Level

EXIT
To Upper
Basilica
& Bookshop

RELIQUARY CHAPEL

ALTAR

NAVE

Not to Scale

ASSISI

ENTRANCE

Lower Piazza

Stairs to Upper Piazza

BASILICA
INFO OFFICE
& VIDEOGUIDES

←To
Porta
San Francesco

WC

Upper Piazza

1 St. Francis (on ceiling)
2 Stairs to Tomb (2)
3 Obedience (on ceiling)
4 Chastity (on ceiling)
5 Poverty (on ceiling)

6 Francis on a Heavenly Throne
7 Reliquary Chapel
8 GIOTTO – Crucifixion
9 CIMABUE – St. Francis
10 LORENZETTI – Stigmata

the work of the order. Unfortunately, in the process, huge arches were cut out of some frescoed scenes, but others survive.

In the fresco directly above the staircase leading to the tomb, Christ is being taken down from the cross (just the bottom half of his body can be seen, on the left), and it looks like the story is over. Defeat. But in the opposite fresco, we see Francis preaching to the birds, reminding the faithful that the message of the Gospel survives.

These stories directed the attention of the medieval pilgrim to the altar, where he could meet God through the sacraments. The church was thought of as a community of believers sailing toward God. The prayers coming out of the nave (*navis*, or ship) fill the triangular sections of the ceiling—called *vele*, or sails—with spiritual wind. With a priest for a navigator and the altar for a helm, faith propels the ship.

Walk around the altar, stand behind it (toes to the bottom step, facing the entrance), and look up. The three scenes above you represent the creed of the Franciscans: Directly above the tomb of St. Francis, to the right, ❸ *Obedience* (Francis appears twice, wearing a rope harness and kneeling in front of Lady Obedience); to the left, ❹ *Chastity* (in her tower of purity held up by two angels); and straight ahead, ❺ *Poverty*. Here Jesus blesses the marriage as Francis slips a ring on Lady Poverty. In the foreground, two "self-sufficient" yet pint-size merchants (the new rich of a thriving northern Italy) are throwing sticks and stones at the bride. But Poverty, in her patched wedding dress, is fertile and strong, and even bare brambles blossom into a rosebush crown.

St. Francis called money the "devil's dung." The jeweled belt of a rich person was all about material wealth. A bag of coins hung from it, as did a weapon to protect that wealth. The simple rope Franciscan monks use to tie their tunics has three knots that symbolize—and serve as constant reminders of—their vows of obedience, chastity, and poverty.

Now turn around and put your heels to the altar and—bending back like a drum major—look up for a peek at the reward for a life of obedience, chastity, and poverty: ❻ **Francis on a heavenly throne** in a rich, golden robe. He traded a life of earthly simplicity for glory in heaven.

• *Turn to the right and march to the corner, where steps lead down into the...*

❼ Reliquary Chapel

This chapel is filled with fascinating relics. Step in and circle the room clockwise. You'll see the silver chalice and plate that Francis used for the bread and wine of the Eucharist (in a small, dark, windowed case set into the wall, marked *Calice e Patena*). Francis be-

The Franciscan Message

Francis' message caused a stir. Not only did he follow Christ's teachings, he also followed Christ's lifestyle, living as a poor, wandering preacher. He traded a life of power and riches for one of obedience, poverty, and chastity. He was never ordained as a priest, but his influence on Christianity was monumental.

The Franciscan realm (Brother Sun, Sister Moon, and so on) is a space where God, man, and the natural world frolic harmoniously. Francis treated every creature—animal, peasant, pope—with equal respect. He and his "brothers" (*fratelli,* or friars) slept in fields, begged for food, and exuded the joy of nonmaterialism. Franciscan friars were known as the "Jugglers of God," modeling themselves on French troubadours who roved the countryside singing, telling stories, and cracking jokes.

In an Italy torn by rival political factions, Francis promoted peace and the restoration of order. (He set an example by reconstructing the crumbled San Damiano chapel.) While the Church was waging bloody Crusades, Francis pushed ecumenism and understanding. And the Franciscan message had an impact. In 1288, just 62 years after Francis died, a Franciscan became pope (Nicholas IV). Francis' message also led to Church reforms that

ASSISI

lieved that his personal possessions should be simple, but the items used for worship should be made of the finest materials. On the left are the tunic and slippers that Francis donned during his last days. Next, the Veli di Lino is a cloth Jacopa wiped her friend's brow with on his deathbed. Then, see the tunic that was lovingly patched and stitched by followers of the 5-foot, 4-inch-tall St. Francis.

In the corner display case is a small section of the itchy haircloth *(cilizio)*—worn by Francis as penance (the cloth he chose was the opposite of the fine fabric his father sold). It's not sheep's wool, but cloth made from scratchy horse or goat hair. Next is a papal document (1223) legitimizing the Franciscan order and assuring Francis' followers that they were not risking a (deadly) heresy charge. Finally, find a prayer (in a fancy silver stand) that St. Francis wrote for Brother Leo and signed with a T-shaped character—his tau cross. The last letter in the Hebrew alphabet, tav ("tau" in Greek) is symbolic of faithfulness to the end, and Francis adopted it for his signature.

many believe delayed the Protestant Reformation by a century.

The richly decorated Assisi basilica seems to contradict the teachings of the poor monk it honors, but it was built as an act of religious and civic pride to remember the hometown saint. It was also designed—and still functions—as a pilgrimage center and a splendid classroom. Though monks in robes may not give off an "easy-to-approach" vibe, the Franciscans of today are still God's jugglers (and many of them speak English).

Here is Francis' message, in his own words:

The Canticle of the Sun

Good Lord, all your creations bring praise to you!

Praise for Brother Sun, who brings the day. His radiance reminds us of you!

Praise for Sister Moon and the stars, precious and beautiful.

Praise for Brother Wind, and for clouds and storms and rain that sustain us.

Praise for Sister Water. She is useful and humble, precious and pure.

Praise for Brother Fire who cheers us at night.

Praise for our sister, Mother Earth, who feeds us and rules us.

Praise for all those who forgive because you have forgiven them.

Praise for our sister, Bodily Death, from whose embrace none can escape.

Praise and bless the Lord, and give thanks, and, with humility, serve him.

ASSISI

Before leaving the chapel, notice the modern paintings done recently by local artists. Over the entrance, Francis is shown being born in a stable like Jesus (by Capitini). Scenes from the life of Clare and Padre Pio (a Capuchin priest, very popular in Italy, who was sainted in 2002) were painted by Stefanelli and Antonio.

• *Return up the stairs, stepping into the...*

Lower Basilica's Transept

The decoration of this church brought together the greatest Sienese (Lorenzetti and Simone Martini) and Florentine (Cimabue and Giotto) artists of the day. Look around at the painted scenes. In 1300, this was radical art—believable homespun scenes, landscapes, trees, real people.

Study ❽ **Giotto's painting of the Crucifixion,** with the eight sparrow-like angels (adjacent to the reliquary chapel). For the first time, holy people are expressing emotion: One angel turns her head sadly at the sight of Jesus, and another scratches her hands down her cheeks, drawing blood. Mary (lower left), previously in control, has fainted in despair. The Franciscans, with their goal of bringing God to the people, found a natural partner in Europe's first naturalist (and therefore modern) painter, Giotto.

To grasp Giotto's artistic leap, compare his work with the painting to the right, by Cimabue. It's Gothic, without the 3-D architecture, natural backdrop, and slice-of-life reality of Giotto's work. ❾ **Cimabue's St. Francis** (far right) shows the saint with the stigmata—Christ's marks of the Crucifixion. Contemporaries described Francis as being short, with a graceful build, dark hair, and sparse beard. (This is considered the most accurate portrait of Francis—done according to the description of one who knew him.) The sunroof haircut (tonsure) was standard for monks of the day. According to legend, the brown robe and rope belt were inventions of necessity. When Francis stripped naked and ran away from Assisi, he grabbed the first clothes he could, a rough wool peasant's tunic and a piece of rope, which became the uniform of the Franciscan order.

To the left, at eye level under the sparrow-like angels, are paintings of **saints** and their exquisite halos (by Simone Martini or his school). To the right of the door at the same level, see five of Francis' closest **followers**—clearly just simple folk.

Francis' friend, **"Sister Bodily Death,"** was really not all that terrible. In fact, Francis would like to introduce you to her now (above and to the right of the door leading into the reliquary chapel). Go ahead, block the light from the door with this book and meet her. Before his death, Francis added a line to *The Canticle of the Sun:* "Praise for our sister, Bodily Death, from whose embrace none can escape."

• *Now, cross the transept to the other side of the altar (enjoying some of the oldest surviving bits of the inlaid local-limestone flooring—c. 13th century) and find the staircase going up. Immediately above the stairs is* ❿ *Lorenzetti's* Francis Receiving the Stigmata. *(Francis is considered the first person ever to earn the marks of the cross through his great faith and love of the Church.) Make your way up the stairs to the...*

Courtyard

The courtyard overlooks the 15th-century cloister, the heart of this monastic complex. Pope Sixtus IV (of Sistine Chapel fame) had it built as a secure retreat for himself. Balanced and peaceful by design, the courtyard also functioned as a cistern to collect rainwater, supplying enough for 200 monks (today, there are about 40). The Franciscan order emphasizes teaching. This place functioned as a kind of theological center of higher learning, which rotated monks in for a six-month stint, then sent them back home more prepared and better inspired to preach effectively. That explains the complex narrative of the frescoes wallpapering the walls and halls here.

The **treasury** *(Museo del Tesoro)* to the left of the bookstore features ornately decorated chalices, reliquaries, vestments, and altarpieces.

• *From the courtyard, climb the stairs (next to the bookshop) to the...*

Upper Basilica

Built later than its counterpart below, the brighter upper basilica is considered the first Gothic church in Italy (started in 1228). You've followed the intended pilgrims' route, entering the lower church and finish-
ing here. Notice how the pulpit (embedded in the corner pillar) can be seen and heard from every spot in the packed church. The spirit of the order was to fill the church and preach.

See also the design in the round window in the west end (high above the entry). The tiny centerpiece reads "IHS" (the first three letters of Jesus' name in Greek). And, as you can see, this trippy kaleidoscope seems to declare that all light radiates from Jesus.

The windows here are treasures from the 13th and 14th centuries. Those behind the altar are among the oldest and most precious in Italy. Imagine illiterate medieval peasants entranced by these windows, so full of meaning that they were nicknamed "Bibles of the Poor."

But for art lovers, the basilica's draw is that Giotto and his assistants practically wallpapered it circa 1297-1300. Or perhaps the job was subcontracted to other artists—scholars debate it (for more on Giotto, see page 139). Whatever the case, the anatomy, architectural depth, and drama of these frescoes helped to kick off the Renaissance. The gallery of frescoes shows 28 scenes from the life of St. Francis. The events are a mix of documented history and folk legend.

• *Take a walk through Francis' life, via these glorious illustrations. As you stand in front of the altar, facing the front of the church, begin with*

ASSISI

Basilica of St. Francis—Upper Level

Entrance from Bookstore

ALTAR

NAVE

SOUTH WALL

NORTH WALL

❶ Three "postmortem miracles" associated with St. Francis

Not to Scale

❷ Francis' death, funeral, and canonization

❶ A common man spreads his cape before Francis

❷ Francis offers his cape to a needy stranger

❸ Francis is visited by the Lord in a dream

❹ Francis prays to the crucifix

❺ Francis relinquishes his possessions

❻ The pope has a dream

❼ The pope confirms the Franciscan order

❽ A vision of the flaming chariot

❾ A vision of thrones

❿ Exorcism of demons in Arezzo

⓫ St. Francis before the sultan

⓬ Ecstasy of St. Francis

⓭ The crèche at Greccio

⓮ Miracle of the spring

Francis receives the stigmata **⓳**

The apparition at Arles **⓲**

Preaching for Pope Honorius III **⓱**

The knight of Celano invites Francis to his deathbed **⓰**

Sermon to the birds → **⓯**

㉒ Tan patches on ceiling

MAIN ENTRANCE

Stairs to Lower Piazza

To Piazza Comune & the Rest of Assisi

Lawn WITH TAU CROSS & "PAX"

BOSCO (WOODS) ENTRY →

ASSISI

the first fresco on the right. From here, you'll work clockwise (moving to the right) along the north wall. Follow along with the help of the numbered map key. The subtitles in the faded black strip below the frescoes describe each scene in clear Latin—and affirm my interpretation.

❶ **A common man spreads his cape before Francis** in front of the Temple of Minerva on Piazza del Comune. Before his conversion, young Francis was the model of Assisian manhood—handsome, intelligent, and well-dressed, befitting the son of a wealthy cloth dealer. Above all, he was liked by everyone, a natural charmer who led his fellow teens in nights of wine, women, and song. Medieval pilgrims understood the deeper meaning of this scene: The "eye" of God (symbolized by the rose window in the Temple of Minerva) looks over the young Francis, a dandy "imprisoned" in his own selfishness (the Temple—with barred windows—was once a prison).

❷ **Francis offers his cape to a needy stranger.** Francis was always generous of spirit. He became more so after being captured in battle and held for a year as a prisoner of war, then suffering from illness. Charity was a Franciscan forte.

❸ **Francis is visited by the Lord in a dream.** Still unsure of his calling, Francis rode off to the Crusades. One night, he dreams of a palace filled with armor marked with crosses. Christ tells him to leave the army—to become what you might consider the first "conscientious objector"—and go home to wait for a nonmilitary assignment in a new kind of knighthood. He returned to Assisi and, though reviled as a coward, would end up fighting for spiritual wealth, not earthly power and riches.

❹ **Francis prays to the crucifix** in the Church of San Damiano. After months of living in a cave, fasting, and meditating, Francis kneels in the run-down church and prays. The crucifix speaks, telling him: "Go and rebuild my Church, which you can see has fallen into ruin." Francis hurried home and sold his father's cloth to pay for God's work. His furious father dragged him before the bishop.

❺ **Francis relinquishes his possessions.** In front of the bishop and the whole town, Francis strips naked and gives his dad his clothes, credit cards, and a time-share on Capri. Francis raises his hand and says, "Until now, I called you father. From now on, my only father is my Father in Heaven." Notice God's hand blessing the action from above. Francis then ran off into the hills, naked and singing. In this version, Francis is covered by the bishop, symbolizing his transition from a man of the world to a man of the Church. Notice the disbelief and concern on the bishop's advisors' faces; subtle expressions like these wouldn't have made it into other medieval frescoes of the day.

❻ **The pope has a dream.** Francis headed to Rome, seeking

the pope's blessing on his fledgling movement. Initially rebuffing Francis, the pope then dreams of a simple, barefooted man propping up his teetering Church, and then...

❼ The pope confirms the Franciscan order, handing Francis and his gang the 1223 document now displayed in the reliquary chapel.

Francis' life was peppered with visions and miracles, shown in three panels in a row: **❽ vision of the flaming chariot, ❾ vision of thrones,** and **❿ exorcism of demons in Arezzo.**

• *Next see...*

⓫ St. Francis before the sultan. Francis' wandering ministry took him to Egypt during the Crusades (1219). He walked unarmed into the Muslim army camp. They captured him, but the sultan was impressed with Francis' manner and let him go, reportedly whispering, "I'd convert to your faith, but they'd kill us both." Here the sultan gestures from his throne.

⓬ Ecstasy of St. Francis. This oft-painted scene shows the mystic communing with Christ.

⓭ The crèche at Greccio. A creative teacher, Francis invents the tradition of manger scenes.

• *Around the corner, see the...*

⓮ Miracle of the spring. Shown here getting water out of a rock to quench a stranger's thirst, Francis felt closest to God when in the hills around Assisi, seeing the Creator in the creation.

• *Cross over to the far side of the entrance door.*

⓯ Sermon to the birds. In his best-known miracle, Francis is surrounded by birds as they listen to him teach. Francis embraces all levels of creation. One interpretation of this scene is that the birds, which are of different species, represent the diverse flock of humanity and nature, all created and beloved by God and worthy of one another's love.

This image of well-fed birds is an appropriate one to take with you. It's designed to remind pilgrims that, like the birds, God gave us life, plenty of food, feathers, wings, and a world to fly around in. Francis, patron saint of the environment and animals, taught his followers to see God in nature and to count their blessings. A monk here reminded me that even a student backpacker today eats as well as the wealthiest nobleman in the days of Francis.

• *Continue to the south wall for the rest of the panels.*

Despite the hierarchical society of his day, Francis was welcomed by all classes, shown in these three panels: **⓰ the knight of Celano invites Francis to his deathbed; ⓱ preaching for Pope Honorius III,** who listens intently; and **⓲ the apparition at Arles,** which illustrates how Francis could be in two places at once (something only Jesus and saints can pull off). The proponents of Francis, who believed he was destined for sainthood, show him performing the necessary miracles.

⓳ Francis receives the stigmata. It's September 17, 1224, and Francis is fasting and praying on nearby Mount Alverna when a six-winged angel (called a seraph) appears with holy laser-like powers to burn in the marks of the Crucifixion, the stigmata. For the strength of his faith, Francis is given the marks of his master, the "battle scars of love." These five wounds suffered by Christ (nails in palms and feet, lance in side) marked Francis' body for the rest of his life.

The next panels deal with **⓴ Francis' death, funeral, and canonization.** The last panels show **㉑ miracles** associated with the saint after his death, proving that he's in heaven and bolstering his eligibility for sainthood.

Francis died thanking God and singing his *Canticle of the Sun*, in which he refers to the sun as his brother and the moon as his sister. Francis also called his body "Brother Ass" (because of the heavy burdens he asked it to carry)—and conceded on his deathbed that he'd been a bit tough on Brother Ass. Ravaged by an asceticism extreme enough to earn him the stigmata, Francis died in 1226.

Before leaving through the front entrance, look up at the ceiling and the walls near the rose window to see **㉒ large tan patches.** In 1997, when a 5.5-magnitude quake hit Assisi, it shattered the upper basilica's frescoes into 300,000 fragments. An aftershock then shook the ceiling frescoes down, killing two monks and two art scholars who were standing here. Later, the fragments were meticulously picked up and pieced back together.

Leaving the Basilica

Outside, on the lawn, the Latin word *pax* (peace) and the Franciscan tau cross are sculpted from shrubbery. For a drink or snack, the **Bar San Francesco** (facing the upper basilica) is handy, or head to one of my recommended restaurants up the hill. For *pax*, take the high lane back to town, or venture into the 160-acre **Bosco di San Francesco** (San Francesco Woods) to the left of the basilica for some silence and contemplation (€6 suggested donation, picnic area; Tue-Sun 10:00-19:00, closed Mon and Oct-March, last entry one hour before closing, +39 075 813 157, www.fondoambiente.it/luoghi/bosco-di-san-francesco).

More Sights in Assisi

IN THE OLD TOWN

These sights are in the upper town, near the main square or basilica.

▲Roman Forum Museum
(Foro Romano e Collezione Archeologica)

For a look at Assisi's Roman roots, check out the Roman Forum from the town of "Asisum"—beneath today's Piazza del Comune.

You'll enter through a nonde-script doorway (behind the TI, just a few steps off the main square) into a room filled with carved stone capitals, tomb-stones, sarcophagi, and sculpture fragments. From there, you'll follow tunnels back under the square itself, seeing various landmarks that once lined the streets of Asisum: a tribunal for speeches, a fountain, columns, the original Roman road, and much more, all displayed in situ (where it was discovered). A helpful five-minute video (subtitled in English) helps resurrect the rubble.

Cost and Hours: €5, €9 combo-ticket with the next two sights, daily 10:00-18:00, until 17:00 in winter, enter at Via Portica 2.

Pinacoteca

This small, unexciting museum attractively displays its 13th- to 17th-century art (mainly frescoes). There's a damaged Giotto Madonna and a rare secular fresco (to the right of the Giotto art), but it's mainly a peaceful walk through a pastel world—best for art lovers.

Cost and Hours: €3, €9 combo-ticket includes Forum and Rocca Maggiore; April-Oct daily 10:00-18:00, closed Nov-March except by appointment; on the main drag between Piazza del Comune and Basilica of St. Francis at Via San Francesco 12, +39 075 813 8680.

▲Rocca Maggiore

The "big castle" offers a few restored medieval rooms, a good look at a 14th-century fortification, and a fine view of Assisi and the Umbrian countryside. If you're pinching your euros, skip it—the view is just as good from outside the castle.

Cost and Hours: €6, €9 combo-ticket includes Forum and Pinacoteca; daily June-Aug 9:00-20:00, April-May and Sept 10:00-19:30, shorter hours off-season; last entry 45 minutes before closing, Via della Rocca, +39 075 815 5077.

IN THE LOWER TOWN
▲▲Basilica of Santa Maria degli Angeli
(Basilica of St. Mary of the Angels)

This huge basilica, towering above the buildings of Santa Maria degli Angeli—the modern part of Assisi in the flat valley below

the hill town—marks the spot where Francis lived, worked, and died. It's a grandiose church built around a humble chapel—reflecting the monumental impact of this simple saint on his town and the world.

Cost and Hours: Free, Mon-Sat 6:15-12:40 & 14:30-19:30, Sun from 6:45, +39 075 805 1430.

Dress Code: Modest dress is required (no shorts or tank tops).

Visitor Services: A little TI is across the street from the souvenir stands, under the arches (generally Tue-Sun 10:00-12:30 & 15:30-18:00, closed Mon, +39 075 804 4554). As you face the church, there are big pay WCs behind the bushes on your right.

Getting There: Whether you're traveling by car or by train, it's most practical to visit this sight on the way into or out of town. From Assisi's train station, it's a five-minute walk (exit station left, after 50 yards take the underground pedestrian walkway—*sottopassaggio*—on your left, then walk straight ahead, passing several handy eateries). There's ample well-marked parking next to the train station, and some free (time-limited) spaces tucked behind the basilica.

From the old town, you can reach the basilica on the same Assisi Link bus (line #C) that runs down to the train station (stay on at least one more stop to reach the basilica; confirm with driver). In the opposite direction, buses from the basilica up to the old town run twice hourly. Leaving the church, the stop is on your right, by the side of the building. For more bus details, see "Getting Around Assisi," earlier.

Visiting the Basilica: This grand church was built in the 16th century around the tiny but historic **Porziuncola Chapel** (now directly under the dome) after the chapel became too small to accommodate the many pilgrims wanting to pay homage to St. Francis. Some local monks had given Francis this *porziuncola,* or "small portion," after his conversion—a little land with a fixer-upper chapel. Francis lived here after he founded the Franciscan order, and this was where he consecrated St. Clare as a Bride of Christ. What would humble Francis think of the huge church—Christianity's 10th largest—built over his tiny chapel?

Behind the Porziuncola Chapel on the right, find the **Cappella del Transito,** which marks the site of Francis' death on October 3, 1226. Only 44 years old, Francis died as he'd lived—simply, in a small hut located here. On his last night on earth, he invited some friars to join him in a Last Supper-style breaking of bread. Then he undressed, lay down on the bare ground, and began to recite Psalm 141: "Lord, I cry unto thee." He spoke the last line, "Let the wicked fall into their own traps, while I escape"...and he passed on.

Retrace your steps and follow *Roseto* signs to the rose garden. You'll walk down a passage with gardens on either side (viewable through the windows)—on the left, a tranquil park with a statue of Francis petting a sheep, and on the right, the **rose garden.** Francis, fighting a temptation that he never named, once threw himself onto the roses. As the story goes, the thorns immediately dropped off. Thornless roses have grown here ever since.

Exiting the passage, turn right to find the **Rose Chapel** (Cappella delle Rose), built over the place where Francis lived.

The next hallway has exhibits that change occasionally, but you'll likely see a giant **Nativity scene**—a reminder to pilgrims that Francis first established the tradition of manger scenes as a teaching aid. The bookshop has some works in English and an "old pharmacy" selling herbal cures.

Porziuncola Museum: Continuing on, you'll pass this small museum featuring early depictions of St. Francis by 13th-century artists, a model of Assisi during Francis' lifetime, and religious art and objects from the basilica. On the museum's upper floor are some monks' cells, which provide intriguing insight into the spartan lifestyles of the pious and tonsured (€4, ask for English brochure; Thu-Tue 9:00-13:00 & 14:30-17:00, closed Wed; +39 075 805 1419, www.porziuncola.org).

ON THE OUTSKIRTS

Church of San Damiano (Chiesa di San Damiano)

Located on the slope steeply below the Basilica of St. Clare, this modest church and convent was where Francis received his call and where Clare spent her days as mother superior of the Poor Clares. As you enter, signs point you through a series of simple rooms—including the dining hall where Clare ate with her flock and the room where she died—to a peaceful, flowery courtyard. Drivers can zip right there (watch for the turnoff on the road up to Piazza Matteotti), while walkers descend pleasantly from Assisi for 15 minutes through an olive grove.

In 1206, Francis was inside when he heard the wooden crucifix order him to rebuild the church. (The crucifix in San Damiano is a copy; the original is now displayed in the Basilica of St. Clare.) Francis initially interpreted these miraculous words as a call to rebuild crumbling San Damiano. He sold his father's cloth for money to fix the church. (The church we see today, however, was rebuilt later by others.) Eventually, Francis realized his charge was to revitalize the Christian Church at large.

As he approached the end of his life, Francis came to San Damiano to visit his old friend Clare. She set him up in a simple reed hut in the olive grove, where he was inspired to write his poem *The Canticle of the Sun* (see page 741).

Cost and Hours: Free; convent open daily 10:00-12:00 & 14:00-18:00, until 16:30 in winter, church opens at 6:15; start walking from the Porta Nuova parking lot at the south end of Assisi and follow the signs; +39 075 812 273, www.santuariosandamiano.org.

▲Hermitage (Eremo delle Carceri)

If you want to follow further in St. Francis' footsteps, take a trip up the rugged slopes of nearby Mount Subasio to the humble, peaceful hermitage where Francis and his followers retreated for solitude. Today the spot is marked by a 14th-century friary that's still occupied by Franciscan monks. You'll twist through the head-thumping doorframes and steep stairways of the medieval structure, the highlight of which is the tiny, dank cave where Francis would retire for private prayer.

Emerging at the far side, near a stone bridge, you'll see a tree (held together with braces) dating from Francis' time. This is said to be where Francis preached to the birds. From here, rustic paths lead to open-air "chapels" in the surrounding forest. Be a Franciscan for a little while. Sit peacefully and listen. Pick out the different sounds of nature: wind blowing through the trees, chirping birds, gravel crunching underfoot. And listen for the spaces *between* the sounds. That's where Francis found God.

Cost and Hours: Free; daily 7:30-19:00, until 18:00 in winter; +39 075 812 301, www.santuarioeremodellecarceri.org.

Getting There: Drive, take a taxi, or hike—there is no public transportation. Drivers can follow signs out of Assisi toward Mount Subasio, then park on the switchback just above the entrance. For hikers starting from Assisi's Porta Cappuccino gate, it's a stiff 3-mile, 1.5-hour hike with an elevation gain of about 1,000 feet. You'll walk along a narrow, paved road (with no shoulders) enjoying brisk air and sporadic views. A souvenir kiosk at the entrance sells drinks and sandwiches, and there are WCs just uphill from the friary.

Sleeping in Assisi

Assisi accommodates large numbers of pilgrims on religious holidays (see list on page 1205). Finding a room at any other time should be easy. Few hotels are air-conditioned.

HOTELS AND ROOMS

$$ Hotel Ideale, on a ridge overlooking the valley, offers 13 bright and airy rooms (all with views and balconies), a tranquil garden setting, and free private parking. As it's just off the main road into town, it's a handy pick for timid drivers (RS%, apartments with kitchens available, air-con, Piazza Matteotti 1, +39 075 813 570, mobile +39 333 452 0666, www.hotelideale.it, info@hotelideale.it, hardworking sisters Lara and Ilaria).

Accommodations
1 Hotel Ideale
2 Hotel Umbra
3 Hotel Belvedere
4 Hotel Pallotta
5 Hotel San Rufino
6 Hotel il Duomo
7 Hotel la Rocca
8 Camere Carli
9 Camere Annalisa Martini
10 St. Anthony's Guest House

Eateries & Other
11 Trattoria Pallotta
12 Osteria Piazzetta dell'Erba
13 Trattoria da Erminio
14 Trattoria degli Umbri
15 Hostaria Terra Chiama
16 La Bottega dei Sapori
17 Pizza al Taglio da Andrea
18 Agenzia Viaggi Stoppini (Train & Bus Tickets)

ASSISI

$$ Hotel Umbra, with a peaceful garden oasis in the middle of town, has 24 spacious, dated rooms with great view terraces. It feels a bit like stepping into a time warp, but is well run, friendly, and beautifully located (RS%, family rooms, air-con, elevator, and view sun terrace, most rooms have views, closed Nov-March, just off Piazza del Comune under the arch at Via degli Archi 6, +39 075 812 240, www.hotelumbra.it, info@hotelumbra.it, Laudenzi family).

$ Hotel Belvedere, along the road into town from Porta Nuova, has 12 dated rooms—eight with sweeping views (breakfast extra, elevator, large communal view terrace, 2 blocks past Basilica of St. Clare at Via Borgo Aretino 13, +39 075 812 460, www.assisihotelbelvedere.com, hotelbelvedereassisi@yahoo.it, thoughtful Enrico speaks fluent New Jerseyan).

$ Hotel Pallotta, hidden above a narrow staircase overlooking the main drag, offers seven tight rooms and a beautiful top-floor lounge with rooftop views. The conscientious hosts provide guests with loads of extra niceties, including a loaner Assisi guidebook, laundry service, and free hot drinks and cake at teatime (RS%, a steep block up from Piazza del Comune at Via San Rufino 6, mobile +39 338 740 7574, www.pallottaassisi.it, pallotta@pallottaassisi.it; Stefano and Jenni).

$ Hotels on Via Porta Perlici: This steep and characteristic lane, stretching uphill from the Church of San Rufino, is home to three interchangeable hotels with the same owners (Carlo and Christian). Inexpensive and straightforward, these are nicely located at the top of town (all have air-con, elevators, and pay parking nearby). In order from the bottom to the top, there's **Hotel San Rufino** (11 rooms, breakfast extra, at #7a; +39 075 812 803, www.hotelsanrufino.it, info@hotelsanrufino.it); **Hotel il Duomo** (14 modern rooms with somewhat less character, a bit pricier but breakfast is included, at #13, +39 075 812 742, www.hotelilduomo.it, info@hotelilduomo.it); and **Hotel la Rocca** (at the peaceful top end of town, 32 rooms in a medieval shell, breakfast extra, sunny rooftop terrace, decent restaurant upstairs, at #27, +39 075 812 284, www.hotelarocca.it, info@hotelarocca.it).

$ Camere Carli has six spacious rooms with bizarre floor plans in a solid, minimalist place above an art gallery. The loft rooms are a great value for families (RS%, no breakfast, family rooms, lots of stairs and no elevator, free parking 150 yards away, just off Piazza San Rufino at Via Porta Perlici 1, mobile +39 339 531 1366, www.camerecarli.it, carliarte@live.it, pleasant Franco runs the pottery shop below and speaks limited English).

¢ Camere Annalisa Martini is a cheery home amid vines and roses in the town's medieval core. This is a good budget choice—Annalisa enthusiastically accommodates her guests with a picnic garden, communal refrigerator, and six homey rooms with cheerful peeling wallpaper and flea market furniture (cash only, 3 rooms share 2 bathrooms, laundry service, no breakfast; one block from Piazza del Comune—go downhill toward the Basilica of St. Francis, turn left on Via San Gregorio to #6; +39 075 813 536, mobile +39 347 908 5212, cameremartini@libero.it). Mamma Rosignoli doesn't speak English, but Annalisa does.

SWEET DREAMS IN A CONVENT

Assisi is filled with convents, most of which rent rooms to pilgrims and travelers. While you don't need to be a pilgrim or even a Christian to be welcome, it's just common sense to stay in a convent *only* if you're approaching Assisi with a contemplative mindset. Convents feel institutional, house many groups, and are not particularly cheap—but they come with all the facilities you might need to enjoy a spirit-filled visit to Assisi.

$ St. Anthony's Guest House is where the Franciscan Sisters of the Atonement offer a very warm and tranquil welcome. Their oasis of peace is just above the Basilica of St. Clare. They have 36 beds in 20 sparkling-clean rooms, some with great views—request when you reserve (family rooms available, no problem if couples want to share a bed, elevator, no air-con but fans, 23:00 curfew, likely closed mid-Nov-Feb, library, picnic garden, parking by donation; from the parking cashier in Piazza Matteotti, take the stairs down to the *"tunnel romano,"* walk around the little park, then continue down on the elevator—it's just to the left at Via Galeazzo Alessi 10; +39 075 812 542, www.graymoor.org/italy, atoneassisi@tiscali.it).

AGRITURISMO NEAR ASSISI

$$ Le Mandrie di San Paolo ("The Herd of St. Paul") is a meticulously restored 1,000-year-old stone house renting 13 rustic but comfortable rooms on a hillside high above the valley. Soulful Alex, his brother Andrew, and their team are justifiably proud of their passion for hospitality and connection to the land. They have an olive grove, lots of animals, a beautiful swimming pool, a sauna, a fine restaurant, and spectacular views over Assisi and the valleys of Umbria (apartments and family rooms, mobile +39 349 821 7867, +39 075 806 4070, www.agriturismomandriesanpaolo.it, mandrie10@gmail.com). It's about a 10-minute drive from Assisi, above the village of Viole (a.k.a. San Vitale). Just head southeast of Assisi following signs for *Viole;* when you enter town, turn left before you reach the arch and follow signs up the hill. Their recommended **$$$$** restaurant is a great choice: They produce their own olive oil, cheese, salami, and flour, and fire their ovens with their own wood.

Eating in Assisi

To bump up any meal, consider a glass or bottle of the favorite homegrown red wine, Sagrantino de Montefalco. Sagrantino is Umbria's answer to Brunello (although many wine lovers around here would say that it's vice versa). Before or after dinner, enjoy a drink on the main square facing the Roman temple...or hang out with the local teens with a takeaway beer under the temple's columns.

IN THE TOWN CENTER

$$$ Trattoria Pallotta is a local favorite with white tablecloths and a living-room ambience. It's run by a friendly and hardworking family—with Margarita in charge of the kitchen—and offers delicious, well-presented regional specialties, such as *piccione* (squab, a.k.a. pigeon) and *coniglio* (rabbit). Ask about split courses *(bis)* featuring two local homemade pastas (Wed-Mon 12:00-14:30 & 19:00-21:30, closed Tue, reservations smart, a few steps off Piazza del Comune across from temple/church at Vicolo della Volta Pinta 2, +39 075 815 5273, www.pallottaassisi.it).

$$$ Osteria Piazzetta dell'Erba is a trendy, youthful-feeling restaurant and a solid choice for lunch on a peaceful square or inside under medieval vaulted ceilings (Tue-Sun 12:30-14:30 & 19:30-22:30, closed Mon, reservations smart, just off the main piazza toward the Cathedral of San Rufino at Via S. Gabriele dell'Addolorata 15a, +39 075 815 352, www.osterialapiazzetta.it, chef Matteo).

$$ Trattoria da Erminio has peaceful tables under a terrace on a tiny square and indoor seating under a big, medieval (but air-conditioned) brick vault. Run by Federico and his family for three generations, it specializes in local meat cooked on an open-fire grill. They have good Umbrian wines—before you order, ask for a taste of their specialties (Fri-Wed 12:00-14:30 & 19:00-21:00, closed Thu; from Piazza San Rufino, go a block up Via Porta Perlici and turn right to Via Montecavallo 19a; +39 075 812 506).

$$ Trattoria degli Umbri has a few nice tables just above the fountain overlooking Assisi's main square (the main reason to come here). They serve delightful Umbrian dishes and good lasagna with quality wines by the glass (Fri-Wed 12:00-15:30 & 19:00-22:00, closed Thu, Piazza del Comune 40, +39 075 812 455).

$$ Hostaria Terra Chiama is a bright, modern little place run by Diego and his family, who serve traditional Umbrian dishes with seasonal specials (daily 12:00-15:00 & 19:00-22:30, Via San Rufino 16, +39 075 819 9051).

PICNIC ON THE MAIN SQUARE

There are a few little grocery stores (alimentari) near Piazza del Comune (one is a block uphill from the main square, at Via San Rufino 19), plus bakeries selling pizza by the slice.

La Bottega dei Sapori is handy for assembling a picnic of Umbrian treats: good porchetta sandwiches and specialty items, including truffle paste and olive oil. Sandwich chef Saverio also makes a nice taglieri misti (meat-and-cheese plate, priced by weight) and takes great pride in his locally sourced ingredients and quality wines (daily 9:30-21:00, shorter hours off-season, closed Jan-Feb, Piazza del Comune 34, +39 075 812 294, Fabrizio). You can picnic on any of the benches surrounding the piazza.

Pizza al Taglio da Andrea, facing the Church of San Rufino on Piazza San Rufino, has perhaps the best pizza-by-the-slice in town. Locals also like their torta al testo, the Umbrian flatbread sandwich (daily 8:00-21:00, Via San Rufino 26, +39 075 815 325).

ABOVE THE BASILICA OF ST. FRANCIS

For locations, see the "Assisi" map near the beginning of this chapter.

$$ Locanda del Podestà, tucked inside a medieval gate just above the basilica, is a cozy spot with a traditional menu of tasty grilled Umbrian sausages, *gnocchi della locanda* (with gorgonzola and truffles), and tasty *scottadito* ("scorch your fingers") lamb chops (Thu-Tue 12:00-14:30 & 19:00-21:30, closed Wed, 5-minute walk uphill along Via Cardinale Merry del Val from basilica, Via San Giacomo 6C, +39 075 816 553).

$$$ Le Terrazze di Properzio, just up the street from Podestà, is the place to go to dine with a big view on a lovely terrace. The traditional menu includes seasonal specials. While the interior has a nice atmosphere, I'd skip this restaurant unless you're seated outside—you're paying a premium for the terrace (daily 12:15-14:30 & 19:30-21:30, terrace closed in bad weather, Via Metastasio 9, +39 075 816 868).

COUNTRYSIDE FARM-TO-TABLE DINNER

$$$$ Le Mandrie di San Paolo, in a 1,000-year-old farmhouse a 10-minute drive outside Assisi, makes many of its own ingredients and serves an exquisite dinner to overnight guests and nonguests alike. This is a good example of a "zero-kilometer meal"—all the ingredients are thoughtfully sourced on the property (daily 19:30-21:30, Sat-Sun also open for lunch, reservations preferred, see "Sleeping in Assisi" for location, www.agriturismomandriesanpaolo.it).

Assisi Connections

If the train station's ticket office is closed, you'll find a ticket machine on the platform. Up in Assisi's old town, you can get train information and tickets from Agenzia Viaggi Stoppini (see listing under "Helpful Hints," earlier). That's also the best place to buy bus tickets—except for the FlixBus connection to Siena, which can easily be booked online.

From Assisi by Train to: Rome (4/day direct, 2 hours, more with change in Foligno), **Florence** (7/day direct, 2-3 hours), **Orvieto** (roughly hourly, 2-3 hours, 1-2 transfers), **Siena** (10/day, about 4 hours, most involve 2 changes; bus is faster).

By Bus: FlixBus runs buses to **Rome** (2/day, 3 hours) and **Siena** (3/day, 2 hours, better than the long train ride, https://global.flixbus.com). Be clear on the departure point for your bus: Sometimes it leaves from Santa Maria degli Angeli, in the valley below Assisi (you'll find the stop at the far end of the big, long park in front of the Basilica of Santa Maria degli Angeli); other departures are from Piazza Unità d'Italia, below the Basilica of St. Francis. Don't take the bus to **Florence;** the train is better.

By Plane: Perugia/Assisi Airport is about 10 miles from Assisi (code: PEG, +39 075 592 141, www.airport.umbria.it). Bus service between Assisi and the airport is sporadic—most travelers wind up taking a taxi (about €30).

ORVIETO & CIVITA

While Tuscany is justifiably famous for its many fine hill towns, Umbria, just to the south, has some stellar offerings of its own. Assisi (covered in its own chapter) is a must for nature lovers and Franciscan pilgrims. But if you're after views, wine, and charming villages, you'll find Umbria's best in Orvieto and in Civita di Bagnoregio (which is technically just across the border in Lazio, the same region as Rome).

About a 30-minute drive apart, these hill towns—one big, one small—perch high above scenic plains. Pleasant Orvieto is best known for its colorful-inside-and-out cathedral and its fine Orvieto Classico wine. Tiny Civita di Bagnoregio is a "dead city": It's effectively one big open-air museum with a smattering of accommodations and eateries, perched precariously on a hill pinnacle that you pay to enter. Taken together, Orvieto and Civita make a perfect duet for experiencing what all the hill-town fuss is about.

PLANNING YOUR TIME

Orvieto and Civita deserve at least an overnight, although even a few hours in each is enough to sample what they have to offer. Both are also great places to slow down and relax. Stay in one and side-trip to the other (Orvieto has more restaurants and other amenities and is easier to reach, while Civita really lets you get away from it all). The two are connected by a 30-minute drive or a longer bus ride. Orvieto is conveniently close to Rome (about an hour away by train or expressway).

Orvieto & Civita Area

① Alta Rocca Wine Resort
② Agriturismo Locanda Rosati
③ Tenuta Le Velette Winery & Accommodations
④ Agriturismo Cioccoleta & Neri Winery
⑤ Agriturismo Fattoria di Vibio
⑥ Custodi Winery

Orvieto

Just off the freeway and the main train line, Umbria's grand hill town entices those zipping between Florence and Rome. The town sits majestically on its *tufo* throne a thousand feet above the valley floor. The city's stony streets are a delight to explore. With its brown stone cityscape, atmospheric covered alleys, and well-tended flowerpots, Orvieto is a photographer's dream. Every side street is a still life. The cathedral provides a great sightseeing experience: detailed scenes carved into its outer columns and a priceless chapel slathered in colorful art by Renaissance big shots Luca Signorelli and Fra Angelico.

Orvieto also provides perhaps the easiest introduction to Umbria—that pastoral region that all too often gets overshadowed by

Orvieto's (Very Long) History

For a little town, Orvieto has a very big history. A few centuries before Christ, Orvieto—then called Velzna—was one of a dozen major Etruscan cities. Some historians believe it may have been a religious center—a kind of Etruscan Mecca (they're still looking for archaeological proof—the town and surrounding countryside are dotted with Etruscan ruins).

Imagine the history: From 900 BC to 264 BC, the town was Etruscan Velzna. After a two-year Roman siege, it was destroyed and the ruins left abandoned for six centuries. Rome fell in AD 476, and in the chaos of that power vacuum, with invaders from the north terrorizing the peninsula, people in the valley headed back into the hills in search of safety. They rebuilt over the old Etruscan foundations, and named the settlement Urbs Vetus, meaning "old town" in Latin. Over time, Urbs Vetus became Orvieto.

Orvieto flourished as a Middle Ages regional power. During Orvieto's glory days—from the 11th to 13th century—it was a city-state of about 30,000 people (like Perugia, Assisi, and Siena) and an occasional home to the pope. Today, with only 5,000 people living in less than a square mile atop its hill, and only half of its 50 churches still active, Orvieto is again a small town.

neighboring Tuscany. Orvieto's many excellent restaurants serve up toothsome pastas, flavorful game, and pungent truffles.

Orvieto has three claims to fame: cathedral, Classico wine, and ceramics. Drinking a shot of the local white wine in a ceramic cup as you gaze up at the cathedral lets you experience Orvieto's three C's all at once. (Is the cathedral best in the afternoon, when the facade basks in golden light, or early in the morning, when it rises above the hilltop mist? You decide.) Though loaded with tourists by day, Orvieto is quiet by night, and a visit here comes with a wonderful bonus: close proximity to the unforgettable Civita di Bagnoregio.

Orientation to Orvieto

Orvieto has two distinct parts: the old-town hilltop and the dreary modern town below (called Orvieto Scalo). Whether coming by train or car, you first arrive in the nondescript lower part of town. From there you can drive or take the funicular to the medieval upper town, an atmospheric labyrinth of streets and squares where all the sightseeing action is.

ORVIETO & CIVITA

TOURIST INFORMATION

The well-organized TI is on the cathedral square at Piazza del Duomo 24 (Mon-Fri 9:00-18:00, Sat-Sun until 19:00, +39 0763 341 772, www.liveorvieto.com). The TI has an excellent city map that highlights the *Anello della Rupe* hike around the base of the city, plus maps for longer countryside hikes. The ticket office next door sells combo-tickets and books reservations for Orvieto Underground Tours (see "Tours in Orvieto," later).

Combo-Tickets: Orvieto's sights are covered by a constantly changing array of combo-tickets.

The full-meal deal is the €25 **Carta Unica** combo-ticket, which covers virtually every sight recommended here, including the underground tours. This is a good value only if you plan to do everything covered. It's sold at the ticket office next to the TI on Piazza del Duomo and at most covered sights.

● Tobacco Shop (Bus Tickets)
❷ St. Patrick's Well Tickets
❸ Rupe Hike Access (5)
❹ Romantic Rampart Stroll (2)

ARRIVAL IN ORVIETO

By Train: The train station is at the foot of the hill the old town sits on. There's a convenient baggage-check service downstairs near the big parking lot (see "Helpful Hints," later).

The easiest way to the top of town is by **funicular** (runs about every 10 minutes Mon-Sat 7:15-20:30, less frequent Sun from 8:00). Exiting the train station, it's across the square to the left (look for *Funicolare* sign). Tickets (€1.30) include both the funicular and the connecting bus to Piazza del Duomo.

The funicular brings you up to Piazza Cahen, at the east end of the upper town. As you exit, to your left is a ruined fortress with a garden and a commanding view. Beyond that is a war memorial with more fine views. To your right, down a steep path, is St. Patrick's Well. Farther to the right is a park with the ruins of an Etruscan temple and another sweeping view.

Just in front of you is the small **shuttle bus** waiting to take you to Piazza del Duomo (runs roughly every 10-15 minutes, timed to arriving funiculars). The views from the ruined fortress are worth pausing for—just catch the next bus. Or you can walk to the cathedral (head uphill on Corso Cavour; after about 10 minutes, take a left at the clock tower onto Via del Duomo). The bus drops you in Piazza del Duomo, just steps from the TI and within easy walking distance of most of my recommended sights and hotels.

If you arrive outside the funicular's operating hours, you can reach the upper part of town by **taxi** (an exorbitant €15) or **bus** to Piazza della Repubblica (roughly 2/hour until midnight; buy €1.30 ticket at bar inside station).

By Car: Driving inside the upper town of Orvieto is stressful. It's a maze of narrow lanes, several of which are marked with red "ZTL" circles (if you drive there, you could get an expensive ticket). Consider using one of two parking lots outside the old center. The free option is the big lot **below the train station** (turn right immediately after the autostrada underpass and follow *Tour Bus Parking* signs). From the parking lot, walk through the station and ride the funicular up the hill (see "By Train," earlier).

The other stress-free option is the **Campo della Fiera** garage, which is tucked behind Orvieto's hill (as you approach town, follow signs with a *P*, a little bullseye, and elevator and escalator icons—you'll curl around the left side of Orvieto's ridge, then switchback up to the lot). While you'll pay to use this lot, it's an easier ascent into town—using either an elevator or the series of escalators, which whisk you up to the west end of the old center.

Those comfortable driving in Italian cities (and careful to avoid ZTL zones) can enter Orvieto's old center by driving up Via Posterla and Via Roma, then take your pick of short-term, pay-and-display parking areas: blue-lined spots on Piazza Cahen; a parking lot on Via Roma northwest of Piazza Cahen; blue-lined spots on Piazza Marconi, behind the cathedral; and the private, tree-lined lot with an attendant next to the cathedral (a central choice for overnight stays in the center). Plan on paying at least €1.50/hour or €12/day to park in Orvieto.

HELPFUL HINTS

Market Days and Festivals: On Thursday and Saturday mornings, Piazza del Popolo becomes a busy **farmers market.**

The city's biggest event is **Corpus Domini** (June 8 in 2023, May 30 in 2024), a medieval procession and festival celebrating a miraculous relic (described in the Duomo tour later in this chapter). Corpus Domini events include flag tossing, concerts, and a giant chess game with costumed people as pieces.

Baggage Check: Downstairs at the train station, the bright and helpful **InfoPoint,** run by Valerio, welcomes visitors near the big free parking lot. They offer pay WCs and have a secure bag check—the only one in town (daily 9:00-18:00).

Laundry: The central **Lavagettone** self-service launderette is handy for travelers, but you must bring your own detergent (daily 7:00-22:00, Via Garibaldi 30, www.lavagettone.it).

Bike Rental: Ask the **TI** for bike rental options. In the upper town, you may be able to rent bikes at the **St. Patrick's Well** ticket office, next to the upper funicular station.

After Dark: In the evening, there's little going on other than strolling and eating. The big *passeggiata* scene is down Via del Duomo and Corso Cavour. **Bar Duomo,** filling a little square along Via del Duomo with outdoor tables, is lively late.

Tours in Orvieto

Local Guide

David Tordi loves sharing his passion for his hometown and organizes custom tours with his colleagues focused on art, history, food, and culture (€250/half-day, €350/day, +39 0763 300 491, www.teseotur.com, info@teseotur.com). Another good choice is **Manuela Del Turco** (€130/2.5-hour tour, +39 333 221 9879, manueladel@virgilio.it). **Francesco Pacelli** is a well-regarded archaeologist and teacher (+39 328 191 1316, frapax1978@gmail.com).

Orvieto Underground Tours (Parco delle Grotte)

Beginning from a nondescript ticket office next to the TI, guides weave archaeological history into a good look at about 100 yards of Etruscan and medieval caves. You'll see the remains of an old olive press, an impressive 130-foot-deep Etruscan well shaft, what's left of a primitive cement quarry, and an extensive dovecote (pigeon coop) where the birds were reared for roasting (€7; one-hour English tours usually depart daily at 11:15, 12:30, 16:15, and 17:30; book in advance and confirm schedule for English guide, book tour and depart from ticket office facing the cathedral at Piazza Duomo 23, +39 0763 340 688, www.orvietounderground.it).

Taxi Excursions

For excursions to Civita, **Alessio Colagè Orvieto Transfer,** run by English-speaking Alessio, offers two options from Orvieto for Rick Steves readers: to and from Civita with a one-hour wait (car for up to 3 people-€120, minivan for up to 7-€140, extra hour-€35), or a two-hour visit to Civita and Lake Bolsena (5 hours total, car-€200, minivan-€250, mobile +39 370 318 1469, www.orvietotransfer.it, info@orvietotransfer.it). **Taxis** hang around the Orvieto train station ready to negotiate a little excursion to Civita.

Orvieto Walk

This quickie L-shaped self-guided walk takes you from the Duomo through Orvieto's historic center to the ramparts above the original Etruscan part of town, with vast Umbrian views. Each evening, this route is the scene of the local *passeggiata*.

❶ **Piazza del Duomo:** Start at the cathedral and admire its attention-grabbing facade (see the "Duomo" listing under "Sights in Orvieto" for a full explanation). Imagine how, as World War II raged around Orvieto, the fine reliefs gracing the front of the cathedral were encased in protective *tufa* walls. (Orvieto and its cathedral were spared destruction, perhaps thanks to a "safe cities" designation by a Nazi general who appreciated the town—or one of its women.)

As you face the cathedral, the papal palace (now hosting various museums) is to your right, and the TI and shuttle bus to the funicular are over your right shoulder. A nice gelato shop is around the church to the left.

• *Head left a few steps to the...*

❷ **Clock Tower** and **Via del Duomo:** Also known as the Maurizio Tower, this was built in the 14th century and equipped with an early mechanized clock, originally used to keep track of workers' time while building the cathedral.

The tower marks the start of Via del Duomo, lined with shops selling ceramics. The tradition of fine ceramics in Orvieto goes way back—the clay from the banks of the nearby Tiber is ideal for pottery. During the Renaissance, the town's pottery was brightly painted and highly prized.

At Via dei Magoni, a detour to the left takes you to a unique toy shop: Stroll up this picturesque lane, following signs for **Il Mago di Oz** (The Wizard of Oz, Via Pedota 9). This shop is a wondrous toy land created by eccentric Giuseppe Rosella. Have Giuseppe push a few buttons, and you're far from Kansas.

• *Backtrack to Via del Duomo, and follow it to Orvieto's main intersection, at Corso Cavour. Here you'll find the tall, stark, 11th-century...*

❸ **Tower of the Moor** (Torre del Moro): Eighty such towers, each the pride and security of a powerful noble family, once decorated the town's skyline. Today only a few survive. This tower marks the center of town, serves as a handy orientation tool, and is decorated with the coats of arms of past governors. An elevator leaves you with 173 steps still to go to earn a commanding view (€3.80, daily March-Oct 10:00-19:00, May-Aug until 20:00, shorter hours off-season).

This crossroads divides the town into four quarters (notice the *Quartiere* signs on the corners). In the past, residents of the four districts competed in a lively equestrian competition, parading all over town during the annual Corpus Domini celebration. Historically, the four streets led from here to four landmarks: Piazza del Popolo with its market and fine palazzo, St. Patrick's Well, the Duomo, and the City Hall.

• *Before heading left down Corso Cavour, side-trip a block farther ahead, behind the tower, for a look at the striking...*

❹ **Palazzo del Popolo:** Built of local *tufo*, this is a textbook example of a fortified medieval public palace: a fortress designed to house the city's leadership and military (built atop an Etruscan temple), with a market at its base, fancy meeting rooms upstairs, and aristocratic living quarters on the top level. A lively market still bustles here Thursday and Saturday mornings, selling food, clothes, and household goods.

• *Return to the tower, and turn right down Corso Cavour. Notice the handwritten sign on the door of the recommended L'Oste del Re osteria (#58), explaining that wild boar, an Umbrian specialty, is considered man's best friend. Continue past classic storefronts to...*

❺ **Piazza della Repubblica** and the **Church of Sant'Andrea:** The original vision—though it never came to fruition—was for the City Hall to have five arches flanking the central arch (marked by the flags today). The Church of Sant'Andrea (left of City Hall) sits atop the Etruscan forum that was likely the birthplace of Orvieto, centuries before Christ. Inside is an interesting architectural progression: 11th-century Romanesque (with few frescoes surviving), Gothic (the pointy vaults over the altar), and a Renaissance barrel vault in the apse (behind the altar)—all dimly lit by alabaster windows.

This spot is a layer cake of history: Under the Christian church lie the remains of the Etruscan city, destroyed by the Romans. While fascinating, the ruins can only be visited with a guide (see "Tours in Orvieto," earlier).

• *From Piazza della Repubblica, continue straight downhill on Via Filippeschi—passing a public WC on the left—until you reach a fork. Check out the friendly, traditional Galleria del Pane bakery on the right (at Via Malabranca 6; we'll return to this intersection after a short detour). Walk downhill along Via della Cava about 70 yards to #28, on the right. This is the...*

❻ **Well of the Quarry** (Pozzo della Cava): While renovating their trattoria here in the oldest part of town, the Sciarra fam-

ORVIETO & CIVITA

Orvieto Walk

1. Piazza del Duomo
2. Clock Tower & Via del Duomo
3. Tower of the Moor
4. Palazzo del Popolo
5. Piazza della Repubblica & Church of Sant'Andrea
6. Well of the Quarry
7. Palazzo Filippeschi & Viewpoint
8. Rampart View

ily discovered a vast underground network of Etruscan-era caves, wells, and tunnels. The excavation started in 1984 and continues to this day. A visit to the well makes for a fun subterranean wander (see more details in "Underground Orvieto," later in this chapter), keeping in mind that the whole city sits on top of a honeycomb of tunnels like these.

Outside, Via della Cava, meaning "Quarry Street," was a main source for building material for Orvieto's predecessor, Etruscan Velzna. The street kept getting lower and lower as more and more stones were cut out of it. Downhill is the site of the town's original gate.

• *Climb back up to the fork with the bakery. If you're hungry, pick up a piece of pizza or lumachelle (snail-shaped bread with cheese and bacon inside). Let's continue up Via Malabranca. After about 70 yards, at #22, you'll reach...*

❼ **Palazzo Filippeschi and Viewpoint:** The friendly, noble Filippeschi family sometimes leaves their big green door open so visitors can peek into their classic medieval courtyard, with black travertine columns scavenged from nearby ancient Roman villas. Enjoy a moment of exquisite medieval tranquility. (If the door is closed, just move along.)

Immediately across from the palazzo, belly up to the view-point overlooking a commotion of faded red-tile roofs. This tradition goes back to Etruscan times, when such tiles were molded on a seated tile-maker's thigh—wide to narrow. They nest so that water flows without leaking—handy for both rooftops and plumbing.

• *Continue on, downhill now, as the street crests.*

Over the next 200 yards notice faded frescoes on stucco walls, arches from previous iterations of buildings (left for structural and nostalgic reasons), built-in letterboxes, and the three local building stones—basalt white, black travertine, and brown tufa.

Soon you'll reach a square with the **Church of Sant'Agostino,** which until recently held the Baroque statues that originally lined the nave of the Duomo (they finally gave them back, after 122 years). Just beyond, on the right, is the **Church of San Giovenale**—the oldest in town, with 11th-century frescoes.

• *Finally you'll pop out at a commanding...*

❽ **Rampart View:** You're at the end of Orvieto. The fertility of the land (with its olives, vines, and fruit orchards) is clear. The manicured little forest of cypress trees straight ahead marks the Orvieto cemetery. In the distance to the right is Mount Cetona, guarding the south end of Tuscany.

Go 50 yards along the rampart to the left for the best view of the natural fortification that made this town the choice of Etruscans before the rise of ancient Rome, of stability-starved peasants after the fall of Rome, and of several popes in the high Middle Ages. From this perch you can understand why the city was never taken by force.

• *The walk is over. From here, you can retrace your steps or follow the rampart farther left, down and up, over the original Etruscan town gate and circle back to the center from there.*

Sights in Orvieto

ORVIETO DUOMO

Orvieto's cathedral (Duomo di Orvieto), worth ▲▲▲, has Italy's liveliest church facade. This colorful, prickly Gothic facade, divided by four pillars, has been compared to a medieval altarpiece. The interior features some fine art, including Luca Signorelli's lavishly frescoed Chapel of San Brizio.

The cathedral's historic importance and wealth is thanks to a miracle that happened

ORVIETO & CIVITA

nearby in 1263. According to the story, a skeptical priest named Peter of Prague passed through the town of Bolsena (12 miles from Orvieto) while on a pilgrimage to Rome. He had doubts that the bread used in Communion could really be transformed into the body of Christ. But during Mass, as he held the host aloft and blessed it, the bread began to bleed, running down his arms and dripping onto a linen cloth (a "corporal") on the altar. That miraculously bloodstained cloth is now kept here, in the Chapel of the Corporal (the last stop of our tour).

Cost and Hours: €5 combo-ticket covers the Duomo and MoDo City Museum; buy ticket in building to the right as you face the facade; cathedral open April-Sept Mon-Sat 9:30-19:00, Sun 13:00-17:30; closes one hour earlier March and Oct, shorter hours Nov-Feb; may close for religious services, www.opsm.it.

⊙ Self-Guided Tour

• *After buying your ticket, return to the front of the church. Begin by viewing the...*

Exterior Facade: Study this gleaming mass of mosaics, stained glass, and sculpture (c. 1300, by Lorenzo Maitani and others). Note how it's literally just a facade, ornamenting an otherwise very plain, mostly Romanesque exterior.

At the base of the cathedral, the four broad **marble pillars** carved with biblical scenes tell the history of the world in four acts, from left to right. The relief on the far left shows the ❶ **Creation** (see God creating Eve from Adam's rib, Cain clubbing Abel, the snake tempting Eve, and a dramatic expulsion). Next is the ❷ **Tree of Jesse** (Jesus' family tree—with Jesus on top, and Mary just below, flanked by Old Testament stories). Look up at the roaring lion of St. Mark and the grand facade filling your view—awe-inspiring as intended. In the third panel, with scenes from the ❸ **New Testament,** look for the unique manger scene, and other events from the life of Christ. On the far right is the ❹ **Last Judgment;** see Christ judging on top, with a commotion of sarcophagi popping open and all hell breaking loose at the bottom.

Each pillar is topped with a bronze symbol of one of the Evangelists (left to right): angel (Matthew), lion (Mark), eagle (John), and ox (Luke). The bronze doors are modern, by the Sicilian sculptor Emilio Greco. (A gallery devoted to Greco's work is to the immediate right of the church; see "Museums Near the Duomo," later.)

Stand back and survey the facade, looking for the central theme—it's clear the church is dedicated to the ascension of Mary. In the mosaic below the rose window, Mary is transported to heaven. In the uppermost mosaic, Mary is crowned.

• *Ticket in hand, step inside the cathedral.*

ORVIETO & CIVITA

Orvieto's Duomo

25 Meters
25 Yards

HIGH ALTAR

LOWER LEVEL ENTRY

14 CHAPEL OF THE CORPORAL

13

7 11
8 CHAPEL OF SAN BRIZIO 10
9 12

CHAPEL OF CORPOREAL ENTRY

To Gelato & WC

6

5

NAVE

ENTRY FOR WORSHIPPERS

EXIT

1 2 3 ENTER 4

To Duomo ticket office, Museo Emilio Greco & Cathedral Art Collections (MoDo)

To WC & Umbrian View

B

FACADE

Piazza del Duomo

VIA DEL DUOMO

To Corso Cavour

ETRUSCAN MUSEUM

VIA MAITANI

VIEW

UNDERGROUND ORVIETO TICKETS

1 Creation
2 Tree of Jesse & Old Testament Stories
3 New Testament Stories
4 Last Judgment
5 Marble Floor Patch
6 Pietà
7 Sermon of the Antichrist

8 End of the World (above doorway)
9 Resurrection of the Bodies
10 Last Judgment
11 Elect in Heaven
12 Damned in Hell
13 Bloody Cloth
14 Miracle of Bolsena

ORVIETO & CIVITA

Nave: The nave feels spacious and less cluttered than most Italian churches, even with statues of the apostles positioned at each column. Those statues have only recently returned to the cathedral: In 1897, the people decided they wanted to "un-Baroque" their church, and they moved the apostles out (for 122 years, they sat in the Church of Sant'Agostino across town). Bits of medieval fresco survive in niches once covered by altars and confessionals. From the back of the nave you can

appreciate the fine stained glass above the altar—it's original from the 14th century and some of the oldest in Italy. The stripes of the church are purely decorative, made of locally quarried basalt and black travertine.

The interior is warmly lit by **alabaster windows,** highlighting the black-and-white striped stonework. Why such a big and impressive church in such a little town? First of all, it's not as big as it looks. By lining the nave with striped columns and opening up the side aisles with arcaded chapels, the architect made the space seem longer and bigger than it is. Still, it's a big and rich cathedral—the seat of a bishop.

• *Now walk to the middle front of the church, where (just before the two steps) you'll see a decorative area in the floor the size of a Turkish carpet.*

❺ Marble Floor Patch: This patch in the marble floor marks where the altar stood before the Counter-Reformation. It's a reminder that as the Roman Catholic Church countered the Reformation, it made reforms of its own. For instance, altars were moved back so that the congregation could sit closer to the spectacular frescoes and stained glass. (These decorations were designed to impress commoners by illustrating the glory of heaven—and the Catholic Church needed that propaganda more than ever during the Counter-Reformation.)

Enjoy the richness that surrounds you. This cathedral put Orvieto on the map, and with lots of pilgrims came lots of wealth. The town—perched on its easy-to-defend hilltop—was used off and on for a couple centuries as a papal refuge, whenever the current pope's enemies forced him to flee Rome. Over the **altar,** the brilliant stained glass is the painstakingly restored original, from the 14th century. The fine **organ,** high on the left, has more than 5,000 pipes. Look high up in the right transept at the alabaster **rose window.** Then turn and face down the nave, the way you came in. Note

Italy Is Made of Tuff Stuff

Tuff (*tufo* in Italian) is a light-colored volcanic rock that is common in Italy. A part of Tuscany is even called the "Tuff Area."

The seven hills of Rome are made of tuff, and quarried blocks of this stone can be seen in the Colosseum, Pantheon, and Castel Sant'Angelo. Just outside of Rome, the catacombs were carved from tuff. Sorrento rises above the sea on a tuff outcrop. Orvieto, Civita di Bagnoregio (pictured), and many other hill towns perch on bluffs of tuff.

Italy's early inhabitants, including the Etruscans and Romans, carved caves, tunnels, burial niches, and even roads out of tuff. Blocks of this rock were quarried to make houses and walls. Tuff is soft and easy to carve when it's first exposed to air, but hardens later, which makes it a good building stone.

Italy's tuff-producing volcanoes resulted from a lot of tectonic-plate bumping and grinding. This violent geologic history is reflected in Italy's volcanoes, like Vesuvius and Etna, and earthquakes such as the 2009 quake in the L'Aquila area northeast of Rome.

Tuff is actually just a big hardened pile of old volcanic ash. When volcanoes hold magma that contains a lot of water, they erupt explosively (think heat + water = steam = POW!). The exploded rock material gets blasted out as hot volcanic ash, which settles on the surrounding landscape, piles up, and over time welds together into the rock called tuff.

So when you're visiting an area in Italy of ancient caves or catacombs built out of this material, you'll know that at least once (and maybe more) upon a time, it was a site of a lot of volcanic activity.

how the architect's trick—making the church look bigger from the rear—works in reverse from here. From this angle, the church appears stubbier than it actually is.

• *A few steps to your left as you face the altar, near the first pillar, is a beautiful, white marble statue.*

❻ *Pietà:* The marble pietà (statue of Mary holding Jesus' just-crucified body) was carved in 1579 by local artist Ippolito Scalza. Clearly inspired by Michelangelo's *Pietà*, this exceptional work, with four figures, was sculpted from one piece of marble. Walk around it to notice the texture that Scalza achieved, and how the light plays on the sculpture from every angle.

• *Now face the main altar. To the right is Orvieto's one must-see artistic sight, the...*

Chapel of San Brizio: This chapel features Luca Signorelli's brilliantly lit frescoes of the Day of Judgment and Life after Death (painted 1499-1504). Step into the chapel and you're surrounded by vivid scenes crammed with figures. Although the frescoes refer to themes of resurrection and salvation, they also reflect the turbulent political and religious atmosphere of late-15th-century Italy.

The chapel is decorated in one big and cohesive story. Start with the panel on your left as you enter, and do a quick counterclockwise spin to get oriented to the basic plot: Antichrist (a false prophet), end of the world (above the arch leading to the nave), Resurrection of the Bodies, hell, Judgment Day (Fra Angelico—who worked on the chapel 50 years before Signorelli—painted Jesus above the window), and finally heaven.

Now do a slower turn to take in the full story: In the ❼ **Sermon of the Antichrist** (left wall), a crowd gathers around a man preaching from a pedestal. It's the Antichrist, who comes posing as Jesus to mislead the faithful. This befuddled Antichrist forgets his lines midspeech, but the Devil is on hand to whisper what to say next. Notice how the arm in front of the Antichrist is attached to both figures, suggesting they are joined as one. His words sow wickedness through the world, including executions (upper right). The worried woman in red and light blue (foreground, left of pedestal) gets money from a man for something she's not proud of (perhaps receiving funds from a Jewish moneylender—notice the Stars of David on his purse). Many of the faces in the crowd are probably actual portraits.

Most likely, the Antichrist himself is a veiled reference to Savonarola (1452-1498), the charismatic Florentine monk who defied the pope, drove the Medici family from power, and riled the populace with apocalyptic sermons. Many Italians—including the painter Signorelli—viewed Savonarola as a tyrant and heretic, the Antichrist who was ushering in the Last Days.

In the upper left, notice the hardworking angel. He looks as if he's at batting practice, hitting followers of the Antichrist back to earth as they try to get through the pearly gates. In the bottom left is a self-portrait of the artist, **Luca Signorelli** (c. 1450-1523), well-dressed in black with long golden hair. Signorelli, from nearby Cortona, was at the peak of his powers, and this chapel was his masterpiece. He looks out proudly as if to say, "I did all this in just a few years, on time and on budget," confirming his reputation as a speedy, businesslike painter. Next to him (also in black) is the artist Fra Angelico, who started the chapel decoration five decades earlier but completed only a small part of it: the Last Judgment over the window and the angels around it.

Compare the style of painting between these two masters—Angelico's angels stacked like little wooden dolls next to Signorelli's intertwined naked bodies. You can clearly see the huge effect the Renaissance had on painting in just a few decades.

Around the arch opposite the windows are signs of the ❽ **end of the world:** eclipse, tsunami, falling stars, earthquakes, violence in the streets, and a laser-wielding gray angel.

On the right wall (opposite the Antichrist) is the ❾ **Resurrection of the Bodies.** Trumpeting angels blow a wake-up call, and the dead climb dreamily out of the earth to be clothed with new bodies, some of the randy skeletons finding time for flirting. On the same wall (below the action, at eye level) is a gripping pietà. Also by Signorelli, this pietà gives insight into the artist's genius and personality. Look at the emotion in the faces of the two Marys and consider that Signorelli's son had just died. The small black-and-white Deposition scene (behind Jesus' leg) seems inspired by ancient Greek scenes of a pre-Christian hero's death. In the confident spirit of the Renaissance, the artist incorporates a pagan scene to support a Christian story. This 3-D realism in a 2-D sketch shows the work of a talented master.

The altar wall (with the windows) features the ❿ **Last Judgment.** To the left of the altar (and continuing around the corner, filling half the left wall) are the ⓫ **Elect in Heaven.** They spend eternity posing like bodybuilders while listening to celestial Muzak. To the right (and continuing around the corner on the right wall) are the ⓬ **Damned in Hell,** in the scariest mosh pit ever. Devils torment sinners in graphic detail, while winged demons control the airspace overhead. In the center, a lusty demon turns to tell the frightened woman on his back exactly what he's got planned. (According to legend, this was Signorelli's lover, who betrayed him...and ended up here.) Signorelli's ability to tell a story through human actions and gestures, rather than symbols, inspired his younger contemporary, Michelangelo, who meticulously studied the elder artist's nudes.

In this chapel, Christian theology sits physically and figuratively upon a foundation of Classical logic. Below everything are Greek and Latin philosophers, plus Dante, struggling to reconcile Classical truth with Church doctrine. You can see the intellectual challenge on their faces as they ponder the puzzle of theology that survives the test of reason.

The figures are immersed in fanciful Grotesque (that is, grotto-esque) decor. Dating from 1499, this is one of the first uses of the frilly, nubile, and even sexy "wallpaper pattern" so popular in the Renaissance. (It was inspired by the decorations found in Nero's Golden House in Rome, which had been discovered under street level just a few years earlier and was mistaken for an underground grotto.)

During the Renaissance, nakedness symbolized purity. When attitudes changed during the Counter-Reformation, the male figures in Signorelli's frescoes were given penis-covering sashes. In a 1982 restoration, most—but not all—of the sashes were removed. A little of that prudishness survives to this day, as those in heaven were left with their sashes modestly in place.

• *Exit the cathedral and make a sharp right towards its far end, where you'll find the entrance to the Chapel of the Corporal. Be mindful that this chapel is used for prayer and may be closed during religious services.*

Chapel of the Corporal: The ⓭ **bloody cloth** from the miracle is displayed in the turquoise frame atop the chapel's altar. It was brought from Bolsena to Orvieto, where Pope Urban IV happened to be visiting. The amazed pope proclaimed a new holiday, Corpus Domini (Body of Christ), and the Orvieto cathedral was built (begun in 1290) to display the miraculous relic. For centuries, the precious linen was paraded through the streets of Orvieto in an ornate reliquary (now in the MoDo City Museum).

The room was frescoed in the 14th century with scenes attesting to Christ's presence in the communion wafer and offering a vivid peek at life here at that time. The ⓮ **miracle of Bolsena** (set here in 13th-century Orvieto) is depicted on the chapel's right wall.

• *Our tour is finished. You're surrounded by great sights. Across the square in front of the Duomo are the Etruscan Museum, the TI, and the ticket office for Underground Orvieto tours. Around the side of the church are the Museo Emilio Greco, MoDo City Museum (included in your Duomo ticket), and National Archaeological Museum. Nearby, beyond a small parking lot, a park affords a fine Umbrian view.*

MUSEUMS NEAR THE DUOMO

▲▲MoDo City Museum (Museo dell'Opera del Duomo)

This museum encompasses two different sights: The **Emilio Greco collection** (in Palazzo Soliano, to the right of the cathedral) shows off the work of Emilio Greco, the Sicilian artist who designed the modern doors of Orvieto's cathedral. And the **Cathedral Art Collections** (in Palazzi Papali, behind the cathedral) holds the city's best devotional art. This is the main attraction of the MoDo City Museum and well worth a visit.

Cost and Hours: €5 combo-ticket covers the MoDo City Museum and the Duomo; daily April-Sept 9:30-19:00, March and Oct until 18:00, Nov-Feb until 17:00; Piazza Duomo, +39 0763 343 592, www.opsm.it.

Visiting the MoDo City Museum Branches: You'll buy your ticket inside Palazzo Soliano. It's the building marked *MUSEO*, to the right as you face the cathedral. This building also houses the Museo Emilio Greco. A good plan is to buy a ticket, visit the Greco collection while you're there, then tour the cathedral interior (described earlier). Afterward, enter the Cathedral Art Collections.

Museo Emilio Greco: This fresh little collection of works by Emilio Greco (1913-1995) displays his sketches and about 30 of his bronze statues, showing his absorption with gently twisting and turning nudes. Greco's sketchy outlines of women are simply beautiful. The artful installation of his work in this palazzo, with walkways and a spiral staircase up to the ceiling, is designed to let you view his sculptures from different angles.

• *To find the Cathedral Art Collections, head around the right side of the cathedral and climb the metal staircase.*

Cathedral Art Collections: A complex of medieval palaces called the Palazzi Papali (Papal Palaces) holds some of Orvieto's finest religious sculptures, paintings, and frescoes. The highlight is just inside the upstairs entrance: a marble **Mary and Child** who sit beneath a bronze canopy, attended by exquisite angels. This proto-Renaissance ensemble, dating from around 1300, once filled the niche in the center of the cathedral's facade (where a replica sits today).

Now proceed through several art-filled rooms on this floor. Entering the first large room, look left to see an exquisite *Madonna and Child* from 1322 by the Sienese great **Simone Martini,** who worked in Orvieto. Nearby are saintly wooden statues and fine inlaid woodwork from the original choir. Farther along, you'll find **Luca Signorelli**'s *Mary Magdalene* (1504), then a large room of Baroque paintings from the late 1500s that decorated the side chapels with a harsh Counter-Reformation message. (Think about how dramatically church art evolved in the 200 years from Martini's

ORVIETO & CIVITA

almost 2-D medieval style, to Signorelli's Renaissance humanism, to the bombast of Baroque.)

In the hall with the Baroque paintings, step into the smaller side-room. This is the **Albèri Library,** with delicate black-and-white frescoes done by Signorelli's workshop while he was in town working on the cathedral's Chapel of San Brizio. This hall displays items from the cathedral treasury, including the reliquary used to parade a holy bloodstained cloth on Corpus Domini.

Continuing through the main collection, go back past the entry to one more large hall, with statues of **St. Michael and the dragon,** more altarpieces and statues, and sinopias (preliminary drawings for the frescoes decorating the cathedral's Chapel of the Corporal, with a roughed-up surface so the wet plaster would stick).

Your MoDo ticket also gives you access to the vast space beneath the cathedral. Access it through the entrance at the cathedral's right transept. Under the **cellar vaults** is equipment used for building the cathedral (giant pulley mechanisms and tools) and neatly stacked fragments of sculptures and tiles.

National Archaeological Museum of Orvieto
(Museo Archeologico Nazionale di Orvieto)

If you want to also see the National Archaeological Museum, its entrance hides between the Cathedral Art Collections and the Museo Emilio Greco in the ground floor of Palazzi Papali. This small five-room collection beautifully shows off a trove of well-preserved Etruscan bronzes, terra-cotta objects, and ceramics—many from the necropolis at the base of Orvieto, and some with painted colors surviving from 500 BC. To see the treasure of this museum, ask an attendant for the Golini tombs (named after the man who discovered them in 1836). You'll be escorted to the reconstructed, fourth-century BC tombs, frescoed with scenes from an Etruscan banquet in the afterlife. For background on the Etruscans, see page 650.

Cost and Hours: €4, €5 combo-ticket with Etruscan Necropolis; Tue-Sun 8:30-19:30, closed Mon; +39 0763 341 039, www.musei.umbria.beniculturali.it.

▲Etruscan Museum
(Museo Claudio Faina e Museo Civico)

This 19th-century, Neoclassical nobleman's palace stands on the main square facing the cathedral. Its elegantly frescoed rooms hold an impressive Etruscan collection. The ground floor features the Museo Civico, with fragments of Etruscan sculpture. On the first floor is the Collezione Conti Faina, with Etruscan jewelry and an extensive array of Roman coins (push the brass buttons to rotate the coins so you can see both sides). The top floor features the best of the Etruscan and proto-Etruscan (from the ninth century BC) vases and bronzes, lots of votives found buried in nearby tombs, and fine views of the Duomo.

Cost and Hours: €6; Wed-Mon April-Sept 9:30-18:00, Oct-March 10:00-17:00, closed Tue year-round; +39 0763 341 511, www.museofaina.it.

Teatro Mancinelli

A short walk from the cathedral, on Corso Cavour, Teatro Mancinelli is a fine 19th-century Italian theater (from 1866) with 500 seats, elegant boxes, and frilly Romantic ceiling paintings—all well described in English. Visitors are sometimes allowed to climb upstairs to the foyer for a chance to peek into a private box. The theater hosts the recommended Café del Teatro—buy a drink and you may be able to wander the theater without paying the €2 entry fee (typically open Mon-Sat 8:00-14:00, closed Sun, Corso Cavour 122).

UNDERGROUND ORVIETO

These sights—showing off the remarkable bounty of history beneath your feet—are scattered around (and outside) the old center. For locations, see the "Orvieto" map at the start of this chapter. Also consider the Underground Orvieto Tours listed under "Tours in Orvieto," earlier.

▲▲St. Patrick's Well (Pozzo di San Patrizio)

Modern engineers are impressed by this deep well—175 feet deep and 45 feet wide—designed in the 16th century with a double-helix pattern. The two spiral stairways allow an efficient one-way traffic flow: intriguing now, but critical then. Imagine if donkeys and people, balancing jugs of water, had to go up and down the same stairway. At the bottom is a bridge that people could walk on to scoop up water. Touring the well requires hiking 248 (awkwardly spaced) steps down, then back up. That's lots of exercise (allow 20-30 minutes round-trip) and not much to see...other than some mesmerizing 16th-century engineering.

The well was built because a pope got nervous. After Rome was sacked in 1527 by renegade troops of the Holy Roman Empire, the pope fled to Orvieto. He feared that even this little town (with no water source on top) would be besieged. He commissioned a well, which was started in 1527 and finished 10 years later. It was a huge project. (As it turns out, the town was never besieged, but supporters believe that the well was worth the cost and labor because of its deterrence value—attackers would think twice about besieging a town with a reliable water source.) Even today, when a local is faced with a difficult task, people say, "It's like digging St. Patrick's Well."

Cost and Hours: €5, interesting €2 audioguide; daily May-Aug 9:00-20:00, shorter hours off-season; ticket office immediately to your right as you exit the funicular, you'll walk a few minutes down the path to enter the well; Viale Sangallo, +39 0763 343 768.

▲Well of the Quarry (Pozzo della Cava)

A five-minute walk west of Piazza della Repubblica, this complex of Etruscan-era caves, wells, and tunnels leads down to a fat, cylindrical, beautifully carved 2,500-year-old well. Go ahead, spit (or drop a coin 100 feet down—coins are collected each Christmas for a local charity). Your visit is capped with a review of local pottery-making.

Cost and Hours: €4, €2.50 with St. Patrick's Well ticket; Tue-Sun 9:00-20:00, closed Mon; Via della Cava 28, +39 0763 342 373, www.pozzodellacava.it.

Etruscan Necropolis
(Necropoli Etrusca di Crocifisso del Tufo)

Below town, at the base of the cliff, is a remarkable "city of the dead" that dates back to the sixth to third century BC. The tombs, which are laid out in a kind of street grid, are empty, and there's precious little to see here other than the basic stony construction. But it is both eerie and fascinating to wander the streets of an Etruscan cemetery.

Cost and Hours: €3, €5 combo-ticket with National Archaeological Museum; Thu-Sat 9:00-15:00, Fri and the first two Sun of each month until 19:00, closed Mon-Wed year-round; +39 0763 343 611, www.musei.umbria.beniculturali.it. Drivers will find it on the ring road below town; hikers can reach it via the Rupe path (see next).

VIEW WALKS
▲Hike Around the City on the Rupe

Orvieto's Rupe is a peaceful path that completely circles the town at the base of the cliff upon which it sits. With the help of the TI's city map, you'll see there are five access points from the town for this three-mile walk. The path includes a series of sightseeing stops along the way (marked in purple, allow about two hours round-trip).

From the access points, you'll walk or take stairs down, down, down to the trail that hugs the cliff. The easy-to-follow path is wide and partially paved, though it has some steep, gravelly descents—wear good shoes and be prepared for a climb. On one side you have the cliff, with the town high above. On the other side you have Umbrian views stretching into the distance. The path is peaceful, with few other people and only the sound of the wind and birds to accompany you. It makes for a delightful evening walk (not lit after dark).

I'd leave Orvieto at Piazza Marconi and walk left (counterclockwise) three-quarters of the way around the town (there's a fine view down onto the Etruscan Necropolis midway), then ride the escalator and elevator back up to the town from the big Campo della Fiera parking lot. If you're ever confused about the path, follow signs for *Anello della Rupe*.

▲Shorter Romantic Rampart Stroll

Thanks to its dramatic hilltop setting, several fine little walks wind around the edges of Orvieto. My favorite after dark, when it's lamp-lit and romantic, is along the ramparts at the far west end of town. Start at the Church of San Giovenale (near the end of my self-guided Orvieto Walk). With your back to the church, go a block to the right to the end of town. Then head left along the ramparts, with cypress-dotted Umbria to your right, and follow Vicolo Volsinia to the Church of San Giovanni Evangelista, where you can reenter the old-town center near several recommended restaurants.

NEAR ORVIETO
Wine Tasting

Orvieto Classico wine is justly famous. Two inviting wineries sit just outside Orvieto on the scenic Canale route to Bagnoregio; if you're side-tripping to Civita, it's easy to stop at either or both for a tasting (call ahead for a reservation). Two more wineries lie to the north where the soil changes from *tufo* to clay, which changes the character of the wines. For locations, see the "Orvieto and Civita Area" map near the beginning of this chapter.

Between Orvieto and Bagnoregio: For a tour of a historic winery with Etruscan cellars, make an appointment to visit **Te-**

nuta Le Velette, where the Bottai family offers a warm welcome. Their wines are considered to be some of the best in the region. Reserve ahead, especially on weekends (no drop-ins; €8-25 for tour and tasting—price varies depending on wines, number of people, and food requested; Mon-Fri 8:30-12:00 & 14:00-18:00, Sat 8:30-12:30, closed Sun; also has accommodations—see listing later in this chapter, +39 0763 29090, www.tenutalevelette.com, booking@tenutalevelette.com). From their sign (a 5-minute drive past Orvieto at top of switchbacks just before Canale, on road to Bagnoregio), cruise down a long tree-lined drive, then park at the striped gate.

Custodi is another respected family-run winery that produces Orvieto Classico, grappa, and olive oil on a modern 140-acre estate. Helpful Chiara and Laura Custodi speak English. Reserve ahead for a tour of their cantina, an explanation of the winemaking process, and a tasting of four wines (€20/person for wines only, daily 8:30-12:30 & 15:30-18:30 except closed Sun afternoon, Viale Venere S.N.C. Loc. Canale; on the road from Orvieto to Civita, a half-mile after Le Velette, it's the first building before Canale; +39 0763 29053, mobile +39 338 316 0405, www.cantinacustodi.com).

To the North: In the rolling hills just north of Orvieto, **Neri** rests amid postcard-pretty estate grounds, with an ancient manor house and grand views of Orvieto and the countryside. Their wines are simple and traditional (tour and tastings from €15, reservations preferred, daily 9:30-17:00; just down the road from recommended Agriturismo Cioccoleta at Località Bardano 28—head north from Orvieto following signs to *Sferracavallo* and *Bardano;* +39 0763 316 196, mobile +39 393 331 3844, www.cantineneri.it, visite@neri-vini.it, Enrico).

Sleeping in Orvieto

Orvieto's high season (with higher hotel prices) is roughly May to early July, September, and October. You'll save a little money off-season.

IN THE TOWN CENTER

$$$ Grand Hotel Italia is businesslike, with a stay-awhile lobby and terrace. While not as "grand" as it once was, it brings predictable modern amenities to this small town. The 45 overpriced rooms are well located in the heart of Orvieto, a block off the main drag and near the market square (RS%, air-con, elevator, off-site pay parking—reserve ahead, Via di Piazza del Popolo 13, +39 0763 342 065, www.grandhotelitalia.it, hotelita@libero.it).

$$ Hotel Duomo is centrally located and modern, with splashy art in 17 rooms and a friendly welcome. It's tucked a few steps off the cathedral square, but double-paned windows keep the sound of

Orvieto Hotels & Restaurants

ETRUSCAN NECROPOLIS

LA RUPE PATH

Cliffs

SANT' AGOSTINO

SAN GIOVENALE

Piazza S. Giovenale

STRADA DELLE CONC

V. CACCIA

PALAZZO FILIPPESCHI

BAKERY

V. MAGALOTTI

VIA PECORELLI

P

12

Piazza della Repubblica

COMMENDA

WC

17

LOGGIA

CITY HALL

SANT' ANDREA

11

PORTA MAGGIORE

WELL OF THE QUARRY

V. RANIERI

V. DRITTA DI MARCH.

VIA MALCORINI

To Bolsena & Viterbo

STRADA DI PORTA ROMANA

SAN GIO. EVANG.

Piazza de' Ranieri

29

ESCALATOR TO PARKING GARAGE

V. GARIBALDI

VIA COZZA

5

Piazza San Gio.

UPPER ELEVATOR

VIA RIPA MEDICI

SAN LODO.

Campo della Fiera

P

LOWER ELEVATOR

ESCALATOR TO PIAZZA DE' RANIERI

To Bolsena & Viterbo

VIA DELLA SEGHERIA

10

PORTA ROMANA

VIA D. ALBERICI

Accommodations
1. Grand Hotel Italia
2. Hotel Duomo
3. Hotel Corso
4. La Magnolia B&B
5. B&B Michelangeli
6. Affittacamere Valentina
7. Hotel Posta
8. Villa Mercede
9. Istituto S.S. Salvatore
10. Casa Sèlita B&B

Eateries & Other
11. Trattoria la Palomba
12. L'Antica Trattoria dell'Orso
13. Trattoria del Moro Aronne

the church bells well-muffled (RS%, family rooms, air-con, elevator, private pay parking, sunny terrace, a block from the Duomo at
Vicolo di Maurizio 7, +39 0763 341 887, www.orvietohotelduomo.
com, orvietohotelduomo@gmail.com; Gianni and Maura Mas-
saccesi don't speak much English, daughter Elisa and son-in-law
Diego do). They have another three rooms in a nearby annex (lower
prices, breakfast at the main hotel).

$$ Hotel Corso is friendly, with 18 fresh and flowery rooms—
a few with balconies and views. Their sunlit little terrace is enjoy-

⑭	Trattoria la Grotta & Grocery	㉒	To La Musa Gelateria
⑮	Trattoria da Carlo	㉓	Caffè ClanDestino
⑯	Trattoria Antico Bucchero	㉔	Café Barrique
⑰	Pizzeria Charlie	㉕	Café del Teatro
⑱	Enoteca al Duomo	㉖	Bar Palace
⑲	L'Oste del Re	㉗	Bar Duomo
⑳	Caffè Montanucci	㉘	Grocery
㉑	Pasqualetti Gelateria (2)	㉙	Launderette

able, but the location—halfway between the center of town and the funicular—is less convenient than others (RS%, family rooms, ask for quieter room off street, air-con, elevator, reserved pay parking, Corso Cavour 339, +39 0763 342 020, www.hotelcorso.net, info@ hotelcorso.net, Carla).

$ La Magnolia B&B is a great value where friendly Serena offers lots of welcoming touches. Its seven unique rooms—some mini-apartments with kitchens and some with frescoed ceilings and nice terraces—are cheerfully decorated and centrally located.

The three units facing the busy street are air-conditioned and have double-paned windows (RS%, family rooms, no elevator, washing machine, Via del Duomo 29, +39 0763 342 808, mobile +39 349 462 0733, www.bblamagnolia.it, info@bblamagnolia.it).

$ B&B Michelangeli offers two comfortable and well-appointed apartments hiding along a residential lane a few blocks from the tourist scene. It's run by eager-to-please Francesca, who speaks limited English but provides homey touches and free tea, coffee, and breakfast supplies. From the Corso, follow Via Michelangeli, a street full of wood sculptures made by her famous artistic family (fully equipped kitchen, washing machine, private pay parking, Via dei Saracinelli 20—ring bell labeled *M. Michelangeli*, mobile +39 347 089 0349, www.bbmichelangeli.com).

$ Affittacamere Valentina rents six clean, airy, well-appointed rooms, all with big double beds and antique furniture. It's in the heart of Orvieto, on a quiet street behind the palace on Piazza del Popolo (RS%, no breakfast, air-con, pay parking, Via Vivaria 7, +39 0763 341 607, mobile +39 328 734 1272, www.affittacamerevalentina.com, camerevalentina@gmail.com). Welcoming Valentina also rents four apartments in the center that work well for families.

$ Hotel Posta is a centrally located, long-ago-elegant palazzo renting 20 quirky, clean, cheap rooms with dark wood floors and vintage furniture. It feels a little institutional, but it's well run, and the rooms without private bath are among the cheapest in town (breakfast extra, elevator, Via Luca Signorelli 18, +39 0763 341 909, www.hotelpostaorvieto.it, hotelposta@orvietohotels.it, Alessia).

$ Villa Mercede, a good value and excellent location, is owned by a religious institution and offers 26 cheap, simple rooms, each with a big modern bathroom and many with glorious Umbrian views (family rooms, elevator, free parking, a half-block from Duomo at Via Soliana 2, reception upstairs, +39 0763 341 766, www.villamercede.it, info@villamercede.it).

$ Istituto SS. Salvatore rents 17 spotless rooms, shared with a convent, which come with a peaceful terrace garden and the best views in town (family rooms, elevator, pay parking, just off Piazza del Popolo at Via del Popolo 1, +39 0763 342 910, www.istitutosansalvatore.com, istitutosansalvatore@gmail.com).

Just Outside the Town Center: A peaceful country house, **$ Casa Sèlita B&B** offers easy access to Orvieto (best for drivers, but workable for adventurous train travelers who want an *agriturismo*-style experience). It's nestled in an orchard just below the town cliffs; to get to town, you'll climb an uphill path through their olive orchard (with a view terrace along the way) to reach the Campo della Fiera parking lot, with its handy escalator taking you the rest of the way up into Orvieto. Its three rooms with terraces are airy and fresh, with dark hardwood floors, fluffy down comforters, and modern baths. Enjoy the views from the relaxing garden. Conscientious Sèlita is a gracious host (cash only, air-con, free parking, closed mid-Nov-Easter, Strada di Porta Romana 8, ask for directions—GPS can be tricky, mobile +39 339 225 4000, www.casaselita.com, info@casaselita.com).

NEAR ORVIETO

All of these (except the last one) are within a 20-minute drive of Orvieto, in different directions, and require a car—see the "Orvieto and Civita Area" map, near the beginning of this chapter.

$$$ **Alta Rocca Wine Resort,** is a fancy "country resort" and spa, located 15 minutes north of Orvieto. They produce their own olive oil and wine and rent 30 modern and air-conditioned rooms and a few apartments. This place has *luna di miele* (honeymoon) written all over it and only allows kids 14 and up (2 pools, panoramic view restaurant, wellness center with Jacuzzi and steam room, massages and spa treatments available, winery visit and wine tasting upon request, gym, hiking paths to private lake, +39 0763 344 210 or +39 0763 393 437, www.altaroccawineresort.com, info@altaroccawineresort.com).

$$$ **Agriturismo Locanda Rosati,** where you'll be greeted by friendly host Giampiero Rosati, rents 11 tastefully decorated rooms in a pleasant, homey atmosphere. The peaceful, flower-lined grounds are perfect for a retreat (RS%, family rooms, full traditional dinners for €40 on request, air-con, swimming pool, 5 miles from Orvieto on the road to Viterbo, tricky to find—use GPS for directions, +39 0763 217 314, www.locandarosati.it, info@locandarosati.it).

$$ **Tenuta Le Velette** is a sprawling, historic, family-run estate and winery. The Bottai family rents six fully furnished apartments and villas scattered over their expansive and scenic grounds. Rooms range in size—accommodating from 2 to 14 people—but they all nestle in perfect Umbrian rural peace and tranquility. See the website for details on their various villas (2-night minimum, discount for weekly stay, pool, 10 minutes from Orvieto—drive toward Bagnoregio-Canale and follow *Tenuta Le Velette* signs, +39 0763 29090, www.tenutalevelette.com, cecilialevelette@libero.it). They also offer wine tastings (see description under "Near Orvieto," earlier in this chapter).

$$ **Agriturismo Cioccoleta** ("Little Stone") has eight rooms with cozy country decor, each named after one of the grapes grown in the *agriturismo*'s vineyards. It's run by friendly Angela, who takes great pride in the farmhouse her family restored, and offers sweeping views of Orvieto and the pastoral countryside (RS%,

ORVIETO & CIVITA

fans, 3 miles north of Orvieto at Località Bardano 34 in Bardano, +39 0763 316 011, mobile +39 349 860 9780, www.cioccoleta.it, info@cioccoleta.it).

Farther Out: Northeast of Orvieto, **$$$ Agriturismo Fattoria di Vibio** produces olive oil and honey, sells organic products, and offers classes and spa services. In August, its 14 rooms rent at peak prices and have a minimum-stay requirement. The rest of the year, no minimum stay is required, although rates drop dramatically for longer visits. Its two cottages sleep from four to six people and rent only by the week (panoramic pool, expensive restaurant, farthest cottage is 20 miles from Orvieto, www.fattoriadivibio.com, info@fattoriadivibio.com).

Eating in Orvieto

Orvieto is a foodie town with a surprising number of great restaurants hidden just off the main drag. Pigeon dishes are featured on many Orvieto menus: Look for—or avoid—*piccione*.

TRATTORIAS IN THE CENTER

$$$ Trattoria la Palomba features excellent game and truffle specialties in a wood-paneled dining room. Giampiero, Enrica, and Giovanna have been enthusiastically taking care of their diners since 1965, offering a fine value, high quality, and classy conviviality. Truffles are shaved right at your table—try the *umbricelli al tartufo* (homemade pasta with truffles) or *spaghetti dell'Ascaro* (with truffles). Their *filetto alla cardinale* and mixed-cheese plates are popular. As slow-foodies, they use organic and locally sourced ingredients (reservations smart, Thu-Tue 12:30-14:00 & 19:30-22:00, closed Wed and July, off Piazza della Repubblica at Via Cipriano Manente 16, +39 0763 343 395).

$$$ L'Antica Trattoria dell'Orso offers well-prepared Umbrian cuisine paired with fine wines in a homey, bohemian-chic, peaceful atmosphere. Owner Stefano and chef Hania offer attentive service and a good value (gluten-free options; Mon-Sat 12:00-15:00 & 19:30-22:00, closed Nov, Feb, and Sun year-round; just off Piazza della Repubblica at Via della Misericordia 18, +39 0763 341 642).

$$ Trattoria del Moro Aronne is a long-established family bistro run by Cristian and his mother, Rolanda, who lovingly prepare homemade pasta and market-fresh Umbrian specialties. Consider their *nidi*—folds of fresh pasta enveloping warm, gooey pecorino cheese sweetened with honey. Three small and separate dining areas make the interior feel intimate. While not particularly atmospheric, this place is known locally as an excellent value (Wed-

ORVIETO & CIVITA

Mon 12:30-14:30 & 19:30-22:00, closed Tue, Via San Leonardo 7, +39 0763 342 763).

$$ Trattoria la Grotta prides itself on serving only the freshest food and finest wine. The decor is Signorelli-mod, and the ambience is quiet, with courteous service. They've been at it for more than 50 years, and promise diners a free coffee, grappa, *limoncello*, or vin santo with this book (Wed-Mon opens at 12:00 for lunch and at 19:00 for dinner, closed Tue, Via Luca Signorelli 5, +39 0763 341 348).

$$ Trattoria da Carlo, hiding on its own little *piazzetta* between Via Corso Cavour and Piazza del Popolo, is a cozy spot with a bright, white-tiled interior and inviting tables outside. Animated and opinionated Carlo—a young, likeable loudmouth—holds court, chatting up his diners as much as he cooks, while his mama scuttles about taking orders, busing dishes, and lovingly rolling her eyes at her son's big personality. Carlo likes big flavors and putting a modern twist on traditional dishes (daily 12:00-15:00 & 19:00-24:00, often closed Sun dinner, Vicolo del Popolo 1, +39 0763 343 916).

$$ Trattoria Antico Bucchero, elegant under a big, white vault, makes for a nice memory with its delicious food—especially game and wild boar (Thu-Tue 12:00-15:00 & 19:00-23:00, closed Wed, also closed Sun in July-Aug; seating indoors and on a peaceful square in summer, air-con, a half-block south of Corso Cavour, between Torre del Moro and Piazza della Repubblica at Via de Cartari 4, +39 0763 341 725; Piero and Silvana, plus sons Fabio and Pericle).

$$ Pizzeria Charlie is a local favorite. Its noisy dining room and stony courtyard are reminiscent of a beer hall, and popular with families and students for casual dinners of wood-fired gourmet pizzas. In a quiet courtyard guarded by a medieval tower, it's a block southwest of Piazza della Repubblica (Wed-Mon 19:00-23:00, closed Tue, Via Loggia dei Mercanti 14, +39 0763 344 766).

$$$ Enoteca al Duomo is to the left of the Duomo and has pleasant outdoor seating with a cathedral view. They serve wines by the glass and a vast selection of Italian wines by the bottle, and a full menu of local dishes in a contemporary wine-bar atmosphere (daily 10:00-22:00, closed Feb, Piazza del Duomo 13, +39 0763 344 607).

FAST AND CHEAP EATS

$ L'Oste del Re is a simple osteria on Corso Cavour, where Maria Grazia and Claudio offer pasta, bruschetta, enticing meat-and-cheese plates, and hearty, made-to-order sandwiches to eat in a small dining room or take out (Fri-Wed 10:00-15:00 & 19:00-

ORVIETO & CIVITA

22:00, closed Thu; no evening hours Oct-April; Corso Cavour 58, +39 0763 343 846).

$ **Caffè Montanucci,** the dominant hangout on the main street—for good reason—lays out an appetizing display of pastas and main courses behind the counter. Choose one (or two—called a *bis*), find a seat in the modern interior or sunny courtyard, and they'll bring it out on a tray. You'll eat among locals on lunch break. They also have good *caffè*, simple sandwiches, and tasty sweets all day (daily 7:00-24:00, meals for lunch only, Corso Cavour 21, +39 0763 341 261).

Panini **and a Picnic:** Scattered around town you'll find many *alimentari* (grocers) selling cured meats, cheese, and other staples. If you're feeling gamey, order prosciutto or salami made from *cinghiale* (cheen-gee-AH-lay; wild boar), a surprisingly mild-tasting local favorite. They're usually willing to make you a simple sandwich of bread, cold cuts, and/or cheese for a few euros.

Elsewhere along the Corso Cavour, you'll find places selling fruit, vegetables, and other picnic items. The fortress/garden, to the right as you face the funicular, is a great spot to enjoy your meal.

Groceries: While a small *alimentari* might have what you need for a picnic, two slightly larger **Pam Local** markets are tucked away two minutes from the Duomo (both Mon-Sat 8:00-20:00, Sun from 9:00, one at Corso Cavour 100 and the other just past recommended Trattoria la Grotta at Via Luca Signorelli 23).

Gelato: For dessert, *gelateria* **Pasqualetti,** next to the cathedral, is a favorite (daily, may close in cold weather, closed Dec-Feb; one location is next to left transept of church, Piazza del Duomo 14; another branch is a few steps off the main drag at Via del Duomo 10). Closer to the funicular, **La Musa** has a nice variety of creative flavors (daily, Corso Cavour 351).

CAFÉ SCENE ON CORSO CAVOUR AND NEARBY

Orvieto has a charming, traffic-free, pedestrian-friendly vibe. To enjoy it, be sure to spend a little time savoring *la dolce far niente*— the art of doing nothing—while sitting at a café. There are inviting places all over town, but these are either on or very near Corso Cavour, the main strolling drag, and offer the best people-watching.

Caffè Montanucci is the town's venerable place for a coffee and pastry, but has no on-street seating (Corso Cavour 21, described earlier for lunch). **Caffè ClanDestino** is well located, with plenty of streetside seating and endless little bites served with your drink (Corso Cavour 40). **Café Barrique** is less crowded, less trendy, and quieter, with nice outdoor tables and good free snacks with your drink (Corso Cavour 111).

Café del Teatro, at Teatro Mancinelli (described earlier), can be a fun experience. Drink streetside, at the bar, or in the theater lobby (Corso Cavour 122). If you buy a drink you might be free to wander around the theater without paying the entry fee.

On Piazza del Popolo: A sunny, relaxed perch, **Bar Palace** faces a big square that's generally quiet except on market day and on nice evenings, when young locals gather here.

Cafés Facing the Cathedral: Several cafés on Piazza del Duomo invite you to linger over a drink with a view of Orvieto's amazing cathedral.

Orvieto Connections

From Orvieto by Train to: Rome (every 1-2 hours, 1-1.5 hours), **Florence** (6/day, 2.5 hours), **Siena** (12/day, 2.5 hours, change in Chiusi), **Assisi** (roughly hourly, 2-3 hours, 1-2 transfers), **Milan** (2/day direct, 5.5 hours; otherwise about hourly with a transfer in Florence, Bologna, or Rome, 4.5-5 hours). The train station's Buffet della Stazione is surprisingly good if you need a quick focaccia sandwich or pizza picnic for the train ride.

Tip for Drivers: If you're thinking of driving to Rome, consider stashing your car in Orvieto instead. You can easily park the car, safe and free, in the big lot below the Orvieto train station (for up to a week or more), and zip effortlessly into Rome by train.

Civita di Bagnoregio

Perched on a pinnacle in a grand canyon, the 2,500-year-old, traffic-free village of Civita di Bagnoregio is Italy's ultimate hill town. Civita's only connection to the town of Bagnoregio (ban-yoh-REH-joh)—and the world—is a long pedestrian bridge. In the last decade, the old, self-sufficient Civita (chee-VEE-tah) has died—the last of its lifelong residents have passed on, and the only employment here is in serving gawking sightseers. But Civita remains an amazing place to visit. And it remains popular as a backdrop for movies, soap operas, and advertising campaigns.

Civita's history goes back to Etruscan and ancient Roman times. In the early Middle Ages, Bagnoregio was a suburb of Civita, which had a population of about 4,000. Later, Bagnoregio surpassed Civita in size—especially following a 1695 earthquake, after which many residents fled Civita to live in Bagnoregio, fearing their houses would be shaken off the edge into the valley below. Bagnoregio is dominated by Renaissance-style buildings, while architecturally, Civita remains stuck in the Middle Ages.

Despite being a "dead city," Civita can be very crowded—especially on the weekends and at lunchtime. The best way to enjoy

Civita is early or late in the day, when you have the village to yourself. While Bagnoregio lacks the pinnacle-town romance of Civita, it's a healthy, vibrant community. In Bagnoregio, get a haircut, sip a coffee on the square, and walk down to the old laundry (ask, *"Dov'è la lavanderia vecchia?"*).

Planning Your Time: In high season—and especially on weekends—little Civita can be uncomfortably jammed; for a better experience, treat it like a major museum and visit either early or late in the day. If side-tripping by bus from Orvieto, it works well to get up early, take the 8:30 bus, and see Civita in the cool morning calm. (The next bus is at 12:50.) If you take the 12:50 bus, you can make the last bus back (around 17:30), but your time in Civita may feel a little rushed. Note that these are weekday times; buses use a different schedule on Saturdays and do not run on Sundays or holidays. See below for details.

GETTING THERE

To reach Civita from Orvieto, you'll first head for the adjacent town of Bagnoregio. From there, it's a 30-minute walk or 5-minute drive to the base of Civita's pedestrian bridge, followed by a steep 10-minute hike up to the town's main square.

By Bus to Bagnoregio: On weekdays, the blue Cotral bus runs from Orvieto to Bagnoregio about 10 times a day, including some very early departures and a long break mid-morning (45 minutes, no bus on Sun or holidays). Get the detailed schedule at the TI or at www.cotralspa.it (click "Orari," then fill in "Bagnoregio" and "Orvieto" in the trip planner—Italian only) or call +39 06 7205 7205 or +39 800 174 471 (press 7 for English).

Tickets are €2.20 one-way if bought in advance at a bar or

Accommodations
1 Romantica Pucci B&B
2 Hotel Divino Amore

Eateries & Other
3 Il Peperoncino

4 Il Ripi&Go
5 L'Arte del Pane
6 Edicola 76 (Bus Tickets)
7 Tobacco Shop
(Bus Tickets)

CIVITA DI BAGNOREGIO

400 Meters
400 Yards

CIVITA TICKET OFFICE

FOOTBRIDGE

BELVEDERE

MAZZINI

STREET PARKING

PARKING (BIGGEST)

STAIRS

DEAD-END STAIRS

tobacco shop, or €7 one-way if purchased from driver. In Orvieto's upper town, buy your ticket from Silvia at the tobacco shop at Corso Cavour 306, a block up from the funicular (daily 7:00-13:00 & 16:00-20:00)—or pay the premium ticket price on board. If you'll be returning to Orvieto by bus, buy two tickets now (they're harder to get in Bagnoregio).

Buses depart from a courtyard within the former military barracks, a short walk from the upper funicular station at the east end of Orvieto. It's tricky to find: With your back to the funicular, walk to the right, bear left (uphill) with the street, then go right under the arch marked *Caserma Piave*. Angle left through the parking lot to find the blue Cotral bus, under and behind the tall trees. (Note: Lots of buses stop in front of the funicular, but Civita is served by a different bus company, Cotral.)

Buses departing the barracks stop five minutes later at Orvieto's train station—to catch the bus there, wait to the left of the funicular station (as you're facing it); schedule and tickets are available in the tobacco shop/bar in the train station.

To locate both bus stops, see the map on page 762. For information on buses returning to Orvieto, see "Bagnoregio Connections," later.

Getting from Bagnoregio Bus Stop to Civita: By Cotral bus from Orvieto, you'll arrive in Bagnoregio near Piazzale Battaglini, at the opposite end of the old center from Civita. To get to Civita's bridge, it's a 20- to 30-minute, mostly downhill **walk** through the middle of Bagnoregio. The walk itself is enjoyable, as it offers a delightful look at a workaday Italian town. With your back to the arch, walk 200 yards towards the big parking lot and TI (Info-Point, free WCs). Pick up a helpful map and take the stairs behind

ORVIETO & CIVITA

the TI to the main drag, Via Roma. Then follow the brown signs to *Civita*.

If you'd rather not walk, you can take a **shuttle.** It runs to Civita from near the Piazzale Battaglini bus stop—look for white minibuses labeled *EPF Tours.* The shuttle is especially handy for the uphill return—it drops you right at the Orvieto-bound bus stop (usually 1-2/hour, 5 minutes, generally daily 7:30-18:15 but few buses 14:00-15:00 or on Sun off-season, €1.50 one-way, €2 round-trip, pay driver).

By Taxi or Shared Taxi to Civita: If you can share the cost with other travelers, a 30-minute taxi ride from Orvieto to Civita is a reasonable value (basic rate: €50 one-way, €85 round-trip with an hour wait). Alessio Colagè Orvieto Transfer can take groups by car or minivan (see "Tours of Orvieto," earlier in this chapter).

By Car to Bagnoregio and Civita: Driving from Orvieto to Civita takes about 30 minutes. Orvieto overlooks the autostrada (and has its own exit). From the Orvieto exit, the shortest way to Civita is to turn left (below Orvieto), and then simply follow the signs to *Lubriano* and *Bagnoregio*.

A more winding and scenic route takes a few minutes longer: From the Orvieto exit on the autostrada, go right (toward *Orvieto*), then at the first big roundabout, follow signs to *Bolsena* (passing under hill-capping Orvieto on your right). Take the first left (direction: *Bagnoregio*), winding up past great Orvieto views and the recommended Tenuta Le Velette and Custodi wineries en route to Canale, and through farms and fields of giant shredded wheat to Bagnoregio.

Whichever route you take, for a breathtaking view of Civita, just before Bagnoregio follow signs left to *Lubriano,* head into that village, turn right as you enter town, and pull into the first little square by the yellow church (on the left). You'll find an even better view farther into the town, from the tiny square at the next church (San Giovanni Battista). Then return to the Bagnoregio road.

Once in Bagnoregio, you'll drive right up the main street—which seems pedestrian-only, but isn't (follow brown *Civita* signs). As you approach Civita, you'll begin to see pay-and-display parking lots and blue-painted lines along the side of the road (all charge €2/hour). The closest you can get is the lot at the end of the tree-lined stretch of road, right in front of the belvedere (viewpoint)—but this is often full, in which case the larger lot at Piazzale Battaglini likely has space.

Civita di Bagnoregio

Note: Map not to scale; a walk across Civita takes approx. 5 minutes—but don't rush it!

To Lubriano Town

Cliffs

Cliffs

OSTERIA AL FORNO DI AGNESE

ANTICO FORNO TRATTORIA & CIVITA B&B

LOCANDA DELLA BUONA VENTURA

CAMPANILE (BELL TOWER)

ANTICO FRANTOIO OLIVE PRESS & BRUSCHETTERIA

L'ARCO DEL GUSTO

WC

Piazza

CHURCH

ALMA CIVITA

OLD LAUNDRY

ETRUSCAN COLUMNS

MAIN

STRADA

ARCH

BAR LA PIAZZETTA

BAR ENOTECA

TRATTORIA LA CANTINA DE ARIANNA

ANTICA CIVITAS MUSEUM

FOOTBRIDGE

To Bagnoregio

WINE BAR DA PEPPONE & GEOLOGICAL MUSEUM

CAVES & CHAPEL CARVED IN ROCK

PALACE (PRIVATE)

Cliffs

RUINS OF HOUSE OF ST. BONAVENTURE

Trail to Etruscan tunnel under Civita

Walking Across the Bridge to Civita: Whether arriving by foot, shuttle bus, or car, first head out to the belvedere at the very end of Bagnoregio for a superb view (through the little garden). From there, backtrack a few steps (the staircase next to the viewpoint is a dead end) and take the stairs down to the road leading to the bridge. You'll first head downhill, then pay the admission fee and hike up the narrow bridge into town.

Orientation to Civita

Civita charges a €5 **admission fee** to enter the old town (waived for overnight guests). The revenue helps with its extensive maintenance expenses. Buy your ticket from the brown kiosk, just before the bridge, on the left.

Tourist Information: The helpful InfoPoint at Piazzale Battaglini (in Bagnoregio) can answer all your questions. Ask for a map and confirm the shuttle schedule before setting off for Civita.

HELPFUL HINTS

Market Day: A lively market fills the Piazzale Battaglini parking lot each Monday.

Orvieto Bus Tickets: Because the Orvieto-Bagnoregio bus ticket is much cheaper purchased in advance than from the driver, ideally you'll buy both tickets in Orvieto. But if you wind up in Bagnoregio needing a ticket, only two places sell them—and both are closed for several hours in the afternoon. Buy one on arrival so you have it when you need it later. One option is the Edicola 76 **newsstand** across from the gas station near the Bagnoregio bus stop (look for the gray awning at #47; daily 7:30-13:00 & 17:00-20:00 except closed Sun afternoon). The other option in Bagnoregio is La Cornucopia **tobacco shop** on Via Roma (Mon-Sat 8:00-13:00 & 17:00-20:00, closed Sun afternoon, directly upstairs from the Piazzale Battaglini parking lot and TI at Larga Fidenza 6).

Civita Walk

Civita was once connected to Bagnoregio, before the saddle between the separate towns eroded away. Photographs around town show the old donkey path—the original bridge. It was bombed in World War II and replaced in 1966 with the footbridge that you're climbing today.

• *Entering the town, you'll pass through* **Porta Santa Maria,** *a 12th-century Romanesque arch. This stone passageway was cut by the Etruscans 2,500 years ago, when this town was a stop on an ancient trading route. Inside the archway, you enter a garden of stones. Stand in the little square—the town's antechamber—facing the Bar La Piazzetta. Over your right shoulder are the remains of a...*

Renaissance Palace

The wooden door and windows (above the door) lead only to thin air. They were part of the facade of one of five palaces that once graced Civita. Much of the palace fell into the valley, riding a chunk of the ever-eroding rock pinnacle. Today, the door leads to a remaining section of the palace—complete with Civita's first hot tub. It was once owned by the "Marchesa," a countess who married into Italy's biggest industrialist family.

• *A few steps uphill, farther into town (on your left, beyond the Bottega souvenir store), notice the two shed-like buildings.*

Old WC and Laundry (Vecchio Lavatoio)

In the nearer building (covered with ivy), you'll see the town's old laundry, which dates from just after World War II, when water was finally piped into the town. Until a few years ago, this was a lively village gossip center. Now, locals park their mopeds here. Just behind that is another stone shed, which houses a less-than-pristine WC.

• *The main square is just a few steps farther along, but we'll take the scenic circular route to get there, detouring around to the right. Walk past the ruined palace and belly up to the...*

Canyon Viewpoint

Lean over the banister and listen to the sounds of the birds and the bees. Survey old family farms, noticing how evenly they're spaced. Historically, each one owned just enough land to stay in business. Turn left along the belvedere and walk a few steps to the site of the long-gone home of Civita's one famous son, St. Bonaventure, known as the "second founder of the Franciscans" (look for the small plaque on the wall).

• *From here, a lane leads past delightful old homes and gardens, and then to...*

Civita's Main Square

The town church faces Civita's main piazza. Grab a stone seat and observe the scene. They say that in a big city you can see a lot, but in a small town like this you can feel a lot. The generous bench built into the long side of the square, now used as restaurant seating, reminds me of how when I first discovered Civita back in the 1970s and 1980s, the town's old folks would gather here every night. The piazza has been integral to Italian culture since ancient Roman times. While Civita is humble today, imagine the town's former wealth, when mansions of the leading families faced this square, along with the former City Hall (opposite the church). The town's history includes a devastating earthquake in 1695. Notice how stone walls were reinforced with thick bases, and how old stones and marble slabs were recycled and built into walls.

Here in the town square, you'll find **Bar Enoteca** (open daily, local wines and microbrews) and two recommended restaurants. The square hosts wild donkey races on the first Sunday of June and the second Sunday of September. At Christmastime, a living Nativity scene is enacted in this square, and if you're visiting at the end of July or beginning of August, you might catch a play here. The pillars that stand like giants' bar stools are ancient Etruscan. The church, with its campanile (bell tower), marks the spot where an Etruscan temple, and then a Roman temple, once stood. Across from Bar Enoteca, on the side of the former City Hall, is a small, square stone counter. Old-timers remember when this was a meat

ORVIETO & CIVITA

shop, and how one day a week the counter was stacked with fish for sale.

The humble **Geological Museum** tells the story of how erosion is constantly shaping the surrounding "Bad Lands" valley, how landslides have shaped (and continue to threaten) Civita, and how plans are developing to stabilize things (€3; daily April-Oct 10:00-13:30 & 14:00-17:00, shorter hours off-season; +39 328 665 7205, www.museogeologicoedellefrane.it).

• *Now step inside...*

Civita's Church

A cathedral until 1699, the church houses records of about 60 bishops that date back to the seventh century (church open daily 10:00-13:00 & 14:00-16:30, often closed Feb). Inside you'll see Romanesque columns and arches with faint Renaissance frescoes peeking through Baroque-era whitewash. The central altar is built upon the relics of the Roman martyr St. Victoria, who once was the patron saint of the town. St. Marlonbrando served as a bishop here in the ninth century; an altar dedicated to him is on the right. The fine crucifix over this altar, carved out of pear wood in the 15th century, is from the school of Donatello. It's remarkably expressive and greatly venerated by locals. Jesus' gaze is almost haunting. Some say his appearance changes based on what angle you view him from: looking alive from the front, in agony from the left, and dead from the right. Regardless, his eyes follow you from side to side. On Good Friday, this crucifix goes out and is the focus of the midnight procession.

On the left side, midway up the nave above an altar, is an intimate fresco known as *Madonna of the Earthquake,* given this name because—in the great shake of 1695—the whitewash fell off and revealed this tender fresco of Mary and her child. (During the Baroque era, a white-and-bright interior was in vogue, and churches such as these—which were covered with precious and historic frescoes—were simply whitewashed over. Look around to see examples.) On the same wall—just toward the front from the *Madonna*—find the faded portrait of Santa Apollonia, the patron saint of your teeth; notice the scary-looking pincers.

• *From the square, you can follow...*

The Main Street

A short walk takes you from the church to the end of the town. Along the way, you'll pass a couple little eateries (described later, under "Eating in Civita"), olive presses, gardens, a rustic town museum, and valley views. The rock below Civita is honeycombed with ancient tunnels, caverns (housing olive presses), cellars (for keeping wine at a constant temperature all year), and cisterns (for collecting rainwater, since there was no well in town). Many date from Etruscan times.

Wherever you choose to eat (or just grab a bruschetta snack), be sure to take advantage of the opportunity to poke around— every place has a historic cellar. At the trendy **Alma Civita,** no- tice the damaged house facing the main street—broken since the 1695 earthquake and scarred to this day. Just beyond, the rustic **Antico Frantoio Bruschetteria** serves bruschetta in an amazing old space. Whether or not you buy food, venture into their back

room to see an interest- ing collection of old olive presses (if you're not eat- ing here, a €1 donation is requested). The huge olive press in the entry is about 1,500 years old. Until the 1960s, blindfolded don- keys trudged in the circle here, crushing olives and creating paste that filled the circular filters and was put into a second press. Notice the 2,500-year-old sarcophagus niche. The hole in the floor (with the metal grate) was a garbage hole. In ancient times, residents would toss their jewels down when under attack; excavations uncovered a windfall of treasures.

In front is the wellhead of an ancient cistern—designed to col- lect rainwater from neighboring rooftops—carved out of *tufo* and covered with clay to be waterproof.

• *Across the street and down a tiny lane, find...*

Antica Civitas

This is the closest thing the town has to a history museum. The humble collection is the brainchild of Felice, an old farmer who hung black-and-white photos, farm tools, olive presses, and local artifacts in a series of old caves. Climb down to the "warm blood machine" (another donkey-powered grinding wheel) and a view- point. You'll see rooms where a mill worker lived until the 1930s. Felice wants to give visitors a feeling for life in Civita when its tra- ditional economy was strong (€1, generally open 10:00-17:00, some English explanations, +39 320 110 4279).

• *Another few steps along the main street take you to...*

The End of Civita

Here the road is literally cut out of the stone, with a dramatic view of the Bad Lands opening up. To savor the scene, consider pop- ping into the cute **"Garden of Poets"** (immediately on the left just

ORVIETO & CIVITA

outside town; they'll ask for a donation as you exit, or you can purchase something at the Ambrosi family's little shop). Then, look back up at the end of town and ponder the precarious future of Civita. There's a certain stillness here, far from the modern world and high above the valley.

Continue along the path a few steps toward the valley below the town, and you come to some shallow caves used as stables until a few years ago. The third cave, cut deeper into the rock with stairs leading to a barred door, is the **Chapel of the Incarcerated** (Cappella del Carcere). In Etruscan times, the chapel—with a painted tile depicting the Madonna and child—may have been a tomb, and in medieval times, it was used as a jail (which collapsed in 1695).

Although it's closed to the public now, an Etruscan tunnel just beyond the Chapel of the Incarcerated cuts completely through the hill. Tall enough for a woman with a jug on her head to pass through, it may have served as a shortcut to the river below. It was widened in the 1930s so that farmers could get between their scattered fields more easily. Later, it served as a refuge for frightened villagers who huddled here during WWII bombing raids.

• *Hike back into town, taking some time to explore the peaceful back lanes before returning to the modern world.*

Sleeping in Civita or Bagnoregio

Civita has nine B&B rooms up for grabs. Bagnoregio has larger lodgings, and there are plenty of *agriturismi* nearby; otherwise, there's always Orvieto. Off-season, when Civita and Bagnoregio are deadly quiet—and cold—I'd side-trip in from Orvieto rather than spend the night here.

IN CIVITA

$$ Alma Civita is a classic old stone house that has been renovated by a sister-and-brother team, Alessandra and Maurizio (hence the name: Al-Ma). These are Civita's two most comfortable, modern, and warmly run rooms and they also have a recommended restaurant (+39 0761 792 415, mobile +39 347 449 8892, www.almacivita. com, prenotazione@almacivita.com).

$$ Locanda della Buona Ventura rents four overpriced rooms, up narrow stairs, decorated in medieval rustic-chic, and overlooking Civita's piazza. You're not likely to see the owner—the Dallaiti shop across the square functions as the reception (tiny bathrooms, skimpy breakfast, +39 0761 792 025, mobile +39 347 627 5628, info@locandabuonaventura.com).

$ Civita B&B, run by gregarious Franco Sala, has three little rooms above Trattoria Antico Forno, each overlooking Civita's main square. Two are doubles with private bath. The third is a triple (with one double and one kid-size bed), which has its own bathroom across the hall (RS%, family rooms, continental breakfast, Piazza del Duomo Vecchio, +39 076 176 0016, mobile +39 347 611 5426, www.civitadibagnoregio.it, fsala@pelagus.it). Franco also rents a few apartments in Civita, Bagnoregio, and nearby.

IN BAGNOREGIO

$ Romantica Pucci B&B is a haven for city-weary travelers. Its five spacious rooms are indeed romantic, with canopied beds and flowing veils (air-con, free parking, along the main drag at Piazza Cavour 1, +39 0761 792 121, www.hotelromanticapucci.it, info@hotelromanticapucci.it).

$ Hotel Divino Amore has 21 bright, modern rooms, four with perfect views of a miniature Civita. These view rooms, and the 13 with air-conditioning, don't cost extra—but they book up first (closed Jan-March, a block below the main drag at Via Fidanza 25-27, +39 076 178 0882, mobile +39 329 344 8950, www.hoteldivinoamore.com, info@hoteldivinoamore.com, Silvia).

Eating in Civita or Bagnoregio

IN CIVITA

Opening hours are highly unpredictable in this little town—when it's quiet, places can close unexpectedly. Take the hours listed here as rough estimates.

$$ Osteria Al Forno di Agnese is a delightful spot where Manuela and her friends serve visitors simple yet delicious meals and a good selection of local wines on a covered patio hidden just off Civita's main square or in a little dining room in gloomy weather (daily at 11:30 for lunch, peak season also at 19:00 for dinner, +39 0761 792 571, mobile +39 340 1259 721).

$$ Trattoria Antico Forno serves up rustic dishes, homemade pasta, and salads at affordable prices. Try their homemade pasta with truffles (daily 12:30-15:30 & 19:00-22:00—but not always open for dinner, on main square, also rents rooms—see Civita B&B listing earlier, +39 076 176 0016, Franco, daughter Elisabetta, and assistants Nina and Daniela).

$$ Trattoria La Cantina de Arianna is a family affair, with a busy open fire specializing in grilled meat and wonderful bruschetta. It's run by Arianna, her sister, Antonella, and their parents, Rossana and Antonio. After eating, wander down to their cellar, where you'll see traditional winemaking gear and provisions for rolling huge kegs up the stairs. Tap on the kegs in the bottom level to see which are full (daily 12:00-16:30, also dinner from 19:30 on summer evenings and Sat year-round, +39 0761 793 270).

$$ Alma Civita feels like a fresh, new take on old Civita, owned by a sister-and-brother team of longtime residents: Alessandra (an architect) and Maurizio (who runs the restaurant). Choose from one of three seating areas: outside on a stony lane, in the modern and trendy-feeling main-floor dining room, or in the equally modern but atmospheric cellar. Even deeper is an old Etruscan tomb that's now a wine cellar (April-Oct lunch Wed-Mon 12:00-15:15, dinner Fri-Sat only 19:00-21:30, closed Tue; Nov-March Thu-Sun only for lunch plus Sat for dinner; they also rent recommended rooms, +39 0761 792 415).

$ **Antico Frantoio Bruschetteria,** the last place in town, is a rustic, super-atmospheric spot for a bite to eat. The specialty here: delicious bruschetta toasted over hot coals. Peruse the menu, choose your toppings (chopped tomato is super), and get a glass of wine for a fun, affordable snack or meal (roughly 10:00-18:00, mobile +39 371 353 3753, Fabrizio).

Sandwich Shop: If you just want a quick bite, $ **L'Arco del Gusto** can make you a sandwich using local products (daily 10:30-16:30, tucked in an archway near the start of town).

IN BAGNOREGIO

The recommended $$ **Romantica Pucci B&B** offers a small restaurant with tables in its private garden and a cozy interior (closed Mon, see contact details earlier). For good gelato, on your walk to Civita you'll go right past a branch of Orvieto's **Pasqualetti,** on the main drag at Mazzini 32.

Near the Bagnoregio Bus Stop: Several basic eateries are along Via Giacomo Matteotti just below the bus stop in Bagnoregio, including $ **Il Peperoncino,** selling pizza by the slice (closed Wed, #49); $$ **Il Ripi&Go,** a sit-down eatery serving traditional food (closed Wed, #35); and—a half-block past Il Ripi&Go—fresh pastries at $ **L'Arte del Pane** (#5).

Bagnoregio Connections

From Bagnoregio to Orvieto: Cotral buses connect Bagnoregio to Orvieto (about 10/day Mon-Sat only—no buses Sun or holidays, 45 minutes, €2.20 one-way if purchased in advance, €7 one-way from driver). Information: +39 06 7205 7205 or +39 800 174 471 (press 7 for English), www.cotralspa.it (Italian only). For info on coming from Orvieto, see "Getting There" on page 792.

From Bagnoregio to Points South: Cotral buses also run to **Viterbo,** which has good train connections to Rome (about 10/day Mon-Fri, fewer Sat, no buses Sun, 35 minutes).

ROME

Rome is magnificent and overwhelming at the same time. It's a showcase of Western civilization, with astonishingly ancient sights and a modern vibrancy. Rome is Italy's political capital, the spiritual capital of a billion Roman Catholics, and an open-air museum of the evocative remains of the capital of what was the greatest empire in the history of humanity.

As you peel through Rome's fascinating and jumbled layers, you'll find the marble ruins of ancient times, tangled streets of the medieval world, early Christian churches, grand Renaissance buildings and statues, Baroque fountains and church facades, 19th-century apartments, 21st-century traffic, and nearly three million people. And then, of course, there are Rome's stupendous sights.

Visit St. Peter's, the greatest church on earth, and scale Michelangelo's 448-foot-tall dome. Learn something about eternity at the huge Vatican Museums, where the story of creation is as bright as when Michelangelo first painted it in the restored Sistine Chapel. Ramble among the rabble and rubble, doing what I call the Caesar Shuffle through ancient Rome's Colosseum and Forum, mentally resurrecting those tumble-down stones. Peer into the eyes of Roman busts at the National Museum of Rome, and savor Bernini's lifelike sculptures at the sumptuous Borghese Gallery. Wander through the surrounding Villa Borghese Gardens, Rome's biggest public park.

When the museums close and the crowds thin, Rome relaxes. The city, so monumental by day, becomes intimate and approachable. Its neighborhoods feel more like villages, and its famous squares become places to simply hang out. Early in the evening, join the promenade—called the *passeggiata*—up and down the main streets. After a sociable stroll, take a break for an aperitivo—a before-dinner drink.

Rome can be romantic...but hard on the unprepared. If you're careless, you could get pickpocketed. And if you have the wrong attitude, you'll be frustrated by the kind of chaos that only an Italian can understand. On a previous visit, my cabbie struggled with the traffic and said, *"Roma chaos."* I responded, *"Bella chaos."* He agreed.

Make it easy on yourself. If you choose a comfortable hotel for a refuge, pace yourself, enjoy a siesta during midday heat, organize your sightseeing (reserving ahead as needed), and take sensible precautions to protect your valuables, you'll love Rome. Soon you'll be the one at the Trevi Fountain throwing in a coin to ensure your return.

PLANNING YOUR TIME

Rome is wonderful, but it's huge and exhausting. On a first-time visit, many travelers find that Rome is best done quickly—Italy is more charming elsewhere. But whether you're here for a day or a week, you won't be able to see everything, so don't try—you'll keep coming back to Rome. Note major sights where advance reservations are smart or a free Rick Steves audio tour is available.

Rome in a Day: Some people actually "do" Rome in a day. Crazy as that sounds, if all you have is a day, it's one of the most exciting days Europe has to offer. Start at 9:00 at the Colosseum. Then explore the Forum (skip the Palatine Hill), hike over Capitoline Hill, and cap your Caesar Shuffle with a Pantheon visit. After a quick lunch, taxi to the Vatican Museums, then head to St. Peter's Basilica (open until 19:00 April-Sept). Taxi to Campo de' Fiori for dinner, then finish your day lacing together the famous floodlit spots (following my Heart of Rome Walk).

Rome in Two to Three Days: On the first day, do my Caesar Shuffle from the Colosseum to the Roman Forum, then over Capitoline Hill (visiting the Capitoline Museums), and on to the Pantheon. After a siesta, add some sightseeing to suit your interest. In the evening enjoy a sound-and-light show at the Imperial Forums and/or a colorful stroll in Trastevere or the Monti district. On the second day, see Vatican City (St. Peter's, dome climb, Vatican Museums). Have dinner near the atmospheric Campo de' Fiori, and then walk to the Trevi Fountain and Spanish Steps (following my Heart of Rome Walk). With a third day, add the Borghese Gallery and more sights.

ROME

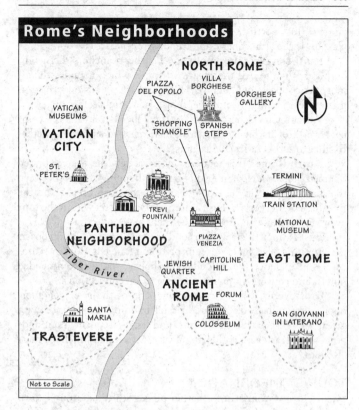

Rome's Neighborhoods

NORTH ROME

PIAZZA DEL POPOLO

VILLA BORGHESE

BORGHESE GALLERY

VATICAN MUSEUMS

VATICAN CITY

"SHOPPING TRIANGLE"

SPANISH STEPS

ST. PETER'S

TERMINI

TRAIN STATION

TREVI FOUNTAIN

NATIONAL MUSEUM

PANTHEON NEIGHBORHOOD

PIAZZA VENEZIA

Tiber River

JEWISH QUARTER

CAPITOLINE HILL

EAST ROME

ANCIENT ROME

FORUM

SANTA MARIA

SAN GIOVANNI IN LATERANO

COLOSSEUM

TRASTEVERE

Not to Scale

Orientation to Rome

Today's Rome sprawls over about 500 square miles, but the city center within the ancient Aurelian Wall is all you need to know—and that's only four square miles. The old core, with most of the tourist sights, sits inside a diamond formed by Termini train station (in the east), the Vatican (west), Villa Borghese Gardens (north), and the Colosseum (south). The Tiber River snakes through the diamond from north to south. At the center of the diamond is Piazza Venezia, a busy square and traffic hub.

ROME BY NEIGHBORHOOD

Think of Rome as a collection of neighborhoods, huddling around major landmarks, and it becomes manageable.

Ancient Rome: In ancient times, this was home to the grandest buildings of a city of a million people. Today, the best of the classical sights stand in a line from the Colosseum (huge stadium) to the ruined Roman Forum (main square and marketplace) over Capitoline Hill to the Pantheon (Roman temple turned into a

ROME

church). Just north of this area, between Via Nazionale and Via Cavour, is the atmospheric and trendy Monti district.

Pantheon Neighborhood: The Pantheon anchors the neighborhood I like to call the Heart of Rome, which includes the atmospheric squares of Campo de' Fiori and Piazza Navona, the dramatic Trevi Fountain, and several historic churches.

Vatican City: Located west of the Tiber River, this is a compact world of its own, with two great, massive sights: St. Peter's Basilica and the Vatican Museums.

North Rome: This modern, classy area hosts the celebrated Spanish Steps, an elegant grid of trendy shopping streets (between the main drag—Via del Corso—and the Spanish Steps), and the Borghese Gallery (gorgeous Bernini sculptures) set within the fun-on-a-sunny-day Villa Borghese Gardens.

East Rome: This neighborhood around Termini Station boasts the stunning National Museum of Rome (ancient Roman sculpture) and includes Piazza della Repubblica, many recommended hotels, and convenient public-transportation connections.

Trastevere: This colorful, wrong-side-of-the-river neighborhood has a village feel. Its red pastel buildings are draped with green ivy, Vespas rule the streets, and locals frequent mom-and-pop cafés. Trastevere is the city at its crustiest...and perhaps most "Roman."

TOURIST INFORMATION

Small city-run tourist information offices scattered around town sell sightseeing passes and maps (typically open daily 9:00-19:00, shorter hours off-season possible). You'll find them at both **airports** (Fiumicino Terminal 3 and Ciampino); **Termini train station** (at the far end of the concourse that runs along track 24—either loop around outside or cut through the department store); directly across from the **Forum** entrance on Via dei Fori Imperiali; between the Pantheon and Trevi Fountain on **Via Minghetti;** and near **Castel Sant'Angelo** (toward the Vatican from the castle).

Rome also has several smaller quasi-TIs, combined with public pay WCs, called (and I am not making this up) **P.Stops.** You'll find them on Piazza di Spagna near the Spanish Steps, in Trastevere at Piazza Sidney Sonnino, and across from the Basilica of San Giovanni Laterano near the Holy Stairs (generally daily 10:00-18:00, some until 20:00, https://pstop.it).

The TI's website is www.turismoroma.it, but a better site for practical information is www.060608.it. That's also the number for Rome's **call center**—the best source of up-to-date tourist information, with English speakers on staff (answered daily 9:00-19:00, +39 06 0608, press 2 for English).

Your hotel will have a freebie map; you'll find better-quality ones at bookstores than at newsstands. See "Getting Around Rome," later, for recommended public transport maps.

An English-language **website**, www.wantedinrome.com, is oriented to those staying longer in Rome and provides insight into news, events, and daily life in the city.

ARRIVAL IN ROME

For a rundown of Rome's train stations and airports, see the "Rome Connections" section at the end of this chapter.

HELPFUL HINTS

Sightseeing Tips: Despite the huge crowds inundating Rome, you'll only find lines a problem at **St. Peter's Basilica** (go early or late to minimize) and **Vatican Museums** (easy to avoid by booking in advance online). Tickets for the **Colosseum,** the **Roman Forum,** and **Palatine Hill** must be reserved in advance (no on-site sales), and for the Colosseum, you must book a specific entrance time. The exquisite **Borghese Gallery** also requires a timed-entry ticket purchased in advance. The **Pantheon** often has a long line that moves fast, but on weekends you'll likely need to book ahead to enter. For any sight, be sure that you're booking on the official website (listed in this book), rather than a third-party scalper site.

Even with a reservation, the above sights can be very crowded. If that's not for you, remember that Rome has many other historical treasures, such as the **Capitoline Museums** and the **Baths of Caracalla,** with fewer to no crowds.

The **Roma Pass,** which you'll see advertised, is only worthwhile if you want a public transit pass (covers 2 or 3 days of transit, entry to 1 or 2 sights, and discounts at others—but you'll still need reservations for the Colosseum and Borghese Gallery).

Closed Days: If you're in Rome on a Sunday, note that the **Vatican Museums** are closed (except for last Sun of the month, when it's free and even more crowded). The **Borghese Gallery** is closed on Mondays, and **St. Peter's Basilica** may be closed on Wednesday mornings for a papal audience.

Decorum: Rome enforces strict laws to protect its historical treasures. Be respectful. Don't climb on ruins, picnic at (or on) ancient or historic sights, or dip your hand in the Trevi Fountain—fines can be expensive.

Bookstores: Borri Books, a large chain store at Termini station, sells English-language books (open daily). A few small, independent bookstores have a more personal touch: The **Anglo-American Bookshop** has great art and history sections (closed Sun, a few blocks south of Spanish Steps at Via della

ROME

Rome

To MAXXI & Parco della Musica

To Foro Italico & Autostrada

PONTE MATTEOTTI

VIA FLAMINIA

VIALE DELLE MILIZIE

Flaminio M

VIA GIULIO CESARE

Lepanto M

S. MARIA DEL POPOLO

Piazza del Popolo

Piazzale degli Eroi

VIA ANDREA DORIA

VIA CANDIA

Ottaviano M

VIA COLA DI RIENZO

VIA M. A. COLONNA

PONTE REG. MARG.

Cipro M

V. VATICANO

Piazza del Risorgimento

MAUSOLEUM OF AUGUSTUS

VIA CRESCENZIO

Piazza Cavour

ARA PACIS

VATICAN MUSEUMS

VIA BORGO PIO

CASTEL SANT' ANGELO

PALACE OF JUSTICE

PONTE CAVOUR

VATICAN CITY

VIA CONCILIAZIONE

Piazza Borg.

PONTE UMBERTO I

SISTINE CHAPEL

ST. PETER'S

St. Peter's Square

Piazza Pio XII

VIA

PONTE S. ANGELO

VIA CORONARI

To Civitavecchia

VIA PORTA CAVALLEGGERI

PONTE VITTORIO EMANUELE

PONTE AMEDEO

V. GIULIA

VIA VITTORIO

CORSO VITTORIO

PANTHEON

Piazza Navona

TUNNEL

EMANUELE

SAN PIETRO STATION

To Termini Station via Trastevere and Ostiense Stations

VIA MURA AURELIE

PONTE MAZZINI

V. MONSERRATO

LUNGOTEVERE

Campo de' Fiori

Largo Argentina

ANITA GARIBALDI STATUE

VILLA FARNESINA

PALAZZO FARNESE

Parco Gianicolense

Tiber River

GHETTO

PONTE SISTO

VIA AURELIA ANTICA

Piazzale Garibaldi

GIUSEPPE GARIBALDI STATUE

SAN PIETRO IN MONTORIO (TEMPIETTO)

Piazza Trilussa

PONTE GARIBALDI

Isola Tiburina

VIA LUNGA

Piazza Belli

PONTE CESTIO

ACQUA PAOLA FOUNTAIN

SANTA MARIA IN TRASTEVERE

TRASTEVERE

SAN PANCRAZIO GATE

ITALIAN INDEPENDENCE WAR MEMORIAL

Villa Doria Pamphilj

PORTA PORTESE

PONTE SUBLICIO

OLD CITY WALLS

VIA DI TRASTEVERE

PORTA PORTESE MARKET

VIA PORTUENSE

LUNG. TESTACCIO

VIA BRANCA

Piazza Testaccio

VIALE DI TRASTEVERE

LONG. PORTUENSE

VIA

TESTACCIO MARKET

TESTAC

To Trastevere Train Station

Monte Testaccio

ROME

ROME

Vite 102—see map on page 826, +39 06 679 5222). In Trastevere, the **Almost Corner Bookshop** stocks an extensive Ital-
ian-interest section (Via del Moro 45—see map on page 919,
+39 06 583 6942, Dermot from Ireland), and the **Open Door
Bookshop** carries the only used books in English in town (Via
della Lungaretta 23—see map on page 919, +39 06 589 6478).

Laundry: Coin launderettes are common in Rome. Your hotelier
can direct you to the closest one (or search on Google Maps
for "laundry").

Best Views: You have good choices: from the rooftop of the Victor
Emmanuel Monument (take the Rome from the Sky elevator
to the top); from the top of the dome of St. Peter's Basilica; and
from the top of Castel Sant'Angelo. One of the best views of
the Roman Forum is from the Farnese Gardens viewpoint on
Palatine Hill. Another is on Capitoline Hill—from two free
overlooks plus the Tabularium (underground galleries) that is
part of the Capitoline Museums.

Best Hangouts: The city's most atmospheric squares are Campo
de' Fiori and Piazza Navona, interesting day and night. For
monuments, it's the Trevi Fountain. The Monti neighborhood, near the Roman Forum, is a popular gathering spot in
the evening (particularly Piazza della Madonna dei Monti)
and a delight to explore any time of day. And the Via dei Fori
Imperiali—from the Victor Emmanuel Monument to the
Colosseum—is an enticing place to stroll and daydream about
ancient Rome.

DEALING WITH (AND AVOIDING) PROBLEMS

Theft Alert: While violent crime is rare in the city center, petty
theft is rampant. Always use your money belt. If you carry a
backpack, never leave it unattended and try to keep it attached
to your body in some way (even when you're seated for a meal).

Be particularly on guard in crowds and wear your day
pack in front, especially when boarding and leaving buses
and subways. You'll find less crowding and commotion—and
less risk—waiting for the end cars of a subway rather than the
middle cars. Thieves are particularly thick on the Metro and
the crowded, made-for-tourists buses #40 and #64.

Thieves strike when you're distracted. Don't trust "kind"
strangers or be deceived by appearance: Sneaky thieves may
pose as businessmen or tourists, moms with babies, or gangs of
children. If a random stranger says, "I like your shoes!"...they
likely are about to hit you up for some scam.

Scams abound: Always be clear about what paper money
you're giving someone, demand clear and itemized bills, and
count your change. Don't give your wallet to self-proclaimed

"police" who stop you on the street, warn you about counterfeit (or drug) money, and ask to see your cash.

Reporting Losses: To report lost or stolen items, file a police report (at Termini station, with *polizia* at track 11 or with carabinieri at track 20; offices are also at Piazza Venezia and at the corner of Via Nazionale and Via Genova). For information on how to replace a passport or report lost or stolen credit cards, see page 1142.

Pedestrian Safety: Your main safety concern in Rome is crossing streets. Use caution. Some streets have pedestrian-crossing signals (red means stop—or jaywalk carefully; green means go...also carefully; and yellow means go...extremely carefully, as cars may be whipping around the corner). But just as often, multilane streets have crosswalks with no signals at all. And even when there are traffic lights, they are provisional: Scooters don't always stop at red lights, and even cars exercise what drivers call the "logical option" of not stopping if they see no oncoming traffic.

Follow locals like a shadow when you cross a street (or spend a good part of your visit stranded on curbs). When you do cross alone, find a gap in the traffic and walk with confidence while making eye contact with approaching drivers—they won't hit you as long as they can tell where you intend to go.

Staying/Getting Healthy: The siesta is a key to survival in summertime Rome. Lie down and contemplate the extraordinary power of gravity in the Eternal City. I drink lots of cold, refreshing water from Rome's many drinking fountains (the Forum has three) which are handy for refilling your bottle and staying hydrated.

Every neighborhood has a **pharmacy** (marked by a green cross); your hotel can help you find the nearest one (or search for "pharmacy" on Google Maps). Bigger pharmacies that stay open late (generally from 7:30 until 22:00 or 23:00) cluster around Termini station: There's one inside the station itself (along northeast side, enter from Via Marsala, +39 06 474 5421); another south of the station, at the corner of Via Cavour (shorter hours, Piazza dei Cinquecento 51, +39 06 488 0019, see map on page 896); and Farmacia Piram, several blocks down from Piazza della Repubblica (Via Nazionale 228, +39 06 488 4437). In the Pantheon neighborhood, Farmacia Senato is between Piazza Navona and the Pantheon (Corso del Rinascimento 50—see map on page 928).

Embassies and hotels can recommend English-speaking **doctors.** Consider MEDline, a 24-hour private home-medical service; doctors speak English and make calls at hotels for

Rome Sightseeing Tips

Rome is doing its best to cope with an ever-increasing number of visitors, but especially in peak season you'll encounter lines, crowds, and exasperating changes to ticketing and tour procedures. These tips will help you use your time and money efficiently, making the Eternal City seem less eternal and more entertaining.

Skip the Colosseum: While it sounds like a sacrilege, a visit to the interior of the Colosseum may not be worth suffering through the mob scene. Half the thrill of the Colosseum is seeing it from outside (free and easy at any time).

Advance Tickets and Reservations: Some sights require advance booking, while at others it's necessary to avoid long lines. For specifics, see page 807 and sight listings.

Forum/Palatine Hill: These two sights share an admission ticket.

Unless you buy a Full Experience ticket (see page 840), you must see them together on a single visit (don't exit the Forum and try to reenter at Palatine Hill).

Roma Pass: I'd skip this pass; it's little more than a glorified transit pass that includes entrance to one or two sights and discounts to others.

Sights with Fewer Crowds: Can't get reservations to the main sights (or just can't stand crowds)? Rome has many magnificent attractions without the hordes. Try the Baths of Caracalla, National Museum of Rome, or Trajan's Market. Even in peak season, you'll often be all alone with the wonders of the ancient world,

about €150 (+39 06 808 0995, https://users.libero.it/medline). Another 24-hour private clinic that makes house calls is International Medical Center '84, Via Firenze 47, +39 06 488 2371, https://imc84.com. Anyone is entitled to emergency treatment at public hospitals. The hospital closest to Termini station is Policlinico Umberto I (entrance for emergency treatment at Viale del Policlinico 155, translators available, Metro: Policlinico).

GETTING AROUND ROME

You can see a lot of Rome on foot, and I've grouped your sightseeing into walkable neighborhoods. Make it a point to visit sights in a logical order.

To connect sights beyond walking distance, you can ride the Metro or a city bus, or take a taxi. As Rome is a great taxi town

ROME

wondering, "Where is everyone?"

Check Sight Hours: Rome's sights have notoriously variable hours from season to season. It's smart to check each sight's website in advance. On holidays, expect shorter hours or closures.

Churches: Many churches, which have divine art and free entry, open early (around 7:00-7:30), close for lunch (roughly 12:00-15:30), and close late (about 19:00). Kamikaze tourists maximize their sightseeing hours by visiting churches before 9:00 or late in the day; during the siesta, they see major sights that stay open all day (St. Peter's, Colosseum, Forum, Capitoline Museums, Pantheon, and National Museum of Rome). Dress modestly for churches.

Picnic Discreetly: Public drinking and eating are not allowed at major sights. To avoid a fine, choose an empty piazza or a park for your picnic.

Morning Magic: When I want to reconnect with the city, I walk through the historical center before Rome wakes up. In the early morning, I've never met more than six people at the Trevi Fountain, and Rome shows its calm, majestic face. It's a great way to get energized for the day ahead.

Miscellaneous Tips: I carry a water bottle and refill it at Rome's many public drinking spouts. Because public restrooms are scarce, use WCs at museums, restaurants, and bars.

(most rides cost €8-12), especially for couples and families, I'd rely more on taxis than public transit.

To find the city's many small streets and alleys, map apps work better than paper maps; Google Maps is excellent for navigation by foot, and has up-to-date public transit info (see below).

Public Transportation

Rome's public transportation system is cheap and efficient, but also confusing and crowded. The three Metro lines are relatively sane and straightforward, but serve a limited area. Buses are more chaotic—there are no posted timetables or maps, and stop names are announced only in the newest vehicles. But they run frequently and go everywhere. If you're in town for more than a day or two, mastering a couple key bus routes serving your neighborhood is worth the effort and will make you feel like a Roman.

Maps and Route Planning: The website www.atac.roma.it has a journey planner in English that will help you sort through the thicket of routes, as well as downloadable network maps. Google Maps works well for transit route planning around Rome; if you're online, it offers updated, fairly accurate estimates of wait times for the next bus, and how long it'll take to get to your destination in current traffic.

There's no official paper map of the system, but Edizioni Lozzi produces a frequently updated "Roma Metro Bus" map (at bookstores), which includes a booklet with details on all bus routes. For information by phone, call ATAC at +39 06 57003.

Buying Tickets

All public transportation uses the same ticket. It costs €1.50 and is valid for one Metro ride—including transfers underground—plus unlimited city buses and trams during a 100-minute period. Passes good on buses and the Metro are sold in increments of 24 hours (€7), 48 hours (€12.50), 72 hours (€18), and one week (€24—about the cost of three taxi rides).

You can purchase tickets and passes from machines at Metro stations and a few major bus stops, and from some newsstands and tobacco shops (*tabacchi*, marked by a black-and-white *T* sign). Tickets are not sold on board. It's smart to stock up on tickets early—that way you don't have to run around searching for an open tobacco shop when you spot your bus approaching.

Validate your ticket by sticking it in the Metro turnstile (magnetic strip-side up, arrow-side first) or in the machine when you board the bus (magnetic-strip-side down, arrow-side first)—watch others and imitate. It'll return your ticket with your expiration time printed. To get through a Metro turnstile with a transit pass, tap the card against the turnstile's sensor. On buses and trams, you need to validate your pass only on your first time using it.

If you need help from a real person, ATAC runs a small ticket office at Termini station. Follow signs for *Metro Linea B*, then *ATAC ticket office* (daily until 20:00).

By Metro

The Roman subway system (Metropolitana, or "Metro") is simple, clean, cheap, and fast. The two lines you need to know—A and B—intersect at Termini station. **Line A** serves the Vatican area, Piazza del Popolo, Spanish Steps/Villa Borghese, Baths of

Diocletian, Termini station, and San Giovanni in Laterano. **Line B** connects the Tiburtina train and bus stations with Termini and the Colosseum and Forum/Palatine Hill, and Testaccio trains run less frequently, so allow a bit more time to complete your journey. The Metro runs from 5:30 to 23:30 (Fri-Sat until 1:30 in the morning; note line A may close around 21:00 while it undergoes repairs).

Within Metro stations, signage is limited and not very intuitive, and electronic signs are often broken. So, before descending, be clear on which line you'll take and which direction you're headed (i.e., the end station of your line). The subway's first and last compartments are generally the least crowded, and the least likely to harbor pickpockets.

By Bus

The Metro is handy, but it won't get you everywhere—you often have to take the bus (or tram). Bus routes are listed at each stop.

Route and system maps aren't posted, but with some knowledge of major stops, you can wing it without one (for help, see "Maps and Route Planning," earlier). Rome's few tram lines function for all intents and purposes identically to buses.

Buses—especially the touristy #40 and #64—are havens for thieves and pickpockets. These two lines can be nose-to-armpit crowded during peak times...and while you're sniffing that guy's pit, his other hand could be busily rifling through your pockets. Assume any commotion is a thief-created distraction. If one bus is packed, there's likely a second one on its tail with far fewer crowds and thieves. Or read the signs posted at stops to see if a different, less crowded bus route can get you to or near your destination.

On buses, tickets must be inserted in the yellow box with the digital readout (magnetic-strip-side down, arrow-side first; be sure to retrieve your ticket after it's spit out). Do this as you board, otherwise you're cheating. Inspectors fine even innocent-looking tourists €55. You don't need to validate a ticket or pass on the bus if you've already validated it elsewhere in the transit system. Bus

Rome's Public Transportation

To MAXXI
To Foro Italico
Flaminio
Lepanto
Piazza del Popolo
Tiber River
Ottaviano
Line A
Valle Aurelia
Cipro
VATICAN MUSEUMS
To Battistini
VATICAN
ST. PETER'S
#64
To Civitavecchia
San Pietro Station
Piazza del Risorgimento
CASTEL SANT'ANGELO
MAUSOLEUM OF AUGUSTUS
ARA PACIS
PANTHEON
Piazza Navona
Largo Argentina
Campo de' Fiori
GHETTO
TRASTEVERE
Piazzale Garibaldi
TEMPIETTO
S. MARIA IN TRASTEVERE
Piazza Mastai
Piazza Belli
PORTA PORTESE
Piramide
TESTACCIO
Porta San Paolo Stn.
Gianicolense-Ravizza Station
Trastevere Station
To Fiumicino (da Vinci) Airport from Termini via express train
Tiber River
Garbatella
MONTEMARTINI MUSEUM
ST. PAUL'S OUTSIDE THE WALLS
Basilica San Paolo
Marconi
To Ostia Antica

Not to Scale

Tiny arrows (↗) indicate one-way routes. Not all shown.

Legend:
━M━ Metro Line A
━M━ Metro Line B
━M━ Metro Line C
--#64-- Bus Route
┿#8 Tram
─── Rail
Ⓑ 118 Bus Hubs, End Points

ROME

ROME

etiquette (not always followed) is to board at the front or rear doors and exit at the middle.

Regular bus lines start running at about 5:30, and during the day major routes run every 10-15 minutes. After 23:30 (and sometimes earlier) and on Sundays, buses are less frequent. Night buses are marked with an *N* and an owl symbol on the bus-stop signs. Frustratingly, the exact frequency of various bus routes is difficult to predict (and not printed at bus stops). At major stops, an electronic board shows the number of minutes until the next buses arrive; otherwise, use your phone to check Google Maps or the ATAC journey planner.

These are the most important bus routes for tourists:

Bus #64: This bus cuts across the city, linking Termini station with the Vatican, stopping at Piazza della Repubblica (sights), Via Nazionale (recommended hotels), Piazza Venezia (near Forum), Largo Argentina (near Pantheon and Campo de' Fiori), St. Peter's Basilica (get off just past the tunnel), and San Pietro station. Ride it for a city overview and to watch pickpockets in action. The #64 can get horribly crowded.

Bus #40: This express bus, which mostly follows the #64 route (but ends near the Castel Sant'Angelo on the Vatican side of the river), is especially helpful—fewer stops and (somewhat) fewer crowds.

The following routes conveniently connect Trastevere with other parts of Rome:

Bus #H: This express bus, linking Termini station and Trastevere, makes a stop near Piazza Repubblica and at the bottom of Via Nazionale (for Trastevere, get off at Sonnino/S. Gallicano, just after crossing the Tiber River). It doesn't run on Sundays.

Tram #8: This tram connects Piazza Venezia and Largo Argentina with Trastevere (get off at Piazza Belli, just over the river) and runs further to the Trastevere train station.

Bus #23: This bus links the Vatican with Trastevere and Testaccio, stopping at the Vatican Museums (nearest stop is on Via Leone IV), Castel Sant'Angelo (Sforza Pallavicini), Trastevere (Lungotevere de Cenci/Arenula, on opposite side of Ponte Garibaldi), Porta Portese (Sunday flea market at Emporio stop), Piramide (Ostiense stop; Metro and gateway to Testaccio), and all the way south to St. Paul's Outside the Walls. **Bus #280** follows much the same route from Trastevere to Piramide.

Other useful routes include:

Bus #49: Piazza Cavour/Castel Sant'Angelo, Piazza Risorgimento (Vatican), and Vatican Museums.

Bus #81: San Giovanni in Laterano, Largo Argentina, and Piazza Risorgimento (Vatican).

Buses #85 and #87: Piazza Navona (#87 only), Pantheon, Via del Corso (#85 only), Piazza Venezia, Forum, Colosseum, San Clemente, and San Giovanni in Laterano.

Bus #492: Travels east-west across the city, connecting Tiburtina (train and bus stations), Largo Santa Susanna (near Piazza della Repubblica), Piazza Barberini, Piazza Venezia, Largo Argentina (near Pantheon and Campo de' Fiori), Piazza Cavour (Castel Sant'Angelo), and Piazza Risorgimento (St. Peter's Basilica and Vatican).

Tram #3: Zips from the Colosseum to San Giovanni in Laterano (and onward to Valle Giulia) in one direction, and to Piramide/Testaccio (and onward to Trastevere, though a 15-minute walk from the touristic heart) in the other.

Elettrico **Minibuses:** Cute electric minibuses take circular routes past major sights and are great for transport or simple joyriding (though they're so small, it can be hard to find a seat). They run Mon-Sat only, 7:05-20:15. *Elettrico* #117 connects San Giovanni in Laterano, Colosseo, Via Cavour, Via Nazionale, and Trevi Fountain. *Elettrico* #119 connects Piazza Venezia, Via del Corso, Trevi Fountain, Piazza di Spagna, Piazza del Popolo, and Piazza Augusto Imperatore.

By Taxi

I use taxis in Rome more often than in other cities. They're reasonable and useful for efficient sightseeing in this big, hot metropolis.

Three or four companions with more money than time should taxi almost everywhere. Taxis start at €3, then charge about €1.50 per kilometer (surcharges: €1.50 on Sun, €3.50 for nighttime hours of 22:00-6:00, one regular suitcase or bag rides free, tip by rounding up—€1 or so). Sample fares: Termini area to Vatican-€15; Termini area to Colosseum-€8; Termini area to the Borghese Gallery-€10; Colosseum to Trastevere-€12 (or look up your route at www.worldtaximeter.com).

Calling a Cab: You can always hail a cab on the street. But Romans generally walk to the nearest taxi stand (many are marked on this book's maps) or ask a passerby or a clerk in a shop, *"Dov'è una fermata dei taxi?"* (doh-VEH OO-nah fehr-MAH-tah DEH-ee TAHK-see). Easiest of all, have your hotel or restaurant call a taxi for you. (It's routine for Romans to ask the restaurant to call a taxi when they're ready to go.) The meter starts when the call is

ROME

received. To call a cab on your own, dial +39 06 3570, +39 06 4994, or +39 06 6645, or use the official city taxi line, +39 06 0609.

You can also use the Free Now app, which orders an official white taxi at regular taxi rates, with the convenience of paying via the app.

Avoid Scams: Beware of corrupt taxis. First, only use official Rome taxis. They're white, with a taxi sign on the roof and a maroon logo on the door that reads *Roma Capitale*.

When you get in, make sure the meter *(tassametro)* is turned on (you'll see the meter either on the dashboard or up by the rearview mirror). If the meter isn't on, get out and find another cab. Check that the meter is reset to the basic drop charge (should be around €3, or around €5 if you phoned for the taxi). You'll rarely pay more than €12-15 for a ride in town. Keep an eye on the fare on the meter as you near your destination; some cabbies turn the meter off instantly when they stop and tell you a higher price.

By law, every cab must display a multilingual official price chart—usually on the back of the seat in front of you. If the fare doesn't seem right, point to the chart and ask the cabbie to explain it.

At the train station or airport, avoid hustlers conning naive visitors into unmarked, rip-off "express taxis" (for tips on taking a taxi from the airport, see page 946). If you encounter problems with a taxi, making a show of writing down the taxi number (to file a complaint) can motivate a driver to quickly settle the matter.

Taxi Alternative: Uber works in Rome as it does in the US, but only at the more expensive Uber Black level.

Tours in Rome

🎧 To sightsee on your own, download my free audio tours, including my Heart of Rome, Jewish Ghetto, and Trastevere neighborhood walks, and my tours of the Pantheon, Colosseum, Roman Forum, St. Peter's Basilica, Vatican Museums, and Sistine Chapel.

ON FOOT

You can either hire a local to serve as your personal guide, or sign up for a group tour with a tour company, joining up to 50 fellow travelers. Private guides are good but pricey (around €180 for a three-hour tour). Tour companies are cheaper (€30/person), but quality and organization are unreliable. If you do hire a private Italian guide, consider inviting others from your hotel to join you and split the cost. This ends up costing about the same per person as going on a scheduled tour from one of the walking-tour companies listed below—and you'll likely get a better guide.

Local Guides

I've worked with and enjoyed each of these licensed independent local guides. They're native Italians, speak excellent English, and enjoy tailoring tours to your interests. Prices (roughly €60/hour) flex with the day, season, and demand. Arrange your date and price by email. **Carla Zaia** (carlaromeguide@gmail.com); **Cristina Giannicchi** (+39 338 111 4573, www.crisromanguide.com, crisgiannicchi@gmail.com); **Sara Magister** (a.magister@iol.it); **Giovanna Terzulli** (gioterzulli@gmail.com); **Alessandra Mazzoccoli** (www.romeandabout.com, alemazzoccoli@gmail.com); and **Massimiliano Canneto** (a Catholic guide with a Vatican forte, but does all of Rome, massicanneto@gmail.com).

Francesca Caruso, who works almost full-time with my tours when in Rome, has contributed generously to this book (www.francescacaruso.com, francescainroma@gmail.com); she offers private tours for €300/half-day. Popular with my readers, Francesca understandably books up quickly; if she's busy, she'll recommend one of her colleagues. At her website you can listen to the many interviews I've enjoyed with Francesca on my public radio program.

Walking-Tour Companies

Rome has many highly competitive tour companies, each offering a series of themed walks through various slices of the city. Three-hour guided walks generally cost €25-30 per person. Guides are usually native English speakers, often American expats. Before your trip, spend some time on these companies' websites to get to know your options, as each company has a particular teaching and guiding personality. Some are highbrow and more expensive. Others are less scholarly. It's sometimes required, and always smart, to book a spot in advance (easy online).

These companies are each well established, creative, and competitive. Each offers a 10 percent discount with most online bookings for Rick Steves travelers.

Walks of Italy (RS%—enter "RICKWALKSROME," US +1 888 683 8670, +39 06 9480 4888, www.walksofitaly.com).

Europe Odyssey (RS%, +39 06 8854 2416, mobile +39 388 121 5318, www.europeodyssey.com, Rahul).

Through Eternity (RS%—look for "Group Tours Rome" and enter "RICKSTEVES," US tel. +1 800 267 7581, www.througheternity.com, office@througheternity.com, Rob).

The Roman Guy (RS%—enter "ricksteves," ask about e-bike tours, US tel. +1 888 290 5595, theromanguy.com, Sean Finelli).

Miles & Miles Private Tours, described under "Car & Minibus Tours," below, also offers walking tours (www.milesandmiles.net). They are a great value, especially if a car is used.

ROME

Rome at a Glance

▲▲▲**Colosseum** Huge stadium where gladiators fought. **Hours:** Daily 9:00 until one hour before sunset: April-Aug until 19:15, Sept until 19:00, Oct until 18:30, off-season closes as early as 16:30. See page 840.

▲▲▲**Roman Forum** Ancient Rome's main square, with ruins and grand arches. **Hours:** Same hours as Colosseum. See page 845.

▲▲▲**Capitoline Museums** Ancient statues, mosaics, and expansive view of Forum. **Hours:** Daily 9:30-19:30. See page 858.

▲▲▲**Pantheon** The defining domed temple. **Hours:** Daily 9:00-19:00, closed for Mass Sat at 17:00 and Sun at 10:30. See page 866.

▲▲▲**St. Peter's Basilica** Most impressive church on earth, with Michelangelo's Pietà and dome. **Hours:** Church—daily 7:00-19:00, Oct-March until 18:30, often closed Wed mornings; dome—daily 7:00-17:00. See page 872.

▲▲▲**Vatican Museums** Four miles of the finest art of Western civilization, culminating in Michelangelo's glorious Sistine Chapel. **Hours:** Mon-Sat 9:00-18:00 (Fri-Sat until 22:30 late April-Oct), closed Sun—except last Sun of month, when it's open 9:00-14:00. See page 879.

▲▲▲**Borghese Gallery** Bernini sculptures and paintings by Caravaggio, Raphael, and Titian in a Baroque palazzo. **Hours:** Tue-Sun 9:00-19:00, closed Mon. See page 891.

▲▲▲**National Museum of Rome** Greatest collection of Roman sculpture anywhere. **Hours:** Tue-Sun 9:00-19:45, closed Mon. See page 897.

▲▲**Trajan's Column, Market, and Forum** Tall column with narrative relief, forum ruins, and museum with entry to Trajan's Market. **Hours:** Forum and column always viewable; museum open daily 9:30-19:30. See page 862.

▲▲**St. Peter-in-Chains** Church with Michelangelo's *Moses.* **Hours:** Daily 7:15-12:30 & 15:00-19:00, Oct-March until 18:00. See page 865.

▲▲**Museo dell'Ara Pacis** Shrine marking the beginning of Rome's golden age. **Hours:** Daily 9:30-19:30. See page 895.

ROME

▲▲**Dolce Vita Stroll** Evening *passeggiata,* where Romans strut their stuff. **Hours:** Roughly Mon-Sat 17:00-19:00 and Sun afternoons. See page 825.

▲▲**Catacombs of Priscilla** Underground tomb just outside city walls. **Hours:** Fri-Sun 9:00-12:00 & 14:00-17:00, closed Mon-Thu but may be open during busy times, closed one random month a year. See page 895.

▲**Palatine Hill** Ruins of emperors' palaces, Circus Maximus view, and museum. **Hours:** Same hours as Colosseum. See page 855.

▲**Mamertine Prison** Ancient prison where Saints Peter and Paul were held. **Hours:** Daily 9:00-17:00, may stay open later in summer. See page 859.

▲**Arch of Constantine** Honors the emperor who legalized Christianity. See page 844.

▲**The Roman House at Palazzo Valentini** Remains of an ancient house and bath. **Hours:** Wed-Mon 10:00-19:00, closed Tue, may have shorter hours off-season. See page 865.

▲**Piazza del Campidoglio** Square atop Capitoline Hill, designed by Michelangelo, with a museum, grand stairway, and Forum overlooks. See page 857.

▲**Victor Emmanuel Monument** Gigantic edifice celebrating Italian unity, with Rome from the Sky elevator ride up to 360-degree city view. **Hours:** Daily 9:30-19:30. See page 860.

▲**Trevi Fountain** Baroque hot spot into which tourists throw coins to ensure a return trip to Rome. See page 869.

▲**Castel Sant'Angelo** Hadrian's Tomb turned castle, prison, papal refuge, now museum. **Hours:** Tue-Sun 9:00-19:30, closed Mon. See page 889.

▲**Baths of Diocletian/Basilica S. Maria degli Angeli** Once ancient Rome's immense public baths, now a Michelangelo church. **Hours:** Mon-Sat 10:00-13:00 & 16:00-18:30, Sun until 19:00, may be open midday in summer. See page 899.

ROME

Car and Minibus Tours

Miles & Miles Private Tours offers tours with good English-speaking Italian driver/guides and fine air-conditioned cars and minibuses. Their basic line-up for groups of up to eight people includes a five-hour "History and Fun" tour (a fine first day by car with a broad overview and a chance to get out when you like, €350), "Squares and Fountains" (three-hour walking tour starting at Piazza Farnese, €250), and day trips from Rome into Umbria, including Civita di Bagnoregio (9 hours with hotel pickup, €600). They also provide walking tours, shore excursions (from Civitavecchia and other ports), and unguided long-distance transportation; if traveling with a small group or a family from Rome to Florence, the Amalfi Coast, or elsewhere, consider paying extra for this convenience (RS%—mention Rick Steves when booking direct, then show this book; +39 331 466 4900, www.milesandmiles.net, info@milesandmiles.net).

ON WHEELS
Hop-On, Hop-Off Bus Tours

Several different agencies run hop-on, hop-off, double-decker bus tours around Rome. These tours make the same 90-minute, eight-stop loop through the traf-fic-congested town center with about four pickups at each stop per hour. Buses provide an easy way to see the city from above the congestion (choose open or with canopy), but you'll likely feel trapped rather than enter-tained. The lazy recorded narra-tion does little more than iden-

tify the sightseeing icons you drive by and misses the opportunity to fill the time with worthwhile information. You can join one (and pay as you board; usually around €20) at any stop; Termini station and Piazza Venezia are handy hubs.

Car and Driver Service

Autoservizi Monti Concezio, run by gentle, capable, and English-speaking Ezio (pronounced Etz-io), offers private cars or minibuses with driver/guides (car-€40/hour, minibus-€45/hour, 3-hour minimum for city sightseeing, transfers between cities are more expensive, +39 335 636 5907 or +39 349 674 5643, info@tourservicemonti.it).

Walks in Rome

Take a refreshing early evening walk (Dolce Vita Stroll) and enjoy the thriving local scene, best at night (Heart of Rome Walk).

DOLCE VITA STROLL

All over the Mediterranean world, people are out strolling in the early evening in a ritual known in Italy as the *passeggiata*, worth ▲▲ (see the sidebar on page 903). Rome's *passeggiata* is both elegant (with chic people enjoying fancy window shopping in the grid of streets around the Spanish Steps) and a little crude (with young people on the prowl). The major sights along this walk are covered later in this section.

Romans' favorite place for a chic evening stroll is along Via del Corso. Join in as you walk from Piazza del Popolo (Metro: Flaminio) down a wonderfully traffic-free section of Via del Corso, and up Via Condotti to the Spanish Steps. Historians can continue to Capitoline Hill. Although busy at any hour, this area really attracts crowds from around 17:00 to 19:00 each evening (Fri and Sat are best), except on Sunday, when it occurs earlier in the afternoon. Leave before 18:00 if you plan to visit the Ara Pacis (Altar of Peace, last entry at 18:30).

As you stroll, you'll see shoppers, flirts, and people watchers filling this neighborhood of some of Rome's most fashionable stores. The most elegance survives in the grid of streets between Via del Corso and the Spanish Steps. If you get hungry during your stroll, see "Eating in Rome," later, for neighborhood wine bars and restaurants.

○ Self-Guided Walk: To reach **Piazza del Popolo,** where the stroll starts, take Metro line A to Flaminio and walk south to the square. Delightfully car-free, Piazza del Popolo is marked by an obelisk that was brought to Rome by Augustus after he conquered Egypt. (It used to stand in the Circus Maximus.) In medieval times, this area was just inside Rome's main entry.

If starting your stroll early enough, the Baroque church of **Santa Maria del Popolo** is worth popping into (next to gate in old wall on north side of square). Inside, look for Raphael's Chigi Chapel (second on left as you face the main altar) and two paintings by Caravaggio (in the Cerasi Chapel, left of altar).

From Piazza del Popolo, stroll down **Via del Corso.** While many Italians shop online or at the mall these days, and the elegance of this street has been replaced by international chains targeting local teens, this remains a fine place to feel the pulse of Rome at twilight.

Historians can side-trip right down Via Pontefici past the fascist architecture to see the massive, round-brick **Mausole-**

Dolce Vita Stroll

Piazzale Flaminio M Flaminio

SANTA MARIA DEL POPOLO

Piazza del Popolo

TERRAZZA

V.L. SAVOIA

WALK BEGINS

FERD. SAVOIA

Villa Borghese Gardens

Galoppatoio

SANTA MARIA DEI MIRACOLI

SANTA MARIA IN MONTESANTO

V. FONT

V. LAURINA

VIA MARGUTTA

VILLA MEDICI

VIA DI RIPETTA

VIA GESU E MARIA

VIA DEL BABUINO

M Spagna

LUNGOTEVERE IN AUGUSTA

VIA SAN GIACOMO

CANOVA

VIA DEI GRECI

FREZZA

Tiber River

PONTEFICI

VIA VITTORIA

ARA PACIS

VIA CROCE

1

4

Piazza di Spagna

T Spagna

WC M

TRINITÀ DEI MONTI

SPANISH STEPS

PONTE CAVOUR

MAUSOLEUM OF AUGUSTUS

Piazza Imperatore

VIA CARROZZE

VIA CONDOTTI

WALK ENDS FOR (WINDOW) SHOPPERS

VIA SISTINA

TOMACELLI

VIA BORGOGNONA

T

VIA DUE MACELLI

Piazza Borghese

3

VIA FRATTINA

PROPA.

Piazza S. Lorenzo

2

VIA VITE

To Barberini M

VIA FONT. BORGHESE

POST

ANGLO AMERICAN BOOKSHOP

V. MERCEDE

EXTENDED WALK FOR HISTORY BUFFS

VIA DELLA SCROFA

Piazza Parlamento

V. CON.

VIA DEL TRITONE

PREFETTI

T

PALD.

CAMPO MARZIO

CHIGI

VIA

PARLIAMENT

B #85 & 492

SABINA

TREVI FOUNTAIN

Piazza di Montecitorio

Piazza Colonna

MURATTE

UMILTA

DATARIA

PALAZZO DEL QUIRINALE

Piazza di Pietra

VIA DELLA SCROFA

Piazza Rotonda

CARAVITA

VIA DEL CORSO

Piazza del Quirinale

PANTHEON

SANT' IGNAZIO

SANTA MARIA SOPRA MINERVA

Piazza del Collegio Romano

L'ANTICA BIRRERIA PERONI

GALLERIA DORIA PAMPHLIJ

200 Meters

200 Yards

BATT.

VIA 4 NOV.

CORSO VITT. EMANUELE II

VIA PLEBISCITO

Piazza Venezia

B #40 & 64

TRAJAN'S COLUMN

VIA MAG.

TRAJAN'S MARKET

Largo Argentina

SAN MARCO

T

To Colosseum M

VIA D'ARA COELI

B #64

VICTOR EMMANUEL MONUMENT

CAPITOLINE HILL

VIA DEI FORI IMPERIALI

GRAND STAIRCASE

Piazza del Campodoglio

WALK ENDS FOR HISTORY BUFFS

FORUM

Eateries
1 Ristorante il Gabriello
2 Ginger
3 Caffè Vitti
4 Via della Croce Eateries

ROME

um of Augustus, ringed with cypress trees. This long-neglected sight, honoring Rome's first emperor, has finally been restored and is newly open to visitors (€5, Tue-Sun 9:00-19:00, closed Mon, shorter hours in winter, book online far in advance at www.mausoleodiaugusto.it). Beyond it, next to the river, is Augustus' **Ara Pacis,** enclosed within a protective glass-walled museum (described later). From the mausoleum, walk down Via Tomacelli to return to Via del Corso and the 21st century.

From Via del Corso, window shoppers should take a left down **Via Condotti** to join the parade to the **Spanish Steps,** passing big-name boutiques. The streets that parallel Via Condotti to the south (Borgognona and Frattina) are also elegant and filled with high-end shops. A few streets to the north hides the narrow Via Margutta, filled with pricey artisan and antique shops.

History Buffs: Another option is to ignore Via Condotti and forget the Spanish Steps. Stay on Via del Corso, which has been straight since Roman times, and walk a half-mile down to the Victor Emmanuel Monument. Climb Michelangelo's stairway to his glorious (especially when floodlit) square atop Capitoline Hill. Stand on the balcony (just past the mayor's palace on the right), which overlooks the Forum. As the horizon reddens and cats prowl the unclaimed rubble of ancient Rome, it's one of the finest views in the city.

HEART OF ROME WALK

Rome's most colorful neighborhood features narrow lanes, intimate piazzas, fanciful fountains, and some of Europe's best people-watching. During the day, this walk—worth ▲▲▲—shows off the colorful Campo de' Fiori market and trendy fashion boutiques as it meanders past major monuments such as the Pantheon and the Spanish Steps.

But the sunset brings unexpected magic. A stroll in the cool of the evening is made memorable by the romance of the Eternal City at its best. Sit so close to a bubbling fountain that traffic noise evaporates. Jostle with kids to see the gelato flavors. Watch lovers straddling more than the bench. Jaywalk past *carabinieri* in bullet-proof vests. And marvel at the ramshackle elegance that softens this brutal city for those who were born here and can't imagine living anywhere else. These are the flavors of Rome, best enjoyed after dark.

This walk is equally pleasant in reverse order. You could ride the Metro to the Spanish Steps and finish at Campo de' Fiori, near many recommended restaurants.

Getting There: Kick off this walk in one of Rome's most colorful spots, Campo de' Fiori. It's a few blocks west of Largo Argentina, a major transportation hub. Buses #40, #64, and #492,

ROME

and tram #8 stop at Largo Argentina and/or along Corso Vittorio Emanuele II (a long block northwest of Campo de' Fiori). A taxi from Termini station costs about €14.

Length of This Walk: Allow one to three hours for this mile-long walk, depending on whether you linger and tour the Pantheon. To lengthen this walk, continue from the Spanish Steps to Piazza del Popolo.

Tours: ☊ Download my free Heart of Rome Walk audio tour.

❍ Self-Guided Walk

❶ **Campo de' Fiori:** In the morning, this bohemian piazza hosts a fruit-and-vegetable market. In the evening, the cafés and res-

taurants that line the square predominate. On weekend nights, beer-drinking young people (mostly American students) pack the medieval square, transforming it into a vast Roman street party.

With the neighborhood feel of Campo de' Fiori, it's hard to believe you're in a major capital city of nearly three million people. Rome has no skyscrapers, no central business district, and no obvious downtown. It's more a collection of urban villages, like this square. Romans jealously guard their laidback lifestyle, and nowhere is it clearer than in Campo de' Fiori.

In ancient times, it was a pleasant meadow—literally a *campo de' fiori*, or "field of flowers." Then the Romans built a massive entertainment complex, the Theater of Pompey, right next to it. The complex covered several city blocks, stretching from here to Largo Argentina (and including the spot where Julius Caesar was stabbed to death).

In medieval times, Christian pilgrims passed through the *campo* on their way to the Vatican, and a thriving market developed. As popes modernized the city in Renaissance and Baroque times, this square kept its local flavor.

Today's Romans live amid the eclectic heritage of their ancestors. For example, at the east end of the square (behind the statue of the heretic Bruno), see how the ramshackle apartments are built right into the older parts. Find the pinkish-beige brick building, midway up, and the two white columns incorporated into it. Those ancient columns were once part of that Theater of Pompey.

Lording over the center of the square is the statue of **Giordano Bruno,** an intellectual who was burned on this spot in 1600. The pedestal shows scenes from Bruno's trial and execution, and an

inscription translates, "And the flames rose up." The statue, facing a Vatican administration building, was erected in 1889, a time when the new state of Italy and the Vatican were feuding. Vatican officials protested the heretic in their midst, but they were overruled by angry neighborhood locals. This district is still known for its free spirit and antiauthoritarian demonstrations.

The square is surrounded by fun eateries, and is great for people-watching. Bruno faces the bustling **Forno** (in the left corner of the square), where takeout *pizza bianca* is sold hot from the oven.

• *If Bruno did a hop, step, and jump forward, then turned left, in a block he'd reach...*

❷ **Piazza Farnese:** While the higgledy-piggledy Campo de' Fiori feels free and easy, the 16th-century Renaissance Piazza Farnese, named for the family whose palace dominates it, seems to stress order. The Farnese family was nouveau riche and needed to make a statement. They hired Michelangelo to help design their palace. He created the jutting roofline (the cornice), and made the window in the very center a little wider than the others. This gave the whole facade a pleasant symmetry and focused attention on the balcony, from where Farnese nobles gave speeches.

Note the flags over the entrance and the security presence. The palazzo now houses the French embassy. The twin fountains decorating the square date from the third century and were made with repurposed stone tubs from the ancient Baths of Caracalla. Rome is famous for its fountains. In times past, they were functional, providing neighborhoods with a water supply. These particular fountains are fed by an ancient aqueduct, the Acqua Vergine. It's the same source that feeds the Trevi Fountain and others that we'll see along this walk. After 2,000 years, the aqueduct is still bringing the water of life into the city.

• *Walk back to Campo de' Fiori, cross the square, and continue a couple of blocks down...*

❸ **Via dei Baullari to Corso Vittorio Emanuele II:** As you slalom through the crowds, notice the crush of cheap cafés, bars, and restaurants—the center of medieval Rome is morphing into a playground for tourists, students, and locals visiting from the suburbs. High rents are driving families out and changing the character of this district. That's why the Campo de' Fiori market increasingly sells more gifty edibles than basic fruits and vegetables.

After a couple of blocks, you reach the busy boulevard, Corso Vittorio Emanuele II. In Rome, any road big enough to have city buses like this is post-unification: constructed after 1870. Look left and right down the street—the facades are mostly 19th-century neo-Renaissance, built after this main thoroughfare sliced through the city. Traffic in much of central Rome is limited to city buses, taxis, motorbikes, "dark cars" (limos and town cars of VIPs), deliv-

Heart of Rome Walk

- Piazza Cavour
- V. DI FONT
- ARA PACIS
- MAUSOLEUM OF AUGUSTUS
- PALACE OF JUSTICE
- PONTE CAVOUR
- Piazza Augusto Imperatore
- VIA DI RIPETTA
- Tiber River
- Piazza Borghese
- LUNGOTEVERE MARZIO
- PONTE UMBERTO
- CLEMENTINO
- VIA DELLA SCROFA
- Piazza Ponte Umberto I
- MONTE BRIANZO
- PREFETTI
- To Ponte Sant'Angelo
- PALAZZO ALTEMPS
- SANT' APOLLINARE
- SANT' AGOSTINO
- STELLETTA
- CAMPO
- UFFICI GIOLITTI
- VIA DEI CORONARI
- VIA ZANARDELLI
- VIEW INTO ANCIENT STADIUM
- VIA SANT' AGOSTINO
- VIA DELLE COPPELLE
- VIA IN AQUIRO
- LA MADDE-LENA
- Piazza Fico
- VOLPE
- TRE SCALINI
- Piazza Navona
- SAN LUIGI
- CARABINIERI
- VIA GIUSTINIANI
- Piazza della Rotonda
- SALVATORE ITALY'S SENATE
- CHIESA NUOVA
- SANT' AGNESE
- FOUR RIVERS FOUNTAIN
- SANT' EUSTACHIO
- MONTE-FORTE
- PANTHEON
- Piazza della Chiesa Nuova
- V. DEL GOVERNO VECCHIO
- PALAZZO PAMPHILJ
- Piazza Pasquino
- SANT' IVO
- CAFFÉ SANT' EUSTACHIO
- Piazza Sant'Eustachio
- To Vatican City & St. Peter's
- CORSO VITTORIO
- PANTALEO
- CITY MUSEUM
- CORSO DEL RINASCIMENTO
- ARGENTINA
- VIA DE' CESTARI
- MINGHETTI STATUE
- EMANUELE II
- Largo Argentina
- LARGO ARGENTINA RUINS
- VIA D. BAULLARI
- SANT' ANDREA DELLA VALLE
- WALK BEGINS
- BRUNO STATUE
- Campo de' Fiori
- VIA MONSERRATO
- Piazza Farnese
- V. CHIAVARI
- Largo Pallaro
- To Ghetto
- VIA GIULIA
- PALAZZO FARNESE
- To Trastevere
- VIA GIUBBONARI

ROME

1. Campo de' Fiori
2. Piazza Farnese
3. Via dei Baullari to Corso Vittorio Emanuele II
4. Pasquino Statue
5. Piazza Navona
6. Pantheon
7. Caffè Tazza d'Oro
8. Piazza Capranica
9. Piazza di Montecitorio
10. Piazza Colonna & Via del Corso
11. Trevi Fountain
12. Palazzo di Propaganda Fide
13. Column of the Immaculate Conception
14. Spanish Steps

ROME

ery vans, residents, and disabled people with permits (a.k.a. friends of politicians). This is one of the increasingly rare streets where any vehicle is welcome.

• *Cross Corso Vittorio Emanuele II, and enter a square with a statue of Marco Minghetti, an early Italian prime minister. Angle left at the statue, walking along the left side of the skippable City Museum of Rome, down Via di San Pantaleo. A block down, at the corner, over your right shoulder you'll find a beat-up old statue.*

❹ **Pasquino:** Pasquino—a third-century-BC statue that was discovered near here—is one of Rome's "talking statues." For 500 years, this statue has served as a kind of community billboard, allowing people to complain anonymously when it might be dangerous to speak up. And, to this day, you'll see the board next to old Pasquino strewn with political posters, strike announcements, and grumbling graffiti. The statue looks worn down by centuries of bitching.

• *Facing Pasquino, turn left and head up Via di Pasquino. You'll soon emerge into a place where all the layers of Rome are on display: ancient, medieval, Baroque, and contemporary.*

❺ **Piazza Navona:** This long, oblong square is dotted with fountains, busy with outdoor cafés, lined with palazzos and churches, and thronged with happy visitors. By its shape you might guess that this square started out as a racetrack, part of the training grounds built here by Emperor Domitian around AD 80. That was the same year the Colosseum opened: Rome was at its peak.

But much of what we see today came in the 1600s, when the whole place got a major renovation. At the time, the popes were trying to put some big scandals behind them, and beautification projects like this were a peace offering to the public.

Three Baroque fountains decorate the piazza. The first fountain, at the southern end, features a Moor wrestling with a dolphin. In 17th-century Rome, Moors (North Africans) represented all that was exotic and mysterious. In the fountain at the northern (far) end, Neptune slays a giant octopus.

The most famous fountain, though, is in the center: the **Four Rivers Fountain** by Gian

Lorenzo Bernini, the man who in the mid-1600s remade Rome in the Baroque style. It's topped with an Egyptian-style obelisk—another of the themes we'll see along this walk. Obelisks were popular with Roman emperors because Egyptian society saw its rulers as divine—an idea Roman rulers liked to promote.

Get close to admire Bernini's four enormous statues at the base. As the water of the world gushes everywhere, these four burly river gods represent the four quarters of the world.

Piazza Navona is Rome's most interesting night scene, with street music, artists, fire-eaters, local Casanovas, gelato, and outdoor cafés that are worthy of a splurge if you've got time to sit and enjoy Italy's human river.

• *Leave Piazza Navona directly across from* **Tre Scalini** *(famous for its tartufo, a rich, chocolate gelato concoction), and go east down Corsia Agonale, past rose peddlers and palm readers. Ahead of you (across the busy street) stands the stately Palazzo Madama, where the* **Italian Senate** *meets. (Hence, security is high.) Jog left around this building, and follow the brown Pantheon sign straight down Via del Salvatore.*

After a block, you'll pass (on your left) the Church of San Luigi dei Francesi, with its très *French decor and precious Caravaggio paintings. If it's open, pop in. Otherwise, continue along, following the crowd to...*

❻ **The Pantheon:** Perhaps the most magnificent building surviving from ancient Rome is this temple to the "pantheon" (literally, all the gods). The 40-foot, single-piece granite columns of the Pantheon's entrance show the scale the ancient Romans built on. The columns support a triangular Greek-style roof with an inscription that proclaims, "M. Agrippa built this." In

fact, the present structure was built (fecit) by Emperor Hadrian (AD 120), who gave credit to the builder of an earlier temple. This impressive entranceway gives no clue that the greatest wonder of the building is inside—a domed room that inspired later domes, including Michelangelo's St. Peter's and Brunelleschi's Duomo in Florence.

If the Pantheon is open, pop in for a look around (for details on the interior, see page 866). Afterward, consider detouring to several interesting churches nearby (see page 868).

If the Pantheon is closed, just stand for a while under the portico, which is romantically floodlit and moonlit at night.

• *To continue this walk, with your back to the Pantheon, veer to the right, uphill toward the yellow sign on Via Orfani that reads* Casa del Caffè—*you've reached the...*

❼ **Caffè Tazza d'Oro:** This is one of Rome's top coffee shops, dating back to the days when this area was licensed to roast coffee beans. Locals come here for a shot of espresso or, when it's hot, a refreshing *granita di caffè con panna* (coffee and crushed ice with whipped cream).

• *From here, our walk continues past some interesting landmarks to the Trevi Fountain. To get there more directly, you could opt to take a* **shortcut** *by bearing right at the coffee shop onto Via de' Pastini, which leads through Piazza di Pietra (with some surviving chunks of the Temple of Hadrian), then across busy Via del Corso, where it becomes the touristy, pedestrianized Via delle Muratte and heads straight for the fountain.*

To stick with me for the slightly longer version, bear left at the coffee shop and continue up Via degli Orfani to the next square...

❽ **Piazza Capranica:** This square is home to the big, plain Florentine-Renaissance-style Palazzo Capranica (directly opposite as you enter the square). Its stubby tower was once much taller, but when a stronger government arrived, the nobles were all ordered to shorten their towers. Like so many of Rome's churches, the church on the square—Santa Maria in Aquiro—is older than its Baroque-era facade. Notice the circular little shrine on the street corner (between the palace and the apartment building). For centuries, worshipful spots like this have made pilgrims (and, today, tourists) feel welcome.

• *Leave the piazza to the right of the palazzo, heading down Via in Aquiro. The street jogs to the left and into a square called...*

❾ **Piazza di Montecitorio:** This square, home to Italy's Parliament, is marked by an **Egyptian obelisk** from the sixth century BC. It adorned a temple in Egypt for half a millennium before Emperor Augustus brought it to Rome as a trophy proclaiming his victory over Mark Antony and Cleopatra. Made of red granite, the obelisk stands 70 feet tall—or well over 100 feet when you include the base.

In Augustus' day, the obelisk acted as a sundial and calendar, aligned to cast a shadow across the solarium altar on the emperor's birthday. Today, the obelisk still functions as a sundial. Follow the zodiac markings in the pavement to the square's next big sight—the Italian Parliament. This impressive building is where the legislature's lower chamber (the equivalent of the US House of Representatives) attempts to govern the nation.

• *One block to your right is Piazza Colonna, where we're heading* *next—unless you like gelato. A one-block detour to the left (past Hotel Nazionale) brings you to a famous Roman gelateria, **Giolitti**.*

🔟 **Piazza Colonna and Via del Corso:** The square features a massive **column** that has stood here since the second century AD.

The column's shaft is 12 feet across, almost 100 feet tall, and stands on a 30-foot base, which rests on a platform. It's a particularly imposing-looking column because it doesn't taper at the top. The whole thing is carved from the finest white marble in the world, from Carrara—the favorite quarry of the ancient Romans and of Michelangelo.

This isn't a single piece of marble. It's 28 cylindrical blocks stacked atop each other like a pile of 10-ton checkers. A carved frieze winds from the bottom to the top, telling the story of Emperor Marcus Aurelius heroically battling barbarians around AD 170.

Beyond Piazza Colonna runs noisy **Via del Corso,** Rome's main north-south boulevard. In ancient times, this was the Via Flaminia, the highway that stretched from the Roman Forum to the Adriatic coast. For 2,000 years, all travelers from northern Europe first entered Rome and headed downtown on this street. In the Middle Ages, the street brought pilgrims to the Vatican.

The street was renamed "corso" for a famous medieval horse race that took place here during the crazy Carnevale season leading up to Lent. In 1854, Via del Corso became one of Rome's first gas-lit streets. It still hosts some of the city's most chic stores. Every evening, the pedestrian-only stretch of the Corso is packed with people on parade, taking to the streets for their *passeggiata*.

Before crossing the street, look left (to the obelisk marking Piazza del Popolo—the ancient north gate of the city) and right (to the Victor Emmanuel Monument).

• *Cross Via del Corso to enter a big palatial building with columns, the **Galleria Alberto Sordi** shopping mall. To the left are convenient WCs. Go to the right and exit out the back. (If you're here after 21:00, when the mall is closed, circle around the right side of the Galleria on Via dei Sabini.) At any time, be on guard for pickpockets, who thrive in the nearby*

ROME

Trevi Fountain crowds. Once out the back, the tourist kitsch builds as you head up Via de Crociferi to the roar of the water, lights, and people at the...

⓫ Trevi Fountain: The Trevi Fountain is the ultimate showcase for Rome's love affair with water.

Architect Nicola Salvi conceived this liquid Baroque avalanche in 1762, cleverly incorporating the palace behind the fountain as a theatrical backdrop. Centerstage is the enormous figure known simply as the "Ocean." He symbolizes water in every form. The statue stands in his shell-shaped chariot, surfing through his wet dream. Water gushes from 24 spouts and tumbles over 30 different kinds of plants. Winged horses represent cresting waves. They're led by Tritons who blow on their conch shells. *Drammatico!*

The square that faces the fountain has a lively atmosphere. The magic is enhanced by the fact that no streets directly approach it. You can hear the excitement as you draw near, and then—*bam!*—you're there. Enjoy the scene. Romantics toss a coin over their shoulder into the fountain. Legend says it will assure your return to Rome. Every year I go through this tourist ritual...and so far it's working.

• *Facing the Trevi Fountain, walk along its right side up Via della Stamperia. Cross busy Via del Tritone. At the McDonald's, angle left as you continue about 30 yards up Via del Nazareno to #9, where you'll pass a fence on the left, with an exposed bit of that ancient Acqua Vergine aqueduct. At the T-intersection ahead, turn right on Via Sant'Andrea delle Fratte. After you cross another street, the street you're on becomes Via di Propaganda. Up ahead, you'll pass alongside the...*

⓬ Palazzo di Propaganda Fide: At #1, on the right, the white-and-yellow entrance marks the palace from which the Catholic Church "propagated," or spread, its message to the world. Back in the 1600s, this "Propaganda Palace" was the headquarters of the Catholic Church's P.R. department—a priority after the Reformation. The building was designed by that dynamic Baroque duo, Bernini and Borromini (with his concave lines). It flies the yellow-and-white flag signifying that it is still owned by the Vatican.

• *The street opens up into a long piazza. You're approaching the Spanish Steps. But first, pause at the...*

⓭ Column of the Immaculate Conception: Atop a tall column stands a bronze statue of Mary. She wears a diadem of stars for a halo, and stands on a crescent moon atop a globe of the earth, which is crushing a satanic serpent.

Picture the festive scene here every December 8, the feast day of the Immaculate Conception. The pope attends, the fire department brings out a ladder truck, and fresh flowers are placed high on Mary's statue. (You may see wilted remains of a flower wreath in Mary's hand.) This is the traditional event that kicks off Rome's Christmas season—the locals all go home and decorate their trees on this December day.

To Mary's immediate left stands the Spanish embassy to the Vatican. Rome has double the embassies of a normal capital because here countries need two: one to Italy and one to the Vatican. And because of this 300-year-old embassy, the square and its famous steps are called "Spanish."

• *Just 100 yards past Mary, you reach the climax of our walk, the...*

⓮ Spanish Steps: The wide, curving staircase is one of Rome's iconic sights. Its 138 steps lead sharply up from Piazza di Spagna.

Partway up, the steps fan out around a central terrace, forming a butterfly shape. The design culminates at the top in an obelisk framed between two Baroque church towers.

For decades the steps were a favorite Roman hangout (see photo), but recently the city banned anyone from sitting on them. You can walk up and down the steps, but if you sit, you'll face a €250 fine.

At the foot of the steps is the aptly named Sinking Boat Fountain. It was built by Gian Lorenzo Bernini's father, Pietro. This fountain is powered by that same Acqua Vergine aqueduct. Because the water pressure here is low, the water can't shoot high in the air. So Bernini designed the fountain to be low key—a sinking boat filled with water.

The piazza is a thriving scene both day and night. From here you can window-shop along Via Condotti, which stretches away from the steps. But before you head off, take a final 360-degree spin of the piazza. It features many of the themes we've enjoyed on this walk—fountains, obelisks, public spaces, statues, and gelato. Most of all, it's a glimpse at today's Rome—a city where friends and families live much the same kind of life as their ancient cousins.

• *Our walk is finished. To reach the top of the steps sweat-free, take the free elevator just inside the Spagna Metro stop (to the left, as you face the steps; elevator closes at 23:30). You'll find a pay WC in the middle of the square just beyond the fountain. And in the opposite direction, the nearby McDonald's (as you face the Spanish Steps, go right one block) is big and lavish, with a handy WC. When you're ready to leave, you can zip home on the Metro (usually open until 23:30) or grab a taxi at the north or south ends of the piazza.*

Sights in Rome

I've clustered Rome's sights into walkable neighborhoods. Save transit time by grouping your sightseeing according to location. For example, in one great day you can start at the Colosseum, then go to the Forum, then Capitoline Hill, and from there either to the Pantheon or back to the Colosseum (by way of additional ruins along Via dei Fori Imperiali).

A 🎧 in the listing means the walk or tour is also available as a free audio tour (via my Rick Steves Audio Europe app—see page 26).

For general tips on sightseeing, see the Practicalities chapter. Rome's good city-run information website, www.060608.it, lists current opening hours.

Reserve Ahead: Most sights in Rome—even small ones—allow prebooking online. At a few key sights, reservations are either required or highly recommended: the Colosseum (combo-ticket with the Roman Forum and Palatine Hill), Borghese Gallery, Vatican Museums (with the Sistine Chapel), and on weekends, the Pantheon. See listings for details on booking.

Beware of Scalper Sites: Before purchasing tickets online, make sure that you are on the sight's official website. Sometimes scalper websites come up first when you do an online search, and they might even have the word "official" on the page. Make sure you use the legitimate official website, listed in this book, when booking tickets online. If the prices are significantly higher than what I list here, you're probably on a third-party site.

Avoid Free-Entry Crowds: State museums in Italy are free to enter once or twice a month, usually on a Sunday, and the Vatican Museums are free on the last Sunday of the month. Free days are actually bad news—they attract crowds. In peak season, I'd check websites in advance and make a point to avoid their free days. Rome's state museums include the Colosseum, Roman Forum, Palatine Hill, Borghese Gallery, National Museum of Rome, Castel Sant'Angelo, and Baths of Caracalla. Note that sights that require reservations still need to be prebooked on free days.

ANCIENT ROME

The core of ancient Rome, where the grandest monuments were built, is between the Colosseum and Capitoline Hill. Among the ancient forums, a few modern sights have popped up. I've listed these sights generally from south to north, starting with the biggies—the Colosseum and Forum—and continuing up to Capitoline Hill and Piazza Venezia. As a pleasant conclusion to your busy day, consider my relaxing self-guided walk back south along the broad, parklike main drag—Via dei Fori Imperiali—with some enticing detours to nearby sights (described in the "Imperial Forums" listing, later).

ROME

ANCIENT CORE
▲▲▲Colosseum (Colosseo)

This 2,000-year-old building is the classic example of Roman engineering. Used as a venue for entertaining the masses, this colossal, functional stadium is one of Europe's most recognizable landmarks. Whether you're playing gladiator or simply marveling at the remarkable ancient design and construction, the Colosseum gets a unanimous thumbs-up.

Cost: €18 combo-ticket covers the Colosseum and the Roman Forum/Palatine Hill and is valid for 24 hours. Buy it online well in advance to get a timed-entry reservation for the Colosseum. Do not show up without a reserved entry. A Full Experience ticket costs €24, is valid for two consecutive days, and covers the Colosseum, Palatine Hill/Roman Forum, and some minor sights at these archaeological areas, plus access to the Colosseum's arena floor.

Hours: Daily 9:00 until one hour before sunset—April-Aug until 19:15, Sept until 19:00, Oct until 18:30, off-season closes as early as 16:30; last entry one hour before closing, audioguide-€5.50, Metro: Colosseo.

Information: Call center: +39 06 3996 7700 (English spoken, daily 10:00-15:00), www.parcocolosseo.it.

Mandatory Advance Ticketing: Tickets must be reserved in advance (no on-site sales), and for the Colosseum, you must book a specific entrance time (even for those with free tickets, such as kids 17 and under). Book online at Coopculture.it (select English, and click on "Ticketing"; you'll be emailed a ticket/QR code to use at entry). You can also book by phone (see call center details above, under "Information").

If you want to join an official English-language tour, it's best to book it in advance with your admission, as these typically sell out.

Although it's possible to make a same-day reservation, don't wait too long to book. Spaces are limited and can sell out. If the time slot you want is unavailable, try booking a different type of ticket (such as one that includes an audioguide or a tour).

When to Go: Try to get an early-morning or late-afternoon time slot. At midday, the Colosseum can be so crowded that even reservation holders can face long waits. Generally, crowds are thinner in the afternoon (especially after 16:00 in summer).

Colosseum

MONTI

To St. Peter-in-Chains Church (Moses Statue)

VIA EUDOSSIANA

VIA TERME DI TITO

Not to Scale

VIA ANNIBALDI

Parco del Colle Oppio

VIA NICOLA SALVI

To Forum/Palatine, Trajan's Forum & Piazza Venezia

STAIRS

Colosseo Ⓜ Ⓑ

To San Clemente & San Giovanni in Laterano

BIKE RENTAL ■

VIA DEI FORI IMPERIALI Ⓑ

Ⓑ

TEMP. EXHIBITS

UPPER LEVEL

PERMANENT EXHIBIT

GUIDED TOURS DESK ■

WC

ENTER

BOOK-STORE

EMPEROR'S BOX

STAIRS DOWN

✝

ARENA LEVEL

ARENA FLOOR (RECONSTRUCTED)

STAIRS UP

⊠ ELEVATOR

WC

FORUM

FORMER 100' TALL "COLOSSAL STATUE"

TEMPLE OF VENUS & ROME

Piazza del Colosseo

BOOK-STORE ■

VESTAL VIRGINS BOX

VIA SACRA

EXIT ONLY

To Forum/Palatine Entrance

Ⓑ

Ⓣ

ARCH OF CONSTANTINE

Ⓑ

VIA DI SAN GREGORIO

VIA CELIO VIBENNA

PALATINE HILL

Parco del Celio

To Palatine/Forum Entrance & Circus Maximus

Getting There: The Colosseo Metro stop on line B is just across the street from the monument. Buses #51, #75, #85, #87, and #118 stop along Via dei Fori Imperiali near the Colosseum entrance (buses don't run on this street on Sun but still stop nearby), one of the Forum/Palatine Hill entrances, and Piazza Venezia. Tram #3 stops behind the Colosseum.

Getting In: There's a single entry point (across from the Forum), where you'll need to show your ticket/QR code to get inside. Be sure to arrive 15 minutes before your appointed time.

Tours: 🎧 My free Colosseum **audio tour,** covering much the same information as provided here, is just the right amount of detail for a casual visitor.

For more in-depth commentary, stop at the **Guided Tours** desk, which you'll find inside the turnstiles. You can choose between a fact-filled audioguide (€5.50/1 hour) or a handheld vid-eoguide that senses where you are in the site and plays related clips (€6/50 minutes) but can be hard to see in bright sunlight. Official guided tours in English depart regularly (€10), but these usually sell out—book in advance with your admission.

Private guides stand outside the Colosseum looking for busi-ness (€25-30/2-hour tour of the Colosseum, Forum, and Palatine Hill). If booking a private guide on the spot, make sure that your tour will start right away and that the ticket you receive covers all three sights: the Colosseum, Forum, and Palatine Hill.

Length of This Tour: Allow an hour. If you're short on time, you can see the entire interior from a single viewpoint.

Baggage: Small bags are no problem. Larger bags and back-packs are not allowed, and there is no bag check. Spray cans and glass bottles are prohibited.

Restoration: The arena is being cleaned from top to bottom, given permanent lighting, and outfitted with new shops and ser-vices. These ongoing renovations may affect your visit.

Services: A WC (often crowded) is inside the Colosseum, and there are also water fountains.

Background: Built when the Roman Empire was at its peak in AD 80, the Colosseum represents Rome at its grandest. The Flavian Amphitheater (the Colosseum's real name) was an arena for gladiator contests and public spectacles. When killing became a spectator sport, the Romans wanted to share the fun with as many people as possible, so they stuck two semicircular theaters together to create a freestanding amphitheater, the largest in the empire.

The sheer size of the Colosseum is impressive, even in our era of mega-stadiums. With four oversized stories, it's 160 feet high, nearly a third of a mile around, and makes an oval-shaped footprint that covers six acres.

Imagine the Colosseum in its glory days. The whole thing was a brilliant white, highlighted with brightly painted trim. Monu-mental statues of Greek and Roman gods (Zeus, Venus, Hercules), also in bright colors, stood in the arches of the middle two stories. The top of the structure was studded with wooden beams stick-ing straight up, to hold a canvas awning that shaded the spectators inside.

The stadium could accommodate 50,000 roaring fans (that's 100,000 thumbs). As Romans arrived for the games, they'd be greeted outside by a huge bronze statue of the emperor Nero—100 feet tall, gleaming in the sunlight—standing where the cypress trees stand today, between the Colosseum and the Metro stop.

Visiting the Colosseum: Once past the turnstiles, signs direct you to the official visitors' route; depending on current policies, you may be expected to stick to this, or you may be able to explore in whatever order you like. Even if you aren't required to, following the official route ensures you will see everything. (If following signs, you want the "long route," which includes the upstairs—with the best views.)

As you pass into the interior, imagine being an ancient spectator arriving for the games. Fans could pour in through ground-floor entrances; there were 76 numbered ones in addition to the emperor's private entrance on the north side. Your ticket (likely a pottery shard) was marked with your entrance, section, row, and seat number. You'd pass by concession stands selling fast food and souvenirs, such as wine glasses with the names of famous gladiators. A hallway leading to the seats was called a *vomitorium*. At exit time, the Colosseum would "vomit" out its contents, giving us the English word. It's estimated that a capacity crowd could enter and exit in just 15 minutes.

The games took place in this oval-shaped **arena,** 280 feet long by 165 feet wide. When you look down into the arena, you're seeing

the underground passages beneath the playing surface (which can be visited only on a private tour). The arena was originally covered with a wooden floor, then sprinkled with sand (*arena* in Latin). The bit of reconstructed floor gives you an accurate sense of the original arena level and the subterranean warren where animals and prisoners were held. As in modern stadiums, the spectators ringed the playing area in bleacher seats that slanted up from the arena floor. Around you are the big brick masses that supported the tiers of seats.

The **games** pitted men against men, men against beasts, and beasts against beasts. The program began in the morning with a few warm-up acts. First came the animals, things like watching dogs bloody themselves attacking porcupines. At lunchtime came Act Two. This is when criminals and POWs were executed, often in creative ways. They might be thrown to the lions—naked and unarmed. Or they were dressed up like classical heroes and forced to star in a play featuring their own death.

Finally, in the afternoon, came the main event: the gladiators. Trumpets would blare, drums would pound, and the gladiators would enter the arena from the west end, parade around to the music, and pause at the south side. There, they'd acknowledge the Vestal Virgins sitting in their special box seats on the 50-yard line. (They got season tickets as a reward for their unique contribu-

ROME

tion to Roman society—chastity.) After a nod to the Virgins, the gladiators continued on to the emperor's box. There, they'd raise their weapons, salute, and shout *Ave, Caesar!*—"Hail Caesar! We who are about to die salute you!" (Though some scholars doubt they actually said that.)

In an age without a hint of a newsreel, it was hard for local Romans to visualize and appreciate the faraway conquests of their empire. The Colosseum spectacles were a way to bring home the environments, animals, and people of these conquered lands, parade them before the public, and make them real. Imagine never having seen an actual lion, and suddenly one jumps out to chase a prisoner in the arena. Seeing the king of beasts slain by a gladiator reminded the masses of man's triumph over nature.

Don't miss the **permanent exhibit,** with lots of ancient artifacts found on-site, architectural illustrations, and fascinating reconstruction models (all well described in English). You'll learn about pulleys and hoists, ancient pastimes, and Roman seating hierarchy. The huge, cutaway model of the intact Colosseum is worth lingering over.

▲Arch of Constantine

This well-preserved arch, which stands between the Colosseum and the Forum, commemorates a military coup and, more important,

the acceptance of Christianity by the Roman Empire. When the ambitious Emperor Constantine (who had a vision that he'd win under the sign of the cross) defeated his rival Maxentius in AD 312, Constantine became sole emperor of the Roman Empire and legalized Christianity. The arch is free to see—always open and viewable.

Roman Forum and Palatine Hill

Though I've covered them separately, the Forum and Palatine Hill are organized as a single sight with one admission. You'll need to see both sights in a single visit.

Cost and Hours: €18 combo-ticket includes the Colosseum and Palatine Hill (must buy in advance; you'll also prebook an entry time for the Colosseum). A €24 Full Experience ticket adds some smaller sights (which may have shorter hours and random closed days) and is valid for two days. Same hours as Colosseum, audioguide-€5, Metro: Colosseo, +39 06 3996 7700, information: www.parcocolosseo.it, tickets: www.coopculture.it.

▲▲▲Roman Forum (Foro Romano)

This is ancient Rome's birthplace and civic center, and the common ground between Rome's famous seven hills. As just about anything important that happened in ancient Rome happened here, it's arguably the most important piece of real estate in Western civilization. While only a few fragments of that glorious past remain, history seekers find plenty to ignite their imaginations amid the half-broken columns and arches.

Getting In: There are three main entrances to the Forum/Palatine Hill sight: 1) from the Colosseum (the most crowded)—nearest the Arch of Titus, where my guided walk starts; 2) from Via dei Fori Imperiali; and 3) from Via di San Gregorio—at the south end of Palatine Hill, which is least crowded. At busy times, turnstiles farther up Via dei Fori Imperiali, near the Arch of Septimius Severus, are sometimes open.

Tours: ∩ Download my free Roman Forum audio tour, which offers a concise introduction to the sight. Audioguides or a downloadable app may be available to further decipher the rubble.

Services: The information center, located across from the Via dei Fori Imperiali entrance, has a bookshop, small café, food stand, and WCs (daily 9:30-19:00). Bookstalls nearby sell a variety of colorful books with plastic overlays that restore the ruins (prices negotiable).

⊙ Self-Guided Tour: As you begin this Forum tour, see things with "period eyes." We imagine the structures in ancient Rome as mostly white, but ornate buildings and monuments like the Arch of Titus were originally more colorful. Through the ages, builders scavenged stone from the Forum, and the finest stone—

Roman Forum

- **1** Arch of Titus
- **2** Basilica of Constantine
- **3** Via Sacra
- **4** Temple of Antoninus Pius & Faustina
- **5** Temple of Vesta
- **6** House of the Vestal Virgins
- **7** Caligula's Palace
- **8** Temple of Castor & Pollux
- **9** The Forum's Main Square
- **10** Temple of Julius Caesar
- **11** Basilica Aemilia
- **12** The Curia
- **13** Rostrum
- **14** Arch of Septimius Severus
- **15** Temple of Saturn
- **16** Column of Phocas

the colored marble—was cannibalized first. If any was left, it was generally the white stone. Statues that filled the niches were vividly painted, but the organic paint rotted away as statues lay buried for centuries. Lettering was inset bronze and eyes were inset ivory. Even seemingly intact structures, like the Arch of Titus, have been reassembled. Notice the columns are half smooth and half fluted. The fluted halves are original; the smooth parts are reconstructions—intentionally not trying to fake the original.

• *Start at the Arch of Titus, which rises above the rubble on the Colosseum end of the Forum.*

❶ **Arch of Titus** (Arco di Tito): The Arch of Titus commemorated the Roman victory over the province of Judaea (Israel) in AD

70. The Romans had a reputation as benevolent conquerors who tolerated local customs and rulers. All they required was allegiance to the empire, shown by worshipping the emperor as a god. No problem for most conquered people, who already had half a dozen gods on their prayer lists anyway. But Israelites believed in only one god, and it wasn't the emperor. Israel revolted. After a short but bitter war, the Romans defeated the rebels, took Jerusalem, destroyed their temple (leaving only a fragment of one wall's foundation—today's revered "Wailing Wall"), and brought home 50,000 Jewish slaves...who were forced to build this arch (and the Colosseum).

• *Walk down Via Sacra into the Forum. Imagine Roman sandals on these original basalt stones—the oldest street you'll ever walk. Many of the stones under your feet were walked on by Caesar Augustus 2,000 years ago. After about 50 yards, turn right and follow a path uphill to the three huge arches of the...*

❷ **Basilica of Constantine** (Basilica Maxentius): Yes, these are big arches. But they represent only one-third of the original Basilica of Constantine, a mammoth hall of justice. The arches were

ROME

Rome: Republic and Empire (500 BC-AD 500)

Ancient Rome lasted for a thousand years, from about 500 BC to AD 500. During that time, Rome expanded from a small tribe of barbarians to a vast empire, then dwindled slowly to city size again. For the first 500 years, when Rome's armies made her ruler of the Italian peninsula and beyond, Rome was a republic governed by elected senators. Over the next 500 years, a time of world conquest and eventual decline, Rome was an empire ruled by a military-backed dictator.

Julius Caesar bridged the gap between republic and empire. This ambitious general and politician, popular with the people because of his military victories and charisma, suspended the Roman constitution and assumed dictatorial powers in about 50 BC. A few years later, he was assassinated by a conspiracy of senators. His adopted son, Augustus, succeeded him, and soon "Caesar" was not just a name but a title.

Emperor Augustus ushered in the Pax Romana, or Roman peace (AD 1-200), a time when Rome reached her peak and controlled an empire that stretched even beyond Eurail—from England to Egypt, Turkey to Morocco.

matched by a similar set along the Via Sacra side (only a few squat brick piers remain). Between them ran the central hall, which was spanned by a roof 130 feet high—about 55 feet higher than the side arches you see. (The stub of brick you see sticking up began an arch that once spanned the central hall.) The hall itself was as long as a football field, lavishly furnished (with colorful inlaid marble, a gilded bronze ceiling, and statues), and filled with strolling Romans. At the far (west) end was an enormous marble statue of Emperor Constantine on a throne. (Pieces of this statue, including a hand the size of a man, are on display in Rome's Capitoline Museums.)

This "basilica" was not a church but a Roman hall of justice. In a society that was as legal-minded as America is today, you needed a lot of lawyers—and a big place to put them. Citizens came here to work out matters like inheritances and building permits, or to sue somebody.

• *Now backtrack downhill and stroll deeper into the Forum, turning right along the...*

❸ **Via Sacra:** Stroll through the trees, down this main drag of the ancient city. Imagine being an out-of-town visitor during Rome's heyday—maybe from Gaul (modern France) or Londinium (modern London). You know a little Latin, but nothing would have prepared you for the bustle of Rome—a city of a million people, by far the biggest in Europe. This street would be swarming with tribunes, slaves, and courtesans. Chariots whizzed by. Wooden stalls lined the roads, where merchants peddled their goods.

On your right, you'll pass a building with a green door still swinging on its fourth-century hinges—the original bronze door to a temple that survived because it became a church shortly after the fall of Rome. This ancient temple is still in use, sometimes hosting modern exhibits. No wonder they call Rome the Eternal City.

• *Just past the ancient temple, 10 huge columns stand in front of a much newer-looking church. This colonnade was part of the...*

❹ **Temple of Antoninus Pius and Faustina:** The Senate built this temple to honor Emperor Antoninus Pius (AD 138-161) and his deified wife, Faustina. (The lintel's inscription calls them *"divo"* and *"divae."*) The 50-foot-tall Corinthian (leafy) columns must have been awe-inspiring to out-of-towners who grew up in thatched huts. Although the temple has been inhabited by a church, you can still see the basic layout—a staircase led to a shaded porch (the columns), which admitted you to the main building (now a church), where the statue of the god sat.

Picture a Roman priest climbing these steps to make an offering to the god inside. And imagine these columns with gilded capitals, supporting brightly painted statues in a triangular pediment, and the whole building capped with a gleaming bronze roof. The stately gray rubble of today's Forum is a faded black-and-white photograph of a 3-D Technicolor era.

The building is a microcosm of many changes that occurred after Rome fell. In medieval times, the temple was pillaged. Note the diagonal cuts high on the marble columns—a failed attempt by scavengers to cut through the pillars to pull them down for their precious stone. (They tried using vinegar and rope to cut the marble...but because vinegar also eats through rope, they abandoned the attempt.) In 1550, a church was housed inside the ancient temple. The green door shows the street level at the time of Michelangelo. The long staircase was underground until excavated in the 1800s.

• *With your back to the colonnade, walk straight ahead—jogging a bit to the right to stay on the path. The path leads to two sights associated with Rome's Vestal Virgins. Head for the three short columns connected by a wall, all that's left of the...*

❺ **Temple of Vesta:** This is perhaps Rome's most sacred spot. Notice that the temple remains are curved. Originally, this temple was circular, like a glorified farmer's hut—the kind Rome's first families lived in. Although we think of the Romans as decadent, in fact they prided themselves on their family values. People venerated their parents, grandparents, and ancestors, even keeping small statues of them in sacred shrines in their homes. This temple represented those family values on a large scale; its fire symbolized the "hearth" of the extended family that was Rome. As long as the sacred flame burned, Rome would stand. The flame was tended by six priestesses known as the Vestal Virgins.

• *Backtrack a few steps up the path, behind the Temple of Vesta. You'll find a few stairs that lead up to a big, enclosed field with two rectangular brick pools (just below the hill). This was the courtyard of the...*

❻ House of the Vestal Virgins: The Vestal Virgins lived in a two-story building surrounding a long central courtyard with two pools at one end. Rows of statues depicting leading Vestal Virgins flanked the courtyard. This place was the model—both architecturally and sexually—for medieval convents and monasteries.

Chosen from noble families before they reached the age of 10, the six Vestal Virgins each served a 30-year term. Honored and revered by the Romans, the Vestals even had their own box seats opposite the emperor in the Colosseum. The statues that line the courtyard honor dutiful Vestals.

Their sacred duty was to be ceremonial homemakers, tending the temple-home of the goddess Vesta. They brought water from a sacred spring, cooked sacred food, polished the ritual silverware, and—most importantly—made sure the hearth fire never went out.

As the name implies, a Vestal took a vow of chastity. If she served her term faithfully—abstaining for 30 years—she was given a huge dowry and allowed to marry. But if they found any Virgin who wasn't, she was strapped to a funeral car, paraded through the streets of the Forum, taken to a crypt, given a loaf of bread and a lamp...and buried alive. Many Vestals suffered the latter fate.

• *Looming just beyond this field is Palatine Hill—the corner of which may have been...*

❼ Caligula's Palace (Palace of Tiberius): Emperor Caligula (ruled AD 37-41) had a huge palace on Palatine Hill overlooking

the Forum. It actually sprawled down the hill into the Forum (some supporting arches remain in the hillside).

Caligula was not a nice person. He tortured enemies, stole senators' wives, and parked his chariot in handicap spaces. But Rome's luxury-loving emperors only added to the glory of the Forum, with each one trying to make his mark on history.

• *Return to the three short columns of the Temple of Vesta. Just downhill, you can't miss three very tall columns just beyond.*

❽ Temple of Castor and Pollux: These three columns—all that remain of a once-prestigious temple—have become the most photographed sight in the Forum. The temple was one of the city's oldest, built in the fifth century BC. It commemorated the Roman victory over the Tarquin, the notorious Etruscan king who once oppressed them. After the battle, the legendary twin brothers Castor and Pollux watered their horses here, at the Sacred Spring of Juturna (which has been excavated nearby). As a symbol of Rome's self-governing republic, the temple was often used as a meeting place of senators, and its front steps served as a podium for free speech.

• *Just beyond, the path spills into a flat, open area that stretches before you. This was the center of the ancient Forum.*

❾ The Forum's Main Square: The original Forum, or main square, was this flat patch about the size of a football field, stretching to the foot of Capitoline Hill. Surrounding it were temples, law courts, government buildings, and triumphal arches.

Rome was born right here. According to legend, twin brothers Romulus (Rome) and Remus were orphaned in infancy and raised by a she-wolf on top of Palatine Hill. Growing up, they found it hard to get dates. So they and their cohorts attacked the nearby Sabine tribe and kidnapped their women. After they made peace, this marshy valley became the meeting place and then the trading center for the scattered tribes on the surrounding hillsides.

Ancient Rome's population exceeded one million, more than any city until London and Paris in the 19th century. All those Roman masses lived in tiny apartments as we would live in tents at a campsite, basically just to sleep. The public space—their Forum, today's piazza—is where they did their living. Consider how, to this day, the piazza is still such an important part of any Italian town. Since Roman times, the piazza has reflected and accommodated the gregarious and outgoing nature of the Italian people.

The Forum is now rubble, but imagine it in its prime: blindingly brilliant marble buildings with 40-foot-high columns and shining metal roofs; rows of statues painted in realistic colors;

processional chariots rattling down Via Sacra. Mentally replace tourists in T-shirts with tribunes in togas. Imagine the buildings towering and the people buzzing around you while an orator gives a rabble-rousing speech from the Rostrum. If things still look like just a pile of rocks, at least tell yourself, "But Julius Caesar once leaned against these rocks."

• *And speaking of Julius Caesar, at the near end of the main square (the end closest to the Colosseum) find the foundations of a temple now sheltered by a peaked wood-and-metal roof.*

❿ Temple of Julius Caesar (Tempio del Divo Giulio, or Ara di Cesare): On March 15, in 44 BC, Julius Caesar (100-44 BC) was stabbed 23 times by political conspirators. After his assassination, Caesar's body was cremated on this spot (under the metal roof). Afterward, this temple was built to honor him. Peek behind the wall into the small apse area, where a mound of dirt usually has fresh flowers—given to remember the man who, more than any other, personified the greatness of Rome.

Although he was popular with the masses, not everyone liked Caesar's urban design or his politics. When he assumed dictatorial powers, he was ambushed and stabbed to death by a conspiracy of senators, including his adopted son, Brutus *("Et tu, Brute?")*.

The funeral was held here, facing the main square. The citizens gathered, and speeches were made. Mark Antony stood up to say (in Shakespeare's words), "Friends, Romans, countrymen, lend me your ears. I come to bury Caesar, not to praise him." When Caesar's body was burned, his adoring fans threw anything at hand on the fire, requiring the fire department to come put it out. Later, Emperor Augustus dedicated this temple in his name, making Caesar the first Roman to become a god.

• *Continue past the Temple of Julius Caesar, to the open area between the columns of the Temple of Antoninus Pius and Faustina (which we passed earlier) and the boxy brick building (the Curia). You can view these ruins of the Basilica Aemilia from a ramp next to the Temple of Antoninus Pius and Faustina, or (if the path is open) walk among them.*

⓫ Basilica Aemilia: Notice the layout. This was a long, rectangular building. The stubby columns all in a row form one long, central hall flanked by two side aisles. Medieval Christians required a larger meeting hall for their worship services than Roman temples provided, so they used the spacious Roman basilica as the model for their churches. Cathedrals from France to Spain to England, from Romanesque to Gothic to Renaissance, all have the same basic floor plan as a Roman basilica.

• *Now head for the big, well-preserved brick building with the triangular roof—the Curia. It's just to the right of the big triumphal arch at the foot of Capitoline Hill. While often closed, the building is impressive even from outside.*

⓬ The Curia (Senate House): The Curia was the most important political building in the Forum. Since the birth of the republic, this was the site of Rome's official center of government. Three hundred senators, elected by the citizens of Rome, donned their togas, tucked their scrolls under their arms, and climbed the steps into this great hall. Inside, they gave speeches, debated policy, and created the laws of the land. They sat with their backs to the walls, surrounding the big hall on three sides, in three rows of seats. At the far end sat the Senate president—and later, the emperor—on his podium. The vast room still echoes with stirring speeches and passionate debates.

The present Curia building dates from AD 283, when it replaced an earlier Senate building. It's so well preserved because it was used as a church since early Christian times. In the 1930s, it was restored as a historic site.

• *Go back down the Senate steps and find the 10-foot-high wall just to the left of the big arch, marked...*

⓭ Rostrum: Nowhere was Roman freedom of speech more apparent than at this "Speaker's Corner." The Rostrum was a raised platform, 10 feet high and 80 feet long, decorated with statues, columns, and the prows of ships.

On a stage like this, Rome's orators, great and small, tried to draw a crowd and sway public opinion. Picture the backdrop these speakers would have had—a mountain of marble buildings piling up on Capitoline Hill. Mark Antony rose to offer Caesar the laurel-leaf crown of kingship, which Caesar publicly (and hypocritically) refused—while privately becoming a dictator. Men such as Cicero—a contemporary of Julius Caesar—railed against the corruption and decadence that came with the city's newfound wealth. (Cicero paid the price: he was executed, and his head and hands were nailed to the Rostrum.)

In later years, when emperors ruled, it took real daring to speak out against the powers-that-be. Rome's democratic spirit was increasingly squelched. Eventually, the emperor and the army—not the Senate and the citizens—held ultimate power, and Rome's vast empire began to rot from within.

• *In front of the Rostrum are* **trees** *bearing fruits that were sacred to the ancient Romans: olives (provided food, oil for light, and preservatives), figs (tasty), and wine grapes (made a popular export product). Now turn your attention to the big arch to the right of the Rostrum, the...*

Rome Falls

Remember that Rome lasted 1,000 years—500 years of growth, 200 years of peak power, and 300 years of gradual decay. The fall had many causes, among them the barbarians who pecked away at Rome's borders. Christians blamed the fall on moral decay. Pagans blamed it on Christians. Socialists blamed it on a shallow economy based on the spoils of war. (Republicans blamed it on Democrats.)

Whatever the reasons, the far-flung empire could no longer keep its grip on conquered lands, and it pulled back. Barbarian tribes from Germany and Asia attacked the Italian peninsula and even looted Rome itself in AD 410, leveling many of the buildings in the Forum. In 476, when the last emperor checked out and switched off the lights, Europe plunged into centuries of ignorance, poverty, and weak government—the Dark Ages.

But Rome lived on in the Catholic Church. Christianity was the state religion of Rome's last generations. Emperors became popes (both called themselves "Pontifex Maximus"), senators became bishops, orators became priests, and basilicas became churches. The glory of Rome remains eternal.

⓮ Arch of Septimius Severus: In imperial times, the Rostrum's voices of democracy would have been dwarfed by images of the empire, such as the huge six-story-high Arch of Septimius Severus (AD 203). The reliefs commemorate the African-born emperor's battles in Mesopotamia. Near ground level, see soldiers marching captured barbarians back to Rome for the victory parade. More and more, Rome's economy was based on slave power and foreign booty rather than on domestic production. And despite efficient rule by emperors like Severus, Rome's empire began to crumble under the weight of its own corruption, disease, and decaying infrastructure.

• *As we near the end of Rome's history, we're also nearing the end of our tour. Our next stop is the Temple of Saturn. You can see it from here—it's the eight big columns just up the slope of Capitol Hill. Or you could make your way to it for a closer look.*

⓯ Temple of Saturn: These columns framed the entrance to the Forum's oldest temple (497 BC). Inside was a humble, very old wooden statue of the god Saturn. The statue's claim to fame was its pedestal, which held the gold bars, coins, and jewels of Rome's state treasury, the booty collected by conquering generals.

Even older than the Temple of Saturn is the **Umbilicus Urbis**, which stands nearby (next to the Arch of Septimius Severus). A humble brick ruin marks this historic "Navel of the City." The spot was considered the center of the cosmos, and all distances in the empire were measured from here.

• *Now turn your attention from the Temple of Saturn, one of the Forum's first buildings, to one of its last monuments. Find a lone, tall column standing in the Forum in front of the Rostrum. It's fluted and topped with a leafy Corinthian capital. This is the...*

⓰ Column of Phocas: This is the Forum's last monument (AD 608), a gift from the powerful Byzantine Empire to a fallen empire—Rome. Given to commemorate the pagan Pantheon's becoming a Christian church, it was a symbolic last nail in ancient Rome's coffin. After Rome's 1,000-year reign, the city was looted by Vandals, the population of a million-plus shrank to about 10,000, and the once-grand city center—the Forum—was abandoned, slowly covered up by centuries of silt and dirt. In the 1700s, an English historian named Edward Gibbon overlooked this spot from Capitoline Hill. Hearing Christian monks singing at these pagan ruins, he looked out at the few columns poking up from the ground, pondered the decline and fall of the Roman Empire, and thought, "Hmm, that's a catchy title..."

• *Your tour is over. If you want to see Palatine Hill, don't leave the Forum complex; you won't be allowed back in without a new ticket. Instead, return to the Arch of Titus.*

If you'd rather exit the Forum, refer to your map for possible exit locations. If heading for Capitoline Hill, your best escape is likely on the west side (behind #16 on the Roman Forum map in this chapter).

▲Palatine Hill (Monte Palatino)

Palatine Hill is nearly empty of tourists, but it's jam-packed with history—"the huts of Romulus," the huge Imperial Palace, a view of the Circus Maximus—but only the barest skeleton of rubble is left to tell the story.

We get our word "palace" from this hill, where the emperors chose to live. It was once so filled with palaces that later emperors had to build out. (Looking up at it from the Forum, you see the substructure that supported these long-gone palaces.) The Palatine

Museum contains statues and frescoes that help you imagine the luxury of the imperial Palatine. From the pleasant garden, you'll get an overview of the Forum. On the far side, unless excavations are blocking the viewpoint, look down into an emperor's private stadium and then beyond at the grassy Circus Maximus, once a chariot course. Imagine the cheers, jeers, and furious betting.

While many tourists consider Palatine Hill just extra credit after the Forum, it offers insight into the greatness of Rome that's well worth the effort. (And, if you're visiting the Colosseum or Forum, you've got a ticket whether you like it or not.)

Cost and Hours: Covered by same tickets and open same hours as Roman Forum, listed earlier.

Getting In: There are three entrances to the combined Palatine/Forum sight; see the map on page 846. The easiest for our tour is the entrance on Via di San Gregorio, 150 yards from the Colosseum. Upon entering, follow the path to the left as it winds to the top (stairs partway along offer a shortcut). Alternatively, if you sightsee the Forum first, you'll walk up from the Arch of Titus to Palatine Hill.

Expect Changes: Parts of Palatine Hill are often closed off due to ongoing archaeological work.

South of the Ancient Core
Baths of Caracalla (Terme di Caracalla)

Inaugurated by Emperor Caracalla in AD 216, this massive bath complex—supplied by its own branch of an aqueduct—could accommodate 1,600 visitors at a time. Today it's just a shell—a huge shell—with all of its sculptures and most of its mosaics moved to museums.

This sight is dramatic in part because nothing was built around or on top of it. It's stood here, in ruins, for 1,500 years. You'll see a two-story roofless brick building surrounded by a garden, bordered by ruined walls. The two large rooms at either end of the building were used for exercise. In between the exercise rooms was a pool flanked by two small mosaic-floored dressing rooms.

Cost and Hours: €8; open Mon 9:00-14:00, Tue-Sun 9:00 until one hour before sunset: April-Aug until 19:15, Sept until 19:00, Oct until 18:30, off-season closes as early as 16:30; last entry one hour before closing, audioguide-€5, good €8 guidebook, Metro: Circo Massimo, then a 5-minute walk south along Via delle Terme di Caracalla; +39 06 3996 7700, www.coopculture.it.

Capitoline Hill

Of Rome's famous seven hills, this is the smallest, tallest, and most famous—home of the ancient Temple of Jupiter and the center of city government for 2,500 years. There are several ways to get to the top of Capitoline Hill. If you're coming from the north (from Piazza Venezia), take Michelangelo's impressive stairway to the right of the big, white Victor Emmanuel Monu-

ment. Coming from the southeast (the Roman Forum), take the steep staircase near the Arch of Septimius Severus. From near Trajan's Forum along Via dei Fori Imperiali, take the winding road. All three converge at the top, in the square called Campidoglio (kahm-pee-DOHL-yoh).

▲Piazza del Campidoglio

This square atop the hill, once the religious and political center of ancient Rome, is still the home of the city's government. In the 1530s, the pope called on Michelangelo to reestablish this square as a grand center. Michelangelo placed the ancient equestrian statue of Marcus Aurelius as its focal point—very effective. (The original statue is now in the adjacent museum.) The twin buildings on either side are the Capitoline Museums. Behind the replica of the statue is the mayoral palace (Palazzo Senatorio).

Michelangelo intended that people approach the square from his grand stairway off Piazza Venezia. From the top of the stairway, you see the new Renaissance face of Rome, with its back to the Forum. Michelangelo gave the buildings the "giant order"—huge pilasters make the existing two-story buildings feel one-storied and more harmonious with the new square. Notice how the statues atop these buildings welcome you and then draw you in.

The terraces just downhill (past either side of the mayor's palace) offer grand views of the Forum. To the left of the mayor's palace is a copy of the famous she-wolf statue on a column. Farther down is *il nasone* ("the big nose"), a refreshing water fountain (see photo). Block the spout with your fingers, and water spurts up for drinking. Romans joke that a cheap Roman boy takes his date out for a drink at *il nasone*.

▲▲▲Capitoline Museums (Musei Capitolini)

Some of ancient Rome's most famous statues and art are housed in the two palaces (Palazzo dei Conservatori and Palazzo Nuovo) that flank the equestrian statue in the Campidoglio. They're connected by an underground passage that leads to the Tabularium, an ancient building with a panoramic overlook of the Forum.

Cost and Hours: €15, daily 9:30-19:30, last entry one hour before closing, videoguide-€7, good children's audioguide-€5, +39 06 0608, www.museicapitolini.org.

Visiting the Museum: You'll enter at the Palazzo dei Conservatori (on your right as you face the equestrian statue), cross underneath the square (beneath the Palazzo Senatorio, the mayoral palace, not open to public), and exit from the Palazzo Nuovo (on your left). This enjoyable museum complex claims to be the world's oldest, founded in 1471 when a pope gave ancient statues to the citizens of Rome. Many of the museum's statues have gone on to become instantly recognizable cultural icons, including the 13th-century *Capitoline She-Wolf* (the little statues of Romulus and Remus were added in the Renaissance). Don't miss the *Boy Extracting a Thorn* and the enchanting *Commodus as Hercules*. Behind Commodus is a statue of his dad, Marcus Aurelius, on a horse. The only surviving equestrian statue of a Roman emperor, this was the original centerpiece of the square (where a copy stands today). Christians in the Dark Ages thought that the statue's hand was raised in blessing, which probably led to their misidentifying him as Constantine, the first Christian emperor. While most pagan statues were destroyed by Christians, "Constantine" was spared.

The museum's second-floor café, **Caffè Capitolino,** has a splendid patio offering city views. It's lovely at sunset (public entrance for those without a museum ticket off Piazzale Caffarelli and through door #4).

The **Tabularium,** built in the first century BC, once held the archives of ancient Rome. (The word Tabularium comes from "tablet," on which Romans wrote their laws.) You won't see any tablets, but you'll get a stunning view of the Forum from the windows.

Capitoline Hill & Piazza Venezia

1. Piazza del Campidoglio
2. Capitoline Museums
3. Copy of She-Wolf Statue
4. "Il Nasone" Water Fountain
5. Mussolini's Balcony

The **Palazzo Nuovo** houses mostly portrait busts of forgotten emperors. But it also has two must-see statues: the *Dying Gaul* and the *Capitoline Venus* (both on the first floor up).

▲Mamertine Prison (Carcer Tullianum Museum)

This 2,500-year-old cistern-like prison on Capitoline Hill is where, according to Christian tradition, the Romans imprisoned Saints Peter and Paul. Today it's a small but impressive archaeological site using the latest technology to illustrate what you might unearth when digging in Rome: a pagan sacred site, an ancient Roman prison, an early Christian pilgrimage destination, or a medieval church. After learning the context using the included videoguide, and browsing artifacts (including the skeletons of those executed with their hands still tied behind their backs), you can walk to the bottom of this dank cistern under an original Roman stone roof—marvel at its engineering. Amid fat rats and rotting corpses, unfortunate prisoners of the emperor awaited slow deaths here. It's said that a miraculous fountain sprang up inside so Peter could convert and baptize his jailers, who were also subsequently martyred. This pricey sight is a good value for pilgrims and antiquities wonks.

Cost and Hours: €10, includes videoguide, €24 combo-ticket includes Colosseum and Roman Forum/Palatine Hill, daily 9:00-17:00, may stay open later in summer, Clivo Argentario 1, +39 06 698 961.

Piazza Venezia

This vast square, dominated by the big, white Victor Emmanuel Monument, is a major transportation hub and the focal point of modern Rome. With your back to the monument (you'll get the best views from the terrace by the guards and eternal flame), look down Via del Corso, the city's axis, surrounded by Rome's classiest shopping district. In the 1930s, Benito Mussolini whipped up Italy's nationalistic fervor from a balcony above the square (it's the less-grand building on the left). Mussolini lied to his people, mixing fear and patriotism to push his country to the extreme right and embroil the Italians in expensive and regrettable wars. In 1945, they shot Mussolini and hung him from a meat hook in Milan.

With your back still to the monument, circle around the left side to reach two staircases leading up Capitoline Hill. One is Michelangelo's grand staircase up to the Campidoglio. The steeper of the two leads to **Santa Maria in Aracoeli,** a good example of the earliest style of Christian church. The contrast between this climb-on-your-knees ramp to God's house and Michelangelo's elegant stairs illustrates the changes Renaissance humanism brought civilization.

▲Victor Emmanuel Monument

This oversized monument to Italy's first king, built to celebrate the 50th anniversary of the country's unification in 1861, was part of Italy's push to overcome the new country's strong regionalism and create a national identity. Today, the monument is appreciated for the views it provides over the city (especially from the top of its pricey elevator), and it also holds a humble museum for Italian patriots.

The scale of the monument is over the top: 200 feet high, 500 feet wide. The 43-foot-long statue of the king on his high horse is

one of the biggest eques-
trian statues in the world.
The king's moustache
forms an arc five feet long,
and a person could sit
within the horse's hoof. At
the base of this statue, Italy's Tomb of the Unknown
Soldier (flanked by Italian
flags and armed guards) is

watched over by the goddess Roma (with the gold mosaic background). With its gleaming white sheen (from a recent scrubbing)
and enormous scale, the monument provides a vivid sense of what
Ancient Rome looked like at its peak—imagine the Forum filled
with shiny, grandiose buildings like this one.

Cost and Hours: Free to climb stairs of monument, €12 to
ride Rome from the Sky elevator and enter Risorgimento Museum
(access to museum limited to small groups entering twice hourly,
www.risorgimento.it). Open daily 9:30-19:30, last elevator ticket
sold 45 minutes before closing, a few WCs scattered throughout,
+39 06 0608, https://vive.beniculturali.it.

Jewish Quarter
From the 16th through the 19th century, Rome's Jewish population
was forced to live in a cramped ghetto at an often-flooded bend of
the Tiber River. While the medieval Jewish ghetto is long gone,
this area—between Capitoline Hill and the Campo de' Fiori—is
still home to Rome's synagogue and fragments of its Jewish heritage.

The Imperial Forums
Though the original Roman Forum is the main attraction for today's tourists, there are several more ancient forums nearby, known
collectively as "The Imperial Forums." The forums stretch in a line
along Via dei Fori Imperiali, from Piazza Venezia to the Colosseum. The boulevard was built by the dictator Benito Mussolini
in the 1930s—supposedly so he could look out his office window
on Piazza Venezia and see the Colosseum, creating a military parade ground and a visual link between the glories of the imperial
past with what he thought would be Italy's glorious imperial future.
Today, the once-noisy boulevard is a pleasant walk, since it is closed
to private vehicles—and, on Sundays, to all traffic.

The ruins are out in the open, never crowded, and free to look
down on from street level at any time, any day.

For an overview of the archaeological area, take this walk from

The Imperial Forums

VIA BATTISTI

100 Meters
100 Yards

MUSEUM OF
IMPERIAL
FORUMS

ROMAN
HOUSE

S. MARIA
DI LORETO

SS. NOME
DI MARIA

Largo
Magnanapoli

To
Piazza della
Repubblica

VIA 4 NOV.

To
Termini

VIA PANISPERNA

WALK
BEGINS

TRAJAN'S
COLUMN

MILIZIE
TOWER

Piazza
Venezia

CAESAR'S
FORUM
SHOW

BASILICA
ULPIA

WALKWAY

TRAJAN'S
MARKET

N

TRAJAN'S
FORUM

B

MONTI

VICTOR
EMMANUEL
MONUMENT

VIA
DEI

TRAJAN

AUGUSTUS'
FORUM

VIA BACCINA

STA. MARIA
ARACOELI

JULIUS
CAESAR

AUGUSTUS

NERVA'S
FORUM

CAPITOLINE
HILL

CAESAR'S
FORUM

NERVA

FORI IMPERIALI

BLEACHERS

VIA
MADONNA
D. MONTI

PALAZZO
NUOVO

SANTI LUCA
E MARTINA

WALL

Piazza
Campodoglio

MAMERTINE
PRISON

SANTA MARIA
ARACOELI

B

B

MEDIEVAL
TOWER

To
Cavour

VIA CAVOUR

VIA DEI FORI IMPERIALI WALK
STANDING RUINS
ORIGINAL FOOTPRINT
RUINS (BELOW STREET LEVEL)

ROMAN
FORUM

WALK ENDS

To
Colosseum,
Colosseo M
&

ROMAN FORUM
ENTRANCE

Piazza Venezia down Via dei Fori Imperiali to the end of the Imperial Forums.

◆ Self-Guided Walk: Start at Trajan's Column, the colossal pillar that stands alongside Piazza Venezia.

Trajan's Column: The world's grandest column from antiquity (rated ▲▲) anchors the first of the forums we'll see—Trajan's Forum. The 140-foot column is decorated with a spiral relief of 2,500 figures trumpeting the emperor's exploits. It has stood for centuries as a symbol of a truly cosmopolitan civilization. At one point, the ashes of Trajan and his wife were held in the base, and the sun glinted off a polished bronze statue of Trajan at the top. Since the 1500s, St. Peter has been on top. (Where's the original bronze statue of Trajan? Spaghetti pots.) Built as a stack of 17 marble doughnuts, the

ROME

column is hollow (note the small window slots) with a spiral staircase inside, leading up to the balcony.

The **relief** unfolds like a scroll, telling the story of Rome's last and greatest foreign conquest, Trajan's defeat of Dacia (modern-day Romania). Originally, the entire story was painted in bright colors. If you were to unwind the scroll, it would stretch over two football fields—it's far longer than the frieze around the Parthenon in Athens.

• *Now, start heading toward the Colosseum, walking along the left side of Via dei Fori Imperiali. You're walking alongside...*

Trajan's Forum: The dozen-plus gray columns mark one of the grandest structures in Trajan's Forum—the Basilica Ulpia, the largest law court of its day. Nearby stood two libraries that contained the world's knowledge in Greek and Latin. (The internet of the day, contained in two big buildings.)

Rome peaked under Emperor Trajan (ruled AD 98-117), when the empire stretched from England to the Sahara, from Spain to the Fertile Crescent. A triumphant Trajan returned to Rome with his booty and shook it all over the city. Most was spent on this forum, complete with temples, law courts, and the monumental column trumpeting his exploits. To build his forum, Trajan cut away a ridge that once connected the Quirinal and Capitoline hills, creating this valley. This was the largest forum ever, and its opulence astounded even jaded Romans. Looking at this, you can only think that for every grand monument here, there was untold hardship and suffering in the Barbarian world.

• *Most astounding of all was Trajan's Market. That's the big, semicircular brick structure nestled into the cutaway curve of Quirinal Hill. If you want a closer look, a pedestrian pathway leads you right up among the ruins.*

Trajan's Market: This structure was part shopping mall, part warehouse, and part administration building and/or government offices. For now the conventional wisdom holds that at ground level, the 13 tall (shallow) arches housed shops selling fresh fruit, vegetables, and flowers to people who passed by on the street. The 26 arched windows (above) lit a covered walkway lined

with shops that sold wine and olive oil. On the roof (now lined with a metal railing) ran a street that likely held still more shops and offices, making about 150 in all. Shoppers could browse through goods from every corner of Rome's vast empire—exotic fruits from Africa, spices from Asia, and fish-and-chips from Londinium.

Above the semicircle, the upper floors of the complex housed bureaucrats in charge of a crucial element of city life: doling out free grain to unemployed citizens, who lived off the wealth plundered from distant lands. Better to pacify them than risk a riot. Above the offices, at the very top, rises a (leaning) tower added in the Middle Ages.

• *Return to the main street and continue toward the Colosseum for about 100 more yards.*

You're still walking alongside Trajan's Forum, but the ruins you see in this section are from the medieval era. These are the foundations of the old neighborhood that was built atop the ancient city. In modern times, that neighborhood was cleared out to build the new boulevard.

You'll soon reach a bronze **statue of Trajan** himself. Though the likeness is ancient, this bronze statue is not. It was erected by the dictator Benito Mussolini when he had the modern boulevard built. Notice the date on the pedestal—Anno XI. That would be "the 11th year of the Fascist Renovation of Italy"—i.e., 1933.

Across the street is a similar statue of **Julius Caesar.** It marks the first of these imperial forums, **Caesar's Forum,** built by Julius in 46 BC as an extension of the Roman Forum. Near Julius stand the three remaining columns of his forum's Temple of Venus—the patron goddess of the Julian family.

• *Continue along (down the left side). As Trajan's Forum narrows to an end, you reach a statue of Emperor Augustus that indicates...*

The Forums of Augustus and Nerva: The statue captures **Emperor Augustus** in his famous hailing-a-cab pose (a copy of the original, which you can see at the Vatican Museums). In fact, this is his "commander talking to his people" pose. Behind him was the Forum of Augustus. It separated fancy "downtown Rome" from the workaday world beyond.

Farther along is a statue of **Emperor Nerva,** trying but failing to have the commanding presence of Augustus. Behind Nerva, you can get a closer look at his forum.

• *You've reached the end of the Imperial Forums. You're at the intersection of Via dei Fori Imperiali and busy Via Cavour. Nearby is the colorful neighborhood of Monti, with fun eateries. A few blocks up busy Via Cavour is the Cavour Metro stop. From there, you could turn right to find St. Peter-in-Chains Church. Across Via dei Fori Imperiali is an entrance to the Roman Forum; 100 yards farther down Via dei Fori Imperiali (on the left) is a TI with a handy café and WC.*

Near the Imperial Forums

Several worthwhile sights sit north of Via dei Fori Imperiali from the Roman Forum—and offer a break from the crowds. If you'll be here in the evening, consider taking in a sound-and-light show (see page 902).

▲The Roman House at Palazzo Valentini
(Le Domus Romane di Palazzo Valentini)

For a quality (air-conditioned) experience, duck into this underground series of ancient spaces at the base of Trajan's Column. The 50-minute tour with good English narration and evocative lighting features scant remains of an elegant ancient Roman house and bath. The highlight is a small theater where you'll learn the entire story depicted by the 2,600 figures that parade around the 650-foot relief carved onto Trajan's Column.

Cost and Hours: €12; Wed-Mon 10:00-19:00, closed Tue, last entry one hour before closing, may have shorter hours off-season; departures hourly but not all in English—check online, limited group sizes—reservations smart (€1.50 fee), +39 06 2276 1280, www.palazzovalentini.it.

▲▲St. Peter-in-Chains Church (San Pietro in Vincoli)

A church was first built on this spot in the fifth century, to house the chains that once restrained St. Peter. Today's church, restored in the 15th century, is famous for its Michelangelo statue of Moses, intended for the (unfinished) tomb of Pope Julius II. Check out the chains under the high altar, then focus on mighty Moses. (Note this isn't the famous St. Peter's—that's in Vatican City.)

Pope Julius II commissioned Michelangelo to build a massive tomb, with 48 huge statues, topped with a grand statue of this egomaniacal pope. The pope had planned to have his tomb placed in the center of St. Peter's Basilica. When Julius died, the work had barely begun, and no one had the money or necessary commitment to Julius to finish the project.

In 1542, some of the remnants of the tomb project were brought to St. Peter-in-Chains and pieced together by Michelangelo's assistants. Some of the best statues ended up elsewhere, such as the *Prisoners* in Florence and the *Slaves* in the Louvre. *Moses* and the Louvre's *Slaves* are the only statues Michelangelo personally completed for the project. Flanking *Moses* are the Old Testament sister-wives of Jacob, Leah (to our right) and Rachel, both begun by Michelangelo but probably finished by pupils.

The powerful statue of Moses—mature Michelangelo—is worth studying. Moses has received the Ten Commandments. As he holds the stone tablets, his eyes show a man determined to stop his tribe from worshipping the golden calf and idols...a man determined to win salvation for the people of Israel. Why the horns? Centuries ago, the Hebrew word for "rays" was mistranslated as "horns."

ROME

Pantheon Neighborhood

Cost and Hours: Free, daily 7:15-12:30 & 15:00-19:00, Oct-March until 18:00, modest dress required; the church is a 10-minute uphill walk from the Colosseum, or a shorter, simpler walk (but with more steps) from the Cavour Metro stop; +39 06 9784 4950.

PANTHEON NEIGHBORHOOD

Besides being home to ancient sites and historic churches, the area around the Pantheon is another part of Rome with an urban village feel. Wander narrow streets, sample the many shops and eateries, and gather with the locals in squares marked by bubbling fountains.

Exploring this area is especially nice in the evening, when restaurants bustle and streets are jammed with foot traffic. For a self-guided walk in this neighborhood from Campo de' Fiori to the Trevi Fountain (and ending at the Spanish Steps), see my "Heart of Rome Walk," earlier.

▲▲▲Pantheon

For the greatest look at the splendor of Rome, antiquity's best-preserved interior is a must. Built two millennia ago, this influential domed temple served as the model for Michelangelo's dome of St. Peter's and many others.

Cost and Hours: Free, daily 9:00-19:00, closed for Mass Sat at 17:00 and Sun at 10:30; reservations may be required on weekends—book at http://pantheon.cultura.gov.it, +39 06 6830 0230, www.pantheonroma.com.

When to Go: Avoid midday, when the Pantheon is packed. If you show up right when it opens, you'll have it all to yourself.

Dress Code: Short shorts and bare shoulders are not allowed.

Tours: The Pantheon offers an audioguide (through an app) and guided tours; neither is worth the high price. 🎧 Instead, download my free Pantheon audio tour.

Visiting the Pantheon: The Pantheon was a Roman temple dedicated to all (pan) of the gods (theos). The original temple was built in 27 BC by Emperor Augustus' son-in-law, Marcus Agrippa. In fact, the inscription below the triangular pediment proclaims (in Latin), "Marcus Agrippa, son of Lucio, three times consul, made this." But after a couple of fires, the structure we see today was completely rebuilt by Emperor Hadrian around AD 120. After the fall of Rome, the Pantheon became a Christian church (from "all the gods" to "all the martyrs"), which saved it from architectural cannibalism and ensured its upkeep through the Dark Ages.

The dome is what makes this building unique—and perhaps the most influential architectural design in art history. The Pantheon's dome was the model for the Florence cathedral dome, which launched the Renaissance, and for Michelangelo's dome of St. Peter's, which capped it all off. Even the US Capitol in Washington, DC, was inspired by this dome.

Wander into the **portico** with its forest of 16 enormous **columns.** They're 40 feet tall and 15 feet around, made of red-and-gray granite. Whereas many ancient columns are a stack of cylindrical drums, these columns are each a single piece of stone. Imagine how impressive this portico was in its heyday, when the ceiling was covered with shiny bronze plating. Check out the giant doorway—it's considered original. The **doors** are 23 feet tall and made of bronze. The magnificent, soaring **dome,** the largest made until the Renaissance, is set on a circular base. The mathematical perfection of this dome-on-a-base design is a testament to Roman engineering; it's as high as it is wide—

142 feet. To picture it, imagine a basketball wedged inside a waste-basket so that it just touches bottom.

The dome is made from concrete, a Roman invention. It gets lighter and thinner as it reaches the top. The base of the dome is 23 feet thick and made from heavy concrete mixed with travertine, while near the top, it's less than five feet thick and made with a lighter volcanic rock (pumice) mixed in. Note the square indentations in the surface of the dome. This **coffered ceiling** reduces the weight of the dome without compromising strength. The walls are strengthened by brick relieving arches ("blind" arches)—visible in the exposed brickwork in a few of the interior niches and easy to see from outside.

Both Brunelleschi and Michelangelo studied this dome before building their own, in Florence and the Vatican, respectively. (The grandiose vision for St. Peter's Basilica was to place the dome of the Pantheon atop the Forum's Basilica of Constantine.)

At the top, the **oculus** is the building's only light source. It's completely open and almost 30 feet across. The 1,800-year-old **floor**—with 80 percent of its original stones surviving—has holes in it and slants toward the edges to let rainwater drain. Although some of the floor's marble has been replaced, the design—alternating circles and squares—is original.

While its ancient statuary is long gone, today the Pantheon's interior holds decorative sculptures and the tombs of important people from more recent centuries. The artist **Raphael** (1483-1520) lies in a stone coffin to the left of the main altar, in a lighted glass niche.

In his will, Raphael asked to be buried in the Pantheon, and he himself commissioned the Madonna and Child statue above his tomb. City fathers were glad to honor the man who'd done so much to beautify Rome with paintings, frescoes, and tapestries (which you can see in today's Vatican Museums and elsewhere). Facing each other across the rotunda are the tombs of modern Italy's first two kings, members of the House of Savoy: **Victor Emmanuel II** and **Umberto I.** Beneath Umberto's tomb lies that of his queen (and first cousin), Margherita.

▲▲Churches near the Pantheon

The following churches are free to visit; modest dress is recommended. The **Church of San Luigi dei Francesi** has a magnificent chapel with paintings by Caravaggio (free, Mon-Sat 9:30-12:45 & 14:30-18:30, Sun from 11:30, between Pantheon and north end of Piazza Navona, www.saintlouis-rome.net). The only Gothic church in Rome is the **Church of Santa Maria sopra Minerva,** with a little-known Michelangelo statue, *Christ Bearing the Cross* (free, daily 9:00-12:00 & 16:00-19:00; on a little square behind the Pantheon, to the east, www.santamariasopraminerva.it). The **Church of Sant'Ignazio,** several blocks east of the Pantheon, is a riot of Baroque illusions with a false dome (free, daily 9:00-19:00, www.chiesasantignazio.it). A few blocks away, across Corso Vittorio Emanuele, is the rich and Baroque **Gesù Church,** headquarters of the Jesuits in Rome (free, generally Mon-Sat 7:30-12:30 & 17:00-19:30, Sun 9:00-12:30 & 17:00-20:00, interesting daily ceremony at 17:30, www.chiesadelgesu.org).

▲Trevi Fountain

The bubbly Baroque fountain, worth ▲▲ by night, is a minor sight to art scholars...but a major nighttime gathering spot for teens on the make and tourists tossing coins. Those coins are collected daily to feed Rome's poor.

For more on the fountain, see page 836.

VATICAN CITY

Vatican City, the world's smallest country, contains St. Peter's Basilica (with Michelangelo's exquisite *Pietà*) and the Vatican Museums (with Michelangelo's Sistine Chapel). The shop (with info/ticket desk), just to the left of St. Peter's Basilica as you're facing it, can answer questions (www.vaticanstate.va).

Planning Your Time: Consider the following time estimates while planning your visit. At a brisk pace, seeing St. Peter's Square takes 15 minutes; the basilica interior requires an hour (plus the line to get inside); the dome climb is an hour; and the museums take at least 2.5 hours. The entrances to St. Peter's and the Vatican Museums are a 15-minute walk apart (follow the outside of the Vatican wall, which links the two sights). From the Sistine Chapel—in the deepest recesses of the Vatican Museums—to the entrance of St. Peter's is about 30 minutes). The nearest Metro stop—Ottaviano—still involves a 10-minute walk to either sight. Budget time for lunch and walking.

When to Go: The basilica's security line tends to be shorter before 9:30 and late in the day, especially after 16:00 (just as sunbeams begin working their magic on the altar). The basilica is

Vatican City & Nearby

closed (and the square is jammed) on Wednesday mornings during the papal audience, until roughly 13:00.

At the Vatican Museums, crowds are generally lighter on weekdays after 14:00 (the later, the better) and on Wednesday mornings, when most tourists are at St. Peter's attending the papal audience. The worst days are Saturdays, the last Sunday of the month (a free-entry day), Mondays, rainy days, and any day before or after a holiday closure.

St. Peter's Square

St. Peter's Square, with its ring of columns, symbolizes the arms of the church welcoming everyone—believers and nonbelievers—in its motherly embrace. It was designed a century after Michelangelo by the Baroque architect Gian Lorenzo Bernini, who did much of the work that we'll see inside. Numbers first: 284 columns, 56 feet high, in stern Doric style. Topping them are Bernini's 140 favorite saints, each 10 feet tall. The "square" itself is actually elliptical, 660 by 500 feet (roughly the same dimensions as the Colosseum). Though large, it's designed like a saucer, a little higher around the edges, so that even when full of crowds (as it often is), it allows those on the periphery to see above the throngs.

The **obelisk** in the center is 90 feet of solid granite weighing more than 300 tons. It once stood about 100 yards from its current location, in the center of the circus course (to the left of where St. Peter's is today). Think for a second about how much history this monument has seen. Originally erected in Egypt more than 2,000 years ago, it witnessed the fall of the pharaohs to the Greeks and then to the Romans. Then the emperor Caligula plundered the obelisk and relocated it to imperial Rome, where it stood impassively watching the slaughter of Christians at the racecourse and the torture of Protestants by the Inquisition (in the yellow-and-rust-colored building just outside the square, to the left of the church). Today, it watches over the church, a reminder that each civilization builds on the previous ones. The puny cross on top reminds us that Christian culture has cast but a thin veneer over our pagan origins.

▲▲▲St. Peter's Basilica (Basilica San Pietro)

There is no doubt: This is the richest and grandest church on earth. To call it vast is like calling Einstein smart. Plaques on the floor show you where other, smaller churches would end if they were placed inside. The ornamental cherubs would dwarf a large man. Birds roost inside, and thousands of people wander about, heads craned heavenward, hardly noticing each other. Don't miss Michelangelo's *Pietà* (behind bulletproof glass) to the right of the entrance. Bernini's altar work and twisting, towering canopy are brilliant.

Cost and Hours: Free, daily 7:00-19:00, Oct-March until 18:30. The church closes on Wednesday mornings during papal audiences (until roughly 13:00). Masses occur daily throughout the day. Info: +39 06 6988 2019, www.vaticanstate.va.

Getting There: Take the Metro to Ottaviano, then walk 10 minutes south on Via Ottaviano. The #40 express bus drops off at Piazza Pio, next to Castel Sant'Angelo—a 10-minute walk from St. Peter's. The more crowded bus #64, beloved by pickpockets, stops just outside St. Peter's Square to the south (get off the bus after it crosses the Tiber, at the first stop past the tunnel; backtrack toward the tunnel and turn left when you see the rows of columns; the return bus stop is adjacent to the tunnel). Bus #492 heads through the center of town, stopping at Largo Argentina, and gets you near Piazza Risorgimento (get off when you see the Vatican walls). A few other handy buses (see page 818) get you to the general Vatican area. A taxi from Termini train station costs about €15.

Church Services: Mass, generally in Italian, is said varyingly in the south (left) transept, the Blessed Sacrament Chapel (on right side of nave), or at the main altar. Confirm times on the signboard as you enter. Typical schedule: Mon-Sat at 8:30, 9:00, 10:00, 11:00, 12:00, and at 17:00 (in Latin, at the main altar); Sun and holidays at 9:00, 10:30 (in Latin), 12:30, 13:00, 16:00, 17:00 (vespers), and 18:00.

Tours: ∩ Download my free St. Peter's Basilica **audio tour.** You can "rent" an **audioguide** (€5 for the church, €15 adds the dome), but you'll probably be told to download their app onto your

ROME

St. Peter's Basilica

Not to Scale

Vatican Gardens

APSE

MAIN ALTAR

DOME ENTRANCE

WINTER CRYPT ENTRANCE

TREASURY MUSEUM

VATICAN MUSEUMS (GRAY AREA)

NAVE

SISTINE CHAPEL

GROUP EXIT FROM SISTINE CHAPEL (LIKELY CLOSED)

Courtyard

DOME CLIMB EXIT

NARTHEX

EXIT ENTRANCE STEPS

SWISS GUARD (LAST-MINUTE POPE TICKETS)

AUDIOGUIDES, WC & BAGGAGE CHECK

PLATFORM

Route to church entrance

St. Peter's Square

1. Holy Door
2. Charlemagne's Coronation Site
3. Michelangelo's Greek-Cross Church
4. St. Andrew Statue; View of Dome; Crypt Entrance
5. St. Peter Statue (with Kissable Toe)
6. Pope John XXIII
7. Main Altar (under Bernini's Canopy & over Peter's Tomb)
8. BERNINI – Dove Window & Throne of St. Peter
9. Peter's Crucifixion Site
10. RAPHAEL – Mosaic Copy of The Transfiguration
11. MICHELANGELO – Pietà
12. Tomb of Pope John Paul II
13. Blessed Sacrament Chapel
14. Treasury Museum
15. Dome Entrance

ROME

phone and activate it with a code. At the same desk, ask about **guided tours** of the basilica, which leave sporadically.

To see St. Peter's original grave, you can take a *Scavi* (excavations) tour into the **Necropolis** under the basilica (€13, 1.5 hours, ages 15 and up only). Book at least two months in advance by email (scavi@fsp.va) for the fastest reply; go to www.scavi.va (select "Excavations Office") for details. No response means they're booked.

Dome Climb: You can take an elevator or climb 231 stairs to the roof, then climb another 323 steps to the top of the dome. The entry to the elevator is just outside the north (right) side of the basilica—look for signs to the *cupola*. If you're climbing the dome without your travel partner, confirm with the staff where you'll exit before you split up (€10 for elevator to roof, then take stairs; €8 to climb stairs all the way, allow an hour to go up and down, daily 7:00-17:00, last entry one hour before closing if you take the stairs the whole way).

Baggage Check: The free bag check (mandatory for bags larger than a purse or day pack) is inside security, but outside the basilica (to the right as you face the entrance).

Vatican Museums Tickets: The shop on St. Peter's Square (on the left as you face the basilica—see "Visitor Information," earlier) has a ticket/info desk that can help you book same-day, timed-entry tickets for the Vatican Museums. While they essentially have access to the same tickets that you can book online, if you show up without a reservation, stopping by this desk before making the hike over to the museums could save you time in line. (For other ticketing options, see "Vatican Museums," later.)

Services: WCs are on both sides of St. Peter's Square (by the shop and just outside security), near the baggage check down the steps by the church entrance, and on the roof.

⊘ Self-Guided Tour

To sample the basilica's highlights, follow these points:

The **narthex** (portico) is itself bigger than most churches. Its huge white columns date from the first church (fourth century). Five famous bronze doors lead into the church. Made from the melted-down bronze of the original door of Old St. Peter's, the central door was the first Renaissance work in Rome (c. 1450). It's only opened on special occasions.

The far-right entrance is the ❶ **Holy Door,** opened only during Holy Years (and special "Jubilee" years designated by the pope). On Christmas Eve every 25 years, the pope knocks three times with a silver hammer and the door opens, welcoming pilgrims to pass through.

Looking down the nave, we get a sense of the splendor of ancient Rome that was carried on by the Catholic Church. The floor plan, with a central aisle (nave) flanked by two side aisles, is based on that of ancient Roman basilicas—large halls built to accommodate business and legal meetings. In fact, many of the stones used to build St. Peter's were scavenged from the ruined law courts of ancient Rome.

On the floor near the central doorway is a round slab of porphyry stone in the maroon color of ancient Roman officialdom. This is the spot where, on Christmas night in AD 800, the king of the Franks ❷ **Charlemagne was crowned** Holy Roman Emperor.

Stand at the very back of the nave and survey the heavenly expanse. It's a riot of marble, gold, stucco, mosaics, columns of stone, and pillars of light. As the symbol of global Catholicism, this church is appropriately big. Size before beauty: The golden window at the far end is two football fields away. The dove in the golden window has the wingspan of a 747 (OK, maybe not quite, but it *is* big). The church covers six acres. The babies at the base of the pillars along the main hall (the nave) are adult-size. The lettering in the gold band along the top of the pillars is seven feet high. Really. The church has a capacity of 60,000 standing worshippers (or 1,200 tour groups).

• *Now, walk straight up the center of the nave toward the altar.*

Michelangelo was 71 when asked to take over the church project and cap it with a dome. He agreed, intending to put the dome over Donato Bramante's original ❸ **Greek-cross floor plan.** In optimistic Renaissance times, this symmetrical arrangement symbolized perfection—the orderliness of the created world and the goodness of man (who was created in God's image). But Michelangelo was a Renaissance Man in Counter-Reformation times. The Church, struggling against Protestants and its own corruption, opted for a plan designed to impress the world with its grandeur—the Latin cross of the Crucifixion, with its nave extended to accommodate the grand religious spectacles of the Baroque period.

Park yourself in front of the ❹ **statue of St. Andrew** to the left of the altar, the guy holding an X-shaped cross. (Note that the **entrance to the crypt** is usually here; in winter it's by the dome entrance.) Like Andrew, gaze up into the dome, and also like him, gasp.

The **dome** soars higher than a football field on end, 448 feet from the floor of the cathedral to the top of the lantern. It glows

with light from its windows, the blue-and-gold mosaics creating a cool, solemn atmosphere. In this majestic vision of heaven (not painted by Michelangelo), we see (above the windows) Jesus, Mary, and a ring of saints, rings of more angels above them, and, way up in the ozone, God the Father (a blur of blue and red, unless you have binoculars).

Look closely at the niche. If you line up the cross on the altar with the dove in the window, you'll notice that the niche below the cross is just off-center compared with the rest of the church. Why? Because Michelangelo built the church around the traditional location of the tomb, not the actual location—about two feet away—discovered by modern archaeology.

Back in the nave—on the right side, roughly facing the crypt entrance—sits a bronze ❺ **statue of St. Peter** under a canopy. This is one of a handful of pieces of art that were in the earlier church. In one hand he holds keys, the symbol of the authority given him by Christ, while with the other hand he blesses us. His big right toe has been worn smooth by the lips of pilgrims and foot fetishists. If the statue is accessible, stand in line and kiss it, or, to avoid foot-and-mouth disease, touch your hand to your lips, then rub the toe. This is simply an act of reverence with no legend attached, though you can make one up if you like.

• *Circle to the right around the statue of Peter to find the lighted glass niche.*

❻ **Pope John XXIII,** whose papacy lasted from 1958 to 1963, is nicknamed "the good pope." He is best known for initiating the landmark Vatican II Council (1962-1965) that instituted major reforms, bringing the Church into the modern age. In 2000, during the beatification process (a stop on the way to sainthood), Church authorities checked his body, and it was surprisingly fresh. So they moved it upstairs, put it behind glass, and now old Catholics who remember him fondly enjoy another stop on their St. Peter's visit. Pope John was canonized in 2014.

Sitting over St. Peter's tomb, the ❼ **main altar** (the white marble slab with cross and candlesticks) beneath the dome and canopy is used only when the pope himself says Mass. He sometimes conducts the Sunday morning service when he's in town, a sight worth seeing.

The tiny altar would be lost in this enormous church if it weren't for Gian Lorenzo Bernini's seven-story bronze canopy (God's "four-poster bed"), which "extends" the altar upward and reduces the perceived distance between floor and ceiling. The corkscrew columns echo the marble ones that surrounded the altar/tomb in Old St. Peter's. Some of the bronze used here was taken and melted down from the ancient Pantheon.

Bernini (1598-1680), the Michelangelo of the Baroque era,

is the man most responsible for the interior decoration of the church. His ❽ **dove window** shines above the smaller front altar used for everyday services. The Holy Spirit, in the form of a six-foot-high dove, pours sunlight onto the faithful through the ala-baster windows, turning into artificial rays of gold and reflecting off swirl-ing gold clouds, angels, and winged babies. Dur-ing a service, real sunlight passes through real clouds of incense, mingling with Bernini's sculpture.

Beneath the dove is the centerpiece of this structure, the so-called **Throne of St. Peter,** an oak chair built in medieval times for a king. Subsequently, it was encrusted with tradition and encased in bronze by Bernini as a symbol of papal authority. In the apse, Mass is said daily for pil-grims, tourists, and Roman citizens alike.

• *To the left of the main altar is the* **south transept.** *It may be roped off for worship, but anyone can step past the guard if you say you're there "for prayer." At the far end, left side, find the dark "painting" of St. Peter crucified upside down.*

This marks (according to tradition) ❾ **Peter's crucifixion site.** Peter had come to the world's greatest city to preach Jesus' mes-sage of love to the pagan, often hostile Romans. During the reign of Emperor Nero, he was arrested and brought to Nero's Circus so all of Rome could witness his execution. When the authorities told Peter he was to be crucified just like his Lord, Peter said, es-sentially, "I'm not worthy" and insisted they nail him on the cross upside down.

Around the corner on the right (heading back toward the cen-tral nave), pause at the mosaic copy of Raphael's epic painting of ❿ *The Transfiguration.* The original is now beautifully displayed in the Pinacoteca of the Vatican Museums. This and all the other "paintings" in the church are actually mosaic copies made from thousands of colored chips the size of your little fingernail. Because smoke and humidity would damage real paintings, since the 1700s church officials have replaced the paintings with mosaics (a.k.a. the "art of eternity") produced by the Vatican Mosaic Studio.

• *Back near the entrance of the church, in the far corner, behind bullet-proof glass, is the sculpture everyone has come to see, the* Pietà.

Michelangelo was 24 years old when he completed this ⓫ *pi-età*—a representation of Mary with the body of Christ taken from the cross. It was his first major commission, done for Holy Year 1500.

ROME

Michelangelo, with his total mastery of the real world, captures the sadness of the moment. Mary cradles her crucified son in her lap. Christ's lifeless right arm drooping down lets us know how heavy this corpse is. Mary looks at her dead son with sad tenderness. Her left hand turns upward, asking, "How could they do this to you?"

• *In the chapel to the left is the* **⓬** ***Tomb of Pope John Paul II.***

John Paul II (1920-2005) was one of the most beloved popes of recent times. During his papacy (1978-2005), he was the highly visible face of the Catholic Church as it labored to stay relevant in an increasingly secular world. The first non-Italian pope in four centuries, he oversaw the fall of communism in his native Poland. He survived an assassination attempt, and he publicly endured his slow decline from Parkinson's disease with great stoicism.

When John Paul II died in 2005, hundreds of thousands lined up outside the church, waiting up to 24 hours to pay their respects. He was sainted in April 2014, just nine years after his death. St. John Paul II lies beneath a painting of the steadfast St. Sebastian, his favorite saint.

You're welcome to step through the metalwork gates into the **⓭ Blessed Sacrament Chapel** (Capella di Santissimo Sacramento), an oasis of peace reserved for prayer and meditation (on right side of church, about midway to the altar). Mass is sometimes said here.

The **⓮ Treasury Museum** (Museo-Tesoro), on the left side of the nave near the altar, contains the room-size tomb of Sixtus IV by Antonio Pollaiuolo, a big pair of Roman pincers used to torture Christians, an original corkscrew column from Old St. Peter's, and assorted jewels, papal robes, and golden reliquaries—a marked contrast to the poverty of early Christians.

The foundation of Old St. Peter's, the **Crypt** (Grotte/Tombe), contains tombs of popes and memorial chapels. In summer, the crypt entrance is usually beside the statue of St. Andrew, to the left of the main altar (near #4 on the map); in winter, it's by the dome entrance. Stairs lead you down to the floor level of the previous church, where you'll pass the sepulcher of Peter. This lighted niche with an icon is not Peter's actual tomb, but part of a shrine that stands atop Peter's tomb. Nearby is the chapel where Pope John Paul II was buried before being moved upstairs in 2011. Continue

ROME

your one-way visit until it spills you out, usually near the cloak-room, or possibly outside. (Save this for last.)

To cap your visit with the best view of Rome, head to the **⓯ dome entrance** along the right (north) side of the church. The line begins to form out front, at the church's right door (as you face the church). Look for *cupola* signs.

There are two levels: the rooftop of the church and the very top of the dome. Climb or take an elevator to the first level, on the church roof just above the facade. From the roof, you can also go inside the gallery ringing the interior of the dome and look down inside the church. Notice the dusty top of Bernini's seven-story-tall canopy far below. Study the mosaics up close—and those huge letters! It's worth the elevator ride for this view alone.

From this level, continue all the way up to the top of the dome. The staircase actually winds between the outer shell and the inner one. It's a sweaty, crowded, claustrophobic 15-minute, 323-step climb, but worth it. Admire the arms of Bernini's colonnade encircling St. Peter's Square. Find the big, white Victor Emmanuel Monument, with the two statues on top; and the Pantheon,

with its large, light, shallow dome. The large rectangular building to the left of the obelisk is the Vatican Museums complex, stuffed with art. Look down into the square at the tiny pilgrims buzzing like electrons around the nucleus of Catholicism.

▲▲▲Vatican Museums (Musei Vaticani)

The four miles of displays in this immense museum complex—from ancient statues to Christian frescoes to modern paintings—culminate in the Raphael Rooms and Michelangelo's glorious Sistine Chapel.

Cost and Hours: €21 for timed-entry ticket (book in advance to avoid long lines), €12 for age 6-18, prices include €4 online reservation fee, free for kids 5 and under, free on the last Sun of each month (when it's very crowded). Open Mon-Sat 9:00-18:00 (Fri-Sat until 22:30 late April-Oct), closed Sun—except last Sun of month, when it's open 9:00-14:00; last entry is generally two hours before closing, and staff start ushering you out about 30 minutes before closing.

Closed Days: The museums are closed on many holidays (mainly religious ones); check the current hours and calendar on the museum website.

Vatican City

The tiny independent country of Vatican City is contained entirely within Rome. (Its 100 acres could fit eight times over in New York's Central Park.) The Vatican has its own postal system, armed guards, beautiful gardens, helipad, mini train station, and radio station (KPOP). It also has two huge sights: St. Peter's Basilica and the Vatican Museums. Politically powerful, the Vatican is the religious capital of 1.3 billion Roman Catholics. If you're not a Catholic, become one for your visit.

The pope is both the religious and secular leader of Vatican City. For centuries, the Vatican was the capital of the Papal States, and locals referred to the pontiff as "King Pope." Because of the Vatican's territorial ambitions, it didn't always have good relations with Italy. Even though modern Italy was created in 1870, the Holy See didn't recognize it as a country until 1929.

Vatican Gardens: To walk through the manicured Vatican Gardens (with views over Rome and a good look at St. Peter's dome), book a guided tour several days in advance at www.museivaticani.va (€39, about 3 hours, daily except Wed and Sun, includes entry to Vatican Museums; tours usually start at 9:00 or 11:00 at Vatican Museums tour desk). Same-day tickets are occasionally available (ask at the ticket/info desk inside the shop in St. Peter's Square). A 45-minute open-bus tour through the gardens is offered in good weather (€37, includes audioguide and entry to Vatican Museums).

General Audience Tickets: For the Wednesday audience at

Information: +39 06 6988 4676, www.museivaticani.va.

Advance Reservations: You're crazy to come without a reservation. The Vatican Museums can be extremely crowded, with waits of up to two hours just to buy tickets. Bypass these long lines by reserving an entry time at their website. For sights covered by my self-guided tour, select the ticket called "Vatican Museums and Sistine Chapel." You'll receive a QR code via email; show the code to get a paper ticket when you arrive.

9:30, a (free) ticket gets you closer to the papal action (though anyone can enjoy a look via jumbo-screens). Reserve tickets (available a month or two in advance) by sending a request by mail or fax (access the form at Vatican.va—select "Prefecture of the Papal Household" at the bottom of the page). You'll then pick up the tickets at St. Peter's Square before the audience (available Tue 15:00-19:00 and Wed from 7:30; usually under Bernini's colonnade).

Another option is to email the Bishops' Office for US Visitors to the Vatican three months to three weeks prior to your requested date; you'll pick up tickets the afternoon before your visit (www.pnac.org, visitorsoffice@pnac.org).

Finally, starting the Monday before the audience, Swiss Guards hand out tickets from their station near the basilica exit (see the "St. Peter's Square" map in this chapter). Don't go through security—just march up, ask nicely, and say *"danke."* While this is perhaps easiest, I'd reserve in advance to guarantee a ticket.

General Audience Tips: Dress modestly (shoulders covered, no short shorts or tank tops—long pants or knee-length skirts are safest) and arrive early to clear security (no big bags). To get a seat (much less a good one), be there a couple of hours early—there are far fewer seats than ticket holders. If you just want to see the pope, get a good photo, and don't mind standing, you can show up later (though still at least 30 minutes early) and take your place in the standing-room section in the back half of the square. The entire event, including prayers, singing, and blessings, lasts about 1.5 hours. The service gets underway as the Popemobile appears, winding through the adoring crowd (the best places—seated or standing—are near the cloth-covered wooden fences that line the Popemobile route). Around 10:00, the Pope's multilingual message begins (you can leave at any time).

(You can also print out the attached voucher—but you'll still have to swap it for a paper ticket.) For strategies on when to book your visit for the Vatican Museums (and how to fit it in with your St. Peter's sightseeing), see page 880.

Same-Day Tickets: If you didn't book tickets in advance, you have a few options. First, try **booking a ticket on your phone,** using the Vatican website listed above, to see if there are any day-of slots. Or you can visit the **shop** on St. Peter's Square (see details under "Vatican City," earlier). The **Opera Romana Pellegrinaggi** (a.k.a., Roma Cristiana), a private pilgrimage tour company, sells same-day tickets (€30, entrances almost hourly, office in front of St. Peter's Square, Piazza Pio XII 9, +39 06 698 961, www.operaromanapellegrinaggi.org).

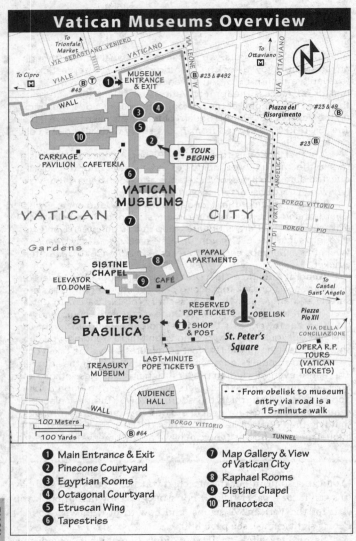

Vatican Museums Overview

1 Main Entrance & Exit
2 Pinecone Courtyard
3 Egyptian Rooms
4 Octagonal Courtyard
5 Etruscan Wing
6 Tapestries
7 Map Gallery & View of Vatican City
8 Raphael Rooms
9 Sistine Chapel
10 Pinacoteca

Hawkers peddling skip-the-line access swarm the Vatican area, offering guided tours—but museum staff advise against accepting their offers (while legitimate, the tour caliber is often low—use them only as a last resort to get in).

Dress Code: While modest dress (no shorts, above-knee skirts, or bare shoulders) is technically required throughout the Vatican Museums, this dress code is most strictly enforced inside the Sistine Chapel.

Getting There: The Ottaviano Metro stop is a 10-minute walk from the entrance. Bus #49 from Piazza Cavour/Castel Sant'Angelo stops at Piazza Risorgimento and continues right to the entrance. Bus #23 from Trastevere hugs the west bank of the Tiber and stops on Via Leone IV, just downhill from the entrance. Bus #492 heads from the city center past Piazza Risorgimento and the Vatican walls, and stops on Via Leone IV. Bus #64 stops on the other side of St. Peter's Square, a 15- to 20-minute walk (facing the church from the obelisk, take a right through the colonnade and follow the Vatican wall). Or take a taxi from the city center—they are reasonable (hop in and say, "moo-ZAY-ee vah-tee-KAH-nee").

Getting In: Approaching the exterior entrance (the big white door), you'll see three lines: individuals without reservations (far left), individuals with reservations (usually shorter and faster), and groups (on the right). Make sure you get in the correct entry line. All visitors must pass through a metal detector (no pocketknives allowed).

With a reservation, the guard will scan your QR code and let you enter via the reserved ticket-holder line. Inside, after the security check, go to any window on the left to show your QR code and pick up your ticket, then go up the steps and enter the museum. (Or, you can skip the ticket-window line by going upstairs and processing your QR code on a machine.)

Without a reservation, enter via the far-left line. Once you clear security, go upstairs to buy your ticket.

Tours: A €7 **audioguide** is available at the top of the spiral ramp/escalator and can be prepaid when you book tickets online. Confirm the drop-off location when renting. ∩ Download my free Vatican Museums and Sistine Chapel **audio tours.** The Vatican offers **guided tours** in English that are easy to book on their website (€34, includes admission; show your QR code to a guard to the right of the entrance, then once inside go to the Guided Tours desk in lobby, up a few stairs). For **private tour** companies and guides, see page 820.

Services: The museum's "checkroom" (to the right after security) takes only bigger bags, not day bags. The post office, with stamps that make collectors drool, is upstairs. WCs are mainly at the entrance/exit, plus a few scattered within the collection.

❷ Self-Guided Tour

Our tour starts in the large open-air "Pinecone Courtyard." This vast space sums up the Vatican's vast collection: Pinecone—ancient, a 2,000 year-old offering to Isis. Bronze sphere—modern, created in 1990. And the courtyard around it—Renaissance, designed by Bramante.

We'll begin our museum visit as civilization did, in **Egypt and Mesopotamia.** Backtrack inside and up the stairs to the right to find linen-wrapped mummies, stiff statues, and early writing on clay tablets. (Occasionally, the stairs up to Egypt are closed off, and crowds are routed through the courtyard to a door to the right of the pine cone. If so, just follow the masses until you reach the Octagonal Courtyard with the *Apollo Belvedere* and *Laocoön* figures. Tour the museum from there to the "Sarcophagi," where you'll find the entrance to the Egyptian rooms.)

After a stop at a view balcony, make your way to the Octagonal Courtyard, decorated with some of the best **Greek and Roman statues** in captivity. The *Apollo Belvedere* is a Roman copy (2nd century AD) of a Hellenistic original that followed the style of the great Greek sculptor Praxiteles. It fully captures the beauty of the human form. The anatomy is perfect, his pose is natural. Instead of standing at attention, face-forward with his arms at his sides (Egyptian-style), Apollo is on the move, coming to rest with his weight on one leg.

Laocoön was sculpted some four centuries after the golden age (5th-4th century BC), after the scales of "balance" had been tipped. Whereas *Apollo* is a balance between stillness and motion, this is textbook Hellenism...unbridled motion. *Apollo* is serene, graceful, and godlike, while *Laocoön* is powerful, emotional, and gritty. The figures (carved from four blocks of marble pieced together seamlessly) are powerful, not light and graceful. The poses are as twisted as possible, accentuating every rippling muscle and bulging vein.

The centerpiece of the next hall is the *Belvedere Torso* (just a 2,000-year-old torso, but one that had a great impact on the art of Michelangelo). Finishing off the classical statuary are two fine fourth-century porphyry sarcophagi. These royal purple tombs were made (though not used) for the Roman emperor Constantine's mother (Helena, on left) and daughter (Constanza, on right).

Overachievers may first choose to pop into the **Etruscan Wing**—labeled *Museo Gregoriano Etrusco.* Otherwise, after long halls of tapestries, old maps, broken penises, and fig leaves, you'll come to what most people are looking for: the Raphael Rooms and Michelangelo's Sistine Chapel.

Raphael Rooms: The highlight of the Raphael Rooms, frescoed by Raphael and his assistants, is the restored *School of Athens*. It is remarkable for its blatant pre-Christian classical orientation, especially considering it originally wallpapered the apartments of Pope Julius II. Raphael honors the great pre-Christian thinkers—Aristotle, Plato, and company—who are portrayed as the leading artists of Raphael's day. There's Leonardo da Vinci, whom Raphael worshipped, in the role of Plato. Michelangelo broods in the foreground, added later. When Raphael snuck a peek at the Sistine Chapel, he decided that his arch-competitor was so good that he had to put their personal differences aside and include him in this tribute to the artists of his generation. And the "school" building is actually an early version of St. Peter's Basilica (under construction at the time).

Sistine Chapel: Next is the brilliantly restored Sistine Chapel. This is the pope's personal chapel and also the place where, upon the death of the ruling pope, a new pope is elected.

The Sistine Chapel is famous for Michelangelo's pictorial culmination of the Renaissance, showing the story of creation, with a powerful God weaving in and out of each scene through that busy first week. This is an optimistic and positive expression of the High Renaissance and a stirring example of the artistic and theological maturity of the 33-year-old Michelangelo, who spent four years on this work.

The ceiling shows the history of the world before the birth of Jesus. We see God creating the world, creating man and woman, destroying the earth by flood, and so on. God himself, in his purple robe, actually appears in the first five scenes. Along the sides (where the ceiling starts to curve), we see the Old Testament prophets and pagan Greek prophetesses who foretold the coming of Christ. Dividing these scenes and figures are fake niches (a painted 3-D illusion) decorated with nude statue-like figures with symbolic meaning.

In the central panel of the *Creation of Adam,* God and man take center stage in this Renaissance version of creation. Adam, newly formed in the image of God, lounges dreamily in perfect naked innocence. God, with his entourage, swoops in with

The Sistine Ceiling

WALL

DAVID & GOLIATH

JUDITH & HOLOFERNES

ZACHARIAH

WALL

JOEL

DRUNKENNESS OF NOAH

DELPHICA

ZORO-BABEL

THE FLOOD

JOSIAH

ERYTHRAEA

SACRIFICE OF NOAH

ISAIAH

OZIAS

TEMPTATION AND EXPULSION

EZEKIAS

EZEKIEL

CREATION OF EVE

CUMAEA

ROBOAM

CREATION OF ADAM

ASA

PERSICA

SEPARATION OF LAND FROM WATER

DANIEL

WALL

SALMON

CREATION OF SUN, MOON & PLANETS

JESSE

JEREMIAH

SEPARATION OF LIGHT FROM DARKNESS

LIBICA

Detail box indicates area of photo on facing page

DEATH OF HAMAN

JONAH

BRAZEN SERPENT

LAST JUDGMENT WALL

ENTRY DOOR FROM RAPHAEL ROOMS & MODERN RELIGIOUS ART...

☆ To use this diagram: face the Last Judgment & hold the book up to the ceiling.

ROME

a swirl of activity (which—with a little imagination—looks like a cross-section of a human brain...quite a strong humanist statement). Their reaching hands are the center of this work. Adam's is limp and passive; God's is strong and forceful, his finger twitching upward with energy. Here is the very moment of creation, as God passes the spark of life to man, the crowning work of his creation.

This is the spirit of the Renaissance. God is not a terrifying giant reaching down to puny and helpless man from way on high. Here they are on an equal plane, divided only by the diagonal bit of sky. God's billowing robe and the patch of green upon which Adam is lying balance each other. They are like two pieces of a jigsaw puzzle, or two long-separated continents, or like the yin and yang symbols finally coming together—uniting, complementing each other, creating wholeness. God and man work together in the divine process of creation.

When the ceiling was finished and revealed to the public, it simply blew 'em away. It both caps the Renaissance and turns it in a new direction. In perfect Renaissance spirit, it mixes Old Testament prophets with classical figures. But the style is more dramatic, shocking, and emotional than the balanced Renaissance works before it. This is a very personal work—the Gospel according to Michelangelo—but its themes and subject matter are universal. Many art scholars contend that the Sistine ceiling is the single greatest work of art by any one human being.

Later, after the Reformation wars had begun and after the Catholic army of Spain had sacked the Vatican, the reeling Church began to fight back. As part of its Counter-Reformation, a much older Michelangelo was commissioned to paint the *Last Judgment* (behind the altar).

It's Judgment Day, and Christ—the powerful figure in the center, raising his arm to spank the wicked—has come to find out who's naughty and who's nice. Beneath him, a band of angels blows its trumpets Dizzy Gillespie-style, giving a wake-up call to the sleeping dead. The dead at lower left leave their graves and prepare to be judged. The righteous, on Christ's right hand (the left side of the picture), are carried up to the glories of heaven. The wicked on the other side are hurled down to hell, where demons wait to torture them. Charon, from the underworld of Greek mythology, waits below to ferry the souls of the damned to hell.

When *The Last Judgment* was unveiled to the public in 1541, it caused a sensation. The pope is said to have dropped to his knees and cried, "Lord, charge me not with my sins when thou shalt come on the Day of Judgment."

And it changed the course of art. The complex composition, with more than 300 figures swirling around the figure of Christ, went far beyond traditional Renaissance balance. The twisted figures shown from every imaginable angle challenged other painters to try and top this master of 3-D illusion. And the sheer terror and drama of the scene was a striking contrast to the placid optimism of, say, Raphael's *School of Athens*. Michelangelo had Baroque-en all the rules of the Renaissance, signaling a new era of art.

Exiting the Vatican Museums: To return to the museum's main entrance/exit, leave the Sistine through the side door next to the screen (on the left, with your back to the altar). You'll soon find yourself facing the **Long March back to the museum's entrance** (about 15 minutes away) and the Pinacoteca. Along this corridor (located one floor below the long corridor that you walked to get here), you'll see some of the wealth amassed by the popes, mostly gifts from royalty. The elaborately decorated library that branches off to the right contains rare manuscripts. The corridor eventually sends you looping through various shops and food courts (keep following signs for exit) until you spill out onto a lawn.

As you leave, enjoy one last view of the Vatican grounds and Michelangelo's magnificent dome. Then go in peace.

▲Castel Sant'Angelo

Built in ancient times as a tomb for the emperor Hadrian, used through the Middle Ages as a castle, prison, and place of last refuge for popes under attack, and today a museum, this giant pile of ancient bricks is packed with history. The structure itself is striking, the opulent papal rooms are dramatic (and cool inside during the summer), and the views up top are some of the best in Rome.

Cost and Hours: €12, more with special exhibits, Tue-Sun 9:00-19:30, closed Mon, last entry one hour before closing, near Vatican City, 10-minute walk from St. Peter's Square at Lungotevere Castello 50, Metro: Lepanto or bus #40 or #64, café, +39 06 681 9111, www.castelsantangelo.beniculturali.it.

Visiting the Castle: Ancient Rome allowed no tombs within its walls, so Emperor Hadrian grabbed the most commanding position across the river and built this towering tomb. In the year 590, the archangel Michael appeared above the mausoleum to signal the end of a plague. The tomb became a fortified palace, renamed for the "holy angel." Castel Sant'Angelo spent the Dark Ages as a fortress and prison, but was connected to the Vatican via an elevated corridor in the 13th century (since Rome was repeatedly plundered by invaders, Castel Sant'Angelo was a handy place of last refuge for popes). In anticipation of long sieges, rooms were decorated with papal splendor.

A one-way route circulates visitors through the medieval and then the ancient parts of the monument. After the ticket booth, head upstairs to the **rampart** with its four bastions (named for the evangelists: Matthew, Mark, Luke, and John). Then climb a ramp and cross a **bridge** that traverses the sacred chamber in the center. Next, you reach a sunny courtyard with a 16th-century statue of St. Michael. Climbing to another rampart, you'll find the armory and later enter medieval rooms built for the pope. The **papal library** was painted by followers of Raphael. Eventually you reach the **rooftop terrace** with the statue of the Archangel Michael sheathing his sword—and one of the best views anywhere of Rome and St. Peter's Basilica.

NORTH ROME
▲Villa Borghese Gardens

Rome's somewhat scruffy three-square-mile "Central Park" is great for its quiet shaded paths and for people-watching plenty of

modern-day Romeos and Juliets. The best entrance is at the head of Via Veneto (Metro: Barberini, then 10-minute walk up Via Veneto and through the old Roman wall at Porta Pinciana, or catch a cab to Via Veneto— Porta Pinciana). There you'll find a cluster of buildings with a café, a kiddie arcade, and bike

rental (€4/hour, includes lock to allow sightseeing stops). Rent a bike or, for romantics, a pedaled rickshaw (*risciò*, €12/hour). Follow signs to discover the park's cafés, fountains, statues, lake, and prime picnic spots. Some sights require paid admission, including the Borghese Gallery, Rome's zoo, and the National Gallery of Modern Art (19th-century art).

You can also enter the gardens from the top of the Spanish Steps (facing the church, turn left and walk down the road 200 yards beyond Villa Medici, then angle right on the small pathway into the gardens), and from Piazza del Popolo (in the northeast corner of the piazza, stairs lead to the gardens via a terrace with

North Rome

To MAXXI &
Parco della
Musica #2

#19

**ETRUSCAN
MUSEUM**
Villa
Giulia

**NATIONAL
GALLERY OF
MODERN ART**

VIA DELLE BELLE ARTI

VIA ALDROVANDI

VIA G. PAISIELLO

Bioparco
#19

**BIOPARCO
(ZOO)**

ENTRANCE

To
Catacombs
of Priscilla

V. GIARDINO ZOOLOGICO

VIA FLAMINIA

Flaminio

Piazzale
del Fiocco

TEMPLE

Villa

Borghese

Gardens

V. UCCELLIERA

Pinciana
#95 & 910 B

**BORGHESE
GALLERY**

VIA PINCIANA

Piazzale
Flaminio #2

S. MARIA
D. POPOLO

**PORTA DEL
POPOLO**

**Piazza
del Popolo**

**PUPPET
THEATER**

VIALE DEL MURO

TORTO

**TEMPIETTO
DI DIANA**

Piazzale
delle
Canestre

**ANCIENT
CITY WALLS**

VIA MUSEO BORGHESE

TERRAZZA
Pincio

Galoppatoio
(Track)

CAFÉ AND
BIKE RENTAL

**PORTA
PINCIANA**

Tiber
River

LUNGOTEVERE

VIA DI RIPETTA

VIA DEL BABUINO

VIA MARGUTTA

**"SHOPPING
TRIANGLE"**

VIA VITT

**VILLA
MEDICI**

VIA TRINITA

Spagna M

TUNNEL

VIA PINCIANA

VIA LUDOVISI

VIA VENETO

VIA BONCOMPAGNI

VIA PIEMONTE

**ST.
PATRICK'S**

**MAUSOLEUM
OF AUGUSTUS**

**ARA
PACIS**

PONTE
CAVOUR

VIA DELLA SCROFA

VIA DEL CORSO

Spagna M

VIA CONDOTTI

**TRINITÀ
DEI MONTI**

**SPANISH
STEPS**

VIA DUE MACELLI

VIA SISTINA

VIA VENETO

**US
EMBASSY**

**CAPUCHIN
CRYPT**

Piazza
Barberini

M Barberini

VIA XX SETTEMBRE

To Termini
Station

PANTHEON

Piazza
Parlamento

PARLIAMENT

VIA DEL TRITONE

SABINA
MURATTE

VIA DELL'UMILTA

**TREVI
FOUNTAIN**

**PALAZZO DEL
QUIRINALE**

Piazza
del
Quirinale

VIA QUIRINALE

VIA 4 FONTANE

VIA NAZIONALE

Piazza
Collegio
Rom.

**GALLERIA
DORIA
PAMPHILIJ**

**Piazza
Venezia**

V. 4 NOV.

XXIV MAGGIO

VIA PLEBISCITO

Largo
Magnanapoli

To Forum & Colosseum

N

400 Meters
400 Yards

grand views out to St. Peter's Basilica—bikes and Segways can be rented nearby).

▲▲▲Borghese Gallery (Galleria Borghese)

This plush museum, filling a cardinal's mansion in the park, offers one of Europe's most sumptuous art experiences. You'll enjoy a collection of world-class Baroque sculpture, including Bernini's *David* and his excited statue of Apollo chasing Daphne, as well as paintings by Caravaggio, Raphael, Titian, and Rubens. The museum's mandatory reservation system keeps crowds to a manageable size.

Cost and Hours: €17, Tue-Sun 9:00-19:00, closed Mon. The museum may be open late one night per week—check online.

Information: +39 06 32810 (tickets and information), www.galleriaborghese.it.

Advance Reservations Required: Reservations are mandatory. As slots can book up, it's better to reserve sooner rather than later. It's easiest to book online at www.tosc.it; after booking you'll be emailed a voucher with a bar code that lets you enter at your appointed time. You can also reserve with a real person over the telephone (+39 06 32810, press 2 for English, phones answered Mon-Fri 9:00-18:00, Sat 9:00-13:00, closed Sat in Aug and Sun year-round).

Getting In: You can get into the Borghese starting 10 minutes before your appointed time, but you may need to wait in a short line to enter (arriving late could result in forfeiting your reservation). For crowd control, they may direct you to start either on the ground floor (where this tour begins), or in the Pinacoteca on the upper floor. This tour works equally well in either order.

Getting There: The museum, at Piazzale del Museo Borghese 5, is set idyllically but inconveniently in the vast Villa Borghese Gardens. A **taxi** drops you along Via Pinciana, 100 yards from the museum. (Tell the cabbie you want "Galleria Borghese," not "Villa Borghese.") To go by **public transit,** take bus #910 from Termini train station/Piazza della Repubblica to the Puccini stop, walk to the park, turn left, and use the first park entrance (but note that #910 runs back to Termini by a different, less convenient route). Bus #53 runs to the Via Pinciana stop from Largo Chigi (not far from Trevi Fountain) and the Barberini Metro station. You can also go by **foot** (20 minutes) from the Barberini Metro stop: Walk 10 minutes up Via Veneto, enter the park, and turn right, following signs another 10 minutes to the Borghese Gallery.

Tours: Guided English tours may be available (€8; book this along with your entry reservation). Or consider the museum's excellent 1.5-hour audioguide (€5), which covers more than this tour.

Length of This Tour: This tour takes about an hour, but the Borghese rewards lingerers. With less time, focus on the ground-floor sculptures, especially Bernini.

Services: Baggage check is free, mandatory, and strictly enforced. Even small purses must be checked. There's a WC in the staircase between the two floors.

Budget most of your time for the more interesting ground

Borghese Gallery—Ground Floor

Stairs up to Pinacoteca & down to Entrance

ROOM VI

ROOM V

ROOM IV

⑩

ROOM III

⑦

⑤

④

CHAPEL

⑥

ROOM II

ROOM VII

③

⑧

MAIN ENTRY HALL ①

START

ROOM I

ROOM VIII

②

⑨

PORTICO

Not to Scale

To Basement (Info, Shop, Café, Bag Check, WC)

① Main Entry Hall
② CANOVA – Pauline Borghese as Venus
③ BERNINI – David
④ BERNINI – Apollo and Daphne
⑤ BERNINI – The Rape of Proserpina
⑥ UNKNOWN – Diana the Hunter; other marbles
⑦ BERNINI – Aeneas, Anchises, and Ascanius
⑧ "Theater of the Universe"
⑨ CARAVAGGIO – Various
⑩ Stairs up to Pinacoteca

floor, but set aside 30 minutes for the paintings of the Pinacoteca upstairs (highlights are marked by the audioguide icons). It's hard to believe that a family of cardinals and popes would display so many works with secular and sensual—even erotic—themes. But the Borgheses felt that all forms of human expression, including pagan myths and physical passion, glorified God.

The essence of the collection is the connection of the Renaissance with the classical world. As you enter, notice the second-century Roman reliefs with Michelangelo-designed panels above either end of the portico. The villa was built in the early 17th century by the great art collector Cardinal Scipione Borghese, who wanted to prove that the glories of ancient Rome were matched by the Renaissance.

In the main entry hall, high up on the wall, is a thrilling first-century Greek sculpture of a horse falling. The Renaissance-era rider was added by Pietro Bernini, father of the famous Gian Lorenzo Bernini.

Each room seems to feature a Baroque masterpiece. In Room I is *Pauline Borghese as Venus,* for which Napoleon's sister went the full monty for the sculptor Canova, scandalizing Europe. With the famous nose of her conqueror brother, she strikes the pose of Venus as conqueror of men's hearts. Notice the contrasting textures that Canova (1757-1822) gets out of the pure white marble. The mythological pose, the Roman couch, the an-

cient hairdo, and the calm harmony make Pauline the epitome of the Neoclassical style.

In Room II, Gian Lorenzo Bernini's *David* twists around to put a big rock in his sling. He purses his lips, knits his brow, and winds his body like a spring as his eyes lock onto the target: Goliath, who's somewhere behind us, putting us right in the line of fire. Compared with Michelangelo's *David,* this is unvarnished realism—an unbalanced pose, bulging veins, unflattering face, and armpit hair. Michelangelo's *David* thinks, whereas Bernini's acts. Bernini slays the pretty-boy *David*s of the Renaissance and prepares to invent Baroque.

The best one of all is in Room III: Bernini's ***Apollo and Daphne***. It's the perfect Baroque subject—capturing a thrilling, action-

filled moment. In the mythological story, Apollo—made stupid by Cupid's arrow of love—chases after Daphne, who has been turned off by the "arrow of disgust." Just as he's about to catch her, she calls to her father to save her. Magically, her fingers begin to sprout leaves, her toes become roots, her skin turns to bark, and she transforms into a tree. Frustrated Apollo will end up with a handful of leaves. Walk slowly around the statue. It's more air than stone.

But don't stop here. In Room IV, admire Bernini's *The Rape of Proserpina*, proof that even at the age of 24 the sculptor was

the master of marble. The statues in the niches are classical originals. **Diana the Hunter** is a rare Greek original, with every limb and finger intact. Over in Room VI, Bernini's first major work for Cardinal Borghese—***Aeneas, Anchises, and Ascanius***—reveals the then-20-year-old sculptor's astonishing aptitude for portraying human flesh, though the statue lacks the Baroque energy of his more mature work. And in Room VIII is a fabulous collection of paintings by **Caravaggio,** who brought Christian saints down to earth with gritty realism.

Upstairs, in the Pinacoteca (Painting Gallery), are busts and paintings by Bernini, as well as paintings by Raphael, Titian, Correggio, and Domenichino.

▲▲Museo dell'Ara Pacis (Museum of the Altar of Peace)

On January 30, 9 BC, soon-to-be-emperor Augustus led a procession of priests up the steps and into this newly built "Altar of Peace." They sacrificed an animal on the altar and poured an offering of wine, thanking the gods for helping Augustus pacify barbarians abroad and rivals at home. This marked the dawn of the Pax Romana (c. AD 1-200), a golden age of good living, stability, dominance, and peace *(pax)*. The Ara Pacis (AH-rah PAH-chees) hosted annual sacrifices by the emperor until the area was flooded by the Tiber River. For an idea of how high the water could get, find the measure *(idrometro)* scaling the right side of the church closest to the entrance. Buried under silt, it was abandoned and forgotten until the 16th century, when various parts were discovered and excavated. Mussolini gathered the altar's scattered parts and reconstructed them in a building here in 1938. Today, the Altar of Peace stands in a pavilion designed by American architect Richard Meier (opened 2006).

Cost and Hours: €10.50, more with special exhibits, tightwads can look in through huge windows for free, daily 9:30-19:30, last entry one hour before closing, videoguide-€7, a long block west of Via del Corso on Via di Ara Pacis, on the east bank of the Tiber near Ponte Cavour, Metro: Spagna plus a 10-minute walk down Via dei Condotti, +39 06 0608, www.arapacis.it.

▲▲Catacombs of Priscilla (Catacombe di Priscilla)

While most tourists and nearly all tour groups go out to the Appian Way to see the famous catacombs of San Sebastiano and San Callisto (7.5 miles south of downtown, easiest by taxi), the Catacombs of Priscilla are more central, less commercialized, and less crowded—they just feel more intimate, as catacombs should. You enter from a convent and explore the result of 250 years of tunneling that occurred from the second to the fifth centuries. Visits are by 30-minute guided tour only (English-language tours go whenever a small group gathers—generally every 20 minutes or so). You'll see a few thousand of the 40,000 niches carved here, along with some beautiful frescoes, including what is considered the first depiction of Mary nursing the Baby Jesus.

Cost and Hours: €8.50, €5.50 for kids 7-15, free for kids 6 and under, Fri-Sun 9:00-12:00 & 14:00-17:00, closed Mon-Thu but may be open during busy times, closed one random month a year—check website or call first, Via Salaria 430, +39 06 8620 6272, www.catacombepriscilla.com.

Getting There: The catacombs are on the northeast edge of

ROME

Near Termini Station

US EMBASSY

To Spanish Steps

V.D. ARTISTI

VIA VENETO

V.D. SAN BASILIO

V. BISO

CAPUCHIN CRYPT

SANTA MARIA VITTORIA

V. PURIFICAZIONE

VIA SISTINA

Barberini

MOSES FOUNTAIN

GROC.

Piazza Barberini

VIA BARBERINI

SANTA SUSANNA

Piazza di San Bernardo

SAN BERNARDO

VIA DEL TRITONE

V. AVIG.

VIA D. QUATTRO FONTANE

PALAZZO BARBERINI

V. TRAFORO

BOCC.

V. RASELLA

FOUR FOUNTAINS

VIA DEI GIARDINI

VIA FIRENZE

V. LAV.

V. VARLONE

VIA DEPRETIS

#40 & 64

To Trevi & Pantheon

Quirinal Gardens

SAN CARLO

PHARMACY

VIA NAPOLI

PALAZZO DEL QUIRINALE

SANT' ANDREA

VIA VENEZIA

VIA PALERMO

VIA DATARIA

VIA FERRARA

PALAZZO DELLE ESPOSIZIONI

VIA GENOVA

To Trevi & Pantheon

Piazza del Quirinale

V. MILANO

SCUDERIE DEL QUIRINALE

VIA NAZIONALE

To Piazza Venezia

4 NOVEMBRE

Largo Magnanapoli

VIA DEI SERPENTI

VIA PANISPERNA

VIA CAVOUR

To Piazza Venezia

MONTI

the city but well served by direct buses (30 minutes from Termini or 40 minutes from Piazza Venezia) or a €15 taxi ride. From Termini, take bus #92 or #310 from Piazza Cinquecento or Metro B1 (direction: Jonio) to Libia or Sant'Agnese/Annibaliano stop. From Piazza Venezia, along Via del Corso or Via Barberini, take bus #63 or #83. Tell the driver "Piazza Crati" and "kah-tah-KOHM-bay" and you'll be let off near Piazza Crati (at the Nemorense/Crati stop). From there, walk through the little market in Piazza Crati, then down Via di Priscilla (about 5 minutes). The entrance is in the orange building on the left at the top of the hill.

ROME

EAST ROME
Near Termini Train Station

Most of these sights are within a 10-minute walk of the station.

▲▲▲National Museum of Rome
(Museo Nazionale Romano Palazzo Massimo alle Terme)

The National Museum's main branch, at Palazzo Massimo, houses the greatest collection of ancient Roman art anywhere. Think of this museum as a walk back in time. As you gaze at the same marble statues that the Romans swooned over, the history of ancient

Rome comes alive—from Julius Caesar's murder to Caligula's incest to Vespasian's Colosseum to the coming of Christianity.

Cost and Hours: €10, €12 combo-ticket covers three other branches—all skippable; open Tue-Sun 9:00-19:45, closed Mon, last entry one hour before closing; audioguide may be available, about 100 yards from Termini station at Largo di Villa Peretti 2, Metro: Repubblica or Termini, +39 06 3996 7700, www.museonazionaleromano.beniculturali.it.

Visiting the Museum: The museum is rectangular, with rooms and hallways built around a central courtyard. The ground-floor sculptures follow Rome's history as the city changes from a republic to a dictatorial empire. The first-floor exhibits take Rome from its peak through its slow decline. The second floor houses rare frescoes and fine mosaics, and the basement presents coins and everyday objects. Take advantage of the thoughtfully written information panels throughout. As you tour this museum, note that in Italian, room is *sala* and hall is *galleria*.

On the first floor, along with statues and busts showing such emperors as Trajan and Hadrian, you'll see the best-preserved Roman copy of the Greek *Discus Thrower*. Statues of athletes like this commonly stood in the baths, where Romans cultivated healthy bodies, minds, and social skills, hoping to lead well-rounded lives. Other statues on this floor originally stood in the pleasure gardens of the Roman rich—surrounded by greenery with the splashing sound of fountains, all painted in bright, lifelike colors. Though created by Romans, the themes are mostly Greek, with godlike humans and human-looking gods.

The second floor contains frescoes and mosaics that once decorated the walls and floors of Roman villas. They're remarkably realistic and unstuffy, featuring everyday people, animals, flowery patterns, and geometrical designs. The Villa Farnesina frescoes—in black, red, yellow, and blue—are mostly architectural designs, with fake columns, friezes, and garlands. The Villa di Livia frescoes, owned by the wily wife of Augustus, immerse you in a leafy green garden full of birds and fruit trees, symbolizing the gods.

Finally, descend into the basement to see fine gold jewelry, the mummified body of an eight-year-old girl, and vault doors leading into the best coin collection in Europe, with fancy magnifying glasses maneuvering you through cases of coins from ancient Rome to modern times.

▲Baths of Diocletian/Church of Santa Maria degli Angeli (Terme di Diocleziano/Basilica S. Maria degli Angeli)

Of all the marvelous structures built by the Romans, their public baths were arguably the grandest, and the Baths of Diocletian were the granddaddy of them all. Built by Emperor Diocletian around AD 300 and sprawling over 30 acres—roughly five times the size of the Colosseum—these baths could cleanse 3,000 Romans at once. They functioned until AD 537, when barbarians attacked and the city's aqueducts fell into disuse, plunging Rome into a thousand years of poverty, darkness, and BO. Today, tourists can visit one grand section of the baths, the former main hall. This impressive remnant of the ancient complex was later transformed (with help from Michelangelo) into the Church of Santa Maria degli Angeli.

Cost and Hours: Free, Mon-Sat 10:00-13:00 & 16:00-18:30, Sun until 19:00, may be open midday in summer, entrance facing the fountain on Piazza della Repubblica, Metro: Repubblica, www.santamariadegliangeliroma.it.

▲Church of Santa Maria della Vittoria

This church, originally a poor Carmelite church, was slathered with Baroque richness in the 17th century. It houses Bernini's best-known statue, the swooning *St. Teresa in Ecstasy.* Note that the church may be closed for repair work.

Cost and Hours: Free (anyone collecting money at the door is not affiliated with the church), pay €0.50 for light, Mon-Sat 8:30-12:00 & 15:30-18:00, Sun 15:30-18:00, about 5 blocks northwest of Termini train station at Via XX Settembre 17, Metro: Repubblica.

Visiting the Church: Inside the church, you'll find *St. Teresa* to the left of the altar. Teresa has just been stabbed with God's arrow of fire. Now, the angel pulls it out and watches her reaction. Teresa swoons, her eyes roll up, her hand goes limp, she parts her lips...and moans. The smiling, cherubic angel understands just how she feels. Teresa, a 16th-century Spanish nun, later talked of the "sweetness" of "this intense pain," describing her oneness with God in ecstatic, even erotic, terms.

Bernini, the master of multimedia, pulls out all the stops to make this mystical vision real. Actual sunlight pours through the alabaster windows, and bronze sunbeams shine on a marble angel holding a golden arrow. Teresa leans back on a cloud and her robe ripples from within, charged with her spiritual arousal. Bernini

ROME

has created a little stage-setting of heaven. And watching from the "theater boxes" on either side are members of the family who commissioned the work.

Shopping in Rome

Even if you're not aiming to buy anything, shopping is a way to connect with contemporary Rome. Shop hours are generally 10:00-19:00; some also have a midday closure. Stores often are closed on Sundays, summer Saturday afternoons, and winter Monday mornings. Produce or flea markets typically close by 13:30.

Department Stores

The shopping complex under Termini train station is a convenient place to peruse clothes, bags, shoes, and perfume at several major Italian chain stores (most open daily 8:00-22:00).

A good upscale department store is **La Rinascente** (Via del Tritone 61). Besides deluxe brands, it has a fine design section with great and often affordable ideas for gifts, a magnificent rooftop terrace for a romantic *aperitivo*, good restaurants, free bathrooms, and a section of an ancient aqueduct in the basement (worth a quick visit). You'll find another branch on Piazza Fiume (east of the Borghese Gallery).

The **Galleria Alberto Sordi** is an elegant 19th-century "mall" (across from Piazza Colonna). **UPIM** is a popular midrange department store (many branches, including inside Termini train station, Via Nazionale 111, and Piazza Santa Maria Maggiore). **Oviesse/OVS,** a cheap clothing outlet, is near the Vatican Museums (on the corner of Via Candia and Via Mocenigo, Metro: Cipro) and also near Piazza Barberini (Via del Tritone 172, Metro: Barberini).

Affordable Shopping

The shopping area all along **Via del Corso** features moderately priced goods, with prices increasing as you head toward Piazza di Spagna (by the Spanish Steps). **Via Nazionale** also features a range of reasonably priced shops, especially for clothes and shoes. Near the bottom of Via Nazionale, in the **Monti** neighborhood near the Roman Forum, Via del Boschetto and Via dei Serpenti are more unique, with a mix of clothing shops and designer bric-a-brac. **Via Cola di Rienzo,** near the Vatican, is good for midrange clothes. Cheapskates scrounge through the junky but dirt-cheap shops in the gritty area around **Piazza Vittorio.**

Boutique Shopping: Rome's "Shopping Triangle"

The triangular-shaped area between the Spanish Steps, Piazza Venezia, and Piazza del Popolo (along Via del Corso, see map on

ROME

page 826) contains Rome's highest concentration of upscale boutiques and fashion stores. For top fashion, stroll the streets around the Spanish Steps, including **Via dei Condotti, Via Borgognona** (for the big-name shops), and **Via del Babuino** (more big names and a few galleries). For antiques and vintage items, wander **Via dei Coronari** (between Piazza Navona and the bend in the river), **Via Giulia** (between Campo de' Fiori and the river), **Via dei Banchi Vecchi** (parallel to Via Giulia), and the super-chic **Via Margutta,** with art galleries too (hidden parallel to Via del Babuino and running from the Spanish Steps to Piazza del Popolo). For dozens of stores selling affordable apparel aimed mainly at a younger crowd, try **Via Giubbonari** near Campo de' Fiori.

Near Campo de' Fiori

Two worthwhile parallel shopping streets run northwest (toward the river) from Piazza Farnese, just a block south of Campo de' Fiori: Via Monserrato/Via dei Banchi Vecchi and Via Giulia. (Streets in the opposite direction—to the southeast—are sleepier, with fewer shops.)

Heading away from Piazza Farnese on low-key **Via Monserrato,** you'll see several antique, furniture, and home-decorating shops. Hollywood (#107) is a treat for cinephiles, with movie posters and rare DVDs; next door, at #108, is a fascinating old-time cobbler, with a crowded workbench crammed into a tiny shop.

Flea Markets

For antiques and fleas, the granddaddy of markets is the **Porta Portese** *mercato delle pulci* (flea market). This Sunday-morning market is long and spindly, running between the actual Porta Portese (a gate in the old town wall) and the Trastevere train station. While the shopping gets old (and the vendor food shouldn't be consumed), the people-watching is endlessly entertaining (6:30-13:00 Sun only, on Via Portuense and Via Ippolito Nievo; to get to the market, catch bus #75 from Termini train station or tram #8 from Piazza Venezia, get off on Viale di Trastevere, and walk toward the river—and the noise).

At the **Via Sannio** market, you'll find new and used clothing and leather goods, some handicrafts, and random items that were probably stolen. You won't find antiques (Mon-Sat 9:00-13:30, closed Sun, behind Coin department store, just outside the walls of San Giovanni in Laterano, Metro: San Giovanni).

For something a bit hipper, visit the weekend **Mercato Monti** in the Monti district. This flea market has an emphasis on vintage clothes and housewares and up-and-coming designers (Sat-Sun 10:00-20:00, closed July-Aug, Hotel Palatino, Via Leonina 46, Metro: Cavour, www.mercatomonti.com).

Open-Air Produce Markets

For a fun and colorfully authentic experience, wander through the easygoing neighborhood produce markets that clog certain streets and squares every morning (7:00-13:30) except Sunday. Consider the huge **Mercato Trionfale** (three blocks north of Vatican Museums at Via Andrea Doria). Another great food market is the **Mercato Esquilino** (near Termini station at Via Filippo Turati, Metro: Vittorio Emanuele). The covered **Mercato di Testaccio** sells produce and housewares and is a hit with photographers and people-watchers (Metro: Piramide). Smaller but equally charming slices of everyday Roman life are at markets on these streets and squares: **Piazza delle Coppelle** (near the Pantheon), **Via Balbo** (near Termini train station), and **Via della Pace** (near Piazza Navona). And **Campo de' Fiori,** despite having become quite touristy, is still a fun scene.

Nightlife in Rome

For most visitors, the best after-dark activity is simply to grab a gelato and join in the *passeggiata,* the evening stroll through the medieval lanes that connect Rome's romantic, floodlit squares and fountains. Head for Piazza Navona, the Pantheon, Campo de' Fiori, Trevi Fountain, the Spanish Steps, Via del Corso, Trastevere (around the Santa Maria in Trastevere Church), or Monte Testaccio.

Sound-and-Light Shows

The Imperial Forums area hosts two atmospheric and inspirational sound-and-light shows that give you a chance to fantasize about the world of the Caesars. During each of these "nighttime journeys through ancient Rome," you spend about an hour with a headphone dialed to English, listening to an artfully crafted narration synced with projections on ancient walls, columns, and porticos. The final effect is worth the price tag (€15, both for €25, nightly mid-April–mid-Nov—bring your warmest coat, confirm the schedule and prebook on website, shows can sell out on busy weekends, +39 06 0608, www.viaggioneifori.it). If you plan to see both, do Caesar first and allow 80 minutes between starting times.

Caesar's Forum Stroll: Starting at Trajan's Column, this tour leads you to eight stops along a wooden sidewalk of a few hundred yards, while an hour's narration tells the dramatic story of

The *Passeggiata*

Throughout Italy, early evening is time to stroll. While else-where in Italy this ritual is called the *passeggiata,* in Rome it's a cruder, big-city version called the *struscio* (meaning "to rub").

Many of Italy's youth live with their parents even into their 30s. They spend a lot of time being trendy and hanging out. Like American kids once gathered at the mall, working-class suburban youth converge on the old center, as there's little to keep them occupied in Rome's dreary outskirts (which lack public spaces). The hot *vroom-vroom* motor scooter is their symbol; haircuts and fashion are follow-the-leader.

In a more genteel small town, the *passeggiata* comes with sweet whispers of *"bella"* and *"bello"* ("pretty" and "hand-some"). In Rome, the admiration is a little cruder and oriented toward consumption—they say *"buona"* and *"buono"*—roughly meaning "tasty."

You can be a spectator, sipping a drink at a sidewalk table, but it's more fun to stroll along with everyone else.

Julius Caesar. You'll be on the ground level of an archaeological site that is otherwise closed to the public, giving you views you'd never see otherwise. The tour departs every 20 minutes from dark until nearly midnight.

Forum of Augustus Show: From your perch on wooden bleachers overlooking the remains of a vast forum, you'll learn the story of Augustus through images projected on an ancient firewall that survives to provide a fine screen for modern-day spectacles. Showings are on the hour from dark until 22:00 or 23:00. Enter on Via dei Fori Imperiali just before Via Cavour (you'll see the bleach-ers along the boulevard).

Museums and Art Exhibitions

Some **museums** have later opening hours (especially on Sat in summer), offering a good chance to see art in a cooler, less-crowded environment. See the "Rome at a Glance" sidebar on page 822 for suggestions.

Performances and Film

Check out the current listings of concerts, operas, dance, and films. Posters around town also advertise upcoming events. For the most up-to-date events calendar, check these English-language web-sites: www.wantedinrome.com and www.angloinfo.com.

Contemporary Music Scene

Music lovers will seek out the mega-music complex of the Rome **Auditorium** (Auditorium Parco della Musica), designed by con-temporary architect Renzo Piano and hosting concerts by both

ROME

Italian and international artists (€20-60 tickets, check availability in advance—concerts often sell out, Viale Pietro de Coubertin 30, take Metro to Flaminio and then catch tram #2 to Apollodoro, from there it's a 5-minute walk east, just beyond the elevated road, tram/Metro runs until 23:30, box office +39 02 6006 0900, www.auditorium.com).

Classical Music and Opera

The **Teatro dell'Opera** has an active schedule of opera and classical concerts. In the summer, the productions move to the Baths of Caracalla, where ancient ruins make an evocative backdrop. You'll brush shoulders with locals in all their finery, so pull your fanciest outfit from your backpack (tickets from €25, online reservations encouraged, box office takes phone reservations beginning 5 days prior at +39 06 481 7003; Piazza Beniamino Gigli 7, a block off Via Nazionale, Metro: Repubblica; www.operaroma.it).

Opera da Camera di Roma is a cute, tourist-oriented, greatest-hits-of-opera performance in various smaller venues around Rome. While their advertising may make the show seem grander than it is, it's still a charming hour-plus of music—and it comes with a glass of wine. You'll enjoy a revue of the most popular Italian arias and Neapolitan songs in a casual and fun-loving atmosphere. Buy the cheapest tickets and request the Rick Steves upgrade (RS%—use code "RickSteves"; check schedule and book on their website, +39 320 530 7112, www.operadacameradiroma.com).

Tourist-oriented musical events take place at the Episcopal **Church of St. Paul's Within the Walls.** The music ranges from orchestral concerts to full operatic performances to candlelit "Luminaria" concerts. Check the church website (under "Music") to see what's on (arrive 30-45 minutes early for best seat, Via Napoli 58 at corner of Via Nazionale, Metro: Repubblica, +39 06 482 6296, www.stpaulsrome.it).

Jazz

Rome has a small but vibrant jazz scene. **Alexanderplatz** is the venerable club in town (Via Ostia 9, Metro: Ottaviano, +39 06 8678 1296, www.alexanderplatzjazz.com). **TramJazz,** a creative venture by the public transit company, combines dinner, music, and a journey through the city in a vintage cable car for a mostly local crowd (€75, daily at 21:00, 3 hours, leaves from Piazza di Porta Maggiore—reached by tram #5 or #14 from Termini station, book well ahead, www.tramjazz.com).

Bars and Nightspots

I've listed some fun neighborhoods worth exploring after dark, along with a few bars and *enoteche* (wine bars) in each. All of these places are recommended in the "Eating in Rome" section, where you'll find more details on each.

Heart of Rome, near the Pantheon: The scene here is touristy but delightful. The monuments—especially the Pantheon and Trevi Fountain—are magically floodlit at night. Not far from the Trevi Fountain, **L'Antica Birreria Peroni** is a big, boisterous beer hall. Farther south, Campo de' Fiori and the surrounding streets become one big, rude street party around 22:00. One good place to sample the youthful energy, as well as some craft beers, is the rollicking **Open Baladin** pub.

North Rome, near the Spanish Steps and Via del Corso: A babel of international tourists, this glitzy zone is bustling after dark. For many, just hanging out around the Spanish Steps is enough to fill an evening.

Near the Colosseum and Forum, in Monti: The best plan in this lively village-Rome zone is to pop the top off a brew and hang out at the fountain on Piazza della Madonna dei Monti. To join the after-dark scene, buy a drink at the shop on the uphill side of the square (cheap bottles of wine with plastic glasses, beer, fruit, and munchies) and be part of what becomes the hottest bar in the area. There are plenty of makeshift benches around the fountain. For more details, see the Monti section of "Eating in Rome."

Sleeping in Rome

Choosing the right neighborhood in Rome is as important as choosing the right hotel. All of my recommended accommodations are in safe areas convenient to sightseeing. Most central hotels near **ancient Rome** are close to the Colosseum and Roman Forum (with the trendy Monti area nearby). The most romantic ambience is in neighborhoods near the **Pantheon,** which encompass the Campo de' Fiori and the Jewish Ghetto. Hotels near **Vatican City** put St. Peter's and the Vatican Museums at your doorstep. The **Termini train station** neighborhood is a hub of good, midrange hotels that are handy for public transit and services, although the area is not particularly charming. Finally, the bohemian **Trastevere** neighborhood is a good choice for living like a Roman (or a young American expat) when in Rome for a few days.

Off-season, it's common for hotels in Rome to cut their prices up to 50 percent, although prices at hostels and cheaper hotels won't fluctuate much. Room rates are lowest in sweltering August. Book any accommodations well in advance, especially if you'll be traveling during peak season (April-June and Sept-early Nov) or if your trip coincides with a major holiday or festival (see the appendix).

Sleeping at Convents: Rome has many convents that rent out rooms. At convents, the beds are twins and English is often

Hotels & Restaurants near Ancient Rome

Accommodations

1. Hotel Lancelot
2. Nerva Boutique Hotel
3. Hotel Paba
4. Casa Il Rosario
5. Hotel Antica Locanda
6. Hotel Rosetta

Eateries

7. Barzilai Bistrot
8. Taverna Romana
9. Taverna dei Fori Imperiali
10. Alle Carrette Pizzeria
11. Trattoria Valentino
12. Antico Forno ai Serpenti
13. Enoteca Cavour 313
14. Analemma & Pizzeria la Boccaccia
15. Fáfiuché
16. Zia Rosetta
17. Fatamorgana Gelateria
18. Trattoria Luzzi
19. Rist. Pizzeria Naumachia
20. Li Rioni

in short supply, but the price is right. I've listed three nun-run places in this chapter: Casa Il Rosario (near Piazza Venezia), the expensive but divine Casa di Santa Brigida (near Campo de' Fiori), and Suore di Santa Elisabetta (near Termini station). For a longer list of convents, see the Church of St. Patrick's website (www. stpatricksamericanrome.org)—select "Resources" and then "Convent Accommodations."

NEAR ANCIENT ROME

This area is central, so you'll find these hotels are a short walk from the Colosseum and Roman Forum, as well as restaurants and shopping in the Monti district (described on page 922). All except Hotel Lancelot are within a 10-minute walk of the Cavour Metro stop.

$$$$ Hotel Lancelot is a comfortable refuge east of the Colosseum—a 60-room hotel with an elegant feel at a fair price. Located in a pleasant, low-key residential neighborhood, it's quiet and safe, with a shady courtyard, restaurant, bar, and tiny communal sixth-floor terrace. It's well run by the Khan family, who serve a good €25 dinner—a tasty way to connect with your hotel neighbors and the friendly staff. No wonder it's popular with returning guests (family rooms, some view rooms, air-con, elevator, wheelchair accessible, cheap parking, 10-minute walk behind Colosseum near San Clemente Church at Via Capo d'Africa 47, +39 06 7045 0615, www.lancelothotel.com, info@lancelothotel.com). Faris and Lubna speak the Queen's English.

$$$$ Nerva Boutique Hotel is a snazzy slice of tranquility with 20 small, stylish, and often discounted rooms. It sits on a quiet, ideally located side street that faces the Roman Forum and backs onto the enjoyable Monti neighborhood (RS%—use code "RICKSTEVES," air-con, elevator, Via Tor de' Conti 3, +39 06 678 1835, www.hotelnerva.com, info@hotelnerva.com, Antonio and Paolo).

$$$ Hotel Paba is homey, chocolate-box-tidy, and lovingly cared for by Alberta Castelli. It's just two blocks from the Forum. You'll take a vintage elevator to reach the seven rooms. Although some overlook busy Via Cavour, it's quiet enough (RS%, email reservations preferred, big beds, no breakfast, air-con, elevator, Via Cavour 266, second floor, +39 06 4782 4497, www.hotelpaba.com, info@hotelpaba.com).

$$ Casa Il Rosario is a peaceful, well-run Dominican convent renting 40 rooms with monastic simplicity to both pilgrims and tourists in a steep but pleasant corner of the Monti neighborhood. Doubles have two single beds that can be pushed together (RS%—use code "ricksteves," cheaper single rooms with shared bath, reserve several months in advance, some rooms with air-con and others with fans, elevator, small garden and rooftop terrace, midnight curfew, near bottom of Via Nazionale at Via Sant'Agata dei Goti 10, bus #40 or #170 from Termini, +39 06 679 2346, www.casailrosarioroma.it, info@casailrosarioroma.it).

$$ Hotel Antica Locanda is a gem on a small street in the heart of the Monti neighborhood. The 15 rooms—each named for a composer or an artist—come with romantically rustic, stylish furnishings. The rooftop terrace is great for sunbathing or relaxing with a sunset drink (air-con, Via del Boschetto 84, +39 06 484 894, www.anticalocandaroma.it, anticalocandaroma@gmail.com).

$$ Hotel Rosetta, a homey, basic, and family-run *pensione*, rents 11 dated rooms. It's pretty minimal, with no lounge and no breakfast, but its convenient location makes it a fine budget option (air-con, up one flight of stairs, Via Cavour 295, +39 06 4782 3069, www.rosettahotel.com, info@rosettahotel.com, Antonietta and Francesca).

PANTHEON NEIGHBORHOOD

Winding, narrow lanes filled with foot traffic and lined with small shops and tiny trattorias...this part of Rome still feels like a village. As in a real village, buses and taxis are the only practical way to connect with other destinations. The atmosphere doesn't come cheap, but this is a great place to be—especially at night, when Romans and tourists gather in the floodlit piazzas.

This neighborhood has two main transportation hubs: Piazza delle Cinque Lune (just north of Piazza Navona) has a TI, a taxi stand, and (just around the corner) handy buses #81 and #87. Largo Argentina has buses to almost everywhere, a taxi stand, and the tram to Trastevere (#8). Peruse my recommended buses on page 818, and you'll likely find a few (#81, #87, #492, and others) that stop near your hotel.

There are two expensive **Co-op supermarkets** in the neighborhood. One is a half-block from the Pantheon toward Piazza Navona (daily until 22:00, Via Giustiniani 18b). A larger Co-op, with a good bakery and sandwich section, is three blocks from the Pantheon, near Largo Argentina (daily until 21:00, Corso Vittorio Emanuele II 42; for Co-op locations see the map on page 928).

Near Largo Argentina and Campo de' Fiori

Each of these places is romantically set deep in the tangled back streets near the idyllic Campo de' Fiori and, for many, worth the extra money. This area is connected to Termini station by bus along Via Nazionale (#40 or #64). From the airport, consider taking the regional train to Trastevere station and then the #8 tram to Largo Argentina.

$$$$ Relais Teatro Argentina, a six-room gem, is steeped in tasteful old-Rome elegance, but has all the modern comforts. It feels cozy like a B&B (despite the busy streets surrounding it) and couldn't be more centrally located (air-con, 3 flights of stairs, breakfast in room or on balcony, Via del Sudario 35, +39 06 9893 1617, www.relaisteatroargentina.com, info@relaisteatroargentina.com, kind Paolo and Carlotta).

$$$ Arch Rome Suites, in a tranquil palace on the site of the former Baths of Agrippa, is just a few steps from the Pantheon and near the Jewish Ghetto. It rents 12 spacious, modern, and cozy rooms—some with balconies and views (family rooms, air-con, elevator, Via dell'Arco della Ciambella 19, +39 06 4549 8947, www.archromesuites.it, info@archromesuites.com, friendly Marika and Omar).

$$$ Casa di Santa Brigida overlooks the elegant Piazza Farnese. With soft-spoken sisters gliding down polished hallways, and pearly gates instead of doors, this lavish 20-room convent makes exhaust-stained Roman tourists feel like they've died

ROME

Hotels in the Pantheon Neighborhood

To Piazza del Popolo
To Spanish Steps
Tiber River
PONTE UMBERTO
Piazza Ponte Umberto I
#81, 87 & 492
VIA D'ORSO
VIA BRIANZO
Piazza Nicosia
VIA CLEMENTINO
To M Barberini
VIA SANT'ANDREA
7
ANCIENT STADIUM ENTRANCE
PARLIAMENT
UFF. VICARIO
VIA DEL TRITONE
TREVI FOUNTAIN
CORONARI
T
VIA D. COPPELLE
5
Piazza di Montecitorio
Piazza Colonna
VIA DEL CORSO
SABINA
SAN LUIGI
AQUIRO
Piazza di Pietra
MURATTE
TRE SCALINI
SALV. GIUST.
VIA DELLA SCROFA
SAL. CRESC.
Piazza Rotonda
PASTINI
SEMINARIO
Piazza Navona
PANTHEON
SANT' IGNAZIO
S. APOST.
Piazza Pasquino
Piazza Sant' Eust.
6
S. CHIARA
Piazza Collegio Rom.
CITY MUSEUM
SANTA MARIA SOPRA MINERVA
GALLERIA DORIA PAMPHILJ
CORSO VITTORIO EMANUELE II
ARGENTINA
CESTARI
To Colosseum & M
2
VIA PLEBISCITO
Piazza Venezia
3
Campo de' Fiori
CHIAVARI
V. M. D. FARINA
1
T B
LARGO ARGENTINA RUINS
GESÙ
Piazza Farnese
PALAZZO FARNESE
V. GIUBBONARI
VIA D. BOTT. OSCURE
VIA DI SAN MARCO
T B
ARACELI
T
VICTOR EMMANUEL MONUMENT
4
SPECCHI
VIA ARENULA
VIA DEL PORTICO D'OTTAVIA
CAPITOLINE HILL
Piazza del Campidoglio
200 Meters
200 Yards
GHETTO

1 Relais Teatro Argentina
2 Arch Rome Suites
3 Casa di Santa Brigida
4 Hotel Smeraldo
5 Hotel Nazionale
6 Albergo Santa Chiara
7 Hotel Portoghesi

and gone to heaven. You won't have a double bed or a TV in your room, but you can luxuriate in the inn's public spaces or on its lovely roof terrace (book well in advance, air-con, elevator, tasty €25 dinners—reserve ahead, roof garden, plush library, Via di Monserrato 54, +39 06 6889 2596, www.brigidine.org, casabrigidaroma@brigidine.org, many of the sisters are from India and speak English—pray you get to work with wonderful Mother Gertrude).

$$$ Hotel Smeraldo, with 66 rooms, is clean and a reasonable deal in a good location. Sixteen of the rooms are in an annex across the street, but everyone has breakfast in the main building. They have a rooftop bar for afternoon *aperitivi* (air-con, elevator, roof terrace, midway between Campo de' Fiori and Largo Argentina at Via dei Chiavari 20, +39 06 687 5929, www.smeraldoroma. com, info@smeraldoroma.com, Massimo and Walter).

Close to the Pantheon

These places are buried in the pedestrian-friendly heart of ancient Rome, each within about a five-minute walk of the Pantheon. They're an easy walk from many sights but are a bit distant from major public transportation arteries (though buses do run nearby). To get close, arrive and depart by taxi.

$$$$ **Hotel Nazionale,** a four-star landmark, is a 16th-century palace that shares a well-policed square with the Italian Parliament building. Its 100 forgettable rooms are augmented by lush public spaces, fancy bars, a uniformed staff, and a marble-floored breakfast room. It's a big, stuffy, impersonal hotel, but it's a worthy splurge if you want security, comfort, and the heart of Rome at your doorstep (RS%—use code "RICK," family rooms, air-con, elevator, Piazza Montecitorio 131, +39 06 695 001, www. hotelnazionale.it, info@hotelnazionale.it).

$$$$ **Albergo Santa Chiara,** remarkably central just a few steps behind the Pantheon, is big, solid, and hotelesque. Flavia, Silvio, and their fine staff offer marbled elegance (but somewhat dated furnishings) and all the hotel services. Its ample public lounges are dressy and professional, and its 96 rooms are quiet and spacious (RS%—use code "RICK," family rooms, air-con, elevator, behind the Pantheon at Via di Santa Chiara 21, +39 06 687 2979, www.albergosantachiara.com, info@albergosantachiara.com).

$$$$ **Hotel Portoghesi** is a classic hotel with 27 colorful rooms in the medieval heart of Rome. It's peaceful, quiet, and comes with a delightful roof terrace—though you pay for the location (family rooms, breakfast on roof, air-con, elevator, Via dei Portoghesi 1, +39 06 686 4231, www.hotelportoghesiroma.it, info@ hotelportoghesiroma.it).

NEAR VATICAN CITY

Sleeping near the Vatican costs a little more, but some enjoy calling this relaxed, residential neighborhood home. The tree-lined streets are wider than in the historical center, so it feels less claustrophobic. Although it's handy to the Vatican, everything else is a long way away. Fortunately, it's well served by public transit, especially the Metro (line A). Most of these listings are within a 10-minute walk of either the Cipro or Ottaviano Metro stops.

$$$$ **Hotel dei Consoli,** family-run with 28 rooms, is a lesser value pleasantly located on a side street. Breakfast is served on its leafy rooftop terrace, with a view to St. Peter's—a nice way to start the day (RS%, air-con, elevator, Via Varrone 2D, +39 06

ROME

Hotels & Restaurants near Vatican City

ROME

6889 2972, www.hoteldeiconsoli.com, info@hoteldeiconsoli.com, friendly Laura and mom Amalia).

$$$$ Tmark Hotel Vaticano, facing the Vatican Museums, features four stars, 24 spacious rooms, and all the modern comforts (air-con, elevator, Viale Vaticano 99, +39 06 3974 5562, www.tmarkhotelvaticano.it, info@tmarkhotelvaticano.it).

$$$$ Hearth Hotel, a block from the Vatican wall, has 22 small, modern, efficient, and characterless rooms (RS%—use code "rick steves," air-con, elevator, Via Santamaura 2, +39 06 3903 8383, www.hearthhotel.com, info@hearthhotel.com).

$$$ Hotel Museum is located steps from the Vatican Museums. It has 31 modest but comfortable rooms and large public spaces, including a piano lounge, pool table, and rooftop terrace (family rooms, air-con, elevator, down the stairs directly in front of Vatican

Accommodations

1. Hotel dei Consoli
2. Tmark Hotel Vaticano
3. Hearth Hotel
4. Hotel Museum
5. Casa Valdese

Eateries & Other

6. Il Colibrì
7. Be.Re. & L'Insalata Ricca
8. Duecento Gradi
9. Gelateria Old Bridge
10. Forno Feliziani
11. Tre Pupazzi
12. Vecchio Borgo
13. Mercato Trionfale
14. Supermarket (2)

Museums, Via Tunisi 8, +39 06 9727 6695, www.hotelmuseum.it, info@hotelmuseum.it).

$$ Casa Valdese is a well-managed, Protestant church-run hotel that's a good value and feels a bit institutional. Its 33 renovated but basic rooms come with the bonus of two breezy, communal roof terraces with incredible views (family rooms, air-con, elevator, Via Alessandro Farnese 18, Metro: Lepanto, +39 06 321 5362, www.casavaldeseroma.it, reception@casavaldeseroma.it).

NEAR TERMINI STATION

While this neighborhood is not as atmospheric as other areas of Rome, the hotels near Termini train station are less expensive, and the Metro and buses link you easily to the rest of the city. My rec-

Hotels near Termini Station

To Spanish Steps

V.D. ARTISTI
VIA VENETO
V. BISO
B

CAPUCHIN CRYPT

V. DI SAN BASILIO

SANTA MARIA VITTORIA

VIA SISTINA
V. PURIFICAZIONE
❷

Barberini
M

VIA BARBERINI

SANTA SUSANNA

Piazza di San Bernardo

MOSES FOUNTAIN

GROC.

Piazza Barberini
T

PALAZZO BARBERINI

❼

SAN BERNARDO

VIA DEL TRITONE
V. AVIG.
BOCC.
VIA D. QUATTRO FONTANE

VIA XX. SETTEMBRE

❺

VIA FIRENZE

❹

❶

V. TRAFORO
V. RASELLA
VIA DEI GIARDINI

FOUR FOUNTAINS

B

V. IN.
V. ARCIONE

Quirinal Gardens

VIA DEPRETIS

#40 & 64
B

To Trevi & Pantheon

SAN CARLO

PHARMACY

VIA NAPOLI

❸

PALAZZO DEL QUIRINALE

VIA QUIRINALE
VIA FERRARA

SANT' ANDREA

VIA NAZIONALE

VIA DATARIA

To Trevi & Pantheon

Piazza del Quirinale

PALAZZO DELLE ESPOSIZIONI

V. MILANO

VIA VENEZIA
GENOVA
VIA PALERMO

❻
T

SCUDERIE DEL QUIRINALE

VIA NAZIONALE

VIA CAVOUR

❶ Hotel Cellini	❾ Hotel Domus Nova Bethlem
❷ Hotel Modigliani	❿ Hotel Montreal
❸ IQ Hotel	⓫ Suore di Sta. Elisabetta
❹ Hotel Aberdeen	⓬ Hotel Astoria Garden
❺ Hotels Oceania & Nardizzi Americana	⓭ The Beehive
❻ Hotel Italia	⓮ Hotel Robinson
❼ The RomeHello	⓯ YellowSquare Hostel
❽ Hotel Raffaello	

ommendations are within a 10-minute walk of the station (some are actually closer to the Repubblica Metro stop).

West of the Station

Most of these hotels are on or near Via Firenze, a safe, handy, central, and relatively quiet street that's a 10-minute walk from Termini and the airport train, and two blocks beyond Piazza della Repubblica. The Defense Ministry is nearby, so you've got heavily armed guards watching over you all night.

The neighborhood is served by two Metro stops: Repubblica (line A) and Termini (intersection of lines A and B). Virtually all the city buses that rumble down Via Nazionale (#60, #64, #70, and the #40 express) take you to Piazza Venezia (near the Forum).

These neighborhood supermarkets are all open daily until late (for locations see the map on page 938): **Co-op** (Via Nazionale 213, at the corner of Via Venezia), **Carrefour Express** (corner of Via Napoli and Via del Viminale), and **Sapori & Dintori** (downstairs from the inner atrium at Termini station). There are many smaller grocery stores, as well.

$$$$ Hotel Cellini feels like the guest wing of a gorgeous Neoclassical palace. It offers 13 rooms, "ortho/anti-allergy beds," four-star comforts and service, and a small, breezy terrace where you

ROME

can enjoy breakfast (RS%, air-con, elevator, Via Modena 5, third floor, +39 06 4782 5204, www.hotelcellini.it, info@hotelcellini.it; Barbara, Gaetano, and Donato).

$$$$ Hotel Modigliani, a delightful 23-room place, is energetically run in a clean, bright, minimalist yet in-love-with-life style that its artist namesake would appreciate. It has a vast and plush lounge, a garden, and a newsletter introducing you to each of the staff (RS%, air-con, elevator; from Tritone Fountain on Piazza Barberini, go 2 blocks up Via della Purificazione to #42; +39 06 4281 5226, www.hotelmodigliani.com, info@hotelmodigliani.com, Giulia and Marco).

$$$$ IQ Hotel, in a modern blue building facing the Opera House, feels almost Scandinavian in its efficiency, without a hint of the Old World. It lacks charm, but more than compensates with modern amenities. Its 90 rooms are fresh and spacious, the roof garden comes with a play area and foosball, and vending machines dispense bottles of wine (RS%, family rooms, breakfast extra, air-con, elevator, cheap self-service laundry, gym, Via Firenze 8, +39 06 488 0465, www.iqhotelroma.it, info@iqhotelroma.it, Diego).

$$$ Hotel Aberdeen, which combines quality and friendliness, is warmly run by Annamaria, with support from sister Laura, cousin Cinzia, and staff member Costel. The 37 comfy rooms, on the ground floor and one floor up, are a fine value (RS%—use "Rick Steves reader reservations" link, family rooms, air-con, Via Firenze 48, +39 06 482 3920, www.hotelaberdeen.it, info@hotelaberdeen.it).

$$$ Hotel Oceania is a peaceful slice of air-conditioned heaven. The 24 rooms are spacious, quiet, and tastefully decorated, and the elegant sitting room has a manor-house feel. Stefano runs a fine staff, serves wonderful coffee, provides lots of thoughtful extra touches, and works hard to maintain a caring family atmosphere (RS%—use code "RICKSTEVES," family rooms, elevator, TV lounge, Via Firenze 38, third floor, +39 06 482 4696, www.hoteloceania.it, info@hoteloceania.it; Kira and Roberto round out the staff).

$$ Hotel Nardizzi Americana, with a small rooftop terrace, 34 slightly scruffy rooms, and a laid-back atmosphere, is another decent value (RS%—email reservation for discount, family rooms, air-con, elevator, Via Firenze 38, fourth floor, +39 06 488 0035, www.hotelnardizzi.it, info@hotelnardizzi.it; friendly Stefano, Fabrizio, Mario, and Giancarlo).

$$ Hotel Italia enjoys a handy locale on a side street next to the Ministry of the Interior. It has a nice, harmonious feeling and 35 modest but comfortable rooms plus four newer, more expensive "residenza" rooms on the third floor (RS%, family rooms, air-con, elevator, Via Venezia 18, just off Via Nazionale, +39 06 482 8355, www.hotelitaliaroma.it, info@hotelitaliaroma.it; Andrea, Sabrina, and Abdul). They offer eight similar annex rooms across the street for the same price as the main hotel.

¢ **The RomeHello** hostel is, as its slogan brags, "more than just a bed." It's a modern, quiet, and friendly hostel run with a mission to employ locals and provide a comfortable home for travelers, with about 200 beds in doubles, triples, and dorms. The public areas and guest kitchen feel like a computer-generated image of a hostel utopia (Via Torino 45, +39 06 9686 0070, www.theromehello.com, ciao@theromehello.com).

Southwest of the Station

These good-value places cluster around the Basilica of Santa Maria Maggiore. Most are a five-minute walk from the Cavour Metro stop.

$$$ Hotel Raffaello, with a professional staff, offers 41 rooms in a grand 19th-century building on the edge of the Monti district. This formal hotel comes with generous public spaces and a breakfast room fit for aristocrats (family rooms, air-con, elevator, Via Urbana 3, +39 06 488 4342, www.hotelraffaello.it, info@hotelraffaello.it).

$$ Hotel Domus Nova Bethlem, owned by the Oblate Sisters of Baby Jesus, is a spacious, institutional-feeling hotel. The 38 high-ceilinged rooms are modest yet classy, and guests have access to a peaceful and leafy courtyard garden (RS%, air-con, elevator, expensive pay parking, Via Cavour 85A, +39 06 4782 4414, www.dnbhotel.com, info@dnbhotel.com).

$$ Hotel Montreal is a basic three-star place with 27 rooms on a big, noisy street a block southeast of Santa Maria Maggiore (RS%, family rooms, air-con, elevator, small garden terrace; Via Carlo Alberto 4, 1 block from Metro: Vittorio Emanuele, 3 blocks from Termini train station, +39 06 445 7797, www.hotelmontrealroma.it, info@hotelmontrealroma.it, Fabrizio).

$ Suore di Santa Elisabetta is a heavenly Polish-run convent with a serene garden, roof terrace with grand views, and 37 rooms. All doubles have twin beds. Often booked long in advance, with such tranquility it's a super value (family rooms, cheaper rooms with shared bath, fans but no air-con, elevator for top floors, guest kitchen, Wi-Fi in lounge only, 23:00 curfew; a block southwest of Santa Maria Maggiore at Via dell'Olmata 9, Metro: Termini or Vittorio Emanuele; +39 06 488 8271, www.csse-roma.com, select "Casa per ferie" for English, ist.it.s.elisabetta@libero.it).

ROME

Sleeping Cheaply, Northeast of the Station

The cheapest beds in town are beyond Termini train station, to the northeast: Standing so that the tracks dead-end into your back,

Accommodations

❶ Residenza Arco dei Tolomei & Arco del Lauro B&B

❷ Hotel Santa Maria

❸ Hotel San Francesco

Eateries & Other

❹ Taverna Trilussa

❺ Dar Sor Olimpio al Drago

❻ Trattoria de Gli Amici

❼ La Prosciutteria Cantina dei Papi

❽ Pizzeria "Ai Marmi"

❾ Pizzeria Dar Poeta

❿ Trapizzino Vineria di Roma

⓫ Grattachecca Stand

⓬ Almost Corner Bookshop

⓭ Open Door Bookshop

this neighborhood is to your right (Metro: Termini). The streets quiet down a block or so away from the station, and these hotels feel plenty safe.

$$ Hotel Astoria Garden is a modern and comfortable 54-room hotel (air-con, elevator, Via V. Bachelet 6, +39 06 446 9908, www.hotelastoriagarden.it, hotelastoriagarden@gmail.com).

$ The Beehive gives vagabonds—old and young—a cheap, clean, and comfy home in Rome (air-con in some rooms, breakfast extra, private garden terrace, *aperitivo* with pizza in the afternoon, 2 blocks from Termini train station at Via Marghera 8, +39 06 4470 4553, www.the-beehive.com, info@the-beehive.com).

$ Hotel Robinson is your dreary, bare-bones-basic budget

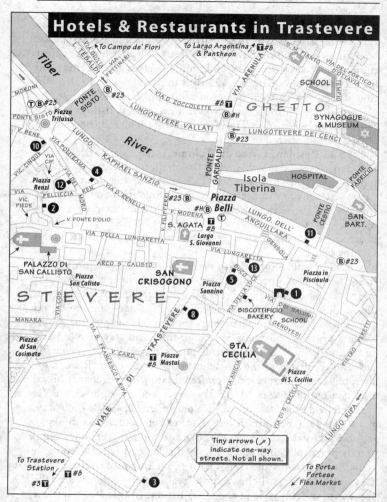

Hotels & Restaurants in Trastevere

option, just a few steps from the station. Tucked away from the commotion on an interior courtyard, it has 20 small and simple rooms (RS%—includes breakfast and air-con when you pay in cash, apartment also available, Via Milazzo 3, +39 06 491 423, www.hotelrobinsonrome.com, info@hotelrobinsonrome.com).

¢**YellowSquare Hostel** is hip yet sane, with loads of activities (Via Palestro 44, +39 06 446 3554, https://yellowsquare.it/roma).

TRASTEVERE

Colorful and genuine, with uneven cobbles and remnants of its tumbledown past, Trastevere is a treat for travelers looking for a more residential, bohemian atmosphere. (🎧 Download my free

Trastevere Walk **audio tour** to explore the neighborhood.) It's also very trendy among American college students and young expats, who fill its bars and restaurants. The heart of Rome and its ancient ruins are just across the river, and tram #8 makes getting there and back a snap. Convenient bus #23 runs to the Vatican area, bus #H runs directly to Termini (none on Sun), and tram #3 goes to the Colosseum. From the airport, you can reach these listings by taking the regional train to Trastevere train station, and the #8 tram downhill from there.

$$$$ Residenza Arco dei Tolomei is the most poetic Trastevere experience imaginable, with six small, unique, antique-filled rooms, some boasting fragrant balconies. In this quiet and elegant setting, you can pretend you're visiting aristocratic relatives (reserve well in advance, air-con, from Piazza Piscinula a block up Via dell'Arco de' Tolomei at #27, +39 06 5832 0819, www.bbarcodeitolomei.com, info@bbarcodeitolomei.com, Marco and Gianna Paola).

$$$$ Hotel Santa Maria sits like a lazy hacienda in the middle of Trastevere. Surrounded by a medieval skyline, you'll feel as if you're on some romantic stage set. Its 20 small but well-equipped, air-conditioned rooms—former cells in a cloister—are mostly on the ground floor, as are a few suites for up to six people. The rooms circle a gravelly courtyard of orange trees and stay-awhile patio furniture. Privacy is limited and noises travel, but it's generally peaceful compared to the bustle just outside the door (RS%, family rooms, email reservations preferred, air-con, free loaner bikes, face church on Piazza Maria Trastevere and go right down Via della Fonte d'Olio 50 yards to Vicolo del Piede 2, +39 06 589 4626, www.hotelsantamariatrastevere.it, info@hotelsantamaria.info).

$$$ Hotel San Francesco, big and modern yet welcoming, stands practically and efficiently at the far end of Trastevere. It rents 24 trim rooms and comes with an inviting roof terrace (May-Oct only). It's a good choice for a "real" hotel—compared to the more casual B&B style of the other listings in this area—but is a bit farther from the action (email reservations preferred, air-con, elevator, on-site restaurant, Via Jacopa de' Settesoli 7, +39 06 5830 0051, www.hotelsanfrancesco.net, hotelsanfrancesco@gmail.com).

$$$ Arco del Lauro B&B rents six tight, whitewashed, straightforward rooms around a dim, quiet back courtyard. Consider it the less expensive version of the Residenza Arco dei Tolomei, which is upstairs. The lower prices make up for the lack of public spaces and mostly offsite management (one family room, includes small breakfast at nearby café, air-con, from Piazza Piscinula a block up Via dell'Arco de' Tolomei at #29, +39 346 244 3212, www.arcodellauro.it, info@arcodellauro.it, Lorenza and Daniela).

Eating in Rome

Romans take great pleasure in dining well. Embrace this passion over a multicourse meal at an outdoor table, watching a parade of passersby while you sip wine with loved ones.

Roman meals are lengthy social occasions. Simple, fresh, seasonal ingredients dominate the dishes. The *cucina* is robust, strongly flavored, and unpretentious—much like the people who've created it over the centuries. It is said that Roman cooking didn't come out of emperors' or popes' kitchens, but from the *cucina povera*—the home cooking of the common people. This may explain the Romans' fondness for meats known as the *quinto quarto* ("fifth quarter"), such as tripe, tail, brain, and pigs' feet, as well as their interest in natural preservatives like chili peppers and garlic.

Rome belongs to the warm, southern region of Lazio, which produces a rich variety of flavorful vegetables and fruit that are the envy of American supermarkets. Rome's proximity to the Mediterranean also allows for a great variety of seafood.

EATING TIPS

Kitchens close at most restaurants between lunch and dinner; if it's a quality restaurant, it won't reopen before 19:00. If a smaller restaurant is booked up later in the evening (from 20:30 or so), they may accommodate walk-ins if you're willing to eat quickly.

Choosing Restaurants: I've listed restaurants that I enjoy. Many are in characteristic and touristy (and therefore pricey) areas such as Piazza Navona, Campo de' Fiori, and Trastevere. Others are tucked away from the tourist crush.

I'm impressed by how small the price difference can be between a mediocre Roman restaurant and a fine one. You can pay about 20 percent more for double the quality. If I had $100 for three meals in Rome, I'd spend $50 for one and $25 each for the other two, rather than $33 on all three. For splurge meals, I'd consider Gabriello (near the Spanish Steps) and Taverna Trilussa (in Trastevere), described later.

Rome's fabled squares—most notably Piazza Navona, near the Pantheon, and Campo de' Fiori—are lined with the outdoor tables of touristy restaurants with enticing menus and formal-vested waiters. The atmosphere is super romantic but restaurants in these areas are notorious for surprise charges, forgettable food, microwaved ravioli, and bad service. I enjoy the view by savoring just a drink or dessert on a famous square, but I dine with locals on nearby low-rent streets, where the proprietor needs to serve a good-value meal and nurture a local following to stay in business.

If you're set on eating—or just drinking and snacking—on a famous piazza, you don't need a guidebook listing to choose a spot;

enjoy the ritual of slowly circling the square, observing both the food and the people eating it, and sit where the view and menu appeal to you.

The *Aperitivo* Tradition: For a fun drink and snacks in a memorable Roman setting, consider partaking in an *aperitivo* buffet. Bars all over town serve up a buffet of small dishes, from about 18:00 to 21:00, and anyone buying a drink (generally €8-12) is entitled to one or two heavy appetizers.

Picnicking: A good budget option is to assemble a picnic and dine with Rome as your backdrop. Buy ingredients for your picnic at one of Rome's open-air produce markets (mornings only; see page 902), an *alimentari* (corner grocery store), a *rosticcerie* (cheap food to go), or a *supermercato,* such as Conad or Co-op. You'll find handy late-night supermarkets near the Pantheon (Via Giustiniani), Spanish Steps (Via Vittoria), Trevi Fountain (Via del Bufalo), and Campo de' Fiori (Via di Monte della Farina). Note that Rome discourages people from picnicking or drinking at historic monuments (such as at the Pantheon) in the old center. Violators can be fined. You'll be OK if you eat *with* a view rather than *in* the view and remain discreet.

ANCIENT ROME: NEAR THE COLOSSEUM AND FORUM

Within a block of the Colosseum and Forum, you'll find convenient eateries catering to weary sightseers, most offering neither memorable food nor good value. To get your money's worth, stick with one of my recommendations, even if it means a 10-minute walk from the ruins. For locations, see the map on page 906.

Monti

Behind the Imperial Forums, nestled in the tight and cobbled lanes between Via Nazionale and Via Cavour, is the characteristic (and trendy) Monti neighborhood. While young American expats gravitate to Trastevere, the Monti crowd is predominantly Roman. It's just a few steps farther from the ancient sites than the battery of forgettable touristy restaurants, but that extra effort opens up a world of characteristic dining experiences. From the Forum, head up Via Cavour and then left on Via dei Serpenti; the action centers on Piazza della Madonna dei Monti and nearby lanes.

$$ Barzilai Bistrot, a family-run wine bar with a kitchen under stout timbers, feels like the neighborhood hangout. The bar is inviting if you just want a nice glass of wine with a plate of meat and cheese. Or consider the full menu, mixing Italian and international influences—from pastas to burgers (daily 9:00-24:00, Sun until 18:00, no reservations, Via Panisperna 44, +39 06 487 4979).

$$ Taverna Romana is small, simple, and a bit chaotic—with an open kitchen and servers scurrying to and fro. This family-run eatery's *tonnarelli cacio e pepe* (cheese-and-pepper pasta) is a favorite. Book ahead at busy times (daily 12:30-14:45 & 19:00-22:45, Via della Madonna dei Monti 79, +39 06 474 5325, www.monti79.it).

$$$ Taverna dei Fori Imperiali serves typical, slightly higher-priced Roman cuisine in a snug interior that bustles with energy (Wed-Mon 12:30-15:00 & 19:30-22:30, closed Tue, reserve for dinner, Via della Madonna dei Monti 9, +39 06 679 8643, www. latavernadeiforiimperiali.com).

$$ Alle Carrette Pizzeria—simple, rustic, and family-friendly—serves great wood-fired pizza. It's just 200 yards from the Forum, tucked down a sleepy dead-end lane with outdoor tables just off Via Cavour. It's cheap and fast (daily 12:00-15:30 & 19:00-24:00, Vicolo delle Carrette 14—or enter from Via della Madonna dei Monti 95, +39 06 679 2770).

$$ Trattoria Valentino is a classic time warp hiding under its historic (and therefore protected) *Birra Peroni* sign. They specialize in *scamorza* (grilled cheese with various toppings), list the day's pastas on a chalkboard, and serve a variety of meat dishes (Mon-Sat 13:00-14:45 & 19:30-23:00, closed Sun, Via del Boschetto 37, +39 06 488 0643).

$ Antico Forno ai Serpenti, a hip bakery with a few simple tables, puts out a small selection of *panini*, baked potatoes, and lasagna. They also bake good bread and pastries and do breakfasts (order at the counter, daily 7:00-22:00, Via dei Serpenti 122, +39 06 4542 7920).

$$ Enoteca Cavour 313 is a quality wine bar with a menu ranging from Lazio specialties and salads to high-quality *affettati* (cold cuts) and cheese. You'll be served with a mellow ambience under lofts of wine bottles, enjoying spacious-for-Rome seating (Mon-Sat 12:30-14:45 & 18:00-23:30, closed Sun, 100 yards off Via dei Fori Imperiali at Via Cavour 313, +39 06 678 5496, Angelo).

Monti *Aperitivo:* Look for bars hosting the *aperitivo*—a happy hour where, for the cost of a drink (€8-12), you get access to a buffet of simple dishes. It's a basic dinner (the Italian equivalent of macaroni and cheese, Spam, and Jello) in a fun scene with a drink. A good example, just a block off Monti's main square, is **Analemma,** which has a casual, youthful scene and a nightly buffet with a drink for about €10 (18:30-22:00, Via Leonina 77).

Monti Food Crawl

The streets of Monti are crowded with fun and creative places offering inexpensive quality snacks and light meals to eat on tiny informal tables or to take away. For a fun movable feast, drop in for

Roman Cuisine

Here are some Roman specialties worth seeking out. For more on Italian food, including salumi, cheeses, pizza, and pasta, see the "Eating" section of the Practicalities chapter.

Antipasti (Appetizers)

Antipasto misto: Marinated or grilled vegetables (eggplant, artichokes, peppers, mushrooms), cured meats, cheeses, or seafood (anchovies, octopus).

Fritti: Battered or breaded fried snacks—often olives stuffed with meat, potato croquettes, or mozzarella balls. Other classics are *supplì* (rice balls with tomato sauce and mozzarella) and *fiori di zucca* (squash blossoms filled with mozzarella and anchovies).

Prosciutto e melone: Cantaloupe wrapped in thin-sliced ham.

Primo Piatto (First Course)

Bucatini all'amatriciana: Thin pasta tubes with a sauce of tomatoes, *guanciale* (cured pork cheek), *pecorino romano*, and hot chili peppers.

Gnocchi alla romana: Dumplings made from semolina (not potatoes) and baked with butter and cheese.

Pasta alla gricia: Guanciale (cured pork cheek) and *pecorino romano* cheese.

Pasta cacio e pepe: Simply *pecorino romano* cheese and fresh-ground black pepper.

Penne all'arrabbiata: Spicy tomato sauce with chili peppers (*peperoncini*) and garlic over penne.

Rigatoni con la pajata: Pasta topped with a stew of calf intestines.

Spaghetti alla carbonara: Pasta prepared with raw eggs, *guanciale* (cured pork cheek), *pecorino romano,* and black pepper.

Spaghetti alle vongole: Pasta served with small clams in the shell.

Stracciatella alla romana: Meat broth with whipped eggs, topped with parmesan; Rome's version of "egg drop soup."

Secondo Piatto (Second Course)

Abbacchio alla scottadito: Baby lamb chops grilled and eaten as finger food.

Anguillette in umido: Stewed baby eels from Lake Bracciano.

Coda alla vaccinara: Oxtail braised with garlic, wine, tomato, and celery.

Filetti di baccalà: Battered and fried salt cod (like fish-and-chips minus the chips).

Involtini di vitello al sugo: Veal cutlets rolled with prosciutto, celery, and cheese in a tomato sauce.

Saltimbocca alla romana: "Jump-in-the-mouth"—thinly sliced veal layered with prosciutto and sage, then lightly fried.

Trippa alla romana: Tripe braised with onions, carrots, and mint.

Contorni (Side Dishes)

You may want to order a side dish if your second course is not served with a vegetable. Note that olive oil and wine vinegar are typically the only salad dressings.

Carciofi: Artichokes served either *alla romana* (simmered with garlic and mint) or *alla giudia* (flattened and fried).

Fave al guanciale: Fava beans simmered with cured pork cheek and onion.

Misticanza: Mixed green salad.

Puntarelle: Curly chicory served with a dressing of oil, vinegar, and anchovy.

Dolci (Desserts)

Dessert can be a seasonal fruit, such as *fragole* (strawberries) or *pesche* (peaches), or even cheese, such as *pecorino romano* (made from ewe's milk) or *caciotta romana* (combination of ewe's and cow's milk).

Bignè: Cream-puff-like pastries filled with *zabaione* (egg yolks, sugar, and Marsala wine).

Crostata di ricotta: A cheesecake-like dessert with ricotta, sweet Marsala wine, cinnamon, and bits of chocolate.

Grattachecca: Sweetened shaved ice. Vendors at little booths scrape shavings off ice blocks, then flavor them with syrups, such as *limoncocco* (lemon and coconut with fresh chunks of coconut).

Roman Pizza

Roman-style pizza is made with a very thin and crispy dough called *scrocchiarella* (thinner and less chewy than Neapolitan-style pizza). In Rome, *pizza bianca* (white pizza) can mean a pizza made without tomato sauce, but can also simply mean a chunk of flat, crispy bread, or a sandwich made with that bread (similar to what's called a *panino* in other parts of Italy).

Local Wines

Rome is located in the region of Lazio, which produces several pleasant white wines and a few reds. Frascati, the region's dominant wine, is an affordable, drink-able, dry white made from trebbiano (from the hills just south of Rome) and malvasia grapes. Castelli Romani, light and fairly dry, is made from trebbiano grapes and is similar to Marino, Colli Albani, and Velletri wines. Torre Ercolana is a dense, balanced, medium-bodied red made from the region-al cesanese grape, as well as cabernet and merlot (known as Lazio's best-quality red, aged at least five years).

a bite to whatever casual places you see that appeal. Here are some ideas:

Wine with *Aperitivo* (dinner only): **$$ Fáfiuché** is an intimate yet vibrant family-run wine bar with a fun-loving vibe and no pretense. They serve a broad selection of wines and beers inside or at tables on the cobblestones outside. Andrea, Maria, and their son Gianmarco offer serious dishes from Apulia and Piedmont. And, if you're assembling a mobile dinner, they put out an inviting buffet for your choice of affordable tapas plates (Mon-Sat 18:30-21:00, closed Sun, Via della Madonna dei Monti 28).

Pizza by the Slice on the Square: The hole-in-the-wall **$ Pizzeria la Boccaccia** is good for a takeaway slice. Point at what you like and mime how big of a rectangle you want (pricing by the *etto*, or 100 grams, daily, Via Leonina 73). Take it a block away to the main square (Piazza della Madonna dei Monti), buy a beer at the convenience store (top of the square), and make the piazza scene.

Gourmet Sandwich and Veggie Juice: Gourmet *rosette*—sandwiches on rose-shaped buns—are the specialty at **$ Zia Rosetta.** They're perfect for a light bite to take away or eat in. A fun, healthy, and creative menu includes salads and *centrifughe*—fresh-squeezed, vitamin-bomb fruit and veggie juices (Mon-Wed 11:00-16:00, Thu-Sun until 22:00, Via Urbana 54).

Gelato: Hiding on the welcoming little square just above Zia Rosetta, **Fatamorgana** features some of the most creative gelato combinations I've seen in Italy, along with more conventional flavors. Portions are small but good quality—everything is organic and gluten-free (Piazza degli Zingari 5).

Behind the Colosseum

A pleasant little residential zone just up the street from the back of the Colosseum (the opposite direction from the Forum) features a real neighborhood feel and a variety of restaurants that capably serve tired and hungry sightseers.

$ Trattoria Luzzi is a well-worn, no-frills eatery serving simple food in a high-energy—sometimes chaotic—environment (as they've done since 1945). With good prices, big portions, and proximity to the Colosseum, it draws a crowd, so reserve ahead or expect a short wait at lunch and after 19:30 (Thu-Tue 12:00-24:00, closed Wed, Via Celimontana 1, +39 06 709 6332).

$$ Ristorante Pizzeria Naumachia, next door to Trattoria Luzzi, is another solid bet with slightly higher (but still reasonable) prices, a bit more refinement, and tasty pastas and pizza (daily 11:00-23:00, Via Celimontana 7, +39 06 700 2764).

$$ Li Rioni, a pizzeria, is open only for dinner, when its over-the-rooftops interior and terrace out front are jammed with Romans watching the busy chef plunge dough into its wood-fired oven, then pull out crispy-crust Roman-style pizzas (Wed-Mon 19:30-24:00, closed Tue, Via dei SS. Quattro 24, +39 06 7045 0605).

PANTHEON NEIGHBORHOOD

I've listed the restaurants in this central area based on which landmark they're closest to: Campo de' Fiori, Piazza Navona, the Trevi Fountain, or the Pantheon itself.

On and near Campo de' Fiori

By day, Campo de' Fiori hosts a colorful fruit-and-veggies market (with an increasing number of tourist knickknacks; Mon-Sat until around 13:30, closed Sun). Combined with a sandwich and a sweet from **Forno Campo de' Fiori,** the bakery in the west corner of the square (behind the fountain), you can assemble a nice picnic.

In the evening, Campo de' Fiori offers a characteristic setting—although it can be overrun by tourists out drinking.

$$$ Emma bills itself as a pizzeria, but it's so much more. Tucked down a quiet side street near Campo de' Fiori, it has an enticing menu, often supplemented with seasonal additions. The prices are a bit high, but the quality is also a step above—as evidenced by the higher ratio of Romans to visitors for this very touristy part of town. Reserve ahead (daily 12:30-15:30 & 19:00-23:00, Via del Monte della Farina 28, +39 06 6476 0475, https://emmapizzeria.com).

$$ Enoteca L'Angolo Divino is an inviting little wine bar run by Massimo Crippa, a sommelier who beautifully describes a fine array of wines along with the best accompanying meats, cheeses, and pastas. With tiny tables, a tiny menu, great wines by the glass, intriguing walls of wine bottles, smart advice, more locals than tourists, and a smooth jazz vibe, this place can leave you with a lifelong memory (daily 17:00-24:00 plus Tue-Sat 11:00-14:00, a block off Campo de' Fiori at Via dei Balestrari 12, +39 06 686 4413).

$ Antico Forno Roscioli is an attractive upscale bakery with a few stools, selling a tempting array of breads, pizzas, and pastries (Mon-Sat 7:30-20:00, Sun 8:30-18:00, Via dei Chiavari 34).

$ Filetti di Baccalà is a cheap and basic Roman classic, where nostalgic regulars cram in at wooden tables and savor €6 fried cod finger-food fillets and raw, slightly bitter *puntarelle* greens (slathered with anchovy sauce, available in spring and winter). Study what others are eating, and order from your grease-stained server by pointing at what you want. Sit in the fluorescently lit interior or try to grab a seat out on the little square, a quiet haven a block east of Campo de' Fiori (Mon-Sat 17:00-23:00, closed Sun, Largo dei Librari 88, +39 06 686 4018). If you're not into greasy spoons, avoid this place.

$$ Open Baladin is a busy, modern, and spacious brewpub

Restaurants in the Pantheon Neighborhood

On and Near Campo de' Fiori
1. Forno Campo de' Fiori
2. Emma
3. Enoteca L'Angolo Divino
4. Antico Forno Roscioli
5. Filetti di Baccalà
6. Open Baladin Pub

Near Piazza Navona
7. Vivi Bistrot
8. Cul de Sac
9. L'Insalata Ricca
10. Rist. Pizzeria "da Francesco"
11. Pizzeria da Baffetto
12. Chiostro del Bramante

ROME

<u>Near Trevi Fountain</u>
- ⑬ To Hostaria Romana
- ⑭ Origano
- ⑮ L'Antica Birreria Peroni

<u>Close to the Pantheon</u>
- ⑯ Enoteca Corsi, Pane Pane Vino ar Vino & L'Antico Caffee della Pigna
- ⑰ Da Gino al Parlamento
- ⑱ Ristorante la Campana
- ⑲ Osteria delle Coppelle & Osteria da Mario

- ⑳ Ginger
- ㉑ Miscellanea

<u>Picnicking & Gelato</u>
- ㉒ Frullati Pascucci
- ㉓ Supermarket (2)
- ㉔ Cremeria Monteforte
- ㉕ Giolitti Gelateria
- ㉖ Gelateria Artigianale Corona

featuring a few dozen Italian craft beers on tap and a menu of burgers, salads, and freshly cooked potato chips. As burger bars are trendy in Italy, prices are somewhat high. It's a nice break if you're parched and ready for pub grub (Mon-Fri 12:00-15:00 & 18:00-late, Sat-Sun 12:00-late, Via degli Specchi 5, +39 06 683 8989).

Near Piazza Navona

Piazza Navona and the streets just to the west are jammed with an amazing array of restaurants. The places lining the piazza itself are traditional and touristy. Instead, survey the scene on the two streets heading west from the square. Here are my favorites in that zone:

$$ Vivi Bistrot is in the Museum of Rome building at the south end of Piazza Navona, with two window tables overlooking the square and quasi-outdoor tables filling the entranceway. This cheery and modern little restaurant serves salads, pastas, and burger plates with a focus on organic ingredients (Tue-Sun 10:00-24:00, closed Mon, Piazza Navona 2, +39 06 683 3779).

$$ Cul de Sac, a long and skinny trattoria lined with wine bottles, is packed with an enthusiastic crowd enjoying a wide-ranging menu, from pasta to homemade pâté. They have fun sampler plates of *salumi* and cheese, good wines by the glass, and fine outdoor seating. It's jammed with regulars, and they don't take reservations—come early to avoid a wait (daily 12:00-23:00, a block off Piazza Navona on Piazza Pasquino 73, +39 06 6880 1094).

$$ L'Insalata Ricca, a popular local chain, specializes in filling salads and also serves pasta, pizzas, and €12 meal deals. It's a couple of blocks toward Largo Argentina, just across busy Corso Vittorio Emanuele (daily 12:00-24:00, Largo dei Chiavari 85, +39 06 6880 3656).

$$$ Ristorante Pizzeria "da Francesco," bustling and authentic, has a 50-year-old tradition, a hardworking young waitstaff, great indoor seating, and a few tables stretching along the quiet street. Their blackboard explains the daily specials (daily 12:00-16:00 & 19:00-24:00, Piazza del Fico 29, +39 06 686 4009, www.dafrancesco.it). While a bit overpriced, it's very popular. Reservations are required for evening seatings at 19:00, 20:30, or 22:00.

$ Pizzeria da Baffetto is famous among visiting Italians and therefore generally comes with a ridiculous line. The pizzas are great, the service is surly, and the tables are tightly arranged amid the mishmash of sketches littering the walls. The pizza-assembly kitchen keeps things energetic, and the pizza oven keeps the main room warm. Streetside tables are less congested and sweaty, but also less memorable (daily 12:00-15:30 & 18:00-late, order "M" or "D"—medium or large, Via del Governo Vecchio 114, +39 06 686 ¹617).

$$ Chiostro del Bramante ("Bramante's Cloister") is a museum café serving light lunches in a unique setting—overlooking the tranquil open-air *chiostro*. Gaze out as the Renaissance master Bramante brings symmetry to your meal. With not a hint of tourism, it's a refined and elegant place, and fine for a predinner drink too. Enter just to the left of the church entrance and tell the ticket-window staff that you're just going to the café (daily 10:00-20:00, meals served 12:00-15:00, Arco della Pace 5, +39 06 6880 9035).

Near the Trevi Fountain

The streets surrounding the Trevi Fountain are littered with mediocre restaurants catering exclusively to tourists. Skip them and walk a few blocks away to one of these. Also consider nearby **Hostaria Romana,** behind the fountain near the Palazzo del Quirinale (walk along Via Rasella to reach the restaurant; see the listing on page 940).

$$$ Origano is a bustling, modern bistro (and café) located three blocks away from the Trevi Fountain. It serves well-priced traditional Roman specialties and wood-fired pizza in an often chaotic setting (daily 12:00-24:00, Via di Sant'Andrea delle Fratte 25, +39 06 6992 0907, Germana).

$$ L'Antica Birreria Peroni is Rome's answer to a German beer hall. Serving hearty mugs of the local Peroni beer and lots of just plain fun beer-hall food and Italian classics, the place is a hit with Romans for a cheap night out (Mon-Sat 12:00-24:00, closed Sun, midway between Trevi Fountain and Capitoline Hill, a block off Via del Corso at Via di San Marcello 19, +39 06 679 5310).

Close to the Pantheon

Eating on the square facing the Pantheon is a temptation, and I'd consider it for breakfast or just to relax and enjoy the Roman scene over a drink. But if you walk a block or two away, you'll get less view and better value. Here are some suggestions:

$$$ Enoteca Corsi, a wine shop that grew into a thriving restaurant, is a charming local scene with the family table in back, where the kids do their homework. The Paiella family serves straightforward, traditional cuisine to an appreciative crowd of office workers. The board lists daily specials (gnocchi on Thursday, fish on Friday, and so on). Friendly Manuela and her staff offer fine wine at a third of the price you'd pay in normal restaurants—buy from their shop and pay a corking fee. Show this book for a free glass of homemade *limoncello* for dessert (Mon-Sat 12:00-15:30, Wed-Fri also 19:15-22:30, closed Sun, a block toward the Pantheon from the Gesù Church at Via del Gesù 87, +39 06 679 0821).

$$ Next to Enoteca Corsi are two other good lunch-only options popular with local office workers: **Pane Pane Vino ar Vino**

ROME

Resources for Foodies

For those looking to take their Roman culinary endeavors seriously, there's no shortage of in-depth advice. Here is a sampling:

KatieParla.com: Food author Katie Parla's website has all the latest on the Roman food scene. She also offers private tours and top-notch tastings and has an easy-to-use app, Katie Parla's Rome (works without internet connection).

Eat Italy: Food writer Elizabeth Minchilli's excellent app lists a wide range of good eateries and food-oriented shops. It covers many cities—including Rome (and works without internet connection). Her website also features recipes and private food tours (www.elizabethminchilliinrome.com).

Eating Europe: This tour company leads fun and insightful walks through Rome's colorful Testaccio and Trastevere neighborhoods, interspersing history, tradition, and local food culture into visits of some of Rome's best food spots. Groups of about eight people makes around seven tasty stops—enough for lunch or dinner (€79-99, RS%—10 percent discount with promo code "ricksteves," 3-4 hours, daily, morning and evening departures, www.eatingeurope.com).

Vino Roma: This small wine "school" is run by several sommeliers who offer evening tasting classes (€50/person) designed to help you understand and enjoy Italian wine. They also lead several neighborhood walks (www.vinoroma.com).

Local Aromas: Giuliana and her daughters Benedetta and Valeria offer excellent private food and market tours (www.localaromas.com).

is a creative little sandwich bar (Via del Gesù 84) and **L'Antico Caffee della Pigna** is a timeless old café serving pastas, salads, and sandwiches (Piazza della Pigna 57).

$$ Da Gino al Parlamento, tucked away on a tiny street behind the Parliament, has been a favorite since 1963. Photos on the wall recall the days when it was the haunt of big-time politicians. Siblings Carla and Fabrizio serve up traditional Roman favorites. They offer four seatings: 13:00, 14:30, 20:00, and 22:00. Reserve ahead, even for lunch, as you'll be packed in with savvy locals (closed Sun, behind Piazza del Parlamento and just off Via di Campo Marzio at Vicolo Rosini 4, +39 06 687 3434, www.ristoranteparlamento.roma.it).

$$$ Ristorante la Campana is a classic—an authentic slice of old Rome appreciated by well-dressed locals. Claiming a history dating to 1518, this place feels unchanged over the years. It serves typical Roman dishes and daily specials, plus it has a self-service *antipasti* buffet, which makes a nice €12 lunch (Tue-Sun 12:30-

15:00 & 19:30-23:00, closed Mon, inside seating only, just off Via della Scrofa and Piazza Nicosia at Vicolo della Campana 18, +39 06 687 5273, www.ristorantelacampana.com).

$$$ Osteria delle Coppelle, a slapdash, trendy place, serves traditional dishes to a local crowd and a fun (if overpriced) selection of €3 *cicchetti* (small plates) that lets you enjoy a variety of Roman and other Italian dishes as tapas. It has a rustic interior and jumbled exterior seating on mismatched furniture, with a much classier dining section in the back (daily 12:30-15:30 & 19:00-late, Piazza delle Coppelle 54, +39 06 4550 2826). They run a fun "speakeasy" bar which opens nightly at 22:00—but don't tell anyone. On the same charming square, the more old-school **Osteria da Mario,** with classic tables inside or out, is also worth considering.

$$$ Ginger, one block from the Pantheon, has a spacious and bright interior and seating on a delightful square. The menu selection—pastas, *panini*, salads, and smoothies—is healthy, organic, and a bit pricey. They may have tables when other places nearby are jammed (daily 8:00-23:00, Piazza di S. Eustachio 54, +39 06 6830 8559). A second location is four blocks in front of the Spanish Steps (see listing later, under "North Rome").

$$ Miscellanea is run by much-loved Miki, who's on a mission to keep foreign students well fed. He offers €4-5 sandwiches, pizza-like bruschetta, and a long list of hearty salads, along with pasta and other staples—it's a good value for a cheap and filling dinner in a convenient location. Miki (and his son Romeo) often tosses in a fun little extra (like their "sexy wine") if you have this book on the table (daily 9:00-24:00, just behind the Pantheon at Via della Palombella 37, +39 06 6813 5318).

Picnicking Close to the Pantheon

It's fun to picnic with a view of the Pantheon. (Remember to be discreet.) Here are some options:

$ Frullati Pascucci, a hole-in-the-wall convenient for takeaway, has been making refreshing fruit *frullati* and frappés (like smoothies and shakes), plus fruit salads, for more than 80 years. Add an inexpensive sandwich to make a healthy light meal (Mon-Sat 6:00-23:00, closed Sun, north of Largo Argentina at Via di Torre Argentina 20, +39 06 686 4816).

For picnic goodies, try the **Co-op** supermarket. There's a very expensive but handy one a half block from the Pantheon (daily 8:30-22:00, Via Giustiniani 18b) and another one three blocks away (daily until 21:00, Corso Vittorio Emanuele II 42).

Gelato Close to the Pantheon

Several fine *gelaterie* are within three or four blocks of the Pantheon.

Cremeria Monteforte is known for its traditional gelato and super-creamy sorbets *(cremolati)*. The fruit flavors are especially refreshing—think gourmet slushies (closed Mon, faces the west side of the Pantheon at Via della Rotonda 22).

San Crispino serves small portions of tasty gourmet gelato. Because of their commitment to natural ingredients, the colors are muted; ice cream purists know that bright colors are artificial and used to attract children (a block in front of the Pantheon at Piazza della Maddalena 3).

Giolitti is Rome's most famous and venerable ice-cream establishment (although few would say it has the best gelato). Take-away prices are reasonable, and it has elegant Old World seating (just off Piazza Colonna and Piazza Montecitorio at Via Uffici del Vicario 40).

Gelateria Artigianale Corona feels like a time warp and is nothing fancy, but it serves honest, homemade gelato with an array of creative flavors (just south of Largo Argentina at Largo Arenula 27).

NEAR VATICAN CITY

As in the Colosseum area, some eateries near the Vatican prey on exhausted tourists. Avoid the restaurant pushers handing out fliers: They're usually hawking places with bad food and expensive menu tricks. Instead, tide yourself over with a slice of pizza or at any of these eateries (see map on page 912), and save your euros for a better meal elsewhere.

Handy Lunch Places near Piazza Risorgimento

These listings are a stone's throw from the Vatican wall. They're mostly fast and cheap, with a good *gelateria* nearby.

$$ Il Colibrì, run by the Ricci brothers, has noisy streetside seating and a quiet interior (daily 10:30-15:30 & 19:00-24:00, at corner of Via Leone IV and Via Famagosta 69, +39 06 3751 4767).

$ Be.Re., facing the Vatican wall, feels trendy and serves a variety of microbrews. It's an outpost of the Trapizzino chain, which means they sell little doughy "pizza pockets" with toasted crusts and a variety of fillings—plus *supplì* and other dishes (daily 10:00-late, Via Vespasiano 2, +39 06 9442 1854).

$ L'Insalata Ricca, next door, is another branch of the popular chain that serves hearty salads and pastas (daily 12:00-23:30, across from the Vatican walls at Piazza Risorgimento 5, +39 06 3973 0387).

$ Duecento Gradi, also nearby, is a good bet for fresh and creative sandwiches—though at €5-8 they're expensive by Roman standards. Munch your lunch sitting down (€1 extra) or take it away (daily 11:00-24:00, Piazza Risorgimento 3, +39 06 3975 4239).

Gelateria Old Bridge scoops up hearty portions of fresh gelato for tourists and nuns alike—join the line (just off Piazza Risorgimento across from the Vatican walls at Viale dei Bastioni di Michelangelo 3).

Other Options in the Vatican Area

Most of these listings are near the Vatican Museums and Cipro Metro stop. The Borgo Pio eateries are near St. Peter's Basilica.

Viale Giulio Cesare and **Via Candia:** These streets are lined with cheap *pizza rustica* shops and self-serve places. **$ Forno Feliziani** (closed Sun, Via Candia 61) is a fancy version with nicely presented pizza by the slice and simple cafeteria-style dishes that you can eat in or take out.

Covered Market: Turn your nose loose in the wonderful **Mercato Trionfale,** one of the city's best market halls. It's more of a sight than a place to eat. Almost completely untouristy (with lots of vendors, but no real prepared-food stands aside from a bakery and a sandwich counter), it's located just three blocks north of the Vatican Museums (Mon-Sat roughly 7:00-14:00, Tue and Fri some stalls stay open until 19:00, closed Sun, corner of Via Tunisi and Via Andrea Doria). If the market is closed, try one of these grocery stores (both open daily until 20:30): **Co-op,** with a big bakery section and tables where you can eat pizza by the slice (to the northwest at Via Andrea Doria 46), or the smaller **Carrefour Express** (closer to the Vatican at Via Sebastiano Veniero 16).

Eating Close to St. Peter's: The pedestrian-only Borgo Pio—a block from Piazza San Pietro—has restaurants worth a look, such as the traditional **$$ Tre Pupazzi** (Mon-Sat 12:00-15:00 & 19:00-23:00, closed Sun, at corner of Via Tre Pupazzi and Borgo Pio, +39 06 6880 3220). At **$ Vecchio Borgo,** across the street, you can get pasta, pizza by weight, and veggies to go or to eat at simple tables (daily 9:30-22:30, Borgo Pio 27a).

NORTH ROME
Near the Spanish Steps and Ara Pacis

To locate these restaurants, see the map on page 826.

$$$$ Ristorante il Gabriello is inviting and small—modern under medieval arches—and provides a peaceful and local-feeling respite from all the top-end fashion shops in the area. Claudio serves with charisma, while his brother Gabriello cooks creative Roman cuisine using fresh, organic products from his wife's farm. Italians normally just trust their waiter and say, "Bring it on." Tourists are understandably more cautious, but you can be trusting here. Invest €55—not including wine—in "Claudio's Extravaganza," created especially for my readers (not on the menu). Specify whether you'd prefer fish, meat, or both. (Be warned: Romans think raw shellfish is the ultimate in fine dining. If you don't, make that clear.) While

ROME

you're likely to dine surrounded by my readers here (especially if eating before 21:00), the atmosphere is fun and convivial (dinner only, Mon-Sat 19:00-23:00, closed Sun, reservations smart, air-con, dress respectfully—no shorts, 3 blocks from Spanish Steps at Via Vittoria 51, +39 06 6994 0810, www.ilgabriello.com).

$$ Ginger, four blocks in front of the Spanish Steps, is modern and bright. It feels stylish with a pinch of posh and pretense (daily 8:00-23:00, Via Borgognona 43, +39 06 9603 6390). A sister location near the Pantheon is described earlier.

$$$ Caffè Vitti, delightfully set on a fine traffic-free square, has been serving its neighborhood for over a century. The food won't win any awards—and you pay for the location—but it offers a delightful chance to enjoy a meal (good salads, pizza) or a cocktail on a quiet and characteristic square. Sit outside and people-watch amidst a professional Roman crowd. The *aperitivi* come with a little tray of munchies (daily 6:30-24:00, Piazza San Lorenzo in Lucina 33, +39 06 687 6304).

Via della Croce Stand-Up Food Crawl

Two blocks north of the Spanish Steps, touristy Via della Croce is a fun street to graze for a light meal or snack. As you peruse this street from Via del Corso, you'll pass these enticing stops for a bite:

Grano Frutta e Farina (#49) sells hard-to-resist pizza by the weight. Consider a tasting plate with a tiny bit of each pizza.

Focacci Deli (#43) makes sandwiches on request. Choose from their long, enticing counter of meats and cheeses.

Antica Enoteca (#76) is an inviting bar for a glass of wine in wonderful surroundings.

Venchi (#25) can make your gelato and chocolate dreams come true.

Pompi (#82), the self-proclaimed "kingdom of tiramisù," features several flavors (classic, strawberry, pistachio, chocolate-banana, and more).

Pastificio (#8), with a history going back to World War I, serves up two fresh €4.50 pasta dishes each day; a glass of water or wine is included when you eat at the stools along the wall.

NEAR TERMINI STATION

With a constant swarm of hungry, well-worn travelers, Rome's train station and the streets on either side of it are a nightmare of mostly low-end eateries. A few places stand out as options to consider:

At the Station

$-$$ Terrazza Termini is a bright, spacious, and safe-feeling food court, with several decent mall-type eateries, free Wi-Fi and charging stations, and plenty of places to sit. To find it, ride the escalator up from near track 15. In the afternoon, you'll notice competing *aperitivo* deals (17:00-20:00, around €7 for a drink and access to buffet, **Eccellenze della Costiera** is best).

$-$$ Mercato Centrale (at the far end of the corridor that runs along track 24, facing Via Giovanni Giolitti) is a thriving, upscale food market hall with a great vibe and plenty of foodie options (daily 8:00-24:00).

Near Recommended Via Firenze Area Hotels

$$$ Target Restaurant seems to be the favorite recommendation of every hotel receptionist on Via Firenze. It has a sleek and dressy ambience, capable service, and food that's reliably good, but pricey (free *aperitivo* with this book, daily 12:00-15:30 & 19:00-24:00, closed Sun at lunch, reserve to specify seating outside or inside—avoid getting seated in basement, Via Torino 33, +39 06 474 0066, www.targetrestaurant.it).

$$ Café Pasticceria Dagnino, a time warp from the 1960s set in a classic and stately old arcade, has a big selection at its *tavola calda* counter. It's known for its fine pastry section and Sicilian treats—savory and sweet, from arancini to cannoli. A hit with local office workers, it's fast, reasonably priced, and reliable, with good seating inside, upstairs, and outside in the mall (daily 7:00-23:00, Galleria Esedra, enter at Via Torino 95, +39 06 481 8660).

$ Caffè Torino Tavola Calda is another workers' favorite for a quick, cheap lunch. They have good, fresh, hot dishes ready to go for a fine price. Head back past the bar to peruse their enticing display, point at what you want, then grab a seat and the young waitstaff will serve you (Mon-Fri 6:00-16:00, closed Sat-Sun, Via Torino 40, +39 06 487 0000).

$ Il Forno degli Amici, handy if your hotel is on Via Firenze, is a little hole-in-the-wall selling salads by the weight, pizza by the slice, sandwiches, and bakery items (Mon-Sat until 21:00, closed Sun, Via Firenze 51).

On Via Flavia

For a serious meal near the station, it's worth walking 10 minutes to the quiet and residential-feeling Via Flavia, where you'll find almost no tourism and a cluster of fine dining options.

$$$ Ristorante la Pentolaccia, upscale and romantic, is a dressy but still tourist-friendly place with tight seating and traditional Roman cooking—consider their daily specials. This is a local hangout, and reservations are smart. To start things off with a free bruschetta, place this book on your table (daily 12:00-15:00 & 18:00-23:00, a block off Via XX Settembre at Via Flavia 38, +39 06

Restaurants near Termini Station

1. Terrazza Termini
2. Mercato Centrale
3. Target Restaurant
4. Café Pasticceria Dagnino
5. Caffè Torino Tavola Calda
6. Il Forno degli Amici
7. Ristorante la Pentolaccia, La Bottega Ristorante & Punturi
8. I Colori del Vino Enoteca
9. Hostaria Romana
10. Groceries (3)

483 477, www.lapentolaccia-restaurant.it, Vincenzo gives a warm welcome).

$$$ La Bottega Ristorante, next door, feels bigger—almost industrial. In the Punturi family since 1919, it's a bright, contemporary, and easygoing place serving Roman and Mediterranean cuisine, and good wine by the glass (nightly from 17:00, Via Flavia 46, +39 06 487 0391).

$ Punturi—owned by the same people, and next door—is a high-end *rosticceria* cooking up super casual dishes sold by the weight and eaten on plastic at its fast-food-type seating (Mon-Sat 8:30-20:30, closed Sun, Via Flavia 46).

$$$ I Colori del Vino Enoteca is a classy wine bar that feels like a laboratory of wine appreciation. It has a creative menu of *affettati* (cold cuts) and cheeses, and a great list of fine wines by the glass. Helpful, English-speaking Marco carries on a long family tradition of celebrating the fundamentals of good nutrition: fine wine, cheese, meat, and bread. They also have a menu with more standard restaurant items (Mon-Sat 12:00-15:00 & 18:00-23:00, closed Sun, may close Sat at quiet times, Via Aureliana 15 at corner of Via Flavia, +39 06 474 1745). This is a great stop after dinner for a dessert wine (which comes with a plate of cookies).

Between Piazza Barberini and Trevi Fountain

$$$ Hostaria Romana, near the Quirinale, is a busy bistro with a hustling and fun-loving gang of waiters and makes a good choice on your way to or from Trevi Fountain. The upstairs is a tight, tidy, glassed-in terrace, while the cellar has noisy walls graffitied by happy eaters. As its menu specializes in traditional Roman dishes, it's a good place to try *saltimbocca alla romana* or *bucatini all'amatriciana.* Their €12 *antipasto della casa* plate, with a variety of vegetables and cheeses, makes a hearty start to your meal (Mon-Sat 12:30-15:00 & 19:15-23:00, closed Sun and Aug, reservations smart, midway between Piazza Barberini and Trevi Fountain at Via del Boccaccio 1, +39 06 474 5284, www.hostariaromana.it).

TRASTEVERE

Restaurants line the streets of colorful Trastevere. It's a favorite dining neighborhood for both Romans and tourists—more rustic than the downtown zone, but just a short walk across the river. (🎧 Download my free Trastevere Walk **audio tour** to combine sight-seeing with dinner.) It has become extremely touristy and attracts large numbers of young, hip, sometimes rowdy Americans. But if you venture away from the central square (Piazza di Santa Maria in Trastevere) into the back streets you'll find places that serve with sincerity and charm. For locations, see the map on page 919.

$$$$ Taverna Trilussa is your best bet for dining memorably in Trastevere. Brothers Massimo and Maurizio offer quality without pretense. With a proud 100-year tradition, this place has the right mix of style and informality. The service is fun-loving (they're happy to let you split plates into smaller portions to enjoy a family-style meal), yet professional. The menu celebrates local classics and seasonal specials—as well as their award-winning *pasta amatriciana*—and comes with a big wine selection. The spacious dining hall is strewn with eclectic Roman souvenirs. And outdoors, Trilussa has an actual hedged-in terrace rather than just tables jumbled together on the sidewalk. While the food is on the pricey side, you're paying for an all-around memorable dining experience (dinner only, Mon-Sat from 19:30, closed Sun, reservations smart, Via del Politeama 23, +39 06 581 8918, www.tavernatrilussa.it).

$$$ Dar Sor Olimpio al Drago, with a small, romantic dining room (no outdoor seating), has a friendly staff and an enticing menu—both typical Roman and modern Italian. The chef enjoys exercising a little creative license (Mon-Fri 18:00-23:00, Sat-Sun 12:30-16:00 & 18:30-23:00, Piazza del Drago 2, +39 339 885 7574).

$$ Trattoria de Gli Amici employs people with developmental disabilities (who are helped and mentored by volunteers) to offer delightful meals in a charming atmosphere. Be a part of that community service mission and enjoy traditional Roman cuisine with a modern twist while surrounded by contemporary art in a medieval building or on a romantic square (daily 12:00-23:00, Piazza Sant'Egidio 6, +39 06 580 6033).

$$ La Prosciutteria Cantina dei Papi is a cozy and friendly place celebrating the wine, cheese, and meats of Lazio and Tuscany. They serve hearty *taglieri* (easily splittable boards) of regional delights (€5-15) and fine wine by the big or little bottle. If you're in the mood for *porchetta* and mortadella, look no further. Nothing's hot and you order at the counter (daily 12:00-24:00, Via della Scala 71, +39 06 6456 2839).

Classic Pizzerias in Trastevere

$$ Pizzeria "Ai Marmi" is a noisy festival of pizza. Tight marble-slab tables (hence the nickname "the Morgue") fill the seating area in front of the oven and pizza-assembly line. It's a classic Roman scene whether you enjoy the chaos inside, sit at a sidewalk table, or take the famously good, thin, and crispy €8-10 pizza to go. They also serve fried cod, rice balls with mozzarella *(supplì),* and bean dishes. Expect brusque service and a long line between 20:00 and 22:00 (Thu-Tue 18:30 until very late, closed Wed, cash only, tram #8 from Piazza Venezia to first stop over bridge, just beyond Piazza Sonnino at Viale di Trastevere 53, +39 06 580 0919).

$$ Pizzeria Dar Poeta, tucked in a back alley and a hit with local students, cranks out €9 wood-fired pizzas and calzones. These pizzas are easily splittable. If you're extra hungry, pay an extra euro for *pizza alta* (thicker crust). Choose between their sloppy, cramped interior or the lively tables outside on the cobblestones (daily 12:00-24:00; call to reserve, arrive before 19:00, or expect a wait; 50 yards directly in front of Santa Maria della Scala Church at Vicolo del Bologna 45, +39 06 588 0516).

$ Trapizzino Vineria di Roma is a modern cousin to these classic pizzerias. It's a bar with just two items on the menu: a variety of €4 *trapizzini* (pizza-like wraps with freshly toasted crusts) and €2 *supplì* (the Roman answer to arancini—Sicily's fried rice balls). They also serve a good variety of Lazio wine. It's a fast and cheap option if you're in the mood for something like pizza—but a bit different (Tue-Sun 12:00-late, closed Mon, Piazza Trilussa 46, +39 06 581 7312). They have other locations around Rome, including in Testaccio; near the Vatican wall; and at the Mercato Centrale food court inside Termini station.

Rome Connections

BY TRAIN

Rome's primary train station, centrally located **Termini,** has high-speed connections to other Italian cities and fast trains to the airport. Rome's other major station is called **Tiburtina.** Most trains you'll ride depart from Termini, but it's always smart to confirm whether your train departs from Termini or Tiburtina (or one of Rome's even smaller stations).

Termini Train Station

Termini, Rome's main train station (www.romatermini.com), is a buffet of tourist services. At the head of the tracks are two atriums.

The inner atrium, open at both ends, houses shops and eateries. The outer atrium, with glass walls, houses ticket windows and ticket machines plus a good-sized bookstore. (Note that ticket windows can be jammed with travelers—find the small red kiosk, take a number, and wait. Better yet, use the machines.) Outside the station is a large square where city buses depart. A basement shopping area extends beneath both atriums.

For security, entry to the train platforms themselves is restricted to ticket holders. Entrances are from the inner atrium and from the halls to the sides of the tracks. You may need to show your ticket, but there are no metal detectors and lines are generally short.

The Leonardo Express train to Fiumicino Airport runs from track 23 or 24—that's on the far right, as you face the tracks (see "By Plane," later).

Eating: In general, the best places in the station to sit are in its eateries (open long hours daily). A snack bar and a good self-service cafeteria (Ciao) are perched one floor above the ticket windows in the outer atrium, accessible from the side closest to track 24. For good-quality sandwiches to go, try VyTA in the inner atrium across from track 1. The large Sapori & Dintori supermarket is on the basement shopping level, below the inner atrium (go down the escalators on the Via Marsala side). For something more substantial, try the Terrazza Termini food court near track 15, or the Mercato Centrale at the far end of the corridor near track 24 (see listings on page 936).

Services: A long hall runs along Via Giovanni Giolitti, on the southwest side of the station (near track 24). Here you'll find the **TI** (look for counters at the far end, just before the Mercato Centrale; daily 9:30-19:00), travel agencies, several car-rental desks, a medical center, and baggage storage *(deposito bagagli)*. (This hallway is connected to the main part of the station by a long, slick Coin department store; you can walk through the store, or go around outside.)

ROME

In the hall along Via Marsala, on the northeast side of the station (near track 1), you'll find a **pharmacy.**

Pay **WCs** are down the escalators from the inner atrium, and also inside both the Terrazza Termini and Mercato Centrale food courts.

Warning: The station has some sleazy sharks with official-looking business cards; avoid anybody selling anything unless they're in a legitimate shop at the station. Other shady characters linger around the ticket machines—offers to help usually come with the expectation of a "tip." There are no official porters; if someone wants to carry your bags or help you find your platform, they are simply angling for some cash.

Getting Between Termini and Rome Hotels

From Termini, many of my recommended hotels are easily accessible by foot or by Metro (for those in the Colosseum and Vatican neighborhoods). The Termini Metro station, where Metro lines A and B intersect, is beneath the station (take the escalator down and look for the red *M*). City buses leave from the square directly in front of the outer atrium. Buses to the airport leave from the streets on both sides of the station. Taxis queue in front and outside exits on both the north and south sides; if there's a long taxi line in front, try a side exit instead. Avoid con men hawking "express taxi" services in unmarked cars (only use official white taxis with the maroon *Roma Capitale* logo).

Train Connections

Unless otherwise specified, the following connections are for Trenitalia.

From Termini by Train to: Fiumicino Airport (Leonardo Express; 2/hour, 32 minutes—see details under "By Plane," later), **Venice** (hourly, 4 hours, 1 direct night train, 7.5 hours; Italo: 4/day, 4 hours, reservations required), **Florence** (2-3/hour, 1.5 hours; Italo: 2/hour, 1.5 hours), **Siena** (1-2/hour, 1 change, 3-4 hours), **Orvieto** (every 1-2 hours, 1.5 hours; regional trains are half the price and only slightly slower than Intercity trains), **Assisi** (4/day direct, 2 hours; more with change in Foligno), **Pisa** (1-2/hour, 3 hours, some change in Florence), **La Spezia** (7/day direct, 3-4 hours), **Milan** (1-3/hour, 3.5 hours; Italo: 1-2/hour), **Naples** (1-4/hour, 1 hour on Frecciarossa, 2 hours on Intercity, 2.5 hours and much cheaper on regional trains; Italo: hourly, 70 minutes), **Pompeii** (connect in Naples; see page 1015), **Sorrento** (Italo train/bus combination, 2/day, 3.5 hours), **Civitavecchia** cruise-ship port (regional trains roughly hourly, 80 minutes; faster but pricier trains every 2 hours, 40-50 minutes), **Brindisi** (3/day, 5 hours), **Bern** (3/day, 6.5 hours, change in Milan), **Munich** (4/day, 10 hours, change in Verona or Padua; 1 direct night train, 11.5 hours), **Nice** (2/day, 9 hours, change in Milan), **Paris** (2/day, 11.5 hours, change in Turin; 1 night train, 13.5 hours, change in Milan), **Vienna** (3/day, 12 hours, 1-2 changes; 1 direct night train, 14 hours).

Tiburtina Train Station

Tiburtina, Rome's second-largest train station (www.stazioneromatiburtina.it), sits in the city's northeast corner (alongside a Metro stop and the intercity bus station). It's a pass-through station: Fast trains along the Milan-Naples line stop here and continue on quickly. A few of these fast trains now stop only at Tiburtina, but most stop at both Tiburtina and Termini. Use the station that's most convenient for you.

A massive top-level concourse (up several escalators) connects the platforms and is lined with all the expected services. The Tiburtina bus station is a five-minute walk to the west (described later, under "By Bus").

Getting Between Tiburtina and Downtown Rome: Tiburtina is on Metro line B, four stops from Termini. Note that when going *to* Tiburtina, Metro line B splits—you want a train signed *Rebibbia*, not *Jonio*. Bus #492 runs conveniently between Tiburtina, several city-center stops (including Piazza Barberini, Piazza Venezia, and Piazza Navona), and the Vatican neighborhood (as you emerge from the train station's front door, the city bus stop is just to the left).

Smaller Stations

Rome has about a dozen small train stations that are usually only useful if you're staying nearby. The ones you're most likely to use are **San Pietro** (south of Vatican City; bus #64 connects it to Piazza Venezia and Termini; if you're staying near the Vatican and taking a regional train, get off here); **Trastevere** (a few minutes' ride on tram #8 from Trastevere and Piazza Venezia); and **Ostiense** (5 minutes from the Piramide Metro stop via an underground walkway).

BY BUS

Long-distance buses use **Autostazione Tiburtina,** 200 yards west of the Tiburtina train and Metro station. Buses are typically slower than trains, but fares are cheap (as little as €5 to Naples or Florence). Buses are also handy for destinations poorly served by rail, or for making a direct connection instead of having to change trains (such as to Siena or Sorrento).

To reach the bus station from Tiburtina train station, follow signs to exit toward *P.le Stazione Tiburtina* (from inside, it's past track 1); you may also see signs for *Bus Regionali*. You'll end up on a square with local bus stops on your left; the long-distance bus station is straight ahead, around the row of trees (look for the large, fenced-in area with bus platforms). The station is mostly outdoors, chaotic, and crowded, with limited seating. Ticket-window lines can be slow, so buy your ticket online in advance if possible. If your bus departure platform isn't listed on the digital board, ask one of the drivers or at a ticket desk for help.

From Rome by Bus to: Siena (9/day, 3 hours, https://global.flixbus.com), **Sorrento** (1-2/day, 4 hours; this is a cheap and easy way to go straight to Sorrento, buy tickets at www.marozzivt.it—in Italian only, at the Tiburtina ticket office, travel agencies, or on board for a €3.50 surcharge; +39 080 579 0111), **Naples** (every 1-2 hours, 3 hours, https://global.flixbus.com), and **Florence** (every 1-2 hours, 4 hours, https://global.flixbus.com).

BY PLANE

Rome's two airports—**Fiumicino** (a.k.a. Leonardo da Vinci, code: FCO) and the small **Ciampino** (code: CIA)—share the same website (www.adr.it).

Fiumicino Airport

Rome's major airport is manageable. Terminals T1, T2, and T3 are all under one roof—walkable end to end in 20 minutes. T5 is a separate building requiring a short shuttle trip. (T4 is still being built.) The T1-2-3 complex has ground transport, a TI (in T3, daily 9:00-17:30, longer in summer), ATMs, banks, luggage storage, shops, and bars.

Getting Between Fiumicino Airport and Downtown Rome

In either direction, give yourself lots of time to allow for traffic delays, travel between your hotel and the train/bus station, finding your train or bus, and walking to the terminal.

By Train: Trenitalia's slick, direct, first-class-only Leonardo Express train connects the airport train station (called Fiumicino Aeroporto) and Rome's central Termini station in 32 minutes for €14. At either station, buy your ticket from a Trenitalia machine, a ticket office *(biglietteria)*, or a newsstand near the platform. Machines sell open tickets that can be used on any train (even if it asks you to select a specific one). You must validate your ticket before boarding by stamping it in a green-and-gray machine near the track. Trains run at least twice hourly in both directions from roughly 6:00 to 23:00 (up to 4/hour in busy times).

From the airport's arrival gate, follow signs to the train icon or *Stazione/Railway Station.* Make sure the train you board is going to the central "Roma Termini" station, as trains from the airport serve other destinations too.

ROME

Returning from Termini train station *to* the airport, trains usually depart from track 23 or 24. Check the departure boards for "Fiumicino Aeroporto" and confirm with an official or a local on the platform that the train is indeed going to the airport.

You can access most of the airport's terminals from the airport train station. If your flight leaves from terminal T5 (where most American air carriers flying direct to the US depart), catch the T5 shuttle bus *(navetta)* on the sidewalk in front of T3—it's too far to walk with luggage.

Cheaper (€8) local trains also run between the airport and some of Rome's smaller train stations (including Trastevere, Ostiense, and Tiburtina). If you're staying in Trastevere or the Pantheon area, it can be simpler and cheaper to take the local train to Trastevere station, then walk out to the street and take the #8 tram downhill to your hotel. The train to Tiburtina is useful if you have a long-distance bus to catch.

Only a couple of long-distance trains per day serve the airport. To connect to other Italian cities, you'll usually have to change at Termini or Tiburtina.

By Bus: Various bus companies—including Cotral (www.cotralspa.it), Terravision (www.terravision.eu), SIT (www.sitbusshuttle.com), T.A.M. (www.tambus.it), and Schiaffini (www.romeairportbus.com)—connect Fiumicino and Termini train station. The SIT bus also stops near the Vatican. I'd just hop on whichever one is departing first (every 10-15 minutes at peak times). While cheaper than the train (about €7 one-way), buses take twice as long (about an hour, depending on traffic) and can fill up (allow plenty of extra time). At the airport, the bus station is at the far end of terminal T3.

By Airport Shuttle: Shared shuttle van services can be economical for one or two people. Consider Rome Airport Shuttle (€25 for one person, extra people—€6 each, by reservation only, +39 06 4201 4507 or 06 4201 3469, www.airportshuttle.it).

By Taxi: A taxi between Fiumicino and downtown Rome takes 45 minutes in normal traffic (for taxi tips, see page 819) and costs €50. (Add a €2-5 tip for good service.) From the airport, be sure to catch an official taxi at the taxi stand. Avoid unmarked, unmetered taxis; these drivers will try to tempt you away from the taxi-stand lineup by offering an immediate (rip-off) ride. Rome's official taxis are white, with a "taxi" sign on the roof and a maroon *Roma Capitale* logo on the door. Cabs based in Fiumicino (the town near the airport) are allowed to charge €60 for the ride to downtown Rome.

Signs stating the Rome and Fiumicino price caps are posted next to the taxi stand. It's best to use the Rome city cabs and establish the price before you get in.

When departing Rome, your hotel can arrange a taxi to the airport at any hour. Alternatively, they sometimes work with comparably priced private car services, which are usually just fine (if not nicer than a regular cab).

Ciampino Airport

Rome's smaller airport handles charter flights and some budget airlines (including most Ryanair flights).

Getting Between Ciampino Airport and Downtown Rome: Bus companies Terravision, Schiaffini, and SIT will take you to Rome's Termini train station (about €5, 2/hour, 45 minutes). Atral runs a quicker route (25 minutes, www.atral-lazio.com) to the Anagnina Metro stop, where you can connect to the stop nearest your hotel (departs every 40 minutes). City bus #520 runs from Ciampino to the Subaugusta Metro stop for a single transit ticket.

The fixed price for any official **taxi** (with the maroon *Roma Capitale* logo on the door) is €31 to downtown (within the old city walls, including most of my recommended hotels).

Rome Airport Shuttle also offers **shared van rides** to and from Ciampino (€25 for one person, listed earlier).

BY CAR

A car is a worthless headache in Rome. If you're visiting Rome as part of a longer trip, avoid a pile of stress and save money by parking at the huge, easy, free, and relatively safe lot behind the train station in the hill town of Orvieto (follow *P* signs from the autostrada) and catching a cheap *regionale* train to Rome (every 1-2 hours, 1.5 hours).

Or, if Rome is the first stop of your trip and you plan to rent a car for the rest of Italy, you could sightsee Rome, then take the train to Orvieto and rent a car there (Hertz has an office down the street from the train station). If you absolutely must drive and park a car in Rome, there's a large underground garage at the Villa Borghese Gardens near the Spagna Metro station, just outside the restricted downtown zone (€20/day, Viale del Galoppatoio 33, www.sabait.it).

Alternatively, use one of the more than two dozen park-and-ride lots at Rome's outlying Metro stations (€5/24 hours). These vary in size and convenience; one of the largest is at the Anagnina Metro station, just inside Rome's ring expressway along the Via Tuscolana (southeast of downtown). For details, search for "park and ride" *(parcheggi di scambio)* at www.atac.roma.it.

For general information on train travel in Italy, see page 1185.

ROME

BY CRUISE SHIP

Hundreds of cruise ships dock each year at the small, manageable port city of **Civitavecchia** (chee-vee-tah-VEH-kyah), about 45 miles northwest of Rome. For more details, see my *Rick Steves Mediterranean Cruise Ports* guidebook.

Getting to Rome: Trains are generally the fastest (and most economical) way to day-trip into Rome. Trains connect Civitavecchia with several stations in Rome, including Ostiense (two Metro stops from the Colosseum), San Pietro (a short walk from Vatican City), or Termini (the main transit hub, but farther from key sights). Trains depart frequently for Rome and take 40-80 minutes. You can buy train tickets at Civitavecchia's station, or the "Tourist Information" travel agency at the station, which also sells other transportation tickets.

To reach Civitavecchia's train station, take a free shuttle bus from your ship to the Largo della Pace transit hub. City bus service from the hub to the train station is fast and reliable (€2, 6/hour, 10 minutes, buy tickets from kiosk before boarding). Or you can walk (about 25 minutes) or take a taxi (€15-20).

By Seasonal Express Train for Cruisers: When there are enough ships in port to justify it, a special "Civitavecchia Express" train offers round-trips to San Pietro station designed for cruise travelers (departs once or twice each morning with one return trip from San Pietro in the afternoon). The €15 round-trip ride is comfortable, air-conditioned, and limited to cruise passengers, and can save you up to 20 minutes each way (https://civitavecchia.portmobility.it). Buy tickets at Trenitalia.com, at the station's ticket window (not available at self-service machines), at the station's "Tourist Information" travel agency, or on the train.

More Options: Organized tours into Rome are offered by Can't Be Missed Tours (RS%, +1 607 7542 7981, www.cantbemissedtours.com) and Miles & Miles Private Tours (see page 824). Several private companies offer cheap **bus transfers** from the transit hub to Rome or Rome's airports (try Civita Tours, +39 346 217 7803, www.civitatours.com).

NAPLES

Napoli

If you like Italy as far south as Rome, go farther south—it gets better. If Italy is getting on your nerves, stop at Rome. Italy intensifies as you plunge deeper. Naples is Italy in the extreme—its best (birthplace of pizza) and its worst (home of the Camorra, Naples' "family" of organized crime).

Before Italy unified in the late 1800s, Naples was the country's richest city. But Naples' fortunes nosedived when the capital of modern Italy was established in Rome. Things got so bad that many of its residents emigrated. The Italy America knows—pizza, spaghetti, and "O Sole Mio"/"Santa Lucia"—came from 19th-century Naples, as brought to the US by all those immigrants.

Today, Naples impresses visitors with one of Europe's top archaeological museums (showcasing the artistic treasures of Pompeii), fascinating churches that convey the city's unique personality and powerful devotion, an underground warren of Greek and Roman ruins, fine works of art (including pieces by Caravaggio, who lived here for a time), and evocative Nativity scenes (called *presepi*). Of course, Neapolitans make great pizza and tasty pastries (try the crispy, ricotta-stuffed *sfogliatella*). But more than anything, Naples has a brash and vibrant street life—"Italy in your face" in ways both good and bad. Walking through its colorful old town is one of my favorite experiences anywhere in Europe. For a grand overlook, head to the hilltop viewpoint (San Martino) for sweeping views of the city and its bay.

Naples is southern Italy's leading city, the third-largest city in Italy, and Europe's most densely populated city, with more than one million people and few open spaces or parks. While in many ways it feels like an urban jungle, Naples surprises the observant

Naples Area

Map legend:
- Main Rail Line
- High Speed Rail Line
- Circumvesuviana Rail Line
- Bus
- Year-Round Boats

↑ To Rome

Naples

Vesuvius

To Rome ←

Ercolano

POMPEII RUINS

HERCULANEUM RUINS

Pompei Scavi Station

Pompei (Town)

Salerno

To Palermo →

Bay of Naples

Amalfi

Positano

Sorrento

Amalfi Coast

Capri

Gulf of Salerno

10 Kilometers
10 Miles

Paestum (Town)
PAESTUM RUINS

traveler with its impressive knack for living, eating, and raising children with good humor and decency. Overcome your fear of being run down or ripped off long enough to talk with people. Enjoy a few smiles and jokes with the man running the neighborhood tripe shop, or the woman taking her daycare class on a walk through the traffic.

The pulse of Italy throbs in Naples. Like Cairo or Mumbai, it's shocking and captivating at the same time, the closest thing to "reality travel" that you'll find in Western Europe. But this tangled mess still somehow manages to breathe, laugh, and sing—with a joyful Italian accent. Thanks to its reputation as a dangerous place, Naples doesn't get nearly as many tourists as it deserves. While the city has its problems, it has improved

a lot in recent years. And even though it remains a bit edgy, I feel comfortable here. Naples richly rewards those who venture in.

Naples is also the springboard to an array of nearby sightseeing treats (covered in the next three chapters and easy to reach by train, bus, or boat): Just beyond Naples are the remarkable ruins of Herculaneum and Pompeii, and the brooding volcano that did them both in, Mount Vesuvius. A few more miles down the road

NAPLES

is the pleasant resort town of Sorrento and the offshore escape isle of Capri. Next comes the dramatic scenery of the Amalfi Coast. Plunging even farther south, you'll reach the Greek temples of Paestum.

PLANNING YOUR TIME

Naples is an ideal day trip either from Rome or from the comfortable home base of Sorrento, each just over an hour away. Or you can stow your bag at the station and see Naples in a few hours while you change trains here on the way between Rome and Sorrento. For some, a little Naples goes a long way. If you're not comfortable in chaotic and congested cities, think twice before spending the night here. But those who are intrigued by the city's sights and street life enjoy overnighting in Naples.

On a quick visit, start with the Archaeological Museum (closed Tue), follow my self-guided Naples Walk, and celebrate your survival with pizza. With more time, dip into more churches, go underground to see Greek and Roman ruins, trek to Capodimonte to see art treasures, or ascend San Martino for the view. Spend an early evening strolling Naples' romantic Lungomare harborside promenade.

For a blitz tour from Rome, you could have breakfast on an early Rome-Naples express train (usually daily 7:35-8:45), zip to Pompeii by bus or train, return to Naples and hit the Archaeological Museum, and be back in Rome before you turn into a zucchini. That's exhausting, but more memorable than a fourth day in Rome.

Yes, Naples is huge. But if you stick to my suggestions and grab a cab when you're lost or tired, it's fun. Treat yourself well in Naples; the city is cheap by Italian standards. Splurging on a sane and comfortable hotel is a worthwhile investment.

On summer afternoons, Naples' street life slows and many churches, museums, and shops close as the temperature soars. The city comes back to life in the early evening.

Orientation to Naples

Naples is set deep inside the large, curving Bay of Naples, with Mount Vesuvius looming just five miles away. Although Naples is a sprawling city, its fairly compact core contains the most interesting sights. The tourist's Naples is a triangle, with its points at the Centrale train station in the east, the Archaeological Museum to the west, and Piazza del Plebiscito (with the Royal Palace) and the port to the south. Steep hills rise above this historic core, including San Martino, capped with a mighty fortress.

Planning Your Time in the Region

Give the entire area—including Sorrento and Naples—a minimum of three days. If you use Sorrento as your sunny springboard, you can spend a day in Naples, a day exploring the Amalfi Coast, and a day split between Pompeii and the town of Sorrento. While Paestum (Greek temples), Mount Vesuvius, Herculaneum (an ancient Roman site like Pompeii), and the island of Capri are fine destinations, they are worthwhile only if you have more time.

The **Campania ArteCard** regional pass may save you a few euros, but it also saves the time and hassle of buying tickets. Consider it if you're here for two or three days, use public transportation, and visit multiple major sights (such as Pompeii, Herculaneum, Paestum, Naples' Archaeological Museum, and several other museums in Naples). The **three-day Campania** version (€32) is good if you'll be visiting both Naples and Sorrento; it includes free entry to two sights, a 50 percent discount off others, and transportation within Naples, on the Circumvesuviana train (but not the Campania Express), the Metropolitana, and on Amalfi Coast buses. The **seven-day Campania** version (€34) covers five sights and discounts on others, but no transportation. If you're focusing on Naples, the **three-day Napoli** version (€21) covers transportation within Naples and three city sights, plus discounts on others, but doesn't cover outlying ancient sites. The card is sold at participating sights and at some Naples TIs; you can also buy an electronic version online (cards activate on first use, expire 3 or 7 days later at midnight, www.campaniartecard.it).

TOURIST INFORMATION

Central Naples has various small TIs, none of them particularly helpful—just grab a map and browse the brochures. The main branch, open all year, is in the city center on Spaccanapoli, across from the **Church of Gesù Nuovo** (Mon-Sat 9:00-18:00, likely closed Sun, +39 081 551 2701). Seasonally, you may also find TI branches at the **Centrale train station,** at the **cruise port,** and at the **airport**—look around when you arrive. For information online, the best overall website is www.inaples.it.

ARRIVAL IN NAPLES

No matter how you arrive, expect some chaos. Instead of getting frustrated, consider it part of the charm of Naples—as most locals do. If you're connecting to another destination from Naples, see the "Getting Around the Region" sidebar on page 1008.

By Train

Naples has several train stations, but all trains coming into town stop at either Napoli Centrale station or Garibaldi station—which are essentially the same place, with Centrale on top of Garibaldi. Stretching in front of this station complex is the vast Piazza Garibaldi, with an underground shopping mall and Metro entrance.

Centrale station, on the ground floor, is the slick, modern main station, with intercity connections across Italy. Baggage check (*deposito bagagli,* run by Kipoint) is near track 2; pay WCs are down the stairs across from track 13. A nice Food Hall Napoli is located near tracks 2-8; other shops and eateries are mainly concentrated on the underground level. In high season, a TI may be set up somewhere in the station; the inStazione desk is a private agency but can be helpful in a pinch. Out the front door to the left, you'll find a big bookstore (La Feltrinelli) and a good supermarket (Sapori & Dintorni).

Garibaldi station, on the lower level, is used exclusively by the narrow-gauge Circumvesuviana commuter train and the Campania Express (options you can use to connect to Sorrento or Pompeii; to get here from Centrale, follow signs to *Circumvesuviana* and *Linee Vesuviane*). Note that this is not the terminus for the Circumvesuviana; that's one stop farther downtown, at the station called Porta Nolana.

To add to the confusion, **"Stazione Piazza Garibaldi,"** or "Napoli S.G." for short, is a stop on Trenitalia's Metropolitana (part of Naples' Metro line 2—see next); these tracks are downstairs near the middle of Centrale station (follow signs for *M Linea 2*). In addition to stops in Naples, some of these trains go all the way out to Pompei (the modern town) and Salerno.

Getting Downtown: Arriving at either station, the best bet for reaching most sights and hotels is either the Metro or a taxi. **Metro** lines 1 and 2 are both downstairs—in separate areas—and signposted throughout the Centrale and Garibaldi stations. Line 1 (direction: Piscinola) is handy for city-center stops, including the cruise port (Municipio), the main shopping drag (Toledo and Dante), and the Archaeological Museum (Museo). Line 2 is slightly quicker for reaching the Archaeological Museum (direction: Campi Flegrei/Pozzuoli/Formina, go one stop to Piazza Cavour, then walk 5 minutes). For tips on navigating the Metro, see "Getting Around Naples," later.

Long rows of white **taxis** line up out front. Ask the driver to charge you the fixed rate *(tariffa predeterminata),* which varies from €9 for the old center to €15 for the most distant hotel I list.

By Plane or Cruise Ship

For information on Naples' airport, cruise ship terminal, and ferry docks, see the end of this chapter.

Naples

VIA STELLA

VIA MATERDEI

To Capodimonte Sights

VICO LUNGO

VIA STA. TERESA

SANTA TERESA

SANITÀ

VIA FORIA

Cavour (Line 2)

VIA SETTEMBRINI

Piazza Cavour

PORTA SAN GENNARO

MADRE ART MUSEUM

ARCHAEO-LOGICAL MUSEUM

VIA SALVATOR ROSA

VIA M. LONGO

VIA DUOMO

VIA DONNA

Museo (Line 1)

DUOMO

VIA B. M. CONST.

GALLERIA PRINCIPE

VIA CONTE DI RUVO

VIA PESSINA

VIA BELLINI

NAPOLI SOTTER-RANEA

S. PAOLO

S. GREG. ARMENO

S. LORENZO MAGGIORE

SALITA PONCORVO

BELLINI THEATER

VIA SAPIENZA

V. ATRI

Piazza Bellini

VIA DEI TRIBUNALI

SAN DOM.

CAPPELLA SANSEVERO

VIA S. BIAGIO

D'AURIA SHOP

V. PORT'ALBA

Dante (Line 1)

PORTA D'ALBA

Piazza San Dom. Maggiore

NILE STATUE

NAPOLI

VIA TARSIA

Piazza Dante

GESÙ NUOVO

VIA B. CROCE

MARADONA CHAPEL

VIA PALADINO

VIA GRAN ARCHIVIO

Montesanto (Line 2)

Piazza Sette Settembre

Piazza Gesù Nuovo

SPACCA

VIA S.G. PIGNA

V. CAND.

VIA CAPASSO

To Vomero District

MONTESANTO FUNICULAR

SANTA CHIARA

VIA MADDALONI

CLOISTER

S. CHIARA

VIA PIGNASECCA

Piazza Monte

CALATA TRINITÀ MAGGIORE

STREET MARKET

VIA TOLEDO

VIA B. SCURA

MONTOLIVETO

V. DONNALBINA

CORSO UMBERTO I

Piazza Carità

FASCIST BLDG.

VIA BATT.

POST

V. SEDILE DI PORTO

CSN Shuttle to Pompeii

CALATA PORTA DI MASSA (CAR FERRY TERMINAL)

Piazza Bovio

Università (Line 1)

BNL BANK

Piazza Matteotti

VIA S. FELICE

VIA A. DEPRETIS

VIA S. MARIA

VIA A. DIAZ

VIA MEDINA

VIA COLOMBO

VIA A. D. GASPERI

Piazza Immacolatella

Toledo (Line 1)

VIA PORTA E. MONTE

VIA PORTA DI TAPPIA

SPANISH QUARTER

V. S. GIACOMO

VICO TOFA

BANCO DI NAPOLI

VIA IMBRIANI

Piazza Municipio

Municipio (Line 1)

PINTAURO

V. D'AFFLITTO

BANCA INTESA SANPAOLO

CSN Shuttle to Pompeii

CASTEL NUOVO

CAFFÈ BEVERELLO

CAFFÈ MORENO

V. S. BRIG.

GALLERIA UMBERTO I

CENTRALE FUNICULAR

GRAN CAFFÈ GAMBRINUS

V. S. CARLO

TEATRO SAN CARLO

Alibus (to Airport)

STAZIONE MARITTIMA (CRUISE TERMINAL)

To Chiaia District & Lungomare

VIA CHIAIA

ROYAL PALACE

VIA AM. FERD. ACTON

MOLO BEVERELLO DOCK (HYDROFOIL & FAST FERRY)

V. SERRA

Piazza del Plebiscito

TUNNEL TO LUNGOMARE

GALLERIA BORBONICA

SAN FRANCESCO DI PAOLA

V. CONSOLE

V. ACTON

To Castel dell'Ovo, Chiaia District, Lungomare Harborside Promenade & Posillipo Hill

NAPLES

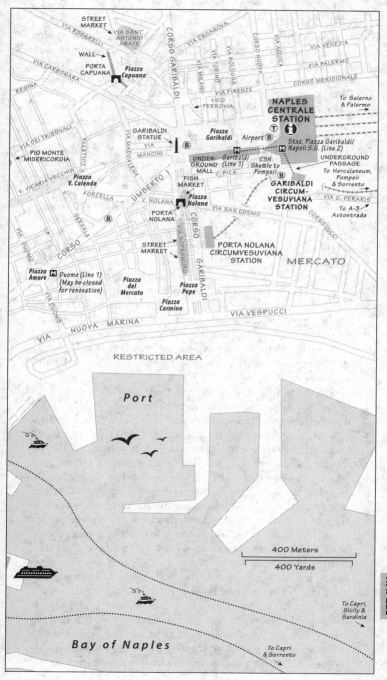

HELPFUL HINTS

Theft Alert: While most travelers visit Naples safely, err on the side of caution. Be aware that thieves and con artists hang out close to where travelers tumble into Naples: the train station and the port. Although the train station itself has been nicely spruced up, its glow doesn't extend far. Remember that poor and chaotic does not necessarily mean dangerous. Don't let your first impression of the station area get in your way of enjoying Naples—the city changes drastically as you move farther away. Touristy Spaccanapoli, Capodimonte, and the posh Via Toledo shopping boulevard are more upscale—though even in its nicest areas, Naples can strike many visitors as a bit scruffy.

Stick to busy streets and beware the odd gang of hoodlums. A third of the city is unemployed, and past local governments have set an example of corruption that the Mafia would be proud of. As in most big cities, consider any jostle or commotion a possible thief-team smokescreen. Keep a low profile, carry only the bare minimum, and leave heavy bags at your hotel or at the left-luggage office in Centrale station.

Walk with confidence, as if you know where you're going and what you're doing. Use the sidewalk (even if the locals don't) and carry your belongings on the side away from the street—thieves on scooters have been known to snatch bags as they swoop by. Keep valuables buttoned up (or secure them at your hotel).

Perhaps your biggest risk of theft is while catching or riding the Circumvesuviana commuter train. While I ride the Circumvesuviana comfortably and safely, each year I hear of travelers who get ripped off on this ride. You won't be mugged—but you may be conned or pickpocketed. At the train station, carry your own bags—there are no official porters. If you're connecting from a long-distance express, you'll be going from a relatively secure compartment into an often-crowded and dingy train. Be ready for this very common trick: A team of thieves blocks the door at a stop, pretending it's stuck. While everyone rushes to try to open it, an accomplice picks their pockets. Wear your money belt, and avoid the Circumvesuviana train late at night when it's plagued by intimidating ruffians. For peace of mind, sit in the front car, where there is a driver who may be able to monitor activity.

Traffic Safety: In Naples, red lights are timed short, and pedestrians need to be wary, particularly of motor scooters that zip among the cars. Even on "pedestrian" streets, stay alert to avoid being sideswiped by scooters (or even cars) that nudge their way through the crowds. Smart tourists jaywalk in the shadow of bold locals, who generally ignore crosswalks. Wait for a break in traffic, cross with confidence, and make eye contact with approaching drivers and motor scooters. The traffic will slow to let you pass.

Free Entry Days: State museums in Italy, including the Archaeological Museum and Capodimonte Museum, are free to enter once or twice a month, usually on a Sunday. Check in advance and if possible, avoid going on a free day, which can attract huge crowds.

Bookstore: La Feltrinelli, conveniently located at Centrale station, carries a small selection of English-language books (daily 8:00-20:00, near track 24, also accessible from outside the station).

Laundry: Lav@Sciuga, a block from the Università Metro stop, is convenient but has just a few washing machines (Mon-Fri 9:00-17:00, Sat until 13:00, closed Sun, Via Sedile di Porto 54, mobile +39 327 754 6639).

GETTING AROUND NAPLES

Sightsee Naples with help from its subway (Metro), funiculars, and taxis. (There are also public buses, but these generally aren't useful for travelers.) For general transit information, maps, and fares, visit www.unicocampania.it. For schedules, your only option is the Italian-only site www.anm.it. Google Maps works as well as anything for journey planning.

Tickets and Passes: Most of Naples' public transportation system—Metro, funiculars, and buses—use the same ticket, which must be stamped as you enter (in yellow or blue machines). Tickets are sold at tobacco stores, some newsstands, clunky machines at Metro stations (these accept coins, small bills, or credit cards, but can be tricky to operate), and occasionally at station windows. Basically, anywhere you see a queue near the station, people are buying tickets.

A €1.10 single ticket *(corsa singola)* covers any ride on bus, funicular, or Metro line 1, with no transfers; for Metro line 2 you need the €1.30 version. (This ticket is a long, printed receipt with a QR code that needs to be punched at the machine—fold your ticket in half and insert.) A *giornaliero* day pass costs €3.50 (or €4.50 including Metro line 2), and pays for itself quickly, but can be hard to find; many tobacco stores don't sell them. A weekly ticket (Mon-Sun) costs €12.50, or €16 including Metro line 2. Several versions of the Campania ArteCard (see sidebar on page 952) include free public transport in Naples.

By Metro (Metropolitana): Naples' subway has three main lines *(linea)*. Station entrances and signs to the Metro are marked by a red square with a white *M*.

Line 1 is very useful for tourists. Starting from Centrale train station (stop name: Garibaldi), it heads to Università (the university), Municipio (at Piazza Municipio, just above the harbor and cruise terminal), Toledo (south end of Via Toledo, near Piazza del Plebiscito), Dante (Piazza Dante), and Museo (Archaeological Museum). Four stops beyond Museo is the Vanvitelli stop, near the hilltop San Martino sights; the end of the line is Piscinola. Many of line 1's stations are huge and elaborate, designed by prominent artists and architects; Naples is proud of them, and locals are excited to tell you about their favorite.

Line 2 (part of Trenitalia, the Italian national rail system) is most useful for getting quickly from the Centrale train station to Piazza Cavour (a 5-minute walk from the Archaeological Museum)

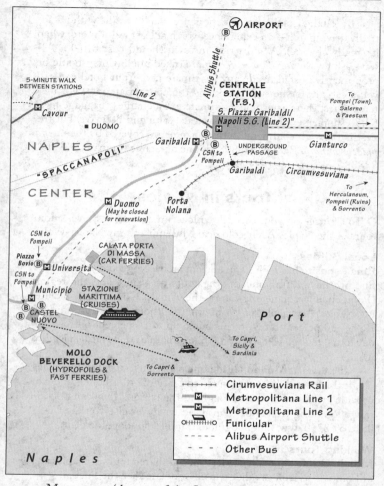

or Montesanto (the top of the Spanish Quarter and Spaccanapoli street, and base of one funicular up to San Martino). Note that the train station stop on this line is called "Napoli S.G." (for Stazione Piazza Garibaldi). Some trains on this line run all the way out into the suburbs (including to modern Pompei and Salerno).

By Funicular: Central Naples' three funiculars *(funicolare)* carry commuters and sightseers into the hilly San Martino neighborhood just west of downtown. All three converge near Piazza Fuga, a short walk from the hilltop fortress and monastery/museum. The Centrale line runs from the Spanish Quarter, just near Piazza del Plebiscito and the Toledo Metro stop; the Montesanto line from the Montesanto Metro stop and Via Pignasecca market zone; and the Chiaia line from near the Piazza Amadeo Metro stop.

By Taxi: A taxi lets you experience Naples traffic without actually driving in it—an experience worth at least ▲ (or more, when it's really chaotic). A short ride in town should cost €10-15. Always ask for the *tariffa predeterminata* (fixed rate), which should be prominently posted inside any legitimate taxi. Your hotel can call you a cab and make sure you know the appropriate rate. For metered rides, there are some legitimate extra charges (baggage fees, €2.50 supplement after 22:00 or all day Sun and holidays) but the destinations I recommend in this chapter are covered by the *tariffa predeterminata*. Radio Taxi 8888 is one reputable company (+39 081 8888).

Tours in Naples

🎧 To sightsee on your own, download my free Rick Steves audio tours of the Naples Archaeological Museum and my Naples Walk.

Local Guides
Pina Esposito has a Ph.D. in ancient archaeology and art and does fine private walking and driving tours of Naples and the region (Pompeii, Herculaneum, Capri, the Amalfi Coast, etc.), including Naples' Archaeological Museum (€60/hour, 2-hour minimum, RS%—10 percent off with this book, up to 20 percent off for full-day tours, mobile +39 338 763 4224, annamariaesposito1@virgilio.it).

The team at **Mondo Guide** offers private tours of the Archaeological Museum (€120/2 hours) and city (€240/4 hours) and can provide guides or drivers throughout the region. They can also arrange kayaking trips, boat trips, and whatever else you need (+39 081 751 3290, www.mondoguide.it, info@mondoguide.com).

Walking Tours
Mondo Guide offers my readers special shared tours of Naples and of Pompeii, as well as other trips. For details, see the sidebar.

Hop-On, Hop-Off Bus Tours
CitySightseeing Napoli tour buses make two different hop-on, hop-off loops through the city. Only the red line, which loops around the historical center and stops at the Archaeological Museum, is particularly helpful. It will also give you a sense of greater Naples that this chapter largely ignores (€23, ticket valid 24 hours, 2/hour, buy from driver or from kiosk at Piazza Municipio in front of Castel Nuovo near the port, scant recorded narration, +39 081 551 7279, www.napoli.city-sightseeing.it). The blue line takes you out along the seafront pedestrian promenade to Posillipo Hill—a more upscale part of the city that Neapolitans love.

Cruise-Ship Excursions

Convenient for cruise-ship passengers, the **Can't Be Missed** tour company takes you from the port of Naples on an all-day coach trip for up to 20 passengers along the Amalfi Coast that includes a stop in Sorrento and a guided tour of Pompeii (€89, meet at 8:00 in front of port, bus leaves at 8:30, returns at 15:45, Pompeii ticket extra, mobile +1 607 542 7981, www.cantbemissedtours.com, RS%—10 percent off when you use promo code "RICKSTEVES" on their website).

Archaeological Museum Tour

Naples' Archaeological Museum (Museo Archeologico), worth ▲▲▲, is one of the world's great museums of ancient art. It boasts supersized statues as well as art and decorations from Pompeii and Herculaneum, the two ancient burgs that were buried in ash by the eruption of Mount Vesuvius in AD 79. For lovers of antiquity, this museum alone makes Naples a worthwhile stop.

When Pompeii was excavated in the late 1700s, Naples' Bourbon king bellowed, "Bring me the best of what you find!" The finest art and artifacts ended up here, leaving the ancient sites themselves barren (though still impressive). It's here at the Archaeological Museum that you can get up close and personal with the ancient world.

ORIENTATION

Cost and Hours: €15, sometimes more for temporary exhibits; Wed-Mon 9:00-19:30, closed Tue. Avoid lines by purchasing your ticket online. Early and temporary closures are noted on a board near the ticket office: The Secret Room tends to have shorter hours (sometimes closing in the early afternoon), and additional rooms can be closed in July and August.

Information: +39 081 442 2149, www.museoarcheologiconapoli. it.

Getting There: From Centrale station, you can reach the museum by Metro or taxi. **Metro** line 2 is quickest: At the station, buy a single transit ticket at a newsstand or tobacco shop—specify you want line 2 since the price and ticket are different from line 1. Follow signs downstairs to *Metro Linea 2*, then fold and punch your ticket in the small blue boxes near the escala-

Mondo Guide Tours of Pompeii, Naples, the Amalfi Coast, and Capri for My Readers

Mondo Guide, a big Naples-based company, offers "shared tours" for Rick Steves readers. These allow you the luxury of a private, professional guide at a fraction of the usual cost, because you'll be sharing the expense with other travelers using this book. Tours run from April through October and include **Pompeii,** a walking tour of **Naples,** and two longer-distance trips from Sorrento: an **Amalfi Coast** van tour and a private boat to the **isle of Capri.** The Pompeii and Naples tours are timed so you can do both on the same day. Mondo also offers shore excursions for cruise passengers arriving in Naples or Salerno. I don't receive a cut from the tours; I set this up with Mondo Guide to help my readers have the most economical experience in this region.

Reservations are required. For specifics and to sign up, go to SharedTours.com (Mondo +39 081 751 3290, mobile +39 340 460 5254, www.mondoguide.it, sharedtours@mondoguide.com). On the website, use your credit-card number to reserve a spot. You'll then pay cash for the tour. If you must cancel, email more than three days in advance or you'll be billed.

Each tour requires a minimum of six participants. You'll be sent an email confirmation as soon as they're sure your tour will run. If there's not enough demand to justify the trip, they'll notify you three days before the departure date (giving you time to come up with alternative plan). Confirmed departures are continually updated on the website.

Pompeii Tour: This two-hour guided walk brings to life the ruins of the excavated city (€20, Pompeii entry extra—your guide will collect money and buy tickets, daily at 11:00; meet in Pompeii at Hotel/Ristorante Suisse, a 5-minute walk from the train station—exiting the station, turn right, pass the Porta Marina entrance, and continue down the hill to the restaurant, on the right).

Historic Naples Walk: Naples is a challenge to enjoy and understand; on this three-hour walk, a local Neapolitan guide helps you uncover the true character of the city (€30; daily at 15:00; meet at the steps of the Naples Archaeological Museum—you can

tor going down to the tracks. Take a train in the direction of Pozzuoli, Campi Flegrei, or Formina (attendants may ask and confirm which direction you're going). Ride one stop to Piazza Cavour. Exit and walk five minutes uphill through the park. Look for a grand old red building up a flight of stairs at the top of the block.

You can also take the Metro's slightly cheaper line 1 five stops from Centrale station to Museo—it's only a little slower, and drops you closer to the museum.

do the museum on your own before joining your guide).

Full-Day Amalfi Coast Minibus Tour from Sorrento: The Amalfi Coast can be complicated and time-consuming to visit on your own, making a shared minibus the simplest and most affordable way to enjoy the sights. (Small groups use an eight-seat minibus with only a driver; larger groups use a 19-seat minibus with a driver and a guide.) This nine-hour trip saves time and money and maximizes your experience. It begins in Sorrento and heads south for the breathtaking (and lightly narrated) drive, several photo stops, and an hour or two on your own in each of the three main towns—Positano, Amalfi, and Ravello—before returning to Sorrento. Lunch isn't included; to save time for exploring, grab a quick lunch in one of the towns (€65, daily at 9:00; meet in Sorrento in front of Hotel Antiche Mura, at Via Fuorimura 7, a block inland from Piazza Tasso).

Full-Day Capri Boat Trip from Sorrento: To sidestep the hassles of taking public boats from Sorrento for a Capri side trip, Mondo offers a trip to the island on a small private boat (12 people maximum), which includes an early visit to the Blue Grotto sea cave when conditions allow (€15, optional) and about four hours of free time to explore the island on your own. After your time on land, the boat takes you on a lightly narrated trip around the island with drinks, snacks, and a chance to swim if the weather cooperates (€120, daily at 8:00, pickup at Sorrento hotel, may be cancelled in bad weather).

Shore Excursions from Naples or Salerno: Mondo Guide offers all-day itineraries from the port of Naples or the port of Salerno that combine three big sights in the region and the scenic Amalfi Coast— from Naples, a guided visit to Pompeii with an hour of free time each in Sorrento and Positano; from Salerno, a guided visit to Pompeii with an hour of free time each in Sorrento and Amalfi town (€80, daily at 8:00-8:30 from the main exit of the Naples cruise terminal building or from your ship in Salerno).

Figure about €13 for a **taxi** from the train station to the museum.

Visitor Information: The shop (behind the ticket desk) sells a worthwhile *National Archaeological Museum of Naples* guidebook for €13.

Tours: The self-guided tour in this chapter covers all the basics. For more detail, the decent **audioguide** (€5, leave ID at ticket desk) focuses largely on the provenance of the artifacts and

how they ended up here. For a **guided tour,** book Pina Esposito (see "Tours in Naples," earlier).

🎧 Download my free Archaeological Museum **audio
tour.**

Baggage Check: Bag check is obligatory and free.

Eating: The museum's **$ Mann Caffè** has both a counter and table
service, and a full menu. There are also a few good places to
grab a meal within a 10-minute walk; see page 1007.

❺ SELF-GUIDED TOUR

Entering the museum, cross the atrium, and stand at the base of
the grand staircase. To your right, on the ground floor, are the
larger-than-life statues of the Farnese Collection, starring the *Toro
Farnese* and the *Farnese Hercules.* Up the stairs on the mezzanine
level are mosaics and frescoes from Pompeii, including the Secret
Room of erotic art. On the top floor are more artifacts from Pompeii, a scale model of the doomed city, and bronze statues from
Herculaneum. WCs are behind the staircase.

• *From the base of the* ❶ *grand staircase, turn right through the door
marked* Collezione Farnese *and head for the far end, walking through
a rich collection of ancient portrait* ❷ *busts.*

    Pause at the busts of **Caracalla** *(a third of the way down, on the
left), and marvel at how he evolved from idealistic youth to cruel tyrant (and nemesis of Russell Crowe in the movie* Gladiator*). Admire
the* **Seated Agrippina** *(two-thirds of the way down) with her typical
hairstyle, realistic face, and pensive look. Nearby, look in* **Vespasian**'s
*right ear and see how the huge head was hollowed out in medieval times.
Now, continue to the end and jog right, then left, entering Room 13.*

Ground Floor: The Farnese Collection

The Farnese Collection statues are not from Pompeii, but from
Rome. Today they're displayed in this grand hall of huge, bright,
and wonderfully restored statues excavated from Rome's Baths of
Caracalla. Peruse the larger-than-life statues filling the hall. They
were dug up in the 1540s at the behest of Alessandro Farnese (by
then Pope Paul III) while he was building the family palace on
the Campo de' Fiori in Rome. His main purpose in excavating the
baths was to scavenge quality building stone. The sculptures were a
nice extra and helped the palace come in under budget on decorations. In the 1700s, the collection ended up in the hands of Charles,
the Bourbon king of Naples (whose mother was a Farnese). His
son, the next king, had it brought to Naples.

• *Quick—look down to the left end of the hall. There's a woman being
tied to a snorting bull.*

    The tangled ❸ *Toro Farnese* tells a thrilling Greek myth. At
13 feet, it's the tallest ancient marble group ever found, and the

Naples Archaeological Museum

Second Floor (2)

VILLA PAPIRI — 13, 14

ANCIENT NAPLES

STAIRS — 9

ATLAS

CEILING FRESCO

POMPEII

OBJECTS — 10

MODEL — 11

POMPEII — 12

GREAT HALL

FRESCOES

Mezzanine (1)

SECRET ROOM — 8, 7

MOSAICS — 6

STAIRS

N — Not to Scale

⊠ Elevator

Ground Floor (0)

CAFÉ

WC STAIRS WC

TOUR BEGINS — 1

2

3

Garden of the Camelias

ATRIUM

Garden of the Fountains

SCULPTURES

FARNESE COLLECTION — 4, 5

GEMS

15

TICKETS

SHOP

BAGGAGE CHECK

ENTRANCE

168, 178 & C63
(to Capodimonte Museum)

B PIAZZA MUSEO

To Cavour Metro Station

GALLERIA PRINCIPE

NAPLES

1 Grand Staircase
2 Hall of the Busts
3 Toro Farnese
4 Farnese Hercules
5 Farnese Cup
6 Various Mosaics
7 Dancing Faun & Battle of Alexander
8 Secret Room
9 Great Hall
10 Metal, Ivory & Glass Objects
11 Model of Pompeii
12 Frescoes
13 Papyrus Scrolls
14 Bronze Statues
15 Doriforo (might have moved)

largest intact statue from antiquity. A third-century AD copy of a lost bronze Hellenistic original, it was carved out of one piece of marble. Michelangelo and others "restored" it at the pope's request—meaning that they integrated surviving bits into a new work. Some pieces were actually carved by Michelangelo: the head of the woman in back, the torso of the aunt under the bull, and the dog. (Imagine how the statue would stand out if it were thoughtfully lit and not surrounded by white walls.)

Here's the tragic story behind the statue: Once upon an ancient Greek time, King Lycus was bewitched by Dirce. He abandoned his pregnant wife, Antiope (standing regally in the background). The single mom gave birth to twin boys. When they grew up, they killed their deadbeat dad and tied Dirce to the horns of a bull to be bashed against a mountain. Captured in marble, the action is thrilling: cape flailing, dog snarling, hooves in the air. You can almost hear the bull snorting. And in the back, Antiope oversees this harsh ancient justice with satisfaction.

At the opposite end of the hall stands the ❹ *Farnese Hercules*. The great Greek hero is exhausted. He leans wearily on his club

(draped with his lion skin) and bows his head. He's just finished the daunting Eleventh Labor, having traveled the world, fought men and gods, freed Prometheus from his rock, and carried Atlas' weight of the world on his shoulders. Now he's returned with the prize: the golden apples of the gods, which he cups behind his back. But, after all that, he's just been told he has to return the apples and do one final labor: descend into hell itself. Oh, man.

The 10-foot colossus is a third-century AD Roman marble copy (signed by "Glykon") of a fourth-century BC Greek bronze original (probably by Lysippos). The statue was enormously famous in its day. Dozens of copies—some marble, some bronze—have been found in Roman villas and baths. This version was unearthed in Rome's Baths of Caracalla in 1546, along with the *Toro Farnese*.

The *Farnese Hercules* was equally famous in the 16th-18th centuries. Tourists flocked to Rome to admire it, art students studied it from afar in prints, Louis XIV made a copy for Versailles, and petty nobles everywhere put small-scale knock-offs in their gardens. This curly-haired version of Hercules became the modern world's image of the Greek hero.

• *Behind Hercules is a doorway into the impressive Farnese gem collection (Gemme Farnese, Rooms 9 and 10). You'll see cameos and the ancient cereal bowl-shaped* ❺ **Farnese Cup,** *which features a portrait thought to be of Cleopatra. When you're ready to move on, backtrack to the main entry hall with its grand staircase—perhaps stopping briefly to admire the magnificent sarcophagi in adjacent rooms—then head up to the mezzanine level (turn left at the lion and go under the* Mosaici *sign), and enter Room 57.*

Mezzanine: Pompeiian Mosaics and the Secret Room

These ❻ **mosaics**—mostly of animals, battle scenes, and geometric designs—were excavated from the walls and floors of Pompeii's ritzy villas. The *Chained Dog* once graced a home's entryway. The colorful mosaic columns (to your right in adjoining Room 58) shaded a courtyard, part of an ensemble of wall mosaics and bubbling fountains. In Room 59, admire the realism of the tambourine-playing musicians, the drinking doves, and the skull—a reminder of impending death.

Continue a few steps into Room 60, with objects taken from one of Pompeii's greatest villas, the House of the Faun. The 20-inch-high statue was the house's delightful centerpiece, the ❼ *Dancing Faun.* This rare surviving Greek bronze statue (from the fourth century BC) is surrounded by some of the best mosaics of that age. (Find the wild-eyed little cat, who's caught a bird.)

A museum highlight, just beyond the statue, is the grand *Battle of Alexander,* a second-century-BC copy of the now-lost original

Greek fresco, done a century earlier. It decorated a floor in the House of the Faun and was found intact. (The damage you see occurred as this treasure was moved from Pompeii to the king's collection here.) Alexander (left side of the scene, with curly hair and sideburns) is about to defeat the Persians under Darius (central figure, in chariot with turban and beard). This pivotal victory allowed Alexander to quickly overrun much of Asia (331 BC). Alexander is the only one without a helmet...a confident master of the battlefield while everyone else is fighting for their lives, eyes bulging with fear. Notice how the horses, already in retreat, add to the scene's propaganda value. Notice also the shading and perspective, which Renaissance artists would later work so hard to accomplish. (A modern reproduction of the mosaic is now back in Pompeii, at the House of the Faun.)

Farther on, the ❽ **Secret Room** (*Gabinetto Segreto*, Room 65) contains a sizable assortment of erotic frescoes, well-hung pottery, and perky statues that once decorated bedrooms, meeting rooms, brothels, and even shops at Pompeii and Herculaneum. These bawdy statues and frescoes—many of them once displayed in Pompeii's grandest houses—were entertainment for guests. (By the time they made it to this museum, in 1819, the frescoes could be viewed only with permission from the king—see the letters in the glass case just outside the door.) The Roman nobles commissioned the wildest scenes imaginable. Think of them as ancient dirty jokes. If you're easily offended, or find scatological humor juvenile, skip this room.

At the entrance, you're enthusiastically greeted by big stone penises that once projected over Pompeii's doorways. A massive phallus was not necessarily a sexual symbol, but a magical amulet used against the "evil eye." It symbolized fertility, happiness, good luck, riches, straight A's, and general wellbeing.

Circulating counterclockwise through this section, look for the following: the fresco—high up—of a faun playfully pulling the sheet off a woman (#12), only to be surprised to find both sets of genitalia. A few steps farther, see horny "pygmies" from Africa in action (#27). There's a toga with an embarrassing bulge (#34). A particularly high-quality statue depicts a goat and a satyr engaging in a sex act (#36). And, watching over it all with remarkable aplomb, is Venus, the patron goddess of Pompeii (#39).

The back room is furnished and decorated the way an ancient brothel might have been. The 10 frescoes on the wall functioned as both a menu of services offered and as a kind of *Kama Sutra* of sex positions. The glass cases contain more phallic art, including dangling mobiles used as party favors at rowdy banquets.

• *So, now that your travel buddy is finally showing a little interest in art...finish up your visit by climbing the stairs to the top floor.*

At the top of the stairs, pause and get oriented to our final sights. Directly ahead is a doorway (marked Salone Meridiana*) that leads into a big, empty hall. To the left of this grand hall is a series of rooms with more artifacts from Pompeii. To the right are rooms of statues from Herculaneum. Keep this general layout in mind, because occasionally door-*

ways and routes are altered, and you may have to improvise a bit to find your way.

Top Floor: Frescoes, Statues, Artifacts, and a Model of Pompeii

First, step into the Salone Meridiana. This was the ❾ **great hall** of the university (17th and 18th centuries) until the building became the royal museum in 1777. Walk to the center. The sundial in the floor (angling off to the right, from 1791) still works. Look up to the far-right corner of the hall and find the tiny pinhole. At noon (13:00 in summer), a ray of sun enters the hall and strikes the sundial, showing the time of the year...if you know your zodiac.

Now, back where you entered, go into the series of rooms to the left of the grand hall, with ❿ **Metal, Ivory, and Glass Objects** found in Pompeii. You enter through a doorway marked *Vetri e Avori*, which leads into Room 89. Browse your way to the far end, with the stunning *Blue Vase* (Room 85), decorated with cameo Bacchuses harvesting grapes. Turn left, then right, to find the huge, room-filling ⓫ **model of Pompeii,** a 1:100 scale model of the ruins (Room 96). Face the model from the side labeled *plastico di Pompei.* This is how tourists enter today, up the street, and spilling into the large rectangular forum with the Temple of Jupiter at one end. Farther up in the model are the city's two amphitheater-shaped theaters. This was all that had been excavated when the model was made in 1879. Another model (displayed on the wall) shows the site in 2004, after more excavations, when they'd dug up as far as the huge oval-shaped arena. Video screens capture images from the 1879 model and reconstruct buildings in 3-D as they would have appeared before the eruption.

Continue on (through Rooms 83-80—turn right, then left) and enter Room 75 (marked *Affreschi*) to see the museum's impressive collection of (nonerotic) ⓬ **frescoes** taken from the walls of Pompeii villas. Pompeiians loved to decorate their homes with scenes from mythology (Hercules' labors, Venus and Mars in love), landscapes, everyday market scenes, and faux architecture. To the left (in Room 78), find the famous dual portrait of baker Terentius Neo and his wife—possibly two of the 2,000 victims when Vesuvius erupted.

• *Browse through more frescoes and objects from Pompeii in this labyrinth of rooms until, eventually, you end up back near the great hall. From here, facing the hall entrance, turn left and find the entrance to the wing labeled* La Villa dei Papiri.

These artifacts came from the Herculaneum holiday home of Julius Caesar's father-in-law. ⓭ In Room 114, find the glass cases holding two blackened examples of the 2,000 **papyrus scrolls** that gave the villa its name. The half-burned scrolls were unrolled and (with luck) read after excavation in the 1750s. Apparently Caesar's father-in-law was an educated man who appreciated everything from Greek philosophy to Latin history.

Continuing into Room 116, enjoy some of the villa's ⑭ **bronze statues.** Look into the lifelike blue eyes of the intense *Corridore*

(runners), bent on doing their best. The *Five Dancers*, with their inlaid-ivory eyes and graceful poses, decorated a portico. The next room (117) has more fine works: *Resting Hermes* (with his tired little heel wings) is taking a break. Nearby, the *Drunken Faun* (singing and snapping his fingers to the beat, a wineskin at his side) is clearly living for today. This statue epitomizes the *carpe diem* lifestyle of the Epicurean philosophy followed by Caesar's father-in-law and so many other Romans living in Herculaneum and Pompeii on that fateful morning of August 24, AD 79, when Vesuvius changed everything.

• *Ka-pow. The artistic explosion you've just experienced in this mighty museum is now over. To exit, return to the ground floor. You may be able to leave the way you came in. Or you may be routed to another exit, past the café and around the museum courtyard to the gift shop. Either way, for extra credit, look for one more sight on your way out. (He tends to get moved around; if you can't find him ask a guard, "Dov'è il Doriforo?")*

⑮ Doriforo

This seven-foot-tall "spear-carrier" (the literal translation of *doriforo*) just stands there, as if holding a spear. What's the big deal about this statue, which looks like so many others?

It's a marble replica made by the Romans of one of the most-copied statues of antiquity, a fifth-century-BC bronze Greek original by Polyclitus. This copy once stood in a Pompeii gym, where it inspired ancient athletes by showing the ideal proportions of Greek beauty. So full of motion, and so realistic in its *contrapposto* pose (weight on one foot), the *Doriforo* would later inspire Donatello and Michelangelo, helping to trigger the Renaissance. And so the glories of ancient Pompeii, once buried and forgotten, live on today.

Naples Walk

Naples, a living medieval city, is its own best sight. Couples artfully make love on Vespas surrounded by more smiles per cobblestone than anywhere else in Italy. Sure, Naples has its important sights. But to capture its essence, take this walk through the core of the city.

A SLICE OF NEAPOLITAN LIFE

This self-guided walk, worth ▲▲▲, takes you from the Archae-ological Museum through the heart of town. Allow at least two hours for the full two-part walk, plus time for pizza and sight-seeing stops. If your time is short, from Piazza Carità—near the middle of the walk—you can head down Via Toledo to the Toledo Metro stop to zip back to the train station.

🎧 You can also download my free Naples City Walk audio tour.

Part 1: Archaeological Museum to Piazza Carità

Start at the Archaeological Museum, at the top of Piazza Cavour (Metro: Cavour or Museo; for directions on getting here, see page 961). From here, we'll ramble down a fine boulevard before cutting into the medieval heart of the city.

❶ **Archaeological Museum:** The palatial building, built in the mid-1700s, captures the glory of Naples at its peak, and is a great introduction to the Naples we'll see. Back then, the city was rich from sea trade and home to erudite nobles from abroad. They built a magnificent capital of buildings like this one. On this walk we'll see that grand city they built...and its remnants following centuries of decline.

• *From the door of the Archaeological Museum, cross the street, veer right, and enter the arched doorway of the beige-colored Galleria Principe di Napoli mall. (If the entrance is blocked, simply loop around the block to another entrance or pick up our walk behind the Galleria.)*

❷ **Galleria Principe di Napoli:** There's no better example of Naples' grandeur—and decline—than this elegant 19th-century shopping mall. You'll enjoy a soaring skylight, carved woodwork, ironwork lanterns, playful cupids, an elegant atmosphere...and empty shops. Built with great expectations, the galleria was named for the first male child of the royal Savoy family, the Prince of Naples. Malls like these were popular in Paris and London. In the US, we call this

NAPLES

Naples Walk

To Capodimonte Sights

VIA MATERDEI
VIA STELLA
VIA VILLARI
VIA PAGANO
VIA CROCELLE
VIA VERGINI
VIA FORIA

SANITÀ

SANTA TERESA
Cavour (Line 2)

Piazza Cavour

VIA SETTEMBRINI

VIA SALVATOR ROSA
VIA STA. TERESA

ARCHAEO-LOGICAL MUSEUM ①

Museo (Line 1) M

VIA M. LONGO
PORTA SAN GENNARO
MADRE ART MUSEUM

VIA DUOMO

GALLERIA PRINCIPE
② WALK BEGINS

VIA CONTE DI RUVO

NAPOLI SOTTERANEA

DUOMO

S. PAOLO

VIA DONNA

BELLINI THEATER

③ Piazza Bellini

VIA SAPIENZA
VIA ATRI

S. LORENZO MAGGIORE

V. PORT ALBA
④ Piazza Dante
PORTA D'ALBA
VIA DEI TRIBUNALI
S. GREG ARMENO
⑬
VIA S. BIAGIO
D'AURIA SHOP

SANTA PONGORO

GESÙ NUOVO

SAN DOM.
CAPPELLA SANSEVERO
NILE STATUE
"SPACCA NAPOLI"

Montesanto (Line 2) M

⑤
Dante (Line 1) M

Piazza Sette Settembre ⑥
Piazza Gesù Nuova ⑩
Piazza San Dom. Maggiore ⑪
⑫

MARADONA CHAPEL

MONTESANTO FUNICULAR
To Vomero District

⑦ VIA MADDALONI
SANTA CHIARA

VIA B. CROCE
VIA S.G. PIGNATELLI
VIA CAPASSO

V. SCURA
⑩
CLOISTER
S. CHIARA

V. CAND.

CORSO UMBERTO I

⑧
VIA PIGNASECCA
TOLEDO
Piazza Monte.
CALATA TRINITÀ MAGGIORE
V. DONNALBINA
VIA SEDILE DI PORTO

STREET MARKET
Piazza Carità ⑨
FASCIST BLDG.
POST
CSN Shuttle to Pompeii
CALATA PORTA DI MASSA (CAR FERRY TERMINAL)

BNL BANK
Piazza Matteotti
Piazza Bovia
Università (Line 1) M

VIA S. MARIA
VIA A. DIAZ
VIA S. FELICE
VIA A. DEPRETIS
VIA A.G. GASPERI
VIA COLOMBO

SPANISH QUARTER
Toledo (Line 1) M

VIA PORTA E. MONTE
To Piazza Plebiscito
To Piazza Municipio
To Piazza Municipio
Piazza Immacola-tella

decorative style Art Nouveau; in Italy it's "Liberty Style," named for a British department store that was in vogue at a time when Naples was nicknamed the "Paris of the South." (Parisian artist Edgar Degas even left Paris to adopt Naples—which he considered more cosmopolitan and sophisticated—as his hometown.) Despite its grandeur, the mall never took off. Ambitious renovations in recent years have failed to attract much business, leaving the mall in a state of disrepair. Falling debris occasionally closes the entire structure.

• *Leaving the gallery through the opposite end, walk one block downhill on a pedestrian street. You'll pass alongside the palatial golden facade of the Academy of Fine Arts, fronted by tropical plants and (usually) busy with students at its outdoor cafés. At Via Conte di Ruvo, turn left, passing the fine* **Bellini Theater** *(also in Liberty Style). All along our walk,*

NAPLES

Part 1

❶ Archaeological Museum
❷ Galleria Principe di Napoli
❸ Piazza Bellini
❹ Piazza Dante
❺ Via Toledo
❻ Piazza Sette Settembre
❼ Spaccanapoli
❽ Via Pignasecca
❾ Piazza Carità

Part 2

❿ Piazza Gesù Nuovo
⓫ Piazza San Domenico Maggiore
⓬ Statue of the Nile
⓭ Via San Gregorio Armeno
⓮ Via Vicaria Vecchia
⓯ Eateries

be sure to enjoy the architecture of the late 19th century, when Naples was the last stop on Romantic Age travelers' Grand Tour of Europe. After one block, turn right on Via Santa Maria di Costantinopoli. Walking between two grand churches, continue directly downhill to a small park with a statue in the center called...

❸ **Piazza Bellini:** Suddenly you're in neighborhood Napoli. The statue honors the opera composer Vincenzo Bellini, whose career was launched in Naples in the early 1800s, when opera itself was being born. Just past the statue, peer down into the sunken area to see Naples' ancient origins as a fifth-century-BC Greek colony called Neapolis—literally, "the new city." These tuff blocks without mortar were part of a tower in the city wall. (And you're standing on land that, back then, was outside of the town.) You can see how the street level has risen from the rubble of centuries.

Now look around at the city of today. Survey the many balconies—and the people who use them as a "backyard" in this densely packed city. The apartment blocks were originally the palaces of noble families, as indicated by the stately family crests above grand doorways. For 2,500 years, laundry has blown in the breeze right here.

• *Walk 30 yards downhill on the right side. Stop at the horseshoe-shaped* **Port'Alba gate** *(just beyond the bottom of the square, on the right). Spin slowly 360 degrees and take in the scene. The proud tile across the street (upstairs, between the two balconies) shows Piazza Bellini circa 1890. Don't ignore the graffiti; try to figure out the issues that artists are calling attention to.*

Pass through the gate, down Via Port'Alba, and stroll through this pleasant passage lined with book stalls. You emerge into a big square called...

❹ Piazza Dante: This square is marked by a statue of Dante, the medieval poet. Fittingly, half the square is devoted to bookstores. Old Dante looks out over an urban area that was once grand, then chaotic, and is now slowly becoming grand again.

Along one side is a grandiose, orange-and-gray **pseudo-facade** of columns and statues designed by Luigi Vanvitelli, an architect who made his mark on the city in the late 1700s. Vanvitelli remade an existing Jesuit monastery into this new school, representing the power of the Bourbon monarchy when Naples was at its peak. Originally, a statue of the king stood in the square. But in 1799, the Bourbon monarchy was toppled when Napoleon invaded. The king's statue was removed and replaced with the generic figure of Dante. And note the name that was later added to the big facade—Victor Emmanuel (Vittorio Emanuele). These suggest the next phase of Naples' history—its decline—which we'll see in just a bit.

The Neapolitan people are survivors. A long history of corrupt and greedy colonial overlords (German, Norman, French, Austrian, Spanish, Napoleon, etc.) has taught Neapolitans to deal creatively with authority. Many credit this aspect of Naples' past for the strength of organized crime here.

• *Before moving on, note the red* "M" *that Dante seems to be gesturing to. This marks the* **Dante Metro station,** *the best of Napoli's art-splashed Metro stations. (To take a look, go down three flights of escalators and then back up; you'll need a ticket, unless you can sweet-talk a guard.) Then, exit Piazza Dante at the far (bottom) end, walking downhill on...*

❺ Via Toledo: The long, straight street heading downhill from Piazza Dante is Naples' principal shopping drag. It originated as a military road built by the Spanish viceroys (hence the name) who made Naples great in the 16th century. Back then, Via Toledo skirted the old town wall to connect the Spanish military headquarters (now the museum where you started this walk) with the Royal Palace (down by the bay). As you stroll, peek into the many lovely atriums, which provide a break from the big street.

After a couple hundred yards, you'll reach the triangular ❻ **Piazza Sette Settembre.** This public space recalls the event that precipitated Naples' swift decline. On September 7, 1860, from the white marble balcony of the Neoclassical building overlooking the square, the famous revolutionary Giuseppe Garibaldi celebrated his conquest of Naples. He declared Italy united and Victor Emmanuel II its first king. And a decade later, that declaration became reality when Rome also fell to unification forces. It was the start of a glorious new era for Italy, Rome, and the Italian people. But not for Naples.

Naples' treasury was confiscated to subsidize the industrial expansion of the north, and its bureaucrats were transferred to the new capital in Rome. Within a few decades, Naples went from being a thriving cultural and political capital to a provincial town, with its economy in shambles and its dialect considered backward.

• *Continue straight on Via Toledo. A block past Piazza Sette Settembre you'll come to Via Maddaloni, which marks the start of the long, straight, narrow street nicknamed...*

❼ **Spaccanapoli:** Via Maddaloni is the modern name for the beginning of this thin street that, since ancient times, has bisected the city. The name Spaccanapoli translates as "split Naples." Look left down the street (toward the train station), and right (toward San Martino hill), and you get a sense of how Spaccanapoli divides this urban jungle of buildings.

• *At this point in our walk, take a moment to plan your next move. From here, our walk loops to the right, through the edge of the intense residential Spanish Quarter neighborhood to Piazza Carità before cutting over to the Spaccanapoli district. (If you were to side-trip to the Royal Palace and Piazza del Plebiscito-area sights—described later in "Sights in Naples"—you'd do that from here...but that makes this walk very long.)*

At the Spaccanapoli intersection, go right (toward the church facade on the hill), heading up Via Pasquale Scura. After about 100 yards,

you hit a busy intersection where the street begins to climb steeply uphill.
Stop. You're on one of Naples' most colorful open-air market streets...

❽ Via Pignasecca: Take in the colorful scene at the intersection. Then, turn left down Via Pignasecca and stroll this colorful
market strip. You'll pass fish stalls, tripe ven-
dors, butchers, produce stands, cheap clothes
stores, street-food vendors, and much more.
There's more activity during the morning,
but afternoon offers better light for photography.

This is a taste of Naples' famous **Spanish Quarter** (its center is farther down Via
Toledo but this area provides a good sampling).

The Spanish Quarter is a classic world of
basso (low) living. The streets—which were
laid out in the 16th century for the Spanish
military barracks outside the city walls—are
unbelievably narrow (and cool in summer), and the buildings rise
five stories high. In such tight quarters, life—flirting, fighting,
playing, and loving—happens in the road. This is *the* cliché of life
in Naples, as shown in so many movies. The Spanish Quarter is
Naples at its most characteristic. The shopkeepers are friendly, and
the mopeds are bold (watch out). Concerned locals will tug on their
lower eyelids, warning you to be wary. Hungry? Pop into a grocery
shop and ask the clerk to make you his best prosciutto-and-mozza-
rella sandwich (it should cost you about €4).

• *Turn left and follow Via Pignasecca as it leads back to Via Toledo at
the square called...*

❾ Piazza Carità: This square, built for an official visit by Hitler to Mussolini in 1938, is full of stern, straight, obedient lines.
The big building belonged to an insurance company. (For the

best example of fascist architecture in
town, take a slight detour from here:
With your back to Via Toledo, leave
Piazza Carità downhill on the right-
hand corner and walk a block to the
Poste e Telegrafi building. There you'll
see several government buildings with
stirring reliefs singing the praises of
lobotomized workers and a totalitarian
society.)

In Naples—long a poor and rough
city—rather than being heroic, people
learn from the cradle the art of survival. The modern memorial statue in the

center of this square celebrates Salvo d'Acquisto, a rare hometown hero. In 1943, he was executed after falsely confessing to sabotage... saving 22 fellow Italian soldiers from a Nazi revenge massacre.

• *We're at the midpoint of this walk. Need a WC? Pop into the Burger King. Running out of time and energy? If you end the walk here, you'll find many cafés and wine bars nearby, and it's a short stroll down Via Toledo to the Toledo Metro station.*

To continue, face the fascist-style building and take the street on its left side. You'll angle through a downhill square called Piazza Monteoliveto. At the bottom of the square, cross the busy street, then angle up Calata Trinità Maggiore to the fancy column in the piazza at the top of the hill.

Part 2: Piazza Gesù Nuovo to Centrale Station

• *You're back on the straight-as-a-Greek-arrow Spaccanapoli, former-ly the main thoroughfare of the Greek city of Neapolis. (Spaccanapoli changes names several times: Via Maddaloni, Via B. Croce, Via S. Bi-agio dei Librai, and Via Vicaria Vecchia.) Linger for a moment on...*

❿ **Piazza Gesù Nuovo:** This square is marked by a towering 18th-century Baroque monument to the Counter-Reformation.

Although the Jesuit order was powerful in Naples because of its Spanish her-itage, locals never attacked Protestants here with the full fury of the Spanish Inquisition.

If you'd like, you can visit two bulky old church-es, starting with the dark, fortress-like, 17th-century **Church of Gesù Nuovo,** followed by the simpler **Church of Santa Chiara** (in the courtyard across the street; both described under "Sights in Naples"). There's also a **TI** on this square.

• *Continue along the main drag for another 200 yards. Since this is a university district, you may see students and bookstores. As this neigh-borhood is also famously superstitious, look for incense-burning women with carts full of good-luck charms for sale.*

Passing Palazzo Venezia—the embassy of Venice to Naples when both were independent powers—you'll emerge into the next square...

⓫ **Piazza San Domenico Maggiore:** This square is marked by another ornate 17th-century monument built to thank God for ending the plague. From this square, you can detour left along the right side of the castle-like church, then follow yellow signs, taking the first right and walking one short block to the remark-

Still Naples After All These Years

For three centuries (1500-1800), Naples was one of the world's richest and most sophisticated cities. The remnants we see today are an elegant reminder of that golden age, and a fascinating case study in what went wrong.

500 BC-AD 500—Greek-Speaking Romans: Naples got its start as Neapolis ("new city"), a thriving Greek colony. Even when conquered by the Romans, the city never fully adopted the Latin language and Roman ways. Actually, those sophisticated Hellenist traditions were exactly what the Romans admired about Naples and made them want to vacation there. For the next 2,000 years, this pattern would repeat itself: The city, living under foreign rule, would evolve independently from the rest of the Italian peninsula.

500-1500—Independence Despite Foreign Rule: The city powered on relatively unchanged after the fall of Rome, ruled as the independent Duchy of Naples under Ostrogoths, Byzantines, and Lombards. Next, in late-medieval times, it was the Germans and French (or "Angevins") who possessed it as the Kingdom of Naples. As sea trade became more important to the European economy, Naples was suddenly smack-dab in the geographical heart of commerce—the Mediterranean.

1500-1800—Golden Age: In 1502, Spain conquered Naples, and their combined wealth made Naples one of the great cities on Earth. With a population of 300,000, Naples was eclipsed only by Paris. Deputies of the Spanish king called viceroys presided over the city, and proceeded to use Spain's New World wealth to beautify Naples.

When Spain's monarchy passed to the Austrian Habsburgs and Spanish Bourbons, the cosmopolitan nature of Naples was only enhanced. Naples was home to nobles and royalty from across Europe. Baroque culture thrived, with artists like Caravaggio and Bernini, thinkers like Giordano Bruno, composers like

able Baroque **Cappella Sansevero** (described under "Sights in Naples").

• *After touring the chapel, return to Via B. Croce (a.k.a. Spaccanapoli), turn left, and continue your cultural scavenger hunt. At the intersection of Via Nilo, find the...*

⓬ Statue of the Nile (on the left): A reminder of the multiethnic makeup of Greek Neapolis, this statue is in what was the Egyptian quarter. Locals like to call this statue *The Body of Naples*, with the overflowing cornucopia symbolizing the abundance of their fine city. (I once asked a Neapolitan man to describe the local women, who are famous for their beauty, in one word. He replied, simply, "Abundant.") This intersection is considered the center of old Naples.

Scarlatti, and a new art form called opera. Naples took on the "look" it retains today, with palatial Neoclassical buildings in pastel colors and lavishly ornamented churches.

Despite its veneer of sophistication, trouble was brewing. In 1656, a vicious bubonic plague (Europe's last) killed off half the population. Trade routes shifted west as Europe industrialized, but Naples languished, remaining feudal and agricultural, with the church owning much of the land. The gap between rich foreign elites and homegrown poor grew.

1800-2000: Napoleon conquered the city. Then the monarchy was restored under a medieval-era political arrangement called the Kingdom of the Two Sicilies (uniting Naples and Sicily). The city was still rich, thanks to its Spanish Bourbon rulers, but it was increasingly backward, left behind by a more industrialized and democratic Europe.

Meanwhile, sweeping down from the north, there was a movement for Italian nationhood. Naples—with its legacy of independence from the rest of the peninsula—resisted. But in 1860, Naples was forcefully united with the new nation-state of Italy. Its vast wealth was confiscated and taken to the capital in Rome.

This began a century-plus of decline. There was no foreign wealth and no local economy. An estimated four million southern Italians fled, emigrating to northern Italy and the US. During World War II, Naples suffered Italy's worst bombings. The postwar economic recovery in northern Italy never trickled south, which remained under the thumb of the feudal-style Camorra (the Naples-based Mafia).

Today: The lack of a postwar economic recovery is a boon to tourists. It preserved an independent way of life that dates back centuries. Visitors today enjoy a rare sight—a city that has been continuously inhabited, independent-minded, and self-sustaining for 2,500 years.

• *Directly opposite the statue, inside of Bar Nilo, is the...*

"Chapel of Maradona": The small "chapel" on the right wall is dedicated to Diego Maradona, an Argentinian soccer star who played for Naples in the 1980s—pushing the team to its greatest success. Locals consider soccer almost a religion, and this guy was practically a deity. You can even see a "hair of Diego" and a teardrop from the city when he went to another team for more money. Unfortunately, his reputation was later sullied by problems he'd had with organized crime, drugs, and police. However, when he passed away in 2020 (at age 60), Naples was overwhelmed with grief. New street-art murals of Maradona popped up all over the city—in many cases, alongside a portrait of a bishop. This is San Gennaro, the city's third-century patron saint—and his juxtaposition with Maradona indicates where the soccer star still ranks in the hearts of Neapolitans.

Meanwhile, the coffee bar has posted a quadrilingual sign (though, strangely, not in English) threatening that those who take a picture without buying a cup of coffee may find their camera damaged...*Capisce?*

• *Continue another 100 yards. You may pass gold and silver shops. Some say stolen jewelry ends up here, is melted down immediately, and gets resold in some other form as soon as it cools. Look for* compro oro *("I buy gold") signs—a sign of Naples' economic woes. (Locals used to blame the 2008 economic crisis; now they blame Covid.) Continue to a tiny square at the intersection with...*

❸ **Via San Gregorio Armeno:** Stroll up this tiny lane toward the fanciful tower that arches over the street. The street is lined with stalls selling lots of souvenir kitsch, as well as some of Naples' most distinctive local crafts. Among the many figurines on sale, find items relating to *presepi* (Nativity scenes). Just as many Americans keep an eye out year-round for Christmas-tree ornaments, Italians regularly add pieces to the family *prese-*

pe, the centerpiece of their holiday decorations. You'll see elaborate manger scenes made of bark and moss, with niches to hold baby Jesus or mother Mary. You'll also see lots of jokey figurines caricaturing local politicians, soccer stars, and other celebrities. (Some of the highest-quality *presepi* pieces are sold at the D'Auria shop, a little farther down Spaccanapoli, on the right at #87. Expressive figures are made from terra-cotta, wood, and cloth, often fetching over €250. They even sell the classy *campane* version, under a glass bell.)

Another popular Naples souvenir sold here—and all over—is the *corno,* a skinny, twisted, red horn that resembles a chili pepper. The *corno* comes with a double symbolism for fertility: It's a horn of plenty, and it's also a phallic symbol turned upside-down. Neapolitans explain that fertility isn't sexual; it provides the greatest gift a person can give—life—and it ensures that one's soul will live on through the next generation. In today's Naples, just as in yesterday's Pompeii (where bulging erections greeted visitors at the entrance to a home), fertility is equated with good luck.

(By the way, a bit farther up Via San Gregorio Armeno, you'll find the underground **Napoli Sotterranea archaeological site**, along Via dei Tribunali, which also has some of the city's best **pizzerias**—both are described later.)

• *Continue down Spaccanapoli another 100 yards until you hit busy Via Duomo. Consider detouring five minutes north (left) up Via Duomo to visit Naples'* **Duomo***; just around the corner from that is the* **Pio Monte della Misericordia Church***, with a fine Caravaggio painting (both described later). But for now, continue straight, crossing Via Duomo. Here, Spaccanapoli is named...*

🄬 **Via Vicaria Vecchia:** Here along Via Vicaria Vecchia, the main "sight" is the vibrant street life. It's grittier and less touristy, but just as atmospheric as what we've been seeing. The street and side-street scenes intensify. The area is said to be a center of the Camorra (the Naples-based version of the Sicilian Mafia), but as a tourist, you won't notice. Paint a picture with these thoughts: Naples has the most intact street plan of any surviving ancient Greek or Roman city. Imagine this city during those times (and retain these images as you visit Pompeii), with streetside shop fronts that close up after dark, and private homes on upper floors. What you see today is just one more page in a 2,000-year-old story of a city: all kinds of meetings, beatings, and cheatings; kisses, near misses, and little-boy pisses.

You name it, it occurs right on the streets today, as it has since ancient times. People ooze from crusty corners. Black-and-white death announcements add to the clutter on the walls. Widows sell cigarettes from buckets. For a peek behind the scenes in the shade of wet laundry, venture down a few side streets. Buy two carrots as a gift for the woman on the fifth floor, if she'll lower her bucket to pick them up. The neighborhood action seems best at about 18:00.

At the tiny fenced-in triangle of greenery, hang out for a few minutes to just observe the crazy motorbike action and teen scene.

• *From here, veer right onto Via Forcella. You emerge into Piazza Vincenzo Calenda, where there's a round fence protecting another chunk of that ancient* **Greek wall** *of Neapolis. Hungry? Turn right here, on Via Pietro Colletta, and close out the walk with three typical Neapolitan...*

🄯 **Eateries:** Step into the North Pole at the recommended **Polo Nord Gelateria** (on the right, at #41). The oldest *gelateria* in Naples has had four generations of family working here since

1931. Before you order, sample a few flavors, including their *bacio*, or "kiss," flavor (named after the national chocolate-and-praline candy)—all are made fresh daily.

Two of Napoli's most competitive **pizzerias** are nearby. **Trianon da Ciro** (across the street from Polo Nord) has been serving them up hot and fast for almost a century. A half-block farther, on the right, is the place where some say pizza was born—at **Antica Pizzeria da Michele.** (For more on both, see "Eating in Naples," later.)

Return to Centrale Station: It's easy to return to Centrale station. Continue downhill on Via Pietro Colletta until you hit the grand boulevard, Corso Umberto I. Turn left and walk 15 minutes to the train station. Or cross the street and hop on any bus; they all go to the station.

Sights in Naples

Naples' best sights are the Archaeological Museum and my self-guided Naples Walk, both covered earlier. For extra credit, consider these sights.

ON OR NEAR SPACCANAPOLI

These sights are linked—in this order—on the second half of my Naples Walk.

▲Church of Gesù Nuovo

This church's unique pyramid-grill facade survives from a fortified 15th-century noble palace. Step inside for a brilliant Neapolitan Baroque interior. The second chapel on the right features a much-adored **statue of St. Giuseppe Moscati** (1880-1927), a Christian doctor famous for helping the poor. In 1987, Moscati became the first modern doctor to be canonized. Sit and watch a steady stream of Neapolitans taking turns to pay their respects.

Continue to the third chapel (past Moscati's vertical tombstone) and enter the **Sale Moscati.** Look high on the walls of this long room to see hundreds of ex-votos—tiny red-and-silver plaques of thanksgiving for prayers answered with the help of St. Moscati (each has a symbol of the ailment cured). Naples' practice of using ex-votos, while incorporated into its Catholic rituals, goes back to its pagan Greek roots. Rooms from Moscati's nearby apartment are on display, and a glass case shows possessions and photos of the great doctor.

NAPLES

Just before leaving the Sale Moscati, notice the big bomb casing that hangs high in the left corner. It fell through the church's dome in 1943, but caused almost no damage...yet another miracle.

Cost and Hours: Free, daily 6:45-13:00 & 16:00-19:30, Piazza del Gesù Nuovo, www.gesunuovo.it.

Church of Santa Chiara

Dating from the 14th century, this church is from a period of French royal rule under the Angevin dynasty. Consider the stark contrast between this church (Gothic) and the Gesù Nuovo (Baroque), across the street. Inside, look for the faded Trinity on the back wall (on the right as you face the door, under the stone canopy), which shows a dove representing the Holy Spirit between the heads of God the Father and Christ (c. 1414). This is an example of the fine frescoes that once covered the walls. Most were stuccoed over during Baroque times or destroyed in 1943 by Allied bombs. Continuing down the main aisle, you'll step over a huge inlaid-marble Angevin coat of arms on the floor. The altar is adorned with four finely carved Gothic tombs of Angevin kings. A chapel stacked with Bourbon royalty is just to the right.

Cost and Hours: Free, daily 7:30-13:00 & 16:30-20:00, Piazza del Gesù Nuovo, www.monasterodisantachiara.it. Its tranquil cloistered courtyard, around back, is not worth its €6 entry fee.

▲▲Cappella Sansevero

This small chapel is a Baroque explosion mourning the body of Christ, who lies on a soft pillow under an incredibly realistic veil.

It's also the personal chapel of Raimondo de Sangro, an eccentric Freemason, containing his tomb and the tombs of his family. Like other 18th-century Enlightenment figures, Raimondo was a wealthy man of letters, scientist and inventor, and patron of the arts—and he was also a grand master of the Freemasons of the Kingdom of Naples. His chapel—filled with Masonic symbolism—is a complex ensemble, with statues representing virtues such as self-control, religious zeal, and the Masonic philosophy of freedom through enlightenment.

Cost and Hours: €8, buy tickets at office at the corner—or reserve ahead online (€2 fee), open Wed-Mon 9:30-19:00, closed Tue, Via de Sanctis 19, +39 081 551 8470, www.museosansevero.it.

Crowd-Beating Tips: This popular sight often has a very long line and can sell out. To be on the safe side, it's best (and worth the

NAPLES

extra fee) to prebook a timed entry. If you're just showing up, the least crowded time to visit is after 16:00—the later the better.

Visiting the Chapel: Pick up the free floor plan, which identifies each of the statues lining the nave. Once inside, study the incredible *Veiled Christ* in the center. Carved out of marble, it's like no other statue I've seen (by Giuseppe "Howdeedoodat" Sammartino, 1753). The Christian message (Jesus died for our salvation) is accompanied by a Masonic message (the veil represents how the body and ego are obstacles to real spiritual freedom). As you walk from Christ's feet to his head, notice how the expression on Jesus' face goes from suffering to peace.

Raimondo's mom and dad are buried on either side of the **main altar.** To the right of the altar, marking his father's tomb, a statue representing *Despair* or *Disillusion* struggles with a marble rope net (carved out of a single piece of stone), symbolic of a troubled mind. The flames on the head of the winged boy represent human intellect—more Masonic symbolism, showing how knowledge frees the human mind. To the left of the main altar is a statue of *Modesty*, marking the tomb of Raimondo's mother (who died after his birth, and was only 20). The veiled woman fingers a broken tablet, symbolizing an interrupted life.

Raimondo de Sangro himself lies buried in a side altar (on the right). Among his inventions was the deep-green pigment used on the ceiling fresco. The inlaid M. C. Escher-esque maze on the floor around de Sangro's tomb is another Masonic reminder of how the quest for knowledge gets you out of the maze of life. This tilework once covered the floor of the entire chapel.

Your Sansevero finale is downstairs: two mysterious...**skeletons.** Perhaps another of the mad inventor's fancies: Inject a corpse with a fluid to fossilize the veins so that they'll survive the body's decomposition. While that's the legend, investigations have shown that the veins were artificial, and the models were created to illustrate how the circulatory system works.

▲Napoli Sotterranea ("Underground Naples")

This archaeological site, a manmade underground maze of passageways and ruins from Greek and Roman times, can only be toured with a guide. You'll descend 121 steps under the modern city to explore two underground areas. One is the old Greek tuff quarry used to build the city of Neapolis, which was later converted into an immense cistern by the Romans. The other is an excavated portion of the Greco-Roman theater that once seated 6,000 people. The space has been encroached upon by modern development—some current residents' windows literally look down into the theater ruins. The tour involves a lot of stairs, as well as a long, narrow 20-inch-wide walkway—lit only by candlelight—that uses an ancient water channel (a heavyset person could not comfortably fit through this, and claustrophobes will be miserable). Although there's not much to see, the experience is fascinating and includes a little history from World War II—when the quarry/cistern was turned into a shelter to protect locals from American bombs.

Cost and Hours: €10, includes 1.5-hour tour, tours in English offered daily every two hours from 10:00 to 18:00. If the ticket-buying line is long, talk to an attendant: They *might* be able to move you into the next English-language tour. Bring a light sweater. +39 081 296 944, www.napolisotterranea.org.

Getting There: The site is at Piazza San Gaetano 68, along the lively Via dei Tribunali pizza zone, and just a couple of blocks uphill from Spaccanapoli's statue of the Nile. The entrance is immediately to the left of the Church of San Paolo Maggiore (look for the *Sotterranea* signs).

▲Duomo

Naples' historic cathedral, built by imported French Anjou kings in the 14th century, boasts a breathtaking Neo-Gothic facade. Step

into the vast interior to see the mix of styles along the side chapels—from pointy Gothic arches to rounded Renaissance ones to gilded Baroque decor.

Cost and Hours: Free, Mon-Sat 8:30-13:30 & 14:30-20:00, Sun 8:30-13:30 & 16:30-19:30, Via Duomo.

Visiting the Church: The cathedral honors St. Gennaro, Naples' patron saint. The **main altar** at the front is ringed by carved wooden seats, filled three times a year by clergy to witness the Miracle of the Blood. Thousands of Neapolitans cram into this church for a peek at two tiny vials with the dried blood of St. Gennaro. As the clergy roots—or even jeers—for the miracle to occur, the blood temporarily liquefies. Neapolitans take this ritual with deadly seriousness, and believe that if the blood remains solid, it's terrible luck for the city. Sure enough, on the rare occasion that the miracle fails, locals can point to a terrible event soon after—such as an earthquake, an eruption of Mount Vesuvius, or an especially disappointing soccer loss.

The stairs beneath the altar take you to a **crypt** with the relics of St. Gennaro and a statue of the bishop who rescued the relics from a rival town and returned them to Naples. These relics are said to have stopped the lava from a 1631 Vesuvius eruption from destroying the city.

The cathedral has two large side chapels (flanking the nave, about halfway to the transept)—each practically a church in its own right. While interesting, they charge separate admissions and have shorter hours than the larger cathedral, and are skippable for most visitors. You can see most of the one on the left—the **Chapel of Santa Restituta**—for free. It stands on the site of the original, early Christian church that predated the cathedral. You'll find some 14th-century golden mosaics up at the front-left chapel-within-the-chapel. (I'd skip paying admission for the sixth-century baptismal font under mosaics.)

Pio Monte della Misericordia

This small church (near the Duomo, and run by a charitable foundation) displays one of the best works by Caravaggio, *The Seven Works of Mercy*. Upstairs is a ho-hum art gallery. The price is steep, but it may be worth it for Caravaggio fans.

Cost and Hours: €8 (ticket booth across the street), Mon-Sat 10:00-18:00, Sun 9:00-14:30, Via dei Tribunali 253, +39 081 446 944, www.piomontedellamisericordia.it.

Visiting the Church: Caravaggio's *The Seven Works of Mercy* hangs over the main altar in a darkened gray chapel. The painting is well-lit, allowing Caravaggio's characteristically dark canvas to really pop. In one crowded canvas, the great early-Baroque artist illustrates seven virtues: burying the dead (the man carrying a corpse by the ankles); visiting the imprisoned and feeding the hungry (Pero breastfeeding her starving father—a scene from a famous Roman story); sheltering the homeless (a pilgrim on the Camino de Santiago, with his floppy hat, negotiates with an innkeeper); caring for the sick and clothing the naked (St. Martin offers part of his cloak to the injured man in the foreground); and giving drink to the thirsty (Samson chugs from a jawbone in the background)—all of them set in a dark Neapolitan alley and watched over by Mary, Jesus, and a pair of angels.

Caravaggio painted this work in Naples in 1607 while in exile from Rome, where he had been sentenced to death for killing a man in a duel. Three years later Caravaggio died from an unknown illness on his way back to Rome to receive a pardon from the Pope.

MADRE

MADRE, a museum of contemporary art, displays works by Jeff Koons, Anish Kapoor, Francesco Clemente, and other big names in the art world. Aficionados of modern art consider it one of the better collections in the country. Some descriptions are in English—you'll need them.

Cost and Hours: €8; Wed-Mon 10:00-19:30—Sun until

20:00, closed Tue, last entry one hour before closing; Via Settembrini 79, +39 081 1973 7254, www.madrenapoli.it.

NEAR THE PORT
This cluster of important sights can be found between the big ceremonial square, Piazza del Plebiscito, and the cruise ship terminal. If touring the entire neighborhood, I'd see it in the order described here. For locations, see the map on page 954.

Getting There from Spaccanapoli: Walking down toward this area on Via Toledo (from the midpoint of my self-guided walk), you'll pass two more big, boxy, fascist-style banks: first, the chalky-white **BNL bank,** and then, past the Toledo Metro stop, the even more imposing **Banco di Napoli** at Via Toledo 178. A bit farther down is the **Banca Intesa Sanpaolo** (filling an older palace rather than a fascist-style building); it hosts Caravaggio's blood-spurting *The Martyrdom of Saint Ursula* in a small art gallery (see signs for entry details). Also along here, on a parklike little piazza on your right, is the easy-to-miss **Centrale funicular** up to the San Martino mountaintop. As you near Piazza del Plebiscito, you'll go through a congested area with popular bars and pizza windows. Push on until you reach the gigantic, semicircular square facing the orange-ish palace. To trace this route, see the map on page 1002.

▲Piazza del Plebiscito
This square celebrates the 1860 vote (*plebiscito,* plebiscite) in which
Naples became a part of a unified Italy. Dominating the top of the square is the Church of San Francesco di Paola, with its Pantheon-inspired dome and broad, arcing colonnades. If it's open, step inside to ogle the vast interior—a Neoclassical re-creation of
one of ancient Rome's finest buildings.
• *Opposite is the...*

Royal Palace (Palazzo Reale)
Having housed Spanish, French, and even Italian royalty, this building displays statues of all those who stayed here. From the square in front of the palace, look for eight kings in the niches, each from a different dynasty (left to right): Norman, German, French, Spanish, Spanish, Spanish, French (Napoleon's brother-in-law), and, finally, Italian—Victor Emmanuel II, King of Savoy. The statues were done at the request of V. E. II's son, so his dad is

the most dashing of the group. As far as palaces go, the interior is relatively unimpressive.

Cost and Hours: €10, skip the painfully dry €5 audioguide (each room has excellent panel descriptions in English; Thu-Tue 9:00-20:00, closed Wed, last entry one hour before closing; +39 848 082 408, www.coopculture.it).

Visiting the Palace: The palace's grand Neoclassical staircase leads up to a floor with 30 plush rooms. You'll follow a one-way route featuring the palace theater, paintings by "the Cara-
vaggio Imitators," Neapolitan
tapestries, fine inlaid-stone
tabletops, chandeliers, gilded
woodwork, and more. The
rooms do feel quite grand, even
if they lack the personality and
sense of importance of Europe's
better palaces. As a less-visited

sight, wandering through the rooms at leisure makes you feel like royalty yourself. Don't miss the huge, tapestry-laden Hercules Hall or the chance to dance on the wooden floor of the wide-open ball-room. Ask a guard (nicely) to open the terrace garden balcony door to enjoy sweeping views of the Bay of Naples. On the way out, step into the royal chapel, with an altar made entirely of precious stones and a fantastic Nativity scene—a commotion of 18th-century ce-ramic figurines.

Hanging Gardens: This beautiful garden terrace, overlooking the Bay of Naples, costs extra and can be seen only a few times a day (with an attendant). If your visit happens to coincide with one of these times—and the weather's fine—it's worth adding on.

• *Continue 50 yards past the Royal Palace (toward the trees) to enjoy a...*

Fine Harbor View

While boats busily serve Capri and Sorrento, Mount Vesuvius smol-ders ominously in the distance. Look back to see the vast "Bour-bon red" palace—its color inspired by Pompeii. The hilltop above Piazza del Plebiscito is San Martino, with its Carthusian monas-tery-turned-museum and the fortress called Castel Sant'Elmo (the Centrale funicular to the top is just across the square and up Via Toledo). The promenade you're on continues to Naples' romantic harborfront—the fishermen's quarter (Borgo Marinaro)—a forti-fied island connected to the mainland by a stout causeway, with its fanciful, ancient Castel dell'Ovo (Egg Castle) and trendy har-borside restaurants. From there, the Lungomare harborside prom-enade—described later—continues past the Santa Lucia district, stretching out along the Bay of Naples. This long promenade, running along Via Francesco Caracciolo to the Mergellina district and beyond, is a delightful people-watching scene on balmy nights.

• *Head back through the piazza and pop into (on the left)...*

Gran Caffè Gambrinus

This coffeehouse, facing the piazza, takes you back to the elegance of 1860. It's a classic place to sample a crispy *sfogliatella* pastry, or perhaps the mushroom-shaped, rum-soaked bread-like cakes called *babà*, which come in a huge variety. Stand at the bar *(banco)*, pay double to sit *(tavola)*, or just wander around as you imagine the café buzzing with the ritzy intellectuals, journalists, and artsy bohemian types who munched on *babà* here during Naples' 19th-century heyday (daily 7:00-24:00, Piazza del Plebiscito 1, +39 081 417 582).

• *A block away, tucked behind the palace, you can peek inside the Neo-classical...*

Teatro di San Carlo

Built in 1737, 41 years before Milan's La Scala, this is Europe's oldest opera house and Italy's second-most-respected (after La Scala). The original theater burned down in 1816, and was rebuilt within the year. Guided 35-minute visits in English basically just show you the fine auditorium with its 184 boxes—each with a big mirror to reflect the candlelight (€9; tours in English usually run daily at 11:30 and 15:30, additional departures in Italian; schedule can change so check online or call to confirm; theater box office +39 081 797 2331, tour info +39 081 7972 412, www.teatrosancarlo.it).

• *Beyond Teatro di San Carlo and the Royal Palace is the huge, harbor-front...*

Castel Nuovo

This imposing castle now houses government bureaucrats and the **Civic Museum.** It feels like a mostly empty shell, with a couple of dusty halls of Neapolitan art, but the views over the bay from the upper terraces are impressive (€6, Mon-Sat 9:00-18:00, closed Sun, last entry one hour before closing, +39 081 795 7722). The castle also hosts frequent special events and exhibits.

• *Head back to Teatro di San Carlo, cross the street, and go through the tall yellow arch into...*

▲Galleria Umberto I

This Victorian iron-and-glass shopping mall opened in 1890 to reinvigorate the district after a devastating cholera epidemic occurred here. Gawk up, then walk left to bring you back out on Via Toledo.

• *Just up the street and behind Piazza del Plebiscito is an interesting subterranean experience.*

▲Galleria Borbonica

Beneath Naples' Royal Palace was a vast underground network of caves, aqueducts, and cisterns that originated as a quarry in the 15th century. In the mid-1800s, when popular revolutions were threatening royalty across Europe, the understandably nervous king of Naples, Ferdinand II, had this underground world expanded to create an escape tunnel from the palace to his military barracks nearby. In World War II, it was used as an air-raid shelter; after the war, the police used it to store impounded cars and motorcycles. Today, enthusiastic guides take the curious on a fascinating 70-minute, 500-yard-long guided walk through this many-layered world littered with disintegrating 60-year-old vehicles upon which Naples sits.

Cost and Hours: €10 English-language tours leave Fri-Sun at 10:00, 12:00, 15:00, and 17:00; +39 081 764 5808, www.galleriaborbonica.com. The most convenient entry is just behind Piazza del Plebiscito—up Via Gennaro Serra and down Vico del Grottone to #4 (to avoid that entrance's 90 steep steps, enter at Via Morelli 61).

NORTH OF SPACCANAPOLI
▲▲Sanità District

While the characteristic Spaccanapoli and Spanish Quarter are being tamed, today's clear winner for wild-and-crazy Neapolitan life in the streets is the gritty Sanità District, north of the Archaeological Museum.

A big part of the attraction of Naples is its *basso* living (life in the streets). Many locals with enough money to move to the sanity of the suburbs choose instead to keep living where the action is—in a cauldron of flapping laundry, police sirens, broken cobblestone lanes, singing merchants, sidewalks clogged with makeshift markets, and walls crusted with ancient posters and graffiti.

One of Naples' most historic and colorful zones, Sanità is sometimes called "the living *presepe*" for the way people live stacked on top of each other in rustic conditions, as if in an elaborate manger scene. (Because organized crime is still strong in this quarter, development is slow.) Literally "the healthy place" (named for the freshness of the air, originally so high above the dense city), this is *the* place for a photo safari.

While the reason to visit Sanità is simply to swim through its amazing river of life, there are two remarkable burial sites in the district: the Catacombs of San Gaudioso (at the Basilica Santa Maria della Sanità) and the Cemetery of the Fountains.

Visiting the Sanità District: Check to be sure your valuables are zipped or buttoned safely away. From near the Porta San Gennaro gate (just west of Via Duomo, two blocks east of Metro: Cavour, six blocks east of Archaeological Museum), leave Via Foria and head up Via Crocelle. Venture a block up Via Crocelle and then three blocks up Via dei Vergini through a thriving daily market scene. Pop into the courtyard of the Palazzo dello Spagnuolo (#19 on the left) to peek at an extravagant 18th-century staircase.

Then dog-leg left on Via Arena della Sanità and continue uphill (past another massive staircase in the courtyard at #6) to Piazza Sanità, at the base of Capodimonte, where you'll stand before the Basilica Santa Maria della Sanità, which sits atop the **Catacombs of San Gaudioso.** Because this area was just outside the old city walls, the dead were buried here (entrance inside the church, €9 ticket also includes Catacombs of San Gennaro—described later, hourly English tours run daily 10:00-13:00, www.catacombedinapoli.it).

From here you have three options: Browse back down the way you just came; continue 10 minutes up Via Sanità and Via Fontanelle to the Cemetery of the Fountains (described next); or ride a free elevator (just past the church, under the high viaduct) up to the modern world and Capodimonte (described later).

▲Cemetery of the Fountains (Cimitero delle Fontanelle)

A thousand years ago, cut into the hills at the high end of Napoli was a quarry. Then, in the 16th century, churches with crowded cemeteries began moving the bones of their long dead here to make room for the newly dead. Later these caves housed the bones of plague victims and the city's paupers. In the 19th century, many churches again emptied their cemeteries and added even more skulls to this vast ossuary. Then a cult of people appeared whose members adopted the skulls. They named the skulls, put them in little houses, brought them flowers, and asked them to intervene with God for favors from the next life. Today, the quirky caves—stacked with human bones and dotted with chapels—are open to the public.

Cost and Hours: Free to enter but tips accepted, daily 10:00-17:00, Via Fontanelle 77, +39 081 795 6160.

Getting There: It's located in a sketchy-feeling neighborhood at the top end of Sanità. You can get here by hopping in a taxi; riding the Metro to the Materdei stop and following the brown signs for 10 minutes; or hiking 10 minutes from the Basilica Santa Maria della Sanità up Via Sanità and Via Fontanelle (described earlier).

ON CAPODIMONTE

Capodimonte, about a mile due north from the Archaeological Museum, is one of Naples' three hills. It's home to an excellent art museum (and its surrounding park) and, not far away, tourable catacombs.

Getting There: Reaching Capodimonte is easiest by taxi (figure €15 from the city center). Various public buses run from near Piazza Dante and the National Archaeological Museum up to Capodimonte, including #168, #178, and #C63—these stop near the catacombs (hop off when you get to the huge, domed church) before continuing up to the museum and park.

▲Capodimonte Museum (Museo di Capodimonte)

This hilltop is home to Naples' top art museum. Its pleasant collection has lesser-known (but still masterful) works by Michelangelo, Raphael, Titian, Caravaggio, and other huge names. It fills the Bourbons' cavernous summer palace, set in the midst of a sprawling hilltop park overlooking Naples, and part of the museum showcases the palace's history and furnishings. Most visitors to Naples understandably prefer to focus on the city's vibrant street life, characteristic churches, and ancient artifacts. But for art lovers and royalty buffs, Capodimonte rates ▲▲.

Cost and Hours: €12, Thu-Tue 8:30-19:30, closed Wed, last entry one hour before closing, avoid lines by purchasing your ticket online (additional fee possible), fine audioguide-€5, café, Via Miano 2, +39 081 749 9111, http://capodimonte.cultura.gov.it. Some rooms may close earlier, items can be out on loan, and special exhibits are frequent; for the latest, check the website.

Nearby: While people visiting the Capodimonte Museum are understandably focused on its paintings, don't overlook the expansive **Capodimonte Park** surrounding it. Once a hunting ground for royalty, the park is now a pleasure garden—beloved by Neapolitans—with elegant paths and lovely gardens sprouting trees and exotic plants from around the world. If you've planned ahead, this is a lovely spot for a picnic.

Visiting the Museum: The gigantic collection sprawls through the massive building, and the curator enjoys rearranging things, loaning and borrowing works, and so on—so it's hard to get a handle on exactly what's on view, and where. Room numbers—sometimes marked above doors—can be difficult to read and are often missing entirely, so they're of limited usefulness for navigating the collection. Still, here's an outline that should point you in the general direction of some interesting pieces.

• *After buying your ticket, pick up the free map and head up several flights of stairs (or ride the elevator) to the "first" floor. You'll step into a room marked...*

Tiziano (Room 2): The museum has a fine selection of works by Titian (1488-1576). At the far end, look for *Portrait of Pope Paul III.* It depicts Alessandro Farnese, the local bigwig whose family married into Bourbon royalty; later, as Pope Paul III, he was responsible for bringing great art to Naples. (Nearby, you'll see another—much younger—Titian portrait of Farnese, before he was pope.) Also in this room, look for one of many versions of Titian's *Danaë,* where—as told in the Greek myth—the sensuous central character looks up at a cloud containing the essence of Zeus (a shower of coins), about to impregnate her. Enjoy the cupid's surprised look at the action as the courtesan awaits her union. Finally, find Titian's poignant portrait of a penitent Mary Magdalene, with finely detailed tears running down her cheeks (1565).

• *Proceeding into the next room, turn left into the darkened...*

Room 4: The lights pop on as you enter, so you can see large charcoal drawings by Raphael (Moses shields his eyes from the burning bush, 1514) and Michelangelo (a group of soldiers, 1546; and *Venus and Love,* 1534).

• *Exiting this room back the way you came, look left down a very long hall of fancy weapons (marked* Armeria Borbonica*), but continue straight ahead, then turn left into a room labeled...*

Masaccio: Here you'll find works by this Renaissance pioneer. If it's not out on loan, you should see a section of his altarpiece (1426) showing a primitive attempt at 3-D: Masaccio has left out Jesus' neck to create the illusion that he's looking down on us.

In the next few rooms, look for some more interesting pieces: Mantegna's medallion-like *Portrait of Ludovico Gonzaga,* c. 1461, a very small but finely executed profile portrait; and Giovanni Bellini's *Circumcision of Christ.* (Bellini was Titian's master.)

• *Next you'll proceed into a section marked...*

Collezione Farnese: The core of the museum's collection sprawls through several rooms. As you explore this zone, keep an eye out for these highlights, which may appear in roughly this order:

You'll spot several works by **Raphael,** including a portrait of the man who will become Pope Paul III, back when he was "just" Alessandro Farnese. You may spot some pieces by **El Greco,** too.

Parmigianino's *Antea* (1531-1535)—one of the collection's highlights—addresses us with an unblinking, dilated gaze. She wears a mink stole (astonishingly lifelike, with disgusting little teeth), gold chain, and hair brooch—items commonly presented by a lover. By wearing the gifts, Antea signals her acceptance of her suitor's advances.

The Misanthrope (1568) is a remarkable work by **Pieter Bruegel the Elder.** The painting suggests the pointlessness of giving up on life and becoming a hermit; cut off from the world and lost in thought, the title figure doesn't even notice that he's about to step on a trail of thorns. Behind him, a wild-eyed young man is stealing the misanthrope's money pouch (Hey! I saw that guy on the Circumvesuviana!).

Annibale Carracci's *Hercules at the Crossroads* (1596) presents the hero with a choice: virtue (on the left, nature and letters, but a steep uphill climb) or vice (on the right, scantily clad women, music, theater masks, and an easy, flat path). While his foot points one way, he looks the other...his mind not yet made up.

• *At the end of the Collezione Farnese, turn left to enter the...*

Royal Apartments: It's easy to forget that this museum is set in a royal palace. Originally a simple hunting lodge, in the 18th century the king decided it could be a grand palace. Several dynasties enjoyed its regal ballrooms and imposing reception rooms while amassing their impressive collections of art. From here on out, you'll pass through some of the opulent apartments of this building, decorated with stunning period details and furniture.

The **grand hall** in the corner (Room 31) comes with a massive bronze chandelier hanging over an ancient Roman inlaid-marble floor, which originally decorated the palace of Roman Emperor Tiberius on Capri (installed here in 1877).

The following rooms tell stories of three Bourbon kings with portraits and objects from their reign. At the opposite corner of this wing, imagine attending a regal ball in the grand *Salone delle Feste* (Room 42).

Branching off from here (Rooms 38-40), look for the **Collezione delle Ciccio,** which is filled with royal porcelain—considered white gold—from all corners of Europe: Naples, Vienna, Paris (Sèvres), and Meissen (Germany).

From here, depending on which areas are open, you may circle through even more apartments (perhaps seeing several rooms decorated in the Napoleon-pleasing Neoclassical style—a reminder that Napoleon's older brother once ruled the Kingdom of Napoli). Or you may be routed back to the Collezione Farnese.

• *Either way, when done at this level, head back to where you entered and climb up four flights of stairs (or take the elevator) to the...*

Second Floor: Here you'll find art from private collections and paintings mostly from local churches. First you'll see a cycle of **Flemish tapestries** (depicting the Battle of Pavia). Then, as you pass through a few halls of Gothic altarpieces, watch out for a few highlights:

Near the end of the **altarpiece corridor,** in Room 65, on the right is a fine altarpiece from Nottingham, England. Carved out of alabaster in the 15th century, it shows expressive scenes from the Passion of Christ.

At the far end of this corridor (just past Nottingham) is a darkened room (Room 66) with **Simone Martini**'s lavish and delicate portrait from 1317 of San Ludovico di Tolosa crowning Roberto king of Naples.

Now proceed down a long line of adjoining rooms. In Room 67, find Colantonio's painting *San Girolamo nello Studio* (c. 1445), in which the astonishing level of detail—from the words on the page of the open book, to the balled-up pages tucked away at the bottom of the frame—drives home the message: Only through complete devotion and meticulous dedication can you hope to accomplish great things...like pulling a thorn out of a lion's paw.

Finally, near the end of this wing, watch for another of the museum's top pieces, **Caravaggio's** *The Flagellation*. Typical of his *chiaroscuro* (light/dark) style, Caravaggio uses a ribbon of light to show us only what he wants us to see: a broken Christ about to be whipped, and the manic fury of the man (on his left) who will do the whipping. This scene could be set in a Naples alley. Compare this with most of the paintings we've seen so far—of popes, saints, and aristocrats. Caravaggio was given refuge in Naples while fleeing a murder trial in Rome. (They put him to work painting. Of the eight canvases he painted during this period, three remain in Naples.) Caravaggio was revolutionary in showing real life rather than idealized scenes—helping common people to better relate to these stories.

The Rest of the Museum: There's so much more to see, including many temporary exhibits. Elsewhere on the second floor, you'll find both Baroque and contemporary works. As in all great collections, more works of art are in storage than can be displayed at any given moment—and the curator enjoys surprising visitors by pulling items out from time to time, hoping to encourage dialogue about lesser-known artists, and get you thinking about what might be hiding in other museum storerooms.

▲▲Catacombs of San Gennaro

Behind the towering modern church of Madre del Buon Consiglio (Mother of Good Counsel) are tucked the most impressive ancient catacombs south of Rome. It started as a pagan tomb of little consequence, but then St. Agrippino, the local bishop, was buried here in the third century. Later, in the fifth century, the bones of St. Gennaro (patron of Naples) were moved here. Suddenly a site of special reverence—complete with miracles—it became a place where Neapolitans wanted to be buried as well. Today, the catacombs are run by a nonprofit organization of earnest young people who conduct walking tours. These half-mile walks survey more than a thousand burial niches on two levels that date from the second to sixth centuries (many with frescoes surviving...barely).

Cost and Hours: €9 ticket includes Catacombs of San Gaudioso—described earlier, at busy times it's wise to prebook on-line, included English-language tours depart on the hour daily 10:00-17:00, Via di Capodimonte 13, +39 081 744 3714, www.catacombedinapoli.it.

SOUTH OF SPACCANAPOLI
Porta Nolana Open-Air Fish Market

Naples' fish market squirts and stinks as it has for centuries under the darkened Porta Nolana (gate in the city wall), four long blocks down from Centrale station. Of the town's many boisterous out-door markets, this will net you the most photos and memories. From Piazza Nolana, wander under the medieval gate and take your first left down Via So-pramuro, enjoying this wild and entirely edible cultural scaven-ger hunt (Tue-Sun 8:00-14:00,

closed Mon). Stalls display the best catch of the day as water jets caress mounds of mussels and clams.

Two other markets with more clothing and fewer fish are at Piazza Capuana (several blocks northwest of Centrale station and tumbling down Via Sant'Antonio Abate, Mon-Sat 8:00-18:00, Sun 9:00-13:00) and a similar cobbled shopping zone along Via Pignasecca (just off Via Toledo, west of Piazza Carità, described on page 976).

▲▲Harborside Promenade: The Lungomare *Passeggiata*

Each evening, relaxed and romantic Neapolitans in the mood for a scenic harborside stroll do their *vasche* (laps) along the inviting Lungomare harborside promenade and beyond. To join in this el-egant people-watching scene (best after 19:00), stroll down to the waterfront from Piazza del Plebiscito and then along Via Nazario Sauro to the beginning of a delightful series of harborside prom-enades that stretch romantically all the way out of the city. Along the way, you'll enjoy views of Mount Vesuvius and the Bay of Na-ples. The entire route is crowded on weekends and lively any good-weather evening of the week with families, amorous couples, and friends hanging out. Here's a brief rundown of its three sections:

Santa Lucia and Borgo Marinaro: Via Nazario Sauro passes the Santa Lucia district, so called because this is where the song "Santa Lucia" was first performed. (The song is probably so famous in America because immigrants from Naples sang it to remember the old country.) At the fortified causeway, make a short detour out to Borgo Marinaro ("Fisherman's Quarter"), and poke around this fabled island neighborhood. With its striking Castel dell'Ovo and a trendy restaurant scene, you can dine here amid yachts with a view of Vesuvius. From here, follow Via Partenope to Piazza Vittoria.

Piazza Vittoria and Via Francesco Caracciolo: From Piazza Vittoria the strolling action stretches along the Lungomare on Via Francesco Caracciolo all the way to the Mergellina district. The convenient bus #140 starts at Piazza Vittoria, making stops all along the promenade to Posillipo (at the end of the nice strolling stretch). Walk as far as you like away from the city center and, when you're ready to return, just hop on the bus or grab a cab. (From Piazza Vittoria you can shortcut scenically directly back to Piazza del Plebiscito by heading inland through Piazza dei Martiri and down Via Chiaia.)

Mergellina and Via Posillipo: The promenade continues past yacht harbors and rocks popular for swimming and sunbathing, under lavish Liberty Style villas, to tiny coves and inviting fish restaurants. Perched on the hillside at Posillipo (the end of the nice stretch) awaits the delightful **$$$ Ristorante Reginella,** with majestic views (closed Tue, Via Posillipo 45a, +39 081 240 3220)...and the bus #140 stop for your quick return.

Posillipo Hill

More a very long, tree-covered, villa-slathered peninsula than a "hill," this promontory helps define the southern boundary of the Bay of Naples. Only conquered by road-building engineers in the early 19th century, Posillipo's hallmark are its many waterfront villas. While these come in a dizzying array of architectural styles, most Posillipo villas have certain features in common: huge cellars (for protection against both sea storms and invaders); decorative fringes on top (often castle-like crenellations); and watchtowers. These are best seen from the water—giving a look at the spacious, green, and colorful Naples in contrast to the congested, tight lanes of the historical center. Italians, who romanticize Posillipo, recognize many of these villas from their favorite movies and TV shows. Out at the tip of Posillipo is a fine, sprawling park called Parco Virgiliano, which locals call "Lovers' Park" for its restful trails and gorgeous views over the Bay of Naples, with Vesuvius looming on the horizon.

ON SAN MARTINO

The ultimate view overlooking Naples, its bay, and the volcano is from San Martino hill, just above (and west of) the city center. Up top you'll find a mighty fortress, Castel Sant'Elmo (which charges for entry but offers the best views from its ramparts) and the adjacent Baroque San Martino monastery-turned-museum. The surrounding neighborhood (especially Piazza Fuga) has a classy "uptown" vibe compared to the gritty city-center streets below. Cheapskates can enjoy the views for free from the benches on the square in front of the monastery.

Getting There: From Via Toledo, the Spanish Quarter gradually climbs up San Martino's lower slopes, before steep paths take you up the rest of the way. But the easiest way to ascend San Martino is by **funicular.** Three different funicular lines with departures every 10 minutes lead from lower Naples to the hilltop: the Centrale line from near the bottom of Via Toledo; the Montesanto line from the Metro stop of the same name (near the top

of Via Toledo); and the Chiaia line from farther out, near Piazza Amadeo. All three are covered by any regular local transit ticket. Ride any of these three up to the end of the line. All lines converge within a few blocks at the top of the hill—Centrale and Chiaia wind up at opposite ends of the charming Piazza Fuga, while Montesanto terminates a bit closer to the fortress and museum.

Leaving any of the funiculars, head uphill, carefully seeking out the brown signs for *Castel S. Elmo* and *Museo di San Martino* (a few strategically placed escalators make the climb easier). Regardless of where you come up, you'll pass the Montesanto funicular station—angle left (as you face the station) past the municipal police station, and then continue following the signs. You'll reach the castle with its bronze plaque first, and then the monastery/museum (both about a 10-minute walk from Piazza Fuga).

Another convenient—if less scenic—approach is via the Metro's line 1 to the Vanvitelli stop, which is near the upper funicular terminals.

Castel Sant'Elmo

While little more than an empty husk with a decent modern art museum, this 16th-century, Spanish-built, star-shaped fortress boasts commanding views over the city and the entire Bay of Naples. Buy your ticket at the booth, then ride the elevator near the entrance to the upper courtyard and climb up to the ramparts for a slow circle to enjoy the 360-degree views. In the middle of the yard is the likeable little Museo del Novecento, a gallery of works by 20th-century Neapolitan artists (covered by same ticket); the castle also hosts temporary exhibits.

Cost and Hours: €5, half-price after 16:15; open daily 8:30-19:30, last entry one hour before closing; museum closes at 17:00

and is closed Tue; Via Tito Angelini 22, +39 081 229 4401, www.
polomusealecampania.beniculturali.it.

▲▲San Martino Carthusian Monastery and Museum (Certosa e Museo di San Martino)

The monastery, founded in 1325 and dissolved in the early 1800s,
is now a sprawling museum with several parts. The square out front

has city views nearly as
good as the ones you'll pay
to see from inside, and a
few cafés angling for your
business.

Cost and Hours: €6,
Thu-Tue 8:30-17:00, may
be open later in summer,
closed Wed, last entry one
hour before closing, some
rooms (such as the Naval Museum) open at 9:30—don't arrive too
early, audioguide-€5, Largo San Martino 5, +39 081 229 4502.

Visiting the Monastery and Museum: After purchasing your
ticket, step into the **church** across the courtyard. First built in the
mid-1300s, this church (as well as the entire complex) received a
makeover by master Baroque architect Cosimo Fanzago—responsible for most of the big Baroque you've already seen in the city
center. To protect the inlaid marble floor, you're not allowed into
the nave; instead you can enjoy this Baroque explosion with beautifully decorated **chapels** from its main entryway. (The space behind
the altar is accessible later in your visit.)

A variety of museum exhibits, art, and sculpture are housed
in the rest of the complex. The **Naval Museum** has nautical paintings, model boats, and giant ceremonial gondolas that were used
by various royalty. In a series of rooms opposite the Naval Museum
is an excellent collection of *presepi* (Nativity scenes), both life-size
and miniature, including a spectacular one by Michele Cucinel-
lo—the best I've seen in this *presepi*-crazy city. Beyond the *presepi*
is the larger **garden cloister,** where monks would eventually rest in
peace (look for the carved skulls).

Follow *chiesa* signs to access the back of the church and the the
sacristy. Cherub-covered ceilings painted by Naples favorite Luca
Giordano and intricate, inlaid wood cabinets compete for your attention. Return to the cloister and find the terra-cotta-tiled floor to
enter a **painting gallery** (with lots of antique maps and artifacts of
old Naples). Finally, step into the massive **Prior's Quarters** with its
private corner terrace and privileged views of the bay. Another view
terrace is just outside, but the prior had the power view.

NAPLES

Sleeping in Naples

As an alternative to intense Naples, most travelers prefer to sleep in mellow Sorrento, just over an hour away (see the Sorrento chapter). But, if needed, here are a few good options. High season in Naples is spring and late fall. Prices are soft during the hot, slow summer months (July-Sept) and plunge during the pleasantly cool winters.

ON AND AROUND VIA TOLEDO

To see the city's best face, stay in the area that stretches between the Archaeological Museum and the port.

$$$$ Decumani Hotel de Charme is a classy oasis tucked away on a residential lane in the very heart of the city, just off Spaccanapoli. While the street is Naples-dingy, the hotel is an inviting retreat, filling an elegant 17th-century palace with 39 rooms and a stunning breakfast room (air-con, elevator, Via San Giovanni Maggiore Pignatelli 15, Metro: Università; if coming from Spaccanapoli, this lane is one street toward the train station from Via Santa Chiara, +39 081 551 8188, www.decumani.com, info@decumani.com).

$$$ Hotel Piazza Bellini is an artistically decorated hotel with 48 minimalist but solid and comfortable rooms surrounding a peaceful, inviting courtyard. Two blocks below the Archaeological Museum, just off the lively Piazza Bellini, and close to the great pizzerias and restaurants on Via dei Tribunali, it offers modern sanity in a strategic city-center location (air-con, elevator, Via Santa Maria di Constantinopoli 101, Metro: Dante, +39 081 451 732, www.hotelpiazzabellini.com, info@hotelpiazzabellini.com).

$$$ Art Resort Galleria Umberto has 25 rooms in two buildings inside the Umberto I shopping gallery at the bottom of Via Toledo, just off Piazza del Plebiscito. This genteel-feeling place gilds the lily, with an aristocratic setting and decor but older bathrooms. Consider paying about €30 extra for a room overlooking the gallery (air-con, elevator, Galleria Umberto 83, fourth floor—ask at booth for coin to operate elevator if needed, Metro: Toledo, +39 081 497 6224, www.artresortgalleriaumberto.com, booking@hotelgalleriaumberto.com).

$$$ Hotel Il Convento is a good choice for those who want to sleep in the tight tangle of lanes called the Spanish Quarter—quintessential Naples. You're only a couple of short blocks off the main Via Toledo drag, and heavy-duty windows help block out some (if not all) of the scooter noise and church bells. A rare haven of calm in this characteristic corner of town, it has 14 small but comfortable rooms—all with teensy balconies—as well as top-floor rooms with a private garden terrace (family rooms, air-con, elevator; Via Speranzella 137A, Metro: Toledo—from just below Banco di Napoli entrance, walk two blocks up Vico Tre Re a Toledo; +39 081 403 977, www.hotelilconvento.com, info@hotelilconvento.com).

$$ Chiaja Hotel de Charme, with the same owner as the Decumani (listed earlier), rents 33 rooms on the Via Chiaia pedestrian shopping drag near Piazza del Plebiscito. The building has a fascinating history: Part of it was the residence of a marquis, and the rest was one of Naples' most famous brothels (some view rooms, air-con, elevator, Via Chiaia 216, first floor, Metro: Toledo, +39 081 415 555, www.hotelchiaia.it, info@hotelchiaia.it).

AT THE TRAIN STATION

These hotels are less convenient for sightseeing and dining, and the neighborhood gets dodgy as you move away from the station. But they're handy for train travelers, practical for a quick stay, and less expensive.

$$ Hotel Stelle has 38 sterile, identical, newly remodeled rooms with modern furnishings. It feels sane compared to its hectic surroundings, and a back entrance leads directly into the train station (air-con, elevator, Corso Meridionale 60, exit station near track 5, +39 081 1889 3090, www.stellehotel.com, info@stellehotel.com).

$$ Ibis Styles Napoli Garibaldi, with 88 rooms, offers chain predictability and a bright, youthful color scheme a five-minute walk from the station (air-con, elevator, pay parking; Via Giuseppe Ricciardi 33, exit station onto Piazza Garibaldi, then take second left onto Via G. Ricciardi; +39 081 690 8111, www.ibis.com, h3243@accor.com).

$ Grand Hotel Europa, across the seedy street right next to the station, has 89 decent rooms and hallways whimsically decorated with not-quite-right reproductions of famous paintings. The hotel is a decent value, and its 1970s-era vibe (including the Kool-Aid and canned fruit at breakfast) makes for fun memories (RS%, family rooms, air-con, elevator, restaurant, Corso Meridionale 14, across street from station's north exit near track 5, +39 081 267 511, www.grandhoteleuropa.com, info@grandhoteleuropa.com).

Eating in Naples

Yes, Naples is (justifiably) famous for pizza. But the Campania region has other delicious tastes, as well. The abundant sunshine and volcanic soil produce excellent fruits and vegetables; the famous San Marzano tomatoes come from just outside Naples; and Italy's best mozzarella (*di bufala*, from water buffalo milk) also originates in Campania. Pastas with bright, flavorful tomato and other sauces

NAPLES

Naples Hotels & Restaurants

VIA FORIA

VIA MATERDEI
To Capodimonte Sights
VICO LUNGO
14

VIA STA. TERESA
SANTA TERESA

SANITÀ

Cavour (Line 2)

VIA SETTEMBRINI

VIA SALVATOR ROSA

Piazza Cavour

VIA M. LONGO
PORTA SAN GENNARO

MADRE ART MUSEUM

ARCHAEO-LOGICAL MUSEUM

Museo (Line 1)

VIA S.M. CONST.

VIA DUOMO

VIA DONNA

DUOMO

GALLERIA PRINCIPE

VIA CONTE DI RUVO

VIA S. SAPIENZA

VIA S. PAOLO

NAPOLI SOTTER-RANEA

12

22

21

18

S. GREG. ARMENO

S. LORENZO MAGGIORE

BELLINI THEATER

16 11

VIA SOLE

VIA DEI TRIBUNALI

CAPPELLA SANSEVERO

S. BIAGIO

VIA NAPOLI

D'AURIA SHOP

2

Piazza Bellini

SAN DOM.

NILE STATUE

Dante (Line 1)
PORTA D'ALBA

VIA PORT'ALBA

Piazza Dante

Piazza San Dom. Maggiore

MARADONA CHAPEL

13

27

VIA TARSIA

GESÙ NUOVO

SPACCA

15

VIA CAFASSO

Montesanto (Line 2)

Piazza Sette Settembre

Piazza Gesù Nuovo

SANTA CHIARA

VIA GRAN ARCHIVIO

MONTESANTO FUNICULAR

To Vomero District

VIA MADDALONI

CLOISTER

17 1

S. CHIARA

VIA PALADINO

STREET MARKET

Piazza Monte.

19

Piazza Carità

FASCIST BLDG.

CALATA TRINITÀ MAGGIORE

POST

29

CORSO UMBERTO I

VIA SEDILE DI PORTO

CALATA PORTA DI MASSA (CAR FERRY TERMINAL)

BNL BANK

Piazza Matteotti

VIA S. FELICE

CSN Shuttle to Pompeii
Università (Line 1)

Piazza Bovio

Toledo (Line 1)
27
20

VIA A. DIAZ

VIA MEDINA

Piazza Immacolatella

SPANISH QUARTER

VIA PORTA DI TAPPIA

VICO TOFA

BANCO DI NAPOLI

Piazza Municipio

Municipio (Line 1)

4

BANCA INTESA SANPAOLO

CSN Shuttle to Pompeii

CAFFÈ MORENO

PINTAURO

GALLERIA UMBERTO I

CASTEL NUOVO

CAFFÈ BEVERELLO

CENTRALE FUNICULAR

3

Alibus (to Airport)

STAZIONE MARITTIMA (CRUISE TERMINAL)

GRAN CAFFÈ GAMBRINUS

TEATRO SAN CARLO

5

VIA CHIAIA

To Chiaia District & Lungomare

ROYAL PALACE

MOLO BEVERELLO DOCK (HYDROFOIL & FAST FERRY)

TUNNEL TO LUNGOMARE

GALLERIA BORBONICA

SAN FRANCESCO DI PAOLA

Piazza del Plebiscito

23

To Castel dell'Ovo, Chiaia District, Lungomare Harborside Promenade & Posillipo Hill

NAPLES

Accommodations
1 Decumani Hotel de Charme
2 Hotel Piazza Bellini & L'Etto
3 Art Resort Galleria Umberto
4 Hotel Il Convento
5 Chiaja Hotel de Charme
6 Hotel Stelle
7 Ibis Styles Napoli Garibaldi
8 Grand Hotel Europa

Eateries & Other
9 Antica Pizzeria da Michele
10 Pizzeria Trianon da Ciro
11 Gino Sorbillo Pizzeria
12 Pizzeria di Matteo
13 La Figlia del Presidente
14 Pizzeria Starita
15 Tandem Ragù
16 Caffè Bistrot Diaz
17 Taverna a Santa Chiara
18 Trattoria Campagnola
19 Osteria il Garum
20 Trattoria da Nennella
21 La Cantina di Via Sapienza
22 Osteria da Carmela
23 To Ristorante la Scialuppa
24 Mimì alla Ferrovia
25 Da Donato
26 Fratelli Attanasio Bakery
27 Groceries (3)
28 Polo Nord Gelateria
29 Laundry

are a highlight here. And don't miss the classic dessert, the delicate, super-crunchy, ricotta-filled *sfogliatella*.

FANTASTIC, FAMOUS PIZZA

Naples is the birthplace of pizza. Its pizzerias bake just the right combination of fresh dough (soft and chewy, as opposed to Roman-style, which is thin and crispy), mozzarella, and tomatoes in traditional wood-burning ovens. You can head for the famous, venerable places, but these can have long lines stretching out the door, and half-hour waits for a table. If you want to skip the hassle, just ask your hotel for directions to the neighborhood

pizzeria. An average one-person pie (usually the only size available) costs €6-9; most places offer both takeout and eat-in, and pizza is often the only thing on the menu.

Near the Station

These two pizzerias—the most famous—are both a few long blocks from the train station, and near the end of my self-guided Naples Walk.

$ Antica Pizzeria da Michele is for pizza purists. Filled with locals (and tourists), it serves just two varieties: *margherita* (tomato sauce and mozzarella) and *marinara* (tomato sauce, oregano, and garlic, no cheese). Come early to sit and watch the pizza artists in action. A pizza with beer costs around €8. As this place is often jammed with a long line, arrive early or late to get a seat. If there's a mob, head inside to get a number. If it's just too crowded to wait, try the less-exceptional Pizzeria Trianon (described next), which often has room (Mon-Sat 10:30-24:00, closed Sun; look for the vertical red *Antica Pizzeria* sign at the intersection of Via Pietro Colletta and Via Cesare Sersale at #1; +39 081 553 9204).

$ Pizzeria Trianon da Ciro, across the street and left a few doors, has been da Michele's archrival since 1923—and these days, it survives mainly on their overflow. It offers more choices, higher prices, air-conditioning, and a cozier atmosphere; for less chaos, head upstairs (daily 11:00-15:30 & 19:00-23:00, Via Pietro Colletta 42, +39 081 553 9426).

On and near Via dei Tribunali

This street, which runs a couple of blocks north of Spaccanapoli, is legendary for its pizzerias and fun eateries. It's packed with hungry strollers and long lines marking the most popular places.

NAPLES

$ Gino Sorbillo is on all the "best pizza in Naples" lists...as you'll learn the hard way if you show up at peak mealtimes, when huge mobs crowd outside the front door waiting for a table. While many locals believe it doesn't warrant the hype, don't tell the happy travelers eating here (Mon-Sat 12:00-15:30 & 19:00-24:00, closed Sun, Via dei Tribunali 32, +39 081 446 643). Relatives run similarly named places on the same street at #35 (a good option for its specialty: fried pizza) and #37.

$ Pizzeria di Matteo is popular for its fried takeout treats. People waiting out front line up at the little window to snack on deep-fried goodies—*arancini* (with rice, gooey cheese, peas, and sausage), *melanzane* (eggplant), *frittatine* (balls of mac and cheese plus sausage), and *crocché* (croquettes)—for €1-2 apiece (sometimes closed Sun, Via dei Tribunali 94, +39 081 455 262).

Nearby: $ La Figlia del Presidente is a short walk south from the two legendary joints listed above, and is quickly establishing its own loyal clientele. Push your way through the locals gathered around the door and get a number, then patiently wait for a slice of heaven. Or you can dine in the big, plain, high-ceilinged cellar (Tue-Sat 12:00-15:30 & 19:00-23:30, Mon 12:00-15:30, closed Sun, Via Grande Archivio 24, +39 081 286 738).

Near the Archaeological Museum

If you've had enough of crowds at the museum, head a few blocks north for world-class pizza without the throngs of people.

$ Pizzeria Starita has been in business for over 100 years, first as a cantina (featured in a Sophia Loren flick) then offering pizza since the 1950s. The fourth generation currently runs this bustling, friendly eatery just off the normal tourist circuit. Neapolitans think less is more with regard to pizza, but Starita offers both modern and traditional toppings (Tue-Sun 12:00-15:30 & 19:00 until late, closed Mon, no reservations—just show up and add your name to the wait list, from the museum walk 10 minutes up Via Santa Teresa degli Scalzi to the intersection with Via Materdei—the pizzeria is a few steps down on the left at #27, Metro: Museo, +39 081 557 3682).

OTHER RESTAURANTS

If you want a full meal rather than a pizza, consider these options.

Between Spaccanapoli and Via Toledo

$$ Tandem Ragù Restaurant, tiny with a few charming tables inside and out, features a fun menu specializing in Neapolitan *ragù* (beef, pork, or vegetarian options). The *scarpetta* (little shoe) dishes are simply various *ragù*s with baskets of bread for dunking (Tue-

Sun 12:00-23:00, closed Mon, Via Giovanni Paladino 51, 50 yards off Spaccanapoli, below the statue of the Nile, +39 081 1900 2468).

$$ Caffè Bistrot Diaz, close to the famous pizzerias on atmospheric Via dei Tribunali, has a short menu of Neapolitan classics that are executed very well. Locals say it's so tasty because *mamma* is cooking in the kitchen. The indoor seating is modern and nondescript; outdoor tables squeeze into a tight piazza in front of a church (Mon-Sat 7:00-22:00, closed Sun, Via dei Tribunali 25, +39 081 292 383).

$$ Taverna a Santa Chiara is your classic little eatery buried deep in the old center of Naples. It's convivial, warmly run, and simple. Just 100 yards from the tourist commotion of Spaccanapoli, it provides a fun and easygoing break (daily 12:00-16:00 & 19:00-24:00, closed Sun at dinner, Via Santa Chiara 6, +39 081 048 4908).

$$ Trattoria Campagnola is a classic family place with a daily home cooking-style chalkboard menu on the back wall, mamma busy cooking in the back, and wine on tap. Here you can venture away from pastas, be experimental with a series of local dishes, and not go wrong (daily 12:30-16:00 & 19:30-23:00, opposite the famous pizzerias at Via Tribunali 47, +39 081 459 034 but no reservations).

$$ Osteria il Garum is great if you'd like to eat on a classic Neapolitan square. It's named for the ancient fish sauce that was widely used in Roman cooking. These days, mild-mannered Luigi and his staff inject their pricey local cuisine with centuries of tradition, served in a cozy split-level cellar or outside on a covered terrace facing a neighborhood church. It's just between Via Toledo and Spaccanapoli, a short walk from the Church of Gesù Nuovo (Wed-Mon 12:00-15:30 & 19:00-23:30, closed Tue, Piazza Monteoliveto 2A, +39 081 542 3228).

$$ Trattoria da Nennella is fun-loving chaos buried in the Spanish Quarter, with red-shirted waiters barking orders, a small festival anytime someone puts a tip in the bucket, and the fruit course served in plastic bidets. There's one price—€15 per person—and you choose three courses plus a fruit. House wine and water is served in tiny plastic cups, the crowd is ready for fun, and the food's good. You can sit indoors or on a cobbled terrace under a trellis. No reservations are taken, so put your name on the list when you arrive—the line moves pretty fast (Mon-Sat 12:00-15:00 & 19:00-23:00, closed Sun, leave Via Toledo a block down from the BNL bank and walk up Vico del Teatro Nuovo three short blocks to the corner, Vico Lungo del Teatro Nuovo 103, +39 081 414 338).

$ La Cantina di Via Sapienza is a lunch-only hole-in-the-wall, serving up traditional Neapolitan fare in an interior that feels like a neighborhood joint (but has also been discovered by tourists).

It's a block north of the congested, pizzeria-packed Via dei Tribunali, and a good alternative if those places are just too crowded and your heart isn't set on pizza (Mon-Sat for lunch only, closed Sun, Via Sapienza 40, +39 081 459 078).

Near the Archaeological Museum

$$ Osteria da Carmela serves up traditional Neapolitan classics only mama could make—like *ragù*, *polpetti*, and tasty fried fish—with a dash of Old World charm, as well as a sprinkle of modern class. Affordable house wine and fine cheeses complete the meal. Tables are limited, so reservations are smart (Mon-Sat 12:00-15:30 & 19:00-24:00, closed Sun, Via Conte di Ruvo 11, +39 081 549 9738, www.osteriadacarmela.it).

$$ L'Etto is *not* the place to go for traditional Neapolitan cooking. This stylish restaurant, with a whisper of pretense in its white-minimalist interior and outside at its long row of sidewalk tables, focuses on a wide variety of creatively assembled, nutritious bowls, plus some trendy cocktails (daily 12:30-15:30 & 19:30-22:30, longer hours on weekends, facing Piazza Bellini at Via S. Maria di Costantinopoli 102, +39 081 1932 0967).

A Romantic Splurge on the Harbor

$$$$ Ristorante la Scialuppa ("The Rowboat") is a great bet for a fine local meal on the harbor. Located in the romantic Santa Lucia district, you'll walk across the causeway to the Castel dell'Ovo in the fisherman's quarter (the castle on the island) just off Via Partenope. They boast fine indoor and outdoor seating facing the marina, attentive waitstaff, a wonderful assortment of *antipasti*, great seafood, and predictably high prices. Reservations are smart (Tue-Sun 12:30-15:00 & 19:30-23:30, closed Mon, Piazzetta Marinari 5, +39 081 764 5333, www.ristorantelascialuppa.net).

Near the Station

$$ Mimì alla Ferrovia is a classic neighborhood *trattoria;* stepping inside, surrounded by well-dressed, in-the-know-locals, you know you're in for a good meal. The menu consists of well-executed Neapolitan classics. It's run by a father-and-son team, who combine a passion for tradition with a willingness to innovate. Their ricotta is heavenly (Mon-Sat 12:00-15:30 & 19:00-23:00, closed Sun, Via Alfonso d'Aragona 19, +39 081 553 8525).

$$ Da Donato, a traditional, family-run *trattoria* on a glum street near the station, serves delicious food in an unpretentious atmosphere. The best approach is for two people to share the astonishing *antipasti* sampler—*degustazione "fantasia" della Casa Terra e Mare.* You'll get more than a dozen small portions, each more delicious than the last. A version without seafood is cheaper (Tue-Sun

NAPLES

Getting Around the Region

For specifics, check the "Connections" sections of each chapter. Confirm times and prices locally.

By Bus: CitySightseeing's fleet of bright red buses with audio commentary offer easy trips from Naples to the ruins at Pompeii (see page 1015), along the popular Amalfi Coast (see page 1081), and even up to the town of Ravello (see page 1107). Crowded SITA buses also traverse the Amalfi Coast; see page 1080.

By Train: The dingy, crowded **Circumvesuviana** commuter train—popular with locals, tourists, and pickpockets—links Naples, Herculaneum, the Pompeii ruins, and Sorrento. The most important Circumvesuviana station in Naples (called "Garibaldi") is underneath Naples' Centrale station; follow the signs downstairs to *Stazione Garibaldi* and then *Circumvesuviana* and/or *Linee Vesuviane* signs to the Circumvesuviana ticket windows and turnstiles (stand in line or get your ticket at a newsstand). Buy your ticket, confirm the time and track, insert your ticket at the turnstiles, and head down another level to the platforms.

The Circumvesuviana is covered by the Campania ArteCard (see page 952), but not by rail passes. For Pompeii or Herculaneum, take any Circumvesuviana train marked *Sorrento*—they all stop at both (usually depart from platform 3). Sorrento-bound trains depart twice hourly and take about 15 minutes to reach Ercolano Scavi (for the Herculaneum ruins, €2.20 one-way), 35 minutes to reach Pompei Scavi-Villa dei Misteri (for the Pompeii ruins, €2.90 one-way), and 60 minutes to reach Sorrento, the end of the line (€3.90 one-way). Express trains to Sorrento marked *DD* (6/day) reach Sorrento 15 minutes sooner (and stop at Herculaneum and Pompeii). For schedules, see the Italian-only website www.eavsrl.it.

On the platform, double-check with a local that the train goes to Sorrento (avoid lines that branch out to other destinations). When returning to Naples on the Circumvesuviana, validate your ticket before boarding and get off at the next-to-the-last station, Garibaldi (Centrale station is just up the escalator).

Pricier **Campania Express trains,** operated by Circumvesuviana, use the same tracks and stops. They run only four times a day, but are less crowded and have air-conditioning (€15 one-way in high season to any destination: Herculaneum, 10 minutes; Pompeii, 30 minutes; Sorrento, 1 hour; mid-March-Oct only, not covered by Campania ArteCard, buy tickets at http://ots.eavsrl.it or at the station).

Trenitalia (Italy's national railway) runs **Metropolitana** trains—part of Naples' Metro line 2—to Pompei town, from which it's a short shuttle bus ride or long walk to the ruins (trains run 1-2/hour, 45 minutes, covered by Campania ArteCard; see details on page 952). Metropolitana trains stop downstairs in Naples' Centrale station (near the center of the station—look for *Metro linea 2*) and conveniently also link to the Naples Archaeological Museum (Piazza Cavour stop). After Pompei town, these continue to Salerno (for boats and buses to Amalfi), though there are faster options. Note that the Metropolitana is *not* convenient for reaching Herculaneum or Sorrento.

By Taxi: The 30-mile taxi ride from Naples directly to your Sorrento hotel costs about €110 (ask the driver for the nonmetered *tariffa predeterminata*). A cab on Capri runs about €70/hour. Taxis on the Amalfi Coast are generally expensive, and often overcharge, but can be convenient, especially with a larger group. See "Getting Around the Amalfi Coast—By Taxi" on page 1082.

By Boat: Major companies include Caremar (www.caremar.it), SNAV (www.snav.it), Gescab (a.k.a. NLG Jet, www.gescab.it), Navigazione Libera del Golfo (www.navlib.it), Alilauro (www.alilauro.it), Travelmar (www.travelmar.it), and Alicost (www.alicost.it). Each company has different destinations and prices; some compete for the same trips. Some lines (like Sorrento-Capri) run all year; others (on the Amalfi Coast, for example) only in summer. Trips can be cancelled in bad weather. Faster watercraft cost a little more than slow car ferries. A hydrofoil, sometimes called a "jet boat," skims between Naples and Sorrento—it's swifter, safer from pickpockets, more scenic, and more expensive than the Circumvesuviana train.

For schedules, check online (www.capritourism.com; click "Shipping Timetable"), or ask at any TI or at Naples' Molo Beverello boat dock. (The handy departure board on the rooftop of the Molo Beverello terminal shows all the upcoming departures.) Most boats charge €2 or so for luggage. When you arrive, note the return times—the last boat usually leaves before 19:00. The preset price for a taxi between Naples' Centrale train station and its port (Molo Beverello) is €11, or you can take Metro line 1 to the Municipio stop and walk to the port.

By Shared Trips: Mondo Guide is sometimes able to play "matchmaker" between travelers looking for an efficient, direct car connection instead of a complicated train or bus connection. By splitting the cost with others headed the same way, this can become reasonable. For details, see www.sharedtrips.com.

12:30-14:30 & 19:30-22:00, closed Mon, two blocks from Piazza Garibaldi—turn down Via Silvio Spaventa to #39, +39 081 287 828).

PASTRY

To get the full overview of Neapolitan pastries at good prices, visit the bakery outlet of **Fratelli Attanasio** on a small alley near the train station—with your back to the station building, it's off the far-right corner of the big square. Come early for the best selection (Tue-Sun 6:30-19:30, closed Mon, Vico Ferrovia 1, +39 081 285 675).

PICNICS

A good supermarket for picnic supplies is **Sapori & Dintorni,** in the train-station complex (Mon-Sat 8:00-20:30, Sun 8:00-15:00, enter from outside, to the right of bookstore). By Piazza Dante is a small **Superò** that's convenient to hotels near this stretch of Via Toledo (Mon-Sat 8:30-20:30, Sun 8:30-14:00, at corner of Via Tarsia and Vico San Domenico Soriano). By the Toledo Metro stop a small **Conad** is handy to hotels near Galleria Umberto I and the Spanish Quarter (daily 8:00-21:00, Via Roberto Bracco 4).

Naples Connections

BY TRAIN

See the "Getting Around the Region" sidebar for information on getting to **Herculaneum,** the ruins at **Pompeii, Pompei Town,** and **Sorrento** by train.

By Train to: Rome (Trenitalia: 1-5/hour, 70 minutes on Frecciarossa, 2 hours on Intercity, 2.5 hours and much cheaper on regional trains; Italo: hourly, 70 minutes), **Civitavecchia** (at least hourly, 3 hours, most change in Rome), **Florence** (Trenitalia: at least hourly, 3 hours, most change in Pisa or Rome; Italo: hourly, 3 hours), **Salerno** (Trenitalia: at least hourly, 35-45 minutes, change in Salerno for bus or boat to Amalfi; *regionale* trains are cheaper but Intercity and Freccia express trains have a first class section for a little extra; avoid slower Metropolitana trains that leave from the same platforms as Metro's line 2; Italo: 4/day, 45 minutes), **Paestum** (12/day, 1.25 hours, direction: Sapri or Reggio), **Brindisi** (4/day, 5-6 hours, change in Caserta; from Brindisi, ferries sail to Greece), **Milan** (Trenitalia: 2/hour, 5 hours; Italo: 1-2/hour), **Venice** (Trenitalia: almost hourly, 5.5 hours, some change in Bologna or Rome; Italo: 3/day, 5.5 hours, reservations required), **Palermo** (2/day direct, 9.5 hours, also an overnight train). Any train listed on the schedule as leaving Napoli PG or Napoli-Garibaldi departs not from Napoli Centrale, but from the adjacent Garibaldi station.

BY BOAT

Ferries and cruise ships dock next to each other in the shadow of the old fortress (Castel Nuovo), a short walk from the old town sightseeing action. Naples has great ferry connections to Sorrento, Capri, and other nearby destinations. Cruise ships use the giant Stazione Marittima cruise terminal, hydrofoils and faster ferries use the Molo Beverello dock (to the west of the terminal), and slower car ferries leave from Calata Porta di Massa, east of the terminal. The entire port area is currently a big construction zone, and has been torn up for years; hopefully it will be tidied up in time for your visit.

Whether arriving by ferry or cruise ship, you can get to the city center by taxi, Metro, or on foot; the Alibus shuttle bus runs to the airport (see "By Plane," next).

A **taxi** stand is in front of the port area. Expect to pay €12-15 to connect the port to the train station or the Archaeological Museum.

Straight ahead across the road from the cruise terminal (on the right side of the big fortress) is Piazza Municipio, with the handy Municipio **Metro** stop. From here, line 1 zips you right to the Archaeological Museum (Museo stop) or, in the opposite direction, to the train station (Garibaldi stop). A €1.10 single ticket *(corsa singola)* covers rides on line 1. You can buy tickets at any tobacco shop or some cafés: Caffè Moreno is between the two buildings of the cruise terminal, and Caffè Beverello is along the busy street on the waterfront. Remember to validate your ticket as you enter the Metro station.

On foot, it's a seven-minute **walk**—past the gigantic Castel Nuovo, then to the left—to Piazza del Plebiscito and the old city center.

From Naples by Boat to: Sorrento (6/day, more in summer, departs roughly every 2 hours starting at 9:00, few or no boats on winter weekends, leaves from Molo Beverello, 40 minutes), **Capri** (roughly hourly, more in summer, hydrofoil: 45 minutes from Molo Beverello; ferries: 60-90 minutes from Calata Porta di Massa). Sometimes seasonal boats go to **Positano** and **Amalfi,** on the Amalfi Coast—ask. For a map showing boat connections, see page 1041. For timetables, visit www.capritourism.com and click "Shipping Timetable."

BY PLANE

Naples International Airport (Aeroporto Internazionale di Napoli, a.k.a. Capodichino, code: NAP) is close to town (+39 081 789 6767, www.aeroportodinapoli.it). In summer, you may find a TI here. Alibus **shuttle buses** zip you in 10 minutes from the airport to Naples' Centrale train station, and then head to the port/Piazza

Municipio for boats to Capri and Sorrento (buses run daily 6:00–23:00, 4/hour, 20–30 minutes to the port, €5 on board). The shuttle bus departs from a stop located straight out the airport exit, past the rental car lots. If you take a **taxi** to or from the airport, ask the driver for the fixed price (€18 to the train station, €21 to the port, €25 to the Chiaia district near the waterfront).

To reach **Sorrento** from Naples Airport, take the direct Curreri bus (see page 1062). A taxi to Sorrento costs about €110.

POMPEII & NEARBY

Pompeii • Herculaneum • Vesuvius

Stopped in their tracks by the eruption of Mount Vesuvius in AD 79, Pompeii and Herculaneum offer the best look anywhere at what life in Rome must have been like around 2,000 years ago. These two cities of well-preserved ruins are yours to explore. Of the two sites, Pompeii is grander, while Herculaneum is smaller, more intimate, and more intact. Pompeii is easily reached from Naples on the CitySightseeing bus or by either the Circumvesuviana commuter, Campania Express, or Trenitalia Metropolitana trains; Herculaneum is best reached by train. Vesuvius, still smoldering ominously, rises up on the horizon. It last erupted in 1944, and is still an active volcano. Buses from the train stations at Herculaneum or Pompeii drop you a half-hour hike below its crater rim.

Pompeii

A once-thriving commercial port of 20,000, Pompeii (worth

▲▲▲) grew from Greek and Etruscan roots to become an important Roman city. Then, on August 24, AD 79, everything changed. Vesuvius erupted and began to bury the city under 20 feet of hot volcanic ash. For the archaeolo-

Pompeii & Nearby

- —·—·— Main Rail Line
- ++++++ Circumvesuviana Rail Line
- – – – – Bus
- ········· Boat

10 Kilometers
10 Miles

To Rome

Capodichino

Naples

Ercolano Scavi Station

PARKING & TICKETS

Mt. Vesuvius
1277M

TRAIL (20-30 MIN. HIKE TO RIM)

HERCULANEUM RUINS

POMPEII RUINS

Pompei (Town)

Bay of Naples

Pompei Scavi Station

Pompei Station (Trenitalia)

To Salerno, Paestum & Palermo

To Capri   To Sorrento

To Sorrento & Amalfi Coast

gists who excavated it centuries later, this was a shake-and-bake windfall, teaching them volumes about daily Roman life. Pompeii was accidentally rediscovered in 1599; excavations began in 1748.

GETTING TO POMPEII

By Train from Naples or Sorrento Directly to the Ruins: Pompeii is roughly midway between Naples and Sorrento on the crowded, run-down **Circumvesuviana commuter train** line (2/hour, 35 minutes from Naples, 30 minutes from Sorrento, either trip costs €2.90 one-way, not covered by rail passes, no air-con, Italian-only website: www.eavsrl.it). In the Naples station, you'll find these downstairs (follow signs for *Circumvesuviana* as well as for *Linee Vesuviane*—both lead to the same tracks). Get off at the **Pompei Scavi-Villa dei Misteri** stop; from Naples, it's the stop after Villa Regina. DD express trains (6/day) bypass several stations but do stop at Pompei Scavi, shaving 10 minutes off the trip from Naples.

Less-frequent **Campania Express trains** use the same tracks and stops, but are less crowded and have air-conditioning (4/day, 30 minutes from Naples, 25 minutes from Sorrento, either trip costs €8 one-way, mid-March-Oct only, http://ots.eavsrl.it). Due to return times, it may work best to take the Campania Express *to* Pompeii and a different train back to Naples. For train details, see page 1008.

From the Pompei Scavi train station, it's just a two-minute

walk to the ruin's Porta Marina entrance: Leaving the station, turn right and walk down the road about a block (entrance on left).

By Train from Naples to Pompei Town (with Bus Transfer to Pompeii Ruins): Trenitalia (Italy's national railway) operates the **Metropolitana** train from Naples to the town center of Pompei (with one "i"), which is a short bus ride (or long walk) from the Pompeii archaeological site. This train is part of Naples' Metro line 2, which stops under Centrale station (at the stop called Stazione Piazza Garibaldi, or "Napoli S.G." for short). It also reaches the Piazza Cavour stop near the Archaeological Museum—handy for those who want to directly connect Pompeii to its greatest artifacts.

In Pompei town, the Metropolitana is coordinated with a **BusLink shuttle bus** that runs to the ruins. The bus is also operated by Trenitalia, so the entire train-bus trip shows up on their online schedules (1-2/hour, 70 minutes, €4.10, search for "Pompei Scavi"; train to Pompei town only: 1-2/hour, 45 minutes, €2.90, search for "Pompei"; www.trenitalia.com).

If you decide to **walk** to the archaeological site, it's actually quite pleasant (allow 25-30 minutes to the main Porta Marina entrance, or 15-20 minutes to the Anfiteatro entrance): Head straight out from the train station to the big church tower, which marks the tidy main piazza of modern Pompei. From there, turn left and you'll soon be walking along the outer gate of the Pompeii site, passing various entrances along the way (see map).

By Shuttle Bus from Naples: CitySightseeing Italy offers a convenient, clean, and stress-free shuttle bus from Naples to Pompeii. The bus departs from three pick-up points in Naples: At the Piazza Municipio end of the Castel Nuovo, at Piazza Bovio near the Università Metro stop, and at Centrale station (stop located across the street and left when exiting, near the Hotel D'Anna). Tickets can be purchased online, but be aware that each bus has a specific return time about 4.5 hours after arrival; no return-trip changes are allowed. Early morning departures beat the heat at Pompeii, but traffic congestion can delay your arrival and cut into your sightseeing time. Check the most recent details on their website (generally 3/day in summer, 2/day off-season, 30-minute ride from the train station when traffic is light, €10 one-way, €18 round-trip, +39 081 551 7279, www.city-sightseeing.it). Skip the option to purchase your Pompeii entrance ticket through CitySightseeing—you'll pay more than buying it yourself online (details later).

By Car: Parking is available at Camping Zeus, next to the Pompei Scavi train station (€3/hour, €20/day); several other campgrounds/parking lots are nearby.

Day-Tripping from Rome: It's possible to day-trip to Pompeii from Rome, if you start early and plan on a long day. Figure about 2.5-3 hours for transportation each way, plus time at the site.

First, take the express train to Naples. In Naples, transfer either to the Circumvesuviana or Campania Express train (which drops you at the ruins) or to the Trenitalia Metropolitana train (which takes you to the modern town of Pompei, where you'll board a shuttle bus to the site). Or, time your train trip from Rome to catch the CitySightseeing shuttle bus from Naples to Pompeii. All of these options are outlined above.

ORIENTATION TO POMPEII

Cost: €16, includes special exhibits. Consider the Campania Arte-Card (see page 952) if visiting other sights in the region. Avoid crowded free entry days (usually once a month on a Sunday).

Hours: Daily 9:00-19:30, Nov-March until 17:00, last entry 1.5 hours before closing.

Information: +39 081 857 5347, general info at www.pompeiisites.org, tickets at www.ticketone.it.

Crowd-Beating Tips: To skip ahead of everyone, purchase your ticket online at www.ticketone.it (€1.50 surcharge). If you're buying onsite and there's a very long ticket line at the Porta Marina entrance, continue walking three minutes to the ticket booth near Hotel Vittoria (called Piazza Esedra or Porta Marina Inferiore; there's rarely a line). Buy your ticket, then either enter here or—to start my tour directly—return to Porta Marina, and walk right in.

Visitor Information: You may get a flimsy map of the site with your ticket, and you'll see QR codes here and there encouraging you to access online maps. But this book's map should suit your needs.

Some buildings and streets are bound to be closed for restoration when you visit. Use your map to find your way. Street names and building numbers are clearly marked throughout the site.

The bookshop sells a couple of books with plastic overlays that allow you to re-create Pompeii from the ruins (€18; if you buy from a street vendor, pay no more than that). Another good book is the €6 *Pompeii (Brief) Guide,* with excellent photos and additional walking routes.

Ignore the "info point" kiosk at the train station, which is a private agency selling tours.

Tours: Here are several ways to enjoy an organized and educational visit to Pompeii.

Simply follow the **self-guided** tour in this chapter (or, better, enjoy the audio version with my free 🎧 Rick Steves Audio Europe app). Both cover the basics and provide plenty of information for do-it-yourselfers.

Join a **Mondo Guide shared tour** for Rick Steves readers. This is your best budget bet for a tour with an actual guide (€20, doesn't include Pompeii entry, daily at 11:00, reservations required; meet at Hotel/Ristorante Suisse, just down the hill from the Porta Marina entrance; for details, see page 962).

Hire guide **Antonio Somma** for a private or shared tour. Antonio and his team of guides offer good two-hour tours of Pompeii for €120 (mobile +39 393 406 3824, +39 081 850 1992, www.tourspompeiiguide.com, info@pompeitour.com).

Other Options: Audioguides are available from a kiosk near the ticket booth at the Porta Marina entrance (€8, €13 for 2, ID required).

When you step off the train, you'll likely be accosted by touts for the "info point" kiosk, which sells €15 tours that depart whenever enough people sign up. Private guides (around €120/2 hours) of varying quality cluster near the ticket booth and may try to herd you into a group with other travelers, which is fine if it makes the price more reasonable. It's unethical for a guide to double charge by combining two groups into one tour. Instead, tourists should enjoy the savings and tip higher.

Rated Risqué: Parents, note that the ancient brothel and its sexually explicit frescoes are included on tours; let your guide know if you'd rather skip that stop.

Length of This Tour: Allow two hours, or three if you visit the theater and amphitheater. With less time, focus on the Forum, Baths of the Forum, House of the Vettii, House of the Faun, and brothel.

Baggage Check: Use the free baggage check near the turnstiles at the site entrance (just yards from the station). The train station also offers pay luggage storage (downstairs, by the WC).

Services: There's a pay WC at the train station. The Pompeii site has four free WCs—at the entrance, in the cafeteria, in the Antiquarium museum, and near the end of this tour, uphill from the theaters.

Eating: These **$** eateries offer reasonably priced meals (though your cheapest bet may be to bring your own food for a discreet picnic).

The **Ciao cafeteria,** within the site, serves good sandwiches, pizza, and pasta. You're welcome to picnic here if you buy a drink. **Bar Sgambati,** the café/restaurant at the train station, has air-conditioning, Wi-Fi, sandwiches to go, and pastas and pizzas. **Marius Juice Shop** (run by local guide Antonio Somma's family) sells sandwiches to go, and is located between Bar Sgambati and the Porta Marina entrance.

A second cluster of eateries around the ticket booth near Hotel Vittoria dishes out handy slices of pizza, salads, and pasta.

Starring: Roofless (collapsed) but otherwise intact Roman buildings, plaster casts of hapless victims, some erotic frescoes, and the dawning realization that these ancient people were not that different from us.

BACKGROUND

Pompeii, founded in 600 BC, eventually became a booming Roman trading city. Not rich, not poor, it was middle class—a perfect example of typical Roman life. Most streets would have been lined with stalls and jammed with customers from sunup to sundown. Chariots vied with shoppers for street space. Two thousand years ago, Rome controlled the entire Mediterranean—making it a kind of free-trade zone—and Pompeii was a central and bustling port.

There were no posh neighborhoods in Pompeii. Rich and poor mixed it up as elegant houses existed side by side with simple homes. While nearby Herculaneum would have been a classier place to live (a smaller, seaside resort with traffic-free streets, fancier houses, and far better drainage), Pompeii was the place for action and shopping. It served an estimated 20,000 residents with more than 40 bakeries, 130 bars, restaurants and hotels, and 30 brothels. With most of its buildings covered by brilliant white ground-marble stucco, Pompeii in AD 79 was an impressive town.

As you tour Pompeii, remember that its best art is safeguarded in the Archaeological Museum in Naples (described in the Naples chapter). Visiting the museum before or after going to Pompeii will help put this fascinating sight into context.

◑ SELF-GUIDED TOUR

• Just past the ticket-taker, start your approach up to the...

❶ Porta Marina

The city of Pompeii was born on the hill ahead of you. This was the original town gate. Before Vesuvius blew and filled in the harbor,

the sea came nearly to here. Notice the two openings in the gate (ahead, up the ramp). Both were left open by day to admit major traffic. At night, the larger one was closed for better security.

• *Pass through the Porta Marina and continue up to the top of the street, pausing at the three large stepping-stones in the middle.*

❷ Pompeii's Streets

Every day, Pompeiians flooded the streets with gushing water to clean them. These stepping-stones let pedestrians cross with-

out getting their sandals wet. Chariots traveling in either direction could straddle the stones (all had standard-size axles). A single stepping-stone in a road means it was a one-way street, a pair indicates an ordinary two-way, and three (like this) signifies

a major thoroughfare. The basalt stones are the original Roman pavement. The sidewalks (elevated to hide the plumbing—you'll see ancient plumbing revealed throughout the site) were paved with bits of broken pots (an ancient form of recycling) and studded with reflective bits of white marble. These "cats' eyes" helped people get around after dark, either by moonlight or with the help of lamps.

• *Continue straight ahead, don your mental toga, and enter the city as the Romans once did. The road opens up into the spacious main square: the Forum. Stand at the right end of this rectangular space (near the centaur statue) and look toward Mount Vesuvius.*

❸ The Forum (Foro)

Pompeii's commercial, religious, and political center stands at the intersection of the city's two main streets. While it's the most ruined part of Pompeii, it's grand nonetheless. Picture the piazza surrounded by two-story buildings on all sides. The pedestals that line the square once held statues of VIPs and various gods (now safely displayed in the museum in Naples). In Pompeii's heyday, its citizens gathered here in the main square to shop, talk politics,

Pompeii Tour

VESUVIUS (IN DISTANCE)

PATH

CITY WALLS

UNEXCAVATED AREA

PORTA VESUVIO

PORTA DI ERCOLANO

VIA VESUVIO

VIA VETTII

VIA NOLA

HOUSE OF THE VETTII 12

HOUSE OF THE FAUN

PIPES

VIA MERCURIO

VIA CONSOLARE

CITY WALLS

8

9 10

FORTUNA

11

TABERNA HEDONES

To Garden of the Fugitives & Amphitheater

WC

VIA

CAFETERIA

7

AUGUSTALI

13

14

VIA TEATRI

VIA ABBONDANZA

HOUSE OF MENANDER

WC

TEMPLE OF JUPITER

WALK ENDS

VIA STABIANA

Private Buses to Vesuvius

PORTA MARINA ENTRANCE

B

TICKETS

WC

POMPEI SCAVI TRAIN STATION

WALK BEGINS

6

FORUM

2

3

5

ANTIQUARIUM

4

VIA ABBONDANZA

TEMPLE OF ISIS

THEATER

TEATRO PICCOLO

1

EXIT

CITY WALLS

PORTA DI STABIA

VIALE DELLE GINESTRE

Piazza Esedra

TICKETS

PIAZZA ESEDRA ENTRANCE (PORTA MARINA INFERIORE)

To Pompei (Town)

HOTEL/RIST. SUISSE (MONDO TOURS STARTING POINT)

HOTEL VITTORIA

SS-18

VIA PLINIO

CIRCUMVESUVIANA LINE

To Sorrento

N

200 Meters

200 Yards

1 Porta Marina

2 Pompeii's Streets

3 Forum

4 Basilica

5 Via Abbondanza

6 Forum Granary; Plaster Casts of Victims

7 Baths of the Forum

8 Fast-Food Joint

9 House of the Tragic Poet

10 Aqueduct Arch

11 House of the Faun

12 House of the Vettii

13 Bakery & Mill

14 Brothel

and socialize. Business took place in the important buildings that lined the piazza.

The Forum was dominated by the **Temple of Jupiter,** at the far end (marked by a half-dozen ruined columns atop a stair-step base). Jupiter was the supreme god of the Roman pantheon—you might be able to make out his little white marble head at the center-rear of the temple. To the left of the temple is a fenced-off area, the **Forum granary,** where many artifacts from Pompeii are stored (and which we'll visit later).

At the near end of the Forum (behind where you're standing) is the **curia,** or City Hall. Like many Roman buildings, it was built with brick and mortar, then covered with marble walls and floors. To your left (as you face Vesuvius and the Temple of Jupiter) is the **basilica,** or courthouse.

Since Pompeii was a pretty typical Roman town, it has the same layout and components that you'll find in any Roman city—main square, curia, basilica, temples, axis of roads, and so on. All power converged at the Forum: religious (the temple), political (the curia), judicial (the basilica), and commercial (this piazza was the main marketplace). Even the power of the people was expressed here, since this is where they gathered to vote. Imagine the hubbub of this town square in its heyday.

Look beyond the Temple of Jupiter. Five miles to the north looms the ominous backstory to this site: **Mount Vesuvius.** Mentally draw a triangle up from the two remaining peaks to reconstruct the mountain before the eruption. When it blew, Pompeiians had no idea that they were living under a volcano, as Vesuvius hadn't erupted for 1,200 years. Imagine the wonder—then the horror—as a column of pulverized rock roared upward, and then ash began to fall. The weight of the ash and small rocks collapsed Pompeii's roofs later that day, crushing people who had taken refuge inside buildings instead of fleeing the city.

• *As you face Vesuvius, the basilica is to your left, lined with stumps of columns. Step inside.*

❹ Basilica

Pompeii's basilica was a first-century palace of justice. This ancient law court has the same floor plan later adopted by many Christian churches (which are also called basilicas). The big central hall (or nave) is flanked by rows of columns marking off narrower side aisles. Along the side walls are traces of the original stucco imitating marble.

The columns—now stumps all about the same height—were not ruined by the volcano. Rather, they were left unfinished when Vesuvius blew. Pompeii had been devastated by an earthquake in AD 62, and was just in the process of rebuilding the basilica when Vesuvius erupted, 17 years later. The half-built columns show off the technology of the day. Uniform bricks were stacked around

a cylindrical core. Once finished, they would have been coated with marble-dust stucco to simulate marble columns—an economical construction method found throughout Pompeii (and the Roman Empire).

Besides the earthquake and the eruption, Pompeii's buildings have suffered other ravages over the years, including Spanish plunderers (c. 1800), 19th-century souvenir hunters, WWII bombs, creeping and destructive vegetation, another earthquake in 1980, and modern neglect. The fact that the entire city was covered by the eruption of AD 79 actually helped preserve it, saving it from the sixth-century barbarians who plundered many other towns into oblivion.

• *Exit the basilica and cross the short side of the square to where the city's main street hits the Forum. Stop at the three white stones that stick up from the cobbles.*

❺ Via Abbondanza

Glance down Via Abbondanza, Pompeii's main street. Lined with shops, bars, and restaurants, it was a lively, pedestrian-only zone.

The three "beaver-teeth" stones are traffic barriers that kept chariots out. On the corner at the start of the street (just to the left), take a close look at the dark travertine column standing next to the white one. Notice that the marble drums of the white column are not chiseled entirely round—another construction project left unfinished when Vesuvius erupted.

• *Our tour will eventually end a few blocks down Via Abbondanza after making a big loop. But now, head toward Vesuvius, cutting across the Forum. To the left of the Temple of Jupiter is the...*

The Eruption of Vesuvius

At about 1:00 in the afternoon on August 24, AD 79, Mount Vesuvius erupted, sending a mushroom cloud of ash, dust, and rocks 12 miles into the air. It spewed for 18 hours straight, as winds blew the cloud southward. The white-gray ash settled like a heavy snow on Pompeii, its weight eventually collapsing roofs and floors, but leaving the walls intact. And though most of Pompeii's 20,000 residents fled that day, about 2,000 stayed behind.

Although the city of Herculaneum was closer to the volcano—about four miles away—at first it largely escaped the rain of ash, due to the direction of the wind. However, 12 hours after Vesuvius awoke, the type of eruption suddenly changed. The mountain let loose a superheated avalanche of ash, pumice, and gas. This red-hot "pyroclastic flow" sped down the side of the mountain at nearly 100 miles per hour, engulfing Herculaneum and cooking its residents alive. Several more flows over the next few hours further entombed Herculaneum, burying it in nearly 60 feet of hot material that later cooled into rock, freezing the city in time. Then, at around 7:30 in the morning, another pyroclastic flow headed south and struck Pompeii, dealing a fatal blow to those who'd remained behind.

❻ Forum Granary

A substantial stretch of the west side of the Forum was the granary and ancient produce market. Today, it houses thousands of artifacts excavated from Pompeii. You'll see lots of crockery, pots, pans, jugs, and containers used for transporting oil and wine. You'll also see casts of a couple of victims (and a dog) of the eruption. These casts show Pompeiians eerily captured in their last moments, hands covering their mouths as they gasped

for air. They were quickly suffocated by a superheated avalanche of gas and ash, and their bodies were encased in volcanic debris. While excavating, modern archaeologists detected hollow spaces underfoot, created when the victims' bodies decomposed. By gently filling the holes with plaster, the archaeologists created molds of the Pompeiians who were caught in the disaster.

A few steps to the left of the granary is a tiny alcove that contained the **Mensa Ponderaria,** a counter where standard units (such as today's liter or gallon) were used to measure the quantities of liquid and solid food that were sold. And just to the right of the granary is the remains of a public toilet. You can imagine the many seats, lack of privacy, and constantly flushing stream running through the room.

• *Exit the Forum by crossing it again in front of the Temple of Jupiter and turning left. Go under the arch. In the road are more "beaver-teeth" traffic blocks. On the pillar to the right, look for the pedestrian-only road sign (two guys carrying an amphora, or ancient jug; it's above the REG VII INS IV sign). The modern cafeteria (on the left) is the only eatery inside the archaeological site. Twenty yards past the cafeteria, on the left-hand side at #24, is the entrance to the...*

❼ Baths of the Forum (Terme del Foro)

Pompeii had six public baths, each with a men's and a women's section. You're in the men's zone. The leafy courtyard at the entrance was the gymnasium. After working out, clients could relax with a hot bath *(caldarium)*, warm bath *(tepidarium)*, or cold plunge *(frigidarium)*.

The first big, plain room you enter served as the **dressing room.** Holes on the walls were for pegs to hang clothing. High up, the window (with a faded Neptune underneath) was originally covered with a less-translucent Roman glass. Walk over the nonslip mosaics into the next room.

The ***tepidarium*** is ringed by mini statues or *telamones* (male caryatids, figures used as supporting pillars), which divided the lockers. Clients would un-dress and warm up here, perhaps relaxing on one of the bronze cow-footed benches near the bronze heater while waiting for a massage. Look at the ceil-ing—half crushed by the eruption and half intact, with its fine blue-and-white stucco work.

Next, admire the engineering in the steam-bath room, or ***caldarium.*** The double floor was heated from below—so it was nice for bare feet (look into the grate across from where you entered to see the brick support towers). The double walls with brown terra-cotta tiles held the heat. Romans soaked in the big tub, which was filled with hot water. Opposite the big tub is a fountain, which spouted water onto the hot floor, creating steam. The lettering on the fountain reminded those enjoying the room which two politi-cians paid for it...and how much it cost them. (On the far right, the Roman numerals indicate they paid 5,250 *sestertii*). To keep condensation from dripping annoyingly from the ceiling, fluting (ribbing) was added to carry water down the walls.

• *Today's visitors exit the baths through the original entry (at the far end of the dressing room). Hungry? Immediately across the street (at #8) is an ancient...*

❽ Fast-Food Joint

After a bath, it was only natural to want a little snack. So, just across the street is a fast-food joint, marked by a series of rectangular marble counters. Most ancient Romans didn't cook for themselves in their tiny apartments, so to-go places like this were commonplace. The holes in the counters held the pots for food. Each container was like a thermos, with a wooden lid to keep the soup hot, the wine cool, and so on. You could dine in the

back or get your food to go. Notice the groove in the front doorstep and the holes out on the curb. The holes likely accommodated cords for stretching awnings over the sidewalk to shield the clientele from the hot sun, while the grooves were for the shop's folding accordion doors. Look at the wheel grooves in the pavement, worn down through centuries of use. Nearby are more stepping-stones for pedestrians to cross the flooded streets.

• *Just a few steps uphill from the fast-food joint, at #5 (behind a glass wall), is the...*

❾ House of the Tragic Poet (Casa del Poeta Tragico)

This house is typical Roman style. The entry is flanked by two family-owned shops (each with a track for a collapsing accordion door). The home is like a train running straight away from the street: atrium (with skylight and pool to catch the rain), den (where deals were made by the shopkeeper), and garden (with rooms facing it and a shrine to remember both the gods and family ancestors). In the entryway is the famous "Beware of Dog" *(Cave Canem)* mosaic.

When it's open, today's visitors enter the home by the back door (circle around to the left). On your way there, look for the modern exposed pipe on the left side of the lane; this is the same as ones used in the ancient plumbing system, hidden beneath the raised sidewalk. The richly frescoed dining room is off the garden. Diners lounged on their couches (the Roman custom) and enjoyed frescoes with fake "windows," giving the illusion of a bigger and airier room. Next to the dining room is a humble BBQ-style kitchen with a little closet for the toilet (the kitchen and bathroom shared the same plumbing).

• *Return to the fast-food place and continue about 10 yards downhill to the big intersection. From the center of the intersection, look left to see a giant arch, framing a nice view of Mount Vesuvius.*

⑩ Aqueduct Arch—Running Water

Water was critical for this city of 20,000 people, and this arch was part of Pompeii's water-delivery system. A 100-mile-long aque-

duct carried fresh water down from the hillsides to a big reservoir perched at the highest point of the city wall. Since overall water pressure was disappointing, Pompeiians built arches like the brick one you see here (originally covered in marble) with hidden water tanks at the top. Located just below the altitude of the main tank, these smaller tanks were filled by gravity and provided each neighborhood with reliable pressure. Look closely at the arch and you'll see 2,000-year-old pipes (made of lead imported all the way from Cornwall in Britannia) embedded deep in the brick.

If there was a water shortage, democratic priorities prevailed: First the baths were cut off, then the private homes. The last to go were the public fountains, where all citizens could get drinking and cooking water.

• *If you're thirsty, fill your water bottle from the modern fountain. Then turn right and continue straight downhill one block (50 yards), to #2 on the left.*

⑪ House of the Faun (Casa del Fauno)

Stand across the street and marvel at the grand entry with *"HAVE"* (hail to you) as a welcome mat. Go in. Notice the two shrines above the entryway—one dedicated to the gods, the other to this wealthy family's ancestors. (Contemporary Neapolitans still carry on this practice; you'll notice little shrines embedded in walls all over Naples.)

You are standing in Pompeii's largest home, where you're greeted by the delightful small bronze **statue of**

the *Dancing Faun,* famed for its realistic movement and fine pro-portion. (The original is in Naples' Archaeological Museum.) With 40 rooms and 27,000 square feet, the House of the Faun covers an entire city block. Just think of how vibrant and luxurious this house would have seemed before the eruption.

At the far end of the first garden is the famous floor mosaic of the *Battle of Alexander.* (The original is also at the museum in Naples.) In 333 BC, Alexander the Great beat Darius and the Per-sians. Romans had much respect for Alexander, the first great em-peror before Rome's. While most of Pompeii's nouveau riche had notoriously bad taste and stuffed their palaces with over-the-top, mismatched decor, this guy had class. Both the faun (an ancient copy of a famous Greek statue) and the Alexander mosaic show an appreciation for history.

The house's back courtyard is lined with pillars rebuilt after the AD 62 earthquake. Take a close look at the brick, mortar, and fake-marble stucco veneer.

• *Leave the House of the Faun through its back door in the far-right corner, past a tiny guard's station. (If closed, exit out the front and walk around to the back.) Turn right and walk about a block until you see metal cages over the sidewalk protecting exposed stretches of ancient lead water pipes. Continue east and take your first left, walking about 20 yards to the entrance (on your left) to the...*

⑫ House of the Vettii

This is Pompeii's best-preserved home, retaining many of its mosa-ics and frescoes. The House of the Vettii was the bachelor pad of two wealthy merchant brothers. In the entryway, it's hard to miss the huge erection. This was not pornography. This was a symbol of success: The penis and sack of money balance each other on the goldsmith scale above a fine bowl of fruit. Translation? Only with a balance of fertility and money can you enjoy true abundance.

Step into the atrium with its replica wooden ceiling open to the sky and a lead pipe to collect water for the house cistern. The pool was flanked by two large moneyboxes (one survives, the foot-print of the other shows how it was secured to the ground). The brothers wanted all who entered to know how successful they were. A variety of rooms give an intimate peek at elegant Pompeiian life. The dark room to the right of the entrance (as you face out) is filled with exquisite frescoes. Notice more white "cat's eye" stones embedded in the floor. Imagine these glinting like little eyes as the brothers and their friends wandered around by oil lamp late at night, with their sacks of gold, bowls of fruit, and enormous...egos.

• *Our next stop, the Bakery, is located about 150 yards south (downhill) from here. To get there, return to the street in front of the House of the Vettii. Walk downhill along Vicolo dei Vetti. Go one block, to where you dead-end at a T-intersection with Via della Fortuna. Go a few steps left and then right at the first corner. Continue down this gently curving road to #22 (on the left).*

⓭ Bakery and Mill

The stubby stone towers are flour grinders. Grain was poured into the top and donkeys or slaves, treading in a circle, pushed wooden bars that turned the stones that ground the grain. The powdered grain dropped out the bottom as flour—flavored with tiny bits of rock. Nearby, the thing that looks like a modern-day pizza oven was...a brick oven. Each neighborhood had a bakery just like this.

• *Continue down the curvy road to the next intersection. As you walk consider the destructive power of all the plants and vines that you see around. Also, notice the chariot grooves worn into the pavement. When the curvy road reaches the intersection with Via degli Augustali, turn left. Ahead, in 50 yards, at #44 (on the left), is the **Taberna Hedones**, an ancient tavern with an original floor mosaic still intact.*

Our next stop is the site's most popular attraction. (Consequently, even though it's just 50 yards from here, we'll have to circle all the way around to reach it from the other side.) Proceed beyond the Taberna Hedones and turn right at the next big street. Follow it downhill, turning right when you reach the wide Via Abbondanza (this is the "main drag" we saw higher up, earlier). Walk along here, passing the entrance to #8 (Terme Stabiane) and carrying on a bit farther. Eventually you'll come to a narrow lane on the right where there's usually a big commotion of visitors. Head up here and get in line to enter #18—one of many Pompeii brothels.

⓮ Brothel (Lupanare)

You'll find the biggest crowds in Pompeii at a place that was likely also quite popular 2,000 years ago—the brothel. Prostitutes were nicknamed *lupe* (she-wolves), alluding to the call they made when attracting business. The brothel was a simple place, with beds and pillows made of stone and then covered with mattresses. The ancient graffiti includes tallies and exotic names of the sex workers, indicating how they came from all corners of the Mediterranean (it also served as feedback from satisfied customers). The faded frescoes above the cells may have been a kind of menu for services offered. Note the idealized women (white, which was considered beautiful; one wears an early bra) and the rougher men (dark, considered horny). The bed legs came with little disk-like barriers to keep critters from crawling up, the tiny rooms had curtains for doors, and the prostitutes provided sheepskin condoms.

• *Leaving the brothel, go right, then take the first left, and continue going downhill two blocks to return to Via Abbondanza. This walk is over.*

*The **Forum**—and exit—are to the right. If you exit now, you'll be* *routed through the shop and the **Antiquarium**—a fine museum with a variety of artifacts, on three floors, from ancient Pompeii. While all the best stuff is in Naples' Archaeological Museum, here you can see a few frescoes, pottery, statues, and other decor. The most interesting things here are several more casts of Pompeiians frozen in time (plus a horse).*

The Rest of the Archaeological Site

These extra stops are worth the time and energy (if you have any left). To locate them, refer to your map. You can weave them together easily, starting by heading left down Via Abbondanza.

Temple of Isis

This temple served Pompeii's Egyptian community. The little white stucco shrine with the modern plastic roof housed holy water from the Nile. Isis, from Egyptian myth, was one of many foreign gods adopted by the eclectic Romans. Pompeii must have had a synagogue, too, but it has yet to be excavated.

Theater

Originally a Greek theater (Greeks built theirs with the help of a hillside), this was the birthplace of the Greek port here in 470 BC. During Roman times, the theater sat 5,000 people in three sets of seats, all with different prices: the five marble terraces up close (filled with romantic wooden seats for two), the main section, and the cheap nosebleed section (surviving only on the high end, near the trees). The square stones above the cheap seats once supported a canvas rooftop. The high-profile boxes, flanking the stage, were for guests of honor. From this perch, you can see the gladiator barracks—the colonnaded courtyard beyond the theater. They lived in tiny rooms, trained in the courtyard, and fought in the nearby amphitheater. Check out the adjacent and well-preserved smaller Teatro Piccolo.

House of Menander (Casa di Menandro)

Once owned by a wealthy Pompeiian, this house takes its current name from a fresco of the Greek playwright Menander on one of the walls. Admire the grand atrium (with frescoes depicting scenes from Homer's *Iliad* and *Odyssey,* and an altar to the family gods), the wall frescoes, and the mosaics. The cloister-like back courtyard leads to a room with skeletons (not plaster casts) of eruption victims from this house. Farther back, a passage leads to the servants' quarters.

Viewpoint

You're at ground level—post eruption. To the right (inland), the farmland shows how locals lived on top of the ruins for centuries without knowing what was underneath. To the left, you can see the entire ancient city of Pompeii spread out in front of you and appreciate the magnitude of the excavations.

Garden of the Fugitives

There's no better reminder in Pompeii of the horror caused by a volcanic eruption (and how we all might act given the same circumstances) than this "garden." Archaeologists identified this house as belonging to a middle-class merchant family. Plaster casts of this fleeing ("fugitive") family are placed exactly as the bodies were found after the eruption: lined up in single file as they attempted to escape several cubic feet of already fallen ash. Their exit was stopped by a sudden wave of hot gas and volcanic material, likely traveling over 100 miles per hour. Frozen in time, servants cannot be distinguished from their masters.

Amphitheater

If you can, climb to the upper level of the amphitheater (though the stairs are often blocked). With Vesuvius looming in the background, mentally replace the tourists below with gladiators and wild animals locked in combat. Walk along the top of the amphitheater and look down into the grassy rectangular area surrounded by columns. This is the **Palaestra,** an area once used for athletic training. (If you can't get to the top of the amphitheater, you can see the Palaestra from outside—in fact, you can't miss it, as it's right next door.) Facing the other way, look for the bell tower that tops the roofline of the modern city of Pompei, where locals go about their daily lives in the shadow of the volcano, just as their ancestors did 2,000 years ago.

• *If it's too crowded to bear hiking back along uneven lanes to the entrance, you can slip out the site's "back door," next to the amphitheater. Exiting, turn right and follow the site's wall all the way back to the entrance (see map on page 1017).*

Or, to head directly to the Archaeological Museum in Naples, consider this alternative: Exit here, turn left, walk to the big church tower in the center of modern Pompei, turn right, and carry on down to the train station. Here you can catch a Trenitalia Metropolitana train (described earlier) that will take you, in about 50 minutes, directly to the Piazza Cavour Metro stop in downtown Naples—just a five-minute walk from the museum.

Herculaneum

Smaller, less crowded, and not as ruined as its famous big sister, Herculaneum (worth ▲▲, Ercolano in Italian—also the name of the modern town) offers a closer, more intimate peek into ancient Roman life. It lacks the grandeur of Pompeii (there's barely a colonnade), but it's a refreshingly uncrowded "Back Door" alternative to its more famous sibling.

GETTING TO HERCULANEUM

Ercolano Scavi, the nearest train station to Herculaneum, is about 20 minutes from Naples and 50 minutes from Sorrento on the same Circumvesuviana train that goes to Pompeii (for details on the Circumvesuviana, see page 1008; Trenitalia trains stop in Ercolano at a station that's farther from the site, and isn't recommended).

Walking from the Ercolano Scavi train station to the ruins takes 10 minutes: Leave the station and turn right, then left down the main drag; continue straight, eight blocks gradually downhill to the end of the road, where you'll run right into the grand arch that marks the entrance to the ruins. (Skip Museo MAV.) Pass through the arch and continue 200 yards down the path—taking in the bird's-eye first impression of the site to your right—to the ticket office in the modern building.

ORIENTATION TO HERCULANEUM

Cost: €13, covered by the Campania ArteCard (see page 952). Avoid crowded free entry days (usually once a month on a Sunday).

Hours: Daily mid-March-mid-Oct 9:30-19:30, off-season 8:30-17:00, ticket office closes 1.5 hours earlier.

Information: +39 081 777 7008, http://ercolano.beniculturali.it.

Closures: Like Pompeii, various sections of Herculaneum can be closed unexpectedly.

Tours: The audioguide provides more information, but it's pricey (€10, €16 for 2, ID required); this book's tour covers the basics for a targeted visit.

Length of This Tour: Allow two hours, including time to visit the Antiquarium museum.

Baggage Storage: Herculaneum is harder than Pompeii for those with luggage, but not impossible. Herculaneum's train station has lots of stairs and no baggage storage, but you can roll wheeled luggage down to the ruins and store it for free in a locked area in the ticket office building (pick up bags at least 30 minutes prior to site closing). To get back to the station, consider splurging on a €5 taxi (ask the staff to call one for you).

Services: There's a free WC in the ticket office building, and others near the site entry.

Eating: Vending machines and café tables are near the entry to the site. There are also several eateries on the way from the train station.

● SELF-GUIDED TOUR

Caked and baked by the same AD 79 eruption that pummeled Pompeii (see sidebar on page 1024), Herculaneum is a small community of intact buildings with plenty of surviving detail. While Pompeii was initially smothered in ash, Herculaneum was spared at first—due to the direction of the wind—but got slammed about 12 hours after the eruption started by a superheated ava-

lanche of ash and hot gases roaring off the volcano. The city was eventually buried under nearly 60 feet of ash, which hardened into tuff, perfectly preserving the city until excavations began in 1748.

After leaving the ticket building, go through the turnstiles and walk the path below the site to the entry point. Look seaward and note where the shoreline is today; before the eruption, it was where you are standing, a quarter-mile inland. This gives you a sense of how much volcanic material piled up. The present-day city of Ercolano looms just above the ruins. The modern buildings don't look much different from their ancient counterparts.

• *Before entering the site, watch on your left for two buildings that house worthwhile museums. The bigger one (farther along) is the most worthwhile.*

Antiquarium: This houses some stunning original pieces from Herculaneum (you'll see replicas of some of these as we tour the site), as well as several slice-of-life items that help capture what ordinary life might have been like here 2,000 years ago. The exhibit ("Splendori da Ercolano") was intended to be temporary, but it appears to be semi-permanent—so hopefully you'll find these items:

As you enter, you face the **Hydra of Lerna,** a sculpted bronze fountain that features the seven-headed monster defeated by Hercules—the city's namesake—as one of his 12 labors. Beyond that, **Room 1** displays the original marble deer from the House of the Deer; a marble statue of Demeter; a detailed statue of Bacchus from the blacksmith's shop; and several small everyday items. Circling into **Room 2**, you see even more items that help resurrect life at ancient Herculaneum. Look for the tiny, precise surgeon's tools (a row of scalpels); a very rusty key; and a carbonized rope and wicker basket. You'll also find jewelry, including golden snake bracelets, amulets, and combs. Finally, in **Room 3**, you'll see a carbonized wooden table, juxtaposed with a (replica) fresco showing a very similar table in an ancient home. Another fresco shows a wealthy woman being dressed for the day, displayed with actual pieces of jewelry and perfume bottles.

• *There's one more, very compact museum (the small, red-brick building just before the Antiquarium), the...*

Boat Exhibit (Padiglione Barca): In this space you'll find an ancient, 30-foot, wooden fishing boat (with three sets of oars on each side) that was found on the beach in front of Herculaneum in 1982.

• *Now let's head into Herculaneum itself.*

Herculaneum Excavation Site: Go down the stairs and cross the modern bridge into the site, looking down into the moat-like **ditch.** On one side, you see Herculaneum's seafront wall. On the other is the wall that you just walked on, a solidified ash layer from the volcano that shows how deeply the town was buried.

After crossing the bridge, stroll straight up the **street.** As at Pompeii, Herculaneum's streets were ruts that sat well below the sidewalk level, so they could be flushed easily with water for quick cleaning. You can duck into any number of houses along here, but I've called out some of the more interesting.

At the end of the street find the **College of the Augustali** (Sede degli Augustali, #24). Decorated with frescoes of Hercules (for whom this city was named), it belonged to an association of freed slaves working together to climb their way up the ladder of Roman society. Here and farther on, look around doorways and ceilings to spot ancient wood charred by the pyroclastic flows. Most buildings were made of stone, with wooden floors and beams (which were preserved here by the ash but rarely survive at ancient sites).

Leave the building through the back and go to the right, down the lane. The adjacent *thermopolium* (#19) was the Roman equivalent of a lunch counter or fast-food joint, with giant jars for wine, oil, and snacks. Most of the buildings along here were shops, with apartments above.

A few steps on, the **Bottega ad Cucumas** wine shop (#14, on the right) still has charred remains of beams, and its drink list remains frescoed on the outside wall (under glass).

Take the next right, go halfway down the street, and on the left find the **House of Neptune and Amphitrite** (Casa di Nettuno e Anfitrite, #7). Outside, notice the intact upper floor and imagine it going even higher. Inside, you'll see vivid, intact mosaics and a unique "frame" made of shells.

Back outside, continue downhill to the intersection, then head left for a block and proceed straight across the street into the don't-miss-it **sports complex** (*palaestra;* #4). First you'll see a row of "marble" columns, which (look closer) are actually made of rounded bricks covered with a thick layer of plaster, shaped to look like carved marble. While important buildings in Rome had solid marble columns, these imitations are typical of ordinary buildings.

Continuing deeper into the complex, look for the hole in the hillside and walk through one of the triangular-shaped entrances to find a replica of the **Hydra of Lerna** (the original is in the Antiquarium).

Return through the sports complex and turn downhill. Just before the path goes underground, on the right, is the **House of the Deer** (Casa dei Cervi, #21). It's named for the statues of deer being attacked by dogs in the garden courtyard (these are copies; the originals are in the Antiquarium). As you wander through the rooms, notice the colorfully frescoed walls. Ancient Herculaneum, like all Roman cities of that age, was filled with color, rather than the stark white we often imagine (even the statues were painted).

You can see more of these colors, this time bright orange, across the street in the **House of Relief of Telephus** (Casa del Rilievo del Telefo, #2).

Continue downhill through the archway. The **Suburban Baths** illustrate the city's devastation (Terme Suburbane, #3; enter near the side of the statue on the terrace, sometimes closed). After you descend into the baths, look back at the steps. You'll see the original wood charred in the disaster, protected by the wooden planks you just walked on. At the bottom of the stairs, in the waiting room to the right, notice where the floor collapsed under the sheer weight of the volcanic debris. (The sunken pavement reveals the baths' heating system: hot air generated by wood-burning furnaces and circulated between the different levels of the floor.) A doorway in front of the stairs is still filled with solidified ash. Despite the damage, elements of refinement remain intact, such as the delicate stuccoes in the *caldarium* (hot bath).

Back outside, make your way down the steps to the sunken area just below. As you descend, you're walking across what was formerly Herculaneum's beach. Looking back, you'll see **arches** that were part of boat storage areas. Archaeologists used to wonder why so few victims were found in Herculaneum. But during excavations in 1981, hundreds of skeletons were discovered here, between the wall of volcanic stone behind you and the city in front of you. Some of Herculaneum's 4,000 citizens tried to escape by sea, but were overtaken by the pyroclastic flows.

• *Thankfully, your escape is easier. Either follow the sound of water and continue through the tunnel (you'll climb up and pop out near the site entry), or, more scenically, backtrack and exit the same way you entered.*

Vesuvius

The 4,000-foot-high Vesuvius, mainland Europe's only active volcano, has been sleeping restlessly since 1944. While Europe has other dangerous volcanoes, only Vesuvius sits in the middle of a three-million-person metropolitan area that would be impossible to evacuate quickly.

Many tourists don't know that you can easily visit the summit. Up top, it's desolate and lunar-like, and the rocks are newly born. Walk the entire accessible part of the crater lip for the most interesting views; the far end overlooks Pompeii. Be still. Listen to the wind and the occasional cascades of rocks tumbling into the crater. Any steam? Vesuvius could blow again. (Don't worry—there'd likely be at least a few hours or days of warning.)

Note: You may need to **reserve a time slot** in advance via www.vivaticket.it (search for "Vesuvio"). If you're considering an ascent, check before you go to ensure you have the proper access.

GETTING TO VESUVIUS

By Car or Taxi: Drivers take the exit *Torre del Greco* and follow signs to *Vesuvio*. Just drive to the end of the road and pay to park. A taxi costs €90 round-trip from Naples, including a 2-hour wait; it's about €70 from Pompeii.

By Bus from Pompeii: From near the Pompei Scavi train station on the Circumvesuviana line (just outside the main entrance to the Pompeii ruins), you have three bus services to choose from, each taking about three hours (40 minutes up, 40 minutes down, and about 1.5 hours at the summit).

The cheapest option is the **public bus** operated by EAV (€3.10 each way, pay on board, 8/day, blue bus departs from in front of train station).

The old-fashioned **Vesuvius Trolley Tram** (Tramvia del Vesuvio) uses the main road up (€25 round-trip plus €12 summit admission, 6/day, tickets sold at and tram departs from Pompei Scavi train station, +39 081 777 3247, www.tramvianapoli.com).

Busvia del Vesuvio winds you up a bumpy back road to the crater rim (Via Boscotrecase) in a cross between a shuttle bus and a monster truck. The walk up to the rim at the end is about the same, but you approach it from the other direction. It's a fun, more scenic way to go, but not for the easily queasy (€22 includes summit admission, hourly April-Oct Mon-Sat 9:00-15:00, until later June-Aug, buy tickets at "info point" at Pompei Scavi train station, www.busviadelvesuvio.com).

By Bus from Herculaneum: The quickest trip up is on the **Vesuvio Express.** These small buses leave from the Ercolano Scavi train station (on the Circumvesuviana line, where you get off for the Herculaneum ruins; €10 round-trip plus €12 summit admission, daily from 9:30, runs every 45 minutes based on demand, 20 minutes each way—about 2.5 hours total, office on square in front of train station, +39 081 777 76 52, www.vesuvioexpress.it).

ORIENTATION TO VESUVIUS

Cost and Hours: €12 covers national park entry and the park guide's orientation; may need to prebook at www.vivaticket.it (search for "Vesuvio")—arrive within 30 minutes before or after your appointed time or you won't be let in; ticket office open daily July-Aug 9:00-18:00, April-June and Sept until 17:00, closes earlier off-season. Bad weather can occasionally close the trail.

Information: The ticket office is 200 yards downhill from the parking lot. +39 081 865 3911, www.vesuviopark.it (official site) or www.guidevesuvio.it (more helpful site run by guides).

When to Go: Early morning visitors enjoy the freshest air and snare the best parking spots. The mountain is open all year, but spring and fall are the most comfortable times to visit. Yellow broom flowers blossom in May and June.

VISITING VESUVIUS

Bring sunscreen, water, a light jacket in summer, and a hat and warm coat in winter. By bus, taxi, or private car, you'll reach the volcano crater up a good but windy road from Torre del Greco (between Herculaneum and Pompeii). As you drive up, you'll pass the remnants of the pre-AD 79 mountain (on your left, now called Monte Somma) and lava flows from the most recent 1944 eruption. No matter how you travel up, you'll land at the parking lot.

Backtrack 200 yards downhill to enter the site. Use the pay WC, as there's none at the summit. From the parking lot, it's a moderately steep half-mile, 25-minute hike (with a 600-foot elevation gain) up a dirt access road to the top. Say "no thank you" to the gentleman passing out walking sticks in return for a tip—you don't need one.

At the rim, a sweeping view of the Bay of Naples is on your right; on your left, fenced off, there's a fearsome drop into the crater. Mountain guides orient you and then set you free.

SORRENTO & CAPRI

Just an hour south of Naples, serene Sorrento makes an ideal home base for exploring this fascinating region. From this easy-to-enjoy town, you can take day trips to Naples, Pompeii, the Amalfi Coast, the Greek temples at Paestum, and the romantic island of Capri. And every night you can return "home" to Sorrento, to enjoy its elegant strolling scene and sort through its many fine restaurant options.

Sorrento

Wedged on a ledge under the mountains and over the Mediterranean, spritzed by lemon and olive groves, Sorrento is an attractive resort of 20,000 residents and, in summer, just as many tourists. It's as well located for regional sightseeing as it is a fine place to stay and stroll. The Sorrentines have gone out of their way to create a relaxed place for tourists to come and spend money. As 90 percent of the town's economy is tourism, everyone seems to speak fluent English and work for the Chamber of Commerce. This gateway to the Amalfi Coast has a pedestrianized old quarter, lively shopping streets, and a spectacular cliffside setting. Residents are proud of the many world-class romantics who've vacationed here, such as famed tenor Enrico Caruso, who chose Sorrento as the place to spend his last months.

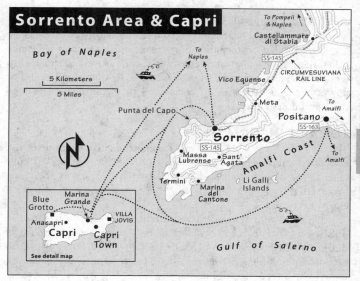

PLANNING YOUR TIME

Sorrento itself has no world-class sights, but it can easily give you a few pleasant hours. More importantly, Sorrento is a fine base for visiting nearby destinations, all reachable within an hour or so: Naples (by boat or train); Pompeii, Herculaneum, and Mount Vesuvius (by train, plus a bus for Vesuvius); the Amalfi Coast (by bus or boat); and the island of Capri (just 30 minutes by boat).

Sorrento hibernates in winter. Many places close down in November—others after the New Year—and stay closed until the town reawakens in March.

Orientation to Sorrento

Downtown Sorrento is long and narrow. Piazza Tasso marks the town's center. The main drag, Corso Italia, runs parallel to the sea through Piazza Tasso and then out toward the cape, where the road's name becomes Via Capo. Nearly everything mentioned here (except Marina Grande and the hotels on Via Capo) is within a 10-minute walk of the station. The town is perched on a cliff (some hotels have elevators down to sundecks on the water); the best real beaches are a couple of miles away.

Sorrento has two separate port areas. Marina Piccola is a functional harbor with boats to Naples and Capri, as well as cruise-ship tenders. Despite its name, Marina Grande, below the other end of downtown is a little fishing enclave, with recommended restaurants and more charm.

SORRENTO & CAPRI

TOURIST INFORMATION

The TI's two "Ask Me" InfoPoints are at the **train station** (in the converted caboose out front; daily 10:00-13:00 & 16:00-19:00, closed Nov-March) and on **Piazza Tasso** at #25, under the clock tower (slightly longer hours). They have maps and can help with basic questions.

Unless it's off-season, there's rarely any reason to trek to the TI's head office, in the entryway to the recommended **Terrazza delle Sirene** view restaurant (Mon-Sat 9:00-19:00, Sun until 18:00 except closed Sun April-May; Nov-March Mon-Fri 8:30-16:00, closed Sat-Sun; Via Luigi de Maio 35, +39 081 807 4033, http://incampania.com).

The privately run website SorrentoInsider.com also has lots of good practical information.

ARRIVAL IN SORRENTO

By Train or Bus: Sorrento is the last stop on the Circumvesuviana train line from Naples. In front of the train station is the town's main bus stop, as well as taxis waiting to overcharge you (€15 minimum). All recommended hotels—except those on Via Capo—are within a 10-minute walk. (For details on taking the bus to Via Capo, see "Sleeping in Sorrento," later.) As you exit the station, the huge mural to your left, at the end of the street, shows beloved Italian singer-songwriter Lucio Dalla, who died in 2012.

By Boat: Passenger boats and cruise-ship tenders dock at Marina Piccola. From there it's a short, steep walk up to the town center. I like to ride the elevator up; it's to the right, about a five-minute walk along the base of the cliff (follow *lift/acensore* signs, €1.10, www.sorrentolift.it; faster, cheaper, and more predictable than a bus). The elevator takes you to the Villa Comunale city park. Exit through the park's iron gate and bear left; Piazza Tasso is about four blocks away. With a bit more bother, minibuses from the port can take you up to town (buy €1.30 ticket at newsstand or tobacco shop, look for stop marked *Fermata Riservata/EAV Bus*, ask driver to drop you at or near Piazza Tasso); for more on buses, see "Getting Around Sorrento," later. You can also climb the stairs from the port.

By Car: The public Achille Lauro underground parking garage is centrally located, just a couple of blocks in front of the train station, and good for a short stay (€2/hour for first 3 hours, then €3/hour, €51/24 hours, on Via Correale). Overnight rates are lower at other garages (around €30), such as the Autoparco Vallone dei Mulini, across from the recommended Hotel Antiche Mura.

HELPFUL HINTS

SORRENTO & CAPRI

Church Services: At Santa Maria delle Grazie (perhaps the most beautiful Baroque church in town), cloistered nuns sing from above and out of sight during a Mass each morning at 7:30 (on Via Santa Maria delle Grazie at Piazza Sant'Antonino).

Baggage Storage: The underground parking lot Parcheggio de Curtis, just downhill from the train station, moonlights as a convenient place to store luggage (daily 7:30-23:30, shorter hours off-season, Via E. de Curtis 5, just before Corsa Italia).

Laundry: A handy 24-hour self-service launderette, **Rosy Laundry,** is a 10-minute walk past the train station (daily, Corso Italia 321g, across from Esso gas station, +39 331 912 1122).

Haircuts: A fun hair salon for men, **Satisfhair,** is run by hairless Luca and Tony and makes for a happy memory (€19 for a good cut, closed Sun-Mon, Via S. Maria della Pieta 17, +39 081 878 3476).

Guided Tours of Pompeii, Naples, the Amalfi Coast, and Capri: Naples-based **Mondo Guide** offers affordable tours of these destinations, including an Amalfi Coast drive that starts from Sorrento (meet in front of the Hotel Antiche Mura; kindly do not use hotel facilities if you are not a guest). You'll team up with fellow Rick Steves readers to split the cost. For details, see page 962.

Local Guides: For excursions around Sorrento and to Amalfi, **Giovanna Donadio** is a knowledgeable, upbeat guide (€120/half-day, €180/day, same price for any size group, +39 338 466 0114, giovanna_dona@hotmail.com). She does a food-themed walk, and can also escort six to eight people from Sorrento on a well-organized full day of fun on Capri (€200 plus public transportation expenses and admissions).

GETTING AROUND SORRENTO

Distances are short in Sorrento. If taking a bus seems too complicated, use the elevator, stairs, and your feet.

By Bus: Local EAV buses run from the train station (bays 7-8) to the port (Marina Piccola), the fishing village (Marina Grande), Via Capo, and Meta beach until at least 20:00 (1-3/hour, buy €1.30 ticket from tobacco shop or newsstand and stamp it on bus, drivers reluctantly sell tickets for €1.60, www.eavsrl.it). Stops are usually marked by a blue sign saying *Fermata a Richiesta* with a stylized

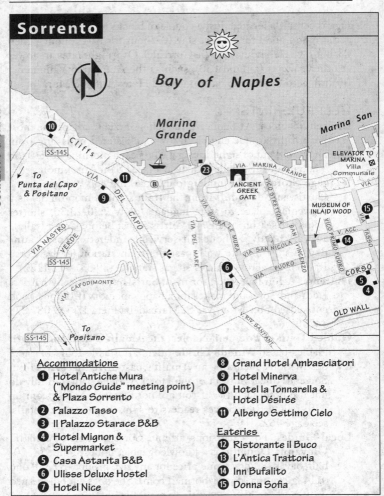

SORRENTO & CAPRI

Sorrento

Bay of Naples

Marina Grande

Marina San

To Punta del Capo & Positano

To Positano

ELEVATOR TO MARINA Villa Communale

ANCIENT GREEK GATE

MUSEUM OF INLAID WOOD

OLD WALL

Accommodations
1. Hotel Antiche Mura ("Mondo Guide" meeting point) & Plaza Sorrento
2. Palazzo Tasso
3. Il Palazzo Starace B&B
4. Hotel Mignon & Supermarket
5. Casa Astarita B&B
6. Ulisse Deluxe Hostel
7. Hotel Nice
8. Grand Hotel Ambasciatori
9. Hotel Minerva
10. Hotel la Tonnarella & Hotel Désirée
11. Albergo Settimo Cielo

Eateries
12. Ristorante il Buco
13. L'Antica Trattoria
14. Inn Bufalito
15. Donna Sofia

EAV. Check the destination display on the front of the bus (*Porto* for Marina Piccola, *Stazione* for the train station, *Massa Lubrense* for Via Capo hotels), wave to flag down the driver, and let them know where you are going.

By Scooter: Several places near the station rent motor scooters for about €35 per day, including **Europcar** (Corso Italia 210p, +39 081 878 1386, www.sorrento.it) and **Penisola Rent** (Piazza Lauro 44, +39 081 362 2189, www.penisolarent.com). Don't rent a vehicle in summer unless you enjoy traffic jams.

By Taxi: Taxis line up at the station and Piazza Tasso, but even short rides in town will cost at least €15-20. Thanks to traffic and one-way roads, you'll get to most central locations faster by

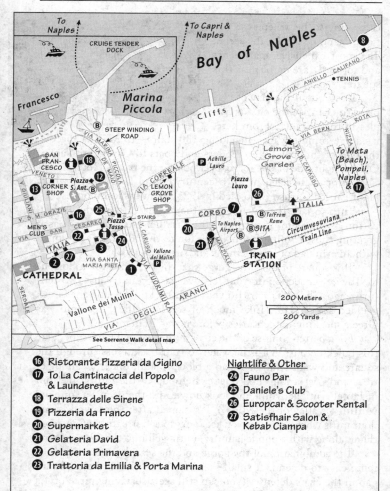

16 Ristorante Pizzeria da Gigino

17 To La Cantinaccia del Popolo & Launderette

18 Terrazza delle Sirene

19 Pizzeria da Franco

20 Supermarket

21 Gelateria David

22 Gelateria Primavera

23 Trattoria da Emilia & Porta Marina

<u>Nightlife & Other</u>

24 Fauno Bar

25 Daniele's Club

26 Europcar & Scooter Rental

27 Satisfhair Salon & Kebab Ciampa

walking. If you do use a taxi, don't ask the price, just be sure it has a meter (all official taxis do).

Sorrento Walk

Get to know Sorrento with this lazy self-guided town stroll that ends down by the waterside at the small-boat harbor, Marina Grande.

• *Begin on the main square. Stand under the flags between the sea and the town's main square...*

❶ Piazza Tasso: As in any southern Italian town, this piazza is Sorrento's living room. It may be noisy and congested, but locals want to be where the action is...and be part of the scene. The most expensive apartments and top cafés are on or near this square.

Look out at the Bay of Naples. You can see the city of Naples in the distance. From here, it's a five-minute walk—including 130 stairs—to Marina Piccola, the harbor for cruise-ship tenders and boats to Capri and Naples. On the right side of the gorge, overlooking the bay, is Hotel Excelsior Vittoria. This elegant, 19th-century Grand Tour hotel is where tenor Enrico Caruso (who died in 1921) spent his last months.

Turn to face the square. A statue of St. Anthony the Abbot, patron of Sorrento, is surrounded by traffic. He faces north as if greeting those coming from Naples (on festival days, he's equipped with an armload of fresh lemons and oranges).

This square bridges the gorge that divides downtown Sorrento. The newer section (to your left) was farm country just two centuries ago. The older part (to your right) retains its ancient Greek gridded street plan. (Like much of southern Italy, Sorrento was Greek-speaking for centuries before it was Romanized.)

For a better glimpse of the city's gorge-gouged landscape, take this quick detour: With the water to your back, cross through the square and walk straight ahead a block inland, under a canopy of trees and past a long taxi queue. Belly up to the railing in front of Hotel Antiche Mura and look down into the deep **Vallone dei Mulini** ("Valley of the Mills"). It's named after the sawmills and flour mills whose remains you see, next to the stream that powered them (along with a public laundry) until well into the 19th century.

The combination of the gorge and the seaside cliffs made Sorrento easy to defend. A small section of wall closed the landward gap in the city's defenses (you can still see a surviving piece of it a few blocks away, near Hotel Mignon).

Sorrento's name may come from the Greek word for "siren," the legendary half-bird, half-woman that sang an intoxicating lullaby. According to Homer, the sirens lived on an island near here. All those who sailed by the sirens succumbed to their incredible musical charms...and to death when they shipwrecked on the island. But Homer's hero Ulysses was determined to hear the song and restrain his manhood. He put wax in his oarsmen's ears and had himself lashed to the mast of his ship and survived their song. The sirens, thinking they had lost their powers, threw themselves into the sea, and the place became safe to inhabit. Ulysses' odyssey was all about the westward expansion of Greek culture, and to the ancient Greeks, places like Sorrento were the wild, wild west.

Sorrento Walk

Bay of Naples

To Naples

CRUISE TENDER DOCK

To Capri & Naples

200 Meters
200 Yards

Marina Piccola

Marina San Francesco

Cliffs

VIA MARINA PICCOLA

VIA DE MAIO

STEEP WINDING ROAD

ELEVATOR TO MARINA PICCOLA

To Marina Grande

Villa Comunale Park

Piazza d. Vittoria

To ⑩

WALK ENDS

⑨

VIA S. FRANCESCO

VIA PR. GIULIANI

V. DONORSO

SAN FRANCESCO

TERRAZZA DELLE SIRENE

Piazza S. Ant.

SANT' ANTONIO

⑧

CORNER SHOP

STA. MARIA DELLE GRAZIE

VIA D. ARCHI

VIA CORREALE

LEMON GROVE SHOP

To Train Station

STAIRS

CORSO ITALIA

VIA PAOLO

VIA S. M. GRAZIE

MUSEUM OF INLAID WOOD

V. ACC.

VIA

SAN

⑦

VIA D. CESAREO

①

i

②

Piazza Tasso
WALK BEGINS

VIA TASSO

⑥

⑤

③

VIA S.M. PIETA

PALAZZO CORREALE

P *Vallone dei Mulini*

VICO PRIMO FUORO

④

CATHEDRAL

SAN VINCENZO

CORSO ITALIA

V. BERSALE

VIC. SANT'ANIELLO

HOTEL ANTICHE MURA

OLD WALL

Vallone dei Mulini

ARANCI

To Punta del Capo & Positano

VIA DEGLI

To Meta (Beach), Pompeii & Naples

N

SORRENTO & CAPRI

① Piazza Tasso
② Statue of Torquato Tasso
③ Via Santa Maria della Pietà
④ Cathedral
⑤ Corso Italia & Old Town
⑥ Sorrento Men's Club
⑦ Via San Cesareo
⑧ Statue & Basilica of St. Anthony the Abbot
⑨ Villa Comunale
⑩ To Ancient Greek Gate & Marina Grande

• *Back at Piazza Tasso, head to the far-left inland corner of the square. You'll find a...*

② **Statue of Torquato Tasso:** The square's namesake, a Sorrento native, was a lively Renaissance poet—but today he seems only to wonder which restaurant to choose for dinner. Directly behind the statue, pop into the **Fattoria Terranova** shop, one of many fun, family-run, and touristy boutiques. They sell regional goodies and offer free biscuits and tastes of liqueurs, and the shop makes all of its organic products on an *agriturismo* outside the city. The gifty edibles spill into the courtyard of **Palazzo Correale,** at #18 next door. Duck in through the archway to get a feel for an 18th-century aristocratic palace's courtyard. Its patio walls are lined with characteristic tiles from 1772.

• *As you're leaving the courtyard, on your immediate left you'll see the narrow...*

❸ **Via Santa Maria della Pietà:** Here, just a few yards off the noisy main drag, is a street that goes back centuries before Christ. About 100 yards down the lane, at #24 (on the left), find a 13th-century palace (no balconies back then...for security reasons), now an elementary school. A few steps farther on, you'll see a tiny shrine across the street. Typical of southern Italy, it's where the faithful pray to their saint, who contacts Mary, who contacts Jesus, who contacts God. This shrine is a bit more direct—it starts right with Mary.

• *Continue down the lane (passing a recommended kebab shop and trattoria) to reach the delightful...*

❹ **Cathedral:** Walk through the wrought-iron gate, which leads to the church patio. The church is free to enter (daily 8:00-12:30 & 16:30-21:00, except during Masses). Step inside the main door and examine the impressive *intarsio* (inlaid-wood) interior doors. They show religious scenes and depict this very church. Take a cool stroll down the right-hand side of the nave, checking out the intricate inlaid Stations of the Cross. You'll find even more inlaid wood on the side entrance doors. They show scenes of the town and its industry, as well as an old-town map (find Piazza Tasso, trace the fortified walls, and notice the Greek grid street plan). These doors were made to celebrate Pope John Paul II's visit in 1992. Notice the fine inlaid-marble seat of the bishop nearby and how the church's elegance matches that of the town. Before exiting, on the right find the *presepe* (manger scene) with its lovingly painted terracotta figures, each with an expressive face. This takes Bethlehem on that first Christmas and sets it in Sorrento—with pasta, mozzarella, salami, local lemons, the gorge with the Valley of the Mills, and even Mount Vesuvius in the background.

• *Cross the open plaza—where the end of the narrow street you just walked down meets the main drag.*

❺ **Corso Italia and the Old Town:** In the evening, this traffic-free road hosts a wonderful *passeggiata*. Look up to find the cathedral bell tower, then down to see the scavenged ancient Roman columns at its base. Now go left down Via P. Reginaldo Giuliani, following the old Greek street plan. Locals claim the ancient Greeks laid out the streets east-west for the most sunlight and north-south for the prevailing and cooling breeze. Pause at the poster board on your right to see who's died lately. Traditionally, Italian women wore black when a relative died (1 year for an uncle, aunt, or sibling; 2-3 years for a husband or parent). Men got off easy, just wearing a black memorial button.

• *One block ahead, on your right, the 14th-century loggia (called Sedil Dominova) is home to the...*

❻ **Sorrento Men's Club:** Once the meeting place of the town's nobles, for generations now the Sedil Dominova has been a retreat

for retired working-class men. Strictly no women—and no phones.

Italian men venerate their mothers. (Italians joke that Jesus must have been a southern Italian because his mother believed her son was God, he believed his mom was a virgin, and he lived at home with her until he was 30.) But Italian men have also built into their culture ways to be on their own. Here, men play cards and gossip under a finely frescoed, 16th-century domed ceiling, with marvelous 3-D scenes.

• *Turn right for a better view of the Men's Club and a historical marker describing the building. Then continue along...*

❼ **Via San Cesareo:** This touristy pedestrian-only shopping street eventually leads back to Piazza Tasso. It's lined with competitive little shops where you can peruse (and sample) lemon products. Notice the huge ancient doorways with their tiny doors—to let the right people in, carefully, during a more dangerous age.

• *After a block, take a left onto Via degli Archi, go under the arch, and then hang a right (under another arch) to the square with the...*

❽ **Statue and Basilica of St. Anthony** (Sant'Antonino): Sorrento's town saint humbly looms among the palms, facing the basil-

ica dedicated to him (free to enter). Step inside the basilica and descend into the crypt (stairs beside main altar), where you'll find a chapel and reliquary containing a few of Anthony's bones surrounded by lots of votives.

In English he is known as St. Anthony the Abbot or St. Anthony the Great (not to be confused with the later St. Anthony of Padua). Locals have long turned to St. Anthony when faced with challenges and hard times. Exploring the room, you'll find countless tokens of appreciation to the saint for his help. Before tourism, fishing was the big employer. The back walls feature paintings of storms with Anthony coming to the rescue. Circle behind the altar with Anthony's relics and study the shiny ex-votos (religious offerings) thanking the saint for healthy babies, good employment, surviving heart attacks and lung problems, and lots of strong legs.

• *Back outside, follow the road that skirts the piazza with St. Anthony's statue (don't go down the street with the line of trees and Porto signs). Watch on the left for The Corner Shop, where Giovanni sells a wide variety of wines,* limoncello, *pastas, and other regional products. Soon after, on the right you'll see the trees in front of the Imperial Hotel Tramontano, and to their right a path leading to the...*

❾ Villa Comunale: This fine public park overlooks the harbor. Belly up to the banister to enjoy the view of Marina Piccola and the Bay of Naples. Notice Naples' skyline and the boats that commute from here to there in 35 minutes. Imagine the view in AD 79 when Vesuvius blew its top and molten mud flowed down the mountain, burying Pompeii. From here, steps zigzag down to the harbor, where lounge chairs, filled by vacationers working on tans, line the sundecks (there's also the elevator to the harbor). The Franciscan church fronting this square faces a fine modern statue of Francis across the street.

Pop through the archway next to the church to see a dreamy little **cloister.** It's local Gothic—a 13th-century mix of Norman, Gothic, and Arabic styles, all around an old pepper tree. This is an understandably popular spot for weddings and concerts.

At the left side of the cloister, stairs lead to a **photo exhibit:** *The Italians* shows off the work of local photographer Raffaele Celentano, who artfully captures classic Italian scenes from 1990 to 2016 in black and white (€5, daily 10:00 until sunset, closed Jan-Feb, great prints for sale, fun photo-op through the grand tree on their deck, www.gallery-raffaele-celentano.com).

• *From here, you can quit the walk and stay in the town center, or continue another few minutes downhill to the waterfront at Marina Grande. If you take the elevator down, the road to the right leads to Marina Piccola, where boats depart to Capri and other nearby towns. Piers and beaches to the left do not connect to the next stop on this walk.*

❿ To continue to **Marina Grande,** return to the road and keep going downhill. At the next square (Piazza della Vittoria, with a dramatic WWI memorial and another grand view), cut over to the road closest to the water. After winding steeply down for a few minutes, it turns into a wide stairway, then makes a sharp and

steep switchback (take the right fork to continue downhill). Farther down, just before reaching the waterfront, you pass under an...

Ancient Greek Gate: This gate fortified the city of Sorrento. Beyond it was Marina Grande, technically a separate town with its own proud residents—it's said that even their cats look different. Because Marina Grande dwellers lived outside the wall and were more susceptible to rape, pillage, and plunder, Sorrentines believe that they come from Saracen (pirate) stock. Sorrentines still scare their children by saying, "Behave—or the pirates will take you away."

• Now go all the way down the steps into Marina Grande, Sorrento's "big" small-boat harbor.

Marina Grande: Until recently, this little community was famously traditional, with its economy based on its fishing fleet. To this day, fathers pass their houses and fishing-boat stalls down to their sons.

Two recommended restaurants are on the harbor. **Trattoria da Emilia** has an old newspaper clipping, tacked near the door, about Sophia Loren filming here. **Porta Marina** is smaller, less fancy, and more local but with food every bit as tasty as that of its competition.

• From here, where the road hits the beach, a minibus returns to Piazza Tasso and the train station once an hour. Or you can walk back up.

Sights in Sorrento

▲▲Strolling

On balmy evenings Sorrento offers one of Italy's most enchant-

ing *passeggiata* scenes. The old-town stretch of Corso Italia is always traffic-free. Each night in summer and on weekends off-season, the police also close off the stretch east of Piazza Tasso to traffic, making

Sorrento's whole main drag a thriving people scene. The *passeggiata* peaks at about 22:00 in the warmest months. Take time to enjoy the old-town streets between Corso Italia and the sea. The views from Villa Comunale, the public park next to Imperial Hotel Tramontano, are worth the detour.

Lemon Products Galore

Via San Cesareo is lined with hardworking rival shops selling a mind-boggling array of lemon products and offering samples of lots of sour goodies. You'll find *limoncello*, lemon biscuits, lemon pasta, lemon drops, lemon chocolate, lemon perfume, lemon soap, and on and on. Poke around for a pungent experience (and read the "Lemons" sidebar, later). A few produce stands are also mixed in.

▲Lemon Grove Garden (Agruminato)

This lemon and orange grove, lined with shady, welcoming paths, was rescued from development by the city of Sorrento and turned into a park. The family that manages it has seasoned green thumbs and descends from the family that started working here decades ago, when the grove was still in private hands. The garden is dotted with benches, tables, and an inviting little tasting (and buying) stand. You'll get a chance to sniff and taste the varieties of lemons and enjoy free samples of *limoncello*, along with other homemade liqueurs made from mandarins, licorice, or fennel. Check out how they've grafted orange-tree branches onto a lemon tree so that both fruits grow on the same tree.

Cost and Hours: Free, daily 10:00 until sunset, closed in rainy weather, +39 081 878 1888, www.igiardinidicataldo.it. Enter the garden on Corso Italia (where painted tiles show lemon fantasies, across from the recommended Pizzeria da Franco at #265) or at the intersection of Via Capasso and Via Rota (next to Hotel la Meridiana).

Eating: For a cheap and relaxing meal, get a big-enough-to-split *saltimbocca* sandwich to go from the recommended **Pizzeria da Franco** (across the street on Corso Italia) and enjoy it in the lemon grove.

Nearby: The entrepreneurial family's small "factory"—where you can see how they use the lemons, and buy a tasty gelato, *granita*, or lemonade—is just west of the Achille Lauro parking garage entrance at Via Correale 27, next to a smaller lemon grove that's not open to the public.

Museum of Inlaid Wood (Museobottega della Tarsialignea)

Sorrento doesn't have much in the way of museums, but if you want to get out of the heat and crowds, this is a good place to do it. The life's work of an older couple, the museum is not only a collection

Lemons

Around here, *limoni* are ubiquitous: screaming yellow painted on ceramics, dainty bottles of *limoncello,* and lemons the size of softballs at the fruit stand.

The Amalfi Coast and Sorrento area produce several different kinds of lemons. The gigantic, bumpy "lemons" are actually citrons, called *cedri,* and are more for show—they're pulpier than they are juicy, and make a good marmalade. The juicy *sfusato sorrentino,* grown only in Sorrento, is shaped like an American football, while the *sfusato amalfitano,* with knobby points on both ends, is less juicy but equally aromatic. These two kinds of luscious lemons are used in sweets such as *granita* (shaved ice doused in lemonade), *limoncello* (a candy-like liqueur with a big kick, called *limoncino* in the Cinque Terre), *delizia al limone* (a dome of fluffy cake filled and slathered with a thick whipped lemon cream), *spremuta di limone* (fresh-squeezed lemon juice), and, of course, gelato or *sorbetto al limone.*

of inlaid wood but also a painting gallery featuring scenes of 19th-century Sorrento, antique maps, and portraits, and a fine decorative arts collection. The basement displays modern examples of inlaid wood. While pricey, it's serious, thoughtfully presented, and bursting with local pride.

Cost and Hours: €8, daily 10:00-18:30, Nov-March until 17:00, Via San Nicola 28, +39 081 877 1942, www.museomuta.it.

▲Swimming and Sunbathing

If you require immediate tanning, you can rent a chair on a pier by the port. There are no great beaches in Sorrento—the gravelly, jam-packed private beaches of **Marina Piccola** are more for partying than pampering, and there's just a tiny spot for public use. The elevator in Villa Comunale city park (next to the Church of San Francesco) gets you down for €1. There's another humble beach at **Marina Grande.**

The classic, sandy Italian beach two miles away at **Meta** is generally overrun with teenagers from Naples. The local bus goes from the station to Meta beach (last stop, schedule posted for hourly returns; you can also get there on the Circumvesuviana but the Meta stop is a very long walk from the beach). At Meta, you'll find pizzerias, snack bars, and a little free section of beach, but the place is mostly dominated by several sprawling private-beach complexes—if you go, pay for a spot in one of these, such as Lido

Metamare (lockable changing cabins, lounge chairs, +39 081 532 2505). It's a very Italian scene—locals complain that it's "too local" (that is, inundated with riffraff)—with light lunches, a playground, a manicured beach, loud pop music...and no international tourists.

More relaxing beaches are west of Sorrento. Tarzan might take Jane to the wild and stony beach at **Punta del Capo,** a 15-minute bus ride from Sorrento (on the same bus, but in the opposite direction, toward Massa Lubrense; 2/hour, get off at stop on Via Capo just after the Maxim Gorky house, then walk 10 minutes down Calata Punta del Capo, past ruined Roman Villa di Pollio).

Another good choice is **Marina di Puolo,** a tiny fishing town popular in the summer for its sandy beach, surfside restaurants, and beachfront disco (to get here, stay on the bus a bit farther beyond the Punta del Capo stop above—ask driver to let you off at Marina di Puolo—then follow signs and hike down about 15 minutes).

More Activities

Sorrento Food Tours: Tamara—a US expat with many years of experience in Italian food and wine—and her colleagues dish up a fast-paced parade of local edibles interspersed with lots of food history, stopping at eight places in three hours (€75, 15 percent discount for Rick Steves readers, use code "ricksteves"; departures at 10:30 and 16:00 with demand, maximum 14 people; +39 331 304 5666, www.sorrentofoodtours.com, info@sorrentofoodtours.com).

Motorboat Rental: You can rent motorboats big enough for four people (with your back to the ferry-ticket offices, it's to the left around the corner at Via Marina Piccola 43; +39 081 807 2283, www.nauticasicsic.com).

Nightlife in Sorrento

PUBS AND CLUBS

Sorrento is a fun place to enjoy a drink or some dancing after dinner. The crowd is older, and British vacationers have paved the way for you (many have holidayed here annually for decades). Several Irish-style pubs on Corso Italia have big screens and show European soccer.

The **Fauno Bar,** which dominates Piazza Tasso with tables spilling onto the square, is a fine place to make the scene over a drink any time of day.

Terrazza delle Sirene (also known by its old name of **Foreigners' Club**) offers live Neapolitan songs, Sinatra-style classics, and jazzy elevator music with an ocean view nightly at 20:00 throughout the summer. It's just right for old-timers feeling frisky (Via Luigi de Maio 35, entrance just past the TI, +39 081 877 3263).

Daniele's Club is run by DJ Daniele, who tailors music to the audience (including karaoke, if you ask nicely). The scene, while sloppy, is generally comfortable for the 30-to-60-year-old crowd. If you're alone, there's a pole you can dance with (no cover charge, try their signature cocktail, "Come Back to Sorrento," a mojito made with *limoncello;* no food, nightly from 21:30, down the steps from the flags at Piazza Tasso 10, +39 081 877 3992).

THEATER SHOW

At **Teatro Armida,** a hardworking troupe puts on *The Sorrento Musical,* a folk-music show that treats visitors to a schmaltzy dose of Neapolitan Tarantella music and dance—complete with "Funiculì Funiculà" and "Santa Loo-chee-yee-yah." The 75-minute Italian-language extravaganza features a cast playing guitar, mandolin, saxophone, and tambourines, and singing operatically from Neapolitan balconies...complete with Vesuvius erupting in the background. Your €30 ticket includes a drink before the show (€60 with 4-course dinner at attached Basilico Italia restaurant; RS%— Maurizio promises my readers a €5 discount if you buy directly at the box office and show this book, 2 tickets/book; shows run 3-5 nights/week May-Oct at 21:00, bar opens 30 minutes before show, dinner starts at 20:00 and must be reserved in advance—in person or by email; box office open long hours daily, theater seats 500, between Piazza Tasso and the train station at Corsa Italia 219, +39 081 877 2048, www.basilicoitalia.it, info@basilicoitalia.it).

Sleeping in Sorrento

Given the location, hotels here often have beautiful views, and many offer balconies. At hotels that offer sea views, ask for a room *"con balcone, con vista sul mare"* (with a balcony, with a sea view). *"Tranquillo"* is taken as a request for a quieter room off the street.

Hotels listed are either near the train station and city center (where balconies overlook city streets) or on cliffside Via Capo (with sea-view balconies). Via Capo is a 20-minute walk—or short bus ride—from the station.

You should have no trouble finding a room anytime except in August, when the town is jammed with Italians and prices often rise above the regular high-season rates.

IN THE TOWN CENTER

$$$$ Hotel Antiche Mura, with 50 rooms and four-star elegance, offers all the amenities, including an impressive breakfast buffet. Just a block off the main square, it's quieter than some central hotels because it's perched on the edge of a dramatic ravine. The pool and sundeck, surrounded by lemon trees, make a peaceful oasis (RS%, some rooms with balconies, family rooms, air-con, elevator, pay parking, closed Jan-mid-March, a block inland from Piazza Tasso at Via Fuorimura 7, +39 081 807 3523, www.hotelantichemura. com, info@hotelantichemura.com, Luigi).

$$$$ Palazzo Tasso, nicely located near the center, has 12 small, sleek, fashionably designed modern rooms; there's no public space and breakfast is at a nearby bar (some rooms with balconies, air-con, elevator, open all year, Via Santa Maria della Pietà 33, +39 081 807 1594, mobile +39 348 592 1019, www.palazzotasso.com, info@palazzotasso.com, Elena).

$$$$ Plaza Sorrento is a contemporary-feeling, upscale refuge in the very center of town (next door to Antiche Mura but with less expansive grounds). Its 65 rooms mix mod decor with wood grain, and the rooftop swimming pool is inviting (RS%, some rooms with balconies, air-con, elevator, closed Jan-mid-March, Via Fuorimura 3, +39 081 878 2831, www.plazasorrento.com, info@plazasorrento.com).

$$$ Il Palazzo Starace B&B, conscientiously run by Massimo, offers seven tidy, modern rooms in a little alley off Corso Italia, one block from Piazza Tasso (RS%—use code "RSWEL," some rooms with balconies, family room, air-con, lots of stairs, luggage dumbwaiter but no elevator, ring bell around corner from Via Santa Maria della Pietà 9, +39 081 807 2633, mobile +39 349 290 7932, www.palazzostarace.com, info@palazzostarace.com).

$$$ Hotel Mignon rents 22 soothing blue rooms with beautiful, tiled public spaces, a rooftop sundeck, and a small garden surrounded by a lemon grove (RS%—use code "2022RSE" on their website, most rooms have balconies but no views, air-con, closed Jan-mid-March; from the cathedral, walk a block farther up Corso Italia and look for the hotel up a small gated lane to your left; Via Sersale 9, +39 081 807 3824, www.sorrentohotelmignon.com, info@sorrentohotelmignon.com, Paolo).

$$$ Casa Astarita B&B, hiding upstairs in a big building facing the main pedestrian street, has a crazy-quilt-tiled entryway and six bright, tranquil, creatively decorated rooms (three with little balconies). Noise from a nearby bar can spill over...bring earplugs (RS%—use code "RICK23," air-con, open year-round, 50 yards past the cathedral at Corso Italia 67, +39 081 877 4906, mobile +39 331 948 9738, www.casastarita.com, info@casastarita.com, Annamaria and Alfonso).

$$$ Ulisse Deluxe Hostel is basically a hotel, with 56 well-equipped, marble-tiled rooms and elegant public areas, but it also has two single-sex dorm rooms with bunks—hence the name (RS%, family rooms, breakfast buffet extra, air-con, elevator, spa and pool use extra, pay parking, closed Jan-mid-Feb, Via del Mare 22, +39 081 877 4753, www.ulissedeluxe.com, info@ulissedeluxe. com, Chiara). It's a five-minute walk from the old-town action:

From Corso Italia, walk down the stairs just beyond the hospital *(ospedale)* to Via del Mare. Go downhill along the right side of the big parking lot to find the entrance.

$$ Hotel Nice rents 24 simple, straightforward rooms 100 yards in front of the train station on the main drag. It's worth considering only for its very handy-to-the-train-station location. Alfonso promises a quiet room—double-paned windows help dim the hum from the busy street—if you request it when you book by email (RS%, air-con, elevator, sundeck terrace, closed Nov-March, Corso Italia 257, +39 081 878 1650, www.hotelnice.it, info@hotelnice.it).

AT THE EAST END OF TOWN

$$$$ Grand Hotel Ambasciatori is a sumptuous five-star hotel with 100 rooms, a cliffside setting, a sprawling garden, and a pool. This is Humphrey Bogart land, with impressive public spaces, a relaxing stay-awhile ambience, and a free elevator to its "private beach"—actually a sundeck built out over the water (RS%, some view rooms, balconies in all rooms, air-con in summer, elevator, pay parking, closed Nov-March, Via Califano 18, +39 081 878 2025, www.ambasciatorisorrento.com, ambasciatori@manniellohotels.com). It's a short walk from the town center (10-15 minutes from the train station or Piazza Tasso).

WITH A VIEW, ON VIA CAPO

These cliffside hotels are outside of town, toward the cape of the peninsula (from the train station, go straight out Corso Italia, which turns into Via Capo). Once you're set up, commuting into town by bus or on foot is easy. Hotel Minerva is my favorite Sorrento splurge, while Hotel Désirée is a super budget bet with comparable views. If you're in Sorrento to stay put and luxuriate, especially with a car, these accommodations are perfect (although I'd rather luxuriate in Positano—see next chapter).

Getting to Via Capo: From the train station, it's a gradually uphill 20-minute walk (last part is a bit steeper), a €25 taxi ride, or a cheap bus ride (direction: Massa Lubrense). Either take the Sorrento city bus (about 2/hour), or look for one of the long-distance SITA buses that stop on Via Capo on their way to Massa Lubrense (about every 40 minutes; some buses heading for Positano/Amalfi also work—check with the driver; SITA day pass valid). Get off at the Hotel Belair stop for the hotels listed here.

Getting from Via Capo into Town: Buses work great once you get the hang of them (and it's particularly gratifying to avoid the taxi racket). To reach downtown Sorrento from Via Capo, catch any bus heading downhill from Hotel Belair (about 2/hour, buses run all day and evening). Or ask your hotel to call a taxi.

$$$$ Hotel Minerva is a sun-worshipper's temple. The road-level entrance (on a busy street) leads to an elevator that takes you to the fifth-floor reception. Getting off, you'll step onto a spectacular terrace with outrageous Mediterranean views. Bright common areas, a small rooftop swimming pool, and a cold-water Jacuzzi complement 63 large, tiled, colorful rooms with views, half with balconies (3-night peak-season minimum, air-con, pay parking, closed Dec-March, Via Capo 30, +39 081 878 1011, www.minervasorrento.com, info@minervasorrento.com).

$$$$ Hotel la Tonnarella is an old-time Sorrentine villa-turned-boutique-hotel, with several terraces, stylish tiles, and warm wood trim. Eighteen of its 24 rooms have views of the sea, and you can pay extra for a terrace (air-con, pay parking, small beach with private elevator access, closed Nov-March, Via Capo 31, +39 081 878 1153, www.latonnarella.it, info@latonnarella.it).

$$$ Albergo Settimo Cielo ("Seventh Heaven") is an old-fashioned, family-run cliffhanger sitting 300 steps above Marina Grande. The reception is just off the waterfront side of the road, and the elevator passes down through four floors with 50 clean but spartan rooms—all with grand views, and many with balconies. The rooms feel dated for the price—you're paying for the views (family rooms, air-con in summer, parking, inviting pool, sun terrace, closed Nov-March, Via Capo 27, +39 081 878 1012, www.hotelsettimocielo.com, info@hotelsettimocielo.com; Giuseppe, sons Stefano and Massimo, and daughter Serena).

$$ Hotel Désirée is more modest, with reasonable rates, humbler vistas, and no traffic noise. The 22 basic rooms have high, ravine-facing or partial-sea views, and half come with balconies (all the same price). There's a fine rooftop sunning terrace. Owner Corinna (a committed environmentalist), daughter Cassandra, and receptionist Antonio serve an organic breakfast and are helpful with tips on exploring the peninsula (family rooms, air-con, lots of stairs and no elevator, laundry services, free parking, shares driveway and beach elevator with La Tonnarella, closed early Nov-Feb except open at Christmas, Via Capo 31, +39 081 878 1563, www.desireehotelsorrento.com, info@desireehotelsorrento.com).

Eating in Sorrento

GOURMET SPLURGES

In a town proud to have no McDonald's, consider eating well for a few extra bucks. Both of these places are worthwhile splurges run by a hands-on boss with a passion for good food and exacting service. The first is gourmet and playful. The second is classic. Both are romantic. Be prepared to relax and stay awhile.

$$$$ Ristorante il Buco, once the cellar of an old monastery, is now a dressy restaurant—with spacious seating—that serves delightfully presented and creative modern Mediterranean dishes. Peppe holds a Michelin star, and he and his staff love to explain their sophisticated dishes (with an emphasis on seafood). They offer lots of fine wines by the glass. Reserve ahead (RS%; extravagant five- and six-course fixed-price meals for €95-150; Thu-Tue 12:30-14:30 & 19:30-22:30, closed Wed and Jan; just off Piazza Sant'Antonino—facing the basilica, go under the grand arch on the left and immediately enter the restaurant at II Rampa Marina Piccola 5; +39 081 878 2354, www.ilbucoristorante.it).

$$$$ **L'Antica Trattoria** enjoys a sedate, *romantico,* candlelit ambience, tucked away in its own little world. The cuisine is traditional Italian but with modern flair. Run by the same family since 1930, the restaurant has a trellised garden outside and intimate nooks inside. Aldo and sons will take care of you while Vincenzo— the Joe Cocker-esque resident mandolin player—entertains. Reservations are smart (RS%—10 percent discount on a fixed-price meal or a free *limoncello* if ordering à la carte, €50-90 fixed-price meals, good vegetarian and kids' options; daily 12:00-23:30, closed Jan-Feb; air-con, Via Padre R. Giuliani 33, +39 081 807 1082, www. lanticatrattoria.it).

MIDPRICED RESTAURANTS

$$$ **Inn Bufalito** specializes in all things buffalo: *mozzarella di bufala* (and other buffalo-milk cheeses), steak, sausage, salami, carpaccio, and buffalo-meat pasta sauce on homemade pasta. The smartly designed space has a modern, borderline-trendy, casual atmosphere and a fun indoor-outdoor vibe (don't miss the seasonal specialties on the blackboard, Thu-Tue 12:00-23:00, closed Wed and Jan-March, Vico I Fuoro 21, +39 081 365 6975).

$$$ At **Donna Sofia,** the six-course tasting menu is a meal you won't forget (€80, minimum 2 people, includes water and *limoncello*). The à la carte options are strong on seafood and include affordable gourmet pizzas. Owners Mario (who lived in New York when young) and his wife Lina (who makes the desserts) serve in a comfy modern dining room and on an upstairs patio. Photos of Sophia Loren (the restaurant's namesake) decorate the walls, and diners watch the open kitchen at work. Reservations are smart for dinner (Wed-Mon 12:00-15:00 & 19:00-23:00, closed Tue; Via Tasso 43, +39 081 877 3532, www.ristorantedonnasofia.com).

$$ **Ristorante Pizzeria da Gigino,** lively and congested with a sprawling interior and tables spilling onto the alley, makes huge, tasty Neapolitan-style pizzas in their wood-burning oven. Their *linguine gigino* and the seafood salad are favorites (daily 12:00-23:00, closed Jan-mid-March, just off Piazza Sant'Antonino at Via degli Archi 15, +39 081 878 1927, Antonino).

$$ La Cantinaccia del Popolo, rustic and informal, draws a spirited crowd anxious to taste Annalisa's cooking. Her husband Peppe seems well fed, so you know the food is good. Peruse the counter of antipasti displayed under hanging prosciutto, but save room for delicious pasta that's stylishly served in large metal skillets (Tue-Sun 12:00-15:30 & 18:00-23:30, closed Mon and mid-Jan-mid-Feb, no reservations but Peppe pours free homemade wine while you wait, a couple of blocks past the train station at Vico Terzo Rota 3, +39 366 101 5497).

With a Sea View: $$$ Terrazza delle Sirene (also known by its old name, the **Foreigners' Club**) has some of the best sea views in town (with a sprawling terrace under breezy palms), live music nightly at 20:00 (May-mid-Oct), and affordable—if uninspired—meals. It's a good spot for dessert or an after-dinner *limoncello*. You might see wedding banquets here ("snack" menu with light meals, daily, bar opens at 9:30, meals served 11:00-23:00, closed off-season, Via Luigi de Maio 35, +39 081 877 3263). If you'd enjoy eating along the water (rather than just with a water view), see "Harborside in Marina Grande," later.

CHEAP EATS

Pizza: There's nothing fancy about **$ Pizzeria da Franco,** Sorrento's favorite place for basic, casual pizza in a fun atmosphere. Join locals and tourists on benches for great pizzas served on waxed paper in square tins. It's packed to the rafters with a youthful crowd that doesn't mind the plastic cups. Consider their *saltimbocca,* a baked sandwich with top-quality prosciutto and mozzarella on pizza bread—splittable and perfect to go (daily 11:00-late, just across from Lemon Grove Garden, Corso Italia 265, +39 081 877 2066).

Kebabs: The little hole-in-the-wall **$ Kebab Ciampa** has a loyal following among eaters who appreciate Andrea's fresh bread and homemade sauces. This is your best cheap, non-Italian meal in town. Choose beef or chicken and garnish with fries and/or salad (Thu-Tue 17:00-late, closed Wed, near the cathedral at Via Santa Maria della Pietà 23, enter around corner on small side street, +39 081 807 4595).

Picnics: Get groceries at the large **Dodeca** supermarket at Corso Italia 223 (Mon-Sat 8:30-20:00, Sun 9:30-13:00) or at **Carrefour** underneath Hotel Mignon (Via Sersale 5, Mon-Sat 8:00-20:30, Sun from 8:30).

Gelato: Near the train station, **Gelateria David** has many repeat customers (so many flavors, so little time; they make 155 different flavors but have about 30 at any one time). Mario makes his gelato on-site, like his grandfather Augusto Davide, who started the store in 1957. Before choosing a flavor, sample *Profumi di Sor-*

rento (an explosive sorbet of mixed fruits), "Sorrento moon" (white almond with lemon zest), or *brontolo*—salty pistachio (daily 8:00-24:00, shorter hours off-season, closed Dec-Feb, almost in view of the train station at Via Marziale 19, +39 081 807 3649). Mario also offers gelato-making classes (€12/person, 5-person minimum, 1 hour, call or email ahead to reserve, www.gelateriadavidsorrento. it, info@gelateriadavidsorrento.itinfo@gelateriadavidsorrento.it).

At **Gelateria Primavera,** Antonio and Alberta whip up 70 exotic flavors...and still have time to make pastries for the pope and other celebrities—check out the nostalgic photos in their inviting back room, proving this is a Sorrento institution (daily 9:00-24:00, just west of Piazza Tasso at Corso Italia 142, +39 081 807 3252).

HARBORSIDE IN MARINA GRANDE

For a decent lunch or dinner *con vista*, head down to either of these restaurants by Sorrento's small-boat harbor, Marina Grande. To get to Marina Grande, follow the directions from Villa Comunale on my self-guided Sorrento Walk, earlier. It's about a 15-minute stroll from downtown. You can also take the hourly minibus from Piazza Tasso or the station. Be prepared to walk back (last bus leaves at 20:00) or spring for a pricey taxi.

$$ Trattoria da Emilia, at the city-side end of the Marina Grande waterfront, is good for straightforward, typical Sorrentine home cooking, including fresh fish, lots of fried seafood, and *gnocchi di mamma*—potato dumplings with meat sauce, basil, and mozzarella (daily 12:00-15:00 & 18:30-22:00, closed Nov-Feb, no reservations taken, indoor and outdoor seating, Via Marina Grande 62, +39 081 807 2720).

$$ Porta Marina serves fresh-as-can-be seafood in a modest location next door to Trattoria da Emilia, with views every bit as good as more expensive places nearby. Servers will tell you the catch of the day—always the best option—but if grilled octopus is on the menu then think no more (daily, 12:00-21:30, Via Marina Grande 64, +39 349 975 4761).

Sorrento Connections

It's impressively fast to zip by boat from Sorrento to many coastal towns and islands during the summer—in fact, it's quicker and easier by fast boat than by car or train (see "By Boat," later, and the map on page 1041).

BY TRAIN AND BUS

At the newsstand in the train station, Ilaria and Gianluigi sell all these tickets and can explain your options (daily from 7:00).

From Sorrento to Naples, Pompeii, and Herculaneum by

Train: The run-down **Circumvesuviana commuter train** runs twice hourly between Naples and Sorrento with crowds, pickpockets, and no air-conditioning (schedules posted widely, www.eavsrl.it). Fares are cheap: Pompeii (35 minutes, €2.40); Herculaneum (55 minutes, €2.90); and Naples (75 minutes, €3.90). If there's a line at the official ticket windows, go to the adjacent snack bar or downstairs to the newsstand.

Four **"Campania Express"** trains per day are no faster than the regular Circumvesuviana but have newer cars with air-conditioning, reserved seats, and some luggage space (€15 in high season to Pompeii, Herculaneum, or Naples; online sales at http://ots.eavsrl.it or buy at the station). For more details, see "Getting Around the Region" on page 1008 of the Naples chapter.

From Sorrento to Naples Airport: Curreri buses make the trip in 75 minutes (€10, online reservations wise, 8/day from 6:30-16:30, no service Dec 25 and Jan 1, departs from bay 5 in front of train station, +39 081 801 5420, www.curreriviaggi.it). From Naples Airport to Sorrento, eight buses depart between 9:00 and 19:30 (ask the info desk in the arrivals hall to point you toward the bus departure lot).

From Sorrento to the Amalfi Coast: See page 1079.

From Sorrento to Rome: Most people ride the train to Naples, then catch the Frecciarossa or Italo express train to Rome. Another option is the Sorrento-Rome bus: It's cheaper although the departure times can be inconvenient—confirm them in advance (daily at 6:00 and 16:00; off-season Mon-Fri at 6:00, Sat-Sun at 16:00; 4 hours; departs Sorrento from Corso Italia 259B, by Bar Kontatto, a block from the train station, and runs to Tiburtina bus station in Rome; buy tickets at train station newsstand, on website in Italian only, or on board for a surcharge; +39 080 579 0111, www.marozzivt.it).

BY BOAT

The number of boats that run per day varies: The frequency indicated here is for roughly mid-May through mid-October, with more boats per day in the peak of summer and fewer off-season. Check all schedules locally with the TI, your hotel, or online (use the individual boat-company websites—see below—or visit www.capritourism.com, select English, and click "Shipping timetable"). Some ferry companies sell tickets online for an extra fee, but buying tickets at the port is easy (and keeps your departure options open, especially valuable if you're watching the weather); next-day tickets typically go on sale starting the evening before. All boats take several hundred people each and (except for the busiest days) rarely fill up.

From Sorrento to Capri: Boats run at least hourly. Your options are a fast **ferry** (*traghetto* or *nave veloce*, takes cars, 4/day, 30 minutes, Caremar, +39 081 1896 6690, www.caremar.it) or a slightly faster and pricier **hydrofoil** (*aliscafo*, over 20/day, 25 minutes, Gescab, +39 081 807 1812, www.gescab.it). To visit Capri when it's least crowded, buy your ticket at 8:00 and take the 8:30 hydrofoil (try to depart by 9:45 at the very latest). If you make a reservation, it's not changeable. These early boats can be jammed, but it's worth it once you reach the island.

From Sorrento to Other Points: Naples (6/day, more in summer, departs roughly every 2 hours starting at 7:20, few or no boats on winter weekends, arrives at Molo Beverello, 40 minutes), **Positano** (mid-April-mid-Oct only, 4-6/day, 35 minutes), **Amalfi** (mid-April-mid-Oct only, 4-6/day, 1 hour).

Getting to Sorrento's Port (Marina Piccola): It's a 5-minute walk from Piazza Tasso. Go down the steep stairs starting under the flags, then down the road. For fewer stairs, head to the Villa Comunale public park (see my self-guided Sorrento Walk, earlier), where you can pay €1.10 to ride the elevator down (from the bottom, it's a 5-minute walk to the port). Otherwise, catch the minibus from the station or Piazza Sant'Antonino (specify that you're going to the *porto*; buses run 3/hour).

Capri

Capri was made famous as the vacation hideaway of Roman emperors Augustus and Tiberius. In the 19th century, it was the haunt

of Romantic Age aristocrats on their Grand Tour of Europe. Later it was briefly a refuge for Europe's artsy gay community: Irish playright Oscar Wilde, English poet D. H. Lawrence, and company hung out here back when being gay could land you in jail...or worse. And these

days, the island is a world-class tourist trap, packed with gawky, nametag-wearing visitors searching for the rich and famous—and finding only their prices.

About 12,000 people live on Capri (although many winter in Naples), and during any given day in high season, the island hosts another 20,000 tourists. The "Island of Dreams" is a zoo in July and August—overrun with tacky group tourism at its worst. At other times of year, though still crowded, it can provide a relaxing and scenic break from the cultural gauntlet of Italy. Even with its crowds, commercialism, fame, and glitz, Capri is a flat-out gorgeous place: Chalky white limestone cliffs rocket boldly from the shimmering blue-and-green surf, and the Blue Grotto sea cave glows with reflected sunlight. Strategically positioned gardens, villas, and viewpoints provide stunning vistas of the Sorrento Peninsula, Amalfi Coast, Vesuvius, and Capri itself.

PLANNING YOUR TIME

This is the best see-everything-in-a-day plan from Naples or Sorrento:

- Take an early hydrofoil to Capri (from Sorrento, buy ticket at 8:00, boat leaves around 8:30 and arrives around 8:50—smart). You'll land at Marina Grande; yes, Capri's port has the same name as the small-boat harbor at Sorrento.
- At the port, select from three boating options: Enjoy the scenic circle-the-island tour with a visit to the Blue Grotto (1.5-2 hours); circle the island without Blue Grotto stop (1 hour); or just visit the Blue Grotto. (There are generally spaces available for departures every few minutes.)
- Arriving back at Marina Grande, catch a bus to Anacapri, which has two or three hours' worth of sightseeing.
- In Anacapri, see the town, ride the chairlift to Monte Solaro and back (or hike down), stroll out from the base of the chairlift to Villa San Michele for the view, and eat lunch.
- Afterward, catch a bus to Capri town, which is worth an hour of browsing.
- Finally, ride the funicular from Capri town down to the harbor and laze on the free beach or wander the yacht harbor while waiting for your boat back to Sorrento.

If you're heading to Capri specifically to see the Blue Grotto, be sure to check weather and sea conditions for the day of your visit. If the tide is too high or the water too rough, the grotto can be closed. Ask the TI or your hotelier. Note that the grotto is also closed in winter. If the Blue Grotto is closed or you're not keen on seeing it, you can still enjoy a leisurely day on the island seeing the sights in Anacapri and Capri town. Or, for the same amount of time and less money, you can skip the Blue Grotto and enjoy circling the entire island by boat (an experience I find even more fun than the famed grotto).

Stormy weather can keep vessels in port. Take care not to get stranded on the island. The website for the sturdy Caremar car ferries, which are the last to be cancelled, shows whether boats are sailing (www.caremar.it).

Efficient travelers can see Capri on the way between destinations: Sail from Sorrento, check your bag at the harbor, see Capri, and take a boat directly from there to Naples or to the Amalfi Coast (or vice versa).

If you buy a one-way boat ticket to Capri (there's no round-trip discount), you'll have maximum schedule flexibility and can take any convenient hydrofoil or ferry back. When you arrive on Capri, double-check the last return trip time at the port ticket office or at www.capritourism.com (it's usually between 18:30 and 19:30). During July and August, however, it's wise to get a round-trip ticket (ensuring you a spot). On busy days, be 20 minutes early for the boat, or you can be bumped.

Starting your day as early as is reasonably possible is key to an enjoyable trip to Capri. Legions of day-trippers on big bus tours come from as far as Rome, combining with cruise-ship excursion groups to create a daily rush hour in each direction (arriving between 10:00 and 11:00, leaving around 17:00) and packing the island through the early afternoon. If you arrive before them, the entire trip to and into the Blue Grotto might take just a half-hour (10 minutes there, 10 minutes in the dinghy going inside, and 10 minutes back); arrive later and you might face a two-hour delay.

GETTING TO CAPRI

For instructions on getting to Capri by **scheduled ferry,** see the "Connections" sections of the Sorrento and Naples chapters, and the "Getting Around the Amalfi Coast" section of the Amalfi Coast chapter.

Another option is to visit Capri by **tour boat.** Consider **Mondo**

Guide, which offers my readers a no-stress, all-day itinerary for €120: You'll be picked up at your Sorrento hotel around 8:00 and driven to the port, where you'll board a small boat (maximum 12 people, shared with other Rick Steves readers) and be taken across to Capri, anchoring by the Blue Grotto (optional entry fee to hop in one of the little rowboats to go inside). Then you'll continue to Marina Grande for about four hours of free time on the island—just enough to head to Anacapri for sightseeing and the Monte Solaro chairlift (island transportation and admissions on your own). Finally, you'll reboard the boat for a lightly narrated circle around the island and pass through the iconic Faraglioni Rocks (includes drinks, a snack, and—conditions permitting—a chance to swim from the boat). For some travelers, the tour may be worth the approximately €45 extra (compared to the cost of doing everything on your own) for a hassle-free, more personalized experience. The trip only goes if enough people sign up, and reservations are required—book online at MondoGuide.it. For details on Mondo and their tours, see page 962. **Tempio Travel**—based at the Sorrento train station—offers a similar trip at a similar price (+39 081 878 2103, www.tempiotravel.com, or drop by their office).

Orientation to Capri

First thing—pronounce it right: Italians say KAH-pree, not kah-PREE like the song (or the pants). The island is small—just four miles by two miles—and is separated from the Sorrentine Peninsula by a five-mile-wide strait. Capri has only two towns to speak of: Capri and Anacapri. The island also has some scant Roman ruins and a few interesting churches and villas. But its chief attraction is its famous Blue Grotto, and its best activity beyond the boat rides is the chairlift from Anacapri up the island's Monte Solaro ("the sunny mount").

TOURIST INFORMATION

Capri's English-speaking TI has three tiny offices in Marina Grande, Capri town, and Anacapri. Their well-organized website has schedules and practical information in English (www.capritourism.com). All have free maps and are open daily in summer (shorter hours on Sun; Mon-Fri only in winter).

The **Marina Grande TI** is in the port office building at the base of the breakwater (+39 081 837 0634).

The **Capri town TI** works out of a closet-like space under the bell tower on Piazza Umberto I and is less crowded than its sister at the port (+39 081 837 0686).

The **Anacapri TI** is at Piazza Vittoria 5, next to the WC near the chairlift entrance (+39 081 837 1524).

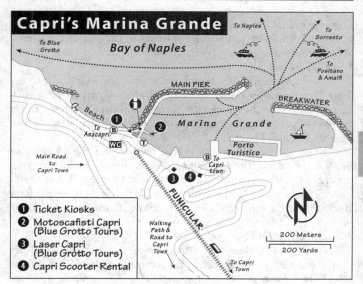

Capri's Marina Grande

Bay of Naples

To Naples
To Sorrento
To Blue Grotto
To Positano & Amalfi

MAIN PIER
BREAKWATER
Beach
Marina Grande
To Anacapri
Porto Turistico

Main Road to Capri Town
To Capri town

WC
FUNICULAR

Walking Path & Road to Capri Town

To Capri Town

1 Ticket Kiosks
2 Motoscafisti Capri (Blue Grotto Tours)
3 Laser Capri (Blue Grotto Tours)
4 Capri Scooter Rental

200 Meters
200 Yards

SORRENTO & CAPRI

ARRIVAL IN CAPRI

Get oriented on the boat before you dock, as you near the harbor with the island spread out before you. The port is a small community of its own, called **Marina Grande,** connected by a funicular and buses to the rest of the island. **Capri town** fills the ridge high above the harbor. The ruins of Emperor Tiberius' palace, **Villa Jovis,** cap the peak on the left. To the right, the dramatic *"Mamma mia!"* road arcs around the highest mountain on the island **(Monte Solaro),** leading up to **Anacapri** (the island's second town, just out of sight). Notice the old zigzag steps below that road. Until 1874, this was the only connection between Capri and Anacapri. (Though it's quite old, it's nowhere near as old as implied by its nickname, "The Phoenician Stairway.") The white house on the ridge above the zig-zags is **Villa San Michele** (where you can go later for a grand view).

Arrival at Marina Grande: Remember that you're arriving with a boatload of other tourists with similar plans. You'll need some patience as you get your bearings. Find the base of the **funicular railway** (signed *funicolare*) that runs up to Capri town, and stand facing it, with your back to the water.

The fourth little clothing-and-souvenir shop to the right of the funicular provides **baggage storage** (€3/bag, look for the awning sign, daily 9:00-18:00, +39 081 837 4575, shorter hours or closed in winter).

Across from the Bar Grotta Azzura are ticket windows for **funicular and bus tickets** (not sold by drivers) and for **boat tickets** to Naples and Sorrento. (Notice the grand electronic departure board on the terminal building listing all boats leaving in the next couple of hours.) Adjacent is the **stop for buses** to the rest of the island. Across the street is a pay **WC,** and a little farther on is Marina Grande's pebbly public beach.

Two companies offer **boat trips** around the island and to the Blue Grotto: **Laser Capri** and **Motoscafisti Capri.** Motoscafisti Capri's ticket shed is along the pier; Laser Capri has two ticket windows along the waterfront. Both offer similar services (see "Sights in Capri," later).

From the port, you can take a boat to the Blue Grotto or around the island, the funicular to Capri town, or a bus to Anacapri or other destinations. The steep paved footpath that connects the port area with Capri town starts a block inland from the ferry dock (follow the signs to *Capri centro;* allow 30 minutes to walk up).

HELPFUL HINTS

Cheap Tricks: A cheap day trip to Capri is tough, as you'll pay about €20 each way just to get there and about €35 to see the Blue Grotto. That's €75 already. But if you picnic and ride buses rather than enjoying restaurants and taxis, you'll find your time on the island itself to be relatively inexpensive. Many of Capri's greatest pleasures are free.

Tread Lightly: Be conscious of your personal impact on this island. More than 2.3 million annual visitors put a strain on local resources. Consider taking any trash out with you and carrying a metal water bottle.

Best Real Hike: Serious hikers love the peaceful and scenic three-hour Fortress Hike, which takes you entirely away from the tourists. You'll walk under ruined forts along the rugged coast, from the Blue Grotto to the *faro* (lighthouse). From there, you can take a bus back to Anacapri (3/hour). The TI has a fine map/brochure. Hiking guru Giovanni Visetti has a great free map of the whole island on his website (www.giovis.com).

Free Beach: Marina Grande has a free pebbly beach (pay at the bar for a shower).

Local Guides: Sorrento-based **Giovanna Donadio** leads good Capri tours (see page 1043). Capri resident **Anna Leva** seems to know everybody and every trick (groups of 2-15 people: €160/half-day, €240/day, +39 339 712 7416, www.capritourinformation.com, annaleva@hotmail.it).

GETTING AROUND CAPRI

By Bus and Funicular: Tickets for the island's buses and funicular cost €2 per ride (no transfers allowed). Think about how many tickets you'll need and save time by buying them all at once at the port kiosk. (Tickets are also available throughout the island at newsstands, tobacco shops, and main bus stops.) The €7 all-day bus pass is available only at the terminals. Validate your ticket when you board.

Schedules are clearly posted at all bus stations. Public buses are orange, while gray and blue buses are for private tour groups. Public buses from the port to Capri town, and from Capri town to Anacapri, are frequent (4/hour, 10 minutes). The direct bus between the port and Anacapri runs less often (2/hour, 25 minutes) but is worth the wait if you're following my suggested visit as outlined in "Planning Your Time" at the start of this section. From Anacapri, branch bus lines run to the parking lot above the Blue Grotto and to the lighthouse (*faro;* 3/hour). Buses are teeny (because of the island's narrow roads) and often packed, the aisles filled with people standing. At most stops, you'll see ranks for passengers to line up in. Locals are allowed to cut the line. If the driver changes the bus's display to read *completo* (full), you'll need to wait for the next one.

By Taxi: Taxis have fixed rates, listed at www.capritourism. com (Marina Grande to Capri town–€17; Marina Grande to Anacapri–€23). You can hire a taxi for about €70 per hour—negotiate.

By Scooter: If you're an experienced scooter rider, this is the perfect way to have the run of the island. (For novice riders, Capri's steep and narrow roads aren't a good place to start.) **Capri Scooter** rents bright-yellow scooters with 50cc engines—strong enough to haul couples. Rentals come with a map and instructions with parking tips and other helpful information (€15/hour, €55/day, RS%— 10 percent discount on rentals of 2 hours or more with this book; includes helmet, gas, and insurance; daily April-Oct 9:30-18:00, may open in good weather off-season, at Via Don Giobbe Ruocco 55, Marina Grande, +39 338 360 6918).

Sights in Capri

ON THE WATER

You have three boat-tour options: circle the island with a stop at the Blue Grotto, circle only, or Blue Grotto only.

▲▲▲Capri Boat Circle (Giro dell'Isola)

For me, the best experience on Capri is to take the scenic boat trip around the island. It's cheap, comes with good narration and lots of curiosities, and there are plenty of departures from Marina Grande.

Both **Laser Capri** and **Motoscafisti Capri** run trips that circle the island and pass stunning cliffs, caves, and views that most miss when they go only to the Blue Grotto (€20; Motoscafisti Capri— +39 081 837 7714, www.motoscafisticapri.com; Laser Capri—+39 081 837 5208, www.lasercapri.com). The circular tour comes with a live guide and takes about an hour. You'll see quirky sights (a solar-powered lighthouse, tiny statues atop desolate rocks, holes in the cliffs with legends going back to Emperor Tiberius' times), pop into various caves and inlets, power through a tiny hole in the famed Faraglioni Rocks, hear stories of celebrity-owned villas, and marvel at a nonstop parade of staggering cliffs.

With both companies, you can stop at the Blue Grotto at no extra charge (this adds about an hour; check schedules to find out which departures allow a Blue Grotto stop). You can also sail just to the grotto and back (10 minutes each way), but this costs the same as circling the island.

All boats leave daily from 9:00 until at least 13:00 (or later, depending on when the Blue Grotto rowboats stop running—likely 16:00 in summer).

▲▲Blue Grotto (Grotta Azzurra)

Thousands of tourists a day visit Capri's Blue Grotto. I did—early (when the light is best), without the frustration of crowds, and with

choppy waves nearly making entrance impossible...and it was great.

The actual cave experience isn't much: a short dinghy ride through a three-foot-high entry hole to reach a 60-yard-long cave, where the sun reflects brilliantly blue on its limestone bottom. But the experience— getting there, getting in, and

getting back—is a scenic hoot. You get a fast ride and scant narration on a 30-foot boat partway around the gorgeous island; along the way, you see bird life and dramatic limestone cliffs. You'll understand why Roman emperors appreciated the invulnerability of the island—it's surrounded by cliffs, with only one good access point, and therefore easy to defend.

Just outside the grotto, your boat idles as you pile into eight-foot dinghies that hold up to four passengers each. Next, you'll be taken to a floating ticket counter to pay the grotto entry fee. From there, your ruffian rower will elbow his way to the tiny hole, then pull fast and hard on the cable at the low point of the swells to squeeze you into the grotto (keep your head down and hands in the boat). Then your man rows you around, spouting off a few descriptive lines and singing "O Sole Mio." Depending on the strength of the sunshine that day, the blue light inside can be brilliant.

The grotto was actually an ancient Roman *nymphaeum*—a retreat for romantic hanky-panky. Many believe that, in its day, a tunnel led here directly from the palace, and that the grotto experience was enlivened by statues of Poseidon and company, placed half-underwater as if emerging from the sea. It was ancient Romans who smoothed out the entry hole that's still used to this day.

When dropping you off, your boatman will fish for a tip—it's optional, and €1 is enough (you've already paid plenty). If you don't want to return by boat, ask to be let off at the little dock, where stairs lead up to a café and the Blue Grotto bus stop.

Cost: The €15 entry fee (separate from the €20 ride from Marina Grande and back) includes €10 for the rowboat service plus €5 for admission to the grotto itself. Though some people swim in for free from the little dock after the boats stop running (about 17:00), it's illegal and can be dangerous.

Timing: When waves or high tide make entering dangerous, the boats don't go in—the grotto can close without notice, sending tourists (flush with anticipation) home without a chance to squeeze through the little hole.

If you're coming from Capri's port (Marina Grande), allow 1-2 hours for the entire visit, depending on the chaos at the caves. Going with the first trip (around 9:00) will get you there at the same time as the boatmen in their dinghies—who hitch a ride behind your boat—resulting in less chaos and a shorter wait at the entry point.

If you arrive on the island later in the morning—when the Blue Grotto is already jammed—you could try waiting to visit until about 15:00, when most of the tour groups have vacated. But this may only work by bus (not boat). Confirm that day's closing time with a TI before making the trip.

Going by Bus: To save money, buy the island bus day pass at Marina Grande (€7) and take the **bus** via Anacapri to the small dock next to the grotto entrance. You'll lose time but see a beautiful, calmer side of the island (roughly 3/hour, 10 minutes; buses depart only from the Anacapri bus station at Piazza della Pace—not from the bus stop at Piazza Vittoria 200 yards away). If you're coming from Marina Grande or Capri town and want to transfer to the Blue Grotto buses, don't get off when the driver announces "Anacapri." Instead, ride one more stop to Piazza della Pace. At the Piazza della Pace bus station, notice the two lines: "Grotta Azzurra" for the Blue Grotto, and "Faro" for the lighthouse.

Getting Back from the Blue Grotto by Bus: Even if you've come to the grotto by sea, you can ask your boatman to row you over to the dock and drop you there (for a small tip). From the dock, climb up the stairs to the stop for the bus to Anacapri (you'll still have to pay the full boat fare).

ANACAPRI TOWN AND NEARBY

More interesting than the island's namesake town, Anacapri has two or three hours' worth of sights. Though Anacapri sits higher up on the island ("ana" means "upper" in Greek) than Capri town, there are no sea views at street level in the town center.

When visiting Anacapri by bus, note that there are two stops: at Piazza Vittoria, in the center of town at the base of the Monte Solaro chairlift; and 200 yards farther along at Piazza della Pace (pronounced "PAH-chay"), a larger bus station near the cemetery. Piazza Vittoria gets you closer to the main sights (chairlift and Villa San Michele), while Piazza della Pace is where you transfer to the Blue Grotto bus. When leaving Anacapri for Marina Grande, buses can be packed. Your best chance of getting on board is to catch the bus from Piazza della Pace (the first stop). Another option is to catch a bus to Capri town, visit sights there, then take the funicular down to Marina Grande. Bus tickets can be purchased at the "Moda Mare" souvenir store directly opposite the bus stop in Piazza Vittoria.

Via Orlandi

Anacapri's pedestrianized main drag takes you through the charming center of town. It's just a block or so from either bus stop. (From Piazza Vittoria, the street is right there—just go down the lane to the right of the Anacapri statue. From Piazza della Pace, cross the street and go down the small pedestrian lane called Via Filietto.) Anacapri's **TI** is at Piazza Vittoria, next to the WC by the chairlift.

To see the town, stroll along Via Orlandi for a few minutes. Signs propose a quick circuit that links the Casa Rossa, St. Michael's Church, and peaceful side streets. You'll also find shops and eateries, including good choices for quick, inexpensive pizza, *saltimbocca* (prosciutto and mozzarella on baked pizza bread—great for a filling picnic), *panini,* and other goodies. These two **$** options are both open daily in peak season: **Sciué Sciué** (same price for informal seating or takeaway, at #73, +39 081 837 2068) and **Pizza e Pasta** (takeaway only, lots of benches nearby, just before the church at #157, +39 328 623 8460).

Of the sights below, the first two are in the heart of town (on or near Via Orlandi), while the next two are a short walk away.

Museo Casa Rossa (Red House Museum)

This "Pompeiian-red," eccentric home, a hodgepodge of architectural styles, is the former residence of John Clay MacKowen, a Louisiana doctor and ex-Confederate officer who moved to Capri in the 1870s and married a local woman. (MacKowen and the Villa San Michele's Axel Munthe—see later—loathed each other, and even tried to challenge each other to a duel.) Its small collection of 19th-century paintings of scenes from around the island recalls a time before mass tourism. Don't miss the second floor, with more paintings and four ancient, sea-worn statues, which were recovered from the depths of the Blue Grotto in the 1960s and 1970s.

Cost and Hours: €3.50; discounted to €1 with ticket stub from Blue Grotto, Villa San Michele, or Monte Solaro chairlift; Tue-Sun 10:00-13:30 & 17:30-20:00; shorter hours April-May and Oct; closed Nov-March and Mon year-round; Via Orlandi 78, +39 081 838 7260, http://www.museocasarossa.it.

▲Church of San Michele

This Baroque church in the village center has a remarkable majolica floor showing paradise on earth in a classic 18th-century Neapolitan style. The entire floor is ornately tiled, featuring an angel (with flaming sword) driving Adam and Eve from paradise. The devil is wrapped around the trunk of a beautiful tree. The animals—happily ignoring this momentous event—all have human expressions. For the best view, climb the spiral stairs from the postcard desk. Services are held only during the first two weeks of Advent, when the church is closed to visitors.

Cost and Hours: €2, daily 9:00-19:00; Oct-Nov and mid-Dec-March usually 10:00-14:00, closed late Nov-mid-Dec; in town center just off Via Orlandi—look for *San Michele* signs, +39 081 837 2396, www.chiesa-san-michele.com.

▲Villa San Michele and Grand Capri View

This is the mansion of Axel Munthe, Capri's grand personality, an idealistic Swedish doctor who bought the property (then run-down) in 1887 and lived here until 1946. Munthe was the personal physician of Sweden's Queen Victoria, who often stayed here with him. Munthe enjoyed the avant-garde and permissive scene at Capri, during an era when Europe's leading artists and creative figures gathered here and the island's many gay visitors could be honest about their sexual orientation.

At the very least, walk the path from Piazza Vittoria past the villa to a superb, free viewpoint over Capri town, Marina Grande, and—in the distance—Mount Vesuvius and Sorrento. Paying to enter the villa lets you see a few rooms with period furnishings (follow the one-way route, good English descriptions); an exhibit on Munthe; and one of this region's most delightful gardens, with a chapel, the Olivetum (a tiny museum of native birds and bugs), and a view that's slightly better than the free one outside. Throughout the gardens and the house, you'll see a smattering of original ancient objects unearthed here—and lots and lots of copies. A café (also with a view) serves affordable sandwiches.

Cost and Hours: €10, daily 9:00-18:00, closes earlier Oct-April, +39 081 837 1401, www.villasanmichele.eu.

Getting There: From Piazza Vittoria, walk up the grand staircase and turn left onto Via Capodimonte. At the start of the shopping street, on your right, pass the deluxe Capri Palace Hotel—venture in if you can get past the treacherously eye-catching swimming pool windows (behind the pillars). After lots of overpriced shops, just before the villa, notice the Swedish consulate. In honor of Munthe, Swedes get into the villa for free.

▲▲Chairlift up to Monte Solaro

From Anacapri, you can ride the chairlift *(seggiovia)* to the 1,900-foot summit of Monte Solaro for a commanding view of the Bay of Naples. Work on your tan as you float over hazelnut, walnut, chestnut, apricot, peach, kiwi, and fig trees, past a montage of tourists (mostly from cruise ships; when the grotto is closed—as it often is—they bring passengers here instead). Prospective smoochers should know that the lift seats are all single. As you ascend, consider how Capri's real estate has been priced out of the locals' reach. The ride takes 13 minutes each way, and you'll want at least 30 minutes on top, where there are picnic benches and a café with WCs.

Cost and Hours: €9 one-way, €12 round-trip, daily 9:30-17:00, last run down at 17:30; March-April until 16:00, Nov-Feb until 15:30, +39 081 837 1438, www.capriseggiovia.it. Note that the lift gets more crowded with tour groups in the afternoon.

Getting There: From the Piazza Vittoria bus stop, just climb the steps and look right.

At the Summit: You'll enjoy the best panorama possible: lush cliffs busy with seagulls enjoying the ideal nesting spot. Even if skies aren't clear, the views are spectacular, with clouds surfing over the cliffs. Find the Faraglioni Rocks—with tour boats squeezing through every few minutes—which are an icon of the island. The pink building nearest the rocks was an American R&R base during World War II. Eisenhower and Churchill met here. On the peak closest to Cape Sorrento, you can see the distant ruins of Emperor Tiberius' palace, Villa Jovis. Pipes from the Sorrento Peninsula bring water to Capri (demand for fresh water here long ago exceeded the supply provided by the island's three natural springs). The Li Galli Islands mark the Amalfi Coast in the distance. Cross the bar terrace for views of Mount Vesuvius and Naples.

Hiking Down: A highlight for hardy walkers (provided you have strong knees and good shoes) is the 40-minute downhill hike from the top of Monte Solaro, through lush vegetation and ever-changing views, past the 14th-century Chapel of Santa Maria Cetrella (at the trail's only intersection, it's a 10-minute detour to the right), and back into

Anacapri. The trail starts downstairs, past the WCs (last chance). Down two more flights of stairs, look for the sign to *Anacapri e Cetrella*—you're on your way. While the trail is well established, you'll encounter plenty of uneven steps, loose rocks, and few signs.

Lighthouse near Anacapri

The lighthouse *(faro)*, at the rocky, arid, and desolate southwestern corner of the island, is a favorite place to enjoy the sunset. This area has a private beach, pool, small restaurants, and a few fishermen. Reach it by bus from Anacapri (3/hour, departs from Piazza della Pace stop).

CAPRI TOWN AND NEARBY

This cute but extremely clogged and touristy shopping town is worth a brief visit, if only for window shopping.

Piazza Umberto I

If you arrive by the funicular, it drops you just around the corner from Piazza Umberto I, the town's main square (named after the second king of Italy). With your back to the funicular, the bus stop is 50 yards straight ahead down Via Roma. The **TI** is under the bell tower on Piazza Umberto (see "Tourist Information," earlier). The footpath to the port starts just behind the TI (follow signs to *Il Porto*, 15-minute walk). A WC and baggage storage are down the stairs by the TI.

Imagine the days when, rather than fancy cafés, the square was filled with a public market. Today, Capri town is traffic-free with only electric service minitrucks scooting here and there. While a coffee costs €1 at any bar, it's €5 at a table on the square.

To the left of City Hall (Municipio, lowest corner), a narrow, atmospheric lane leads into the medieval part of town, which has plenty of eateries and is the starting point for the 45-minute hike to Villa Jovis.

Cathedral

Capri town's multidomed Baroque cathedral, which faces the square, is worth a quick look. Its multicolored marble floor at the altar dates from the first century AD—it was scavenged from Emperor Tiberius' villa and laid here in the 19th century.

"Rodeo Drive"

The lane to the left of the cathedral (past Bar Tiberio, under the wide arch) is a fashionable shopping strip that's justifiably been dubbed "Rodeo Drive" by residents. Walk a few minutes down the street (past Gela- teria Buonocore at #35, with its tempting fresh waffle cones—you'll smell them as you approach) to Quisisana Hotel, the island's top old-time hotel (formerly a 19th-century sanitorium). From there, head left for fancy shops and villas, and right for gardens and views. Between the lane and the sea is a huge monastery (Certosa di San Giacomo, described later; access to the left).

Giardini di Augusto

To the right and downhill, a five-minute walk leads to this lovely public garden (€1.50, use machines, daily 9:00-19:30, Nov-March until 17:30, free to enter off-season, no picnicking). While the garden itself is modest, it boasts great views over the famous Faraglioni Rocks—handy if you don't have the time, money, or interest to access the higher vantage points near Anacapri (Monte Solaro, Villa San Michele).

Monastery of San Giacomo

One of the most historic buildings on the island is the Certosa di San Giacomo (€6, Tue-Sun 10:00-16:00, later in summer, closed Mon, Via Certosa 10, +39 081 837 6218). The stark monastery has an empty church and a sleepy cloister. But the finest piece of art on Capri is over the church's front entrance: an exquisite 14th-century fresco of Mary and the baby Jesus by the Florentine Niccolo di Tommaso. Today, the monastery hosts the **Museo Diefenbach,** a small collection of dark and moody paintings by eccentric German artist Karl Wilhelm Diefenbach, who walked around naked in Capri in the early 1900s, when this was a gay, political, and avant-garde place.

Villa Jovis and the Emperor's Capri

Even before becoming emperor, Augustus loved Capri so much that he traded the family-owned Isle of Ischia to the (then-independent) Neapolitans in exchange for making Capri his personal property. Emperor Tiberius spent a decade here, AD 26-37. (Some figure he did so in order to escape being assassinated in Rome.)

Emperor Tiberius' ruined villa, Villa Jovis, is reachable only by a scenic 45-minute hike from Capri town. You won't find any statues or mosaics here—just an evocative, ruined complex of terraces clinging to a rocky perch over a sheer drop to the sea...and a lovely view. You can make out a large water reservoir for baths, the foundations of servants' quarters, and Tiberius' private apartments (fragments of marble flooring still survive). The ruined lighthouse dates from the Middle Ages.

Cost and Hours: €6, Wed-Mon 10:00-18:00, closed Tue, shorter hours and closed off-season—check at Capri TI.

Capri Connections

From Capri's Marina Grande by Boat to: Sorrento (ferry: 4/day, 30 minutes, www.caremar.it; hydrofoil: up to 20/day, 20 minutes, www.gescab.it), **Naples** (roughly hourly, more in summer, hydrofoil: 50 minutes, arrives at Molo Beverello; ferries: 60-90 minutes, arrive at Calata Porta di Massa), **Positano** (mid-April-mid-Oct, 6/day, 40 minutes). Confirm the schedule carefully at TIs or www.capritourism.com (under "Shipping Timetable")—the last boats back to the mainland usually leave around 18:00-20:00. For a steep price, you can always hire a water taxi (weather permitting).

AMALFI COAST & PAESTUM

Amalfi Coast Tour • Positano • Ravello • Paestum

With its stunning scenery, hill- and harbor-hugging towns, and historic ruins, Amalfi is Italy's coast with the most. The breathtaking trip from Sorrento to Salerno is one of the world's great bus or taxi rides. It will leave your mouth open and your camera's memory card full. You'll gain respect for the 19th-century Italian engineers who built the roads—and even more for the 21st-century drivers who squeeze past each other here daily. Cantilevered garages, hotels, and villas cling to the vertical terrain, and beautiful but out-of-reach coves tease from far below. As you hyperventilate, notice how the Mediterranean, a sheer 500-foot drop below, really twinkles. All this beautiful scenery apparently inspires local Romeos and Juliets, with the latex evidence of late-night romantic encounters littering the roadside turnouts. Over the centuries, the spectacular scenery and climate have been a siren call for the rich and famous, luring Roman emperor Tiberius, Richard Wagner, Sophia Loren, Gore Vidal, and others to the Amalfi Coast's special brand of *la dolce vita*.

The two main Amalfi Coast towns (Positano and Amalfi) are pretty, but they're also touristy, congested, and overpriced. (Many visitors prefer side-tripping in from Sorrento.) Most beaches here are private, pebbly, and expensive. Check and understand your bills in this greedy region.

In Paestum, farther south, you can see one of the world's best collections of 2,500-year-old Greek temples, a worthwhile museum with artifacts from the site, and the remains of a Roman town.

Amalfi Coast

The Amalfi Coast is one of those places with a "must see" reputation. Staggeringly picturesque and maddeningly touristy, it can be both rewarding and frustrating. As an antidote to intense Naples, it's the perfect place for a romantic break—if done right and if you can afford it. These towns are the big three sights of the Amalfi Coast: Positano is like a living Gucci ad and has good overnight options; Amalfi evokes a day when small towns with big fleets were powerhouses on the Mediterranean; and Ravello is fun for that tramp-in-a-palace feeling.

PLANNING YOUR TIME

On a quick visit, use Sorrento (see previous chapter) as your home base and do the Amalfi Coast as a day trip. But for a small-town vacation from your vacation, spend a few more days on the coast, sleeping in Positano.

Trying to decide between staying in Sorrento or Positano? Sorrento is larger, with useful services and the best transportation connections and accommodations. Tiny Positano is more touristy, but also more chic and picturesque, with a decent beach.

Naples or Paestum can also work as a base for an Amalfi Coast day trip, if you get an early start and the timetables align. From Naples, you have two options by public transport: train to Salerno, then bus (or boat) to Amalfi town; or, Circumvesuviana train to Sorrento, then bus to Positano and/or Amalfi. (You can go out one way and return the other.) From Paestum, you can take the train to Salerno, then the bus (or boat) to Amalfi or Positano.

GETTING AROUND THE AMALFI COAST

The real thrill here is the scenic drive between Sorrento and Salerno. The stretch from Positano to Amalfi is the best. This is treacherous stuff—even if you have a car, you may want to take the bus or hire a driver. Brave souls enjoy seeing the coast by scooter or motorbike (rent in Sorrento).

Next, I've outlined your options by bus, boat, and taxi. Many travelers do the Amalfi Coast as a round-trip by bus, but a good strategy is to go one way by land and return by boat. For example, take the bus along the coast to

AMALFI COAST

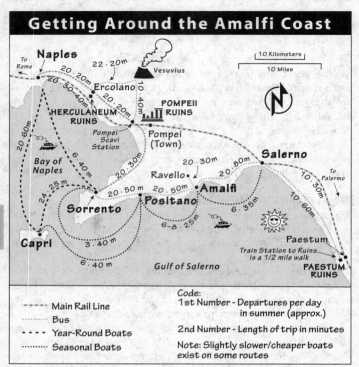

Getting Around the Amalfi Coast

To Rome
Naples
To Rome
22 · 20m
Vesuvius
20 · 20m
20 · 20m
Ercolano
20 · 30 · 40m
20 · 20m
10 · 40m
HERCULANEUM RUINS
POMPEII RUINS
Pompei Scavi Station
20 · 60m
Pompei (Town)
Bay of Naples
6 · 40m
20 · 30m
20 · 30m
20 · 80m
Salerno
24 · 25m
20 · 50m
Ravello•
10 · 30m
To Palermo
20 · 50m 20 · 50m **Amalfi**
Sorrento
Positano
10 · 60m
6 · 35m
6-8 · 25m
3 · 40m
Capri
Paestum
Train Station to Ruins is a 1/2 mile walk
6 · 40m
Gulf of Salerno
PAESTUM RUINS

10 Kilometers
10 Miles

- - - - - Main Rail Line
.... Bus
- - - Year-Round Boats
.... Seasonal Boats

Code:
1st Number - Departures per day in summer (approx.)
2nd Number - Length of trip in minutes
Note: Slightly slower/cheaper boats exist on some routes

Positano and/or Amalfi, then catch the ferry back. Ferries run less often in spring and fall, and some don't run at all off-season (mid-Oct-mid-April). Boats don't run in stormy weather at any time of year. If boats aren't running directly between Amalfi or Positano and Sorrento, check if you can change boats in Capri.

Looking for exercise? Consider an Amalfi Coast hike (see "Hikes" in the Amalfi Town section, later in this chapter). Numerous trails connect the main coastal towns with villages on the hills. Get a good map before you venture out (local hiker and orienteer Giovanni Visetti has posted free maps and itineraries at www.giovis.com).

By Public Bus

SITA buses from Sorrento to Amalfi, via Positano, are the most common, inexpensive way to see the coast (for schedules, see www.sitasudtrasporti.it or—easier to read—www.positano.com). From Sorrento, the first bus leaves at 6:30; from 8:30 they run roughly every half-hour until 17:00, then hourly until 22:00 in summer or until 20:00 in winter (50 minutes to Positano; another 50 minutes to Amalfi). To reach Ravello (the hill town beyond Amalfi) or Salerno (at the far end of the coast), transfer in Amalfi. When checking the schedule, note that *giornaliero* (G) means daily, *scolastico* (S) means school bus, *feriale* (F) denotes Monday-Saturday, and *festivo* (H) is for Sundays and holidays.

Individual tickets are inexpensive (€2-4). All rides are covered by the 24-hour Costiera SITA Sud pass (€10), which may not save you money but does save time buying tickets. Tickets are sold at tobacco shops and newsstands, not by drivers.

In Sorrento, SITA buses leave from *stalli* (bays) 1-3 at the train station (10 steps down, then join the line). In warm months, look for an extra ticket sales desk under an umbrella.

Leaving Sorrento, grab a seat on the right for the best views. If you return by bus, it's fun to sit directly behind the driver for a box seat with a view over the twisting hairpin action. Sitting toward the front will also help minimize carsickness. If you're unlucky enough to land the occasional bus whose windows are covered by advertising, either sit right up front, or try your luck with the next departure.

Avoiding Crowded Buses: Amalfi Coast public buses are routinely unable to handle demand during summer months and holidays (perhaps because the fares are so cheap). Generally, if you don't get on one bus, you're well positioned to catch the next one. From Sorrento, aim to leave on the 8:30 bus at the latest—earlier if possible. Departures between 9:00 and 11:00 can be frustratingly crowded.

Note that an eight-seater minibus and driver costs about €350 for the day: If you can organize a small group, €50 per person is a very good deal. (For options, see "By Taxi," later.)

When to Stop in Positano: Summer congestion can be so bad—particularly in July and August—that some Amalfi-Sorrento buses don't even stop in Positano (because they fill up in Amalfi). Those trying to get back from Positano to Sorrento are stuck taking an extortionist taxi or hopping a boat...if one's running. When day-tripping from Sorrento to Amalfi, it's safest to make your Positano stop on the outbound leg, then come straight home from Amalfi, where the bus originates. Or consider the hop-on, hop-off bus as an alternative.

By Tour Bus

CitySightseeing's bright red hop-on, hop-off buses travel from Sorrento to Positano to Amalfi and back. While more expensive than public buses, they can be much less crowded and come with a recorded commentary. You'll pay €15 for your outgoing ride (buy tickets onboard) and €6 for the return trip (on the same day). Buses run from the Sorrento train station—confirm times locally (+39 081 1825 7088, www.city-sightseeing.it).

By Boat

A few passenger boats per day link Positano and Amalfi with Sorrento, Capri, and Salerno (generally April-Oct only). The last daily departure can be as early as midafternoon and is never much later than 18:00. Check schedules carefully: Frequency varies from month to month, and boats may be cancelled in bad weather (especially at Positano, where there's no real pier). The companies operating each route change frequently, compete for passengers, and usually claim to know nothing about their rivals' services. The best sources for timetables are www.positano.com (under "Ferry Schedules") and www.capritourism.com (under "Shipping Timetable"). Go to the dock to confirm times and buy tickets. For a summary of sample routes, frequencies, and travel times, see the "Getting Around the Amalfi Coast" map.

If you're going to Capri from Positano, save time and money by finding a boat that goes directly to the Blue Grotto (rather than dropping you at the port in Capri to catch another boat from there). Here's another useful trick: If no boats are going directly between Sorrento and Positano/Amalfi, you can usually still connect the two sides of the peninsula via Capri.

By Taxi

Given the hairy driving, impossible parking, crowded public buses, and potential fun, you might consider splurging to hire your own car and driver for your Amalfi day.

The English-speaking **Monetti family** car-and-driver service—Raffaele, daughter Carolina, and cousin Gianpaolo—have taken excellent care of my readers' transit needs for decades. Sample trips and rates: all-day Amalfi Coast (Positano, Amalfi, Ravello, usually with stops in each town and lunch in Ravello), 8 hours, €350; Pompeii and Paestum, 10 hours, €480; transfer between Naples airport or train station and Sorrento, €160. These prices are for up to three people; you'll pay more for a larger eight-seater van. Though based in Sorrento, they can also pick you up from other places. Payment is cash only (as with most of the car services listed). Reserve directly by email (or by phone on short notice)—don't rely on a web search for the name Monetti, as that might lead you to an impersonator trying to siphon off their business (Raffaele's mobile +39 335 602 9158 or +39 338 946 2860, "office" run by his English-speaking

Finnish wife, Susanna, www.monettitaxi17.com, monettitaxi17@libero.it). If you get into any kind of serious jam in the area, you can call Raffaele for help.

Francesco del Pizzo is another smooth and honest Sorrento-based driver. A classy man who speaks English well, Francesco enjoys explaining things as he drives (9 hours or so in a car with up to 4 passengers, €320; up to 8 passengers in a minibus, €360; +39 333 238 4144, francescodelpizzo@yahoo.it).

Anthony Buonocore, an Amalfi native, specializes in cruise shore excursions, as well as trips anywhere in the region in his eight-person Mercedes van (rates vary, special deals for early booking and in low season, +39 349 441 0336, www.amalfitransfer.com, buonocoreanthony@yahoo.it).

Rides Only: If you're hiring a cabbie off the street for a ride and not a tour, a one-way trip from Sorrento to Positano might cost about €90 (to Amalfi, €150). All Sorrento taxis are white minivans (taking up to eight passengers), sport a taxi sign on top, and use a meter (fares will vary a bit depending on traffic). If there's no meter, it's not an official taxi.

By Shared Minibus

While hiring your own driver is convenient, it's also expensive. To bring the cost down, split the trip—and the bill—with other travelers using this book. Naples-based **Mondo Guide** offers a nine-hour minibus trip that departs from Sorrento and heads down the Amalfi Coast, with brief stops in Positano, Amalfi, and Ravello, before returning to Sorrento (€65/person). They also offer Rick Steves readers shared tours in Pompeii and Naples. For details, see page 962.

Amalfi Coast Tour

The wildly scenic Amalfi Coast drive from Sorrento to Salerno, worth ▲▲▲, is one of the all-time great white-knuckle rides, whether you tackle it by bus, taxi, or shared minibus.

Gasp from the right side of the car or bus as you go out and from the left as you return to Sorrento. (Those on the wrong side really miss out.) Traffic is so heavy that private tour buses are only allowed to go in one direction (southbound from Sorrento). Summer traffic is infuriating. Fluorescent-vested police are posted at tough bends during peak hours to help fold in side-view mirrors and keep things moving. Here's a loose, self-guided tour of what you're seeing as you travel from west to east.

❍ **Self-Guided Tour:** Leaving **Sorrento,** the road winds up into the hills past lemon groves and hidden houses. The gray-green trees are olives. (Notice the green nets slung around the trunks; these are unfurled in October and November, when the ripe olives drop naturally, for an easy self-harvest.) Dark, green-leafed trees planted in dense groves are the source of the region's lemons (many destined to become *limoncello* liqueur) and big, fat citrons (*cedri,* mostly used for marmalade). The black nets over the orange and lemon groves create a greenhouse effect, trapping warmth and humidity for maximum tastiness, while offering protection from extreme weather (preserving the peels used for *limoncello*).

Atop the ridge outside Sorrento, look to your right: The two small islands are the **Li Galli Islands,** where some say the sirens in Homer's *Odyssey* lived. The largest of these islands was once owned by the famed ballet dancer Rudolf Nureyev; it's now a luxury residence, rented to wealthy visitors for upward of $100,000 per week (bring your own yacht or arrive by helicopter).

When Nureyev bought the island, the only building standing was the stony watchtower—the first of many you'll see all along the coast. These were strategically placed within sight of one another so that a relay of rooftop bonfires could quickly spread word of a pirate attack.

The limestone cliffs that plunge into the sea were traversed by a hand-carved trail that became a modern road in the mid-19th century. Fruit stands sell produce from farms and orchards just over the hill. Limestone absorbs heat and rainwater, making this south-facing coastline a fertile suntrap, with temperatures as much as 10 degrees higher than in nearby Sorrento. The chalky, reflective limestone, which extends below the surface, accounts for the uniquely colorful blues and greens of the water. With the favorable climate, bougainvillea, geraniums, oleander, and wisteria grow like weeds here in the summer. Notice the nets pulled tight against the cliffs—they're designed to catch rocks that often tumble loose after heavy rains.

The dramatic, exotic-looking town of **Positano** is the main stop along the coast. The town is built on a series of man-made terraces, which were carefully carved out of the steep rock, then filled with fertile soil carried here from Sorrento on the backs of donkeys. You can read the history of the region in Positano's rooftops—a mix of Roman-style red terra-cotta tiles and white domes inspired by the Saracens (see sidebar).

If you're getting off here, stay on through the first main stop by the round-domed yellow church (Chiesa Nuova), which is a very long walk above town. Instead, get off at the second main stop,

The Saracens

Along Italy's coast, you'll hear about the Saracens. To understand who they were, go back in time and across the sea to Spain in 1492. That's when Ferdinand and Isabel—Spain's foremost Catholic monarchs—defeated the last Moorish stronghold of Granada. The conquered Muslims were allowed to settle in the mountains to the south. But over time, Catholic intolerance forced most Muslims across the Mediterranean to North Africa.

In the 16th century, the North African coast from Tunisia to Morocco was somewhat united and known as the Barbary States. The displaced Moors (chased from Spain), along with indigenous Berber tribes, were often referred to as Saracens, a term perhaps derived from Arabic, meaning "marauder." Saracens raided Christian ships, capturing and reselling cargo and holding crews for ransom. Christian kingdoms paid bribes to keep shipping lanes open. The Barbary Coast Saracens were loosely aligned with the Ottoman Empire, but that wasn't much help when European powers (plus the United States in its first overseas show of strength) had enough of the raids and declared war. Saracen influence came to an end after their defeat in the Barbary War of 1815, but the Saracen legacy lives on along the Italian coast, with everything from watchtowers to restaurants named after them.

Sponda, then head downhill toward the start of my self-guided Positano Walk (later in this chapter). Sponda is also the best place to catch the onward bus to Amalfi. If you're coming on a smaller minibus, you'll twist all the way down—seemingly going in circles—to Piazza dei Mulini and the start of the walk.

Just south of Positano, **St. Peter's Hotel** (Il San Pietro di Positano, camouflaged below the tiny St. Peter's Church) is just about the poshest stop on the coast. In the adjacent gorge, notice the hotel's terraced gardens (where produce is grown for their restaurant) above an elevator-accessible beach and dock.

Just around the bend, **Praiano** comes into view. Less ritzy or charming than Positano or Amalfi, it's notable for its huge Cathedral of San Gennaro, with a characteristic majolica-tiled roof and dome—a reminder of this region's respected ceramics industry. In spindly Praiano, most of the homes are accessible only by tiny footpaths and staircases. Near the end of town, just before the big tunnel, watch on the left for the big *presepe* (manger scene) embedded into the cliff face. This Praiano-in-miniature was carved by one local man over several decades. At Christmastime, each house is filled with little figures and twinkle lights.

Just past the tunnel, look below and on the right to see another

AMALFI COAST

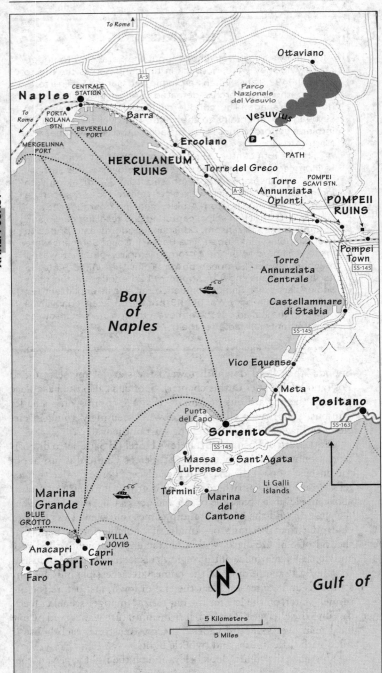

AMALFI COAST

To Rome

Ottaviano

A-3

Parco
Nazionale
del Vesuvio

Naples
CENTRALE
STATION

PORTA
NOLANA
STN.

Barra

Vesuvius

P

PATH

BEVERELLO
PORT

To Rome

MERGELINNA
PORT

Ercolano

Torre del Greco

HERCULANEUM
RUINS

A-3

Torre
Annunziata
Oplonti

POMPEI
SCAVI STN.

POMPEII
RUINS

Pompei
Town

SS-145

Bay
of
Naples

Torre
Annunziata
Centrale

Castellammare
di Stabia

SS-145

Vico Equense

Meta

Positano

SS-163

Punta
del Capo

Sorrento

SS-145

Massa
Lubrense

Sant'Agata

Li Galli
Islands

Termini

Marina
del
Cantone

Marina
Grande

BLUE
GROTTO

VILLA
JOVIS

Anacapri

Capri
Town

Capri

Faro

N

Gulf of

5 Kilometers

5 Miles

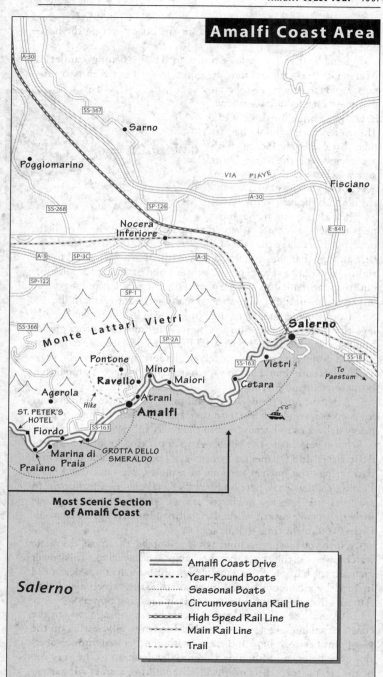

Amalfi Coast Area

AMALFI COAST

Most Scenic Section of Amalfi Coast

Salerno

Legend	
─────	Amalfi Coast Drive
- - - -	Year-Round Boats
··········	Seasonal Boats
+++++++	Circumvesuviana Rail Line
═══════	High Speed Rail Line
═ ═ ═ ═	Main Rail Line
- · - · -	Trail

Saracen watchtower. (Yet another caps the little point on the horizon.)

A bit farther along, look down to see the fishing hamlet of **Marina di Praia** tucked into the gorge *(furore)* between two tunnels.

If you're driving—or being driven—consider a detour down here for a coffee break or meal. This serene, tidy nook has its own little pebbly beach with great views of the stout bluffs and watchtower that hem it in. A seafront walkway curls around the bluff all the way to the tower.

Just after going through the next tunnel, watch for a jagged rock formation on its own little pedestal. Locals see the face of the Virgin Mary in this natural feature and say that she's holding a flower (the tree growing out to the right). Also notice several caged, cantilevered parking pads sticking out from the road. This stretch of coastline is popular for long-term villa rentals—Italians who want to really settle into Amalfi life.

Look down and left for the blink-or-you'll-miss-it fishing village that's aptly named **Fiordo** ("fjord"), filling yet another gorge. You'll see humble homes burrowed into the cliff face, tucked so far into the gorge that they're entirely in shadow for much of the year. Today these are rented out to vacationers; the postage-stamp beach is uncrowded and inviting.

After the next tunnel, in the following hamlet, keep an eye out for donkeys with big baskets on their backs—the only way to make heavy deliveries to homes high in the rocky hills.

Soon you'll pass the big-for-Amalfi parking lot of the **Grotta dello Smeraldo** ("Emerald Grotto"), a cheesy roadside attraction that wrings the most it can out of a pretty, seawater-filled cave. Passing tourists park here and pay €5 to take an elevator down to sea level, pile into big rowboats, and get paddled around a genuinely impressive cavern while the boatman imparts sparse factoids. Unless you've got time to kill, skip it.

Now you're approaching what might be the most dramatic watchtower on the coast, perched atop a near-island. This tower guarded the harbor of the Amalfi navy until the fleet was destroyed in 1343 by a tsunami caused by an earthquake, which also led to Amalfi's decline (it was once one of Italy's leading powers).

Around the next bend you're treated to stunning views of the coastline's namesake town—**Amalfi.** The white villa sitting on the low point between here and there (with another watchtower at its tip) once belonged to Sophia Loren. Now look up to the very top of the steep, steep cliffs overhead. The hulking former Monastery of Santa Rosa occupies this prime territory. Locals proudly explain that the *sfogliatella* dessert so beloved throughout the Campania region was first created at this monastery. (Today it's a luxury resort, where you can pay a premium to sleep in a tight little former monk's cell.)

Now the bus pulls to a halt—at the end of the line, the waterfront of Amalfi town. Spend some time enjoying this once-powerful, now-pleasant city, with its fine cathedral, fascinating paper museum, and fun-to-explore tangle of lanes (covered later in this chapter).

From Amalfi, you can transfer to another bus to head up to **Ravello** (described later), capping a cliff just beyond Amalfi, or onward to the big city of **Salerno.** Alternatively, buses and boats take you back to Positano and Sorrento.

If you're continuing the trip southward (on the bus to Salerno or Ravello), look up to the left as you leave Amalfi—the white house that clings to a cliff (Villa Rondinaia) was home for many years to writer Gore Vidal. Soon you'll pass through the low-impact, less touristy town of **Atrani** (described later in this chapter). From here, you'll enjoy fine (though slightly less thrilling) scenery all the way to Salerno.

Positano

Specializing in scenery and sand, the easygoing town of Positano hangs halfway between Sorrento and Amalfi town on the most spectacular stretch of the coast. According to legend, the Greek god Poseidon created Positano for Pasitea, a nymph he lusted after, but some think the town's name comes from Poseidon himself.

In the early Middle Ages, Positano was part of the Amalfi Republic, famed for its bold sailors and hearty fleet. But after a big 1343 tsunami and the pirate raids of the Middle Ages, its wealth and power declined. Positano flourished again as a favorite under the Bourbon royal family in the 1700s, when many of its fine mansions were built. Until the late 1800s, the only access was by donkey path or by sea. In the 20th century, Positano became a haven for artists and writers escaping Communist Russia and Nazi Germany. In 1953, American writer John Steinbeck's essay on the town popularized Positano among tourists, and soon after it became a trendy stop. That was when the town gave the world "Moda

AMALFI COAST

Positano

MAIN COASTAL ROAD →

One-way street

SS-163

VIA GUGLIELMO MARCONI

SS-163

VIALE PASITEA

Chiesa Nuova (B)

9

VIA BOSCARIELLO

P

P

6

VIALE PASITEA

5

VIA FORNILLO

VIA TRARA

N

100 Meters
100 Yards

VIA POSITANESI

11

SCENIC VIEWPOINT

Fornillo Beach

WALK ENDS

To Sorrento

Positano"—a leisurely *dolce vita* lifestyle of walking barefoot; wearing bright, happy, colorful clothes; and sporting skimpy bikinis.

Today, the village, a breathtaking ▲▲▲ sight from a distance, is a pleasant gathering of cafés and expensive stores draped over an almost comically steep hillside. Terraced gardens and historic houses cascade downhill to the stately Church of Santa Maria Assunta and a broad, pebbly beach. Positano is famous for its fashions—and many of its shops are women's clothing boutiques (linen is a particularly popular item).

The "skyline" looks like it did a century ago. Notice the town's characteristic Saracen-inspired rooftop domes. Filled with sand, these provide low-tech insulation—to help buildings, in the days before central air, stay cool in summer and warm in winter. Traditionally, they were painted white in summer and black in winter.

For decades, it's been practically impossible to get a building permit in Positano. Landowners who want to renovate can't make external changes. Endless staircases are a way of life for the hardy locals. Only one street in Positano allows motorized traffic; the rest are narrow pedestrian lanes. While Positano has 4,000 residents, an average of 12,000 tourists visit daily from Easter through October. But because hotels don't take large groups (bus access is too difficult), this town—unlike Sorrento—has been spared the worst

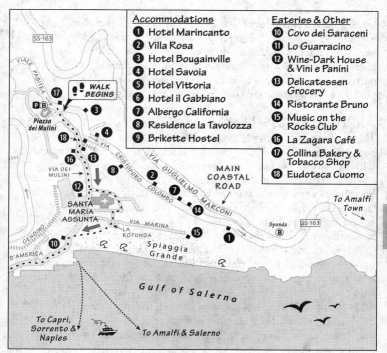

AMALFI COAST

ravages of big-bus tourism. In winter, hotels shut down and the town once again belongs to the locals.

Consider seeing Positano as a day trip from Sorrento: Take the bus out and the afternoon ferry home, but be sure to check boat schedules when you arrive—the last ferry often leaves before 18:00 and doesn't always run in spring and fall. Or spend the night to enjoy the magic of Positano after dark. The town has a local flavor at night, when the grown-ups stroll and the kids play soccer on the church porch.

Orientation to Positano

Squished into a ravine, with narrow alleys that cascade down to the harbor, Positano requires you to stroll, whether you're going up or heading down. The center of town has no main square (unless you count the beach). There's little to do here but eat, window shop, and enjoy the beach and views...hence the town's popularity.

Tourist Information: There's no full-time TI. In summer, the town sets up information stands at the Sponda bus stop, Piazza dei Mulini, and the beach.

Local Guide: Positano native **Lucia Ferrara** (a.k.a. "Zia Lucy") brings substance to this glitzy town. During the day, she leads guided hiking tours, including the "Path of the Gods" high above town (up to 10 people, about 4 miles, 5 hours, €55/person, includes picnic). In the evening, if there's enough demand, she leads a Positano town walking tour (3 hours, departs at 17:00, €30/person). She also offers food tours, and can guide in Amalfi town (+39 339 272 0971, www.zialucy.com).

ARRIVAL IN POSITANO

The main coastal highway winds above the town. Regional SITA buses stop at two scheduled bus stops located at either end of town: **Chiesa Nuova** (at Bar Internazionale, near the Sorrento end of town; use this one only if you're staying at Brikette Hostel) and **Sponda** (nearer Amalfi town). Although both stops are near roads leading downhill through the town to the beach, Sponda is closer and less steep; from this stop, it's a scenic 20-minute downhill stroll/shop/munch to the beach.

Neither bus stop has easy **baggage storage.** Positano does have porter services: A porter can meet you at the Sponda bus stop and watch your bags for €5 apiece—but you have to call them in advance (try Positano Porter, +39 089 875 310). A last resort is to get off at the Sponda stop and roll your bags all the way down to Piazza dei Mulini, where the porters tend to hang out.

If you're catching the SITA bus from Positano, be aware that it may leave from the Sponda stop five minutes before the printed departure time. There's simply no room for the bus to wait, so in case the driver is early, you should be, too. Buy tickets at the tobacco shop in the town center (on Piazza dei Mulini).

To skip the walk up to the stop, take one of the dizzy little **shuttle buses** (marked *Interno Positano*) that constantly loop through Positano, connecting the lower town with the two bus stops up on the highway (2/hour, €1.30 at tobacco shop on Piazza dei Mulini, €1.80 on board, catch it at Piazza dei Mulini). The Collina bakery is just across from the shuttle bus stop, with a fine, breezy terrace to enjoy while you wait.

Coming from the **ferry,** you can give luggage to one of the porter services or lug everything uphill yourself. Follow crowds up wide stairs to the large church, then follow the trellis to Piazza dei Mulini. You'll be doing the reverse of my Positano Walk (described next).

Drivers must go with the one-way flow, entering the town only at the Chiesa Nuova bus stop (closest to Sorrento) and exiting at Sponda (a 20-minute one-way loop). Driving is a headache here. Parking is even worse.

Positano Walk

This short, self-guided stroll downhill will help you get your bearings from top to bottom.

• *Start at...*

Piazza dei Mulini: This "square" is the town center's main junction—as close to the beach as vehicles can get—and the lower stop for the little shuttle bus. The **Collina bakery** is a nice place for gelato or pastries.

Dip into the little yellow **Church of the Holy Rosary** (by the bus stop), with a serene 12th-century interior. Up front, to the right of the main altar, find the delicately carved fragment of a Roman sarcophagus (first century BC). Positano sits upon the site of a sprawling Roman villa, and we'll see a few reminders of that age as we walk.

In summer, look for a popular *granita* stand at the top of the lane (across from the church), where the family has been following the same secret lemon slush recipe for generations.

Now continue downhill into town, passing a variety of **shops**—many selling linen and ceramics. These industries boomed when tourists discovered Positano. The beach-inspired Moda Positano fashion label was born as a break from the rigid dress code of the 1950s. (For tips on shopping for linen, see "Shopping," under "Sights in Positano," later). Positano also considers itself an artists' colony, and you'll see many **galleries** featuring the work of area artists.

• *Wander downhill to the "fork" in the road (stairs to the left, road to the right). You've reached...*

Midtown: At **Eudoteca Cuomo** (#3), butchers Pasquale and Rosario stock fine local red wines and are happy to explain their virtues. They also make homemade sausages, salami, and *panini*—good for a quick lunch. The smaller set of stairs leads to the recommended **Delicatessen grocery,** where Emilia can fix you a good picnic.

La Zagara (across the lane from the steps, at #10, with a leafy terrace) is a pricey pastry shop by day and a restaurant by night. Tempting pastries such as the rum-drenched *babà* (a southern Italian favorite) fill the window display. A bit farther downhill, **Brunella** (on the right, at #24) is respected for traditional quality, and Positano-made linens.

Across the street, the ritzy **Hotel Palazzo Murat** fills what was once a grand Benedictine monastery. Napoleon, fearing the power of the Church, had many such monasteries closed during his rule here. This one became a private palace, named for his brother-in-law, who was briefly the King of Naples. Glance into the plush courtyard to appreciate the scene. Continuing on, under a fragrant wisteria trellis, you'll pass "street merchants' gulch," where artisans display their goodies.

• *Continue straight down. You'll run into a fork at the big church. For now, turn right and go downstairs to Piazza Flavio Gioia, facing the big...*

Church of Santa Maria Assunta: This church, which sits upon Roman ruins, was once the abbey of Positano's 12th-century Benedictine monastery. Originally Romanesque, it got an extreme Baroque makeover in the 18th century, when the town was booming and the coast was clear of pirate attacks.

Step **inside** and find these items: In the first chapel on the left is a fine manger scene *(presepe)*. Its original 18th-century figurines give you an idea of the folk costumes of the age. Above the main altar is the Black Madonna, an icon-like Byzantine painting likely brought here from Constantinople by monks in the 12th century. But locals prefer a more romantic origin story for the gilded painting: Saracen pirates had it on their ship as plunder. A violent storm hit—sure to sink the evil ship. The painting of Mary spoke, saying, *"Posa, posa"* (lay me down), and the ship glided safely to this harbor. The pirates were so stricken they became Christians. Locals kept the painting, and the town became known as *Posa-tano* (recalling Mary's command).

To the right of the altar, a small freestanding display case holds a silver-and-copper bust of St. Vitus (along with his bones, now holy relics). He's the town patron, who brought Christianity here in about AD 300. In the adjacent niche (on the right) is a rare 1599 painting by Fabrizio Santafede of Baby Jesus being circumcised, considered the finest historic painting in town.

Back outside, you'll see the **bell tower,** dating from 1707. Above the door, it sports a Romanesque relief scavenged from the original church. The scene—a wolf mermaid with seven little fish—was a reminder to worshippers of how integral the sea was to their livelihood. Nicknamed "our pagan protector," it's a good example of how early Christians incorporated pagan elements into their worship. Notice the characteristic shallow, white "insulation domes" on rooftops in front of the church.

• *Backtrack up the steps, where you'll see a phone-booth-like, glass-walled ticket office for the...*

Roman Villa Complex: The entire town center of today's Positano—from this church all the way up to Piazza dei Mulini, where we started this walk—sits upon the site of a huge Roman villa complex, buried when Mount Vesuvius erupted in AD 79. In 2004, archaeologists made an exciting find under the church crypt: a surviving room from the villa. Now a 30-minute guided tour of the excavated remains (limited to 10 people at a time) will take you down a safe, well-lit stairway to see the walls and floor of

AMALFI COAST

what might have been a dining room. The walls are frescoed with decorations not unlike those at Pompeii. Artifacts from the excavation are nicely displayed, and the guide explains the history of the church directly above you, as well as its crypt (pricey at €15, tours daily April-Oct 9:00-21:00, Nov-March until 14:00, Piazza Flavio Gioia 7, +39 331 208 5821, https://marpositano.it).

• *Now circle around the church, and continue descending the steps to the right (following* beach/spiaggia *signs). You'll eventually come to the little square with concrete benches facing the beach, called...*

La Rotonda: This is the town gathering point in the evening, as local boys hustle tourist girls into the nearby nightclub. Step down to beach level. Residents traded their historic baptistery font with Amalfi town for the two iron lions you see facing the beach. Around the staircase, you'll also see some original Roman columns, scavenged from the buried villa. Look up and admire the colorful majolica tiles so typical of church domes in this region.

Positano's **beach,** called Spiaggia Grande, is almost completely private now. It's atmospherically littered with a commotion of fishing boats and recreational craft. The big kiosk on the beach sells excursions to Capri and elsewhere.

Looking out over the beach from this point, you can see three of the **watchtowers** built centuries ago to protect the Amalfi Coast from Saracen pirates: one on the far-left horizon, just below Praiano; a small one on the Li Galli Islands, ahead and right; and the rectangular one far to the right, marking the far end of Fornillo Beach. Defenders used these towers—strategically situated within sight of each other—to relay smoke signals. In more recent times, the tower on the right (near Fornillo Beach) was a hangout for artists, who holed up inside for inspiration. (The people of Positano pride themselves on being artists rather than snazzy jet-setters like those in Capri.)

As you face out to sea, on the far-left side of the beach (below Rada Restaurant) is **Music on the Rocks,** a chic club that's the only remaining piece of the 1970s scene, when Positano really rocked. While it's dead until very late, you're welcome to peek in at the cool troglo-disco interior, or go upstairs to the Fly Bar for the priciest cocktails in town.

• *Now turn right and wander across the beach. Behind the kiosks that sell boat tickets, find the steps to the **path** that climbs up and over, past a 13th-century lookout fort from Saracen pirate days, to the next beach. It's a worthwhile little five-minute walk through a shady ravine to...*

Fornillo Beach: This is where locals go for better swimming and to escape some of the tourist crowds. Via Positanesi d'America is the lane (lit at night) leading to the beach. It's named for the people who emigrated to America between the 1860s and the 1940s (more than 50 percent of Positano's population) and sent money back to build this path. (Some locals remember when priests used to say at Mass, "And now, let's pray for Positanesi d'America.")

• *Our walk is over. Time to relax. When you're ready to return, go back the way you came to the main beach. Although tempting, Via Fornillo continues straight up the cliffside with a whopping 200-plus stairs...not for the faint of heart.*

Sights in Positano

Beaches

Positano's pebbly and sandy primary beach, **Spiaggia Grande,** is colorful with umbrellas as it stretches wide around the cove. It's mostly private (pay €20-100 to enter, includes lounge chair and umbrella, most expensive near Music on the Rocks). There's a tiny free section near the middle, close to where the boats take off. Look for the pay showers. The nearest WC is beneath the steps to the right (as you face the water).

Fornillo Beach, a less-crowded option just around the bend (to the west) of Spiaggia Grande, is favored by residents, with more affordable chair/umbrella rentals (€15-20) and a wider free area. It has a mellow Robinson Crusoe vibe, with a sturdy Saracen tower keeping watch overhead. This beach has a few humble snack bars and lunch eateries. Note that its position, tucked back in the rocks, means it gets shade earlier in the day than the main beach.

Boat Trips

Boats serving Positano pull up to the dock at the west end of Spiaggia Grande (to the right as you face the sea; booths sell tickets). Also consider renting a rowboat, or see whether they can talk you into taking a boat tour. Passenger boats run to Amalfi, Capri, Salerno, and Sorrento; see "Getting Around the Amalfi Coast" on page 1079.

Shopping

Linen: Garments made of **linen** (especially women's dresses) are popular items in Positano. To find a good-quality piece that will last, look for "Made in Positano" (or at least "Made in Italy") on the label, and check the percentage of linen; 60 percent or more is good quality and 100 percent is best. Two companies with top reputations and multiple outlets are **Brunella** and **Pepito's** (each has shops on Via Colombo, near the top of town; along Viale Pasitea, a main drag; and along claustrophobic Via del Saracino, near the bottom of town, parallel to the beach).

Ceramics: One of the oldest ceramics stores in Positano, **Ceramica Assunta** carries colorful Solimene dinnerware and more at two locations (Via Cristoforo Colombo 97 and 137).

Custom Sandals: Positano has a tradition of handmade sandals, crafted to your specifications while you wait (prices start at about €70). One good shop, La Botteguccia, faces a tranquil little square (Piazzetta del Saracino); around the corner, in front of the Capricci restaurant, you'll see Carmine Todisco, who loves to explain how his grandfather shod Jackie O.

Nightlife

The big-time action in the old town center is the impressive club **Music on the Rocks,** literally carved into the rocks on the beach (opens at 23:00 mid-April-Oct, but the party starts even later; there's often a €15-30 cover charge on weekends and in summer, which includes a drink; closed off-season; Via Grotte Dell'Incanto 51, +39 089 875 874, www.musicontherocks.it).

Sleeping in Positano

Most of these hotels are on Via Cristoforo Colombo, which leads from the Sponda bus stop down into the village (ideal for arrival by bus). Most places close in the winter (Dec-Feb or longer). Expect to pay at least €30 per day to park.

$$$$ **Hotel Marincanto** is a somewhat impersonal four-star hotel with 32 beautiful rooms and a bright breakfast terrace practically teetering on a cliff. Suites seem to be designed for a *luna di miele*—honeymoon (air-con, elevator, pool, stairs down to a private beach, pay parking, closed Nov-March, Via Cristoforo Colombo 50, reception on bottom floor, +39 089 875 130, www.marincanto. it, info@marincanto.it). This is the closest hotel to the Sponda bus stop, 50 yards away.

$$$$ **Villa Rosa** decorates its 12 spacious rooms plus one apartment with—you guessed it—roses. Most rooms have views plus a terrace, which is the perfect place to have your breakfast served (air-con, no elevator, closed Nov-March, Via Cristoforo Colombo 127, +39 089 811 955, www.villarosapositano.it, info@ villarosapositano.it).

$$$$ **Hotel Bougainville** rents 16 comfortable rooms, half with balconies. Everything's bright, modern, and tasteful (rooms without views are cheaper, air-con, small elevator, closed Nov-March, Via Cristoforo Colombo 25, +39 089 875 047, www. bougainville.it, info@bougainville.it).

$$$$ **Hotel Savoia,** run by the friendly D'Aiello family, has 39 sizeable, breezy, bright, simple, tiled rooms (RS%, most rooms with balcony or terrace, some cheaper nonview rooms, air-con, elevator, closed Nov-March, Via Cristoforo Colombo 73, +39 089 875 003, www.savoiapositano.it, info@savoiapositano.it).

$$$$ **Hotel Vittoria** sits just west of the town center with 20 open, spacious rooms and arched ceilings that feel right out

of Positano's 1950s boom era. Sprawling up a cliffside, they offer their own free porter service (tips appreciated). All rooms have balconies, most with views overlooking the town (buffet breakfast, uphill from Fornillo Beach on Via Fornillo 19, +39 089 875 049, www.hotelvittoriapositano.it, info@hotelvittoriapostiano.it).

$$$$ Hotel il Gabbiano lies west of the busy town center and has 19 simple but tasteful rooms plus one apartment. All have a view terrace. From here you can explore the many eateries downhill (past the curve) along Viale Pasitea without having to trek into the main part of town (air-con, elevator, closed Nov-March, Viale Pasitea 310, +39 089 875 306, www.ilgabbianopositano.com, info@ilgabbianopositano.com).

$$$$ Albergo California has 15 spacious rooms (all with lofty views), a grand terrace draped with vines, and full breakfasts. The Cinque family—including Maria, Bronx-born son John, and grandchildren Giuseppe and Maria—will welcome you (air-con, pay parking, closed Nov-Feb, Via Cristoforo Colombo 141, +39 089 875 382, www.hotelcaliforniapositano.it, info@hotelcaliforniapositano.it).

$$$ Residence la Tavolozza is an attractive six-room hotel (doubles only), warmly run by Celeste (cheh-LEHS-tay) and English-speaking daughters Francesca and Paola. Each cheerily tiled room comes with a view, a terrace, and silence (lavish à la carte breakfast extra, air-con, confirm by phone if arriving late, closed Dec-Feb, Via Cristoforo Colombo 10, +39 089 875 040, www.latavolozzapositano.it, info@latavolozzapositano.it).

$ Brikette Hostel is your best budget option in this ritzy town. Its 35 dorm beds are pricey by hostel standards, but you're in Positano. It has a great sun and breakfast terrace and a youthful ambience (private and family rooms available, breakfast extra, cheap dinners, air-con, usually open all year, leave bus at Chiesa Nuova stop and backtrack uphill 500 feet to Via G. Marconi 358, www.hostel-positano.com, hostelpositano@gmail.com, Cristiana). The hostel isn't reachable by phone; email instead.

Eating in Positano

Down at the beach, several interchangeable restaurants with view terraces leave people fat and happy, albeit with skinnier wallets (figure €15-20 pastas and *secondi*, plus pricey drinks and sides, and a cover charge). Little distinguishes one place from the next; all are scenic, convenient, and overpriced. **$$$ Covo dei Saraceni** offers the best value on the beach, with good pizza and tables overlooking the action (daily, on the far right as you face the sea, where Via Positanesi d'America starts).

A local favorite for its great views, **$$$ Lo Guarracino** is on the path to Fornillo Beach, with good food at prices similar to the beachfront places (daily 12:00-15:30 & 18:30-22:30, closed Nov-March, follow path behind the boat-ticket kiosks 5 minutes to Via Positanesi d'America 12, +39 089 875 794). **$$ Wine-**

Dark House, tucked around the base of the stairs below the church, fills a cute little piazzetta at the start of Via del Saracino. They serve good pastas and *secondi* and excellent local wines, and are popular with Positano's youngsters for their long list of sandwiches (Wed-Mon 10:00-15:30 & 18:30-22:30, closed Tue, Via del Saracino 6, +39 089 811 925).

Picnics: If a picnic dinner on your balcony or the beach sounds good, sunny Emilia at the **Delicatessen** grocery store can supply the ingredients: *antipasto misto*, pastas, home-cooked dishes, and sandwiches made to order. She'll heat it up for you and throw in the picnic ware. Come early for the best selection (all sold by weight, daily 7:00-22:00, shorter hours off-season, Via dei Mulini 5, +39 089 875 489). **Vini e Panini** (a.k.a. "The Wine Shop"), another small grocery, is a block from the beach just behind the church steps. Daniela, the fifth-generation owner, speaks English and happily makes sandwiches to order. Choose between the "Caprese" (mozzarella and tomato) and the "Positano" (mozzarella, tomato, and prosciutto), or create your own. They also have a nice selection of well-priced regional wines (daily 8:00-20:00, until 22:00 in summer, closed mid-Nov-mid-March, +39 089 875 175).

"Uptown": The unassuming, family-run **$$$ Ristorante Bruno** is handy to my listed hotels on Via Cristoforo Colombo. While expensive, it has nice views and is worth considering if you want a meal without hiking down into the town center (daily 12:00-23:00, closed Nov-Feb, near the top of Via Cristoforo Colombo at #157, +39 089 875 179).

Amalfi Town

After Rome fell, the town of Amalfi was one of the first to trade goods—coffee, carpets, and paper—between Europe and points east. Its heyday was the 10th and 11th centuries, when it was a powerful maritime republic—a trading power with a fleet that controlled this region and rivaled Pisa, Genoa, and Venice. The Republic of Amalfi founded a hospital in Jerusalem and claims to have founded the Knights of Malta order—even giving them the Amalfi

AMALFI COAST

cross, which became the famous Maltese cross. Amalfi minted its own coins and established "rules of the sea"—the basics of which survive today.

In 1343, this little powerhouse was suddenly destroyed by a tsunami caused by an undersea earthquake. That disaster, com-

pounded by devastating plagues, left Amalfi a humble backwater. Much of the culture of this entire region was driven by this town—but because it fell from power, Amalfi doesn't always get the credit it deserves. Today its 5,000 residents live off tourism. The coast's namesake is not as picturesque as Positano or as well connected as Sorrento, but it has a real-life feel and a vivacious bustle.

Though generally less touristy than Positano, Amalfi is still packed during the day with big-bus tours (whose drivers pay €80 an hour to park while their groups shop for *limoncello* and ceramics). Amalfi's charms reveal themselves early and late in the day, when the crowds dissipate.

Orientation to Amalfi Town

Amalfi's waterfront is the coast's biggest transport hub. Right next to each other at Piazza Flavio Gioia are the bus station, ferry docks, and a parking lot (€5/hour; if the lot is full, park in the huge Lunarossa garage, burrowed into the hillside just past town and just before the tunnel leading into Atrani). The waterfront hub is overlooked by a statue of local boy Flavio Gioia, the purported inventor of the magnetic compass.

Amalfi's **TI** is just 100 yards up the main road heading east, right before the post office and overlooking the beach (daily 9:00-17:00; Nov-March Mon-Sat until 14:00, closed Sun; pay WC in same courtyard, Corso della Repubbliche Marinare 27; facing the sea, it's to the left; +39 089 871 107, http://incampania.com).

HELPFUL HINTS

Don't Get Stranded: If you're day-tripping to Amalfi from elsewhere in the region, check locally to confirm when the last return bus or boat to Sorrento or Salerno leaves in the evening (in winter this can be as early as 19:00). Don't plan to leave on the last bus or boat of the day in peak season: If that bus or boat is full, your only way home might be a €100 taxi ride.

Baggage Storage and Bus Tickets: You can store your bag safely

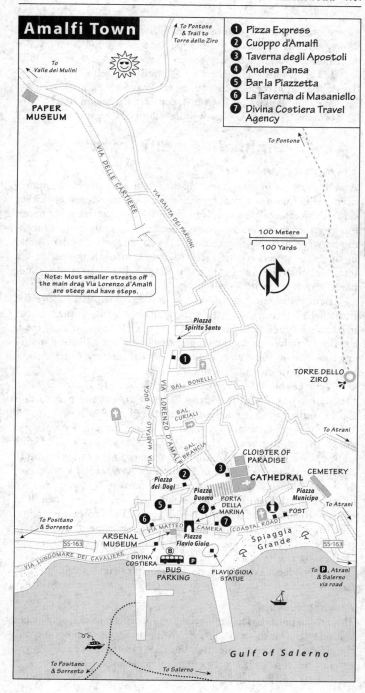

Amalfi Town

1. Pizza Express
2. Cuoppo d'Amalfi
3. Taverna degli Apostoli
4. Andrea Pansa
5. Bar la Piazzetta
6. La Taverna di Masaniello
7. Divina Costiera Travel Agency

To Pontone & Trail to Torre dello Ziro

To Valle dei Mulini

PAPER MUSEUM

VIA DELLE CARTIERE

VIA SALITA DEI PARIONI

To Pontone

100 Meters
100 Yards

N

AMALFI COAST

Note: Most smaller streets off the main drag Via Lorenzo d'Amalfi are steep and have steps.

Piazza Spirito Santo

TORRE DELLO ZIRO

SAL. BONELLI

VIA LORENZO D'AMALFI

SAL. CURIALI

VIA MASTALO II DUCA

SAL. BRANCIA

To Atrani

CLOISTER OF PARADISE

CEMETERY

CATHEDRAL

Piazza dei Dogi

Piazza Duomo

Piazza Municipo

PORTA DELLA MARINA

To Atrani

POST

To Positano & Sorrento

VIA MATTEO CAMERA (COASTAL ROAD)

ARSENAL MUSEUM

Piazza Flavio Gioia

Spiaggia Grande

SS-163

SS-163

VIA LUNGOMARE DEI CAVALIERE

DIVINA COSTIERA

BUS PARKING

FLAVIO GIOIA STATUE

To P., Atrani & Salerno via road

Gulf of Salerno

To Positano & Sorrento

To Salerno

at the **Divina Costiera Travel Office** facing the waterfront square, across from the bus parking area (€5/4 hours, daily 8:00-20:00, closed Feb, Piazza Flavio Gioia 3, +39 089 871 181). They also sell tickets for the bus to Ravello.

Speedboat Charters: To hire your own boat for a tour of the coastline from Amalfi (or to Capri), consider **Premium Boat Charter** (+39 329 460 3771, www.premiumboatcharter.com).

Sights in Amalfi Town

AMALFI TOWN

Amalfi's one main street runs up from the waterfront through a deep valley, with stairways to courtyards and houses on either side. It's worth walking uphill to the workaday upper end of town. Super-atmospheric, narrow, stepped side lanes branch off, squeezing between hulking old buildings. If you hear water under a grate in the main street, it's the creek that runs through the ravine—a reminder that the town originally straddled the stream but later paved it over to create a main drag.

Before you enter the town, notice the colorful tile above the Porta della Marina gateway, showing off the trading domain of the maritime Republic of Amalfi. Just to the left, along the busy road, a series of arches marks the long, narrow, vaulted halls of Amalfi's arsenal—where ships were built in the 11th century. One of these is now the little Arsenal Museum.

Venture into town, and you'll quickly come to Piazza Duomo, the main square, with the cathedral—the town's most important sight—and a spring water-spewing statue of St. Andrew.

As you get farther away from the water, Amalfi becomes less glitzy and more traditional. The Paper Museum is a 10-minute walk up Via Lorenzo d'Amalfi, the main drag. On the way up to the museum, don't miss the huge, outdoor *presepi* (Nativity scenes) on your left. From the museum, the road narrows and you can turn off onto a path leading to the shaded Valle dei Mulini; it's full of paper-mill ruins that recall this once proud and prosperous industry. The ruined castle clinging to the rocky ridge above Amalfi is Torre dello Ziro, a good lookout point for intrepid hikers (see "Hikes," later).

As you return downhill, be sure to explore up the winding and narrow lanes and arcaded passages on either side of the main street.

Arsenal Museum

This small, underground museum just across the road from the bus station tells a bit about Amalfi's maritime glory years. Stepping into the single long room under the dramatic vaulted stone ceiling, you can just tell that 1,000 years ago, they made ships here.

Cost and Hours: €4; Wed-Thu 10:00-13:00 & 16:00-18:00, Fri-Sun until 20:00, closed Mon-Tue; Piazza Flavio Gioia, +39 089 873 6204, https://arsenalediamalfi.it.

Cathedral

This church is "Amalfi Romanesque" (a mix of Moorish and Byzantine flavors, built c. 1000-1300), with a fanciful Neo-Byzantine facade from the 19th century. Climb the imposing stairway, which functions as a mini Spanish Steps-style hangout zone and a handy outdoor theater. The 1,000-year-old bronze door at the top was given to Amalfi by a wealthy local merchant who had it made in Constantinople. Visitors are directed on a one-way circuit through the cathedral complex with four stops: the cloister, original basilica, crypt, and cathedral.

Cost and Hours: €3, daily 10:00-17:00, open later in summer, closed Jan-March. The cathedral—but not the rest of the complex—can be entered free for prayer or discreet visits daily 7:30-10:00 & 17:00-19:30; it's closed 10:00-17:00 except as part of the paid visit; +39 089 871 324, www.parrocchiaamalfi.com. There's a fine, free WC at the top of the steps (through unmarked green door, just a few steps before ticket booth, ask for key at desk).

Visiting the Cathedral: You'll follow a self-guided, one-way tour of the complex, beginning in a courtyard of 120 graceful columns—the **"Cloister of Paradise."** This was the cemetery for nobles in the 13th century (note their stone sarcophagi). Don't miss the fine view of the bell tower and its majolica tiles.

The original ninth-century church, known as the **Basilica of the Crucifix,** boasts a fine 13th-century wooden crucifix. Today the basilica is a museum filled with the cathedral's art treasures. The Angevin Mitre (Mitra Angioina), with a "pavement of tiny pearls" setting off its gold and gems, has been worn by bishops since the 14th century. Also on display (waist-high, facing the altar) is a carved wooden decoration from a Saracen pirate ship that wrecked just outside of town in 1544 during a freak storm. The church is dedicated to St. Andrew, whom believers credit with causing the storm and saving the town from certain pillage and plunder.

Down the stairs to the right of the basilica's altar is the **Crypt of St. Andrew.** Just as Venice needed St. Mark to get on the pilgrimage map, Amalfi needed St. Andrew—one of the apostles who, along with his brother Peter, left their fishing nets to become the original "fishers of men." Under the huge bronze statue, you'll see a reliquary holding what are believed to be Andrew's remains (kneel at the back of the crypt for a better view). These were brought here from Constantinople in 1206 during the Crusades—an indication of the wealth and importance of Amalfi back then.

Climb the stairs up into the **cathedral** itself. Behind the main altar is a painting of St. Andrew martyred on an X-shaped cross flanked by two Egyptian granite columns supporting a triumphal arch. Before leaving, check out the delicate mother-of-pearl crucifix (right of door in back).

▲Paper Museum (Museo della Carta)

This excellent little museum—worth ▲▲▲ for paper enthusiasts—makes for a good excuse to break free from the crowds and walk up the main drag to a quieter, more local part of town. Paper has been an important industry here since Amalfi's glory days in the Middle Ages. Millworkers would pound rags into pulp in a big vat, pull it up using a screen, and air-dry each sheet (the same technique used to make artisan paper today—look for it at shops in town). At this cavernous, cool museum (an actual paper mill from the 13th century), a multilingual guide collects groups at the entrance (no particular times) for a 25-minute tour. The guide recounts the history and process of papermaking and turns on the museum's vintage machinery. You'll see how the Amalfi River (which you can still hear rumbling underfoot) powered this important industry, and you'll learn the origins of the term "watermark." Kids can dip a screen into the rag pool and make a sheet of paper. It's amazing to think this factory produced paper through 1969 (when it was replaced by a modern facility up the valley).

Cost and Hours: €4.50; daily 10:00-19:00, shorter hours and closed Mon Nov-Jan, closed Feb, last entry 40 minutes before closing; a 10-minute walk up the main street from the cathedral—follow signs to *Museo della Carta* at Via delle Cartiere 23; +39 089 830 4561, www.museodellacarta.it.

HIKES

Amalfi is the starting point for several fine hikes, two of which I've described here. The TI hands out photocopies of Giovanni Visetti's trail maps (or download them from his engaging website, www. giovis.com). The best book on local hikes is Julian Tippett's *Sorrento Amalfi Capri Car Tours and Walks* (2015), with useful color-coded maps and info on public transportation to the trailheads. Lucia Ferrara, a great guide based in Positano, leads hikes around Amalfi (see her listing on page 1091).

Hike #1: Pontone

This loop trail leads up the valley past paper-mill ruins, ending in the tiny town of Pontone; you can get lunch there, and head back down to the town of Amalfi (allow 3 hours total). Bring a good map, since it's easy to veer off the main route. Start your hike by following the main road (Via Lorenzo d'Amalfi) away from the sea.

After the Paper Museum, jog right, then left to join the trail, which runs through the shaded woods along a babbling stream. Heed the signs that warn people to stay away from the ruins of paper mills (no matter how tempting they look), since many are ready to collapse on unwary hikers. Continue up to Pontone, where **Trattoria l'Antico Borgo** offers wonderful cuisine and a great view (Via Noce 4, +39 334 748 6611). After lunch, return to Amalfi via a steep stairway.

If you're feeling ambitious and have good shoes, before you head back to Amalfi, add a one-hour detour from Pontone (30 minutes each way) to visit the ridge-hugging **Torre dello Ziro** (a map and trail description are at www.giovis.com). You'll be rewarded with a spectacular view from the headland between Amalfi and Atrani.

Hike #2: Atrani

For an easier walk, head to the nearby town of Atrani. This village, just a 15-minute stroll beyond Amalfi town, is a world apart; its 1,500 residents consider themselves definitely *not* from Amalfi. Leave Amalfi via the main road and stay on the water side until the promenade ends. Cross the street, continue a few more yards, then go up the whitewashed staircase just past the pizzeria. From here, twist up through old lanes to a paved route that takes you over the hill and drops you into Atrani in about 15 minutes.

With relatively few tourists, a delightful town square, and a free, sandy beach (if you drive here, pay for parking at harbor), Atrani has none of Amalfi's trendy resort feel. Piazza Umberto I is the core of town, with cafés, restaurants, and little grocery stores that can make sandwiches. A whitewashed staircase leads up to the serene and beautiful town church (under the clock face).

To save time and sweat on the return walk, follow the promenade just above water level toward Amalfi. Then walk up through the restaurant terrace and find the big, long tunnel next to the parking garage—this will deposit you in the middle of Amalfi.

From Atrani, you could theoretically continue up to **Ravello** (described later in this chapter). But unless you're part mountain goat, you'll probably prefer catching the bus to Ravello from Amalfi town instead.

AMALFI COAST

Eating in Amalfi Town

Quick Bites: Walk five minutes up the main drag; on the right, past the first archway, is **$ Pizza Express,** with honest pies, calzones, and heated sandwiches to go (Thu-Tue 11:00-21:00, closed Wed, Via Capuano 48, +39 329 046 9403). The **Cuoppo d'Amalfi** fried-fish stand at Piazza dei Dogi (described below) is another good option.

On the Main Square, Piazza Duomo: Several pricey places face the cathedral steps. The best of the bunch is tucked just around the left side of the grand staircase, up a smaller flight of stairs: **$$$$ Taverna degli Apostoli,** with colorful outdoor tables and cozy upstairs dining room in what was once an art gallery. The menu is brief but thoughtful, going beyond the old standbys, and everything is well executed (Thu-Tue 12:00-16:00 & 19:00-24:00, closed Wed, cash only, Supportico San Andrea 6, +39 089 872 991). For dessert, the **Andrea Pansa** pastry shop and café, to the right as you face the cathedral steps, is the most venerable place in town—a good spot to try *sfogliatella* (the delicate pastry invented at a nearby monastery) and other desserts popular in southern Italy (daily 7:30-24:00).

Near the Main Square, on Piazza dei Dogi: If you walk straight ahead from the cathedral stairs, go up the little covered lane, and hook right at the fork, you'll pop out in atmospheric little Piazza dei Dogi. Slightly less trampled and more neighborhood-feeling than Piazza Duomo, this has several decent (if forgettable) restaurants aimed squarely at pleasing tourists. The **$ Cuoppo d'Amalfi** fried-fish shop, on the right as you enter the square, fills cardboard cones with all manner of deep-fried sea life. **$$$ Bar la Piazzetta** has tables right in the middle of the square, and **$$$ La Taverna di Masaniello,** tucked at the corner of the square leading to the port, also has good food.

Amalfi Town Connections

Amalfi is connected by bus and boat to all other nearby towns. In season, boats run to Sorrento, Capri, Positano, and Salerno. Amalfi is the terminus for SITA buses to Sorrento (via Positano), Ravello, and Salerno. CitySightseeing buses from Sorrento terminate in Amalfi as well. For details see "Getting Around the Amalfi Coast" on page 1079.

Ravello

The Amalfi Coast's version of a hill town, Ravello (a 30-minute bus ride from Amalfi town) sits atop a lofty perch 1,000 feet above the sea. It boasts an interesting church, two villas with stunning gardens, and breathtaking views that have attracted celebrities for generations. Gore Vidal, Richard Wagner, D. H. Lawrence, M. C. Escher, Henry Wadsworth Longfellow, Tennessee Williams, and Greta Garbo all succumbed to Ravello's charms and called it home.

The town is like a lush and peaceful garden floating in a world all its own. It seems to be made entirely of cafés, stonework, old villas-turned-luxury hotels, tourists, and grand views. Ravello feels like a place to convalesce.

AMALFI COAST

GETTING TO RAVELLO

Ravello and Amalfi town are connected by bus along a very windy road (hourly, 30-minute trip, €1.30). Coming from Amalfi, buy your bus ticket at the Divina Costiera travel office facing the waterfront square, or at any tobacco shop. Wait for the bus under the big awning by the statue on the waterfront, just to the left of the statue as you face the water. Coming from Positano or Sorrento, you'll change buses in Amalfi. From Naples or Paestum, you'll change twice (in Salerno and Amalfi), making for a long day.

When returning from Ravello to Amalfi, line up early, since the buses are often crowded (buy ticket in tobacco shop; catch bus 100 yards off main square, by the recommended Ristorante da Salvatore).

Orientation to Ravello

To see the sights listed here, start at the bus stop and walk through the tunnel to the main square, where you'll find Villa Rufolo on the left and the church on the right. Villa Cimbrone is a 10-minute walk from the square (follow the signs).

If you have time for only one villa, consider this: Villa Rufolo is easier to reach (facing the main square) and has a stunning terrace garden. Villa Cimbrone is a 10-minute up-and-down hike from the square, but it's bigger and more rugged and offers even grander views in both directions along the coast.

Tourist Information: From the bus stop, to find the TI, face the church, then walk up the stepped lane to the left and into the Giardino del Vescovo (Bishop's Garden) behind the church (TI open daily 10:00-18:00, closes earlier Nov-April, Viale Richard Wagner 4, +39 089 857 096). The independent website www.ravello.com has helpful information.

Sights in Ravello

Piazza Duomo

Though Ravello is perfectly peaceful today, the weathered watchtower of Villa Rufolo—which once kept an eye out for fires and invasions—is a reminder that it wasn't always postcards and *limoncello*.

The fine umbrella pines on the square provide a shady meeting place for strollers ending up here on the piazza. Opposite the church is a fine view of the terraced hillside and the community of Scala (which means "steps"—historically a way of life there). The terraces—supporting grapevines and lemon trees—mostly date from the 16th century. To the left of the church, Viale Richard Wagner climbs past the TI to the top of town for sea views and ruined villas that are now luxury hotels. The town center is essentially traffic-free.

Duomo

Ravello's cathedral, overlooking the main square, feels stripped-down and Romanesque. The facade of the cathedral is plain because the earlier, fancy west portal was destroyed in a 1364 earthquake. Inside, you'll find tastefully restrained decoration and a floor that slopes upward. The key features of this church are its 12th-century bronze doors (from Constantinople), with 54 biblical scenes; the carved marble pulpit supported by six lions; and the chance to get a close-up look at the relic of holy blood (in the chapel left of main altar). The geometric designs show Arabic influence. In the afternoon, the church's front doors are locked; to enter, you'll need to pay to visit the museum on Viale Richard Wagner, around the left side. The humble museum is two rooms of well-described carved marble that evoke the historical importance of the town.

Cost and Hours: €3 for the museum—which also gets you into the church, daily 12:00-17:00; in the morning and early evening, the church is free to enter.

Villa Rufolo

The villa, built in the 13th-century ruins of a noble family's palace, presents wistful gardens among stony walls, with oh-my-God views. The Arabic/Norman gardens seem designed to frame commanding coastline vistas (you can enjoy some of the same view, without the entry fee, from the bus parking lot just below the villa). It's also one of the venues for Ravello's annual arts festival (July-Sept, www.ravellofestival.com) and music society performances (April-June and Sept-Oct, www.ravelloarts.org). Musicians perch on a bandstand on the edge of the cliff for a combination of wonderful music and dizzying views. Wagner visited here and was impressed enough to set the second act of his opera *Parsifal* in the villa's magical gardens. By all accounts, the concert on the cliff is a sublime experience.

Cost and Hours: €7, daily 9:00-20:00, Oct-April until sunset, may close earlier for concerts, +39 089 857 621, www.villarufolo.it.

Visiting the Villa: From Piazza Duomo, enter through the stout watchtower to buy your ticket and pick up the English booklet explaining the sight. Then, walk through part of the sprawling villa ruins. Check out the short video in the tiny theater at the base of the tower and the exhibit upstairs. The palace itself has little to show, but the gardens and views are magnificent and invite exploration.

▲Villa Cimbrone

This villa offers another romantic garden, this one built upon the ruins of an old convent. Located at the seaward end of Ravello, it was created in the 20th century by Englishman William Beckett. His mansion is now a five-star hotel. The longish walk out rewards you with dreamy landscaping around a villa set on a bluff over the ocean. At the far end, above a sublime café on the lawn, "the Terrace of Infinity" dangles high above the sea.

Cost and Hours: €10, daily 9:00-sunset, +39 089 857 459, www.hotelvillacimbrone.com.

Getting There: Facing the cathedral on Piazza Duomo, exit the square to the right and follow signs. You'll climb up and down (and up and down) the stepped lanes, enjoying a quieter side of Ravello, before reaching the villa at the point.

Visiting the Villa: Buy your ticket and pick up the free map/guide of the gardens. Across from the ticket booth, duck into the old monastery. Then pass the rose-garden terrace and head up the "main boulevard," which leads straight to the stunning Terrace of Infinity, with 360-degree views up and down the coast. If you have the interest and energy, loop back along the more rugged downhill slope (facing the adjacent town of Scala). Tiny lizards scurry underfoot, while mythological statues (Mercury's Seat, Temple of Bacchus, Eve's Grotto) strike their poses before a stunning and serene backdrop.

▲Hike Down to Amalfi Town

Enthusiastic walkers, who have good knees and don't mind lots of uneven stairs, enjoy taking the bus up to Ravello and then making the descent back to Amalfi on foot (there are several ways down). If you plan on this, study your route in advance, get a good map (the free, downloadable one at www.giovis.com will do in a pinch), wear good shoes, allow extra time to give your knees a break, and visit the Ravello TI to check that the paths are open.

The steepest, quickest route starts from Ravello's Villa Cimbrone. From the villa, retrace your steps back toward town. Take the first left, just by the arched entrance gate, onto Via Santa Barbara (this "via" is actually a stairway signposted *Amalfi/Minori*). The stepped path winds its way below the cliff. Pause here to look back up at the rock with a big white mansion—Villa La Rondinaia, where American author Gore Vidal lived for many years. Continue downward, mostly on stone stairs, about 40 minutes to the town of Atrani, where several bars on the main square offer well-deserved refreshments. From here, it's about a 15-minute walk back to Amalfi (see "Hike #2" under "Sights in Amalfi," earlier).

Another route down starts below the Church of Santa Maria a Gradillo (a couple hundred yards down Via Roma from Piazza Duomo). Look for a set of steps called Via Sigilgaida, signposted for *Amalfi*. This path, which has some short stretches on the road (take care), leads you down to Pontone (see "Hike #1" under "Sights in Amalfi"). At Pontone, you can continue directly to Amalfi, or take a fairly level detour through the evocative, ruin-filled Valle delle Ferriere.

Eating in Ravello

Several no-brainer, interchangeable restaurants face Piazza Duomo and line the surrounding streets. To enjoy this fine setting, just take your pick. You can also grab a takeaway lunch at one of the little groceries and sandwich shops that line Via Roma (running off Piazza Duomo). Enjoy your meal at the panoramic benches at the far end of Piazza Duomo (facing the cathedral), or facing even better views just outside of town, near the bus stop and Ristorante da Salvatore. (Picnicking isn't allowed inside the two villas.)

$$$$ Ristorante da Salvatore, near the Ravello bus stop (at the other end of the little tunnel from the Duomo), serves a serious sit-down lunch with great views. Pino, the English-speaking owner of this formal restaurant, serves nicely presented, traditional Amalfi cuisine from a fun, if pricey, menu. Their pasta with potatoes and calamari is a favorite. Be adventurous when ordering and share dishes (Tue-Sun 12:30-15:00 & 19:30-22:00, closed Mon, Via della Repubblica 2, smart to call ahead for reservations—+39 089 857 227).

$$ Trattoria Cumpà Cosimo, a classic indoor family-run restaurant, is a good choice for a quicker, less expensive lunch. For a special treat, get their *piatto misto* with five different pastas for €20 (daily 12:00-15:30 & 18:00-24:00, Via Roma 44, +39 089 857 156).

Paestum

The archaeological park at Paestum (PASTE-oom) includes one of the best collections of Greek temples anywhere—and certainly the most accessible to Western Europe. Serenely situated, Paestum is surrounded by fields and wildflowers. Not quite a village, it also has a bus stop, a church, a TI, a straggle of houses, and a handful of eateries.

This city was founded as Poseidonia by Greeks in the sixth century BC and became a key stop on an important trade route. In the fifth century BC, the Lucanians, a barbarous inland tribe, conquered Poseidonia and tried to adopt the cultured ways of the Greeks. By the time of the Romans, who took over in the third century BC and built a fine town on the site, the name Poseidonia had been simplified to Paestum. The final conquerors of Paestum, malaria-carrying mosquitoes, kept the site wonderfully deserted for nearly a thousand years. The temples were never buried—just ignored. Rediscovered in the 18th century, Paestum today offers the only well-preserved Greek ruins north of Sicily.

While most visitors do Paestum as a day trip (it's 1.25 hours from Naples by convenient direct train), it's not a bad place to overnight. Accommodations offer great value, and you could use Paestum as a base for day trips to Naples or the Amalfi Coast. With more time, there's a beach nearby, and local buffalo-milk dairies that you can visit.

Tourist Information: There's a small TI window at the train station (daily 9:00-13:00 & 14:00-18:00) and a bigger one next to the Paestum Archaeological Museum (daily 9:00-13:00 & 14:00-16:00, +39 0828 811 016).

GETTING TO PAESTUM

A dozen slow milk-run trains to Paestum run directly from Naples via Salerno; from elsewhere, you'll need to transfer at one of those two points. For those transferring in Salerno, see the "Salerno Connections" map, which shows train, bus, and boat stops as well as a few handy eateries if you need to grab a bite. Confirm train schedules at www.trenitalia.it and bus schedules at www. sitasudtrasporti.it (or—easier to read—www.positano.com).

From Naples

Direct trains run from Naples' Centrale station to Paestum for €7 (12/day, 1.25 hours, direction: Sapri or Reggio; only the more expensive Intercity trains have a first-class section). Buy tickets online, or from ticket windows or machines at the station. For a day trip from Naples, it's wise to get an early start—especially in warm weather. As of this printing, trains left Naples at 6:50, 7:35, 7:50, and 8:50, then not until 11:45. In the cooler shoulder season, consider arriving for lunch, visiting the museum, then seeing the temples bask in warm afternoon light.

From Sorrento

For a day trip, the smart (if dull) approach is to go bright and early by Circumvesuviana **train** to Naples (70 minutes), catch a direct Naples-Paestum train, and take the same route back (about 3 hours each way). While it's technically possible to do one leg of the trip via an Amalfi Coast SITA **bus,** this makes for a very long day marred by worry about making connections. By **car** from Sorrento, Paestum is 60 miles and at least 3 hours (depending on traffic) via the Amalfi Coast road, but a smooth 2 hours by autostrada. To reach Paestum from Sorrento via the autostrada, drive toward Naples, catch the autostrada (direction: Salerno), skirt Salerno (direction: Reggio), exit at Battipaglia, and drive straight through the roundabout.

From Positano via Salerno

First take a SITA **bus** (2 hours, change in Amalfi) or **boat** (70 minutes) to Salerno, where you can catch the **train** on its way from Naples (30 minutes from Salerno to Paestum). Buses from Amalfi to Salerno terminate at the Salerno train station; boats arrive at a dock a few short blocks from the train station (about a 10-minute, mostly level walk). Once in Salerno, buy your Paestum train ticket at ticket machines or the ticket office in the train station. Note: To start your day trip by bus, you'll need to leave Positano at the crack of dawn—7:00 at the latest—to make the last morning train in Salerno. Check return times from Paestum to Positano carefully in advance; the last possible connection may leave Paestum as early as 16:20.

If you're in a pinch—for example, you've arrived in Salerno during the midday lull in the train schedule—you could take **local CSTP/BusItalia bus #34** from Salerno to Paestum (about hourly, fewer on Sun, 1 hour). It departs from Piazza della Concordia— look for bus shelter between the big parking lot and the main road. This looks convenient to the port, but the closest ticket sales point is the tobacco shop a block in front of the train station. In Paestum, this bus drops you only slightly closer to the ruins than does the train.

To **drive** from Positano to Paestum, you can either follow the Amalfi Coast road to Salerno, or cross back over the peninsula toward Sorrento and then take the expressway. Either way, allow at least 2.5 hours.

Returning from Paestum

Paestum's **train** station is unstaffed but you can buy tickets at machines.

To return to Salerno on local **bus** #34, buy a ticket from one of the bars in Paestum, then go to either of the intersections that flank the ruins (see the "Paestum" map), flag down any northbound bus, and confirm "Salerno?" The last stop is the Salerno waterfront; from here you can catch a boat to Amalfi or Positano, or walk up to the train station to catch an Amalfi-bound SITA bus or a train.

Orientation to Paestum

If you arrive by **train,** cross under the tracks, exit the tiny station, and walk through the ancient city gate; the ruins are a half-mile walk straight ahead, up a dusty road. When you hit the street with hotels and shops, turn right to find the museum and archaeological park entrance. If you'd rather not walk, English-speaking Patrizia Pecora runs a great team of local **taxi** drivers available for transport to hotels or to the ruins (€10-15, +39 392 444 9020). **Buses** from Salerno stop near a corner of the ruins (at a little bar/café). **Drivers** park in the lot by the museum and La Basilica pizzeria (€3). The street between the ruins and museum has been closed off to cars.

Baggage Storage: There's no official baggage storage at the train station or museum. If you're desperate, you can try nicely asking at one of the bars along the main road (they may want a small payment) or at a restaurant you've already patronized.

Local Guide: For an insider's knowledge, Silvia Braggio and her team specialize in Paestum and give a fine two-hour walk of the site and museum (RS%—special €100 rate for my readers, arrange in advance, +39 347 643 2307, www.silviaguide.it, silvia@silviaguide.it). Ask about rounding out the day with a visit to a buffalo farm or another nearby sight. Silvia also offers walking tours of Pompeii and Herculaneum.

Sights in Paestum

PAESTUM ARCHAEOLOGICAL PARK AND MUSEUM

While Paestum is famous for its marvelous Greek temples, most of the structures you see are Roman. Five elements of Greek Paestum survive: three misnamed temples, a memorial tomb, and a circular meeting place (the Ekklesiasterion). The rest, including the wall that defines the site, are the remains of the later Roman town.

Paestum was once a seaport (the ocean is now about a mile away—the wall in the distance, which stretches about three miles, is about halfway to today's coastline). Only about a fifth of the site has been excavated. The original Greek city, which archaeologists figure had a population of about 13,000, was first conquered by Lucanians (distant relatives of the Romans, who spoke a language related to Latin), and then by the Romans (who completely made it over and built the wall you see today).

The remaining Greek structures survive because the Romans were superstitious—they respected sacred areas and didn't mess with temples and tombs. While most old Christian churches are built upon Roman temples (it tends to be what people do when they conquer another culture), no Roman temple is built upon a Greek

Paestum

ROMAN CITY WALLS

HOTEL DEI TEMPLI
VIA TAVERNELLE SP-276
BISTROT 73
ANTICHE MURA
IL GRANAIO DEI CASABELLA

B #34 To/From Salerno

To Agriturismo Seliano & Salerno

N

100 Meters
100 Yards

SITE TOUR BEGINS

P

LA BASILICA CAFE

TEMPLE OF CERES

WC

NORTH ENTRY

VIA SACRA

GREEK MEMORIAL TOMB

EKKLESIASTERION

TICKETS

MUSEUM

AMALFI COAST

VIA MAGNA GRECIA

TOUR ENDS

SANCTUARY OF FORTUNA VIRILIS (POOL)

AMPHITHEATER

UNEXCAVATED AREA

FORUM

Roman Road to Port

To Paestum Train Station (8-minute walk)

CURIA

VIA SACRA

Rose Garden

SOUTH ENTRY

WC

TEMPLE OF NEPTUNE

ANCIENT RESIDENTIAL AREA

TEMPLE OF HERA

CITY WALLS

STANDING RUINS
ORIGINAL FOOTPRINT

RESTAURANT NETTUNO

P

VIA NETTUNO

B #34 To/From Salerno

To Beach & Barlotti Buffalo Farm

ROMAN CITY WALLS SP-189

To Hotel Villa Rita

temple. The three Greek temples that you'll see here today have stood for about 2,500 years.

Cost: €12, Dec-Feb-€6, free (and packed) first Sun of each month. Tickets are valid for three days and also cover a nearby archaeological site at Velia.

Hours: Daily 9:00-19:30, last entry one hour before closing.

Information: +39 0828 811 023, www.museopaestum. beniculturali.it.

Getting In: The site and museum have separate entrances. The museum, across the street from the ruins, is in a cluster with the TI and a small early-Christian basilica.

Visitor Information: The following self-guided tours provide all the information you need for both the site and the museum. Skip the museum bookshop's dull audioguide. Renovations are in progress at the museum and ruins; expect changes. You'll enjoy the coolest temperatures in the morning, but the best light and smallest crowds late in the day.

Length of This Tour: Allow two hours to see the ruins and the museum (about an hour for each).

▲▲Paestum Archaeological Site

This tour starts at the site's northern gate (by the museum), visits the Temple of Ceres, goes through the center of the Roman town past the Greek Memorial Tomb, circles around the other two Greek temples, and then leaves the site through the southern gate to walk down the modern road to the Ekklesiasterion (which faces the museum).

◉ Self-Guided Tour

• *Buy your ticket at the museum, then head to the right to find the site's northern gate. (Note that entry is sometimes permitted only through the southern gate: If that's the case, enter the ruins and stroll less than five minutes up to the northern gate and Temple of Ceres to begin this tour.)*

Stand in front of the...

Temple of Ceres: All three Paestum temples have inaccurate names, coined by 19th-century archaeologists who based their "discoveries" on wishful thinking. (While the Romans made things easy by leaving lots of inscriptions, the Greeks did not.) Those 1800s archaeologists wanted this temple to be devoted to Ceres, the goddess of agriculture. However, all the little votive statues found later, when modern archaeologists dug here, instead depicted a woman with a big helmet: Athena, goddess of wisdom and war. (The Greeks' female war goddess was also the goddess of wisdom—thinking... strategy...female. The Romans' masculine war god was Mars—just fighting.) Each temple is part of a sanctuary—an open, sacred space around the temple. Because regular people couldn't go into the temple, the altar logically stood outside.

The Temple of Ceres dates from 500 BC. It's made of locally quarried limestone blocks. Good roads and shipping didn't come along until the Romans, so the Greeks' buildings were limited to local materials. The wooden roof is long gone. Like the other two temples, this one was once painted white, black, and red, and has an east-west orientation—facing the rising sun. This temple's *cella* (interior room) is gone, cleared out when it was used as a Christian church in the sixth century. In medieval times, Normans scavenged stones from here; chunks of these temples can be found in Amalfi's cathedral.

Walk around to the back side of the Temple of Ceres. The capitals broke in a modern earthquake, so a steel bar provides necessary support. Each of the Paestum temples is Doric style—with three stairs, columns without a base, and shafts that narrow at the top to a simple capital of a round, then a square, block. While there were no carved reliefs, colorful frescoes once decorated the pediments.

As you walk away, look back at the temple. Traditionally, Greeks would build a sanctuary of Athena on a city's highest spot (like the Parthenon in Athens, on the Acropolis). Paestum had no hill, so the Greeks created a mound. The hill was more impressive in its time because the level of the Greek city was substantially lower than the Roman pavement stones you'll walk on today.

• *Follow the path down from behind the temple, and turn left to walk on the paving stones of Via Sacra toward the other Greek temples. After about 100 yards, to the left of the road, you'll see a little half-buried house with a tiled roof.*

Greek Memorial Tomb (Heroon): This tomb (from 500 BC) also survived because the Romans respected religious buildings. But the tomb was most inconveniently located, right in the middle of their growing city. So the practical Romans built a perimeter wall around it (visible today), added a fine tiled roof, and then buried the tomb.

There's a mystery here. Greeks generally buried their dead outside the city (as did Romans)—there are over a thousand ancient tombs outside Paestum's walls—yet this tomb was parked smack-dab in the center of town. When it was uncovered in 1952, no bodies were found inside. The tomb instead held nine perfectly preserved vases (now in the museum). Archaeologists aren't sure what the tomb's purpose was. Perhaps it was a memorial dedicated to some great hero (like a city founder). Or perhaps it was a memorial to those lost when a neighboring community had to evacuate and settle as refugees here.

• *Continue walking down Via Sacra, the main drag of...*

Roman Paestum: Roman towns were garrison towns: rectangular with a grid street plan and two main streets cutting north-south and east-west, dividing the town into four equal sections. They were built by military engineers with a no-nonsense standard design. New excavations (on the left) have uncovered Roman-era lead piping. City administration buildings were on the left, and residential buildings were on the right.

Shortly after the road turns into a dirt path, you'll come to a big **Roman pool** (on the left) that archaeologists believe was a sanctuary dedicated to Fortuna Virilis, goddess of luck and fertility. The strange stones likely supported a wooden platform for priests and statues of gods. Imagine young women walking down the ramp at the far end and through the pool, hoping to conceive a child.

The next big square on the left was the **Roman forum** and ancient Paestum's main intersection. The road on the right led directly (and very practically) to the port. It made sense to have a direct connection to move freight between the sea and the center of town.

Until 2007, the vast field of ruins on the right (between the forum and the next temple) was covered in vegetation. It's since been cleared and cleaned of harmful lichen, which produce acids that dissolve limestone. Study the rocks: Yellow lichen is alive, black is dead. Even the great temples of Paestum were covered in this destructive lichen until 2000, when a two-year-long project cleaned them for the first time.

• *Ahead on the left are the so-called...*

Temples of Neptune and Hera: The **Temple of Neptune** dates from 450 BC and employs the Greek architectural trick where the base line is curved up just a tad to overcome the illusion of sagging caused by a straight base. The Athenians built their Parthenon (with a similar bowed-up base line) just 30 years after this. Many think this temple could have been their inspiration.

The adjacent **Temple of Hera,** dating from 550 BC, is the oldest of Paestum's three temples and one of the oldest Greek temples still standing anywhere. Notice the change 100 years makes in the architectural styles: Archaic Doric in 550 BC versus Classic Doric in 450 BC.

Archaeologists now believe the "Temple of Neptune" was actually devoted to a different god. Votive statues uncovered here suggest that Hera was the focus (perhaps this was a new-and-improved version of the adjacent, simpler, and older Temple of Hera). Or perhaps it was a temple to Zeus, Hera's husband, to honor the couple together.

Together, the two temples formed a single huge sanctuary, with altars outside the temples on the far (east) side. Walk between the temples, then hook right to get a good look at the front of the Temple of Hera. Notice how over-built this temple appears. Its columns and capitals are closer together than necessary, as if the builders lacked confidence in their ability to span the distance between supports. Square pillars mark the corners of the *cella* inside. Temples with an odd number of columns (here, nine) had a single colonnade crossing in the center inside to support the wooden roof. More modern temples (such as the Temple of Neptune) had six columns, with two colonnades passing through the *cella*. This left a line of vision open through the middle so that worshippers could see the big statue of the god.

By the way, in 1943, Allied paratroopers dropped in near here during the famous "Landing of Salerno," when the Allies (who had already taken Sicily) invaded mainland Italy. Paestum was part of their first beachhead. The Temple of Hera served as an Allied military tent hospital. From here, the Allies pushed back the Nazis, marching to Naples, Cassino, and finally to Rome.

• *With the Temple of Hera at your back, turn left then right to leave the site (using the exit straight across from the Temple of Neptune). Now turn left onto the modern road...*

Via Magna Grecia: The king of Naples had this Naples-to-Paestum road built in 1829 to inspire his people with ancient temples. While he was modern in his appreciation of antiquity, his road project destroyed a swath of the ancient city, as you'll see as you pass by half of a small **amphitheater.**

• *Just past the amphitheater, you'll find the...*

Ekklesiasterion: Immediately across the street from the museum is what looks like a sunken circular theater. This rare bit of ancient Greek ruins was the Ekklesiasterion, a meeting place where the Greeks would get together to discuss things and vote. Archaeologists believe that the Greek agora (market) was next to here, where the museum stands today.

• *Across the street is the...*

▲▲Paestum Archaeological Museum

Paestum's museum offers the rare opportunity to see artifacts—dating from prehistoric to Greek to Roman times—at the site where they were discovered. These beautifully crafted works (with good English descriptions throughout) help bring Paestum to life. Not everything you see here is from Paestum, though, as the museum also collects artifacts from other nearby sites.

❷ Self-Guided Tour

Before stepping into the museum, notice the proud fascist architecture meant to imitate the structure of the temples you've just seen. Though the building dates from 1954, it was designed in 1938. It seems to command that you *will* enjoy this history lesson.

The exhibit is on several levels. As you follow this tour, expect some location changes due to a recent renovation. You'll likely find mostly Greek pieces on the ground floor (artifacts from the Temple of Hera in front, frescoes from tombs in the back), Paleolithic to Iron Age artifacts on the mezzanine level, and Roman art on the top floor (statues, busts, and inscriptions dating from the time of the Roman occupation). While Roman art is not unique to Paestum, the Greek collection is—so that's what you should focus on.

• *Before exploring the collection, notice the display case (tucked into the far-right corner near the entrance) with the **huge book** turned to a page with a fine drawing by the Italian artist Giovanni Piranesi, showing his visit to Paestum in 1777. Then look for these museum highlights.*

Temple Reliefs: The museum's center room is designed like a Greek temple inner *cella* and only opened for temporary exhibitions. If it's open, look at the large carvings overhead (known as metopes) that wrap around this inner sanctum. They once adorned a sanctuary of the goddess Hera five miles away. This sanctuary, called Heraion del Sele, was discovered and excavated in 1934. Some of the carvings show scenes from the life of Hercules. You'll get a chance to see the details later in this visit.

• *Along the back wall of this room, find the glass case holding nine perfectly preserved...*

Vases: One ceramic and eight bronze, with artistic handles, these vases were found in Paestum's Greek Memorial Tomb. Greek bronzes are rare because Romans often melted them down to make armor. These were discovered in 1952, filled with still-liquid honey and sealed with beeswax. The honey (as you can see in the display cases below) has since crystallized. Honey was a standard part of a funeral because, to ancient Greeks, honey symbolized immortality...it lasts forever.

• *Enter the room at the far end of the main hall, filled with ancient Greek...*

Votive Offerings: These were dug up at Heraion del Sele (not at Paestum) like the temple reliefs seen earlier. Such offerings are a huge help to modern archaeologists, since the figures that worshippers brought to a temple are clues as to which god the temple honored. These votives depict a woman with a crown on a throne—clearly Hera. The clay votives were simple, affordable, and accessible to regular people.

• *Now continue ahead into the large room (broken up by pillars and interior walls) that holds...*

Relics from the Temples at Paestum: This room displays smaller pieces. Displays tell in which temple each relic was found (videos unfortunately are only in Italian). The Temple of Ceres is often referred to as the Temple of Athena or as the northern *(settentrionale)* sanctuary. The Temples of Neptune and Hera are spoken of as the southern *(meridionale)* sanctuaries.

In a glass case nearby, find the seated statue of **Zeus.** This painted clay Zeus dates from 520 BC. The king of the gods was so lusty with his antics, he's still smirking.

Farther into the room, you can't miss the display case of a statue's **torso** emblazoned with swastikas—a reminder that this symbol (carrying completely different meanings) predated Hitler by millennia.

Across the room, look for the short fragment of a **frieze** with lion heads. Paestum's three temples were once adorned with decorations, such as these ornamental spouts that spurted rainwater out of lions' mouths. Notice the bits of the surviving black, red, and white paint. Reconstructions on the adjacent wall show archaeologists' best guesses as to how the original decorations might have looked.

• *Look out the museum's back window for a good, if distant...*

View of Paestum's Walls: The walls of ancient Paestum reach halfway to the mountain—a reminder that most of the site is still private property and yet to be excavated. The town up on the mountainside is Capaccio, established in the eighth century when inhabitants of the original city of Paestum were driven out by malaria and the city was abandoned.

• *Walk along the corridor at the back of the museum, which shows...*

Objects from Tombs: More than 1,000 tombs have been identified outside the ancient city's wall. About 100 were found

decorated with frescoes or containing objects such as these.

• *At the far end of the corridor, turn left to see...*

The Tomb of the Diver: This is the museum's treasure and the most precious Paestum find. Dating from 480 BC, it's not only the sole ancient Greek tomb fresco in the museum—it's the only one ever found in southern Italy. Discovered in 1968, it has five frescoed slabs (four sides and a lid; the bottom wasn't decorated). The Greeks saw death as a passage: diving from mortality into immortality...into an unknown world. Archaeologists believe that the pillars shown on the fresco represent the Pillars of Hercules at Gibraltar, which in ancient times defined the known world. The ocean beyond the Mediterranean was the great unknown...like the afterlife. The Greek banquet makes it clear that this was an aristocratic man.

• *After the Tomb of the Diver, the next room displays...*

Lucanian Tomb Frescoes: The many other painted slabs in the room date from a later time, around 350 BC, when Paestum fell under Lucanian rule. These frescoes are cruder than their earlier Greek counterpart. The people who conquered the Greeks tried to appropriate their art and style, but they lacked the Greeks' distinctive light touch. Still, these offer fascinating glimpses into ancient life here at Paestum. At the entrance to this room, study the tomb and skeleton of an ancient warrior, who was buried with his armor.

• *Beyond this room, you'll find yourself back at the entrance. Before you leave, go up the stairs by the bookshop for a glimpse at the mezzanine level, which focuses on prehistoric archaeology. Also see the temple friezes at eye level now, with explications of what's happening in almost every scene. The back wall of the mezzanine displays **bronze vases**, mostly from Gaudo, a half-mile from Paestum.*

MORE SIGHTS IN PAESTUM
Barlotti Caseificio Buffalo Farm

This part of Italy is known for its mozzarella cheese made from buffalo milk. A convenient place to appreciate buffalo mozzarella and other buffalo products is at Barlotti Caseificio, a working buffalo farm about a mile from the Paestum ruins (a 25-minute walk from the museum). Visitors can look around for free, lunch on a buffalo burger or buffalo-cheese ravioli in the café, or buy buffalo gelato and buffalo-based cosmetics in the shop (open daily year-round, shop and gelato counter 8:00-20:00, lunch 12:00-15:00, guided tours available, Via Torre di Paestum 1, +39 0828 811 146, www.barlotti.it).

Sleeping in Paestum

Paestum at night, with views of the floodlit ruins, is magic. Accommodations here offer great value. You can sleep in a mansion for the same price you'd pay for a closet in Positano. For locations see the "Paestum" map earlier in this section.

$$ Hotel Villa Rita is a tidy, quiet country hotel set on two acres of attractive grounds with grassy lawns. A 15-minute walk from the museum and a 20-minute walk from the beach, it has 22 rooms, a kid-friendly swimming pool, and rental bikes (RS%, air-con, lunch or dinner available, free parking, closed Nov-March, Via Nettuno 9, +39 0828 811 081, www.hotelvillarita.it, info@hotelvillarita.it, Luigi and his children Rita and Arnaldo).

$$ Il Granaio dei Casabella, a converted old granary with 14 attractive, reasonably priced rooms, is a 10-minute walk from the museum at the end of the little restaurant strip. It has a beautiful garden and pretty common areas, and four rooms have temple views (RS%, family rooms, air-con, free parking, closed Dec-Feb, 300 yards west of the #34 bus stop closest to Salerno, Via Tavernelle 84, +39 0828 721 014, www.ilgranaiodeicasabella.com, info@ilgranaiodeicasabella.com, hospitable Celardo family).

$$ Hotel dei Templi, with 11 good rooms, is a few doors from Il Granaio dei Casabella (air-con, lots of stairs, pay parking, Via Tavernelle 64, +39 0828 811 747, www.hoteldeitempli.it, info@hoteldeitempli.it).

Outside Town: An offbeat option for drivers, **$$ Agriturismo Seliano** has a huge dining room and lounge with a fireplace, a pool, and 14 spacious rooms on a peaceful, once-elegant farm estate that's been in the same family for 300 years (air-con, closed Nov-March; two miles north of ruins—*Azienda Agrituristica Seliano* sign directs you off the main road down a long, potholed dirt driveway; Via Seliano, +39 0828 723 634, www.agriturismoseliano.it, seliano@agriturismoseliano.it). If you stay here, reserve dinner too—it's served at one long table and made with produce fresh from the garden. They can also organize cooking classes. The place is run by Cecilia, an English-speaking baroness, and her family, including a half-dozen nice and friendly dogs.

Eating in Paestum

Picnics in the ruins aren't allowed. Several eateries cluster around the museum. **$ La Basilica,** facing a pretty little garden between the parking lot and TI, is the most straightforward and reasonable option, with good pizzas and other lunch fare (open daily 12:00-15:00 & 19:00-22:00, Via Magna Grecia 881, +39 0828 811 301).

At the south end of the ruins, **$$$ Ristorante Nettuno** is more elegant, with white tablecloths, a grand piano, and views of the temples; it's built into a surviving tower from the Roman city walls. It has limited hours, though, serving only dinners in summer (mid-June-mid-Sept from 19:30) and lunches in spring and fall (March-mid-June and mid-Sept-Oct 12:00-15:30; closed Tue and Nov-Feb; Via Nettuno 2, +39 0828 811 028).

AMALFI COAST

Just north of the ruins, outside the Roman city wall, Via Tavernelle has been partly blocked off to traffic, creating a fun little restaurant row with casual indoor and outdoor tables. Consider **$$$ Bistrot 73,** with wonderful pasta dishes (at #48, +39 342 526 1393), or **$$$ Antiche Mura,** which accompanies fine grilled meats with an impressive wine list (at #20, +39 0828 199 8535).

ITALIAN HISTORY

Italy has a lot of history, so let's get started.

ORIGINS OF ROME (c. 753 BC-450 AD)

A she-wolf breastfed two human babies, Romulus and Remus, who grew to build the city of Rome in 753 BC—you buy that? Closer to fact, farmers and shepherds of the Latin tribe settled near the mouth of the Tiber River, a convenient trading location. The crude settlement was sandwiched between two sophisticated civilizations—Greek colonists to the south (Magna Graecia, or "Great Greece"), and to the north (Etruria—present-day Tuscany/Umbria) the Etruscans, whose origins and language have long puzzled historians (for more on the Etruscans, see page 650). Baby Rome was both dominated and nourished by these societies.

According to legend, when the son of an Etruscan king raped a Roman woman (509 BC), her defenders led a revolt, driving out the Etruscans and replacing them with elected Roman senators and (eventually) a code of law (Laws of the Twelve Tables, 450 BC). The Roman Republic was born.

THE ROMAN REPUBLIC EXPANDS (c. 509 BC-AD 1)

Located at the midpoint of the peninsula, Rome was perfectly situated for trading salt and wine. Roman businessmen, backed by a disciplined army, expanded throughout the Italian peninsula, establishing a Roman infrastructure as they went. Rome soon swallowed up its northern Etruscan neighbors, conquering them by force and absorbing their culture.

Next came Magna Graecia, with Rome's legions defeating the Greek general Pyrrhus after several costly "Pyrrhic" victories (c. 275 BC). Rome now ruled a united federation stretching from Tuscany to the tip of the Italian peninsula, with a standard currency, a system of roads (including the Via Appia), and a standing army of a half-million soldiers ready for the next challenge: Carthage.

Carthage (modern-day Tunisia) and Rome fought the three bitter Punic Wars for control of the Mediterranean (264-201 BC and 146 BC). The balance of power hung precariously in the Second Punic War (218-201 BC), when Hannibal of Carthage crossed the sea to Spain with a huge army of men and elephants. He marched 1,200 miles overland, crossed the Alps, and forcefully penetrated Italy from the rear. Almost at the gates of the city of Rome, he was finally turned back. The Romans prevailed, and, in the mismatched Third Punic War, they burned the city of Carthage to the ground (146 BC).

The well-tuned Roman legions easily subdued sophisticated Greece in three Macedonian Wars (215-146 BC). Though Rome conquered Greece, Greek culture dominated the Romans. From hairstyles to statues to temples to the evening's entertainment, Rome was forever "Hellenized," becoming the curators of Greek culture, passing it down to future generations.

By the first century BC, Rome was master of the Mediterranean. Booty, cheap grain, and thousands of captured slaves poured in, transforming the economic model from small farmers to unemployed city dwellers living off tribute from conquered lands. The Republic had changed.

CIVIL WARS AND THE TRANSITION TO EMPIRE
(First Century BC)

With easy money streaming in and traditional roles obsolete, Romans bickered among themselves over their slice of the pie. Wealthy landowners (patricians, the ruling Senate) wrangled with the middle and working classes (plebeians) and with the growing population of slaves, who demanded greater say-so in government. In 73 BC, Spartacus—a Greek-born soldier-turned-Roman slave who'd been forced to fight as a gladiator—escaped to the slopes of Mount Vesuvius, where he amassed an army of 90,000 angry slaves. After two years of fierce fighting across Italy, the Roman legions crushed the revolt and crucified 6,000 rebels along the Via Appia as a warning.

Amid the chaos of class war and civil war, charismatic generals who could provide wealth and security became dictators—men such as Sulla, Crassus, Pompey...and Caesar. Julius Caesar (100-44 BC) was a cunning politician, riveting speaker, conqueror of Gaul, author of *The Gallic Wars,* and lover of Cleopatra, queen of Egypt. In his four-year reign, he reformed and centralized the government around himself. Disgruntled Republicans feared that he would make himself king. At his peak of power, they surrounded Caesar

Italy Almanac

Official Name: Repubblica Italiana (Italian Republic)

Locals Call It: Italia

Size: 116,000 square miles, including the islands of Sicily, Sardinia, and others. Population is 62 million.

Geography: Italy is shaped like a boot, 850 miles long and 150 miles wide, jutting into the central Mediterranean. (By comparison, Florida is 500 miles long.) The terrain is generally mountainous or hilly, with the Alps in the north and a north-south "spine" of the Apennine Mountains. The highest point is Mont Blanc (15,771 feet), on the border with France. Outside the Alps, the highest point on the peninsula is Corno Grande (9,554 feet). Italy has 5,000 miles of coastline. Major rivers include the Po (the longest at 400 miles), Arno, Adige, and Tiber. Italy has three active volcanoes: Vesuvius, Etna, and Stromboli.

Latitude and Longitude: 43°N and 12°E (similar to Oregon and Maine).

Regions: Italy is divided into 20 regions (including Tuscany, Umbria, Veneto, and Lazio). Locally, there are some 8,200 "communes," each with a community council and mayor.

Major Cities: Rome (the capital, 2.8 million), Milan (1.3 million), and Naples (1 million).

Economy: The Gross domestic product is $2.3 trillion; the GDP per capita is $38,200. About 74 percent of the economy consists of service jobs (especially tourism), 24 percent is industry (textiles, chemicals), and 2 percent is agriculture (fruit, vegetables, olives, wine, plus fishing). There are 12,500 miles of train lines (mostly government-run) and 4,300 miles of expressway (autostrada).

Government: Italy is a republic, with three branches of government. The chief executive is Prime Minister Mario Draghi. The bicameral legislature is elected by (mostly) direct voting. Since World War II, the fragmented country has had 66 national governments.

Flag: Three vertical bands of green, white, and red.

Italian Inventions: Opera, cologne, thermometer, barometer, pizza, wireless telegraph, espresso machine, typewriter, batteries, nitroglycerin, yo-yos...and the ice-cream cone.

Museums: 3,800.

The Average Gio: The average Italian is 46 years old, has 1.4 kids, is nominally Roman Catholic, and will live to the ripe old age of 82 (1 in 5 Italians is older than 65). Every day, he or she consumes two servings of pasta, a half-pound of bread, and two glasses of wine. Despite Italian cuisine, Gio isn't fat—only 20 percent of Italians are considered obese.

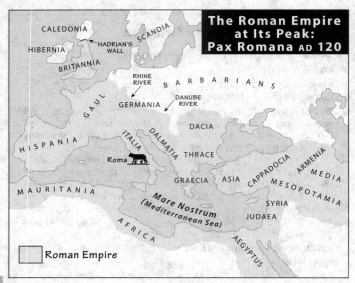

in the Senate on the Ides of March (March 15, 44 BC) and stabbed him to death.

Julius Caesar died, but the concept of one-man rule lived on in his adopted son. Named Octavian at birth, he defeated rival Mark Antony (another lover of Cleopatra, 31 BC) and was proclaimed Emperor Augustus (27 BC). Augustus outwardly followed the traditions of the Republic, while in practice he acted as a dictator with the backing of Rome's legions and the rubber-stamp approval of the Senate. He established his family to succeed him (making the family name "Caesar" a title) and set the pattern of rule by emperors for the next 500 years.

THE ROMAN EMPIRE (c. AD 1-500)

In his 40-year reign, Augustus ended Rome's civil wars and ushered in the Pax Romana: 200 years of prosperity and relative peace. Rome ruled an empire of 54 million people, stretching from Scotland to northern Africa, from Spain to the Euphrates River. Conquered peoples were welcomed into the fold of prosperity, linked by roads, common laws, common gods, education, and the Latin language. The city of Rome, with more than a million inhabitants, was decorated with Greek-style statues and monumental structures faced with marble. It was the marvel of the known world.

The empire prospered on a (false) economy of booty, slaves, and cheap imports. On the Italian peninsula, traditional small farms were swallowed up by large farming and herding estates. In this "global economy," the Italian peninsula became just one province among many in a worldwide Latin-speaking empire, ruled by an emperor who was likely born elsewhere. The empire even survived the often turbulent and naughty behavior of emperors such as Caligula (r. 37-41) and Nero (r. 54-68).

DECLINE AND FALL (AD 200-500)

Rome peaked in the second century AD under the capable emperors Trajan (r. 98-117), Hadrian (r. 117-138), and Marcus Aurelius (r. 161-180). For the next three centuries, the Roman Empire declined, shrinking in size and wealth, a victim of corruption, disease, an overextended army, a false economy, and the constant pressure of "barbarian" tribes pecking away at its borders. By the third century, the army had become the real power, handpicking figurehead emperors to do its bidding: In a 40-year span, 15 emperors were first saluted and then assassinated by fickle generals.

Trying to stall the disintegration, Emperor Diocletian (r. 284-305) split the empire into two administrative halves under two equal emperors. Constantine (r. 306-337) solidified the divide by moving the capital of the empire from decaying Rome to the new city of Constantinople (330, present-day Istanbul). Almost instantly, the once-great city of Rome became a minor player in imperial affairs. (The eastern "Byzantine" half of the empire would thrive and live on for another thousand years.) Constantine also legalized Christianity (313), and the once-persecuted cult soon became virtually the state religion, the backbone of Rome's fading hierarchy.

By 410, "Rome" had shrunk to just the city itself, surrounded by a protective wall. Barbarian tribes from the north and east poured in to loot and plunder. The city was sacked by Visigoths (410) and vandalized by Vandals (455), and the pope had to plead with Attila the Hun for mercy (451). The peninsula's population fell to six million, trade and agriculture were disrupted, schools closed, and the infrastructure collapsed. Peasants huddled near powerful lords for protection from bandits, planting the seeds of medieval feudalism.

In 476, the last emperor sold his title for a comfy pension, and Rome fell like a huge column, kicking up dust that would plunge Europe into a thousand years of darkness. For the next 13 centuries, there would be no "Italy," just a patchwork of rural dukedoms and towns, victimized by foreign powers. Italy lay in shambles, helpless.

INVASIONS (AD 500-1000)

In 500 years, Italy suffered through a full paragraph of invasions: Lombards (568) and Byzantines (under Justinian, 536) occupied the north. In the south, Muslim Saracens (827) and Christian Normans (1061) established thriving kingdoms. Charlemagne, king of

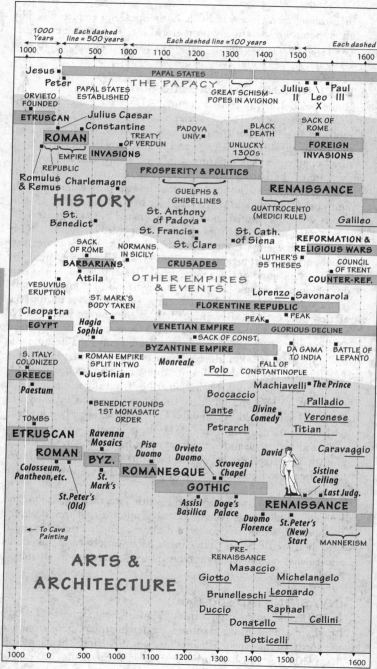

HISTORY

1000 Years

Each dashed line = 500 years

Each dashed line =100 years

Each dashed

| 1000 | 0 | 500 | 1000 | 1100 | 1200 | 1300 | 1400 | 1500 | 1600 |

Jesus

PAPAL STATES

THE PAPACY

Peter

PAPAL STATES ESTABLISHED

GREAT SCHISM - POPES IN AVIGNON

Julius II

Leo X

Paul III

ORVIETO FOUNDED

ETRUSCAN

Julius Caesar

Constantine

TREATY OF VERDUN

PADOVA UNIV.

BLACK DEATH

SACK OF ROME

ROMAN

EMPIRE

INVASIONS

UNLUCKY 1300s

FOREIGN INVASIONS

REPUBLIC

Romulus & Remus

Charlemagne

PROSPERITY & POLITICS

RENAISSANCE

HISTORY

GUELPHS & GHIBELLINES

QUATTROCENTO (MEDICI RULE)

St. Benedict

St. Anthony of Padova

Galileo

St. Francis

St. Clare

St. Cath. of Siena

REFORMATION & RELIGIOUS WARS

SACK OF ROME

NORMANS IN SICILY

CRUSADES

LUTHER'S 95 THESES

COUNCIL OF TRENT

BARBARIANS

OTHER EMPIRES & EVENTS

COUNTER-REF.

VESUVIUS ERUPTION

Attila

Lorenzo

Savonarola

ST. MARK'S BODY TAKEN

FLORENTINE REPUBLIC

Cleopatra

Hagia Sophia

PEAK

PEAK

EGYPT

VENETIAN EMPIRE

GLORIOUS DECLINE

SACK OF CONST.

S. ITALY COLONIZED

BYZANTINE EMPIRE

DA GAMA TO INDIA

BATTLE OF LEPANTO

ROMAN EMPIRE SPLIT IN TWO

Monreale

FALL OF CONSTANTINOPLE

GREECE

Justinian

Polo

Paestum

Machiavelli

The Prince

Boccaccio

Palladio

TOMBS

BENEDICT FOUNDS 1ST MONASATIC ORDER

Dante

Divine Comedy

Veronese

ETRUSCAN

Ravenna Mosaics

Petrarch

Titian

ROMAN

Pisa Duomo

Orvieto Duomo

David

Caravaggio

BYZ.

Colosseum, Pantheon, etc.

St. Mark's

ROMANESQUE

Scrovegni Chapel

Sistine Ceiling

St. Peter's (Old)

GOTHIC

RENAISSANCE

Last Judg.

← To Cave Painting

Assisi Basilica

Doge's Palace

Duomo Florence

St. Peter's (New) Start

MANNERISM

PRE-RENAISSANCE

ARTS & ARCHITECTURE

Masaccio

Giotto

Michelangelo

Brunelleschi

Leonardo

Duccio

Raphael

Cellini

Donatello

Botticelli

| 1000 | 0 | 500 | 1000 | 1100 | 1200 | 1300 | 1400 | 1500 | 1600 |

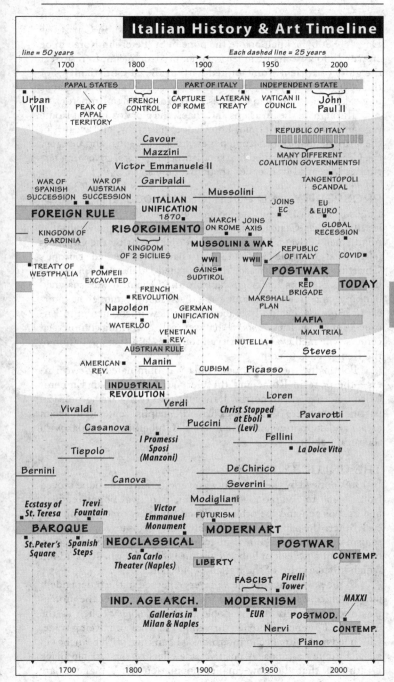

Italian History & Art Timeline

the Germanic Franks, defeated the Lombards, and on Christmas Day, AD 800, he knelt before the pope in St. Peter's in Rome to be crowned Holy Roman Emperor, an empty title meant to resurrect the glory of ancient Rome united with medieval Christianity. For the next thousand years, Italians would pledge nominal allegiance to weak, distant German kings as their Holy Roman Emperor.

Through all the invasions and chaos, the glory of ancient Rome was preserved in the pomp, knowledge, hierarchy, and wealth of the Christian Church. Strong popes (Leo I, 440-461, and Gregory the Great, 590-604) ruled like small-time emperors, governing territories in central Italy called the Papal States.

PROSPERITY AND POLITICS (AD 1000-1300)

Italy survived Y1K, and the economy picked up. Sea-trading cities like Venice, Genoa, Pisa, Naples, and Amalfi grew wealthy as middlemen between Europe and the Orient. During the Crusades (e.g., First Crusade 1097-1130), Italian ships ferried Europe's Christian soldiers eastward, then returned laden with spices and highly marked-up luxury goods from the Orient. Trade spawned banking, and Italians became capitalists, loaning money at interest to Europe's royalty. Italy pioneered a new phenomenon in Europe—municipalities *(comuni)* that were self-governing commercial centers. The medieval prosperity of the cities laid the foundation of the Renaissance to come.

Politically, the Italian peninsula was dominated by two rulers—the pope in Rome and the German Holy Roman Emperor (with holdings in the north). Italy split into two warring political parties: supporters of the popes (called Guelphs, centered in urban areas) and supporters of the emperors (Ghibellines, popular with the rural nobility).

THE UNLUCKY 1300s

In 1309, enticed by the fast-rising power of France, the pope moved from Rome to Avignon. At one point, two rival popes reigned, one in Avignon and the other in Rome, and they excommunicated each other. The papacy eventually returned to Rome (1377), but the schism created a breakdown in central authority that was exacerbated by an outbreak of bubonic plague (Black Death, 1347-1348), which killed a third of the Italian population.

In the power vacuum, new players emerged in the independent cities. Venice, Florence, Milan, and Naples were under the protection and leadership of local noble families *(signoria)* such as the Medici in Florence. Florence thrived in the wool and dyeing trade, which led to dominance in international banking, with branches in all of Europe's capitals. A positive side effect of the terrible Black Death was that the now-smaller population got a bigger share

Typical Church Architecture

History comes to life when you visit a centuries-old church. Even if you wouldn't know your apse from a hole in the ground, learning a few simple terms will enrich your experience. Note that not every church has every feature, and a "cathedral" isn't a type of church architecture, but rather a designation for a church that's a governing center for a local bishop.

Aisles: Long, generally low-ceilinged arcades that flank the nave

Altar: Raised area with a ceremonial table (often adorned with candles or a crucifix), where the priest prepares and serves the bread and wine for Communion

Apse: Space behind the altar, sometimes bordered with small chapels

Barrel Vault: Continuous round-arched ceiling that resembles an extended upside-down U

Choir: Intimate space reserved for clergy and choir, located within the nave near the high altar and often screened off

Cloister: Covered hallways bordering a square or rectangular open-air courtyard, traditionally where monks and nuns got fresh air

Facade: Exterior of the church's main (west) entrance, usually highly decorated

Groin Vault: Arched ceiling formed where two equal barrel vaults meet at right angles

Narthex: Area (portico or foyer) between the main entry and the nave

Nave: Long central section of the church (running west to east, from the entrance to the altar) where the congregation sits or stands during the service

Transept: One of the two parts forming the "arms" of the cross in a traditional cross-shaped floor plan; runs north-south, perpendicularly crossing the east-west nave

West Portal: Main entry to the church (on the west end, opposite the main altar)

Top 10 Italians

Romulus: Breastfed on wolf milk, this legendary orphan founded the city of Rome (traditionally in 753 BC). Over the next seven centuries, his descendants dominated the Italian peninsula, ruling from Rome as a Republic.

Julius Caesar (100-44 BC): After conquering Gaul (France), subduing Egypt, and winning Cleopatra's heart, Caesar ruled Rome with king-like powers. In an attempt to preserve the Republic, senators stabbed him to death, but the concept of one-man rule lived on.

Augustus (born Octavian, 63 BC-AD 14): Julius' adopted son became the first of the Caesars that ruled Rome during its 500 years as a Europe-wide power. He set the tone for emperors both good (Trajan, Hadrian, Marcus Aurelius) and bad (Caligula, Nero, and dozens of others).

Constantine (c. 280-337 AD): Raised in a Christian home, this emperor legalized Christianity, almost instantly turning a persecuted sect into a Europe-wide religion. With the Fall of Rome, the Church was directed by strong popes and so guided Italians through the next thousand years of invasions, plagues, political decentralization, and darkness.

Lorenzo (the Magnificent) de' Medici (1449-1492): Soldier, poet, lover, and ruler of Florence in the 1400s, this Renaissance Man embodied the "rebirth" of ancient enlightenment. Lorenzo's wealthy Medici family funded Florentine artists who pioneered a new realism in painting and sculpture.

Michelangelo Buonarroti (1475-1564): His statue of David—slayer of an ignorant brute—stands as a monumental symbol of Italian enlightenment. Along with fellow geniuses Leonardo da Vinci and

of the land, jobs, and infrastructure. By century's end, Italy was poised to enter its most glorious era since antiquity.

THE RENAISSANCE (1400s-1600s)

The Renaissance (Rinascimento)—the "rebirth" of ancient Greek and Roman art styles, knowledge, and humanism—began in Italy (c. 1400) and spread through Europe over the next two centuries. Many of Europe's most famous painters, sculptors, and thinkers—Michelangelo, Leonardo, Raphael, etc.—were Italian.

It was a cultural boom that changed people's thinking about every aspect of life. In politics, it meant an eventual rebirth of Greek ideas of democracy. In religion, it meant a move away from Church dominance and toward the assertion of man (humanism) and a more personal faith. Science and secular learning were revived after centuries of superstition and ignorance. In architecture,

Raphael, Michelangelo mastered the visual arts of the Italian Renaissance: painting, sculpture, and architecture. Their innovations spread northward, influencing the rest of Europe.

Giovanni Lorenzo Bernini (1598-1680): The "Michelangelo of Baroque" kept Italy a major exporter of sophisticated trends. Bernini's ornate statues and architectural projects decorated palaces of the rising power brokers in France, even as Italy was reverting to an economically stagnant patchwork of foreign-ruled states.

Victor Emmanuel II (1820-1878): As the only Italian-born ruler on the peninsula, this king of Sardinia played a central role in Italian unification. Aided by the general Garibaldi, writer Mazzini, and politician Cavour (with a soundtrack by Verdi), he became the first ruler of a united, democratic Italy, in September 1870. (The preceding proper nouns have since come to adorn streets and piazzas throughout Italy.)

Benito Mussolini (1883-1945): An inspiration for Hitler, he derailed Italy's fledgling democracy, becoming dictator of a fascist state and leading the country to defeat in World War II. No public places honor Mussolini, but many streets and piazzas throughout Italy bear the name of Giacomo Matteotti (1885-1924), a politician whose outspoken opposition to Mussolini got him killed.

Federico Fellini (1920-1993): Fellini's films (*La Strada, La Dolce Vita, 8 1/2*) chronicle Italy's postwar years in gritty black and white—the poverty, destruction, and disillusionment of the war followed by the optimism, decadence, and materialism of the economic boom. He captured the surreal chaos of Italy's abrupt social change from traditional Catholicism to a secular, urban world presided over by Mafia bosses and weak government.

HISTORY

it was a return to the balanced columns and domes of Greece and Rome. In painting, the Renaissance meant 3-D realism.

Italians dotted their cities with publicly financed art that celebrated Greek gods and emulated Roman-style domed buildings. They preached Greek-style democracy and explored the natural world. The cultural boom was financed by thriving trade and lucrative banking. During the Renaissance, the peninsula once again became the trendsetting cultural center of Europe.

FOREIGN INVASIONS (1500s)

In May 1498, Vasco da Gama of Portugal landed in India, having found a sea route around Africa. Italy's monopoly on trade with the East was broken. Portugal, France, Spain, England, and Holland—nation-states under strong central rule—began to overtake decentralized Italy. Italy's once-great maritime cities now traded in an economic backwater, just as Italy's bankers (such as the Medici in Florence) were going bankrupt. While the Italian Renaissance was all the rage throughout Europe, it declined in its birthplace. Italy—culturally sophisticated but weak and decentralized—was ripe for the picking by Europe's rising powers.

Several kings of France invaded (1494, 1495, and 1515)—initially invited by Italian lords to attack their rivals—and began divvying up territory for their noble families. Italy also became a battleground in religious conflicts between Catholics and the new Protestant movement. In the chaos, the city of Rome was brutally sacked by foreign mercenaries (1527).

FOREIGN RULE (1600-1800)

For the next two centuries, most of Italy's states were ruled by foreign nobles, who treated them as prizes in Europe's dynastic wars. Italy ceased to be a major player in Europe, politically or economically. Italian intellectual life was often cropped short by a conservative Catholic Church trying to fight Protestantism. Galileo, for example, was forced by the Inquisition to renounce his belief that the earth orbited the sun (1633). But Italy did export Baroque art (Bernini) and the budding new medium of opera.

The War of the Spanish Succession (1713)—in which Italy did not participate—gave much of northern Italy to Austria's ruling family, the Habsburgs (who now wore the crown of Holy Roman Emperor). In the south, Spain's Bourbon family ruled the Kingdom of Naples (known after 1816 as the Kingdom of the Two Sicilies), making it a culturally sophisticated but economically backward area, preserving a medieval, feudal caste system.

In 1720, a minor war (the War of Austrian Succession) created a new state at the foot of the Alps, called the Kingdom of Sardinia (a.k.a. the Kingdom of Piedmont, or Savoy). Ruled by the Savoy family, this was the only major state on the peninsula that was actually ruled by Italians. It proved to be a toehold to the future.

ITALY UNITES—THE RISORGIMENTO (1800s)

In 1796, Napoleon Bonaparte swept through Italy and changed everything. He ousted Austrian and Spanish dukes, confiscated Church lands, united scattered states, and crowned himself "King of Italy" (1805). After his defeat (1815), Italy's old ruling order (namely, Austria and Spain) was restored. But Napoleon had planted a seed: What if Italians could unite and rule themselves like Europe's other modern nations?

For the next 50 years, a movement to unite Italy slowly grew. Called the Risorgimento—a word that means "rising again"—the movement promised a revival of Italy's glory. It started as a revolutionary, liberal movement—taking part in it was punishable by death. Members of a secret society called the Carbonari (led by

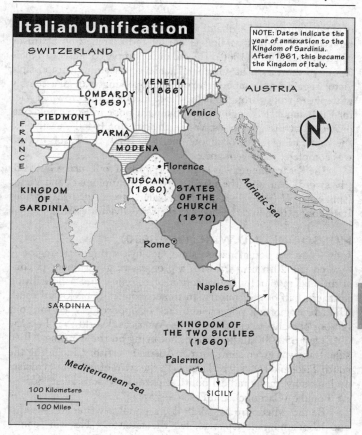

Italian Unification

NOTE: Dates indicate the year of annexation to the Kingdom of Sardinia. After 1861, this became the Kingdom of Italy.

SWITZERLAND

AUSTRIA

VENETIA (1866)

LOMBARDY (1859)

PIEDMONT

PARMA

MODENA

Venice

FRANCE

Florence

TUSCANY (1860)

STATES OF THE CHURCH (1870)

Adriatic Sea

KINGDOM OF SARDINIA

Rome

Naples

SARDINIA

KINGDOM OF THE TWO SICILIES (1860)

Mediterranean Sea

Palermo

SICILY

100 Kilometers
100 Miles

a professional revolutionary named Giuseppe Mazzini) exchanged secret handshakes, printed fliers, planted bombs, and assassinated conservative rulers. Their small revolutions (1820-1821, 1831, 1848) were easily and brutally slapped down, but the cause wouldn't die.

Gradually, Italians of all stripes warmed to the idea of unification. Whether a united dictatorship, a united papal state, a united kingdom, or a united democracy, most Italians could agree that it was time for Spain, Austria, and France to leave.

The movement coalesced around the Italian-ruled Kingdom of Sardinia and its king, Victor Emmanuel II. In 1859, Sardinia's prime minister, Camillo Cavour, cleverly persuaded France to drive Austria out of northern Italy, leaving the region in Italian hands. A vote was held, and several central Italian states (including some of the pope's) rejected their feudal lords and chose to join the growing Sardinian kingdom.

After victory in the north, Italy's most renowned Carbonari

general, Giuseppe Garibaldi (1807-1882), steamed south with a thousand of his best soldiers (I Mille) and marched on Spanish-ruled southern Italy (1860). The old order simply collapsed. In Sicily, in two short months, Garibaldi achieved a seemingly impossible victory against a far superior army. The following year, an assembly of deputies from throughout Italy met in Turin and crowned Victor Emmanuel II "King of Italy." Only the pope in Rome held out, protected by French troops. When the city finally fell—easily—to the unification forces on September 20, 1870, the Risorgimento was complete. Italy went ape.

The Risorgimento was largely the work of four men: Garibaldi (the sword), Mazzini (the spark), Cavour (the diplomat), and Victor Emmanuel II (the rallying point). Today, street signs throughout Italy honor them and the dates of their great victories.

MUSSOLINI AND WAR (1900-1950)

Italy—now an actual nation-state, not just a linguistic region—entered the 20th century with a progressive government (a constitutional monarchy), a collection of colonies, and a flourishing northern half of the country. In the economically backward south (the Mezzogiorno), poverty and lack of opportunity led millions of poor peasants to emigrate to the Americas. World War I (1915-1918) left 650,000 Italians dead, but being on the winning Allied side, Italy was given some former Austrian territory, including the south Tirol and the city of Trieste. In the swirl of postwar cynicism and anarchy, many radical political parties—Communist, Socialist, Popular (Catholic), and Fascist—rose up.

Benito Mussolini (1883-1945), a popular writer for socialist and labor-union newspapers, led the fascists. ("Fascism" comes from Latin *fasci*, the bundles of rods that symbolized unity in ancient Rome.) Though only a minority (6 percent of the parliament in 1921), they intimidated the disorganized majority with organized violence by black-shirted fascist gangs. In 1922, Mussolini seized the government (see "The March on Rome" sidebar) and began his rule as dictator for the next two decades.

Mussolini solidified his reign among Catholics by striking an agreement with the pope (Lateran Treaty, 1929), giving Vatican City to the papacy, while Mussolini ruled Italy with the implied blessing of the Catholic Church. Italy responded to the great worldwide Depression (1930s) with big public works projects (including Rome's subway), government investment in industry, and an expanded army.

Mussolini allied his country with Hitler's Nazi regime, drawing an unprepared Italy into World War II (1940). Italy's lame army was never a factor in the war, and when Allied forces landed in Sicily (1943), Italians welcomed them as liberators. The Italians

The March on Rome

In October 1922, Benito Mussolini, head of the newly formed Fascist Party, boldly proposed a coup d'état, saying: "Either the government will be given to us, or we will take it by marching on Rome." Throughout Italy, black-shirted fascists occupied government buildings in their hometowns. Others grabbed guns, farming hoes, and kitchen knives and set off to converge on the outskirts of Rome. (Estimates of the size of the fascist band range from 300 to the 300,000 of fascist legend.) Mussolini sent the government an ultimatum to surrender. Though the fascists were easily outmanned and outgunned by government forces, the show of force intimidated the king, Victor Emmanuel III, into avoiding a nasty confrontation. He invited Mussolini to Rome. Mussolini arrived the next day (by first-class train), was made prime minister, then marched his black-shirted troops triumphantly through the streets of Rome.

toppled Mussolini's government and surrendered to the Allies, but Nazi Germany sent troops to rescue Mussolini. The war raged on as Allied troops inched their way north against German resistance. Italians were reduced to dire poverty. In the last days of the war (April 1945), Mussolini was captured by the Italian resistance. They shot him and his girlfriend and hung their bodies upside down in a public square in Milan.

POSTWAR ITALY

At war's end, Italy was physically ruined and extremely poor. The nation rebuilt in the 1950s and 1960s with Marshall Plan aid from the United States. Many Italian men moved to northern Europe to find work; many others left farms and flocked to the cities. Over time, Italy regained its standing among nations, joining NATO and what would later become the European Union.

However, the government remained weak, changing on average once a year, shifting from right to left to centrist coalitions. Afraid of another Mussolini, the authors of the postwar constitution created a feeble executive branch; without majorities in both houses of parliament, nothing could get done. All Italians acknowledged that the real power lay in the hands of backroom politicians and organized crime—a phenomenon called *Tangentopoli*, or "Bribe City." The country remained strongly divided between the rich, industrial north and the poor, rural south.

Italian society changed greatly after the liberal reforms of the Catholic Church at the Vatican II conference (1962-1965). The once-conservative Catholic country legalized divorce and contraception, and the birth rate plummeted. In the 1970s, Italy suffered a wave of violence from left- and right-wing domestic terrorists and organized crime, punctuated by the assassination of former Prime Minister Aldo Moro (1978). In the early 1990s, the judiciary undertook a reasonably effective campaign to rid politics of corruption and Mafia ties. The Mafia still exists but is much less powerful.

Italy entered the 21st century buoyed by a growing economy and living standards that were nearly on par with its European neighbors.

ITALY TODAY

That turnaround made Italy a magnet for immigration, especially from Albania, North Africa, and Eastern Europe. The influx brought with it cheap labor but also pressures on social services and cultural norms. Like other European nations, Italy ran up big deficits, and its debt load became the second worst in the euro zone, behind only Greece.

Italy is used to political merry-go-rounds, more recently involving coalition governments; it's had 69 governments since World War II. And while Italy remains the third-largest economy in the eurozone (and world's eighth-largest exporter), unemployment seems stuck at around 10 percent—with youth unemployment hovering around 30 percent.

As you travel through Italy today, you'll encounter a fascinating country with a rich history and a per-capita income that comes close to its neighbors to the north. Despite its ups and downs, Italy remains committed to Europe...yet it's as wonderfully Italian as ever.

To learn more about Italian history, consider *Europe 101: History and Art for the Traveler,* written by Rick Steves and Gene Openshaw (available at www.ricksteves.com).

PRACTICALITIES

This chapter covers the practical skills of European travel: how to get tourist information, pay for things, sightsee efficiently, find good-value accommodations, eat affordably but well, use technology wisely, and get between destinations smoothly. For more information on these topics, see RickSteves.com/travel-tips.

Travel Tips

Travel Advisories: Before traveling, check updated health and safety conditions, including restrictions for your destination, on the travel pages of the US State Department (www.travel.state.gov) and Centers for Disease Control and Prevention (www.cdc.gov/travel). The US embassy website for Italy is another good source of information (see page 1142).

Covid Vaccine/Test Requirements: It's possible you'll need to present proof of vaccination against the coronavirus and/or a negative Covid-19 test result to board a plane to Europe or back to the US. Carefully check requirements for each country you'll visit well before you depart, and again a few days before your trip. See the websites listed above for current requirements.

ETIAS Registration: The European Union may soon require US and Canadian citizens to register online with the European Travel Information and Authorization System (ETIAS) before entering Italy and other Schengen Zone countries (quick and easy process). For the latest, check www.etiasvisa.com.

Tourist Information: Before your trip, scan the website of the Italian national tourist office (www.italia.it) for a wealth of travel information. If you have a specific question, try contacting one of their US offices (New York: +1 212 245 5618, newyork@enit.it; Los Angeles: +1 310 820 1898, losangeles@enit.it).

In Italy, a good first stop in every town is generally the tourist information office (abbreviated **TI** in this book). TIs are in business to help you spend money in their town—which can color their advice—but I still swing by to pick up a city map and get info on public transit, walking tours, special events, and nightlife. While Italian TIs are about half as helpful as those in other countries, their information is twice as important. Some TIs have information on the entire country or at least the region, so you can pick up maps and other info for destinations you'll be visiting later in your trip.

Be wary of travel agencies or special information services that masquerade as TIs but serve fancy hotels and tour companies. They're selling things you don't need.

Emergency and Medical Help: For any emergency service—ambulance, police, or fire—call **112** from a mobile phone or landline (operators typically speak English). If you get sick, do as the locals do and go to a pharmacist for advice. Or ask at your hotel for help—they'll know the nearest medical and emergency services.

Theft or Loss: To replace a passport, you'll need to go in person to an embassy (see next). If your credit and debit cards disappear, cancel and replace them (see "Damage Control for Lost Cards" on page 1148). File a police report, either on the spot or within a day or two; you'll need it to submit an insurance claim for lost or stolen items, and it can help with replacing your passport or credit and debit cards. For more information, see RickSteves.com/help.

US Embassies and Consulates: Embassy in Rome—+39 06 46741, passport and nonemergency consular services, by appointment only (Via Vittorio Veneto 121). Consulates in Milan—+39 02 290 351 (Via Principe Amedeo 2/10); Florence—+39 055 266 951 (Lungarno Vespucci 38); and Naples—+39 081 583 8111 (Piazza della Repubblica). For all, see http://it.usembassy.gov.

Canadian Embassies: Rome—+39 06 854 442 911 (Via Zara 30); Milan—+39 02 626 94238 (Piazza Cavour 3). For both, see www.italy.gc.ca. After-hours emergency in Ottawa +1 613 996 8885.

Avoiding Theft and Scams: Although violent crime is rare in Italy, petty theft is common in large cities and heavily touristed sights. With sweet-talking con artists meeting you at the station and well-dressed pickpockets on buses, tourists face a gauntlet of rip-offs. Pickpockets don't want to hurt you—they usually just want your money and gadgets. Green or sloppy tourists are prone to scams.

Thieves strike when you're distracted. Don't trust overly kind strangers. Keep nothing important in your pockets, and be especially careful with expensive cell phones—maintain a firm grip when you're using one. Be on guard while boarding and leaving buses and subways. Thieves jam up the door, then stop and turn while others crowd and push from behind. You'll find less crowding and commotion—and less risk—on the end cars of a subway rather than the middle cars. Hold your bags in front with your arms over them. Sneaky thieves pretend to be teenagers on holiday, well-dressed businessmen, or tourists wearing fanny packs and toting cameras and even Rick Steves guidebooks. The best deterrent is to look confident and aware, not confused and afraid.

Watch out for fast-fingered moms with babies and groups of children picking the pockets and handbags of naive tourists. Be particularly aware of groups of young women who seem to have nothing to do. Pickpockets troll tourist crowds around major sights and at train stations. Watch them target tourists who are overloaded with bags or distracted with their phones.

Scams abound. When paying for something, be aware of how much cash you're handing over, demand clear and itemized bills, and count your change. Don't give your wallet to self-proclaimed "police" who stop you on the street, warn you about counterfeit (or drug) money, and ask to see your cash. If a bank machine eats your ATM card, check for a thin plastic insert with a tongue hanging out (thieves use these devices to extract cards).

If you feel you are being scammed or are in a situation that makes you feel threatened, use your camera to document the incident and call the police immediately. This alone may deter criminal behavior.

Don't be scared—just be aware and be smart, and you'll be fine.

Time Zones: Italy, like most of continental Europe, is generally six/nine hours ahead of the East/West Coasts of the US. The exceptions are the beginning and end of Daylight Saving Time: Europe "springs forward" the last Sunday in March (two weeks after most of North America), and "falls back" the last Sunday in October (one week before North America). For a handy time converter, use the world clock app on your phone or download one (see www.timeanddate.com).

PRACTICALITIES

Business Hours: Traditionally, Italy used the siesta plan, with people generally working from about 9:00 to 13:00 and from 15:30-16:00 to 19:00-19:30, Monday through Saturday. Siesta hours are no longer required by law, so offices and many shops stay open through lunch or later into the evening, especially larger stores in tourist areas. Shops in small towns and villages are more likely to close during lunch. Stores are usually closed on Sunday, and often on Monday. Many shops close for a couple of weeks around August 15.

Watt's Up? Europe's electrical system is 220 volts, instead of North America's 110 volts. Most electronics (laptops, phones, cameras) and appliances (newer hair dryers, CPAP machines) convert automatically, so you won't need a converter, but you will need an adapter plug with two round prongs, sold inexpensively at travel stores in the US.

Rip up this book! Turn chapters into mini guidebooks: Break the book's spine and use a utility knife to slice apart chapters, keeping gummy edges intact. Reinforce the chapter spines with clear wide tape; use a heavy-duty stapler; or make or buy a cheap cover (see the Travel Store at RickSteves.com), swapping out chapters as you travel.

Discounts: Discounts for sights are generally not listed in this book. However, youths under 18 and students and teachers with proper identification cards (obtain from www.isic.org) can get discounts at many sights—always ask. Italy's national museums generally offer free admission to children under 18, but some discounts are available only for citizens of the European Union (EU).

Tobacco Shops: Known as *tabacchi* (often indicated with a big *T* sign), these Italian-style minimarts are ubiquitous across the country. They're handy places to pay for street parking and purchase such things as batteries, tickets for city buses and subways, and sometimes postage. If you aren't sure where to buy something, a *tabacchi* is a good place to start.

Online Translation Tips: Google's Chrome browser instantly translates websites; Translate.google.com and DeepL.com are also handy. The Google Translate app converts spoken or typed English into most European languages (and vice versa) and can also translate text it "reads" with your smartphone's camera.

Going Green: There's plenty you can do to reduce your environmental footprint when traveling. When practical, take a train instead of a flight within Europe, and use public transportation within cities. In hotels, use the "Do Not Disturb" sign to avoid daily linen and towel changes (or hang up your towels to signal you'll reuse them). Bring a reusable shopping tote and refillable water bottle (Europe's tap water is safe to drink). Skip printed brochures, maps, or other materials that you don't plan to keep—get your info online instead. To find out how Rick Steves' Europe is offsetting carbon emissions with a self-imposed carbon tax, see RickSteves.com/about-us/climate-smart.

Money

Here's my basic strategy for using money wisely in Europe. I pack the following and keep it all safe in my money belt.

Credit Card: You'll use your credit card for purchases both big (hotels, advance tickets) and small (little shops, food stands). Some European businesses have gone cashless, making a card your only payment option. A "tap-to-pay" or "contactless" card is widely accepted and simple to use.

Debit Card: Use this at ATMs to withdraw a small amount of local cash. Wait until you arrive to get euros (European airports have plenty of ATMs); if you buy euros before your trip, you'll pay bad stateside exchange rates. While most transactions are by card these days, cash can help you out of a jam if your card randomly doesn't work, and can be useful to pay for things like tips and local guides.

Backup Card: Some travelers carry a third card (debit or credit; ideally from a different bank) in case one gets lost or simply doesn't work.

Stash of Cash: I carry $100-200 in US dollars as a cash backup, which comes in handy in an emergency (for example, if your debit card gets eaten by the machine).

BEFORE YOU GO

Know your cards. For credit cards, Visa and MasterCard are universal while American Express and Discover are less common. US debit cards with a Visa or MasterCard logo will work in any European ATM.

Go "contactless." Get comfortable using contactless pay options. Check to see if you already have—or can get—a tap-to-pay version of your credit card (look on the card for the tap-to-pay symbol—four curvy lines), and consider setting up your smartphone for contactless payment (see next section for details). Both options are widely used in Europe and are more secure than a physical credit card: Instead of recording your credit card number, a one-time encrypted "token" enables the purchase and expires shortly afterward.

Know your PIN. Make sure you know the numeric, four-digit PIN for each of your cards, both debit and credit. Request it if you don't have one, as it may be required for some purchases. Allow

---

Exchange Rate

1 euro (€) = about $1.10

To convert prices in euros to dollars, add about 10 percent: €20 = about $22, €50 = about $55. Like the dollar, one euro is broken into 100 cents. Coins range from €0.01 to €2, and bills from €5 to €200 (bills over €50 are rarely used).

Check www.oanda.com for the latest exchange rates.

---

time to receive the information by mail—it's not always possible to obtain your PIN online or by phone.

Report your travel dates. Let your bank know that you'll be using your debit and credit cards in Europe, and when and where you're headed.

Adjust your ATM withdrawal limit. Find out how much you can withdraw daily and ask for a higher daily limit if you want to get more cash at once. Note that European ATMs will withdraw funds only from checking accounts, not savings accounts.

Find out about fees. For any purchase or withdrawal made with a card, you may be charged a currency conversion fee (1-3 percent) and/or a Visa or MasterCard international transaction fee (less than 1 percent). If you're getting a bad deal, consider getting a new card. Reputable no-fee cards include those from Capital One, as well as Charles Schwab debit cards. Most credit unions and some airline loyalty cards have low or no international transaction fees.

IN EUROPE
Using Credit Cards and Payment Apps

Tap-to-Pay or **Contactless Cards:** These cards have the usual chip and/or magnetic stripe, but with the addition of a contactless symbol. Simply tap your card against a contactless reader to complete a transaction—no PIN or signature is required. This is by far the easiest way to pay and has become the standard in much of Europe.

Payment Apps: Just like at home, you can pay with your smartphone or smartwatch by linking a credit card to an app such as Apple Pay or Google Pay. To pay, hold your phone near a contactless reader; you may need to verify the transaction with a face scan, fingerprint scan, or passcode. If you've arrived in Europe without a tap-to-pay card, you can easily set up your phone to work in this way.

Other Card Types: Chip-and-PIN cards have a visible chip embedded in them; rather than swiping, you insert the card into the payment machine, then enter your PIN on a keypad. In Europe, these cards have largely been supplanted by tap-to-pay cards, but you may be asked to use chip-and-pin for certain purchases. **Swipe-and-sign** credit cards—with a swipeable magnetic stripe, and a receipt you have to sign—are increasingly rare.

Will My US Card Work? Usually, yes. On rare occasions, at self-service payment machines (such as transit-ticket kiosks, toll-booths, or fuel pumps), some US cards may not work. Usually a tap-to-pay card does the trick in these situations. Just in case, carry cash as a backup and look for a cashier who can process your payment if your card is rejected. Drivers should be prepared to move on to the next gas station if necessary. (In some countries, gas stations sell prepaid gas cards, which you can purchase with any US card). When approaching a toll plaza or ferry ticket line, use the "cash" lane.

Using Cash

Cash Machines: European cash machines work just like they do at home—except they spit out local currency instead of dollars, calculated at the day's standard bank-to-bank rate. In most places, ATMs are easy to locate—in Italy ask for a *bancomat*. When possible, withdraw cash from a bank-run ATM located just outside that bank.

If your debit card doesn't work, try a lower amount—your request may have exceeded your withdrawal limit or the ATM's limit. If you still have a problem, try a different ATM or come back later.

Avoid "independent" ATMs, such as Travelex, Euronet, Moneybox, Your Cash, Cardpoint, and Cashzone. These have high fees, can be less secure, and may try to trick users with "dynamic currency conversion" (see next).

Dynamic Currency Conversion: When withdrawing cash at an ATM or paying with a credit card, you'll often be asked whether you want the transaction processed in dollars or in the local currency. Always refuse the conversion and *choose the local currency*. While DCC offers the illusion of convenience, it comes with a poor exchange rate, and you'll wind up losing money.

Exchanging Cash: Minimize exchanging money in Europe; it's expensive (you'll generally lose 5 to 10 percent). In a pinch you can find exchange desks at major train stations or airports. Banks generally do not exchange money unless you have an account with them.

Security Tips

Pickpockets target tourists. Keep your cash, credit cards, and passport secure in your money belt, and carry only a day's spending money in your front pocket or wallet.

Before inserting your card into an ATM, inspect the front. If anything looks crooked, loose, or damaged, it could be a sign of a

PRACTICALITIES

card-skimming device. When entering your PIN, carefully block other people's view of the keypad.

Avoid using a debit card for purchases. Because a debit card pulls funds directly from your bank account, potential charges incurred by a thief will stay on your account while your bank investigates.

To access your accounts online while traveling, be sure to use a secure connection (see the "Tips on Internet Security" sidebar, later).

Damage Control for Lost Cards

If you lose your credit or debit card, report the loss immediately to the respective global customer-assistance centers. With a mobile phone, call these 24-hour US numbers: Visa (+1 303 967 1096), MasterCard (+1 636 722 7111), and American Express (+1 336 393 1111). From a landline, you can call these US numbers collect by going through a local operator.

You'll need to provide the primary cardholder's identification-verification details (such as birth date, mother's maiden name, or Social Security number). You can generally receive a temporary card within two or three business days in Europe (see RickSteves.com/help for more).

If you report your loss within two days, you typically won't be responsible for unauthorized transactions on your account, although many banks charge a liability fee.

TIPPING

Tipping in Italy isn't as automatic and generous as it is in the US. For special service, tips are appreciated, but not expected. As in the US, the proper amount depends on your resources, tipping philosophy, and the circumstances, but some general guidelines apply.

Restaurants: In Italy, a service charge *(servizio)* is usually built into your check (look at the bill carefully). If it is included, there's no need to leave an extra tip. If it's not included, it's common to leave about €1 per person (a bit more at finer restaurants) or to round up the bill. If paying with a credit card, be prepared to tip separately with cash or coins; credit card receipts don't often have a tip line. For more details on restaurant tipping, see page 1165.

Taxis: For a typical ride, round up your fare a bit (for instance, if the fare is €4.50, pay €5). If the cabbie hauls your bags and zips you to the airport to help you catch your flight, you might want to toss in a little more.

Services: In general, if someone in the tourism or service industry does a super job for you, a small tip of a euro or two is appropriate...but not required. If you're not sure whether (or how much) to tip, ask a local for advice.

PRACTICALITIES

GETTING A VAT REFUND

Wrapped into the purchase price of your Italian souvenirs is a Value-Added Tax (VAT) of about 22 percent. You're entitled to get most of that tax back if you purchase more than €155 worth of goods at a store that participates in the VAT-refund scheme. Typically, you must ring up the minimum at a single retailer—you can't add up your purchases from various shops to reach the required amount. (If the store ships the goods to your US home, VAT is not assessed on your purchase.)

Getting your refund is straightforward...and worthwhile if you spend a significant amount.

At the Merchant: Have the merchant completely fill out the refund document (they'll ask for your passport; a photo of your passport usually works). Keep track of the paperwork and your original sales receipt. Note that you're not supposed to use your purchased goods before you leave Europe.

At the Border or Airport: Process your VAT document at your last stop in the European Union (such as at the airport) with the customs agent who deals with VAT refunds (allow plenty of extra time to deal with this process). At some airports, you'll have to go to a customs office to get your documents stamped and then to a separate VAT refund service (such as Global Blue or Planet) to process the refund. At other airports, a single VAT desk handles the whole thing. (Note that refund services typically extract a 4 percent fee, but you're paying for the convenience of receiving your money in cash immediately or as a credit to your card.) Otherwise, you'll need to mail the stamped refund documents to the address given by the merchant.

CUSTOMS FOR AMERICAN SHOPPERS

You can take home $800 worth of items per person duty-free, once every 31 days. Many processed and packaged foods are allowed, including cheeses, dried herbs, jams, baked goods, candy, chocolate, oil, vinegar, condiments, and honey. Fresh fruits and vegetables and most meats are not allowed, with exceptions for some canned items. As for alcohol, you can bring in one liter duty-free (it can be packed securely in your checked luggage, along with any other liquid-containing items).

To bring alcohol (or liquid-packed foods) in your carry-on bag on your flight home, buy it at a duty-free shop at the airport. You'll increase your odds of getting it onto a connecting flight if it's packaged in a "STEB"—a secure, tamper-evident bag. But stay away from liquids in opaque, ceramic, or metallic containers, which usually cannot be successfully screened (STEB or no STEB).

For details on allowable goods, customs rules, and duty rates, visit http://help.cbp.gov.

PRACTICALITIES

Sightseeing

Sightseeing can be hard work. Use these tips to make your visits to Italy's finest sights meaningful, fun, efficient, and painless.

MAPS AND NAVIGATION TOOLS

A good map is essential for efficient navigation while sightseeing. The maps in this book are concise and simple, designed to help you locate recommended destinations, sights, hotels, and restaurants. In Europe, simple maps are generally free at TIs and hotels.

You can also use a mapping app on your mobile device, which provides turn-by-turn directions for walking, driving, and taking public transit. Google Maps, Apple Maps, and CityMaps2Go allow you to download maps for offline use; ideally, download the areas you'll need before your trip. For certain features, you'll need to be online—either using Wi-Fi or an international data plan.

PLAN AHEAD

Set up an itinerary that allows you to fit in all your must-see sights. For a one-stop look at opening hours, see this book's "At a Glance" sidebars for each major city (Venice, Milan, Florence, Siena, and Rome). Since the Covid-19 pandemic, hours for museums and sights have been unstable. Both before and during your trip, confirm the latest opening days and times with the TI or on a museum or sight's official website (listed throughout this book).

Don't put off visiting a must-see sight—you never know when a place will close unexpectedly for a holiday, strike, or restoration. Many museums are closed or have reduced hours at least a few days a year, especially on holidays such as Christmas, New Year's *(Capodanno)*, Italian Liberation Day (April 25), Labor Day (May 1), and Ferragosto (Feast of the Assumption, Aug 15). A list of holidays is in the appendix; check for possible closures during your trip. In summer, some sights may stay open late. Off-season hours may be shorter.

Going at the right time helps avoid crowds. This book offers tips on the best times to see specific sights. Try visiting popular sights very early or very late. Evening visits (when possible) are usually more peaceful, with fewer crowds. Late morning is usually the worst time to visit a popular sight.

If you plan to hire a local guide, reserve ahead by email. Popular guides can get booked up.

Study up. To get the most out of the self-guided tours and sight descriptions in this book, read them before you visit.

Covid Changes: What to Expect Post-Pandemic

The Covid-19 pandemic caused many disruptions and changes to the way museums and other sights operate—some of which were temporary, others of which may turn out to be permanent. Depending on what's happening during your visit, hours may be modified; reservations may be required (or strongly recommended) to control crowd flow; and paper maps and audioguides may have been replaced by apps.

For any must-see sight on your list, check in advance on its official website (listed throughout this book) or the TI's website to fully understand the current situation. You may learn that it's required to prebook, for example, or you may be able to download an app so you'll have an up-to-date museum map and audioguide on your phone when you arrive.

RESERVATIONS, ADVANCE TICKETS, AND PASSES

Many popular sights in Europe come with long lines—not to get in, but to buy a ticket. Visitors who buy tickets online in advance (or who have a museum pass covering these key sights) can skip the line and waltz right in. Advance tickets are generally timed-entry, meaning you're guaranteed admission on a certain date and time.

For some sights, buying ahead is required (tickets aren't sold at the sight and it's the only way to get in). At other sights, buying ahead is recommended to skip the line and save time. And for many sights, advance tickets are available but unnecessary: At these uncrowded sights you can simply arrive, buy a ticket, and go in.

Don't confuse the reservation options: available, recommended, and required. Use my advice in this book as a guide. Note any must-see sights that sell out long in advance and be prepared to buy tickets early. If you do your research, you'll know the smart strategy.

Given how precious your vacation time is, I'd book in advance both where it's required (as soon as your dates are firm) and where it will save time in a long line (in some cases, you can do this even on the day you plan to visit). Make reservations well in advance to visit these top sights in Venice (St. Mark's Basilica), Padua (Scrovegni Chapel), Milan *(Last Supper),* Florence (Uffizi Gallery, Accademia, Duomo dome climb), or Rome (Colosseum, Roman Forum, Vatican Museums, Borghese Gallery).

You'll generally be emailed an eticket with a QR or bar code that you'll store on your phone to scan at the entrance (if you prefer, you can print it out). At the sight, look for the ticket-holders line

PRACTICALITIES

rather than the ticket-buying line; you may still have to wait in a security line.

Some cities offer passes (e.g., Florence's Duomo complex passes or Siena's Acropoli pass) that cover admission to several sights. At some popular places (such as Venice's Doge's Palace), you can get in more quickly by buying a ticket or pass at a less-crowded sight (the Correr Museum).

Booking a guided tour can help you avoid lines at many popular sights. So can knowing what days to avoid. State museums in Italy are free to enter (and more crowded) once or twice a month, usually on a Sunday. In peak season, check museum websites for specifics and avoid free entry days when possible.

AT SIGHTS

Here's what you can typically expect:

Entering: You may not be allowed to enter if you arrive too close to closing time. And guards start ushering people out well before the actual closing time, so don't save the best for last.

Many sights have a security check. Allow extra time for these lines. Some sights require you to check day packs and coats. (If you'd rather not check your day pack, try carrying it tucked under your arm like a purse as you enter.) Pocketknives may not be allowed.

Photography: If the museum's photo policy isn't clearly posted, ask a guard. Generally, taking photos without a flash or tripod is allowed. Some sights ban selfie sticks; others ban photos altogether.

Audioguides and Apps: I've produced free, downloadable audio tours for some of Italy's major sights, including those in Venice, Florence, Milan, Rome, Assisi, Naples, and Pompeii; look for the ∩ in this book. For more on my audio tours, see page 26.

Some sights offer audioguides with excellent recorded descriptions in English. In some cases, you'll rent a device to carry around (if you bring your own plug-in earbuds, you'll enjoy better sound). Increasingly, museums and sights instead offer an app you can download with their audioguide (often free; check websites from home and considering downloading in advance as not all sights offer free Wi-Fi hotspots).

Temporary Exhibits: Museums may show special exhibits in addition to their permanent collection. Some exhibits are included in the entry price, while others come at an extra cost (which you may have to pay even if you don't want to see the exhibit).

Expect Changes: Artwork can be on tour, on loan, out sick, or shifted at the whim of the curator. Pick up a floor plan as you enter, and ask the museum staff if you can't find a particular item. Say the title or artist's name, or point to the photograph in this book and ask, *"Dov'è?"* (doh-VEH, meaning "Where is?").

Dates for Artwork: Art historians and Italians refer to the great Florentine centuries by dropping a thousand years. The Trecento (300s), Quattrocento (400s), and Cinquecento (500s) were the 1300s, 1400s, and 1500s. The Novecento (900s) means modern art (the 1900s). In Italian museums, art is dated with *sec* for *secolo* (century, often indicated with Roman numerals), AC (*avanti Cristo*, or BC), and DC (*dopo Cristo*, or AD). OK?

Services: Important sights usually have a reasonably priced on-site café or cafeteria (handy air-conditioned places to rejuvenate during a long visit). The WCs at sights are free and generally clean.

Before Leaving: At the gift shop, scan the postcard rack or thumb through a guidebook to be sure you haven't overlooked something that you'd like to see. Every sight or museum offers more than what is covered in this book. Use the information I provide as an introduction—not the final word.

FIND RELIGION

Churches offer some amazing art (usually free), a cool respite from heat, and a welcome seat.

A modest dress code—no bare shoulders or shorts for anyone, even kids—is enforced at larger churches—such as the Duomos in Florence and Siena, Venice's St. Mark's Basilica, and the Vatican's St. Peter's—but is often overlooked elsewhere. If you're caught by surprise, you can sometimes improvise, using maps to cover your shoulders and a jacket for your knees. A few major churches let you borrow or buy disposable ponchos to cover up in a pinch. (I wear a super-lightweight pair of long pants rather than shorts for my hot and muggy Italian sightseeing.) If your heart's set on seeing a certain church, err on the side of caution and dress appropriately.

Some churches have coin-operated boxes that trigger lights to illuminate works of art. I pop in a coin whenever I can, to improve my experience (and photos), as a small contribution to that church, and as a courtesy to other visitors enjoying this great art. Whenever possible, let there be light.

Sleeping

Extensive and opinionated listings of good-value rooms are a major feature of this book's Sleeping sections. Rather than list accommodations scattered throughout a town, I choose hotels in my favorite neighborhoods that are convenient to your sightseeing.

My recommendations run the gamut, from dorm beds to luxurious rooms with all of the comforts. I like places that are clean, central, relatively quiet at night, reasonably priced, friendly, small

Sleep Code

Hotels in this book are categorized according to the average price of a standard double room with breakfast in high season.

$$$$	**Splurge:**	Most rooms over €170
$$$	**Pricier:**	€130-170
$$	**Moderate:**	€90-130
$	**Budget:**	€50-90
¢	**Backpacker:**	Under €50
RS%	**Rick Steves discount**	

Unless otherwise noted, credit cards are accepted, hotel staff speak basic English, and free Wi-Fi is available. Comparison-shop by checking prices at several hotels (on each hotel's own website, on a booking site, or by email). For the best deal, *book directly with the hotel.* Ask for a discount if paying in cash; if the listing includes **RS%,** request a Rick Steves discount.

enough to have a hands-on owner or manager, and run with a respect for Italian traditions. I'm more impressed by a handy location and a fun-loving philosophy than oversized TVs and a fancy gym. Most of my recommendations fall short of perfection. But if I can find a place with most of these features, it's a keeper.

Book your accommodations as soon as your itinerary is set, especially if you want to stay at one of my top listings or if you'll be traveling during busy times. See the appendix for a list of major holidays and festivals in Italy.

Some people make reservations a few days ahead as they travel. This approach fosters spontaneity, and booking sites make it easy to find available rooms, but—especially during busy times—you run the risk of settling for lesser-value accommodations.

RATES AND DEALS

I've categorized my recommended accommodations based on price, indicated with a dollar-sign rating (see sidebar). Room prices can fluctuate significantly with demand and amenities (size, views, room class, and so on), but relative price categories remain constant.

City taxes vary from place to place (figure €2-5 per person, per night). Some hoteliers will ask to collect the tax in cash to make their bookkeeping and accounting simpler.

Booking Direct: Once your dates are set, compare prices at several hotels. You can do this by checking hotel websites and booking sites such as Hotels.com or Booking.com. After you've zeroed in on your choice, book directly with the hotel itself. This increases the chances that the hotelier will be able to accommodate special needs or requests (such as shifting your reservation). And when you book on the hotel's website, by email, or by phone, the owner avoids the commission paid to booking sites, giving them wiggle room to offer you a discount, a nicer room, or a free breakfast (if it's not already included).

Getting a Discount: Some hotels extend a discount to those who pay cash or stay longer than three nights. And some accommodations offer a special discount for Rick Steves readers, indicated in this guidebook by the abbreviation **"RS%."** Discounts vary: Ask for details when you reserve. Generally, to qualify for this discount, you must book direct (not through a booking site), mention this book when you reserve, show this book upon arrival, and sometimes pay cash or stay a certain number of nights. In some cases, you may need to enter a discount code (which I've provided in the listing) in the booking form on the hotel's website. Rick Steves discounts apply to readers with either print or digital books. Understandably, discounts do not apply to promotional rates.

TYPES OF ACCOMMODATIONS
Hotels

Double rooms listed in this book range from about €50 (very simple, toilet and shower down the hall) to €450 (maximum plumbing and more), with most clustered around €140 (with private bathrooms). Prices are higher in big or heavily touristed cities, and lower off the beaten path. Traveling alone can be expensive: A *camera singola* is often only 25 percent less than a *camera doppia*.

Some hotels can add an extra bed (for a small charge) to turn a double into a triple; some offer larger rooms for four or more people (I call these "family rooms" in the listings). If there's space for an extra cot, they'll cram it in for you. In general, a triple room is cheaper than the cost of a double and a single. Three or four people can economize by requesting one big room.

Arrival and Check-In: Hotels and B&Bs are sometimes located on the higher floors of a multipurpose building with a secured door. In that case, look for your hotel's name on the buttons by the main entrance. When you ring the bell, you'll be buzzed in.

Hotel elevators are common, though small, and some older buildings still lack them. You may have to climb a flight of stairs to reach the elevator (if so, you can ask the front desk for help carrying your bags up).

The EU requires hotels to collect your name, nationality, and ID number. At check-in, the receptionist will normally ask for your passport and may keep it for several hours. If you're not comfortable leaving your passport at the desk, bring a copy to give them instead.

If you're arriving in the morning, your room probably won't be ready. Check your bag safely at the hotel and dive right into sightseeing.

PRACTICALITIES

Using Online Services to Your Advantage

From booking services to user reviews, online businesses play a greater role in travelers' planning than ever before. Take advantage of their pluses—and be wise to their downsides.

Booking Sites

Booking websites such as Booking.com and Hotels.com offer one-stop shopping for hotels. While convenient for travelers, they're both a blessing and a curse for small, independent, family-run hotels. Without a presence on these sites, small hotels become almost invisible. But to be listed, a hotel must pay a sizable commission...and promise that its own website won't undercut the price on the booking-service site.

Here's the work-around: Use the big sites to research what's out there, then book directly with the hotel by email or phone, in which case hotel owners are free to give you whatever price they like. Ask for a room without the commission markup (or ask for a free breakfast if not included, or a free upgrade). If you do book online, be sure to use the hotel's own website. The price will likely be the same as via a booking site, but your money goes to the hotel, not agency commissions.

As a savvy consumer, remember: When you book with an online service, you're adding a middleman who takes a cut. To support small, family-run hotels whose world is more difficult than ever, book direct.

Short-Term Rental Sites

Rental juggernaut Airbnb (along with other short-term rental sites) allows travelers to rent rooms and apartments, often providing more value, space, and amenities than a cookie-cutter hotel. Airbnb fans appreciate feeling part of a real neighborhood and getting into a daily routine as "temporary Europeans." Some places are run by thoughtful hosts, allowing you to get to know a local and keep the money in the community; but beware: others are impersonally managed by large, absentee agencies.

In Your Room: Most hotel rooms have a TV and free Wi-Fi, which can vary in strength and quality. Simpler places rarely have a room phone. Pricier hotels usually come with a small fridge stocked with beverages, called a *frigo bar* (FREE-goh bar; pay for what you use).

Nearly all places offer private bathrooms, which have a tub or shower, a toilet, and a bidet (which Italians use for quick sponge baths). The cord over the tub or shower is not a clothesline. You pull it when you've fallen and can't get up.

Double beds are called *matrimoniale*, even though hotels aren't interested in your marital status. Twins are *due letti singoli*. Con-

Critics of Airbnb see it as a threat to "traditional Europe." Landlords can make more money renting to short-stay travelers, driving rents up—and local residents out. Traditional businesses are replaced by ones that cater to tourists. And the character and charm that made those neighborhoods desirable to the tourists in the first place goes too. Some cities have cracked down, requiring owners to obtain a license and to occupy rental properties part of the year (and staging disruptive "inspections" that inconvenience guests).

As a lover of Europe, I share the worry of those who see residents nudged aside by tourists. But as an advocate for travelers, I appreciate the value Airbnb can provide in offering the chance to stay in a local building or neighborhood with potentially fewer tourists.

User Reviews

User-generated review sites and apps such as Yelp and TripAdvisor can give you a consensus of opinions about everything from hotels and restaurants to sights and nightlife. If you scan reviews of a restaurant or hotel and see several complaints about noise or a rotten location, you've gained insight that can help in your decision-making.

As a guidebook writer, my sense is that there is a big difference between the uncurated information on a review site and the vetted listings in a guidebook. A user review is based on the limited experience of one person, who stayed at just one hotel in a given city and ate at a few restaurants there. A guidebook is the work of a trained researcher who forms a well-developed basis for comparison by visiting many restaurants and hotels year after year.

Both types of information have their place, and in many ways, they're complementary. If something is well reviewed in a guidebook and it also gets good online reviews, it's likely a winner.

vents offer cheap accommodation but have more *letti singoli* than *matrimoniali*.

Breakfast and Meals: Italian hotels typically include breakfast in their room prices. If breakfast is optional, you may want to skip it. While convenient, it's usually pricey for what you get: a simple continental buffet with (at its most generous) bread, croissants, ham, cheese, yogurt, and unlimited *caffè latte*. It's cheaper—and much more Italian—to head to the corner café for a sweet roll and coffee and stand at the counter. If you need a bigger breakfast, have a little picnic in your room before heading out.

Hotels in resort areas may charge you for half-pension, called *mezza pensione*, during peak season. Half-pension means that you

Keep Cool

If you're visiting Italy in the summer, you'll want an air-conditioned room. Most hotel air-conditioners come with a remote control that generally has similar symbols and features: fan icon (click to toggle through wind power, from light to gale); temperature (20 degrees Celsius is comfortable); louver icon (choose steady airflow or waves); snowflake and sunshine icons (cold air or heat); and clock ("O" setting: run X hours before turning off; "I" setting: wait X hours to start). When you leave your room for the day, do as the environmentally conscious Europeans do, and turn off the air-conditioning.

pay for one meal per day per person (lunch or dinner). If half-pension is required, you can't opt out and pay less. If it's an option, it can be worth considering, especially if they charge less per meal than you've been paying for an average restaurant meal (and provided the chef is good).

Checking Out: While it's customary to pay for your room upon departure, it can be a good idea to settle your bill the day before, when you're not in a hurry and while the manager's in.

Hotelier Help: Hoteliers can be a good source of advice. Most know their city well and can assist you with everything from public transit and airport connections to finding a good restaurant, the nearest launderette, or a late-night pharmacy.

Hotel Hassles: Even at the best places, mechanical breakdowns occur: Sinks leak, hot water turns cold, toilets may gurgle or smell, the Wi-Fi goes out, or the air-conditioning dies when you need it most. Report your concerns clearly and calmly at the front desk.

If you find that night noise is a problem (if, for instance, your room is over a nightclub or facing a busy street), ask for a quieter room in the back or on an upper floor.

To guard against theft in your room, keep valuables out of sight. Some rooms come with a safe, and other hotels have safes at the front desk. I've never bothered using one and, in a lifetime of travel, I've never had anything stolen out of my room.

For more complicated problems, don't expect instant results. Above all, keep a positive attitude. Remember, you're on vacation. If your hotel is a disappointment, spend more time out enjoying the place you came to see.

Bed-and-Breakfasts

B&Bs can offer good-value accommodations in excellent locations. Usually converted family homes or apartments, they can range from humble rooms with communal kitchens to high-end boutique accommodations with extra amenities. Boutique B&Bs can be an especially good option, as they are typically less expensive than a big hotel, but often newer and nicer, with more personal service. Because the B&B scene is constantly changing, it's smart to supplement this book's recommendations with your own research.

Short-Term Rentals

A short-term rental—whether an apartment, a house, or a room in a private residence—is a popular alternative, especially if you plan to settle in one location for several nights. For stays longer than a few days, you can usually find a rental that's comparable to—and even cheaper than—a hotel room with similar amenities. Plus, you'll get a behind-the-scenes peek into how locals live.

Many places require a minimum-night stay and have strict cancellation policies. And you're generally on your own: There's no reception desk, breakfast, or daily cleaning service.

Finding Accommodations: Websites such as Airbnb, FlipKey, Booking.com, and VRBO let you browse a wide range of properties. Alternatively, rental agencies such as InterhomeUSA. com or RentaVilla.com can provide a more personalized service (their curated listings are also more expensive). Or try Cross-Pollinate, a booking service for private rooms and apartments in the old centers of Florence, Rome, and Venice; rates start at €35 per person (www.cross-pollinate.com).

Before you commit, be clear on the location. I like to virtually "explore" the neighborhood using Google Street View. Also consider the proximity to public transportation, and how well connected the property is with the rest of the city. Ask about amenities (elevator, air-conditioning, laundry, Wi-Fi, parking, etc.). Reviews from previous guests can help identify trouble spots.

Think about the kind of experience you want: Just a key and an affordable bed...or a chance to get to know a local? Some hosts offer self check-in and minimal contact; others enjoy interacting with you. Read the description and reviews to help shape your decision.

Confirming and Paying: Many places require payment in full before your trip, usually through the listing site. Be wary of owners who want to take your transaction offline; this gives you no recourse if things go awry. Never agree to wire money (a key indicator of a fraudulent transaction).

Apartments or Houses: If you're staying in one place several nights, it's worth considering an apartment or rental house. Apartment or house rentals can be especially cost-effective for groups and families. European apartments, like hotel rooms, tend to be small by US standards. But they often come with laundry facilities and small, equipped kitchens *(cucinetta)*, making it easier and cheaper to dine in.

Making Hotel Reservations

Reserve your rooms as soon as you've pinned down your travel dates. For busy national holidays, it's wise to reserve far in advance (see the appendix).

Requesting a Reservation: For family-run hotels, it's generally best to book your room directly via email or phone. For business-class and chain hotels, or if you'd rather book online, reserve directly through the hotel's official website (not a booking website). Almost all of my recommended hotels take reservations in English.

Here's what the hotelier wants to know:

- Type(s) of room(s) you want and number of guests
- Number of nights you'll stay
- Arrival and departure dates, written European-style as day/month/year (for example, 18/06/24 or 18 June 2024)
- Special requests (en suite bathroom, cheapest room, twin beds vs. double bed, quiet room)
- Applicable discounts (such as a Rick Steves discount, cash discount, or promotional rate)

Confirming a Reservation: Most places will request a credit-card number to hold your room. If the hotel's website doesn't have a secure form where you can enter the number directly, share this info via a phone call.

Canceling a Reservation: If you must cancel, it's courteous—and smart—to do so with as much notice as possible, especially for

Rooms in Private Homes: In small towns, there may be few hotels or apartments, but an abundance of Airbnb rentals and some *affittacamere* (rental rooms). These can be anything from a set of keys and a basic bed to a cozy B&B with your own Tuscan grandmother. Renting a room in someone's home is a good option for those traveling alone, as you're more likely to find true single rooms—with just one single bed, and a price to match. Beds range from air-mattress-in-living-room basic to plush-B&B-suite posh. While you can't expect your host to also be your tour guide—or even to provide you with much info—some are interested in getting to know the travelers who pass through their home.

Other Options: Swapping homes with a local works for people with an appealing place to offer (don't assume where you live is not interesting to Europeans). Good places to start are HomeExchange.com and LoveHomeSwap.com. To sleep for free, Couchsurfing.com is a vagabond's alternative to Airbnb. It lists millions of outgoing members who host fellow "surfers" in their homes.

From: rick@ricksteves.com
Sent: Today
To: info@hotelcentral.com
Subject: Reservation request for 19-22 July

Dear Hotel Central,

I would like to stay at your hotel. Please let me know if you have a room available and the price for:
• 2 people
• Double bed and en suite bathroom in a quiet room
• Arriving 19 July, departing 22 July (3 nights)

Thank you!
Rick Steves

smaller family-run places. Cancellation policies can be strict; read the fine print before you book. Many discount deals require pre-payment and can be expensive to change or cancel.

Reconfirming a Reservation: Always call or email to reconfirm your room reservation a few days in advance. For B&Bs or very small hotels, I call again on my arrival day to tell my host what time to expect me (especially important if arriving late—after 17:00).

Phoning: For tips on calling hotels overseas, see page 1183.

PRACTICALITIES

Agriturismi

Agriturismi—working farms that double as countryside B&Bs—began cropping up in the 1980s to allow small family farms to survive (as in the US, many have been squeezed out by giant agribusinesses). By renting rooms to travelers, farmers receive generous tax breaks that allow them to remain on their land and continue to grow food crops. These B&Bs make a peaceful home base for those exploring rural Italy, and are ideal for those traveling by car—especially families.

It's wise to book several months in advance for high season (late May-mid-Oct). July and August are jammed with Italians and other European vacationers; in spring and fall, it's mostly Americans. Weeklong stays (typically Saturday to Saturday) are preferred at busy times, but shorter stays are possible off-season. To sleep cheaper, try early spring and late fall. Most places are closed in winter (about Nov-Easter).

As the name implies, *agriturismi* are in the countryside, although some are located on the outskirts of a large town or city. Most are family-run. *Agriturismi* vary dramatically in quality—

some properties are rustic, while others are downright luxurious, offering amenities such as swimming pools and riding stables. The rooms are usually clean and comfortable. Breakfast is often included, and *mezza pensione* (half-pension, which in this case means a home-cooked dinner) might be built into the price whether you want it or not. Most places serve tasty homegrown food; some are vegetarian or organic, others are gourmet. Kitchenettes are often available to cook up your own feast.

To qualify officially as an *agriturismo*, the farm must still generate more money from its farm activities, thereby ensuring that the land is worked and preserved. Some farmhouse B&Bs aren't working farms, but are still fine places to stay. Some travelers who are enticed by romanticized dreams of *agriturismi* are turned off when they arrive to actual farm smells and sounds. These folks would be more comfortable with a countryside B&B or villa that offers a bit more upscale comfort. In this book, I've listed both types of rural accommodations; if you want the real thing, make sure the owners call their place an *agriturismo*.

In addition to my listings, local TIs can give you a list of places in their area. For a sampling, visit www.agriturismoitaly.it or search online for *agriturismo*. One booking agency among many is Farm Holidays in Tuscany (closed Sat-Sun, tel. 0564-417-418, www.byfarmholidays.com, info@byfarmholidays.com).

Hostels

A hostel provides cheap beds in dorms where you sleep alongside strangers for about €25-30 per night. Travelers of any age are welcome if they don't mind dorm-style accommodations and meeting other travelers. Most hostels offer kitchen facilities, guest computers, Wi-Fi, and a self-service laundry. Hostels almost always provide bedding, but the towel's up to you (though you can usually rent one). Family and private rooms are often available.

Independent hostels tend to be easygoing, colorful, and informal (no membership required; www.hostelworld.com). You may pay slightly less by booking directly with the hostel. **Official hostels** are part of Hostelling International (HI) and share a booking site (www.hihostels.com). HI hostels typically require that you be a member or else pay a bit more per night.

Eating

The Italians are masters of the art of fine living. That means eating long and well. Lengthy, multicourse meals and endless hours sitting in outdoor cafés are the norm. Americans eat on their way to an evening event and complain if the check is slow in coming. For Italians, the meal is an end in itself, and only rude servers rush you.

Restaurant Code

Eateries in this book are categorized according to the average cost of a higher-end pasta or typical main course. Drinks, desserts, and splurge items can raise the price considerably.

$$$$ **Splurge:** Most main courses over €25
$$$ **Pricier:** €20-25
$$ **Moderate:** €15-20
$ **Budget:** Under €15

Pizza by the slice and other takeaway food is **$;** a basic trattoria or sit-down pizzeria is **$$;** a casual but more upscale restaurant is **$$$;** and a swanky splurge is **$$$$.**

I've written an entire book (with co-author Fred Plotkin) on the subject: *Rick Steves Italy for Food Lovers,* a region-by-region handbook on how to appreciate Italian cuisine like an Italian. This section condenses that book's most valuable tips and insights.

A highlight of your Italian adventure will be this country's cafés, cuisine, and wines. Trust me: This is sightseeing for your palate. Even if you liked dorm food and are sleeping in cheap hotels, your taste buds will relish an occasional first-class splurge. You can eat well without going broke. But be careful: You're just as likely to blow a small fortune on a disappointing meal as you are to dine wonderfully for €25. Rely on my recommendations in the various Eating sections throughout this book.

In general, Italians start their day with a light breakfast (*prima colazione;* coffee—usually cappuccino or espresso—and a pastry, often eaten while standing at a counter). Lunch (*pranzo*) was traditionally the largest meal of the day, eaten at home between 13:00 and 15:00 (earlier in northern Italy, later in the south). Dinner (*cena)* was a lighter affair, often just soup with cold cuts, eaten around 20:00 or 21:00 (maybe earlier in winter).

However, as times have changed, so have eating habits. So, while some Italian families still have a big lunch and a small dinner, others do the reverse. Many Italian urbanites grab a quick lunch in a *tavola calda* bar (cafeteria) or buy a *panino* or *tramezzino* (sandwich). To bridge the gap until dinner, people drop into a bar in the late afternoon for a cocktail *(aperitivo),* often served with snacks.

RESTAURANT PRICING

I've categorized my recommended eateries based on the average price of a typical main course, indicated with a dollar-sign rating (see sidebar). Obviously, expensive specialties, fine wine, appetizers, and dessert can significantly increase your final bill.

PRACTICALITIES

The categories also indicate the personality of a place: **Budget** eateries include street food, takeaway, order-at-the-counter shops, basic cafeterias, and bakeries selling sandwiches. **Moderate** eateries are nice (but not fancy) sit-down restaurants, ideal for a pleasant meal with good-quality food. Most of my listings fall in this category—great for a taste of the local cuisine at a reasonable price.

Pricier eateries are a notch up, with more attention paid to the setting, presentation, and (often inventive) cuisine. **Splurge** eateries are dress-up-for-a-special-occasion swanky—typically with an elegant setting, polished service, and pricey and refined cuisine.

BREAKFAST

Italian breakfasts, like Italian bath towels, can be small: The basic, traditional version is coffee and a roll with butter and marmalade. Many places have yogurt and juice (in season, look for *spremuta d'arancia rossa*—fresh-squeezed juice from Sicilian blood oranges), and possibly also cereal, cold cuts and sliced cheese, and eggs (typically hard-boiled; scrambled or fried eggs are less common). Small budget hotels may leave a basic breakfast in your room (stale croissant, roll, jam, yogurt, coffee).

If you want to skip your hotel breakfast, consider browsing for a morning picnic at a local open-air market. Or do as the Italians do: Step into a bar or café to drink a cappuccino and munch a *cornetto* (croissant) while standing at the counter. While the *cornetto* is the most common pastry, you'll find a range of *pasticcini* (pastries, sometimes called *dolci*—sweets). Look for *otto* (an 8-shaped pastry, often filled with custard, jam, or chocolate), *sfoglia* (filo-dough crust that's fruit-filled, like a turnover), or *ciambella* (doughnut filled with custard or chocolate)—or ask about local specialties.

ITALIAN RESTAURANTS

In Italy, *ristorante* typically means a high-end, sit-down restaurant. A *trattoria* is a notch below a *ristorante* in price, but the food is often just as good, if not better. An *osteria*, which originated as a place to drink wine accompanied by food, is similar. *Trattorie* and *osterie* are generally family-owned and serve home-cooked meals at moderate prices. A *locanda* is an inn, a *cantina* is a wine cellar, and a *birreria* is a brewpub. *Pizzerie, rosticcerie* (delis), *tavola calda* ("hot table") bars, *enoteche* (wine bars), and other alternatives are explained later.

I look for restaurants that are convenient to your hotel and sightseeing. When restaurant-hunting, choose a spot filled with locals, not the place with the big neon signs boasting, "We speak English and accept credit cards." Restaurants parked on famous squares generally serve bad food at high prices to tourists. Venturing even a block or two off the main drag leads to higher-quality food for a better price. Locals eat better at lower-rent locales. Family-run places operate without hired help and can offer cheaper meals.

Most restaurant kitchens close between their lunch and dinner service. Good restaurants don't reopen for dinner before 19:00. If you arrive at opening time, most restaurants will be empty and available—the main push of customers arrives later. Small restaurants with a full slate of reservations for 20:30 or 21:00 often will accommodate walk-in diners willing to eat a quick, early meal, but you aren't expected to linger.

When you want the bill, mime-scribble on your raised palm or request it: *"Il conto, per favore."* You may have to ask more than once. If you're in a hurry, request the check when you receive the last item you order.

Cover and Tipping

Avoid surprises when eating out by familiarizing yourself with two common Italian restaurant charges: *coperto* and *servizio*. You won't encounter them in all restaurants, but both charges, if assessed, by law must be listed on the menu.

The *coperto* (cover) is a minor fee (€1.50-3/person) covering the cost of the linens, cutlery, and typical basket of bread found on your table. (It's sometimes called *pane e coperto*—"bread and cover.") It's not negotiable, even if you don't eat the bread. And it's not a tip. Think of it as a fee paid to the owner entitling you to use the table for as long as you like.

The *servizio* is a 10- to 15-percent "service" charge that goes to the server (similar to the mandatory gratuity that American restaurants often add for groups of six or more). These days, most Italian restaurants don't charge this separately; rather, they include service in their prices—you'll see *servizio compreso* or *servizio incluso* on the menu. (At places that do levy a separate *servizio* charge, you don't need to leave an additional tip.)

Italian servers are well paid and are not as reliant on additional **tips** as servers are back home. Even so, if you're pleased with the service, it's polite to add a small tip *(una mancia)*. This is much smaller than the standard 20 percent in the US. A common tip at a simple restaurant or pizzeria is €1 per person (or simply round up the bill); at a finer restaurant, leave a few euros per person. While you could leave coins on the table, it's classier to simply round up the bill when paying. (For instance, if the bill is €46, hand the server €50 and tell them to keep the change.) If paying with a credit card, be prepared to tip separately with cash or coins; credit card receipts don't have a tip line.

Italian Menu Courses

A full Italian meal consists of multiple courses.

Antipasto: An appetizer such as *salumi* (cured meats including salami and prosciutto), cheeses, bruschetta, grilled veggies, or deep-fried tasties. To get a sampler plate of *salumi* and cheeses in a restaurant, look for *affettato misto* (mixed *salumi*), *antipasto misto* (*salumi*, cheeses, and marinated vegetables), or *tagliere* (a sampler "board"). This could make a light meal in itself.

Primo piatto: A "first dish" generally consisting of pasta, soup, rice (usually risotto), or polenta. If you think of pasta when you think of Italian food, you can dine well here without ever going beyond the *primo.*

Secondo piatto: A "second dish" of meat or fish/seafood. Italians freely admit the *secondo* is the least interesting part of their cuisine.

Contorno: A vegetable side dish may come with the *secondo* but more often must be ordered separately. Typical *contorni* are *insalata mista* (mixed salad), spinach, roasted potatoes, or grilled veggies. This can be an interesting, if overlooked, part of the menu. Vegetarians can skip the *secondo* and order several *contorni* to make a meal.

Dolce: No meal is complete without a sweet. On most menus, you'll find typical Italian desserts such as tiramisu and *panna cotta,* or other local favorites. Servers are accustomed to diners splitting a single dessert—just ask for extra forks. Fruit *(frutta)* is often eaten as a dessert, often in the form of *macedonia* (a mixed-fruit salad). A shot of espresso *(un caffè)* is typically served after dessert. (Or skip the restaurant dessert and wander around licking a cone of gelato.)

Ordering Tips

For most travelers, a complete, multicourse meal is simply too much food—and the euros can add up in a hurry. To avoid overeating (and to stretch your budget), share dishes. A good rule of thumb is for each person to order two courses. For example, a couple can order and share one *antipasto,* one *primo,* one *secondo,* and one dessert; or two *antipasti* and two *primi;* or whatever combination appeals. Small groups can mix *antipasti* and *primi* family-style (skipping *secondi*).

It can be worth paying a little more for an inventive fixed-price meal that shows off the chef's creativity. A *menù turistico* is a made-for-tourists plate of Italian food clichés for one fixed price. But locals have their own, typically more interesting version, usually called a *prezzo fisso* or sometimes *menù del giorno* (menu of the day). For a smaller appetite, some restaurants serve a *piatto unico*, with smaller portions of each course on one plate (for instance, a meat, starch, and vegetable).

Seafood and steak may be sold by weight and priced by the *etto* (100 grams, 3.5 ounces) or the kilo (1,000 grams, 2.2 pounds). The abbreviation *s.q. (secondo quantità)* indicates an item is priced by weight (often used at antipasto buffets). Unless the menu indicates a fillet *(filetto)*, fish is usually served whole with the head and tail. You can always ask your server to select a small fish and fillet it for you. Sometimes, especially for steak, restaurants require a minimum order of four or five *etti* (which diners can share). Make sure you're clear on the price before ordering.

Some dishes come in larger quantities meant to be shared by two people. The shorthand way of showing this on a menu is "X2" (for two), but the price listed could indicate the cost per person.

If you order only a pasta and a salad, the server may bring them in that order, which is the opposite of what you might expect; astute severs ask if you want it *insieme* (een-see-EH-meh; together).

Because pasta and bread are both starches, Italians consider them redundant. If you order only a pasta dish, bread may not come with it; you can request it, but you may be charged extra. On the other hand, if you order a vegetable antipasto or a meat *secondo*, bread is often provided to balance the ingredients.

At places with counter service—such as at a bar or a freeway rest-stop diner—you'll first order and pay at the *cassa* (cashier). Then take your receipt to the counter to claim your food.

When going to an especially good restaurant with an approachable staff, I like to find out what they're eager to serve. Sometimes I'll simply say "Make me happy"...and set a price limit.

BUDGET EATING

Italy offers many budget options for hungry travelers. Self-service cafeterias offer the basics without add-on charges. Travelers on a hard-core budget equip their room with a pantry stocked at the market (fruits and veggies are remarkably cheap), or pick up a sandwich or *döner kebab*, then dine in at picnic prices. Bars and cafés are also good places to grab a meal on the go.

Pizzerias

Italians head to a pizzeria at dinnertime to order a one-person pie. Some shops sell *pizza rustica* (also called *pizza al taglio* or *pizza al trancio*)—thick pizza baked in a large rectangular pan and sold by weight. This, rather than floppy New York-style slices, is the standard option for Italians on the go. If you simply ask for a piece, you may wind up with a gigantic slab and be charged top euro. Instead, clearly indicate how much you want: *un etto*—100 grams— is a hot and cheap snack; *due etti*—200 grams—makes a light meal. Or show the size with your hands: *tanto così* (TAHN-toh koh-ZEE; this much). They may ask if you want it *riscaldata* (ree-skahl-DAH-tah; heated up). The correct answer is *sì*. For

a rundown of common types of pizza, see that section, later. Pizzerias also sell *cecina*, a savory crêpe-like garbanzo-bean flatbread—a cheap snack that pairs well with a glass of red wine.

Bars/Cafés

An Italian bar isn't so much a tavern as an inexpensive café. These neighborhood hangouts serve coffee, light food, and drinks from the cooler. This is where locals go for a breakfast of cappuccino and *cornetto* (croissant). Throughout the day, bars are the place to drop in for a coffee or another drink.

Many bars are small—if you can't find a table, you'll need to stand or find a ledge to sit on outside. Most charge extra for table service. To get food to go, say, *"da portar via"* (for the road). All bars have a WC *(toilette, bagno)* in the back, available to customers...and the discreet public.

Food: For quick meals, bars usually have trays of cheap, pre-made sandwiches (*panini*, on a baguette; *piadine*, on flatbread; *tramezzini*, on crustless white bread; or *toasts*, on, well, toast)—some are delightful grilled. (Others have too much mayo.) In bigger cities, they'll have a variety of salads ready to serve up from under the glass counter. To save time for sightseeing and room for dinner, stop by a bar for a light lunch, such as a ham-and-cheese sandwich—ideally thrown on the grill to heat up.

Ordering: If the bar isn't busy, you can probably just order and pay when you leave. Otherwise, there's a particular procedure: First look around to decide what you want, then go to cashier *(la cassa)* to order and pay. Often, a list with two sets of prices is posted near the cashier: *al banco* (standing at the bar) or *al tavolo* (seated). Unless you really plan to settle in and watch the world go by, have your drink at the bar. If you're not sure, you can ask, "Same price if I sit or stand?": *"Costa uguale al tavolo o al banco?"* (KOH-stah oo-GWAH-lay ahl TAH-voh-loh oh ahl BAHN-koh).

Upon paying, you're handed a receipt *(scontrino)*. Take that to the bartender (whose clean fingers handle no dirty euros) and tell them what you want. It's customary to set a small coin or two on the bar, as a tip, when you place your order. Throughout Italy, you can get cheap coffee at the bar of any establishment, no matter how fancy, and pay the same low, government-regulated price (generally about a euro if you stand).

Tavola Calda Bars and *Rosticcerie*

For a fast and cheap lunch, find an Italian variation on the corner deli: a *rosticceria* ("roasting place," specializing in roasted meats and accompanying sides, such as roasted potatoes or sautéed greens) or a *tavola calda* bar (a "hot table" point-and-shoot cafeteria with a buffet spread of meat and vegetables; sometimes called *tavola fredda,* or "cold table," in the north of Italy). For a healthy light meal, ask for a mixed plate of vegetables with a hunk of mozzarella (*piatto misto di verdure con mozzarella;* pee-AH-toh MEE-stoh dee vehr-DOO-ray). Don't be limited by what's displayed. If you'd like a salad with a slice of cantaloupe and some cheese, they'll whip that up for you in a snap. Belly up to the bar; with a pointing finger, you can assemble a fine meal. If something's a mystery, ask for *un as-saggio* (oon ah-SAH-joh) to get a little taste. To have your choices warmed up, ask for them to be heated (*riscaldata;* ree-skahl-DAH-tah).

Wine Bars

Wine bars *(enoteche)* are a popular, fast, and generally inexpensive option for lunch. Meaning "wine library," an *enoteca* is usually a bar highlighting local wines, accompanied with well-paired light food (such as *salumi* and cheese, a salad, or simple seasonal dishes). A good *enoteca* aims to impress visitors with its wine—look for a blackboard listing today's selection and price per glass. The food prices can add up—be careful with your ordering to keep this a budget choice). For more on Italian cocktails and wines, see page 1178.

Aperitivo Snacks *("Apericena")*

The Italian term *aperitivo* means a predinner drink, but it's also used to describe their version of what we might call happy hour: a light buffet of snacks that many bars serve to customers during the predinner hours (typically around 18:00 or 19:00 until 21:00). The drink itself may not be cheap (typically around €8-12), but some bars lay out an enticing array of *salumi,* cheeses, grilled vegetables, and other *antipasti*-type dishes. (Really good spreads earn the nickname *"apericena"*—a pun combining *aperitivo* and *cena,* dinner.) You're welcome to nibble while you nurse your drink.

The *apericena* is intended as an appetizer course before heading out for dinner: You're invited to have a couple of hearty snacks with each drink you pay for. For light eaters who've had a too-big lunch, this could wind up being enough to skip dinner. Drop by a few bars around this time to scope out their buffets before choosing. Or opt for a place with a big view and simpler snacks—either way, you'll get your money's worth.

Markets, Groceries, and Delis: Assembling a Picnic

Picnicking saves lots of euros and is a great way to sample regional specialties. A picnic can even be an adventure in high cuisine. Be daring. Try the fresh ricotta, *presto* pesto, shriveled olives, and any regional specialties the locals are excited about.

Markets: For the most colorful experience, gather your ingredients in the morning at a produce market. Towns big and small have markets selling everything imaginable for a fantastic picnic, including cheese, meat, bread, sweets, and prepared foods. You'll often find street-food stalls tucked into the marketplace as well (note that many stalls close in the early afternoon).

Groceries and Delis: Another budget option is to visit a supermarket (look for the Conad, Carrefour, Esselunga, and Co-op chains), *alimentari* (neighborhood grocery), or *salumeria* (delicatessen) to pick up *salumi*, cheeses, and other picnic supplies. Some grocery stores, *salumerie,* and any *paninoteca* or *focacceria* (sandwich shop) can make a sandwich to order. Just point to what you want, and they'll stuff it into a *panino.* Almost every grocery store has a deli case with prepared items like stuffed peppers, marinated olives, lasagna, and chicken, all usually sold by weight; if you want it reheated, remember the word *riscaldata* (ree-skahl-DAH-tah). And *rosticcerie* sell cheap food to go—you'll find options such as lasagna, rotisserie chicken, and sides including roasted potatoes and spinach. For more on *salumi* and cheeses, see those sections, later.

Ordering: A typical picnic for two might be fresh rolls, *un etto* (3.5 ounces) of cheese, and *un etto* of meat (sometimes ordered by the slice—*fetta*—or piece—*pezzo*). For two people, I might get *un etto* of prosciutto and *due pezzi* of bread. Add two tomatoes, three carrots, two apples, yogurt, and a liter box of juice. Total: about €10.

If ordering *antipasti* (such as grilled or marinated veggies) at a deli counter, you can ask for *una porzione* in a takeaway container *(contenitore).* Use gestures to show exactly how much you want. To set a price limit of 5 or 10 euros on what you order, say *"Da [cinque/dieci] euro, per favore."* The word *basta* (BAH-stah; enough) works as a question or as a statement.

Shopkeepers are happy to sell small quantities of produce, but it's customary to let the merchant choose for you. Say *"per oggi"* (pehr OH-jee; for today) and he or she will grab you something ready to eat. To avoid being overcharged, know the cost per kilo, study the weighing procedure, and do the math. Remember that a kilo is 2.2 pounds.

ITALIAN CUISINE STAPLES

Much of your Italian eating experience will likely involve the big five: pizza, pasta, *salumi,* cheese, and gelato. Here's a rundown on what you might find on menus and in stores. I've included specifics on regional cuisine throughout this book. For more food help, try a menu translator, such as the *Rick Steves Italian Phrase Book & Dictionary,* which has a menu decoder and plenty of useful phrases for navigating the culinary scene.

Pizza

Here are some of the pizzas you might see at restaurants or at a pizzeria. Note that if you ask for pepperoni on your pizza, you'll get *peperoni* (green or red peppers); instead, try requesting *salsiccia piccante* (spicy sausage) or *salame piccante* (spicy salami).

Bianca: White pizza with no tomatoes
Capricciosa: Prosciutto, mushrooms, olives, and artichokes—literally the chef's "caprice"
Carciofi: Artichokes
Diavola: Spicy hot
Funghi: Mushrooms
Margherita: Tomato sauce, mozzarella, and basil—the red, white, and green of the Italian flag
Marinara: Tomato sauce, oregano, garlic, no cheese
Ortolana or *vegetariana:* "Greengrocer-style," with vegetables
Quattro formaggi: Four different cheeses
Quattro stagioni: "Four seasons," with tomato, mozzarella, and usually one-quarter each of ham, mushrooms, artichokes, and olives
Salsiccia: Sausage
Siciliana: Capers, olives, and often anchovies

Pasta

While we think of pasta as a main dish, in Italy it's considered a *primo piatto*—first course. There are hundreds of varieties of Italian pasta, each one specifically used to highlight a certain sauce, meat,

Eating with the Seasons Across Italy

Italian cooks love to serve fresh produce and seafood at its tastiest. Each region in Italy has its seasonal specialties, which you'll see displayed in open-air markets. To get a plate of the freshest veggies at a fine restaurant, request *"Un piatto di verdure della stagione, per favore."* ("A plate of seasonal vegetables, please.") Italians take fresh, seasonal ingredients so seriously that a restaurant cooking with frozen ingredients *(congelato)* must note it on the menu. Here are a few examples of what's fresh when:

April-May: Calamari (Venice), romanesco (similar to cauliflower), fava beans (Rome), green beans, artichokes

April-May and Sept-Oct: Black truffles

April-June: Asparagus, zucchini flowers, zucchini

May-June: Mussels, cantaloupe, loquats, strawberries

May-Aug: Eggplant, clams

July-Sept: Figs, cherries, peaches, apricots, plums

Oct-Nov: Mushrooms, white truffles, persimmons, chestnuts

Nov-Feb: Radicchio (Venice), cardoon (wild artichoke), *puntarelle* (chicory shoots; Rome)

or regional ingredient. *Pastasciutta* is dry-stored pasta, which is boiled until *al dente* (chewy, "to the tooth") and tossed with a sauce. *Pasta fresca* is fresh pasta cut into noodles and served with sauce, or cut into sheets *(sfoglie),* filled with different ingredients, folded, cooked, and then covered lightly with butter, cream, or broth.

Don't mistakenly assume that dry pasta is inferior to fresh. If prepared well, it can be just as satisfying. There are two general types of dry pasta:

Pasta lunga, also called strand pasta, are noodles long enough to twist around a fork. Spaghetti is the most famous, but *pasta lunga* can be round, such as *capellini* (thin "little hairs"), *vermicelli* ("little worms"), and *bucatini* (long and hollow); or it can be flat, such as *linguine* (narrow "little tongues"), *fettuccine* (wider "small ribbons"), *tagliatelle* (even wider), and *pappardelle* (very wide, best with meat sauces).

Pasta corta ("short pasta") are smaller, designed to be scooped or speared with a fork. They go well with creamy sauces and chunkier meat sauces. The most common are dried tubular pastas called *maccheroni;* these come in endless forms, such as *penne* ("quills") and *maccheroncini* (tiny macaroni). Tubular pastas come either *lisce* (smooth) or *rigate* (grooved—so sauce clings better). Many short pastas are named for their shapes, such as *conchiglie* (shells), *farfalle* (butterflies), or *cavatappi* (corkscrews).

Here's a list of common pasta toppings and sauces. On a menu, these terms are usually preceded by *alla* (in the style of) or *in* (in):

Aglio e olio: Garlic and olive oil

Alfredo: Sweet butter and heaps of Parmigiano-Reggiano cheese

Amatriciana: Guanciale (pork cheek), tomatoes, *pecorino romano* cheese, and chili peppers

Arrabbiata: "Angry," spicy tomato sauce with chili peppers

Bolognese: "Bologna-style" meat and tomato sauce

Boscaiola: "Woodsman-style," with mushrooms and sausage or ham

Brodo: Broth (typical for filled pastas)

Burro e salvia: Butter and sage

Cacio e pepe: Pecorino romano cheese and fresh-ground pepper

Carbonara: Raw egg, *guanciale* (pork cheek), *pecorino romano* cheese, and fresh-ground pepper

Carrettiera: Spicy and garlicky, with olive oil and little tomatoes

Diavola: "Devil-style," spicy hot

Frutti di mare: Seafood

Genovese: Basil ground with Parmigiano-Reggiano cheese, garlic, pine nuts, and olive oil; a.k.a. pesto

Gricia: Cured pork cheek and *pecorino romano* cheese

Marinara: Usually tomato, often with garlic and onions, but can also be a seafood sauce ("sailor's style")

Mollicata: Simple sauce of tomato, onion, red wine, breadcrumbs, and sometimes anchovy

Norma: Tomato, eggplant, basil, and *ricotta salata* (Sicily)

Pajata: Calf intestines (also called *pagliata*)

Pescatora: Seafood ("fisherman style")

Pomodoro: Tomato only

Puttanesca: Tomato sauce with anchovies and/or tuna, olives, capers, and garlic

Ragù: Meaty tomato sauce (more meat in the north; more tomato in the south)

Scoglio: Mussels, clams, and tomatoes

Sorrentina: "Sorrento-style," with tomatoes, basil, and mozzarella (usually over gnocchi)

Sugo di lepre: Rich sauce made of wild hare

Tartufi: Truffles (also called *tartufate*)

Vongole: Clams and spices

Salumi

Salumi (cured meats)—sometimes called *affettati* (sliced meats)—

are an Italian staple. While most American cold cuts are cooked, in Italy they're far more commonly cured by air-drying, salting, and smoking. (While called "raw"—*crudo*—these are perfectly safe to eat.)

The two most familiar types of *salumi* are *salame* and *prosciutto*. *Salame* is an air-dried, sometimes-spicy sausage that comes in many varieties. When Italians say *"prosciutto,"* they usually mean *prosciutto crudo*—the raw ham that air-cures on the hock and is then thinly sliced. Produced mainly in the north of Italy, *prosciutto* can be either *dolce* (sweet) or *salato* (salty). Purists say the best is *prosciutto di Parma*.

Other *salumi* may be less familiar, but no less worth trying:

Bresaola: Air-cured beef

Capocollo: Peppery pork shoulder (also called *coppa*)

Culatello: High-quality, slow-cured prosciutto

Finocchiona: *Salame* with fennel seeds

Guanciale: Tender pork cheek

Lardo: Pork lard made fragrant with herbs and spices; the best is *lardo di Colonnata*

Lonzino: Cured pork loin

Mortadella: A finely ground pork loaf, similar to our bologna

'Nduja: Super-spicy, smoky, soft, spreadable pork sausage with a texture like bright-red pâté

Pancetta: Salt-cured, peppery pork-belly meat, similar to bacon

Salame di Sant'Olcese: What we'd call "Genoa salami"

Salame piccante: Spicy hot, similar to pepperoni

Soppressata: A simple dry *salame* that has some kick, common in the south

Speck: Smoked pork shoulder

Squeamish eaters should avoid *testa in cassetta* (headcheese—organs in aspic) and *lampredotto* (cow stomach).

Cheese

When it comes to cheese (*formaggio* or *cacio*), you're probably already familiar with most of these Italian favorites:

Asiago: Hard cow cheese that comes either *mezzano* (young, firm, and creamy) or *stravecchio* (aged, pungent, and granular)

Burrata: Ball of mozzarella wrapped around a buttery, almost liquid center

Caciocavallo: This misnamed "horse cheese" is a cow's-milk cheese that's pear-shaped so it can be lashed at the top and hung to dry, like a saddlebag

Fontina and **Montasio:** Semihard, nutty, Gruyère-style mountain cheeses

Gorgonzola: Pungent, blue-veined cheese, either *dolce* (creamy) or *piccante* (aged and sharp)

Grana: Generic term for grating cheeses; most common is *grana padano* ("*grana* of the Po")

Mascarpone: Sweet, buttery, spreadable dessert cheese

Mozzarella di bufala: Made from the milk of water buffaloes

Parmigiano-Reggiano: Hard, crumbly, sharp, aged cow cheese with more nuanced flavor than American parmesan

Pecorino: Sheep's cheese, either *fresco* (fresh, soft, and mild) or *stagionato* (aged and sharp, sometimes called *pecorino romano*—a popular grating cheese)

Provolone: Rich, firm, aged cow cheese

Ricotta: Soft, airy cheese made by "recooking" leftover whey

Scamorza: Similar to mozzarella, but often smoked

Gelato

American and Italian ice cream are similar but decidedly not the same. Italy's gelato is denser and creamier (even though it has less butterfat than ice cream) than American versions, and connoisseurs swear it's more flavorful.

A key to gelato appreciation is sampling liberally and choosing flavors that go well together. At a *gelateria,* ask, as Italians do, for a taste: *"Un assaggio, per favore?"* (oon ah-SAH-joh pehr fah-VOH-ray).

Most *gelaterie* clearly display prices and sizes. But in the textbook *gelateria* scam, the tourist orders two or three flavors—and the clerk selects a fancy, expensive chocolate-coated waffle cone, piles it high with huge scoops, and cheerfully charges the tourist €10. To avoid rip-offs, point to the price or say what you want—for instance, a €3 cup: *"Una coppetta da tre euro"* (OO-nah koh-PEH-tah dah tray eh-OO-roh).

The best *gelaterie* display signs reading *artigianale, nostra produzione,* or *produzione propria,* indicating that the gelato is made on the premises. Seasonal flavors are also a good sign, as are mellow hues (avoid colors that don't appear in nature). Gelato stored in covered metal tins (rather than white plastic) is more likely to be homemade. The chain called Grom is the Starbucks of Italian gelato: It's an acceptable choice, but try to find something more local.

Other Italian frozen treats include *sorbetto* (sorbet—made with fruit, but no milk or eggs); *granita* or *grattachecca* (a cup of slushy ice with flavored syrup); and *cremolata* (a gelato-*granita* float). *Caffè affogato* is a scoop of gelato "drowned" in a shot of hot espresso.

Classic gelato flavors include:

After Eight: Chocolate and mint

Bacio: Chocolate hazelnut, named for Italy's popular "kiss" candies

Cassata: With dried fruits

Cioccolato: Chocolate

Crema: Plain (similar to vanilla)
Croccantino: "Crunchy," with toasted peanut bits
Fior di latte: Sweet milk
Fragola: Strawberry
Frutti di bosco: Mixed berries
Gianduia (or *gianduja*): Chocolate-hazelnut
Lampone: Raspberry
Macedonia: Mixed fruits
Malaga: Similar to rum raisin
Nocciola: Hazelnut
Noce: Walnut
Riso: With actual bits of rice mixed in
Stracciatella: Vanilla with chocolate shreds
Tartufo: Super chocolate
Zabaione: Named for the egg yolk-and-Marsala wine dessert
Zuppa inglese: Sponge cake, custard, chocolate, and cream

BEVERAGES

Italian bars serve great drinks—hot, cold, sweet, caffeinated, or alcoholic.

Water, Juice, and Cold Drinks

Italians are notorious water snobs. At restaurants, your server just can't understand why you wouldn't want good water to go with your good food. It's customary and never expensive to order a *litro* or *mezzo litro* (half-liter) of bottled water. Simply ask for *con gas* if you want fizzy water and *senza gas* if you prefer still water. You can ask for *acqua del rubinetto* (tap water) in restaurants, but your server may give you a funny look.

Chilled bottled water—still *(naturale)* or carbonated *(frizzante)*—is sold cheap in stores. Half-liter bottles of mineral water are available everywhere for about €1. (I refill my water bottle with tap water.)

Juice is *succo*, and *spremuta* means freshly squeezed. Order *una spremuta* (don't confuse it with *spumante*, sparkling wine)—it's usually orange juice *(arancia)*, and from February through April it can be made from Sicilian blood oranges *(arance rosse)*.

In grocery stores, you can get a liter of OJ for the price of a Coke or coffee. Look for *100% succo* or *senza zucchero* (without sugar) on the label—or be surprised by something diluted and sugary sweet. Hang on to your water bottles. Buy juice in cheap liter boxes, then drink some and store the extra in your water bottle.

Tè freddo (iced tea) is usually from a can—sweetened and flavored with lemon or peach. Lemonade is *limonata*.

Coffee and Other Hot Drinks

The espresso-based style of coffee so popular in the US was born in Italy. If you ask for *"un caffè,"* you'll get a shot of espresso in a little cup. Most Italian coffee drinks begin with espresso, to which they add varying amounts of hot water and/or steamed or foamed milk. The closest thing to American-style drip coffee is a *caffè americano*—a shot of espresso diluted with hot water. Milky drinks, like cappuccino or *caffè latte,* are served to locals before noon and to tourists any time of day. To an Italian, cappuccino is a morning drink; they believe having milk after a big meal impairs digestion. If they add any milk after lunch, it's just a splash, in a *caffè macchiato*.

Italians like their coffee only warm—to get it very hot, request *"Molto caldo, per favore"* (MOHL-toh KAHL-doh pehr fah-VOH-ray). Any coffee drink is available decaffeinated—ask for it *decaffeinato* (deh-kah-feh-NAH-toh).

If you want a hot drink other than coffee, *cioccolato* is hot chocolate, and *tè* is hot tea.

Cappuccino: Espresso with foamed milk on top (*cappuccino freddo* is iced cappuccino)

Caffè latte: Espresso mixed with hot milk, no foam, in a tall glass (ordering just a "latte" gets you only milk)

Caffè macchiato: Espresso "stained" with a splash of milk, in a small cup

Latte macchiato: Layers of hot milk and foam, "stained" by an espresso shot, in a tall glass. Note that if you order simply a *"macchiato,"* you'll probably get a *caffè macchiato* (see above).

Caffè corto/lungo: Concentrated espresso diluted with a tiny bit of hot water, in a small cup

Caffè americano: Espresso diluted with even more hot water, in a larger cup

Caffè corretto: Espresso "corrected" with a shot of liqueur (normally grappa, *amaro,* or *sambuca*)

Marocchino: "Moroccan" coffee with espresso, foamed milk, and cocoa powder; the similar *mocaccino* has chocolate instead of cocoa

Caffè freddo: Sweet and iced espresso

Caffè hag: Instant decaf

Alcoholic Beverages

Beer: While Italy is traditionally considered wine country, in recent years there's been a huge and passionate growth in the production of craft beer *(birra artigianale)*. Even in small towns, you'll see microbreweries slinging their own brews. What's on tap is often inspired by the same trends you'll find stateside—IPAs, ambers, stouts, saisons, sours, seasonal beers, and so on. You'll also find loc

Ordering Wine

To order a glass of red or white wine, say, *"Un bicchiere di vino rosso/bianco."* House wine comes in a carafe; choose from a quarter-liter pitcher (8.5 oz, *un quarto*), half-liter pitcher (17 oz, *un mezzo*), or one-liter pitcher (34 oz, *un litro*). When ordering, have some fun, gesture like a local, and you'll have no problems speaking the language of the *enoteca. Salute!*

English	Italian
wine	*vino* (VEE-noh)
house wine	*vino della casa* (VEE-noh DEH-lah KAH-zah)
glass	*bicchiere/calice* (bee-kee-EH-ray/KAH-lee-chay)
bottle	*bottiglia* (boh-TEEL-yah)
carafe	*caraffa* (kah-RAH-fah)
red	*rosso* (ROH-soh)
white	*bianco* (bee-AHN-koh)
rosé	*rosato* (roh-ZAH-toh)
sparkling	*spumante/frizzante* (spoo-MAHN-tay/freed-ZAHN-tay)
dry	*secco* (SEH-koh)
fruity	*fruttato* (froo-TAH-toh)
full-bodied	*corposo/pieno* (kor-POH-zoh/pee-EH-noh)
sweet	*dolce* (DOHL-chay)

brews (Peroni and Moretti), as well as imports such as Heineken. Italians drink mainly lager beers. Beer on tap is *alla spina*. Get it *piccola* (33 cl, 11 oz), *media* (50 cl, about a pint), or *grande* (a liter). A *lattina* (lah-TEE-nah) is a can and a *bottiglia* (boh-TEEL-yah) is a bottle.

Cocktails and Spirits: Italians appreciate both *aperitivi* (palate-stimulating cocktails) and *digestivi* (after-dinner drinks designed to aid digestion).

The classic **aperitivo** is the *spritz:* prosecco (or white wine) and soda livened up with either Campari (carmine-red bitters with a secret blend of herbs and orange peel) or Aperol (sweeter, softer, bright-orange bitters with herbal, citrusy undertones). Vermouths (both red and white) from Carpano, Cinzano, Martini, or Riccadonna can be served straight, on the rocks, with a splash of soda, or as part of drinks like Punt e Mes (sweet red vermouth and red wine). Other choices include Americano (vermouth with bitters, brandy, and lemon peel); Garibaldi (also known as Campari-Or-nge, a mixture of Campari and orange juice); and Cynar (bitters ed with artichoke).

gestivo choices fall into three categories. First is the bit-tersweet, syrupy herbal drink called *amaro* (many restaurants have their own brew; popular commercial brands are Fernet Branca and Montenegro). For something sweeter, try *limoncello* (lemon-flavored), *amaretto* (almond), Frangelico (hazelnut), *sambuca* (anise), or Marsala wine. And grappa is a brandy distilled from grape skins and stems; *stravecchio* is an aged, mellower variation. *Acquavite* ("water of life") is similar to grappa, but distilled from fruit such as apples, berries, or plums.

Wine: The ancient Greeks who colonized Italy more than 2,000 years ago called it Oenotria—land of the grape. Centu-

ries later, Galileo wrote, "Wine is light held together by water." Wine *(vino)* is certainly a part of the Italian culinary trinity—grape, olive, and wheat. (I'd add gelato.) Ideal conditions for grapes (warm climate, well-draining soil, and an abundance of hillsides) make the Italian peninsula a paradise for grape growers, winemakers, and wine drinkers.

In most years, Italian winemakers produce more wine than any other country—more than 4 million liters annually. Production is mainly red *(rosso)* and white *(bianco)* wines. Rosé *(rosato)* is less traditional—though as it's become trendy stateside and elsewhere, more Italian vintners are experimenting with it. A sparkling wine is *frizzante* or *spumante;* prosecco is a bubbly white wine from northeastern Italy (though that word is sometimes, incorrectly, used to refer to any Italian sparkling white).

Even if you're clueless about wine, the information on an Italian wine label can help you choose something decent. Terms you may see on the bottle include *classico* (from a defined, select area), *annata* (year of harvest), *vendemmia* (harvest), and *imbottigliato dal produttore all'origine* (bottled by producers).

In general, Italy designates its wines by one of four official categories:

Vino da Tavola (VDT) is table wine, the lowest grade, made from grapes grown anywhere in Italy. It's often inexpensive, but Italy's wines are so good that, for many people, a basic *vino da tavola* is just fine with a meal. And, because it's grown in the same area as the other ingredients you're enjoying, it pairs perfectly with the food. Many restaurants, even modest ones, take pride in their house wine *(vino della casa)*, bottling their own or working with wineries.

Denominazione di Origine Controllata (DOC) meets nation

Regional Wines

In almost every part of Italy, you'll find wine varieties designed to go with the regional cuisine.

Tuscany (Florence, Siena, and Nearby): Many Tuscan wines are made with the native sangiovese grape, including the well-known Chiantis, which range from cheap basket-bottles of table wine (called *fiaschi*) to the hearty Chianti Classico. Vino Nobile di Montepulciano is a high-quality dry ruby red. One of Italy's top reds is the smooth Brunello di Montalcino; a cheaper, younger "baby Brunello" is Rosso di Montalcino. Pricey Super Tuscans blend traditional grapes with locally grown non-Italian grapes (such as cabernet or merlot). The best white choice is the crisp Vernaccia di San Gimignano; trebbiano and vermentino are other local white grapes. Sweet and syrupy, vin santo dessert wine is often served with a cookie for dipping.

Veneto (near Venice): Valpolicella grapes are used to make red table wines as well as rich red Amarone and sweet Recioto dessert wine (both made from dried—*passito*—grapes). Whites include Soave, Pinot Grigio, and Bianco di Custoza. If you like bubbles, try sweet, fizzy Fragolino or prosecco (connoisseurs say the best hails from Valdobbiadene).

Umbria (Assisi, Orvieto, and Nearby): Trebbiano is this region's main white grape; look for golden, dry Orvieto Classico. For reds, consider Sagrantino de Montefalco or Torgiano Rosso Riserva. Wines from the quality producer Lungarotti are worth trying.

Liguria (Italian Riviera, including Cinque Terre): This coastal region produces light, delicate whites from native bosco grapes. Sossese di Dolceacqua is a medium-bodied red. After dinner, try

standards for high-quality wine, produced in a legally controlled geographical area. It's usually good and still quite affordable.

Denominazione di Origine Controllata e Guarantita (DOCG), the highest grade, meets national standards for the highest-quality wine (made with grapes from a defined area whose quality is "guaranteed"). These wines can be identified by the pink or green label on the neck...and the high price. They're a good bet if you want a quality wine. (*Riserva* indicates a DOC or DOCG wine that's been aged for even longer than required.)

Indicazione Geografica Tipica (IGT) is a broad group of wines that don't meet the standard for DOC or DOCG status but have been designated as "typical" of a particular region.

If you're on a tight budget, try looking for a more affordable alternative. For example, in Tuscany, the world-famous Brunello ~~Montalcino (a DOCG) can break the bank, but Rosso di Mon-~~ (a DOC)—made in the same zone with similar grapes, in the potent, amber-colored Sciacchetrà.

Lazio (Rome and Nearby): The majority of wines produced in this region are white, most often made with trebbiano or malvasia grapes; the most popular is Frascati. For a red, try the medium-bodied Torre Ercolana.

Dolomites: While beer is king here, look for reds like the robust Santa Magdalaner and fruity Lagrein Scuro, or whites like Pinot Grigio, Gewürztraminer, and Pinot Blanc. Nosiola is an aromatic local grape used for dessert and sparkling wine.

Piedmont (near Milan and the Lakes): This region specializes in bold, dry reds. Nebbiolo is the main red grape, used in big, tannic Barolo or its elegant "little brother," Barbaresco. For lighter, fruitier reds, try Barbera or Dolcetto. Whites include the dry Gavi and flowery Arneis. For bubbly wines, sample sweet Brachetto, semisweet Moscato d'Asti (slightly fizzy), or dry Asti Spumante.

Campania (Naples, Sorrento, and Nearby): Plentiful sun and volcanic soils provide great wine-growing conditions. Taurasi is an excellent ruby-colored, full-bodied red. Lacryma Christi ("tears of Christ") comes in both a medium-bodied red and a dry and fruity white. Campanian whites include the mineral Greco di Tufo and flavorful Fiano di Avellino.

Sicily: The main red is the full-bodied Nero d'Avola. Corvo, Regaleali, and Planeta are some established producers. White wines use indigenous grapes like grillo, inzolio, and catarrato. Try fruity Bianca d'Alcamo and dry Etna Bianco. Marsala is a (usually) sweet fortified dessert wine.

a similar way, but aged for a shorter period of time—costs half as much.

Staying Connected

One of the most common questions I hear from travelers is, "How can I stay connected in Europe?" The short answer? More easily and affordably than you might think.

The simplest solution is to bring your own device—phone, tablet, or laptop—and use it much as you would at home, following the money-saving tips below, such as getting an international plan or connecting to free Wi-Fi whenever possible. Another option is to buy a European SIM card for your mobile phone. Or you can use European landlines and computers to connect. More details are at RickSteves.com/phoning.

Hurdling the Language Barrier

Many Italians—especially those in the tourist trade and in big cities—speak English. Still, you'll get better treatment if you learn and use Italian pleasantries. In smaller, nontouristy towns, Italian is the norm. Italians have an endearing habit of talking to you even if they know you don't speak their language—and yet, thanks to gestures and thoughtfully simplified words, it somehow works. Don't stop them to tell them you don't understand every word—just go along for the ride. For a list of survival phrases, see the appendix.

Note that Italian is pronounced much like English, with a few exceptions, such as: c followed by e or i is pronounced ch (to ask, *"Per centro?"* "To the center?" you say, pehr CHEHN-troh). In Italian, *ch* followed by e or i is pronounced like the hard c in Chianti (*chiesa*—church—is pronounced kee-AY-zah). Adding a vowel to the English word often gets you close to the Italian one. Give it your best shot. Italians appreciate your efforts.

For more tips on hurdling the language barrier, consider the *Rick Steves Italian Phrase Book* (available at RickSteves. com).

USING YOUR PHONE IN EUROPE

Here are some budget tips and options.

Sign up for an international plan. To stay connected at a lower cost, sign up for an international service plan through your carrier. Most providers offer a simple bundle that includes calling, messaging, and data. Your normal plan may already include international coverage (for example, T-Mobile's covers data and text, but not voice calls).

Before your trip, research your provider's international rates. Activate the plan a day or two before you leave, then remember to cancel it when your trip's over.

Use free Wi-Fi whenever possible. Unless you have an unlimited-data plan, save most of your online tasks for Wi-Fi. Most accommodations in Europe offer free Wi-Fi. Many cafés offer hotspots for customers; ask for the password when you buy something. You may also find Wi-Fi at TIs, city squares, major museums, public-transit hubs, airports, and aboard trains and buses.

Minimize the use of your cellular network. The best way to make sure you're not accidentally burning through data is to put your device in "airplane" mode (which also disables phone calls and texts), and connect to Wi-Fi as needed. When you need to get online but can't find Wi-Fi, simply turn on your cellular network (or turn off airplane mode) just long enough for the task at hand.

with an international data plan, wait until you're on

How to Dial

Here's how to dial from anywhere in the US or Europe, using the phone number of one of my recommended Florence hotels as an example (055 213 154). If a non-Italian number starts with 0, drop it when dialing internationally.

From a US Mobile Phone
Phone numbers in this book are presented exactly as you would dial them from a US mobile phone. For international access, press and hold 0 (zero) to get a + sign, then dial the country code (39 for Italy) and phone number.
▶ To call the Florence hotel from any location, dial +39 055 213 154.

From a US Landline
Replace + with 011 (US/Canada access code), then dial the country code (39 for Italy) and phone number.
▶ To call the Florence hotel from your home landline, dial 011 39 055 213 154.

From a European Landline
Replace + with 00 (Europe access code), then dial the country code (39 for Italy, 1 for the US) and phone number.
▶ To call the Florence hotel from a Spanish landline, dial 00 39 055 213 154.
▶ To call my US office from an Italian landline, dial 00 1 425 771 8303.

From One Italian Phone to Another
To place a domestic call (from an Italian landline or mobile), drop +39 and dial the phone number.
▶ To call the Florence hotel from Rome, dial 055 213 154.

More Dialing Tips
Local Numbers: European phone numbers and area codes can vary in length and spacing, even within the same country. Mobile phones use separate prefixes (for instance, in Italy, landlines begin with 0, and mobile numbers begin with 3).

Toll and Toll-Free Calls: It's generally not possible to dial European toll or toll-free numbers from a US mobile or landline (although you can sometimes get through using Skype). Look for a direct-dial number instead.

Calling the US from a US Mobile Phone, While Abroad: Dial +1, area code, and number.

More Phoning Help: See HowToCallAbroad.com.

PRACTICALITIES

Wi-Fi to Skype or FaceTime, download apps, stream videos, or do other megabyte-greedy tasks. Using a navigation app such as Google Maps over a cellular network can require lots of data, so download maps when you're on Wi-Fi, then use the app offline.

Limit automatic updates. By default, your device constantly checks for a data connection and updates app content. Check your device's menu for ways to turn this off, and change your email settings from "auto-retrieve" to "manual" (or from "push" to "fetch").

Use Wi-Fi calling and messaging apps. Skype, WhatsApp,

Tips on Internet Security

Make sure that your device is running the latest versions of its operating system, security software, and apps. Next, ensure that your device and key programs (like email) are password protected. On the road, use only secure, password-protected Wi-Fi. Ask the hotel or café staff for the specific name of their network, and make sure you log on to that exact one.

If you must access your financial info online, use a banking app rather than accessing your account via a browser, and use a cellular connection, not Wi-Fi. Never log on to personal finance sites on a public computer. If you're very concerned, consider subscribing to a VPN (virtual private network).

FaceTime, and Google Meet are great for making free or low-cost calls or sending texts over Wi-Fi worldwide. Just log on to a Wi-Fi network, then connect with friends, family members, or local contacts who use the same service.

Buy a European SIM Card. If you anticipate making a lot of local calls or need a local phone number, or if your provider's international data rates are expensive, consider buying a SIM card in Europe to replace the one in your (unlocked) US phone or tablet.

In Italy, buy SIM cards at mobile-phone shops. You'll be required to register the SIM card with your passport as an antiterrorism measure (which may mean you can't use the phone for the first hour or two).

There are generally no roaming charges when using a European SIM card in other EU countries, but confirm when you buy.

WITHOUT A MOBILE PHONE

It's less convenient but possible to travel in Europe without a mobile device. You can make calls from your hotel and check email or get online using public computers.

Most **hotels** charge a fee for placing calls. You can use a prepaid international phone card (*carta telefonica prepagata internazionale*—usually available at newsstands, tobacco shops, and train stations) to call out from your hotel.

Some hotels have **public computers** in their lobbies for guests to use; otherwise you may find them at public libraries (ask your hotelier or the TI for the nearest location). On a European keyboard, use the "Alt Gr" key to the right of the space bar to insert the extra symbol that appears on some keys. If you can't locate a special character (such as @), simply copy and paste it from a web page.

MAIL

You can mail one package per day to yourself worth up to $200 duty-free from Europe to the US (mark it "personal purchases"). If you're sending a gift to someone, mark it "unsolicited gift." For details, visit www.cbp.gov, select "Travel," and search for "Know Before You Go." The Italian postal service works fine, but for quick transatlantic delivery (in either direction), consider services such as DHL (DHL.com).

Transportation

Figuring out how to get around in Europe is one of your biggest trip decisions. **Cars** work well for two or more traveling together (especially families with small kids), those packing heavy, and those delving into the countryside. **Trains** and **buses** are best for solo travelers, blitz tourists, city-to-city travelers, and those who want to leave the driving to others. Short-hop **flights** within Europe can creatively connect the dots. Be aware of the potential downside of each option: A car is an expensive headache in any major city; with trains and buses you're at the mercy of a timetable; flying entails a trek to and from a usually distant airport and leaves a larger carbon footprint.

If your itinerary mixes cities and countryside, my advice is to connect cities by train or bus and to explore rural areas by rental car. Arrange to pick up your car in the last big city you'll visit, then use it to lace together small towns and explore the countryside. For more detailed information on transportation throughout Europe, see RickSteves.com/transportation.

TRAINS

To travel by train affordably within Italy, you can simply buy tickets as you go. For travelers ready to lock in dates and times weeks or months in advance, buying nonrefundable tickets online can cut costs in half. Note that the Italy rail pass is generally not a good value, but if your travel extends beyond Italy, there are multicountry rail passes that might be worth checking into. For advice on figuring out the smartest train-ticket or rail-pass options for your trip, visit the Trains & Rail Passes section of my website at RickSteves.com/rail.

Types of Trains

Most trains in Italy are operated by the state-run **Trenitalia** company (www.trenitalia.com, a.k.a. Ferrovie dello Stato Italiane, abbreviated FS). Ticket prices depend on the speed of the train, so it helps to know the different types of trains: pokey Regionale (R or

PRACTICALITIES

PRACTICALITIES

Italy's Public Transportation

SWITZERLAND

To Innsbruck

San Candido

St. Moritz

Brennero

Cast.

Locarno

Geneva

Lugano

Bolzano

Men.

Tirano

Mtn. Lift

Domo-dossola

Varenna

Trento

DOLO-MITES

Chamonix

Pré-Saint-Didier

Stresa

Riva

La Palud

Gallarate

Como

Bergamo

Vicenza

Aosta

Malpensa

Verona

To Lyon & Paris

Milan

Desezano

Modane

Torino

Cremona

Mantova

FRANCE

Parma

Modena

Genoa

Santa Margherita Ligure

Bologna

To Paris

Finale

Vernazza

Florence

Marseille

CINQUE TERRE

Lucca

Ventimiglia

La Spezia

Pisa

To Barcelona

Nice

Livorno

San Gim.

Ligurian Sea

Volterra

Poggi.

Siena

See Hill Towns Public Transportation detail map

ELBA Piombino

C O R S I C A (FRANCE)

Civitavecchia

Mediterranean Sea

Porto Torres

Olbia

100 Kilometers

100 Miles

S A R D I N I A

Chilivani

To Cagliari

To Naples

To Aeolian Islands

Milazzo

Messina

To Naples & Rome

To Tunis

Palermo

Cefalú

Villa San Giovanni

Trapani

Reggio Calabria

To Cagliari

Marsala

S I C I L Y

Enna

Taormina

See detail map

Castelvetrano

Catania

Agrigento

Ionian Sea

Mediterranean Sea

Piazza Armerina

Siracusa

Ragusa

To Tunis

Same scale as main map

REG); medium-speed Regionale Veloce (RV); fast InterCity (IC) and EuroCity (EC); and super-fast Frecce trains.

All trains (except those with Regionale in the name) require seat assignments, which are built into your ticket for a specific date and time. If you're traveling with a rail pass, you'll need to buy a separate seat reservation (see "Rail Passes," later). Regional trains offer only open seating (no assigned seats for love nor money).

The private train company Italo (www.italotreno.it) runs fast trains on major routes serving large cities on the mainland but few small towns. Italo has fewer departures than Trenitalia but its service is comparable to Trenitalia's Frecce service, with similar prices and advance purchase discounts. Be aware that in Naples, Milan, and Rome, a few departures use secondary stations. Italo does not accept rail passes but is a worthy alternative for point-to-point tickets.

Both train companies have call centers for answering general questions (Trenitalia: daily 7:00-24:00, +39 06 6847 5475; Italo: daily 6:00-23:00, +39 06 8937 1892).

Be aware that Trenitalia and Italo don't cooperate. If you buy a ticket for one train line, it's not valid on the other. Both companies tend to ignore the other's schedules.

Schedules

Check schedules at Trenitalia.it and ItaloTreno.it (domestic journeys only) or use their apps; for international trips, use Bahn.com (Germany's excellent all-Europe schedule website, which reflects national railways but not private companies like Italo). At the train station, the easiest way to check schedules is at a ticket machine. Enter the desired date, time, and destination to see all your options. Printed schedules are also posted at the station (yellow posters show departures—*partenze;* white posters show arrivals).

Schedules list the time of departure *(ora),* the type of train *(treni),* and service classes offered *(classi servizi)*—first- and second-class cars, dining car, *cuccetta* berths, and whether you need reservations (usually denoted by an R in a box). The train's destination *(principali fermate destinazioni)* is shown, along with intermediate stops, and notes such as "also stops in..." *(ferma anche a...),* "doesn't stop in..." *(non ferma a...),* "stops in every station" *(ferma in tutte le stazioni),* "delayed..." *(ritardo...),* and so on.

At the station, look at the electronic display to find your train's track *(binario)* number. Remember that your destination may be listed as an intermediate (not final) stop. For example, if you're going from Milan to Florence, you'll notice that virtually all the trains that terminate in Naples or Salerno stop in Florence en route (but most terminating in Rome do not). If you're not sure, ask for help.

Point-to-Point Tickets
Train tickets are a good value in Italy. Typical full fares are shown on the map on page 1191, though ticket prices can vary for the same journey, mainly depending on the time of day, the speed of the train, and advance discounts.

Classes of Service: Frecce and Italo trains each offer several classes of service (e.g., Standard, Premium, Business, Executive). Other trains offer standard first- and second-class seating (with first class costing up to 50 percent more than second). Buying up gives you a little more elbow room, a snack, or perhaps a better chance at seating a group together, if you're buying on short notice.

Advance Discounts: Ticket price levels are Base (full fare, easily changeable or partly refundable before scheduled departure), Economy (one schedule change allowed before departure, for a fee), and Super Economy or Low Cost (sells out quickly, no refunds or exchanges).

For example, traveling Standard class from Rome to Florence on the fastest train costs €50 at Base fare, €39 at Economy fare, or €30 at Super Economy rate. Discounted fares must be purchased at least two days in advance but typically sell out several weeks before departure. Fares labeled *servizi abbonati* are available only for locals with monthly passes—not tourists. Regional trains don't offer advance discounts or seat assignments, so there's little need to buy those tickets in advance.

Speed vs. Savings: For point-to-point tickets, you'll pay more the faster you go. Spending a modest amount of extra time in transit can save money on shorter trips. For example, the regional train from Milano Centrale to Stresa takes just over an hour (67 minutes) and costs €9, while the EC train takes just under an hour (58 minutes)—but costs €19.

On longer mainline routes, fast trains save more time and provide most of the service. For example, speedy Florence-Rome trains run about 3/hour, cost €50 in second class, and make the trip in 1.5 hours, while infrequent InterCity trains (only 1-2/day) cost €37 at full price and take three hours.

Age-Based Discounts: Discounts for kids don't usually beat the Super Economy rate described above. If the cheapest tickets are no longer available, look for deals like "Bimbi Gratis" and "Offerta Famiglia." Other discounts for youths and seniors require purchase of a separate card (€40 Carta Verde for ages 12-26, €30 Carta Argento for ages 60 and over), but the discount is so minor (10-15 percent for domestic travel), it's not worth it for most.

Buying Point-to-Point Tickets

You can buy tickets online, with an app, at train station ticket windows, from ticket machines, or at travel agencies. For long-haul runs or travel on a busy weekend or holiday, it can be cheaper to buy tickets in advance. But because most Italian trains run frequently and there's no deadline to buy tickets, for the most part I prefer to keep my travel plans flexible by purchasing tickets as I go. (You can buy tickets at one station for several trips when you are ready to commit.)

It's easy to buy tickets **online** at Trenitalia.com or ItaloTreno. it. On either website, choose English and be sure to read the pricing info, as many of the cheaper tickets are not refundable or changeable. You can keep the ticket on your mobile device (either as a PDF or with a QR code), or you can print it out. Or download the Trenitalia or Italo **app** to your phone—both have English versions that make ticket-buying a breeze.

If you instead go to the train station to buy tickets, you can avoid ticket-office lines by using the **ticket machines** in station halls. You'll be able to easily purchase tickets for travel within Italy, make seat reservations, and even book a *cuccetta* (koo-CHEH-tah; overnight berth). If you do use the **ticket windows** (e.g., to buy international tickets), be sure you're in the correct line. Key terms: *biglietti* (general tickets), *prenotazioni* (reservations), *nazionali* (domestic), and *internazionali*. Some big stations have counters (close to the tracks) marked "Last Minute," which let you jump the line if your train is departing soon.

Trenitalia's ticket machines are user-friendly and found in all but the tiniest stations in Italy. You can pay with cash (change given when indicated) or by debit or credit card (even for small amounts, but you may need to enter your PIN—even when using "tap-to-pay"). Select English, then your destination. If you don't immediately see the city you're traveling to, keep keying in the spelling until it's listed. You can choose from first- and second-class seats, request tickets for more than one traveler, and pick seats, when applicable. Don't select a discount rate without being sure that you meet the criteria (for example, Americans are not eligible for certain EU or resident discounts).

To buy tickets at the station for **Italo** trains, look for a dedicated service counter (in most major stations) or a red ticket machine labeled *Italo*.

Some **international tickets** can't be bought online or from machines; for these tickets and anything else that requires a real

Rail Pass or Point-to-Point Tickets?

Will you be better off buying a rail pass or point-to-point tickets? It pays to know your options and choose what's best for your itinerary.

Rail Passes

A Eurail Italy Pass lets you travel by train in Italy for three to eight days (consecutively or not) within a one-month period. Italy is also covered (along with most of Europe) by the classic Eurail Global Pass.

Discounted rates are offered for seniors (age 60 and up) and youths (ages 12-27). Up to two kids (ages 4-11) can travel free with each adult-rate pass (but not with senior rates). All rail passes offer a choice of first or second class for all ages.

While most rail passes are delivered electronically, it's smart to get your pass sorted before leaving home. For more on rail passes, including current prices and purchasing, visit RickSteves.com/rail.

Point-to-Point Tickets

Italian train tickets are relatively cheap, and most include seat reservations, making them the best deal for most travelers. Use this map to add up approximate pay-as-you-go fares for your itinerary, and compare that to the price of a rail pass plus reservations. Keep in mind that significant discounts on point-to-point tickets may be available with advance purchase.

Map shows approximate costs, in US dollars, for one-way, second-class tickets on faster trains.

PRACTICALITIES

person, you must go to a ticket window at the station. A good alternative, though, is to drop by a local travel agency. Agencies sell domestic and international tickets and make reservations. They charge a small fee, but the language barrier (and the lines) can be smaller than at the station's ticket windows.

Rail Passes

The single-country Eurail Italy Pass may save you money if you take several long train rides or prefer first-class travel, but for most people it's not a good value. Most train travelers in Italy take relatively short rides on the Milan-Venice-Florence-Rome circuit. For these trips, it can be cheaper to buy point-to-point tickets. Remember that rail passes are valid on Trenitalia trains but not on Italo trains.

Furthermore, a rail pass doesn't offer much hop-on convenience in Italy, since even with a rail pass, seat reservations are required for InterCity, EuroCity, and Frecce trains (€5-10 each; make seat reservations at station ticket machines or windows). Most regional trains (such as Florence-Pisa-Cinque Terre service) don't require (or offer) reservations. Reservations for berths on overnight trains cost extra and aren't covered by rail passes.

If you're also traveling by train in other countries, consider a Eurail Global Pass. Although it covers most of Europe, prices can work for trips as short as three travel days or as long as three months. For more info, see the sidebar.

Train Tips

Validating Tickets: If your ticket includes a seat reservation on a specific train *(biglietto con prenotazione)*, you're all set and can just get on board. The same is true for any ticket bought online or with the Trenitalia or Italo apps (whether open or reserved seating); these tickets are considered already validated.

An open ticket (generally for a *regionale* train) bought from a ticket desk or machine must be validated (date-stamped) before you board (the ticket may say *da convalidare* or *convalida*). To validate it, before getting on the train, stamp your ticket in the machine near the platform (usually marked *convalida biglietti* or *vidimazione*). Once you validate a ticket, you must complete your trip within the stamped timeframe (usually about four hours). If you forget to validate your ticket, go right away to the train conductor—before he comes to you—or you'll pay a fine.

Getting a Seat: If you're taking an unreserved *regionale* train that originates at your departure point (e.g., you're catching the Florence-Pisa train in Florence), arriving at least 15 minutes before the departure time will help you snare a seat.

Baggage Storage: Many Italian stations have *deposito bagagli*

Hill Town Public Transportation

where you can safely leave your bag for a standardized but steep price (€6/5 hours, €12/12 hours, €17/24 hours, payable when you pick up the bag, double-check closing hours; they may ask to photocopy your passport). Due to security concerns, no Italian stations have lockers.

Theft: In big cities, exercise caution and prudence at train stations to avoid thieves and con artists. If someone helps you to find your train or carry your bags, be aware that they are not an official porter; they are simply hoping for some cash. And if someone other than a uniformed railway employee tries to help you use the ticket machines, politely refuse.

Italian trains are famous for their thieves. Never leave a bag unattended. Police do ride the trains, cutting down on theft. Still, for an overnight trip, I'd feel safe only in a *cuccetta* (a bunk in a special sleeping car with an attendant who keeps track of who comes and goes while you sleep—approximately €40 or more).

Strikes: Strikes, which are common, generally last a day (often a Friday). Train employees will simply explain, *"Sciopero"* (SHOH-peh-roh, strike). But in actuality, a minimum amount of "essential" or "guaranteed" *(garantito)* main-line service is maintained (by law) during strikes. When a strike is pending, travel agencies, savvy hoteliers, and remaining station personnel can check to see when the strike will go into effect and which trains will continue to run. Revised schedules may be posted online and in Italian at stations. See Trenitalia.com, choose English, then "Information and Contacts," and then "In Case of Strike."

If your train is cancelled, your reserved-seat ticket will likely be accepted on any similar train running that day (either earlier or later than the original departure time) but you won't have a seat assignment. Tickets for cancelled trains should also be exchangeable without penalty ahead of the original departure time, or can be refunded (have an agent mark it "unused," and check refund deadlines). A rail pass works on any train still operating, but partially used rail passes can't be refunded—so make full use of any pass you have to continue your trip.

BUSES

You can usually get anywhere you want in Italy by bus, as long as you're not in a hurry and plan ahead using bus schedules (pick up at local TIs or bus stations). For reaching small towns, buses are sometimes the only option if you don't have a car. In many hill towns, trains leave you at a station in the valley far below, while buses more likely drop you right into the thick of things. (If the bus stop or station is below town, sometimes an escalator or elevator helps get you up into town.)

Long-distance buses are catching on in Italy as an alternative to the train. Buses are usually cheaper, more modern, and often have free Wi-Fi. They're especially useful on routes poorly served by train, or to allow a direct connection instead of having to change trains (such as from Rome to Siena or Sorrento). Some of the operators you'll see are Flixbus (http://global.flixbus.com) and Marozzi (www.marozzivt.it). In general, orange buses are local city buses, and blue buses are for long distances.

Larger towns have a (usually chaotic) long-distance bus station *(stazione degli autobus* or *autostazione)*, with ticket windows and several stalls (usually labeled *corsia, stallo,* or *binario)*—but to save time, buy your ticket at a travel agent or online; many companies use etickets (they'll scan your emailed QR code as you board). Smaller towns—where buses are more useful—often have a central bus stop *(fermata),* likely along the main road or on the main square, and maybe several more scattered around town. In small towns, buy bus tickets at newsstands or tobacco shops (with the big *T* signs). When buying your ticket, confirm the departure point *("Dov'è la fermata?").*

Before boarding, confirm the destination with the driver. You are expected to stow big bags underneath the bus (if the compartment is closed, ask the driver for help; which compartment you use may depend on your destination). If you'll be continuing on later by bus, upon arrival, double-check that the posted schedule lists your next destination and departure time.

Traveling by bus on Sundays and holidays can be problematic; even from large cities, schedules are sparse, departing buses are jam-packed, and ticket offices are often closed. Plan ahead and buy your ticket in advance. Most travel agencies book bus (and train) tickets for a small fee.

TAXIS AND RIDE-BOOKING SERVICES

Most Italian taxis are reliable and cheap. In many cities, two people can travel short distances by cab for little more than the cost of bus or subway tickets. If you like ride-booking services such as Uber, their apps usually work in Europe just like they do in the US: Request a car on your mobile phone (connected to Wi-Fi or data), and the fare is automatically charged to your credit card. In Italy, however, Uber faces legal challenges, and may not be consistently available (for instance, Uber does not operate in Florence).

RENTING A CAR

It's cheaper to arrange most car rentals from the US, so research and compare rates before you go. Most of the major US rental agencies (including Avis, Budget, Enterprise, Hertz, and Thrifty) have offices throughout Europe. Also consider the two major Europe-based agencies, Europcar and Sixt. Consolidators such as Auto Europe (AutoEurope.com—or the sometimes cheaper AutoEurope.eu) compare rates at several companies to get you the best deal.

Wherever you book, always read the fine print. Check for add-on charges—such as one-way drop-off fees, airport surcharges, or mandatory insurance policies—that aren't included in the "total price."

Rental Costs and Considerations

If you book well in advance, expect to pay $350-500 for a one-week rental for a basic compact car. Allow extra for supplemental insurance, fuel, tolls, and parking. To save money on fuel, request a diesel car.

Manual vs. Automatic: Almost all rental cars in Europe are manual by default—and cars with a stick shift are generally cheaper. If you need an automatic, reserve one specifically. When selecting a car, don't be tempted by a larger model, as it won't be as maneuverable on narrow, winding roads or when squeezing into tight parking lots.

Age Restrictions: Some rental companies impose minimum and maximum age limits. Young drivers (25 and under) and seniors

(69 and up) should check the rental policies and rules section of car-rental websites.

Choosing Pick-Up/Drop-off Locations: Always check the hours of the locations you choose: Many rental offices close from midday Saturday until Monday morning and, in smaller towns, at lunchtime. When selecting an office, confirm the location on a map. A downtown site might seem more convenient than the airport but could actually be in the suburbs or buried deep in big-city streets. Pedestrianized and one-way streets can make navigation tricky when returning a car at a big-city office or urban train station. Wherever you select, get precise details on the location and allow ample time to find it. And be aware that most Italian cities have a "ZTL" (limited traffic zone) that's carefully monitored by cameras. If your drop-off point is near this zone, get clear directions on how to get there to avoid getting a big fine.

Have the Right License: If you're renting a car in Italy, bring your driver's license. You're also technically required to have an International Driving Permit—an official translation of your license (sold at AAA offices for about $20 plus the cost of two passport-type photos; see AAA.com). How this is enforced varies: I've never needed one.

Picking Up Your Car: Before driving off in your rental car, check it thoroughly and make sure any damage is noted on your rental agreement. Rental agencies in Europe tend to charge for even minor damage, so be sure to mark everything. Find out how your car's gearshift, lights, turn signals, wipers, radio, and fuel cap function, and know what kind of fuel the car takes (diesel is common in Europe). When you return the car, make sure the agent verifies its condition with you.

Car Insurance Options

When you rent a car in Europe, the price typically includes liability insurance, which covers harm to other cars or motorists—but not the rental car itself. To limit your financial risk in case of damage to the rental, choose one of these options: Buy a Collision Damage Waiver (CDW; also called "loss damage waiver" or LDW by some firms) with a low or zero deductible from the car-rental company (roughly 30-40 percent extra), get coverage through your credit card (free, but more complicated), or get collision insurance as part of a larger travel-insurance policy.

Basic **CDW** costs $15–30 a day and typically comes with a $1,000-2,000 deductible, reducing but not eliminating your financial responsibility. When you reserve or pick up the car, you'll be offered the chance to "buy down" the deductible to zero (for an additional $10–30/day; this is sometimes called "super CDW" or "zero-deductible coverage").

In Italy, most car-rental companies' rates automatically include CDW coverage. Even if you try to decline CDW when you reserve your car, you may find when you show up at the counter that you must buy it after all (along with mandatory theft insurance, about $15–20 a day).

If you opt for **credit-card coverage,** you must decline all coverage offered by the car-rental company—which means they can place a hold on your card to cover the deductible. In case of damage, it can be time-consuming to resolve the charges. Before relying on this option, quiz your card company about how it works.

For more on car-rental insurance, see RickSteves.com/cdw.

Navigation Options

If you'll be navigating using your phone or a GPS unit from home, remember to bring a car charger and device mount.

Your Mobile Phone: The mapping app on your mobile phone works fine for navigating Europe's roads. To save on data, most apps allow you to download maps for offline use (do this before you need them, when you have a strong Wi-Fi signal). Some apps—including Google Maps—also have offline route directions, but you'll need mobile data access for current traffic. For more on using a mapping app without burning through data, see "Using Your Phone in Europe," earlier.

GPS Devices: If you want a dedicated GPS unit, consider renting one with your car (about $20/day, or sometimes included—ask). These units offer real-time turn-by-turn directions and traffic without the data requirements of an app. The unit may come loaded only with maps for its home country; if you need additional maps, ask. Make sure you know how to use the device—and that the language is set to English—before you drive off.

Paper Maps and Atlases: Even when navigating primarily with a mobile app or GPS, I always have a paper map, ideally a big, detailed regional road map. It's invaluable for getting the big picture, understanding alternate routes, and filling in if my phone runs out of juice. The free maps you get from your car-rental company usually don't have enough detail. It's smart to buy a better map before you go, or pick one up at a local gas station, bookshop, newsstand, or tourist shop.

DRIVING

Driving in Italy can be scary—a video game for keeps, and you only get one quarter. Locals drive fast and tailgate as if it were required. They pass where Americans are taught not to—on blind corners and just before tunnels. Roads have narrow shoulders or none at all. Driving in the countryside is less stressful than driving through

Driving in Italy

urban areas or on busy highways, but stay alert. On one-lane roads, larger vehicles have the right-of-way.

Road Rules: Stay out of restricted traffic zones or you'll risk huge fines. Car traffic is restricted in many city centers. Don't drive or park in any area that has a sign reading *Zona Traffico Limitato* (*ZTL*, often shown above a red circle—see image). If you do, your license plate will likely be photographed and a hefty (€80-plus) ticket mailed to your home without your ever having met a cop. Bumbling in and out of these zones can net you multiple fines. If your hotel is within a restricted area, ask your hotelier to direct you to parking outside the zone. (Although your hotelier can register your car as an authorized vehicle permitted to enter the zone, this usually isn't worth the hassle.) If you get a ticket, it could

zona
traffico limitato

7,30 - 19,30

Driving in Tuscany

m = miles h = hours
Note: Your times may vary based on traffic, construction, and road conditions.

take months to show up (for more about traffic tickets in Italy, see www.bella-toscana.com/traffic_violations_italy.htm).

Be aware of typical European road rules; for example, many countries require headlights to be turned on at all times, and nearly all forbid handheld mobile-phone use. Seatbelts are mandatory, and children under age 12 must ride in child-safety or booster seats. In Europe, you're not allowed to turn right on a red light unless a sign or signal specifically authorizes it, and on expressways it's illegal to pass drivers on the right. Ask your car-rental company about these rules, or check the "International Travel" section of the US State Department website (www.travel.state.gov, search for your country in the "Learn About Your Destination" box, then click "Travel and Transportation").

Drive Defensively: Italians are aggressive drivers. Turn signals are optional. If a driver is tailgating you on the highway, pull to the side to let them pass, even if that means driving on the shoulder. If you're traveling in the right-hand lane on the highway, keep

PRACTICALITIES

an eye out for slow-moving cars that appear out of nowhere. Also, if you brake quickly, it's customary to put on your hazard lights to warn the driver behind you. All this is normal for locals, who may colorfully gesture at you. Don't take it personally.

Motor scooters are very popular, and scooter drivers often see themselves as exempt from rules that apply to automobiles.

Tolls: You'll pay tolls for some stretches of freeway (auto-strada; for costs, use the trip-planning tool at www.autostrade.it or search "European Tolls" on www.theaa.com). When approaching a tollbooth, skip lanes marked *Telepass;* for an attended booth, choose a lane with a sign that shows a hand or coins. Some express-ways (such as those between Milan and the lakes) use automated toll systems that take a photo of your license plate and bill you by mail. When you pick up your rental car, ask how this will be handled so you don't incur late-payment fees (more info at https://apl.pedemontana.com).

While I favor freeways because I feel they're safer and less nerve-racking than smaller roads, savvy local drivers know which toll-free *superstrade* are actually faster and more direct than the au-tostrada (e.g., Florence to Pisa). In some cases, if you have some time to spare, smaller roads can be worth the extra hassle.

Fuel: Fuel is expensive—often about $6.50 per gallon. Diesel cars are more common in Europe than back home, so be sure you know what type of fuel your car takes before you fill up. Diesel costs less, about $6 per gallon. Some pumps are color-coded: Un-leaded pumps *(senza piombo)* are green and labeled "E," while diesel pumps *(gasolio;* often yellow or black) are labeled "B". You'll also see the term *benzina*, which is standard fuel. If you are unsure or need help, stop for full-service gas *(servito)*. To fill up, say *"Pieno"* (pee-EH-noh). Autostrada rest stops can have full- or self-service stations (open daily without a siesta break). Many 24-hour stations are entirely automated. Small-town stations are usually cheaper and offer full service but shorter hours.

Maps and Signage: Learn the universal road signs (see illus-tration). Although roads are numbered on maps, actual road signs give just a city name (if you were heading west out of Venice, the map would be marked "route SR-11"—but you'd follow signs to *Padua*, the next town along this road). Signs are inconsistent: They may direct you to the nearest big city or simply the next town along the route.

Theft: Cars are routinely vandalized and stolen. Thieves eas-ily recognize rental cars and assume they are filled with a tour-ist's gear. Be sure your valuables are out of sight and locked in the trunk, or even better, with you or in your room.

Parking: White lines generally mean parking is free. Yellow lines mean that parking is reserved for residents only (who have

AND LEARN THESE ROAD SIGNS

Speed Limit (km/hr) · Yield · No Passing · End of No Passing Zone

One Way · Intersection · Main Road · Expressway

Roundabout Ahead · Danger · No Entry · All Vehicles Prohibited

No Through Road · Restrictions No Longer Apply · Yield to Oncoming Traffic · No Stopping

Parking · No Parking · Customs or Toll Road · Peace

permits). Blue lines mean you'll have to pay—usually around €1.50 per hour (use machine, leave time-stamped receipt on dashboard). Study the signs. Free zones often have a 30- or 60-minute time limit. Signs showing a street cleaner and a day of the week indicate which day the street is cleaned; there's a €100 tow-fee—incentive to learn the days of the week in Italian.

Zona disco has nothing to do with dancing. Italian cars come equipped with a time disc (a cardboard clock), which you can use in a *zona disco*—set the clock to your arrival time and leave it on the dashboard. (If your rental car doesn't come with a *disco*, pick one up at a tobacco shop or just write your arrival time on a piece of paper and place it on the dashboard.) These are generally used in areas where parking is free but has a time limit.

Garages are safe, save time, and help you avoid the stress of parking tickets. Take the parking voucher with you to pay the cashier before you leave.

FLIGHTS

To compare flights, begin with an online travel search engine: Kayak is the top site for flights to and within Europe, easy-to-use Google Flights has price alerts, and Skyscanner includes many inexpensive flights within Europe. To avoid unpleasant surprises, before you book be sure to read the small print about refunds, changes, and the costs for "extras" such as reserving a seat, checking a bag, or printing a boarding pass.

Flights to Europe: Start looking for international flights about four to six months before your trip, especially for peak-season travel. Depending on your itinerary, it can be efficient and no more expensive to fly into one city and out of another. If your flight requires a connection in Europe, see my hints on navigating Europe's top hub airports at RickSteves.com/hub-airports.

Flights Within Europe: Flying between European cities is surprisingly affordable. Before buying a long-distance train or bus ticket, check the cost of a flight on one of Europe's airlines, whether a major carrier or a no-frills outfit like Easyjet or Ryanair. Be aware that flying with a discount airline can have drawbacks, such as minimal customer service, time-consuming treks to secondary airports, and a larger carbon footprint than a train or bus.

Flying to the US and Canada: Because security is extra tight for flights to the US, be sure to give yourself plenty of time at the airport (see www.tsa.gov for the latest rules).

Resources from Rick Steves

Begin Your Trip at RickSteves.com

My mobile-friendly **website** is *the* place to explore Europe in preparation for your trip. You'll find thousands of fun articles, videos, and radio interviews; a wealth of money-saving tips for planning your dream trip; travel news dispatches; a video library of travel talks; my travel blog; our latest guidebook updates (RickSteves.com/update); and the free Rick Steves Audio Europe app. You can also follow me on Facebook, Instagram, and Twitter.

Our **Travel Forum** is a well-groomed collection of message boards where our travel-savvy community answers questions and shares their personal travel experiences—and our well-traveled staff chimes in when they can be helpful (RickSteves.com/forums).

Our **online Travel Store** offers bags and accessories that I've designed to help you travel smarter and lighter. These include my popular carry-on bags (which I live out of four months a year), money belts, totes, toiletries kits, adapters, guidebooks, and planning maps (RickSteves.com/shop).

Our website can also help you find the perfect **rail pass** for your itinerary and your budget, with easy, one-stop shopping for rail passes, seat reservations, and point-to-point tickets (RickSteves.com/rail).

Rick Steves' Tours, Guidebooks, TV Shows, and More

Small Group Tours: Want to travel with greater efficiency and less stress? We offer more than 40 itineraries reaching the best destinations in this book...and beyond. Each year about 30,000 travelers join us on about 1,000 Rick Steves bus tours. You'll enjoy great guides and a fun bunch of travel partners (with small groups of 24 to 28 travelers). You'll find European adventures to fit every vacation length. For all the details, and to get our tour catalog, visit RickSteves.com/tours or call us at +1 425 608 4217.

Books: This book is just one of many books in my series on European travel, which includes country and city guidebooks, Snapshots (excerpted chapters from bigger guides), Pocket guides (full-color little books on big cities), "Best Of" guidebooks (condensed, full-color country guides), and my budget-travel skills handbook, *Rick Steves Europe Through the Back Door.* A complete list of my titles—including phrase books, cruising guides, and travelogues on European art, history, and culture—appears near the end of this book.

TV Shows and Travel Talks: My public television series, *Rick Steves' Europe,* covers Europe from top to bottom with over 100 half-hour episodes—and we're working on new shows every year (watch full episodes at my website for free). My free online video library, Rick Steves Classroom Europe, offers a searchable database of short video clips on European history, culture, and geography (Classroom.RickSteves. com). And to raise your travel IQ, check out the video versions of our popular classes (covering most European countries as well as travel skills, packing smart, cruising, tech for travelers, European art, and travel as a political act—RickSteves.com/travel-talks).

Audio Tours on My Free App: I've produced dozens of free, self-guided audio tours of the top sights in Europe. For those tours and other audio content, get my free **Rick Steves Audio Europe app,** an extensive online library organized by destination. For more on my app, see page 26.

Radio: My weekly public radio show, *Travel with Rick Steves,* features interviews with travel experts from around the world. It airs on 400 public radio stations across the US. An archive of programs is available at RickSteves. com/radio.

Podcasts: You can enjoy my travel content via several free podcasts. The podcast version of my radio show brings you a weekly, hour-long travel conversation. My other podcasts include a weekly selection of video clips from my public television show, my audio tours of Europe's top sights, and live recordings of my travel classes (RickSteves.com/watch-read-listen/audio/podcasts).

APPENDIX

Holidays and Festivals

In Italy, holidays seem to strike without warning, and every town has a festival honoring its patron saint.

This list includes selected festivals in major cities, plus national holidays observed throughout Italy. Many sights and banks close on national holidays—keep this in mind when planning your itinerary. Before planning a trip around a festival, verify the dates with the festival website, the national tourist office (www.italia. it), or my "Upcoming Holidays and Festivals in Italy" web page at RickSteves.com/europe/italy/festivals.

In Italy, hotels get booked up on Easter weekend, Liberation Day, Labor Day, All Saints' Day, and on Fridays and Saturdays year-round. Some hotels require you to book the full three-day weekend around a holiday. During the Feast of the Assumption, a.k.a. Ferragosto, beach destinations are flooded with vacationing Italians. Cities empty out for much of August, and while tourist attractions remain open, shops and restaurants are often closed until September.

For festivals and events in the Cinque Terre, see page 340.

Jan 1	New Year's Day
Jan 6	Epiphany
Late Feb	Carnevale Celebrations/Mardi Gras, Florence (costumed parades, jousting competitions)
Feb/March	Carnevale, Venice (Mardi Gras, www.carnevale.venezia.it)
March/April	Easter weekend (Good Friday-Easter Monday): April 7-10, 2023; March 29-April 1, 2024; Scoppio del Carro, Florence (fireworks on Easter Sunday)
Mid-April	Vinitaly, Verona (wine festival, www.vinitaly.com)
April 25	Italian Liberation Day; Feast of St. Mark, Venice
May 1	Labor Day
May	Ascension Day: May 18, 2023; May 9, 2024
Late May-early June	Vogalonga Regatta, Venice
May/June	Feast of Corpus Christi: June 8, 2023; May 30, 2024
June 2	Anniversary of the Republic
June 16-17	St. Ranieri Day, Pisa
June 24	St. John the Baptist Day, Florence (parades, dances, boat races); Calcio Storico, Florence (Renaissance ball game played on Piazza Santa Croce)
June 29	Sts. Peter and Paul Day, most fervently celebrated in Rome
June-Aug	Verona opera season
Late June-early Sept	Outdoor cinema season, Florence (contemporary films)
July 2	Palio horse race, Siena
July (third weekend)	Feast and Regatta of the Redeemer, Venice
July-Aug	Stresa Festival, Lake Maggiore (classical music)
Aug 10	St. Lawrence Day, Rome
Aug 15	Feast of the Assumption (Ferragosto)
Aug 16	Palio horse race, Siena
Sept (first weekend)	Historical Regatta, Venice

Early Sept	Festa della Rificolona, Florence (children's procession with lanterns, street performers, parade)
Sept 13	Volto Santo, Lucca (luminaria procession and fair)
Sept 19	St. Januarius Day, Naples
Sept-Oct	Chestnut festivals, most towns, mainly north of Rome (festivals, chestnut roasts)
Late Sept or early Oct	Musica dei Popoli Festival, Florence (global and folk music and dances)
Mid-Oct	Castelrotto Music Festival, Dolomites (Kastelruther Spatzenfest)
Nov 1	All Saints' Day
Nov 21	Feast of Our Lady of Good Health, Venice
Dec	Christmas market, Rome (Piazza Navona); crèches in churches throughout Italy
Dec 8	Feast of the Immaculate Conception
Dec 25	Christmas
Dec 26	St. Stephen's Day

Books and Films

To learn more about Italy past and present, check out a few of these books or films.

APPENDIX

Nonfiction

Absolute Monarchs (John Julius Norwich, 2011). This warts-and-all illustrated guide to the most significant popes in history is a readable best seller.

Ancient Rome: The Rise and Fall of an Empire (Simon Baker, 2007). Baker chronicles the rise and demise of the great Roman Empire and its powerful leaders.

The Architecture of the Italian Renaissance (Peter Murray, 1969). Heavily illustrated, this classic presents the architectural life of Italy from the 13th through the 16th century.

La Bella Figura: A Field Guide to the Italian Mind (Beppe Severgnini, 2005). Severgnini strips down the idealized vision of Italy to reveal its more authentic self—at its best and its worst.

Brunelleschi's Dome: How a Renaissance Genius Reinvented Architecture (Ross King, 2000). The remarkable story of how the dome of Florence's cathedral was designed and built.

Christ Stopped at Eboli: The Story of a Year (Carlo Levi, 1945). Levi recounts the harsh yet beautiful existence he found in exile to a remote region of southern Italy during Mussolini's reign.

City: A Story of Roman Planning and Construction (David Macaulay, 1974). Macaulay's illustrated book about the Eternal City will please both kids and adults.

A Concise History of Italy (Christopher Duggan, 1994). Duggan's history starts with the fall of Rome but zooms in on the political difficulties of unified Italy over the last two centuries.

Delizia!: The Epic History of the Italians and Their Food (John Dickie, 2007). History buffs and foodies alike will enjoy this vibrant exploration of Italy's famed cuisine.

Desiring Italy (Susan Cahill, 1997). In this anthology, 28 women writers offer a mix of fiction, memoirs, and essays about the complexity and allure of Italy.

Excellent Cadavers: The Mafia and the Death of the First Italian Republic (Alexander Stille, 1995). This true account of Sicilian Mafia assassinations in the 1990s is as much thriller as it is history.

A History of Venice (John Julius Norwich, 1977). English Lord Norwich's engaging account spans more than a century, from Venice's fifth-century origins to the arrival of Napoleon.

The House of Medici (Christopher Hibbert, 1974). Florence's first family of the Renaissance included power-hungry bankers, merchants, popes, art patrons—and two queens of France.

Italian Days (Barbara Grizzuti Harrison, 1989). Harrison's appealing travel essays about Italy's varied regions cover everything from architecture to food to history.

Italian Neighbors (Tim Parks, 1992). Parks describes an Englishman's humorous and sometimes difficult attempt to live as a local in a small Italian town.

Italian Renaissance Art (Laurie Schneider Adams, 2013). In this well-written introduction to this pivotal period, Adams focuses on the most important and innovative artists and their best works.

The Italians (John Hooper, 2015). A veteran English correspondent in Italy probes the fascinating paradoxes of contemporary Italian life.

Italy for the Gourmet Traveler (Fred Plotkin, 1996). Plotkin, who's been described as an expert on everything Italian, shares his knowledge of Italy's culinary world in this food/travel guide.

The Lives of the Artists (Giorgio Vasari, 1550). The man who invented the term "Renaissance" offers anecdote-filled biographies of his era's greatest artists, some of whom he knew personally.

Michelangelo and the Pope's Ceiling (Ross King, 2003). The story behind the Sistine Chapel includes Michelangelo's technical difficulties, personality conflicts, and money troubles.

Midnight in Sicily (Peter Robb, 1996). Robb offers a good general history of Sicily, covering its decadent pleasures and its literature, politics, art, and crimes.

The Prince (Niccolò Machiavelli, 1532). The original "how-to" for gaining and maintaining political power, still chillingly relevant after 500 years.

Saints & Sinners (Eamon Duffy, 1997). Everything you always wanted to know about the popes, but were afraid to ask.

The Secrets of Rome: Love and Death in the Eternal City (Corrado Augias, 2005). Augias takes readers back through 27 centuries of Roman history, secrets, and conspiracies.

A Small Place in Italy (Eric Newby, 1994). A young American couple tries to renovate a Tuscan farmhouse in the late 1960s.

The Stones of Florence (Mary McCarthy, 1956). McCarthy applies wit and keen observation to produce a quirky, impressionistic investigation of Florence and its history.

Travelers' Tales Italy (Anne Calcagno, 2001). Calcagno's guide is an excellent compilation of travel writing.

Under the Tuscan Sun (Frances Mayes, 1996). Mayes' best seller describes living *la dolce vita* in the Tuscan countryside (and is better than the movie of the same name).

The Venetian Empire: A Sea Voyage (Jan Morris, 1990). Morris brings a maritime empire to life in this book that illustrates the city's place on a larger historical canvas.

Venice Observed (Mary McCarthy, 1963). This snappy and engaging memoir details the Venetian ethos through the eyes of a sharply critical writer.

Fiction

The Agony and the Ecstasy (Irving Stone, 1958). Stone fictionalizes Michelangelo's struggle to paint the Sistine Chapel (also a 1965 movie starring Charlton Heston).

The Aspern Papers and Other Stories (Henry James, 1894). An American editor travels to Venice in search of letters written to his mistress. Other James works about Italy include *Italian Hours* and *Daisy Miller*.

Beautiful Ruins (Jess Walter, 2012). This comedic romance, which follows an Italian innkeeper's search for lost love over 50 years, is the perfect beach read for the Cinque Terre.

A Bell for Adano (John Hersey, 1944). Hersey's novel about an American major overseeing a town in WWII Sicily won him the Pulitzer Prize in 1945.

Birth of Venus (Sarah Dunant, 2003). Dunant follows the life of a Florentine girl who develops feelings for the boy hired to paint the walls of the family's chapel.

The Day of the Owl (Leonardo Sciascia, 1961). This classic murder mystery set in a mid-20th-century Sicilian village is a fascinating window into the Mafia.

Death at La Fenice (Donna Leon, 1992). This chilling Venetian mystery and the others in Leon's Commissario Brunetti series reveal more about "real" Italy than many memoirs do.

Death in the Mountains: The True Story of a Tuscan Murder (Lisa Clifford, 2008). This fictionalized account of an unsolved murder reveals the hardship of early-20th-century Tuscan farming life.

Death in Venice and Other Tales (Thomas Mann, 1912). The centerpiece of this collection is an eloquent classic that explores obsession, beauty, and death in plague-ridden Venice (also a 1971 film).

The Decameron (Giovanni Boccaccio, 1348). Boccaccio's collection of 100 hilarious, often bawdy tales is a masterpiece of Italian literature and inspired Chaucer, Keats, and Shakespeare.

Divine Comedy (Dante Alighieri, 1321). Dante's epic poem—a journey through hell, purgatory, and paradise—is one of the world's greatest works of literature.

The First Man in Rome (Colleen McCullough, 1990). The author of *The Thorn Birds* describes the early days of the Roman Republic, in the first of a best-selling series of historical fiction.

Galileo's Daughter (Dava Sobel, 1999). Sobel's historical memoir centers on Galileo's correspondence with his oldest daughter and confidante.

I, Claudius (Robert Graves, 1934). This brilliant history of ancient Rome is told by Claudius, the family's laughingstock who becomes emperor himself. The sequel is *Claudius the God* (1935).

I'm Not Scared (Niccolò Ammaniti, 2001). A boy stumbles upon a terrible secret in an abandoned farmhouse in this thriller set in the 1970s Italian South.

Invisible Cities (Italo Calvino, 1972). Marco Polo tells of the fantastical cities he's seen...or is he just describing the many facets of his beloved Venice?

Italian Journey (Johann Wolfgang von Goethe, 1786). In his 18th-century collection of writings, Goethe describes his travels to Rome, Sicily, and Naples.

The Leopard (Giuseppe Tomasi di Lampedusa, 1957). Sicilian aristocrats see their world slipping away during the turmoil of the Risorgimento (also a 1963 movie starring Burt Lancaster).

The Light in the Piazza (Elizabeth Spencer, 1960). A mother and daughter are intoxicated by the beauty of 1950s Florence (also a 1962 movie and an award-winning Broadway musical).

Lucrezia Borgia (Maria Bellonci, 1939). In this historically based tale of court intrigue, a daughter of Pope Alexander VI navigates passions, plots, and controversy in Renaissance Rome.

The Merchant of Venice (William Shakespeare, 1598). In addition to *Merchant*, other Shakespearean plays set in Italy include *Romeo and Juliet* (Verona), *Much Ado About Nothing* (Sicily), *The Two Gentlemen of Verona*, and *The Taming of the Shrew* (Padua).

The Neapolitan Novels (Elena Ferrante, 2012-2015). This popular four-novel series traces two girls' coming of age in mid-20th-century Naples.

The Passion of Artemisia (Susan Vreeland, 2001). This novel is based on the life of Artemisia Gentileschi, one of the rare female post-Renaissance artists who gained fame in her own time.

Pompeii (Robert Harris, 2003). The engineer responsible for Pompeii's aqueducts has a bad feeling about Mount Vesuvius in this historical novel.

A Room with a View (E. M. Forster, 1908). A young Englishwoman visiting Florence finds a socially unsuitable replacement for her snobby fiancé (also a 1985 movie starring Helena Bonham Carter).

The Sixteen Pleasures (Robert Hellenga, 1994). Set during the 1966 floods in Florence, a young student discovers an erotic manuscript banned by the pope and lost for centuries.

A Soldier of the Great War (Mark Helprin, 1991). A young Roman lawyer falls in love with an art student, but World War I rips them apart.

That Awful Mess on the Via Merulana (Carlo Emilio Gadda, 1957). This detective story about a murder and a burglary in an apartment building in central Rome shines a harsh light on fascist Italy.

A Thread of Grace (Mary Doria Russell, 2004). This historical novel fictionalizes the story of how more than 43,000 Jews were saved by Italian citizens during World War II.

Film and TV

1900 (1976). Bernardo Bertolucci's epic tale of early-20th-century Italy follows the relationship between two young men—one rich (Robert De Niro), one poor (Gérard Depardieu).

Ben-Hur (1959). At the height of the Roman Empire, a Jewish prince is enslaved by a friend, and later seeks revenge in a stunning chariot race (the film won a record 11 Oscars).

The Best of Youth (2003). Beginning in the turbulent 1960s, this award-winning miniseries follows the dramatic ups and downs in the lives of two brothers over four decades.

Bicycle Thieves (1948). A poor man looks for his stolen bicycle in busy Rome in this inspirational classic of Italian Neorealism.

Caterina in the Big City (2003). A teenager whose family moves to Rome from a small town is the focus of this bitter comedy about the crisis of contemporary Italian society.

Cinema Paradiso (1988). This Oscar-winning drama about a friendship between a film projectionist and a little boy is a compelling portrayal of post-WWII Sicily and a tribute to movies everywhere.

La Dolce Vita (1960). Director Federico Fellini tells a series of stories that capture the hedonistic days of early 1960s Rome.

Enchanted April (1991). Filmed in Portofino, this languid film follows an all-star British cast as they fall in love, discuss relationships, eat well, and take naps in the sun.

The First Beautiful Thing (2010). A man returns to his hometown in Tuscany to aid his dying mother, a woman determined to live life to the fullest while being a good parent to her children.

Gladiator (2000). An enslaved Roman general (Russell Crowe) fights his way back to freedom in Ridley Scott's Oscar winner.

The Godfather (1969). Francis Ford Coppola's famous film and its two sequels portray the multigenerational saga of a Sicilian family at the center of organized crime in New York.

Golden Door (2006). Poor Sicilian immigrants give up everything for a passage to America, but find a less-than-enthusiastic welcome at Ellis Island.

Gomorrah (2008). This mob drama, which reveals details about the Camorra (Neapolitan mafia), is not for the faint of heart.

The Great Beauty (2013). This thoughtful movie, named Best Foreign Film at the 2014 Academy Awards, showcases Rome in all of its decadence and splendor.

The Italian Job (1969). This classic English film features a crew of thieves attempting a high-stakes gold heist in Turin under the nose of the Mafia.

Life Is Beautiful (1997). In this tragicomic winner of three Oscars, a Jewish man from Tuscany finds imaginative ways to protect his son from the truth after they arrive at a Nazi concentration camp.

Marriage Italian Style (1964). A young Neapolitan prostitute (Sophia Loren) begins a lifelong on-again, off-again relationship with a cynical businessman in this Academy Award-nominated comedy.

Mid-August Lunch (2008). A broke Roman bachelor gets more than he bargained for when he agrees to take care of an elderly lady during a summer holiday to pay off a debt.

Il Postino (1994). Poet Pablo Neruda befriends his Italian postman, who uses a newfound love for Italian poetry to woo a local beauty.

Quo Vadis (1951). A Roman general falls in love with a Christian hostage in this epic that includes the burning of Rome, the crucifixion of St. Peter, and the madness of Nero.

Roman Holiday (1953). Audrey Hepburn plays a princess who es-capes her royal minders, falls for an American newspaperman (Gregory Peck), and discovers Rome on the back of his scooter.

Rome (2005-2007). This BBC/HBO miniseries focusing on Julius Caesar and Augustus intertwines the perspectives of aristocratic and ordinary Romans during the transition from republic to empire.

Spartacus (1960). In this epic directed by Stanley Kubrick, a gladiator (Kirk Douglas) leads a slave revolt in the last days of the Roman Republic.

A Special Day (1977). On the day of Hitler's visit to Rome, the wife of a militant fascist (Sophia Loren) has a fateful meeting with a persecuted journalist (Marcello Mastroianni).

Tea with Mussolini (1999). Franco Zeffirelli's look at pre-war Florence involves proper English ladies, a rich American Jew, and the son of a local businessman—all caught in the rise of fascism.

The Wings of the Dove (1997). Based on the Henry James novel, this romantic drama is a tale of desire that takes full advantage of its Venetian locale.

Conversions and Climate

Numbers and Stumblers

- Europeans write a few of their numbers differently than we do. 1 = 1, 4 = 4, 7 = 7.
- In Europe, dates appear as day/month/year, so Christmas 2024 is 25/12/24.
- Commas are decimal points and decimals commas. A dollar and a half is $1,50, one thousand is 1.000, and there are 5.280 feet in a mile.
- When counting with fingers, start with your thumb. If you hold up your first finger to request one item, you'll probably get two.
- What Americans call the second floor of a building is the first floor in Europe.
- On escalators and moving sidewalks, Europeans keep the left "lane" open for passing. Keep to the right.

Metric Conversions

A **kilogram** equals 1,000 grams (about 2.2 pounds). One hundred **grams** (a common unit at markets) is about a quarter-pound. One **liter** is about a quart, or almost four to a gallon.

A **kilometer** is six-tenths of a mile. To convert kilometers to miles, cut the kilometers in half and add back 10 percent of the original (120 km: 60 + 12 = 72 miles). One **meter** is 39 inches—just over a yard.

APPENDIX

1 foot = 0.3 meter	1 square yard = 0.8 square meter
1 yard = 0.9 meter	1 square mile = 2.6 square kilometers
1 mile = 1.6 kilometers	1 ounce = 28 grams
1 centimeter = 0.4 inch	1 quart = 0.95 liter
1 meter = 39.4 inches	1 kilogram = 2.2 pounds
1 kilometer = 0.62 mile	32°F = 0°C

Roman Numerals

In the US, you'll see Roman numerals—which originated in ancient Rome—used for copyright dates, clocks, and the Super Bowl. In Italy, you're likely to observe these numbers chiseled on statues and buildings. If you want to do some numeric detective work, here's how: In Roman numerals, as in ours, the highest numbers (thousands, hundreds) come first, followed by smaller numbers. Many numbers are made by combining numerals into sets: V = 5, so VIII = 8 (5 plus 3). Roman numerals follow a subtraction principle for multiples of fours (4, 40, 400, etc.) and nines (9, 90, 900, etc.); the number four, for example, is written as IV (1 subtracted from 5), rather than IIII. The number nine is IX (1 subtracted from 10).

Big numbers such as dates can look daunting at first. The easiest way to handle them is to read the numbers in discrete chunks. For example, Michelangelo was born in MCDLXXV: M (1,000) + CD (100 subtracted from 500, or 400) + LXX (50 + 10 + 10, or 70) + V (5) = 1475. It was a very good year.

M = 1000	XC = 90	IX = 9
CM = 900	L = 50	V = 5
D = 500	XL = 40	IV = 4
CD = 400	X = 10	I = duh
C = 100		

Clothing Sizes

When shopping for clothing, use these US-to-European comparisons as general guidelines (but note that no conversion is perfect).

Women: For pants and dresses, add 36 in Italy (US 10 = Italian 46). For blouses and sweaters, add 8 for most of Europe (US 32 = European 40). For shoes, add 30-31 (US 7 = European 37/38).

Men: For shirts, multiply by 2 and add about 8 (US 15 = European 38). For jackets and suits, add 10. For shoes, add 32-34.

Children: Clothing is sized by height—in centimeters (2.5 cm = 1 inch), so a US size 8 roughly equates to 132-140. For shoes up to size 13, add 16-18, and for sizes 1 and up, add 30-32.

Italy's Climate

First line, average daily high; second line, average daily low; third line, average days without rain. For more detailed weather statistics for destinations in this book (as well as the rest of the world), check Wunderground.com.

	J	F	M	A	M	J	J	A	S	O	N	D
Rome												
	55°	57°	63°	68°	75°	84°	90°	86°	81°	73°	64°	59°
	37°	37	43°	46°	55°	63°	66°	64°	61°	54°	46°	39°
	24	22	24	21	24	26	28	31	24	23	22	22
Florence												
	54°	54°	59°	66°	75°	82°	88°	88°	81°	70°	59°	52°
	37°	39°	43°	48°	55°	63°	66°	64°	61°	54°	45°	39°
	25	21	24	23	24	23	27	26	22	22	21	23
Venice												
	42°	46°	53°	62°	70°	76°	81°	80°	75°	65°	53°	46°
	33°	35°	41°	49°	56°	63°	66°	65°	61°	53°	44°	37°
	25	21	24	21	23	22	24	24	25	24	21	23
Naples												
	54°	56°	59°	65°	73°	79°	85°	85°	79°	71°	63°	57°
	39°	40°	43°	47°	54°	60°	64°	64°	60°	53°	46°	41°
	21	18	21	21	25	26	29	27	24	23	19	20

Fahrenheit and Celsius Conversion

For Weather

F°		C°
120	—	50
104	—	40
95	—	35
86	—	30
82	—	28 — perfect weather
68	—	20
50	—	10
32	—	0

For Health

F°		C°
105		40.6
104.5		40.3
104	-------	40
103.5		39.7
103		39.4
102.5		39.2
102		38.9
101.5		38.6
101		38.3
100.5		38.1
100		37.8
99.5		37.5
99		37.2
98.6	—	37 — perfect health

Europe takes its temperature using the Celsius scale, while we opt for Fahrenheit. For a rough conversion from Celsius to Fahrenheit, double the number and add 30. For weather, remember that 28°C is 82°F—perfect. For health, 37°C is just right. At a launderette, 30°C is cold, 40°C is warm (usually the default setting), 60°C is hot, and 95°C is boiling. Your air-conditioner should be set at about 20°C.

APPENDIX

Packing Checklist

Whether you're traveling for five days or five ~~months~~, you won't need more than this. Pack light to enjoy the sweet freedom of true mobility.

Clothing

- ☐ 5 shirts: long- & short-sleeve
- ☐ 2 pairs pants (or skirts/capris)
- ☐ 1 pair shorts
- ☐ 5 pairs underwear & socks
- ☐ 1 pair walking shoes
- ☐ Sweater or warm layer
- ☐ Rainproof jacket with hood
- ☐ Tie, scarf, belt, and/or hat
- ☐ Swimsuit
- ☐ Sleepwear/loungewear

Money

- ☐ Debit card(s)
- ☐ Credit card(s)
- ☐ Hard cash (US $100-200)
- ☐ Money belt

Documents

- ☐ Passport
- ☐ Other required ID: Vaccine card/Covid test, entry visa, etc.
- ☐ Driver's license, student ID, hostel card, etc.
- ☐ Tickets & confirmations: flights, hotels, trains, rail pass, car rental, sight entries
- ☐ Photocopies of important documents
- ☐ Insurance details
- ☐ Guidebooks & maps

Electronics

- ☐ Mobile phone
- ☐ Camera & related gear
- ☐ Tablet/ebook reader/laptop
- ☐ Headphones/earbuds
- ☐ Chargers & batteries
- ☐ Phone car charger & mount (or GPS device)
- ☐ Plug adapters

Toiletries

- ☐ Basics: soap, shampoo, toothbrush, toothpaste, floss, deodorant, sunscreen, brush/comb, etc.
- ☐ Medicines & vitamins
- ☐ First-aid kit
- ☐ Glasses/contacts/sunglasses
- ☐ Face masks & hand sanitizer
- ☐ Sewing kit
- ☐ Packet of tissues (for WC)
- ☐ Earplugs

Miscellaneous

- ☐ Daypack
- ☐ Sealable plastic baggies
- ☐ Laundry supplies: soap, laundry bag, clothesline, spot remover
- ☐ Small umbrella
- ☐ Travel alarm/watch
- ☐ Notepad & pen
- ☐ Journal

Optional Extras

- ☐ Second pair of shoes (flip-flops, sandals, tennis shoes, boots)
- ☐ Travel hairdryer
- ☐ Picnic supplies
- ☐ Disinfecting wipes
- ☐ Water bottle
- ☐ Fold-up tote bag
- ☐ Small flashlight
- ☐ Mini binoculars
- ☐ Small towel or washcloth
- ☐ Inflatable pillow/neck rest
- ☐ Tiny lock
- ☐ Address list (to mail postcards)
- ☐ Extra passport photos

Italian Survival Phrases

Hello. (informal)	Ciao.	chow
Good day.	Buongiorno.	bwohn-**jor**-noh
Do you speak English?	Parla inglese?	**par**-lah een-**gleh**-zay
Yes. / No.	Sì. / No.	see / noh
I (don't) understand.	(Non) capisco.	(nohn) kah-**pees**-koh
Please.	Per favore.	pehr fah-**voh**-ray
Thank you.	Grazie.	**graht**-see-ay
You're welcome.	Prego.	**preh**-go
I'm sorry.	Mi dispiace.	mee dee-spee-**ah**-chay
Excuse me.	Mi scusi.	mee **skoo**-zee
No problem.	Non c'è problema.	nohn cheh proh-**bleh**-mah
Goodbye.	Arrivederci.	ah-ree-veh-**dehr**-chee
one / two / three	uno / due / tre	**oo**-noh / **doo**-ay / tray
four / five / six	quattro / cinque / sei	**kwah**-troh / **cheeng**-kway / **seh**-ee
seven / eight	sette / otto	**seh**-tay / **oh**-toh
nine / ten	nove / dieci	**noh**-vay / dee-**ay**-chee
How much is it?	Quanto costa?	**kwahn**-toh koh-stah
Write it?	Me lo scrive?	may loh **skree**-vay
Is it free?	È gratis?	eh **grah**-tees
Is it included?	È incluso?	eh een-**kloo**-zoh
Where can I buy / find...?	Dove posso comprare / trovare...?	**doh**-vay **poh**-soh kohm-**prah**-ray / troh-**vah**-ray
I'd like / We'd like...	Vorrei / Vorremmo...	voh-**reh**-ee / voh-**reh**-moh
...a room.	...una camera.	**oo**-nah **kah**-meh-rah
...a ticket to ___.	...un biglietto per ___.	oon beel-**yeh**-toh pehr ___
Is it possible?	È possibile?	eh poh-**see**-bee-lay
Where is...?	Dov'è...?	doh-**veh**
...the train station	...la stazione	lah staht-see-**oh**-nay
...tourist information	...informazioni turisti	een-for-maht-see-**oh**-nee too-**ree**-stee
...the bathroom	...il bagno	eel **bahn**-yoh
men / women	uomini, signori / donne, signore	**woh**-mee-nee, seen-**yoh**-ree / **doh**-nay, seen-**yoh**-ray
left / right / straight	sinistra / destra / sempre dritto	see-**nee**-strah / **deh**-strah / **sehm**-pray **dree**-toh
What time does this open / close?	A che ora apre / chiude?	ah kay **oh**-rah **ah**-pray / kee-**oo**-day
At what time?	A che ora?	ah kay **oh**-rah
Just a moment.	Un momento.	oon moh-**mehn**-toh
now / soon / later	adesso / presto / tardi	ah-**deh**-soh / **preh**-stoh / **tar**-dee
today / tomorrow	oggi / domani	**oh**-jee / doh-**mah**-nee

In an Italian Restaurant

I'd like / We'd like...	Vorrei / Vorremmo...	voh-**reh**-ee / voh-**reh**-moh
...to reserve a table for one / two.	...prenotare un tavolo per uno / due. preh-noh-**tah**-ray oon **tah**-voh-loh pehr **oo**-noh / **doo**-ay	
...the menu (in English).	...il menù (in inglese). eel meh-**noo** (een een-**gleh**-zay)	
Is this seat free?	È libero questo posto? eh **lee**-beh-roh **kweh**-stoh **poh**-stoh	
service (not) included	servizio (non) compreso sehr-**veet**-see-oh (nohn) kohm-**pray**-zoh	
cover charge	(pane e) coperto (**pah**-nay ay) koh-**pehr**-toh	
to go	da portar via dah **por**-tar **vee**-ah	
with / without	con / senza kohn / **sehnt**-sah	
and / or	e / o ay / oh	
breakfast / lunch / dinner	(prima) colazione / pranzo / cena (**pree**-mah) koh-laht-zee-**oh**-nay / **prahn**-zoh / **chay**-nah	
fixed-price meal (of the day)	menù (del giorno) meh-**noo** (dehl **jor**-noh)	
specialty of the house	specialità della casa speh-chah-lee-**tah** deh-lah **kah**-zah	
appetizer	antipasto ahn-tee-**pah**-stoh	
first course	primo (piatto) **pree**-moh (pee-**ah**-toh)	
main course	secondo (piatto) seh-**kohn**-doh (pee-**ah**-toh)	
side dishes	contorni kohn-**tor**-nee	
cold cuts / bread / cheese	salumi / pane / formaggio sah-**loo**-mee / **pah**-nay / for-**mah**-joh	
sandwich	panino pah-**nee**-noh	
soup / salad	zuppa / insalata **tsoo**-pah / een-sah-**lah**-tah	
meat / chicken	carne / pollo **kar**-nay / **poh**-loh	
fish / seafood	pesce / frutti di mare **peh**-shay / **froo**-tee dee **mah**-ray	
fruit / vegetables	frutta / verdure **froo**-tah / vehr-**doo**-ray	
dessert	dolce **dohl**-chay	
tap water	acqua del rubinetto **ah**-kwah dehl roo-bee-**neh**-toh	
mineral water	acqua minerale **ah**-kwah mee-neh-**rah**-lay	
still / sparkling	naturale / frizzante nah-too-**rah**-lay / freet-**zahn**-tay	
(orange) juice	succo (d'arancia) **soo**-koh (dah-**rahn**-chah)	
coffee / tea / milk	caffè / tè / latte kah-**feh** / teh / **lah**-tay	
wine / beer	vino / birra **vee**-noh / **bee**-rah	
red / white	rosso / bianco **roh**-soh / bee-**ahn**-koh	
glass / bottle	bicchiere / bottiglia bee-kee-**eh**-ray / boh-**teel**-yah	
Cheers!	Salute! / Cin cin! sah-**loo**-tay / cheen cheen	
The bill, please.	Il conto, per favore. eel **kohn**-toh pehr fah-**voh**-ray	
Do you accept credit cards?	Accettate carte di credito? ah-cheh-**tah**-tay **kar**-tay dee **kreh**-dee-toh	
Delicious!	Delizioso! day-leet-see-**oh**-zoh	

For more user-friendly Italian phrases, check out *Rick Steves Italian Phrase Book* or *Rick Steves French, Italian, & German Phrase Book*.

INDEX

INDEX

MAP INDEX

Our website enhances this book and turns

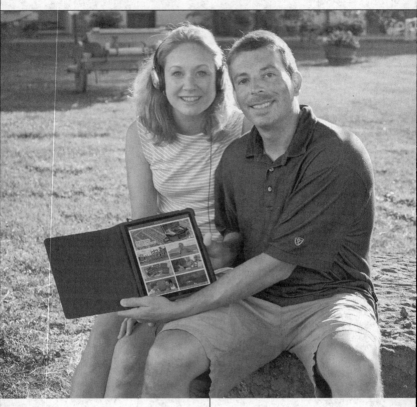

Explore Europe

At ricksteves.com you can browse through thousands of articles, videos, photos and radio interviews, plus find a wealth of money-saving travel tips for planning your dream trip. And with our mobile-friendly website, you can easily access all this great travel information anywhere you go.

TV Shows

Preview the places you'll visit by watching entire half-hour episodes of *Rick Steves' Europe* (choose from all 100 shows) on-demand, for free.

your travel dreams into affordable reality

Radio Interviews

Enjoy ready access to Rick's vast library of radio interviews covering travel tips and cultural insights that relate specifically to your Europe travel plans.

Travel Forums

Learn, ask, share! Our online community of savvy travelers is a great resource for first-time travelers to Europe, as well as seasoned pros.

Travel News

Subscribe to our free Travel News e-newsletter, and get monthly updates from Rick on what's happening in Europe.

Classroom Europe®

Check out our free resource for educators with 500 short video clips from the *Rick Steves' Europe* TV show.

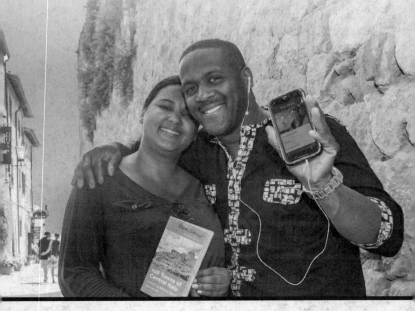

Gear up for your next adventure at ricksteves.com

Light Luggage

Pack light and right with Rick Steves' affordable, custom-designed rolling carry-on bags, backpacks, day packs and shoulder bags.

Accessories

From packing cubes to moneybelts and beyond, Rick has personally selected the travel goodies that will help your trip go smoother.

Shop at ricksteves.com

Save time and energy

This guidebook is your independent-travel toolkit. But for all it delivers, it's still up to you to devote the time and energy it takes to manage the preparation and logistics that are essential for a happy trip. If that's a hassle, there's a solution.

Rick Steves Tours

A Rick Steves tour takes you to Europe's most interesting places with great

with minimum stress

guides and small groups. We follow Rick's favorite itineraries, ride in comfy buses, stay in family-run hotels, and bring you intimately close to the Europe you've traveled so far to see. Most importantly, we take away the logistical headaches so you can focus on the fun.

Join the fun

This year we'll take thousands of free-spirited travelers—nearly half of them repeat customers—along with us on 50 different itineraries, from Athens to Istanbul. Is a Rick Steves tour the right fit for your travel dreams?

Find out at ricksteves.com, where you can also check seat availability and sign up. Europe is best experienced with happy travel partners. We hope you can join us.

See our itineraries at ricksteves.com

BEST OF GUIDES

Full-color guides in an easy-to-scan format. Focused on top sights and experiences in the most popular European destinations

Best of England
Best of Europe
Best of France
Best of Germany
Best of Ireland
Best of Italy
Best of Scotland
Best of Spain

COMPREHENSIVE GUIDES

City, country, and regional guides printed on Bible-thin paper. Packed with detailed coverage for a multi-week trip exploring iconic sights and venturing off the beaten path

Amsterdam & the Netherlands
Barcelona
Belgium: Bruges, Brussels,
  Antwerp & Ghent
Berlin
Budapest
Croatia & Slovenia
Eastern Europe
England
Florence & Tuscany
France
Germany
Great Britain
Greece: Athens & the Peloponnese
Iceland
Ireland
Istanbul
Italy
London
Paris
Portugal
Prague & the Czech Republic
Provence & the French Riviera
Rome
Scandinavia
Scotland
Sicily
Spain
Switzerland
Venice
Vienna, Salzburg & Tirol

HE BEST OF ROME

ne, Italy's capital, is studded with
nan remnants and floodlit-fountain
res. From the Vatican to the Colos-
n, with crazy traffic in between, Rome
nderful, huge, and exhausting. The
ds, the heat, and the weighty history

of the Eternal City where Caesars walked
can make tourists wilt. Recharge by taking siestas, gelato breaks, and after-dark
walks, strolling from one atmospheric
square to another in the refreshing evening air.

d *Pantheon*—which
est dome until the
rly 2,000 years old
ay over 1,500.

of Athens in the Vat-
dies the humanistic
ice.

gladiators fought
mother, entertaining

e *Rome ristorante.*

Rick Steves books are available from your favorite bookseller.
Many guides are available as ebooks.

POCKET GUIDES
Compact color guides for shorter trips

Amsterdam
Athens
Barcelona
Florence
Italy's Cinque Terre
London
Munich & Salzburg
Paris
Prague
Rome
Venice
Vienna

SNAPSHOT GUIDES
Focused single-destination coverage

Basque Country: Spain & France
Copenhagen & the Best of Denmark
Dublin
Dubrovnik
Edinburgh
Hill Towns of Central Italy
Krakow, Warsaw & Gdansk
Lisbon
Loire Valley
Madrid & Toledo
Milan & the Italian Lakes District
Naples & the Amalfi Coast
Nice & the French Riviera
Normandy
Northern Ireland
Norway
Reykjavík
Rothenburg & the Rhine
Sevilla, Granada & Southern Spain
St. Petersburg, Helsinki & Tallinn
Stockholm

CRUISE PORTS GUIDES
Reference for cruise ports of call

Mediterranean Cruise Ports
Scandinavian & Northern European
  Cruise Ports

Complete your library with...

TRAVEL SKILLS & CULTURE
*Study up on travel skills and gain
insight on history and culture*

Europe 101
Europe Through the Back Door
Europe's Top 100 Masterpieces
European Christmas
European Easter
European Festivals
For the Love of Europe
Italy for Food Lovers
Travel as a Political Act

PHRASE BOOKS & DICTIONARIES
French
French, Italian & German
German
Italian
Portuguese
Spanish

PLANNING MAPS
Britain, Ireland & London
Europe
France & Paris
Germany, Austria & Switzerland
Iceland
Ireland
Italy
Scotland
Spain & Portugal

Credits

RESEARCHERS
For help with this edition, Rick relied on...

Cameron Hewitt

Cameron Hewitt was born in Denver, grew up in Central Ohio, and moved to Seattle in 2000 to work for Rick Steves' Europe. Since then, he has spent about 100 days each year in Europe—researching and writing guidebooks, blogging, tour guiding, and making travel TV (described in his memoir, *The Temporary European*). Cameron married his high school sweetheart, Shawna, and enjoys taking pictures, trying new restaurants, and planning his next trip.

Suzanne Kotz

Suzanne, an editor with Rick Steves' Europe, began her travel career riding in a station wagon with her six siblings from Michigan to Florida for spring break. Since then, she's broadened her destinations to include much of Europe and parts of Asia. A librarian by training and a longtime editor of art publications, she's happiest in her Seattle garden or when planning a meal for family and friends.

Gretchen Strauch

Before Gretchen became the online-content editor and an occasional tour guide for Rick Steves' Europe, she lived in Europe for four years: studying philosophy in Scotland, then teaching English in southern Germany—meanwhile exploring the rest of Europe at every opportunity and accruing stories of misadventure that she's been happily retelling ever since.

Cary Walker

Cary discovered international travel during college and has been feeding her wanderlust ever since. A former teacher, she believes that Europe is the best classroom for those who travel with an open mind. When not researching guidebooks or leading Rick Steves' Europe tours, she resides in Dallas, with her husband Brian and three well-traveled stepsons.

Ian Watson

Ian has worked with Rick Steves on his guide-books since 1993, after starting out with Let's Go and Frommer's guides. Originally from western New York, Ian has lived in Europe for many years now, first in Iceland and more recently in southern Germany.

CONTRIBUTOR
Gene Openshaw

Gene has co-authored more than a dozen books with Rick, specializing in Europe's art, history, and culture. In particular, their *Europe 101: History and Art for the Traveler* and *Europe's Top 100 Masterpieces* have helped bring European art to life. Gene also writes for Rick's television shows, produces the audio tours, and is a regular guest on

Rick's radio show. For public TV, Gene has co-authored *Rick Steves Fascism in Europe* and the ambitious six-hour series *Rick Steves Art of Europe.* Outside of the travel world, Gene has composed an opera called *Matter,* a violin sonata, and dozens of songs. His latest book is *Michelangelo at Midlife.* Gene lives near Seattle, where he roots for the Mariners in good times and bad.

ACKNOWLEDGMENTS
Thanks to Risa Laib for her 25-plus years of dedication to the Rick Steves guidebook series.

Avalon Travel
Hachette Book Group
1700 Fourth Street
Berkeley, CA 94710

Printed in Canada by Friesens
27th Edition. First printing November 2022.

ISBN 978-1-64171-459-4

For the latest on Rick's talks, guidebooks, tours, public television series, and public radio show, contact Rick Steves' Europe, 130 Fourth Avenue North, Edmonds, WA 98020, +1 425 771 8303, RickSteves.com, rick@ricksteves.com.

Rick Steves' Europe
Managing Editor: Jennifer Madison Davis
Assistant Managing Editor: Cathy Lu
Editors: Glenn Eriksen, Julie Fanselow, Suzanne Kotz, Rosie Leutzinger, Teresa Nemeth, Jessica Shaw, Carrie Shepherd
Editorial & Production Assistant: Megan Simms
Researchers: Cameron Hewitt, Suzanne Kotz, Gretchen Strauch, Cary Walker, Ian Watson
Contributor: Gene Openshaw
Graphic Content Director: Sandra Hundacker
Maps & Graphics: Orin Dubrow, David C. Hoerlein, Lauren Mills, Mary Rostad, Laura Terrenzio

Avalon Travel
Senior Editor and Series Manager: Madhu Prasher
Associate Managing Editor: Jamie Andrade
Editor: Rachael Sablik
Proofreader: Maggie Ryan
Indexer: Stephen Callahan
Production and Typesetting: Lisi Baldwin, Rue Flaherty, Jane Musser, Ravina Schneider
Cover Design: Kimberly Glyder Design
Maps & Graphics: Kat Bennett

COLOR MAPS

Italy • Venice • Florence • Tuscany & Umbria • Rome

SIGHTS

1. Accademia Gallery
2. Bridge of Sighs
3. Ca' d'Oro
4. Ca' Pesaro Internat'l Gallery of Modern Art
5. Ca' Rezzonico
6. Campanile
7. Clock Tower
8. Correr Museum
9. Doge's Palace
10. Frari Church
11. Jewish Ghetto & Museum
12. La Fenice Opera House
13. La Salute Church
14. Palazzo Grassi
15. Palazzo Mocenigo Costume Museum
16. Peggy Guggenheim Collection
17. Piazzale Roma
18. Punta della Dogana Museum
19. Rialto Bridge & T Fondaco dei Tedeschi Mall
20. St. Mark's Basilica
21. St. Mark's Square
22. San Giorgio Maggiore Church
23. San Polo Church
24. San Zaccaria Church
25. Santa Maria Formosa Church
26. Scala Contarini del Bovolo
27. To Scuola Dalmata di San Giorgio
28. Scuola San Rocco
29. Train Station

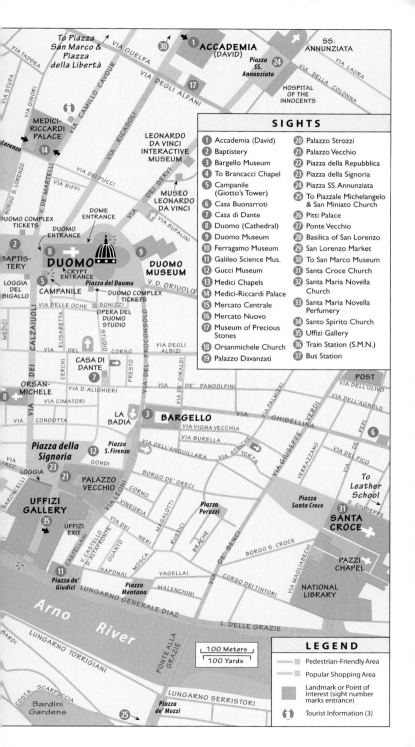

To Piazza San Marco & Piazza della Libertà

30 **1** ACCADEMIA (DAVID)

SS. ANNUNZIATA

Piazza SS. Annunziata **24**

VIA LAURA

VIA GUELFA

VIA TADDEA

VIA STUFA

VIA DEGLI ALFANI

VIA GINORI

VIA CAMILLO CAVOUR

VIA RICASOLI

17

VIA DELLA COLONNA

HOSPITAL OF THE INNOCENTS

MEDICI-RICCARDI PALACE

14

BORGO S. LORENZO

V. DE' MARTELLI

VIA DEI PUCCI

VIA BIFFI

LEONARDO DA VINCI INTERACTIVE MUSEUM

DEI SERVI

VIA BUFALINI

MUSEO LEONARDO DA VINCI

VIA

Lorenzo

DUOMO COMPLEX TICKETS

DOME ENTRANCE

DUOMO ENTRANCE

2

BAPTIS-TERY

8 **DUOMO** ✚

CRYPT ENTRANCE

9

DUOMO MUSEUM

LOGGIA DEL BIGALLO

5 CAMPANILE

Piazza del Duomo

DUOMO COMPLEX TICKETS

V. D. ORIUOLO

VIA DELLE OCHE

BONIZZI

OPERA DEL DUOMO STUDIO

SIGHTS

1 Accademia (David)	**20** Palazzo Strozzi
2 Baptistery	**21** Palazzo Vecchio
3 Bargello Museum	**22** Piazza della Repubblica
4 To Brancacci Chapel	**23** Piazza della Signoria
5 Campanile (Giotto's Tower)	**24** Piazza SS. Annunziata
6 Casa Buonarroti	**25** To Piazzale Michelangelo & San Miniato Church
7 Casa di Dante	**26** Pitti Palace
8 Duomo (Cathedral)	**27** Ponte Vecchio
9 Duomo Museum	**28** Basilica of San Lorenzo
10 Ferragamo Museum	**29** San Lorenzo Market
11 Galileo Science Mus.	**30** To San Marco Museum
12 Gucci Museum	**31** Santa Croce Church
13 Medici Chapels	**32** Santa Maria Novella Church
14 Medici-Riccardi Palace	**33** Santa Maria Novella Perfumery
15 Mercato Centrale	**34** Santo Spirito Church
16 Mercato Nuovo	**35** Uffizi Gallery
17 Museum of Precious Stones	**36** Train Station (S.M.N.)
18 Orsanmichele Church	**37** Bus Station
19 Palazzo Davanzati	

VIA CALZAIUOLI

VIA ELISABETTA

VIA DEL

CORSO

VIA DEI PROCONSOLO

VIA DEGLI ALBIZI

CASA DI DANTE **7**

CERCHI

PRESTO

VIA DE' GIRALDI

POST

VIA DELL'ULIVO

ORSAN-MICHELE

8

VIA D. ALIGHIERI

VIA CIMATORI

LA BADIA **3** **BARGELLO**

VIA

CONDOTTA

VIA

VIA DE' PANDOLFINI

VIA PALMIERI

VIA DELL'AGNOLO

VERDI

VIA GHIBELLINA

6

VIA DEI PEPI

VIA VIGNA VECCHIA

VIA BURELLA

Piazza della Signoria

23

Piazza S. Firenze **12**

GONDI

VIA DELL'ANGUILLARA

VIA STINCHE

VIA GIUSEPPE

VERRAZZANO

VIA DEI FICO

VIA

ACC.

LOGGIA

21

PALAZZO VECCHIO

VIA LEONI

CORNO

BORGO DE' GRECI

TORTA

Piazza Peruzzi

Piazza Santa Croce

To Leather School

VIA GIUSEPPE

SANTA CROCE ✚

31

UFFIZI GALLERY

35

BARONCELLI

UFFIZI EXIT

VINEGRIA

VIA DEI NERI

MAGALOTTI

RUSTICI

BRACHE

BORGO S. CROCE

VIA MAGLIABECHI

PAZZI CHAPEL

CASTELLANI

V. CASTELLO D'ALTAFRONTE

GUANTO

MOSCA

CORSO DEI TINTORI

NATIONAL LIBRARY

11

Piazza de' Giudici

SAPONAI

VAGELLAI

Piazza Mentana

MALENCHINI

LUNGARNO GENERALE DIAZ

L. DELLE GRAZIE

Arno River

LUNGARNO TORRIGIANI

BARDI

COSTA SCARPUCCIA

Bardini Gardens

PONTE ALLA GRAZIE

Piazza de' Mozzi

25

LUNGARNO SERRISTORI

| 100 Meters |
| 100 Yards |

LEGEND

▬▬▬	Pedestrian-Friendly Area
▬▬▬	Popular Shopping Area
■	Landmark or Point of Interest (sight number marks entrance)
✚	Tourist Information (3)

Rome

SIGHTS